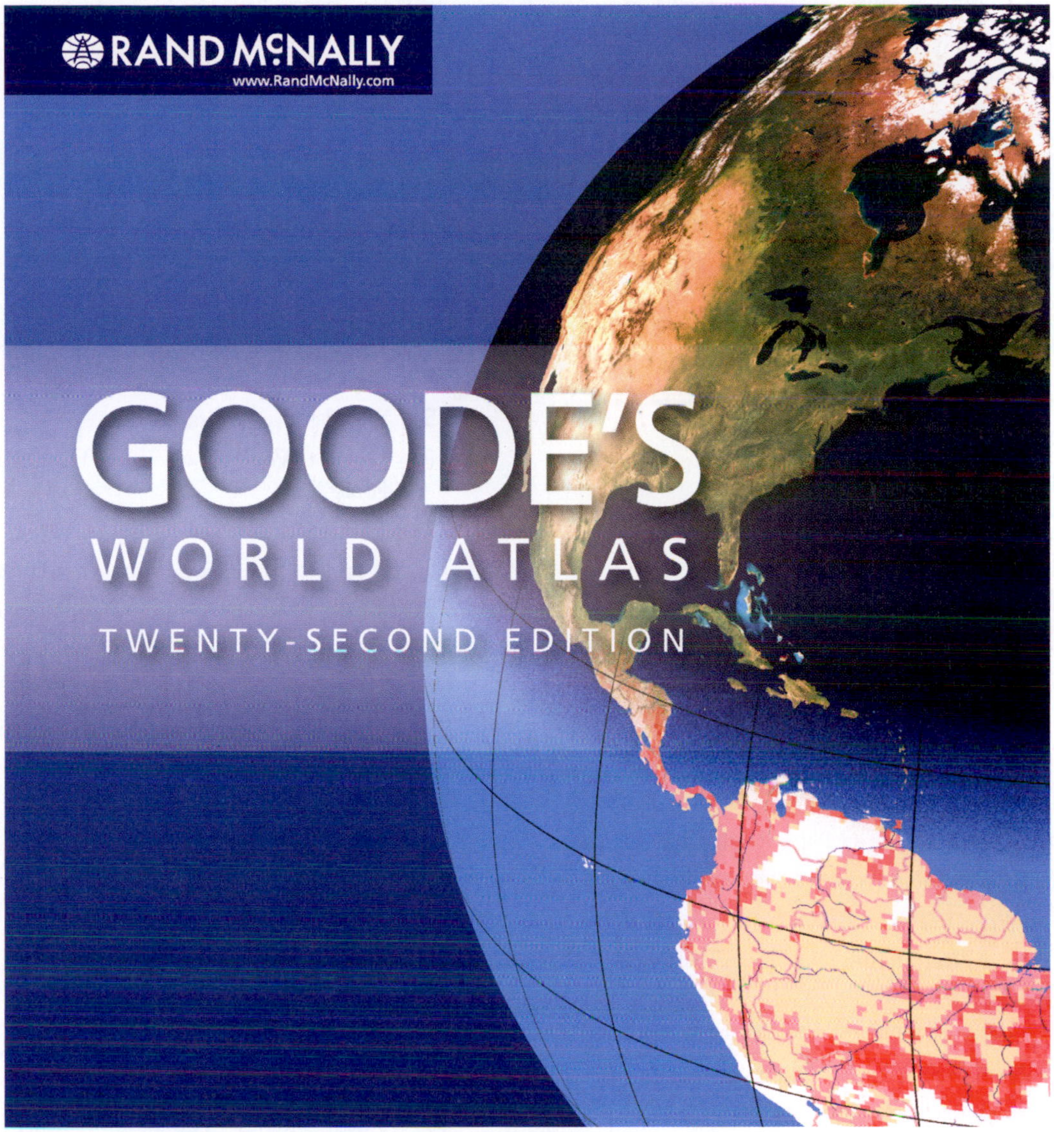

GOODE'S
WORLD ATLAS
TWENTY-SECOND EDITION

Editor

Howard Veregin, Ph.D.

Editorial Advisory Board

Robert W. Christopherson, M.A.
American River College (Emeritus)

Francis Galgano, Ph.D.
Villanova University

Alberto Giordano, Ph.D.
Texas State University, San Marcos

Sallie A. Marston, Ph.D.
University of Arizona

Virginia Thompson, Ph.D.
Towson University

Goode's World Atlas

Copyright ©2010 by Rand McNally

Copyright ©1922, 1923, 1932, 1933, 1937, 1939, 1943, 1946, 1949, 1954, 1957, 1960, 1964, 1970, 1974, 1978, 1982, 1986, 1990, 1995, 2000, 2005 by Rand McNally. All rights reserved.

Formerly Goode's School Atlas

Made in U.S.A.

Library of Congress Catalog Card Number 99-38535

This publication, or any part thereof, may not be reproduced in any form by photographic, electrostatic, mechanical, or any other method, for any use, including information storage and retrieval, without the prior written permission of the publisher.

01 02 03 **WA** 11 10 09

Cover Image

Top half. Blue Marble Next Generation monthly composite image for August. Blue Marble Next Generation images are derived from MODIS data at a spatial resolution of 500 meters. MODIS (Moderate Resolution Imaging Spectroradiometer) sensors on board the Terra and Aqua satellites provide global coverage every one to two days in 36 spectral bands. Source: NASA Visible Earth program (http://visibleearth.nasa.gov/).

Bottom half. Map of humid tropical forest loss for the period 2000-2005, derived from MODIS and Landsat imagery. Humid tropical forest loss is estimated to be over 27 million hectares for this period. Source: Hansen, M.C., Stehman, S.V., Potapov, P.V., Loveland, T.R., Townshend, J.R.G., DeFries, R.S., Pittman, K.W., Stolle, F., Steininger, M.K., Carroll, M., and Dimiceli, C. (2008). Humid tropical forest clearing from 2000 to 2005 quantified using multi-temporal and multi-resolution remotely sensed data. PNAS, 105(27), 9439-9444. (http://globalmonitoring.sdstate.edu/projects/gfm/humidtropics/data.html).

The cover image illustrates how remote sensing data, coupled with geographic information systems for analysis and display, are increasingly being used to map and monitor changes in the global environment.

Interest in geography has increased dramatically in the last few decades.

Perhaps it is because of efforts by those who teach geography or study it. Perhaps, because of instant global communications and the Internet, we're all more aware of global events. Maybe it's globalization, or recent wars, or global terrorism. Perhaps, because of environmental concerns, we feel a responsibility to better understand and manage Earth and its resources.

Whatever the reasons, this renewed interest in geography is serious. Billions of dollars are being spent every year collecting geographic data. Globally, tens of thousands of organizations of all kinds — government, business, academic, non-profit — have recognized that many of the problems they face must be understood geographically.

In emergencies, government agencies at every level need geographic information about the hurricanes, wildfires, earthquakes, tsunamis, storm surges, and floods they must respond to. They also need to know about the geography of political trouble spots, famines, droughts, terrorism, the narcotics trade, energy resources, shipping, war fighting, and a long list of other topics.

But spending for geographic information goes far beyond governments. Geographic information is also essential to understanding commerce, business, history, military campaigns, migrations, exploration, evangelization, cultural diffusion, origins of civilizations, distribution of organisms and their ecology, agriculture, climate change, natural resources, transportation patterns, productivity, epidemiology, conservation, election results, and many, many other topics. Organizations throughout the world recognize this, pay for geographic information, and hire people to manage and analyze it for them.

Geography matters! The community of people who rely on it is growing every day.

Geography today is a multidisciplinary science. Our ability to collect geographic data scientifically is exploding and we have begun to acquire the methods needed to effectively manage this data explosion for the entire planet. This includes new tools like satellite images of Earth, geographic information system (GIS) software to process and display enormous volumes of data, and global positioning system (GPS) devices that can accurately determine locations anywhere on Earth.

Goode's World Atlas is part of this revolutionary growth. The atlas has long been a staple of the college classroom, educating students about important geographic issues of the day. The current 22nd edition, which you hold in your hands, makes extensive use of digital geographic information of the kind I refer to above. It focuses on important contemporary issues like globalization, global climate change, food security, and environmental degradation. It uses GIS to integrate information and render it for cartographic display.

Goode's World Atlas helps us understand our world and our place in it. It helps us interpret stories in the news, understand international conflicts, evaluate foreign competition for jobs, make informed decisions about free trade or immigration, respond to changing oil prices or possible climate change, and think through complex domestic and foreign policy issues.

Goode's World Atlas is an essential guidebook to the new geography, helping us sort through and decipher patterns in a flood of geographic data. It helps us make sense of these data, and it provides authoritative cartographic interpretations of complex geographic issues.

I have studied and worked with geographic information for more than forty years. My experiences have given me insights into what our world was and is, and what we can make of it in the future. I think that geography can give us new eyes with which to see the world, so that — as the poet remarked — after all our traveling we return home and see it for the first time. I believe that Goode's World Atlas is an invaluable component of this learning process. The Atlas continues to evolve and adapt, but remains rooted in its original function — helping us develop geographic understanding and knowledge as a way to make sense of our world.

Jack Dangermond
President, ESRI

Goode's Atlas is named for John Paul Goode, who created the atlas and served as its editor for many editions. Goode was one of the first U.S. academic cartographers. He was born in rural Minnesota in 1862, received his bachelor's degree from the University of Minnesota in 1889, and earned his doctorate in economic geography from the University of Pennsylvania in 1903. He spent much of his professional career at the University of Chicago. Among his many accomplishments he is perhaps best known for the development of the Interrupted Homolosine projection, which he first presented at the Association of American Geographers meeting in 1923, and which has been used extensively in Goode's Atlas and in many other geographic publications to the present day.

The Homolosine is a composite of two projections, the Mollweide (Homolographic) and the Sinusoidal. Goode interrupted the Homolosine over the oceans to minimize distortion of shapes over continental land masses. Lines of latitude on the Homolosine are straight lines, to facilitate analysis of comparative latitudes. Also, the projection is equal area. Goode was a strong proponent of equal area projections and an equally strong opponent of the Mercator projection, widely used in the early part of the 20th century for world maps. As Goode stated in the introduction to the 1st edition of the atlas (1923, p. x), the distortion of area on the Mercator projection is so extreme that "it becomes pedagogically a crime to use Mercator's map" for studies of areal distributions such as population density, rainfall, or sizes of countries.

Under Goode's editorship the atlas doubled in size. The 1st edition of Goode's School Atlas contained 96 pages of maps. The 4th edition (1932), the last edition that Goode would edit before his death, contained 174 pages of maps. Goode introduced many of the thematic map topics that are still found in the atlas today, including world economic maps of agricultural commodities, minerals, energy, and international trade. These topics reflect Goode's interest and training in economic geography.

Goode remained the only name on Goode's School Atlas until the 8th edition (1949), on which Edward B. Espenshade, Jr., was credited with numerous updates and revisions. Espenshade was then named editor for the 9th edition (1953). Espenshade was one of Goode's students and spent his academic career at Northwestern University in Evanston, Illinois. The 9th edition was significant in many respects. It boasted a new title, Goode's World Atlas, and contained many of the features of the modern atlas.

John Paul Goode

In particular, Espenshade made extensive use of maps compiled by experts in specific subdisciplines of geography. Examples include natural vegetation by A. W. Küchler, physiography by Erwin Raisz, climate regions by Glenn Trewartha, and agricultural regions by Derwent Whittlesey. By relying on the research of these and other scholars, Espenshade was able to incorporate the latest advances in the study of geographical phenomena. Espenshade also oversaw the creation of a new reference map series, which included hand-drawn shaded relief for the first time in the atlas. These reference maps were introduced in the 11th edition (1960).

Joel L. Morrison, then at the University of Wisconsin, joined Espenshade as associate editor on the 14th edition (1974). Morrison, who had a distinguished career in academia and the federal government, was affiliated with the atlas through the 19th edition (1995). In the 1970s and 1980s the atlas saw numerous innovations, including the introduction of ocean floor shaded relief maps, reference maps of major world cities, a continent environments map series, and the first use of cartograms.

The 19th edition was Espenshade's last as editor. On that edition, John C. Hudson assumed the role of associate editor. Hudson, a distinguished academic geographer at Northwestern University, then took on the role of editor for the 20th edition. Hudson introduced many new thematic maps, including world ecoregions, origins of plants, refugees, conflicts, and oceanic environments.

Howard Veregin was named editor for the 21st edition. Veregin was on the geography faculty at the University of Minnesota, then moved to Rand McNally where he currently serves as director of geographic information services. Veregin created the Goode's Editorial Board to help reorient the atlas in relation to modern geographic scholarship and pedagogy. With the 22nd edition the atlas became all-digital for the first time, with most maps produced using geographic information systems (GIS) technology. Major innovations for the 22nd edition include a new digital reference map series (the first new series since the 11th edition), many new thematic maps, and an updated design.

Throughout its history Goode's Atlas has adapted to changes in cartographic technology, map design, and geographic curricula. However, it has always maintained the pedagogical foundation that John Paul Goode established in the 1st edition in 1923. It should be seen first and foremost as a work of scholarship, incorporating the latest insights into geographical research and knowledge. It is also a fascinating portrait of almost nine decades of evolution in geography and cartography.

Robert B. McMaster, Ph.D.
Susanna A. McMaster, Ph.D.
University of Minnesota

The 22ⁿᵈ edition of Goode's World Atlas blends dramatic new maps and exceptional cartography with the strong traditions that have made Goode's Atlas a standard for over 85 years.

The 22ⁿᵈ edition features new thematic maps that focus on topics important to modern geography, including global climate change, sea level rise, CO_2 emissions, polar ice fluctuations, forest loss, extreme weather events, infectious diseases, water resources, and energy production. These maps have been produced with the latest digital sources integrated within geographic information systems (GIS) technology to deliver a contemporary portrait of the planet. We have also retained and updated the new maps introduced in the 21ˢᵗ edition, including HIV infection, military power, women's rights, and food aid. Other thematic maps and graphs have been updated using the same standards and quality requirements that have always been a defining feature of Goode's World Atlas.

The 22ⁿᵈ edition also delivers over 160 pages of new, digitally produced reference maps, providing detailed coverage of all continents. We have paid particular attention to expanding our coverage of Africa, Asia, and Central and South America. The new reference maps were produced using state-of-the-art GIS technology to integrate digital data sources and render them for cartographic display. Underlying these maps is Rand McNally's proprietary digital world database, the same trusted source used in many of our other world atlases.

At Rand McNally we take pride in the quality of our cartography and the rigorous standards we set for the research underlying each map. For the 22ⁿᵈ edition we worked closely with our Editorial Advisory Board to select new map topics, assess cartographic approaches, and identify new atlas features. Longtime Goode's users will see numerous changes to the atlas, including the use of more contemporary color palettes and graphic treatments to improve clarity, readability, and aesthetics. In addition we have implemented changes that bring more consistency to each section of the atlas.

Needless to say this atlas would not have been possible without the efforts of a very talented cartographic development team, who conducted basic research, developed new thematic maps, created the new reference maps, designed the maps and page layouts, performed quality assurance, and helped work through countless editorial decisions. I include their names here in alphabetical order.

Robert Argersinger, Greg Babiak, Genna Davis, Marzee Eckhoff, Brett Gover, Justin Griffin, Rob Harris, Michael Healy, Susan Hudson, Valbona Kokoshi, Marc Kugel, Brian Lash, Felix A. Lopez, Andy Lotter, Nina Lusterman, Donna McGrath, Rob Merrill, Joerg Metzner, Angela Mrotek, Darren Raffel, Amy J. Ruggles, Damon Sather, Dave Simmons, Andy Skinner, Jeff Thomas, Raymond T. Tobiaski, Tom Vitacco, Steve Wiertz, Yanyan Zhang

A brief acknowledgment such as this cannot really do justice to the thousands of hours of effort expended by these and other Rand McNally subject matter experts. Nor does this list include Rand McNally employees who worked on previous editions of the atlas, and to whom the current atlas owes much.

I would also like to acknowledge the work of the Editorial Advisory Board, who participated in discussions of the new directions we were planning to take, and made significant contributions in terms of content and design. We are indebted to the Board for helping us refocus Goode's Atlas in relation to modern geographic scholarship and teaching. The Goode's Editorial Advisory Board members are listed on the title page of this atlas.

While Goode's Atlas continues to change with the times, it remains the same accurate and reliable educational resource that J. Paul Goode originally intended it to be. We at Rand McNally remain committed to providing you with the most trusted tools to help you and your students open your classrooms to the world.

Howard Veregin

Howard Veregin, Ph.D., Editor
Skokie, Illinois

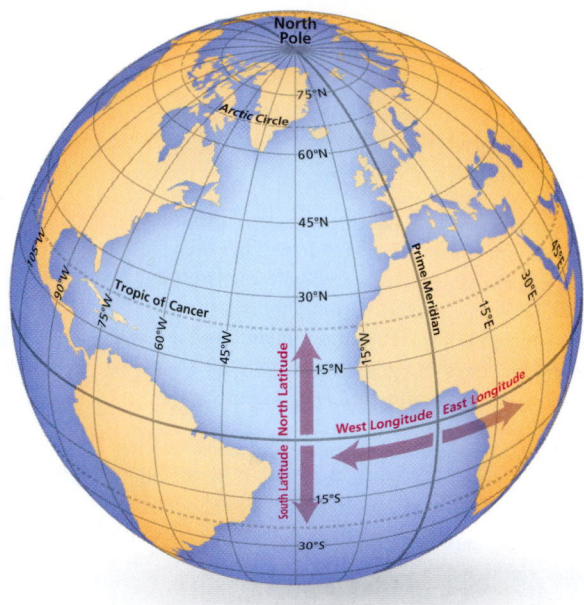

View of Earth centered on 30° N, 30° W

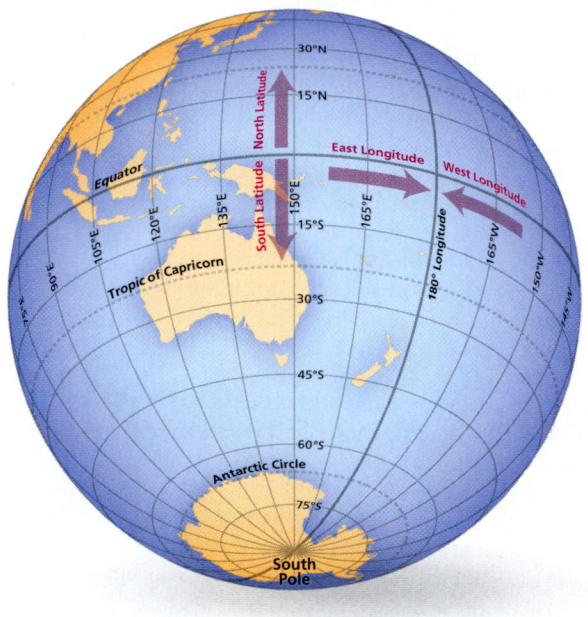

View of Earth centered on 30° S, 150° E

Basic Earth Properties

Earth is essentially spherical in shape. The North and South Poles are aligned with Earth's axis of rotation. The Equator is equidistant between the Poles and divides Earth into northern and southern hemispheres.

Latitude and longitude identify the locations of features on Earth's surface. Latitude is the angle north or south of the Equator. Longitude is the angle east or west of the Prime (Greenwich) Meridian. A meridian is a line of longitude extending from the North Pole to the South Pole. The Prime Meridian is the meridian passing through the Royal Observatory in Greenwich, England. This location for the Prime Meridian was adopted at the International Meridian Conference in Washington, D.C., in 1884.

Latitude and longitude are usually given in degrees, minutes and seconds. There are 60 minutes in a degree and 60 seconds in a minute. The symbols °, ' and " represent degrees, minutes and seconds, respectively. For latitude the symbols N and S indicate degrees north or south of the Equator. The latitude of the Equator is 0° and the latitudes of the North and South Poles are 90° N and 90° S. For longitude the symbols E and W indicate degrees east or west of the Prime Meridian. Longitude ranges from 0° at the Prime Meridian to 180° E or W. The meridian at 180° E is the same as the meridian at 180° W, and this meridian is the approximate location of the International Date Line. This meridian and the Prime Meridian divide Earth into eastern and western hemispheres.

A latitude-longitude coordinate pair defines the location of a feature on Earth. As an example, the Rand McNally building in Skokie, Illinois, has the coordinates 42° 3' 37" N, 87° 45' 39" W. Often the number of seconds are omitted from the coordinates if a high level of precision is not required.

Lines of latitude are also known as parallels. Two parallels of special importance are the Tropic of Cancer and the Tropic of Capricorn, at approximately 23° 30' N and S respectively. This angle coincides with the inclination of Earth's axis relative to its orbital plane around the Sun. The Tropics are the lines of latitude where the noon sun is directly overhead on the solstices. Two other important parallels are the Arctic Circle and the Antarctic Circle, at approximately 66° 30' N and S respectively. These lines mark the most northerly and southerly points at which the Sun can be seen on the solstices.

The Geographic Grid

The geographic grid is the grid of latitude-longitude lines on Earth. The following are some important characteristics of the grid.

Lines of longitude (meridians) are equal in length and meet at the Poles.

Lines of latitude (parallels) are parallel to each other and equally spaced along meridians.

The length of parallels decreases as one gets closer to the Poles. For example, the length of the parallel at 60° latitude is one-half the length of the Equator.

Meridians get closer together with increasing distance from the Equator, and finally converge at the Poles.

Parallels and meridians meet at right angles.

Cartography and Geospatial Technology

Geography's subject matter includes the people, landforms, climate, and other physical and human phenomena that make up Earth's environments and give unique character to different places. Geographers construct maps to visualize how these phenomena vary over geographic space. Maps help geographers understand and explain phenomena and their interactions.

The art and science of mapmaking is known as cartography. Although maps were once drawn by hand, they are now usually created using digital technology. This technology includes GIS (geographic information systems), as well as GPS (global positioning system) and remote sensing. Collectively these are known as geospatial technologies.

GIS is a specialized type of software that enables the integration, processing, analysis, and display of digital geographic information. It combines an underlying database with spatial analysis tools and cartographic rendering capabilities. First developed in the 1960s, GIS has evolved rapidly in the last decade with advances in computer processing power and the increased availability of digital geographic information. Applications of GIS have also diversified rapidly as more users have recognized its utility for solving geographic problems.

In cartography, GIS has redefined how maps are made. Since the underlying data for a map is stored in a database, a map is just one of many possible data representations. Many different maps can be produced from one database, based on different permutations of attributes, for different map scales, geographic areas, or time periods, and using different map treatments. GIS also enhances the efficiency of map production. For example, map symbology can be driven off stored attributes, selection and generalization can be conducted using defined rules, map text can be placed automatically, and index creation can be automated. All of the maps in this edition of Goode's World Atlas are digital, and the vast majority have been created using GIS software.

GIS also greatly enhances the ability to integrate data from a variety of sources and process these data for specific mapping purposes. In this sense GIS is closely related to other geospatial technologies such as GPS and remote sensing. GPS is a satellite-based system for capturing precise information about locations on Earth's surface. Originally developed by and for the military, GPS is now the underlying technology behind personal navigation devices and location-based services. GPS has revolutionized the field of surveying and is used in a wide variety of fields where accurate coordinates are needed.

Remote sensing refers to the collection of data about Earth from satellites and aircraft. Advances in remote sensing have greatly magnified the volume and types of geographic data available for mapping. Many of the maps in this atlas are derived from remote sensing imagery, including the maps of land cover, gravity, sea level change, sea ice, and forest loss. Modern remote sensing systems are designed to focus on specific portions of the electromagnetic spectrum, some of which cannot be seen by the human eye. This capability allows very specific geographic phenomena to be imaged and analyzed.

The diagram below illustrates how geospatial technology can be used to map and monitor changes in the global environment. This edition of Goode's World Atlas reflects this growing awareness and capability by incorporating the latest digital data sources wherever possible.

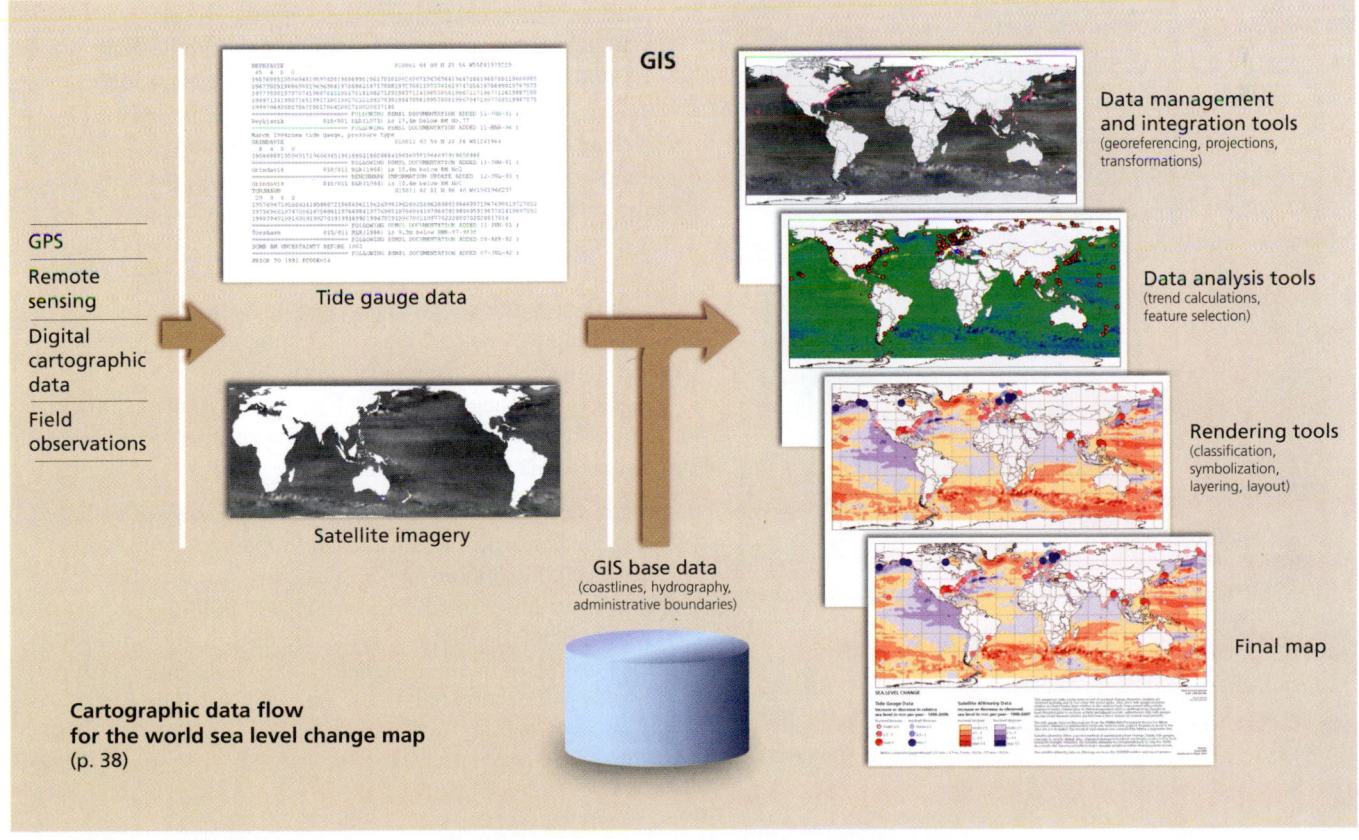

GIS

GPS

Remote sensing

Digital cartographic data

Field observations

Tide gauge data

Satellite imagery

GIS base data
(coastlines, hydrography, administrative boundaries)

Data management and integration tools
(georeferencing, projections, transformations)

Data analysis tools
(trend calculations, feature selection)

Rendering tools
(classification, symbolization, layering, layout)

Final map

Cartographic data flow for the world sea level change map
(p. 38)

1:40,000,000 scale

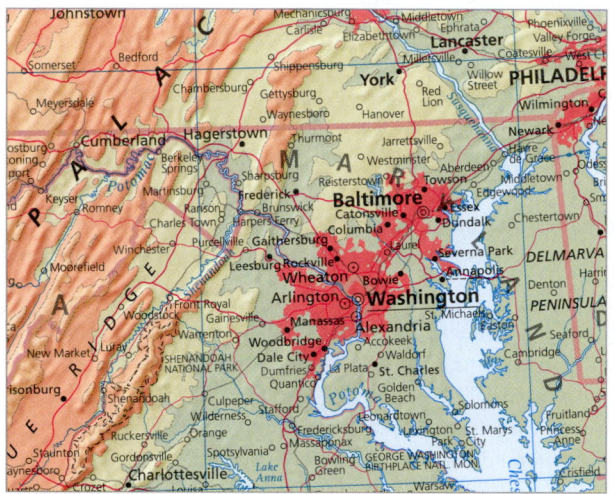

1:4,000,000 scale

1:1,000,000 scale

Map Scale

Map scale is the ratio of distance on a map to distance on Earth's surface. For example, if two towns on a map are separated by a distance of 1 inch, and these towns are actually 1 mile apart, then the scale of the map is 1 inch to 1 mile.

The statement "1 inch to 1 mile" is a verbal scale. Verbal scales are simple and intuitive, but it can be difficult to compare verbal scales for different maps on which different linear units are used, such as kilometers instead of miles. A more flexible way to express map scale is the representative fraction. To construct a representative fraction, the numerator and denominator are first converted to the same units. For example, since there are 63,360 inches in a mile, the verbal scale "1 inch to 1 mile" can be expressed as "1 inch to 63,360 inches". Next the unit names are dropped and the scale is expressed as a ratio, in this case 1:63,360. This means that 1 linear unit on the map represents 63,360 linear units on Earth, whether those units are inches, miles, kilometers, or some other unit of measurement.

Map scale can also be represented in graphical form. Many maps contain a graphic scale (or bar scale) showing real-world units such as miles or kilometers. The bar scale is usually subdivided to allow easy calculation of distance on the map. However, using a bar scale to measure distance can result in significant errors, especially on small-scale maps covering large areas. This is due to the distortion of distances on the map, as discussed in the map projection section below.

Map scale determines the amount of detail that can be portrayed on a map. The maps on this page illustrate this concept. The scale of these maps increases from 1:40,000,000 (top map) to 1:4,000,000 (middle map) to 1:1,000,000 (bottom map). On small-scale maps, only the largest and most important features can be shown, such as large cities, major rivers and lakes, and international boundaries. Features on small-scale maps are also smaller and more generalized than they are on larger-scale maps. For example, on the top map (smallest scale), Washington, D.C., appears as a small dot. On the middle map (larger scale), it is represented by a red blob indicating the built-up area of Washington. The bottom map (largest scale) shows additional detail that could not be shown on the other maps. This change in map content and feature complexity as a function of map scale is known as map generalization.

Maps in Goode's World Atlas have a wide range of scales. The smallest scales are for the world maps, where scales are 1:100,000,000 or smaller. Overview maps of the continents range in scale from 1:16,000,000 to 1:40,000,000 depending on the size of the continent. Regional maps of areas smaller than a whole continent vary from 1:16,000,000 to 1:4,000,000. In addition there are numerous inset maps of cities and islands at a scale of 1:1,000,000.

Map Projections

A map projection is a geometric representation of Earth's surface on a flat surface. Since Earth is roughly spherical, a map projection is needed to produce any flat map, whether a page in this atlas or a computer-generated map of driving directions on www.RandMcNally.com. Hundreds of projections have been developed since the dawn of cartography. A limitation of all of these projections is that they introduce geometric distortion. Some projections distort shape, others distort area, and all distort distance to some degree.

In order to choose an appropriate projection for a particular map, cartographers must pay careful attention to the properties that are distorted and the properties that are preserved by the projection. If shape is preserved, the projection is "conformal." On conformal projections the shapes of geographic features agree with their shapes on Earth. However, a limitation of conformal projections is that they necessarily distort area. This means that the sizes of the geographic features on the map will not be directly comparable. Some will be too large and others too small.

If areas are correctly represented, the projection is "equal area." On equal area projections the sizes of features on the map are directly comparable and in correct proportion to their sizes on Earth. However, in order to achieve this effect, equal area projections distort shape. No projection can preserve both shape and area simultaneously. Some projections preserve neither shape nor area, but instead balance shape and area distortion, creating a compromise projection.

The term "equidistant" is often used for projections that preserve distance. However this can be misleading since distance can only be preserved selectively, such as along specific meridians or parallels. No projection correctly preserves distance in all directions at all locations. Since distance is closely related to scale, one implication is that map scale is often only approximate and may not apply to the entire coverage area of a map. This problem is especially acute for small-scale maps covering large areas.

The projection selected for a particular map depends on the relative importance of different types of distortion, which in turn depends on the purpose of the map. For example, world maps showing phenomena that vary with area, such as population density, often use an equal area projection to give an accurate depiction of the importance of each region.

Map projections are created using mathematical procedures. To illustrate the general principles of projections without using mathematics, we can view a projection as the geometric transfer of information from a globe to a flat projection surface, such as a sheet of paper. If we allow the paper to be rolled in different ways, we can derive three basic types of map projections called cylindrical, conic, and azimuthal.

For cylindrical projections, the sheet of paper is rolled into a tube and wrapped around the globe so that it is tangent (touching) along a circle such as the Equator (see figure below). Information from the globe is transferred to the tube, and the tube is then unrolled to produce the final flat map.

Conic projections use a cone rather than a cylinder. The figure shows the cone tangent to the globe along a line of latitude with the apex of the cone over the North Pole. The line of tangency is called the standard parallel of the projection. Azimuthal projections use a flat projection surface that is tangent to the globe at a single point, such as the North Pole (see figure below).

In general, map distortion increases with distance away from the point or line of tangency. This is why maps of equatorial, mid-latitude, and polar regions often use cylindrical, conic and azimuthal projections, respectively.

The projection surface model is useful for illustrating how projections are developed. However, each of the three projection surfaces actually represents scores of individual projections. There are, for example, many projections with the term "cylindrical" in the name, each of which has the same basic rectangular shape, but different spacings of parallels and meridians.

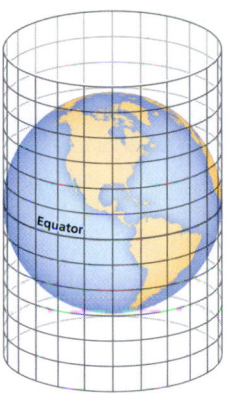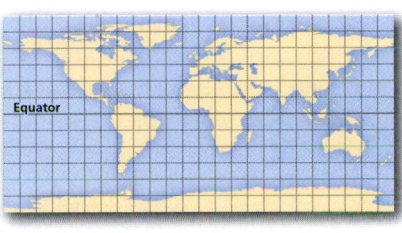

Cylindrical Projection

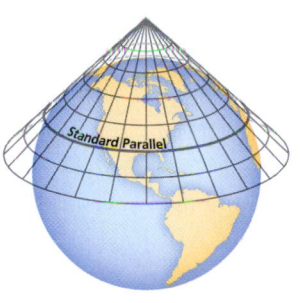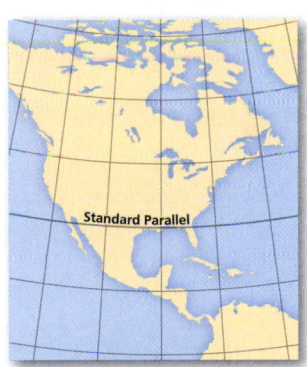

Conic Projection

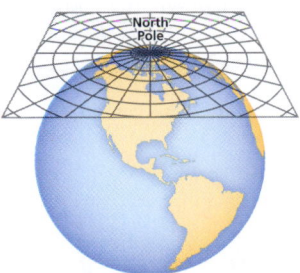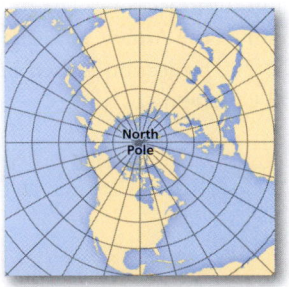

Azimuthal Projection

Map Projections Used in Goode's World Atlas

Of the hundreds of projections that have been developed, only a fraction are in everyday use. The main projections used in Goode's World Atlas are described below.

Lambert Conformal Conic Projection

On this conic projection, spacing between parallels increases with distance away from the standard parallel, which allows the geometric property of shape (but not area) to be preserved. The projection is named after Johann Lambert, an 18th century mathematician who developed some of the most important projections in use today. It became widely used in the United States in the 20th century following its adoption for many state mapping programs. This projection is used extensively in Goode's World Atlas for larger-scale reference maps.

Albers Equal Area Conic Projection

On this conic projection, spacing between parallels decreases with distance away from the standard parallel, which allows the geometric property of area (but not shape) to be preserved. The projection is named after Heinrich Albers, who developed it in 1805. It became widely used in the 20th century, when the United States Coast and Geodetic Survey made it a standard for equal area maps of the United States. This projection is used in Goode's World Atlas for continent thematic maps where the equal area property is important.

Lambert Azimuthal Equal Area Projection

On this azimuthal projection, area is preserved, but at the expense of significant shape distortion as distance from the point of tangency increases. This projection is most appropriate for areas of roughly circular shape. This projection, like the Lambert Conformal Conic, is named after Johann Lambert. It is used in Goode's World Atlas for smaller-scale reference maps.

Stereographic Projection

On this azimuthal projection, shape is preserved, but distortion of area becomes significant as distance from the point of tangency increases. As a result, this projection is often used for areas that are roughly circular in shape. This projection is used in Goode's World Atlas for maps of the polar regions.

Miller Cylindrical Projection

This cylindrical projection is neither conformal nor equal area. However, it is a useful compromise projection to show Earth in a simple, rectangular form. One problem is that polar areas exhibit significant exaggeration of area, a problem common to many cylindrical projections. The projection is named after Osborn Miller, director of the American Geographical Society, who developed it in 1942. The projection is used in Goode's World Atlas for many of the world climate maps.

Lambert Conformal Conic Projection

Albers Equal Area Conic Projection

Lambert Azimuthal Equal Area Projection

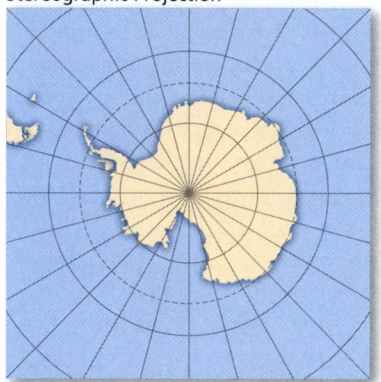

Stereographic Projection

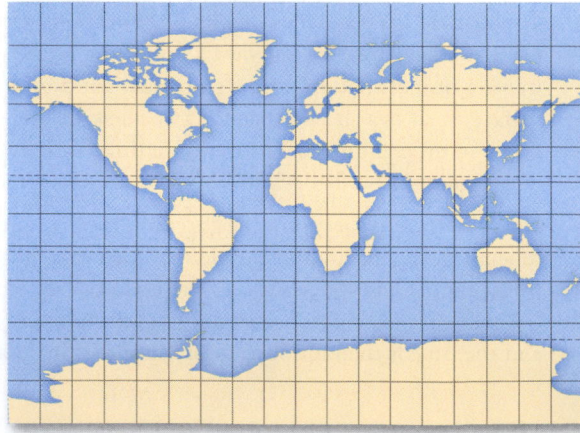

Miller Cylindrical Projection

Plate Carrée Projection

This cylindrical projection is neither conformal nor equal area. Its main utility lies in the fact that it shows lines of latitude as evenly spaced lines on the map. This allows for effective thematic map display for phenomena that are measured at regular intervals of latitude. The projection is used in Goode's World Atlas for world climate change maps.

Sinusoidal Projection

The straight, evenly-spaced parallels on this pseudocylindrical projection resemble the parallels on cylindrical projections. Unlike cylindrical projections, however, meridians are curved and converge at the poles. This causes significant shape distortion in polar regions. The projection is therefore not conformal, although it is equal area. The Sinusoidal is the oldest-known pseudocylindrical projection, dating to the 16th century. It is not used extensively in Goode's World Atlas. However, along with the Mollweide projection, it is the basis for the Goode's Interrupted Homolosine projection described below.

Mollweide Projection

The Mollweide (or Homolographic) projection resembles the Sinusoidal but has less shape distortion in polar areas due to its elliptical form. Like the Sinusoidal projection, it is equal area but not conformal. It is one of several pseudocylindrical projections developed in the 19th century, and is named after Karl Mollweide, an astronomer and mathematician, who developed it in 1805. It is not used extensively in Goode's World Atlas. However, along with the Sinusoidal projection, it is the basis for the Goode's Interrupted Homolosine projection described below.

Goode's Interrupted Homolosine Equal Area Projection

This projection is a fusion of the Sinusoidal projection between 40° 44' N and S, and the Mollweide projection between these parallels and the Poles. The projection is equal area but not conformal. The unique appearance of the projection is due to the introduction of discontinuities in oceanic regions, the goal of which is to reduce distortion for continental land masses. A condensed version of the projection also exists in which the Atlantic Ocean is compressed to help maximize the scale of the map on the page. The Goode's Interrupted Homolosine projection is named after J. Paul Goode of the University of Chicago, who developed it in 1923. Goode was an advocate of interrupted projections and, as editor of Goode's School Atlas, promoted their use in education. This projection is used extensively in Goode's World Atlas for world thematic maps.

Robinson Projection

This pseudocylindrical projection resembles the Mollweide projection except that polar regions are flattened and stretched out. While neither conformal nor equal area, the Robinson projection manages to balance shape and area distortion in an effective way. The projection was developed in 1963 by Arthur Robinson of the University of Wisconsin, at the request of Rand McNally. The Robinson projection is widely used in Goode's World Atlas for world thematic maps where the interrupted nature of the Goode's Homolosine projection would be inappropriate.

Plate Carrée Projection

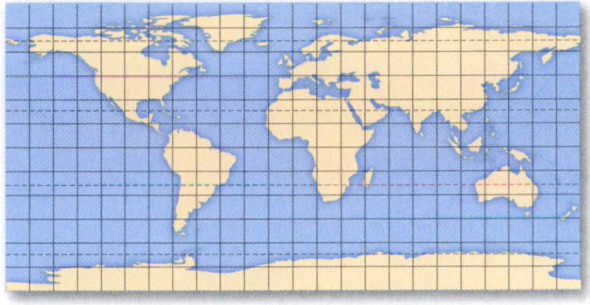

Sinusoidal Projection

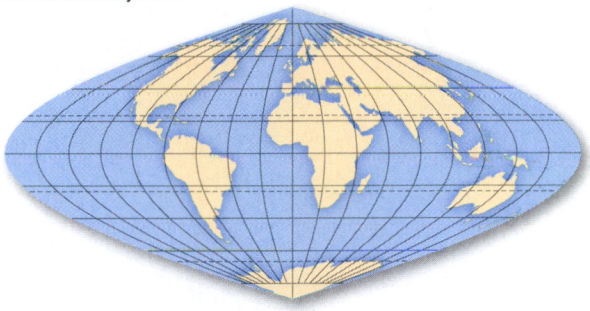

Mollweide Projection

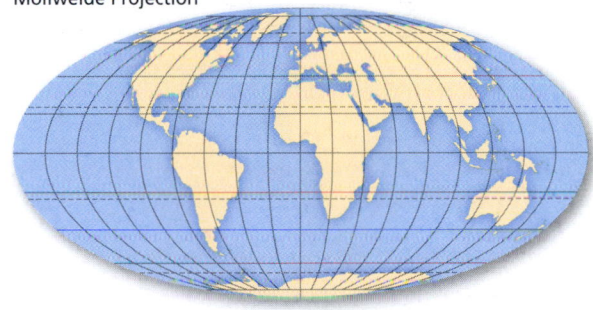

Goode's Interrupted Homolosine Equal Area Projection

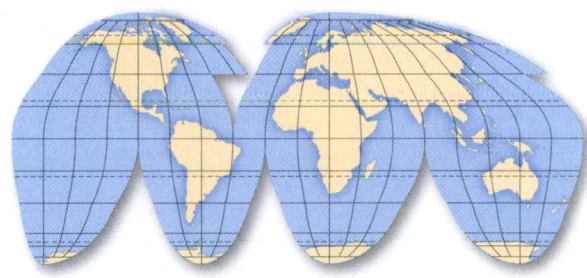

Robinson Projection

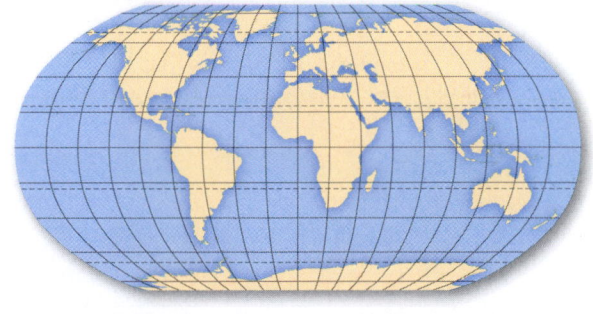

Point symbol map: Detail of Zinc and Coltan (p. 69)

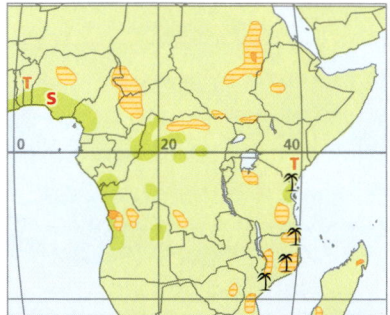

Area symbol map: Detail of Vegetable Oils (p. 64)

Dot map: Detail of Sugar, Spices (p. 62)

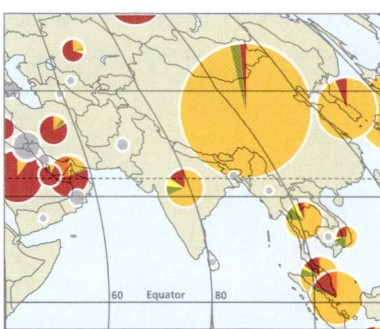

Proportional symbol map: Detail of Exports (p. 77)

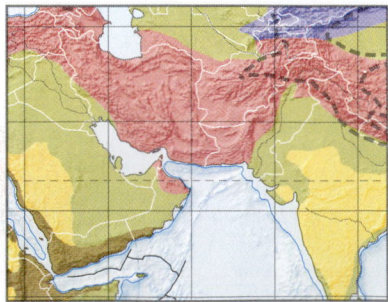

Area class map: Detail of Landforms (pp. 24-25)

Thematic Map Types in Goode's World Atlas

Thematic maps depict a single theme such as population density, agricultural productivity or annual precipitation. The selected theme is presented on a base of locational information, such as coastlines, country boundaries, and major drainage features.

Goode's World Atlas contains many different types of thematic maps. The characteristics of each are summarized below.

Point Symbol Maps

Point symbol maps are perhaps the simplest type of thematic map. They show features that occur at discrete locations. Examples include earthquakes, nuclear power plants, and mineral-producing areas. The Zinc and Coltan map (p. 69) is an example of a point symbol map. Different colors represent the two different materials, and various symbol sizes show relative importance.

Area Symbol Maps

Area symbol maps are useful for delineating regions of interest. For example, the Vegetable Oils maps (p. 64) show major oil-producing regions in different colors. Some point symbols also appear on this map, for less extensive oil crops.

Dot Maps

Dot maps show a distribution using a pattern of dots, where each dot represents a certain quantity or amount. For example, on the Sugar and Spice map (p. 62), each dot represents 20,000 metric tons of sugar produced. The different dot colors represent different sources of sugar (cane vs. beet). Dot maps are an effective way of representing the variable density of geographic phenomena.

Proportional Symbol Maps

Proportional symbol maps portray numeric quantities, such as total toxic chemical releases per state, or the total value of agricultural goods produced by country. The symbols on these maps — usually circles — are drawn such that the size the symbol is proportional to the value at that location. For example, the Exports map (p. 77) shows the value of goods exported by each country in the world, in billions of U.S. dollars. Proportional symbols are frequently subdivided based on the percentage of individual components making up the total. The Exports map uses wedges of different color to show the percentages of various types of exports, such as manufactured articles and raw materials.

Area Class Maps

Area class maps divide Earth into zones based on categories of a particular geographic phenomenon. For example, the Landforms map (pp. 24-25) divides Earth into seven unique structural regions based on landform type and origin. Other examples of area class maps in Goode's World Atlas include soil taxonomy (pp. 44-45), terrestrial biomes (pp. 46-47), and natural vegetation (pp. 42-43).

Flow Line Maps

Flow line maps show flows between locations. Usually the thickness of the flow lines is proportional to the volume of the flow. Flows may be physical commodities like petroleum or less tangible quantities like information. The flow lines on the Communication Network Infrastructure map (pp. 82-83) represent bandwidth usage in gigabits per second. Note that the locations of flow lines may not accurately represent the actual physical route.

Choropleth Maps

Choropleth maps apply distinctive colors to predefined areas, such as counties or states, to represent different quantities in each area. The quantities shown are usually rates, percentages, or densities. For example, the Birth Rate map (p. 50) shows the annual number of births per one thousand people for each country.

Isoline Maps

Isoline maps are used to portray quantities that vary continuously over space. These maps are frequently used for climate variables such as precipitation and temperature. For example, the January Temperature map for the North Polar region (p. 33) contains isolines at intervals of 5° C. Colors are also used to assist map interpretation.

Grid-Based Maps

Grid-based maps rely on data points occurring at regular intervals in a two-dimensional grid. Some grid-based maps are actually digital images, analogous to the pictures captured by digital cameras. These maps are created from a very fine grid of cells called pixels, each of which is assigned a color that corresponds to a specific value or range of values. The population density maps in this atlas (pp. 48-49, for example) are examples of this type. Other grid-based maps are based on data integrated over a coarser grid, such as the map showing temperature change for 5-degree grid cells (p. 38) and the tornado map showing the frequency of tornadoes within 1-degree grid cells (p. 91). Grid-based mapping is increasingly being used to map environmental phenomena observable from remote sensing systems.

Cartograms

Cartograms are maps on which shapes and areas have been deliberately distorted. The cartograms in this atlas draw each country as a rectangle whose size is proportional to the population of the country. This means that the countries with the largest areas are those with the largest populations, regardless of actual country area. Cartograms make explicit the relationship between the mapped variable and the size of the affected population. As an example, consider the HIV cartogram (p. 54). Both Chad and Nigeria have relatively high rates of HIV infection, but Nigeria is much larger than Chad on the cartogram, since Nigeria's population is much larger. This informs the cartogram reader that the population affected by HIV is much larger in Nigeria.

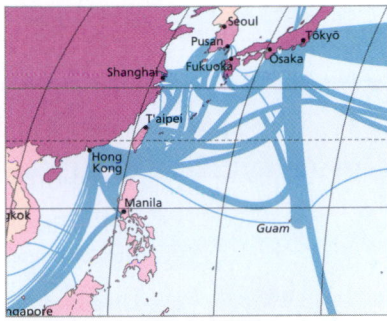

Flow line map: Detail of Communication Network Infrastructure (pp. 82-83)

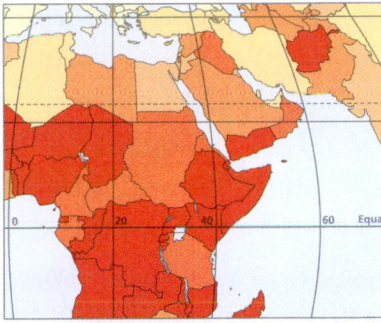

Choropleth map: Detail of Birth Rate (p. 50)

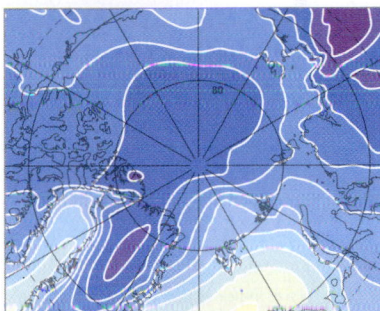

Isoline map: Detail of January Temperature (p. 33)

Grid-based map: Detail of Population Density (pp. 48-49)

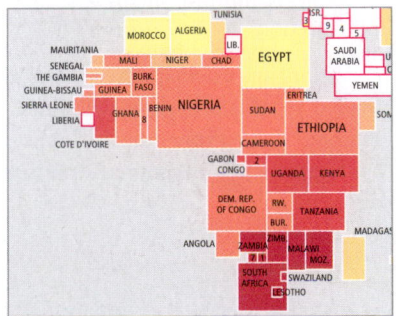

Cartogram: Detail of HIV Infection (p. 54)

Political Boundaries

---- — ━━━	International
━■━■━	Disputed or Unrecognized
---- ━━━	Secondary (State, Provincial, etc.)
-·---	International Boundary over Water
-·---	Secondary Boundary over Water
⌐ ¬	Park, Indian Reservation, Area of Interest
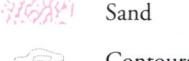	Urbanized Area

Populated Places

TŌKYŌ — National Capital

B̲o̲i̲s̲e̲ — Secondary Capital

1:2,000,000, 1:1,000,000 and 1:500,000 Inset Maps

◉	1,000,000 and over
◎	100,000 to 1,000,000
☉	50,000 to 100,000
•	10,000 to 50,000
○	Under 10,000
□	Neighborhood, Section of City

Other Reference Maps

◉	1,000,000 and over
◎	250,000 to 1,000,000
☉	100,000 to 250,000
•	25,000 to 100,000
○	Under 25,000

Note: Type size indicates the relative importance of the city.
On the continent physical maps, city populations and relative
importance are not differentiated.

Cultural Features

⌣	Dam
⊡	Point of Interest
∴	Ruins
PALESTINE	Cultural or Historic Region

Transportation

———	Major Road
———	Minor Road
———	Railroad
✈	Airport

Land Features

△	Peak, Spot Height
≍	Pass
	Sand
	Contours

Elevation

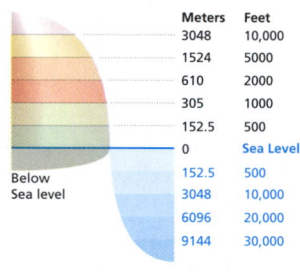

Meters	Feet	
3048	10,000	
1524	5000	
610	2000	
305	1000	
152.5	500	
0	Sea Level	
Below Sea level		
152.5	500	
3048	10,000	
6096	20,000	
9144	30,000	

Note: The 500 foot contour is not
shown on the small-scale oceans
and polar regions maps.

Lakes and Reservoirs

	Fresh Water
	Fresh Water: Intermittent
	Dry Lake
	Salt Water
	Salt Water: Intermittent

Other Water features

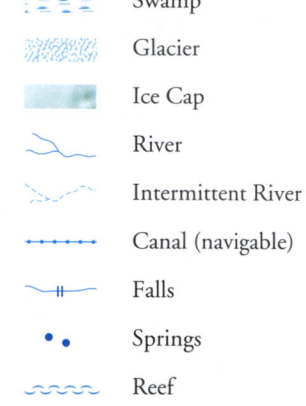

	Swamp
	Glacier
	Ice Cap
	River
	Intermittent River
	Canal (navigable)
	Falls
	Springs
	Reef
→	Warm Ocean Current
→	Cold Ocean Current

The legend above shows the symbols used for reference maps in Goode's World Atlas.

To portray relative areas correctly, uniform map scales have been used wherever possible:

Continents – Between 1:16,000,000 and 1:40,000,000

Countries and regions – Between 1:4,000,000 and 1:16,000,000

World, polar areas and oceans – 1:40,000,000 and smaller

City and island inset maps – 1:500,000, 1:1,000,000 and 1:2,000,000

Elevations on the maps are shown using a combination of shaded relief and hypsometric tints. Shaded relief (or hill-shading) gives a three-dimensional impression of the landscape, while hypsometric tints show elevation ranges in different colors.

The choice of names for mapped features is complicated by the fact that a variety of languages and alphabets are used throughout the world. A local-names policy is used in Goode's World Atlas for populated places and local physical features. For some major features, an English form of the name is used with the local name, e.g., Vienna (Wien) and Naples (Napoli). In countries where more than one official language is used, names are given in the dominant local language. For large physical features spanning international borders, the conventional English form of the name is used. In cases where a non-Roman alphabet is used, names have been transliterated according to accepted practice.

Selected features are also listed in the Index, which includes a pronunciation guide. A list of foreign geographic terms is provided in the Glossary.

THE SOLAR SYSTEM

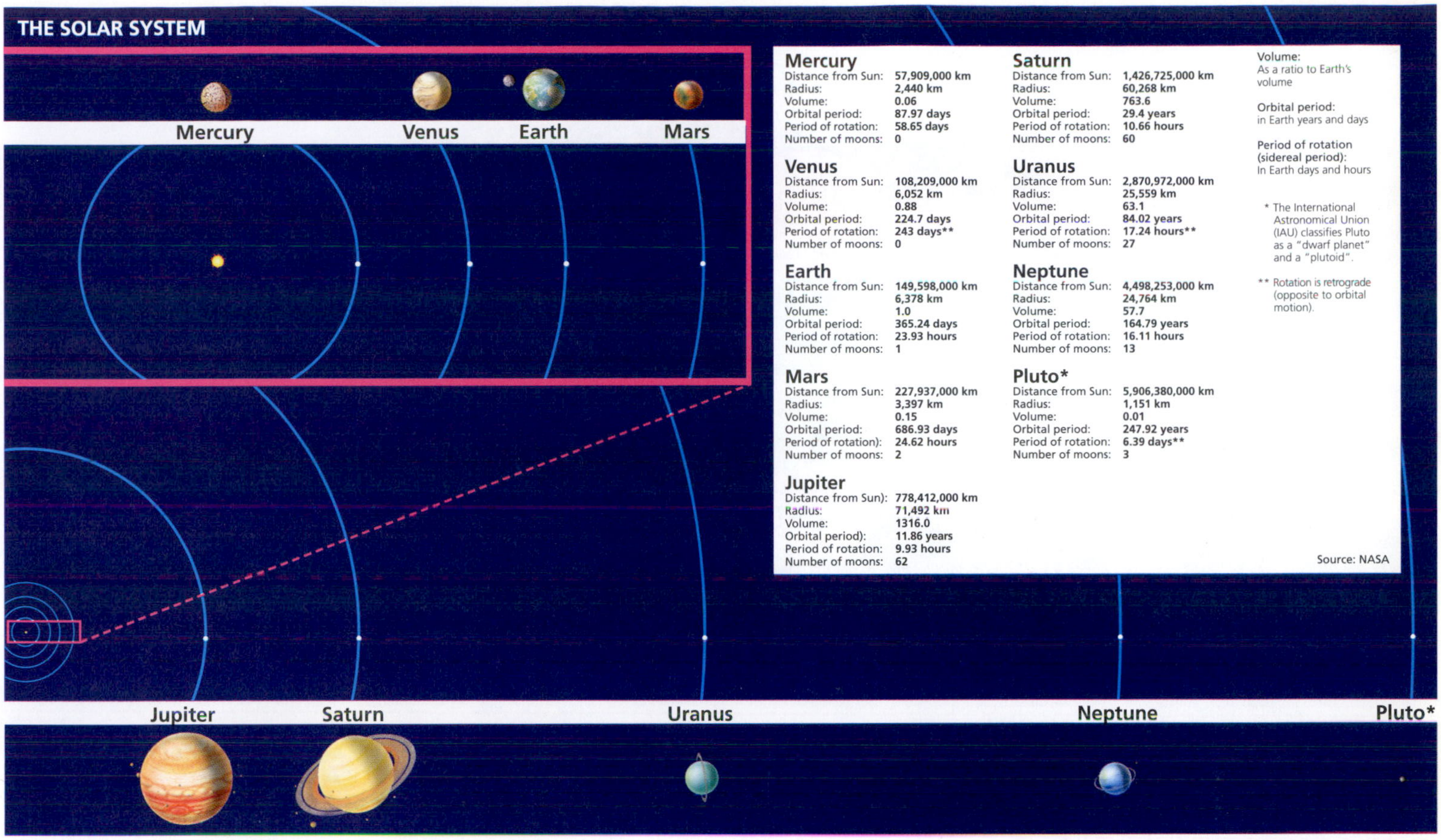

Mercury   Venus   Earth   Mars

Mercury
Distance from Sun:	57,909,000 km
Radius:	2,440 km
Volume:	0.06
Orbital period:	87.97 days
Period of rotation:	58.65 days
Number of moons:	0

Venus
Distance from Sun:	108,209,000 km
Radius:	6,052 km
Volume:	0.88
Orbital period:	224.7 days
Period of rotation:	243 days**
Number of moons:	0

Earth
Distance from Sun:	149,598,000 km
Radius:	6,378 km
Volume:	1.0
Orbital period:	365.24 days
Period of rotation:	23.93 hours
Number of moons:	1

Mars
Distance from Sun:	227,937,000 km
Radius:	3,397 km
Volume:	0.15
Orbital period:	686.93 days
Period of rotation):	24.62 hours
Number of moons:	2

Jupiter
Distance from Sun):	778,412,000 km
Radius:	71,492 km
Volume:	1316.0
Orbital period):	11.86 years
Period of rotation:	9.93 hours
Number of moons:	62

Saturn
Distance from Sun:	1,426,725,000 km
Radius:	60,268 km
Volume:	763.6
Orbital period:	29.4 years
Period of rotation:	10.66 hours
Number of moons:	60

Uranus
Distance from Sun:	2,870,972,000 km
Radius:	25,559 km
Volume:	63.1
Orbital period:	84.02 years
Period of rotation:	17.24 hours**
Number of moons:	27

Neptune
Distance from Sun:	4,498,253,000 km
Radius:	24,764 km
Volume:	57.7
Orbital period:	164.79 years
Period of rotation:	16.11 hours
Number of moons:	13

Pluto*
Distance from Sun:	5,906,380,000 km
Radius:	1,151 km
Volume:	0.01
Orbital period:	247.92 years
Period of rotation:	6.39 days**
Number of moons:	3

Volume:
As a ratio to Earth's
volume

Orbital period:
in Earth years and days

Period of rotation
(sidereal period):
In Earth days and hours

* The International
Astronomical Union
(IAU) classifies Pluto
as a "dwarf planet"
and a "plutoid".

** Rotation is retrograde
(opposite to orbital
motion).

Source: NASA

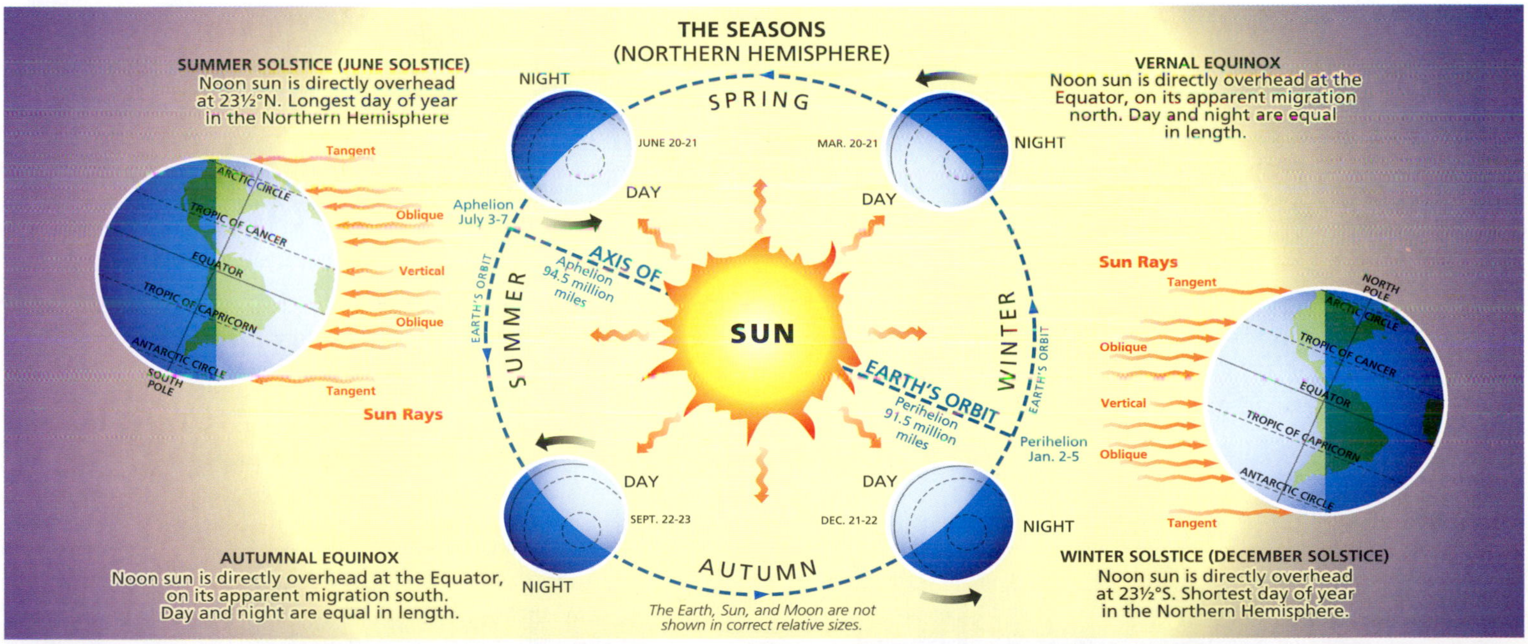

Jupiter   Saturn   Uranus   Neptune   Pluto*

THE SEASONS
(NORTHERN HEMISPHERE)

SUMMER SOLSTICE (JUNE SOLSTICE)
Noon sun is directly overhead
at 23½°N. Longest day of year
in the Northern Hemisphere

VERNAL EQUINOX
Noon sun is directly overhead at the
Equator, on its apparent migration
north. Day and night are equal
in length.

NIGHT — SPRING — NIGHT
DAY — DAY
JUNE 20-21 — MAR. 20-21

Aphelion
July 3-7

AXIS OF

EARTH'S ORBIT

Aphelion
94.5 million
miles

SUN

Tangent
Oblique
Vertical
Oblique
Tangent

ARCTIC CIRCLE
TROPIC OF CANCER
EQUATOR
TROPIC OF CAPRICORN
ANTARCTIC CIRCLE
SOUTH POLE

Sun Rays

SUMMER

WINTER

EARTH'S ORBIT
Perihelion
91.5 million
miles

Perihelion
Jan. 2-5

Sun Rays
Tangent
Oblique
Vertical
Oblique
Tangent

NORTH POLE
ARCTIC CIRCLE
TROPIC OF CANCER
EQUATOR
TROPIC OF CAPRICORN
ANTARCTIC CIRCLE

DAY — DAY
SEPT. 22-23 — DEC. 21-22
NIGHT — AUTUMN — NIGHT

AUTUMNAL EQUINOX
Noon sun is directly overhead at the Equator,
on its apparent migration south.
Day and night are equal in length.

WINTER SOLSTICE (DECEMBER SOLSTICE)
Noon sun is directly overhead
at 23½°S. Shortest day of year
in the Northern Hemisphere.

The Earth, Sun, and Moon are not
shown in correct relative sizes.

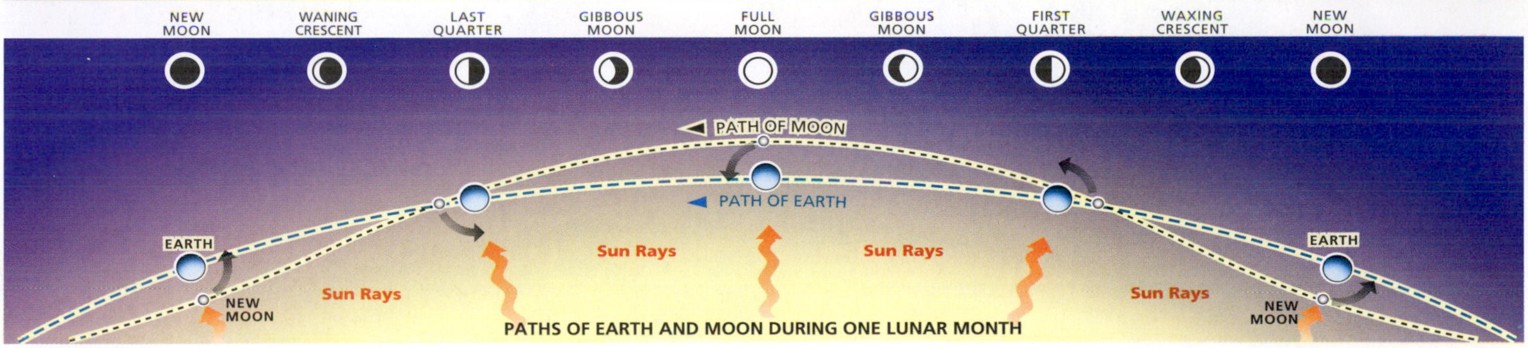

NEW MOON	WANING CRESCENT	LAST QUARTER	GIBBOUS MOON	FULL MOON	GIBBOUS MOON	FIRST QUARTER	WAXING CRESCENT	NEW MOON

PATH OF MOON
PATH OF EARTH

EARTH

NEW MOON

Sun Rays   Sun Rays   Sun Rays

EARTH

NEW MOON

Sun Rays

PATHS OF EARTH AND MOON DURING ONE LUNAR MONTH

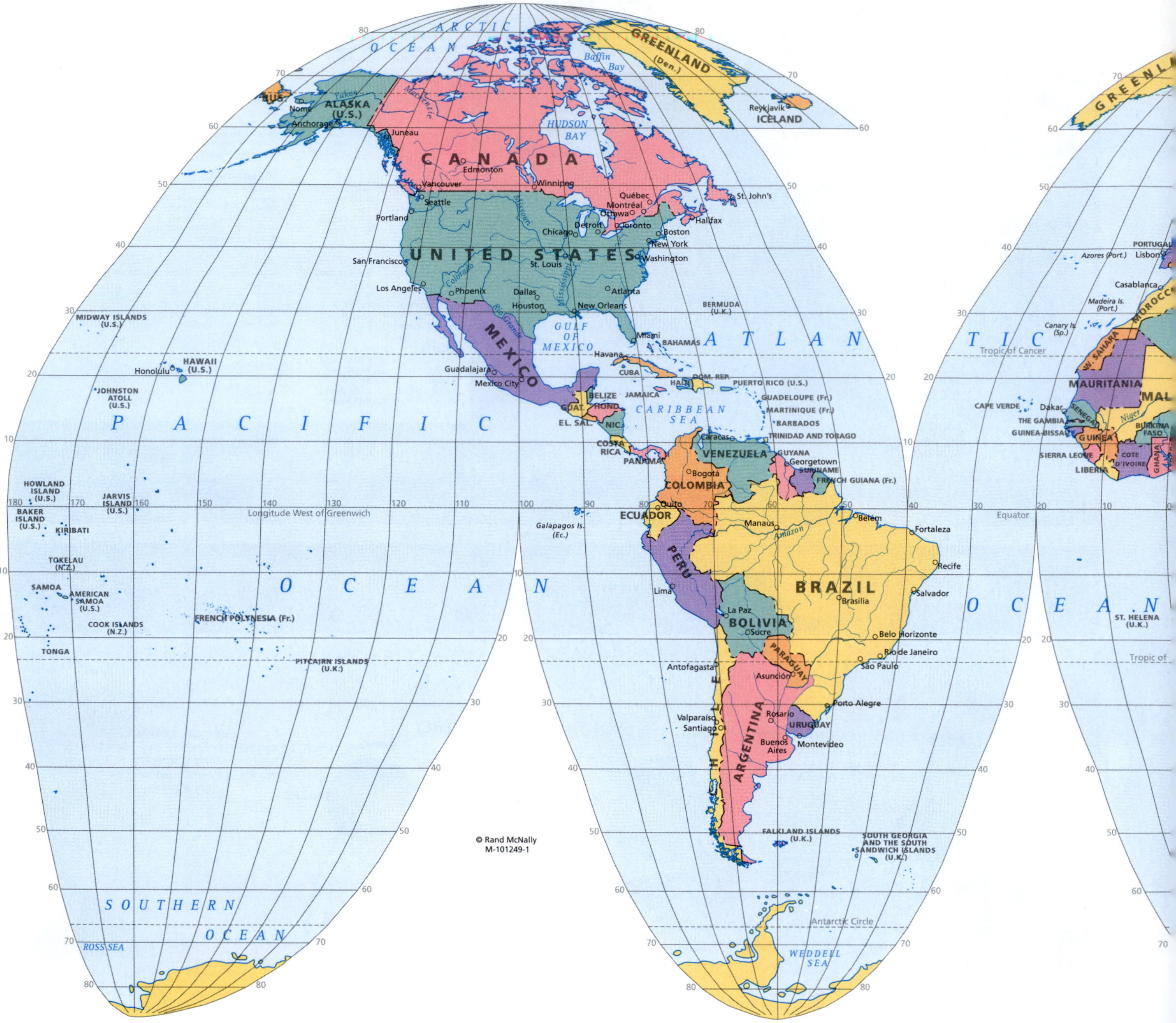

ARCTIC OCEAN · Baffin Bay · GREENLAND (Den.) · Reykjavík · ICELAND · ALASKA (U.S.) · Nome · Anchorage · Juneau · CANADA · Edmonton · HUDSON BAY · Vancouver · Seattle · Winnipeg · Québec · Montréal · Ottawa · St. John's · Portland · Chicago · Detroit · Toronto · Halifax · UNITED STATES · Boston · New York · Washington · San Francisco · St. Louis · ATLANTIC · Los Angeles · Phoenix · Dallas · Atlanta · BERMUDA (U.K.) · Houston · New Orleans · MEXICO · GULF OF MEXICO · Miami · BAHAMAS · Havana · CUBA · HAITI · DOM. REP. · PUERTO RICO (U.S.) · Guadalajara · Mexico City · BELIZE · JAMAICA · GUADELOUPE (Fr.) · GUAT. · HOND. · CARIBBEAN SEA · MARTINIQUE (Fr.) · EL SAL. · NIC. · BARBADOS · COSTA RICA · PANAMA · TRINIDAD AND TOBAGO · Caracas · VENEZUELA · GUYANA · Georgetown · SURINAME · FRENCH GUIANA (Fr.) · COLOMBIA · Bogotá · ECUADOR · Quito · Manaus · Belém · Fortaleza · PERU · Amazon · BRAZIL · Recife · Lima · Brasília · Salvador · BOLIVIA · La Paz · Sucre · Belo Horizonte · PARAGUAY · Rio de Janeiro · Antofagasta · Asunción · São Paulo · Valparaíso · Rosario · Porto Alegre · Santiago · ARGENTINA · URUGUAY · Buenos Aires · Montevideo · FALKLAND ISLANDS (U.K.) · SOUTH GEORGIA AND THE SOUTH SANDWICH ISLANDS (U.K.) · SOUTHERN OCEAN · ROSS SEA · WEDDELL SEA · Antarctic Circle

PACIFIC OCEAN · MIDWAY ISLANDS (U.S.) · HAWAII (U.S.) · Honolulu · JOHNSTON ATOLL (U.S.) · Tropic of Cancer · HOWLAND ISLAND (U.S.) · BAKER ISLAND (U.S.) · KIRIBATI · JARVIS ISLAND (U.S.) · Longitude West of Greenwich · Galápagos Is. (Ec.) · Equator · TOKELAU (N.Z.) · SAMOA · AMERICAN SAMOA (U.S.) · COOK ISLANDS (N.Z.) · FRENCH POLYNESIA (Fr.) · TONGA · PITCAIRN ISLANDS (U.K.)

GREENLAND · PORTUGAL · Lisbon · Azores (Port.) · Casablanca · Madeira Is. (Port.) · MOROCCO · Canary Is. (Sp.) · W. SAHARA · MAURITANIA · MALI · CAPE VERDE · Dakar · SENEGAL · Niger · THE GAMBIA · BURKINA FASO · GUINEA-BISSAU · GUINEA · SIERRA LEONE · CÔTE D'IVOIRE · GHANA · LIBERIA · ATLANTIC OCEAN · ST. HELENA (U.K.) · Tropic of Capricorn

© Rand McNally · M-101249-1

Comparative Land Areas Includes land and inland water. Numbers indicate thousands of square kilometers.

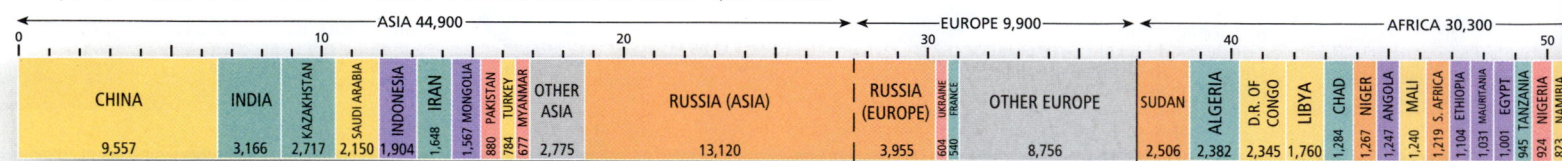

ASIA 44,900 — EUROPE 9,900 — AFRICA 30,300

CHINA	INDIA	KAZAKHSTAN	SAUDI ARABIA	INDONESIA	IRAN	MONGOLIA	PAKISTAN	TURKEY	MYANMAR	OTHER ASIA	RUSSIA (ASIA)	RUSSIA (EUROPE)	UKRAINE	FRANCE	OTHER EUROPE	SUDAN	ALGERIA	D.R. OF CONGO	LIBYA	CHAD	NIGER	ANGOLA	MALI	S. AFRICA	ETHIOPIA	MAURITANIA	EGYPT	TANZANIA	NIGERIA	NAMIBIA
9,557	3,166	2,717	2,150	1,904	1,648	1,567	880	784	677	2,775	13,120	3,955	604	540	8,756	2,506	2,382	2,345	1,760	1,284	1,267	1,247	1,240	1,219	1,104	1,031	1,001	945	924	823

Comparative Populations Estimated population as of January 1, 2009. Numbers indicate millions of people.

ASIA 4,078.8

CHINA	INDIA	INDONESIA	PAKISTAN	BANGLADESH	JAPAN	PHILIPPINES	VIETNAM	TURKEY
1,341.8	1,157.1	238.9	174.5	155.0	127.2	97.0	86.5	76.

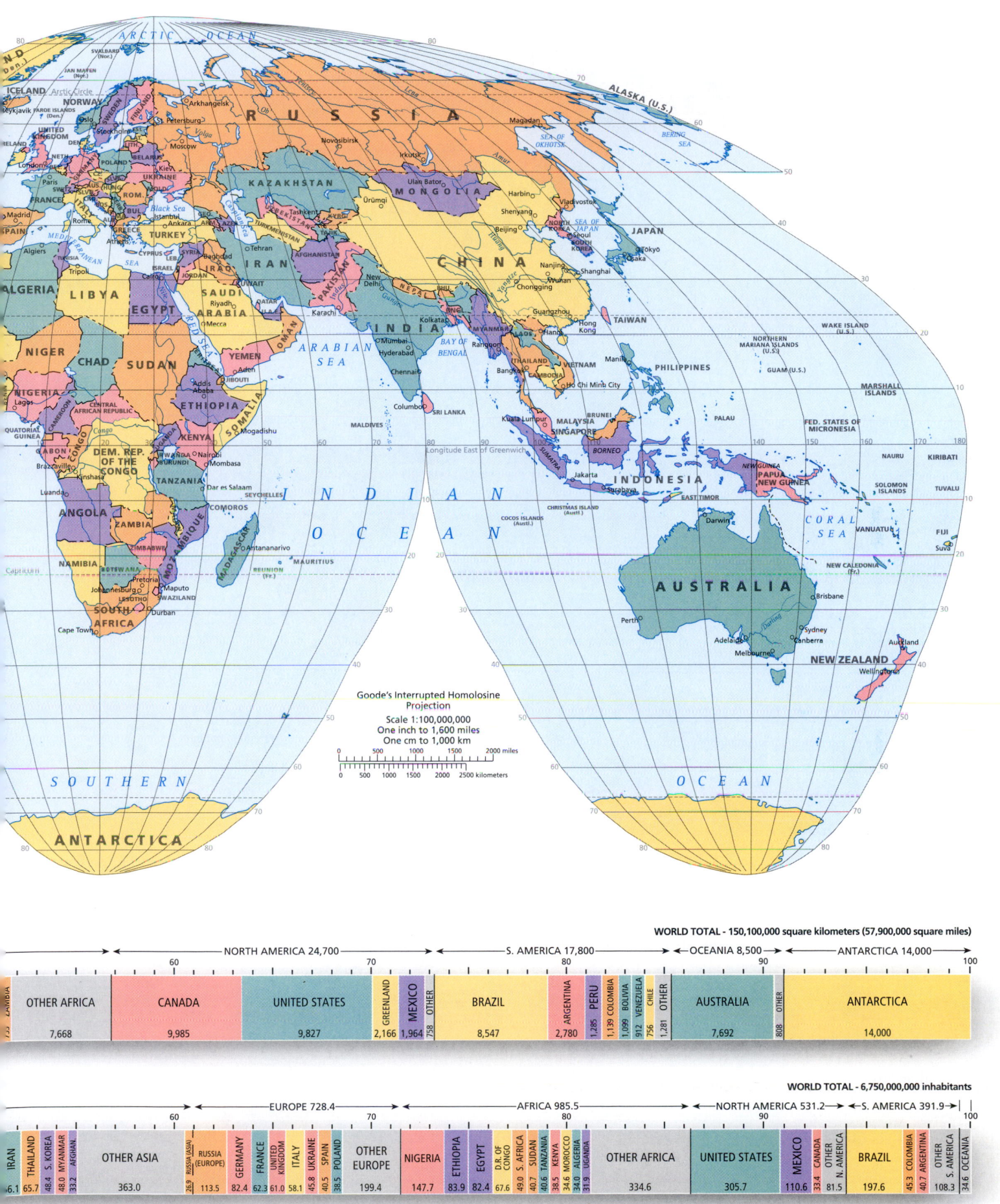

ARCTIC OCEAN

ICELAND · Arctic Circle · ALASKA (U.S.)

NORWAY · RUSSIA

SWEDEN · FINLAND

UNITED KINGDOM · DEN. · POLAND · BELARUS

London · Paris · FRANCE · UKRAINE · KAZAKHSTAN · MONGOLIA · Harbin · Vladivostok · JAPAN

Madrid · Rome · TURKEY · Ankara · UZBEKISTAN · KYRGY · Ürümqi · Beijing · Shenyang · SOUTH KOREA · Seoul · Tokyo · Osaka

SPAIN · GREECE · Athens · CYPRUS · SYRIA · IRAQ · IRAN · AFGHANISTAN · CHINA · Nanjing · Shanghai

ALGERIA · LIBYA · EGYPT · SAUDI ARABIA · Riyadh · Mecca · OMAN · PAKISTAN · New Delhi · NEPAL · Chongqing · Guangzhou · Hong Kong · TAIWAN

NIGER · CHAD · SUDAN · YEMEN · INDIA · Mumbai · Hyderabad · Chennai · MYANMAR · Rangoon · LAOS · Hanoi · WAKE ISLAND (U.S.)

NIGERIA · ETHIOPIA · SOMALIA · Mogadishu · ARABIAN SEA · BAY OF BENGAL · THAILAND · Bangkok · CAMBODIA · VIETNAM · Ho Chi Minh City · Manila · PHILIPPINES · GUAM (U.S.) · NORTHERN MARIANA ISLANDS (U.S.) · MARSHALL ISLANDS

DEM. REP. OF THE CONGO · KENYA · Nairobi · MALDIVES · SRI LANKA · Columbo · MALAYSIA · Kuala Lumpur · SINGAPORE · BRUNEI · PALAU · FED. STATES OF MICRONESIA · NAURU · KIRIBATI

ANGOLA · ZAMBIA · TANZANIA · Dar es Salaam · COMOROS · SEYCHELLES · INDIAN OCEAN · SUMATRA · BORNEO · INDONESIA · Jakarta · Surabaya · EAST TIMOR · PAPUA NEW GUINEA · SOLOMON ISLANDS · TUVALU

NAMIBIA · BOTSWANA · ZIMBABWE · MOZAMBIQUE · MADAGASCAR · Antananarivo · MAURITIUS · RÉUNION (Fr.) · COCOS ISLANDS (Austl.) · CHRISTMAS ISLAND (Austl.) · Darwin · CORAL SEA · VANUATU · FIJI · Suva · NEW CALEDONIA (Fr.)

SOUTH AFRICA · Cape Town · Durban · Johannesburg · Pretoria · LESOTHO · SWAZILAND · Maputo · AUSTRALIA · Brisbane · Perth · Adelaide · Sydney · Canberra · Melbourne · Auckland · NEW ZEALAND · Wellington

SOUTHERN OCEAN

Goode's Interrupted Homolosine Projection
Scale 1:100,000,000
One inch to 1,600 miles
One cm to 1,000 km

0 500 1000 1500 2000 miles

0 500 1000 1500 2000 2500 kilometers

ANTARCTICA

WORLD TOTAL - 150,100,000 square kilometers (57,900,000 square miles)

NORTH AMERICA 24,700 — S. AMERICA 17,800 — OCEANIA 8,500 — ANTARCTICA 14,000

ZAMBIA	OTHER AFRICA	CANADA	UNITED STATES	GREENLAND	MEXICO	OTHER	BRAZIL	ARGENTINA	PERU	COLOMBIA	BOLIVIA	VENEZUELA	CHILE	OTHER	AUSTRALIA	OTHER	ANTARCTICA
	7,668	9,985	9,827	2,166	1,964	758	8,547	2,780	1,285	1,139	1,099	912	756	1,281	7,692	808	14,000

WORLD TOTAL - 6,750,000,000 inhabitants

EUROPE 728.4 — AFRICA 985.5 — NORTH AMERICA 531.2 — S. AMERICA 391.9

IRAN	THAILAND	S. KOREA	MYANMAR	AFGHAN.	OTHER ASIA	RUSSIA (ASIA)	RUSSIA (EUROPE)	GERMANY	FRANCE	UNITED KINGDOM	ITALY	UKRAINE	SPAIN	POLAND	OTHER EUROPE	NIGERIA	ETHIOPIA	EGYPT	D.R. OF CONGO	S. AFRICA	SUDAN	TANZANIA	KENYA	MOROCCO	ALGERIA	UGANDA	OTHER AFRICA	UNITED STATES	MEXICO	CANADA	OTHER N. AMERICA	BRAZIL	COLOMBIA	ARGENTINA	OTHER S. AMERICA	OCEANIA
6.1	65.7	48.4	48.0	33.2	363.0	26.9	113.5	82.4	62.3	61.0	58.1	45.8	40.5	38.5	199.4	147.7	83.9	82.4	67.6	49.0	40.7	40.6	38.5	34.6	34.0	31.9	334.6	305.7	110.6	33.4	81.5	197.6	45.3	40.7	108.3	34.6

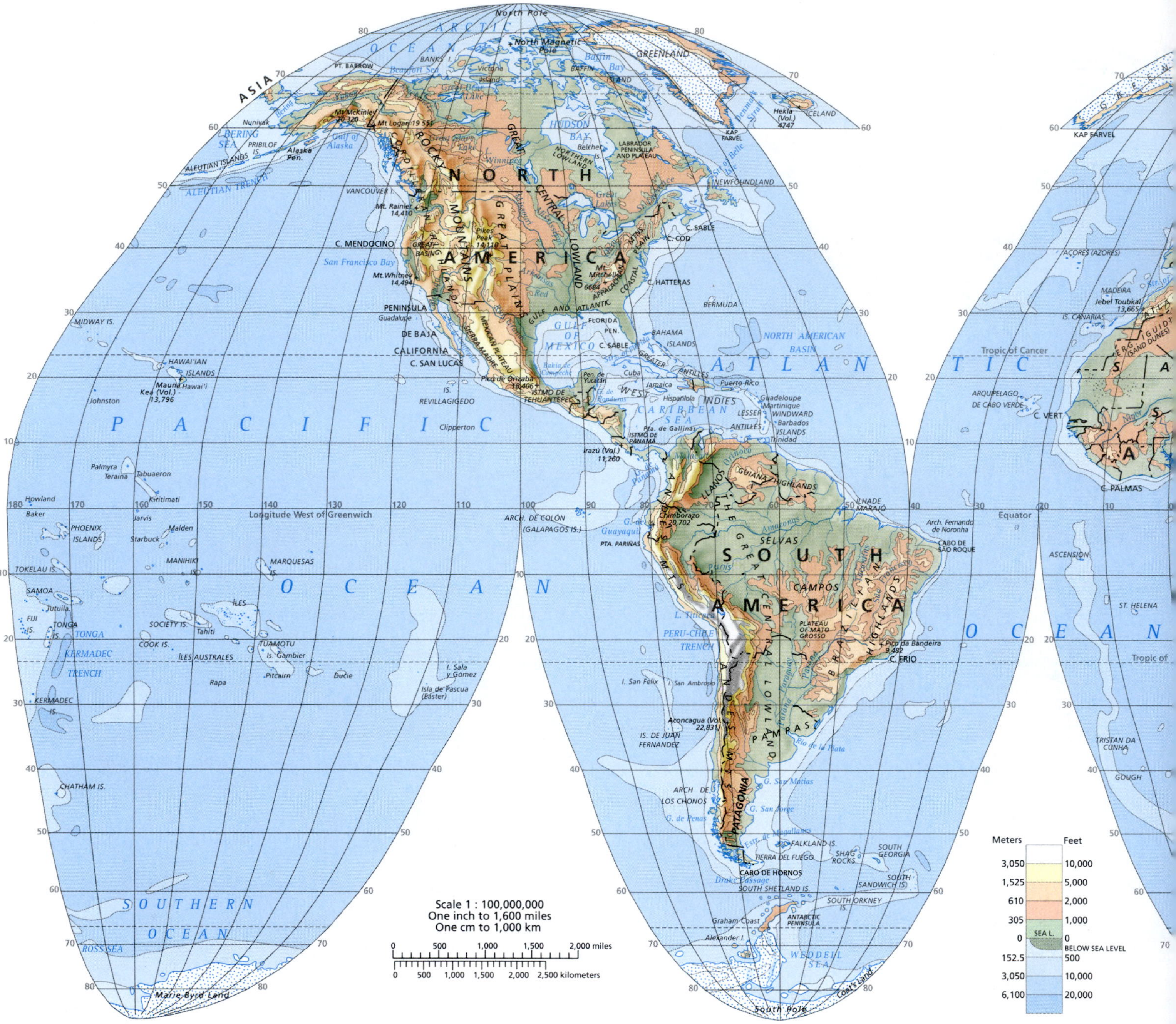

Scale 1 : 100,000,000
One inch to 1,600 miles
One cm to 1,000 km

Meters		Feet
3,050		10,000
1,525		5,000
610		2,000
305		1,000
0	SEA L.	0
152.5	BELOW SEA LEVEL	500
3,050		10,000
6,100		20,000

Land Elevations in Profile

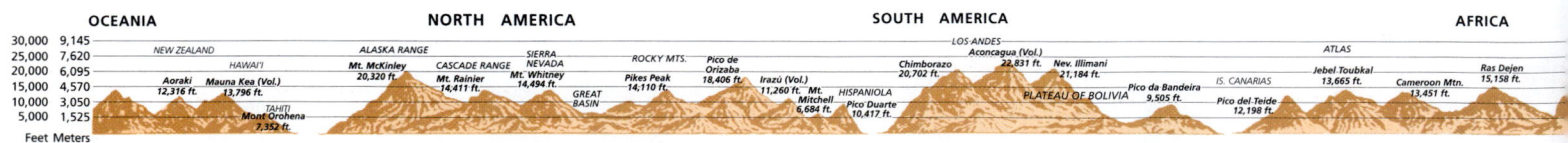

Ocean Depths in Profile

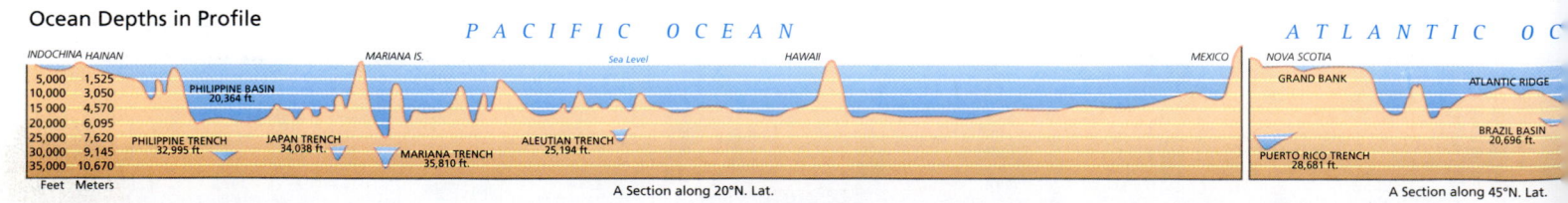

A Section along 20°N. Lat.

A Section along 45°N. Lat.

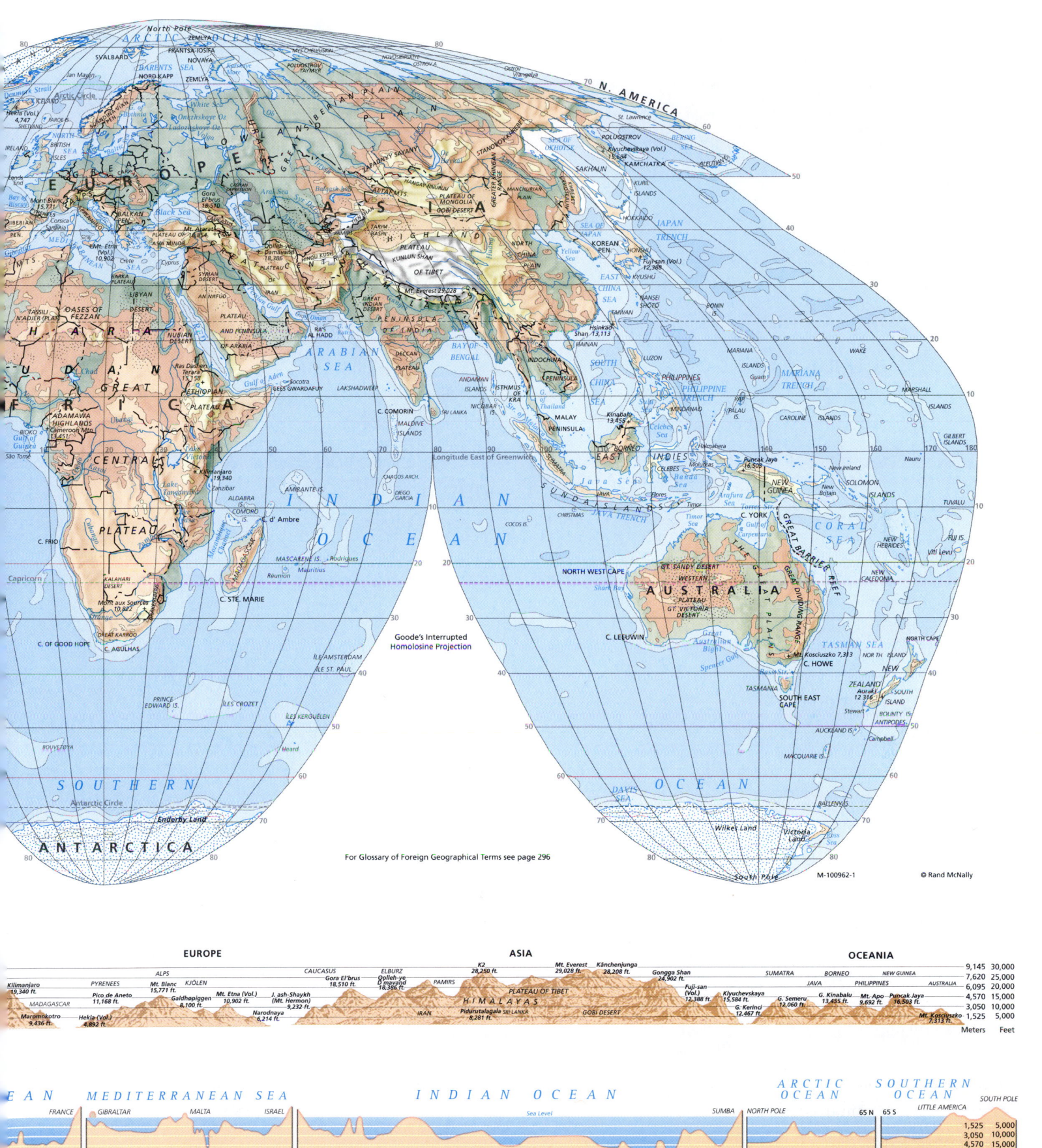

Goode's Interrupted
Homolosine Projection

For Glossary of Foreign Geographical Terms see page 296

M-100962-1   © Rand McNally

EVOLUTION OF THE CONTINENTS

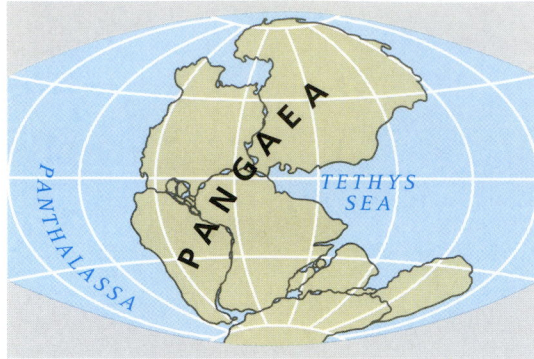

225 million years ago
The supercontinent of Pangaea exists and Panthalassa forms the ancestral ocean. Tethys Sea separates Eurasia and Africa.

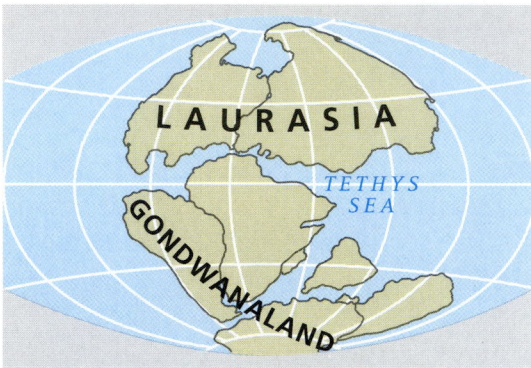

180 million years ago
Pangaea splits, Laurasia drifts north. Gondwanaland breaks into South America/Africa, India, and Australia/Antarctica.

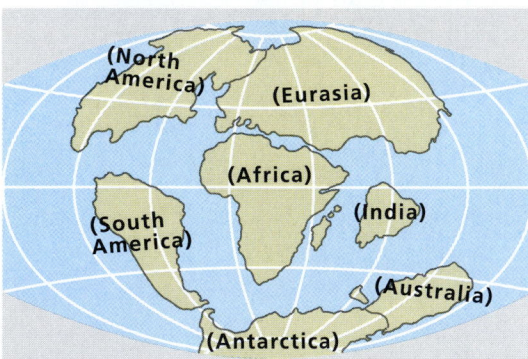

65 million years ago
Ocean basins take shape as South America and India move from Africa and the Tethys Sea closes to form the Mediterranean Sea.

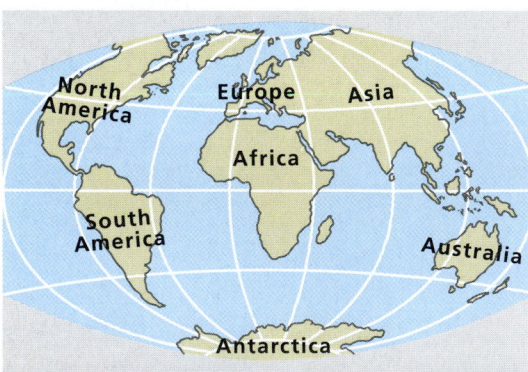

The present day
India has merged with Asia, Australia is free of Antarctica, and North America is free of Eurasia.

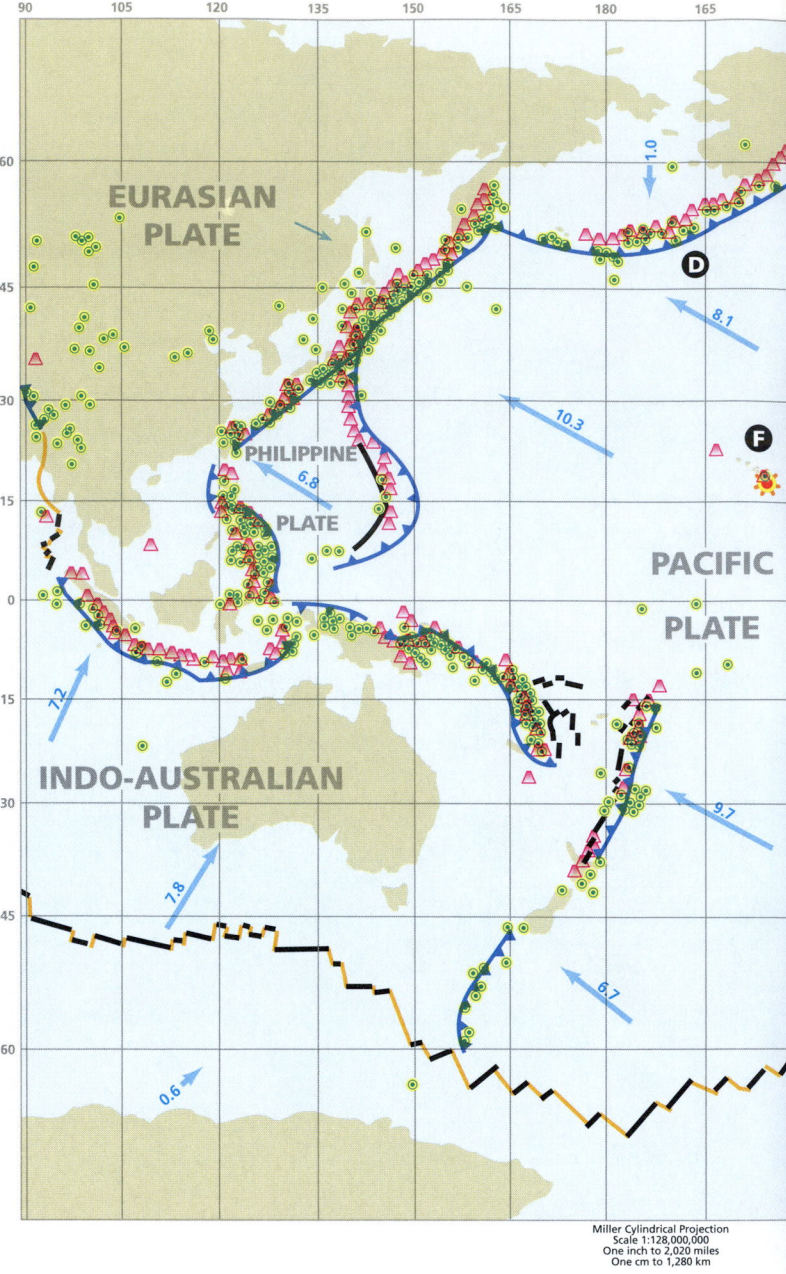

Miller Cylindrical Projection
Scale 1:128,000,000
One inch to 2,020 miles
One cm to 1,280 km

PLATE TECTONICS

Types of plate boundaries
See text at right for explanation

—— Divergent

▲▲▲ Convergent

—— Transform

Other map symbols

→ Direction of plate movement

6.7 → Length of arrow is proportional to the amount of plate movement (number indicates centimeters of movement per year)

⊙ Earthquake of magnitude 7.5 and above (from 10 A.D. to the present)

△ Volcano (eruption since 1900)

 Selected hot spots

Ⓐ Key to text descriptions and diagrams

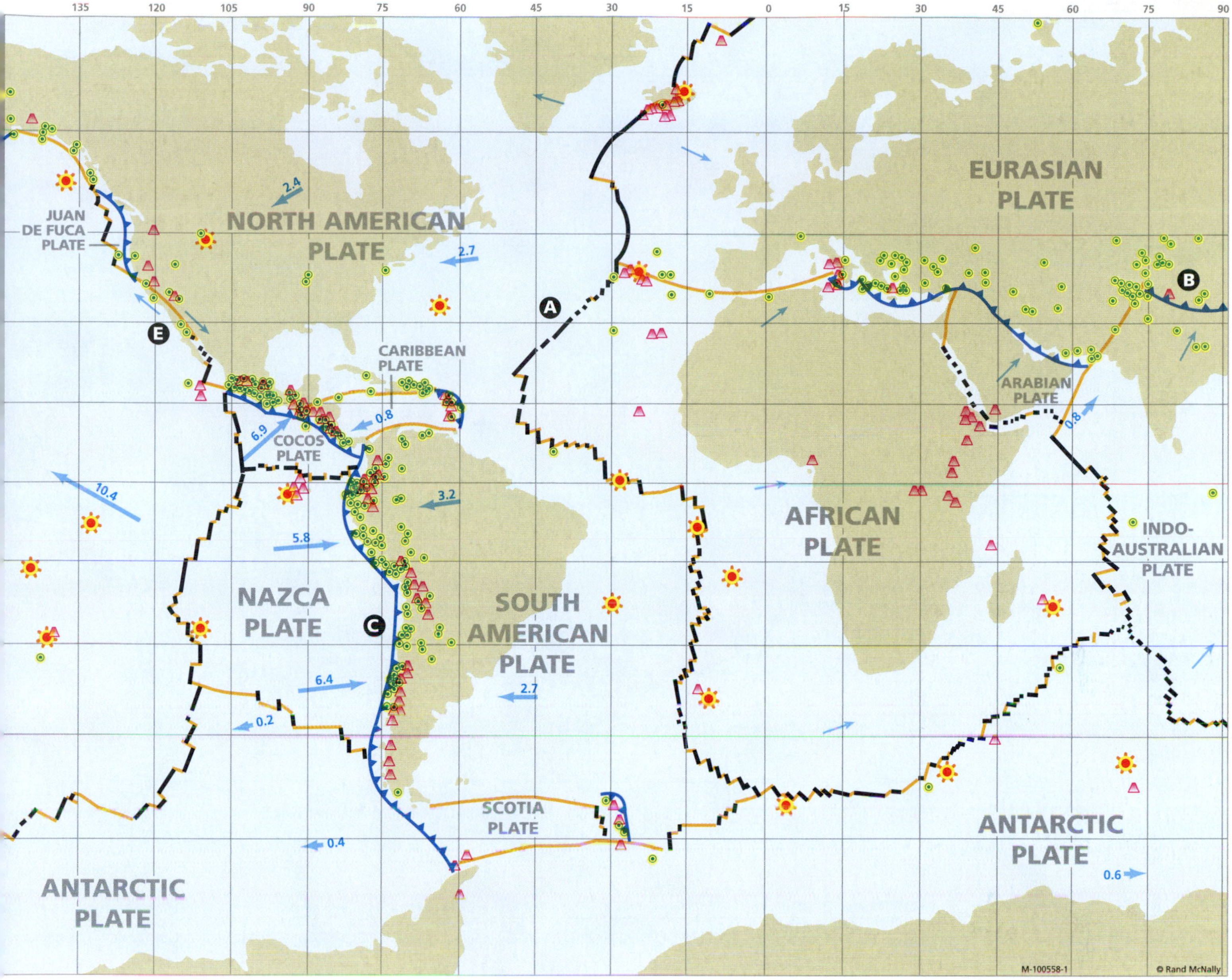

Map labels

EURASIAN PLATE

NORTH AMERICAN PLATE

JUAN DE FUCA PLATE

CARIBBEAN PLATE

COCOS PLATE

NAZCA PLATE

SOUTH AMERICAN PLATE

AFRICAN PLATE

ARABIAN PLATE

INDO-AUSTRALIAN PLATE

ANTARCTIC PLATE

ANTARCTIC PLATE

SCOTIA PLATE

2.4 2.7 0.8 6.9 10.4 5.8 3.2 6.4 0.2 2.7 0.4 0.8 0.6

M-100558-1 © Rand McNally

Body text

Plate tectonic theory describes the motions of the lithosphere, the outer surface of which forms the Earth's crust. The theory originated with scientist Alfred Wegener's work on continental drift in the early part of the 20th century. According to plate tectonic theory, the lithosphere is composed of distinct plates that move relative to each other as a result of convection currents deep within the Earth's mantle. The largest of these plates and their movements are shown on the map above.

There are three main types of plate boundaries.

Divergent plate boundaries occur where two adjacent plates move away from each other. As the plates separate, upwelling magma from the mantle solidifies, and new crust is formed. (See diagram to the right.) These boundaries frequently make up oceanic ridge zones, such as the Mid-Atlantic Ridge (symbol A on map above). This spreading explains why North and South America have separated from Eurasia and Africa over time, as shown on the map series to the left. The Mid-Atlantic Ridge is actually part of a much larger subaqueous divergent boundary system that encircles the Earth.

Convergent plate boundaries occur where two adjacent plates collide with one another. When two continental plates collide, the resulting compression of lithospheric material causes large mountain ranges to form. The Himalayas, for example, were formed by the collision of the Eurasian and Indo-Australian Plates (symbol B on map above).

In other cases one plate is forced (subducted) under the other and the lithospheric material from the descending plate is recycled within the mantle. These areas are called **subduction zones**.

Subduction zones occur when a continental plate collides with an oceanic plate. An example occurs along the west coast of South America

where the Nazca Plate is being subducted under the South American Plate, creating the long, deep Peru-Chile trench and the Andes mountain chain (symbol C on map above). This area is part of a much larger ring of convergent plate boundaries circling the Pacific and known as the Ring of Fire. Volcanoes and earthquakes are common features in this region.

Subduction zones can also occur when two oceanic plates collide. Intense volcanic activity in these areas eventually results in the formation of long, volcanic island chains. (See diagram to the right.) The Aleutian Islands of Alaska are one example (symbol D on map above).

Transform boundaries occur when two plates slide laterally past each other with no divergence or convergence. Commonly they offset the active spreading ridges of divergent boundaries on the ocean floor. The San Andreas fault zone of California is an example of a terrestrial transform boundary (symbol E on map above).

Volcanoes and earthquakes do not occur only at plate boundaries. At certain isolated **hot spots**, upwelling magma rises to the surface to create tall volcanoes. Over time, as the plate moves, long islands chains are formed. The Hawai'ian Islands are one such example (symbol F on map above).

The rate of movement of tectonic plates is very slow, on the order of several centimeters per year. Over geological time, these small movements accumulate and cause fragmentation and reformation of continental land masses, as shown in the map series to the left. The process is still underway, which implies that the arrangement of the continents millions of years from now will be quite different from what it is today.

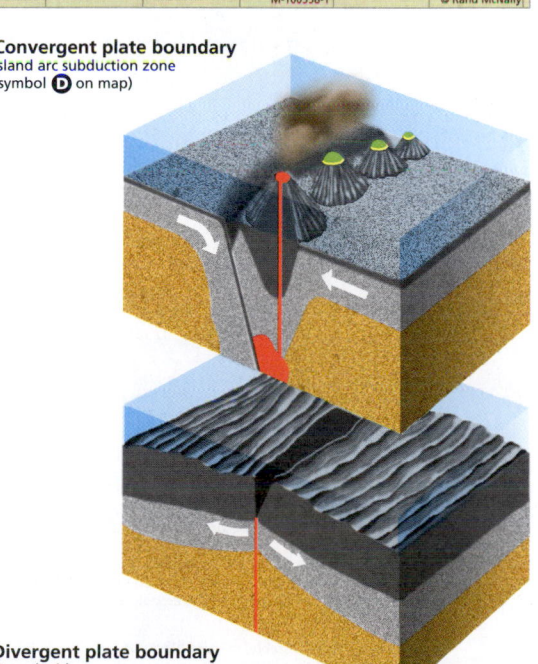

Convergent plate boundary
Island arc subduction zone
(symbol D on map)

Divergent plate boundary
Oceanic ridge
(symbol A on map)

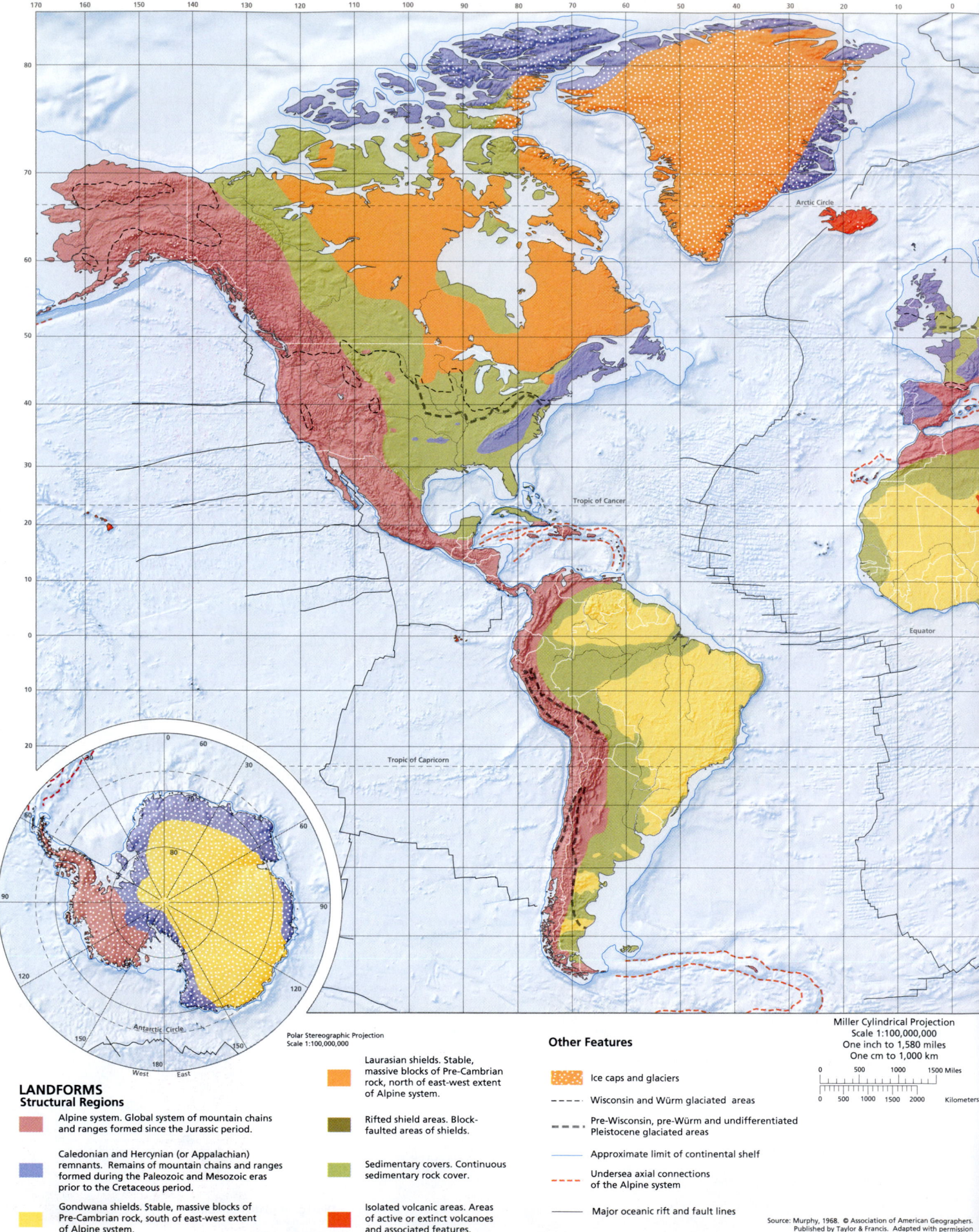

LANDFORMS
Structural Regions

Alpine system. Global system of mountain chains and ranges formed since the Jurassic period.

Caledonian and Hercynian (or Appalachian) remnants. Remains of mountain chains and ranges formed during the Paleozoic and Mesozoic eras prior to the Cretaceous period.

Gondwana shields. Stable, massive blocks of Pre-Cambrian rock, south of east-west extent of Alpine system.

Laurasian shields. Stable, massive blocks of Pre-Cambrian rock, north of east-west extent of Alpine system.

Rifted shield areas. Block-faulted areas of shields.

Sedimentary covers. Continuous sedimentary rock cover.

Isolated volcanic areas. Areas of active or extinct volcanoes and associated features.

Other Features

Ice caps and glaciers

- - - - **Wisconsin and Würm glaciated areas**

- - - - **Pre-Wisconsin, pre-Würm and undifferentiated Pleistocene glaciated areas**

——— **Approximate limit of continental shelf**

- - - - **Undersea axial connections of the Alpine system**

——— **Major oceanic rift and fault lines**

Polar Stereographic Projection
Scale 1:100,000,000

Miller Cylindrical Projection
Scale 1:100,000,000
One inch to 1,580 miles
One cm to 1,000 km

Source: Murphy, 1968. © Association of American Geographers. Published by Taylor & Francis. Adapted with permission of the Association of American Geographers.

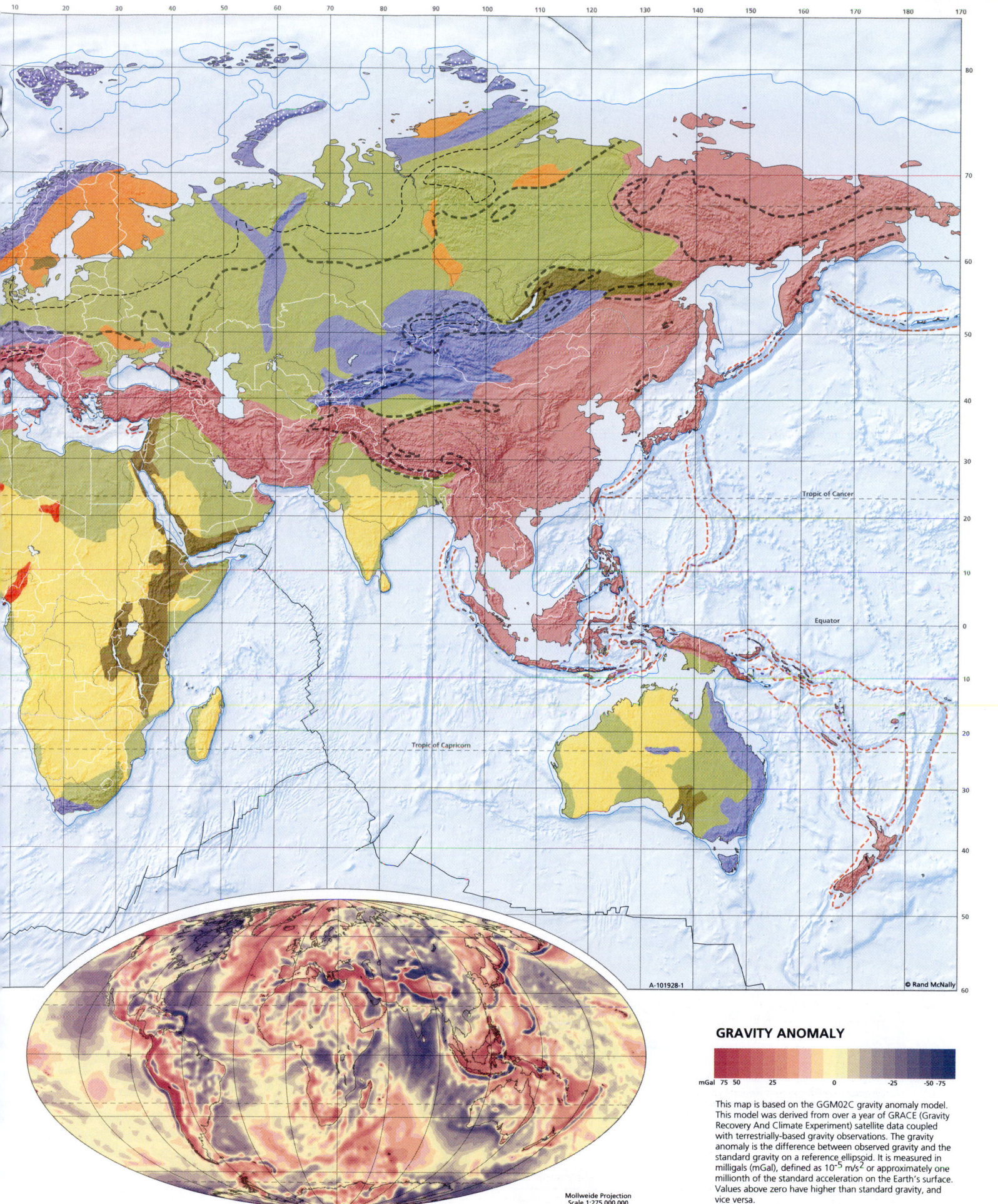

GRAVITY ANOMALY

mGal 75 50   25   0   -25   -50 -75

This map is based on the GGM02C gravity anomaly model.
This model was derived from over a year of GRACE (Gravity
Recovery And Climate Experiment) satellite data coupled
with terrestrially-based gravity observations. The gravity
anomaly is the difference between observed gravity and the
standard gravity on a reference ellipsoid. It is measured in
milligals (mGal), defined as 10^{-5} m/s^2 or approximately one
millionth of the standard acceleration on the Earth's surface.
Values above zero have higher than standard gravity, and
vice versa.

Mollweide Projection
Scale 1:275,000,000
Source: Tapley et al., 2005

A-101928-1

© Rand McNally

Robinson Projection
Scale 1:73,000,000
One inch to 1,200 miles
One cm to 730 km

M-100932-1 © Rand McNally

Robinson Projection
Scale 1:73,000,000
One inch to 1,200 miles
One cm to 730 km

© Rand McNally   M-100927-1

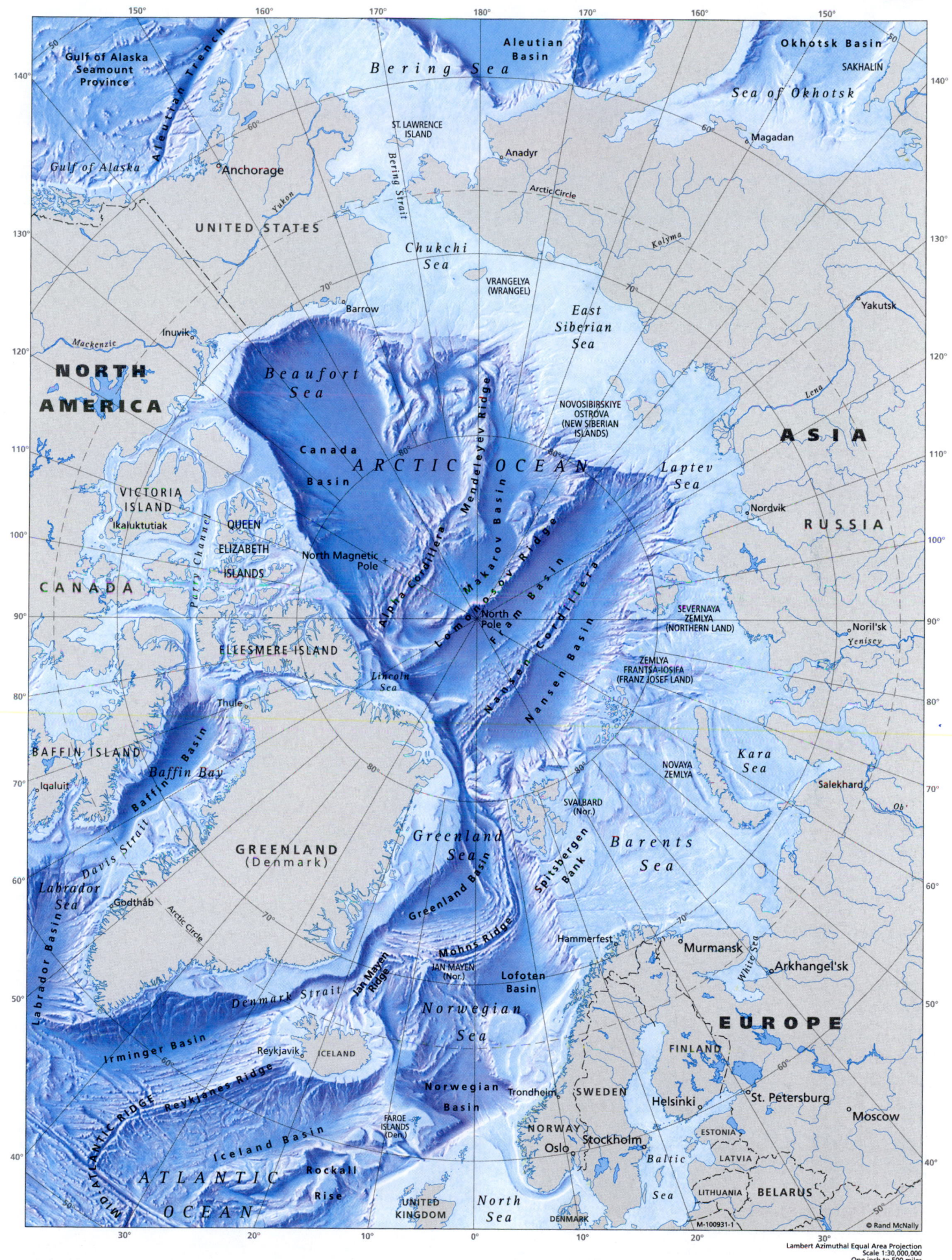

Gulf of Alaska Seamount Province

Aleutian Trench

Bering Sea

Aleutian Basin

Okhotsk Basin

SAKHALIN

Sea of Okhotsk

Gulf of Alaska

°Anchorage

ST. LAWRENCE ISLAND

Magadan

Anadyr

Arctic Circle

Kolyma

°Yakutsk

UNITED STATES

Chukchi Sea

VRANGELYA (WRANGEL)

East Siberian Sea

Lena

°Barrow

NOVOSIBIRSKIYE OSTROVA (NEW SIBERIAN ISLANDS)

°Inuvik

Beaufort Sea

Laptev Sea

NORTH AMERICA

Mackenzie

Canada Basin

A R C T I C   O C E A N

A S I A

Nordvik°

Mendeleyev Ridge

VICTORIA ISLAND

°Ikaluktutiak

QUEEN

Makarov Basin

Makarov Basin

Fram Basin

°Noril'sk

R U S S I A

Parry Channel

ELIZABETH

Alpha Cordillera

Lomonosov Ridge

SEVERNAYA ZEMLYA (NORTHERN LAND)

North Magnetic Pole

ISLANDS

Yenisey

C A N A D A

North Pole

Nansen Cordillera

ELLESMERE ISLAND

Fram

Nansen Basin

ZEMLYA FRANTSA-IOSIFA (FRANZ JOSEF LAND)

Lincoln Sea

°Thule

Kara Sea

BAFFIN ISLAND

Baffin Basin

NOVAYA ZEMLYA

Salekhard°

°Iqaluit

Baffin Bay

Baffin

Davis Strait

SVALBARD (Nor.)

Barents Sea

Labrador Sea

GREENLAND (Denmark)

Greenland Sea

Spitsbergen Bank

°Godthåb

Greenland Basin

Murmansk°

Arctic Circle

Hammerfest°

White Sea

°Arkhangel'sk

Irminger Basin

Jan Mayen Ridge

Mohns Ridge

JAN MAYEN (Nor.)

Lofoten Basin

E U R O P E

Denmark Strait

Norwegian Sea

FINLAND

°Reykjavik   ICELAND

Trondheim°

SWEDEN

Helsinki°

°St. Petersburg

Reykjanes Ridge

Norwegian Basin

NORWAY

ESTONIA

°Moscow

FAROE ISLANDS (Den.)

Oslo°

Stockholm°

Baltic

LATVIA

Iceland Basin

Rockall Rise

LITHUANIA

BELARUS

ATLANTIC OCEAN

UNITED KINGDOM

North Sea

DENMARK

Sea

MID-ATLANTIC RIDGE

M-100931-1

© Rand McNally

Lambert Azimuthal Equal Area Projection
Scale 1:30,000,000
One inch to 500 miles
One cm to 300 km

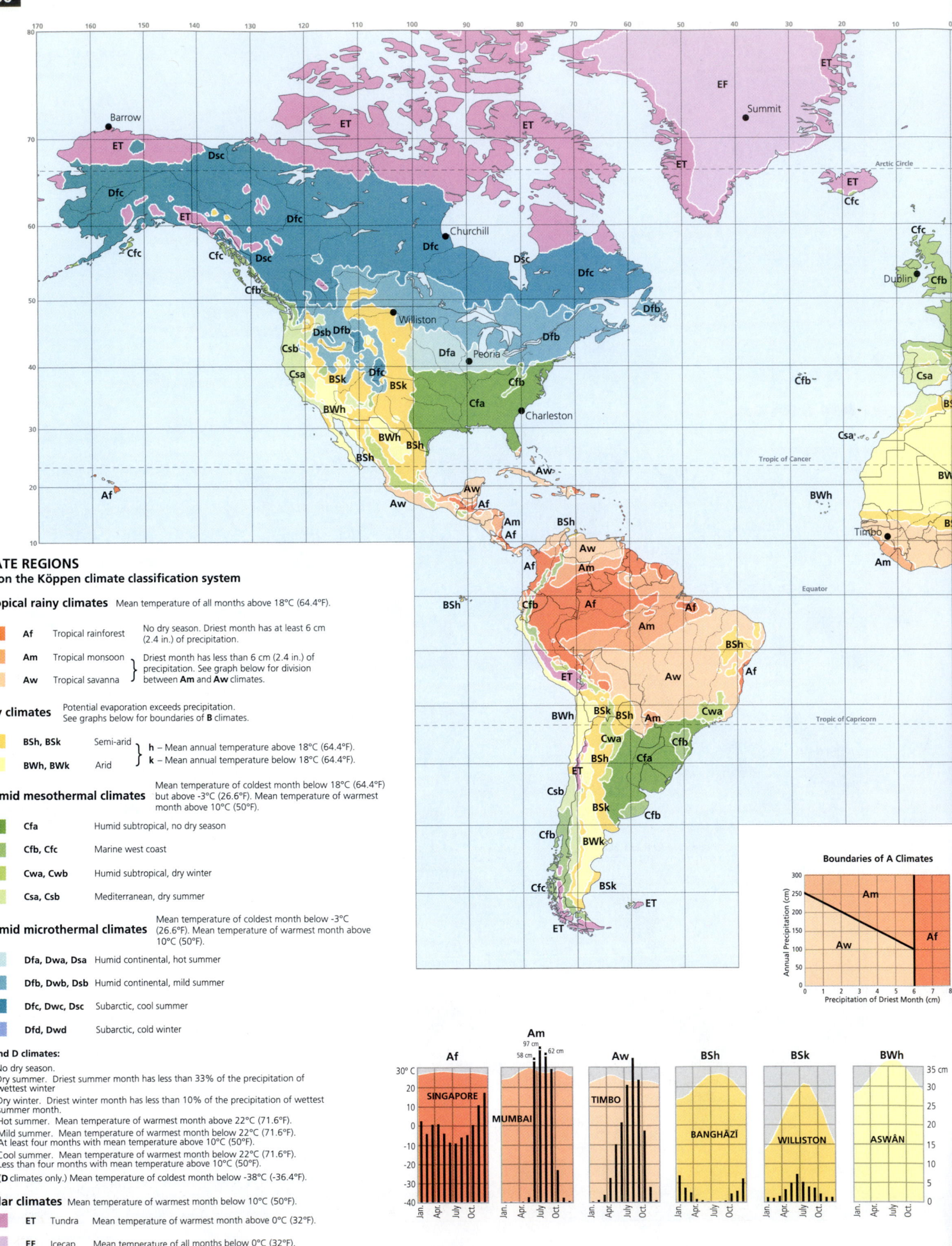

CLIMATE REGIONS
Based on the Köppen climate classification system

A **Tropical rainy climates** Mean temperature of all months above 18°C (64.4°F).

Af	Tropical rainforest	No dry season. Driest month has at least 6 cm (2.4 in.) of precipitation.
Am	Tropical monsoon	Driest month has less than 6 cm (2.4 in.) of precipitation. See graph below for division between **Am** and **Aw** climates.
Aw	Tropical savanna	

B **Dry climates** Potential evaporation exceeds precipitation. See graphs below for boundaries of **B** climates.

BSh, BSk	Semi-arid	**h** – Mean annual temperature above 18°C (64.4°F).
BWh, BWk	Arid	**k** – Mean annual temperature below 18°C (64.4°F).

C **Humid mesothermal climates** Mean temperature of coldest month below 18°C (64.4°F) but above -3°C (26.6°F). Mean temperature of warmest month above 10°C (50°F).

Cfa	Humid subtropical, no dry season
Cfb, Cfc	Marine west coast
Cwa, Cwb	Humid subtropical, dry winter
Csa, Csb	Mediterranean, dry summer

D **Humid microthermal climates** Mean temperature of coldest month below -3°C (26.6°F). Mean temperature of warmest month above 10°C (50°F).

Dfa, Dwa, Dsa	Humid continental, hot summer
Dfb, Dwb, Dsb	Humid continental, mild summer
Dfc, Dwc, Dsc	Subarctic, cool summer
Dfd, Dwd	Subarctic, cold winter

C and D climates:

f - No dry season.

s - Dry summer. Driest summer month has less than 33% of the precipitation of wettest winter

w- Dry winter. Driest winter month has less than 10% of the precipitation of wettest summer month.

a - Hot summer. Mean temperature of warmest month above 22°C (71.6°F).

b - Mild summer. Mean temperature of warmest month below 22°C (71.6°F). At least four months with mean temperature above 10°C (50°F).

c - Cool summer. Mean temperature of warmest month below 22°C (71.6°F). Less than four months with mean temperature above 10°C (50°F).

d - (**D** climates only.) Mean temperature of coldest month below -38°C (-36.4°F).

E **Polar climates** Mean temperature of warmest month below 10°C (50°F).

ET	Tundra	Mean temperature of warmest month above 0°C (32°F).
EF	Icecap	Mean temperature of all months below 0°C (32°F).

Boundaries of A Climates

Am Singapore / Mumbai / Timbo / Banghāzī / Williston / Aswân

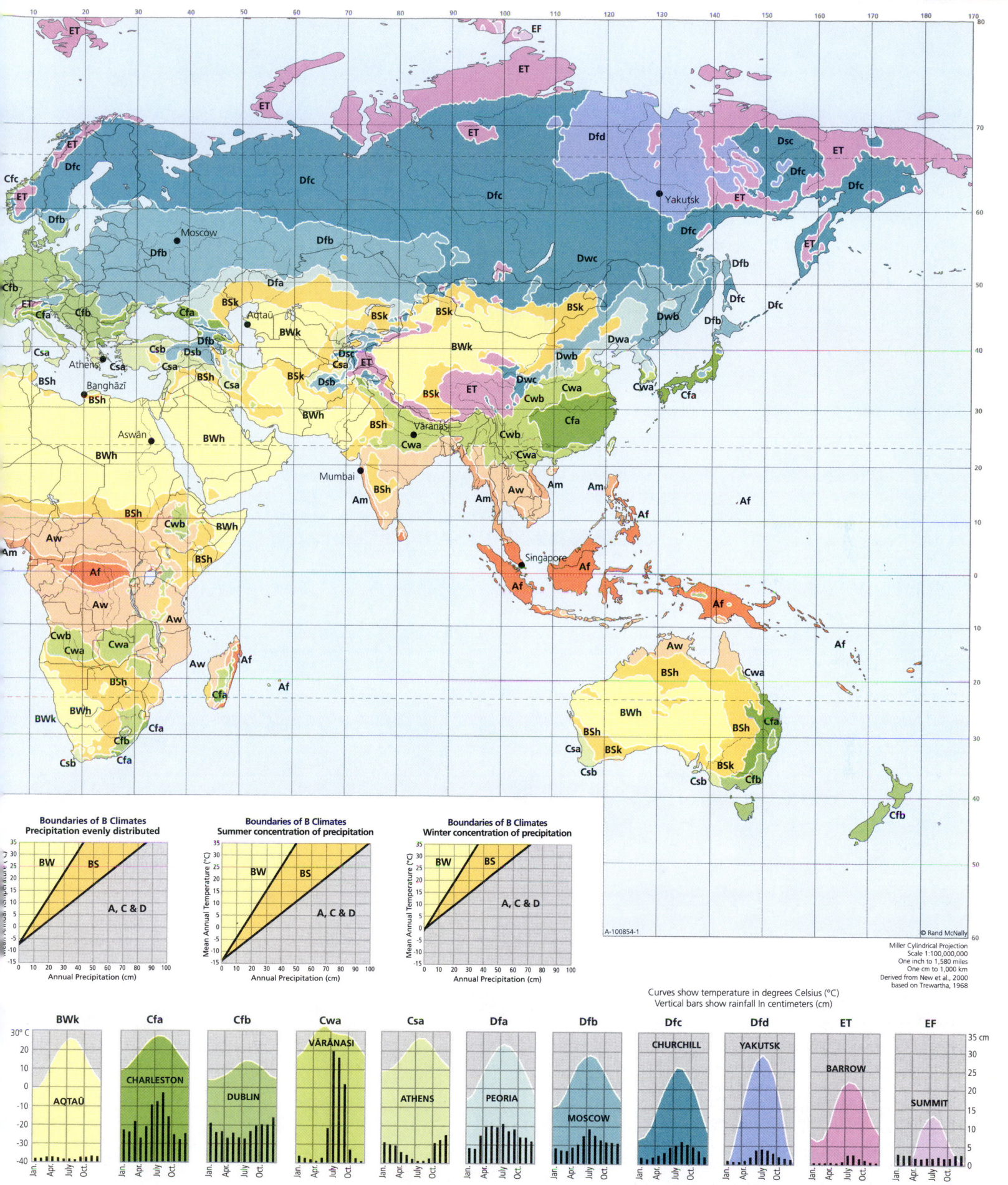

Boundaries of B Climates
Precipitation evenly distributed

BW BS

A, C & D

Annual Precipitation (cm)

Boundaries of B Climates
Summer concentration of precipitation

BW BS

A, C & D

Annual Precipitation (cm)

Boundaries of B Climates
Winter concentration of precipitation

BW BS

A, C & D

Annual Precipitation (cm)

A-100854-1

Miller Cylindrical Projection
Scale 1:100,000,000
One inch to 1,580 miles
One cm to 1,000 km
Derived from New et al., 2000
based on Trewartha, 1968

Curves show temperature in degrees Celsius (°C)
Vertical bars show rainfall In centimeters (cm)

BWk — AQTAŪ
Cfa — CHARLESTON
Cfb — DUBLIN
Cwa — VĀRĀNASI
Csa — ATHENS
Dfa — PEORIA
Dfb — MOSCOW
Dfc — CHURCHILL
Dfd — YAKUTSK
ET — BARROW
EF — SUMMIT

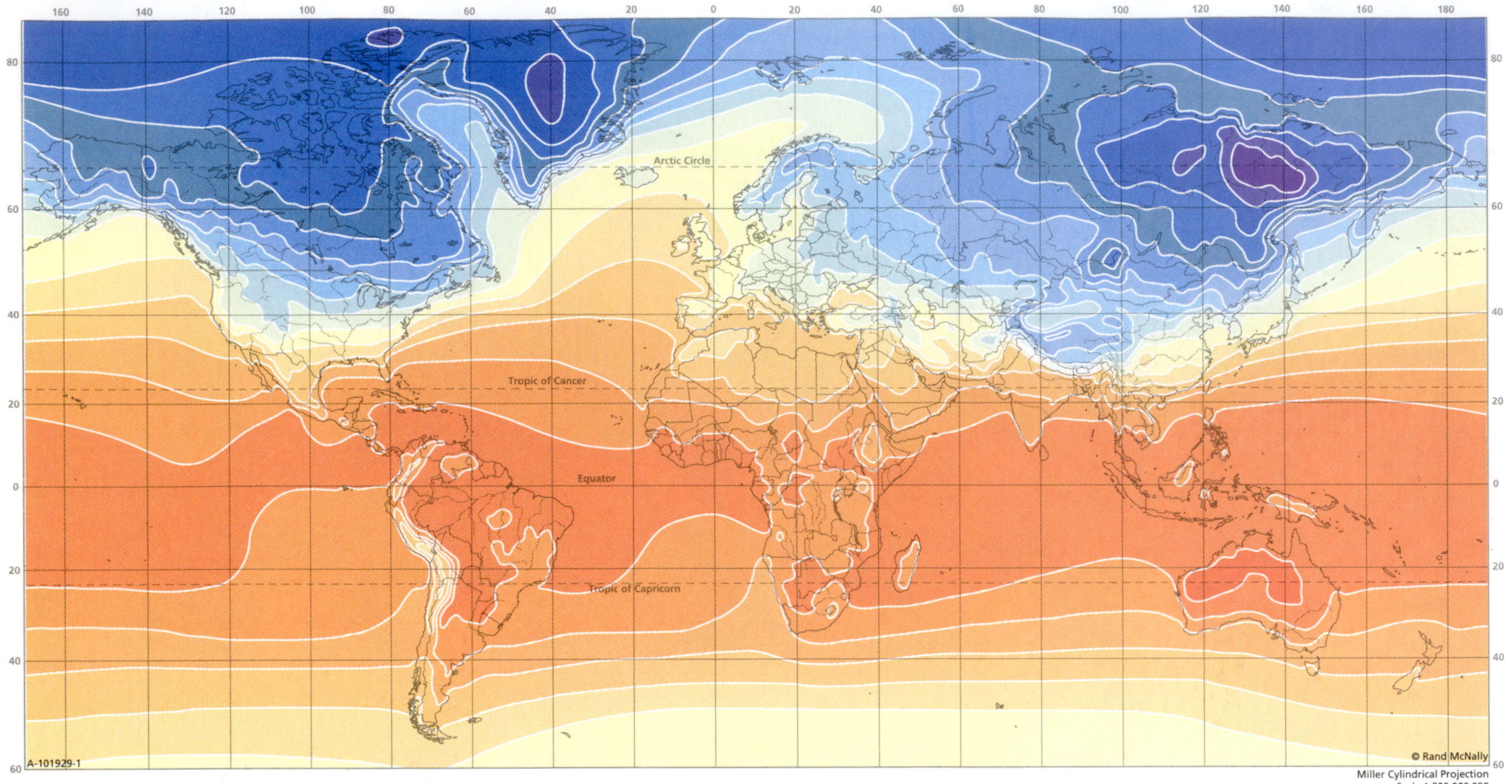

AVERAGE JANUARY TEMPERATURE

°C -45 -40 -35 -30 -25 -20 -15 -10 -5 0 5 10 15 20 25 30

°F -49 -40 -31 -22 -13 -4 5 14 23 32 41 50 59 68 77 86

© Rand McNally
Miller Cylindrical Projection
Scale 1:200,000,000
Sources: New et al., 2000; NOAA

A-101929-1

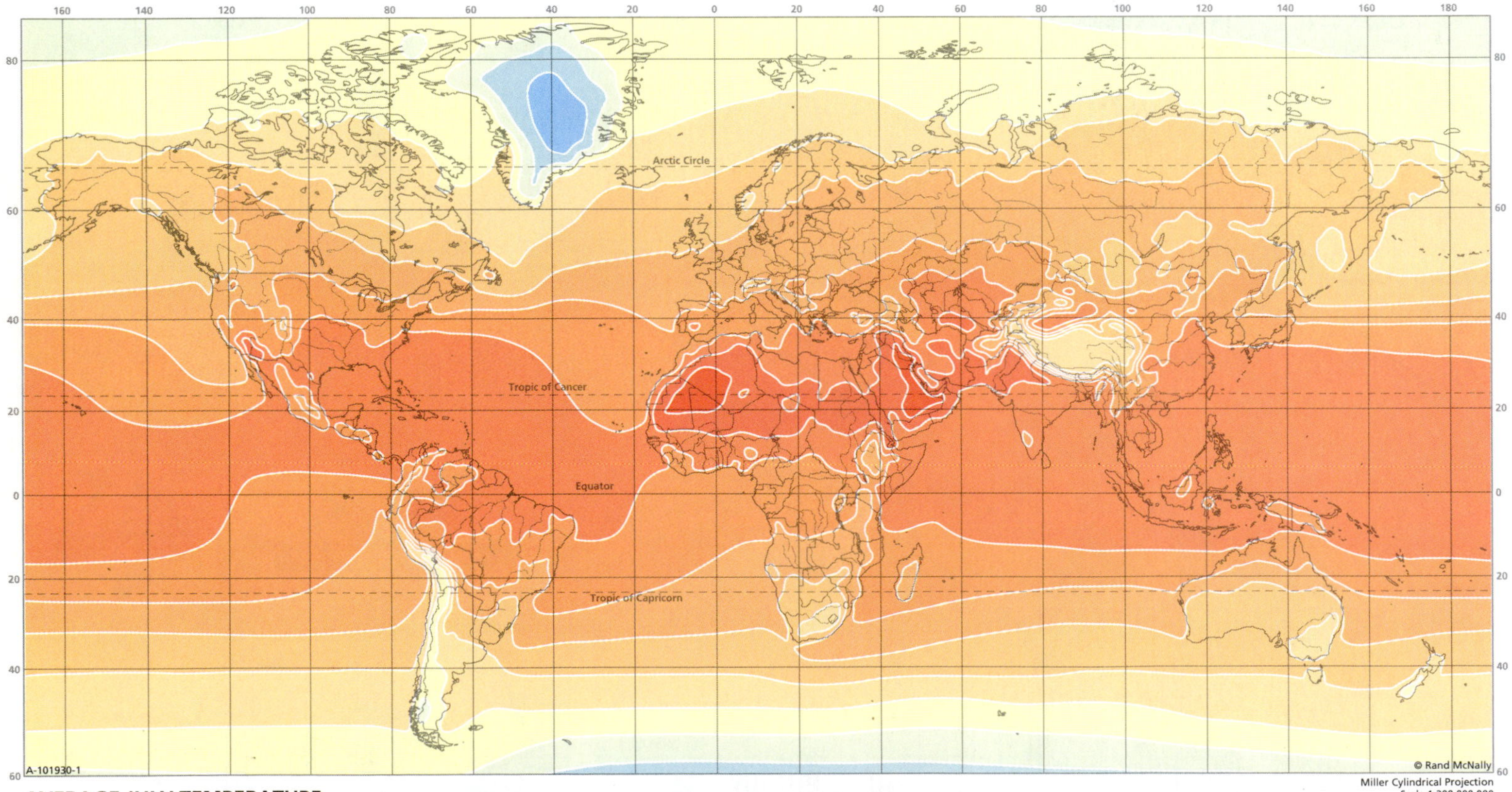

AVERAGE JULY TEMPERATURE

°C -10 -5 0 5 10 15 20 25 30 35

°F 14 23 32 41 50 59 68 77 86 95

© Rand McNally
Miller Cylindrical Projection
Scale 1:200,000,000
Sources: New et al., 2000; NOAA

A-101930-1

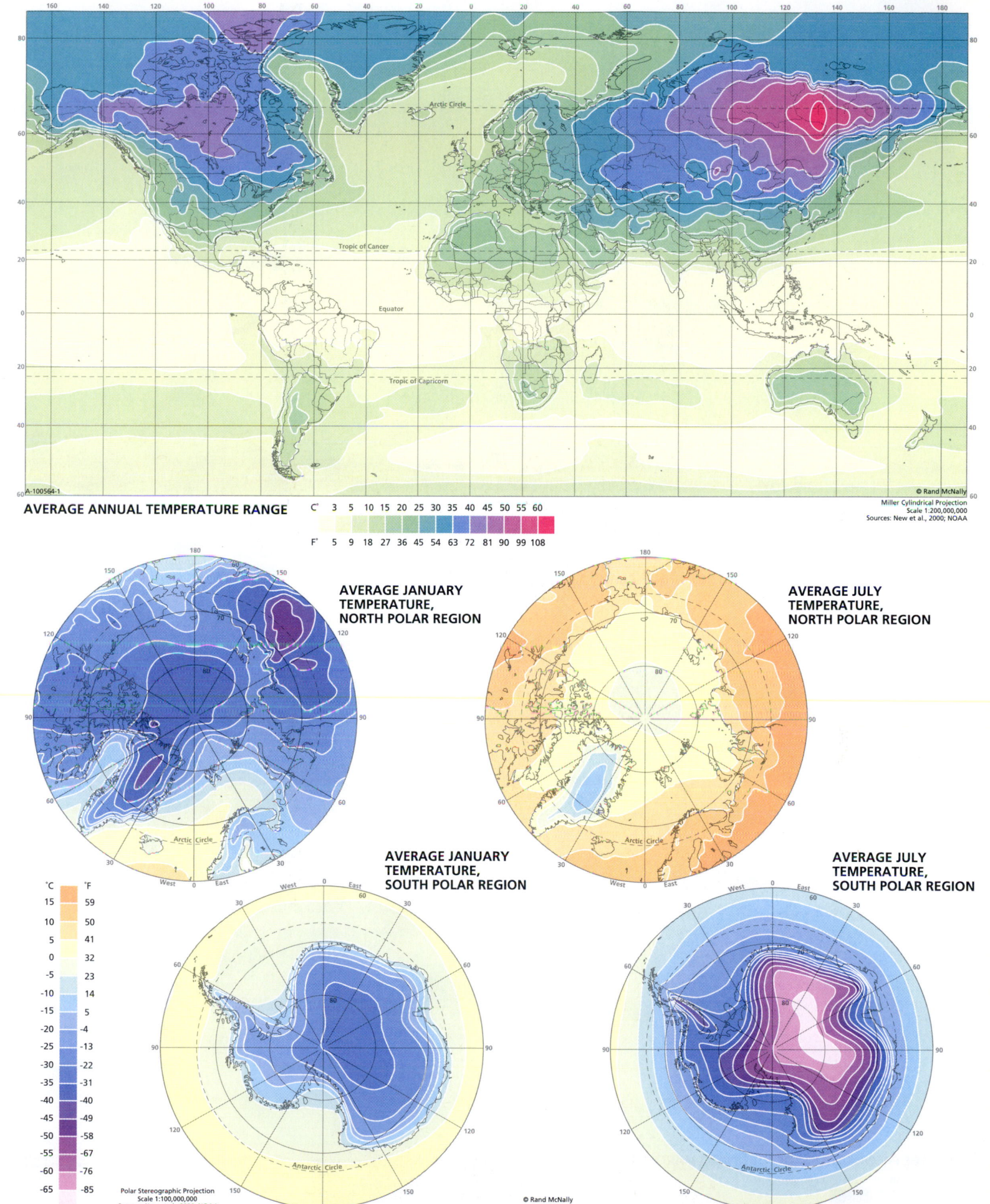

AVERAGE ANNUAL TEMPERATURE RANGE

C° 3 5 10 15 20 25 30 35 40 45 50 55 60
F° 5 9 18 27 36 45 54 63 72 81 90 99 108

Miller Cylindrical Projection
Scale 1:200,000,000
Sources: New et al., 2000; NOAA

A-100564-1

© Rand McNally

AVERAGE JANUARY TEMPERATURE, NORTH POLAR REGION

AVERAGE JULY TEMPERATURE, NORTH POLAR REGION

AVERAGE JANUARY TEMPERATURE, SOUTH POLAR REGION

AVERAGE JULY TEMPERATURE, SOUTH POLAR REGION

°C	°F
15	59
10	50
5	41
0	32
-5	23
-10	14
-15	5
-20	-4
-25	-13
-30	-22
-35	-31
-40	-40
-45	-49
-50	-58
-55	-67
-60	-76
-65	-85

Polar Stereographic Projection
Scale 1:100,000,000
Sources: New et al., 2000; NOAA

© Rand McNally
A-101983-1

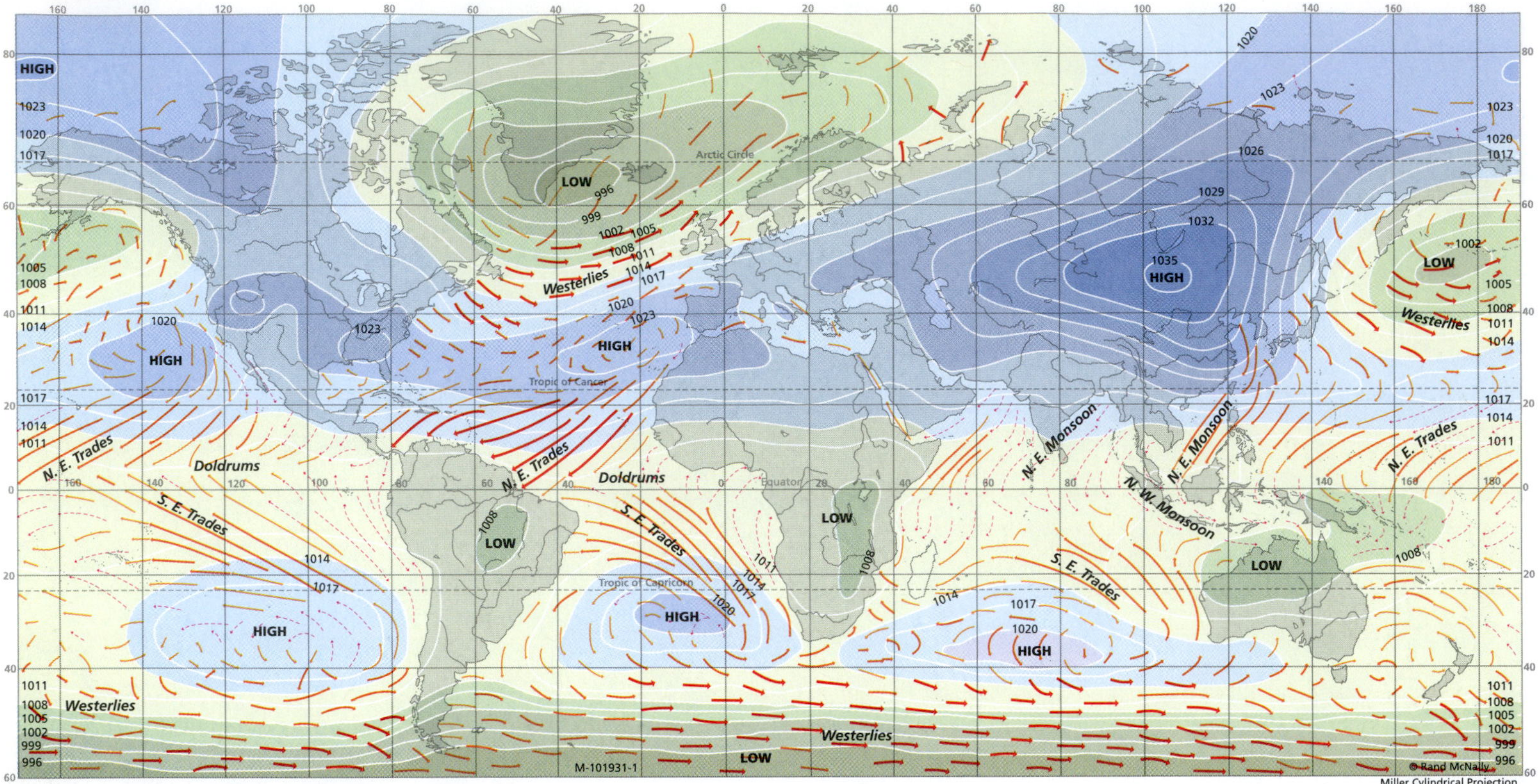

JANUARY PRESSURE AND PREDOMINANT WINDS

Atmospheric Pressure
in millibars (mb)

Normal sea-level pressure (1013.25 mb)

| 1032 | 1026 | 1020 | 1014 | 1008 | 1002 | 996 |

Isobars on map at intervals of 3 millibars

Wind Speed

Kilometers per hour (kph)	Miles per hour (mph)
0-16	0-10
19-24	10-15
24-40	15-25
Over 40	Over 25

Direction of arrow indicates dominant wind direction.
Length of arrow indicates steadiness of wind.

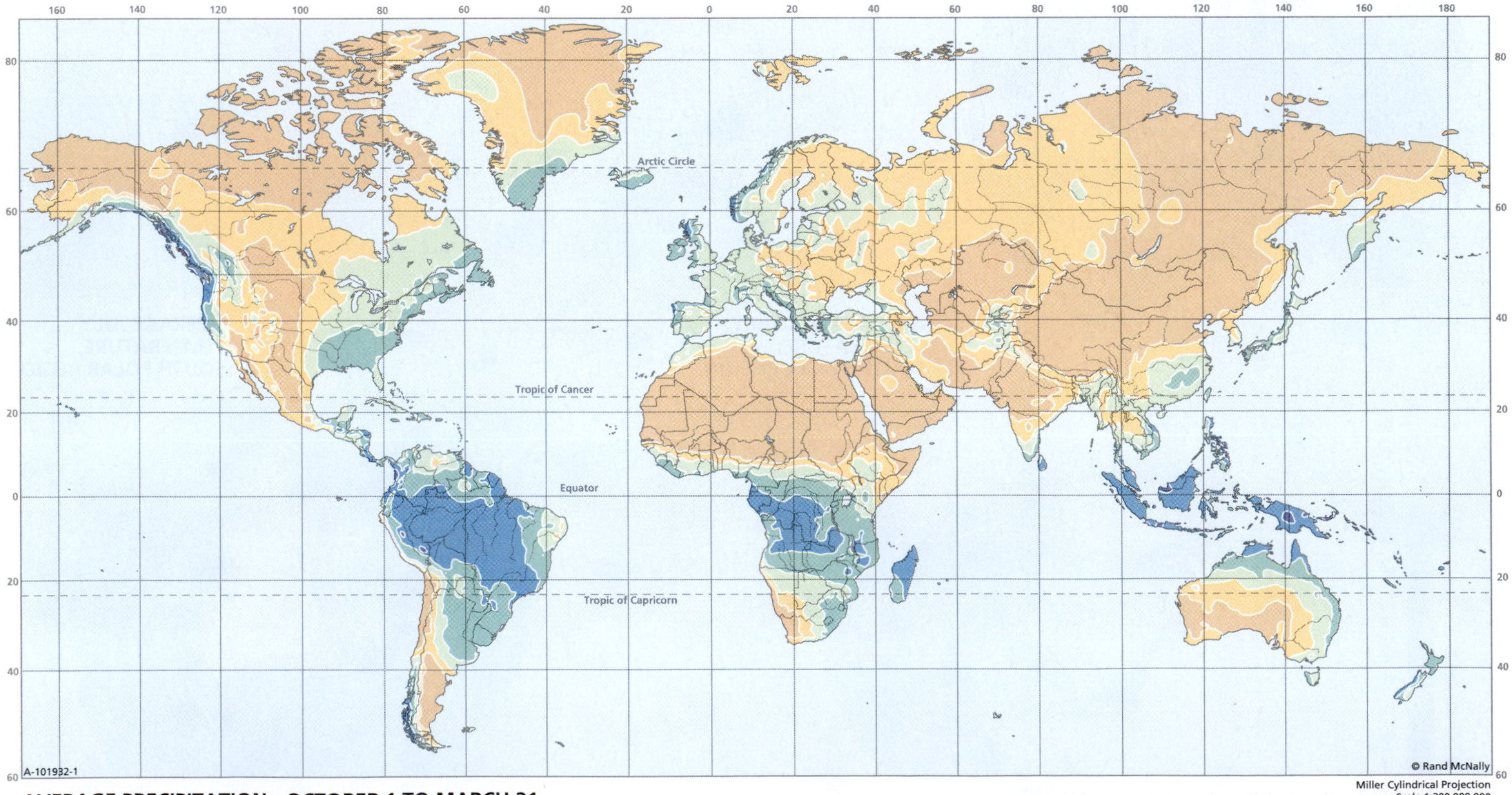

Miller Cylindrical Projection
Scale 1:200,000,000

© Rand McNally

M-101931-1

AVERAGE PRECIPITATION - OCTOBER 1 TO MARCH 31

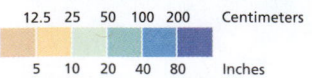

| 12.5 | 25 | 50 | 100 | 200 | Centimeters |
| 5 | 10 | 20 | 40 | 80 | Inches |

Miller Cylindrical Projection
Scale 1:200,000,000
Source: New et al., 2000

© Rand McNally

A-101932-1

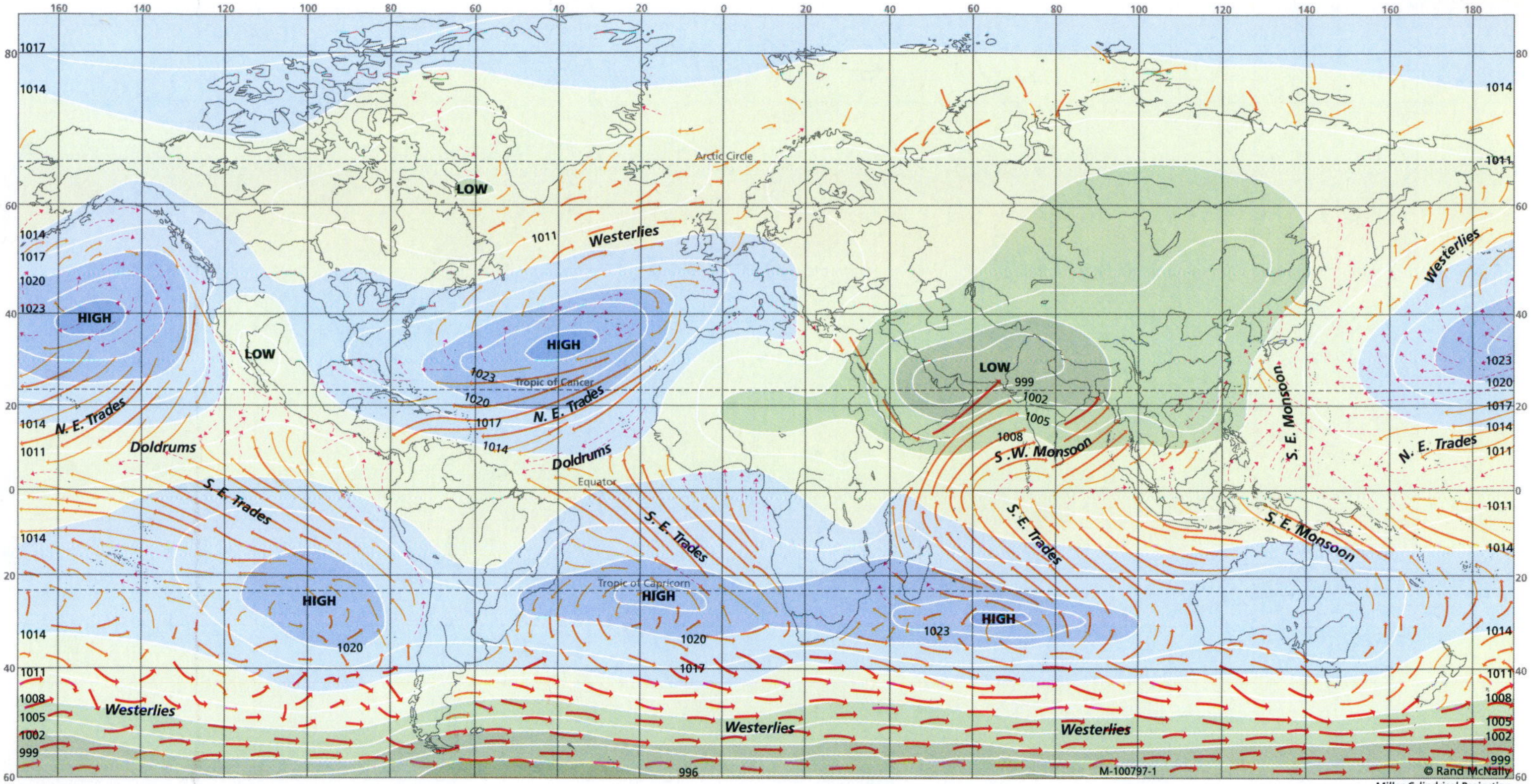

JULY PRESSURE AND PREDOMINANT WINDS

Atmospheric Pressure

in millibars (mb)

Normal sea-level pressure (1013.25 mb)

1026 1020 1014 1008 1002 996

Isobars on map at intervals of 3 millibars

Wind Speed

Kilometers per hour (kph)	Miles per hour (mph)
0–16	0–10
19–24	10–15
24–40	15–25
Over 40	Over 25

Direction of arrow indicates dominant wind direction.
Length of arrow indicates steadiness of wind.

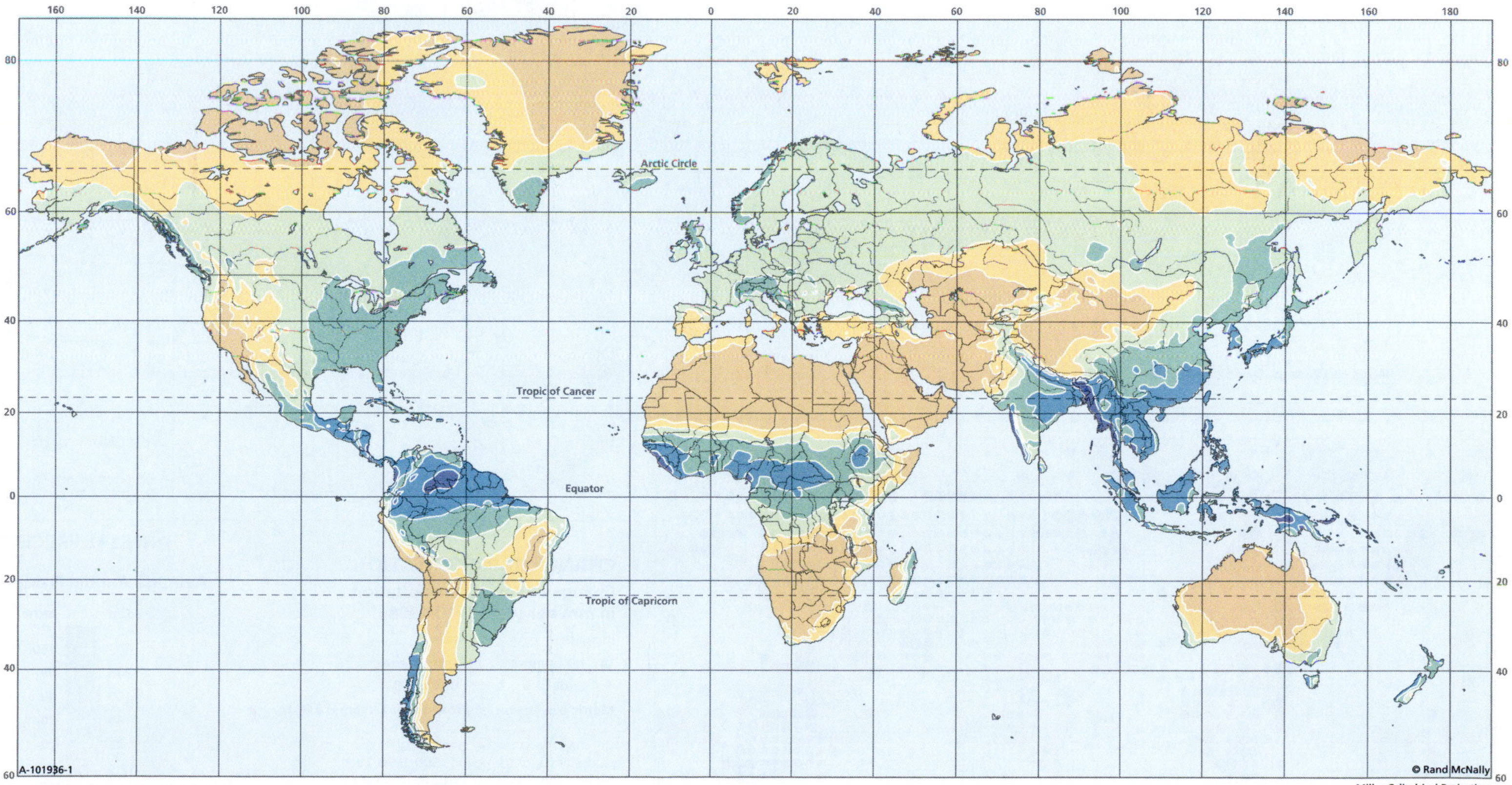

Miller Cylindrical Projection
Scale 1:200,000,000

© Rand McNally

AVERAGE PRECIPITATION - APRIL 1 TO SEPTEMBER 30

12.5 25 50 100 200 Centimeters

5 10 20 40 80 Inches

Miller Cylindrical Projection
Scale 1:200,000,000
Source: New et al., 2000

© Rand McNally

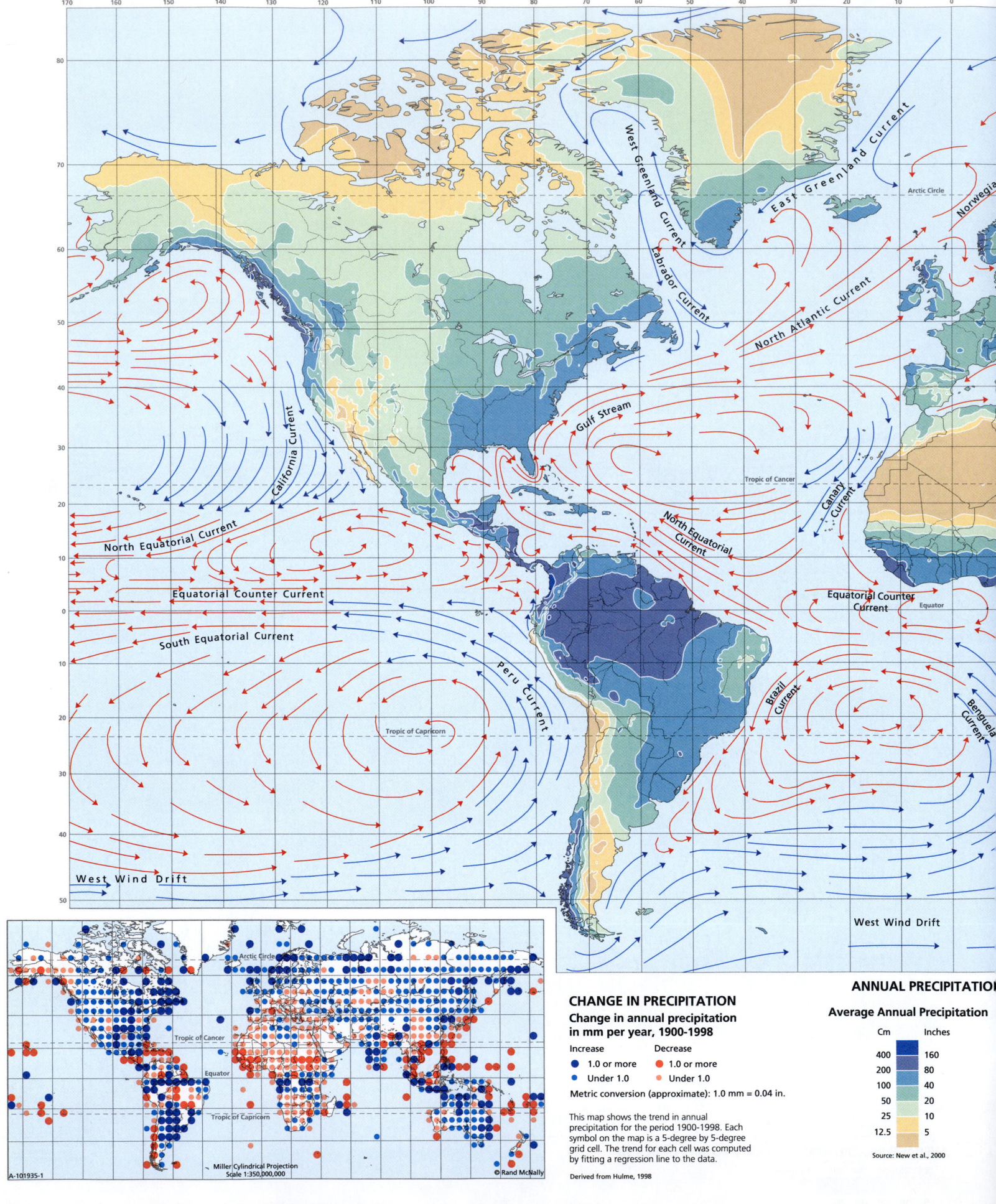

CHANGE IN PRECIPITATION

Change in annual precipitation in mm per year, 1900-1998

Increase
- 1.0 or more
- Under 1.0

Decrease
- 1.0 or more
- Under 1.0

Metric conversion (approximate): 1.0 mm = 0.04 in.

This map shows the trend in annual precipitation for the period 1900-1998. Each symbol on the map is a 5-degree by 5-degree grid cell. The trend for each cell was computed by fitting a regression line to the data.

Derived from Hulme, 1998

ANNUAL PRECIPITATION

Average Annual Precipitation

Cm	Inches
400	160
200	80
100	40
50	20
25	10
12.5	5

Source: New et al., 2000

Miller Cylindrical Projection
Scale 1:350,000,000

© Rand McNally

A-101935-1

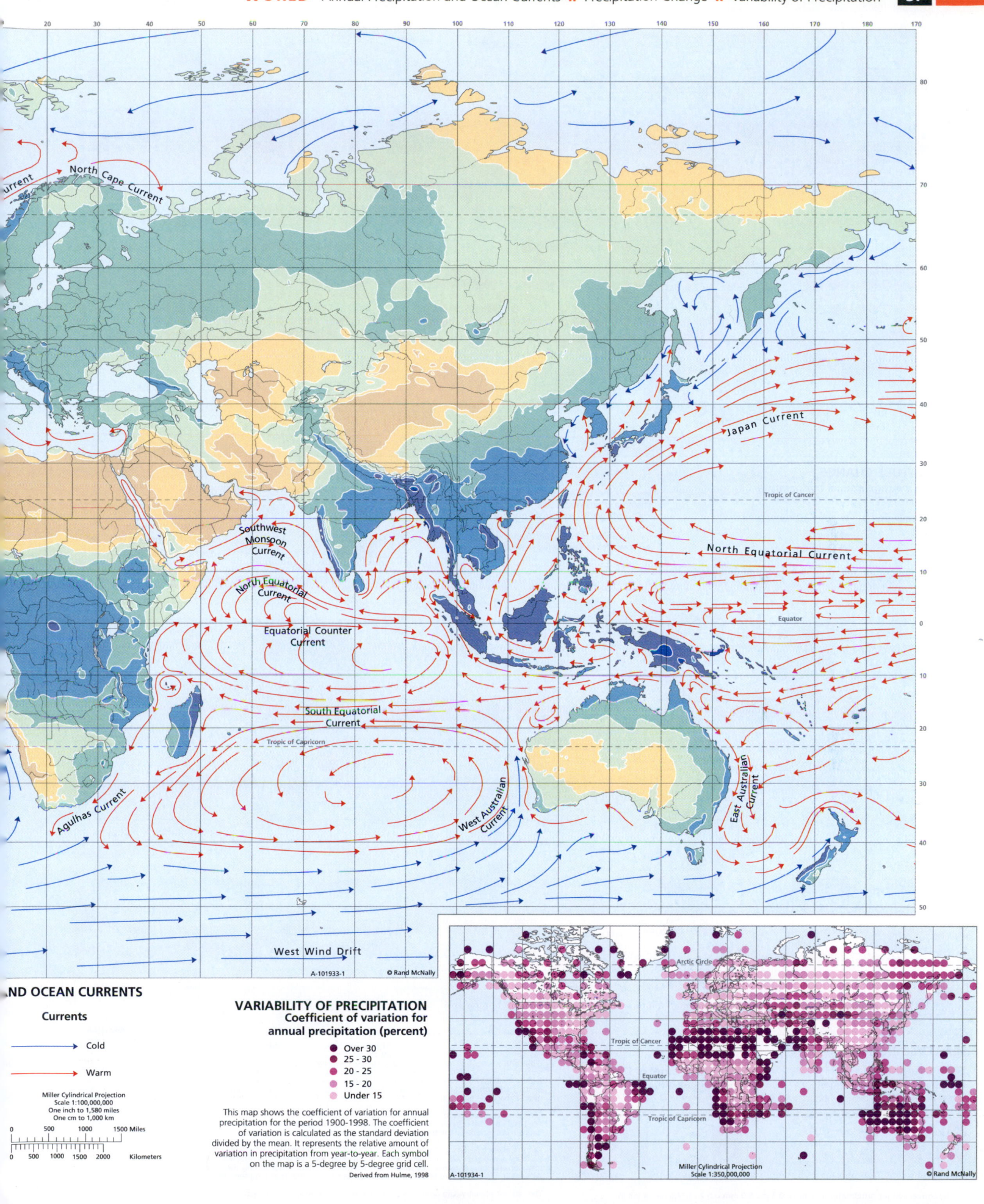

North Cape Current

Japan Current

Tropic of Cancer

Southwest
Monsoon
Current

North Equatorial Current

North Equatorial
Current

Equator

Equatorial Counter
Current

South Equatorial
Current

Tropic of Capricorn

Agulhas Current

West Australian
Current

East Australian
Current

West Wind Drift

A-101933-1   © Rand McNally

...ND OCEAN CURRENTS

Currents

→ Cold

→ Warm

Miller Cylindrical Projection
Scale 1:100,000,000
One inch to 1,580 miles
One cm to 1,000 km

0   500   1000   1500 Miles

0   500 1000 1500 2000
Kilometers

VARIABILITY OF PRECIPITATION
Coefficient of variation for annual precipitation (percent)

● Over 30
● 25 - 30
● 20 - 25
● 15 - 20
● Under 15

This map shows the coefficient of variation for annual
precipitation for the period 1900-1998. The coefficient
of variation is calculated as the standard deviation
divided by the mean. It represents the relative amount of
variation in precipitation from year-to-year. Each symbol
on the map is a 5-degree by 5-degree grid cell.

Derived from Hulme, 1998

Arctic Circle

Tropic of Cancer

Equator

Tropic of Capricorn

Miller Cylindrical Projection
Scale 1:350,000,000

A-101934-1   © Rand McNally

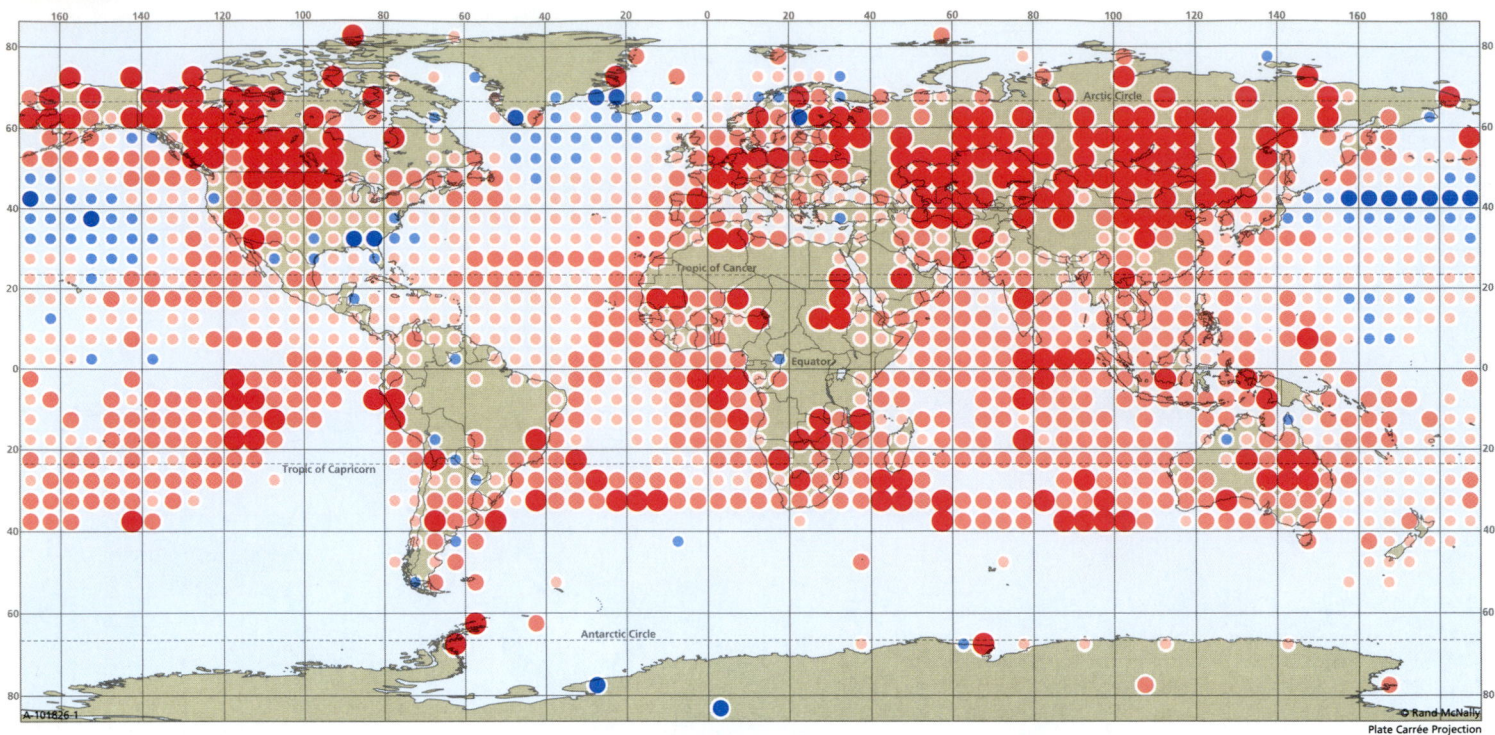

TEMPERATURE CHANGE

Change in average annual temperature
in Celsius degrees (C°) per decade, 1950-2006

Temperature increase
- ● Over 0.2
- ● 0.1 - 0.2
- ● Under 0.1

Temperature decrease
- ● Over 0.1
- ● Under 0.1

Temperature conversion (approximate): 0.1 C° = 0.18 F°; 0.2 C° = 0.36 F°

This map is derived from the HadCRUT3 temperature anomaly dataset. The anomaly for a given year is the difference in temperature from the baseline period of 1961-1990. Each symbol on the map is a 5-degree by 5-degree grid cell. Cells with a gap of 10 years or more in the record are not included. The trend for each cell was computed by fitting a regression line to the data.

Average Annual Global Temperature Trend, 1850-2007

Plate Carrée Projection
Scale 1:200,000,000
Derived from Brohan et al., 2006

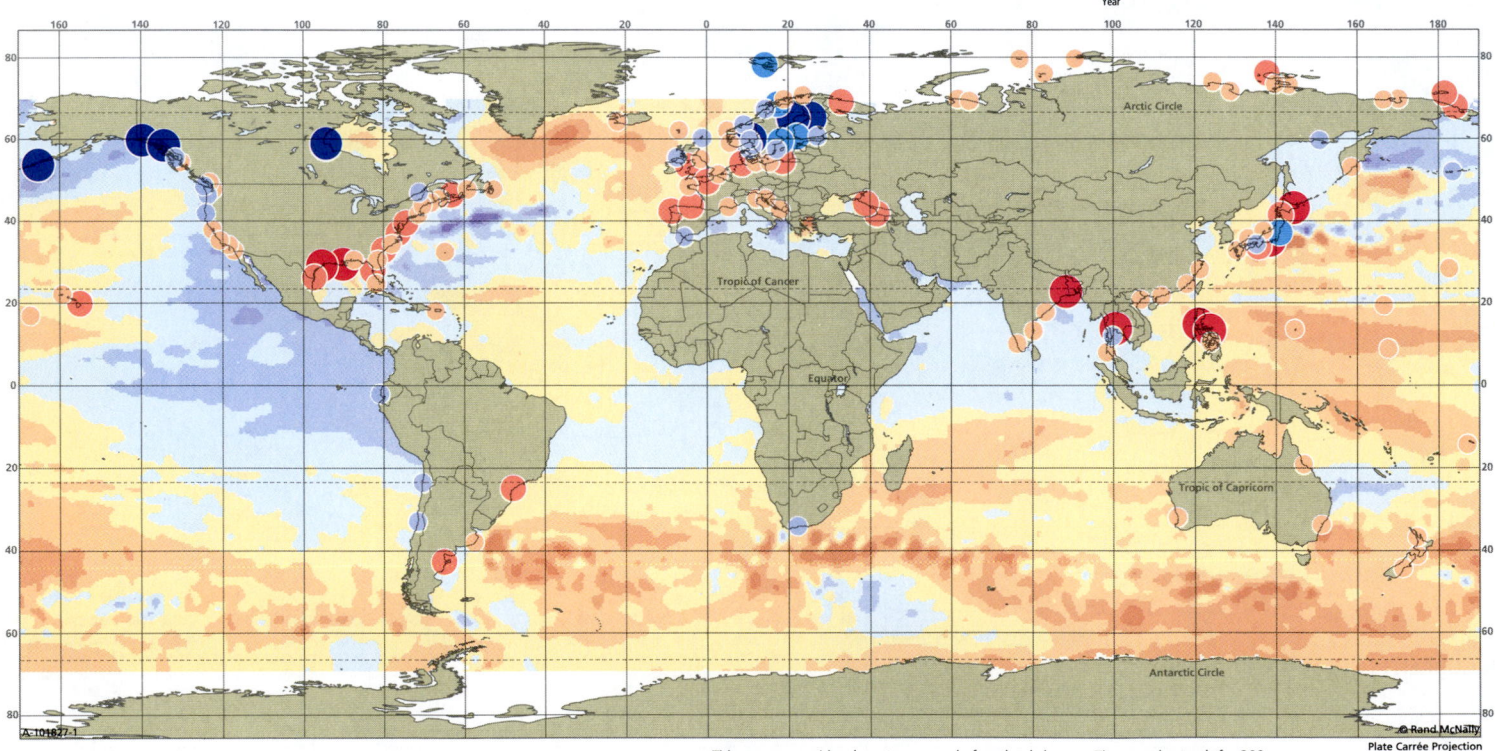

SEA LEVEL CHANGE

Tide Gauge Data
Change in relative sea level
in mm per year, 1950-2006

Sea level increase
- ● Over 5.0
- ● 2.5 - 5.0
- ● Under 2.5

Sea level decrease
- ● Over 5.0
- ● 2.5 - 5.0
- ● Under 2.5

Satellite Altimetry Data
Change in observed sea level
in mm per year, 1992-2007

Sea level increase
- Over 7.5
- 5.0 - 7.5
- 2.5 - 5.0
- Under 2.5

Sea level decrease
- Over 7.5
- 5.0 - 7.5
- 2.5 - 5.0
- Under 2.5

Metric conversion (approximate): 2.5 mm = 0.1 in.; 5.0 mm = 0.2 in.; 7.5 mm = 0.3 in.

Tide gauges provide a long-term record of sea level change. The record extends for 200 years in some cases. However, stations are clustered spatially and do not cover the entire globe. Also, since tide gauges measure relative sea level (water level relative to the land surface), they cannot differentiate changes in water volume (due to thermal expansion and ice melting) from changes in land elevation (due to tectonic activity and glacial isostatic adjustment). Still, tide gauges are important because relative sea level has a direct impact on coastal environments.

The tide gauge data on this map are from the PSMSL-RLR (Permanent Service for Mean Sea Level - Revised Local Reference) network. Stations with gaps of 10 years or more in the data are not included. The trend at each station was computed by fitting a regression line.

Satellite altimetry offers a second method of assessing sea level change. Unlike tide gauges, coverage is nearly global. Also, observed changes in sea level are largely unaffected by land elevation changes. However, the satellite altimetry record extends back to only the 1990s. As a result, the data record reflects major decadal variations rather than long-term trends.

The satellite altimetry data on this map are from the TOPEX/Poseidon and Jason1 sensors.

Plate Carrée Projection
Scale 1:200,000,000
Sources: NOAA Laboratory
for Satellite Altimetry;
Woodworth and Player, 2003

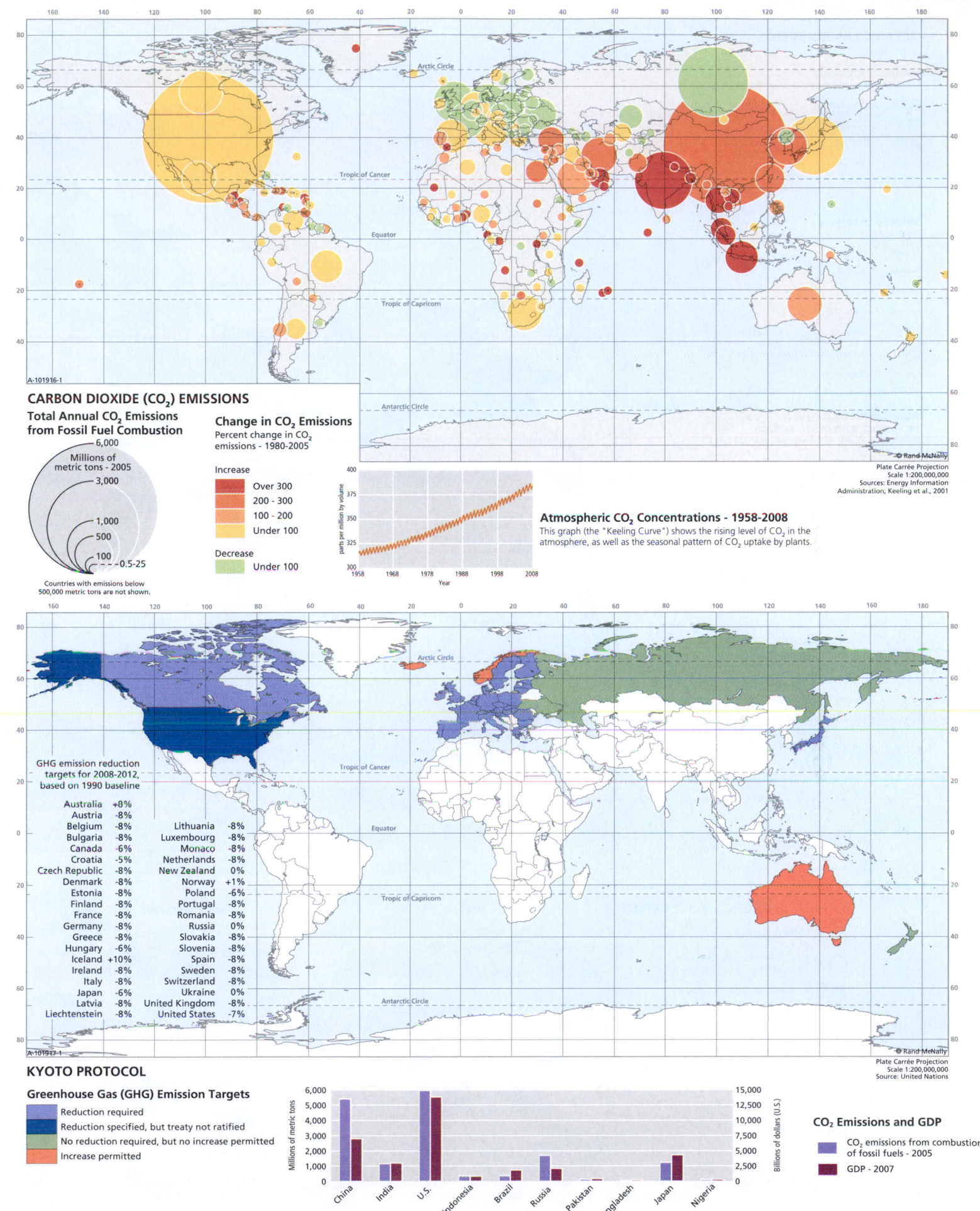

CARBON DIOXIDE (CO₂) EMISSIONS

Total Annual CO₂ Emissions from Fossil Fuel Combustion

Millions of metric tons - 2005

6,000
3,000
1,000
500
100
0.5-25

Countries with emissions below 500,000 metric tons are not shown.

Change in CO₂ Emissions

Percent change in CO₂ emissions - 1980-2005

Increase

Over 300
200 - 300
100 - 200
Under 100

Decrease

Under 100

Atmospheric CO₂ Concentrations - 1958-2008

This graph (the "Keeling Curve") shows the rising level of CO₂ in the atmosphere, as well as the seasonal pattern of CO₂ uptake by plants.

A-101916-1

Plate Carrée Projection
Scale 1:200,000,000
Sources: Energy Information
Administration; Keeling et al., 2001

© Rand McNally

GHG emission reduction targets for 2008-2012, based on 1990 baseline

Australia	+8%		
Austria	-8%		
Belgium	-8%	Lithuania	-8%
Bulgaria	-8%	Luxembourg	-8%
Canada	-6%	Monaco	-8%
Croatia	-5%	Netherlands	-8%
Czech Republic	-8%	New Zealand	0%
Denmark	-8%	Norway	+1%
Estonia	-8%	Poland	-6%
Finland	-8%	Portugal	-8%
France	-8%	Romania	-8%
Germany	-8%	Russia	0%
Greece	-8%	Slovakia	-8%
Hungary	-6%	Slovenia	-8%
Iceland	+10%	Spain	-8%
Ireland	-8%	Sweden	-8%
Italy	-8%	Switzerland	-8%
Japan	-6%	Ukraine	0%
Latvia	-8%	United Kingdom	-8%
Liechtenstein	-8%	United States	-7%

A-101917-1

Plate Carrée Projection
Scale 1:200,000,000
Source: United Nations

© Rand McNally

KYOTO PROTOCOL

Greenhouse Gas (GHG) Emission Targets

Reduction required
Reduction specified, but treaty not ratified
No reduction required, but no increase permitted
Increase permitted

CO₂ Emissions and GDP

CO₂ emissions from combustion of fossil fuels - 2005
GDP - 2007

(World's largest countries, 2000)

China India U.S. Indonesia Brazil Russia Pakistan Bangladesh Japan Nigeria

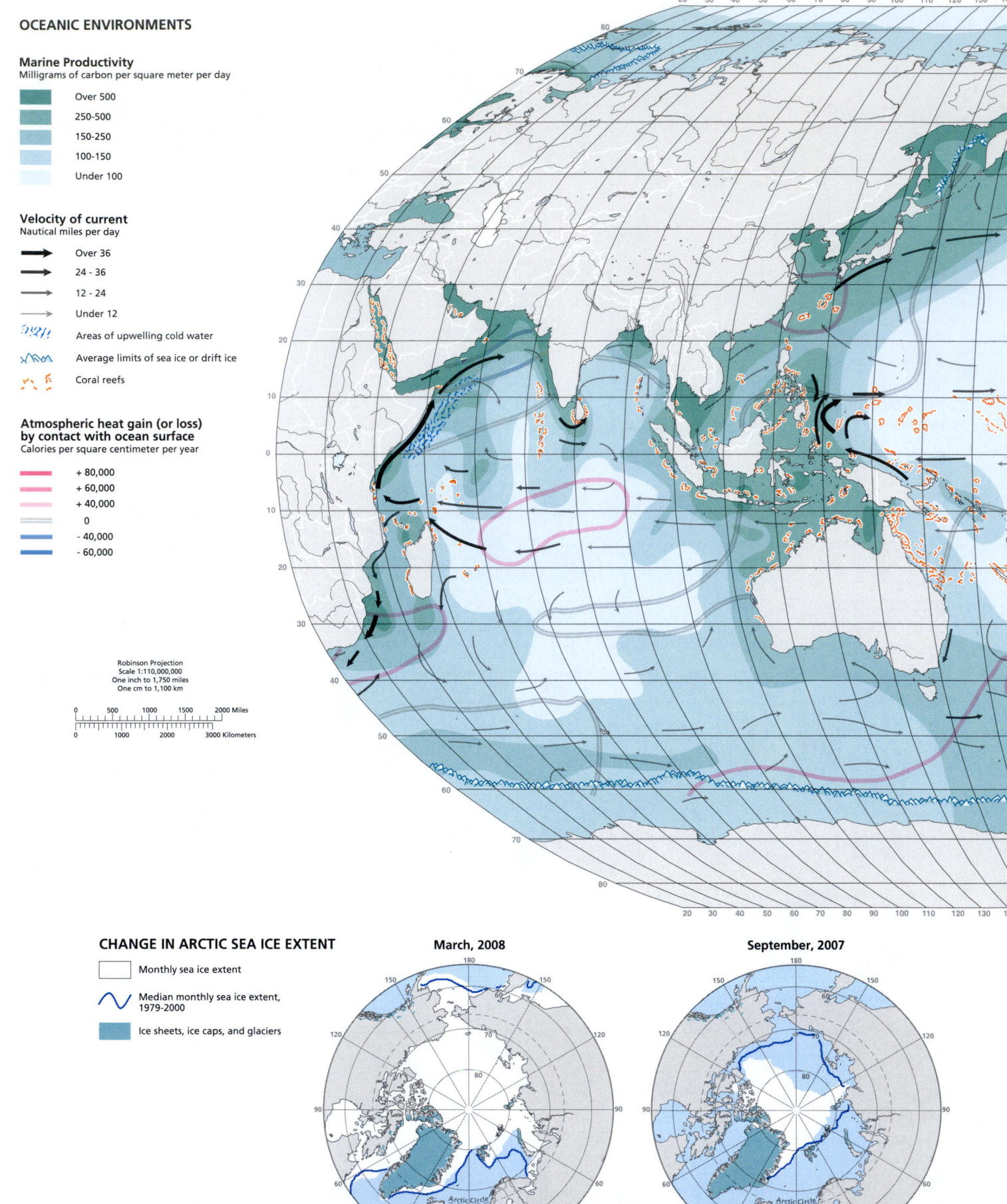

OCEANIC ENVIRONMENTS

Marine Productivity
Milligrams of carbon per square meter per day

- Over 500
- 250-500
- 150-250
- 100-150
- Under 100

Velocity of current
Nautical miles per day

→ Over 36
→ 24 - 36
→ 12 - 24
→ Under 12

〰 Areas of upwelling cold water

〜 Average limits of sea ice or drift ice

Coral reefs

Atmospheric heat gain (or loss)
by contact with ocean surface
Calories per square centimeter per year

- + 80,000
- + 60,000
- + 40,000
- 0
- - 40,000
- - 60,000

Robinson Projection
Scale 1:110,000,000
One inch to 1,750 miles
One cm to 1,100 km

0   500   1000   1500   2000 Miles
0   1000   2000   3000 Kilometers

CHANGE IN ARCTIC SEA ICE EXTENT

☐ Monthly sea ice extent

〜 Median monthly sea ice extent, 1979-2000

■ Ice sheets, ice caps, and glaciers

March, 2008

September, 2007

Polar Stereographic Projection
Scale 1:140,000,000
Source: National Snow and Ice Data Center
© Rand McNally A-101961-1

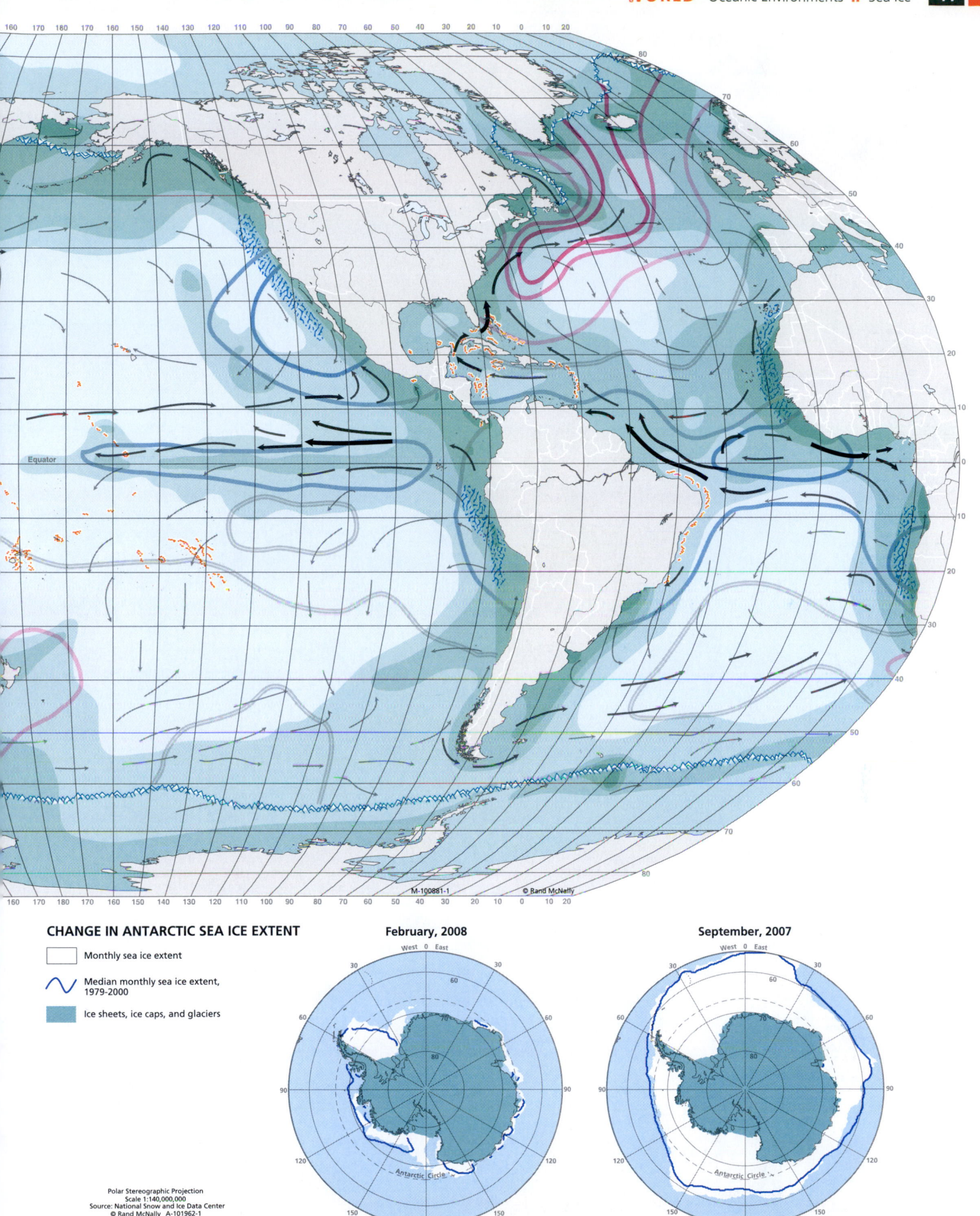

CHANGE IN ANTARCTIC SEA ICE EXTENT

☐ Monthly sea ice extent

〰 Median monthly sea ice extent, 1979-2000

▨ Ice sheets, ice caps, and glaciers

Polar Stereographic Projection
Scale 1:140,000,000
Source: National Snow and Ice Data Center
© Rand McNally A-101962-1

February, 2008

West 0 East

September, 2007

West 0 East

M-100881-1   © Rand McNally

Equator

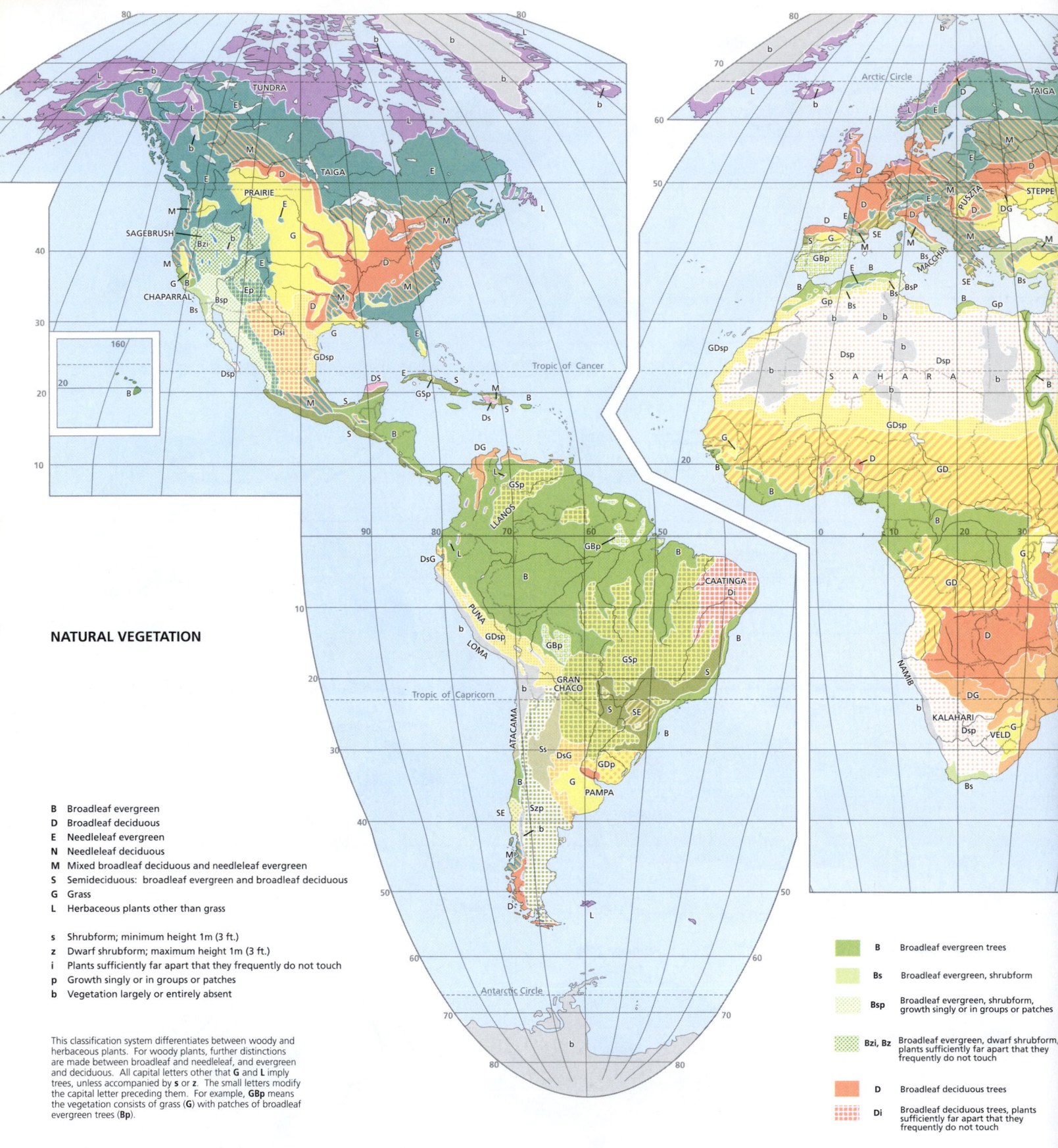

NATURAL VEGETATION

B Broadleaf evergreen
D Broadleaf deciduous
E Needleleaf evergreen
N Needleleaf deciduous
M Mixed broadleaf deciduous and needleleaf evergreen
S Semideciduous: broadleaf evergreen and broadleaf deciduous
G Grass
L Herbaceous plants other than grass

s Shrubform; minimum height 1m (3 ft.)
z Dwarf shrubform; maximum height 1m (3 ft.)
i Plants sufficiently far apart that they frequently do not touch
p Growth singly or in groups or patches
b Vegetation largely or entirely absent

This classification system differentiates between woody and herbaceous plants. For woody plants, further distinctions are made between broadleaf and needleleaf, and evergreen and deciduous. All capital letters other that **G** and **L** imply trees, unless accompanied by **s** or **z**. The small letters modify the capital letter preceding them. For example, **GBp** means the vegetation consists of grass (**G**) with patches of broadleaf evergreen trees (**Bp**).

	B	Broadleaf evergreen trees
	Bs	Broadleaf evergreen, shrubform
	Bsp	Broadleaf evergreen, shrubform, growth singly or in groups or patches
	Bzi, Bz	Broadleaf evergreen, dwarf shrubform, plants sufficiently far apart that they frequently do not touch
	D	Broadleaf deciduous trees
	Di	Broadleaf deciduous trees, plants sufficiently far apart that they frequently do not touch

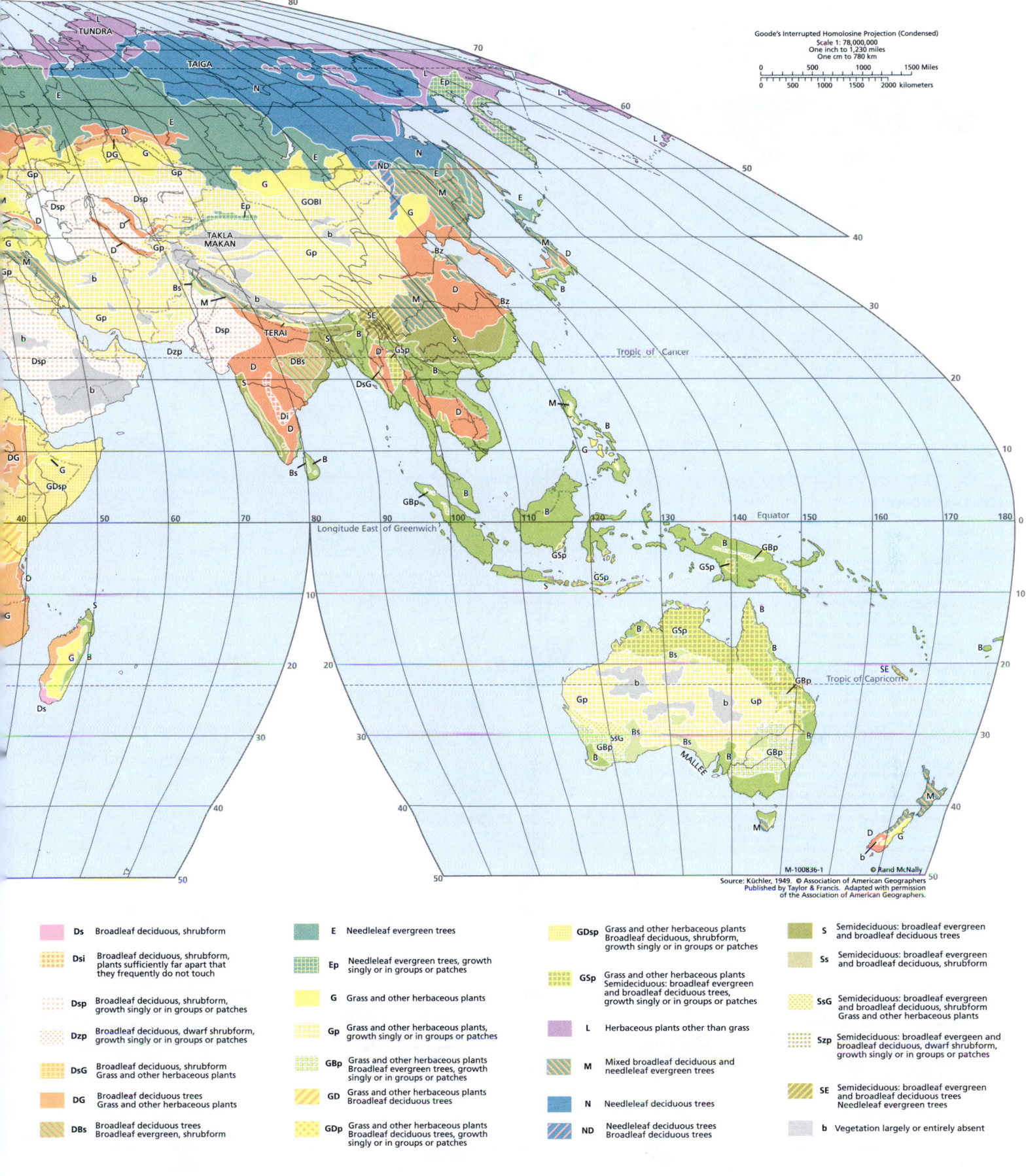

Goode's Interrupted Homolosine Projection (Condensed)
Scale 1: 78,000,000
One inch to 1,230 miles
One cm to 780 km

0   500   1000   1500 Miles
0   500   1000   1500   2000 kilometers

TUNDRA

TAIGA

GOBI

TAKLA MAKAN

TERAI

MALLEE

Tropic of Cancer

Equator

Longitude East of Greenwich

Tropic of Capricorn

M-100836-1

© Rand McNally

Source: Küchler, 1949. © Association of American Geographers
Published by Taylor & Francis. Adapted with permission
of the Association of American Geographers.

Ds	Broadleaf deciduous, shrubform	
Dsi	Broadleaf deciduous, shrubform, plants sufficiently far apart that they frequently do not touch	
Dsp	Broadleaf deciduous, shrubform, growth singly or in groups or patches	
Dzp	Broadleaf deciduous, dwarf shrubform, growth singly or in groups or patches	
DsG	Broadleaf deciduous, shrubform Grass and other herbaceous plants	
DG	Broadleaf deciduous trees Grass and other herbaceous plants	
DBs	Broadleaf deciduous trees Broadleaf evergreen, shrubform	

E	Needleleaf evergreen trees	
Ep	Needleleaf evergreen trees, growth singly or in groups or patches	
G	Grass and other herbaceous plants	
Gp	Grass and other herbaceous plants, growth singly or in groups or patches	
GBp	Grass and other herbaceous plants Broadleaf evergreen trees, growth singly or in groups or patches	
GD	Grass and other herbaceous plants Broadleaf deciduous trees	
GDp	Grass and other herbaceous plants Broadleaf deciduous trees, growth singly or in groups or patches	

GDsp	Grass and other herbaceous plants Broadleaf deciduous, shrubform, growth singly or in groups or patches	
GSp	Grass and other herbaceous plants Semideciduous: broadleaf evergreen and broadleaf deciduous trees, growth singly or in groups or patches	
L	Herbaceous plants other than grass	
M	Mixed broadleaf deciduous and needleleaf evergreen trees	
N	Needleleaf deciduous trees	
ND	Needleleaf deciduous trees Broadleaf deciduous trees	

S	Semideciduous: broadleaf evergreen and broadleaf deciduous trees	
Ss	Semideciduous: broadleaf evergreen and broadleaf deciduous, shrubform	
SsG	Semideciduous: broadleaf evergreen and broadleaf deciduous, shrubform Grass and other herbaceous plants	
Szp	Semideciduous: broadleaf evergeen and broadleaf deciduous, dwarf shrubform, growth singly or in groups or patches	
SE	Semideciduous: broadleaf evergreen and broadleaf deciduous trees Needleleaf evergreen trees	
b	Vegetation largely or entirely absent	

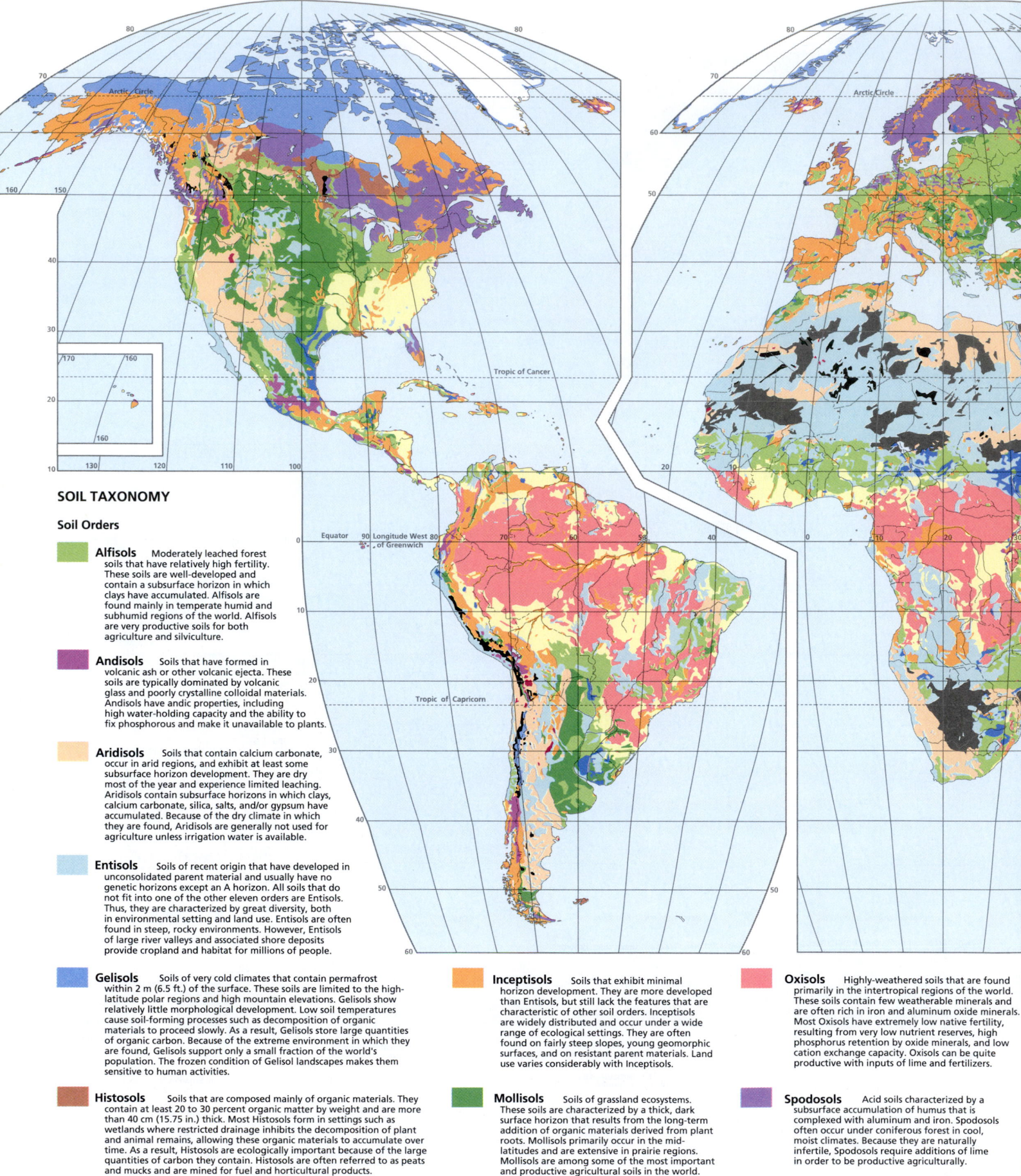

SOIL TAXONOMY

Soil Orders

Alfisols Moderately leached forest soils that have relatively high fertility. These soils are well-developed and contain a subsurface horizon in which clays have accumulated. Alfisols are found mainly in temperate humid and subhumid regions of the world. Alfisols are very productive soils for both agriculture and silviculture.

Andisols Soils that have formed in volcanic ash or other volcanic ejecta. These soils are typically dominated by volcanic glass and poorly crystalline colloidal materials. Andisols have andic properties, including high water-holding capacity and the ability to fix phosphorous and make it unavailable to plants.

Aridisols Soils that contain calcium carbonate, occur in arid regions, and exhibit at least some subsurface horizon development. They are dry most of the year and experience limited leaching. Aridisols contain subsurface horizons in which clays, calcium carbonate, silica, salts, and/or gypsum have accumulated. Because of the dry climate in which they are found, Aridisols are generally not used for agriculture unless irrigation water is available.

Entisols Soils of recent origin that have developed in unconsolidated parent material and usually have no genetic horizons except an A horizon. All soils that do not fit into one of the other eleven orders are Entisols. Thus, they are characterized by great diversity, both in environmental setting and land use. Entisols are often found in steep, rocky environments. However, Entisols of large river valleys and associated shore deposits provide cropland and habitat for millions of people.

Gelisols Soils of very cold climates that contain permafrost within 2 m (6.5 ft.) of the surface. These soils are limited to the high-latitude polar regions and high mountain elevations. Gelisols show relatively little morphological development. Low soil temperatures cause soil-forming processes such as decomposition of organic materials to proceed slowly. As a result, Gelisols store large quantities of organic carbon. Because of the extreme environment in which they are found, Gelisols support only a small fraction of the world's population. The frozen condition of Gelisol landscapes makes them sensitive to human activities.

Histosols Soils that are composed mainly of organic materials. They contain at least 20 to 30 percent organic matter by weight and are more than 40 cm (15.75 in.) thick. Most Histosols form in settings such as wetlands where restricted drainage inhibits the decomposition of plant and animal remains, allowing these organic materials to accumulate over time. As a result, Histosols are ecologically important because of the large quantities of carbon they contain. Histosols are often referred to as peats and mucks and are mined for fuel and horticultural products.

Inceptisols Soils that exhibit minimal horizon development. They are more developed than Entisols, but still lack the features that are characteristic of other soil orders. Inceptisols are widely distributed and occur under a wide range of ecological settings. They are often found on fairly steep slopes, young geomorphic surfaces, and on resistant parent materials. Land use varies considerably with Inceptisols.

Mollisols Soils of grassland ecosystems. These soils are characterized by a thick, dark surface horizon that results from the long-term addition of organic materials derived from plant roots. Mollisols primarily occur in the mid-latitudes and are extensive in prairie regions. Mollisols are among some of the most important and productive agricultural soils in the world.

Oxisols Highly-weathered soils that are found primarily in the intertropical regions of the world. These soils contain few weatherable minerals and are often rich in iron and aluminum oxide minerals. Most Oxisols have extremely low native fertility, resulting from very low nutrient reserves, high phosphorus retention by oxide minerals, and low cation exchange capacity. Oxisols can be quite productive with inputs of lime and fertilizers.

Spodosols Acid soils characterized by a subsurface accumulation of humus that is complexed with aluminum and iron. Spodosols often occur under coniferous forest in cool, moist climates. Because they are naturally infertile, Spodosols require additions of lime in order to be productive agriculturally.

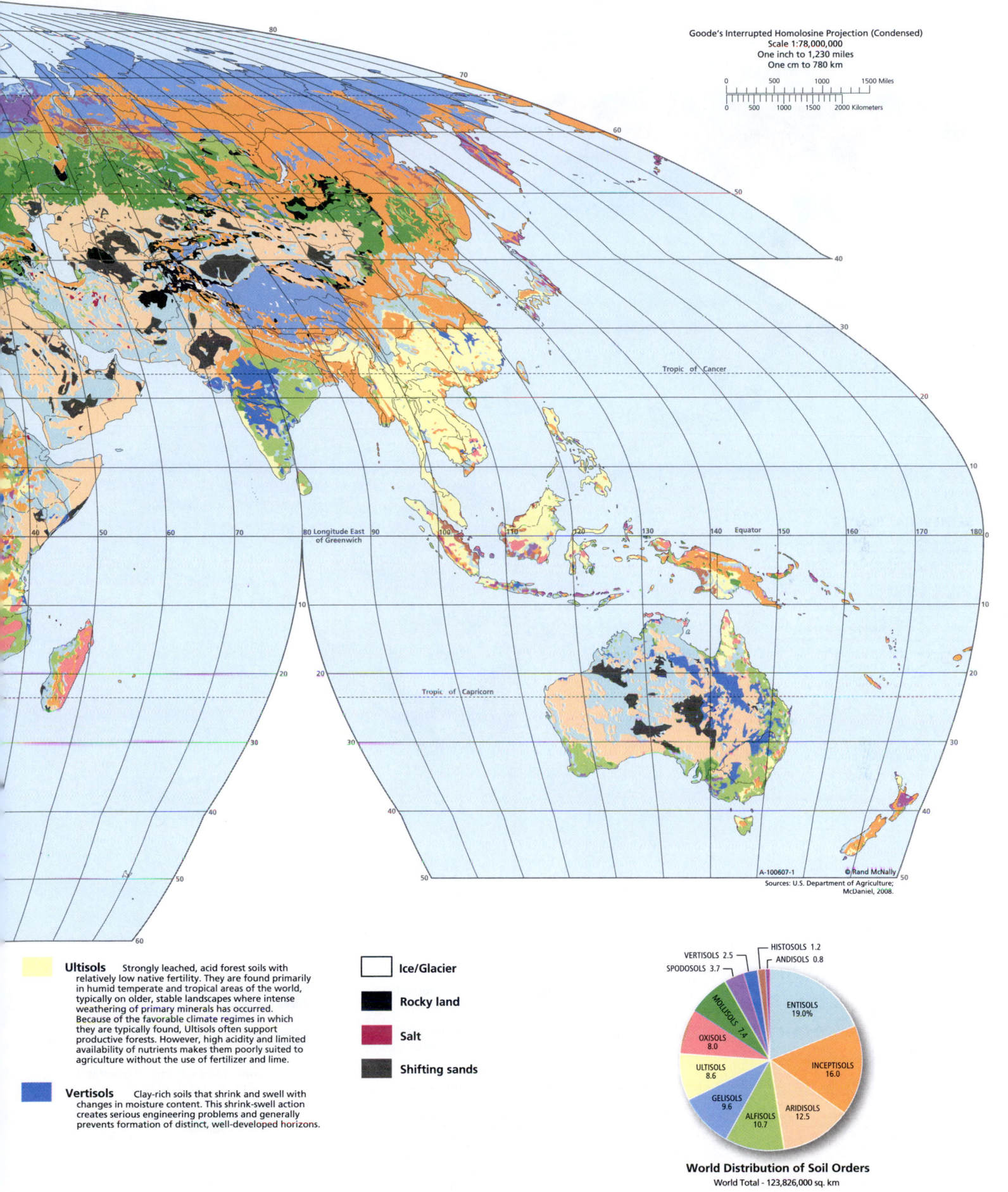

Goode's Interrupted Homolosine Projection (Condensed)
Scale 1:78,000,000
One inch to 1,230 miles
One cm to 780 km

A-100607-1   © Rand McNally

Sources: U.S. Department of Agriculture;
McDaniel, 2008.

Ultisols Strongly leached, acid forest soils with relatively low native fertility. They are found primarily in humid temperate and tropical areas of the world, typically on older, stable landscapes where intense weathering of primary minerals has occurred. Because of the favorable climate regimes in which they are typically found, Ultisols often support productive forests. However, high acidity and limited availability of nutrients makes them poorly suited to agriculture without the use of fertilizer and lime.

Vertisols Clay-rich soils that shrink and swell with changes in moisture content. This shrink-swell action creates serious engineering problems and generally prevents formation of distinct, well-developed horizons.

Ice/Glacier

Rocky land

Salt

Shifting sands

World Distribution of Soil Orders
World Total - 123,826,000 sq. km

HISTOSOLS 1.2
ANDISOLS 0.8
VERTISOLS 2.5
SPODOSOLS 3.7
MOLLISOLS 7.4
OXISOLS 8.0
ULTISOLS 8.6
GELISOLS 9.6
ALFISOLS 10.7
ARIDISOLS 12.5
INCEPTISOLS 16.0
ENTISOLS 19.0%

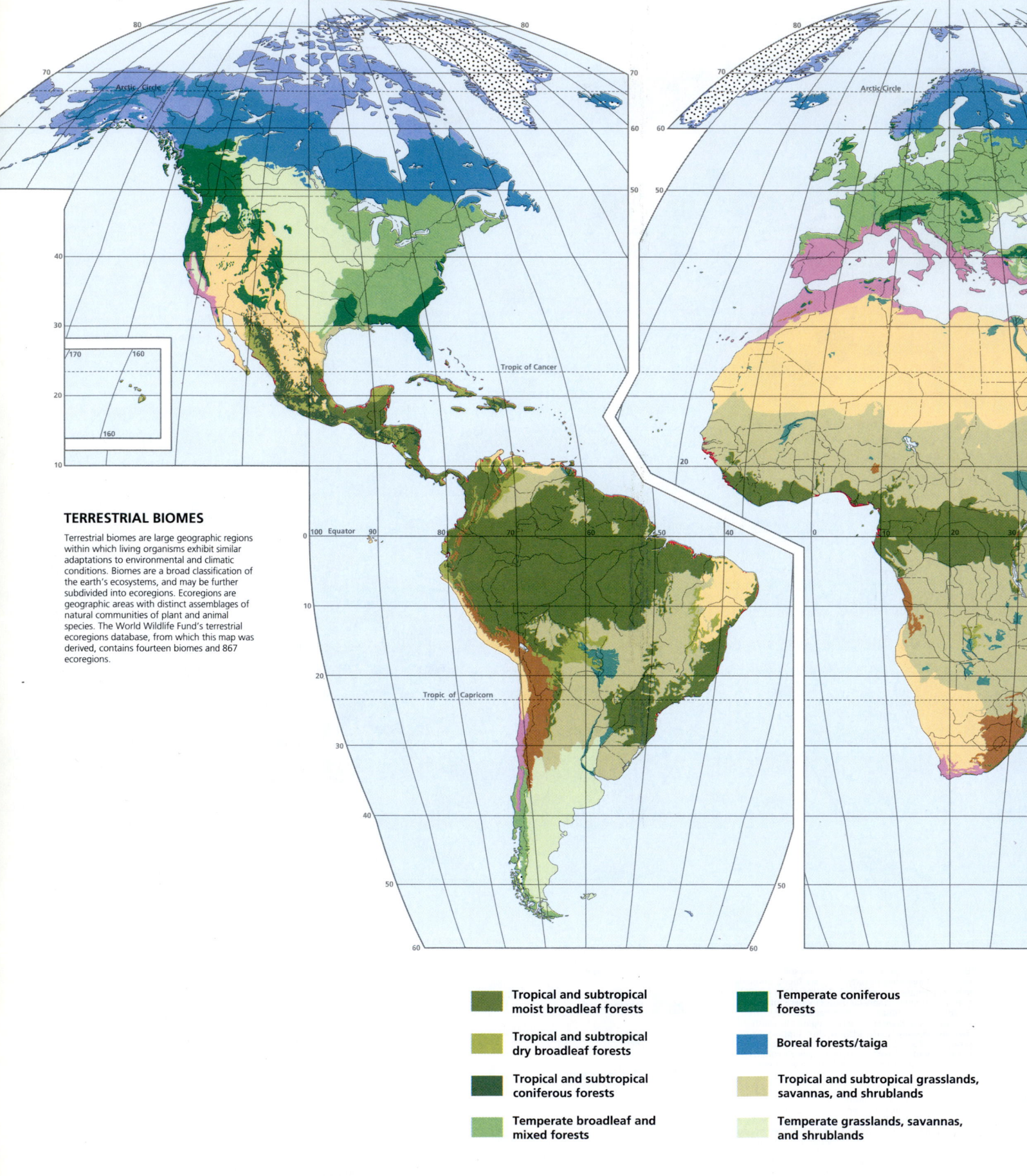

TERRESTRIAL BIOMES

Terrestrial biomes are large geographic regions within which living organisms exhibit similar adaptations to environmental and climatic conditions. Biomes are a broad classification of the earth's ecosystems, and may be further subdivided into ecoregions. Ecoregions are geographic areas with distinct assemblages of natural communities of plant and animal species. The World Wildlife Fund's terrestrial ecoregions database, from which this map was derived, contains fourteen biomes and 867 ecoregions.

Tropical and subtropical moist broadleaf forests

Tropical and subtropical dry broadleaf forests

Tropical and subtropical coniferous forests

Temperate broadleaf and mixed forests

Temperate coniferous forests

Boreal forests/taiga

Tropical and subtropical grasslands, savannas, and shrublands

Temperate grasslands, savannas, and shrublands

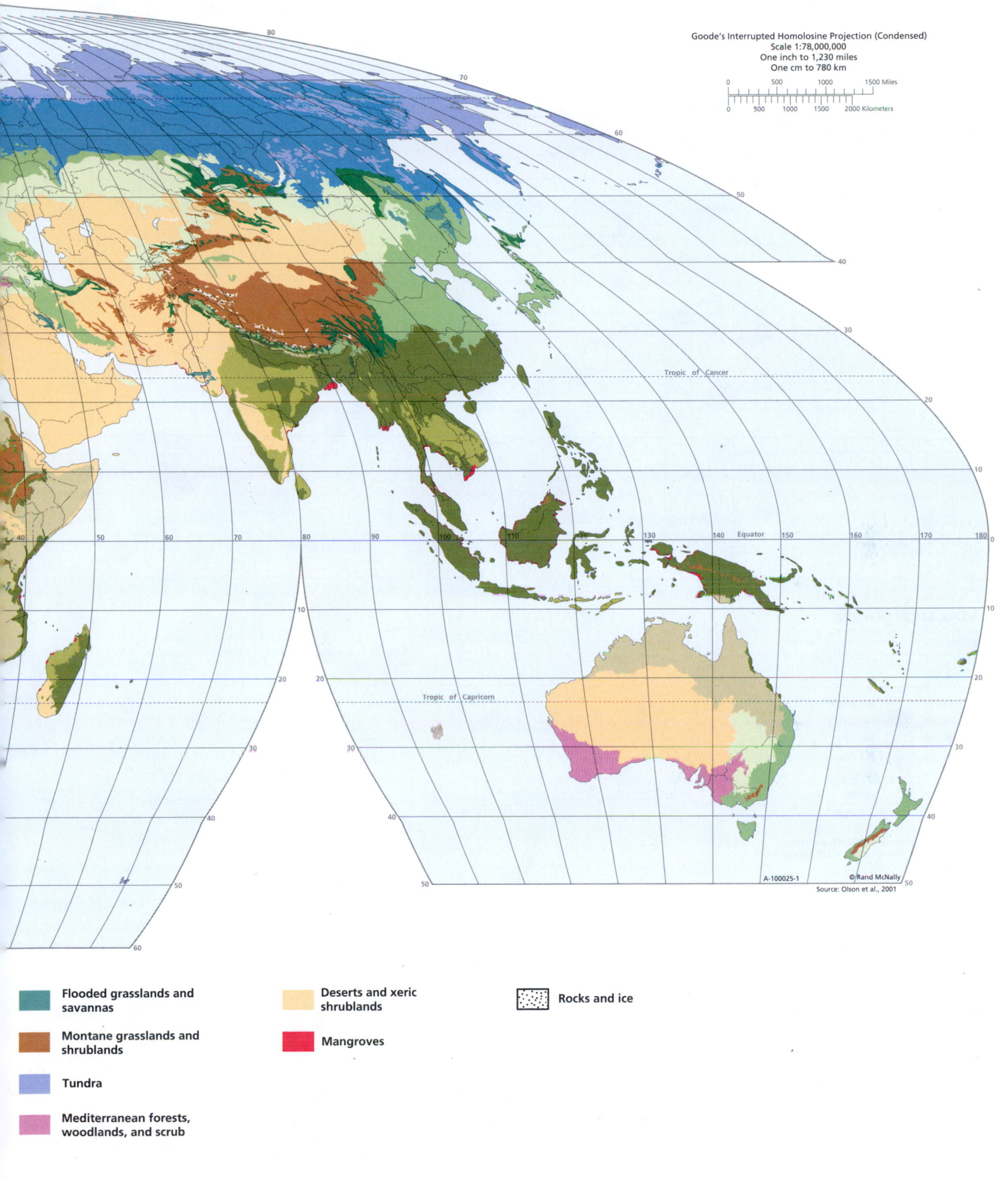

Goode's Interrupted Homolosine Projection (Condensed)
Scale 1:78,000,000
One inch to 1,230 miles
One cm to 780 km

A-100025-1

© Rand McNally

Source: Olson et al., 2001

Flooded grasslands and savannas

Montane grasslands and shrublands

Tundra

Mediterranean forests, woodlands, and scrub

Deserts and xeric shrublands

Mangroves

Rocks and ice

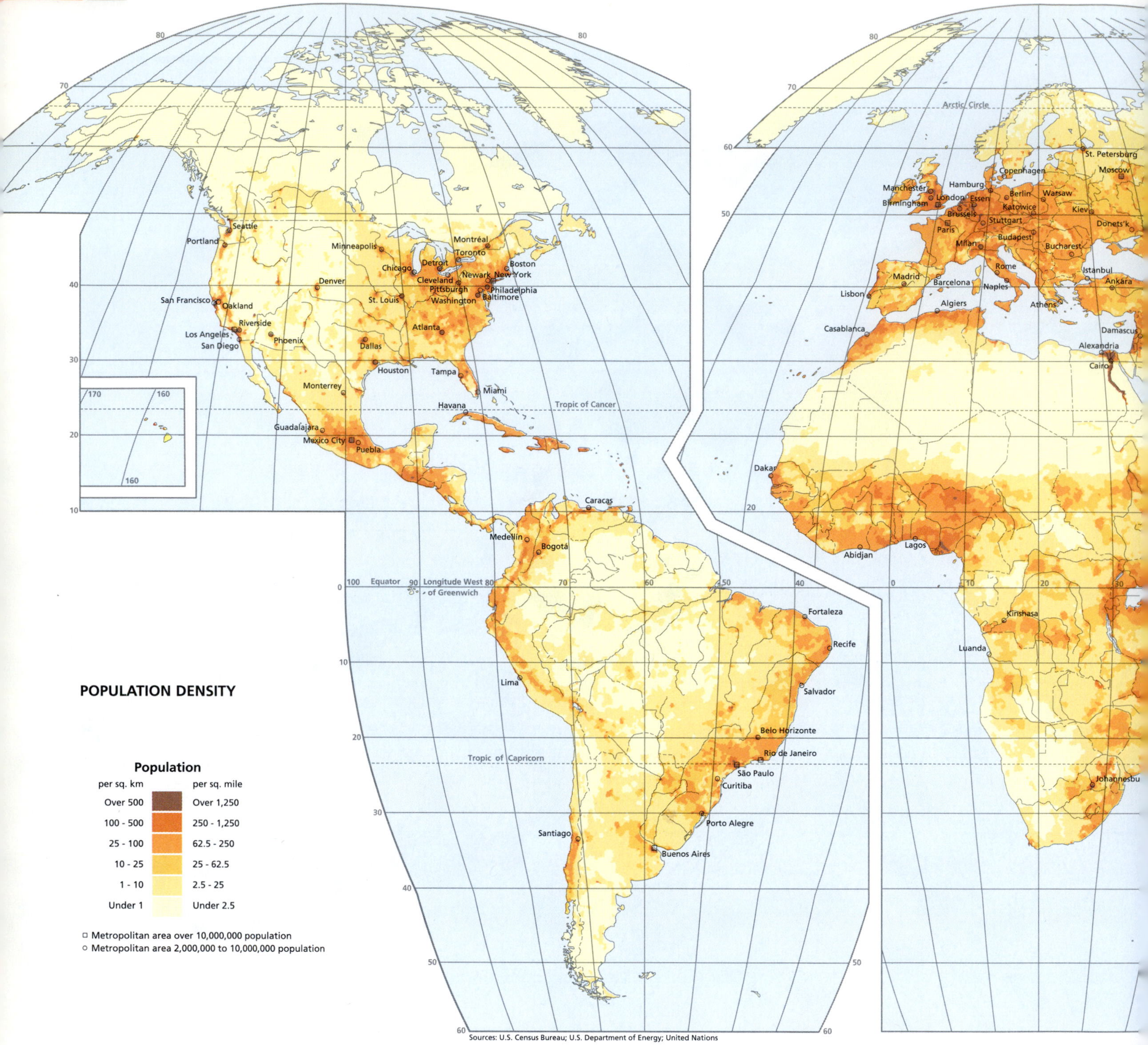

80 70 80 70 60 50 40 30 20 10 Tropic of Cancer 20 100 Equator 90 Longitude West 80 70 60 50 40 of Greenwich 10 20 Tropic of Capricorn 30 40 50 60

Arctic Circle

Seattle
Portland
Minneapolis
Montréal
Toronto
Chicago
Detroit
Boston
Denver
Cleveland
Newark New York
San Francisco
Pittsburgh
Philadelphia
Oakland
St. Louis
Washington
Baltimore
Riverside
Atlanta
Los Angeles
Phoenix
San Diego
Dallas
Houston
Tampa
Monterrey
Miami
Havana
Guadalajara
Mexico City
Puebla

Caracas
Medellín
Bogotá
Lima
Fortaleza
Recife
Salvador
Belo Horizonte
Rio de Janeiro
São Paulo
Curitiba
Porto Alegre
Santiago
Buenos Aires

St. Petersburg
Moscow
Copenhagen
Manchester
Hamburg
Berlin
Warsaw
Birmingham
London Essen
Katowice
Kiev
Brussels
Stuttgart
Donets'k
Paris
Milan
Budapest
Bucharest
Madrid
Rome
Barcelona
Istanbul
Lisbon
Naples
Ankara
Algiers
Athens
Casablanca
Damascus
Alexandria
Cairo
Dakar
Lagos
Abidjan
Kinshasa
Luanda
Johannesbu

POPULATION DENSITY

Population

per sq. km	per sq. mile
Over 500	Over 1,250
100 - 500	250 - 1,250
25 - 100	62.5 - 250
10 - 25	25 - 62.5
1 - 10	2.5 - 25
Under 1	Under 2.5

□ Metropolitan area over 10,000,000 population
○ Metropolitan area 2,000,000 to 10,000,000 population

Sources: U.S. Census Bureau; U.S. Department of Energy; United Nations

Largest Countries of the World 1950, 2000, 2050

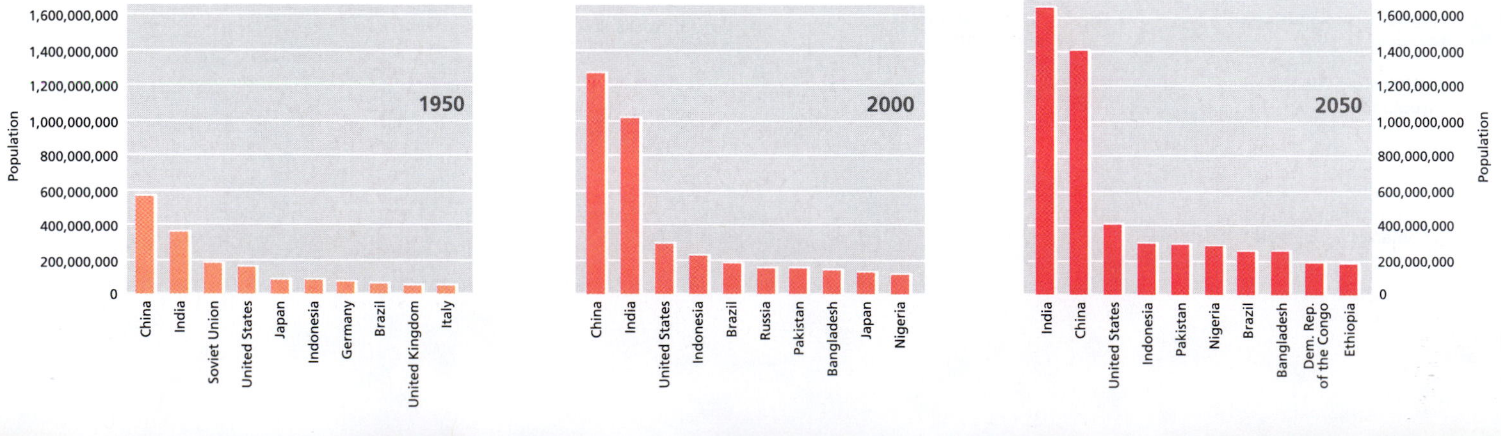

1950

Population: China, India, Soviet Union, United States, Japan, Indonesia, Germany, Brazil, United Kingdom, Italy

2000

Population: China, India, United States, Indonesia, Brazil, Russia, Pakistan, Bangladesh, Japan, Nigeria

2050

Population: India, China, United States, Indonesia, Pakistan, Nigeria, Brazil, Bangladesh, Dem. Rep. of the Congo, Ethiopia

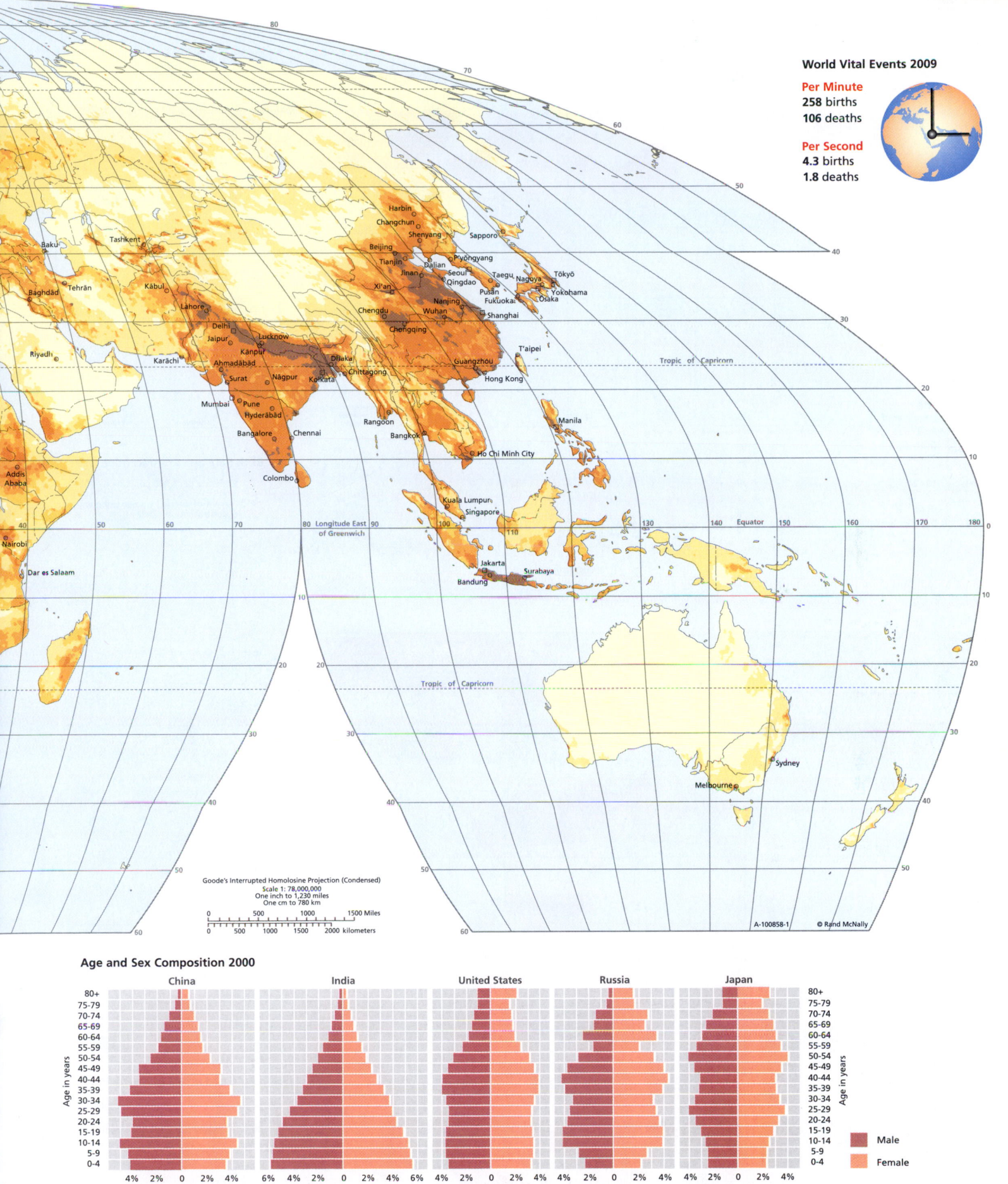

World Vital Events 2009

Per Minute
258 births
106 deaths

Per Second
4.3 births
1.8 deaths

Goode's Interrupted Homolosine Projection (Condensed)
Scale 1: 78,000,000
One inch to 1,230 miles
One cm to 780 km

500   1000   1500 Miles
500   1000   1500   2000 kilometers

A-100858-1   © Rand McNally

Age and Sex Composition 2000

China   India   United States   Russia   Japan

Age in years

■ Male
■ Female

Percent of total population

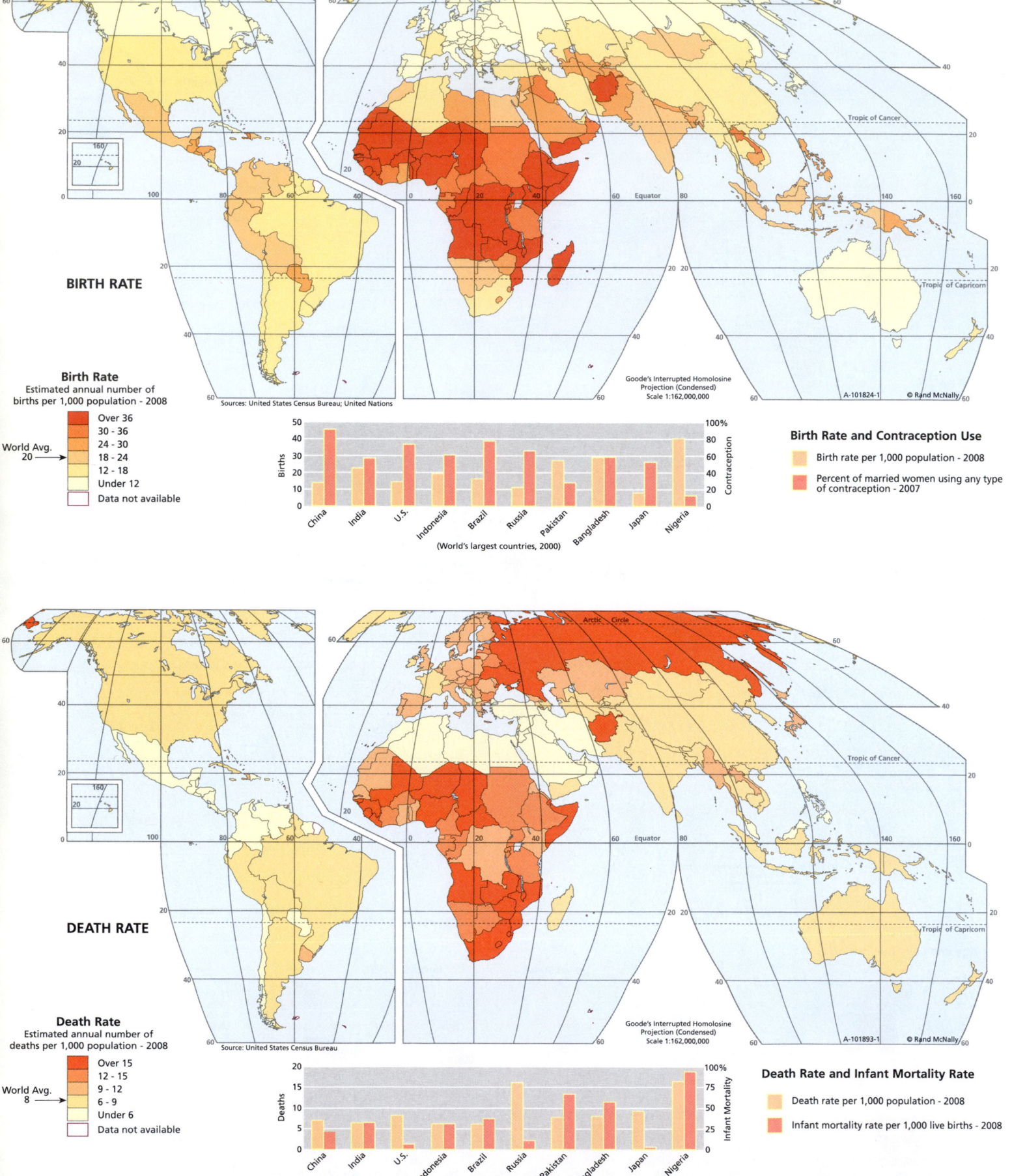

BIRTH RATE

Birth Rate
Estimated annual number of
births per 1,000 population - 2008

World Avg.
20 ➜

	Over 36
	30 - 36
	24 - 30
	18 - 24
	12 - 18
	Under 12
	Data not available

Sources: United States Census Bureau; United Nations

Goode's Interrupted Homolosine
Projection (Condensed)
Scale 1:162,000,000

A-101824-1   © Rand McNally

(World's largest countries, 2000)

Birth Rate and Contraception Use

Birth rate per 1,000 population - 2008

Percent of married women using any type
of contraception - 2007

DEATH RATE

Death Rate
Estimated annual number of
deaths per 1,000 population - 2008

World Avg.
8 ➜

	Over 15
	12 - 15
	9 - 12
	6 - 9
	Under 6
	Data not available

Source: United States Census Bureau

Goode's Interrupted Homolosine
Projection (Condensed)
Scale 1:162,000,000

A-101893-1   © Rand McNally

(World's largest countries, 2000)

Death Rate and Infant Mortality Rate

Death rate per 1,000 population - 2008

Infant mortality rate per 1,000 live births - 2008

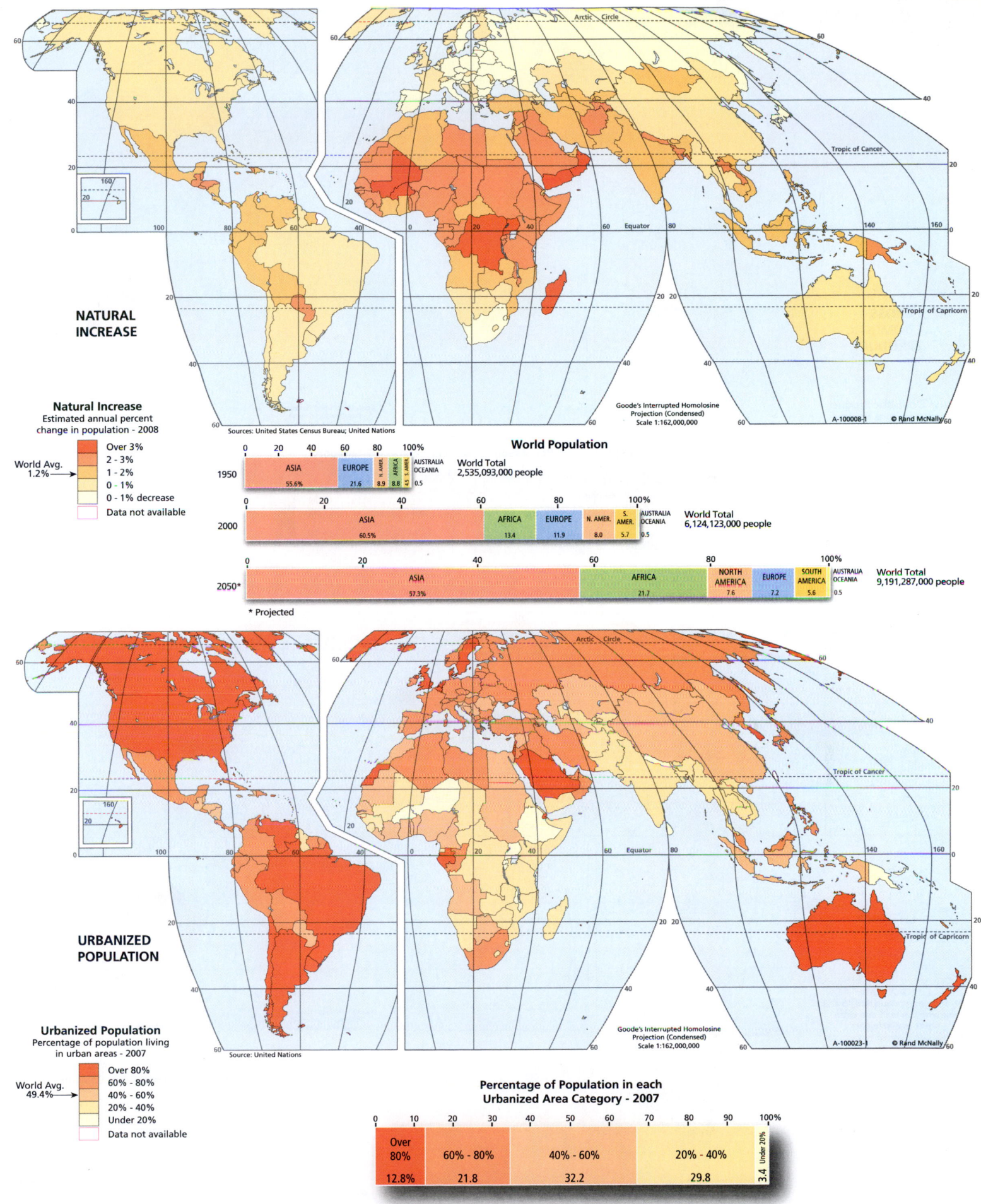

NATURAL INCREASE

Natural Increase
Estimated annual percent
change in population - 2008

World Avg.
1.2%
- Over 3%
- 2 - 3%
- 1 - 2%
- 0 - 1%
- 0 - 1% decrease
- Data not available

Sources: United States Census Bureau; United Nations

Goode's Interrupted Homolosine
Projection (Condensed)
Scale 1:162,000,000

A-100008-1   © Rand McNally

World Population

1950   ASIA 55.6%   EUROPE 21.6   N. AMER. 8.9   AFRICA 8.8   AUSTRALIA/OCEANIA 0.5   S. AMER. 4.5
World Total 2,535,093,000 people

2000   ASIA 60.5%   AFRICA 13.4   EUROPE 11.9   N. AMER. 8.0   S. AMER. 5.7   AUSTRALIA/OCEANIA 0.5
World Total 6,124,123,000 people

2050*   ASIA 57.3%   AFRICA 21.7   NORTH AMERICA 7.6   EUROPE 7.2   SOUTH AMERICA 5.6   AUSTRALIA/OCEANIA 0.5
World Total 9,191,287,000 people

* Projected

URBANIZED POPULATION

Urbanized Population
Percentage of population living
in urban areas - 2007

World Avg.
49.4%
- Over 80%
- 60% - 80%
- 40% - 60%
- 20% - 40%
- Under 20%
- Data not available

Source: United Nations

Goode's Interrupted Homolosine
Projection (Condensed)
Scale 1:162,000,000

A-100023-1   © Rand McNally

**Percentage of Population in each
Urbanized Area Category - 2007**

Over 80%	60% - 80%	40% - 60%	20% - 40%	Under 20%
12.8	21.8	32.2	29.8	3.4

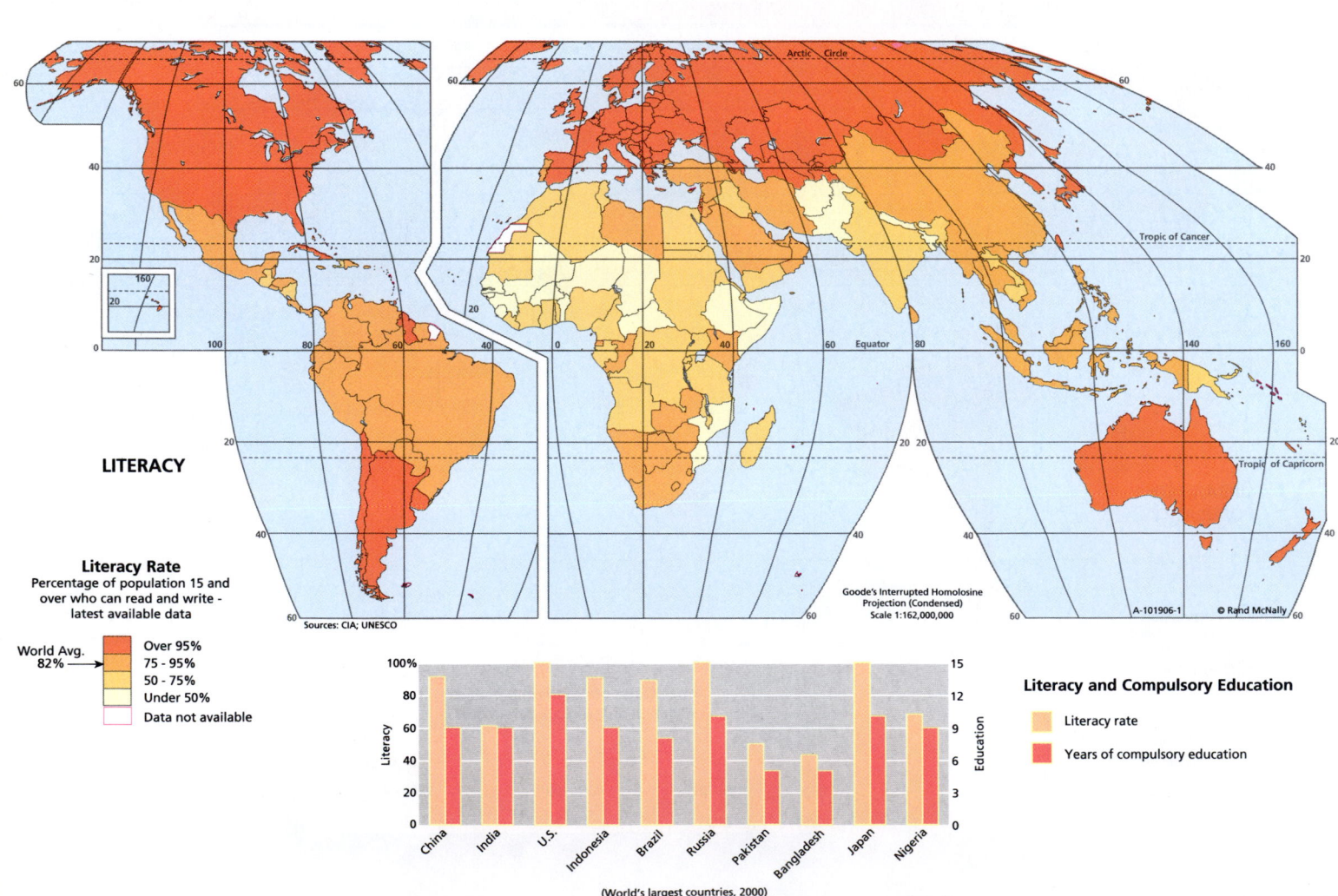

GROSS DOMESTIC PRODUCT

Gross Domestic Product
Annual per capita estimate
in U.S. dollars -
latest available data

World Avg.
$10,000 →

- Over $32,000
- $16,000 - $32,000
- $8,000 - $16,000
- $4,000 - $8,000
- $2,000 - $4,000
- Under $2,000
- Data not available

Source: CIA

Goode's Interrupted Homolosine
Projection (Condensed)
Scale 1:162,000,000

A-101907-1   © Rand McNally

Percentage of World Population in each Per Capita GDP Category

Over $32,000	$16,000-$32,000	$8,000-$16,000	$4,000 - $8,000	$2,000 - $4,000	Under $2,000
11.7%	4.8%	12.6%	27.8%	30.7%	12.5%

LITERACY

Literacy Rate
Percentage of population 15 and
over who can read and write -
latest available data

World Avg.
82% →

- Over 95%
- 75 - 95%
- 50 - 75%
- Under 50%
- Data not available

Sources: CIA; UNESCO

Goode's Interrupted Homolosine
Projection (Condensed)
Scale 1:162,000,000

A-101906-1   © Rand McNally

Literacy and Compulsory Education

- Literacy rate
- Years of compulsory education

(World's largest countries, 2000)

China, India, U.S., Indonesia, Brazil, Russia, Pakistan, Bangladesh, Japan, Nigeria

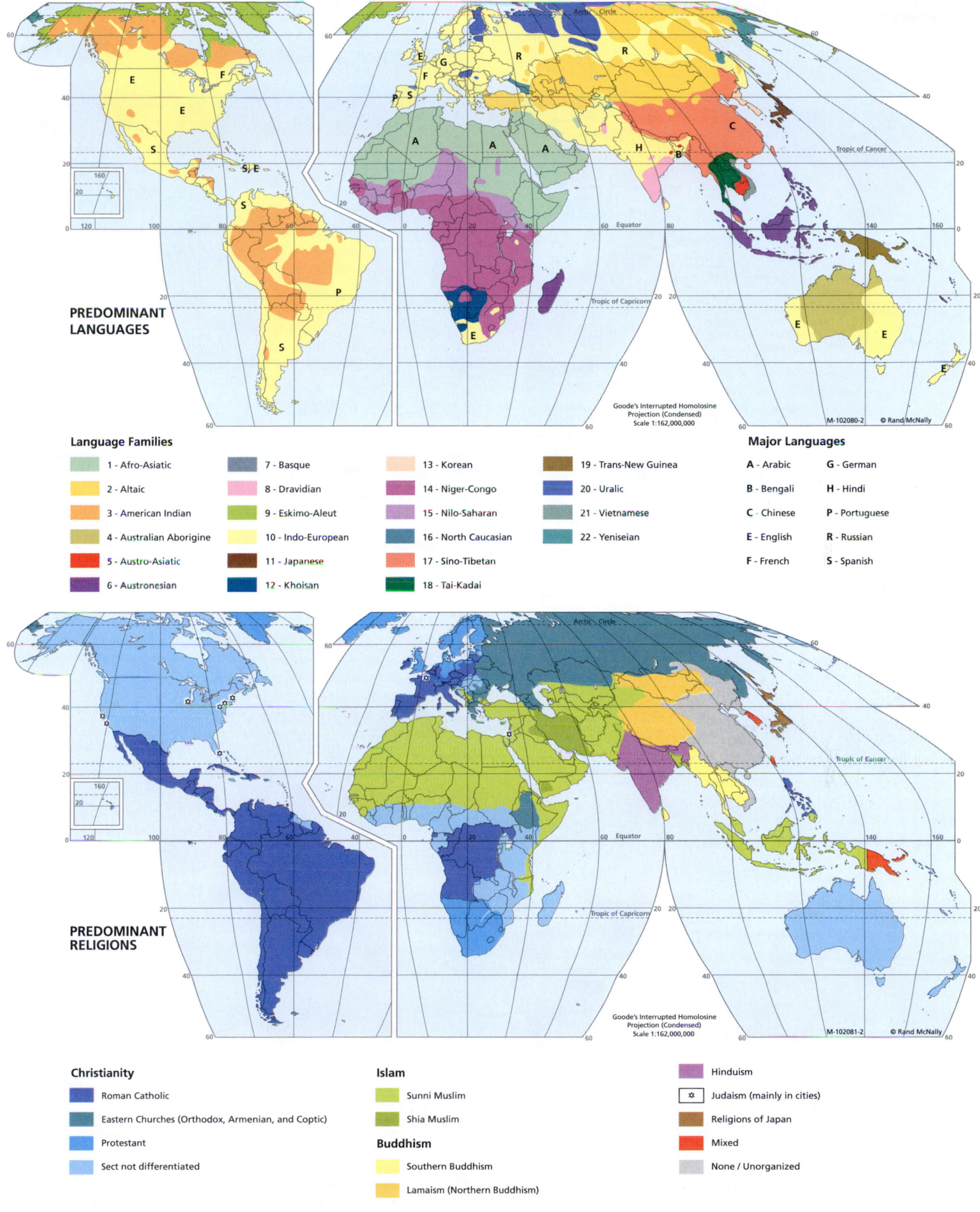

PREDOMINANT LANGUAGES

Goode's Interrupted Homolosine Projection (Condensed)
Scale 1:162,000,000

M-102080-2 © Rand McNally

Language Families

- 1 - Afro-Asiatic
- 2 - Altaic
- 3 - American Indian
- 4 - Australian Aborigine
- 5 - Austro-Asiatic
- 6 - Austronesian
- 7 - Basque
- 8 - Dravidian
- 9 - Eskimo-Aleut
- 10 - Indo-European
- 11 - Japanese
- 12 - Khoisan
- 13 - Korean
- 14 - Niger-Congo
- 15 - Nilo-Saharan
- 16 - North Caucasian
- 17 - Sino-Tibetan
- 18 - Tai-Kadai
- 19 - Trans-New Guinea
- 20 - Uralic
- 21 - Vietnamese
- 22 - Yeniseian

Major Languages

- A - Arabic
- B - Bengali
- C - Chinese
- E - English
- F - French
- G - German
- H - Hindi
- P - Portuguese
- R - Russian
- S - Spanish

PREDOMINANT RELIGIONS

Goode's Interrupted Homolosine Projection (Condensed)
Scale 1:162,000,000

M-102081-2 © Rand McNally

Christianity

- Roman Catholic
- Eastern Churches (Orthodox, Armenian, and Coptic)
- Protestant
- Sect not differentiated

Islam

- Sunni Muslim
- Shia Muslim

Buddhism

- Southern Buddhism
- Lamaism (Northern Buddhism)

- Hinduism
- Judaism (mainly in cities)
- Religions of Japan
- Mixed
- None / Unorganized

HIV INFECTION

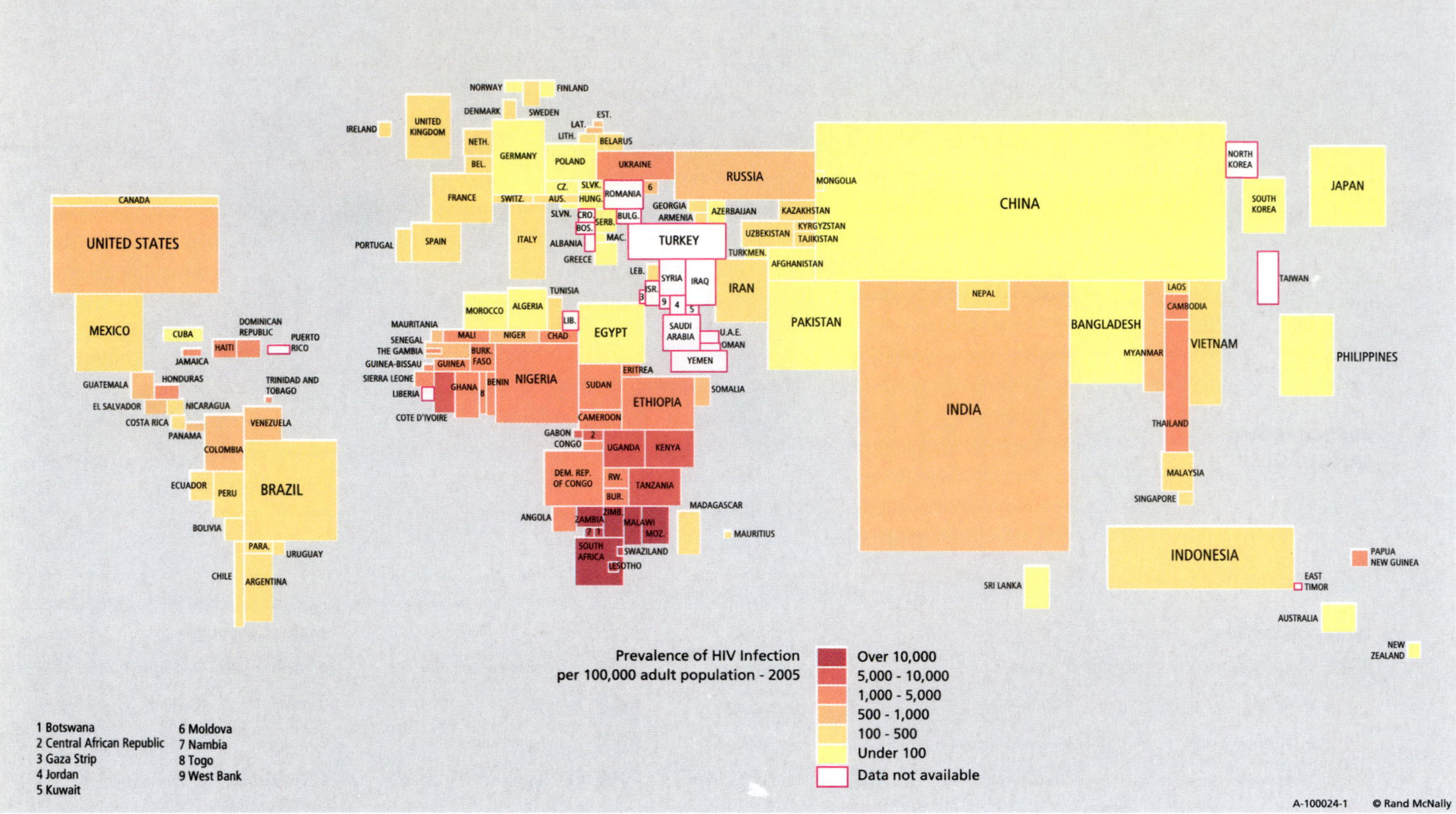

NORWAY FINLAND
IRELAND UNITED KINGDOM DENMARK SWEDEN EST.
NETH. LAT. LITH.
BEL. GERMANY POLAND BELARUS
FRANCE SWITZ. CZ. SLVK. UKRAINE RUSSIA MONGOLIA
AUS. HUNG. ROMANIA 6 GEORGIA CHINA NORTH KOREA
PORTUGAL SPAIN ITALY SLVN. CRO. BULG. AZERBAIJAN KAZAKHSTAN SOUTH KOREA JAPAN
BOS. SERB. ARMENIA KYRGYZSTAN
ALBANIA MAC. TURKEY UZBEKISTAN TAJIKISTAN TAIWAN
GREECE TURKMEN.
LEB. SYRIA IRAQ AFGHANISTAN
TUNISIA ISR. IRAN PAKISTAN BANGLADESH LAOS
MOROCCO ALGERIA LIB. 9 4 5 CAMBODIA PHILIPPINES
CANADA MAURITANIA EGYPT SAUDI U.A.E. NEPAL MYANMAR VIETNAM
UNITED STATES SENEGAL MALI NIGER CHAD ARABIA OMAN INDIA THAILAND
THE GAMBIA BURK. YEMEN
GUINEA-BISSAU GUINEA FASO NIGERIA SUDAN ERITREA MALAYSIA
MEXICO CUBA DOMINICAN SIERRA LEONE GHANA 8 BENIN SOMALIA SINGAPORE
REPUBLIC PUERTO LIBERIA ETHIOPIA
JAMAICA HAITI RICO COTE D'IVOIRE CAMEROON
GUATEMALA HONDURAS TRINIDAD AND GABON 2 UGANDA KENYA
EL SALVADOR TOBAGO CONGO RW.
NICARAGUA DEM. REP. BUR. INDONESIA PAPUA
COSTA RICA VENEZUELA OF CONGO TANZANIA NEW GUINEA
PANAMA ANGOLA MADAGASCAR EAST
COLOMBIA ZAMBIA ZIMB. MALAWI TIMOR
ECUADOR PERU BRAZIL SOUTH MOZ. MAURITIUS
BOLIVIA AFRICA SWAZILAND
PARA. URUGUAY LESOTHO AUSTRALIA
CHILE ARGENTINA SRI LANKA NEW ZEALAND

Prevalence of HIV Infection
per 100,000 adult population - 2005

■	Over 10,000
■	5,000 - 10,000
■	1,000 - 5,000
■	500 - 1,000
■	100 - 500
■	Under 100
▢	Data not available

1 Botswana   6 Moldova
2 Central African Republic   7 Namibia
3 Gaza Strip   8 Togo
4 Jordan   9 West Bank
5 Kuwait

A-100024-1   © Rand McNally

Source: WHO

Size of each country is proportional to its population

▢ = 25,000,000 people

Countries with populations under 1,000,000 are not shown.

TUBERCULOSIS

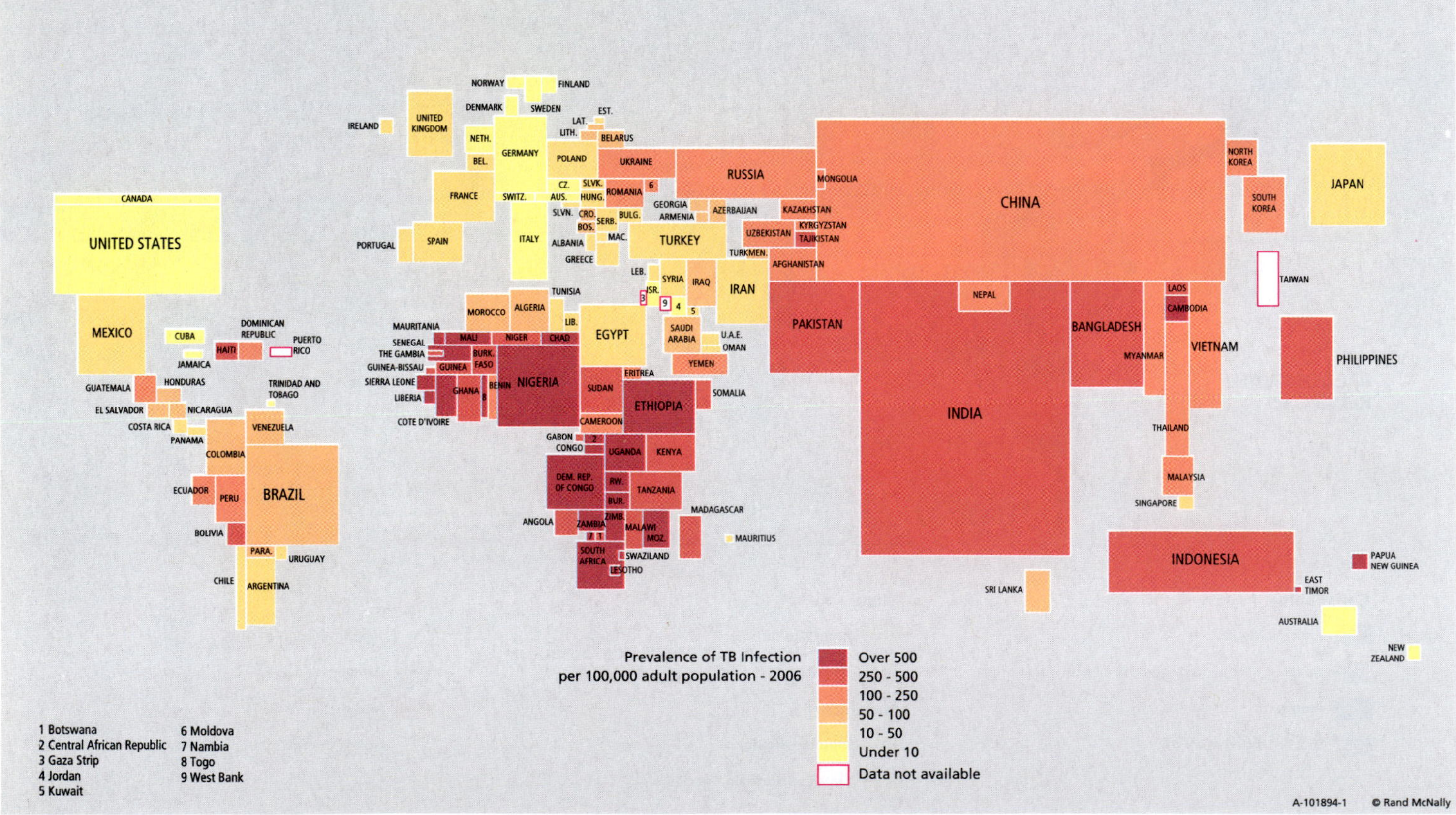

NORWAY FINLAND
IRELAND UNITED KINGDOM DENMARK SWEDEN EST.
NETH. LAT. LITH.
BEL. GERMANY POLAND BELARUS
FRANCE SWITZ. CZ. SLVK. UKRAINE RUSSIA MONGOLIA
AUS. HUNG. ROMANIA 6 GEORGIA CHINA NORTH KOREA
PORTUGAL SPAIN ITALY SLVN. CRO. BULG. AZERBAIJAN KAZAKHSTAN SOUTH KOREA JAPAN
BOS. SERB. ARMENIA KYRGYZSTAN
ALBANIA MAC. TURKEY UZBEKISTAN TAJIKISTAN TAIWAN
GREECE TURKMEN.
LEB. SYRIA IRAQ AFGHANISTAN
TUNISIA ISR. IRAN PAKISTAN BANGLADESH LAOS
MOROCCO ALGERIA LIB. 9 4 5 CAMBODIA
CANADA MAURITANIA EGYPT SAUDI U.A.E. NEPAL MYANMAR VIETNAM PHILIPPINES
UNITED STATES SENEGAL MALI NIGER CHAD ARABIA OMAN INDIA
THE GAMBIA BURK. YEMEN THAILAND
GUINEA-BISSAU GUINEA FASO NIGERIA SUDAN ERITREA
MEXICO CUBA DOMINICAN SIERRA LEONE GHANA BENIN SOMALIA MALAYSIA
REPUBLIC PUERTO LIBERIA ETHIOPIA SINGAPORE
JAMAICA HAITI RICO COTE D'IVOIRE CAMEROON
GUATEMALA HONDURAS TRINIDAD AND GABON 2 UGANDA KENYA
EL SALVADOR TOBAGO CONGO RW.
NICARAGUA DEM. REP. BUR.
COSTA RICA VENEZUELA OF CONGO TANZANIA INDONESIA PAPUA
PANAMA ANGOLA MADAGASCAR NEW GUINEA
COLOMBIA ZAMBIA ZIMB. MALAWI EAST
ECUADOR PERU BRAZIL SOUTH MOZ. MAURITIUS TIMOR
BOLIVIA AFRICA SWAZILAND
PARA. URUGUAY LESOTHO AUSTRALIA
CHILE ARGENTINA SRI LANKA NEW ZEALAND

Prevalence of TB Infection
per 100,000 adult population - 2006

■	Over 500
■	250 - 500
■	100 - 250
■	50 - 100
■	10 - 50
■	Under 10
▢	Data not available

1 Botswana   6 Moldova
2 Central African Republic   7 Namibia
3 Gaza Strip   8 Togo
4 Jordan   9 West Bank
5 Kuwait

A-101894-1   © Rand McNally

Source: WHO

MALARIA

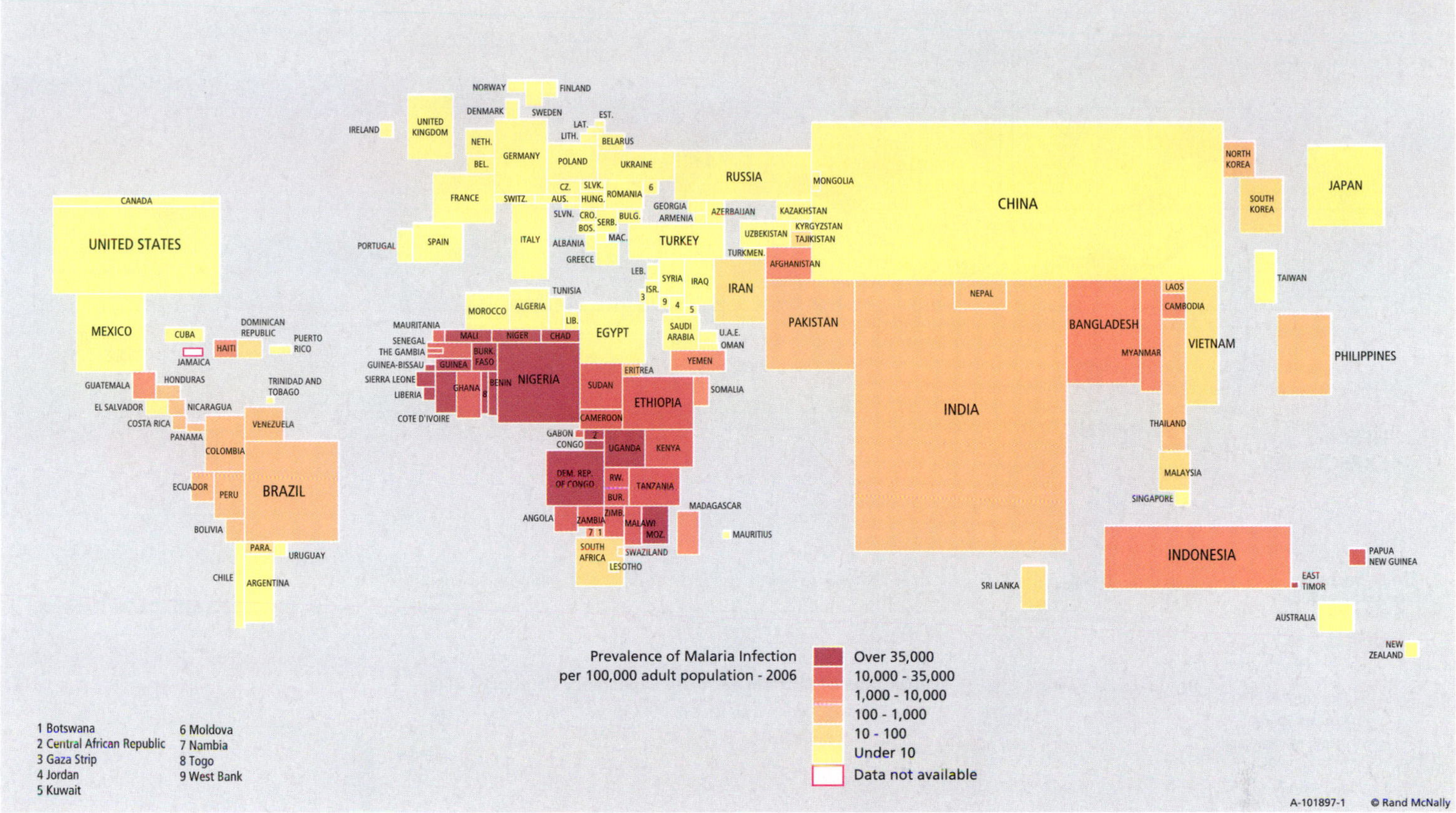

NORWAY FINLAND
IRELAND UNITED KINGDOM
DENMARK SWEDEN
NETH. LAT. EST.
BEL. GERMANY LITH. BELARUS
POLAND UKRAINE
FRANCE SWITZ. CZ. SLVK. ROMANIA 6 RUSSIA MONGOLIA
AUS. HUNG.
SLVN. CRO. SERB. BULG. GEORGIA ARMENIA AZERBAIJAN KAZAKHSTAN
CANADA PORTUGAL SPAIN ITALY ALBANIA MAC. TURKEY UZBEKISTAN KYRGYZSTAN CHINA
GREECE TAJIKISTAN
TURKMEN. NORTH KOREA
JAPAN
UNITED STATES TUNISIA LEB. SYRIA IRAQ AFGHANISTAN SOUTH KOREA
3 ISR. 9 4 5 IRAN
TAIWAN
MAURITANIA MOROCCO ALGERIA LIB. EGYPT SAUDI ARABIA PAKISTAN NEPAL LAOS
MEXICO CUBA DOMINICAN REPUBLIC SENEGAL NIGER CHAD U.A.E. CAMBODIA BANGLADESH
HAITI THE GAMBIA MALI BURK. OMAN
PUERTO RICO GUINEA-BISSAU FASO YEMEN VIETNAM
JAMAICA GUINEA BENIN NIGERIA SUDAN ERITREA MYANMAR PHILIPPINES
GUATEMALA HONDURAS SIERRA LEONE GHANA ETHIOPIA SOMALIA
EL SALVADOR LIBERIA CAMEROON INDIA
NICARAGUA COTE D'IVOIRE THAILAND
COSTA RICA TRINIDAD AND GABON 2
PANAMA TOBAGO CONGO UGANDA KENYA
VENEZUELA DEM. REP. MALAYSIA
COLOMBIA OF CONGO RW. TANZANIA SINGAPORE
ECUADOR PERU BRAZIL BUR. INDONESIA PAPUA NEW GUINEA
BOLIVIA ANGOLA ZAMBIA ZIMB. MADAGASCAR
7 1 MALAWI MAURITIUS EAST TIMOR
PARA. MOZ.
URUGUAY SOUTH SWAZILAND SRI LANKA AUSTRALIA
CHILE AFRICA LESOTHO
ARGENTINA NEW ZEALAND

Prevalence of Malaria Infection
per 100,000 adult population - 2006

- Over 35,000
- 10,000 - 35,000
- 1,000 - 10,000
- 100 - 1,000
- 10 - 100
- Under 10
- Data not available

1 Botswana   6 Moldova
2 Central African Republic   7 Namibia
3 Gaza Strip   8 Togo
4 Jordan   9 West Bank
5 Kuwait

A-101897-1 © Rand McNally

Source: WHO

The maps on these two pages are called **cartograms**. On these cartograms, the size of each country is proportional to its total population. This means that the countries with the largest areas are those with the largest populations. The shapes of countries must be distorted in order to achieve this proportional representation. Here, each country is shown as a rectangle in order to facilitate size comparisons.

One advantage of these cartograms is that they reveal the relationship between the mapped variable and the affected population. Consider the example of Chad and Nigeria. Both have relatively high rates of HIV infection (between 1,000 and 5,000 cases per 100,000 population). But Nigeria is much larger than Chad on the cartogram, which informs the reader that the population affected by HIV is much larger in Nigeria.

PHYSICIANS

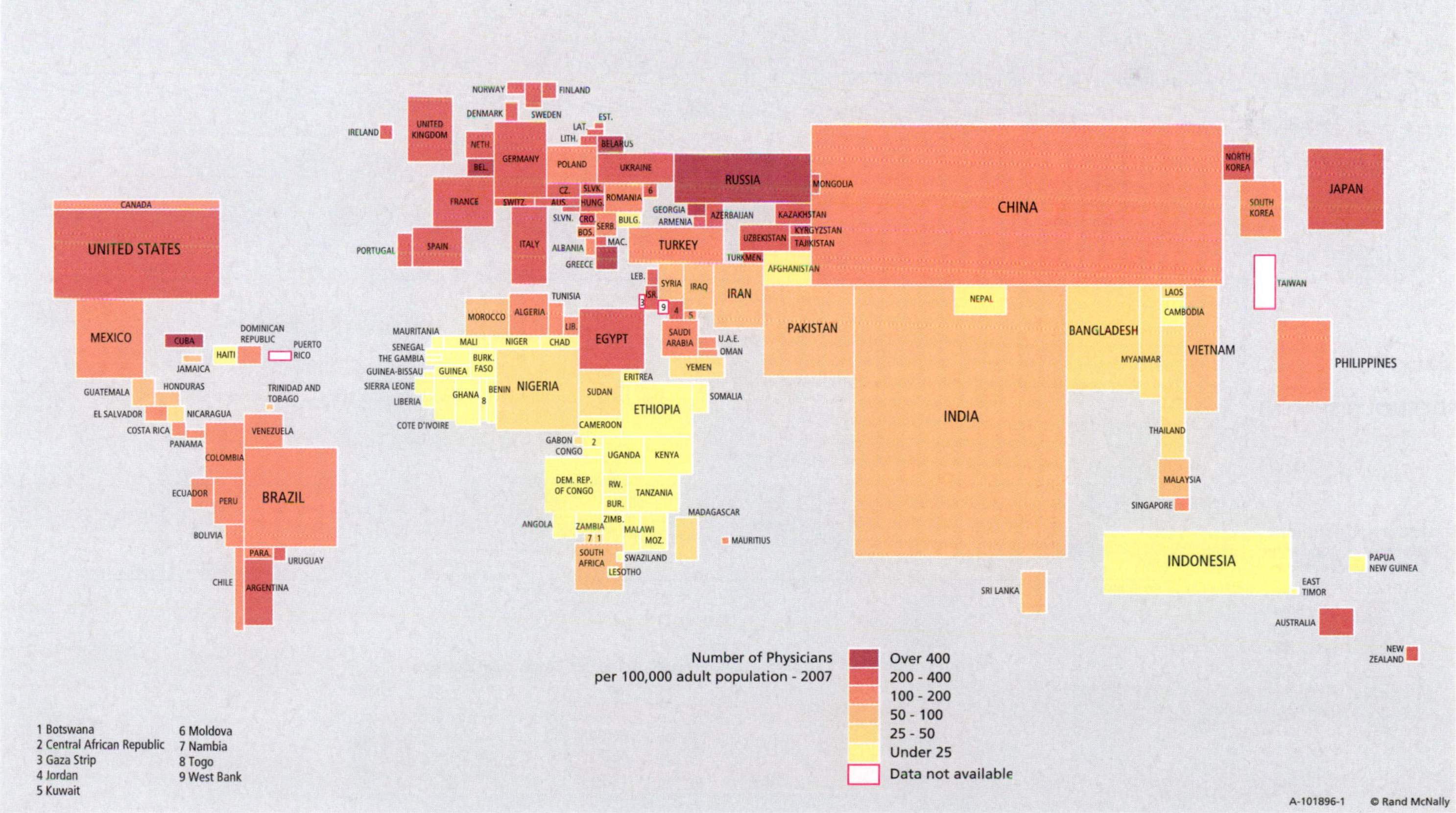

NORWAY FINLAND
IRELAND UNITED KINGDOM DENMARK SWEDEN
NETH. LAT. EST.
BEL. GERMANY LITH. BELARUS
POLAND UKRAINE
FRANCE SWITZ. CZ. SLVK. ROMANIA 6 RUSSIA MONGOLIA
AUS. HUNG.
SLVN. CRO. BOS. SERB. BULG. GEORGIA ARMENIA AZERBAIJAN KAZAKHSTAN
CANADA PORTUGAL SPAIN ITALY ALBANIA MAC. TURKEY UZBEKISTAN KYRGYZSTAN CHINA
GREECE TAJIKISTAN
TURKMEN. NORTH KOREA
JAPAN
UNITED STATES TUNISIA LEB. SYRIA IRAQ AFGHANISTAN SOUTH KOREA
GR. 9 4 5 IRAN
3 TAIWAN
MOROCCO ALGERIA LIB. EGYPT SAUDI ARABIA PAKISTAN NEPAL LAOS
MEXICO DOMINICAN MAURITANIA CAMBODIA
CUBA REPUBLIC SENEGAL MALI NIGER CHAD U.A.E. BANGLADESH
HAITI THE GAMBIA BURK. OMAN
JAMAICA PUERTO GUINEA-BISSAU FASO YEMEN VIETNAM
RICO GUINEA BENIN NIGERIA SUDAN ERITREA MYANMAR PHILIPPINES
GUATEMALA SIERRA LEONE ETHIOPIA SOMALIA
HONDURAS LIBERIA GHANA
EL SALVADOR 8 CAMEROON INDIA
NICARAGUA COTE D'IVOIRE
COSTA RICA GABON 2 THAILAND
PANAMA CONGO UGANDA KENYA
VENEZUELA DEM. REP. MALAYSIA
COLOMBIA OF CONGO RW. TANZANIA SINGAPORE
ECUADOR BUR.
PERU BRAZIL ANGOLA ZAMBIA ZIMB. MADAGASCAR INDONESIA PAPUA NEW GUINEA
BOLIVIA 7 1 MALAWI MAURITIUS
MOZ. EAST TIMOR
PARA. SOUTH SWAZILAND
URUGUAY AFRICA LESOTHO SRI LANKA AUSTRALIA
CHILE ARGENTINA NEW ZEALAND

Number of Physicians
per 100,000 adult population - 2007

- Over 400
- 200 - 400
- 100 - 200
- 50 - 100
- 25 - 50
- Under 25
- Data not available

1 Botswana   6 Moldova
2 Central African Republic   7 Namibia
3 Gaza Strip   8 Togo
4 Jordan   9 West Bank
5 Kuwait

A-101896-1 © Rand McNally

Source: WHO

LIFE EXPECTANCY

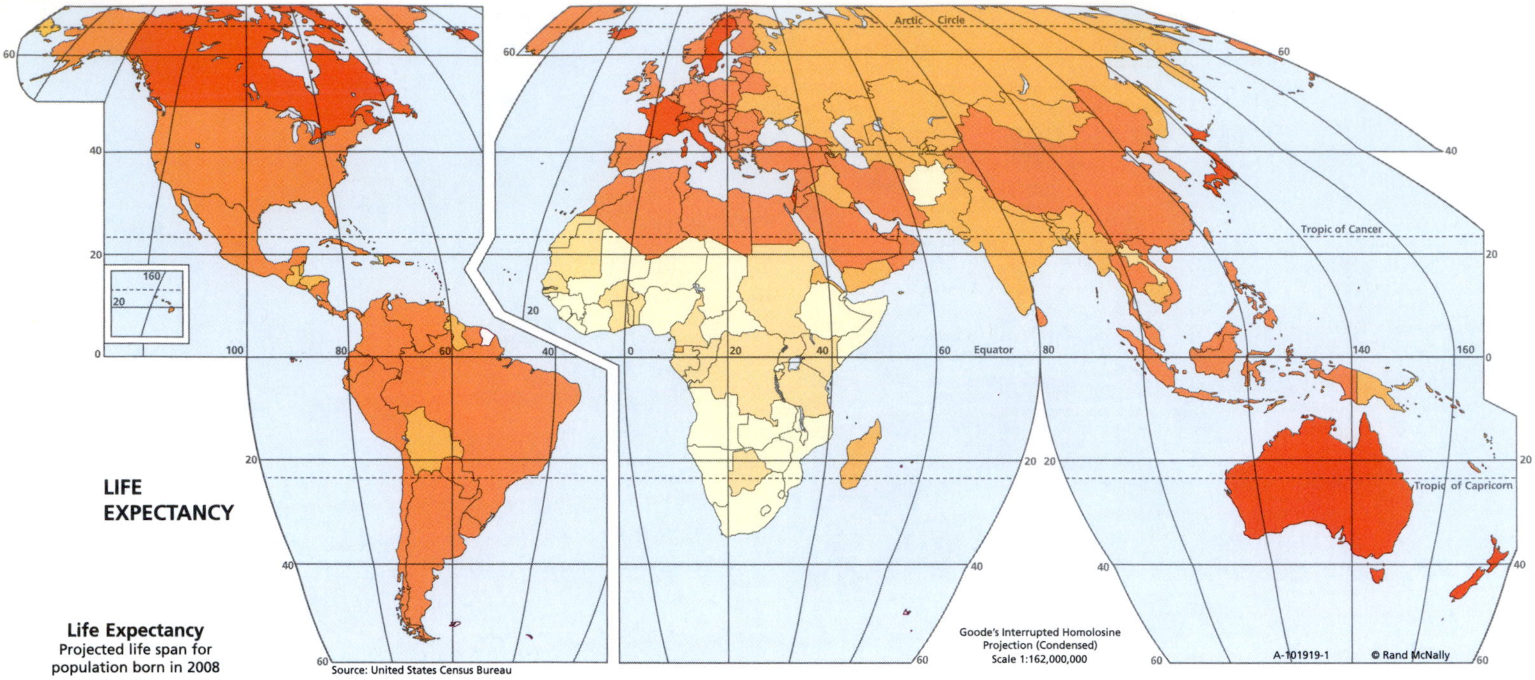

Life Expectancy
Projected life span for
population born in 2008

World Avg. 66 →

- Over 80
- 70 - 80
- 60 - 70
- 50 - 60
- Under 50
- Data not available

Source: United States Census Bureau

Goode's Interrupted Homolosine
Projection (Condensed)
Scale 1:162,000,000

A-101919-1   © Rand McNally

Percentage of Births in each Life Expectancy Category - 2008

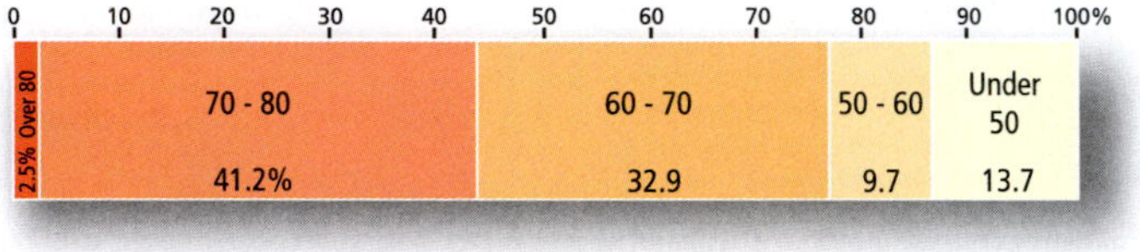

2.5% Over 80	70 - 80	60 - 70	50 - 60	Under 50
	41.2%	32.9	9.7	13.7

UNDERNOURISHMENT

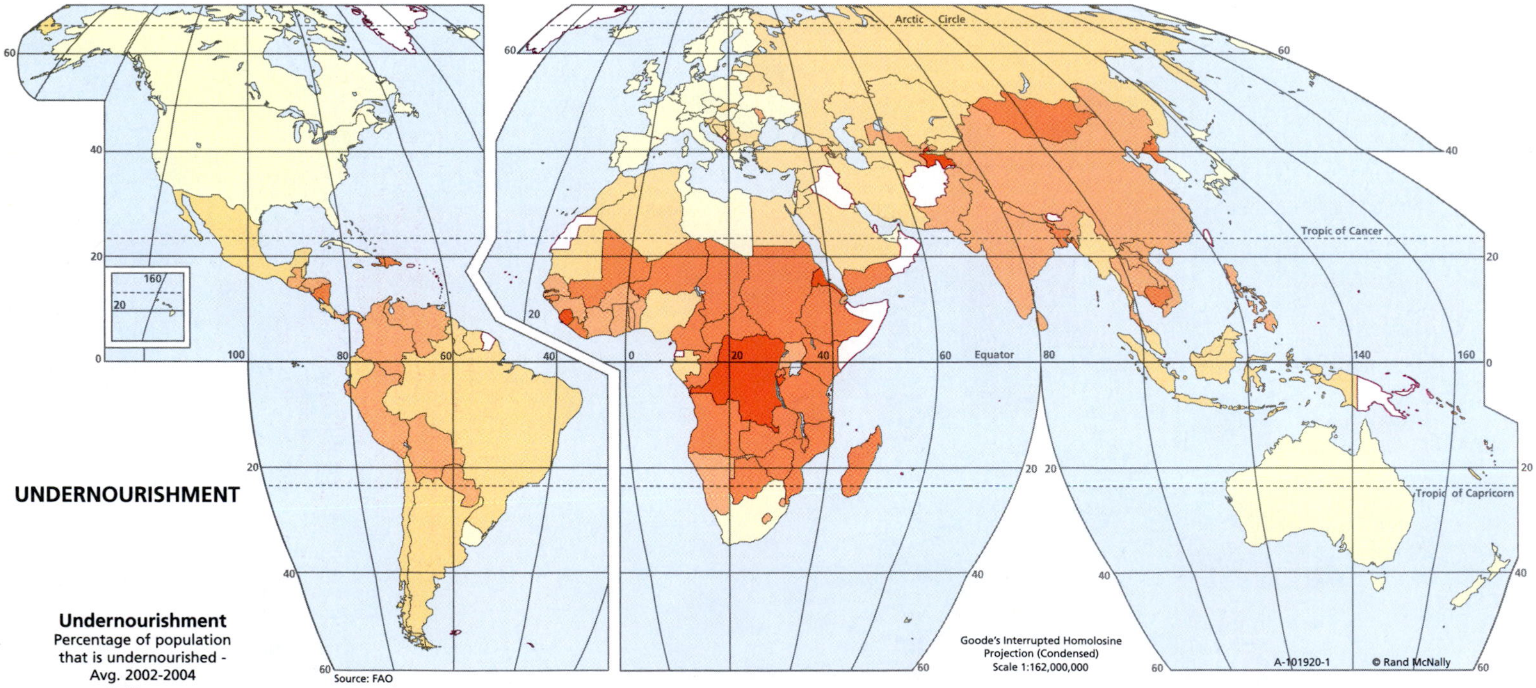

Undernourishment
Percentage of population
that is undernourished -
Avg. 2002-2004

- Over 50%
- 25% - 50%
- 10% - 25%
- 2.5% - 10%
- Under 2.5%
- Data not available

Source: FAO

Goode's Interrupted Homolosine
Projection (Condensed)
Scale 1:162,000,000

A-101920-1   © Rand McNally

Undernourished People   World Total* - 825,900,000 people - Avg. 2002-2004

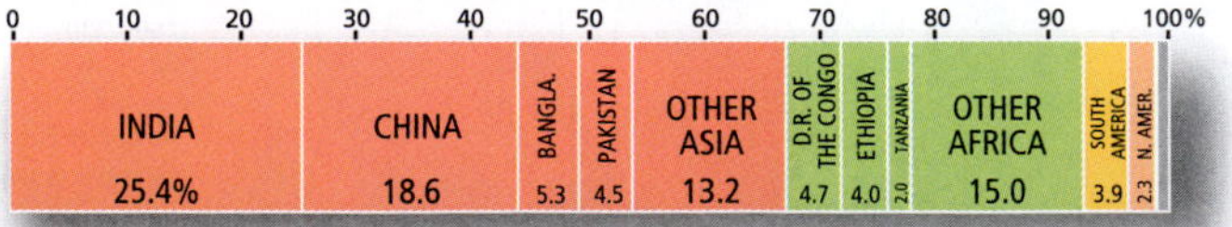

INDIA	CHINA	BANGLA.	PAKISTAN	OTHER ASIA	D.R. OF THE CONGO	ETHIOPIA	TANZANIA	OTHER AFRICA	SOUTH AMERICA	N. AMER.
25.4%	18.6	5.3	4.5	13.2	4.7	4.0	2.0	15.0	3.9	2.3

* Excluding Afghanistan, Bhutan, Equatorial Guinea, Iraq, Papua New Guinea, and Somalia.

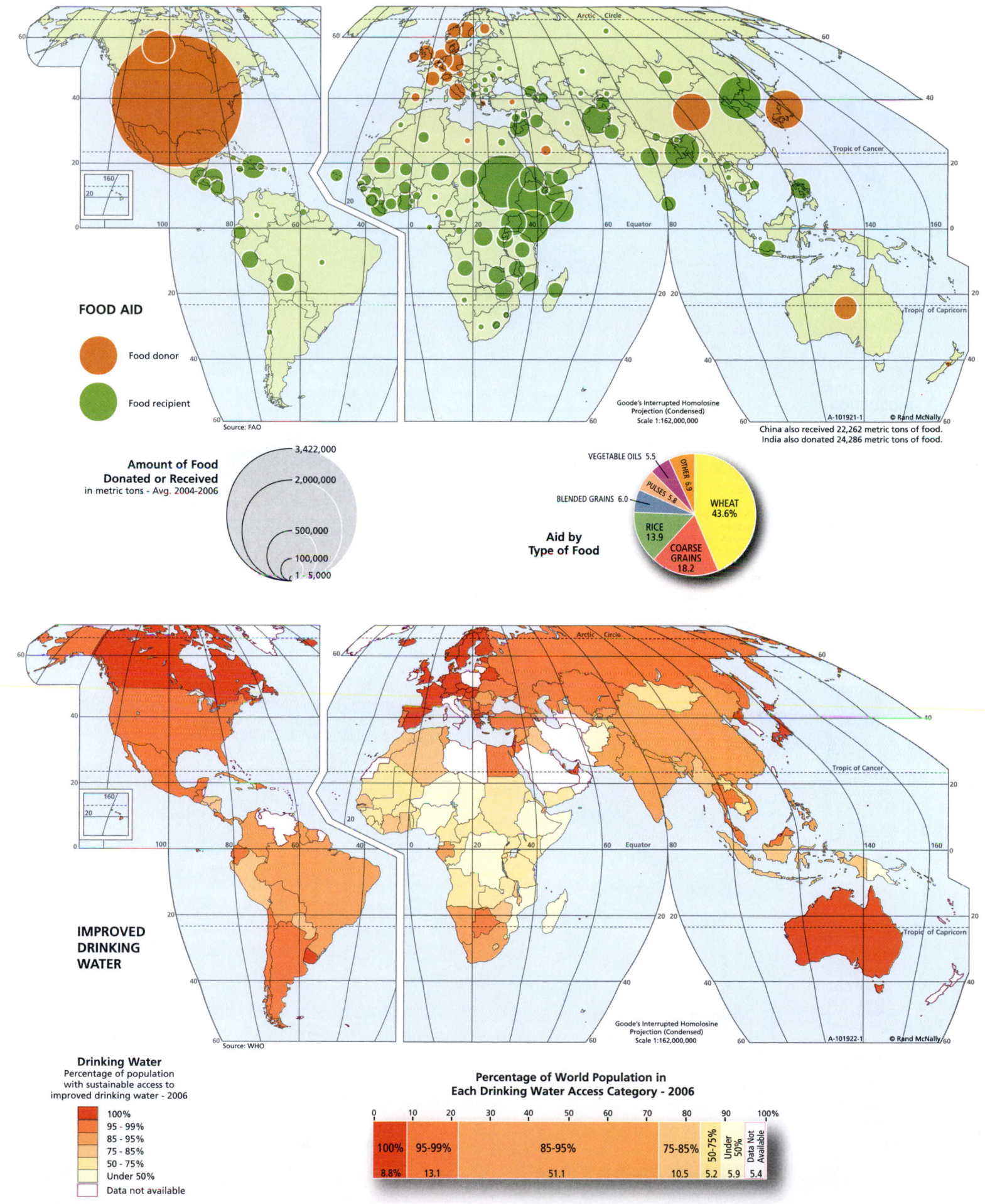

FOOD AID

Food donor

Food recipient

Source: FAO

Goode's Interrupted Homolosine
Projection (Condensed)
Scale 1:162,000,000

A-101921-1   © Rand McNally

China also received 22,262 metric tons of food.
India also donated 24,286 metric tons of food.

**Amount of Food
Donated or Received**
in metric tons - Avg. 2004-2006

3,422,000
2,000,000
500,000
100,000
1 - 5,000

**Aid by
Type of Food**

VEGETABLE OILS 5.5
OTHER 6.9
PULSES 5.8
BLENDED GRAINS 6.0
WHEAT 43.6%
RICE 13.9
COARSE GRAINS 18.2

**IMPROVED
DRINKING
WATER**

Source: WHO

Goode's Interrupted Homolosine
Projection (Condensed)
Scale 1:162,000,000

A-101922-1   © Rand McNally

Drinking Water
Percentage of population
with sustainable access to
improved drinking water - 2006

100%
95 - 99%
85 - 95%
75 - 85%
50 - 75%
Under 50%
Data not available

**Percentage of World Population in
Each Drinking Water Access Category - 2006**

| 0 | 10 | 20 | 30 | 40 | 50 | 60 | 70 | 80 | 90 | 100% |

100%	95-99%	85-95%	75-85%	50-75%	Under 50%	Data Not Available
8.8%	13.1	51.1	10.5	5.2	5.9	5.4

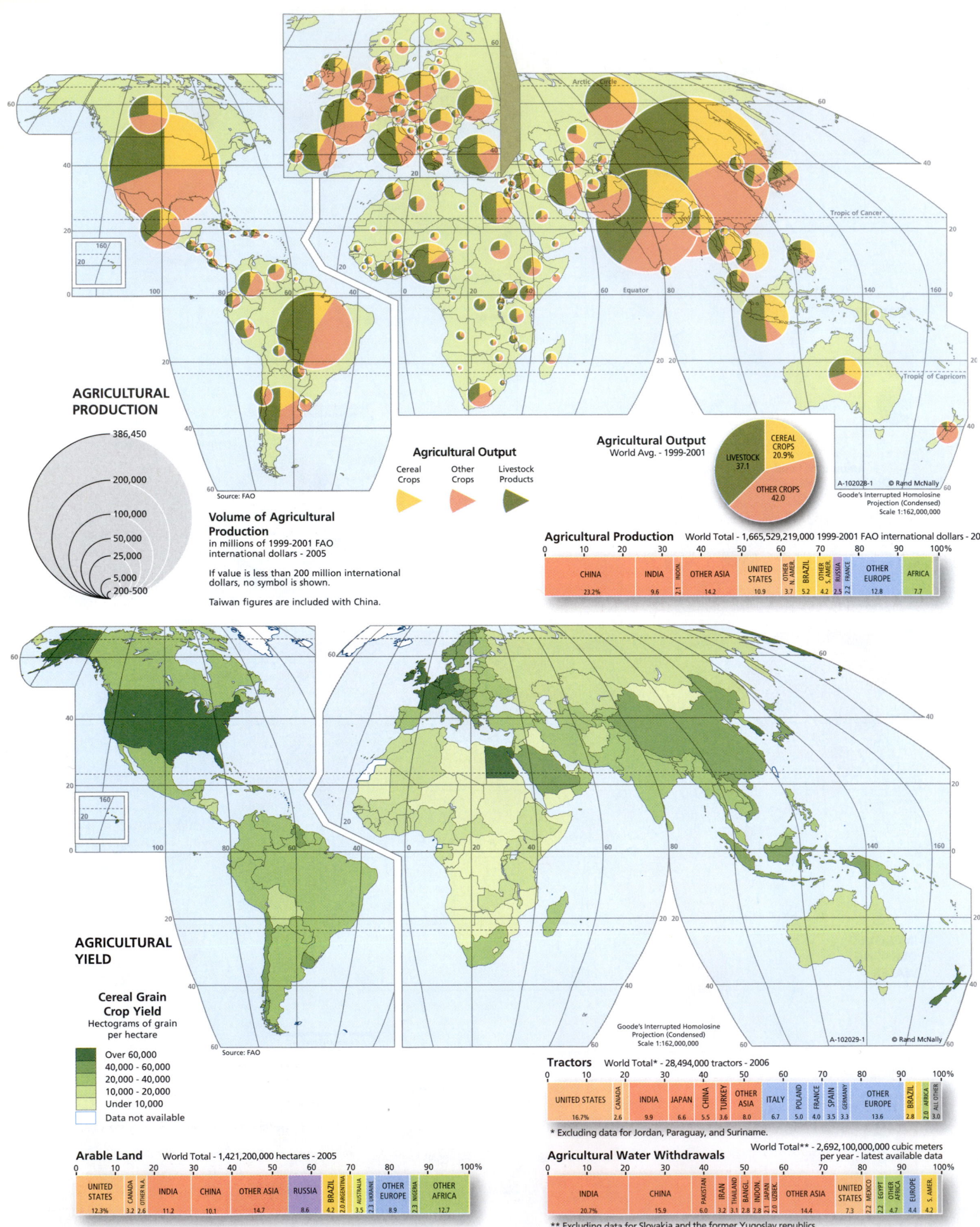

AGRICULTURAL PRODUCTION

386,450

200,000

100,000

50,000

25,000

5,000

200-500

Source: FAO

Volume of Agricultural Production
in millions of 1999-2001 FAO international dollars - 2005

If value is less than 200 million international dollars, no symbol is shown.

Taiwan figures are included with China.

Agricultural Output

Cereal Crops

Other Crops

Livestock Products

Agricultural Output
World Avg. - 1999-2001

CEREAL CROPS 20.9%

LIVESTOCK 37.1

OTHER CROPS 42.0

A-10202B-1 © Rand McNally

Goode's Interrupted Homolosine Projection (Condensed)
Scale 1:162,000,000

Agricultural Production World Total - 1,665,529,219,000 1999-2001 FAO international dollars - 2005

0	10	20	30	40	50	60	70	80	90	100%
CHINA		INDIA	INDON	OTHER ASIA		UNITED STATES	OTHER N. AMER.	BRAZIL	OTHER S. AMER.	RUSSIA	FRANCE	OTHER EUROPE		AFRICA
23.2%		9.6	2.1	14.2		10.9	3.7	5.2	4.2	2.5	2.2	12.8		7.7

AGRICULTURAL YIELD

Cereal Grain Crop Yield
Hectograms of grain per hectare

Over 60,000

40,000 - 60,000

20,000 - 40,000

10,000 - 20,000

Under 10,000

Data not available

Source: FAO

Goode's Interrupted Homolosine Projection (Condensed)
Scale 1:162,000,000

A-102029-1 © Rand McNally

Tractors World Total* - 28,494,000 tractors - 2006

0	10	20	30	40	50	60	70	80	90	100%
UNITED STATES	CANADA	INDIA	JAPAN	CHINA	TURKEY	OTHER ASIA	ITALY	POLAND	FRANCE	SPAIN	GERMANY	OTHER EUROPE	BRAZIL	AFRICA	ALL OTHER
16.7%	2.6	9.9	6.6	5.5	3.6	8.0	6.7	5.0	4.0	3.5	3.3	13.6	2.8	2.0	3.0

* Excluding data for Jordan, Paraguay, and Suriname.

Arable Land World Total - 1,421,200,000 hectares - 2005

0	10	20	30	40	50	60	70	80	90	100%
UNITED STATES	CANADA	OTHER N.A.	INDIA	CHINA	OTHER ASIA	RUSSIA	BRAZIL	ARGENTINA	AUSTRALIA	UKRAINE	OTHER EUROPE	NIGERIA	OTHER AFRICA
12.3%	3.2	2.6	11.2	10.1	14.7	8.6	4.2	2.0	3.5	2.3	8.9	2.3	12.7

Agricultural Water Withdrawals World Total** - 2,692,100,000,000 cubic meters per year - latest available data

0	10	20	30	40	50	60	70	80	90	100%
INDIA		CHINA	PAKISTAN	IRAN	THAILAND	BANGL	INDON	JAPAN	UZBEK	OTHER ASIA	UNITED STATES	MEXICO	OTHER AFRICA	EGYPT	EUROPE	S. AMER.
20.7%		15.9	6.0	3.2	3.1	2.8	2.8	2.1	2.0	14.4	7.3	2.2	4.7	4.7	4.4	4.2

** Excluding data for Slovakia and the former Yugoslav republics.

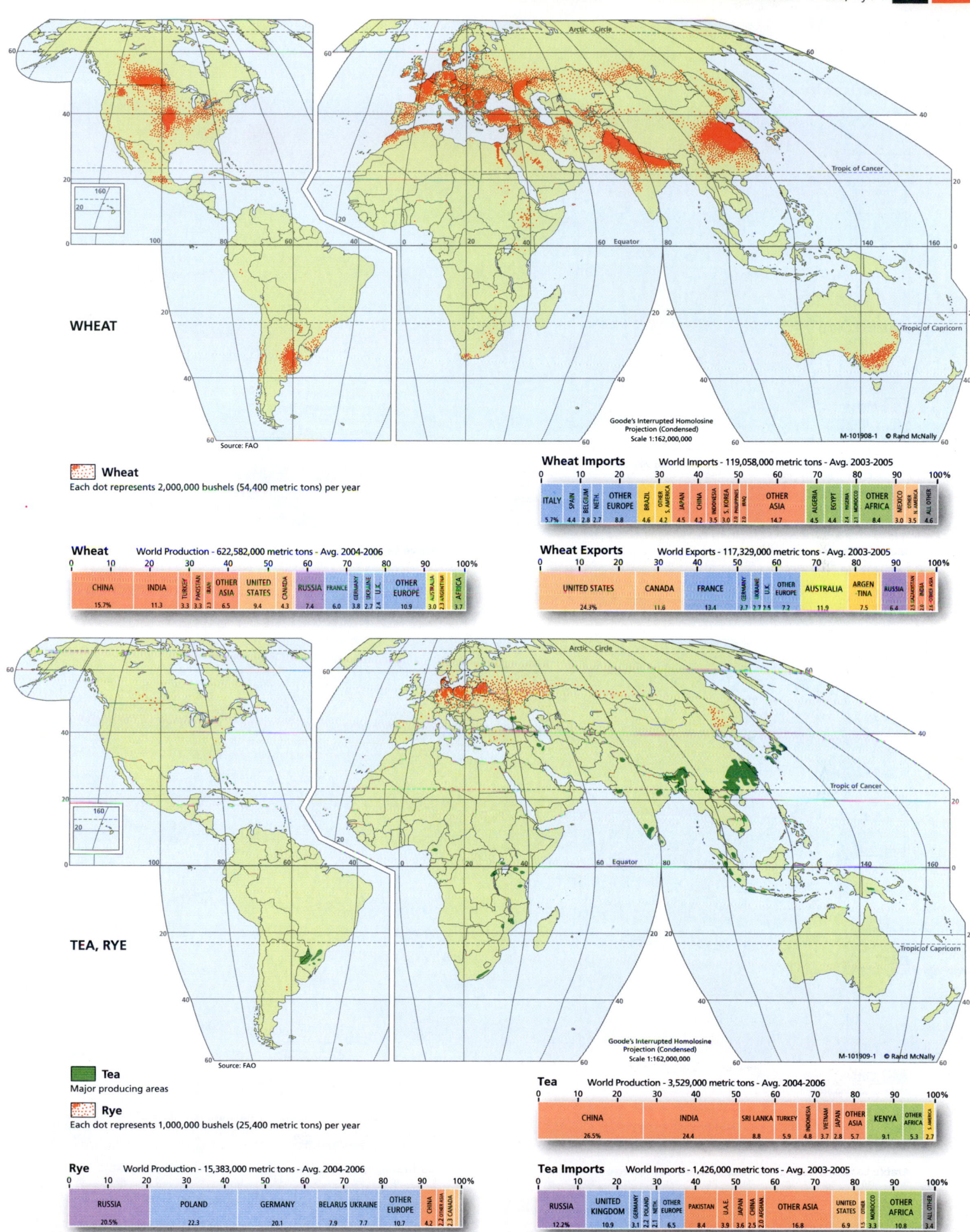

WHEAT

Goode's Interrupted Homolosine
Projection (Condensed)
Scale 1:162,000,000

M-101908-1 © Rand McNally

Source: FAO

Wheat
Each dot represents 2,000,000 bushels (54,400 metric tons) per year

Wheat Imports   World Imports - 119,058,000 metric tons - Avg. 2003-2005

0	10	20	30	40	50	60	70	80	90	100%
ITALY	SPAIN	BELGIUM	NETH.	OTHER EUROPE	BRAZIL	OTHER S. AMERICA	JAPAN	CHINA	INDONESIA	S. KOREA	IRAQ	PHILIPPINES	OTHER ASIA	ALGERIA	EGYPT	NIGERIA	MOROCCO	OTHER AFRICA	MEXICO	OTHER N. AMERICA	ALL OTHER
5.7%	4.4	2.8	2.7	8.8	4.6	4.2	4.5	4.2	3.5	3.0	2.0	2.0	14.7	4.5	4.6	2.4	2.1	8.4	3.0	3.5	4.6

Wheat   World Production - 622,582,000 metric tons - Avg. 2004-2006

0	10	20	30	40	50	60	70	80	90	100%
CHINA	INDIA	TURKEY	PAKISTAN	IRAN	OTHER ASIA	UNITED STATES	CANADA	RUSSIA	FRANCE	GERMANY	UKRAINE	U.K.	OTHER EUROPE	AUSTRALIA	ARGENTINA	AFRICA
15.7%	11.3	3.3	3.3	2.3	6.5	9.4	4.3	7.4	6.0	3.8	2.4		10.9	3.0	2.3	3.7

Wheat Exports   World Exports - 117,329,000 metric tons - Avg. 2003-2005

0	10	20	30	40	50	60	70	80	90	100%
UNITED STATES	CANADA	FRANCE	GERMANY	UKRAINE	U.K.	OTHER EUROPE	AUSTRALIA	ARGENTINA	RUSSIA	KAZAKHSTAN	INDIA	OTHER ASIA
24.3%	11.6	13.4	3.7	2.7	2.5	7.2	11.9	7.5	6.4	2.3	2.0	2.6

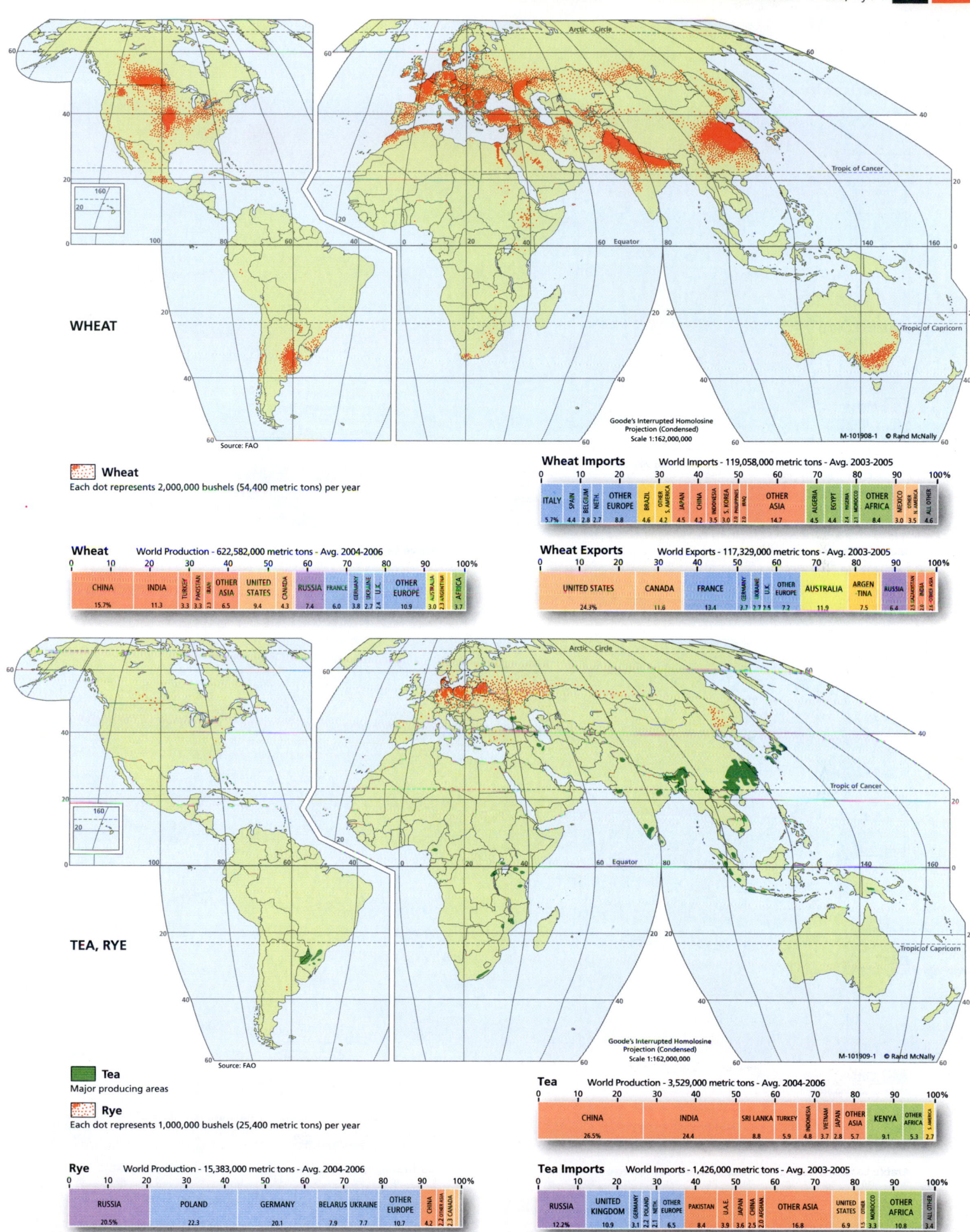

TEA, RYE

Goode's Interrupted Homolosine
Projection (Condensed)
Scale 1:162,000,000

M-101909-1 © Rand McNally

Source: FAO

Tea
Major producing areas

Rye
Each dot represents 1,000,000 bushels (25,400 metric tons) per year

Tea   World Production - 3,529,000 metric tons - Avg. 2004-2006

0	10	20	30	40	50	60	70	80	90	100%
CHINA	INDIA	SRI LANKA	TURKEY	INDONESIA	VIETNAM	JAPAN	OTHER ASIA	KENYA	OTHER AFRICA	S. AMERICA
26.5%	24.4	8.8	5.9	4.8	3.9	2.8	5.7	9.1	5.3	2.7

Rye   World Production - 15,383,000 metric tons - Avg. 2004-2006

0	10	20	30	40	50	60	70	80	90	100%
RUSSIA	POLAND	GERMANY	BELARUS	UKRAINE	OTHER EUROPE	CHINA	OTHER ASIA	CANADA
20.5%	22.3	20.1	7.9	7.7	10.7	4.2	2.2	2.3

Tea Imports   World Imports - 1,426,000 metric tons - Avg. 2003-2005

0	10	20	30	40	50	60	70	80	90	100%
RUSSIA	UNITED KINGDOM	GERMANY	POLAND	NETH.	OTHER EUROPE	PAKISTAN	U.A.E.	JAPAN	CHINA	AFGHAN.	OTHER ASIA	UNITED STATES	MOROCCO	OTHER AFRICA	ALL OTHER
12.2%	10.9	3.1	2.1	2.0	6.5	8.4	3.9	3.6	2.0	2.0	16.8	6.9	3.3	10.8	3.4

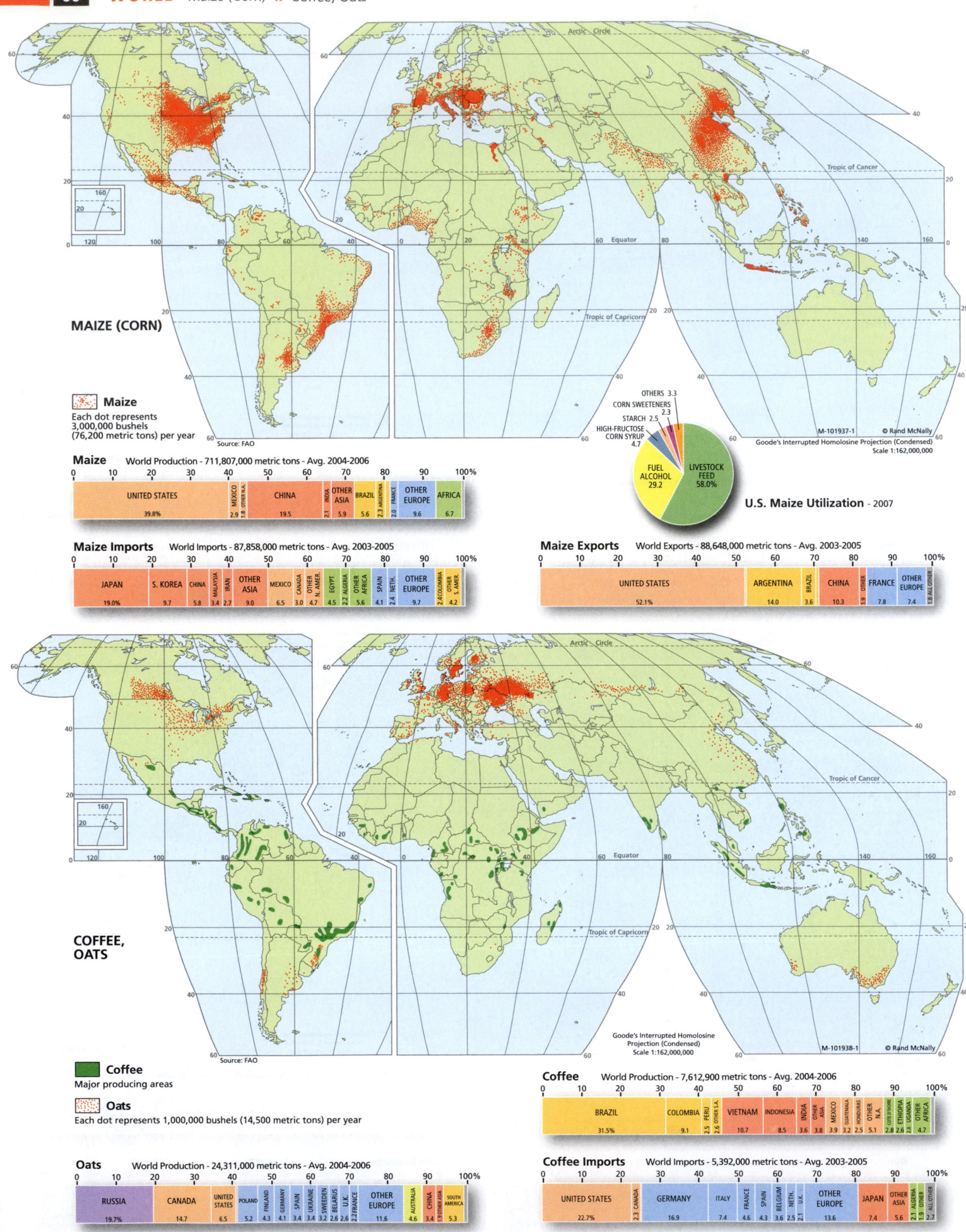

MAIZE (CORN)

Maize
Each dot represents
3,000,000 bushels
(76,200 metric tons) per year

Source: FAO

U.S. Maize Utilization - 2007

Pie chart:
- LIVESTOCK FEED 58.0%
- FUEL ALCOHOL 29.2
- HIGH-FRUCTOSE CORN SYRUP 4.7
- STARCH 2.5
- CORN SWEETENERS 2.3
- OTHERS 3.3

M-101937-1 © Rand McNally
Goode's Interrupted Homolosine Projection (Condensed)
Scale 1:162,000,000

Maize World Production - 711,807,000 metric tons - Avg. 2004-2006

UNITED STATES 39.8%	MEXICO 2.9	OTHER N.A. 1.8	CHINA 19.5	INDIA 2.1	OTHER ASIA 5.9	BRAZIL 5.6	ARGENTINA 2.3	FRANCE 2.0	OTHER EUROPE 9.6	AFRICA 6.7

Maize Imports World Imports - 87,858,000 metric tons - Avg. 2003-2005

JAPAN 19.0%	S. KOREA 9.7	CHINA 5.8	MALAYSIA 3.4	IRAN 2.7	OTHER ASIA 9.0	MEXICO 6.5	CANADA 3.0	OTHER N. AMER. 4.7	EGYPT 4.5	ALGERIA 2.2	OTHER AFRICA 5.6	SPAIN 4.1	NETH. 2.4	OTHER EUROPE 9.7	COLOMBIA 2.4	OTHER S. AMER. 4.2

Maize Exports World Exports - 88,648,000 metric tons - Avg. 2003-2005

UNITED STATES 52.1%	ARGENTINA 14.0	BRAZIL 3.6	CHINA 10.3	1.9	FRANCE 7.8	OTHER EUROPE 7.4	ALL OTHER 1.9

COFFEE, OATS

Source: FAO

Goode's Interrupted Homolosine
Projection (Condensed)
Scale 1:162,000,000

M-101938-1 © Rand McNally

Coffee
Major producing areas

Oats
Each dot represents 1,000,000 bushels (14,500 metric tons) per year

Coffee World Production - 7,612,900 metric tons - Avg. 2004-2006

BRAZIL 31.5%	COLOMBIA 9.1	PERU 2.5	OTHER S.A. 2.6	VIETNAM 10.7	INDONESIA 8.5	INDIA 3.6	OTHER ASIA 3.8	MEXICO 3.9	GUATEMALA 3.2	OTHER N.A. 5.1	COTE D'IVOIRE 2.8	ETHIOPIA 2.6	UGANDA 2.0	OTHER AFRICA 4.7

Coffee Imports World Imports - 5,392,000 metric tons - Avg. 2003-2005

UNITED STATES 22.7%	CANADA 2.3	GERMANY 16.9	ITALY 7.4	FRANCE 4.6	SPAIN 4.3	BELGIUM 3.6	NETH. 2.1	U.K.	OTHER EUROPE 13.6	JAPAN 7.4	OTHER ASIA 5.6	ALGERIA 2.1	OTHER 1.9	ALL OTHER 2.7

Oats World Production - 24,311,000 metric tons - Avg. 2004-2006

RUSSIA 19.7%	CANADA 14.7	UNITED STATES 6.5	POLAND 5.2	FINLAND 4.3	GERMANY 4.1	SPAIN 3.4	UKRAINE 3.2	SWEDEN 2.6	BELARUS 2.6	U.K. 2.2	FRANCE	OTHER EUROPE 11.6	AUSTRALIA 4.6	CHINA 3.4	OTHER ASIA 1.9	SOUTH AMERICA 5.3

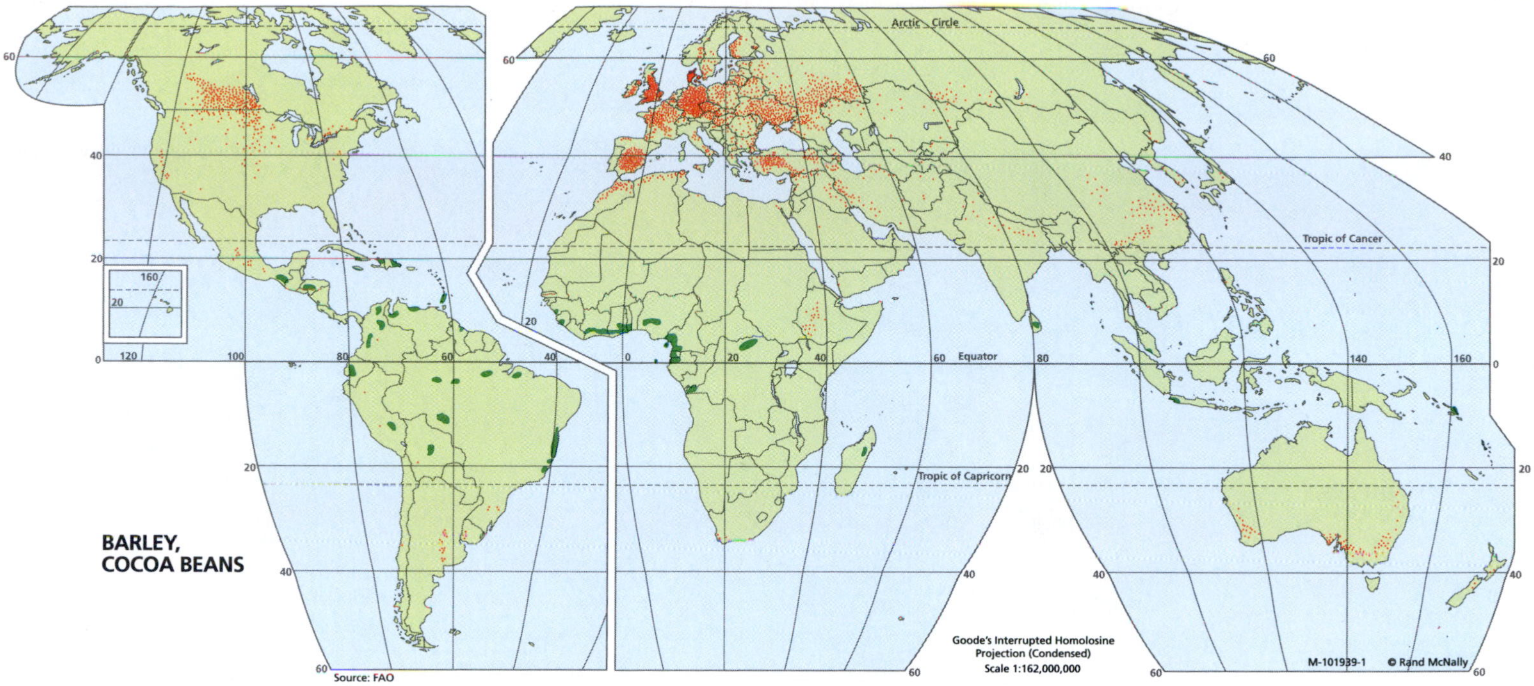

BARLEY, COCOA BEANS

Source: FAO

Goode's Interrupted Homolosine Projection (Condensed)
Scale 1:162,000,000

M-101939-1 © Rand McNally

Barley
Each dot represents 3,000,000 bushels (65,400 metric tons) per year

Cocoa Beans
Major producing areas

Barley World Production - 144,809,000 metric tons - Avg. 2004-2006

RUSSIA	GERMANY	FRANCE	UKRAINE	SPAIN	U.K.	DENMARK	POLAND	OTHER EUROPE	CANADA	UNITED STATES	TURKEY	CHINA	IRAN	OTHER ASIA	AUSTRALIA	AFRICA	ALL OTHER
11.8%	8.4	7.3	7.2	5.4	3.8	2.5	2.4	13.0	8.2	3.7	6.5	2.3	2.0	4.4	4.9	3.9	

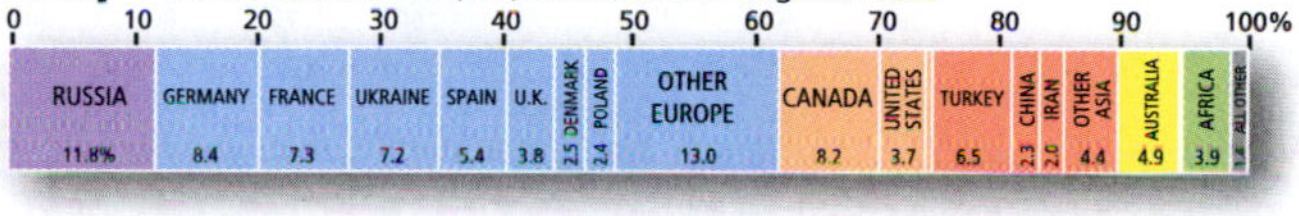

Cocoa Beans World Production - 4,017,000 metric tons - Avg. 2004-2006

COTE D'IVOIRE	GHANA	NIGERIA	CAMEROON	OTHER AF.	INDONESIA	OTHER ASIA	BRAZIL	ECUADOR	OTHER S.A.	N. AMERICA	ALL OTHER
34.6%	18.3	11.1	4.2	2.7	14.9	1.3	5.0	2.3	2.3		

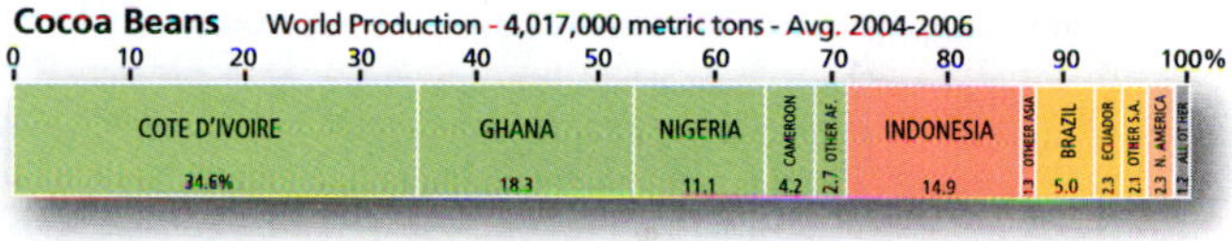

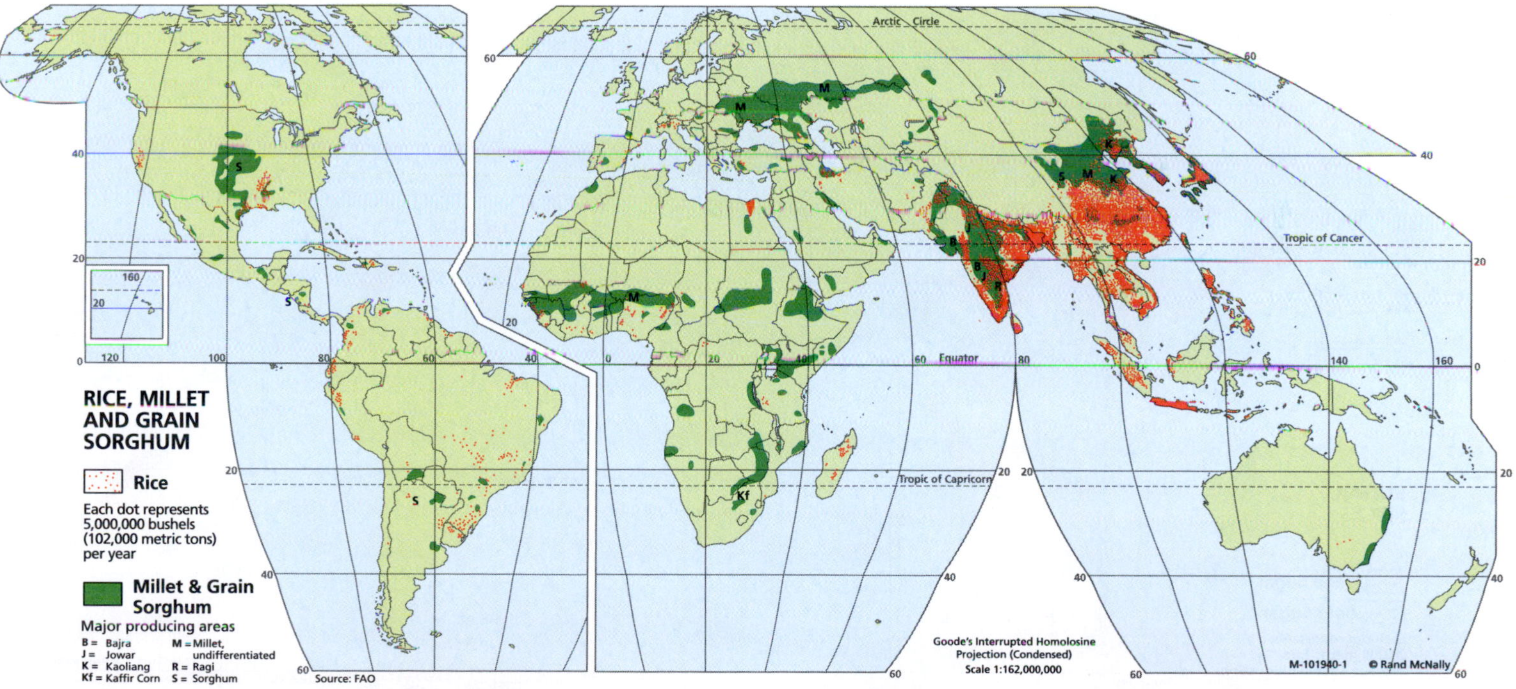

RICE, MILLET AND GRAIN SORGHUM

Rice
Each dot represents 5,000,000 bushels (102,000 metric tons) per year

Millet & Grain Sorghum
Major producing areas

B = Bajra
J = Jowar
K = Kaoliang
Kf = Kaffir Corn
M = Millet, undifferentiated
R = Ragi
S = Sorghum

Source: FAO

Goode's Interrupted Homolosine Projection (Condensed)
Scale 1:162,000,000

M-101940-1 © Rand McNally

Rice World Production - 624,479,000 metric tons - Avg. 2004-2006

CHINA	INDIA	INDONESIA	BANGL.	VIETNAM	THAILAND	MYANMAR	PHILIPPINES	OTHER ASIA	BRAZIL	OTHER S.A.	ALL OTHER
28.9%	21.3	8.7	6.4	5.8	4.7	4.0	2.4	8.4	2.0	3.2	2.5

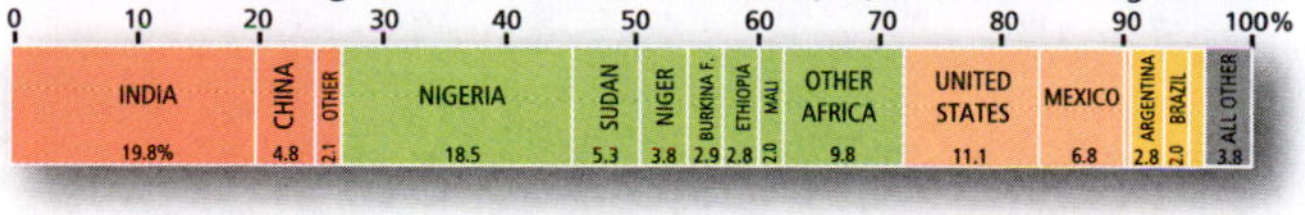

Rice Imports World Imports - 26,906,000 metric tons - Avg. 2003-2005

NIGERIA	SENEGAL	S. AFRICA	COTE D'IVOIRE	OTHER AFRICA	PHILIPPINES	IRAN	BNGL.	S. ARABIA	INDONESIA	JAPAN	N. KOREA	CHINA	IRAQ	OTHER ASIA	BRAZIL	U.K.	OTHER EUROPE	CUBA	OTHER N. AMER.	ALL OTHER
5.2%	3.2	2.8	2.8	15.4	4.1	3.8	3.5	3.5	2.7	2.7	2.4			14.5	3.0	2.1	9.0	2.0	7.9	

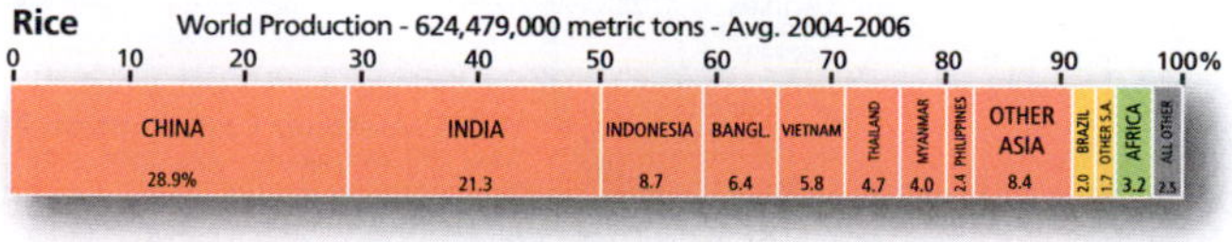

Millet & Grain Sorghum World Production - 88,629,000 metric tons - Avg. 2004-2006

INDIA	CHINA	OTHER	NIGERIA	SUDAN	NIGER	BURKINA F.	ETHIOPIA	MALI	OTHER AFRICA	UNITED STATES	MEXICO	ARGENTINA	BRAZIL	ALL OTHER
19.8%	4.8		18.5	5.3	3.8	2.9	2.8		9.8	11.1	6.8	2.8	2.0	

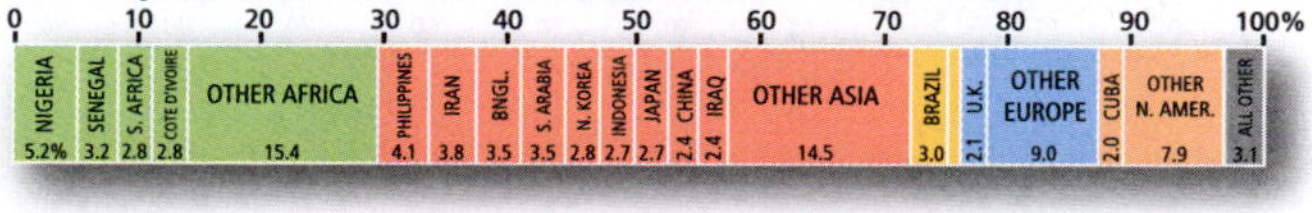

Rice Exports* World Exports - 28,749,000 metric tons - Avg. 2003-2005

THAILAND	VIETNAM	INDIA	PAKISTAN	CHINA	OTHER ASIA	UNITED STATES	EGYPT	ITALY	URUGUAY	OTHER
30.1%	15.2	14.2	7.6	4.8	2.1	12.4	2.9	3.1	2.3	2.3

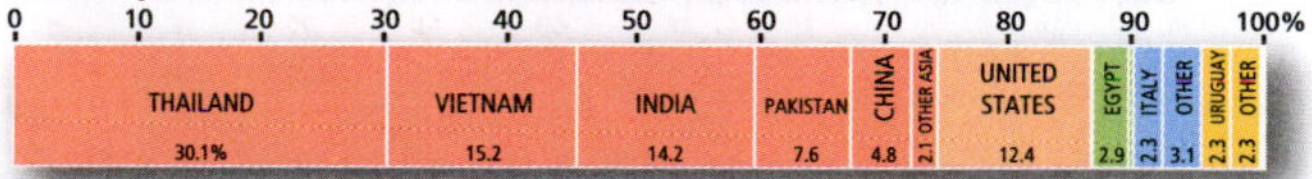

* including reexports

POTATOES, CASSAVA

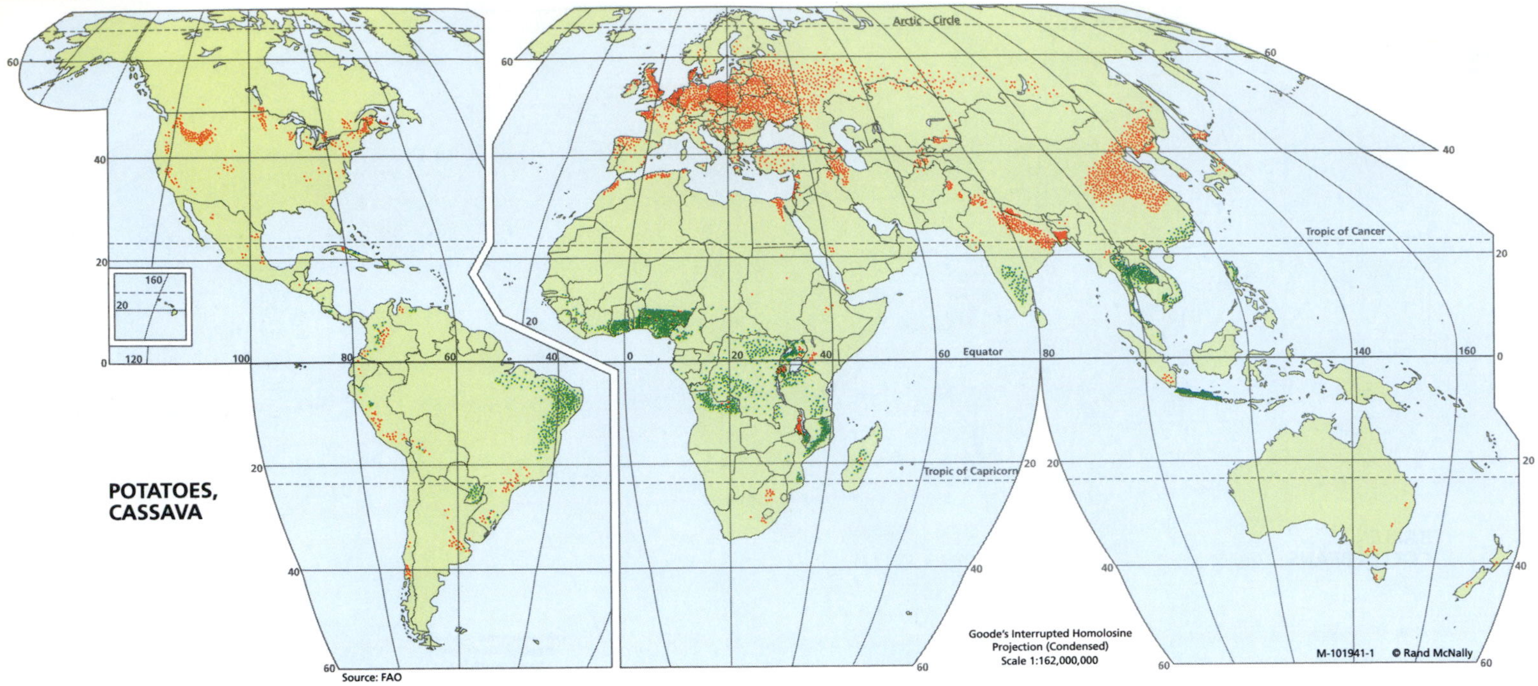

Goode's Interrupted Homolosine
Projection (Condensed)
Scale 1:162,000,000

M-101941-1   © Rand McNally

Source: FAO

Potatoes
Each dot represents 100,000 metric tons average annual production

Cassava
Each dot represents 100,000 metric tons average annual production

Potatoes   World Production - 323,418,000 metric tons - Avg. 2004-2006

	0	10	20	30	40	50	60	70	80	90	100%

CHINA	INDIA	OTHER ASIA	RUSSIA	UKRAINE	GERMANY	POLAND	BELARUS	NETH.	FRANCE	OTHER EUROPE	UNITED STATES	OTHER N.A.	AFRICA	SOUTH AMERICA
22.3%	7.3	11.1	11.5	6.2	3.6	3.4	2.7	2.1	2.3	9.8	6.1	2.2	5.0	4.1

Cassava   World Production - 214,400,000 metric tons - Avg. 2004-2006

	0	10	20	30	40	50	60	70	80	90	100%

NIGERIA	DEM. REP. OF THE CONGO	MOZ.	GHANA	ANGOLA	TANZANIA	UGANDA	OTHER AFRICA	BRAZIL	PARAGUAY	OTHER S.A.	THAILAND	INDONESIA	VIETNAM	INDIA	CHINA	OTHER ASIA
19.6%	7.0	4.6	4.5	4.0	3.1	2.5	9.3	11.9	2.3	1.9	9.5	9.1	3.1	3.0	2.0	1.7

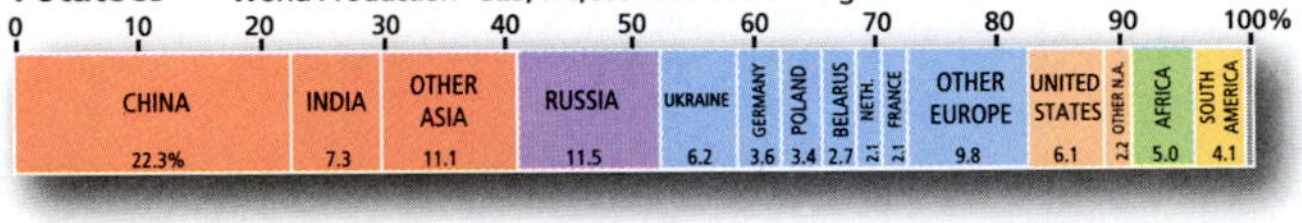

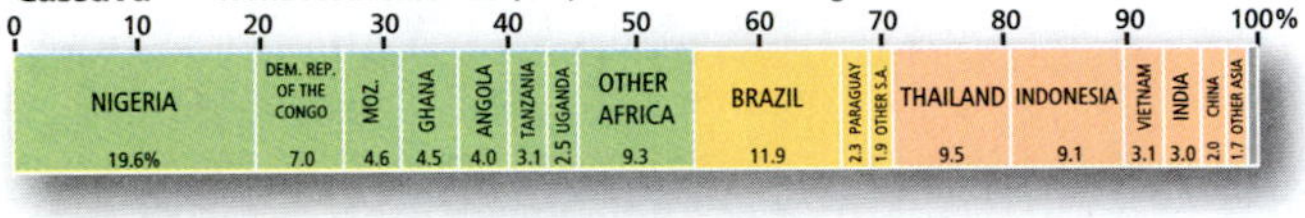

SUGAR, SPICES

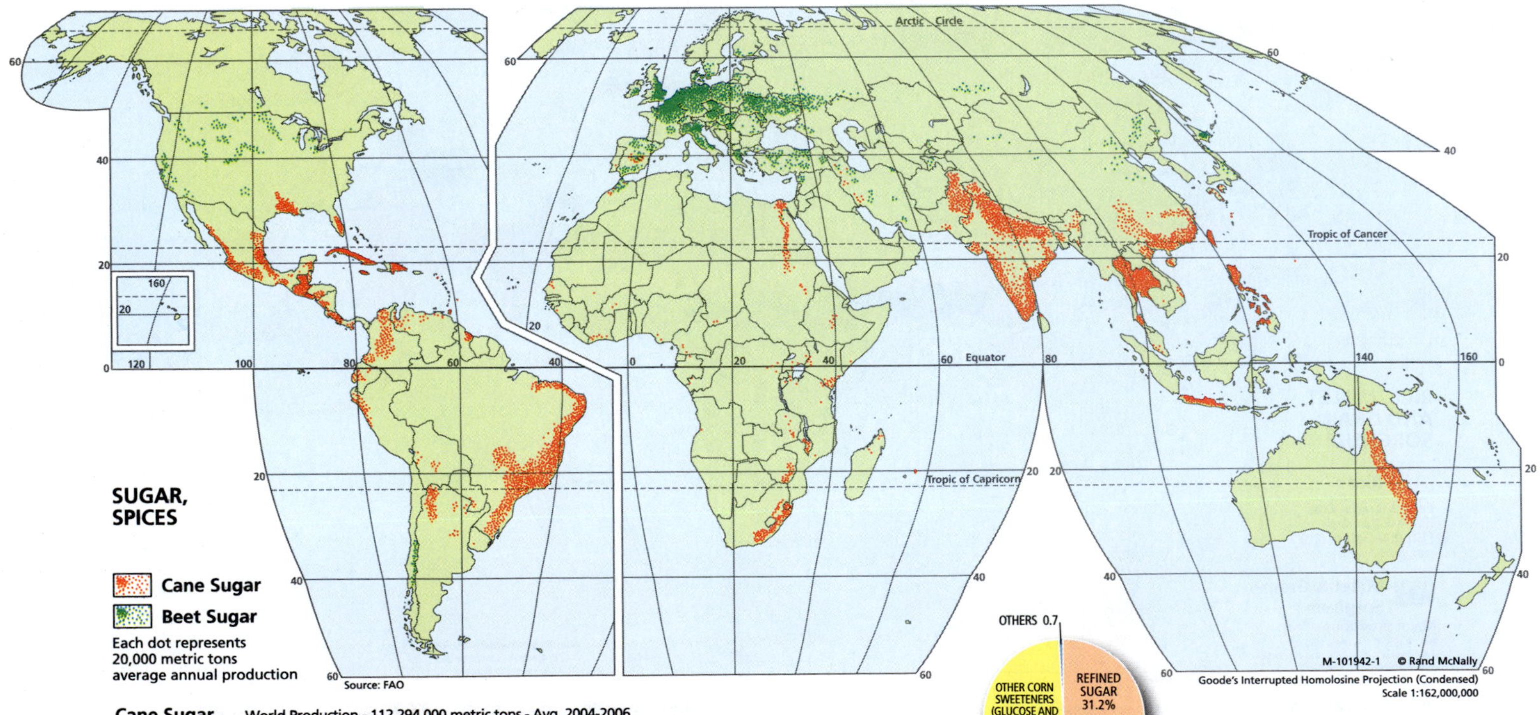

Cane Sugar
Beet Sugar
Each dot represents 20,000 metric tons average annual production

Source: FAO

Goode's Interrupted Homolosine
Projection (Condensed)
Scale 1:162,000,000

M-101942-1   © Rand McNally

OTHERS 0.7

OTHER CORN SWEETENERS (GLUCOSE AND DEXTROSE) 38.6

REFINED SUGAR 31.2%

HIGH FRUCTOSE CORN SWEETENERS 29.5

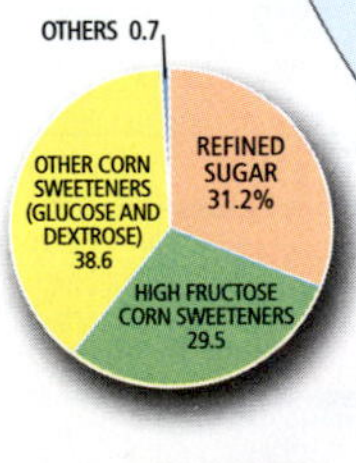

U.S. Sweetener Consumption Per Person
Total - 90.9 kilograms - Avg. 2004-2006

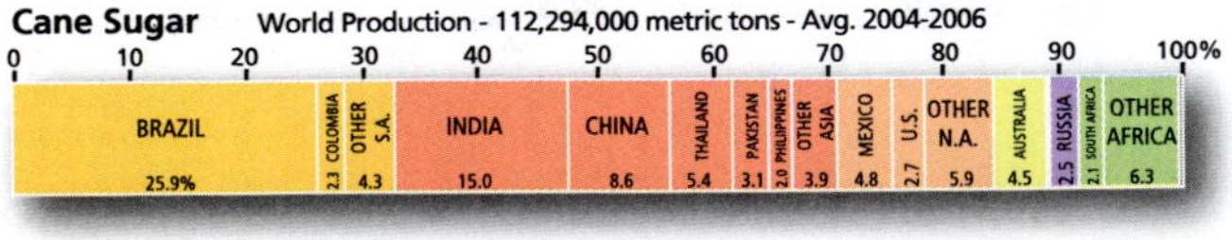

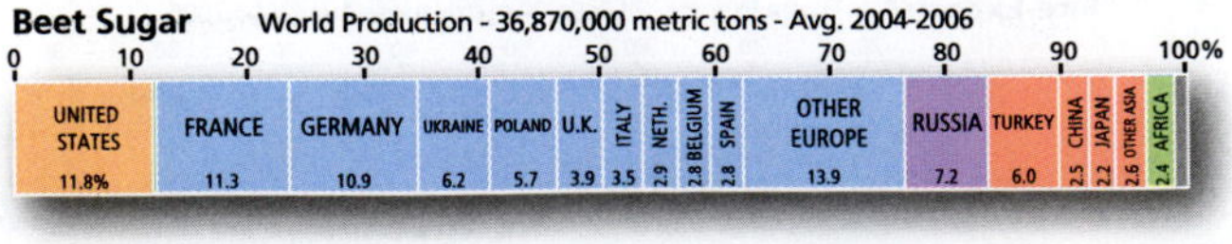

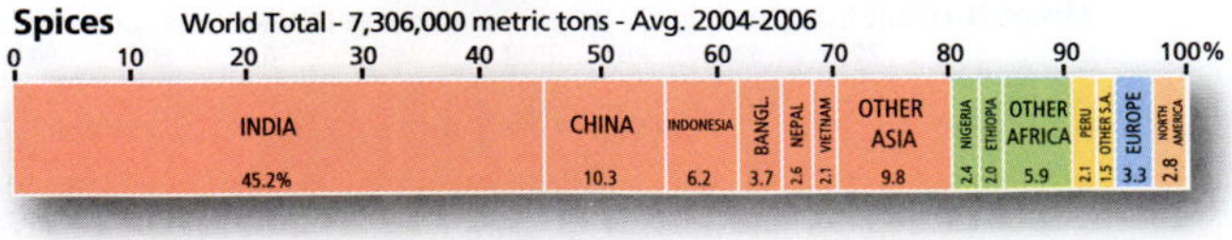

Cane Sugar   World Production - 112,294,000 metric tons - Avg. 2004-2006

	0	10	20	30	40	50	60	70	80	90	100%

BRAZIL	COLOMBIA	OTHER S.A.	INDIA	CHINA	THAILAND	PAKISTAN	PHILIPPINES	OTHER ASIA	MEXICO	U.S.	OTHER N.A.	AUSTRALIA	SOUTH AFRICA	OTHER AFRICA
25.9%	2.3	4.3	15.0	8.6	3.5	2.3	2.0	3.9	4.8	2.7	5.9	4.5	2.1	6.3

Beet Sugar   World Production - 36,870,000 metric tons - Avg. 2004-2006

	0	10	20	30	40	50	60	70	80	90	100%

UNITED STATES	FRANCE	GERMANY	UKRAINE	POLAND	U.K.	ITALY	NETH.	BELGIUM	SPAIN	OTHER EUROPE	RUSSIA	TURKEY	CHINA	JAPAN	OTHER ASIA	AFRICA
11.8%	11.3	10.9	6.2	5.7	3.9	3.5	2.9	2.8	2.8	13.9	7.2	6.0	2.5	2.2	2.6	2.4

Spices   World Total - 7,306,000 metric tons - Avg. 2004-2006

	0	10	20	30	40	50	60	70	80	90	100%

INDIA	CHINA	INDONESIA	BANGL.	NEPAL	VIETNAM	OTHER ASIA	NIGERIA	ETHIOPIA	OTHER S.A.	PERU	OTHER S.A.	EUROPE	NORTH AMERICA
45.2%	10.3	6.2	3.7	2.6	2.1	9.8	2.4	2.6	5.9	2.1	1.5	3.3	2.8

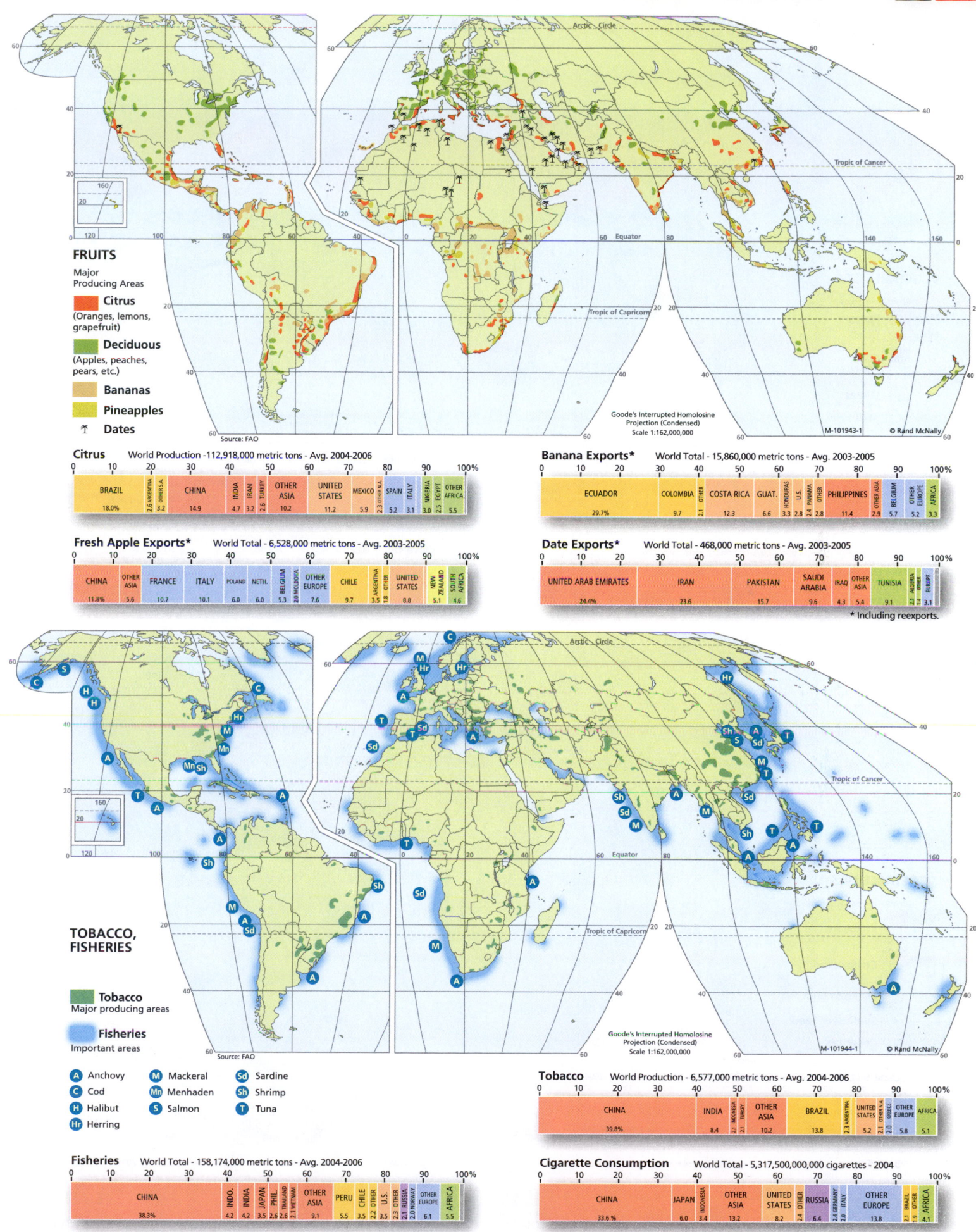

FRUITS

Major Producing Areas

- **Citrus** (Oranges, lemons, grapefruit)
- **Deciduous** (Apples, peaches, pears, etc.)
- **Bananas**
- **Pineapples**
- **Dates**

Source: FAO

Goode's Interrupted Homolosine Projection (Condensed)
Scale 1:162,000,000
M-101943-1   © Rand McNally

Citrus   World Production - 112,918,000 metric tons - Avg. 2004-2006

| BRAZIL 18.0% | ARGENTINA 2.6 | OTHER S.A. 3.2 | CHINA 14.9 | INDIA 4.7 | IRAN 3.2 | TURKEY 2.6 | OTHER ASIA 10.2 | UNITED STATES 11.2 | MEXICO 5.9 | OTHER N.A. 2.3 | SPAIN 5.2 | ITALY 3.1 | NIGERIA 3.0 | EGYPT 2.5 | OTHER AFRICA 5.5 |

Banana Exports*   World Total - 15,860,000 metric tons - Avg. 2003-2005

| ECUADOR 29.7% | COLOMBIA 9.7 | OTHER 2.1 | COSTA RICA 12.3 | GUAT. 6.6 | HONDURAS 3.3 | U.S. 2.8 | PANAMA 2.4 | OTHER ASIA 2.8 | PHILIPPINES 11.4 | OTHER ASIA 2.9 | BELGIUM 5.7 | OTHER EUROPE 5.2 | AFRICA 3.3 |

Fresh Apple Exports*   World Total - 6,528,000 metric tons - Avg. 2003-2005

| CHINA 11.8% | OTHER ASIA 5.6 | FRANCE 10.7 | ITALY 10.1 | POLAND 6.0 | NETH. 6.0 | BELGIUM 5.3 | MOLDOVA 2.0 | OTHER EUROPE 7.6 | CHILE 9.7 | ARGENTINA 3.5 | OTHER 1.8 | UNITED STATES 8.8 | NEW ZEALAND 5.1 | SOUTH AFRICA 4.6 |

Date Exports*   World Total - 468,000 metric tons - Avg. 2003-2005

| UNITED ARAB EMIRATES 24.4% | IRAN 23.6 | PAKISTAN 15.7 | SAUDI ARABIA 9.6 | IRAQ 4.3 | OTHER ASIA 5.4 | TUNISIA 9.1 | ALGERIA 2.1 | OTHER 1.4 | EUROPE 3.1 |

*Including reexports.

TOBACCO, FISHERIES

- **Tobacco** Major producing areas
- **Fisheries** Important areas

Source: FAO

Goode's Interrupted Homolosine Projection (Condensed)
Scale 1:162,000,000
M-101944-1   © Rand McNally

- **A** Anchovy
- **C** Cod
- **H** Halibut
- **Hr** Herring
- **M** Mackeral
- **Mn** Menhaden
- **S** Salmon
- **Sd** Sardine
- **Sh** Shrimp
- **T** Tuna

Tobacco   World Production - 6,577,000 metric tons - Avg. 2004-2006

| CHINA 39.8% | INDIA 8.4 | INDONESIA 2.1 | TURKEY | OTHER ASIA 10.2 | BRAZIL 13.8 | ARGENTINA 2.3 | UNITED STATES 5.2 | OTHER N.A. 2.1 | GREECE 2.0 | OTHER EUROPE 5.8 | AFRICA 5.1 |

Cigarette Consumption   World Total - 5,317,500,000,000 cigarettes - 2004

| CHINA 33.6% | JAPAN 6.0 | INDONESIA 3.4 | OTHER ASIA 13.2 | UNITED STATES 8.2 | OTHER 2.4 | RUSSIA 6.4 | GERMANY 2.4 | ITALY 2.0 | OTHER EUROPE 13.8 | BRAZIL 2.1 | OTHER 1.9 | AFRICA 4.1 |

Fisheries   World Total - 158,174,000 metric tons - Avg. 2004-2006

| CHINA 38.3% | INDO. 4.2 | INDIA 4.2 | JAPAN 3.5 | PHIL. 2.6 | THAILAND 2.6 | VIETNAM 2.1 | OTHER ASIA 9.1 | PERU 5.5 | CHILE 3.5 | U.S. 2.2 | RUSSIA 3.5 | NORWAY 2.1 | OTHER EUROPE 6.1 | AFRICA 5.5 |

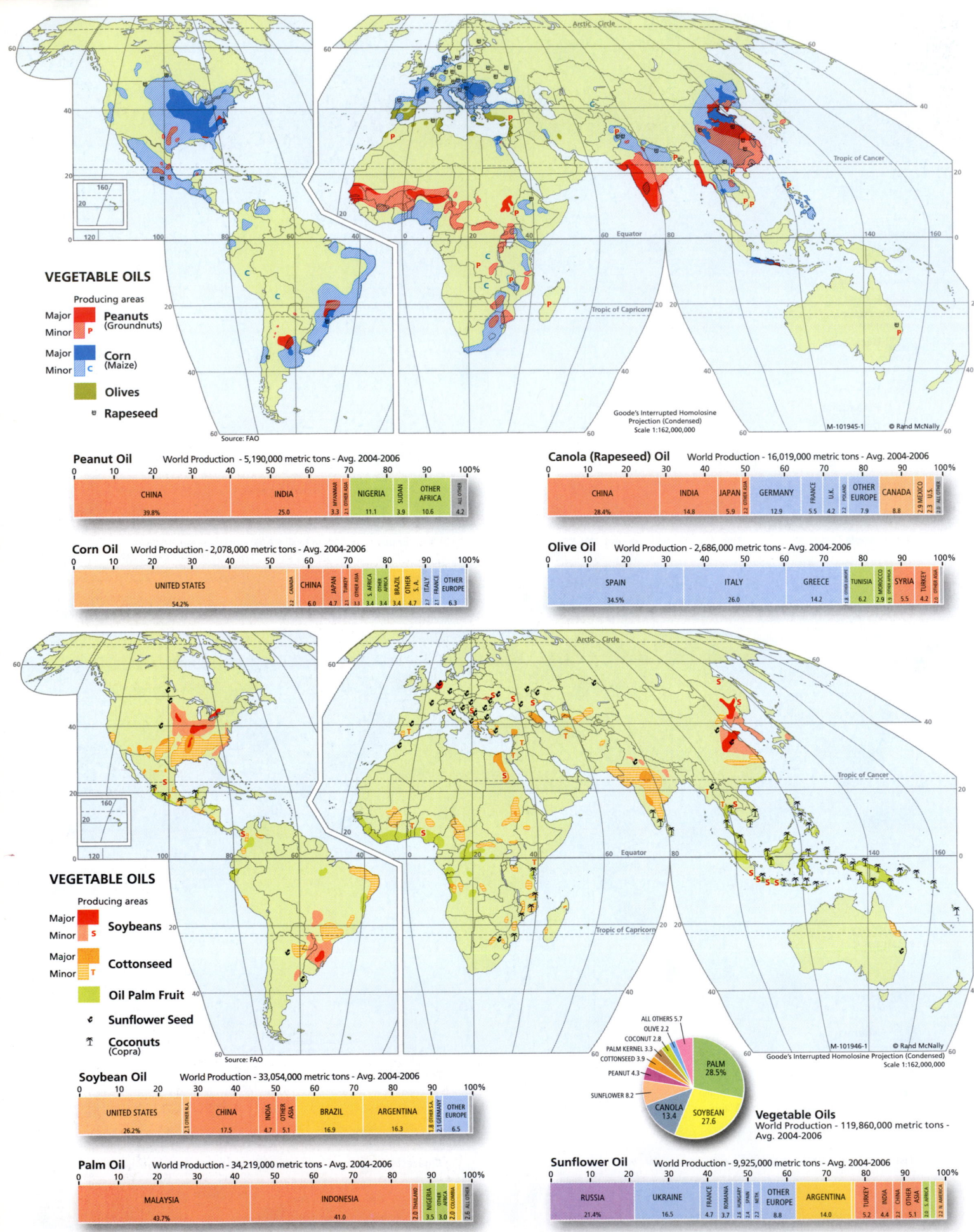

VEGETABLE OILS

Producing areas

Major		**Peanuts**
Minor	P	(Groundnuts)
Major		**Corn**
Minor	C	(Maize)
		Olives
	ш	**Rapeseed**

Source: FAO

Goode's Interrupted Homolosine Projection (Condensed)
Scale 1:162,000,000

M-101945-1 © Rand McNally

Peanut Oil World Production - 5,190,000 metric tons - Avg. 2004-2006

CHINA 39.8% | INDIA 25.0 | MYANMAR 3.3 | OTHER ASIA 2.1 | NIGERIA 11.1 | SUDAN 3.9 | OTHER AFRICA 10.6 | ALL OTHER 4.2

Canola (Rapeseed) Oil World Production - 16,019,000 metric tons - Avg. 2004-2006

CHINA 28.4% | INDIA 14.8 | JAPAN 5.9 | OTHER ASIA 2.2 | GERMANY 12.9 | FRANCE 5.5 | U.K. 4.2 | POLAND 2.2 | OTHER EUROPE 7.9 | CANADA 8.8 | MEXICO 2.9 | U.S. 2.3 | ALL OTHER 2.0

Corn Oil World Production - 2,078,000 metric tons - Avg. 2004-2006

UNITED STATES 54.2% | CANADA 2.2 | CHINA 6.0 | JAPAN 4.7 | TURKEY 2.1 | OTHER ASIA 3.3 | S. AFRICA 3.4 | OTHER AFRICA 3.4 | BRAZIL 3.4 | OTHER S.A. 4.7 | ITALY 2.7 | FRANCE 2.1 | OTHER EUROPE 6.3

Olive Oil World Production - 2,686,000 metric tons - Avg. 2004-2006

SPAIN 34.5% | ITALY 26.0 | GREECE 14.2 | OTHER EUROPE 1.8 | TUNISIA 6.2 | MOROCCO 2.9 | OTHER AFRICA 1.9 | SYRIA 5.5 | TURKEY 4.2 | OTHER ASIA 2.6

VEGETABLE OILS

Producing areas

Major		**Soybeans**
Minor	S	
Major		**Cottonseed**
Minor	T	
		Oil Palm Fruit
	✿	**Sunflower Seed**
	⚘	**Coconuts** (Copra)

Source: FAO

Goode's Interrupted Homolosine Projection (Condensed)
Scale 1:162,000,000

M-101946-1 © Rand McNally

Soybean Oil World Production - 33,054,000 metric tons - Avg. 2004-2006

UNITED STATES 26.2% | OTHER N.A. 2.1 | CHINA 17.5 | INDIA 4.7 | OTHER ASIA 5.1 | BRAZIL 16.9 | ARGENTINA 16.3 | OTHER S.A. 2.1 | GERMANY 2.1 | OTHER EUROPE 6.5

Palm Oil World Production - 34,219,000 metric tons - Avg. 2004-2006

MALAYSIA 43.7% | INDONESIA 41.0 | THAILAND 2.0 | NIGERIA 3.5 | OTHER AFRICA 3.0 | ALL OTHER 2.6

Vegetable Oils World Production - 119,860,000 metric tons - Avg. 2004-2006

- ALL OTHERS 5.7
- OLIVE 2.2
- COCONUT 2.8
- PALM KERNEL 3.3
- COTTONSEED 3.9
- PEANUT 4.3
- SUNFLOWER 8.2
- PALM 28.5
- SOYBEAN 27.6
- CANOLA 13.4

Sunflower Oil World Production - 9,925,000 metric tons - Avg. 2004-2006

RUSSIA 21.4% | UKRAINE 16.5 | FRANCE 4.7 | ROMANIA 3.7 | HUNGARY 2.6 | SPAIN 2.2 | OTHER EUROPE 8.8 | ARGENTINA 14.0 | TURKEY 5.2 | INDIA 4.4 | CHINA 2.2 | OTHER ASIA 5.1 | S. AFRICA 2.0 | N. AMERICA 2.2

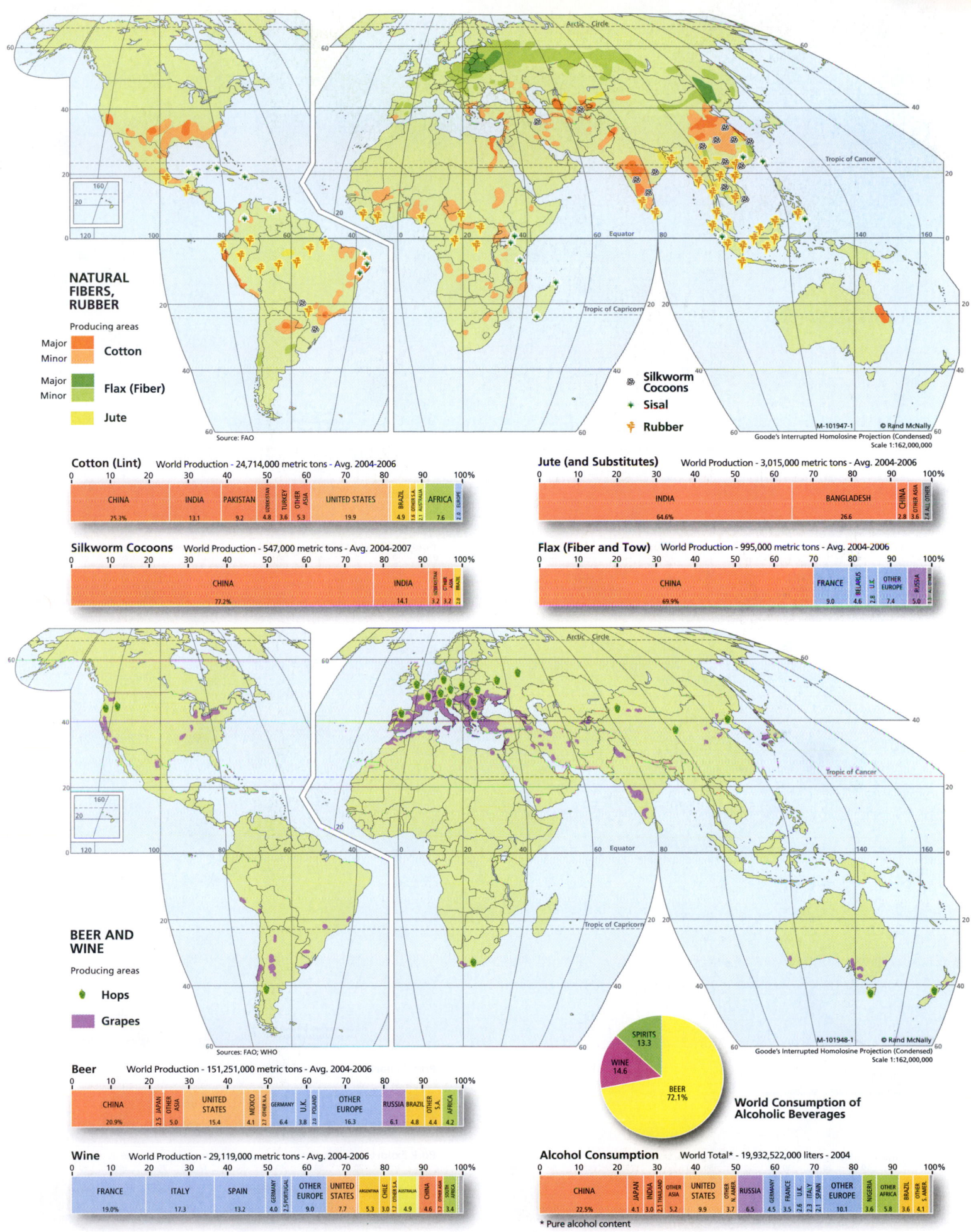

NATURAL FIBERS, RUBBER

Producing areas

Major / Minor — Cotton
Major / Minor — Flax (Fiber)
Jute

⊗ Silkworm Cocoons
✛ Sisal
⚕ Rubber

Source: FAO

M-101947-1 © Rand McNally
Goode's Interrupted Homolosine Projection (Condensed)
Scale 1:162,000,000

Cotton (Lint) World Production - 24,714,000 metric tons - Avg. 2004-2006

| CHINA 25.3% | INDIA 13.1 | PAKISTAN 9.2 | UZBEKISTAN 4.8 | TURKEY 3.6 | OTHER ASIA 5.3 | UNITED STATES 19.9 | BRAZIL 4.9 | OTHER S.A. 1.8 | AUSTRALIA 2.1 | AFRICA 7.6 | EUROPE |

Silkworm Cocoons World Production - 547,000 metric tons - Avg. 2004-2007

| CHINA 77.2% | INDIA 14.1 | UZBEKISTAN 3.2 | OTHER ASIA 3.2 | BRAZIL 2.0 |

Jute (and Substitutes) World Production - 3,015,000 metric tons - Avg. 2004-2006

| INDIA 64.6% | BANGLADESH 26.6 | CHINA 2.8 | OTHER ASIA 3.6 | ALL OTHER 2.4 |

Flax (Fiber and Tow) World Production - 995,000 metric tons - Avg. 2004-2006

| CHINA 69.9% | FRANCE 9.0 | BELARUS 4.6 | U.K. 2.8 | OTHER EUROPE 7.4 | RUSSIA 5.0 | ALL OTHER 1.3 |

BEER AND WINE

Producing areas

🌿 Hops
🟪 Grapes

Sources: FAO; WHO

M-101948-1 © Rand McNally
Goode's Interrupted Homolosine Projection (Condensed)
Scale 1:162,000,000

Beer World Production - 151,251,000 metric tons - Avg. 2004-2006

| CHINA 20.9% | JAPAN 2.5 | OTHER ASIA 5.0 | UNITED STATES 15.4 | MEXICO 4.1 | OTHER N.A. 2.7 | GERMANY 6.4 | U.K. 3.8 | POLAND 2.0 | OTHER EUROPE 16.3 | RUSSIA 6.1 | BRAZIL 4.8 | OTHER S.A. 4.4 | AFRICA 4.2 |

Wine World Production - 29,119,000 metric tons - Avg. 2004-2006

| FRANCE 19.0% | ITALY 17.3 | SPAIN 13.2 | GERMANY 4.0 | PORTUGAL 2.5 | OTHER EUROPE 9.0 | UNITED STATES 7.7 | ARGENTINA 5.3 | CHILE 3.7 | OTHER S.A. 1.7 | AUSTRALIA 4.9 | CHINA 4.6 | OTHER ASIA 1.7 | SOUTH AFRICA 3.4 |

World Consumption of Alcoholic Beverages

SPIRITS 13.3
WINE 14.6
BEER 72.1%

Alcohol Consumption World Total* - 19,932,522,000 liters - 2004

| CHINA 22.5% | JAPAN 4.1 | INDIA 3.0 | THAILAND 2.1 | OTHER ASIA 5.2 | UNITED STATES 9.9 | OTHER N. AMER. 3.7 | RUSSIA 6.5 | GERMANY 4.5 | FRANCE 3.5 | U.K. 2.6 | ITALY 2.3 | SPAIN 2.1 | OTHER EUROPE 10.1 | NIGERIA 3.6 | OTHER AFRICA 5.8 | BRAZIL 3.6 | OTHER S. AMER. 4.1 |

* Pure alcohol content

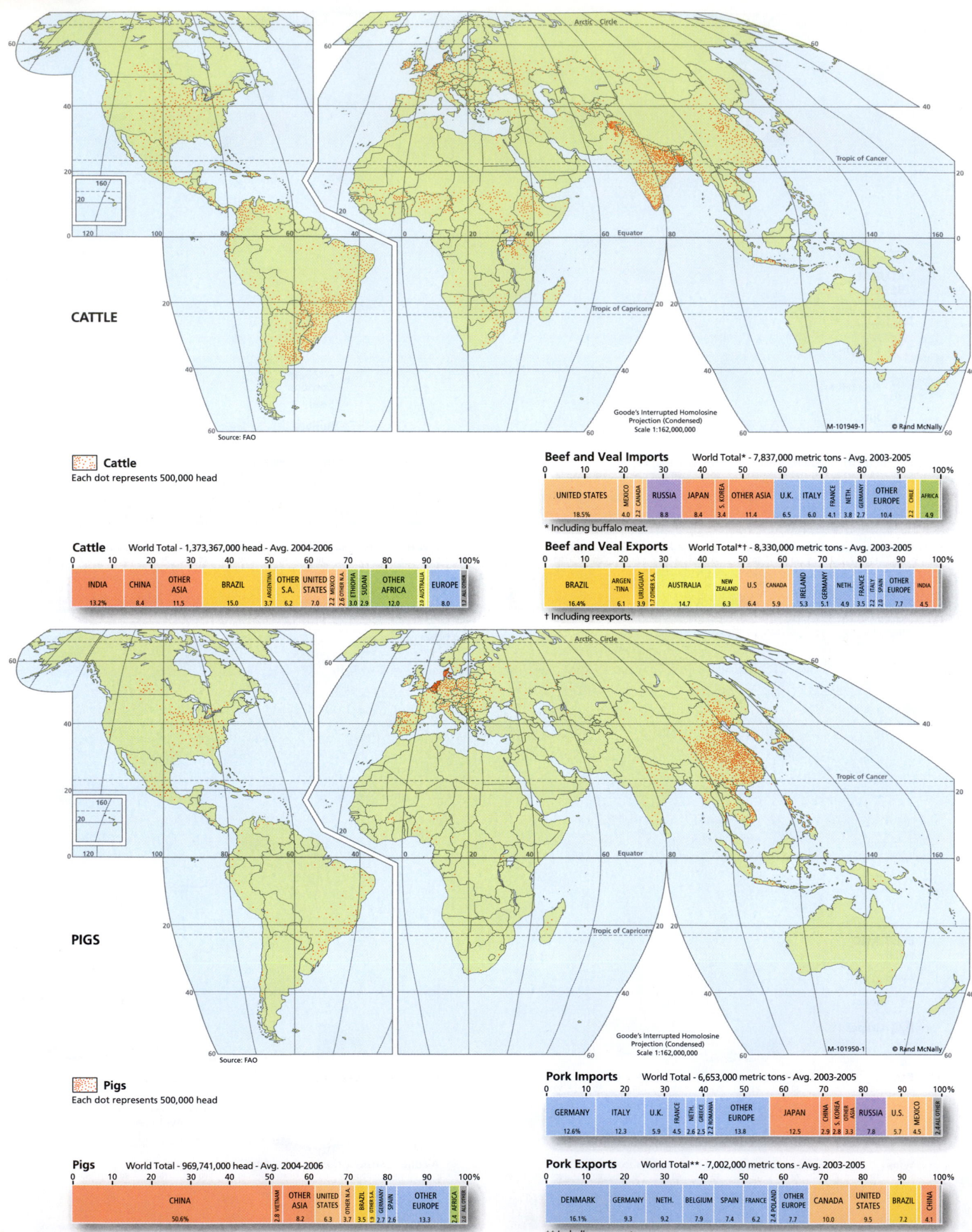

CATTLE

Goode's Interrupted Homolosine
Projection (Condensed)
Scale 1:162,000,000

M-101949-1   © Rand McNally

Source: FAO

Cattle
Each dot represents 500,000 head

Cattle   World Total - 1,373,367,000 head - Avg. 2004-2006

INDIA	CHINA	OTHER ASIA	BRAZIL	ARGENTINA	OTHER S.A.	UNITED STATES	MEXICO	OTHER N.A.	ETHIOPIA	SUDAN	OTHER AFRICA	AUSTRALIA	EUROPE	ALL OTHER
13.2%	8.4	11.5	15.0	3.7	6.2	7.0	2.2	2.6	3.0	2.9	12.0	2.0	8.0	1.7

Beef and Veal Imports   World Total* - 7,837,000 metric tons - Avg. 2003-2005

UNITED STATES	MEXICO	CANADA	RUSSIA	JAPAN	S. KOREA	OTHER ASIA	U.K.	ITALY	FRANCE	NETH.	GERMANY	OTHER EUROPE	CHILE	AFRICA
18.5%	4.0	2.2	8.8	8.4	3.4	11.4	6.5	6.0	4.1	3.8	2.7	10.4	2.2	4.9

* Including buffalo meat.

Beef and Veal Exports   World Total*† - 8,330,000 metric tons - Avg. 2003-2005

BRAZIL	ARGENTINA	URUGUAY	OTHER S.A.	AUSTRALIA	NEW ZEALAND	U.S	CANADA	IRELAND	GERMANY	NETH.	FRANCE	ITALY	SPAIN	OTHER EUROPE	INDIA
16.4%	6.1	3.9	1.7	14.7	6.3	6.4	5.9	5.3	5.1	4.9	3.5	2.2	2.0	7.7	4.5

† Including reexports.

PIGS

Goode's Interrupted Homolosine
Projection (Condensed)
Scale 1:162,000,000

M-101950-1   © Rand McNally

Source: FAO

Pigs
Each dot represents 500,000 head

Pigs   World Total - 969,741,000 head - Avg. 2004-2006

CHINA	VIETNAM	OTHER ASIA	UNITED STATES	OTHER N.A.	BRAZIL	OTHER S.A.	GERMANY	SPAIN	OTHER EUROPE	AFRICA	ALL OTHER
50.6%	2.8	8.2	6.3	3.7	3.5	1.9	2.7	2.6	13.3	2.4	1.8

Pork Imports   World Total - 6,653,000 metric tons - Avg. 2003-2005

GERMANY	ITALY	U.K.	FRANCE	NETH.	GREECE	ROMANIA	OTHER EUROPE	JAPAN	CHINA	S. KOREA	OTHER ASIA	RUSSIA	U.S.	MEXICO	ALL OTHER
12.6%	12.3	5.9	4.5	2.6	2.5	2.2	13.8	12.5	2.9	2.8	3.3	7.8	5.7	4.5	2.4

Pork Exports   World Total** - 7,002,000 metric tons - Avg. 2003-2005

DENMARK	GERMANY	NETH.	BELGIUM	SPAIN	FRANCE	POLAND	OTHER EUROPE	CANADA	UNITED STATES	BRAZIL	CHINA
16.1%	9.3	9.2	7.9	7.4	6.2	2.4	7.7	10.0	9.5	7.2	4.1

** Including reexports.

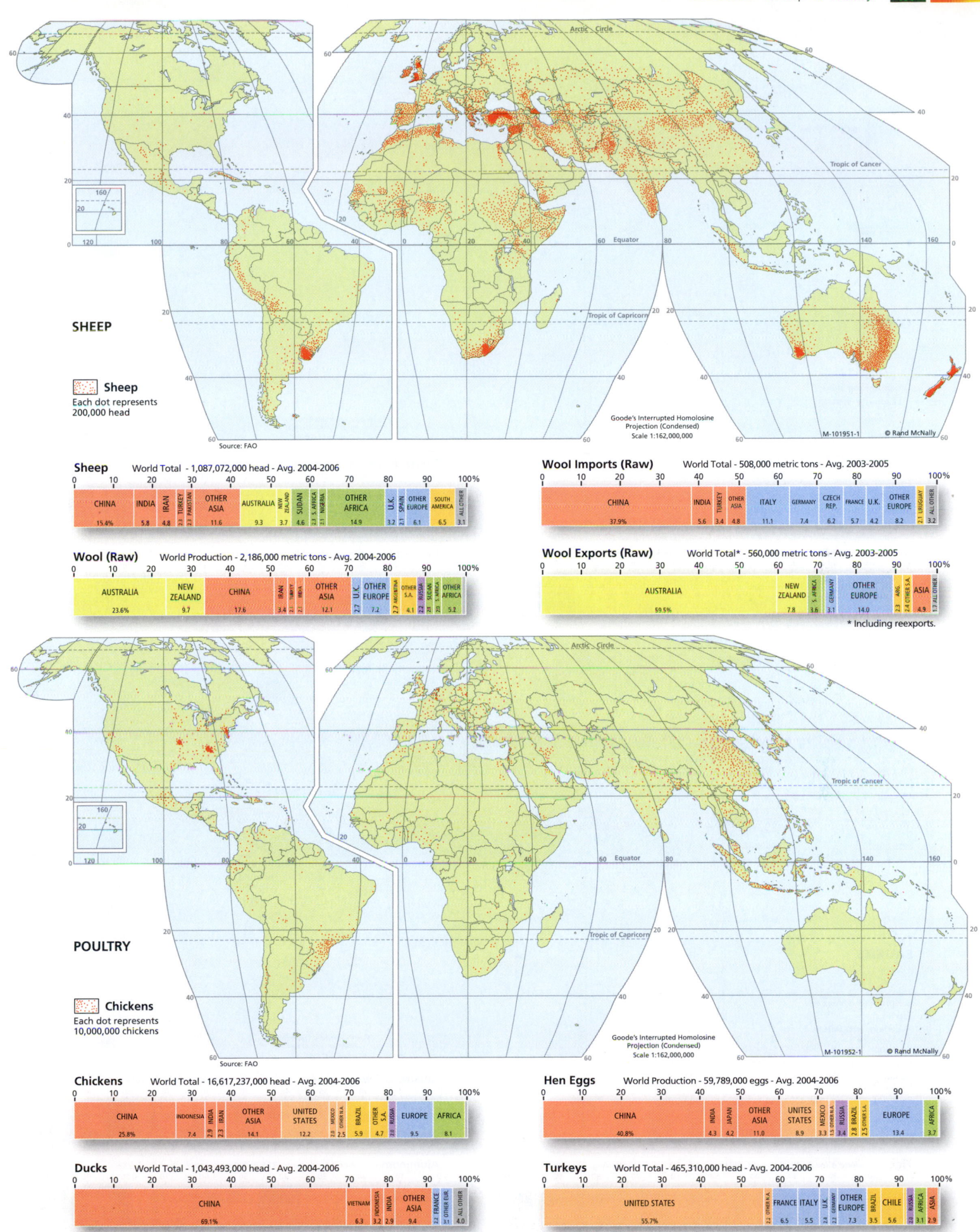

SHEEP

▢ **Sheep**
Each dot represents
200,000 head

Source: FAO

Goode's Interrupted Homolosine
Projection (Condensed)
Scale 1:162,000,000
M-101951-1
© Rand McNally

Sheep World Total - 1,087,072,000 head - Avg. 2004-2006

0	10	20	30	40	50	60	70	80	90	100%

| CHINA 15.4% | INDIA 5.8 | IRAN 4.8 | TURKEY 2.3 | PAKISTAN 2.3 | OTHER ASIA 11.6 | AUSTRALIA 9.3 | NEW ZEALAND 3.7 | SUDAN 4.6 | S. AFRICA 2.3 | NIGERIA 3.1 | OTHER AFRICA 14.9 | U.K. 2.1 | SPAIN | OTHER EUROPE 6.1 | SOUTH AMERICA 6.5 | ALL OTHER 3.1 |

Wool Imports (Raw) World Total - 508,000 metric tons - Avg. 2003-2005

0	10	20	30	40	50	60	70	80	90	100%

| CHINA 37.9% | INDIA 5.6 | TURKEY 3.4 | OTHER ASIA 4.8 | ITALY 11.1 | GERMANY 7.4 | CZECH REP. 6.2 | FRANCE 5.7 | U.K. 4.2 | OTHER EUROPE 8.2 | URUGUAY 2.1 | ALL OTHER 3.2 |

Wool (Raw) World Production - 2,186,000 metric tons - Avg. 2004-2006

0	10	20	30	40	50	60	70	80	90	100%

| AUSTRALIA 23.6% | NEW ZEALAND 9.7 | CHINA 17.6 | IRAN 3.4 | TURKEY 2.1 | INDIA | OTHER ASIA 12.1 | U.K. 2.7 | OTHER EUROPE 7.2 | ARGENTINA 2.7 | RUSSIA 4.1 | S. AFRICA 2.3 | OTHER AFRICA 5.2 |

Wool Exports (Raw) World Total* - 560,000 metric tons - Avg. 2003-2005

0	10	20	30	40	50	60	70	80	90	100%

| AUSTRALIA 59.5% | NEW ZEALAND 7.8 | S. AFRICA 3.6 | GERMANY 3.1 | OTHER EUROPE 14.0 | ARG. 2.3 | OTHER S.A. 2.4 | ASIA 4.9 | ALL OTHER 1.7 |

* Including reexports.

POULTRY

▢ **Chickens**
Each dot represents
10,000,000 chickens

Source: FAO

Goode's Interrupted Homolosine
Projection (Condensed)
Scale 1:162,000,000
M-101952-1
© Rand McNally

Chickens World Total - 16,617,237,000 head - Avg. 2004-2006

0	10	20	30	40	50	60	70	80	90	100%

| CHINA 25.8% | INDONESIA 7.4 | INDIA 2.9 | IRAN 2.3 | OTHER ASIA 14.1 | UNITED STATES 12.2 | MEXICO 2.8 | OTHER N.A. 2.5 | BRAZIL 5.9 | OTHER S.A. 4.7 | RUSSIA 2.0 | EUROPE 9.5 | AFRICA 8.1 |

Hen Eggs World Production - 59,789,000 eggs - Avg. 2004-2006

0	10	20	30	40	50	60	70	80	90	100%

| CHINA 40.8% | INDIA 4.3 | JAPAN 4.2 | OTHER ASIA 11.0 | UNITES STATES 8.9 | MEXICO 3.3 | OTHER N.A. 1.5 | RUSSIA 2.8 | BRAZIL 2.5 | OTHER S.A. | EUROPE 13.4 | AFRICA 3.7 |

Ducks World Total - 1,043,493,000 head - Avg. 2004-2006

0	10	20	30	40	50	60	70	80	90	100%

| CHINA 69.1% | VIETNAM 6.3 | INDONESIA 3.2 | INDIA 2.9 | OTHER ASIA 9.4 | FRANCE 2.2 | OTHER EUR. 3.1 | ALL OTHER 4.0 |

Turkeys World Total - 465,310,000 head - Avg. 2004-2006

0	10	20	30	40	50	60	70	80	90	100%

| UNITED STATES 55.7% | OTHER N.A. 2.2 | FRANCE 6.5 | ITALY 5.5 | U.K. 2.8 | GERMANY 2.2 | OTHER EUROPE 7.3 | BRAZIL 3.5 | CHILE 5.6 | RUSSIA 2.0 | AFRICA 3.1 | ASIA 2.9 |

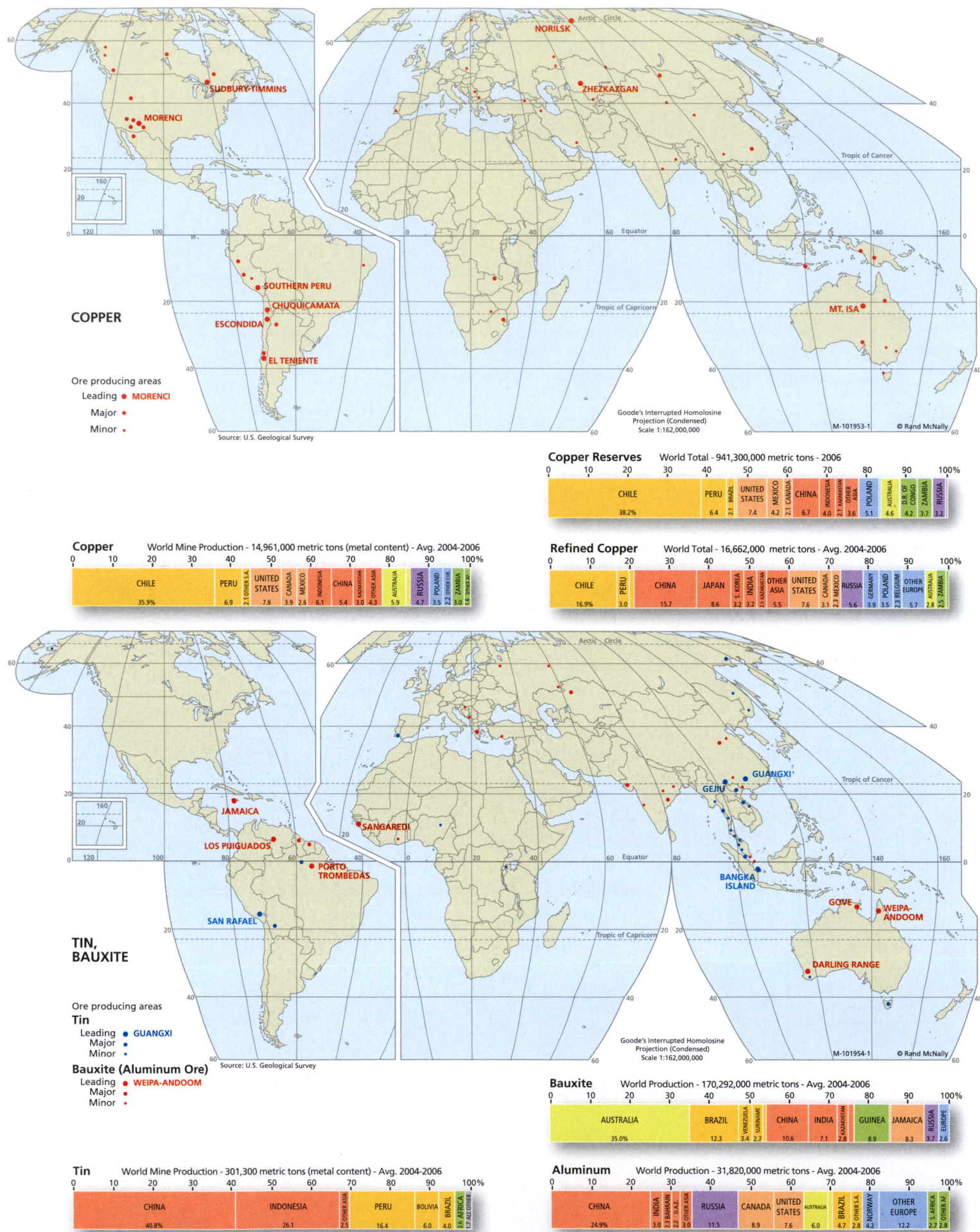

COPPER

NORILSK
SUDBURY-TIMMINS
MORENCI
ZHEZKAZGAN
SOUTHERN PERU
CHUQUICAMATA
ESCONDIDA
EL TENIENTE
MT. ISA

Ore producing areas
Leading ● MORENCI
Major ●
Minor ·

Source: U.S. Geological Survey

Goode's Interrupted Homolosine
Projection (Condensed)
Scale 1:162,000,000

M-101953-1 © Rand McNally

Copper Reserves World Total - 941,300,000 metric tons - 2006

CHILE	PERU	BRAZIL	UNITED STATES	MEXICO	CANADA	CHINA	INDONESIA	KAZAKHSTAN	OTHER ASIA	POLAND	AUSTRALIA	D.R. OF CONGO	ZAMBIA	RUSSIA
38.2%	6.4	2.1	7.4	4.2	2.1	6.7	4.0	2.1	3.6	5.1	4.6	4.2	3.7	3.2

Copper World Mine Production - 14,961,000 metric tons (metal content) - Avg. 2004-2006

CHILE	PERU	OTHER S.A.	UNITED STATES	CANADA	MEXICO	INDONESIA	CHINA	KAZAKHSTAN	OTHER ASIA	AUSTRALIA	RUSSIA	POLAND	OTHER EUR. ZAMBIA OTHER AF.
35.9%	6.9	2.1	7.8	3.9	2.6	6.1	5.4	3.0	4.3	5.9	4.7	3.5	2.2 3.0 1.6

Refined Copper World Total - 16,662,000 metric tons - Avg. 2004-2006

CHILE	PERU	CHINA	JAPAN	S. KOREA	INDIA	OTHER ASIA	UNITED STATES	CANADA	MEXICO	RUSSIA	GERMANY	POLAND	BELGIUM	OTHER EUROPE	AUSTRALIA ZAMBIA
16.9%	3.0	15.7	8.6	3.2	2.3	5.5	7.6	3.1	2.3	5.6	3.9	3.5	2.3	5.7	2.5

TIN, BAUXITE

JAMAICA
LOS PIJIGUADOS
PORTO TROMBEDAS
SAN RAFAEL
SANGAREDI
GEJIU
GUANGXI
BANGKA ISLAND
GOVE
WEIPA-ANDOOM
DARLING RANGE

Ore producing areas
Tin
Leading ● GUANGXI
Major ●
Minor ·
Bauxite (Aluminum Ore)
Leading ● WEIPA-ANDOOM
Major ●
Minor ·

Source: U.S. Geological Survey

Goode's Interrupted Homolosine
Projection (Condensed)
Scale 1:162,000,000

M-101954-1 © Rand McNally

Bauxite World Production - 170,292,000 metric tons - Avg. 2004-2006

AUSTRALIA	BRAZIL	VENEZUELA	SURINAME	CHINA	INDIA	KAZAKHSTAN	GUINEA	JAMAICA	RUSSIA EUROPE
35.0%	12.3	3.4	2.7	10.6	7.1	2.8	8.9	8.3	3.7 2.6

Tin World Mine Production - 301,300 metric tons (metal content) - Avg. 2004-2006

CHINA	INDONESIA	OTHER ASIA	PERU	BOLIVIA	BRAZIL AFRICA ALL OTHER
40.8%	26.1	2.5	16.4	6.0	4.0 2.6 1.7

Aluminum World Production - 31,820,000 metric tons - Avg. 2004-2006

CHINA	INDIA	BAHRAIN	U.A.E.	RUSSIA	CANADA	UNITED STATES	AUSTRALIA	BRAZIL	OTHER S.A. NORWAY	OTHER EUROPE	S. AFRICA OTHER AF.
24.9%	3.0	2.3	2.2	11.5	8.9	7.6	6.0	4.7	2.8 4.2	12.2	2.7 2.8

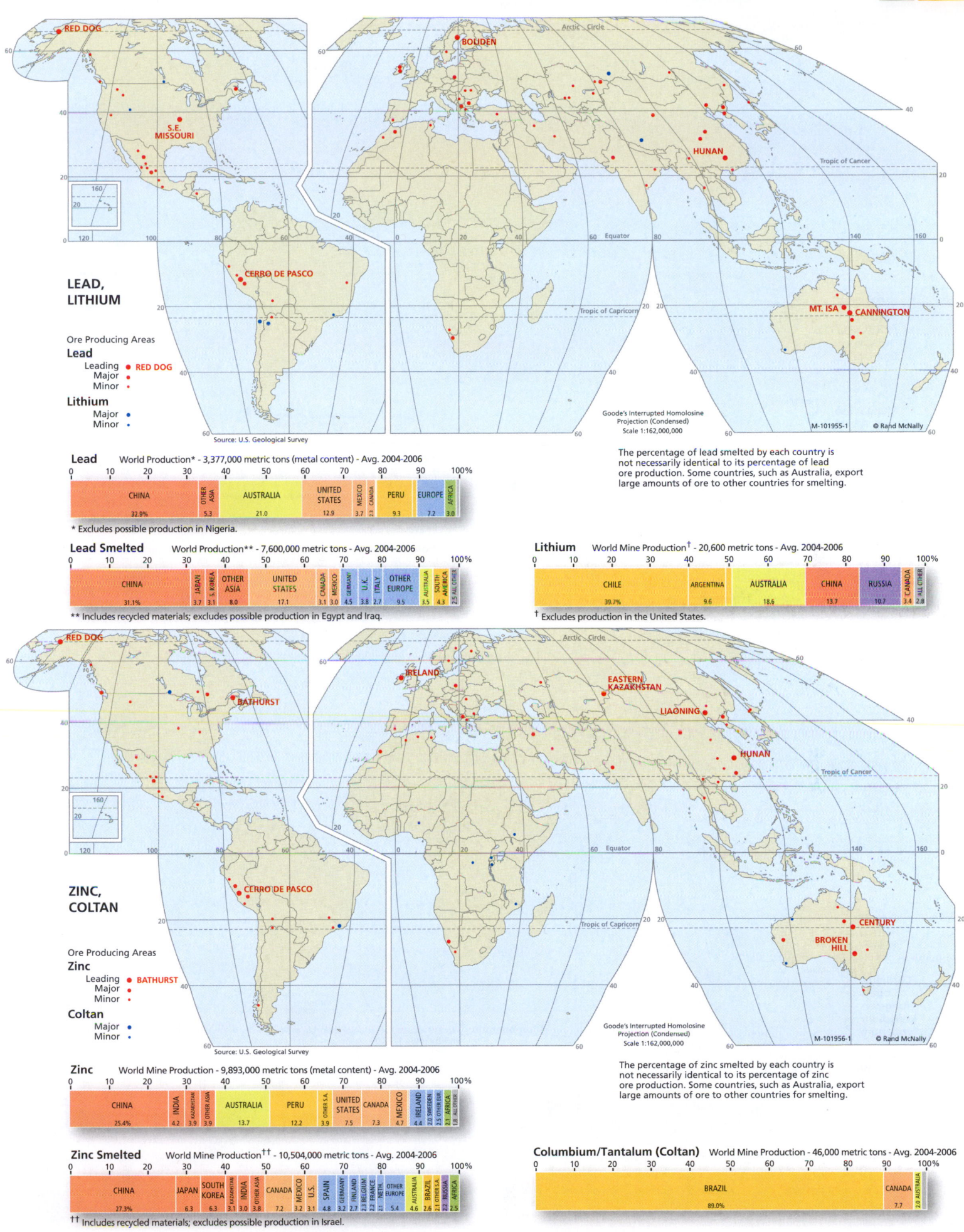

LEAD, LITHIUM

Ore Producing Areas

Lead
Leading ● **RED DOG**
Major ●
Minor ·

Lithium
Major ●
Minor ·

Source: U.S. Geological Survey

Goode's Interrupted Homolosine Projection (Condensed)
Scale 1:162,000,000
M-101955-1 © Rand McNally

The percentage of lead smelted by each country is not necessarily identical to its percentage of lead ore production. Some countries, such as Australia, export large amounts of ore to other countries for smelting.

Lead World Production* - 3,377,000 metric tons (metal content) - Avg. 2004-2006

0	10	20	30	40	50	60	70	80	90	100%
CHINA 32.9%			OTHER ASIA 5.3	AUSTRALIA 21.0		UNITED STATES 12.9	MEXICO 3.7	CANADA 2.3	PERU 9.3	EUROPE 7.2	AFRICA 3.0

* Excludes possible production in Nigeria.

Lead Smelted World Production** - 7,600,000 metric tons - Avg. 2004-2006

0	10	20	30	40	50	60	70	80	90	100%
CHINA 31.1%	JAPAN 3.7	S. KOREA 3.1	OTHER ASIA 8.0	UNITED STATES 17.1	CANADA 3.1	MEXICO 3.0	GERMANY 4.5	U.K. 3.8	ITALY 2.7	OTHER EUROPE 9.5	AUSTRALIA 3.5	SOUTH AMERICA 4.3	ALL OTHER 2.5

** Includes recycled materials; excludes possible production in Egypt and Iraq.

Lithium World Mine Production† - 20,600 metric tons - Avg. 2004-2006

0	10	20	30	40	50	60	70	80	90	100%
CHILE 39.7%				ARGENTINA 9.6	AUSTRALIA 18.6		CHINA 13.7	RUSSIA 10.7	CANADA 3.4	ALL OTHER 2.8

† Excludes production in the United States.

ZINC, COLTAN

Ore Producing Areas

Zinc
Leading ● **BATHURST**
Major ●
Minor ·

Coltan
Major ●
Minor ·

Source: U.S. Geological Survey

Goode's Interrupted Homolosine Projection (Condensed)
Scale 1:162,000,000
M-101956-1 © Rand McNally

The percentage of zinc smelted by each country is not necessarily identical to its percentage of zinc ore production. Some countries, such as Australia, export large amounts of ore to other countries for smelting.

Zinc World Mine Production - 9,893,000 metric tons (metal content) - Avg. 2004-2006

0	10	20	30	40	50	60	70	80	90	100%
CHINA 25.4%		INDIA 4.2	KAZAKHSTAN 3.9	OTHER ASIA 3.9	AUSTRALIA 13.7	PERU 12.2	OTHER S.A. 3.9	UNITED STATES 7.5	CANADA 7.3	MEXICO 4.7	IRELAND 4.4	SWEDEN 2.5	OTHER EUR. 2.1	AFRICA 1.8	ALL OTHER

Zinc Smelted World Mine Production†† - 10,504,000 metric tons - Avg. 2004-2006

0	10	20	30	40	50	60	70	80	90	100%
CHINA 27.3%		JAPAN 6.3	SOUTH KOREA 6.3	KAZAKHSTAN 3.1	INDIA 3.0	OTHER ASIA 3.8	CANADA 7.2	MEXICO 3.2	U.S. 3.4	SPAIN 4.8	FINLAND 3.2	BELGIUM 2.7	FRANCE 2.3	NETH. 2.2	OTHER EUROPE 5.4	AUSTRALIA 4.6	BRAZIL 2.6	RUSSIA 2.1	AFRICA 2.5

†† Includes recycled materials; excludes possible production in Israel.

Columbium/Tantalum (Coltan) World Mine Production - 46,000 metric tons - Avg. 2004-2006

0	10	20	30	40	50	60	70	80	90	100%
BRAZIL 89.0%									CANADA 7.7	AUSTRALIA 2.0	ALL OTHER

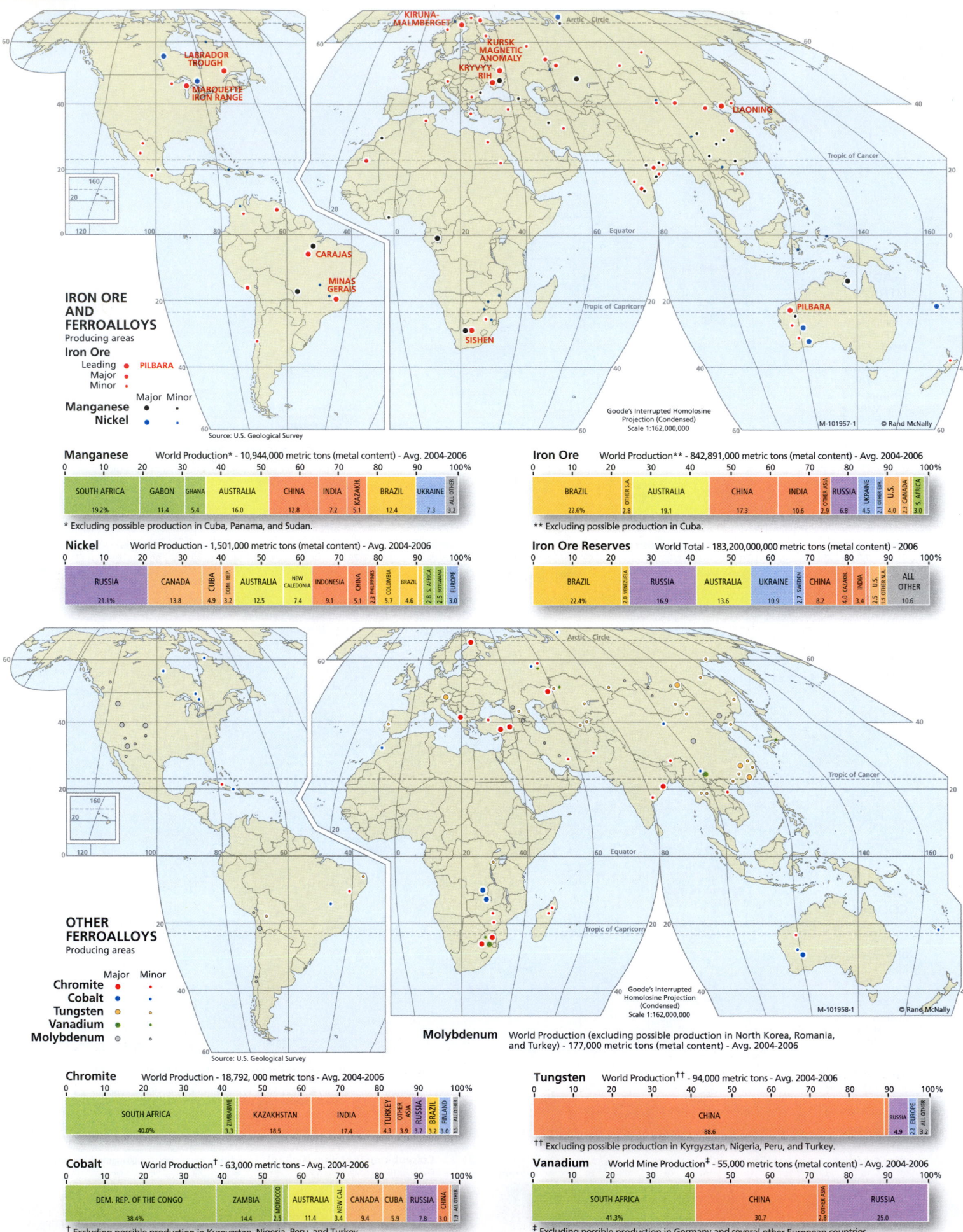

IRON ORE AND FERROALLOYS
Producing areas

Iron Ore
- Leading ● PILBARA
- Major ●
- Minor •

Major Minor
Manganese ● •
Nickel ● •

Source: U.S. Geological Survey

Goode's Interrupted Homolosine
Projection (Condensed)
Scale 1:162,000,000

M-101957-1 © Rand McNally

Manganese
World Production* - 10,944,000 metric tons (metal content) - Avg. 2004-2006

SOUTH AFRICA	GABON	GHANA	AUSTRALIA	CHINA	INDIA	KAZAKH.	BRAZIL	UKRAINE	ALL OTHER
19.2%	11.4	5.4	16.0	12.8	7.2	5.1	12.4	7.3	3.2

* Excluding possible production in Cuba, Panama, and Sudan.

Iron Ore
World Production** - 842,891,000 metric tons (metal content) - Avg. 2004-2006

BRAZIL	OTHER S.A.	AUSTRALIA	CHINA	INDIA	OTHER ASIA	RUSSIA	UKRAINE	OTHER EUR.	U.S.	CANADA	S. AFRICA
22.6%	2.8	19.1	17.3	10.6	2.9	6.8	4.5	2.1	4.0	2.3	3.0

** Excluding possible production in Cuba.

Nickel
World Production - 1,501,000 metric tons (metal content) - Avg. 2004-2006

RUSSIA	CANADA	CUBA	DOM. REP.	AUSTRALIA	NEW CALEDONIA	INDONESIA	CHINA	PHILIPPINES	COLOMBIA	BRAZIL	S. AFRICA	BOTSWANA	EUROPE
21.1%	13.8	4.9	3.2	12.5	7.4	9.1	5.1	2.3	5.7	4.6	2.8	2.5	3.0

Iron Ore Reserves
World Total - 183,200,000,000 metric tons (metal content) - 2006

BRAZIL	VENEZUELA	RUSSIA	AUSTRALIA	UKRAINE	SWEDEN	CHINA	KAZAKH.	INDIA	U.S.	OTHER N.A.	ALL OTHER
22.4%	2.0	16.9	13.6	10.9	2.7	8.2	4.0	3.4	2.5	1.9	10.6

OTHER FERROALLOYS
Producing areas

Major Minor
- **Chromite** ● •
- **Cobalt** ● •
- **Tungsten** ● •
- **Vanadium** ● •
- **Molybdenum** ● •

Source: U.S. Geological Survey

Goode's Interrupted
Homolosine Projection
(Condensed)
Scale 1:162,000,000

M-101958-1 © Rand McNally

Molybdenum
World Production (excluding possible production in North Korea, Romania, and Turkey) - 177,000 metric tons (metal content) - Avg. 2004-2006

Chromite
World Production - 18,792,000 metric tons - Avg. 2004-2006

SOUTH AFRICA	ZIMBABWE	KAZAKHSTAN	INDIA	TURKEY	OTHER ASIA	RUSSIA	BRAZIL	FINLAND	ALL OTHER
40.0%	3.3	18.5	17.4	4.3	3.9	3.7	3.2	1.5	

Tungsten
World Production†† - 94,000 metric tons - Avg. 2004-2006

CHINA	RUSSIA	EUROPE	ALL OTHER
88.6	4.9	2.3	3.2

†† Excluding possible production in Kyrgyzstan, Nigeria, Peru, and Turkey.

Cobalt
World Production† - 63,000 metric tons - Avg. 2004-2006

DEM. REP. OF THE CONGO	ZAMBIA	MOROCCO	AUSTRALIA	NEW CAL.	CANADA	CUBA	RUSSIA	CHINA	ALL OTHER
38.4%	14.4	2.5	11.4	3.4	9.4	5.9	7.8	1.9	

† Excluding possible production in Kyrgyzstan, Nigeria, Peru, and Turkey.

Vanadium
World Mine Production‡ - 55,000 metric tons (metal content) - Avg. 2004-2006

SOUTH AFRICA	CHINA	OTHER ASIA	RUSSIA
41.3%	30.7	2.8	25.0

‡ Excluding possible production in Germany and several other European countries.

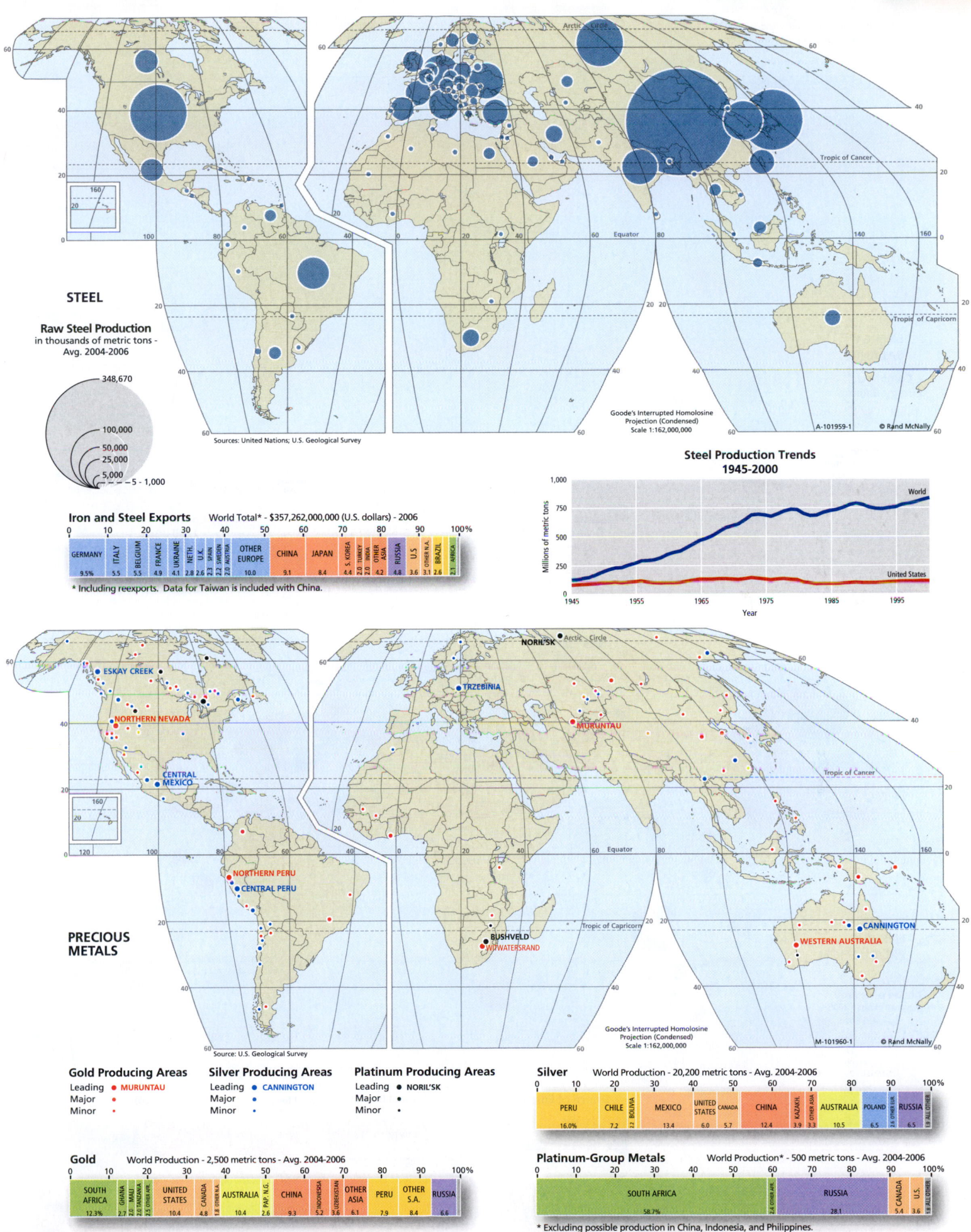

STEEL

Raw Steel Production
in thousands of metric tons -
Avg. 2004-2006

348,670
100,000
50,000
25,000
5,000
5 - 1,000

Sources: United Nations; U.S. Geological Survey

Goode's Interrupted Homolosine
Projection (Condensed)
Scale 1:162,000,000
A-101959-1   © Rand McNally

Iron and Steel Exports   World Total* - $357,262,000,000 (U.S. dollars) - 2006

	0	10	20	30	40	50	60	70	80	90	100%

GERMANY	ITALY	BELGIUM	FRANCE	UKRAINE	NETH.	U.K.	SPAIN	SWEDEN	AUSTRIA	OTHER EUROPE	CHINA	JAPAN	S. KOREA	TURKEY	INDIA	OTHER ASIA	RUSSIA	U.S.	OTHER N.A.	BRAZIL	AFRICA
9.5%	5.5	5.5	4.9	4.1	2.8	2.6	2.3	2.2	2.0	10.0	9.1	8.4	4.4	2.0	2.0	4.2	4.8	3.6	3.1	2.6	2.1

* Including reexports. Data for Taiwan is included with China.

Steel Production Trends 1945-2000

Millions of metric tons
World
United States
Year

PRECIOUS METALS

Source: U.S. Geological Survey

NORIL'SK

ESKAY CREEK
TRZEBINIA
NORTHERN NEVADA
MURUNTAU
CENTRAL MEXICO
NORTHERN PERU
CENTRAL PERU
CANNINGTON
WESTERN AUSTRALIA
BUSHVELD
WITWATERSRAND

Goode's Interrupted Homolosine
Projection (Condensed)
Scale 1:162,000,000
M-101960-1   © Rand McNally

Gold Producing Areas
Leading ● MURUNTAU
Major ●
Minor ●

Silver Producing Areas
Leading ● CANNINGTON
Major ●
Minor ●

Platinum Producing Areas
Leading ● NORIL'SK
Major ●
Minor ●

Silver   World Production - 20,200 metric tons - Avg. 2004-2006

	0	10	20	30	40	50	60	70	80	90	100%

PERU	CHILE	BOLIVIA	MEXICO	UNITED STATES	CANADA	CHINA	KAZAKH.	OTHER ASIA	AUSTRALIA	POLAND	OTHER EUR.	RUSSIA	ALL OTHER
16.0%	7.2	2.2	13.4	6.0	5.7	12.4	3.9	3.3	10.5	6.5	2.6	6.5	

Gold   World Production - 2,500 metric tons - Avg. 2004-2006

	0	10	20	30	40	50	60	70	80	90	100%

SOUTH AFRICA	GHANA	MALI	TANZANIA	OTHER AFR.	UNITED STATES	CANADA	AUSTRALIA	PAP. N.G.	CHINA	INDONESIA	UZBEKISTAN	OTHER ASIA	PERU	OTHER S.A.	RUSSIA
12.3%	2.7	2.1	2.2	2.5	10.4	4.8	10.4	2.6	9.3	5.2	3.6	6.1	7.9	8.4	6.6

Platinum-Group Metals   World Production* - 500 metric tons - Avg. 2004-2006

	0	10	20	30	40	50	60	70	80	90	100%

SOUTH AFRICA	OTHER AFR.	RUSSIA	CANADA	U.S.	ALL OTHER
58.7%	2.4	28.1	5.4	3.6	

* Excluding possible production in China, Indonesia, and Philippines.

Taiwan figures are included with China.

Botswana, Lesotho, Namibia and Swaziland figures are included with South Africa.

Montenegro figures are included with Serbia.

Arctic Circle
Tropic of Cancer
Equator
Tropic of Capricorn
Goode's Interrupted Homolosine Projection (Condensed)
Scale 1:162,000,000
A-100017-1
© Rand McNally

Sources: Energy Information Administration; United Nations

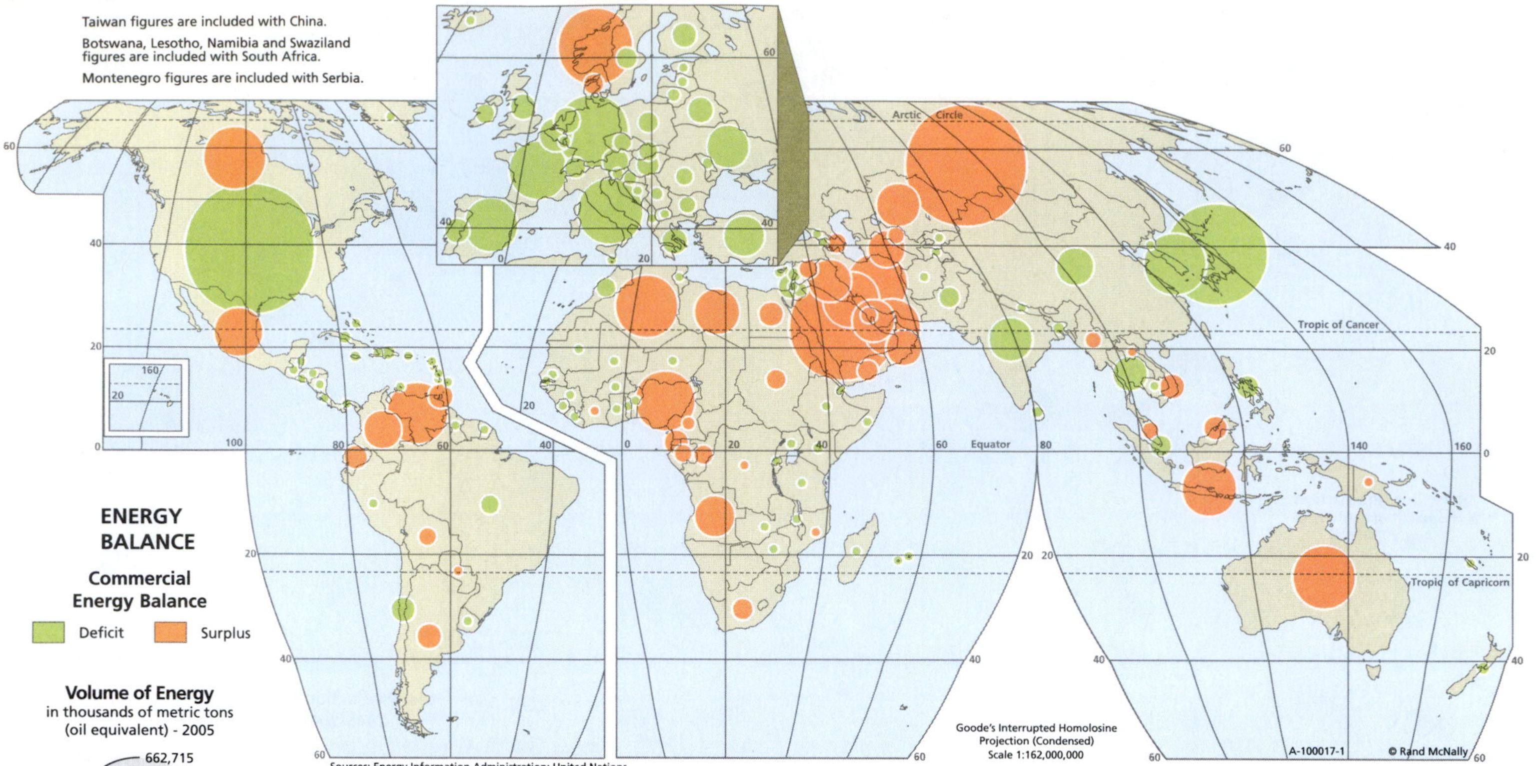

ENERGY BALANCE

Commercial Energy Balance

Deficit Surplus

Volume of Energy

in thousands of metric tons (oil equivalent) - 2005

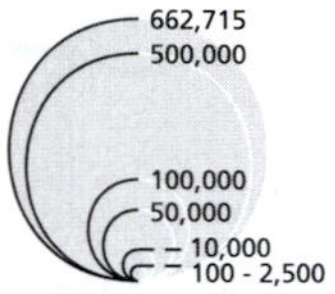

662,715
500,000
100,000
50,000
10,000
100 - 2,500

No symbol is shown if value is less than 100,000 metric tons.

Commercial Energy Consumption

World Total - 9,398,100,000 metric tons (oil equiv.) - 2005

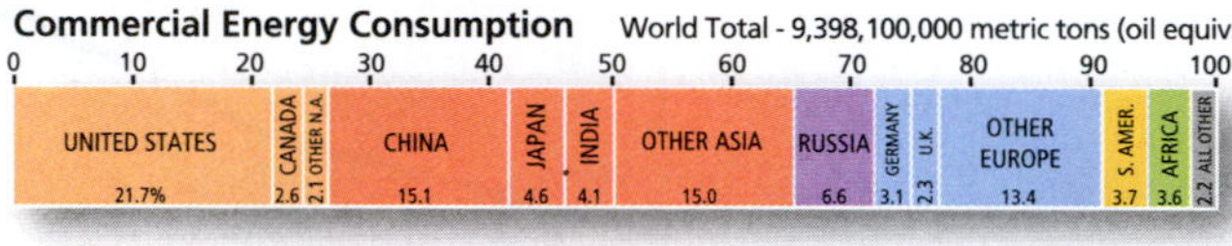

0 10 20 30 40 50 60 70 80 90 100%
UNITED STATES 21.7%
CANADA 2.6
OTHER N.A. 2.1
CHINA 15.1
JAPAN 4.6
INDIA 4.1
OTHER ASIA 15.0
RUSSIA 6.6
GERMANY 3.1
U.K. 2.3
OTHER EUROPE 13.4
S. AMER. 3.7
AFRICA 3.6
ALL OTHER 2.2

Energy Consumption Trends 1980-2030

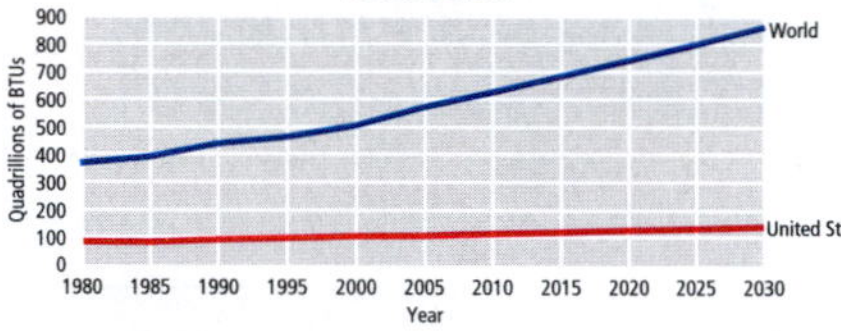

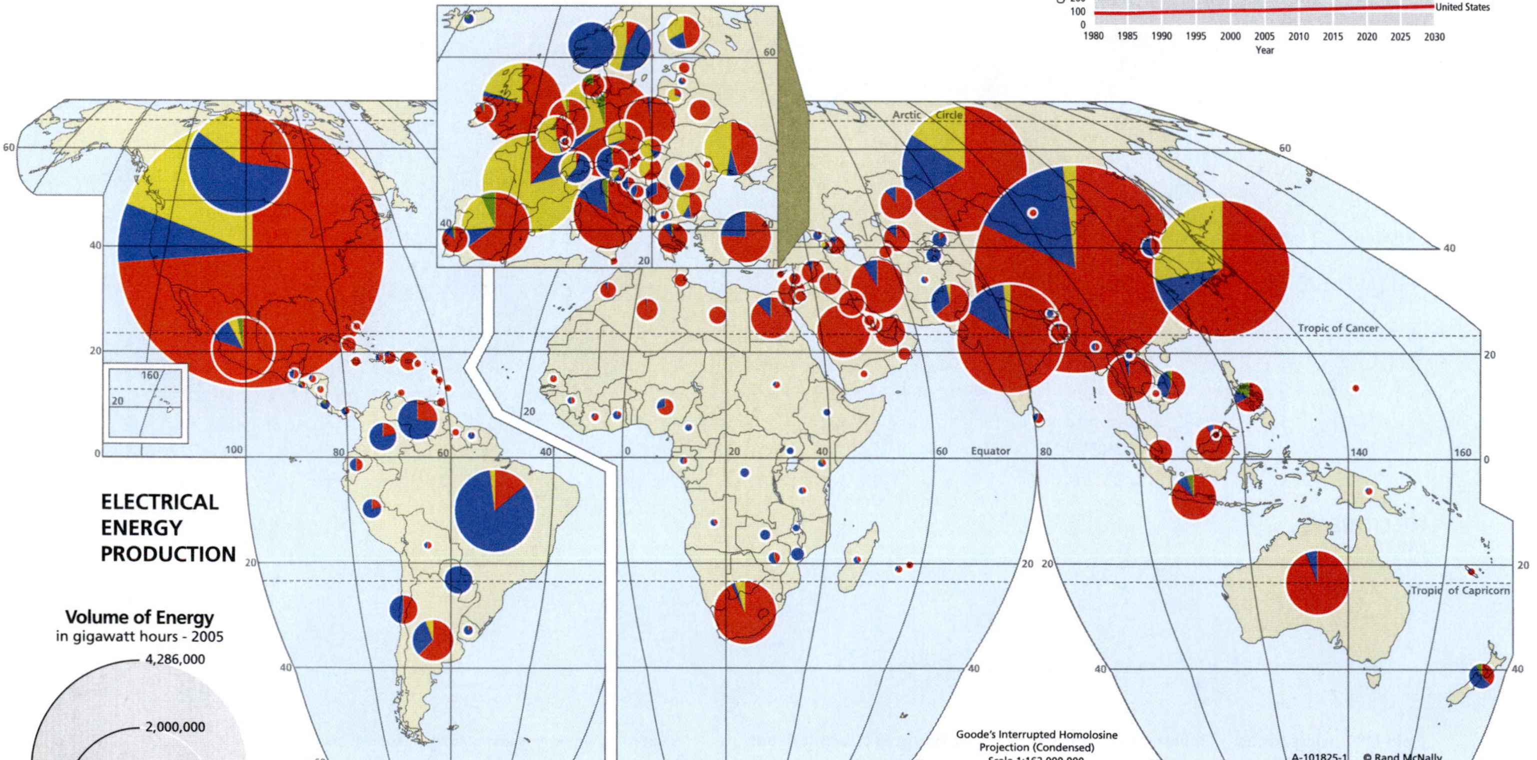

Quadrillions of BTUs
900
800
700
600
500
400
300
200
100
0
World
United States
1980 1985 1990 1995 2000 2005 2010 2015 2020 2025 2030
Year

Arctic Circle
Tropic of Cancer
Equator
Tropic of Capricorn
Goode's Interrupted Homolosine Projection (Condensed)
Scale 1:162,000,000
A-101825-1
© Rand McNally

Source: United Nations

ELECTRICAL ENERGY PRODUCTION

Volume of Energy

in gigawatt hours - 2005

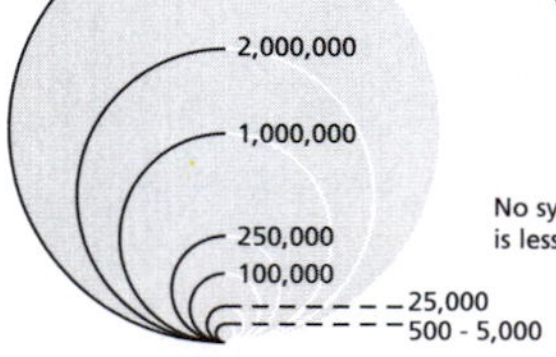

4,286,000
2,000,000
1,000,000
250,000
100,000
25,000
500 - 5,000

No symbol is shown if production is less than 500 gigawatt hours.

Source of Energy

Thermal
Nuclear
Hydro
Other

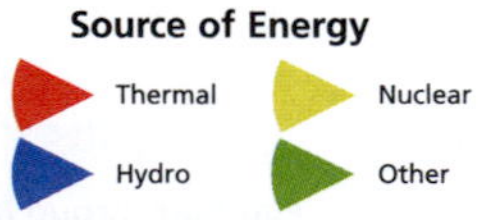

Thermal Energy

World Total - 12,413,000 gigawatt hours - 2005

0 10 20 30 40 50 60 70 80 90 100%
UNITED STATES 25.4%
OTHER N.A. 3.6
CHINA 16.8
JAPAN 5.7
INDIA 4.7
OTHER ASIA 13.3
RUSSIA 5.1
GERMANY 3.2
U.K. 2.5
ITALY 2.0
OTHER EUROPE 8.8
AFRICA 3.7
AUSTRALIA 2.1
ALL OTHER 3.0

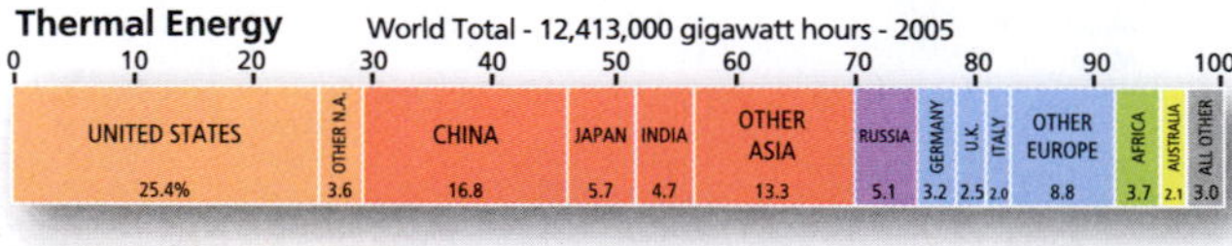

All Energy

World Total - 18,335,000 gigawatt hours - 2005

0 10 20 30 40 50 60 70 80 90 100%
UNITED STATES 23.4%
CANADA 3.4
OTHER N.A. 1.9
CHINA 13.8
JAPAN 6.0
INDIA 3.8
S. KOREA 2.1
OTHER ASIA 9.1
RUSSIA 5.2
GERMANY 3.4
FRANCE 3.1
U.K. 2.2
OTHER EUROPE 12.1
BRAZIL 2.2
OTHER S.A. 2.3
AFRICA 3.0
ALL OTHER 2.9

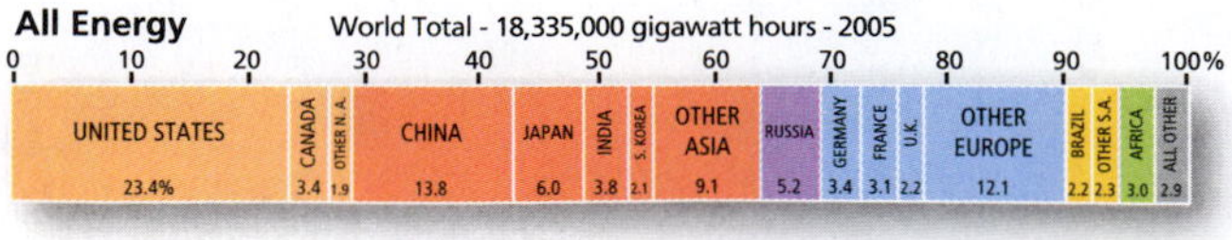

Nuclear Energy

World Total - 2,768,000 gigawatt hours - 2005

0 10 20 30 40 50 60 70 80 90 100%
UNITED STATES 29.3%
CANADA 3.3
FRANCE 16.3
GERMANY 5.9
UKRAINE 3.2
U.K. 2.9
SWEDEN 2.6
SPAIN 2.1
OTHER EUROPE 7.0
JAPAN 11.0
S. KOREA 5.3
OTHER ASIA 2.7
RUSSIA 5.4
ALL OTHER 2.5

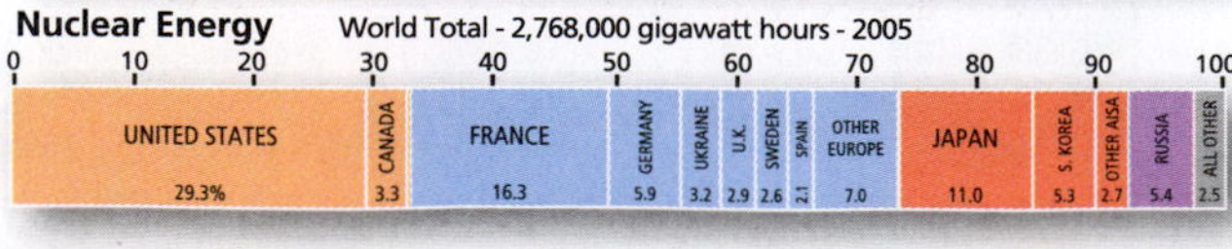

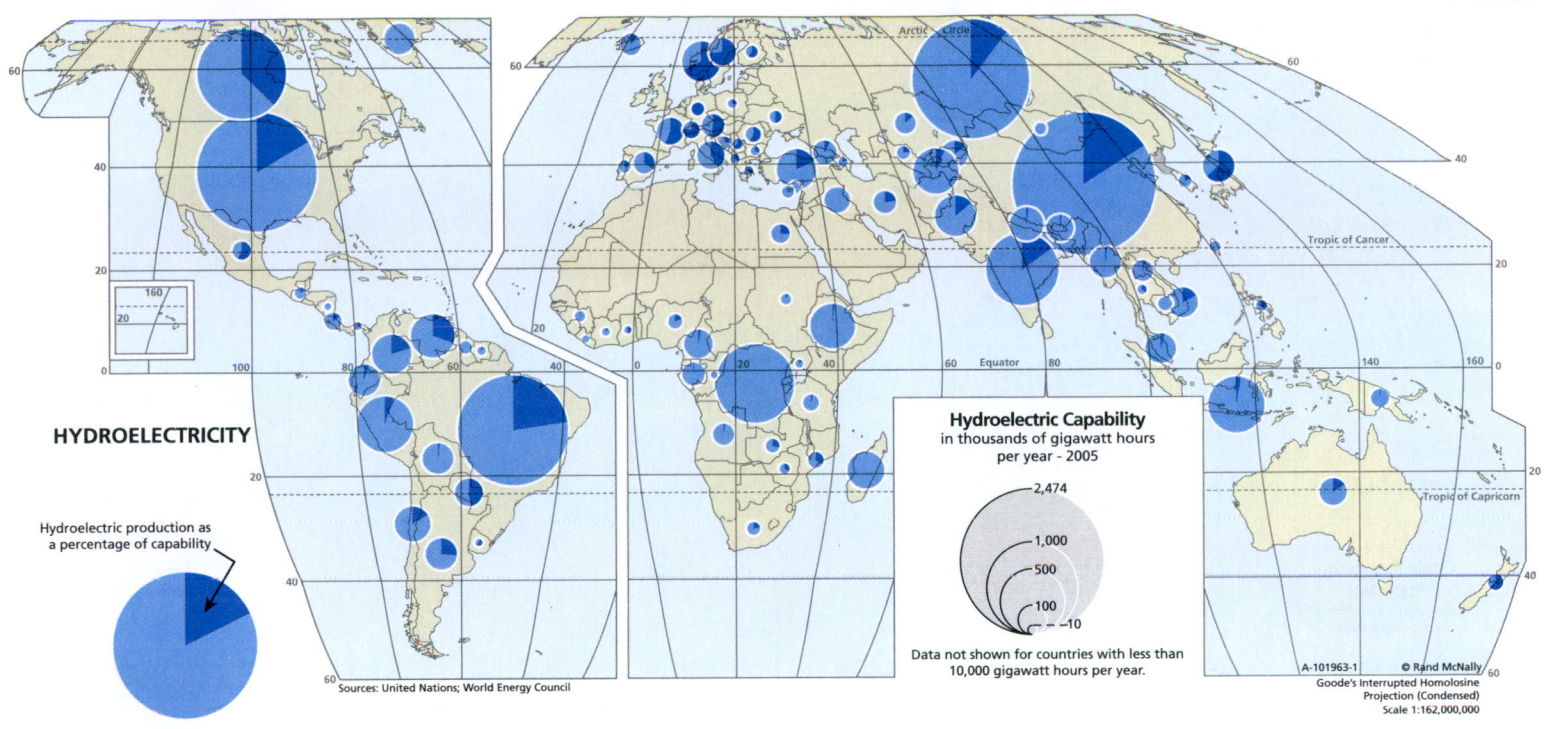

HYDROELECTRICITY

Hydroelectric production as a percentage of capability

Hydroelectric Capability
in thousands of gigawatt hours per year - 2005

2,474
1,000
500
100
10

Data not shown for countries with less than 10,000 gigawatt hours per year.

Sources: United Nations; World Energy Council

A-101963-1 © Rand McNally
Goode's Interrupted Homolosine Projection (Condensed)
Scale 1:162,000,000

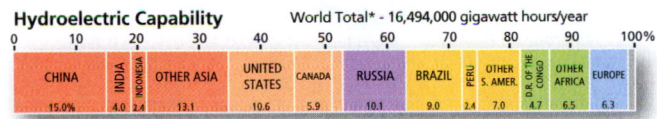

Hydroelectric Capability
World Total* - 16,494,000 gigawatt hours/year

CHINA	INDIA	INDONESIA	OTHER ASIA	UNITED STATES	CANADA	RUSSIA	BRAZIL	PERU	OTHER S. AMER.	D.R. OF THE CONGO	OTHER AFRICA	EUROPE
15.0%	4.0	2.4	13.1	10.6	5.9	10.1	9.0	2.4	7.0	4.7	6.5	6.3

* Technically exploitable capability.

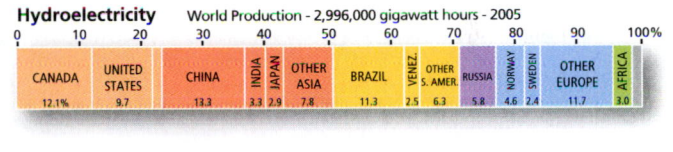

Hydroelectricity
World Production - 2,996,000 gigawatt hours - 2005

CANADA	UNITED STATES	CHINA	INDIA	JAPAN	OTHER ASIA	BRAZIL	VENEZ.	OTHER S. AMER.	RUSSIA	NORWAY	SWEDEN	OTHER EUROPE	AFRICA
12.1%	9.7	13.3	3.3	2.9	7.8	11.3	2.5	6.3	5.8	4.6	2.4	11.7	3.0

ALTERNATIVE ENERGY

Volume of Geothermal Energy*
in gigawatt hours - 2005

35,000
10,000
1,000
500
100
1

Sources: United Nations; World Wind Energy Association

Goode's Interrupted Homolosine Projection (Condensed)
Scale 1:162,000,000

A-101964-1 © Rand McNally

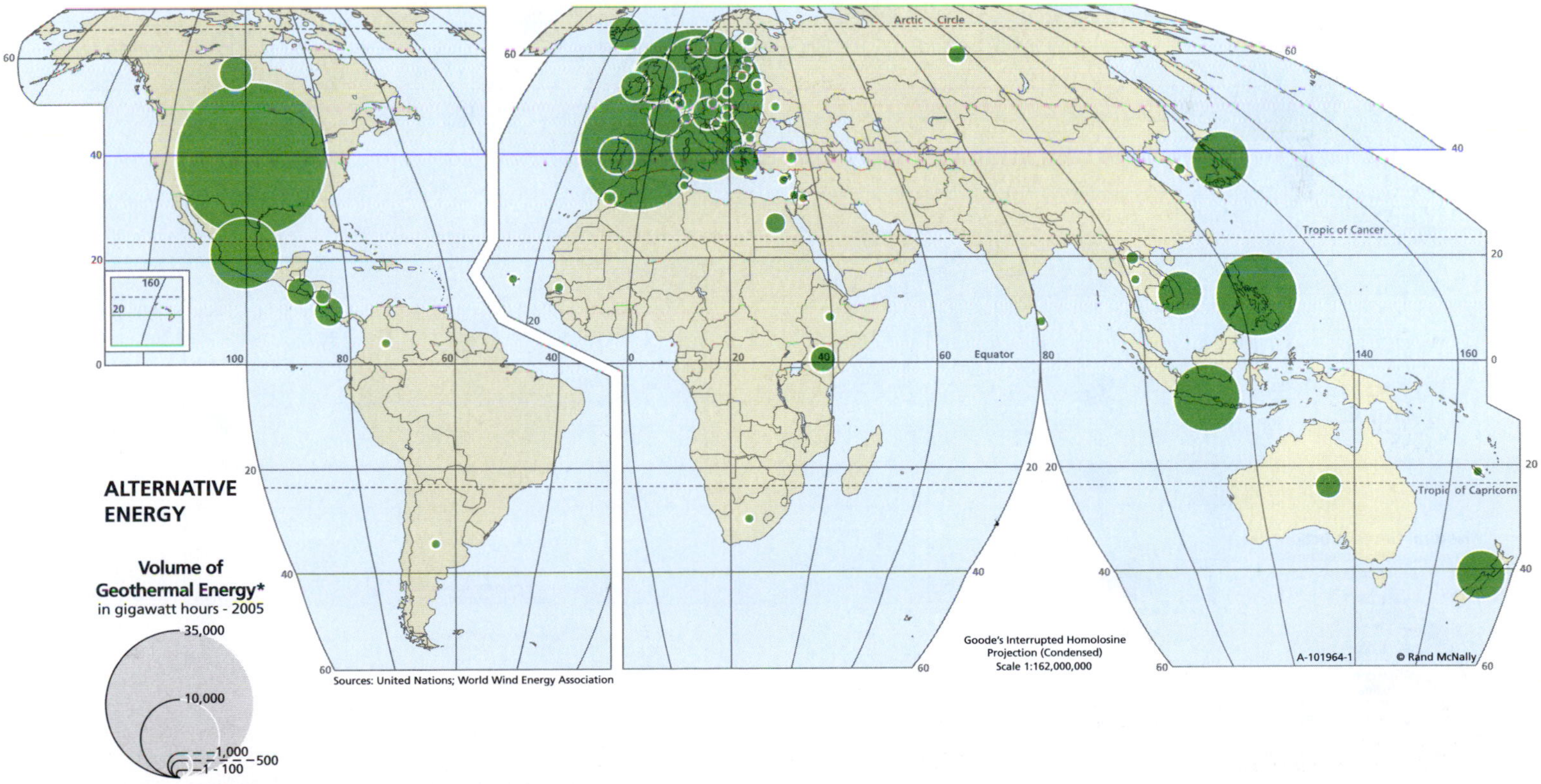

Geothermal Energy
World Production* - 158,000 gigawatt hours - 2005

UNITED STATES	MEXICO	OTHER N.A.	GERMANY	SPAIN	ITALY	DENMARK	OTHER EUROPE	PHIL.	INDON.	JAPAN	N.Z.
22.3%	4.7	2.5	18.0	13.5	4.9	4.2	10.2	6.3	4.2	3.0	2.2

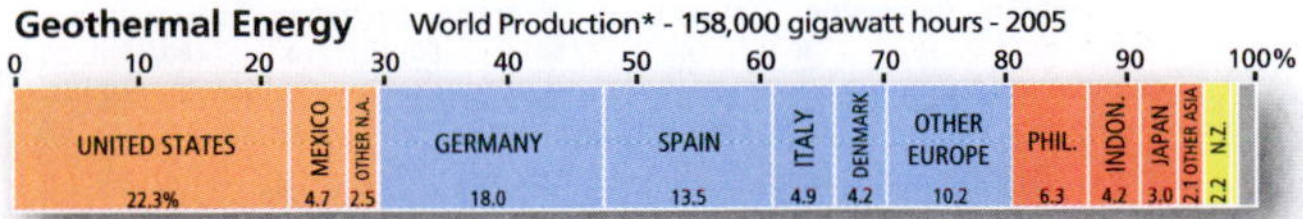

* May include other sources of energy, such as solar or wind energy.

Wind Energy
World Installed Capacity - 59 gigawatts - 2005

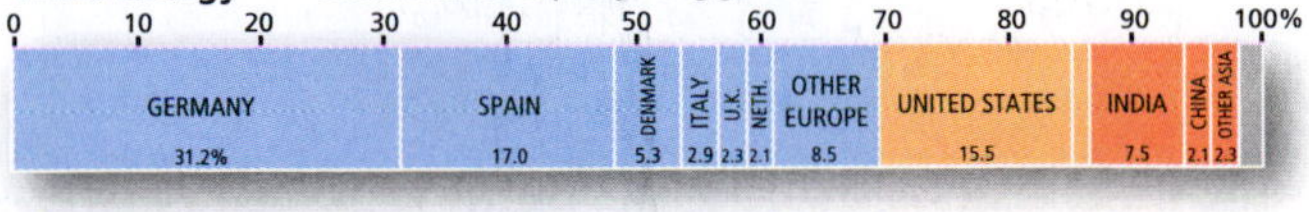

GERMANY	SPAIN	DENMARK	ITALY	U.K.	NETH.	OTHER EUROPE	UNITED STATES	INDIA	CHINA	OTHER ASIA
31.2%	17.0	5.3	2.9	2.3	2.1	8.5	15.5	7.5	2.1	2.3

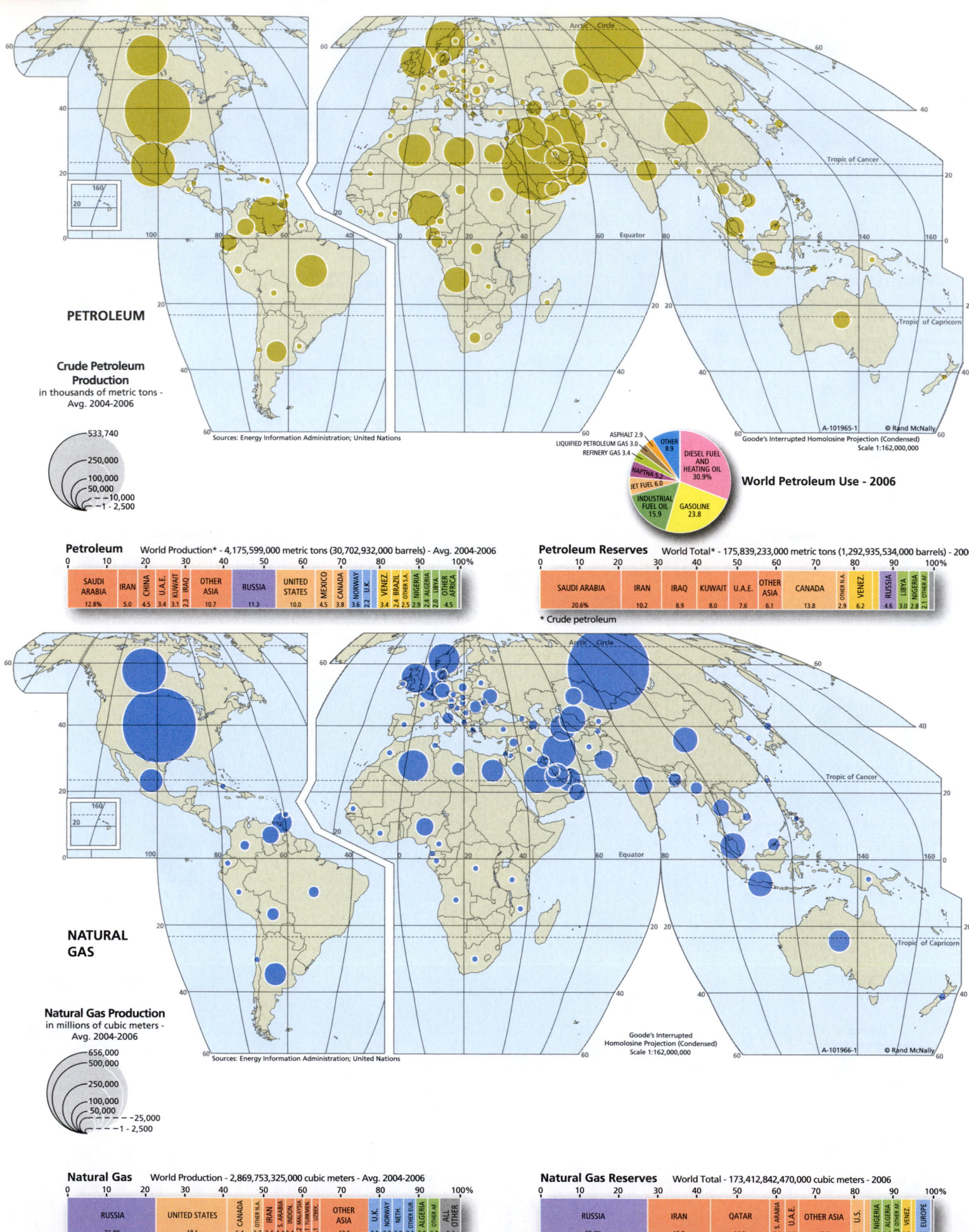

PETROLEUM

Crude Petroleum Production
in thousands of metric tons - Avg. 2004-2006

- 533,740
- 250,000
- 100,000
- 50,000
- 10,000
- 1 - 2,500

Sources: Energy Information Administration; United Nations

A-101965-1   © Rand McNally

Goode's Interrupted Homolosine Projection (Condensed)
Scale 1:162,000,000

World Petroleum Use - 2006

- ASPHALT 2.9
- LIQUIFIED PETROLEUM GAS 3.0
- REFINERY GAS 3.4
- NAPTHA 5.2
- JET FUEL 6.0
- INDUSTRIAL FUEL OIL 15.9
- OTHER 8.9
- DIESEL FUEL AND HEATING OIL 30.9%
- GASOLINE 23.8

Petroleum   World Production* - 4,175,599,000 metric tons (30,702,932,000 barrels) - Avg. 2004-2006

SAUDI ARABIA	IRAN	CHINA	U.A.E.	KUWAIT	IRAQ	OTHER ASIA	RUSSIA	UNITED STATES	MEXICO	CANADA	NORWAY	U.K.	VENEZ.	BRAZIL	OTHER S.A.	NIGERIA	ALGERIA	LIBYA	OTHER AFRICA
12.8%	5.0	4.5	3.4	3.1	2.3	10.7	11.3	10.0	4.5	3.8	3.6	2.2	3.4	2.5		2.9	2.4	2.0	4.5

Petroleum Reserves   World Total* - 175,839,233,000 metric tons (1,292,935,534,000 barrels) - 2006

SAUDI ARABIA	IRAN	IRAQ	KUWAIT	U.A.E.	OTHER ASIA	CANADA	OTHER N.A.	VENEZ.	RUSSIA	LIBYA	NIGERIA	OTHER AF.
20.6%	10.2	8.9	8.0	7.6	6.1	13.8	2.9	6.2	4.6	3.0	2.1

* Crude petroleum

NATURAL GAS

Natural Gas Production
in millions of cubic meters - Avg. 2004-2006

- 656,000
- 500,000
- 250,000
- 100,000
- 50,000
- 25,000
- 1 - 2,500

Sources: Energy Information Administration; United Nations

Goode's Interrupted Homolosine Projection (Condensed)
Scale 1:162,000,000

A-101966-1   © Rand McNally

Natural Gas   World Production - 2,869,753,325,000 cubic meters - Avg. 2004-2006

RUSSIA	UNITED STATES	CANADA	OTHER N.A.	S. ARABIA	IRAN	INDON.	MALAYSIA	TURKMEN.	UZBEK.	OTHER ASIA	U.K.	NORWAY	NETH.	ALGERIA	ALL OTHER
22.4%	18.1	6.4	2.7	3.4	2.4	2.4	2.2	2.1		12.5	3.1	3.0	2.8	3.0	5.2

Natural Gas Reserves   World Total - 173,412,842,470,000 cubic meters - 2006

RUSSIA	IRAN	QATAR	S. ARABIA	U.A.E.	OTHER ASIA	U.S.	NIGERIA	ALGERIA	VENEZ.	EUROPE
27.4%	15.9	14.9	3.9	3.5	13.3	3.3	3.0	2.6	2.5	3.9

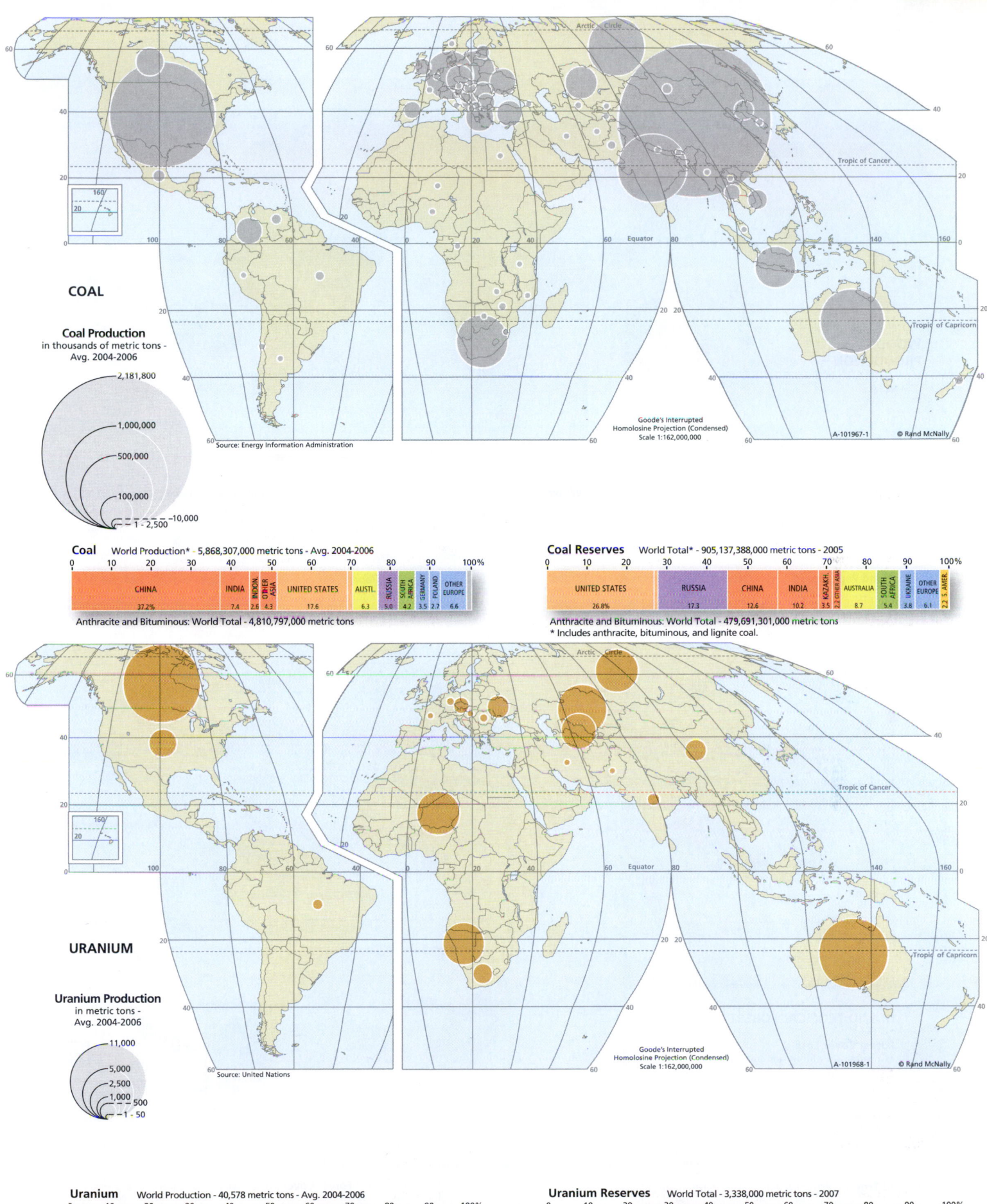

COAL

Coal Production
in thousands of metric tons -
Avg. 2004-2006

2,181,800

1,000,000

500,000

100,000

10,000

1 - 2,500

Source: Energy Information Administration

Goode's Interrupted
Homolosine Projection (Condensed)
Scale 1:162,000,000

A-101967-1   © Rand McNally

Coal World Production* - 5,868,307,000 metric tons - Avg. 2004-2006

	0	10	20	30	40	50	60	70	80	90	100%

CHINA	INDIA	INDON.	OTHER ASIA	UNITED STATES	AUSTL.	RUSSIA	SOUTH AFRICA	GERMANY	POLAND	OTHER EUROPE
37.2%	7.4	2.6	4.3	17.6	6.3	5.0	4.2	3.5	2.7	6.6

Anthracite and Bituminous: World Total - 4,810,797,000 metric tons

Coal Reserves World Total* - 905,137,388,000 metric tons - 2005

	0	10	20	30	40	50	60	70	80	90	100%

UNITED STATES	RUSSIA	CHINA	INDIA	KAZAKH.	OTHER ASIA	AUSTRALIA	SOUTH AFRICA	UKRAINE	OTHER EUROPE	S. AMER.
26.8%	17.3	12.6	10.2	3.5		8.7	5.4	3.8	6.1	2.2

Anthracite and Bituminous: World Total - 479,691,301,000 metric tons
* Includes anthracite, bituminous, and lignite coal.

URANIUM

Uranium Production
in metric tons -
Avg. 2004-2006

11,000

5,000

2,500

1,000

500

1 - 50

Source: United Nations

Goode's Interrupted
Homolosine Projection (Condensed)
Scale 1:162,000,000

A-101968-1   © Rand McNally

Uranium World Production - 40,578 metric tons - Avg. 2004-2006

	0	10	20	30	40	50	60	70	80	90	100%

CANADA	U.S.	AUSTRALIA	KAZAKHSTAN	UZBEK.	OTHER ASIA	NIGER	NAMIBIA	RUSSIA	UKRAINE
27.2%	3.2	21.4	11.0	5.5	2.5	8.2	7.6	8.0	2.0

Uranium Reserves World Total - 3,338,000 metric tons - 2007

	0	10	20	30	40	50	60	70	80	90	100%

AUSTRALIA	KAZAKHSTAN	UZBEK.	OTHER ASIA	UNITED STATES	CANADA	SOUTH AFRICA	NIGER	NAMIBIA	RUSSIA	BRAZIL	UKRAINE
21.7%	11.3	2.2	6.2	10.2	9.9	8.5	7.3	5.3	5.2	4.7	4.0

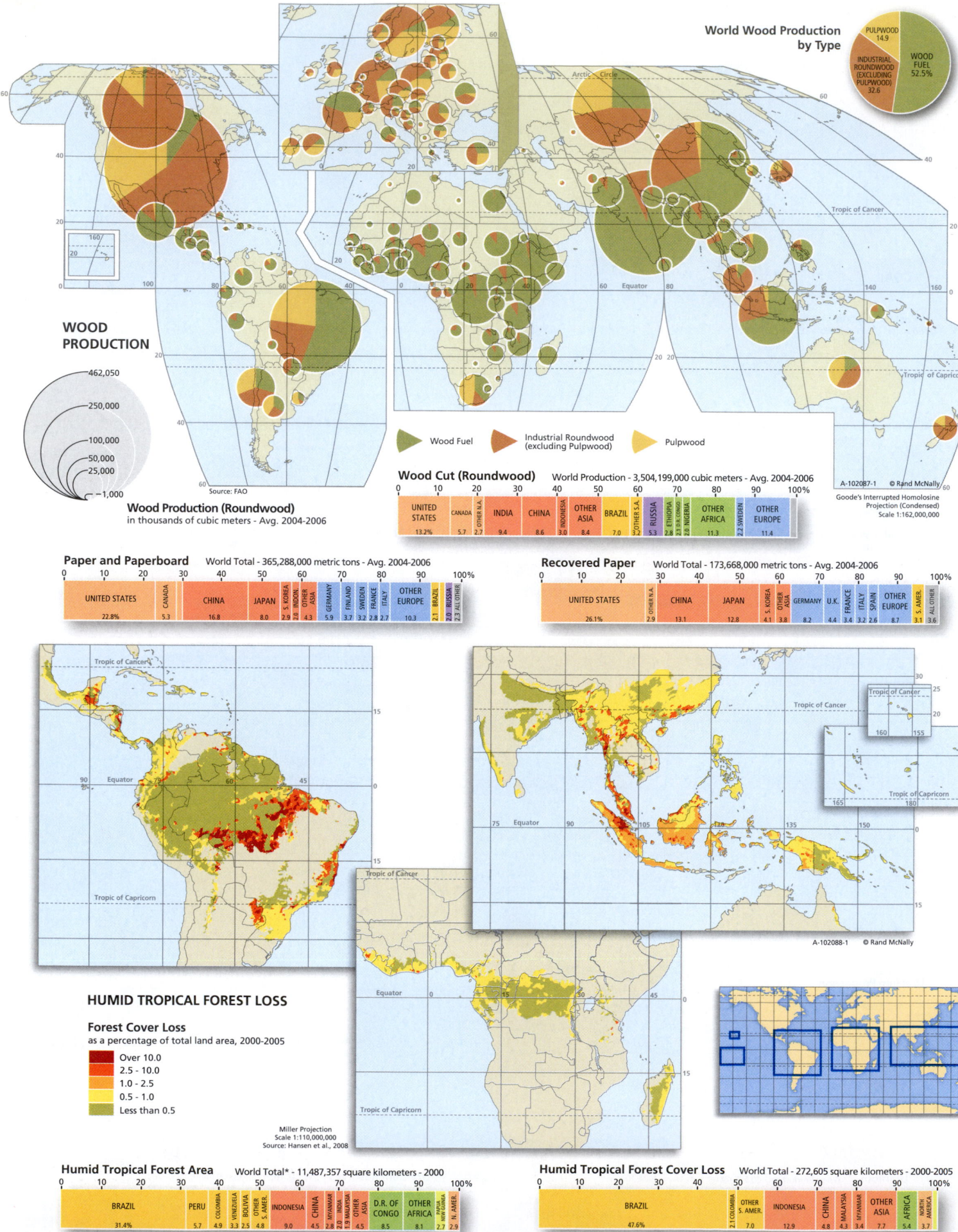

World Wood Production by Type

PULPWOOD 14.9

INDUSTRIAL ROUNDWOOD (EXCLUDING PULPWOOD) 32.6

WOOD FUEL 52.5%

WOOD PRODUCTION

462,050
250,000
100,000
50,000
25,000
1,000

Source: FAO

Wood Production (Roundwood)
in thousands of cubic meters - Avg. 2004-2006

Wood Fuel
Industrial Roundwood (excluding Pulpwood)
Pulpwood

A-102087-1 © Rand McNally

Goode's Interrupted Homolosine Projection (Condensed)
Scale 1:162,000,000

Wood Cut (Roundwood) — World Production - 3,504,199,000 cubic meters - Avg. 2004-2006

UNITED STATES 13.2%	CANADA 5.7	OTHER N.A. 2.7	INDIA 9.4	CHINA 8.6	INDONESIA 3.0	OTHER ASIA 8.4	BRAZIL 7.0	OTHER S.A. 3.2	RUSSIA 5.3	ETHIOPIA 2.8	D.R. CONGO 2.1	NIGERIA 2.0	OTHER AFRICA 11.3	SWEDEN 2.2	OTHER EUROPE 11.4

Paper and Paperboard — World Total - 365,288,000 metric tons - Avg. 2004-2006

| UNITED STATES 22.8% | CANADA 5.3 | CHINA 16.8 | JAPAN 8.0 | S. KOREA 2.9 | INDON. 2.8 | OTHER ASIA 4.3 | GERMANY 5.9 | FINLAND 3.7 | SWEDEN 3.2 | FRANCE 2.8 | ITALY 2.7 | OTHER EUROPE 10.3 | BRAZIL 2.1 | RUSSIA 2.0 | ALL OTHER 2.3 |

Recovered Paper — World Total - 173,668,000 metric tons - Avg. 2004-2006

| UNITED STATES 26.1% | OTHER N.A. 2.9 | CHINA 13.1 | JAPAN 12.8 | S. KOREA 4.1 | OTHER ASIA 3.8 | GERMANY 8.2 | U.K. 4.4 | FRANCE 3.4 | ITALY 3.2 | SPAIN 2.6 | OTHER EUROPE 8.7 | S. AMER. 3.1 | ALL OTHER 3.6 |

A-102088-1 © Rand McNally

HUMID TROPICAL FOREST LOSS

Forest Cover Loss
as a percentage of total land area, 2000-2005

- Over 10.0
- 2.5 - 10.0
- 1.0 - 2.5
- 0.5 - 1.0
- Less than 0.5

Miller Projection
Scale 1:110,000,000
Source: Hansen et al., 2008

Humid Tropical Forest Area — World Total* - 11,487,357 square kilometers - 2000

| BRAZIL 31.4% | PERU 5.7 | COLOMBIA 4.9 | VENEZUELA 3.3 | BOLIVIA 2.5 | OTHER S. AMER. 4.8 | INDONESIA 9.0 | CHINA 4.5 | MYANMAR 2.8 | INDIA 2.0 | MALAYSIA 1.9 | OTHER ASIA 4.5 | D.R. OF CONGO 8.5 | OTHER AFRICA 8.1 | PAPUA NEW GUINEA 2.7 | N. AMER. 9 |

*Defined as areas with tree canopy cover of 25% or more.

Humid Tropical Forest Cover Loss — World Total - 272,605 square kilometers - 2000-2005

| BRAZIL 47.6% | OTHER S. AMER. 7.0 | COLOMBIA 2.1 | INDONESIA 12.9 | CHINA 4.8 | MALAYSIA 4.3 | OTHER ASIA 3.4 | OTHER ASIA 7.7 | AFRICA 5.4 | NORTH AMERICA 3.7 |

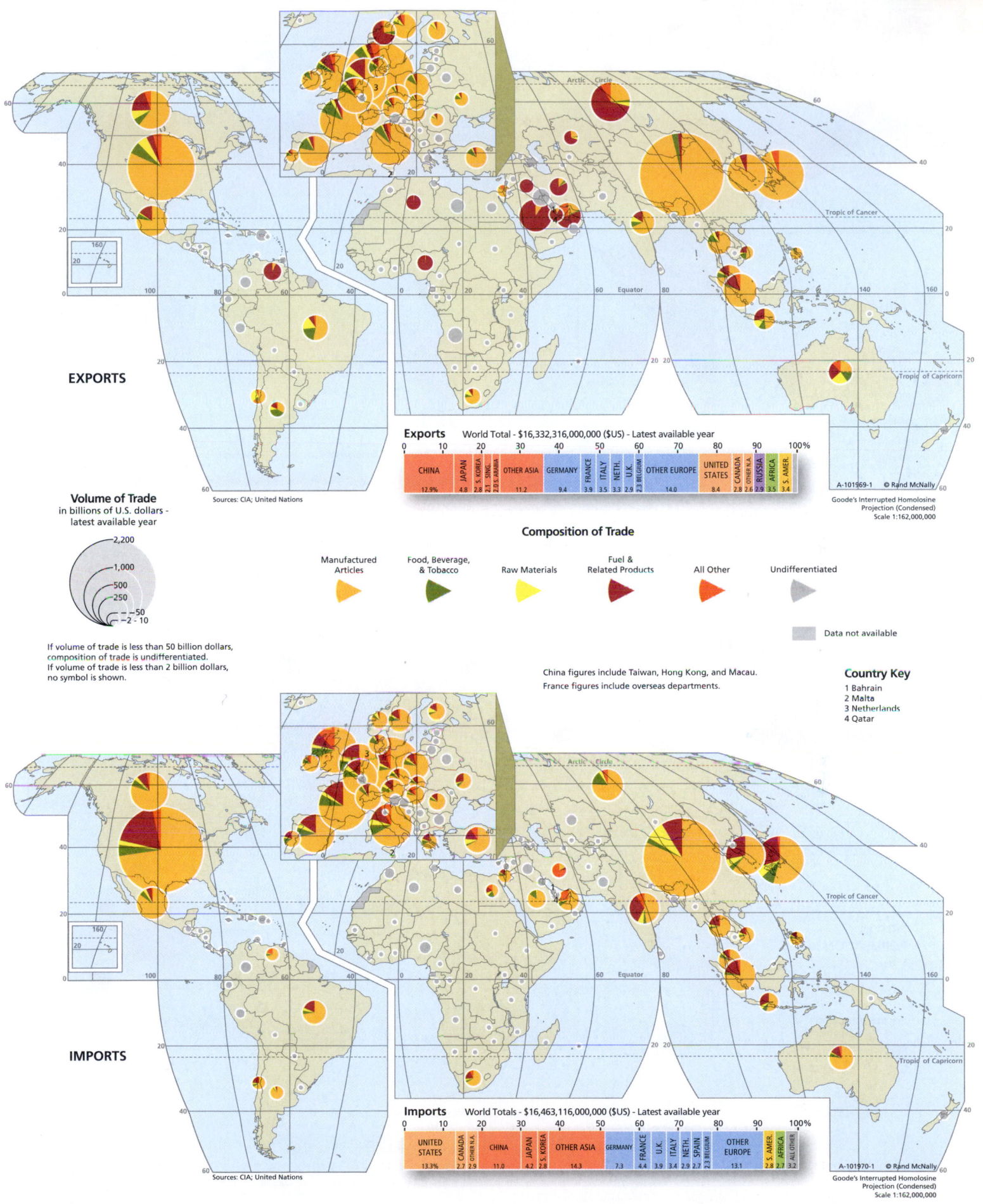

EXPORTS

Volume of Trade
in billions of U.S. dollars -
latest available year

2,200
1,000
500
250
50
2 - 10

If volume of trade is less than 50 billion dollars,
composition of trade is undifferentiated.
If volume of trade is less than 2 billion dollars,
no symbol is shown.

Sources: CIA; United Nations

Exports World Total - $16,332,316,000,000 ($US) - Latest available year

	0	10	20	30	40	50	60	70	80	90	100%

CHINA	JAPAN	S. KOREA	SING.	S. ARABIA	OTHER ASIA	GERMANY	FRANCE	ITALY	NETH.	U.K.	BELGIUM	OTHER EUROPE	UNITED STATES	CANADA	OTHER N.A.	RUSSIA	AFRICA	S. AMER.
12.9%	4.8	2.8	2.1	2.0	11.2	9.4	3.9	3.5	2.9	2.3		14.0	8.4	2.8	2.6	2.9	3.5	3.4

A-101969-1

Goode's Interrupted Homolosine
Projection (Condensed)
Scale 1:162,000,000

Composition of Trade

Manufactured Articles   Food, Beverage, & Tobacco   Raw Materials   Fuel & Related Products   All Other   Undifferentiated

Data not available

China figures include Taiwan, Hong Kong, and Macau.
France figures include overseas departments.

Country Key
1 Bahrain
2 Malta
3 Netherlands
4 Qatar

IMPORTS

Sources: CIA; United Nations

Imports World Totals - $16,463,116,000,000 ($US) - Latest available year

	0	10	20	30	40	50	60	70	80	90	100%

UNITED STATES	CANADA	OTHER N.A.	CHINA	JAPAN	S. KOREA	OTHER ASIA	GERMANY	FRANCE	U.K.	ITALY	NETH.	SPAIN	BELGIUM	OTHER EUROPE	S. AMER.	AFRICA	ALL OTHER
13.3%	2.7	2.9	11.0	4.2	2.8	14.3	7.3	4.4	3.9	3.4	2.9	2.7	2.3	13.1	2.8	2.7	3.2

A-101970-1

Goode's Interrupted Homolosine
Projection (Condensed)
Scale 1:162,000,000

© Rand McNally

DRUG USE

Western Europe†
34,250,000
drug users

Eastern Europe††
8,000,000 drug users

North America*
45,000,000 drug users

Asia
76,500,000
drug users

Africa
46,500,000 drug users

South America**
16,500,000
drug users

Australia, New Zealand, and Oceania
4,750,000 drug users

Cannabis (all forms)

Cocaine (all forms)

Amphetamine-type stimulants
(amphetamines and ecstasy)

Opiates (including heroin)

Data not available

Circles show annual prevalence of drug use - 2006.
Circle size is proportional to number of drug users
per continent.

Country tints show primary drug or drugs of abuse,
based on drug treatment statistics - most current available year.

Other drugs, such as hallucinogens, depressants, and inhalants, are not included.

Source: United Nations

* Includes Canada, the United States, and Mexico.
** Includes Central America and the Caribbean.
† Includes Cyprus and Turkey; excludes Russia, Belarus, Moldova, and Ukraine.
†† Includes Russia, Belarus, Moldova, and Ukraine.

Goode's Interrupted Homolosine
Projection (Condensed)
Scale 1:162,000,000

A-101971-1   © Rand McNally

Cocaine Potential World Production - 984 metric tons - 2006

0	10	20	30	40	50	60	70	80	90	100%
COLOMBIA 62.0%						PERU 28.5			BOLIVIA 9.5	

Opium Potential World Production (Dry Opium) - 6,611 metric tons - 2006

0	10	20	30	40	50	60	70	80	90	100%
AFGHANISTAN 92.3%									BURMA 4.8	

Cannabis World Production - 41,400 metric tons - 2006

0	10	20	30	40	50	60	70	80	90	100%
NORTH AMERICA* 31.0%		SOUTH AMERICA** 24.0		AFRICA 22.0		ASIA 16.0		EUROPE 6.0		

PRISON POPULATION

Prison Population
Rate per 100,000 population

Over 500

250 - 500

100 - 250

50 - 100

0 - 50

Data not available

Source: International Centre for Prison Studies

Goode's Interrupted Homolosine
Projection (Condensed)
Scale 1:162,000,000

A-101972-1   © Rand McNally

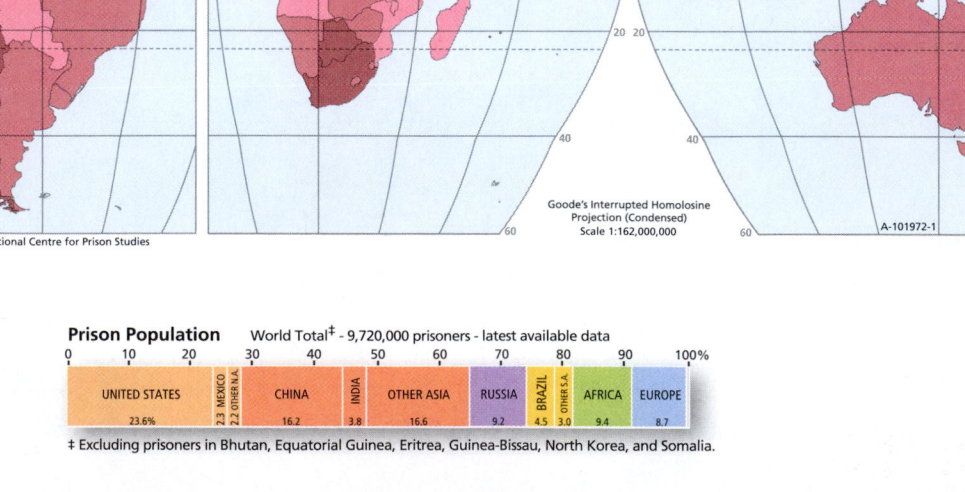

Prison Population   World Total‡ - 9,720,000 prisoners - latest available data

0	10	20	30	40	50	60	70	80	90	100%
UNITED STATES 23.6%		MEXICO 2.3 / OTHER N.A. 2.2	CHINA 16.2	INDIA 3.8	OTHER ASIA 16.6		RUSSIA 9.2	BRAZIL 4.5 / OTHER S.A. 3.0	AFRICA 9.4	EUROPE 8.7

‡ Excluding prisoners in Bhutan, Equatorial Guinea, Eritrea, Guinea-Bissau, North Korea, and Somalia.

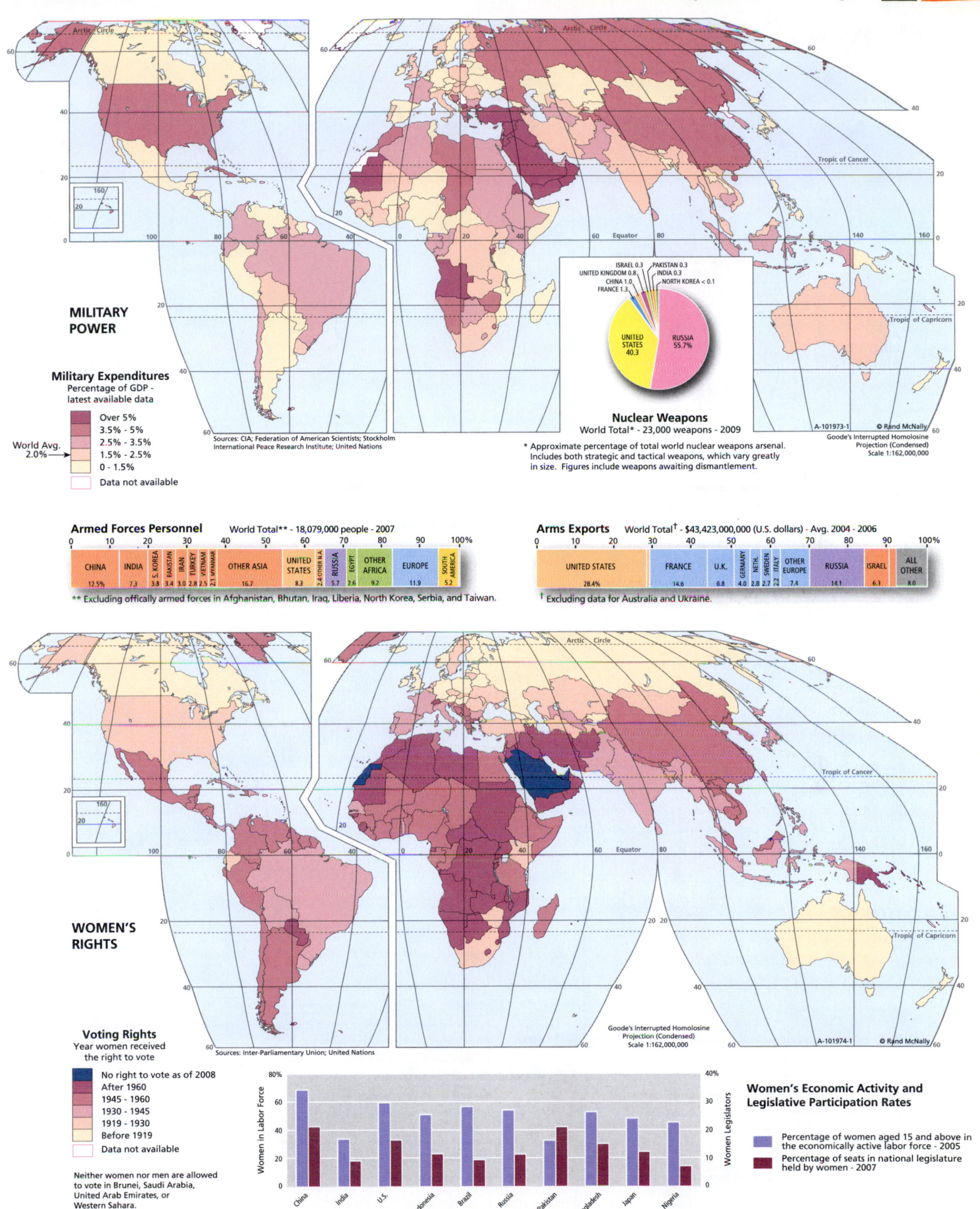

MILITARY POWER

Military Expenditures
Percentage of GDP - latest available data

- Over 5%
- 3.5% - 5%
- 2.5% - 3.5%
- 1.5% - 2.5%
- 0 - 1.5%
- Data not available

World Avg. 2.0% →

Sources: CIA; Federation of American Scientists; Stockholm International Peace Research Institute; United Nations

ISRAEL 0.3 PAKISTAN 0.3
UNITED KINGDOM 0.8 INDIA 0.3
CHINA 1.0 NORTH KOREA < 0.1
FRANCE 1.3

UNITED STATES 40.3
RUSSIA 55.7

Nuclear Weapons
World Total* - 23,000 weapons - 2009

* Approximate percentage of total world nuclear weapons arsenal. Includes both strategic and tactical weapons, which vary greatly in size. Figures include weapons awaiting dismantlement.

Goode's Interrupted Homolosine Projection (Condensed)
Scale 1:162,000,000

A-101973-1 © Rand McNally

Armed Forces Personnel World Total** - 18,079,000 people - 2007

CHINA	INDIA	S. KOREA	PAKISTAN	IRAN	TURKEY	VIETNAM	MYANMAR	OTHER ASIA	UNITED STATES	OTHER N.A.	RUSSIA	EGYPT	OTHER AFRICA	EUROPE	SOUTH AMERICA
12.5%	7.3	3.8	3.4	3.0	2.8	2.5	2.1	16.7	8.3	2.4	5.7	2.6	9.2	11.9	5.2

** Excluding officially armed forces in Afghanistan, Bhutan, Iraq, Liberia, North Korea, Serbia, and Taiwan.

Arms Exports World Total† - $43,423,000,000 (U.S. dollars) - Avg. 2004 - 2006

UNITED STATES	FRANCE	U.K.	GERMANY	NETH.	SWEDEN	ITALY	OTHER EUROPE	RUSSIA	ISRAEL	ALL OTHER
28.4%	14.6	6.8	4.0	2.8	2.7	2.2	7.4	14.1	6.3	8.0

† Excluding data for Australia and Ukraine.

WOMEN'S RIGHTS

Goode's Interrupted Homolosine Projection (Condensed)
Scale 1:162,000,000

A-101974-1 © Rand McNally

Sources: Inter-Parliamentary Union; United Nations

Voting Rights
Year women received the right to vote

- No right to vote as of 2008
- After 1960
- 1945 - 1960
- 1930 - 1945
- 1919 - 1930
- Before 1919
- Data not available

Neither women nor men are allowed to vote in Brunei, Saudi Arabia, United Arab Emirates, or Western Sahara.

Women's Economic Activity and Legislative Participation Rates

- Percentage of women aged 15 and above in the economically active labor force - 2005
- Percentage of seats in national legislature held by women - 2007

Women in Labor Force / Women Legislators

China, India, U.S., Indonesia, Brazil, Russia, Pakistan, Bangladesh, Japan, Nigeria

(World's largest countries, 2000)

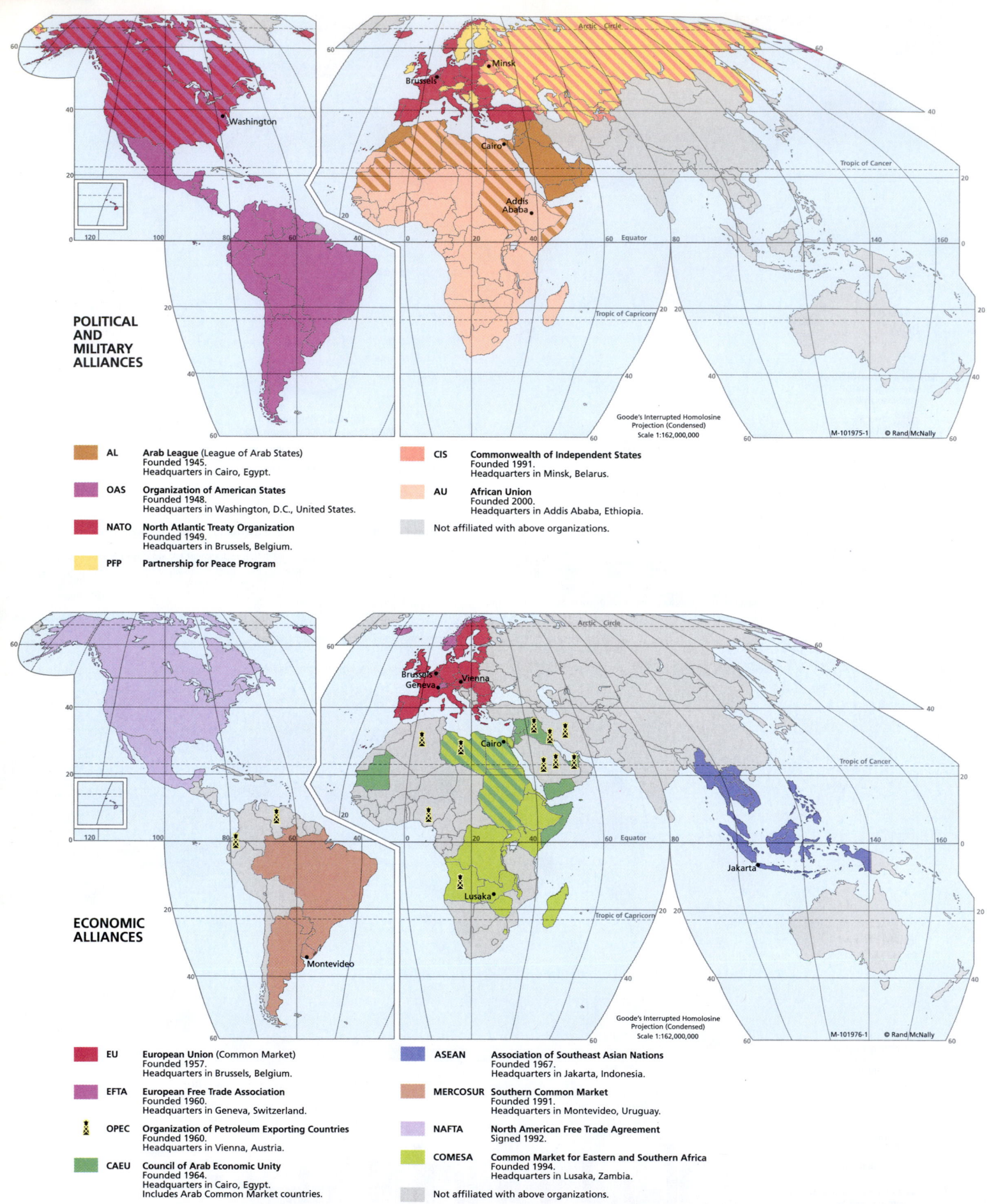

POLITICAL AND MILITARY ALLIANCES

AL	**Arab League** (League of Arab States) Founded 1945. Headquarters in Cairo, Egypt.
OAS	**Organization of American States** Founded 1948. Headquarters in Washington, D.C., United States.
NATO	**North Atlantic Treaty Organization** Founded 1949. Headquarters in Brussels, Belgium.
PFP	**Partnership for Peace Program**
CIS	**Commonwealth of Independent States** Founded 1991. Headquarters in Minsk, Belarus.
AU	**African Union** Founded 2000. Headquarters in Addis Ababa, Ethiopia.
	Not affiliated with above organizations.

Goode's Interrupted Homolosine Projection (Condensed)
Scale 1:162,000,000
M-101975-1 © Rand McNally

ECONOMIC ALLIANCES

EU	**European Union** (Common Market) Founded 1957. Headquarters in Brussels, Belgium.
EFTA	**European Free Trade Association** Founded 1960. Headquarters in Geneva, Switzerland.
OPEC	**Organization of Petroleum Exporting Countries** Founded 1960. Headquarters in Vienna, Austria.
CAEU	**Council of Arab Economic Unity** Founded 1964. Headquarters in Cairo, Egypt. Includes Arab Common Market countries.
ASEAN	**Association of Southeast Asian Nations** Founded 1967. Headquarters in Jakarta, Indonesia.
MERCOSUR	**Southern Common Market** Founded 1991. Headquarters in Montevideo, Uruguay.
NAFTA	**North American Free Trade Agreement** Signed 1992.
COMESA	**Common Market for Eastern and Southern Africa** Founded 1994. Headquarters in Lusaka, Zambia.
	Not affiliated with above organizations.

Goode's Interrupted Homolosine Projection (Condensed)
Scale 1:162,000,000
M-101976-1 © Rand McNally

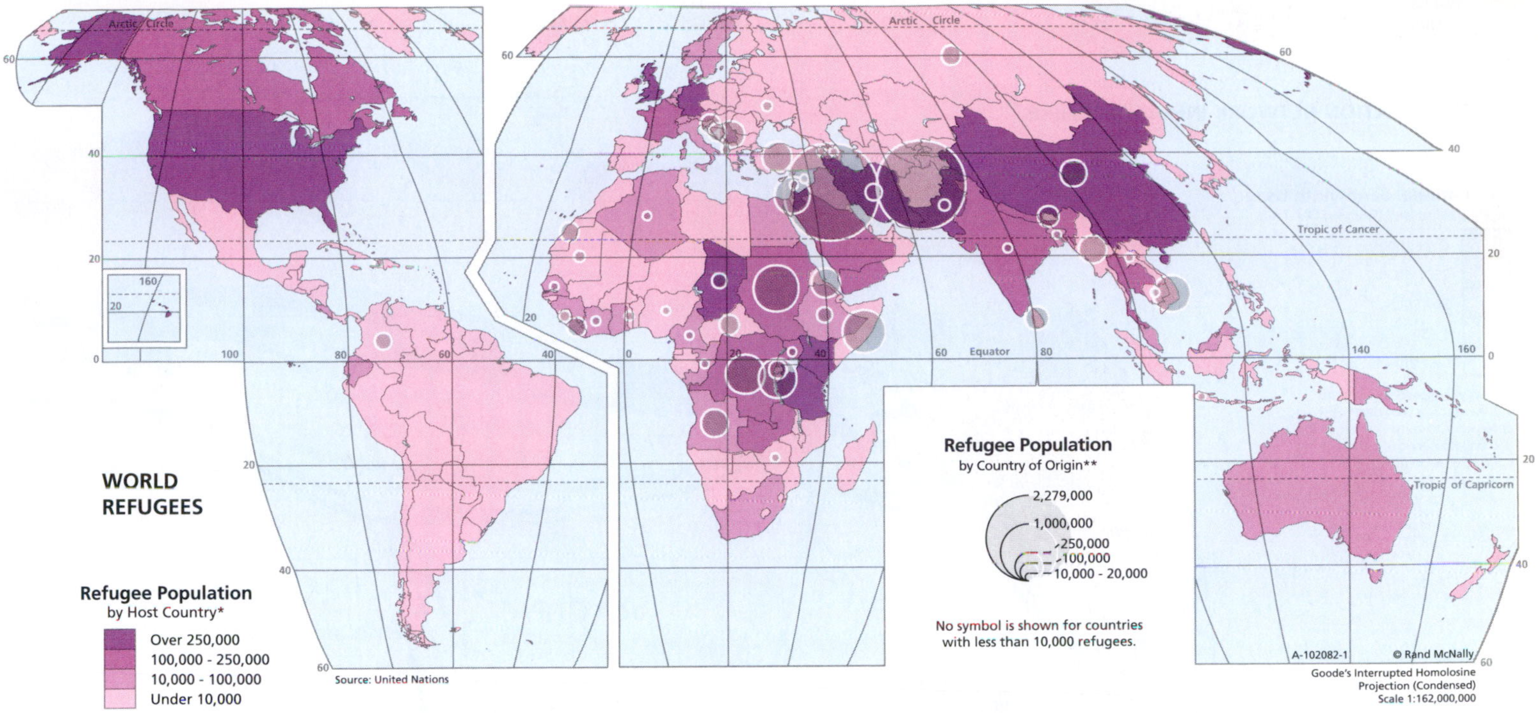

WORLD REFUGEES

Refugee Population
by Host Country*

- ■ Over 250,000
- ■ 100,000 - 250,000
- ■ 10,000 - 100,000
- ■ Under 10,000

Source: United Nations

Refugee Population
by Country of Origin**

- 2,279,000
- 1,000,000
- 250,000
- 100,000
- 10,000 - 20,000

No symbol is shown for countries
with less than 10,000 refugees.

A-102082-1   © Rand McNally

Goode's Interrupted Homolosine
Projection (Condensed)
Scale 1:162,000,000

Refugee Population (by Host Country)* World Total - 9,679,000 - 2007

0	10	20	30	40	50	60	70	80	90	100%

SYRIA	IRAN	PAKISTAN	JORDAN	CHINA	S. ARABIA	OTHER ASIA	GERMANY	U.K.	OTHER EUROPE	TANZANIA	CHAD	KENYA	UGANDA	SUDAN	OTHER AFRICA	U.S.	OTHER N.A.
15.5%	10.0	9.2	5.2	3.1	2.5	7.4	6.0	3.1	7.1	4.5	3.0	2.7	2.4	2.3	10.6	2.9	2.0

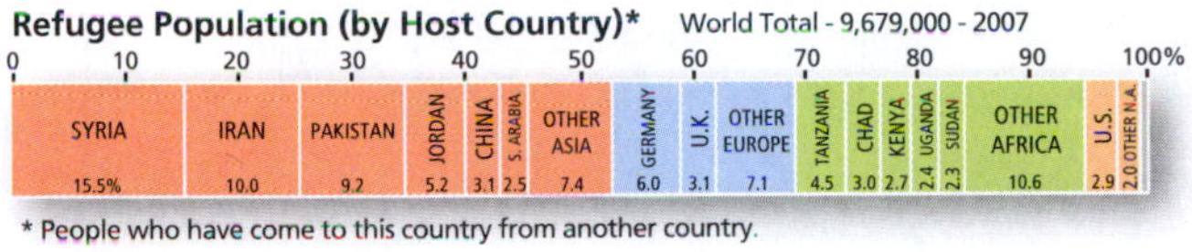

* People who have come to this country from another country.

Refugee Population (by Country of Origin)* World Total - 9,679,000 - 2007

0	10	20	30	40	50	60	70	80	90	100%

IRAQ	AFGHANISTAN	GAZA-STRIP	VIETNAM	TURKEY	MYANMAR	OTHER ASIA	SUDAN	SOMALIA	BURUNDI	D.R. OF THE CONGO	ERITREA	OTHER AFRICA	EUROPE	ALL OTHER
23.5%	19.7	3.5	3.4	2.3	2.0	7.1	5.4	4.7	3.9	3.8	2.2	9.6	4.4	4.6

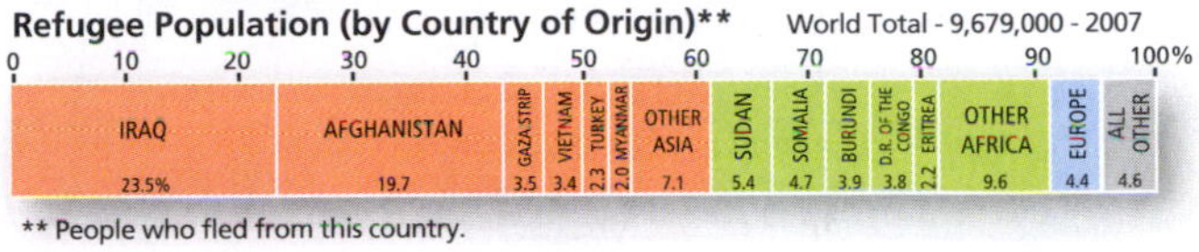

** People who fled from this country.

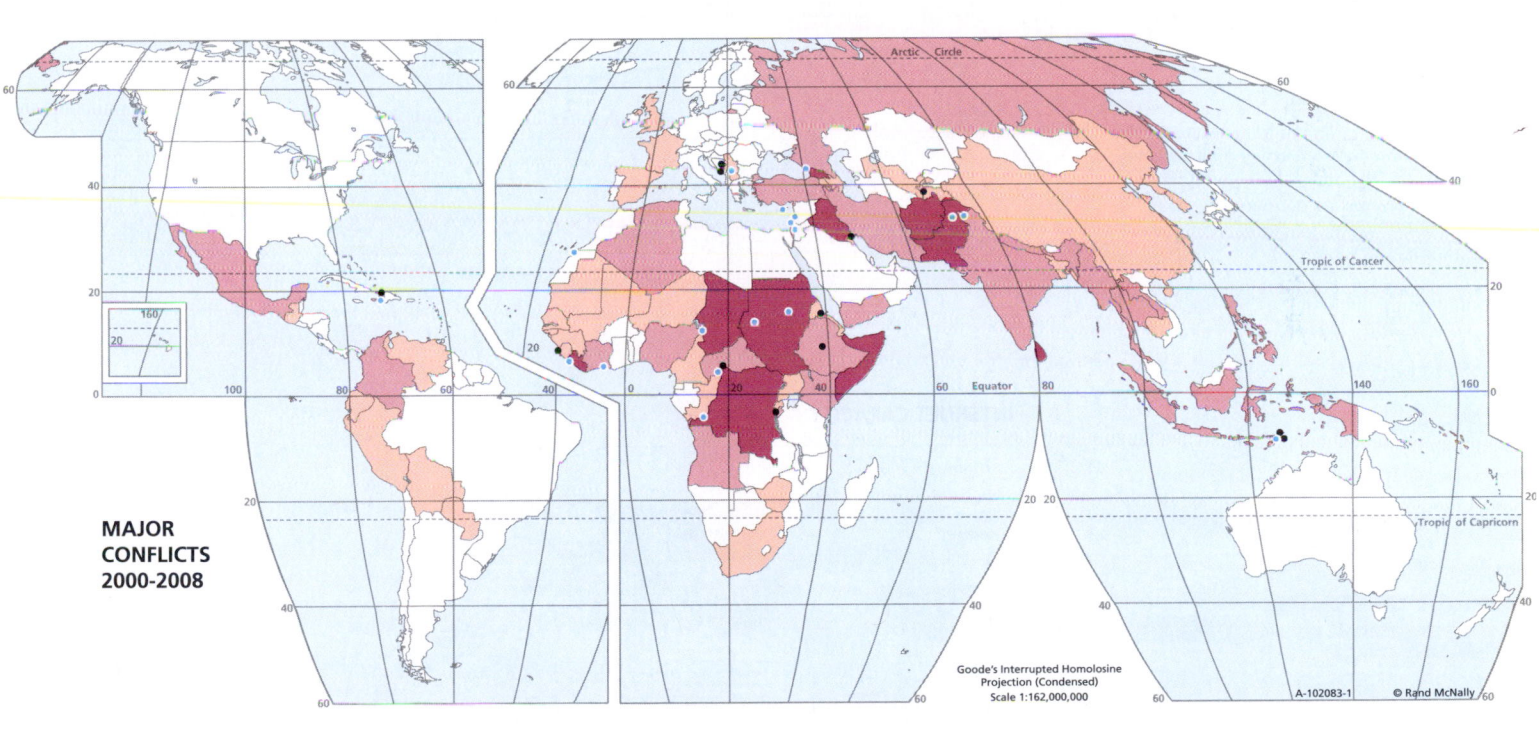

MAJOR CONFLICTS 2000-2008

Goode's Interrupted Homolosine
Projection (Condensed)
Scale 1:162,000,000

A-102083-1   © Rand McNally

- ■ **Very Serious Conflict:** A sustained conflict in which organized, systematic, and continual violent force is used causing massive destruction.
- ■ **Serious Conflict:** Severe crisis where organized violence is used regularly.
- ■ **Hot Spot:** A tense situation in which at least one of the parties uses violence in sporadic incidents.

United Nations Peacekeeping Operations

- • Ongoing Peacekeeping Missions
- ● Completed Peacekeeping Missions

COMMUNICATION NETWORK INFRASTRUCTURE

International Bandwidth Usage
Gigabits per second (Gbps) - 2007

- Over 1000
- 250 - 1000
- 50 - 250
- 1 - 50
- Less than 1

Capacity deployed by carriers, internet service providers (ISPs), and enterprises to carry internet, voice, and private network traffic across international borders.

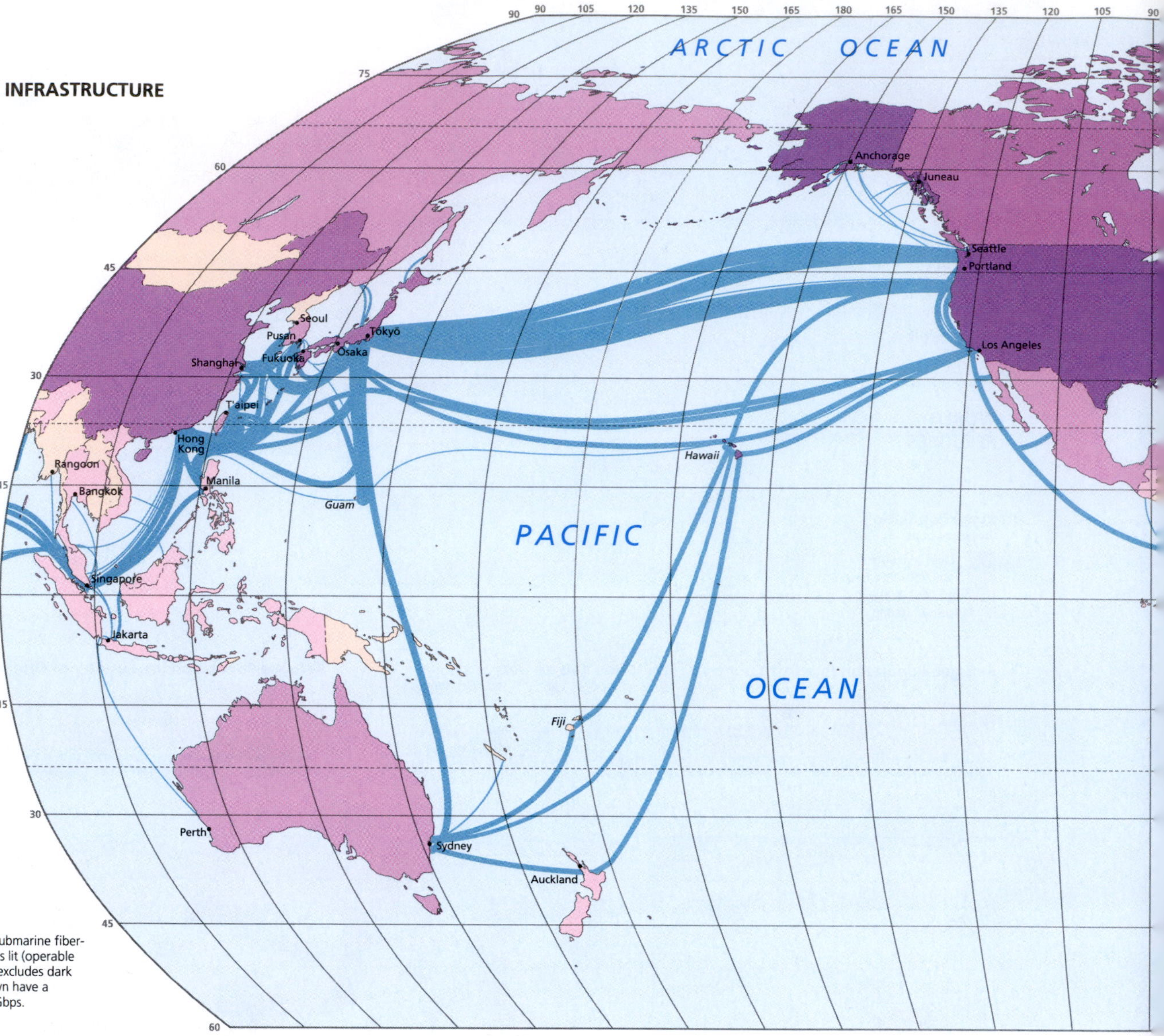

Submarine Cable Capacity
Lit capacity of submarine cables, in Gigabits per second (Gbps) - 2008

- Over 500
- 50 - 500
- 10 - 50

Line thickness is proportional to lit capacity of submarine fiber-optic cables. Lit capacity includes all cable that is lit (operable and capable of transmitting a light signal), but excludes dark fiber (inactive or inoperable cable). Cables shown have a maximum upgradeable capacity of at least 10 Gbps.

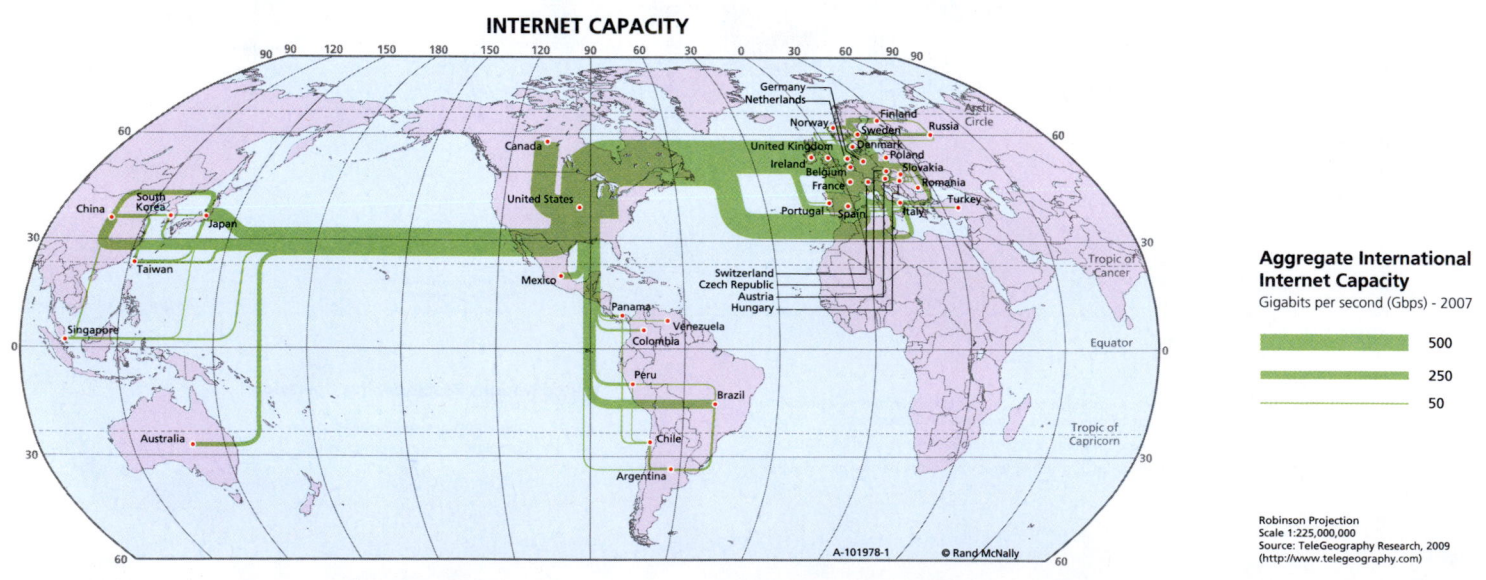

INTERNET CAPACITY

Aggregate International Internet Capacity
Gigabits per second (Gbps) - 2007

- 500
- 250
- 50

Robinson Projection
Scale 1:225,000,000
Source: TeleGeography Research, 2009
(http://www.telegeography.com)

A-101978-1   © Rand McNally

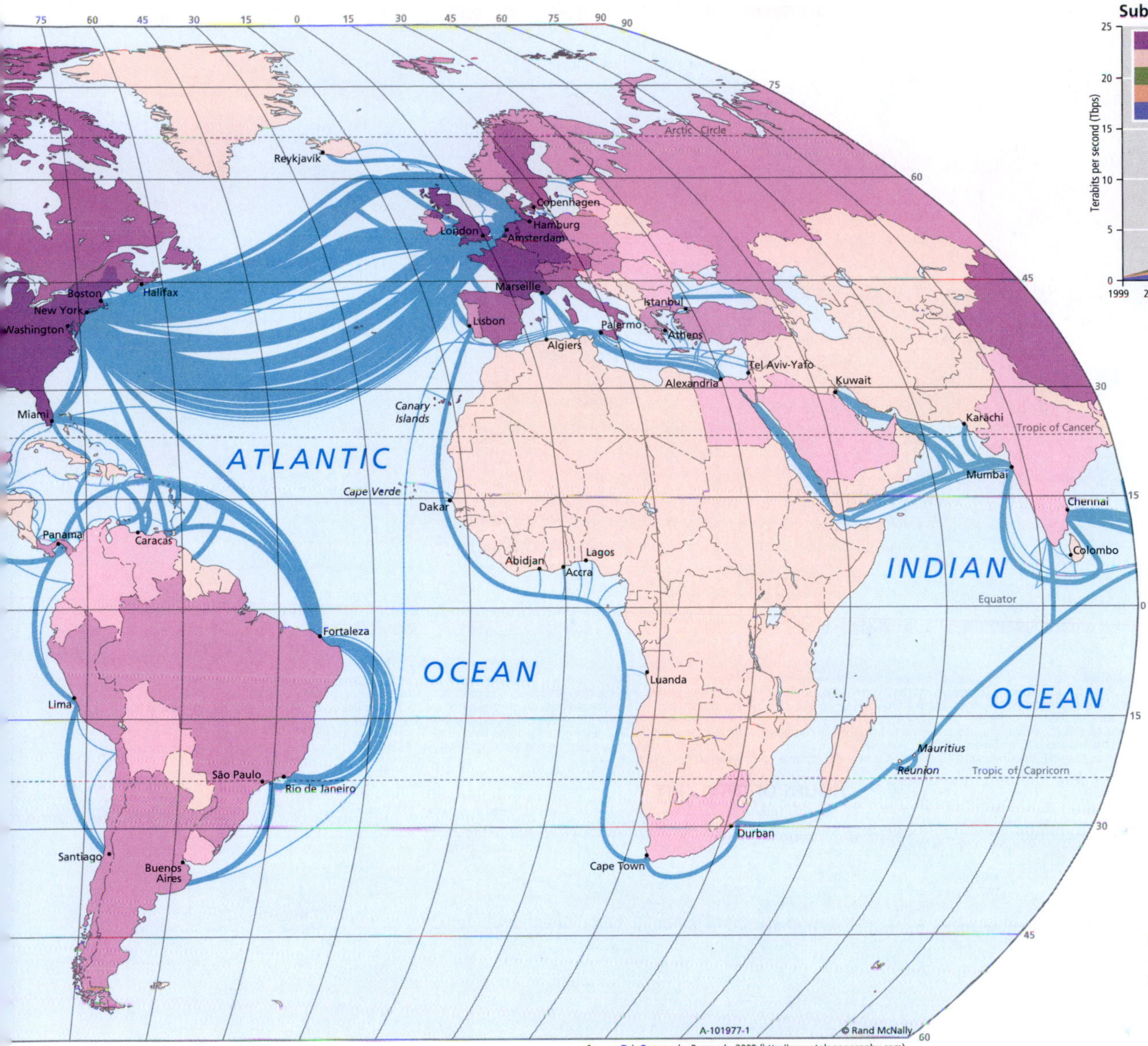

Submarine Cable Capacity by Route

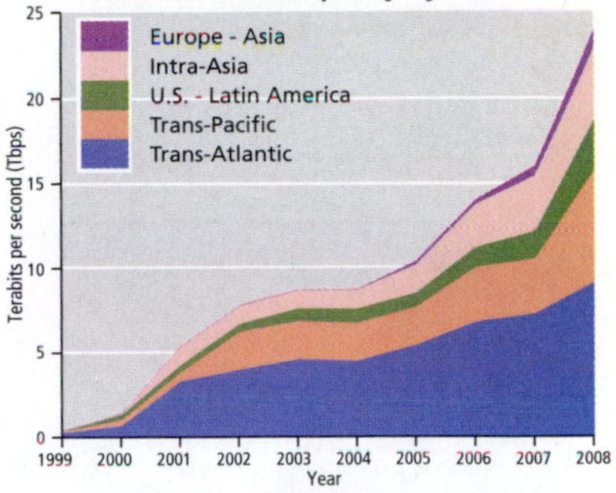

Legend:
- Europe - Asia
- Intra-Asia
- U.S. - Latin America
- Trans-Pacific
- Trans-Atlantic

Terabits per second (Tbps) — *Year* 1999–2008

Figures denote lit capacity of submarine fiber-optic cables. Trans-Pacific capacity excludes cables linking the United States to Australia and New Zealand. Trans-Atlantic capacity excludes cables linking Europe to South America. Intra-Asia capacity includes cables with landings in both Hong Kong and Japan. Europe-Asia capacity reflects available capacity between the Middle East and Europe, and excludes Europe-Asia capacity routed via Russia or the United States.

ATLANTIC OCEAN

INDIAN OCEAN

Robinson Projection
Scale 1:100,000,000
One inch to 1,580 miles
One cm to 1,000 km

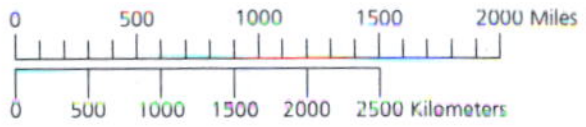

A-101977-1   © Rand McNally

Source: TeleGeography Research, 2009 (http://www.telegeography.com)

SHIPPING LANES

Relative Frequency of Ship Traffic

Highest

Lowest

This map shows the relative frequency of ship traffic over the world's oceans, for the period October 2004 through September 2005. Ship tracks were derived from the World Meteorological Association Voluntary Observing Ships Scheme, comprising over 3000 commercial and research vessels (equivalent to approximately 11% of the world commercial oceangoing fleet).

Robinson Projection
Scale 1:225,000,000
Source: Halpern et al., 2008

A-101980-1   © Rand McNally

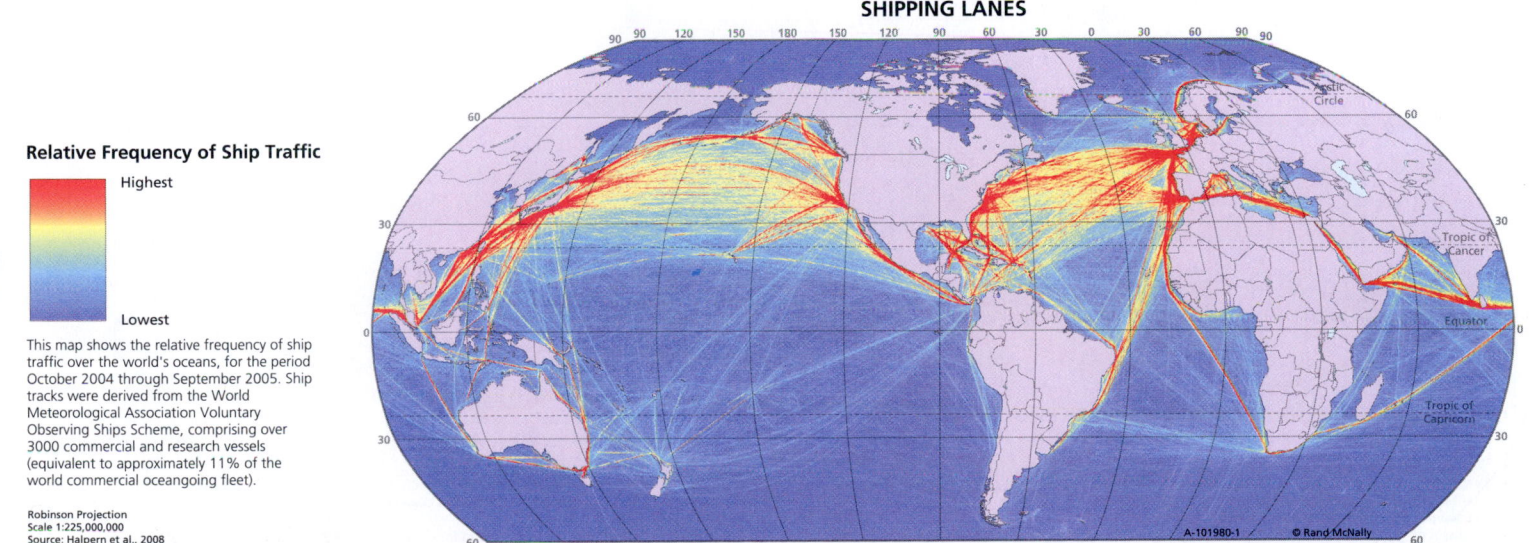

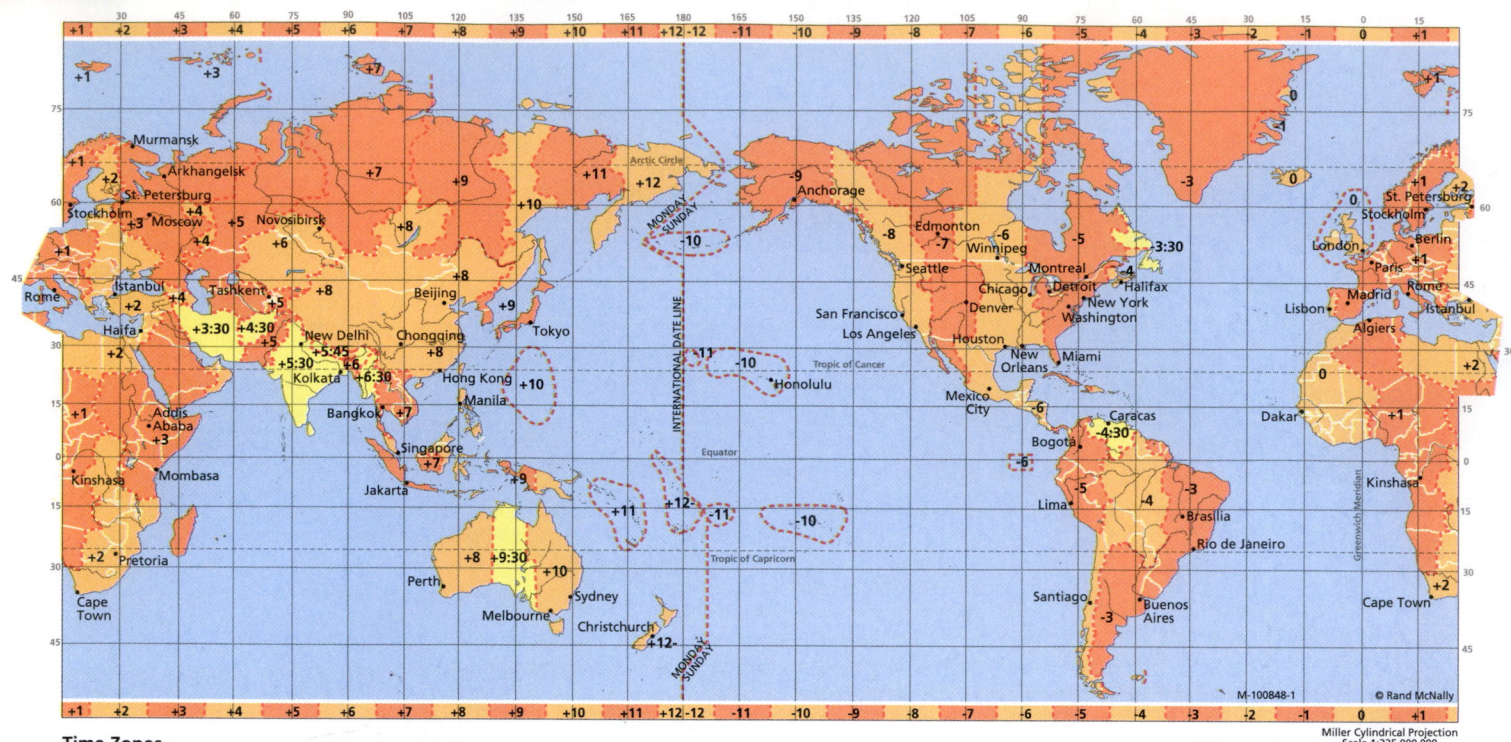

Time Zones

Coordinated Universal Time (UTC) is the standard for international time zones and the official reference for standard time across the world. Although UTC has officially replaced Greenwich Mean Time (GMT), both terms are widely employed and, in casual usage, are essentially synonymous. On the time zone map above, the numbers along the top and bottom edges indicate the time difference, in hours, from UTC. The first time zone, with a value of 0, is centered on the Prime Meridian running through Greenwich, England. To compute standard time at any location, add the value on the map to UTC at Greenwich. For example, Chicago is in time zone UTC -6, which means it is 6 hours earlier than UTC at Greenwich. This means that if it is noon at Greenwich then it is 6 a.m. in Chicago.

To ensure synchronization with the Sun's location, time zone boundaries should follow lines of longitude very precisely. However this is rarely the case, and most time zones boundaries are very irregular. They are often constrained to follow international or internal administrative boundaries, and may be shifted east or west for various reasons. Discontinuities sometimes exist where time changes by more than one hour across a zone boundary, and the UTC difference for some time zones is less than a full hour. To make matters even more complicated, these time zones do not account for Daylight Savings Time, which is observed in some jurisdictions for part of the year.

Miller Cylindrical Projection
Scale 1:225,000,000

HOURS OF DAYLIGHT

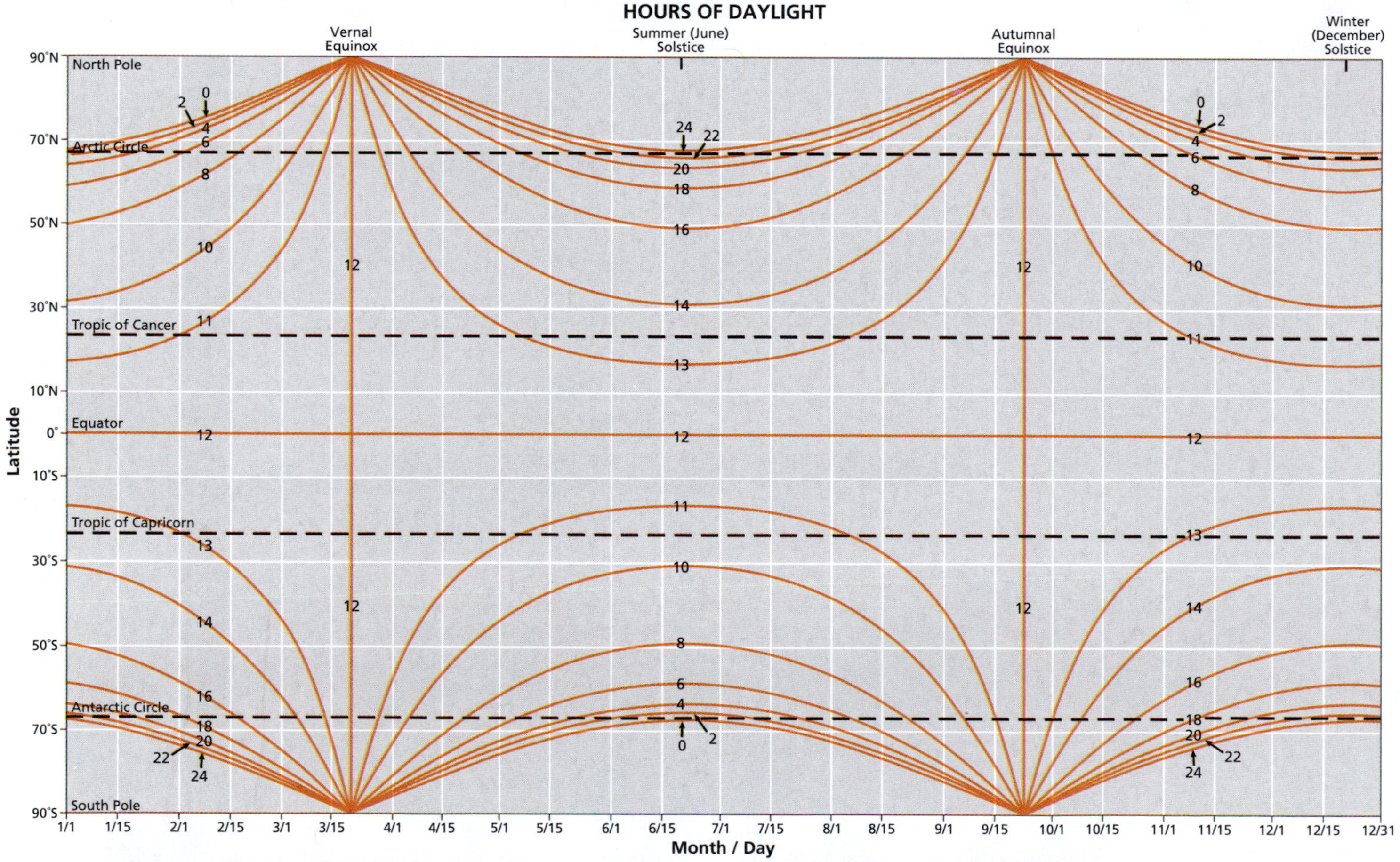

This graph shows hours of daylight at various latitudes for each day of the year. The following are some important patterns evident on the graph.
- The Equator experiences 12 hours of daylight every day of the year.
- Every point on the Earth experiences 12 hours of daylight at the vernal and autumnal equinoxes.
- The greater the distance from the Equator, the greater the variability in daylight length over the year.
- In the northern hemisphere, daylight length is greater than 12 hours between the vernal and autumnal equinoxes (the northern hemisphere summer) and less than 12 hours between the autumnal and vernal equinoxes (the northern hemisphere winter). The opposite pattern occurs in the southern hemisphere.

- Areas north of the Arctic Circle and south of the Antarctic Circle experience an annual pattern with periods of total darkness and periods of continuous daylight.

The data used to create this graph do not account for refraction of the Sun's rays by the Earth's atmosphere, which lengthens the daylight period slightly. The calculations are based on the center of the Sun, and do not account for the size of the solar disk, which also extends the daylight period by several minutes.

ARCTIC OCEAN

GREENLAND
SEA

NORTH SEA

UNITED
KINGDOM
Glasgow

FAROE IS.
(Denmark)

Anadyr

CHUKCHI
SEA

POINT
BARROW

Barrow

QUEEN ELIZABETH
ISLANDS

ELLESMERE
ISLAND

Thule

GREENLAND
(Denmark)

Gunnbjørn Field
12 157 ft.
3700 m

Denmark Strait

ICELAND

Reykjavík

ATLANTIC
OCEAN

BERING
SEA

ST. LAWRENCE
ISLAND

Nome

BROOKS RANGE

UNITED
STATES

ALASKA

Fairbanks

BEAUFORT
SEA

DEVON I.

Godthåb

MELVILLE I.

BANKS
ISLAND

Baffin
Bay

CAPE BREWSTER

NUNIVAK
ISLAND

Bethel

ALASKA RANGE

Mt. McKinley
20 320 ft.
6194 m

Anchorage

Dawson

Whitehorse

Amundsen
Gulf

VICTORIA
ISLAND

Kugluktuk

Arctic Circle

Great Bear
Lake

Yellowknife

Thelon

Gulf of
Boothia

SOUTHAMPTON
ISLAND

Foxe
Basin

Iqaluit

BAFFIN ISLAND

Hudson Strait

Ungava
Bay

Tingmiarmiut

CAPE FAREWELL

CAPE
BAULD

Bristol
Bay

Gulf of
Alaska

Juneau

KODIAK
ISLAND

Kodiak

Yukon

Mt. Logan
19 551 ft.
5959 m

COAST RANGE

Prince Rupert

QUEEN
CHARLOTTE
ISLANDS

Fort St. John

Prince
George

VANCOUVER ISLAND

Vancouver

Seattle

Portland

Eugene

CAPE MENDOCINO

Mackenzie

Great Slave
Lake

Peace

Fraser

Edmonton

Calgary

Lake
Athabasca

Saskatoon

Regina

Thompson

Churchill

Nelson

Lake
Winnipeg

Winnipeg

C A N A D A

Arviat

Hudson

Bay

Kuujjuaq

James
Bay

Albany

Timmins

Lake
Nipigon

Sudbury

Thunder
Bay

Lake Superior

Labrador City

Sept-Îles

Gulf of
St. Lawrence

Québec

MONTRÉAL

St.
Lawrence

CAPE BRETON
ISLAND

Halifax

LABRADOR
SEA

NEWFOUNDLAND

St. John's

CAPE RACE

CAPE SABLE

San Francisco

San Jose

Sacramento

SIERRA NEVADA

ROCKY   MOUNTAINS

Mt. Rainier
14 411 ft.
4392 m

Spokane

CASCADE RANGE

Boise

Snake

Billings

Great Salt
Lake

Salt Lake
City

Fargo

Sioux Falls

Minneapolis

Milwaukee

CHICAGO

Lake Michigan

Detroit

Cleveland

Lake Huron

Lake Erie

Lake Ontario

Ottawa

TORONTO

Buffalo

Pittsburgh

APPALACHIAN MTS.

Boston

NEW YORK

PHILADELPHIA

Washington

Norfolk

Chesapeake Bay

Missouri

Los Angeles

SAN DIEGO

Mt. Whitney
14 494 ft.
4418 m

Las Vegas

PHOENIX

Tucson

Denver

Platte

Colorado

U N I T E D   S T A T E S

Oklahoma
City

Fort Worth

DALLAS

Austin

Kansas
City

Omaha

St. Louis

Ohio

Arkansas

Memphis

Birmingham

Atlanta

Mississippi

Charlotte

Raleigh

CAPE HATTERAS

BERMUDA
(U.K.)

ATLANTIC

OCEAN

SAN ANTONIO

HOUSTON

New Orleans

Jacksonville

Orlando

Tampa

Miami

Gulf of Mexico

BAHAMAS

Rio Grande

Ciudad
Juárez

Chihuahua

Hermosillo

GUADALUPE
(Mex.)

Golfo de
California

BAJA CALIFORNIA

SIERRA MADRE OCCIDENTAL

Torreón

Culiacán

CABO SAN LUCAS

Tropic of Cancer

ISLAS
REVILLAGIGEDO
(Mex.)

MONTERREY

M E X I C O

León

GUADALAJARA

MEXICO CITY

SIERRA MADRE ORIENTAL

Mérida

Bahía de
Campeche

Volcán Pico
de Orizaba
18 406 ft.
5610 m

Yucatan Channel

HAVANA

CUBA

Santiago
de Cuba

JAMAICA

Kingston

HAITI

Port-au-
Prince

DOMINICAN
REPUBLIC

Santo
Domingo

PUERTO RICO
(U.S.)

San Juan

DOMINICA

ST. LUCIA

GUADELOUPE
(Fr.)

MARTINIQUE
(Fr.)

BARBADOS

C A R I B B E A N   S E A

ARUBA
(Neth.)

NETH. ANT.
(Neth.)

GRENADA

TRINIDAD
AND TOBAGO

Acapulco de Juárez

BELIZE

GUATEMALA

Guatemala

EL SALVADOR

HONDURAS

Tegucigalpa

NICARAGUA

Managua

Lago de
Nicaragua

COSTA
RICA

San José

PANAMÁ

PANAMA

Golfo de
Panamá

CARACAS

VENEZUELA

GUYANA

PACIFIC OCEAN

ÎLE CLIPPERTON
(Fr.)

ISLA DEL COCO
(C.R.)

BOGOTÁ

COLOMBIA

Orinoco

Negro

Amazon

BRAZIL

Equator

ECUADOR

PERU

© Rand McNally
A-101611-1

0   200   400   600   800   1000   1200 Miles

0   200 400 600 800 1000 1200 1400 1600 1800 2000 Kilometers

Lambert Azimuthal Equal Area Projection
Scale 1:40,000,000
One inch to 640 miles
One cm to 400 km

| 0 | 200 | 400 | 600 | 800 | 1000 | 1200 Miles |

| 0 | 200 | 400 | 600 | 800 | 1000 | 1200 | 1400 | 1600 | 1800 | 2000 Kilometers |

Lambert Azimuthal Equal Area Projection
Scale 1:40,000,000
One inch to 640 miles
One cm to 400 km

Land Cover

- Evergreen Needleleaf Forest
- Evergreen Broadleaf Forest
- Deciduous Broadleaf Forest
- Mixed Forest
- Woodland
- Wooded Grassland
- Closed Shrubland
- Open Shrubland
- Grassland
- Cropland
- Bare Ground (Desert and Ice)
- Urban and Built Up

A-102092-1
© Rand McNally

0 200 400 600 800 1000 1200 Miles
0 200 400 600 800 1000 1200 1400 1600 1800 2000 Kilometers

Lambert Azimuthal Equal Area Projection
Scale 1:40,000,000
One inch to 640 miles
One cm to 400 km

Source: CIESIN; Hansen et al., 2000

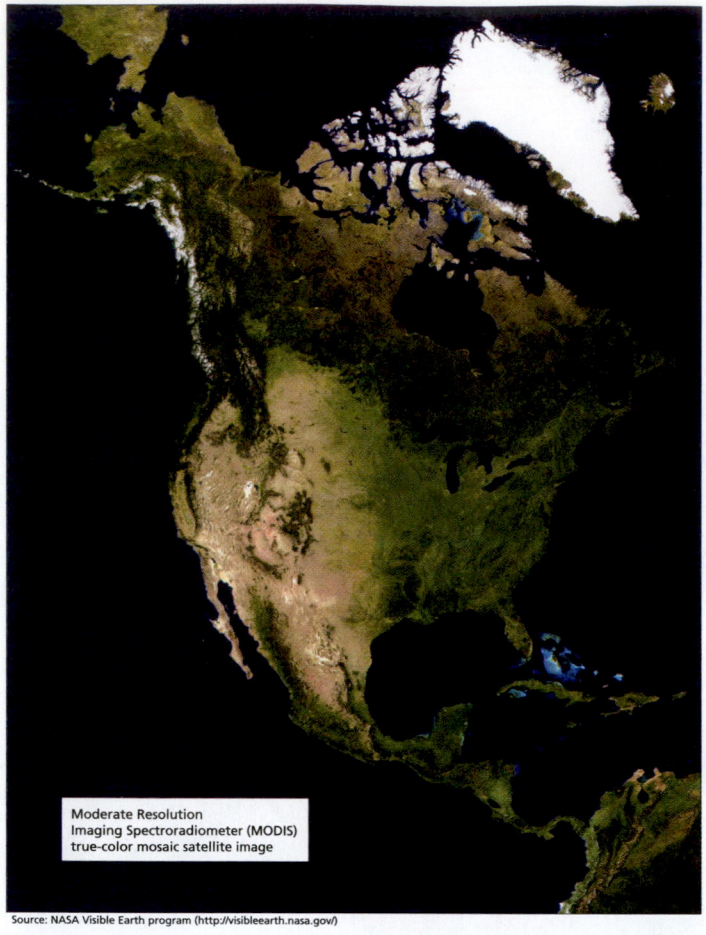

Moderate Resolution
Imaging Spectroradiometer (MODIS)
true-color mosaic satellite image

Source: NASA Visible Earth program (http://visibleearth.nasa.gov/)

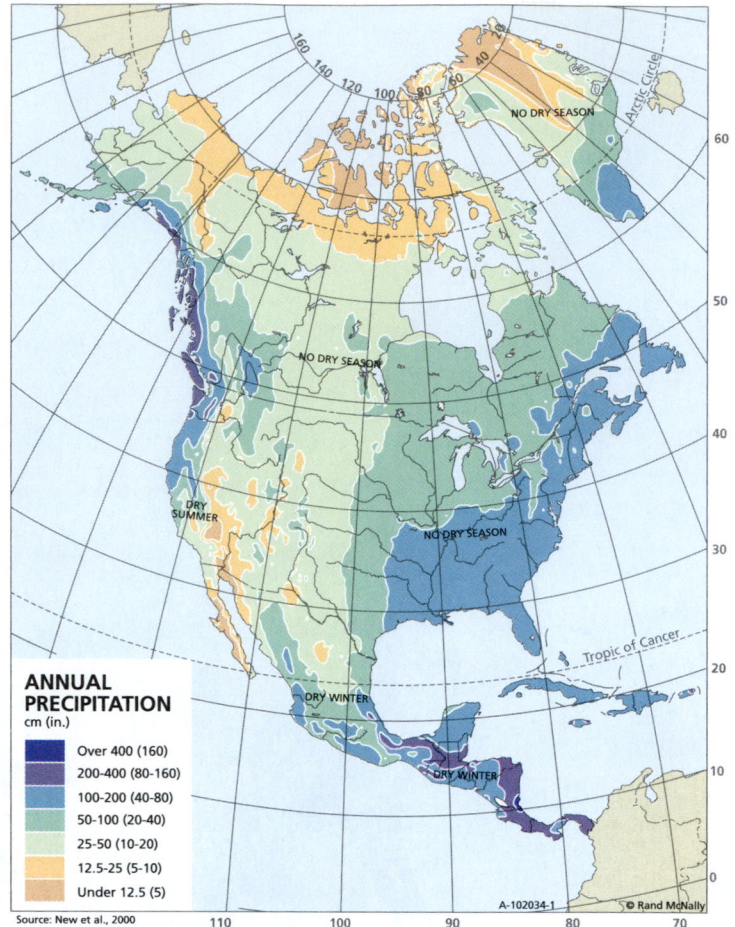

ANNUAL PRECIPITATION
cm (in.)

- Over 400 (160)
- 200-400 (80-160)
- 100-200 (40-80)
- 50-100 (20-40)
- 25-50 (10-20)
- 12.5-25 (5-10)
- Under 12.5 (5)

Source: New et al., 2000

A-102034-1

© Rand McNally

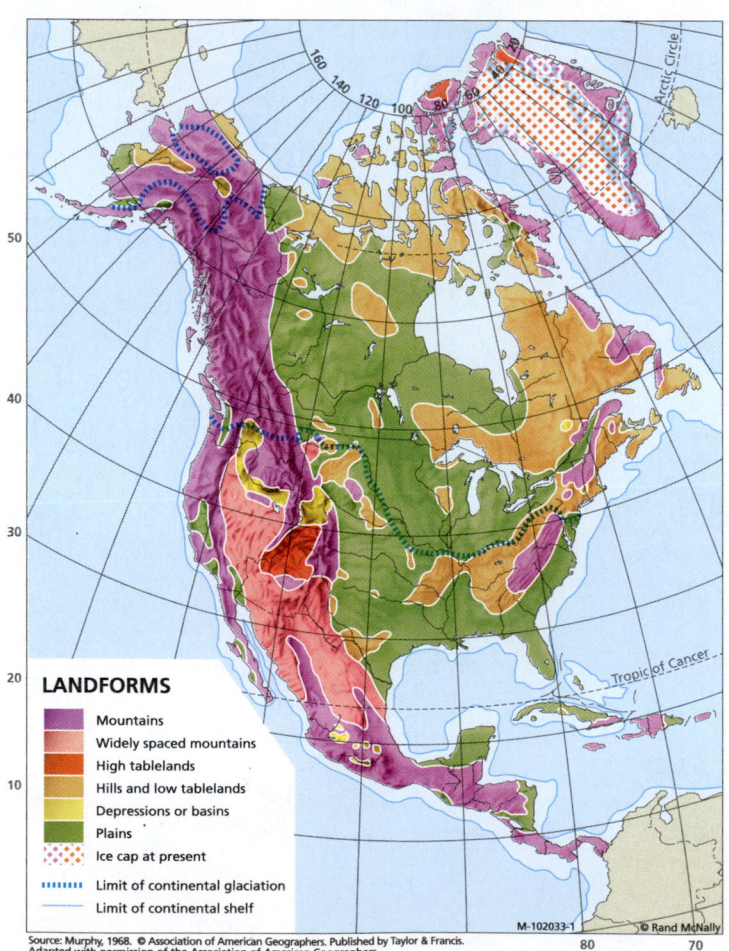

LANDFORMS

- Mountains
- Widely spaced mountains
- High tablelands
- Hills and low tablelands
- Depressions or basins
- Plains
- Ice cap at present
- ······ Limit of continental glaciation
- —— Limit of continental shelf

Source: Murphy, 1968. © Association of American Geographers. Published by Taylor & Francis.
Adapted with permission of the Association of American Geographers.

M-102033-1

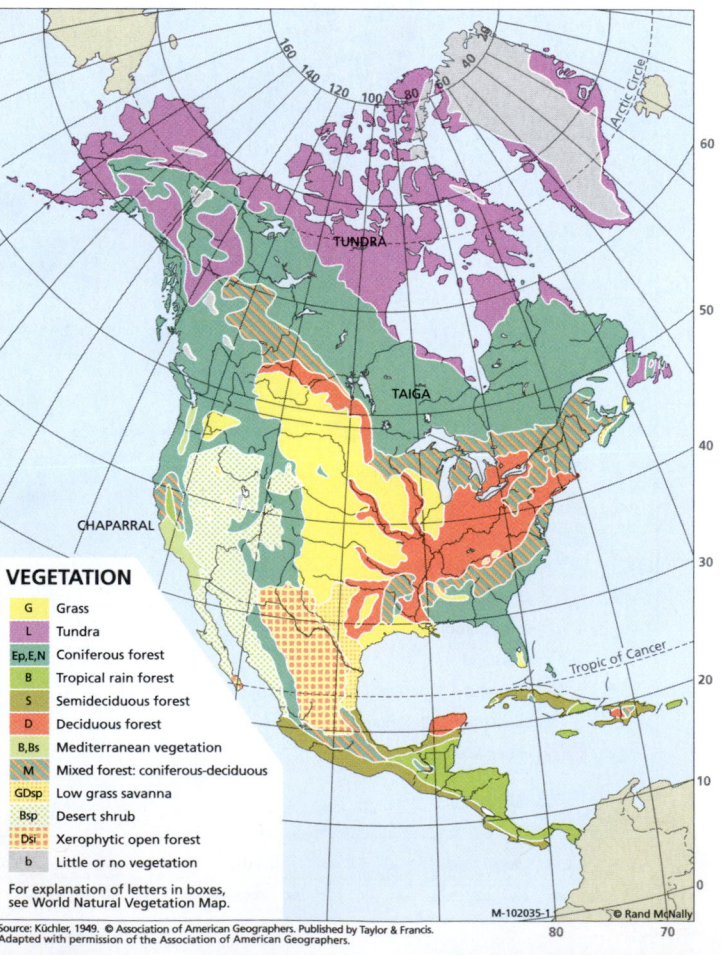

VEGETATION

- G   Grass
- L   Tundra
- Ep,E,N   Coniferous forest
- B   Tropical rain forest
- S   Semideciduous forest
- D   Deciduous forest
- B,Bs   Mediterranean vegetation
- M   Mixed forest: coniferous-deciduous
- GDsp   Low grass savanna
- Bsp   Desert shrub
- Dsl   Xerophytic open forest
- b   Little or no vegetation

For explanation of letters in boxes,
see World Natural Vegetation Map.

Source: Küchler, 1949. © Association of American Geographers. Published by Taylor & Francis.
Adapted with permission of the Association of American Geographers.

M-102035-1

© Rand McNally

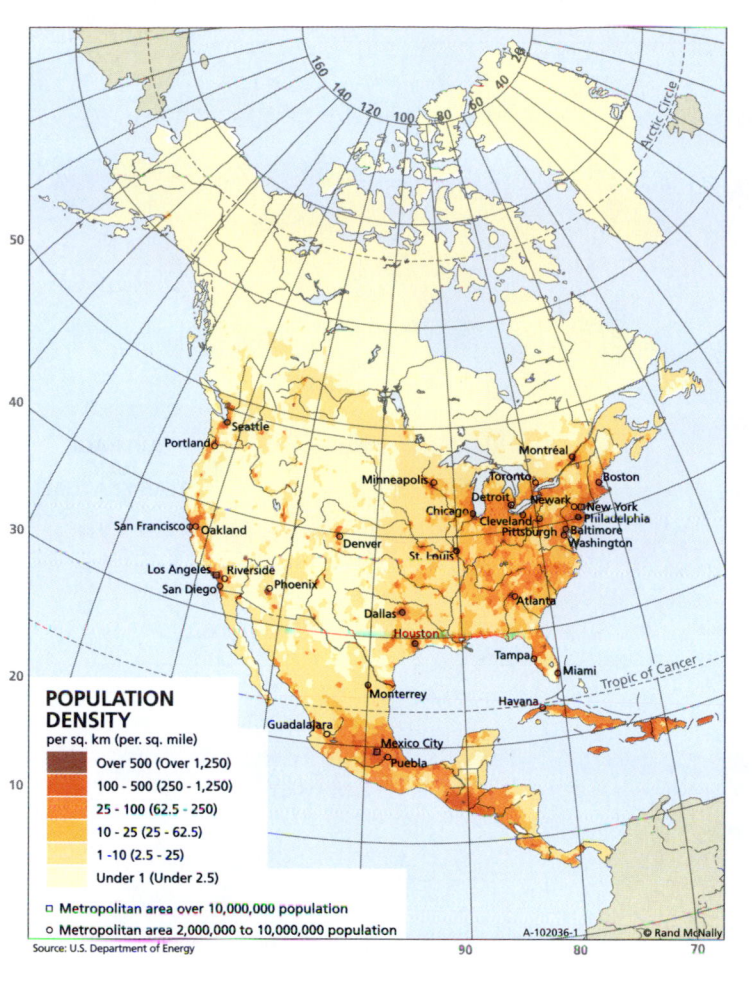

POPULATION DENSITY

per sq. km (per. sq. mile)

- Over 500 (Over 1,250)
- 100 - 500 (250 - 1,250)
- 25 - 100 (62.5 - 250)
- 10 - 25 (25 - 62.5)
- 1 - 10 (2.5 - 25)
- Under 1 (Under 2.5)

□ Metropolitan area over 10,000,000 population
○ Metropolitan area 2,000,000 to 10,000,000 population

Source: U.S. Department of Energy

A-102036-1 © Rand McNally

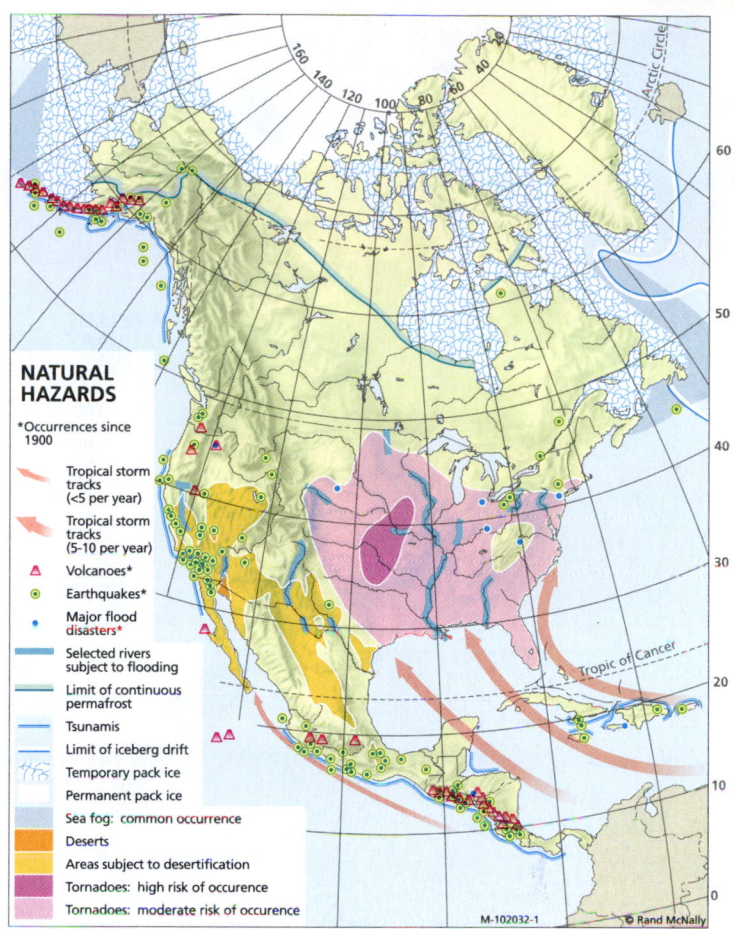

NATURAL HAZARDS

*Occurrences since 1900

- → Tropical storm tracks (<5 per year)
- → Tropical storm tracks (5-10 per year)
- △ Volcanoes*
- ⊙ Earthquakes*
- • Major flood disasters*
- — Selected rivers subject to flooding
- — Limit of continuous permafrost
- — Tsunamis
- — Limit of iceberg drift
- Temporary pack ice
- Permanent pack ice
- Sea fog: common occurrence
- Deserts
- Areas subject to desertification
- Tornadoes: high risk of occurence
- Tornadoes: moderate risk of occurence

M-102032-1 © Rand McNally

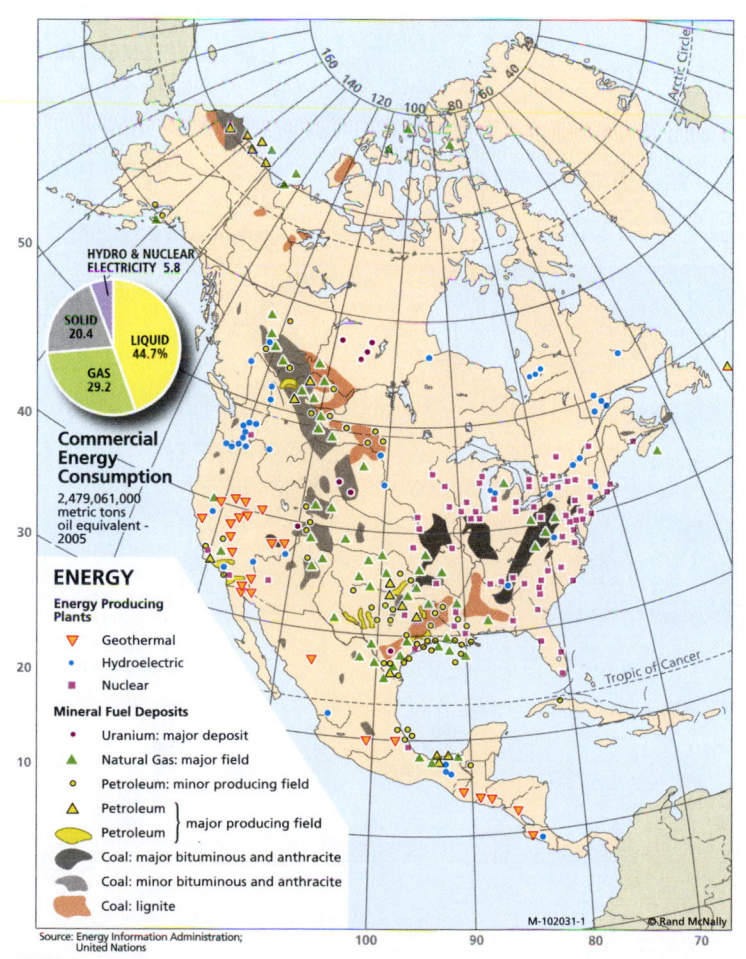

Commercial Energy Consumption

2,479,061,000 metric tons / oil equivalent - 2005

Pie chart:
- HYDRO & NUCLEAR ELECTRICITY 5.8
- SOLID 20.4
- LIQUID 44.7%
- GAS 29.2

ENERGY

Energy Producing Plants

- ▽ Geothermal
- • Hydroelectric
- ■ Nuclear

Mineral Fuel Deposits

- • Uranium: major deposit
- ▲ Natural Gas: major field
- ○ Petroleum: minor producing field
- ▽ Petroleum } major producing field
- Petroleum }
- Coal: major bituminous and anthracite
- Coal: minor bituminous and anthracite
- Coal: lignite

Source: Energy Information Administration; United Nations

M-102031-1 © Rand McNally

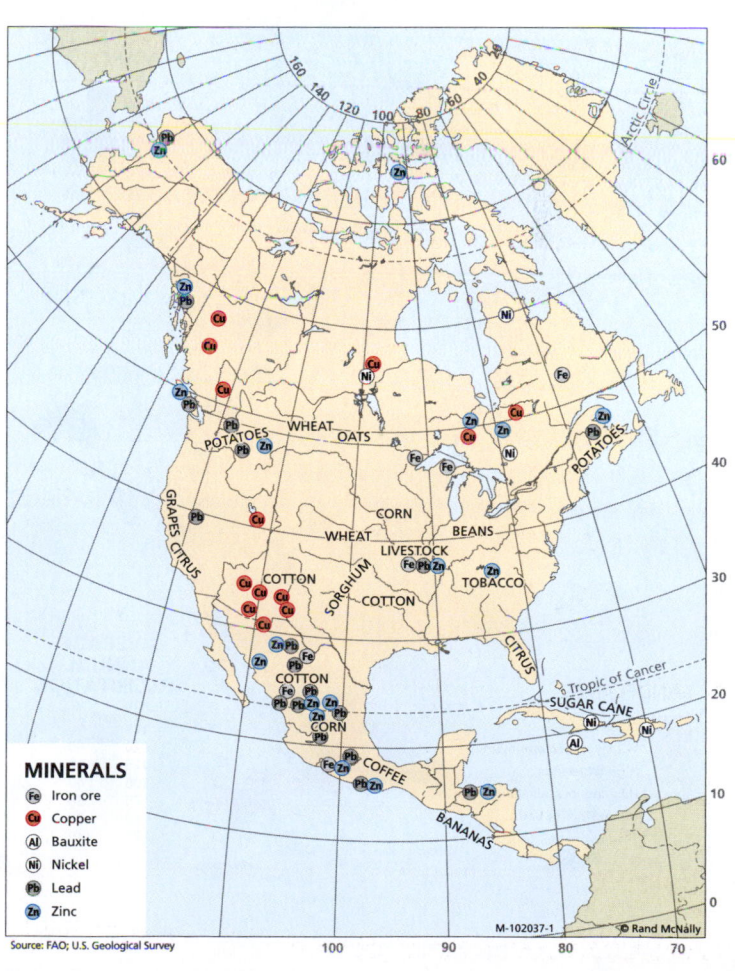

MINERALS

- Fe Iron ore
- Cu Copper
- Al Bauxite
- Ni Nickel
- Pb Lead
- Zn Zinc

Source: FAO; U.S. Geological Survey

M-102037-1 © Rand McNally

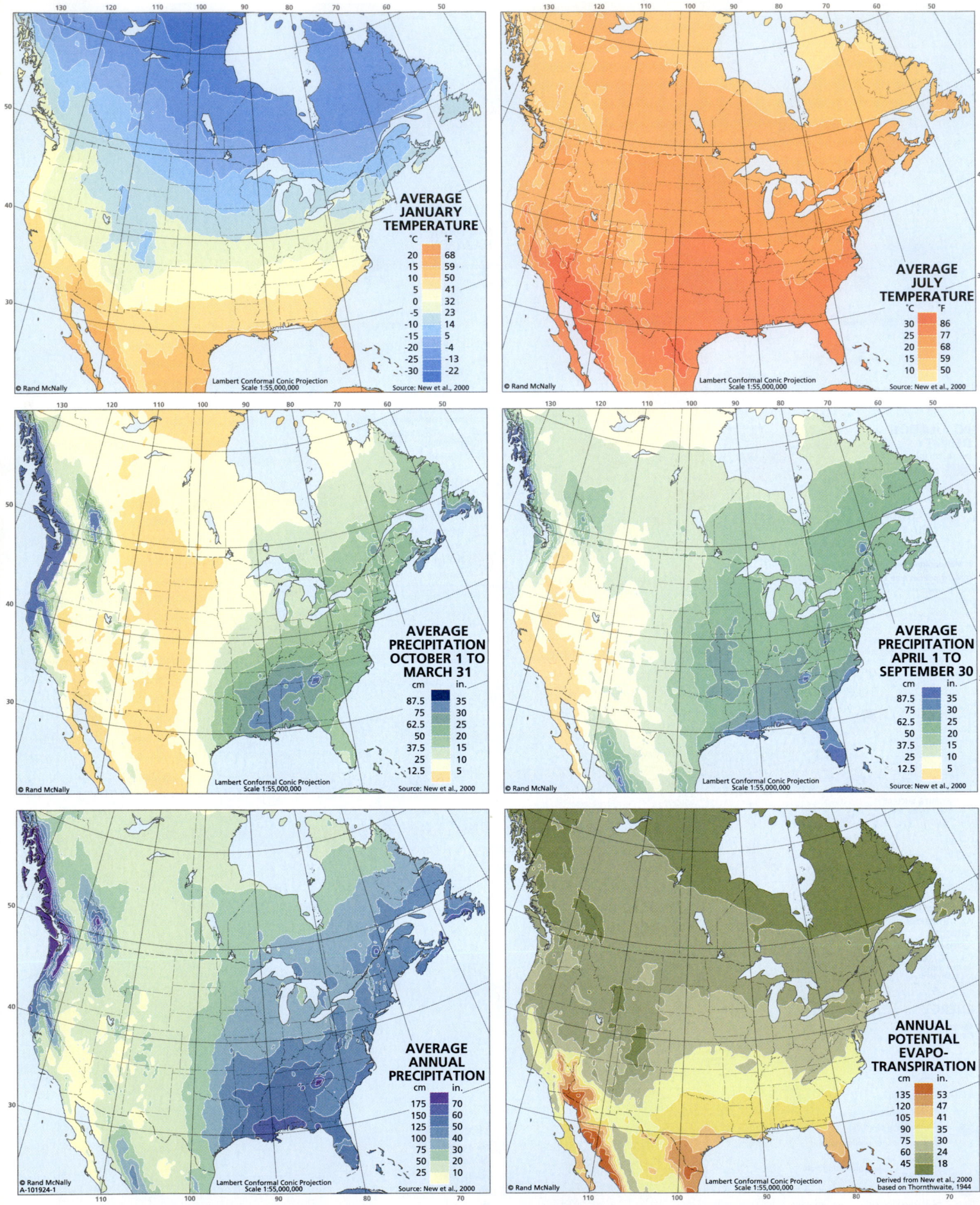

**AVERAGE
JANUARY
TEMPERATURE**

°C	°F
20	68
15	59
10	50
5	41
0	32
-5	23
-10	14
-15	5
-20	-4
-25	-13
-30	-22

© Rand McNally
Lambert Conformal Conic Projection
Scale 1:55,000,000
Source: New et al., 2000

**AVERAGE
JULY
TEMPERATURE**

°C	°F
30	86
25	77
20	68
15	59
10	50

© Rand McNally
Lambert Conformal Conic Projection
Scale 1:55,000,000
Source: New et al., 2000

**AVERAGE
PRECIPITATION
OCTOBER 1 TO
MARCH 31**

cm	in.
87.5	35
75	30
62.5	25
50	20
37.5	15
25	10
12.5	5

© Rand McNally
Lambert Conformal Conic Projection
Scale 1:55,000,000
Source: New et al., 2000

**AVERAGE
PRECIPITATION
APRIL 1 TO
SEPTEMBER 30**

cm	in.
87.5	35
75	30
62.5	25
50	20
37.5	15
25	10
12.5	5

© Rand McNally
Lambert Conformal Conic Projection
Scale 1:55,000,000
Source: New et al., 2000

**AVERAGE
ANNUAL
PRECIPITATION**

cm	in.
175	70
150	60
125	50
100	40
75	30
50	20
25	10

© Rand McNally
A-101924-1
Lambert Conformal Conic Projection
Scale 1:55,000,000
Source: New et al., 2000

**ANNUAL
POTENTIAL
EVAPO-
TRANSPIRATION**

cm	in.
135	53
120	47
105	41
90	35
75	30
60	24
45	18

© Rand McNally
Lambert Conformal Conic Projection
Scale 1:55,000,000
Derived from New et al., 2000
based on Thornthwaite, 1944

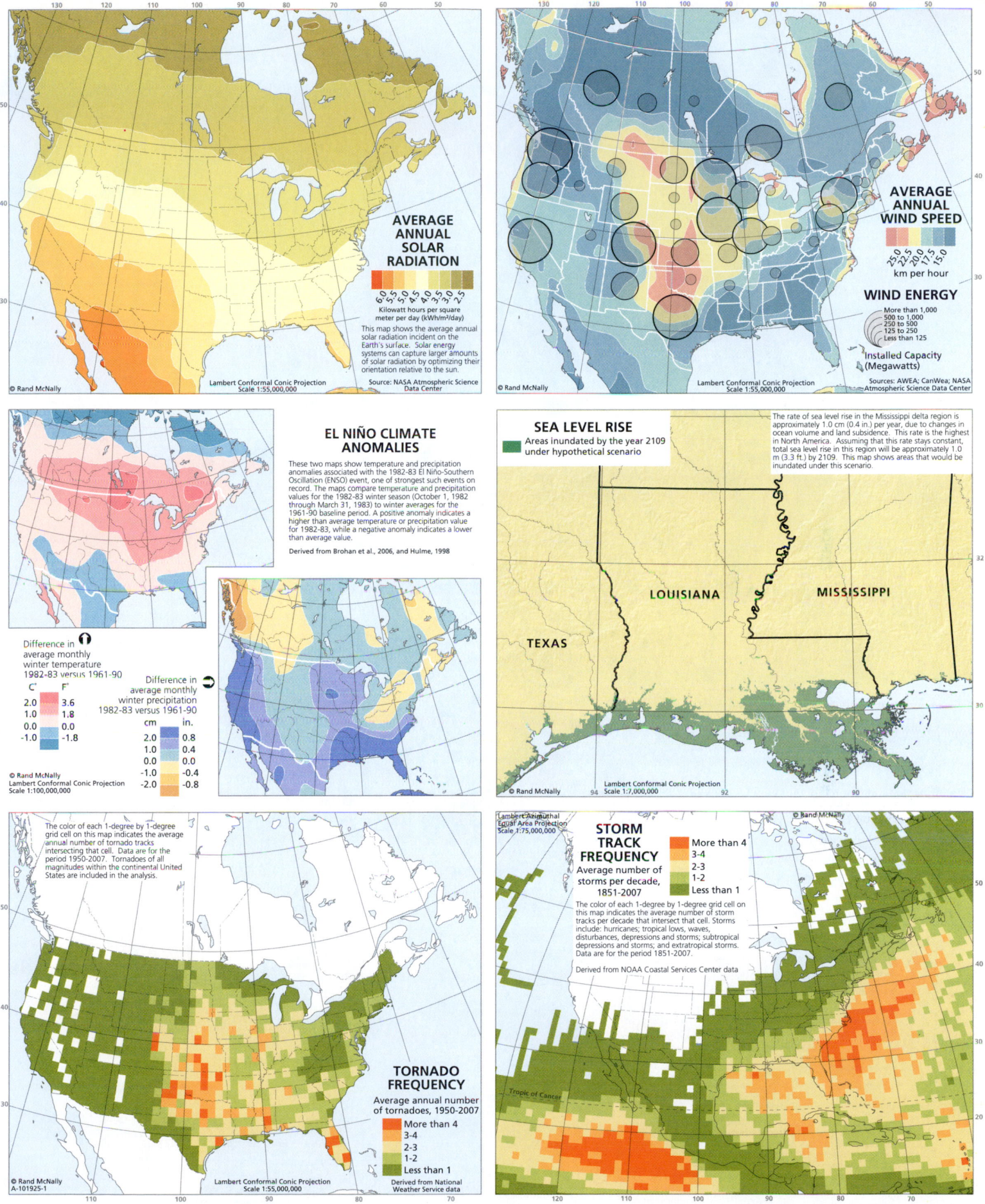

AVERAGE ANNUAL SOLAR RADIATION

Kilowatt hours per square meter per day (kWh/m²/day)

6.0 5.5 5.0 4.5 4.0 3.5 3.0 2.5

This map shows the average annual solar radiation incident on the Earth's surface. Solar energy systems can capture larger amounts of solar radiation by optimizing their orientation relative to the sun.

Source: NASA Atmospheric Science Data Center

Lambert Conformal Conic Projection
Scale 1:55,000,000

© Rand McNally

AVERAGE ANNUAL WIND SPEED

25.0 22.5 20.0 17.5 15.0
km per hour

WIND ENERGY

Installed Capacity (Megawatts)
More than 1,000
500 to 1,000
250 to 500
125 to 250
Less than 125

Sources: AWEA; CanWea; NASA Atmospheric Science Data Center

Lambert Conformal Conic Projection
Scale 1:55,000,000

© Rand McNally

EL NIÑO CLIMATE ANOMALIES

These two maps show temperature and precipitation anomalies associated with the 1982-83 El Niño-Southern Oscillation (ENSO) event, one of strongest such events on record. The maps compare temperature and precipitation values for the 1982-83 winter season (October 1, 1982 through March 31, 1983) to winter averages for the 1961-90 baseline period. A positive anomaly indicates a higher than average temperature or precipitation value for 1982-83, while a negative anomaly indicates a lower than average value.

Derived from Brohan et al., 2006, and Hulme, 1998

Difference in average monthly winter temperature 1982-83 versus 1961-90

C°	F°
2.0	3.6
1.0	1.8
0.0	0.0
-1.0	-1.8

Difference in average monthly winter precipitation 1982-83 versus 1961-90

cm	in.
2.0	0.8
1.0	0.4
0.0	0.0
-1.0	-0.4
-2.0	-0.8

© Rand McNally
Lambert Conformal Conic Projection
Scale 1:100,000,000

SEA LEVEL RISE

Areas inundated by the year 2109 under hypothetical scenario

The rate of sea level rise in the Mississippi delta region is approximately 1.0 cm (0.4 in.) per year, due to changes in ocean volume and land subsidence. This rate is the highest in North America. Assuming that this rate stays constant, total sea level rise in this region will be approximately 1.0 m (3.3 ft.) by 2109. This map shows areas that would be inundated under this scenario.

LOUISIANA

MISSISSIPPI

TEXAS

© Rand McNally
Lambert Conformal Conic Projection
Scale 1:7,000,000

The color of each 1-degree by 1-degree grid cell on this map indicates the average number of tornado tracks intersecting that cell. Data are for the period 1950-2007. Tornadoes of all magnitudes within the continental United States are included in the analysis.

TORNADO FREQUENCY

Average annual number of tornadoes, 1950-2007

More than 4
3-4
2-3
1-2
Less than 1

© Rand McNally
A-101925-1

Lambert Conformal Conic Projection
Scale 1:55,000,000

Derived from National Weather Service data

Lambert Azimuthal Equal Area Projection
Scale 1:75,000,000

© Rand McNally

STORM TRACK FREQUENCY

Average number of storms per decade, 1851-2007

More than 4
3-4
2-3
1-2
Less than 1

The color of each 1-degree by 1-degree grid cell on this map indicates the average number of storm tracks per decade that intersect that cell. Storms include: hurricanes; tropical lows, waves, disturbances, depressions and storms; subtropical depressions and storms; and extratropical storms. Data are for the period 1851-2007.

Derived from NOAA Coastal Services Center data

Tropic of Cancer

NATURAL VEGETATION
Vegetation Types

B   Broadleaf evergreen

D   Broadleaf deciduous

E   Needleleaf evergreen

N   Needleleaf deciduous

G   Grass

L   Herbaceous plants other than grass

O   Woody plants without leaves

s   Shrubform; minimum height 1 m (3 ft.)

z   Dwarf shrubform; maximum height 1 m (3 ft.)

l   Low; maximum height of trees 9 m (30 ft.); maximum height of herbaceous plants 0.5 m (1.5 ft.)

m   Medium height; maximum height of trees 9-23 m (30-75 ft.); maximum height of herbaceous plants 0.5-2 m (1.5-6 ft.)

p   Growth singly or in groups or patches

b   Vegetation largely or entirely absent

This classification system differentiates between woody and herbaceous plants. For woody plants, further distinctions are made between broadleaf and needleleaf, and evergreen and deciduous. All capital letters other than G and L imply trees, unless accompanied by s or z. The small letters modify the capital letter preceding them. For example, GlDsp means that the vegetation consists of low grass (Gl) and of patches of broadleaf deciduous shrubs (Dsp).

Lambert Conformal Conic Projection
Scale 1:14,000,000
One inch to 220 miles
One cm to 140 km

0 50 100 150 200 250 300 350 400 450 500 Miles

0 100 200 300 400 500 600 700 800 Kilometers

Source: Küchler, 1949. © Association of American Geographers. Published by Taylor & Francis.
Adapted with permission of the Association of American Geographers.

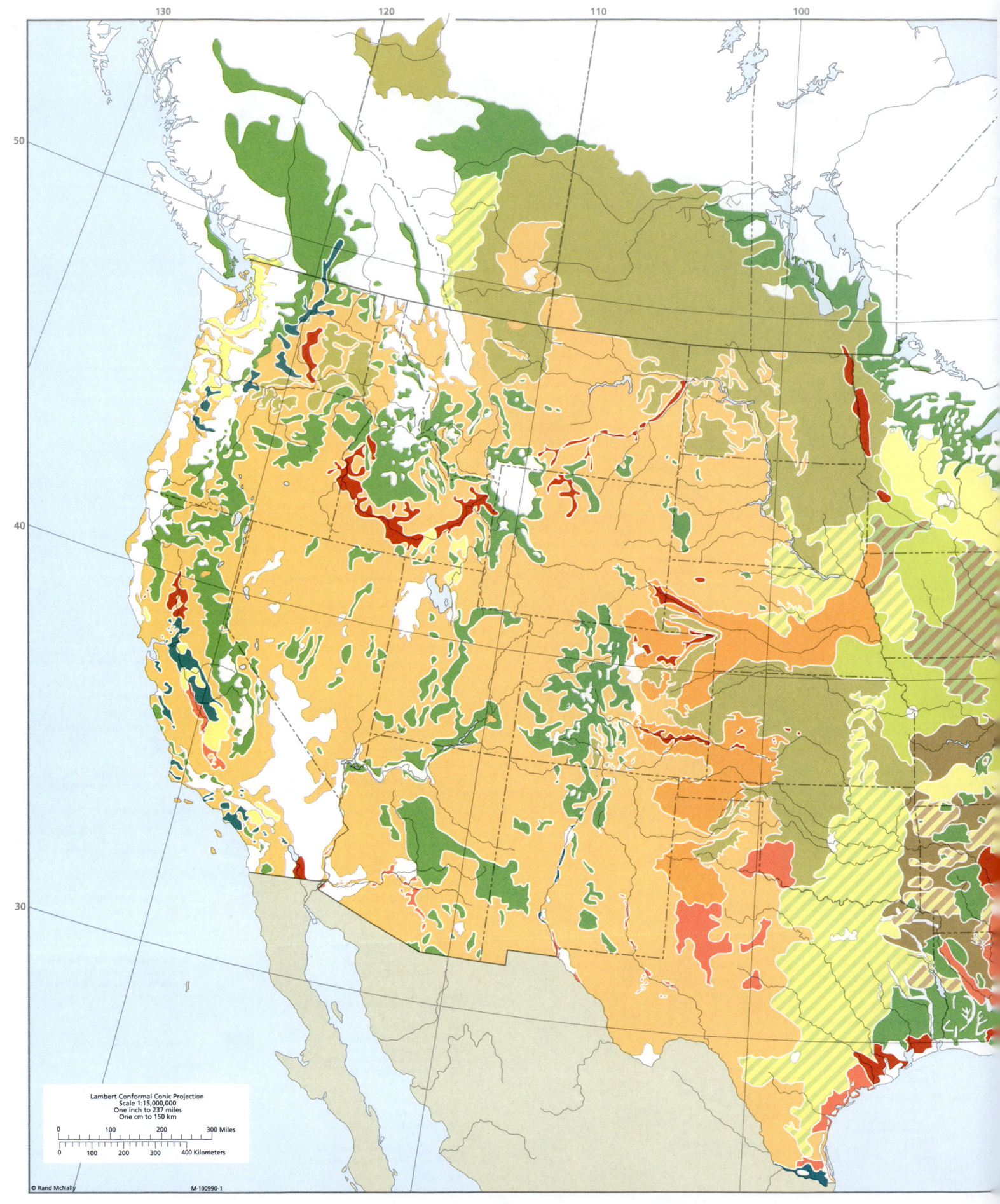

Lambert Conformal Conic Projection
Scale 1:15,000,000
One inch to 237 miles
One cm to 150 km

0   100   200   300 Miles

0   100   200   300   400 Kilometers

© Rand McNally

M-100990-1

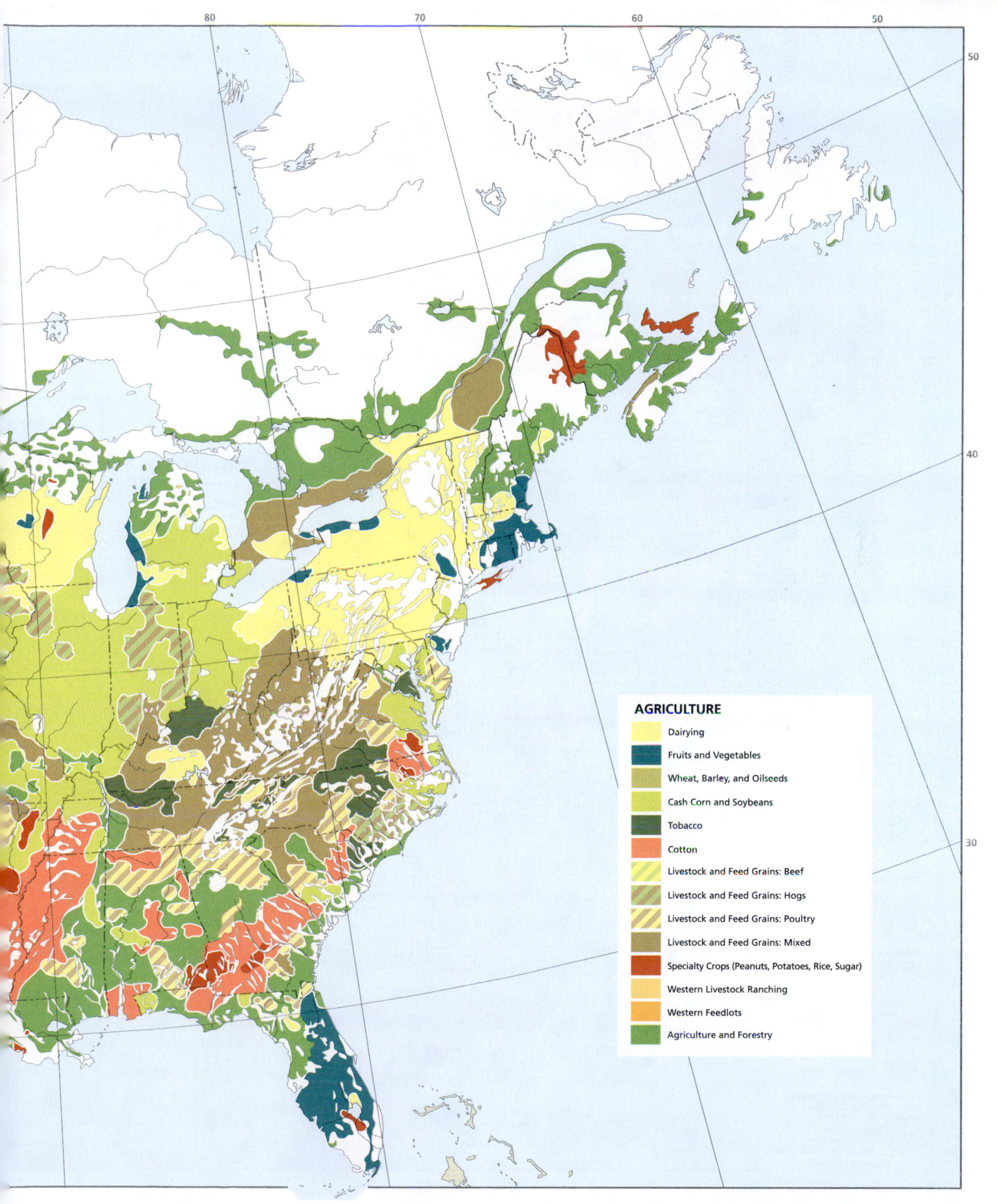

AGRICULTURE

- Dairying
- Fruits and Vegetables
- Wheat, Barley, and Oilseeds
- Cash Corn and Soybeans
- Tobacco
- Cotton
- Livestock and Feed Grains: Beef
- Livestock and Feed Grains: Hogs
- Livestock and Feed Grains: Poultry
- Livestock and Feed Grains: Mixed
- Specialty Crops (Peanuts, Potatoes, Rice, Sugar)
- Western Livestock Ranching
- Western Feedlots
- Agriculture and Forestry

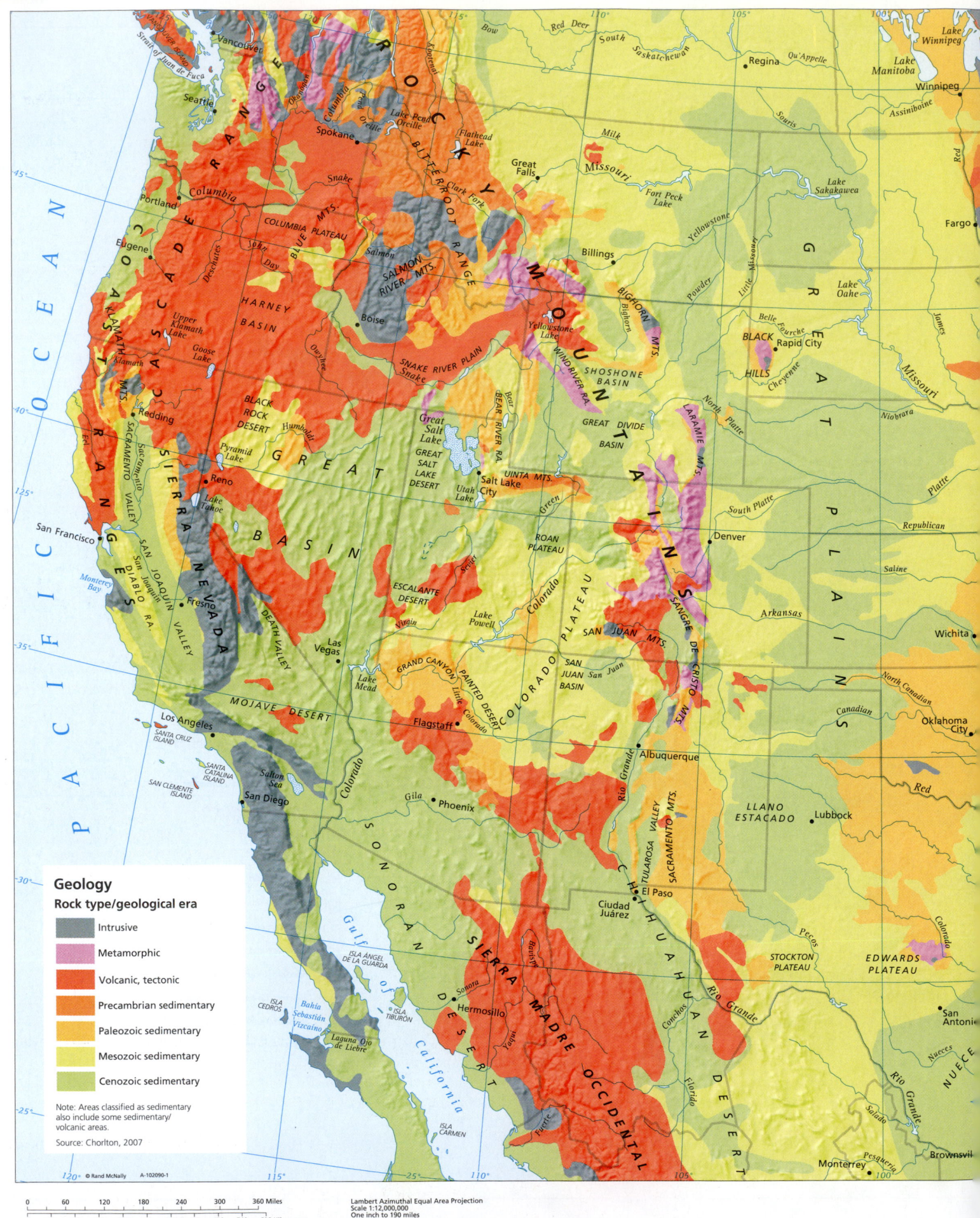

Geology

Rock type/geological era

- Intrusive
- Metamorphic
- Volcanic, tectonic
- Precambrian sedimentary
- Paleozoic sedimentary
- Mesozoic sedimentary
- Cenozoic sedimentary

Note: Areas classified as sedimentary also include some sedimentary/volcanic areas.

Source: Chorlton, 2007

0   60   120   180   240   300   360 Miles
0   60   120   180   240 300 360 420 480 540 600 Kilometers

Lambert Azimuthal Equal Area Projection
Scale 1:12,000,000
One inch to 190 miles
One cm to 120 km

© Rand McNally   A-102090-1

The geological information on this map is highly generalized, and is intended for use at scales of 1:10,000,000 or smaller.

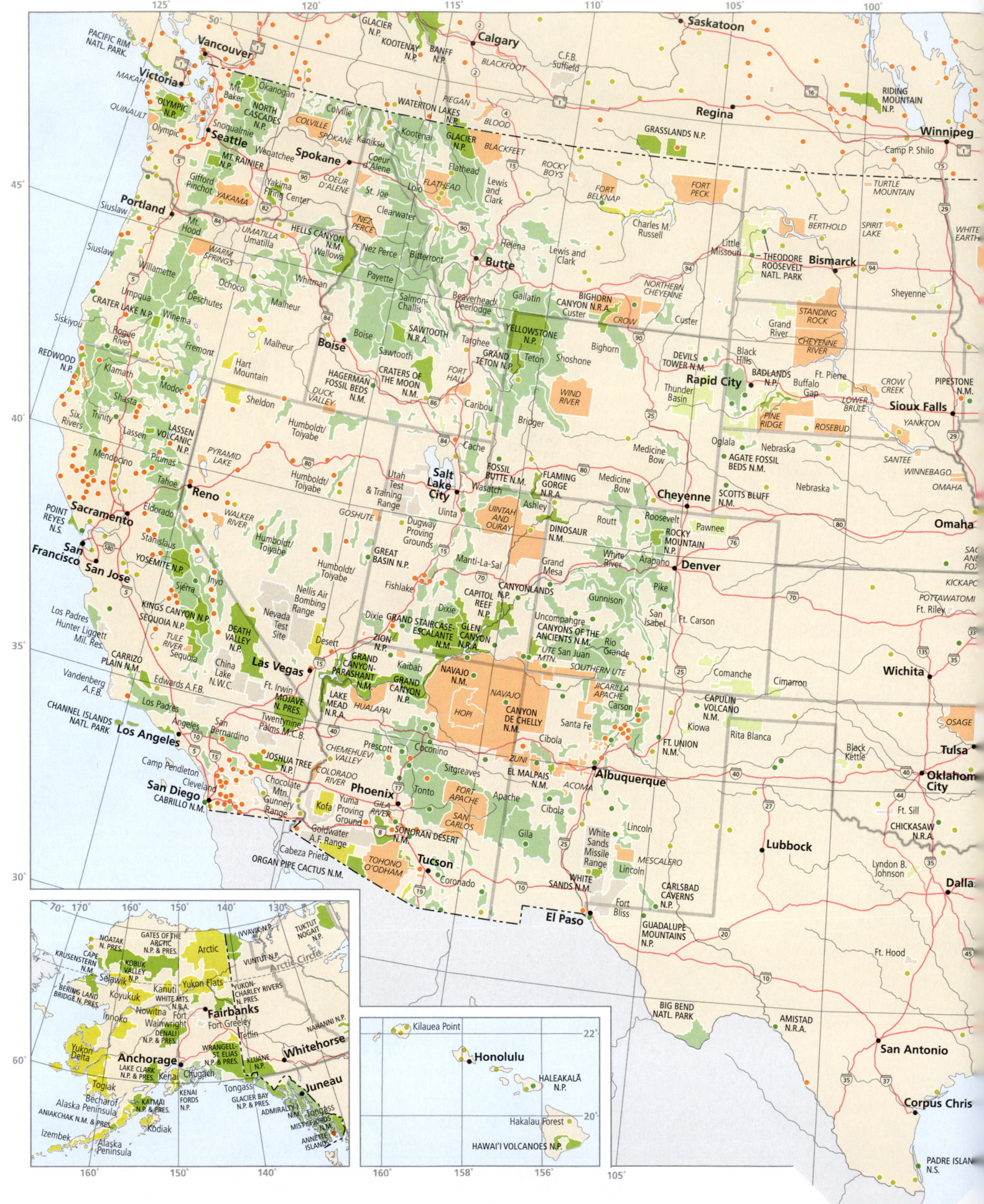

FORILLON NATL. PARK

KOUCHIBOUGUAC NATL. PARK

C.F.B. Gagetown

FUNDY N.P.

Saint John

KEJIMKUJIK NATL. PARK

ACADIA NATL. PARK

LA MAURICIE NATL. PARK

Québec

Portland

White Mountain

Concord

Green Mountain

Boston

Providence

CAPE COD N.S.

Albany

Hartford

RED LAKE

Chippewa

VOYAGEURS N.P.

Thunder Bay

PUKASKWA NATL. PARK

Rouyn-Noranda

Superior

Fond du Lac

ISLE ROYALE N.P.

GRAND PORTAGE N.M.

APOSTLE ISLANDS N.L.

Leech Lake

Chequamegon

Lac Courte Oreilles

Ottawa

L'ANSE

Seney

Hiawatha

PICTURED ROCKS N.L.

Sudbury

C.F.B. Petawawa

St. Lawrence Is. Natl. Park

Ft. Drum

Ottawa

Montréal

Minneapolis

Lac du Flambeau

Nicolet

Stockbridge

Menominee

Oneida

SLEEPING BEAR DUNES N.L.

Manistee

Huron

FATHOM FIVE N.P.

BRUCE PENINSULA N.P.

GEORGIAN BAY IS. N.P.

Toronto

FT. STANWIX NATL. MON.

Ft. Drum

Milwaukee

Isabella

SIX NATIONS

London

Buffalo

CATTARAUGUS

Detroit

POINT PELEE NATL. PARK

ALLEGANY

Allegheny

New York

GATEWAY NATL. REC AREA

FIRE ISLAND N.S.

Chicago

INDIANA DUNES N.L.

Cleveland

CUYAHOGA VALLEY N.P.

Pittsburgh

Philadelphia

Fort Dix

Des Moines

Columbus

Wayne

Baltimore

Washington D.C.

ASSATEAGUE ISLAND N.S.

Kansas City

Indianapolis

Cincinnati

Wayne

Monongahela

SHENANDOAH N.P.

Ft. A.P. Hill

Richmond

Crane Naval Weapons Support Ctr.

Hoosier

George Washington

St. Louis

Mark Twain

Ft. Leonard Wood

Louisville

Ft. Knox

Daniel Boone

Jefferson

Charleston

BOOKER T. WASHINGTON NATL. MONUMENT

Norfolk

Great Dismal Swamp

G.W. CARVER NATL. MON.

Mark Twain

Shawnee

MAMMOTH CAVE N.P.

MT. ROGERS N.R.A.

CAPE HATTERAS N.S.

Ozark

RUSSELL CAVE N.M.

Fort Campbell

Cherokee

GREAT SMOKY MOUNTAINS N.P.

Pisgah

Nashville

Cherokee

Nantahala

Charlotte

Uwharrie

Ft. Bragg

Croatan

CAPE LOOKOUT N.S.

Camp Lejeune Marine Corps Base

Memphis

Holly Springs

William B. Bankhead

Sumter

Columbia

CONGAREE N.P.

Little Rock

Ouachita

White River

HOT SPRINGS N.P.

Francis Marion

Ouachita

Atlanta

Oconee

Ft. Gordon

Birmingham

Talladega

Tombigbee

OCMULGEE N.M.

Charleston

FORT SUMTER NATL. MON.

Jackson

Kisatchie

Bienville

Ft. Benning

Savannah

FORT PULASKI NATL. MON.

Ft. Stewart

Delta

Felsenthal

Ft. Rucker

FORT FREDERICA NATL. MON.

Houston

Sam Houston

Sabine

Homochitto

Desoto

Conecuh

Okefenokee

CUMBERLAND ISLAND N.S.

Jacksonville

Angelina

Davy Crockett

New Orleans

Eglin A.F.B.

Tallahassee

Osceola

CASTILLO DE SAN MARCOS NATL. MON.

FORT MATANZAS NATL. MON.

GULF ISLANDS NATL. SEASHORE

Apalachicola

Ocala

CANAVERAL N.S.

Cape Canaveral Air Force Station

Orlando

St. Petersburg

Tampa

BRIGHTON

Marshall-Loxahatchee

MICCOSUKEE

BIG CYPRESS NATL. PRESERVE

Miami

BISCAYNE NATL. PARK

EVERGLADES NATL. PARK

FEDERAL LANDS AND INTERSTATE HIGHWAYS
Selected highways and Federal Lands

- National Parks, Monuments, Seashores, Preserves, Lakeshores, Recreation Areas
- National Forests
- National Grasslands
- National Wildlife Refuges
- Military Installations
- Indian Reservations
- Interstate Highways
- Other Roads
- U.S. Interstate Highways
- Trans-Canada Highway
- Canadian Autoroute
- Other Canadian Roads

0 60 120 180 240 300 360 Miles
0 60 120 180 240 360 420 480 540 600 Kilometers

Albers Equal Area Conic Projection
Scale 1:12,000,000
One inch to 190 miles
One cm to 120 km

A-100036-1 © Rand McNally

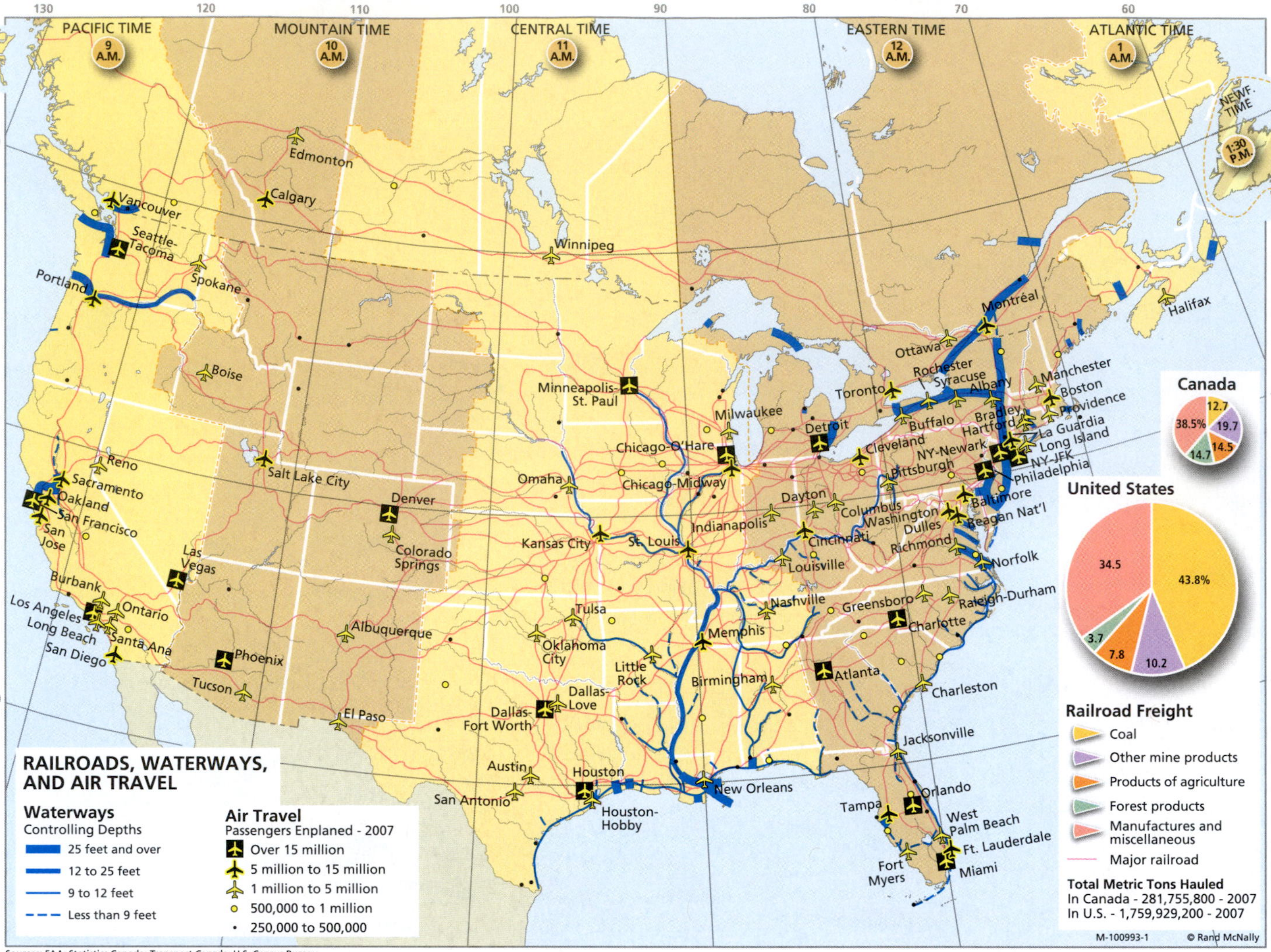

RAILROADS, WATERWAYS, AND AIR TRAVEL

Waterways
Controlling Depths
- ▬ 25 feet and over
- ▬ 12 to 25 feet
- — 9 to 12 feet
- – – Less than 9 feet

Air Travel
Passengers Enplaned - 2007
- ■ Over 15 million
- ✈ 5 million to 15 million
- ✈ 1 million to 5 million
- ○ 500,000 to 1 million
- • 250,000 to 500,000

PACIFIC TIME — 9 A.M.
MOUNTAIN TIME — 10 A.M.
CENTRAL TIME — 11 A.M.
EASTERN TIME — 12 A.M.
ATLANTIC TIME — 1 A.M.
NEWF. TIME — 1:30 P.M.

Canada
38.5% · 12.7 · 19.7 · 14.5 · 14.7

United States
34.5 · 43.8% · 10.2 · 7.8 · 3.7

Railroad Freight
- Coal
- Other mine products
- Products of agriculture
- Forest products
- Manufactures and miscellaneous
- Major railroad

Total Metric Tons Hauled
In Canada - 281,755,800 - 2007
In U.S. - 1,759,929,200 - 2007

Sources: FAA; Statistics Canada; Transport Canada; U.S. Census Bureau

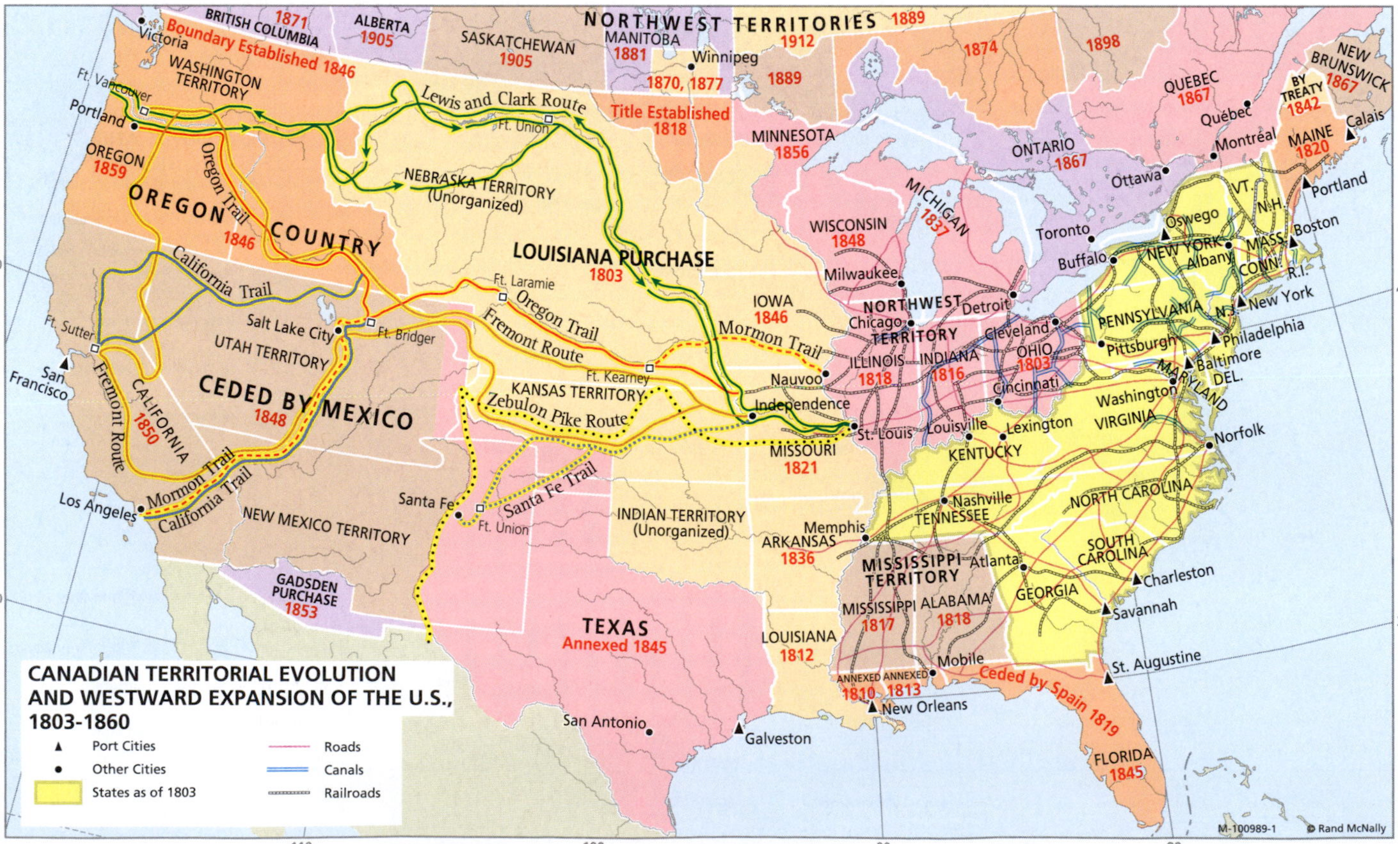

M-100993-1   © Rand McNally

CANADIAN TERRITORIAL EVOLUTION AND WESTWARD EXPANSION OF THE U.S., 1803-1860

- ▲ Port Cities
- • Other Cities
- ▨ States as of 1803
- — Roads
- — Canals
- ···· Railroads

BRITISH COLUMBIA 1871
Boundary Established 1846
ALBERTA 1905
SASKATCHEWAN 1905
MANITOBA 1881
Title Established 1818
NORTHWEST TERRITORIES 1889
1870, 1877
1874
1889
1898
QUEBEC 1867
NEW BRUNSWICK 1867
BY TREATY 1842

WASHINGTON TERRITORY
OREGON COUNTRY
OREGON 1859
OREGON 1846
Lewis and Clark Route
Oregon Trail
California Trail
Fremont Route
NEBRASKA TERRITORY (Unorganized)
LOUISIANA PURCHASE 1803
MINNESOTA 1856
ONTARIO 1867
MAINE 1820
MICHIGAN 1837
WISCONSIN 1848
IOWA 1846
NORTHWEST TERRITORY
Mormon Trail
ILLINOIS 1818
INDIANA 1816
OHIO 1803
PENNSYLVANIA
NEW YORK
VT N.H. MASS. CONN. R.I. NJ

UTAH TERRITORY
CEDED BY MEXICO 1848
CALIFORNIA 1850
Fremont Route
Mormon Trail
California Trail
KANSAS TERRITORY
Zebulon Pike Route
MISSOURI 1821
KENTUCKY
VIRGINIA
MARYLAND DEL.

GADSDEN PURCHASE 1853
NEW MEXICO TERRITORY
Santa Fe Trail
INDIAN TERRITORY (Unorganized)
ARKANSAS 1836
TENNESSEE
NORTH CAROLINA
SOUTH CAROLINA
GEORGIA
MISSISSIPPI TERRITORY
MISSISSIPPI 1817
ALABAMA 1818

TEXAS Annexed 1845
LOUISIANA 1812
ANNEXED 1810 ANNEXED 1813
Ceded by Spain 1819
FLORIDA 1845

Ft. Vancouver, Victoria, Portland, Ft. Sutter, San Francisco, Los Angeles, Salt Lake City, Ft. Bridger, Ft. Laramie, Ft. Kearney, Ft. Union, Nauvoo, Independence, St. Louis, Santa Fe, Ft. Union, Memphis, New Orleans, Mobile, San Antonio, Galveston, St. Augustine, Savannah, Charleston, Norfolk, Washington, Richmond, Baltimore, Philadelphia, Pittsburgh, Cleveland, Detroit, Chicago, Milwaukee, Winnipeg, Toronto, Ottawa, Montréal, Québec, Boston, Albany, New York, Oswego, Buffalo, Calais, Portland

M-100989-1   © Rand McNally

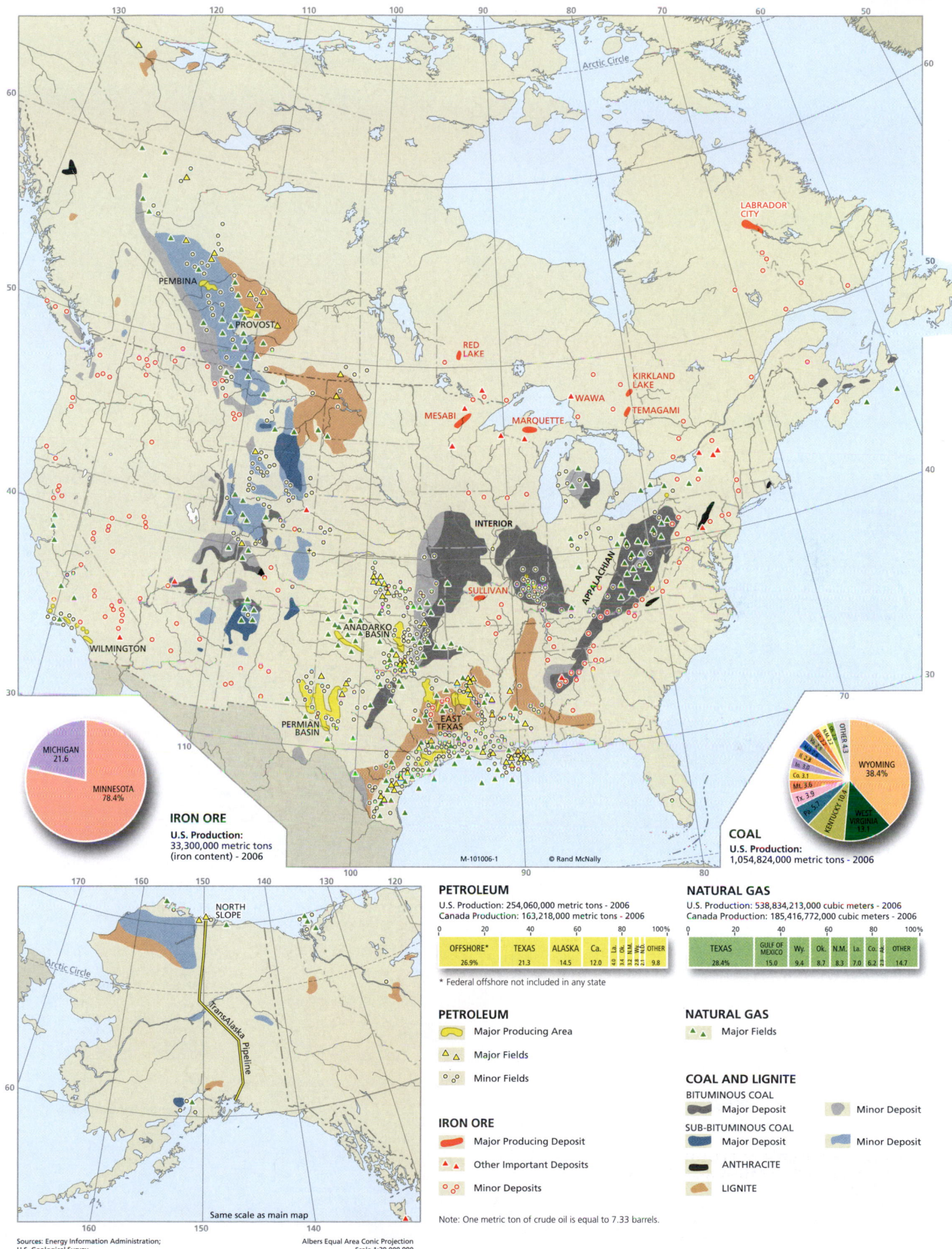

LABRADOR CITY

PEMBINA

PROVOST

RED LAKE

KIRKLAND LAKE

MESABI

WAWA

TEMAGAMI

MARQUETTE

INTERIOR

SULLIVAN

APPALACHIAN

ANADARKO BASIN

WILMINGTON

PERMIAN BASIN

EAST TEXAS

IRON ORE

MICHIGAN 21.6

MINNESOTA 78.4%

U.S. Production:
33,300,000 metric tons
(iron content) - 2006

COAL

WYOMING 38.4%

WEST VIRGINIA 13.1

KENTUCKY 10.4

Wa. 5.7

Tx. 3.9

Mt. 3.6

Co. 3.1

In. 3.0

Il. 2.4

Nd. 2.2

OTHER 4.3

U.S. Production:
1,054,824,000 metric tons - 2006

M-101006-1 © Rand McNally

NORTH SLOPE

Arctic Circle

TransAlaska Pipeline

Same scale as main map

Sources: Energy Information Administration;
U.S. Geological Survey

Albers Equal Area Conic Projection
Scale 1:29,000,000
One inch to 457 miles
One cm to 290 km

PETROLEUM

U.S. Production: 254,060,000 metric tons - 2006
Canada Production: 163,218,000 metric tons - 2006

OFFSHORE* 26.9%	TEXAS 21.3	ALASKA 14.5	Ca. 12.0	4.0	3.4	3.2	2.8	2.1	OTHER 9.8

* Federal offshore not included in any state

NATURAL GAS

U.S. Production: 538,834,213,000 cubic meters - 2006
Canada Production: 185,416,772,000 cubic meters - 2006

TEXAS 28.4%	GULF OF MEXICO 15.0	Wy. 9.4	Ok. 8.7	N.M. 8.3	La. 7.0	Co. 6.2	OTHER 14.7

PETROLEUM

Major Producing Area

Major Fields

Minor Fields

IRON ORE

Major Producing Deposit

Other Important Deposits

Minor Deposits

NATURAL GAS

Major Fields

COAL AND LIGNITE

BITUMINOUS COAL
Major Deposit   Minor Deposit

SUB-BITUMINOUS COAL
Major Deposit   Minor Deposit

ANTHRACITE

LIGNITE

Note: One metric ton of crude oil is equal to 7.33 barrels.

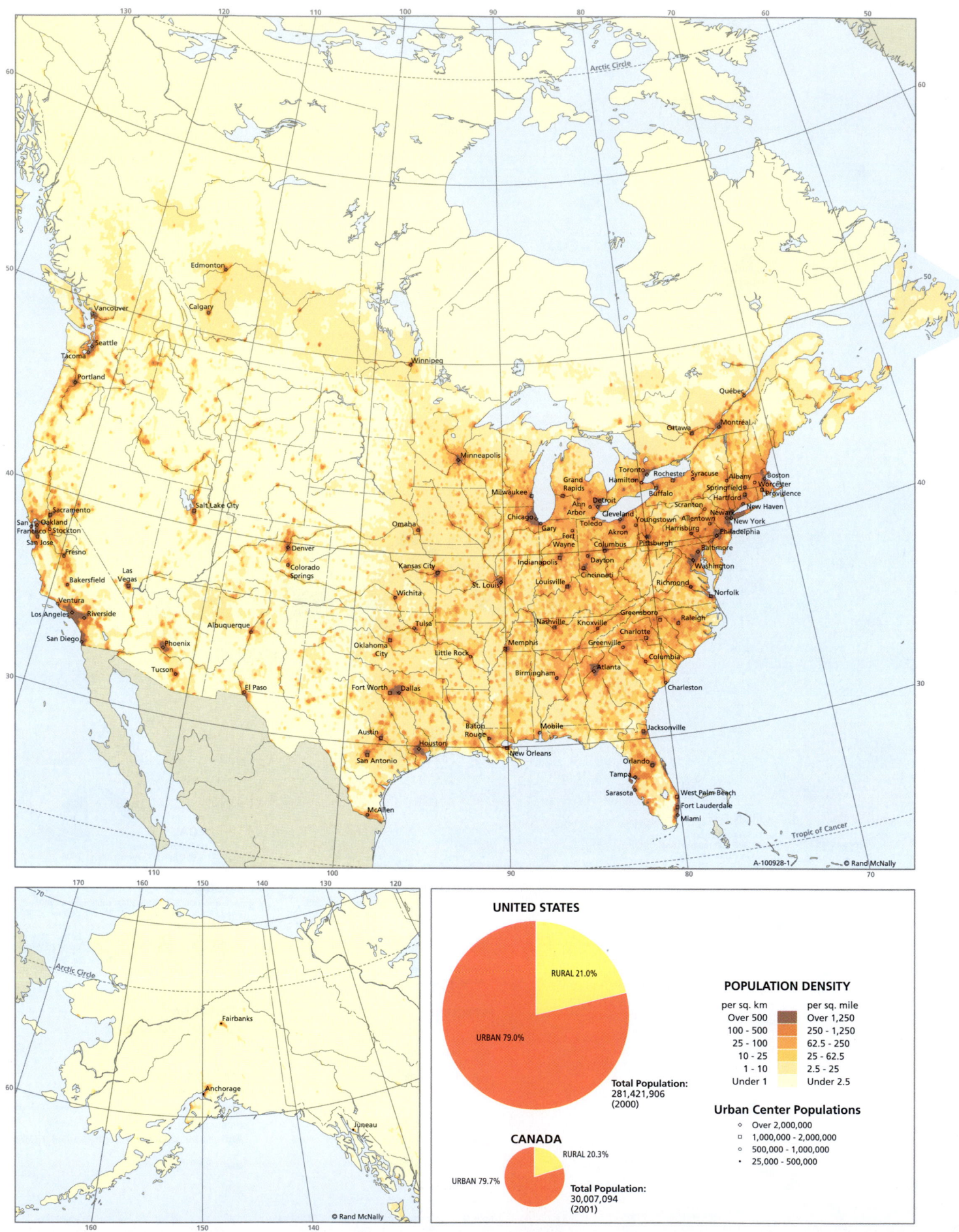

UNITED STATES

RURAL 21.0%

URBAN 79.0%

Total Population:
281,421,906
(2000)

CANADA

RURAL 20.3%

URBAN 79.7%

Total Population:
30,007,094
(2001)

POPULATION DENSITY

per sq. km	per sq. mile
Over 500	Over 1,250
100 - 500	250 - 1,250
25 - 100	62.5 - 250
10 - 25	25 - 62.5
1 - 10	2.5 - 25
Under 1	Under 2.5

Urban Center Populations

◇ Over 2,000,000
□ 1,000,000 - 2,000,000
○ 500,000 - 1,000,000
• 25,000 - 500,000

Sources: Census of Canada; U.S. Census Bureau;
U.S. Department of Energy

Albers Equal Area Conic Projection
Scale 1:29,000,000
One inch to 457 miles
One cm to 290 km

© Rand McNally
A-100928-1

WHITE POPULATION

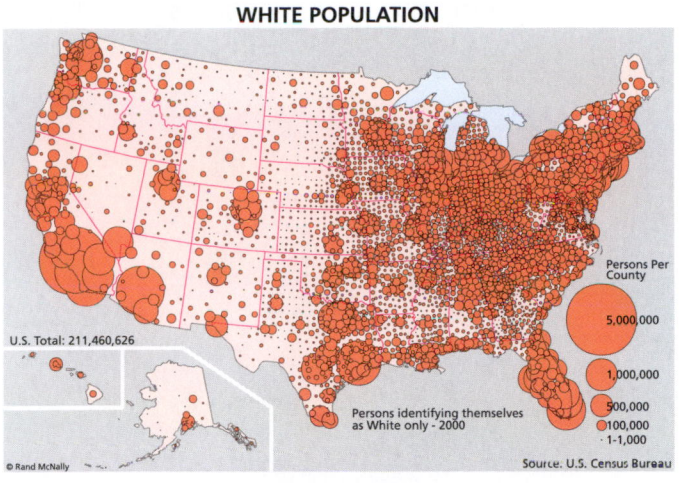

U.S. Total: 211,460,626

Persons Per County

5,000,000
1,000,000
500,000
100,000
· 1-1,000

Persons identifying themselves as White only - 2000

Source: U.S. Census Bureau

© Rand McNally

AFRICAN AMERICAN POPULATION

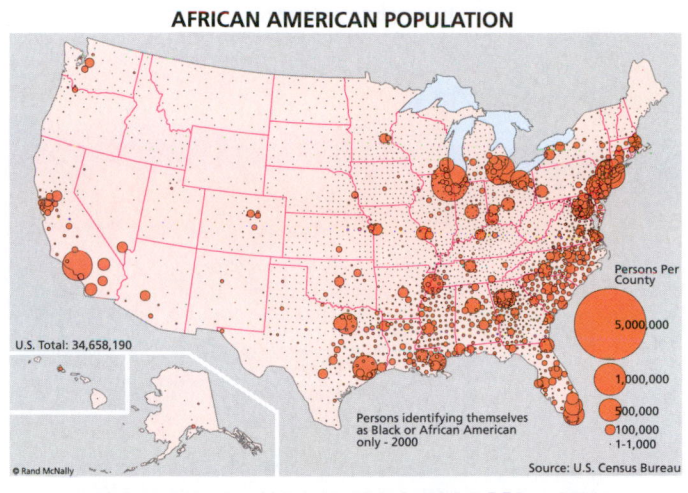

U.S. Total: 34,658,190

Persons Per County

5,000,000
1,000,000
500,000
100,000
· 1-1,000

Persons identifying themselves as Black or African American only - 2000

Source: U.S. Census Bureau

© Rand McNally

ASIAN POPULATION

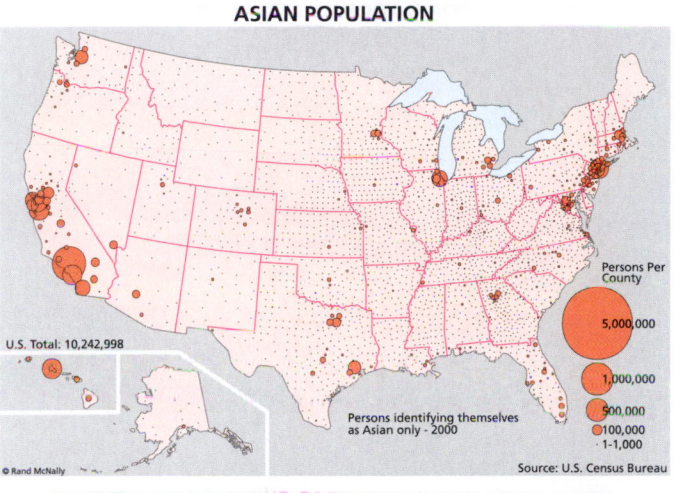

U.S. Total: 10,242,998

Persons Per County

5,000,000
1,000,000
500,000
100,000
· 1-1,000

Persons identifying themselves as Asian only - 2000

Source: U.S. Census Bureau

© Rand McNally

AMERICAN INDIAN AND ALASKA NATIVE POPULATION

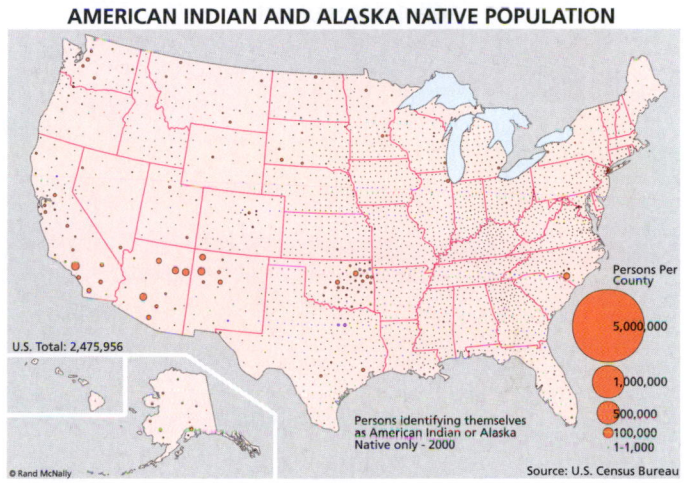

U.S. Total: 2,475,956

Persons Per County

5,000,000
1,000,000
500,000
100,000
· 1-1,000

Persons identifying themselves as American Indian or Alaska Native only - 2000

Source: U.S. Census Bureau

© Rand McNally

NATIVE HAWAIIAN AND PACIFIC ISLANDER POPULATION

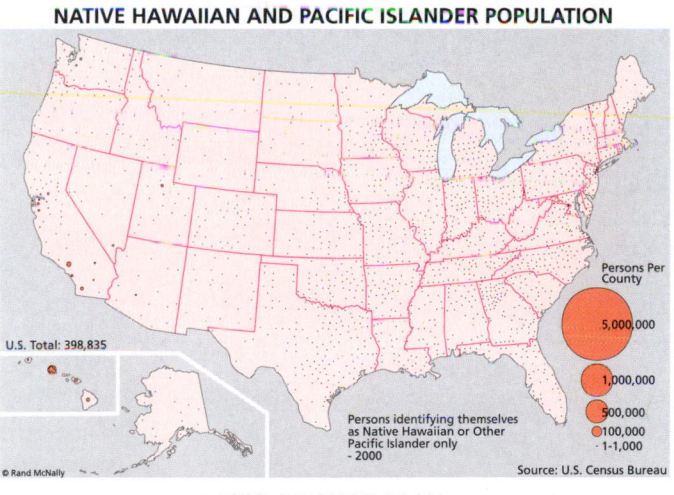

U.S. Total: 398,835

Persons Per County

5,000,000
1,000,000
500,000
100,000
· 1-1,000

Persons identifying themselves as Native Hawaiian or Other Pacific Islander only - 2000

Source: U.S. Census Bureau

© Rand McNally

SOME OTHER RACE

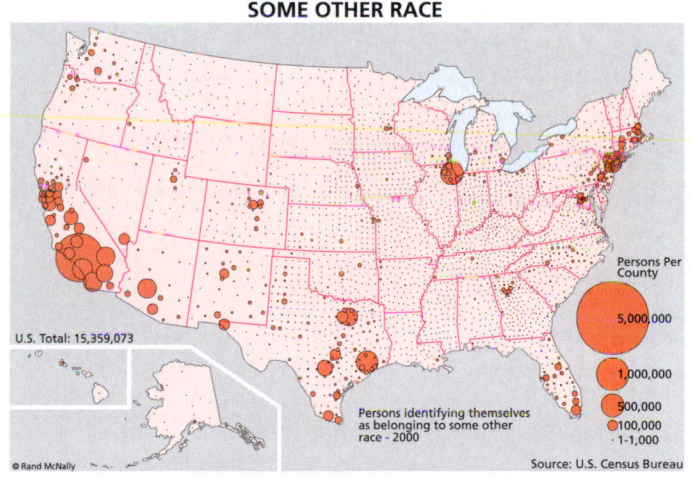

U.S. Total: 15,359,073

Persons Per County

5,000,000
1,000,000
500,000
100,000
· 1-1,000

Persons identifying themselves as belonging to some other race - 2000

Source: U.S. Census Bureau

© Rand McNally

TWO OR MORE RACES

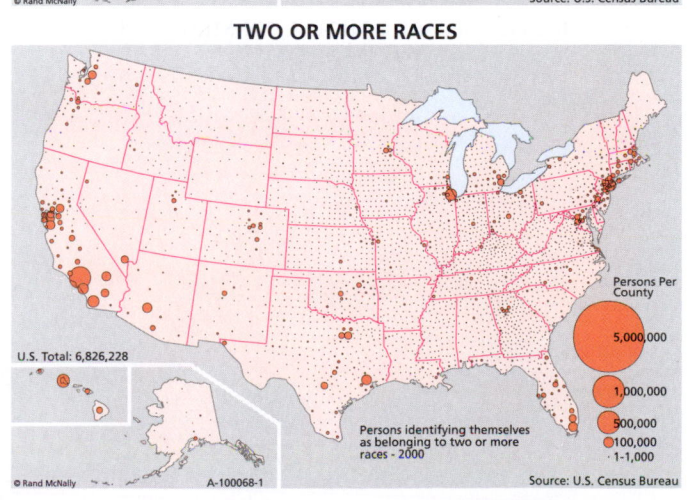

U.S. Total: 6,826,228

Persons Per County

5,000,000
1,000,000
500,000
100,000
· 1-1,000

Persons identifying themselves as belonging to two or more races - 2000

Source: U.S. Census Bureau

© Rand McNally   A-100068-1

HISPANIC POPULATION (ANY RACE)

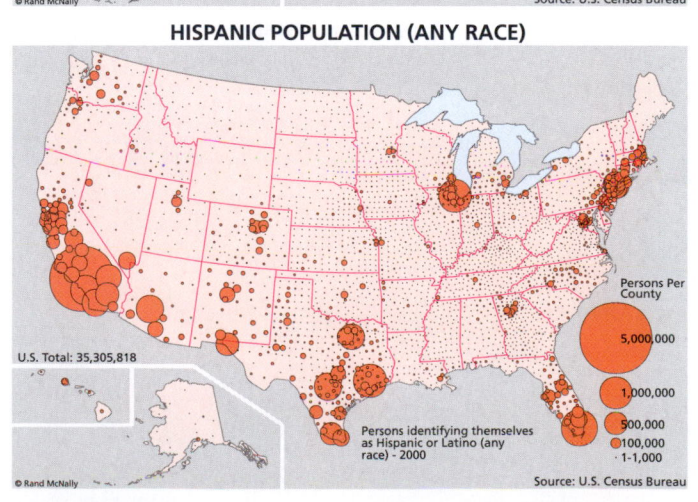

U.S. Total: 35,305,818

Persons Per County

5,000,000
1,000,000
500,000
100,000
· 1-1,000

Persons identifying themselves as Hispanic or Latino (any race) - 2000

Source: U.S. Census Bureau

© Rand McNally

POPULATION CHANGE

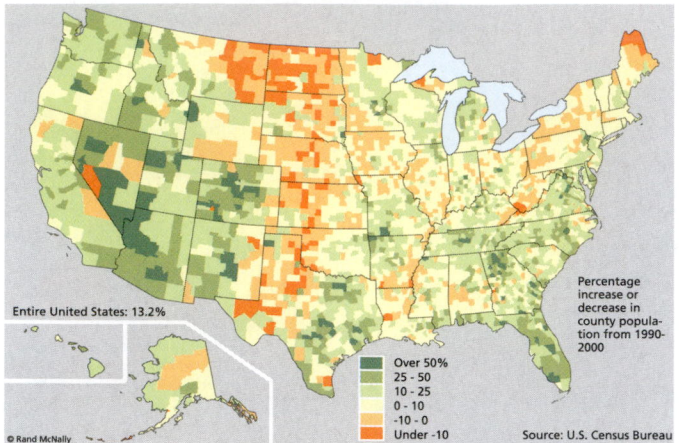

Percentage increase or decrease in county population from 1990-2000

Entire United States: 13.2%

Over 50%
25 - 50
10 - 25
0 - 10
-10 - 0
Under -10

© Rand McNally

Source: U.S. Census Bureau

INTER-STATE POPULATION SHIFTS

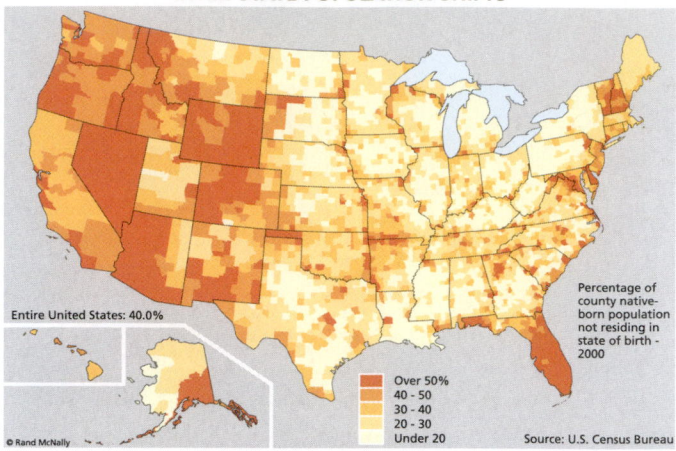

Percentage of county native-born population not residing in state of birth - 2000

Entire United States: 40.0%

Over 50%
40 - 50
30 - 40
20 - 30
Under 20

© Rand McNally

Source: U.S. Census Bureau

POPULATION UNDER 18

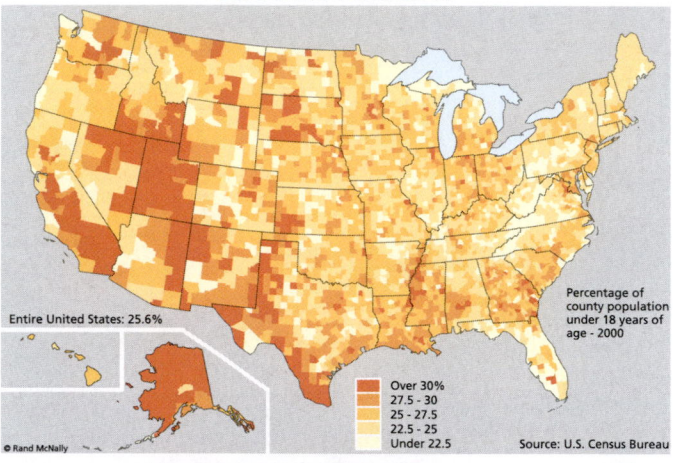

Percentage of county population under 18 years of age - 2000

Entire United States: 25.6%

Over 30%
27.5 - 30
25 - 27.5
22.5 - 25
Under 22.5

© Rand McNally

Source: U.S. Census Bureau

POPULATION 65 AND OVER

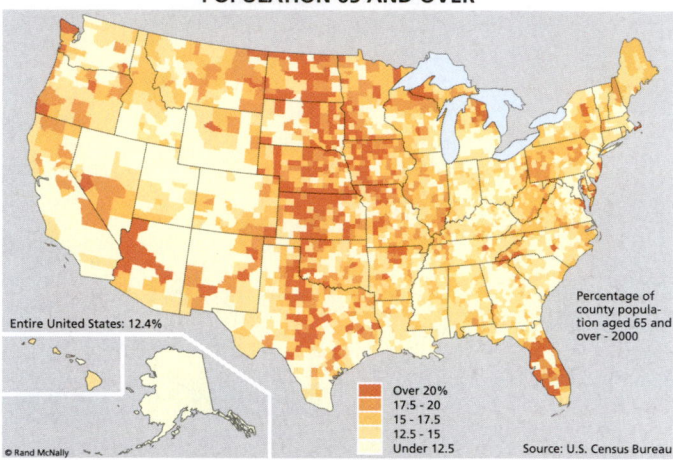

Percentage of county population aged 65 and over - 2000

Entire United States: 12.4%

Over 20%
17.5 - 20
15 - 17.5
12.5 - 15
Under 12.5

© Rand McNally

Source: U.S. Census Bureau

EDUCATIONAL ATTAINMENT RATE

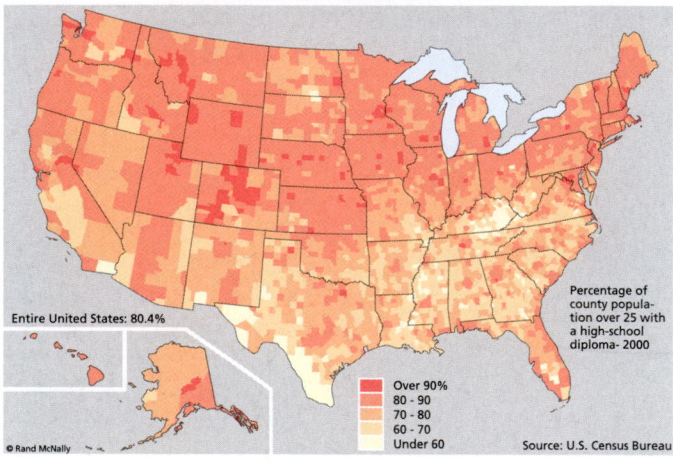

Percentage of county population over 25 with a high-school diploma- 2000

Entire United States: 80.4%

Over 90%
80 - 90
70 - 80
60 - 70
Under 60

© Rand McNally

Source: U.S. Census Bureau

COLLEGE ENROLLMENT RATE

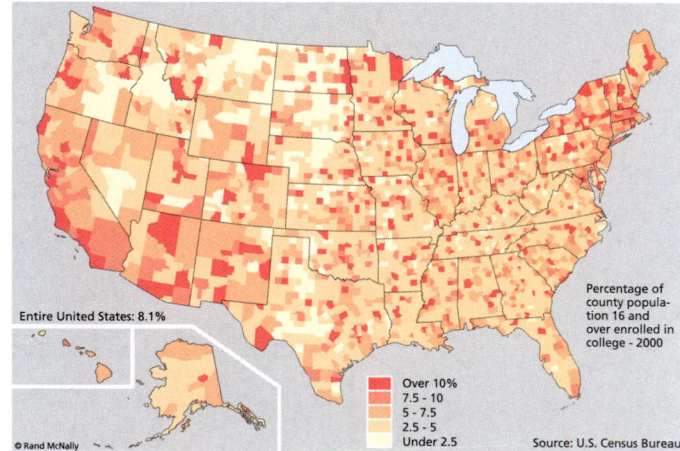

Percentage of county population 16 and over enrolled in college - 2000

Entire United States: 8.1%

Over 10%
7.5 - 10
5 - 7.5
2.5 - 5
Under 2.5

© Rand McNally

Source: U.S. Census Bureau

COMMUTING TIME

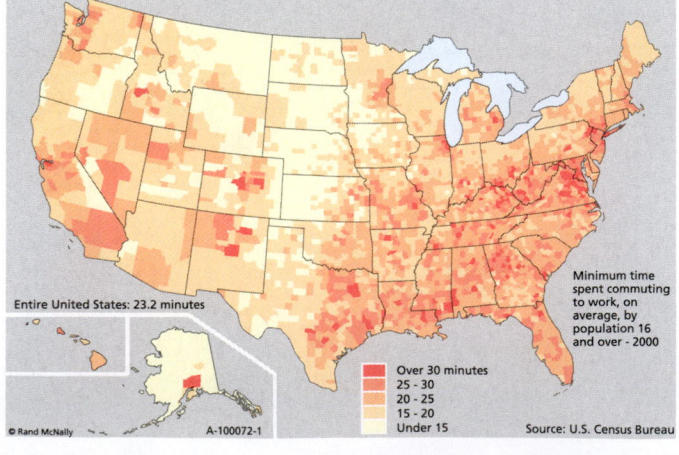

Minimum time spent commuting to work, on average, by population 16 and over - 2000

Entire United States: 23.2 minutes

Over 30 minutes
25 - 30
20 - 25
15 - 20
Under 15

© Rand McNally   A-100072-1

Source: U.S. Census Bureau

MEDIAN DECADE OF HOUSE CONSTRUCTION

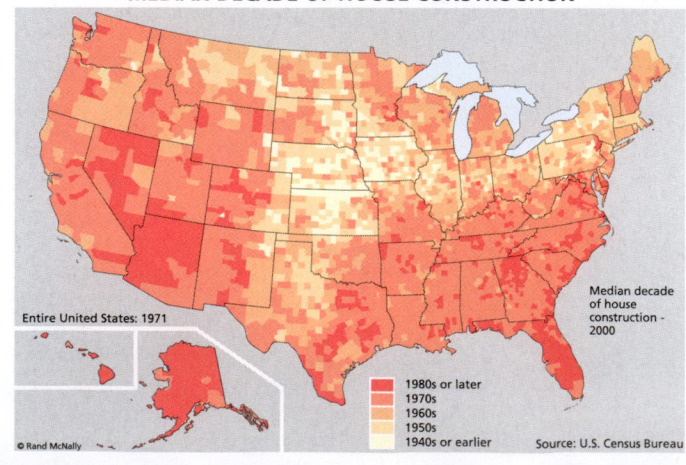

Median decade of house construction - 2000

Entire United States: 1971

1980s or later
1970s
1960s
1950s
1940s or earlier

© Rand McNally

Source: U.S. Census Bureau

WOMEN'S MEDIAN EARNINGS

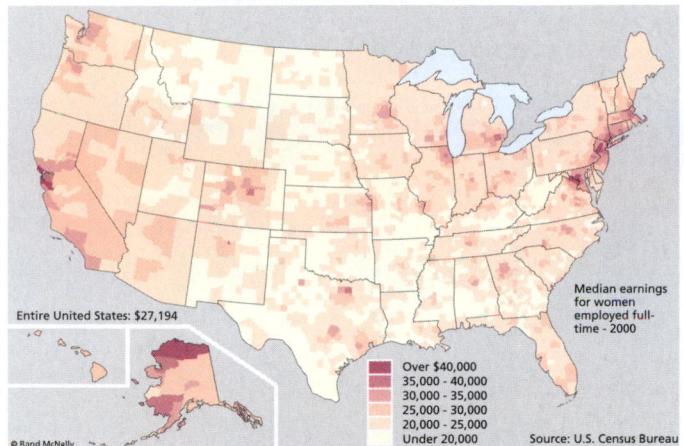

Entire United States: $27,194

Median earnings for women employed full-time - 2000

Over $40,000
35,000 - 40,000
30,000 - 35,000
25,000 - 30,000
20,000 - 25,000
Under 20,000

© Rand McNally

Source: U.S. Census Bureau

MEN'S MEDIAN EARNINGS

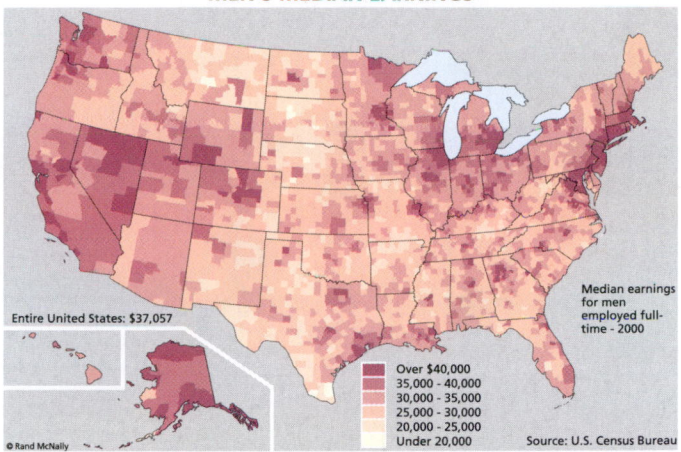

Entire United States: $37,057

Median earnings for men employed full-time - 2000

Over $40,000
35,000 - 40,000
30,000 - 35,000
25,000 - 30,000
20,000 - 25,000
Under 20,000

© Rand McNally

Source: U.S. Census Bureau

RATIO OF WOMEN'S TO MEN'S EARNINGS

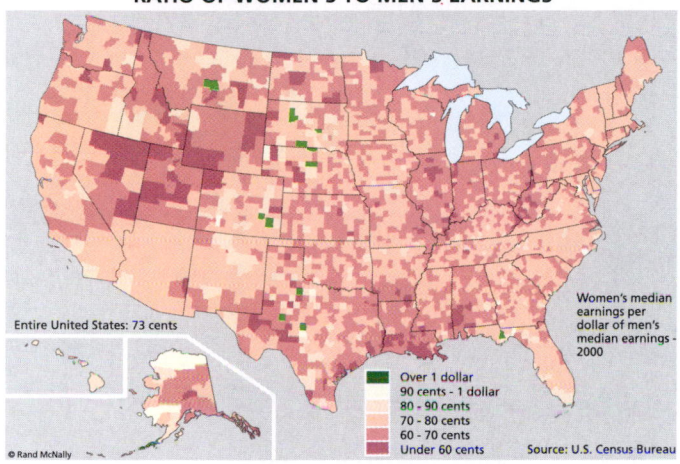

Entire United States: 73 cents

Women's median earnings per dollar of men's median earnings - 2000

Over 1 dollar
90 cents - 1 dollar
80 - 90 cents
70 - 80 cents
60 - 70 cents
Under 60 cents

© Rand McNally

Source: U.S. Census Bureau

MEDIAN HOUSEHOLD INCOME

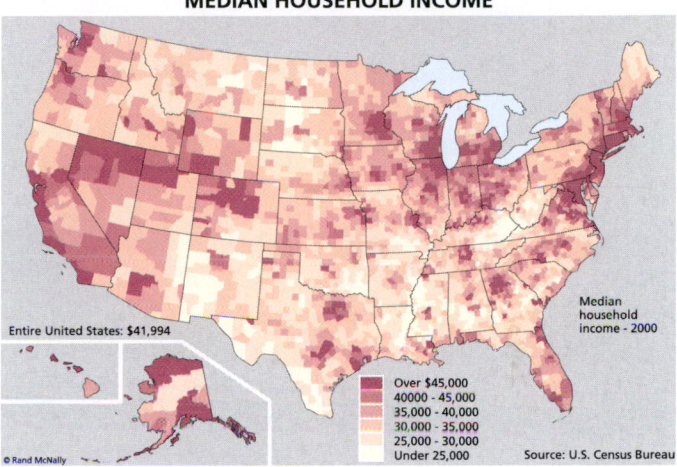

Entire United States: $41,994

Median household income - 2000

Over $45,000
40000 - 45,000
35,000 - 40,000
30,000 - 35,000
25,000 - 30,000
Under 25,000

© Rand McNally

Source: U.S. Census Bureau

HOUSEHOLDS HEADED BY WOMEN

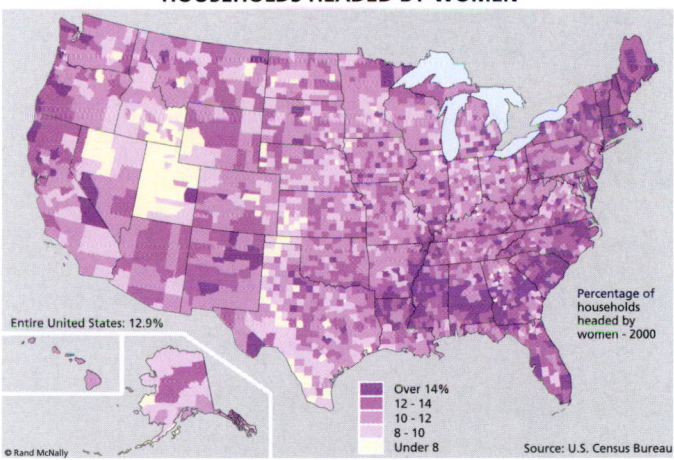

Entire United States: 12.9%

Percentage of households headed by women - 2000

Over 14%
12 - 14
10 - 12
8 - 10
Under 8

© Rand McNally

Source: U.S. Census Bureau

CHILDREN LIVING IN POVERTY

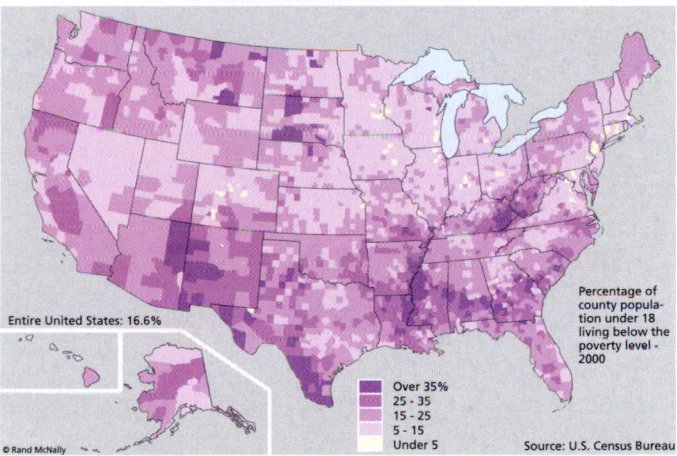

Entire United States: 16.6%

Percentage of county population under 18 living below the poverty level - 2000

Over 35%
25 - 35
15 - 25
5 - 15
Under 5

© Rand McNally

Source: U.S. Census Bureau

UNEMPLOYMENT RATE

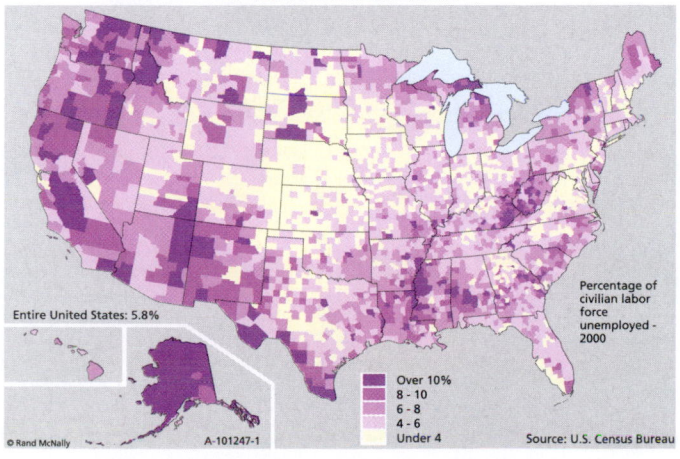

Entire United States: 5.8%

Percentage of civilian labor force unemployed - 2000

Over 10%
8 - 10
6 - 8
4 - 6
Under 4

© Rand McNally

A-101247-1

Source: U.S. Census Bureau

NON-ENGLISH SPEAKING HOUSEHOLDS

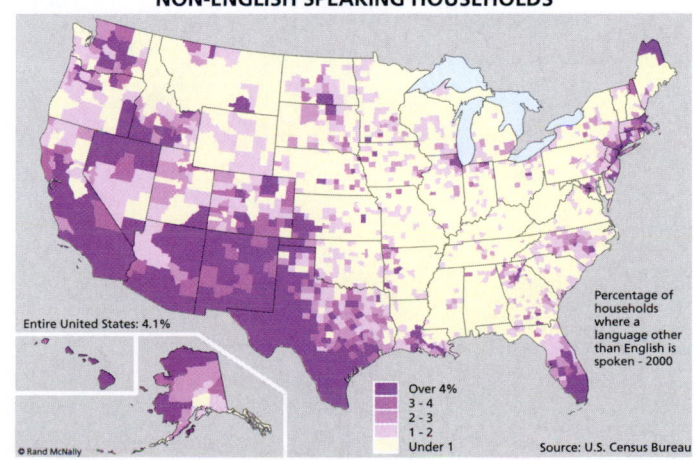

Entire United States: 4.1%

Percentage of households where a language other than English is spoken - 2000

Over 4%
3 - 4
2 - 3
1 - 2
Under 1

© Rand McNally

Source: U.S. Census Bureau

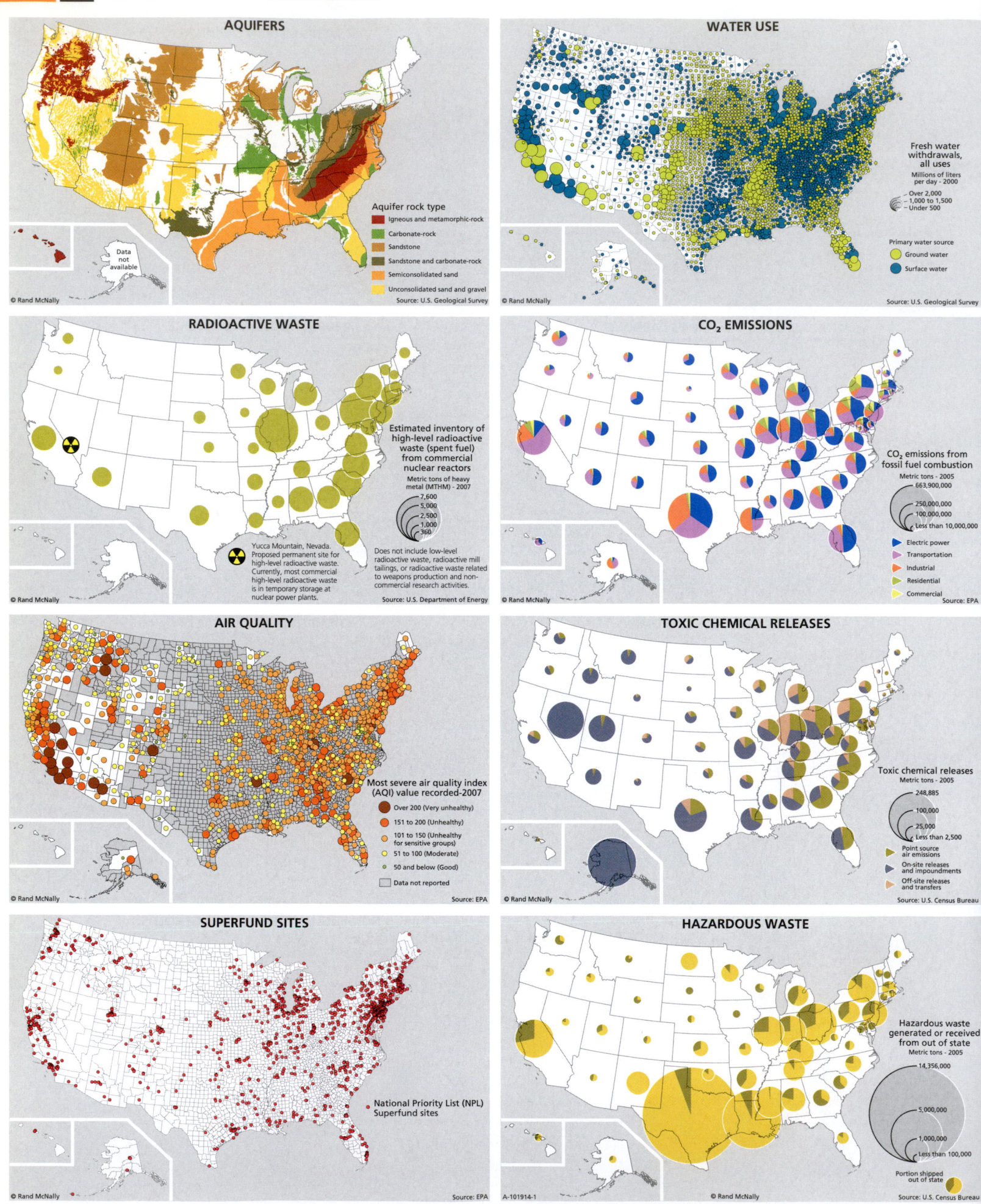

AQUIFERS

Aquifer rock type
- Igneous and metamorphic-rock
- Carbonate-rock
- Sandstone
- Sandstone and carbonate-rock
- Semiconsolidated sand
- Unconsolidated sand and gravel

Data not available

© Rand McNally

Source: U.S. Geological Survey

WATER USE

Fresh water withdrawals, all uses
Millions of liters per day - 2000
- Over 2,000
- 1,000 to 1,500
- Under 500

Primary water source
- Ground water
- Surface water

© Rand McNally

Source: U.S. Geological Survey

RADIOACTIVE WASTE

Estimated inventory of high-level radioactive waste (spent fuel) from commercial nuclear reactors
Metric tons of heavy metal (MTHM) - 2007
- 7,600
- 5,000
- 2,500
- 1,000
- 360

Yucca Mountain, Nevada. Proposed permanent site for high-level radioactive waste. Currently, most commercial high-level radioactive waste is in temporary storage at nuclear power plants.

Does not include low-level radioactive waste, radioactive mill tailings, or radioactive waste related to weapons production and non-commercial research activities.

© Rand McNally

Source: U.S. Department of Energy

CO₂ EMISSIONS

CO₂ emissions from fossil fuel combustion
Metric tons - 2005
- 663,900,000
- 250,000,000
- 100,000,000
- Less than 10,000,000

- Electric power
- Transportation
- Industrial
- Residential
- Commercial

© Rand McNally

Source: EPA

AIR QUALITY

Most severe air quality index (AQI) value recorded-2007
- Over 200 (Very unhealthy)
- 151 to 200 (Unhealthy)
- 101 to 150 (Unhealthy for sensitive groups)
- 51 to 100 (Moderate)
- 50 and below (Good)
- Data not reported

© Rand McNally

Source: EPA

TOXIC CHEMICAL RELEASES

Toxic chemical releases
Metric tons - 2005
- 248,885
- 100,000
- 25,000
- Less than 2,500

- Point source air emissions
- On-site releases and impoundments
- Off-site releases and transfers

© Rand McNally

Source: U.S. Census Bureau

SUPERFUND SITES

National Priority List (NPL) Superfund sites

© Rand McNally

A-101914-1

Source: EPA

HAZARDOUS WASTE

Hazardous waste generated or received from out of state
Metric tons - 2005
- 14,356,000
- 5,000,000
- 1,000,000
- Less than 100,000

Portion shipped out of state

© Rand McNally

Source: U.S. Census Bureau

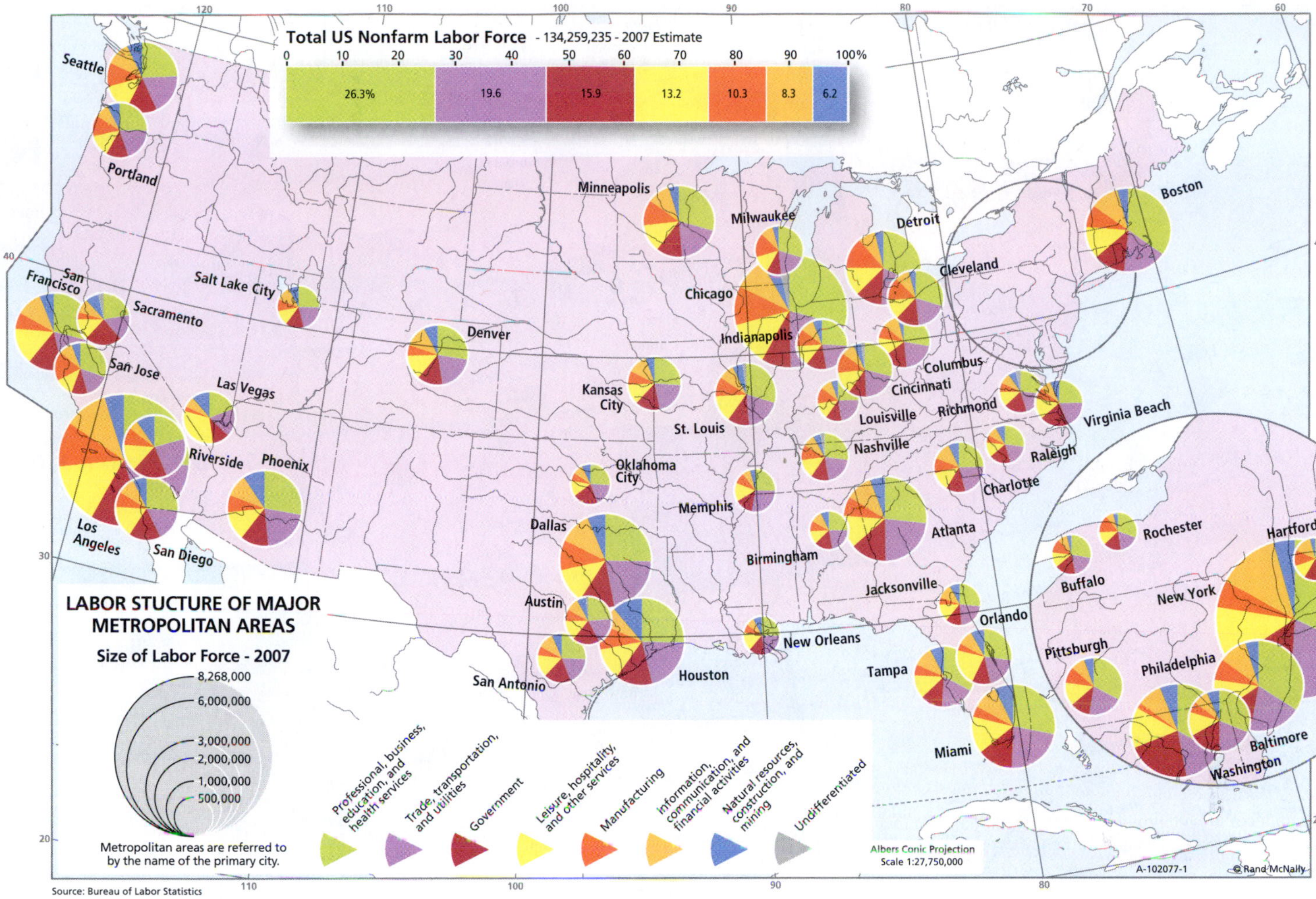

Total US Nonfarm Labor Force - 134,259,235 - 2007 Estimate

0	10	20	30	40	50	60	70	80	90	100%

26.3%	19.6	15.9	13.2	10.3	8.3	6.2

Seattle
Portland
San Francisco
Sacramento
San Jose
Salt Lake City
Las Vegas
Riverside
Phoenix
Los Angeles
San Diego
Denver
Minneapolis
Milwaukee
Chicago
Indianapolis
Detroit
Cleveland
Columbus
Cincinnati
Kansas City
St. Louis
Louisville
Nashville
Richmond
Oklahoma City
Memphis
Dallas
Austin
San Antonio
Birmingham
Atlanta
Charlotte
Raleigh
Virginia Beach
Jacksonville
Orlando
New Orleans
Houston
Tampa
Miami
Boston
Rochester
Buffalo
New York
Pittsburgh
Philadelphia
Hartford
Providence
Baltimore
Washington

LABOR STUCTURE OF MAJOR METROPOLITAN AREAS

Size of Labor Force - 2007

8,268,000
6,000,000
3,000,000
2,000,000
1,000,000
500,000

Metropolitan areas are referred to by the name of the primary city.

- Professional, business, education, and health services
- Trade, transportation, and utilities
- Government
- Leisure hospitality, and other services
- Manufacturing
- Information, communication, and financial activities
- Natural resources, construction, and mining
- Undifferentiated

Albers Conic Projection
Scale 1:27,750,000

A-102077-1 © Rand McNally

Source: Bureau of Labor Statistics

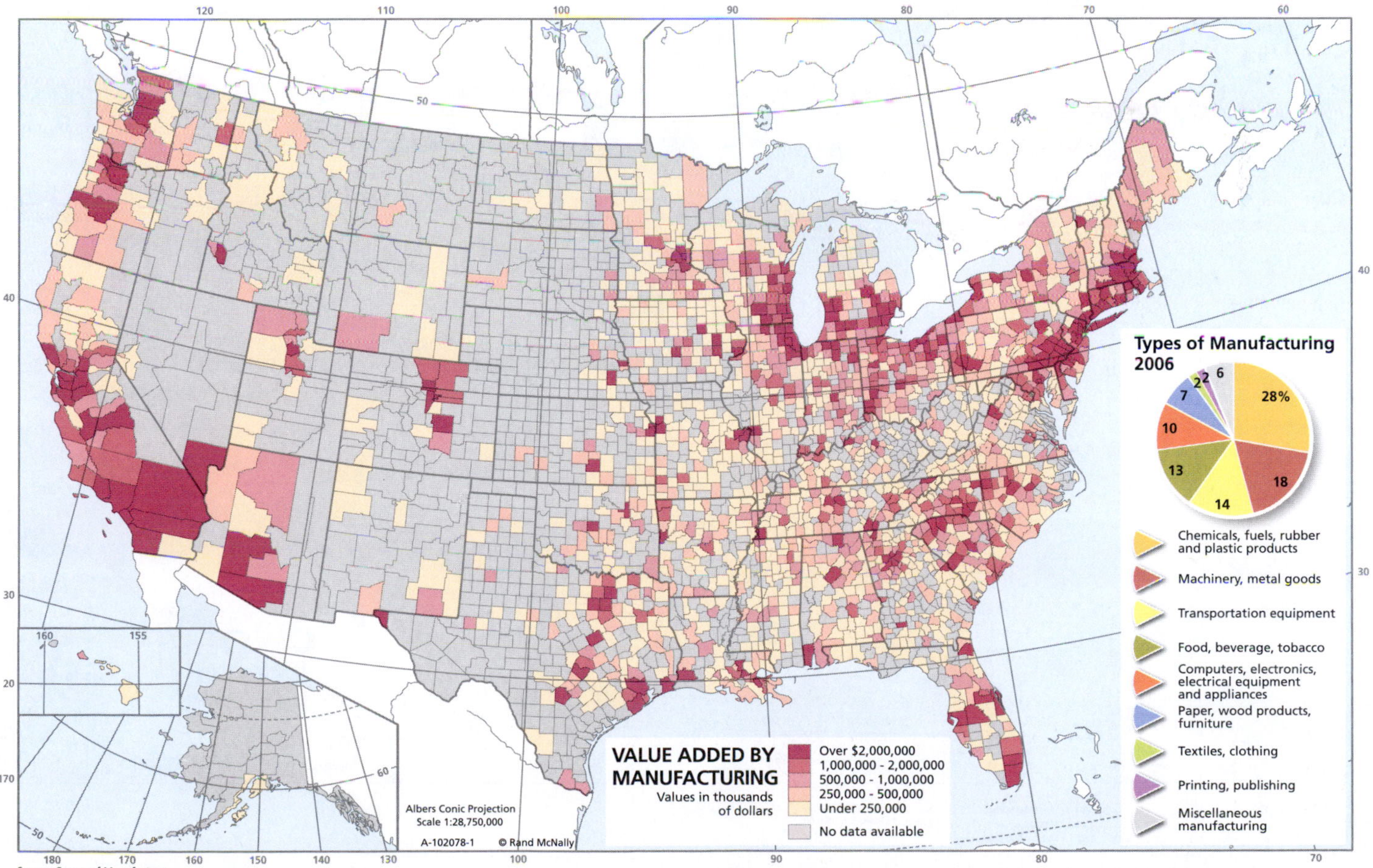

Types of Manufacturing 2006

28%
18
14
13
10
7
2 2 6

- Chemicals, fuels, rubber and plastic products
- Machinery, metal goods
- Transportation equipment
- Food, beverage, tobacco
- Computers, electronics, electrical equipment and appliances
- Paper, wood products, furniture
- Textiles, clothing
- Printing, publishing
- Miscellaneous manufacturing

VALUE ADDED BY MANUFACTURING

Values in thousands of dollars

- Over $2,000,000
- 1,000,000 - 2,000,000
- 500,000 - 1,000,000
- 250,000 - 500,000
- Under 250,000
- No data available

Albers Conic Projection
Scale 1:28,750,000

A-102078-1 © Rand McNally

Source: Census of Manufactures

Lambert Azimuthal Equal Area Projection
Scale 1:12,000,000
One inch to 190 miles
One cm to 120 km

© Rand McNally
A-101613-1

0 60 120 180 240 300 360 Miles

0 60 120 180 240 300 360 420 480 540 600 Kilometers

0   60   120   180   240   300   360 Miles

0   60   120   180   240   300   360   420   480   540   600 Kilometers

Lambert Azimuthal Equal Area Projection
Scale 1:12,000,000
One inch to 190 miles
One cm to 120 km

A
CANADA
ONTARIO
A
QUÉBEC
NEW BRUNSWICK

Lake of the Woods
Lake St. Joseph
Lake Nipigon
Lac Seul
Winnipeg
Rainy
Upper Red Lake
Lower Red Lake
MINNESOTA
Leech Lake
Mille Lacs Lake
Duluth
Minneapolis
Minnesota
Mississippi
Sioux Falls
Omaha
Des Moines
IOWA
S
Topeka
Kansas City
MISSOURI
St Louis
Kansas
Missouri
Lake of the Ozarks
OZARK PLATEAU
Memphis
HOMA
ARKANSAS
BOSTON MTS.
OUACHITA MTS.
Little Rock
Arkansas
Ouachita
Dallas
Sabine
Red
Neches
Trinity
Brazos
Houston
PLAINS
PADRE ISLAND
GALVESTON ISLAND
Toledo Bend Reservoir
LOUISIANA
New Orleans
MISSISSIPPI DELTA
Lake Pontchartrain
Mobile

Lake Nipissing
Sault Ste. Marie
ISLE ROYALE
MICHIPICOTEN ISLAND
KEWEENAW POINT
KEWEENAW PEN.
LAKE SUPERIOR
MICHIGAN
Green Bay
BEAVER ISLAND
DOOR PEN.
WISCONSIN
Lake Winnebago
Wisconsin
Milwaukee
Chicago
Rock
Fox
MANITOULIN ISLAND
Georgian Bay
LAKE HURON
Saginaw Bay
Lake St. Clair
Grand
Muskegon
LAKE MICHIGAN
Detroit
Kankakee
Maumee
LAKE ERIE
Cleveland
ILLINOIS
INDIANA
Columbus
OHIO
Wabash
Indianapolis
Cincinnati
Illinois
Mississippi
Kaskaskia
KENTUCKY
Ohio
Green
Cumberland
Nashville
TENNESSEE
Tennessee
Birmingham
Tombigbee
ALABAMA
Alabama
Tallapoosa
Coosa
GEORGIA
Atlanta
Chattahoochee
Flint
FLORIDA

Ottawa
Matawin
Abitibi
Mississagi
Missinaibi
Lake Abitibi
Réservoir Gouin
Saguenay
Lac Saint-Jean
St. Maurice
Gatineau
Réservoir Cabonga
Ottawa
Montréal
Québec
LES LAURENTIDES
Richelieu
Saint John
Bay of Fundy
N.S.
PEI
NEW
Mt Katahdin 5268 ft 1606 m
MAINE
Penobscot
Mt Washington 6288 ft 1917 m
N.H.
Portland
Gulf of Maine
Lake Champlain
ADIRONDACK MTS.
Ottawa
St. Lawrence
Lake Ontario
Buffalo
NEW YORK
PLATEAU
Allegheny
Genesee
CATSKILL MTS.
Hartford
MASS.
Boston
CAPE COD
NANTUCKET ISLAND
MARTHA'S VINEYARD
CONN. R.I.
LONG ISLAND
New York
Lake Simcoe
Lake Ontario
MOUNTAINS
PENNSYLVANIA
Pittsburgh
Susquehanna
Philadelphia
NEW JERSEY
DELMARVA PENINSULA
CAPE MAY
DEL.
Delaware Bay
Allegheny
Monongahela
WEST VIRGINIA
Spruce Knob 4863 ft 1482 m
Keeney Knob 3927 ft 1197 m
Kanawha
Potomac
MARYLAND
Washington
Chesapeake Bay
CAPE CHARLES
James
VIRGINIA
Roanoke
Norfolk
APPALACHIAN
CUMBERLAND PLATEAU
Mt Rogers 5729 ft 1746 m
BLUE RIDGE
Mt Mitchell 6684 ft 2037 m
Clingmans Dome 6643 ft 2025 m
NORTH CAROLINA
Raleigh
HATTERAS ISLAND
CAPE HATTERAS
Yadkin
Neuse
Charlotte
SOUTH CAROLINA
Lake Marion
Santee
CAPE LOOKOUT
Cape Fear
CAPE FEAR
J. Strom Thurmond Res.
Savannah
Charleston
HILTON HEAD ISLAND
CAPE ROMAIN
Altamaha
Ocmulgee
Oconee
St. Marys
Jacksonville
St. Johns
CAPE CANAVERAL
Suwannee
Apalachicola
CAPE SAN BLAS
Tampa
Tampa Bay
Lake Okeechobee
Miami
CAPE ROMANO
CAPE SABLE
KEY WEST
KEY LARGO
FLORIDA KEYS
Straits of Florida
GULF OF MEXICO
ATLANTIC OCEAN
BAHAMAS
GRAND BAHAMA
ABACO
ELEUTHERA
NEW PROVIDENCE
ANDROS
CAT ISLAND
SAN SALVADOR
MANGROVE CAY
GREAT EXUMA
LONG ISLAND
CROOKED ISLAND
Tropic of Cancer

0   20   40   60   80   100   120 Miles
0   20   40   60   80   100   120   140   160   180   200 Kilometers

Lambert Conformal Conic Projection
Scale 1:4,000,000
One inch to 64 miles
One cm to 40 km

States and Provinces

ALBERTA · SASKATCHEWAN · CANADA · UNITED STATES

MONTANA · IDAHO · WYOMING · UTAH · COLORADO

GREAT PLAINS · ROCKY MOUNTAINS · SNAKE RIVER PLAIN

Selected features and places

Waterton Lakes Natl. Park · Blood Indian Reserve · Cardston · Milk River

Glacier National Park · Mt. Cleveland 10,466 ft. 3190 m · Blackfeet Indian Reservation · Cut Bank · Browning · Shelby · Sunburst · Chester · Havre · Chinook · Harlem · Malta · Bowdoin · Glasgow · Wolf Point · Poplar · Culbertson · Sidney

Lewis Range · Swan Range · Lewis and Clark Ra. · Flathead Lake · Flathead Indian Reservation · Polson · Ronan · Kalispell · Whitefish · Columbia Falls · Evergreen · Hungry Horse Reservoir

Missoula · Lolo · Stevensville · Hamilton · Lolo Pass 5,235 ft. 1596 m · Trapper Peak 10,157 ft. 3096 m · Mt. McGuire 10,082 ft. 3073 m

Great Falls · Ulm · Cascade · Helena · East Helena · Townsend · Deer Lodge · Philipsburg · Anaconda · Butte · Whitehall · Boulder · Three Forks · Manhattan · Belgrade · Bozeman · Livingston · Big Timber

Red Mountain 9,411 ft. 2868 m · Mt. Haggin 10,607 ft. 3233 m · Mt. Edith 9,501 ft. 2896 m · Little Belt Mts. · Big Belt Mts. · Crazy Mts. · White Sulphur Springs

Lewistown · Harlowton · Roundup · Forsyth · Miles City · Billings · Laurel · Columbus · Worden · Lockwood · Hardin · Crow Agency · Colstrip · Baker · Glendive · Terry

MONTANA MOUNTAINS · ABSAROKA RANGE · Mt. Wood 12,320 ft. 3755 m · Granite Peak 12,799 ft. 3901 m · Red Lodge · Yellowstone National Park · West Yellowstone · Mt. Holmes 10,336 ft. 3150 m · Gardiner · Big Sky · Ennis Lake · Hebgen Lake · Koch Peak 11,286 ft. 3440 m

Trout Peak 12,244 ft. 3732 m · Cody · Buffalo Bill Reservoir · Powell · Greybull · Basin · Worland · Thermopolis · Cloud Peak 13,167 ft. 4013 m · BIGHORN MTS. · BIGHORN BASIN · Sheridan · Story · Buffalo · Gillette · Moorcroft · Devils Tower Natl. Mon. · Keyhole Reservoir · Little Bighorn Battlefield Natl. Mon. · Crow Indian Reservation · Northern Cheyenne Ind. Res. · Lame Deer · Ranchester · Kaycee

Francs Peak 13,153 ft. 4009 m · Grand Teton National Park · Grand Teton 13,770 ft. 4197 m · Jackson Lake · Jackson · WIND RIVER RANGE · Gannett Peak 13,804 ft. 4207 m · Fremont Lake · Downs Mountain 13,349 ft. 4069 m · Doubletop Peak 11,682 ft. 3561 m · Dubois · Pinedale · Lander · Riverton · Fort Washakie · Wind River Indian Reservation · Boysen Reservoir · SHOSHONE BASIN · Shoshone · Badwater

Wind River Peak 13,192 ft. 4021 m · South Pass 7,549 ft. 2301 m · Casper · North Platte · Evansville · Glenrock · Douglas · Mills · WYOMING

IDAHO · Salmon · Challis · Borah Peak 12,662 ft. 3859 m · Castle Peak 11,815 ft. 3601 m · LOST RIVER RANGE · LEMHI RANGE · BEAVERHEAD MTS. · PIONEER MTS. · ANACONDA RA. · Tweedy Mountain 11,154 ft. 3400 m · Homer Youngs Peak 10,621 ft. 3237 m · Dillon · Lima Reservoir · Clark Canyon Reservoir

SNAKE RIVER PLAIN · Sun Valley · Ketchum · Hailey · Bellevue · Hyndman Peak 12,009 ft. 3660 m · Craters of the Moon Natl. Mon. · Arco · Idaho Falls · Shelley · Ammon · Rexburg · Rigby · Driggs · St. Anthony · Ashton · Palisades Reservoir

Shoshone · Gooding · Wendell · Jerome · Twin Falls · Kimberly · Buhl · Burley · Rupert · Heyburn · American Falls · American Falls Reservoir · Aberdeen · Pocatello · Chubbuck · McCammon · Fort Hall Ind. Res. · Blackfoot · Blackfoot Reservoir · Lake Walcott

Soda Springs · Montpelier · Meade Peak 9,957 ft. 3035 m · Afton · Fontenelle Reservoir · Kemmerer · Diamondville · Fossil Butte Natl. Mon. · Green River · Rock Springs · Flaming Gorge Reservoir · GREAT DIVIDE BASIN · Rawlins · Hanna · Saratoga · Elk Mountain 11,156 ft. 3400 m · MEDICINE BOW MTS. · Medicine Bow Peak 12,013 ft. 3662 m · Bridger Peak 11,004 ft. 3354 m · Laramie · Wheatland · Seminoe Reservoir · Pathfinder Reservoir · Alcova Reservoir · Glendo Reservoir

Malad City · Preston · Smithfield · Logan · Wellsville · Brigham City · North Ogden · Tremonton · BEAR RIVER RANGE · Bear Lake · Evanston · Fort Bridger · Lyman

GREAT SALT LAKE · Great Salt Lake Desert · Pilot Peak 10,716 ft. 3266 m · Wendover · Tooele · Ogden · South Ogden · Roy · Clearfield · Layton · Kaysville · Bountiful · West Valley · Salt Lake City · Murray · Sandy · West Jordan · Heber · UTAH · UINTA MTS. · Kings Peak 13,528 ft. 4123 m · Uintah and Ouray Ind. Res. · Vernal · Dinosaur Natl. Mon.

COLORADO · Rocky Mountain National Park · Longs Peak 14,255 ft. 4345 m · Haques Peak 13,560 ft. 4133 m · Craig · Steamboat Springs · Yampa

Rand McNally
© Rand McNally A-101621-1

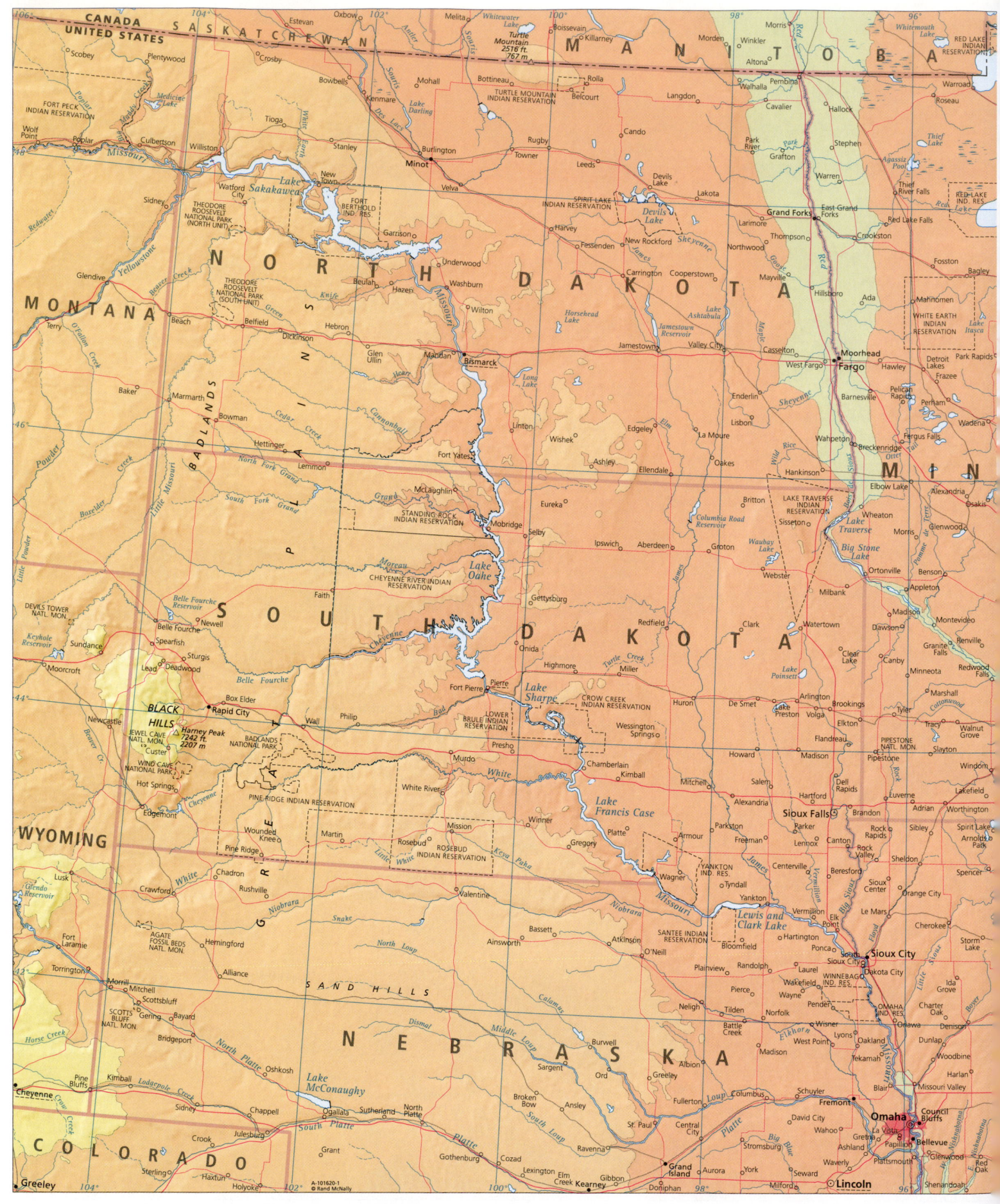

CANADA
UNITED STATES
SASKATCHEWAN

MANITOBA

MONTANA

NORTH DAKOTA

G R E A T   P L A I N S

SOUTH DAKOTA

M I N N

WYOMING

BLACK HILLS

Harney Peak
7242 ft.
2207 m

BADLANDS
NATIONAL PARK

PINE RIDGE INDIAN RESERVATION

S A N D   H I L L S

NEBRASKA

COLORADO

Omaha

Lincoln

A-101620-1
© Rand McNally

| 0 | 20 | 40 | 60 | 80 | 100 | 120 Miles |

| 0 | 20 | 40 | 60 | 80 | 100 | 120 | 140 | 160 | 180 | 200 Kilometers |

Lambert Conformal Conic Projection
Scale 1:4,000,000
One inch to 64 miles
One cm to 40 km

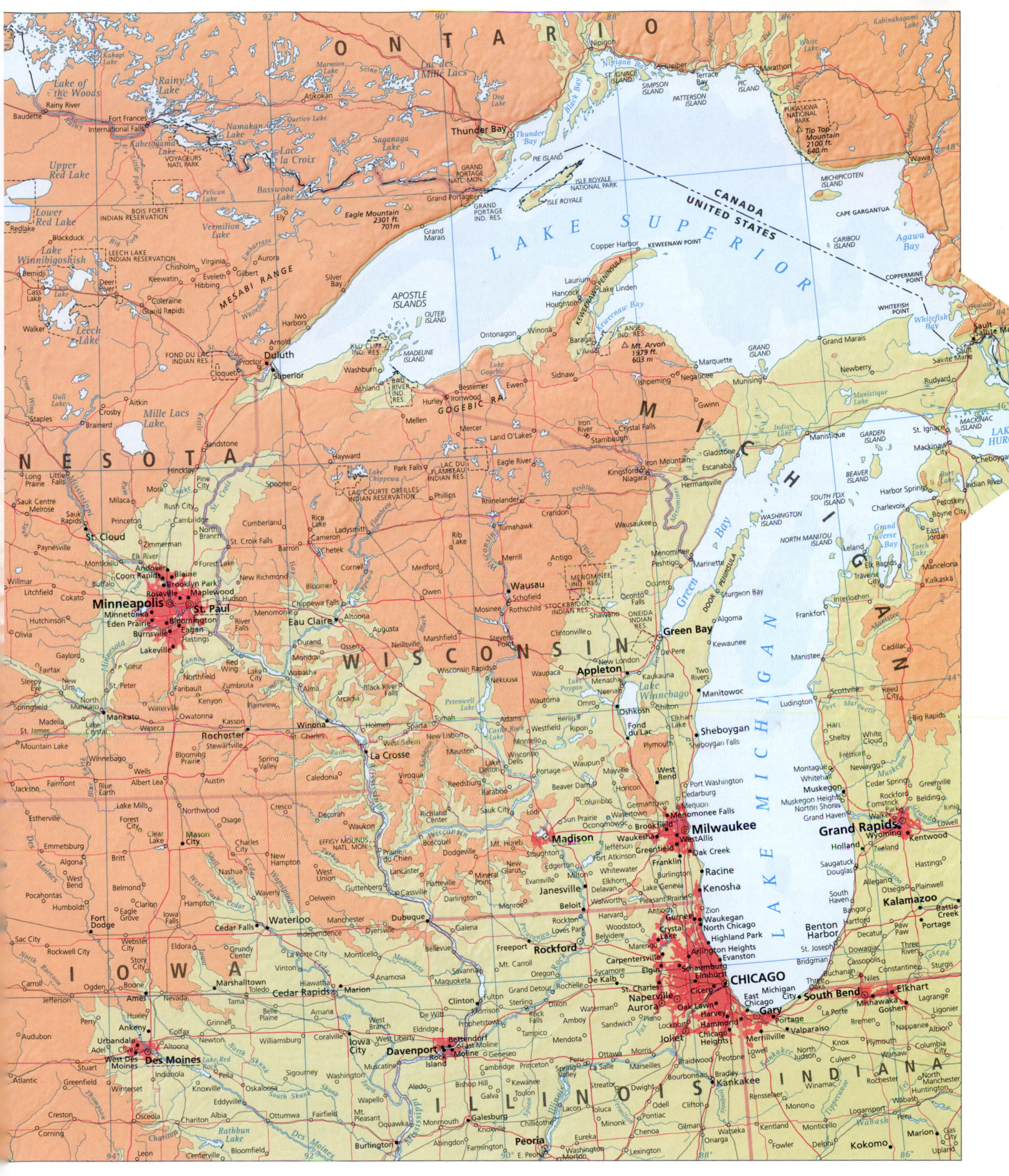

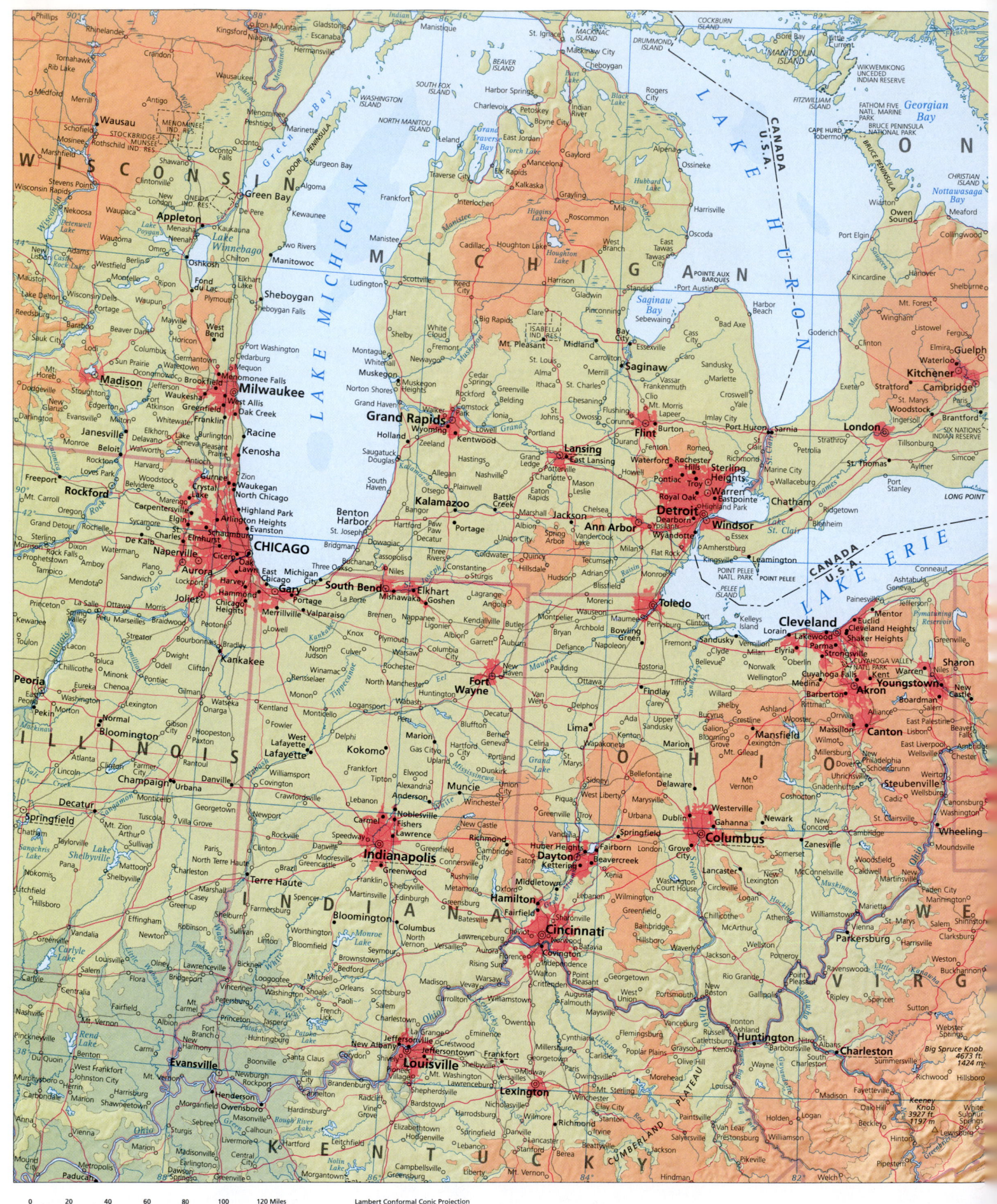

| 0 | 20 | 40 | 60 | 80 | 100 | 120 Miles |
| 0 | 20 | 40 | 60 | 80 | 100 | 120 | 140 | 160 | 180 | 200 Kilometers |

Lambert Conformal Conic Projection
Scale 1:4,000,000
One inch to 64 miles
One cm to 40 km

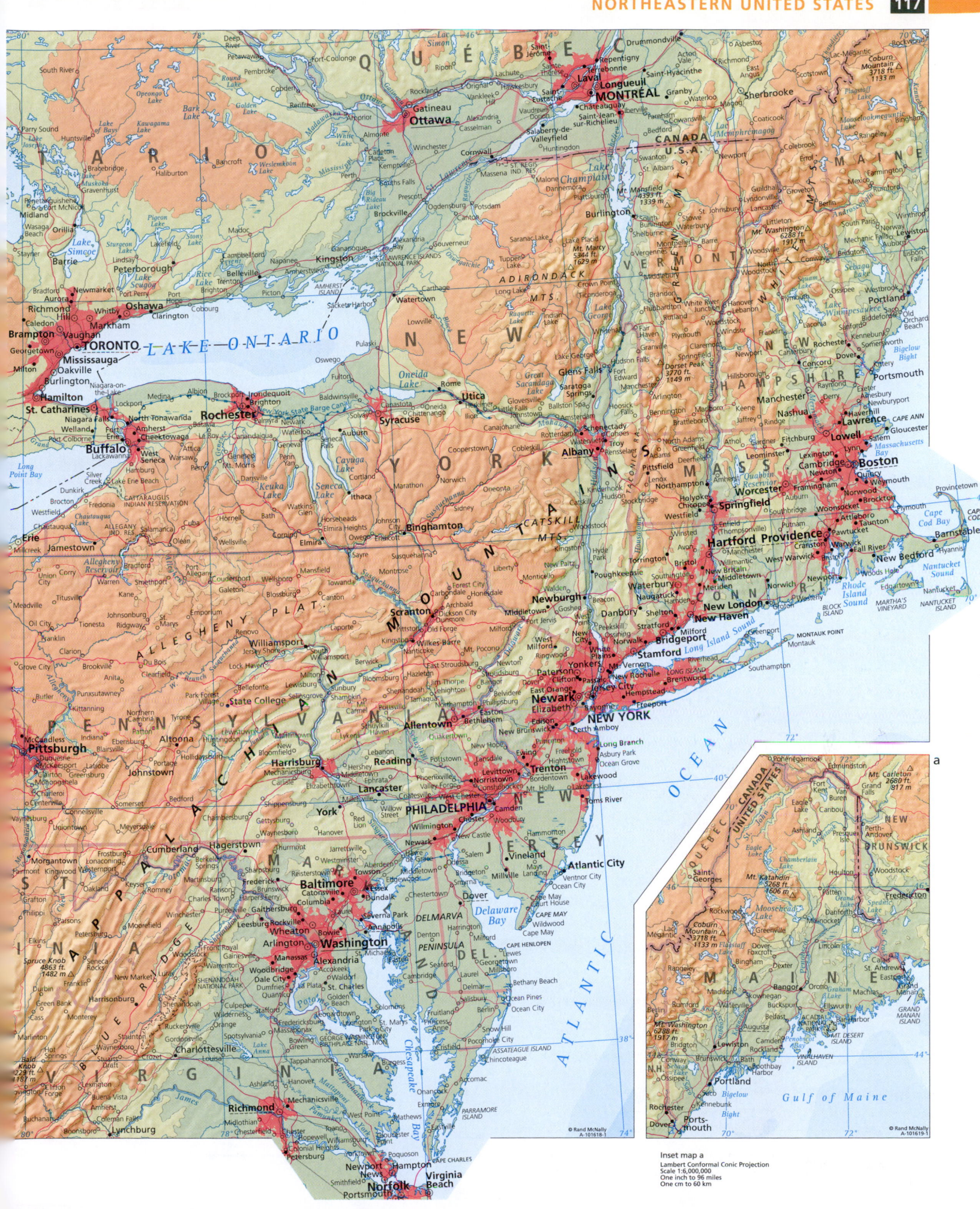

Inset map a
Lambert Conformal Conic Projection
Scale 1:6,000,000
One inch to 96 miles
One cm to 60 km

Inset map a
Lambert Conformal Conic Projection
Scale 1:1,000,000
One inch to 16 miles
One cm to 10 km

Lambert Conformal Conic Projection
Scale 1:4,000,000
One inch to 64 miles
One cm to 40 km

© Rand McNally
A-101623-1

© Rand McNally
A-101622-1

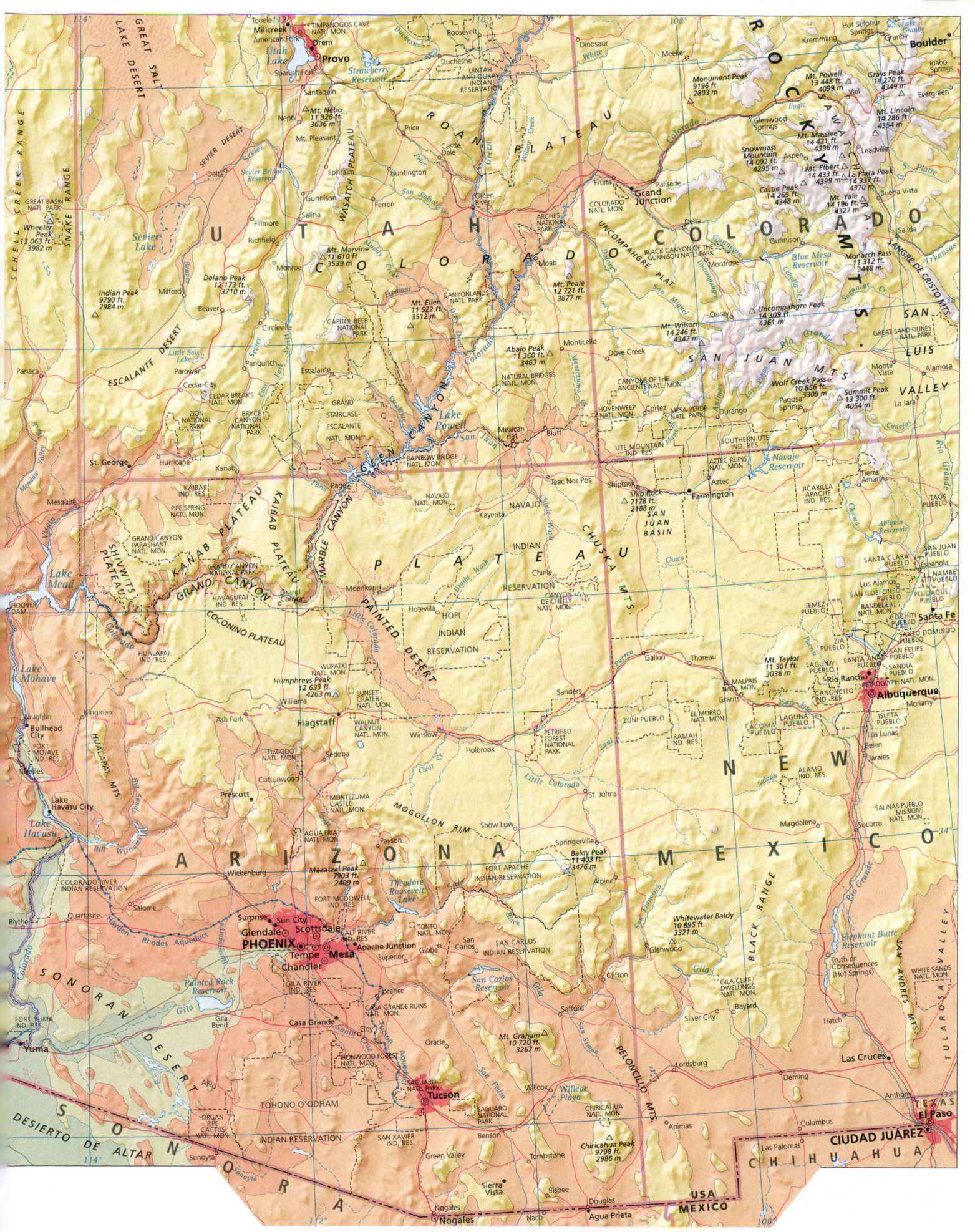

0   20   40   60   80   100   120 Miles

0   20 40 60 80 100 120 140 160 180 200 Kilometers

Lambert Conformal Conic Projection
Scale 1:4,000,000
One inch to 64 miles
One cm to 40 km

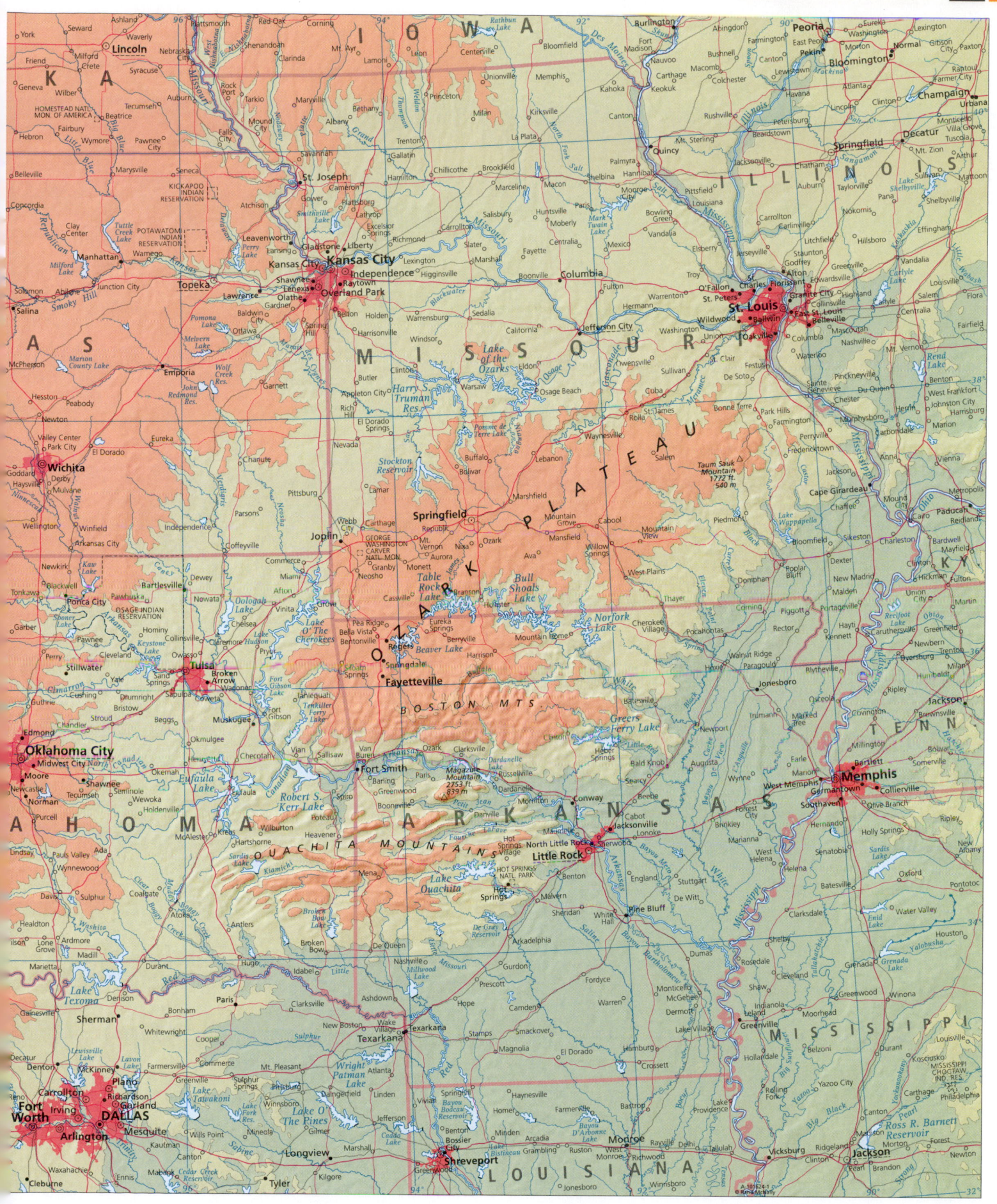

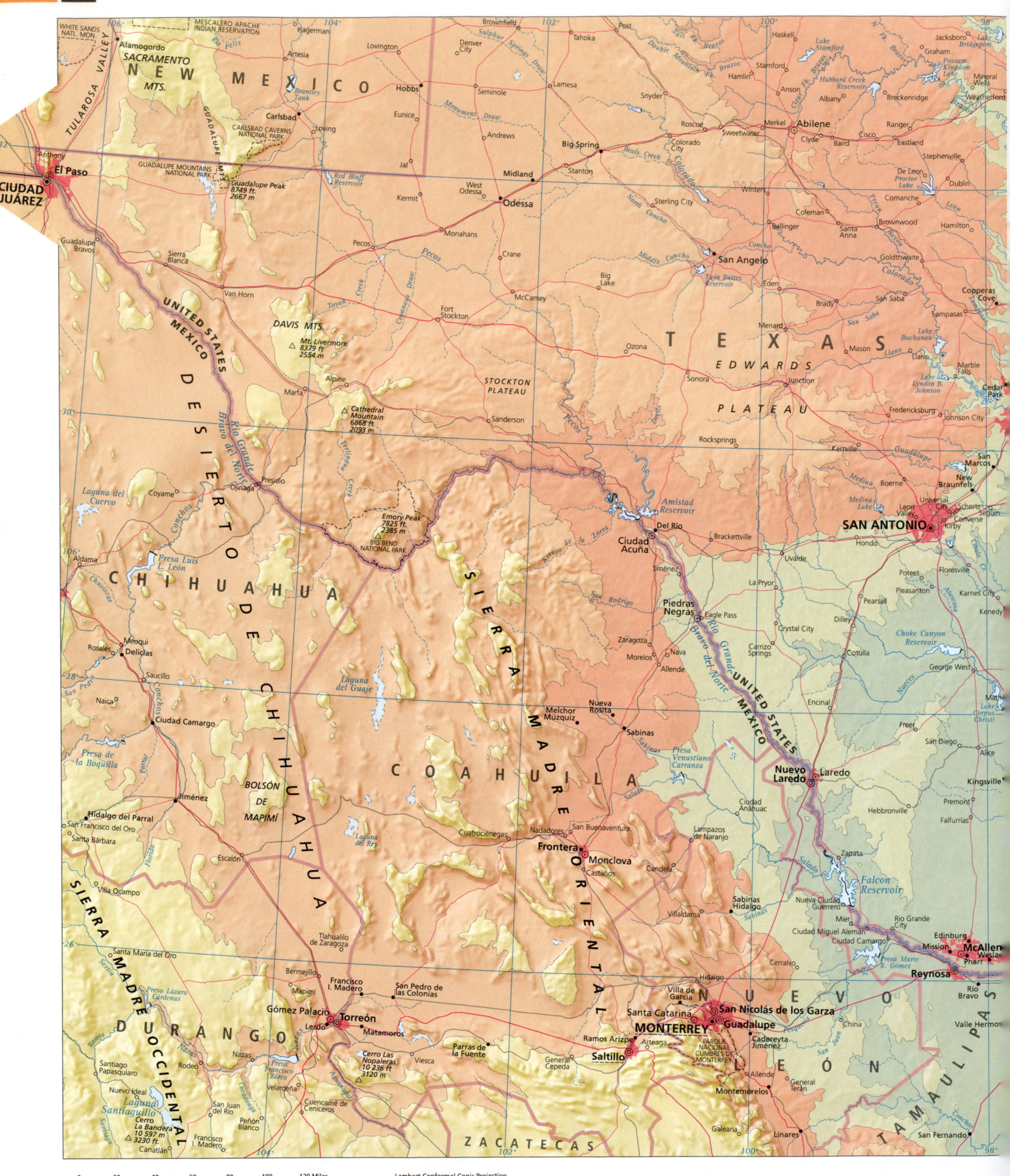

Lambert Conformal Conic Projection
Scale 1:4,000,000
One inch to 64 miles
One cm to 40 km

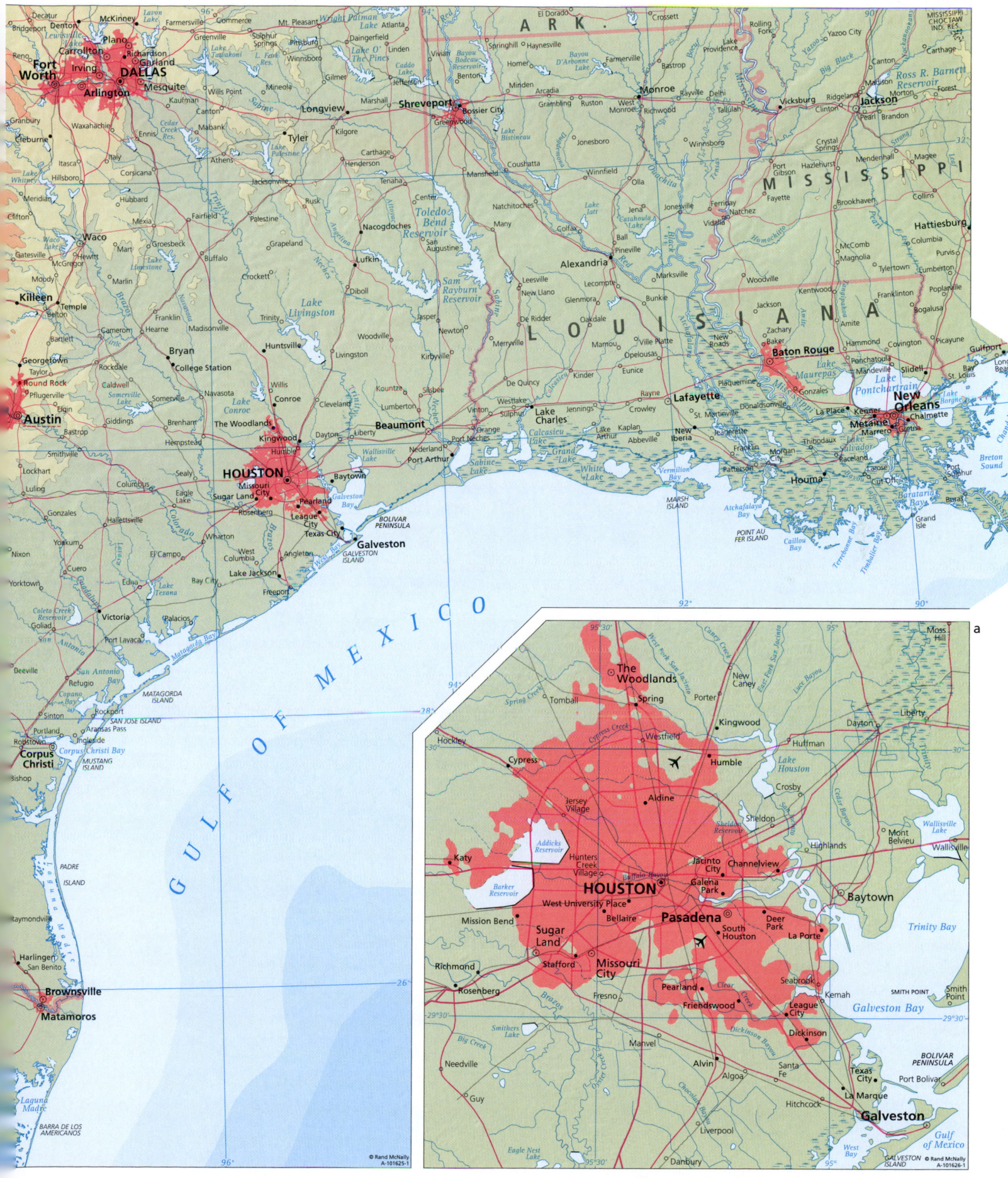

Inset map a
Lambert Conformal Conic Projection
Scale 1:1,000,000
One inch to 16 miles
One cm to 10 km

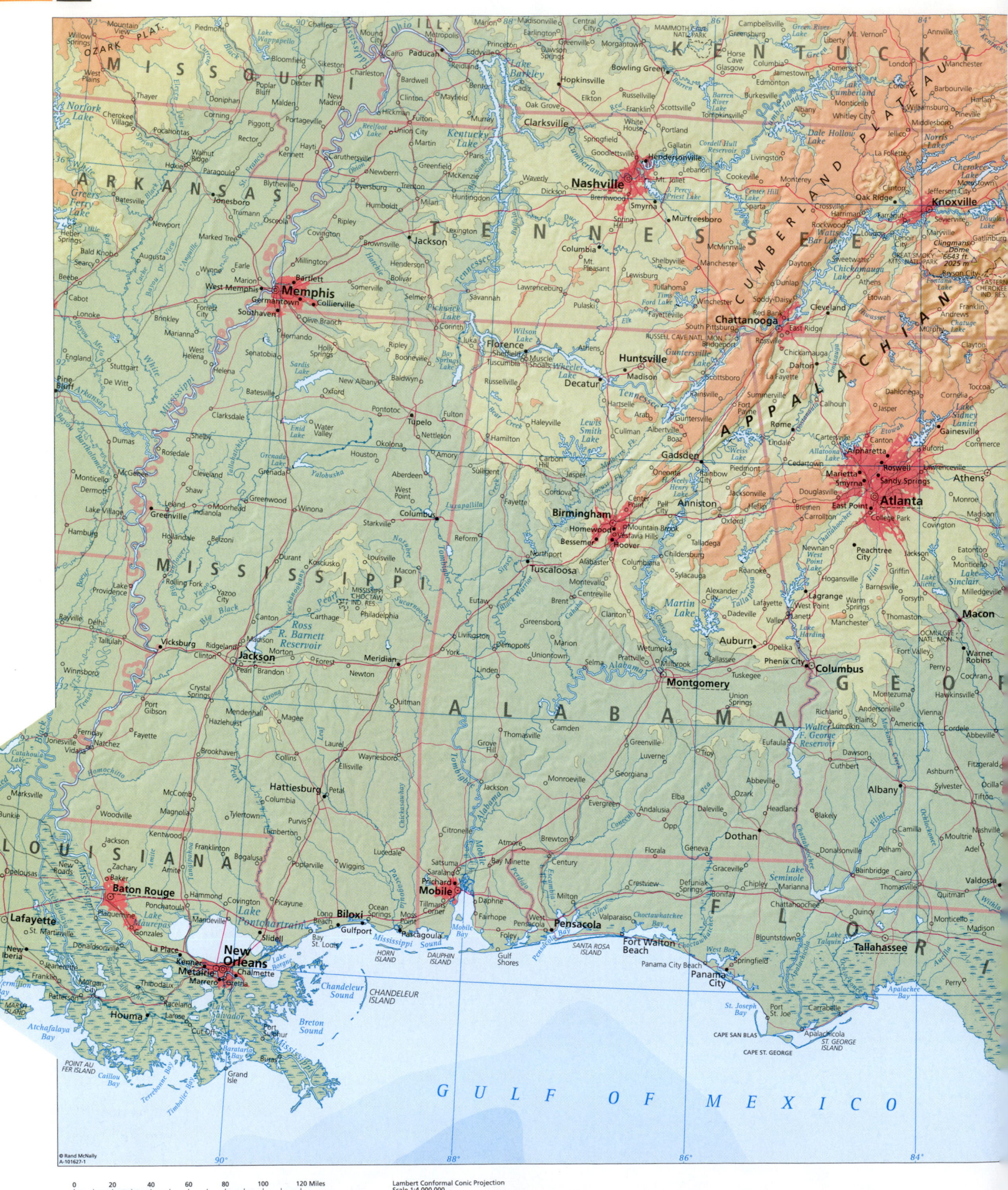

Lambert Conformal Conic Projection
Scale 1:4,000,000
One inch to 64 miles
One cm to 40 km

Inset map a
Lambert Conformal Conic Projection
Scale 1:4,000,000
One inch to 64 miles
One cm to 40 km

Inset map a
Lambert Azimuthal Equal Area Projection
Scale 1:12,000,000
One inch to 190 miles
One cm to 120 km

0 60 120 180 240 300 360 Miles
0 60 120 180 240 360 420 480 540 600 Kilometers

Lambert Azimuthal Equal Area Projection
Scale 1:12,000,000
One inch to 190 miles
One cm to 120 km

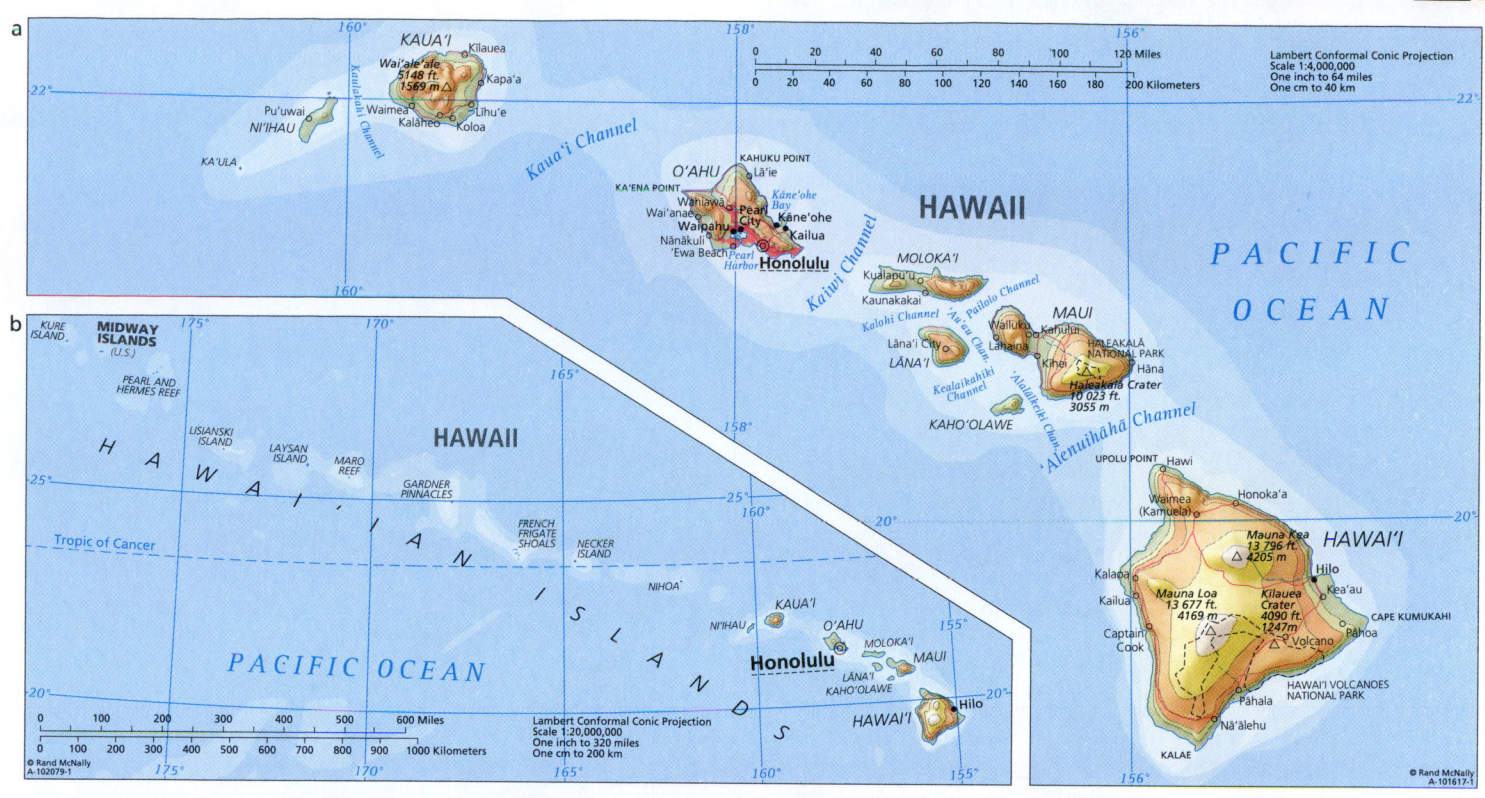

a

b

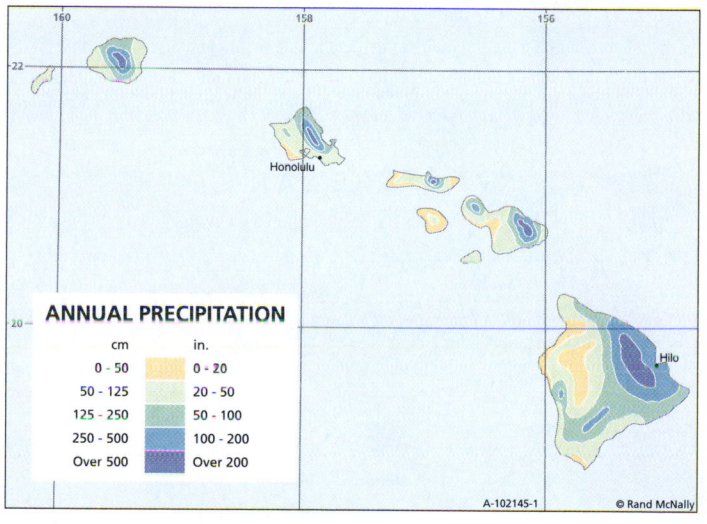

ANNUAL PRECIPITATION

cm	in.
0 - 50	0 - 20
50 - 125	20 - 50
125 - 250	50 - 100
250 - 500	100 - 200
Over 500	Over 200

A-102145-1 © Rand McNally

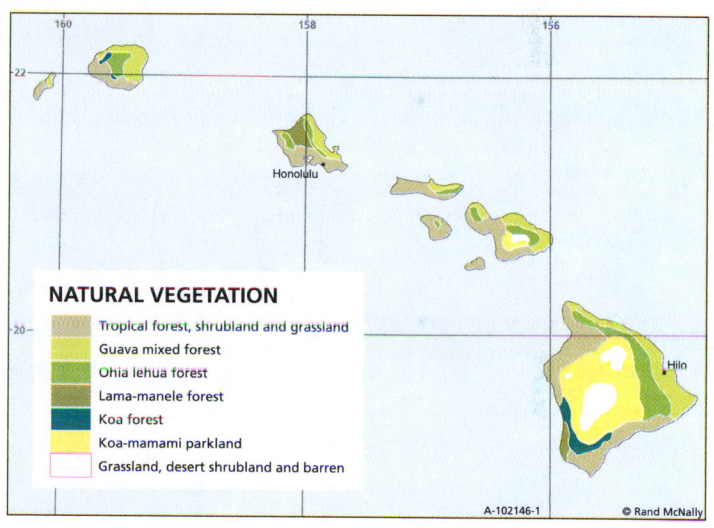

NATURAL VEGETATION

Tropical forest, shrubland and grassland
Guava mixed forest
Ohia lehua forest
Lama-manele forest
Koa forest
Koa-mamami parkland
Grassland, desert shrubland and barren

A-102146-1 © Rand McNally

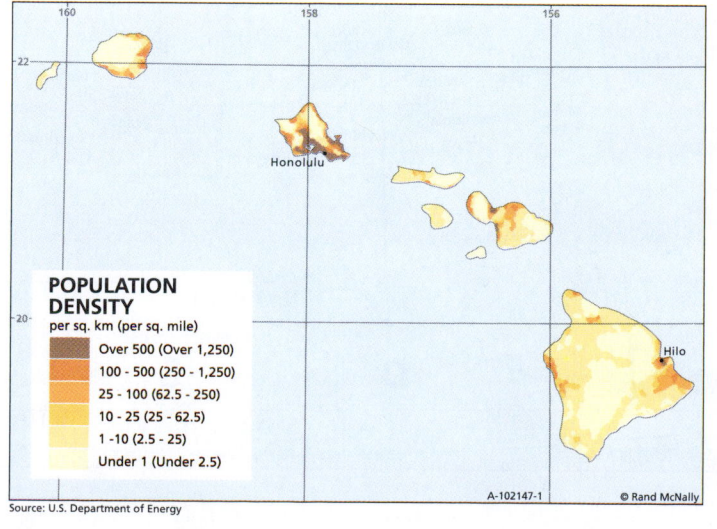

POPULATION DENSITY
per sq. km (per sq. mile)

Over 500 (Over 1,250)
100 - 500 (250 - 1,250)
25 - 100 (62.5 - 250)
10 - 25 (25 - 62.5)
1 -10 (2.5 - 25)
Under 1 (Under 2.5)

Source: U.S. Department of Energy

A-102147-1 © Rand McNally

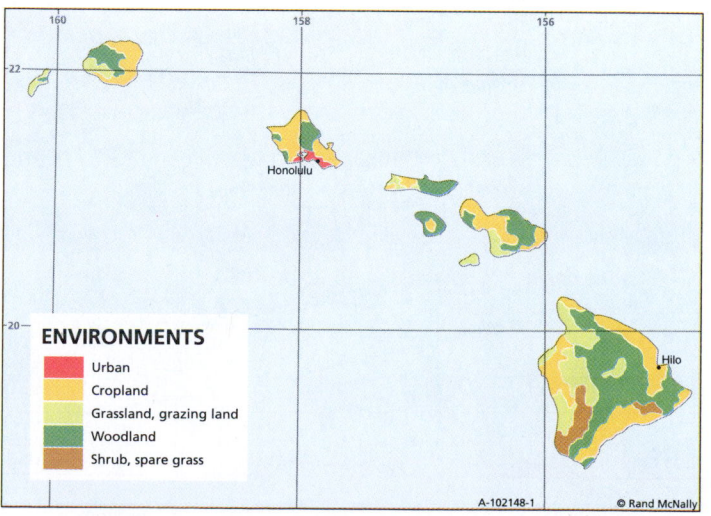

ENVIRONMENTS

Urban
Cropland
Grassland, grazing land
Woodland
Shrub, spare grass

A-102148-1 © Rand McNally

Lambert Azimuthal Equal Area Projection
Scale 1:12,000,000
One inch to 190 miles
One cm to 120 km

a

Saint-Augustin
St. Anthony
CAPE BAULD
LABRADOR
SEA
QUÉBEC
NEWFOUNDLAND
AND LABRADOR
Gulf of
St. Lawrence
GROS MORNE
NATL. PARK
Springdale
Notre Dame
Bay
Corner Brook
Deer Lake
Bishop's
Falls
Gander
Bonavista
Bay
Grand Falls-
Windsor
Bonavista
Stephenville
NEWFOUNDLAND
TERRA NOVA
NATL. PARK
Trinity Bay
Carbonear
Channel-Port
aux Basques
Placentia Bay
St. John's
CAPE RAY
Cabot Strait
Grand Bank
ST. PIERRE
& MIQUELON
(Fr.)
CAPE RACE
CAPE BRETON
HIGHLANDS NATL. PARK
NOVA SCOTIA
Glace Bay
ATLANTIC OCEAN
Sydney
A-101659-1
© Rand McNally

Igloolik
Boothia
Repulse Bay
Nettilling
Lake
PRINCE
CHARLES
ISLAND
AIR FORCE
ISLAND
AUYUITTUQ
NATL. PARK
Pangnirtung
ANGUAK
ISLAND
Cumberland Sound
Foxe
Basin
BAFFIN
ISLAND
Amadjuak
Lake
Arctic Circle
Iqaluit
NUNAVUT
Chesterfield Inlet
SOUTHAMPTON
ISLAND
Coral Harbour
CAPE
DORCHESTER
Cape Dorset
Frobisher Bay
RESOLUTION
ISLAND
Kimmirut
COATS
ISLAND
Foxe
Channel
MANSEL
ISLAND
Hudson Strait
AKPATOK
ISLAND
LABRADOR
SEA
Ivujivik
Salluit
Kangiqsujuaq
Ungava
Bay
Kangiqsualujjuaq
Hebron
York
Factory
Fort Severn
Kangirsuk
PÉNINSULE
Lac
Couture
D'UNGAVA
Povungnituk
Kuujjuaq
Nain
Hopedale
CAPE HARRISON
NEWFOUNDLAND
Inukjuak
OTTAWA
ISLANDS
Lac
Minto
Feuilles
Smallwood
Reservoir
AND LABRADOR
Cartwright
St. Anthony
Hudson
Bay
Lac
Bienville
Schefferville
Happy Valley-
Goose Bay
Churchill
Battle Harbour
Whapmagoostui
BELCHER
ISLANDS
Réservoir
La Grande
Deux
Lac
Caniapiscau
Labrador City
Saint-Augustin
GROS MORNE
NATIONAL PARK
NEWFOUNDLAND
Corner Brook
Deer
Lake
Springdale
James
Bay
Chisasibi
Réservoir
Eastmain-
Opinaca
QUÉBEC
Havre-
Saint-Pierre
CAPE RAY
Channel-Port
aux Basques
Cabot Strait
Glace Bay
Sydney
Severn
AKIMISKI
ISLAND
Eastmain
Eastmain
Réservoir
Manicouagan
ÎLE D'ANTICOSTI
Gulf of
St. Lawrence
Fort Severn
Winisk
Ekwan
Waskaganish
Lac
Mistassini
Sept-Îles
Port-
Cartier
PARC NATL.
FORILLON
ÎLES DE LA
MADELEINE
Attawapiskat
Fort Albany
Chibougamau
Baie-
Comeau
Matane
Gaspé
Bonaventure
CAPE BRETON
HIGHLANDS NATL. PARK
New
Glasgow
Glace Bay
Sydney
ONTARIO
Moosonee
Dolbeau-
Mistassini
Alma
Saguenay
Rimouski
Mont-Joli
Campbellton
Bathurst
Miramichi
PRINCE
EDWARD
ISLAND
Summerside
Charlottetown
Missinaibi
Matagami
Saint-
Félicien
Roberval
Rivière-du-Loup
La Malbaie
Edmundston
KOUCHIBOUGUAC
NATL. PARK
NEW
BRUNSWICK
Moncton
Amherst
Truro
NOVA SCOTIA
Armstrong
Hearst
Kapuskasing
Iroquois
Falls
Lac
Abitibi
La Sarre
Amos
Senneterre
Réservoir
Gouin
La Tuque
Baie-
Saint-Paul
Québec
Lévis
Montmagny
Woodstock
Fredericton
KEJIMKUJIK NATL. PARK
FUNDY
NATL. PARK
Dartmouth
Halifax
Red Lake
Lac
Seul
Sioux Lookout
Geraldton
Timmins
Kirkland
Lake
Rouyn-
Noranda
Val-d'Or
PARC NATIONAL
DE LA MAURICIE
Shawinigan
Trois-Rivières
Victoriaville
Drummondville
Sherbrooke
Granby
Saint John
St. Stephen
Oromocto
Bay of Fundy
Yarmouth
CAPE SABLE
Bridgewater
Shelburne
Kenora
Dryden
Nipigon
Marathon
Wawa
PUKASKWA
NATL. PARK
Chapleau
New
Liskeard
Mattawa
Hawkesbury
Laval
MONTRÉAL
Cornwall
St-
Jean
MAINE
Augusta
Portland
Gulf of
Maine
Rainy
River
Fort
Frances
Atikokan
Thunder
Bay
Lake
Superior
Elliot
Lake
Sudbury
Lake
Nipissing
North
Bay
Pembroke
Renfrew
Ogdensburg
Montpelier
VT.
N.H.
Concord
ATLANTIC
OCEAN
International
Falls
Houghton
Sault
Sainte
Marie
Blind
River
Espanola
Georgian
Bay
Parry
Sound
Smiths
Falls
Brockville
Kingston
Ottawa
Boston
MASS.
Providence
R.I.
Duluth
MICHIGAN
Midland
Orillia
Peterborough
Belleville
Oshawa
Rochester
Albany
Hartford
CONN.
St. Paul
WISCONSIN
Green
Bay
Owen
Sound
Barrie
Lake
Ontario
Niagara
Falls
Buffalo
NEW YORK
Minneapolis
Grand
Rapids
Goderich
Kitchener
TORONTO
Hamilton
St.
Catharines
N.J.
NEW YORK
Milwaukee
Lansing
Sarnia
London
Lake
Erie
Erie
PENN.
Detroit
Windsor
Chatham
Cleveland
Toledo
OHIO
Lake St. Clair

Inset map a
Lambert Azimuthal Equal Area Projection
Scale 1:12,000,000
One inch to 190 miles
One cm to 120 km

A-101658-1
© Rand McNally

Lambert Azimuthal Equal Area Projection
Scale 1:12,000,000
One inch to 190 miles
One cm to 120 km

0   60   120   180   240   300   360 Miles

0   60   120   180   240   300   360   420   480   540   600 Kilometers

LABRADOR SEA

QUÉBEC

NEWFOUNDLAND AND LABRADOR

CAPE BAULD

Strait of Belle Isle

CAP WHITTLE

Gulf of St. Lawrence

Corner Brook

LONG RANGE MTS.

Bell Island

ST. JOHN

Grand Lake

Notre Dame Bay

FOGO ISLAND

CAPE FREELS

Exploits

NEWFOUNDLAND

Bonavista Bay

Trinity Bay

St. George's Bay

St. John's

CAPE SPEAR

Cabot Strait

CAPE RAY

MIQUELON

Placentia Bay

CAPE RACE

ST. PIERRE & MIQUELON (Fr.)

Saint-Pierre

CAPE BRETON ISLAND

NOVA SCOTIA

ATLANTIC OCEAN

A-101661-1 © Rand McNally

a

Inset map a
Lambert Azimuthal Equal Area Projection
Scale 1:12,000,000
One inch to 190 miles
One cm to 120 km

A-101660-1 © Rand McNally

a

Inset map a
Lambert Conformal Conic Projection
Scale 1:1,000,000
One inch to 16 miles
One cm to 10 km

Lambert Conformal Conic Projection
Scale 1:4,000,000
One inch to 64 miles
One cm to 40 km

0 20 40 60 80 100 120 Miles

0 20 40 60 80 100 120 140 160 180 200 Kilometers

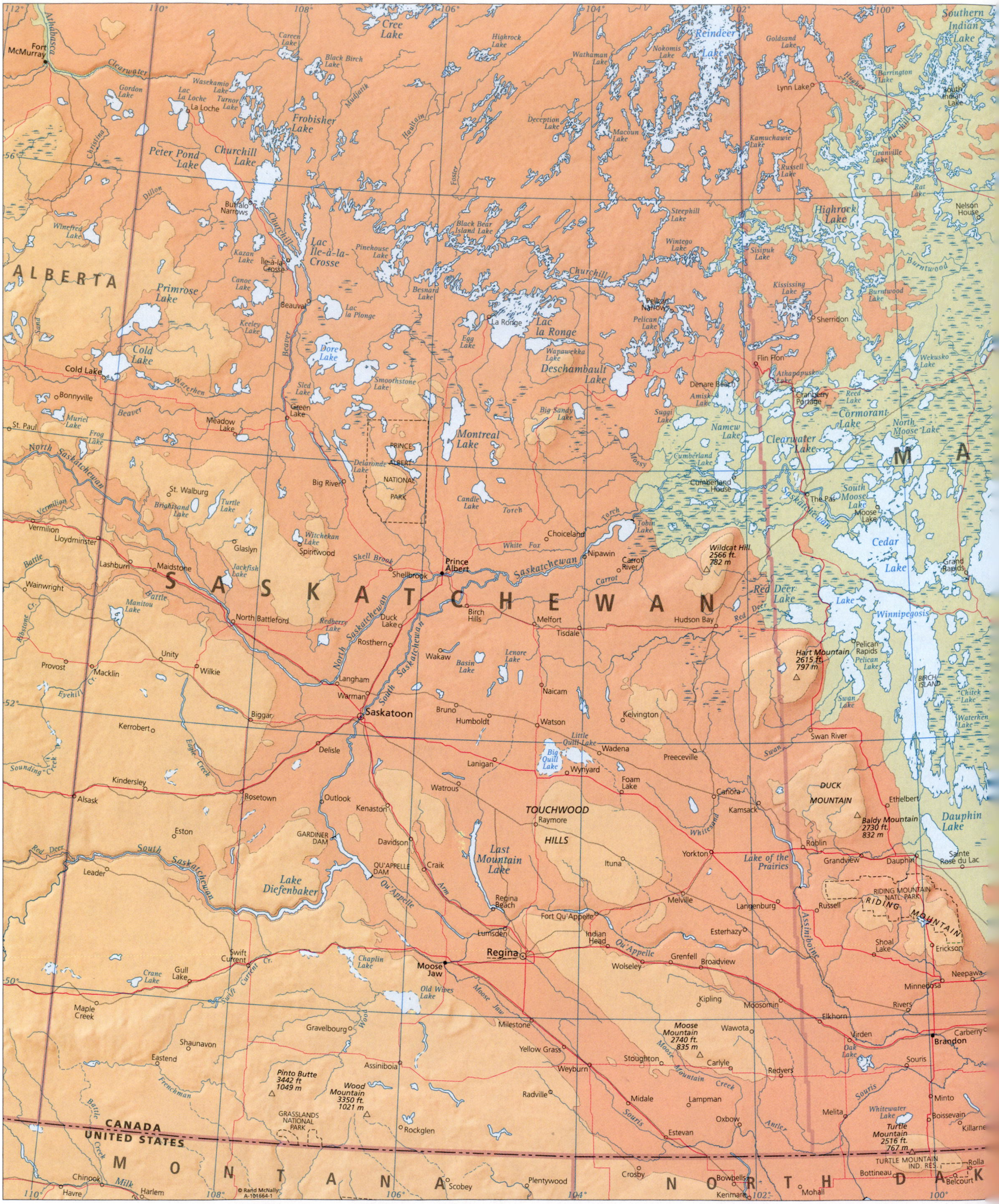

ALBERTA
SASKATCHEWAN
CANADA
UNITED STATES
MONTANA
NORTH DAK
Fort McMurray
Athabasca
Clearwater
Gordon Lake
Lac La Loche
La Loche
Wasekamio Lake
Turnor Lake
Frobisher Lake
Churchill Lake
Peter Pond Lake
Buffalo Narrows
Cree Lake
Careen Lake
Black Birch Lake
Highrock Lake
Wathaman Lake
Nokomis Lake
Reindeer Lake
Goldsand Lake
Lynn Lake
Southern Indian Lake
Barrington Lake
South Indian Lake
Deception Lake
Macoun Lake
Kamuchawie Lake
Russell Lake
Granville Lake
Rat Lake
Nelson House
Highrock Lake
Steephill Lake
Wintego Lake
Sisipuk Lake
Kississing Lake
Burntwood Lake
Burntwood
Sherridon
Winefred Lake
Kazan Lake
Ile-à-la-Crosse
Lac Ile-à-la-Crosse
Pinehouse Lake
Black Bear Island Lake
Churchill
Primrose Lake
Canoe Lake
Beauval
Lac la Plonge
Besnard Lake
La Ronge
Lac la Ronge
Pelican Narrows
Pelican Lake
Keeley Lake
Dore Lake
Egg Lake
Wapawekka Lake
Deschambault Lake
Flin Flon
Wekusko Lake
Cold Lake
Bonnyville
Waterhen
Smoothstone Lake
Sled Lake
Green Lake
Denare Beach
Amisk Lake
Athapapuskow Lake
Cranberry Portage
Reed Lake
Cormorant Lake
St. Paul
Muriel Lake
Frog Lake
Beaver
Meadow Lake
Big Sandy Lake
Suggi Lake
Namew Lake
Clearwater Lake
North Moose Lake
North Saskatchewan
PRINCE ALBERT NATIONAL PARK
Delaronde Lake
Montreal Lake
Cumberland Lake
Cumberland House
Big River
Vermilion
Lloydminster
St. Walburg
Brightsand Lake
Turtle Lake
Candle Lake
Torch
The Pas
South Moose Lake
Moose Lake
Cedar Lake
Glaslyn
Witchekan Lake
Spiritwood
Shell Brook
Choiceland
Tobin Lake
Nipawin
Carrot River
Carrot
White Fox
Wildcat Hill 2566 ft. 782 m
Grand Rapids
Battle
Lashburn
Maidstone
Jackfish Lake
Shellbrook
Prince Albert
Saskatchewan
Red Deer Lake
Red Deer
Wainwright
Manitou Lake
North Battleford
Redberry Lake
Duck Lake
Birch Hills
Melfort
Tisdale
Hudson Bay
Lake Winnipegosis
Rosthern
Pelican Rapids
Pelican Lake
Hart Mountain 2615 ft. 797 m
Provost
Macklin
Unity
Wilkie
Wakaw
Basin Lake
Lenore Lake
Naicam
Langham
Warman
Saskatoon
South Saskatchewan
Eyehill Cr.
Biggar
Bruno
Humboldt
Watson
Kelvington
Swan Lake
Birch Island
Chitek Lake
Waterhen Lake
Kerrobert
Delisle
Lanigan
Little Quill Lake
Big Quill Lake
Wadena
Preeceville
Swan River
Swan
Sounding Creek
Eagle Creek
Kindersley
Alsask
Rosetown
Watrous
Wynyard
Foam Lake
Canora
Kamsack
Whitesand
DUCK MOUNTAIN
Ethelbert
Baldy Mountain 2730 ft. 832 m
Dauphin Lake
Outlook
Kenaston
TOUCHWOOD HILLS
Raymore
Eston
GARDINER DAM
Davidson
Last Mountain Lake
Ituna
Yorkton
Lake of the Prairies
Roblin
Grandview
Dauphin
Sainte Rose du Lac
Red Deer
South Saskatchewan
Leader
QU'APPELLE DAM
Craik
Arm
Lake Diefenbaker
Qu'Appelle
Regina Beach
Melville
Langenburg
Russell
RIDING MOUNTAIN NATL. PARK
RIDING MOUNTAIN
Fort Qu'Appelle
Lumsden
Indian Head
Esterhazy
Assiniboine
Shoal Lake
Erickson
Regina
Swift Current
Swift Current Cr.
Chaplin Lake
Moose Jaw
Grenfell
Broadview
Wolseley
Gull Lake
Crane Lake
Old Wives Lake
Neepawa
Minnedosa
Maple Creek
Kipling
Moosomin
Rivers
Milestone
Wawota
Moose Mountain 2740 ft. 835 m
Elkhorn
Virden
Brandon
Carberry
Gravelbourg
Wood
Shaunavon
Yellow Grass
Oak Lake
Eastend
Stoughton
Carlyle
Souris
Redvers
Frenchman
Assiniboia
Weyburn
Moose Mountain Creek
Pinto Butte 3442 ft. 1049 m
Wood Mountain 3350 ft. 1021 m
Radville
Midale
Lampman
Minto
GRASSLANDS NATIONAL PARK
Melita
Whitewater Lake
Boissevain
Oxbow
Estevan
Antler
Turtle Mountain 2516 ft. 767 m
Killarney
Rockglen
TURTLE MOUNTAIN IND. RES.
Rolla
Battle Creek
Milk
Chinook
Havre
Harlem
Scobey
Plentywood
Crosby
Bowbells
Kenmare
Mohall
Bottineau
Belcourt
© Rand McNally A-101664-1
112° 110° 108° 106° 104° 102° 100°
56° 52° 50°

0 20 40 60 80 100 120 Miles
0 20 40 60 80 100 120 140 160 180 200 Kilometers

Lambert Conformal Conic Projection
Scale 1:4,000,000
One inch to 64 miles
One cm to 40 km

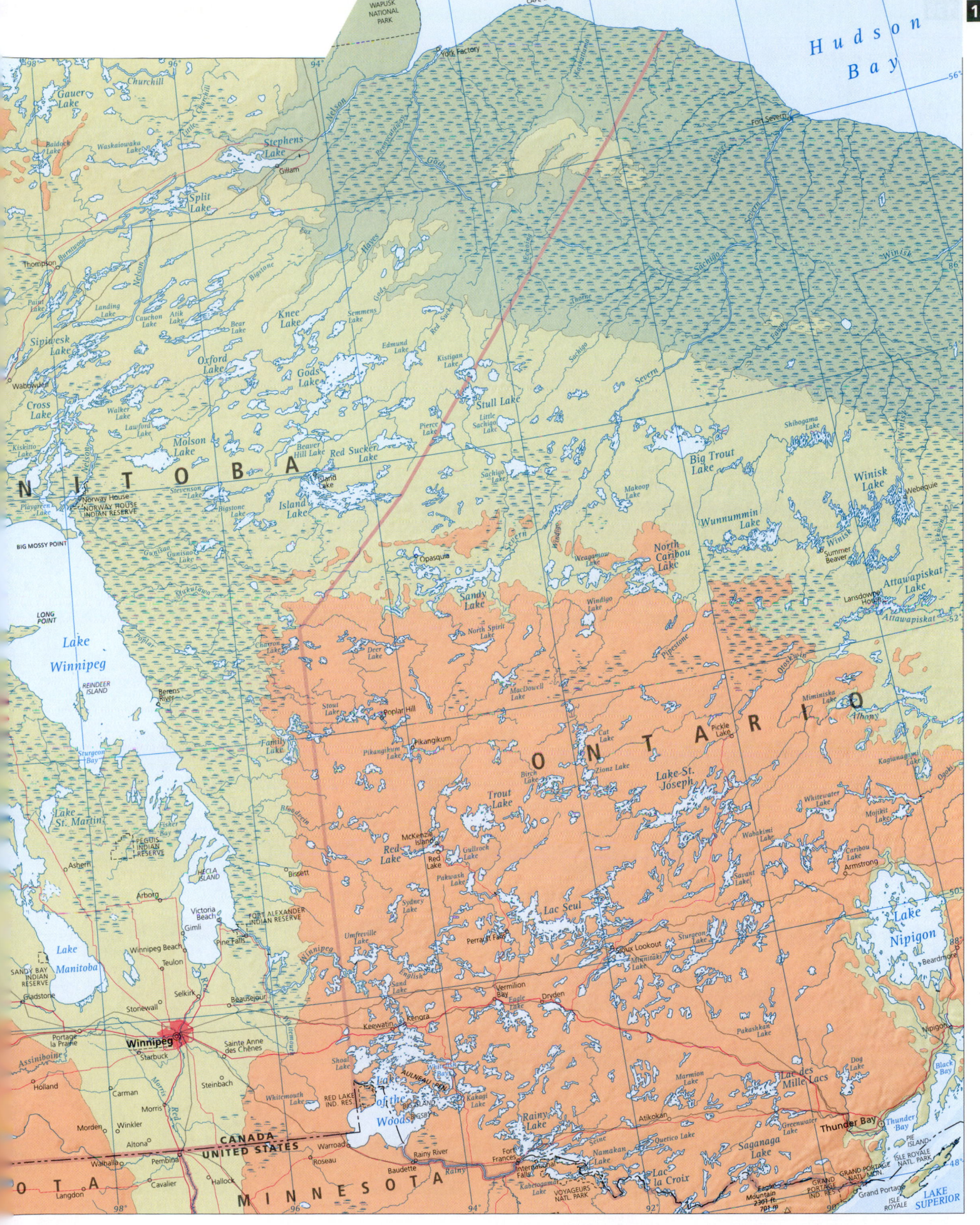

H u d s o n
B a y

CAPE TATNAM

WAPUSK
NATIONAL
PARK

Churchill

Gauer
Lake

Baldock
Lake

Waskaiowaka
Lake

Stephens
Lake

York Factory

Fort Severn

Thompson

Split
Lake

Gillam

Point
Lake

Landing
Lake

Cauchon
Lake

Atik
Lake

Bear
Lake

Knee
Lake

Semmens
Lake

Sipiwesk
Lake

Oxford
Lake

Gods
Lake

Edmund
Lake

Kistigan
Lake

Big Trout
Lake

Shibogama
Lake

Wabowden

Walker
Lake

Lauford
Lake

Molson
Lake

Beaver
Hill Lake

Red Sucker
Lake

Stull Lake

Winisk
Lake

Webeque

Cross
Lake

Kiskitto
Lake

Pierce
Lake

Little
Sachigo
Lake

Summer
Beaver

Stevenson
Lake

Island
Lake

Sachigo
Lake

Makoop
Lake

Wunnummin
Lake

Attawapiskat
Lake

Lansdowne
House

Playgreen
Lake

NORWAY HOUSE
INDIAN RESERVE

Bigstone
Lake

Bland
Lake

Opasquia

Weagamow
Lake

North
Caribou
Lake

Attawapiskat

BIG MOSSY POINT

Gunisao
Lake

Mukutawa

Sandy
Lake

Windigo
Lake

LONG
POINT

Lake
Winnipeg

Poplar

REINDEER
ISLAND

North Spirit
Lake

O N T A R I O

Miminiska
Lake

Berens
River

Deer
Lake

Charron
Lake

MacDowell
Lake

Pigeon

Athany

Sturgeon
Bay

Family
Lake

Stout
Lake

Poplar Hill

Pickle
Lake

Koglunamo
Lake

Pikangikum
Lake

Pikangikum

Cat
Lake

Whitewater
Lake

Lake
St. Martin

Birch
Lake

Zionz
Lake

Lake St.
Joseph

Mojikit
Lake

Fisher
Bay

Trout
Lake

Caribou
Lake

PEGUIS
INDIAN
RESERVE

Bloodvein

McKenzie
Island

Wabakimi
Lake

Armstrong

Ashern

Reds
Lake

Gullrock
Lake

Lake
Nipigon

Arborg

Bissett

Red
Lake

Savant
Lake

Victoria
Beach

HECLA
ISLAND

Pakwash
Lake

Lac Seul

Beardmore

Gimli

FORT ALEXANDER
INDIAN RESERVE

Sydney
Lake

Pine Falls

Sioux Lookout

Sturgeon
Lake

Lake
Manitoba

Umfreville
Lake

Perrault Falls

Minnitaki
Lake

SANDY BAY
INDIAN
RESERVE

Winnipeg Beach

Teulon

English

Eagle
Lake

Pakashkan
Lake

Nipigon

Gladstone

Selkirk

Beauséjour

Vermilion
Bay

Dryden

Stonewall

Keewatin

Kenora

Pakwash
Lake

Portage
la Prairie

Winnipeg

Starbuck

Sainte Anne
des Chênes

Sand
Lake

Dog
Lake

Black
Bay

Assiniboine

Shoal
Lake

Lac des
Mille Lacs

Holland

Carman

Morris

Steinbach

Whitemouth
Lake

SAULTEAUX
IND. RES.

Marmion
Lake

Morden

Winkler

Altona

Whitemouth
Red

Lake
of the
Woods

RED LAKE
IND. RES.

Kakagi
Lake

Rainy
Lake

Atikokan

Saganaga
Lake

Greenwater
Lake

Thunder Bay

Thunder
Bay

PIE
ISLAND

Walhalla

Pembina

CANADA
UNITED STATES

Warroad

Roseau

Rainy River

Fort
Frances

Quetico Lake

Stine

Namakan
Lake

Lac
la Croix

GRAND PORTAGE
NATL. MON.

Langdon

Cavalier

Hallock

M I N N E S O T A

Baudette

Rainy

International
Falls

Kabetogama
Lake

VOYAGEURS
NATL. PARK

Eagle
Mountain
2301 ft
701 m

GRAND
PORTAGE
IND. RES.

Grand Portage

ISLE ROYALE
NATL. PARK

ISLE
ROYALE

LAKE
SUPERIOR

Lambert Conformal Conic Projection
Scale 1:4,000,000
One inch to 64 miles
One cm to 40 km

| 0 | 20 | 40 | 60 | 80 | 100 | 120 Miles |

| 0 | 20 | 40 | 60 | 80 | 100 | 120 | 140 | 160 | 180 | 200 Kilometers |

Lambert Conformal Conic Projection
Scale 1:4,000,000
One inch to 64 miles
One cm to 40 km

LABRADOR SEA

Red Bay 56°
CAPE BAULD
Pistolet Bay
L'ANSE-AUX-MEADOWS
St. Anthony
Strait of Belle Isle
Saint-Augustin
Mutton Bay
CAP DU GROS MÉCATINA
ST. JOHN ISLAND
Roddickton
Hare Bay
GROAIS ISLAND
GREY ISLANDS
Île du Petit Mécatina
Port Saunders
BELL ISLAND
HORSE ISLANDS
CAP WHITTLE
Blue Mountain 2129 ft. 649 m
La Romaine
Natashquan
La-Scie
CAPE ST. JOHN 50°
Notre Dame Bay
NEW WORLD ISLAND
FOGO ISLAND
Fogo
Durrell
ÎLE D' ANTICOSTI
GROS MORNE NATIONAL PARK
Rocky Harbour
Gros Morne 2644 ft. 806 m
Sandy Lake
Springdale
Robert's Arm
Hamilton Sound
Carmanville
CAPE FREELS
POINTE DE L'EST
Bay of Islands
Deer Lake
Pasadena
NEWFOUNDLAND
Botwood
Lewisporte
New-Wes-Valley
Lark Harbour
Corner Brook
Badger
Bishop's Falls
Glenwood
Gander
Hare Bay
Bonavista Bay
AND LABRADOR
Explorts
Grand Falls-Windsor
Gander Lake
Glovertown
Bonavista
Gulf of St. Lawrence
LONG POINT
Buchans
NEWFOUNDLAND
Catalina
52°
Port au Port Bay
Stephenville
Grand Lake
Red Indian Lake
TERRA NOVA NATIONAL PARK
RANDOM ISLAND
GRATES POINT
CAPE ST. GEORGE
Victoria Lake
Jeddore Lake
Shoal Harbour
Bay de Verde 48°
St. George's Bay
Meelpaeg Lake
Trinity Bay
Conception Bay
Pouch Cove
CAPE ANGUILLE
Carbonear
Torbay
Harbour Grace
Wabana
St. John's
CAPE RAY
Channel-Port aux Basques
Isle aux Morts
Burgeo
Hermitage Bay
Harbour Breton
Belle Bay
Bay Roberts
Brigus
CAPE SPEAR
AVALON PENINSULA
Witless Bay
LA GROSSE ÎLE
ÎLE DE L'EST
ÎLE DU CAP AUX MEULES
ÎLES DE LA MADELEINE (Que.)
Cap-aux-Meules
ÎLE DU HAVRE AUBERT
Cabot Strait
BRUNETTE ISLAND
Fortune Bay
BURIN PENINSULA
Fox Harbour
Placentia Bay
MIQUELON
Grand Bank
Marystown
Burin
Branch
St. Mary's Bay
CAPE NORTH
Aspy Bay
Dingwall
CAPE BRETON HIGHLANDS NAT'L PARK
LANGLADE
Fortune
St. Lawrence
CAPE ST. MARY'S
St. Shotts
CAPE RACE
SAINT PIERRE & MIQUELON (Fr.)
Saint-Pierre
Saint-Pierre
Souris
Georgetown
Aïnslie Lake
St. Ann's Bay
Sydney Mines
New Waterford
Glace Bay
Montague
NOVA SCOTIA
North Sydney
Sydney
SCATARIE ISLAND
Murray Harbour
Port Hood
46°
St. Georges Bay
Bras d'Or Lake
St. Peters
Louisbourg
Antigonish
Port Hawkesbury
CAPE BRETON ISLAND
New Glasgow
ISLE MADAME
Chedabucto Bay
Canso
Sheet Harbour
ATLANTIC OCEAN
SABLE ISLAND (N.S.)

Inset map a
Lambert Conformal Conic Projection
Scale 1:1,000,000
One inch to 16 miles
One cm to 10 km

LES LAURENTIDES
Sainte-Anne-de-Beaupré
Beaupré
Saint-Joachim
ÎLE D'ORLÉANS
Château-Richer
Lac-Beauport
Lac Saint-Joseph
L'Ange-Gardien
Saint-Raymond
Lac Saint-Charles
Boischatel
Saint-Pétronille
St. Lawrence
Sainte-Catherine-de-la-Jacques-Cartier
Shannon
Charlesbourg
Beauport
Chute-Panet
Val-Bélair
Loretteville
Vanier
QUÉBEC
Beaumont
L'Ancienne-Lorette
Sillery
Lévis
Sainte-Foy
Pont-Rouge
Cap-Rouge
Saint-Romuald
Saint-Basile
Charny
Saint-Jean-Chrysostome
Neuville
Saint-Rédempteur
Saint-Henri
Portneuf
Saint-Nicolas
Donnacona
Saint-Antoine-de-Tilly
Saint-Apollinaire
Saint-Agapit
Saint-Anselme
Cap-Santé
Sainte-Croix
Rivière-Bois-Clair
Saint-Flavien
Saint-Gilles
Laurier-Station
Dosquet
Saint-Bernard

PACIFIC OCEAN

Gulf of Mexico

UNITED STATES

MEXICO

TEXAS

LOS ANGELES
Long Beach
Anaheim
Oxnard
SAN DIEGO
Oceanside
TIJUANA
Ensenada
Mexicali
PHOENIX
Tucson
Nogales
El Paso
CIUDAD JUÁREZ
Albuquerque
Amarillo
Oklahoma City
Tulsa
Wichita Falls
Fort Smith
Little Rock
Lubbock
Midland
Abilene
Fort Worth
DALLAS
Tyler
Waco
Shreveport
Monroe
Jackson
Memphis
Huntsville
Birmingham
Mobile
Baton Rouge
New Orleans
Lake Charles
Beaumont
HOUSTON
Galveston
Corpus Christi
Brownsville
Matamoros
Reynosa
MONTERREY
Nuevo Laredo
Laredo
Piedras Negras
Monclova
Ciudad Victoria
Ciudad Mante
Ciudad Valles
Tampico
Tuxpan de Rodríguez Cano
Veracruz
Xalapa
Córdoba
San Andrés Tuxtla
Coatzacoalcos
Ciudad del Carmen
Villahermosa
MÉRIDA
Cancún
Chetumal
Belize City
BELIZE
Belmopan
San Cristóbal de las Casas
Tuxtla Gutiérrez
Comitán de Domínguez
Tapachula
GUATEMALA
Quetzaltenango
Guatemala
San Pedro Sula
La Ceiba
Santa Ana
San Salvador
San Miguel
Tegucigalpa
EL SALVADOR
León
Managua

Hermosillo
Ciudad Obregón
Los Mochis
Culiacán
La Paz
CABO SAN LUCAS
Mazatlán
Durango
Torreón
Gómez Palacio
Hidalgo del Parral
Chihuahua
Zacatecas
Aguascalientes
San Luis Potosí
Querétaro
León
Celaya
GUADALAJARA
Puerto Vallarta
Tepic
Zamora de Hidalgo
Uruapan del Progreso
Tecomán
Morelia
Toluca de Lerdo
MEXICO CITY
Puebla de Zaragoza
Iguala
Lázaro Cárdenas
Zihuatanejo
Acapulco de Juárez
Oaxaca de Juárez
Salina Cruz

SIERRA MADRE OCCIDENTAL
SIERRA MADRE ORIENTAL
SIERRA MADRE DEL SUR
Golfo de Tehuantepec
MIDDLE AMERICA TRENCH

Golfo de California
ISLA TIBURÓN
ISLA CEDROS
ISLA GUADALUPE
ISLAS REVILLAGIGEDO (Mex.)
ÎLE CLIPPERTON (Fr.)
ISLAS TRES MARIAS
Tropic of Cancer
YUCATAN PENINSULA
CABO CATOCHE
Bahía de Campeche
ISLA DEL COCO (C.R.)

Inset map a

CARIBBEAN SEA

VENEZUELA
ARUBA (Neth.)
NETHERLANDS ANTILLES (Neth.)
CURAÇAO
BONAIRE
Willemstad
Oranjestad

Inset map a
Lambert Conformal Conic Projection
Scale 1:2,000,000
One inch to 32 miles
One cm to 20 km

© Rand McNally

b

BERMUDA
(U.K.)

ST. GEORGE'S ISLAND — St. George
ST. DAVID'S ISLAND
Harrington Sound
Flatts — Castle Harbour
Town Hill 259 ft. 79 m
Hamilton
Great Sound
SOMERSET ISLAND
HIGH POINT

© Rand McNally
A-101670-1

ATLANTIC OCEAN

KENTUCKY W.VA.
Roanoke
Richmond
MTS. VIRGINIA
Norfolk
Virginia Beach
Chesapeake Bay
Knoxville
Mt. Mitchell 6684 ft. 2037 m
Raleigh
Chattanooga
Charlotte NORTH CAROLINA
TENNESSEE
SOUTH
Fayetteville
Wilmington
CAPE HATTERAS
Atlanta
Columbia CAROLINA
Cape Lookout
Columbus
Charleston
GEORGIA
Cape Fear
Montgomery
Savannah

ALABAMA
Tallahassee
Jacksonville
CAPE SAN BLAS
FLORIDA
St. Johns R.

ATLANTIC OCEAN

Orlando
Cape Canaveral
St. Petersburg Tampa
Lake Okeechobee
West Palm Beach
Fort Lauderdale
CAPE SABLE
Miami
Key West
Nassau
ANDROS
NEW PROVIDENCE
Straits of Florida
MANGROVE CAY
CAT ISLAND
San Salvador

ABACO
GRAND BAHAMA
BAHAMAS
ELEUTHERA
GREAT EXUMA
LONG ISLAND
ACKLINS
CROOKED ISLAND
MAYAGUANA

Tropic of Cancer

HAVANA Matanzas
Pinar del Río
Santa Clara
CABO DE SAN ANTONIO
Golfo de Batabanó
Cienfuegos
ISLA DE LA JUVENTUD
CUBA
Camagüey
Cayo Coco
Cayo Romano
Cayo Guajaba
GREAT INAGUA
TURKS AND CAICOS ISLANDS (U.K.)
Grand Turk

Holguín
Bayamo
Manzanillo
CABO CRUZ
GREATER
Santiago de Cuba
Pico Turquino 6470 ft. 1972 m
Guantánamo
Windward Passage
Cap-Haïtien
PUERTO RICO TRENCH

CAYMAN ISLANDS (U.K.)
George Town
GRAND CAYMAN
Gonaïves
Pico Duarte 10,417 ft. 3175 m
Santiago de los Caballeros
DOMINICAN REPUBLIC
HAITI
HISPANIOLA
San Juan
VIRGIN ISLANDS (U.S.)
BRITISH VIRGIN ISLANDS (U.K.)
ANGUILLA (U.K.)

Montego Bay
Port-au-Prince
Santo Domingo
San Pedro de Macorís
Ponce
Charlotte Amalie
ST. CROIX (U.S.)
ANTIGUA AND BARBUDA

JAMAICA Kingston
Spanish Town
PUERTO RICO (U.S.)
ST. KITTS AND NEVIS
MONTSERRAT (U.K.)
Basse-Terre
GUADELOUPE (Fr.)
GRANDE-TERRE
MARIE-GALANTE

ANTILLES
LEEWARD ISLANDS

WEST INDIES
DOMINICA Roseau
MARTINIQUE (Fr.)
Fort-de-France

HONDURAS
CABO GRACIAS A DIOS
Coco
CARIBBEAN SEA
Castries ST. LUCIA
BARBADOS
Kingstown Bridgetown
ST. VINCENT AND THE GRENADINES

Tegucigalpa

NICARAGUA
ISLA DE PROVIDENCIA (Col.)
GRENADA
ISLA LA BLANQUILLA
Lago de Nicaragua
Bluefields
ISLA DE SAN ANDRÉS (Col.)
TOBAGO
ARUBA (Neth.)
NETHERLANDS ANTILLES (Neth.)
LESSER
ISLA LA ORCHILA
ISLA LA TORTUGA
ISLA DE MARGARITA
TRINIDAD AND TOBAGO
Carúpano
Port of Spain
TRINIDAD
WINDWARD ISLANDS

PUNTA GALLINAS
PEN. DE LA GUAJIRA
Willemstad
CURAÇAO
BONAIRE
Golfo de Paria

COSTA RICA
Volcán Irazú 11,260 ft. 3432 m
Golfo de Venezuela
Punto Fijo
ANTILLES
Cumaná

Puerto Limón
Santa Marta
Punta Fijo
MARACAIBO
Puerto Cabello
CARACAS
Barcelona

San José
Cerro Chirripó 12,530 ft. 3819 m
David
Colón
Barranquilla
Soledad
Pico Cristóbal Colón 18,947 ft. 5775 m
Cabimas
Barquisimeto
Valle de la Pascua
El Tigre
Cumaná

Volcán Barú 11,401 ft. 3475 m
Cartagena
Lago de Maracaibo
Valera
Ciudad Bolívar
Ciudad Guayana

Panama Canal
Sincelejo
Magangué
Mérida
Acarigua
Calabozo
Cerro Mato 6712 ft. 1863 m

ISTMO DE PANAMÁ
Panamá
Monteria
Cauca
Pico Bolívar 16,427 ft. 5007 m
San Fernando de Apure
Orinoco
Embalse de Guri
Golfo de Chiriquí
PEN. DE AZUERO
Golfo de Panamá
Santiago
Ocaña
VENEZUELA
Mt. Roraima 9432 ft. 2875 m
GUYANA

ISLA DE COIBA
PUNTA MARIATO
Cúcuta
San Cristóbal
Apure
Arauca
Angel Falls
Georgetown

CABO CORRIENTES
Barrancabermeja
Bucaramanga
LLANOS
Mazaruni

ISLA DE MALPELO (Col.)
MEDELLÍN
Sogamoso
Tunja
Meta
Vichada
Puerto Ayacucho
GUIANA HIGHLANDS

La Dorada
Nevado del Tolima 17,110 ft. 5215 m
San Fernando de Atabapo
Cerro Marahuaca 8461 ft. 2579 m
PAKARAIMA MTS.
BRAZIL

Manizales
Villavicencio
Guaviare
Caroní
SURINAME

Buenaventura
Ibagué
Palmira
BOGOTÁ
Negro
Boa Vista

CALI
Cartago
COLOMBIA
Nevado del Huila 18,865 ft. 5750 m
Guaviare
Orinoco

0 80 160 240 320 400 480 Miles
0 80 160 240 320 400 480 560 640 720 800 Kilometers

Lambert Azimuthal Equal Area Projection
Scale 1:16,000,000
One inch to 256 miles
One cm to 160 km

Inset map b
Lambert Conformal Conic Projection
Scale 1:1,000,000
One inch to 16 miles
One cm to 10 km

ATLANTIC OCEAN

GULF OF MEXICO

UNITED STATES
FLORIDA

Venice
Port Charlotte
Fort Myers
Cape Coral
Bonita Springs
Naples
Marco Island
CAPE ROMANO

Lake Okeechobee
Clewiston
Belle Glade
Stuart
Jupiter
Riviera Beach
West Palm Beach
Boynton Beach
Boca Raton
Pompano Beach
Fort Lauderdale
Hollywood
Miami Beach
Hialeah
Miami
Homestead
The Everglades
Biscayne Bay
Big Cypress Swamp
Tamiami Canal
Marquesas Keys
Dry Tortugas
CAPE SABLE
Florida Bay
Key Largo
Marathon
Key West
FLORIDA KEYS
Straits of Florida

GREAT SALE CAY
LITTLE ABACO
Cooper's Town
West End
McLeans Town
Freeport
GRAND BAHAMA
Marsh Harbour
ABACO
MOORE'S ISLAND
Sandy Point
SOUTHWEST POINT
Northwest Providence Channel
BIMINI ISLANDS
Alice Town
BERRY ISLANDS
Nicholl's Town
Nassau
NEW PROVIDENCE
ANDROS
Andros Town
Dunmore Town
ELEUTHERA
Governor's Harbour
Rock Sound
EAST END POINT
Arthur's Town
CAT ISLAND
New Bight
Port Howe
HAWKS NEST POINT
B A H A M A
Northeast Providence Channel
Tongue of the Ocean
CISTERN POINT
Exuma Sound
GREAT GUANA CAY
CAPE SANTA MARIA
RUM CAY
EXUMA CAYS
GREAT EXUMA
LITTLE EXUMA
LONG ISLAND
Deadman's Cay
Clarence Town
RAGGED ISLAND RANGE
JUMENTOS CAYS
CAPE VERDE
RAGGED ISLAND
Crooked

Tropic of Cancer

CAY SAL BANK
CAY SAL BANK
CAY SAL
ANGUILLA CAYS
Santaren Channel
Nicholas Channel
Old Bahama Channel
GREAT BAHAMA BANK

HAVANA (LA HABANA)
CIUDAD DE LA HABANA
La Esperanza
Minas de Matahambre
PINAR DEL RIO
Guane
Pinar del Rio
Los Palacios
Candelaria
Artemisa
LA HABANA
Güira de Melena
Güines
Jovellanos
Colón
Matanzas
Cárdenas
Quemado de Güines
Sagua la Grande
MATANZAS
VILLA CLARA
Santa Clara
Caibarién
Yaguajay
CAYO FRAGOSO
ARCH. DE SABANA
ARCH. DE CAMAGÜEY
CAYO COCO
CAYO GUILLERMO
CABO DE SAN ANTONIO
CABO CORRIENTES
CAYOS DE SAN FELIPE
Nueva Gerona
ISLA DE LA JUVENTUD
La Fe
Ensenada de la Siguanea
ARCHIPIÉLAGO DE LOS CANARREOS
CAYO LARGO
PENÍNSULA DE ZAPATA
PUNTA GORDA
Golfo de Batabanó
Ensenada de la Broa
Jagüey Grande
Aguada de Pasajeros
Palmira
Cienfuegos
CIENFUEGOS
Bahía de Cochinos (Bay of Pigs)
Pico San Juan 3740 ft. 1140 m
Trinidad
SANCTI SPÍRITUS
Placetas
Sancti Spíritus
CIEGO DE ÁVILA
Morón
Ciego de Ávila
Esmeralda
CAYO ROMANO
CAYO GUAJABA
CAYO SABINAL
CAMAGÜEY
Camagüey
Minas
Nuevitas
Florida
Vertientes
Presa Zaza
Tunas de Zaza
Júcaro
Golfo de Ana Maria
ARCHIPIÉLAGO DE LOS JARDINES DE LA REINA
San Pedro
Santa Cruz del Sur
Golfo de Guacanayabo
CUBA
Martí
LAS TUNAS
Las Tunas
Puerto Padre
Gibara
Holguín
Banes
PUNTA DE MULAS
HOLGUÍN
Cueto
Mayarí
Sagua de Tánamo
Bahía de Nipe
Bayamo
Jiguaní
GRANMA
Manzanillo
Campechuela
Niquero
CABO CRUZ
SANTIAGO DE CUBA
SIERRA MAESTRA
Palma Soriano
GUANTÁNAMO
Guantánamo
Caimanera
Pico Turquino 6470 ft. 1972 m
Santiago de Cuba
Bahía de Guantánamo

LITTLE CAYMAN
CAYMAN BRAC
GRAND CAYMAN
George Town
CAYMAN ISLANDS (U.K.)
CAYMAN TRENCH

a

ATLANTIC OCEAN

PUERTO RICO (U.S.)
PUNTA AGUJEREADA
Aguadilla
PUNTA HIGÜERO
San Sebastián
Mayagüez
Hormigueros
CABO ROJO
San Germán
Lares
Yauco
Guánica
CABO ROJO
Sabana Grande
Isabela
Hatillo
Arecibo
Manatí
Vega Baja
Florida
Vega Alta
Bayamón
Guaynabo
San Juan
Carolina
Trujillo Alto
Río Grande
CABEZAS DE SAN JUAN
Fajardo
Ceiba
PUNTA PUERCA
El Toro 3524 ft. 1074 m
Cayey
Caguas
Cidra
Juncos
San Lorenzo
SIERRA DE CAYEY
Humacao
PUNTA SANTIAGO
Yabucoa
Maunabo
PUNTA PETRONA
Guayama
Salinas
Santa Isabel
Coamo
Juana Díaz
Ponce
Guayanilla
Peñuelas
CORDILLERA CENTRAL
Cerro de Punta 4390 ft. 1338 m
Grande de Añasco
Canal de la Mona
CABO ROJO
ISLA CAJA DE MUERTOS
CARIBBEAN SEA
ISLA DE CULEBRA
Virgin Passage
Sonda de Vieques
ISLA DE VIEQUES
Pasaje de Vieques
PUNTA ESTE

Montego Bay
Falmouth
Ocho Rios
SOUTH NEGRIL POINT
Savanna-la-Mar
Mandeville
May Pen
Mt. Denham 3235 ft. 986 m
JAMAICA
Spanish Town
Kingston
Blue Mountain Peak 7402 ft. 2256 m
Port Antonio
MORANT POINT
PORTLAND POINT
Portland Bight
NAVASSA I. (U.S.; claimed by Haiti)
Jamaica Channel
PEDRO CAYS (Jam.)
MORANT CAYS (Jam.)
CARIB

© Rand McNally
A-101690-1

Inset map a
Lambert Conformal Conic Projection
Scale 1:2,000,000
One inch to 32 miles
One cm to 20 km

b

ICN

PUERTO RICO TRENCH

ATLANTIC OCEAN

PUERTO RICO (U.S.)

Aguadilla Arecibo
PUNTA HIGÜERO **San Juan**
Bayamón
Mayagüez Cerro de Punta
4390 ft. Caguas Fajardo
1338 m Humacao
CORD. △ CENTRAL
CABO ROJO Ponce Guayama

ISLA DE MONA
ISLA DE VIEQUES

Canal de la Mona

ISLA DE CULEBRA
Charlotte Amalie
ST. THOMAS TORTOLA
ST. JOHN Road Town

VIRGIN ISLANDS (U.S.)
BRITISH VIRGIN ISLANDS (U.K.)

ANEGADA
VIRGIN GORDA

Anegada Passage

SOMBRERO

ANGUILLA (U.K.)
DOG I. SCRUB I.
The Valley
ST. MARTIN
Philipsburg SAINT MAARTEN
NETHERLANDS ANTILLES (Neth.) ST.-BARTHÉLEMY

SABA SINT EUSTATIUS

ST. KITTS AND NEVIS
ST. CHRISTOPHER
Basseterre
Nevis Peak
Charlestown 3232 ft.
NEVIS 985 m

REDONDA

GUADELOUPE (France)

BARBUDA

ANTIGUA AND BARBUDA
Boggy Peak St. John's
1319 ft. ANTIGUA
402 m

MONTSERRAT (U.K.)
Soufrière Hills

POINTE DE LA GRANDE VIGIE
BASSE-TERRE GRANDE-TERRE
LA DÉSIRADE
Pointe-à-Pitre Les Abymes
Soufrière 4813 ft.
1467 m △ **GUADELOUPE** (France)
Basse-Terre Trois-Rivières
MARIE-GALANTE
LES SAINTES Grand-Bourg

Guadeloupe Passage

Dominica Passage

Frederiksted Christiansted
ST. CROIX

ISLA LAS AVES (Venezuela)

VENEZUELAN BASIN

CARIBBEAN SEA

Morne Diablotins Marigot
4747 ft. **DOMINICA**
1447 m
Roseau

Martinique Passage

MAS

SAN SALVADOR (WATLING ISLAND)

SAMANA CAY

CROOKED ISLAND
NORTH EAST POINT

LONG CAY Bight of Acklins

ACKLINS

SALINA POINT

Mayaguana Passage

MAYAGUANA

TURKS AND CAICOS ISLANDS (U.K.)

Kew NORTH CAICOS
PROVIDENCIALES MIDDLE CAICOS EAST CAICOS
WEST CAICOS **CAICOS ISLANDS**
NORTH EAST POINT

Caicos Passage

Turks Island Passage

Grand Turk
TURKS ISLANDS

SEAL CAYS

MOUCHOIR BANK

Mouchoir Passage

Island Passage

MARTINIQUE (France)
Montagne Pelée La Trinité
4583 ft.
1397 m Le Lamentin
Fort-de-France

POINTE DES SALINES
POINTE DU CAP
St. Lucia Channel
Castries

Mt. Gimie **ST. LUCIA**
3117 ft.
950 m Vieux Fort

St. Vincent Passage

Soufrière Georgetown
4049 ft.
1234 m **ST. VINCENT**
Kingstown
BEQUIA
ST. VINCENT AND THE GRENADINES
MUSTIQUE
CANOUAN
UNION I.
GRENADINES
CARRIACOU
RONDE I.

BARBADOS
Speightstown
Mt. Hillaby
1115 ft.
Bridgetown 340 m

PALACCA POINT
Matthew Town
Lake Rosa
GREAT INAGUA

Baracoa
PUNTA DE QUEMADO

Windward Passage

SILVER BANK

Silver Bank Passage

NAVIDAD BANK

Mt. St. Catherine
2756 ft.
840 m Grenville
St. George's
GRENADA

ANTILLES
LESSER
WINDWARD ISLANDS

Port de Paix
ÎLE DE LA TORTUE
CAP DU MÔLE
CAP-HAÏTIEN CABO ISABELA
Monte Cristi Puerto Plata CABO MACORÍS
CAP À FOUX Limbé CABO FRANCÉS VIEJO
Fort-Liberté
Gonaïves Dajabón Mao
HISPANIOLA Santiago de los Caballeros
Golfe de la Gonâve Morne Bonhomme Tamboril Moca
5866 ft. Hinche San Francisco de Macorís Nagua
1788 m La Vega Yuna Sánchez
Saint-Marc Pico Duarte Bahía de Samaná
Terrettes 10,417 ft. Bonao CABO SAMANÁ
ÎLE DE LA GONÂVE 3175 m △ Bahía Escocesa
HAITI Comendador **DOMINICAN REPUBLIC** El Seibo
Port-au-Prince San Juan de la Maguana Villa CABO ENGAÑO
Léogâne Pétion-Ville Alto Bandera Altagracia Higüey
8629 ft. **Santo Domingo**
Petit-Goâve 2630 m Lago Consuelo
GRANDE CAYEMITE Sabana Enriquillo Bajos de Haina La Romana
Jérémie Jacmel Yegua San Pedro de Macorís
Pic Macaya Neiba Azua San Cristóbal ISLA SAONA
POINTE 7700 ft. Baní Bahía de Yuma
FANCHON 2347 m Morne La Selle Barahona
8773 ft. Bahía de Ocoa PUNTA PALENQUE
Aquin 2674 m Pedernales Bahía de la Mona
Les Cayes Enriquillo
Coteaux ÎLE À VACHE CABO FALSO
POINTE ABACOU CABO BEATA
ISLA BEATA

Canal de la Mona

TOBAGO Charlotteville
Scarborough GALERA POINT
El Cerro del Aripo
3084 ft. **TRINIDAD AND TOBAGO**
PENÍNSULA DE PARIA 940 m Morvant
Güiria **Port of Spain** Arima Sangre Grande
TRINIDAD Rio Claro
San Fernando GALEOTA POINT
Point Fortin
Gulf of Paria Serpents Mouth

Canal du Sud
Canal de Saint-Marc

BEAN SEA

B E A N S E A

© Rand McNally A-101689-1

© Rand McNally A-101691-1

DELTA DEL ORINOCO
ISLA TOBEJUBA
VENEZUELA
Tucupita DELTA AMACURO

Pedernales

0 25 50 75 100 125 150 Miles
0 25 50 75 100 125 150 175 200 225 250 Kilometers

Lambert Conformal Conic Projection
Scale 1:5,000,000
One inch to 80 miles
One cm to 50 km

Inset map b
Lambert Conformal Conic Projection
Scale 1:5,000,000
One inch to 80 miles
One cm to 50 km

0   40   80   120   160   200   240 Miles

0   40 80 120 160 200 240 280 320 360   400 Kilometers

Lambert Azimuthal Equal Area Projection
Scale 1:8,000,000
One inch to 128 miles
One cm to 80 km

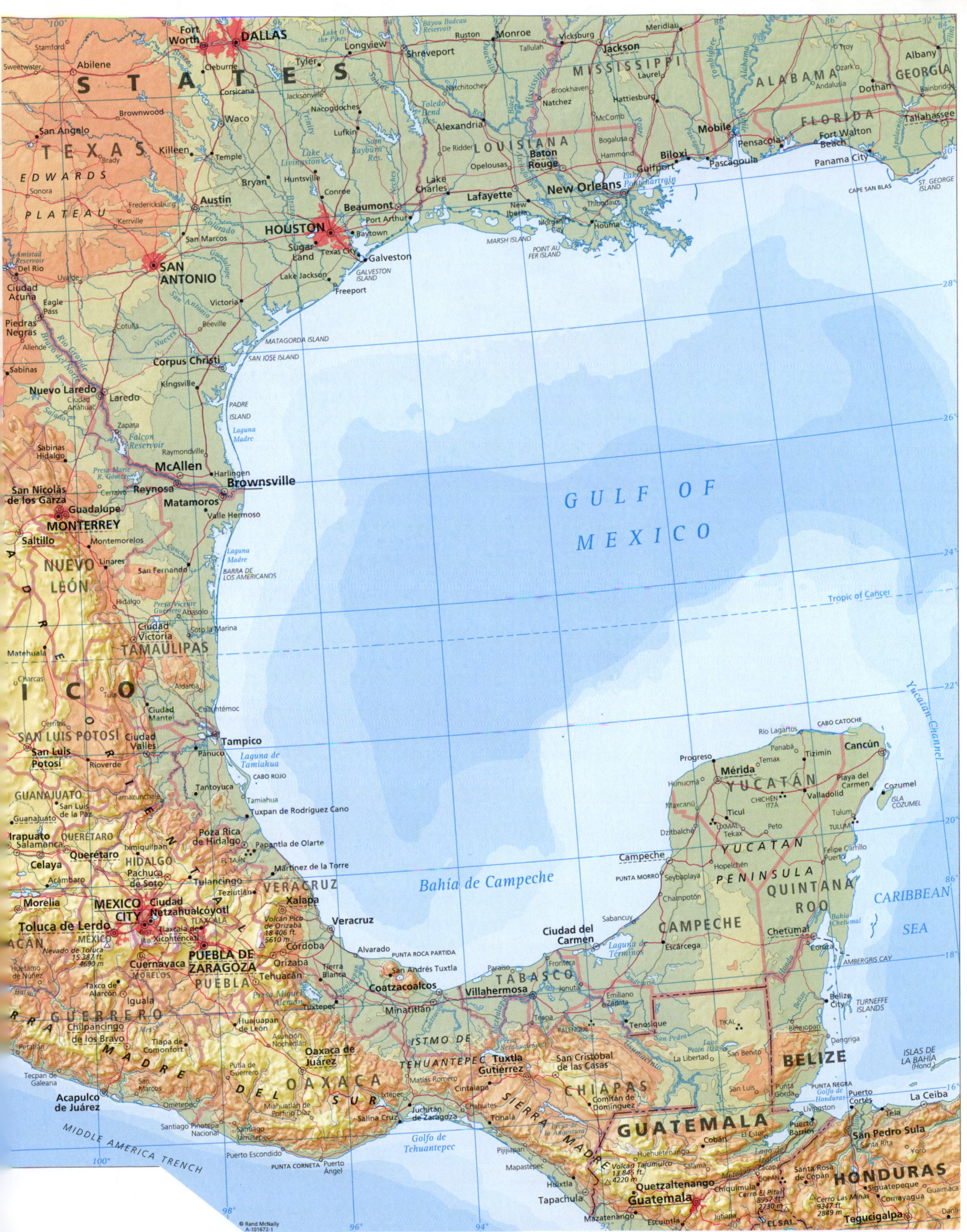

UNITED STATES

Fort Worth DALLAS
Cleburne
Stamford Corsicana Longview Ruston Monroe Vicksburg Jackson Meridian Troy Albany Georgia
Sweetwater Abilene Tyler Shreveport Tallulah MISSISSIPPI Bainbridge
Brownwood Jacksonville Nacogdoches Natchitoches Natchez Brookhaven Hattiesburg ALABAMA Dothan Andalusia Ozark
San Angelo Waco Lufkin Alexandria McComb Mobile Pensacola FLORIDA
Brady EDWARDS De Ridder Opelousas Baton Bogalusa Biloxi Fort Walton Panama City
Sonora PLATEAU Austin Temple Conroe Lake Rouge Gulfport Pascagoula Beach
Fredericksburg Bryan Charles Lafayette New Orleans CAPE SAN BLAS ST. GEORGE
Kerrville HOUSTON Beaumont New Houma ISLAND
Amistad San Marcos Sugar Port Arthur Iberia Morgan POINT AU
Reservoir SAN ANTONIO Land Baytown MARSH ISLAND FER ISLAND
Del Rio Lake Jackson Galveston
Ciudad Uvalde Victoria Texas City GALVESTON
Acuña Cotulla Freeport ISLAND
Eagle Beeville
Pass MATAGORDA ISLAND
Piedras Corpus Christi SAN JOSE ISLAND
Negras
Allende Kingsville
Sabinas PADRE SAN JOSE ISLAND
Nuevo Laredo ISLAND
Ciudad Laredo
Anáhuac
Zapata Laguna
Falcon Madre
Reservoir Raymondville
Sabinas Presa Mari Harlingen
Hidalgo R. Gómez McAllen
San Nicolás Reynosa Brownsville
de los Garza Cerralvo Matamoros
MONTERREY Guadalupe Valle Hermoso
Saltillo Montemorelos Laguna
NUEVO Linares Madre
LEÓN San Fernando BARRA DE
Hidalgo LOS AMERICANOS

GULF OF
MEXICO

Matehuala
Presa Vicente
Guerrero Abasolo
Charcas Aldama
Ciudad Soto la Marina
Victoria
TAMAULIPAS
Tropic of Cancer

Ciudad
Mantel
Cuauhtémoc

SAN LUIS POTOSÍ Ciudad Tampico
San Luis Valles Pánuco Laguna de
Potosí Tamiahua
Rioverde CABO ROJO Progreso Panabá Tizimín Cancún
GUANAJUATO Tantoyuca Tamiahua YUCATÁN Temax Río Lagartos CABO CATOCHE
San Luis Tuxpan de Rodríguez Cano Hunucmá Mérida
Guanajuato de la Paz Maxcanú CHICHÉN Valladolid Cozumel
Irapuato Ixmiquilpan Papantla de Olarte Ticul ITZÁ ISLA
Salamanca QUERÉTARO EL TAJÍN Dzitbalché Peto Tulum COZUMEL
Celaya Querétaro YUCATÁN IXMAL TULUM
Acámbaro Pachuca HIDALGO Tulancingo Campeche PENINSULA Felipe Carrillo
Morelia de Soto Teziutlán Martínez de la Torre PUNTA MORRO Puerto
MEXICO Ciudad Xalapa Seybaplaya QUINTANA
Toluca de Lerdo CITY Netzahualcóyotl Volcán Pico Hopelchén ROO CARIBBEAN
MÉXICO TLAXCALA de Orizaba Veracruz CAMPECHE Champotón Chetumal SEA
Nevado de Toluca Tlaxcala de 18 406 ft. Sabancuy Bahía
15 387 ft. Xicoténcatl 5610 m Córdoba CAMPECHE Chetumal
4690 m PUEBLA DE Orizaba Alvarado PUNTA ROCA PARTIDA Escárcega AMBERGRIS CAY
Cuernavaca ZARAGOZA Tehuacán San Andrés Tuxtla Laguna de Corozal
MORELOS PUEBLA Sierra Paraíso Términos Belize
Taxco de Blanca Coatzacoalcos Frontera TURNEFFE
Alarcón Iguala Tuxtepec Villahermosa Emiliano City ISLANDS
Minatitlán TABASCO Zapata Belmopan ISLAS DE
GUERRERO Huajuapan Teapa Tenosique BELIZE LA BAHÍA
Chilpancingo de León TIKAL Dangriga (Hond.)
de los Bravo Asunción ISTMO DE San Pedro PALENQUE La Libertad San Benito
Petatlán Nochixtlán San Cristóbal Lago Punta Negra
Tlapa de Oaxaca de TEHUANTEPEC de las Casas Petén Golfo de
Comonfort Juárez Tuxtla CHIAPAS Itzá Honduras Puerto
Tecpan de Putla de Gutiérrez Comitán de Punta Cortés
Galeana Guerrero OAXACA Domínguez Gorda Livingston La Ceiba
SIERRA Matías Romero Cintalapa San Luis Tela
Acapulco Santa María Ixtepec SUR Chahuites Tonalá GUATEMALA Cobán El Estor Puerto Tela
de Juárez Nachtipa Salina Juchitán MADRE Huehuetenango Barrios Santa Rita
Santiago Pinotepa Santiago Cruz de Zaragoza Volcán Tajumulco Salamá Quetzaltenango Yoro HONDURAS
Nacional Jamiltepec 13 846 ft. de Copán Santa Rosa
MIDDLE AMERICA TRENCH Puerto Escondido Golfo de 4220 m GUATEMALA El Progreso de Copán Siguatepeque Guaimaca
PUNTA CORNETA Puerto Tehuantepec Guatemala Chiquimula COPÁN 9347 ft. Comayagua
Puerto Ángel Pijijiapan Cerro El Pital 2889 m Tegucigalpa
PUNTA CORNETA Ángel Mapastepec 8957 ft. Cerro Las Minas Danlí
Huixtla Quetzaltenango 2730 m
Tapachula Guatemala EL SAL. Juticalpa
Mazatenango Estancia

© Rand McNally
A-101672-1

Lambert Conformal Conic Projection
Scale 1:4,000,000
One inch to 64 miles
One cm to 40 km

0 20 40 60 80 100 120 Miles
0 20 40 60 80 100 120 140 160 180 200 Kilometers

CAMPECHE BANK

GULF OF MEXICO

PUNTA HOLOHIT

CABO CATOCHE

ISLA CONTOY

Rio Lagartos

Progreso

Chicxulub

Dzemul

Dzilam González

Panabá

Laguna de Yalahau

Puerto Juárez

ISLA MUJERES

Isla Mujeres

Celestún

Hunucmá

Mérida

Motul de Felipe Carrillo Puerto

Temax

Tizimín

Espita

Kantunilkin

Cancún

PUNTA CANCÚN

Estero Celestún

Umán

Izamal

Tunkás

X-Can

Puerto Morelos

CAYOS ARCAS

Maxcanú

Muna

YUCATÁN

Tekit

Valladolid

CHICHÉN ITZÁ

Chichimila

Chemax

COBÁ

Playa del Carmen

Halachó

Ticul

Oxkutzcab

Chikindzonot

Cozumel

Becal

Dzitbalché

UXMAL

Tekax

Y U C A T A N

Peto

ISLA COZUMEL

Tenabo

Hecelchakán

Tzucacab

Tulum

TULUM

Campeche

Bolonchén de Rejón

José Marla Morelos

Laguna Chichancanab

P E N I N S U L A

Bahía de la Ascensión

PUNTA MORRO

Seybaplaya

Hopelchén

Iturbide

Chunhuhux

Felipe Carrillo Puerto

Champotón

Dzibalchén

MEXICO

QUINTANA ROO

Nohbec

Sabancuy

CAMPECHE

Laguna Bacalar

Escárcega

Chetumal

Bahía Chetumal

BANCO CHINCHORRO

ISLA DEL CARMEN

Nuevo Progreso

Ciudad del Carmen

Laguna de Términos

Candelaria

CALAKMUL

Nicolás Bravo

Corozal

Xcalak

Paraíso

Frontera

Palizada

Caledonia

Laguna Mecoacán

Comalcalco

Laguna del Pom

Orange Walk

AMBERGRIS CAY

TABASCO

Cárdenas

Villahermosa

Laguna del Este

San Pedro Tabasco

San Pedro

CARIBBEAN SEA

Pichucalco

Teapa

Macuspana

Emiliano Zapata

Multé

Laguna Chinchil

Chuntuquí

Indian Church

CAY CORKER

Revolución Mexicana

PALENQUE

Palenque

Tenosique

Hill Bank

Belize City

NORTHERN CAY

Petalcingo

Chilón

Piedras Negras

TIKAL

El Encanto

Belmopan

Northern Lagoon

TURNEFFE ISLANDS

Copainalá

Simojovel

Ocosingo

San Pedro

Ciudad Melchor de Mencos

BELIZE

LONG CAY

HALF MOON CAY

Presa Nezahualcóyotl

San Cristóbal de las Casas

Cerro Los Bolones △ 9154 ft. 2790 m

Lago Petén Itzá

Benque Viejo Del Carmen

Middlesex

Dangriga

SOUTH WATER CAY

Presa Chicoasén

Ocozocuautla

Chiapa de Corzo

San Benito

Flores

Ocozocoautla

Tuxtla Gutiérrez

CHIAPAS

La Libertad

Savaxché

Victoria Peak △ 3675 ft. 1120 m

Venustiano Carranza

Las Rosas

Laguna Lacandón

San Luis

Dolores

M A Y A M O U N T A I N S

LAUGHING BIRD CAY

ISLA DE ROATÁN

Villa Flores

Las Margaritas

La Florida

La Pasión

RANGUANA CAY

Roatán

Socoltenango

Comitán de Domínguez

PUNTA NEGRA

SAPODILLA CAYS

ISLA DE UTILA

ISLAS DE LA BAHÍA

Revolución Mexicana

La Trinitaria

Punta Gorda

Utila

Las Delicias

Gulf of Honduras

Presa de la Angostura

Cerro el Triunfo △ 8038 ft. 2450 m

Paso Hondo

CABO TRES PUNTAS

Barillas

Chisec

Chahal

Bahía de Amatique

Puerto Cortés

Baracoa

Colorado

La Ceiba

Chicomuselo

Jacaltenango

Livingston

Santa Isabel

Sarstoon

El Golfete

Pico Bonito △ 7989 ft. 2435 m

Cerro de Huista

Concepción Huista

San Pedro Carchá

El Estor

Puerto Barrios

Choloma

S I E R R A M A D R E

Mapastepec

Motozintla de Mendoza

Cobán

QUIRIGUÁ

Lago de Izabal

Cerro San Ildefonso △ 7310 ft. 2228 m

San Pedro Sula

El Progreso

Pico Pijol △ 7487 ft. 2282 m

Yoro

Olanchito

Huixtla

Volcán Tacaná △ 13 428 ft. 4093 m

San Pedro Sacatepéquez

Santa Cruz del Quiché

Salamá

San Jerónimo

Panzós

La Lima

El Negrito

Aguán

Tapachula

Volcán Tajumulco △ 13 845 ft. 4220 m

Quetzaltenango

Chichicastenango

Zacapa

COPÁN

Santa Bárbara

Lago de Yojoa

Siguatepeque

Minas de Oro

Salamá

Puerto Madero

Volcán Santa María △ 12 375 ft. 3772 m

Chimaltenango

GUATEMALA

Chiquimula

Santa Rosa de Copán

HONDURAS

San Ignacio

Guaimaca

Volcán Tajumulco

Lago de Atitlán

Jalapa

San Luis Jilotepeque

Cerro Las Minas △ 9347 ft. 2849 m

Comayagua

Retalhuleu

Mazatenango

Antigua Guatemala

Guatemala

Villa Nueva

Laguna de Ayarza

La Esperanza

La Paz

Montaña El Chile △ 7402 ft. 2256 m

Champerico

Volcán de Fuego △ 12 346 ft. 3763 m

Escuintla

Barberena

Cuilapa

Jutiapa

Cerro El Pital △ 8957 ft. 2730 m

Metapán

Lago de Güija

CORDILLERA OPALACA

MONTAÑAS DE COMAYAGUA

Chiquimulilla

Chalatenango

Tegucigalpa

Yuscarán

Danlí

Puerto San José

Santa Ana

Apopa

Soyapango

Cojutepeque

San Francisco

Sabanagrande

Güinope

Sonsonate

Nueva San Salvador

San Salvador

Lago de Ilopango

Volcán de San Vicente △ 7156 ft. 2181 m

San Miguel

San Marcos de Colón

Acajutla

PUNTA REMEDIOS

San Vicente

Usulután

La Unión

Choluteca

PACIFIC OCEAN

MIDDLE AMERICA TRENCH

EL SALVADOR

Bahía de Jiquilisco

Laguna de Olomega

Golfo de Fonseca

Volcán Cosigüina △ 2818 ft. 859 m

El Corpus

NICARAGUA

© Rand McNally
A-101673-1

0 20 40 60 80 100 120 Miles

0 20 40 60 80 100 120 140 160 180 200 Kilometers

Lambert Conformal Conic Projection
Scale 1:4,000,000
One inch to 64 miles
One cm to 40 km

0   20   40   60   80   100   120 Miles
0 20 40 60 80 100 120 140 160 180 200 Kilometers

Lambert Conformal Conic Projection
Scale 1:4,000,000
One inch to 64 miles
One cm to 40 km

a

Map labels — Inset map (a)

CARIBBEAN SEA

NICARAGUA

Laguna Páhara
Puerto Cabezas

ISLA DE PROVIDENCIA

SAN ANDRÉS Y PROVIDENCIA
(Colombia)

ISLA DE SAN ANDRÉS · San Andrés

CAYOS DEL ESTE SUDESTE

ISLAS DEL MAÍZ
(Nicaragua)

CAYOS DE ALBUQUERQUE

C A R I B B E A N   S E A

Inset map (a) labels

PUNTA MANZANILLO

Portobelo
Nombre de Dios
Palenque
Miramar
Playa Chiquita

Cerro Bruja 3212 ft 979 m

María Chiquita

COLÓN

Coco Solo
Colón
Cativá
Puerto Pilón

Cristóbal
Rainbow City
Río Rita
Salamanca
La Mesa

GATÚN LOCKS
Margarita
Gatuncillo

Nuevo Chagres
Palmas Bellas
Gatún
Buena Vista

Escobal
Lago Gatún
ISLA BARRO COLORADO
Chilibre
Calzada Larga

Bahía Trinidad
Panama Canal (Canal de Panamá)
Gamboa
Lago Alajuela
Tocumen
Pacora

Lagarterita
Las Cumbres
Paraíso
Pedro Miguel
Juan Díaz

Arenosa
Cerro Cama
PEDRO MIGUEL LOCKS
San Miguelito

Boca del Río Indio
MIRAFLORES LOCKS
Diablo Heights
Panamá

PANAMA
La Zanguenga
Arraiján
Balboa

COCLÉ
Pueblo Nuevo
La Chorrera
Nuevo Arraiján
Vacamonte

Ciri Grande
Bahía de Panamá

Río Indio
Taboga

Lídice
Capira

©Rand McNally
A-101679-1

Main map labels

CARIBBEAN SEA

COSTA RICA

Puerto Limón
Vesta
PUNTA MONA

ISLA COLÓN
ARCHIPIÉLAGO DE BOCAS DEL TORO

CORDILLERA DE TALAMANCA
Cerro Kamuk △ 11 660 ft. 3554 m
Buenos Aires

Almirante
Bocas del Toro
ISLA BASTIMENTOS
ISLA POPA
Laguna de Chiriquí
PEN. VALIENTE
ISLA ESCUDO DE VERAGUAS

Golfo de los Mosquitos

PUNTA MANZANILLO
Nombre de Dios
El Porvenir
Golfo de San Blas
Ticantiquí

Portobelo
Panama Canal (Canal de Panamá)
Colón
Cristóbal
ISTMO DE PANAMÁ
SERRANÍA DE SAN BLAS
PUNTA MOSQUITO

Volcán Barú 11 401 ft 3475 m
Chiriquí
Grande
Bajo Boquete
Volcán
Palmas Bellas
Lago Gatún
Gamboa
Lago Alajuela
Paraíso
Chepo
Mansucum

CORDILLERA CENTRAL
San Miguelito
Chepo
Chepo

P A N A M A

PEN. DE OSA
Golfo Dulce
CABO MATAPALO
Golfito

La Concepción
Dolega
Gualaca
David
Cerro Santiago 9959 ft 2121 m
Santa Fe

Puerto Armuelles, Pedregal
Concepción
Remedios
El Valle
Penonomé
Antón
La Chorrera
Capira
Lídice
San Miguel
Chimán

Bahía de Charco Azul
ISLA SEVILLA
Las Lajas
Las Palmas
Natá
San Carlos
Bejuco

PUNTA BURICA
ISLA BOCA BRAVA
ISLA PARIDA
Golfo de Chiriquí
Soná
Santiago
Montija
Pesé
Aguadulce
Río Hato
San Miguel

Bahía de Parita
ISLA SAN JOSE
Golfo de San Miguel
PUNTA GARACHINÉ
Garachiné

Golfo de Montijo
Monagrillo
Chitré
Guararé
La Palma

ISLA DE COIBA
PENÍNSULA DE AZUERO
Las Tablas
La Palma
Pedasí

ISLA DE CEBACO
Tonosí
PUNTA MALA

ISLA JICARÓN
PUNTA MARIATO

Golfo de Panamá
ARCHIPIÉLAGO DE LAS PERLAS
ISLA DEL REY
SERRANÍA DE SAN BLAS

Bahía de Panamá
San Miguelito
Panamá

Jaqué

SERRANÍA DEL DARIÉN
Acandí
Golfo de Urabá
CABO TIBURÓN
PUNTA CARIBANA

El Real de Santa María
Yaviza
La Palma
Turbo
Apartado

COLOMBIA
CHOCÓ
ANTIOQUIA
Chigorodó
Riosucio
Saláqui

PACIFIC OCEAN

PANAMA BASIN

PUNTA MARZO
Golfo de Cupica
SERRANÍA DE BAUDÓ
Nuquí
Quibdó
Ensenada de Tribugá

ANT.

Scale and projection

0 20 40 60 80 100 120 Miles
0 20 40 60 80 100 120 140 160 180 200 Kilometers

©Rand McNally
A-101677-1

Lambert Conformal Conic Projection
Scale 1:4,000,000
One inch to 64 miles
One cm to 40 km

Inset map a
Lambert Conformal Conic Projection
Scale 1:1,000,000
One inch to 16 miles
One cm to 10 km

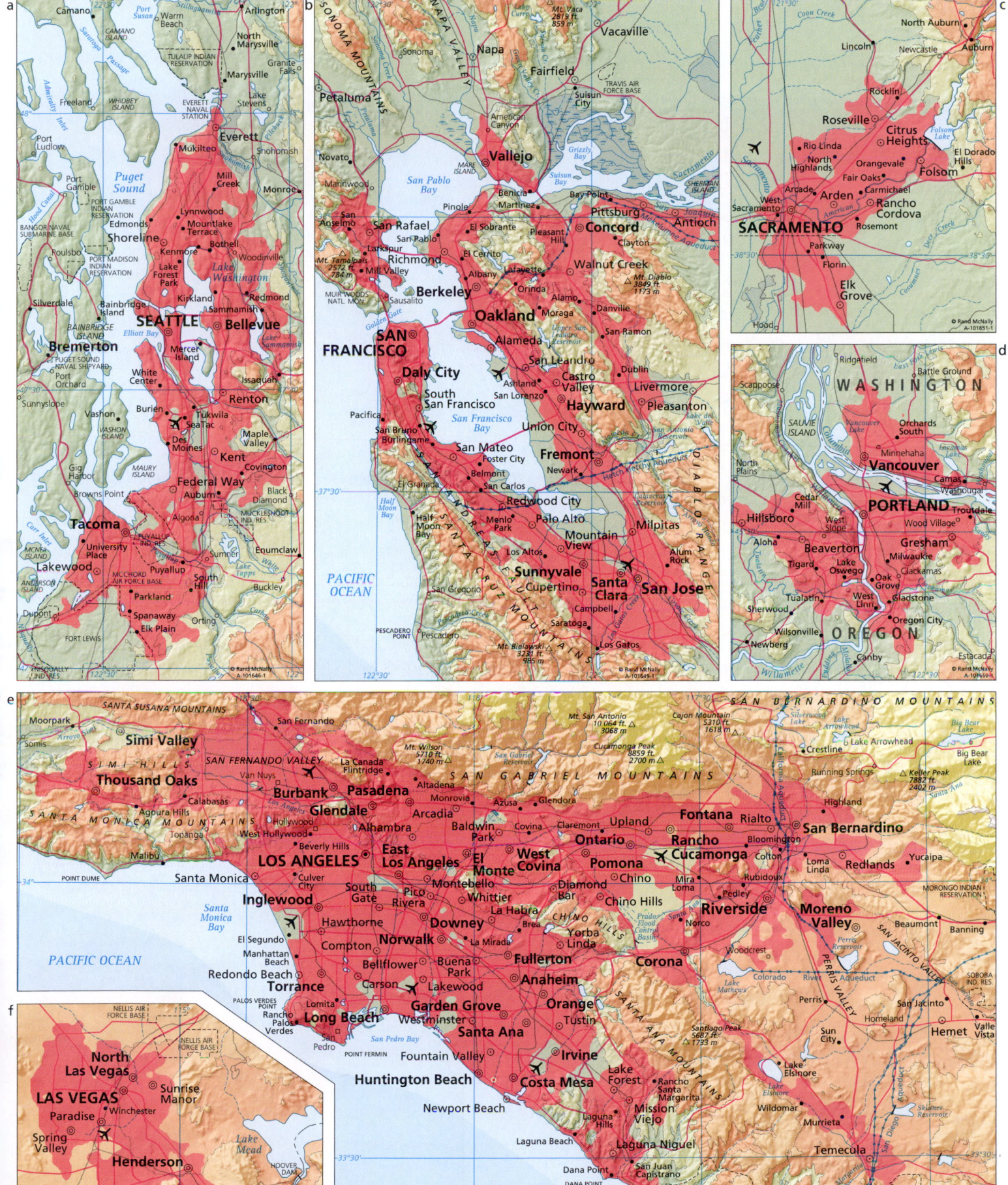

a

Camano
Arlington
Port Susan
Camano Island
North Marysville
Stillaguamish R.
Warm Beach
Granite Falls
Marysville
Lake Stevens
Snohomish
TULALIP INDIAN RESERVATION
EVERETT NAVAL STATION
Everett
Freeland
WHIDBEY ISLAND
Mukilteo
Mill Creek
Monroe
Admiralty Inlet
Port Gamble
Edmonds
Lynnwood
Mountlake Terrace
Bothell
Woodinville
Shoreline
Kenmore
Redmond
BANGOR NAVAL SUBMARINE BASE
Poulsbo
PORT MADISON INDIAN RESERVATION
Kirkland
Sammamish
Lake Washington
SEATTLE
Bellevue
Silverdale
Bainbridge Island
BAINBRIDGE ISLAND
Mercer Island
Issaquah
Bremerton
PUGET SOUND NAVAL SHIPYARD
White Center
Renton
Port Orchard
Sunnyslope
Burien
Tukwila
SeaTac
Maple Valley
Vashon
VASHON ISLAND
Des Moines
Kent
Covington
Black Diamond
Gig Harbor
MAURY ISLAND
Federal Way
Algona
Auburn
Carr Inlet
University Place
Sumner
Buckley
MCNEIL ISLAND
Puyallup
South Hill
Enumclaw
ANDERSON ISLAND
Tacoma
Lakewood
MCCHORD AIR FORCE BASE
Parkland
Spanaway
Elk Plain
Orting
Dupont
FORT LEWIS
NISQUALLY IND. RES.
© Rand McNally
A-101646-1

b

SONOMA MOUNTAINS
Mt. Vaca 2819 ft. 859 m
Vacaville
Napa
NAPA VALLEY
Sonoma
Fairfield
Suisun City
TRAVIS AIR FORCE BASE
Petaluma
American Canyon
Grizzly Bay
Sacramento R.
Novato
MARE ISLAND
Vallejo
Benicia
Bay Point
Pittsburg
Antioch
Marinwood
San Pablo Bay
Martinez
Clayton
Concord
San Anselmo
San Rafael
Pinole
El Sobrante
Pleasant Hill
San Pablo
Larkspur
Richmond
El Cerrito
Lafayette
Walnut Creek
Mt. Tamalpais 2572 ft. 784 m
Mill Valley
Albany
Orinda
Alamo
Mt. Diablo 3849 ft. 1173 m
MUIR WOODS NATL. MON.
Sausalito
Berkeley
Moraga
Danville
Golden Gate
Oakland
San Ramon
SAN FRANCISCO
Alameda
San Leandro
Dublin
Daly City
Castro Valley
Livermore
South San Francisco
Ashland
Pleasanton
Pacifica
San Lorenzo
Hayward
San Bruno
Burlingame
San Mateo
Union City
Foster City
Newark
Fremont
Belmont
El Granada
San Carlos
Half Moon Bay
Redwood City
Half Moon Bay
Menlo Park
Palo Alto
Milpitas
Alum Rock
Los Altos
Mountain View
San Gregorio
Sunnyvale
Cupertino
Santa Clara
Pescadero
Campbell
San Jose
PESCADERO POINT
Saratoga
Mt. Bielawski 3231 ft. 985 m
Los Gatos
PACIFIC OCEAN
© Rand McNally
A-101649-1

c

North Auburn
Lincoln
Newcastle
Auburn
Rocklin
Roseville
Citrus Heights
Folsom Lake
Rio Linda
North Highlands
Orangevale
El Dorado Hills
Folsom
Arcade
Fair Oaks
Carmichael
West Sacramento
SACRAMENTO
Arden
Rancho Cordova
Rosemont
Parkway
Florin
Hood
Elk Grove
© Rand McNally
A-101651-1

d

Ridgefield
Battle Ground
WASHINGTON
Scappoose
Orchards South
Minnehaha
Vancouver
Camas
Washougal
North Plains
SAUVIE ISLAND
Cedar Mill
PORTLAND
Troutdale
Hillsboro
West Slope
Wood Village
Aloha
Beaverton
Gresham
Tigard
Lake Oswego
Milwaukie
Clackamas
Tualatin
Oak Grove
West Linn
Gladstone
Sherwood
Oregon City
Wilsonville
Newberg
Canby
OREGON
Estacada
© Rand McNally
A-101650-1

e

SANTA SUSANA MOUNTAINS
San Fernando
Mt. San Antonio 10,064 ft. 3068 m
Cajon Mountain 5310 ft. 1678 m
SAN BERNARDINO MOUNTAINS
Silverwood Lake
Big Bear Lake
Moorpark
Simi Valley
SIMI HILLS
SAN FERNANDO VALLEY
Mt. Wilson 5710 ft. 1740 m
Cucamonga Peak 8859 ft. 2700 m
Crestline
Lake Arrowhead
Big Bear Lake
Somis
La Cañada Flintridge
SAN GABRIEL MOUNTAINS
Keller Peak 7882 ft. 2402 m
Thousand Oaks
Van Nuys
Altadena
Running Springs
SANTA MONICA MOUNTAINS
Burbank
Pasadena
Monrovia
Azusa
Glendora
Highland
Agoura Hills
Calabasas
Glendale
Arcadia
Topanga
Hollywood
Covina
Claremont
Upland
Fontana
Rialto
Malibu
West Hollywood
Alhambra
Baldwin Park
Rancho Cucamonga
San Bernardino
Beverly Hills
East Los Angeles
El Monte
West Covina
Bloomington
Colton
Loma Linda
Redlands
Yucaipa
POINT DUME
Santa Monica
LOS ANGELES
Ontario
Pomona
Chino
Mira Loma
Rubidoux
Pedley
Santa Monica Bay
Culver City
Montebello
Diamond Bar
Chino Hills
MORONGO INDIAN RESERVATION
PACIFIC OCEAN
Inglewood
South Gate
Pico Rivera
Whittier
La Habra
CHINO HILLS
Norco
Riverside
Beaumont
Banning
Hawthorne
Brea
Yorba Linda
Moreno Valley
El Segundo
Downey
La Mirada
Woodcrest
Manhattan Beach
Norwalk
Buena Park
Fullerton
Corona
Lake Mathews
Perris
SOBOBA IND. RES.
Redondo Beach
Bellflower
Lakewood
Anaheim
San Jacinto
Torrance
Carson
Orange
Tustin
Sun City
Hemet
Lomita
Garden Grove
Valle Vista
PALOS VERDES POINT
Rancho Palos Verdes
Long Beach
Westminster
Santa Ana
SANTA ANA MOUNTAINS
Santiago Peak 5687 ft. 1733 m
San Pedro
POINT FERMIN
San Pedro Bay
Fountain Valley
Irvine
Lake Elsinore
Wildomar
Huntington Beach
Costa Mesa
Lake Forest
Mission Viejo
Rancho Santa Margarita
Murrieta
Newport Beach
Laguna Hills
Temecula
Laguna Beach
Laguna Niguel
Dana Point
DANA POINT
San Juan Capistrano
CAMP PENDLETON MARINE CORPS BASE
PECHANGA INDIAN RESERVATION
San Clemente
© Rand McNally
A-101647-1

f

NELLIS AIR FORCE BASE
North Las Vegas
Sunrise Manor
LAS VEGAS
Winchester
Paradise
Lake Mead
Spring Valley
HOOVER DAM
Henderson
Boulder City
© Rand McNally
A-101648-1

0 5 10 15 20 25 30 Miles
0 5 10 15 20 25 30 35 40 45 50 Kilometers

Lambert Conformal Conic Projection
Scale 1:1,000,000
One inch to 16 miles
One cm to 10 km

a CLEVELAND

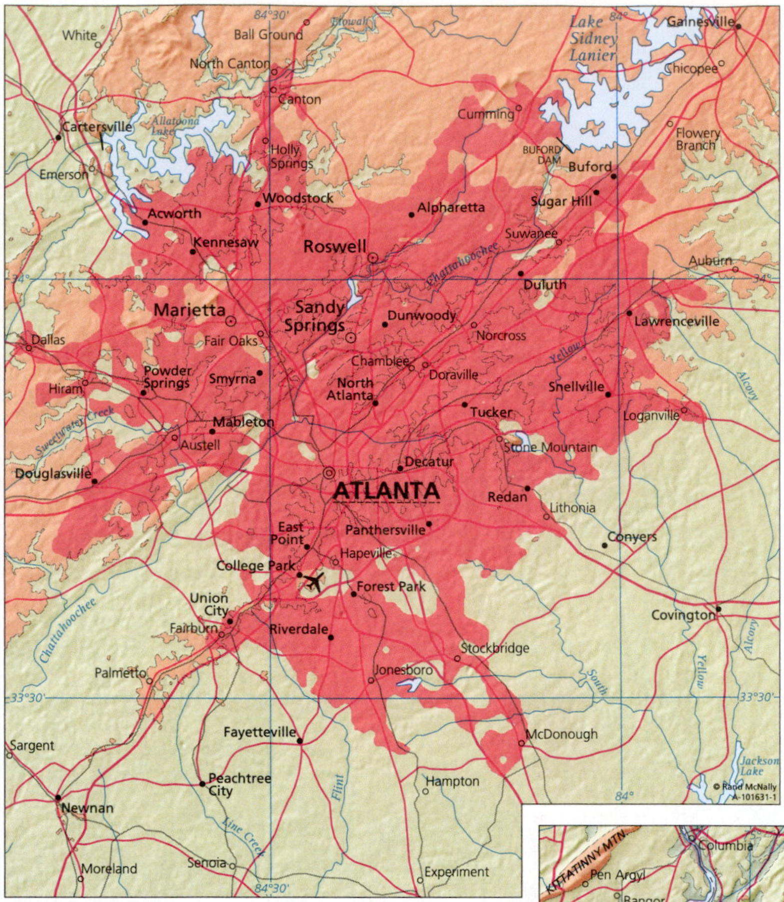

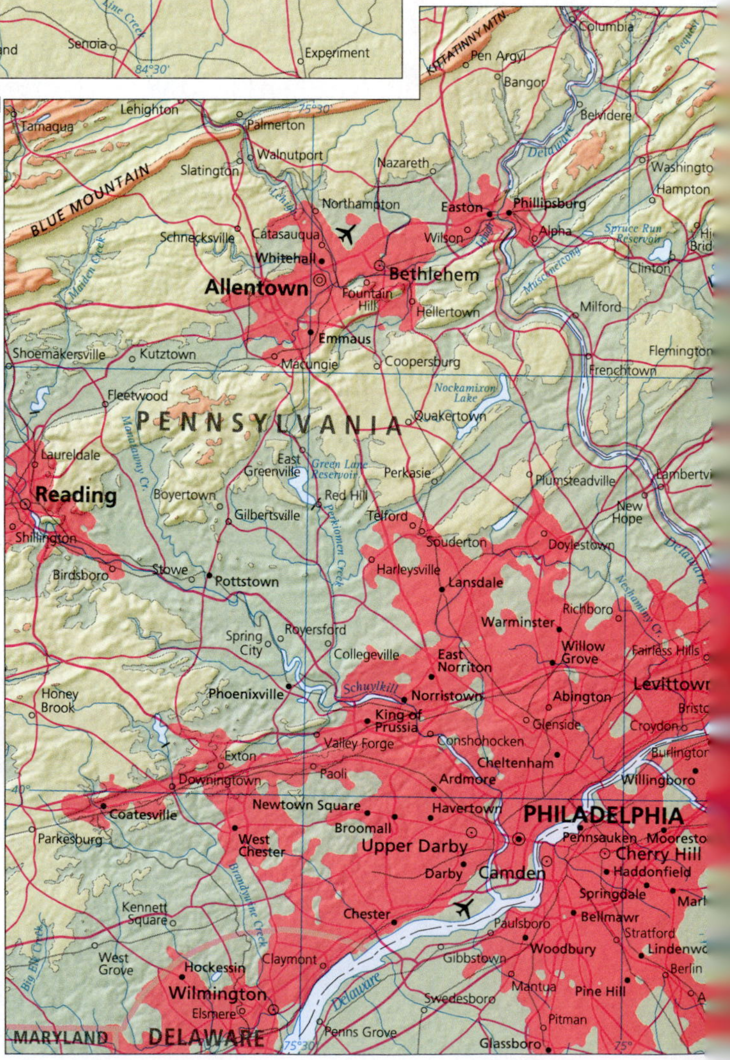

b ATLANTA

c BALTIMORE / WASHINGTON

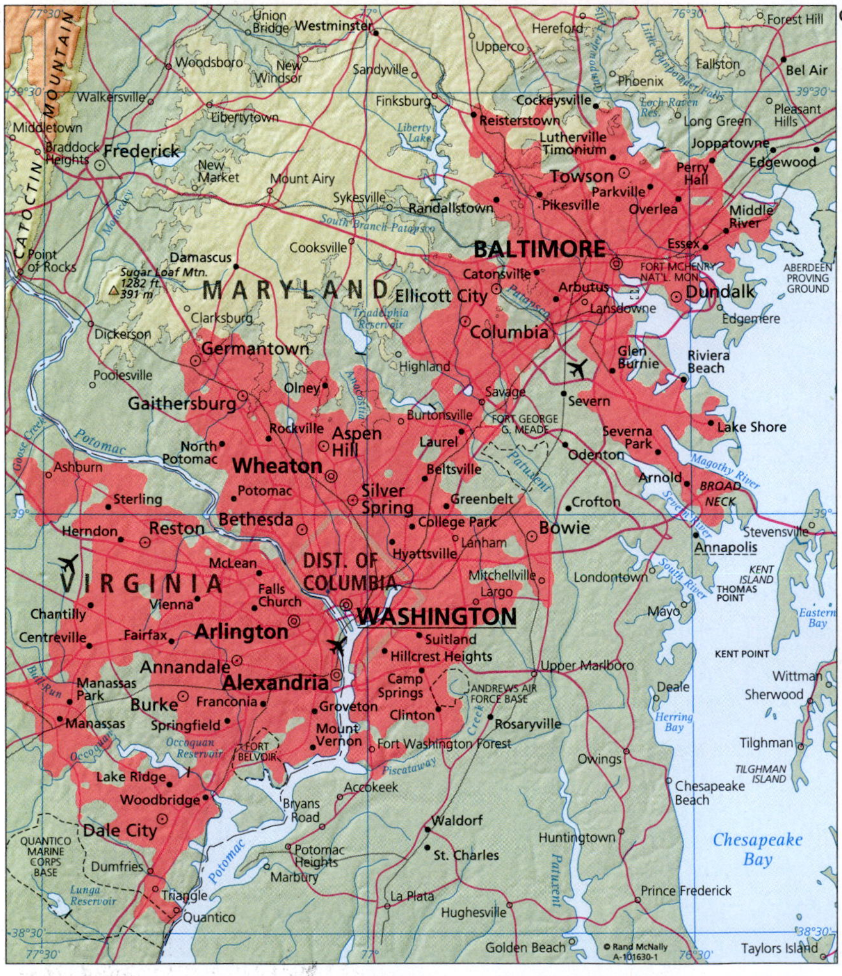

d PHILADELPHIA

Lambert Conformal Conic Projection
Scale 1:1,000,000
One inch to 16 miles
One cm to 10 km

30 Miles
50 Kilometers

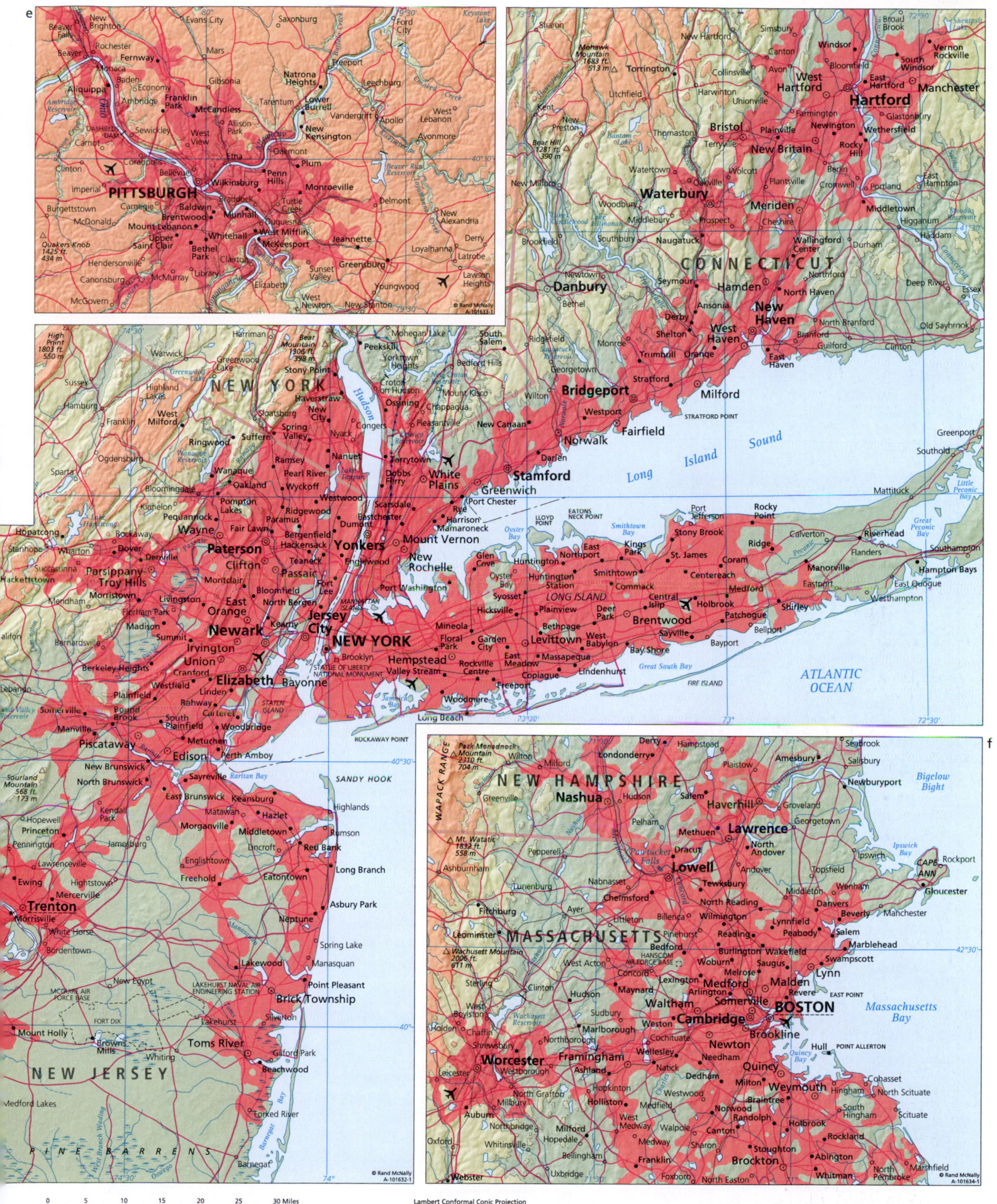

0   5   10   15   20   25   30 Miles

0   5   10   15   20   25   30   35   40   45   50 Kilometers

Lambert Conformal Conic Projection
Scale 1:1,000,000
One inch to 16 miles
One cm to 10 km

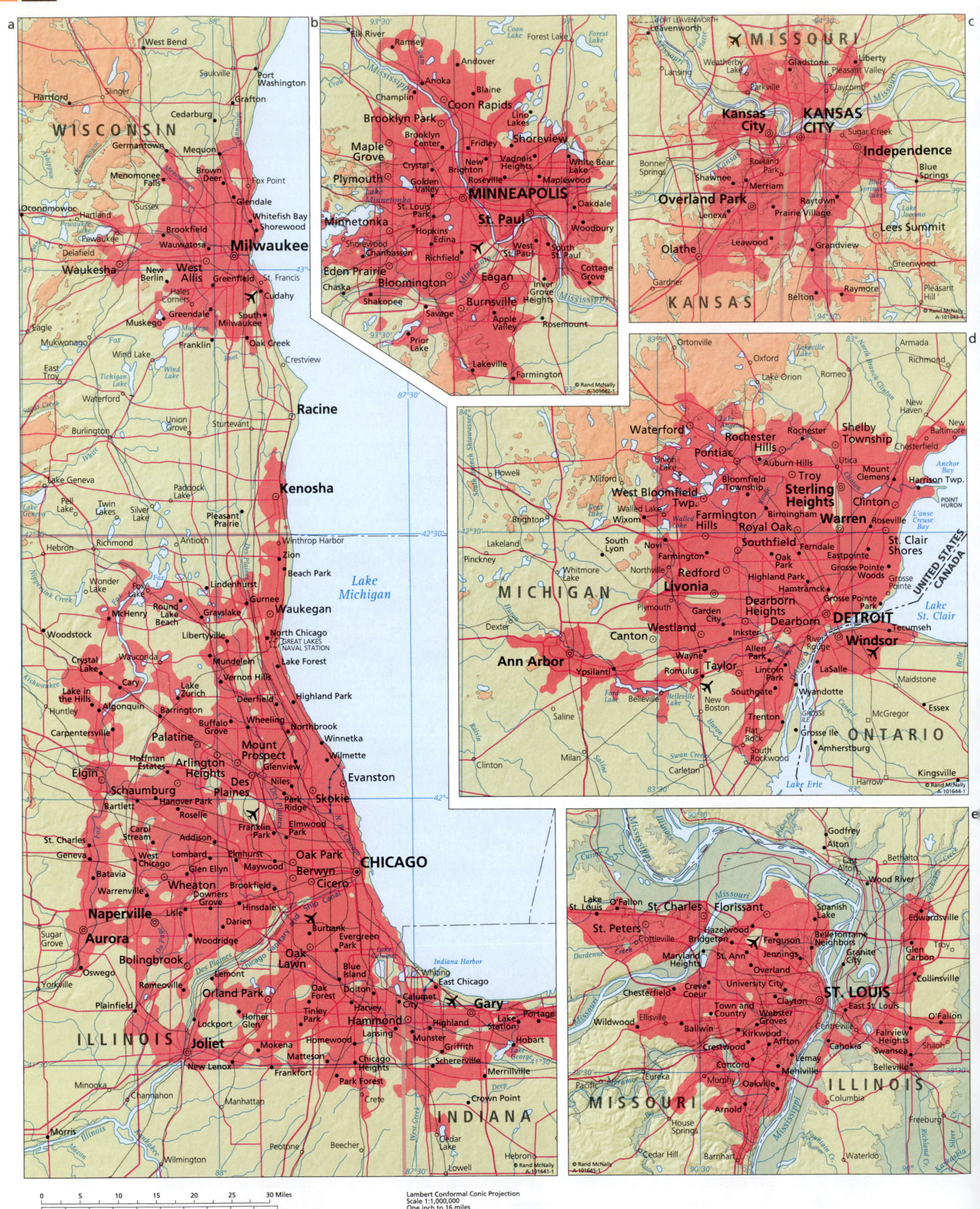

a

West Bend
Saukville
Port Washington
Hartford
Slinger
Cedarburg
Grafton
Germantown
WISCONSIN
Mequon
Menomonee Falls
Brown Deer
Fox Point
Oconomowoc
Hartland
Glendale
Whitefish Bay
Brookfield
Shorewood
Pewaukee
Wauwatosa
Delafield
Milwaukee
Waukesha
West Allis
New Berlin
Greenfield
St. Francis
Eagle
Hales Corners
Cudahy
Mukwonago
Greendale
South Milwaukee
Muskego
Oak Creek
Franklin
East Troy
Wind Lake
Waterford
Crestview
Burlington
Union Grove
Racine
Sturtevant
Lake Geneva
Kenosha
Paddock Lake
Twin Lakes
Silver Lake
Pleasant Prairie
Pell Lake
Hebron
Richmond
Antioch
Winthrop Harbor
Zion
Beach Park
Wonder Lake
Fox Lake
Lindenhurst
Woodstock
McHenry
Round Lake Beach
Gurnee
Waukegan
Grayslake
Crystal Lake
Wauconda
Libertyville
North Chicago
GREAT LAKES NAVAL STATION
Lake in the Hills
Cary
Mundelein
Lake Forest
Huntley
Algonquin
Lake Zurich
Vernon Hills
Carpentersville
Barrington
Deerfield
Highland Park
Elgin
Buffalo Grove
Wheeling
Northbrook
Winnetka
Hoffman Estates
Palatine
Arlington Heights
Glenview
Wilmette
Schaumburg
Mount Prospect
Niles
Evanston
Bartlett
Hanover Park
Des Plaines
Skokie
St. Charles
Roselle
Park Ridge
Geneva
Carol Stream
Addison
Elmwood Park
West Chicago
Lombard
Franklin Park
Batavia
Elmhurst
Maywood
Oak Park
Warrenville
Wheaton
Glen Ellyn
Berwyn
CHICAGO
Naperville
Downers Grove
Brookfield
Cicero
Lisle
Hinsdale
Aurora
Darien
Sugar Grove
Woodridge
Burbank
Evergreen Park
Bolingbrook
Oak Lawn
Oswego
Romeoville
Lemont
Blue Island
Yorkville
Plainfield
Orland Park
Oak Forest
Dolton
Harvey
Whiting
East Chicago
Gary
Lockport
Homer Glen
Tinley Park
Calumet City
Portage
Joliet
Mokena
Homewood
Hammond
Highland
Lake Station
Hobart
New Lenox
Matteson
Chicago Heights
Lansing
Munster
Griffith
Merrillville
Minooka
Frankfort
Park Forest
Schererville
Morris
Channahon
Manhattan
Peotone
Beecher
Crete
Crown Point
Wilmington
Lowell
Cedar Lake
Hebron
ILLINOIS
INDIANA
Lake Michigan

b

Elk River
Ramsey
Andover
Champlin
Anoka
Blaine
Coon Rapids
Brooklyn Park
Lino Lakes
Maple Grove
Brooklyn Center
Fridley
Shoreview
Plymouth
Crystal
New Brighton
Vadnais Heights
White Bear Lake
Golden Valley
Roseville
Maplewood
Minnetonka
St. Louis Park
MINNEAPOLIS
Oakdale
Hopkins
St. Paul
Woodbury
Shorewood
Edina
West St. Paul
Eden Prairie
Richfield
South St. Paul
Chaska
Bloomington
Eagan
Inver Grove Heights
Shakopee
Burnsville
Cottage Grove
Savage
Apple Valley
Rosemount
Prior Lake
Lakeville
Farmington
MISSISSIPPI
Minnetonka (lake)

c

FORT LEAVENWORTH
Leavenworth
MISSOURI
Weatherby Lake
Gladstone
Liberty
Pleasant Valley
Lansing
Parkville
Claycomb
Kansas City
KANSAS CITY
Sugar Creek
Bonner Springs
Independence
Shawnee
Merriam
Blue Springs
Overland Park
Raytown
Lenexa
Prairie Village
Lees Summit
Olathe
Leawood
Grandview
Greenwood
Gardner
KANSAS
Belton
Raymore
Pleasant Hill

d

Ortonville
Oxford
Lakeville
Armada
Richmond
Howell
Lake Orion
Romeo
New Haven
Waterford
Rochester
Rochester Hills
Shelby Township
New Baltimore
Milford
Pontiac
Auburn Hills
Utica
Chesterfield
Anchor Bay
West Bloomfield Twp.
Union Lake
Bloomfield Township
Troy
Mount Clemens
Harrison Twp.
Brighton
Walled Lake
Birmingham
Clinton
POINT HURON
Wixom
Farmington Hills
Sterling Heights
Roseville
L'anse Creuse Bay
Whitmore Lake
South Lyon
Novi
Royal Oak
Warren
St. Clair Shores
Pinckney
Northville
Farmington
Ferndale
Eastpointe
Grosse Pointe Woods
Lakeland
Redford
Highland Park
Hamtramck
Grosse Pointe
Dexter
Southfield
Oak Park
Livonia
Dearborn Heights
DETROIT
Grosse Pointe
Plymouth
Garden City
Dearborn
Windsor
MICHIGAN
Westland
Inkster
Lake St. Clair
Canton
Wayne
Allen Park
River Rouge
Tecumseh
Ann Arbor
Romulus
Taylor
Lincoln Park
Ypsilanti
Southgate
LaSalle
Maidstone
Saline
Belleville
New Boston
Wyandotte
Essex
Milan
Belleville Lake
Trenton
GROSSE ILE
McGregor
Flat Rock
Grosse Ile
Clinton
South Rockwood
Amherstburg
Swan Creek
Carleton
Kingsville
ONTARIO
Harrow
Lake Erie
UNITED STATES
CANADA

e

Godfrey
Alton
Bethalto
Lake St. Louis
O'Fallon
St. Charles
Florissant
Spanish Lake
East Alton
Wood River
St. Peters
Cottleville
Hazelwood
Bellefontaine Neighbors
Edwardsville
Maryland Heights
Bridgeton
Ferguson
Granite City
Glen Carbon
Chesterfield
Creve Coeur
St. Ann
Jennings
Troy
Collinsville
Wildwood
Overland
University City
Town and Country
Clayton
ST. LOUIS
East St. Louis
O'Fallon
Ellisville
Webster Groves
Ballwin
Kirkwood
Fairview Heights
Crestwood
Afton
Cahokia
Swansea
Belleville
Eureka
Concord
Lemay
Pacific
Murphy
Oakville
Mehlville
Columbia
MISSOURI
Arnold
ILLINOIS
House Springs
Barnhart
Freeburg
Cedar Hill
Waterloo

Lambert Conformal Conic Projection
Scale 1:1,000,000
One inch to 16 miles
One cm to 10 km

0 5 10 15 20 25 30 Miles
0 5 10 15 20 25 30 35 40 45 50 Kilometers

© Rand McNally

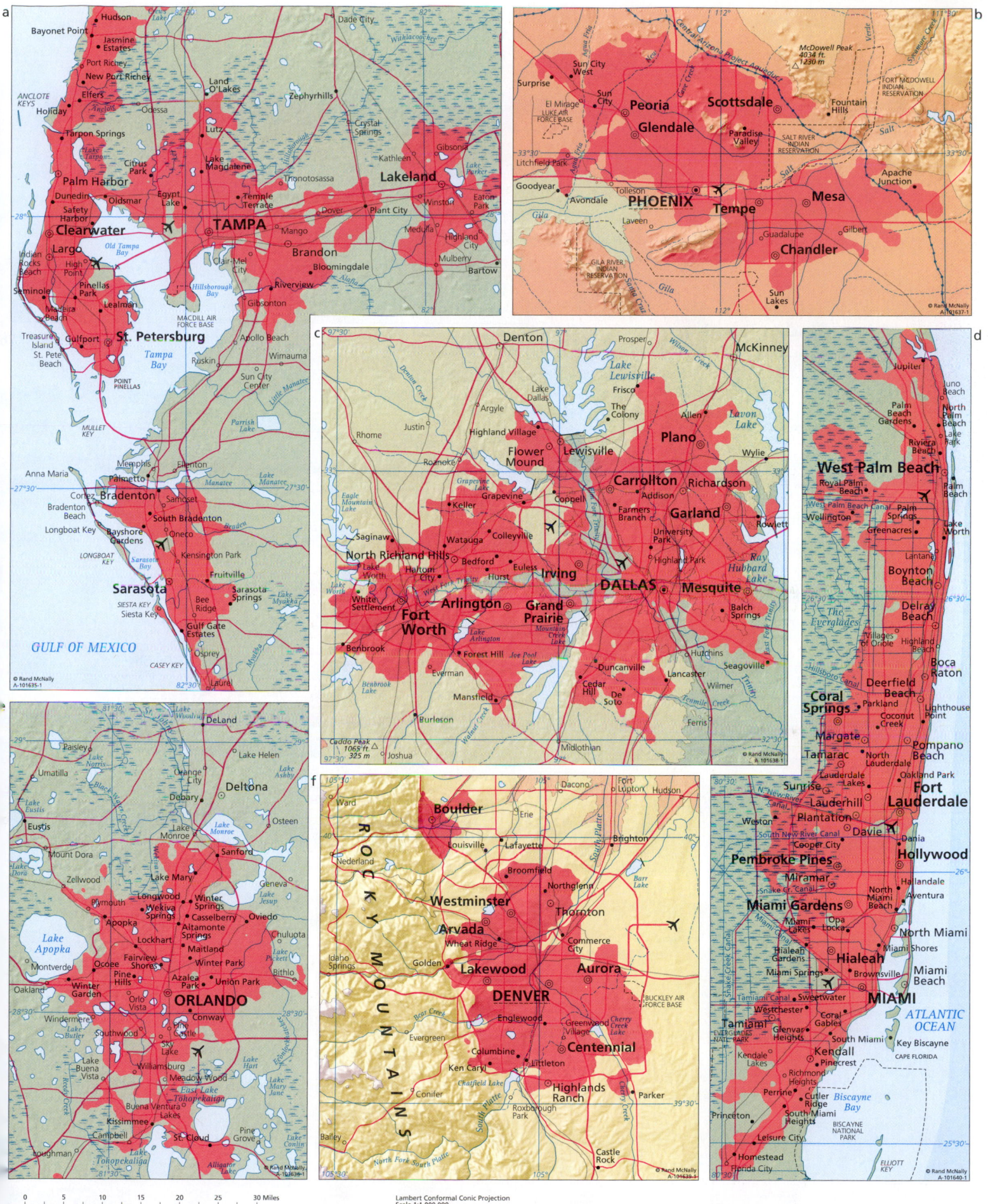

a

Hudson
Bayonet Point
Jasmine Estates
Port Richey
New Port Richey
Elfers
Holiday
ANCLOTE KEYS
Tarpon Springs
Palm Harbor
Dunedin
Oldsmar
Safety Harbor
Clearwater
Largo
Indian Rocks Beach
High Point
Seminole
Pinellas Park
Madeira Beach
Lealman
Treasure Island
Gulfport
St. Pete Beach
St. Petersburg
Dade City
Withlacoochee
Land O'Lakes
Lutz
Zephyrhills
Crystal Springs
Odessa
Citrus Park
Lake Magdalene
Kathleen
Gibsonia
Lakeland
Lake Parker
Egypt Lake
Temple Terrace
Tronotosassa
TAMPA
Dover
Plant City
Winston
Eaton Park
Mango
Brandon
Medulla
Highland City
Bloomingdale
Mulberry
Riverview
Bartow
Gibsonton
MacDILL AIR FORCE BASE
Apollo Beach
Wimauma
Ruskin
Sun City Center
POINT PINELLAS
MULLET KEY
Parrish Lake
Memphis
Ellenton
Palmetto
Bradenton
Cortez
Bradenton Beach
Longboat Key
South Bradenton
Oneco
Samoset
Manatee
Kensington Park
Bayshore Gardens
LONGBOAT KEY
Fruitville
SIESTA KEY
Sarasota
Sarasota Springs
Bee Ridge
Gulf Gate Estates
Osprey
Siesta Key
Anna Maria
GULF OF MEXICO
CASEY KEY
Laurel
© Rand McNally
A-101635-1

b

Agua Fria
Central Arizona Project Aqueduct
McDowell Peak 4034 ft. 1230 m
FORT McDOWELL INDIAN RESERVATION
Surprise
Sun City West
Sun City
Peoria
Scottsdale
Fountain Hills
El Mirage
LUKE AIR FORCE BASE
Glendale
Paradise Valley
SALT RIVER INDIAN RESERVATION
Litchfield Park
Apache Junction
Goodyear
Tolleson
PHOENIX
Tempe
Mesa
Avondale
Gilbert
Laveen
Guadalupe
Chandler
Gila
GILA RIVER INDIAN RESERVATION
Sun Lakes
© Rand McNally
A101637-1

c

Denton
Prosper
Wilson Creek
McKinney
Lake Lewisville
Frisco
Rhome
Argyle
Justin
Highland Village
The Colony
Allen
Lavon Lake
Wylie
Plano
Roanoke
Flower Mound
Lewisville
Keller
Grapevine
Coppell
Carrollton
Richardson
Addison
Garland
Saginaw
Watauga
Colleyville
Farmers Branch
Rowlett
North Richland Hills
Bedford
Euless
University Park
Haltom City
Hurst
Irving
Highland Park
Ray Hubbard Lake
White Settlement
Fort Worth
Arlington
Grand Prairie
DALLAS
Mesquite
Benbrook
Balch Springs
Lake Arlington
Hutchins
Everman
Forest Hill
Duncanville
Lancaster
Seagoville
Cedar Hill
De Soto
Wilmer
Mansfield
Burleson
Ferris
Caddo Peak 1065 ft. 325 m
Joshua
Midlothian
© Rand McNally
A 101638-1

d

Jupiter
Juno Beach
Palm Beach Gardens
North Palm Beach
Riviera Beach
Palm Beach
West Palm Beach
Royal Palm Beach
Palm Springs
West Palm Beach Canal
Wellington
Greenacres
Lake Worth
Lantana
Boynton Beach
THE EVERGLADES
Delray Beach
Villages of Oriole
Highland Beach
Hillsboro Canal
Boca Raton
Deerfield Beach
Coral Springs
Parkland
Lighthouse Point
Coconut Creek
Margate
Pompano Beach
Tamarac
North Lauderdale
Oakland Park
Lauderdale Lakes
Sunrise
Lauderhill
Fort Lauderdale
New River Canal
Plantation
Weston
Davie
Dania
South New River Canal
Cooper City
Hollywood
Pembroke Pines
Hallandale
Miramar
North Miami Beach
Aventura
Miami Gardens
Miami Lakes
Opa Locka
North Miami
Hialeah Gardens
Miami Shores
Hialeah
Brownsville
Miami Beach
Miami Springs
Sweetwater
MIAMI
Westchester
Coral Gables
ATLANTIC OCEAN
Tamiami
Glenvar Heights
South Miami
Key Biscayne
EVERGLADES NATL. PARK
Kendale Lakes
Kendall
Pinecrest
CAPE FLORIDA
Richmond Heights
Cutler Ridge
Biscayne Bay
Perrine
South Miami Heights
Princeton
Leisure City
BISCAYNE NATIONAL PARK
Homestead
ELLIOT KEY
Florida City
© Rand McNally
A-101640-1

e

DeLand
Parsley
Lake Helen
Orange City
Lake Ashby
Umatilla
Lake Norris
Debary
Osteen
Deltona
Eustis
Lake Monroe
Mount Dora
Sanford
Zellwood
Lake Mary
Geneva
Montverde
Longwood
Wekiva Springs
Winter Springs
Lake Jesup
Plymouth
Apopka
Casselberry
Oviedo
Lake Apopka
Lockhart
Altamonte Springs
Chuluota
Ocoee
Fairview Shores
Maitland
Winter Park
Oakland
Pine Hills
Winter Garden
Azalea Park
Union Park
Windermere
Orlo Vista
ORLANDO
Conway
Pine Castle
Southwood
Sky Lake
Lake Butler
Williamsburg
Meadow Wood
Buena Ventura Lakes
Kissimmee
Pine Grove
Campbell
St. Cloud
Loughman
Lake Tohopekaliga
Alligator Lake
East Lake Tohopekaliga
© Rand McNally
A-101636-1

f

Ward
Dacono
Fort Lupton
Hudson
ROCKY MOUNTAINS
Boulder
Erie
Brighton
Nederland
Louisville
Lafayette
Broomfield
Northglenn
Barr Lake
Westminster
Thornton
Idaho Springs
Arvada
Wheat Ridge
Commerce City
Golden
Lakewood
Aurora
BUCKLEY AIR FORCE BASE
DENVER
Englewood
Evergreen
Greenwood Village
Cherry Creek Lake
Centennial
Columbine
Ken Caryl
Littleton
Chatfield Lake
Highlands Ranch
Parker
Conifer
Roxborough Park
Bailey
North Fork South Platte
Castle Rock
© Rand McNally
A-101639-1

0 5 10 15 20 25 30 Miles

0 5 10 15 20 25 30 35 40 45 50 Kilometers

Lambert Conformal Conic Projection
Scale 1:1,000,000
One inch to 16 miles
One cm to 10 km

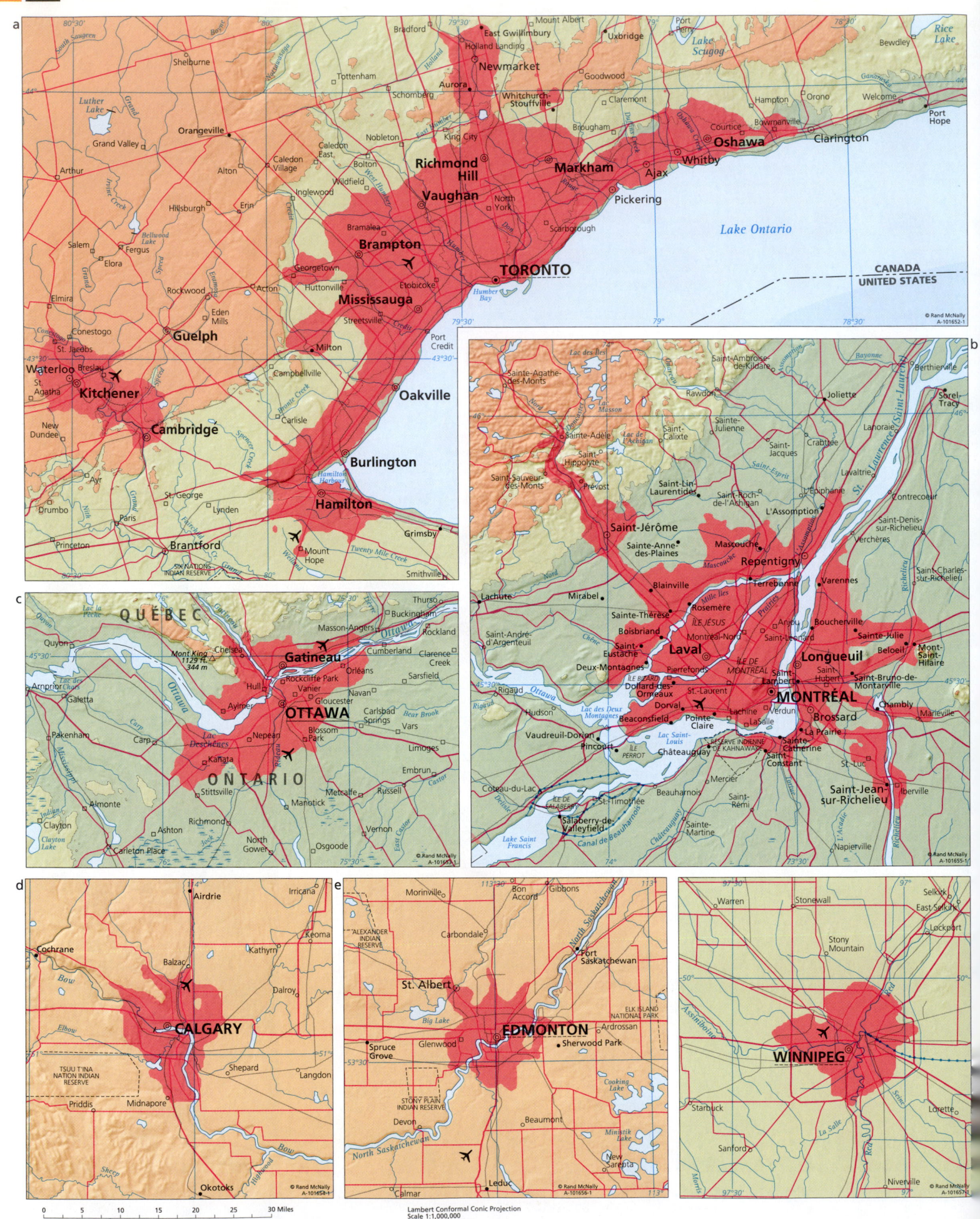

Lambert Conformal Conic Projection
Scale 1:1,000,000
One inch to 16 miles
One cm to 10 km

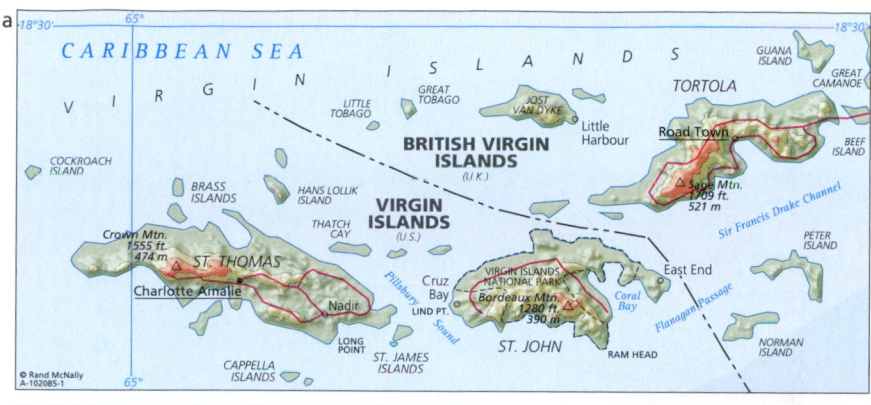

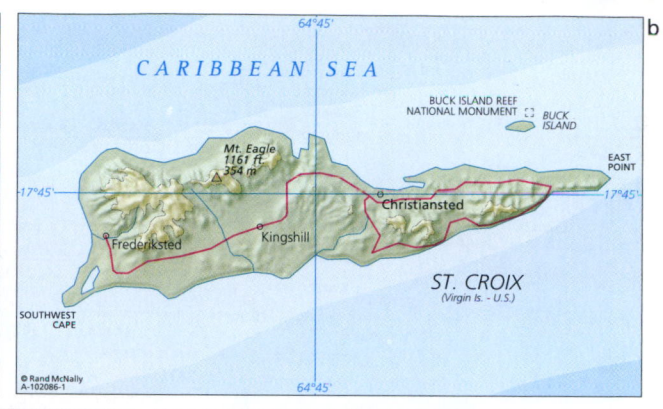

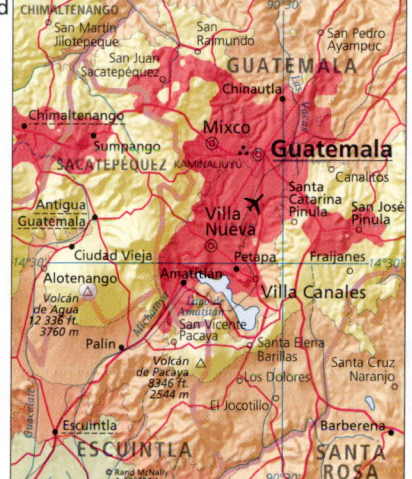

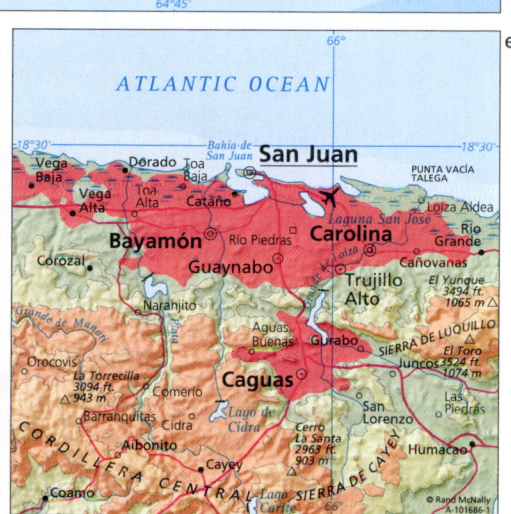

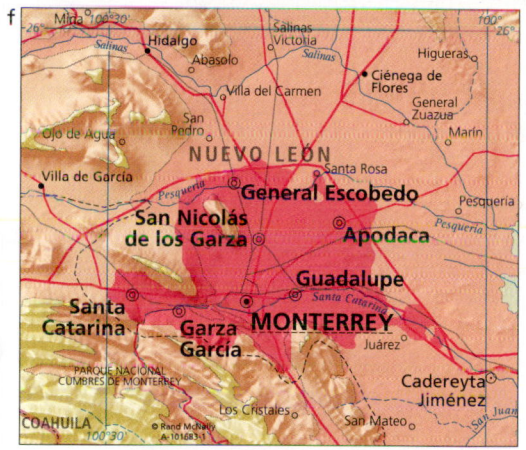

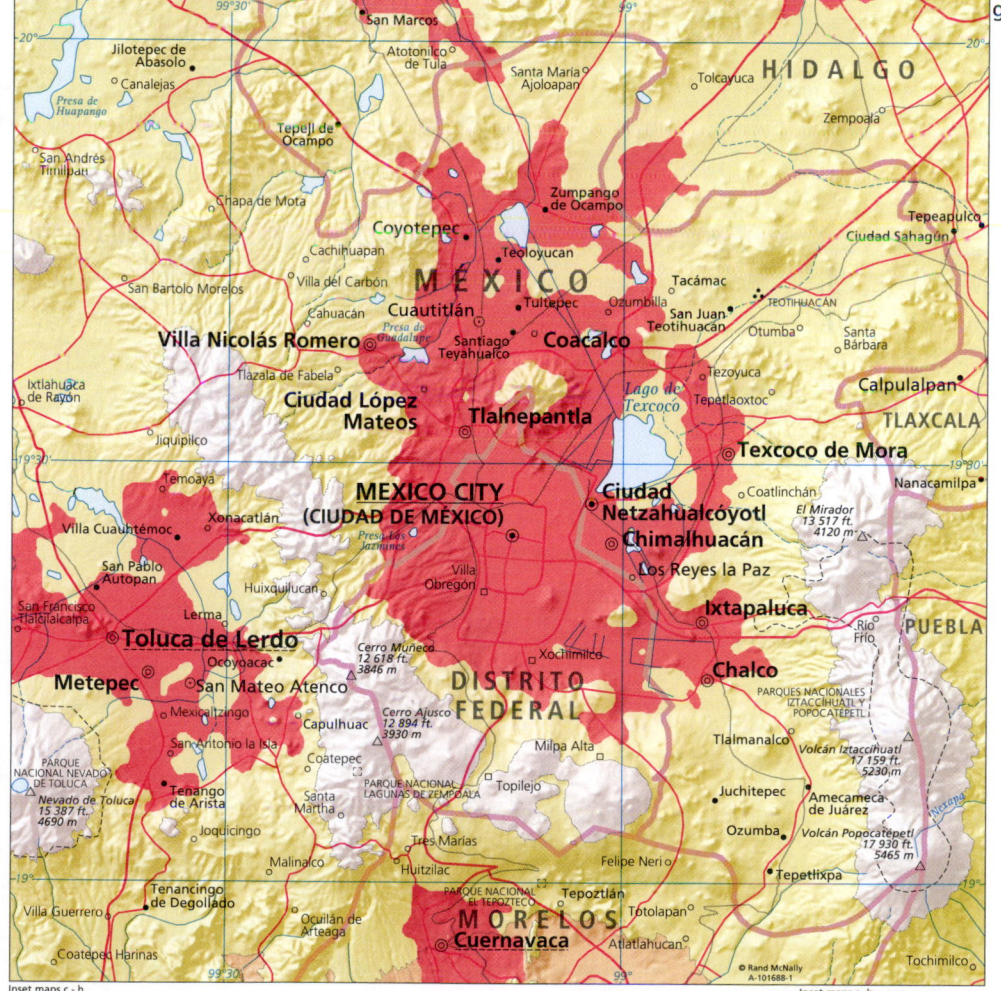

Inset maps c – h
Lambert Conformal Conic Projection
Scale 1:1,000,000
One inch to 16 miles
One cm to 10 km

Inset maps a, b
Lambert Conformal Conic Projection
Scale 1:500,000
One inch to 8 miles
One cm to 5 km

Gulf of Mexico

HAVANA ⊙ CUBA

Mérida

JAMAICA
Kingston

HAITI
Port-au-Prince

DOMINICAN REPUBLIC
Santo Domingo

San Juan

PUERTO RICO (U.S.)

MEXICO

GUADELOUPE (Fr.)
MARTINIQUE (Fr.)

ST. LUCIA
BARBADOS

GUATEMALA HONDURAS
Guatemala
EL SALVADOR NICARAGUA
Managua

COSTA RICA
Panamá
PANAMA

CARIBBEAN SEA

ARUBA (Neth.)

GRENADA
TRINIDAD AND TOBAGO

ATLANTIC OCEAN

BELIZE

ISLA DEL COCO (C.R.)

Barranquilla
Cartagena

MARACAIBO
Barquisimeto
Cúcuta
San Cristóbal

CARÁCAS
Barcelona

Ciudad Bolívar
Ciudad Guayana

VENEZUELA

GUYANA
Georgetown
Paramaribo
SURINAME
Cayenne
FRENCH GUIANA (Fr.)
CABO ORANGE

MEDELLÍN
Bucaramanga
BOGOTÁ
Manizales

LLANOS
Orinoco

Buenaventura
CALI

COLOMBIA
Esmeraldas

Boa Vista

Pico da Neblina
9888 ft.
3014 m

Macapá

Negro

Equator

QUITO
Chimborazo
20 702 ft.
6310 m

ECUADOR
GUAYAQUIL

Cuenca
Loja

Iquitos

Amazon
Santarém

Belém
São Luís
Parnaíba

Fortaleza

Japurá
Putumayo

S E L V A S

MANAUS

ARCHIPIÉLAGO DE COLÓN (GALAPAGOS ISLANDS) (Ec.)

Marañón
Chiclayo
Cajamarca

Trujillo
Pucallpa

Ucayali

Juruá
Purus
Madeira
Tapajós
Xingu

Marabá

Teresina

Campina Grande
Natal
João Pessoa
RECIFE
Caruaru

CABO DE SÃO ROQUE

Rio Branco
Porto Velho

Tocantins
Parnaíba

PERU

Nevado Huascarán
22 133 ft.
6746 m

Huancayo

Lima

Cusco

BOLIVIA
Trinidad

Guaporé

Represa de Sobradinho

São Francisco

Juazeiro

Maceió
Aracaju

SALVADOR

PUNTA CARRETA

Ica

Puno

Arequipa

La Paz
Cochabamba

SANTA CRUZ DE LA SIERRA

Oruro

Sucre
Potosí

Cuiabá

BRASÍLIA

GOIÂNIA

Corumbá

BELO HORIZONTE

Montes Claros

Itabuna

Araguaia

Arica

Iquique

Tarija

GRAN

PARAGUAY

Pico da Bandeira
9505 ft.
2897 m

Campos

Vitória

ILHAS MARTIN VAZ (Braz.)

Tropic of Capricorn

Antofagasta

Salta

CHACO

Asunción
Posadas

SÃO PAULO

Santos

RIO DE JANEIRO
CABO FRIO

San Miguel de Tucumán

Corrientes

CURITIBA

Coquimbo

Santiago del Estero

Salado
Paraná

Santa Maria

Florianópolis

PORTO ALEGRE

A N D E S

CÓRDOBA

Santa Fe

Uruguay

Pelotas

Salto
Paysandú
URUGUAY

Rio Grande

Cerro Aconcagua
22 831 ft.
6959 m

Valparaíso
SANTIAGO

Mendoza

Rosario

BUENOS AIRES

La Plata

MONTEVIDEO

ARCHIPIÉLAGO JUAN FERNÁNDEZ (Chile)

ISLA SAN FÉLIX (Chile)

PAMPA

CABO SAN ANTONIO

PACIFIC OCEAN

Concepción

Neuquén

Bahía Blanca

Mar del Plata

C H I L E

A R G E N T I N A

Negro

Valdivia

Osorno

Puerto Montt

Golfo San Matías

ATLANTIC OCEAN

ARCHIPIÉLAGO DE LOS CHONOS

Monte San Valentín
13 314 ft.
4058 m

Comodoro Rivadavia

Golfo San Jorge

CABO TRES PUNTAS

P A T A G O N I A

FALKLAND ISLANDS (U.K.)

Río Gallegos

Stanley

Punta Arenas

CAPE HORN

Drake Passage

SCOTIA SEA

SOUTH GEORGIA AND THE SOUTH SANDWICH ISLANDS (U.K.)

SOUTH SHETLAND IS.

SOUTH ORKNEY IS. (U.K.)

SOUTHERN OCEAN

ANTARCTIC PENINSULA

Antarctic Circle

© Rand McNally
A-101692-1

0 200 400 600 800 1000 1200 Miles
0 200 400 600 800 1000 1200 1400 1600 1800 2000 Kilometers

Lambert Azimuthal Equal Area Projection
Scale 1:40,000,000
One inch to 640 miles
One cm to 400 km

B R A Z I L

Gulf of Mexico
Havana
CUBA
GREATER
YUCATAN
PENINSULA
MEXICO
BELIZE
GUATEMALA HONDURAS
EL SALVADOR NICARAGUA
Lago de
Nicaragua
COSTA
RICA
PANAMA
ISTMO DE
PANAMA
Golfo de
Panamá
ISLA DEL
COCO
(C.R.)
ISLA DE
MALPELO
(Col.)
PUNTA GALERA
PUNTA PARIÑAS
Archipiélago de Colón
(GALAPAGOS ISLANDS)
(Ec.)

HAITI
HISPANIOLA
DOMINICAN
REPUBLIC
PUERTO RICO TRENCH
ANTILLES PUERTO
RICO
(U.S.)
WEST INDIES
LESSER ANTILLES
GUADELOUPE
(Fr.)
MARTINIQUE
(Fr.)
BARBADOS

Pico Cristóbal Colón
18 947 ft.
5775 m
Maracaibo
Lago de
Maracaibo
Pico Bolívar
16 427 ft.
5007 m
Caracas

TRINIDAD AND
TOBAGO

VENEZUELA
Orinoco
GUYANA
Mt. Roraima
9432 ft.
2875 m
SURINAME
Paramaribo
CABO ORANGE
FRENCH
GUIANA
(Fr.)

Nevado del Tolima
17 110 ft.
5215 m
Bogotá
LLANOS
COLOMBIA
Nevado del Huila
18 865 ft.
5750 m
Cauca
Cavambe
18 996 ft.
5790 m
Quito
ECUADOR
Chimborazo
20 702 ft.
6310 m
Iquitos
Putumayo
Japurá
Negro
Branco
Pico da Neblina
9888 ft.
3014 m
Represa
Balbina
Manaus
Amazon
Equator

Marañón
PUNTA CARRETA
Amazon
S E L V A S
Juruá
Purus
Madeira
Tapajós
Xingu
Belém
Fortaleza
ILHA FERNANDO
DE NORONHA
CABO DE
SÃO ROQUE
PONTA DO SEIXAS

Nevado Huascarán
22 133 ft.
6746 m
PERU
Ucayali
Madre de Dios
Beni
Guaporé
Porto
Velho
B R A Z I L
Represa de
Sobradinho
Recife

Lima
Nevado Illampu
21 066 ft.
6421 m
Nevado Coropuna
20 686 ft.
6305 m
Nevado Sajama
21 463 ft.
6542 m
La Paz
Lago
Titicaca
Altiplano
BOLIVIA
Grande
Paraguay
PLANALTO DO
MATO GROSSO
Brasília
São Francisco
SERRA DO ESPINHAÇO
Pico das Almas
6024 ft.
1836 m
Salvador

Volcán San Pedro
20 161 ft.
6145 m
DESIERTO DE ATACAMA
Volcán Llullaillaco
22 110 ft.
6739 m
CHACO
PARAGUAY
Belo Horizonte
Pico da Bandeira
9505 ft.
2897 m
ILHAS
MARTIN VAZ
(Braz.)

Tropic of Capricorn
ISLA SAN FÉLIX
(Chile)
Nevado Ojos del Salado
22 615 ft.
6893 m
GRAN CHACO
San Miguel
de Tucumán
Cerro General
Manuel Belgrano
20 505 ft.
6250 m
Córdoba
Salado
Asunción
Iguassu
Falls
Paraná
Uruguay
São Paulo
Rio de Janeiro
CABO FRIO

PACIFIC
OCEAN
ARCHIPIÉLAGO
JUAN FERNÁNDEZ
(Chile)
Cerro Aconcagua
22 831 ft.
6959 m
Santiago
A N D E S
Bermejo
A R G E N T I N A
URUGUAY
Montevideo
Lagoa
dos Patos
Porto
Alegre
Río de
la Plata

PUNTA LAVAPIÉ
Buenos
Aires
PAMPA
CABO SAN ANTONIO
Bahía Blanca
Negro
Colorado
Monte Tronador
11 453 ft.
3491 m
ISLA GRANDE
DE CHILOÉ
ARCHIPIÉLAGO
DE LOS CHONOS
Golfo
San Jorge
CABO DOS BAHÍAS
CABO TRES PUNTAS
PATAGONIA
Monte San Valentín
13 314 ft.
4058 m
Golfo San Matías

ATLANTIC
OCEAN

ISLA WELLINGTON
FALKLAND
ISLANDS
(U.K.)
WEST
FALKLAND
EAST
FALKLAND
ISLA DESOLACIÓN
Punta Arenas
TIERRA DEL FUEGO
ISLA SANTA INÉS
ISLA HOSTE
CAPE HORN
(CABO DE HORNOS)
CAPE DISAPPOINTMENT
SOUTH
GEORGIA
SOUTH GEORGIA
AND THE SOUTH
SANDWICH ISLANDS
(U.K.)
SOUTH SANDWICH TRENCH

SCOTIA
SEA
Drake Passage
SOUTH
SHETLAND IS.
(U.K.)
SOUTH
ORKNEY IS.
(U.K.)
SOUTH
SANDWICH IS.
ANTARCTIC PENINSULA
Antarctic Circle
SOUTHERN OCEAN

CARIBBEAN SEA

ATLANTIC
OCEAN

Tropic of Cancer

© Rand McNally
A-101693-1

0   200   400   600   800   1000   1200 Miles
0   200   400   600   800   1000   1200   1400   1600   1800   2000 Kilometers

Lambert Azimuthal Equal Area Projection
Scale 1:40,000,000
One inch to 640 miles
One cm to 400 km

Land Cover

- Evergreen Needleleaf Forest
- Evergreen Broadleaf Forest
- Deciduous Broadleaf Forest
- Mixed Forest
- Woodland
- Wooded Grassland
- Closed Shrubland
- Open Shrubland
- Grassland
- Cropland
- Bare Ground (Desert and Ice)
- Urban and Built Up

0   200   400   600   800   1000 1200 Miles

0   200 400 600 800 1000 1200 1400 1600 1800 2000 Kilometers

Lambert Azimuthal Equal Area Projection
Scale 1:40,000,000
One inch to 640 miles
One cm to 400 km

Source: CIESIN; Hansen et al., 2000

A-102093-1
© Rand McNally

Moderate Resolution
Imaging Spectroradiometer (MODIS)
true-color mosaic satellite image

Source: NASA Visible Earth program (http://visibleearth.nasa.gov/)

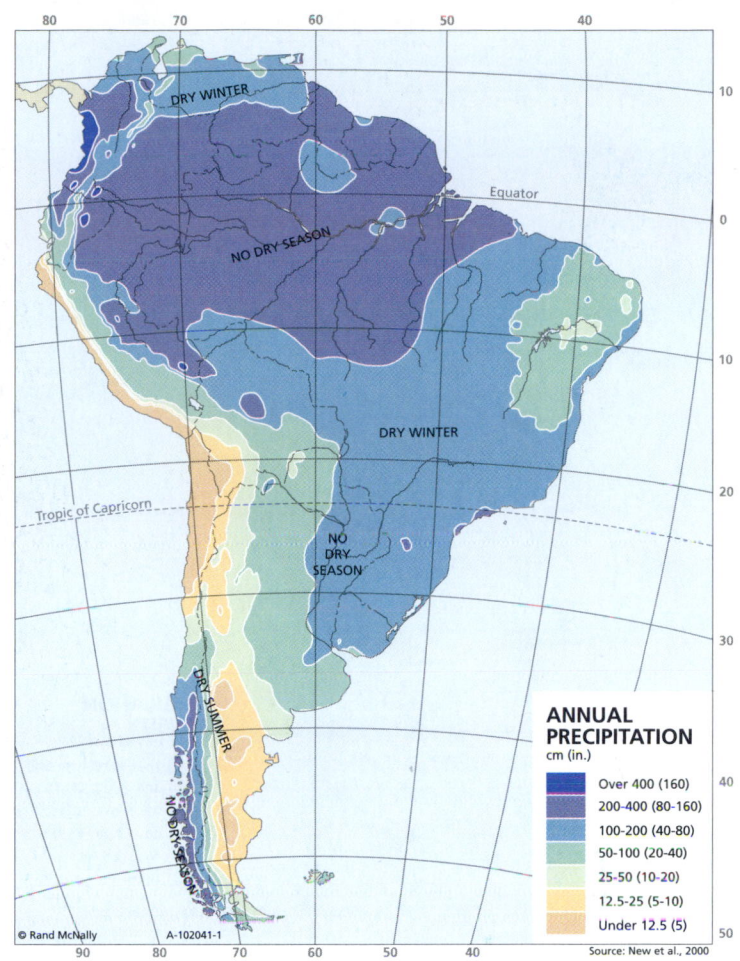

DRY WINTER

Equator

NO DRY SEASON

DRY WINTER

Tropic of Capricorn

NO
DRY
SEASON

DRY SUMMER

NO DRY SEASON

ANNUAL PRECIPITATION
cm (in.)

- Over 400 (160)
- 200–400 (80-160)
- 100–200 (40-80)
- 50–100 (20-40)
- 25–50 (10-20)
- 12.5–25 (5-10)
- Under 12.5 (5)

© Rand McNally   A-102041-1

Source: New et al., 2000

Equator

Tropic of Capricorn

LANDFORMS

- Mountains
- Widely spaced mountains
- High tablelands
- Hills and low tablelands
- Depressions or basins
- Plains
- Limit of continental shelf

© Rand McNally   M-102038-1

Source: Murphy, 1968. © Association of American Geographers. Published by Taylor & Francis.
Adapted with permission of the Association of American Geographers.

LLANOS

Equator

SELVAS

CAATINGA

LOMA
PUNA

ATACAMA

GRAN
CHACO

Tropic of Capricorn

PAMPA

VEGETATION

B	Tropical rain forest
B	Mediterranean vegetation
S	Semideciduous forest
D	Broadleaf deciduous (galleria forest)
SE	Araucaria forest
M	Beech, cedar forest
Dl	Xerophytic open forest
Szp	Desert shrub
G	Tall grass
Gsp	Tall grass, galleria forest
DsG	Low grass, desert shrub
GDsp	Montane grass, tola shrub
b	Little or no vegetation

For explanation of letters in boxes,
see World Natural Vegetation Map.

© Rand McNally   M-102042-1

Source: Küchler, 1949. © Association of American Geographers. Published by Taylor & Francis.
Adapted with permission of the Association of American Geographers.

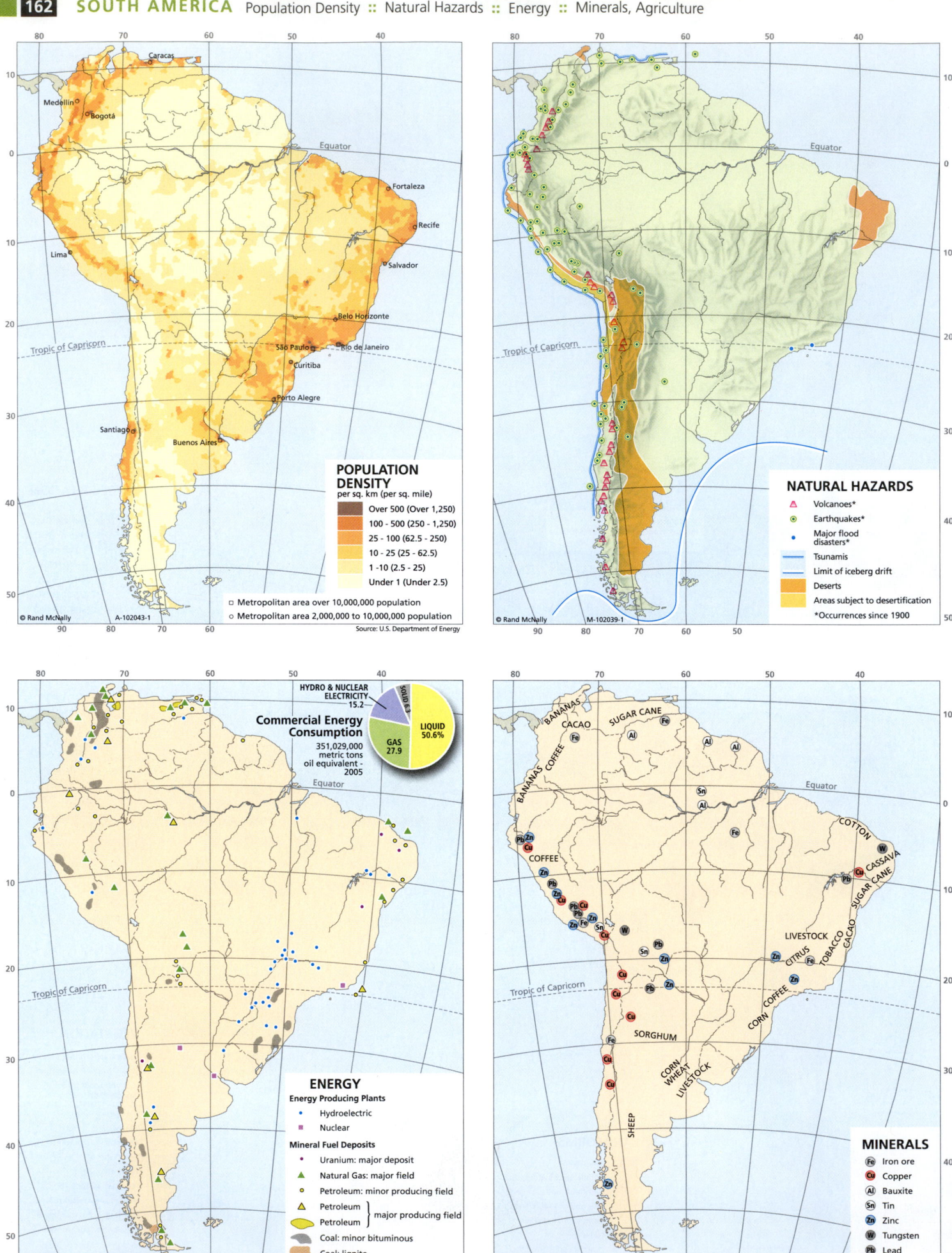

POPULATION DENSITY
per sq. km (per sq. mile)

- Over 500 (Over 1,250)
- 100 - 500 (250 - 1,250)
- 25 - 100 (62.5 - 250)
- 10 - 25 (25 - 62.5)
- 1 - 10 (2.5 - 25)
- Under 1 (Under 2.5)

□ Metropolitan area over 10,000,000 population
○ Metropolitan area 2,000,000 to 10,000,000 population

© Rand McNally   A-102043-1

Source: U.S. Department of Energy

NATURAL HAZARDS
- ▲ Volcanoes*
- ⊙ Earthquakes*
- • Major flood disasters*
- — Tsunamis
- — Limit of iceberg drift
- Deserts
- Areas subject to desertification

*Occurrences since 1900

© Rand McNally   M-102039-1

ENERGY
Energy Producing Plants
- • Hydroelectric
- ■ Nuclear

Mineral Fuel Deposits
- • Uranium: major deposit
- ▲ Natural Gas: major field
- ○ Petroleum: minor producing field
- ▲ Petroleum } major producing field
- ⬤ Petroleum
- Coal: minor bituminous
- Coal: lignite

Commercial Energy Consumption
351,029,000 metric tons oil equivalent - 2005

HYDRO & NUCLEAR ELECTRICITY 15.2
SOLID 6.3
LIQUID 50.6%
GAS 27.9

© Rand McNally   M-102040-1

Source: Energy Information Administration; United Nations

MINERALS
- Fe Iron ore
- Cu Copper
- Al Bauxite
- Sn Tin
- Zn Zinc
- W Tungsten
- Pb Lead

© Rand McNally   M-102044-1

Source: FAO; U.S. Geological Survey

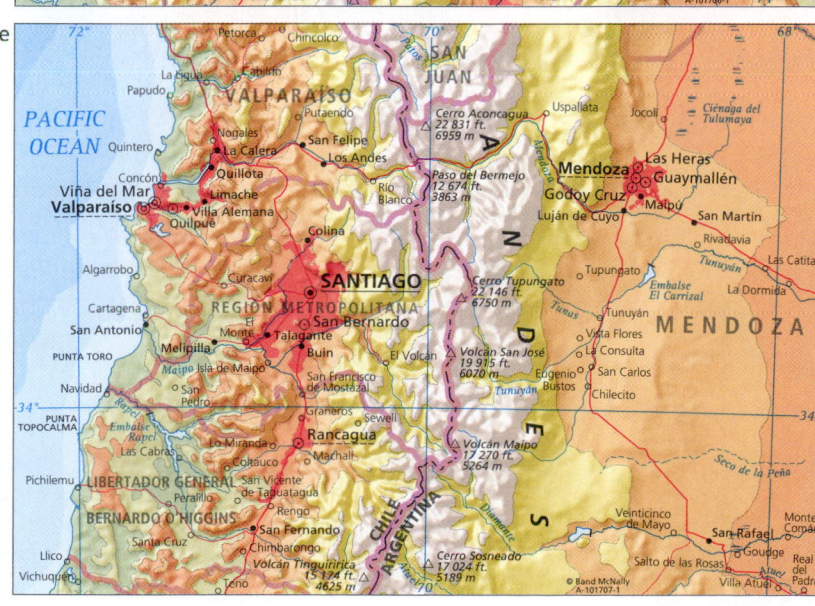

0 20 40 60 80 100 120 Miles
0 20 40 60 80 100 120 140 160 180 200 Kilometers

Lambert Conformal Conic Projection
Scale 1:4,000,000
One inch to 64 miles
One cm to 40 km

COLOMBIAN BASIN

CARIBBEAN
SEA

ISLA DE PROVIDENCIA (Col.)

ISLAS
DEL MAÍZ (Nic.)

CAYOS DEL ESTE SUDESTE
ISLA DE SAN ANDRÉS (Col.)

PUNTA GALLINAS

PENÍNSULA DE
LA GUAJIRA

PENÍNSULA DE
PARAGUANÁ
Punto Fijo

Oranjestad
ARUBA
(Neth.)

NETHERLANDS
ANTILLES
(Neth.)
CURAÇAO BONAIRE
Willemstad

LESSER

ISLAS
LA BLANQUILLA
ISLA LA ORCHILA

Puerto Cumarebo
Coro

San Juan de
los Cayos

ISLA LA TORTUGA

ISLAS
LOS ROQUES

Riohacha
Santa Marta
Maicao

Golfo de
Venezuela

Capatárida
San Luis

Barranquilla
Soledad
Ciénaga

MARACAIBO

Altagracia

CABO DE LA AGUJA

Cartagena
Sabanalarga
Fundación
Plato
Valledupar

Pico Cristóbal Colón
19,947 ft.
5,775 m

Cabimas
Ciudad
Ojeda

Mene Grande

Puerto Cabello
San Felipe
Valencia
Yaritagua
Barquisimeto
El Tocuyo

CARACAS
Los Teques

Guarenas

Puerto
la Cruz

Barcelona
Aragua de
Barcelona

COSTA RICA
Puerto Limón

ISTMO DE PANAMÁ

Volcán Barú
11,401 ft.
3,475 m
Almirante
David
La Chorrera
Portobelo
Colón

Panama Canal

Machiques

Lago de
Maracaibo

Trujillo
Valera

Acarigua
San Carlos
Tinaco

San Juan de
los Morros

Altagracia
de Orituco

Zaraza
Cantaura

Anaco

PANAMA
Panama

Santiago
Chitré
Las Tablas
Soná
PEN. DE
AZUERO

Aguadulce
Penonomé

SERRANÍA DEL DARIÉN

ISLA DEL
REY

Golfo
de Urabá

Acandí
Yaviza
La Palma

San Onofre
Sincelejo
Lorica
Cereté
Montería
San Marcos

El Carmen de Bolívar
Magangué
Mompós
Sahagún
El Banco

Pico
16,427 ft.
5,007 m

Guanare
Guanarito

MÉRIDA

CORDILLERA

Barinas

Arismendi

El Baúl
Calabozo

Las Mercedes

Santa María
de Ipire

PUNTA
BURICA
Golfo de
Chiriquí
ISLA DE COIBA

PUNTA
MALA
PUNTA
MARIATO

Golfo de
Panamá

PUNTA
MARZO

Jaqué
Riosucio
Chigorodó

Caucasia
Ayapel
Nechí
Simití

Ocaña

Cúcuta
San Cristóbal
Rubio
Pamplona
Bucaramanga

La Fría
Ciudad Bolívar

Puerto
Rondón
Tame

ORIENTAL

Puerto Carreño

Cerro Mato
6,112 ft.
1,863 m

Arauca
Guasdualito

Elorza
La Urbana

Capanaparo

VENEZUELA

PACIFIC
OCEAN

ISLA DE MALPELO
(Col.)

Nuquí

Frontino
Ituango
Yarumal
Antioquia
Amalfi

Barrancabermeja
Puerto
Berrío

Floridablanca
Socorro
San Gil

Málaga

Achaguas

Apurito

San Fernando
de Apure

Las Bonitas

Mantecal

Cabruta

CABO CORRIENTES

Quibdó
Istmina

Bolívar
Urao
MEDELLÍN
Itagüí
Santa
Bárbara

Sonsón
Aguadas

Puerto
Triunfo

Chiquinquirá
Honda
La Dorada

Duitama
Tunja
Sogamoso
Paz de Ariporo
Trinidad

Yopal

Orocué

Puerto
Carreño

Cerro Yaví
8,009 ft.
2,441 m

Tomo

Samariapo

L L A N O S

Manizales
Pereira
Cartago
Armenia

Salamina

Nev. del Tolima
17,110 ft.
5,215 m

Zipaquirá
Facatativá

BOGOTÁ

Chávira

Puerto López

San Fernando de Atabapo

Vichada

Sucuaro

Cerro Marahuaca
8,461 ft.
2,579 m

Buenaventura

Sevilla
Ibagué
Tuluá
Buga
Palmira

Girardot
Espinal

Villavicencio
San Martín

Meta

Maroa

CALI
Yumbo
Pradera
Puerto Tejada

Cerro Nevado
14,961 ft.
4,560 m

Uribe

Puerto Limón

Guaviare

Victorino

La Esmeralda

Casiquiare

Pico Tamacuari
7,677 ft.
2,340 m

ISLA GORGONA

Nevado del Huila
18,865 ft.
5,750 m
Popayán

Neiva

San José del Guaviare

Mosquera
Guapi

Timbío

Garzón
Pitalito

San Vicente
del Caguán

COLOMBIA

Inírida

Negro
Tigre

San Carlos
de Río Negro

Cúcui

Pico da Neblina
9,888 ft.
3,014 m

Tumaco
Barbacoas
Bolívar

La Unión

Puerto Rico

Calamar

Guainía

ANDES

Florencia

Miraflores

Uaupés

Içana

Esmeraldas
PUNTA GALERA

San Lorenzo
Tuquerres
Nevado Cumbal
15,630 ft.
4,764 m

CABO
MANGLARES

El Diviso

Pasto
Tulcán
Ipiales

Puerto Asís

Tres Esquinas

Santa
Rita

Apaporis

Mitú

Iauareté

Içana

Taraquá

Tapuruquara

Santo Domingo de los Colorados

CABO PASADO

Bahía de Caráquez

Chone
Calceta

Manta
CABO SAN LORENZO

Portoviejo
Jipijapa
Paján

Atuntaqui
Otavalo
Ibarra
Cayambe

QUITO

Machachi
Latacunga
Quevedo

CORDILLERA

Cayambe
18,996 ft.
5,790 m

Cotopaxi
19,347 ft.
5,897 m

Tena

Puerto Francisco
de Orellana

Nuevo Rocafuerte

Puerto Leguízamo

Lérida

La Chorrera

La Pedrera

Ueuari

Maraã

Japurá

Lago
Amanã

Daule

Ambato
Chimborazo
20,702 ft.
6,310 m

Baños
Puyo

Guaranda
ECUADOR
Riobamba

Tarqui

El Encanto

Arica

Putumayo

Tarapacá

Santo Antônio do Içá

Içá

Amazon (Solimões)

Fonte
Boa

Lago
Tefé

Tefé

GUAYAQUIL

PUNTA SANTA ELENA
Salinas
Santa Elena

Babahoyo
Milagro

Sangay
17,159 ft.
5,230 m

Macas

Andoas

Pebas

Iquitos

Santa Clotilde

Nauta

Caballococha

São Paulo
de Olivença

Leticia

AMAZONAS

Alvarães

ISLA
PUNÁ
Golfo de
Guayaquil

Naranjal

Azogues
Cuenca
Pasaje
Sígsig

Machala
Zaruma
Santa Rosa

Loja
Zamora

Marañón

Intuto

San Joaquín de Omaguas

Benjamín Constant

Jutaí

Iça

Juruá

Concórdia

Carauari

Tumbes
Zorritos
MÁncora

Catamayo

PERU

Requena

Javari

SELVAS

PUNTA PARIÑAS

Sullana

Chulucanas

Piura
Castilla

ANDES

Cerro Bravo
12,359 ft.
3,767 m
Jaén

Moyobamba

Yurimaguas

Lagunas

Ucayali

Eirunepé

Juruá

Fortaleza do Ituxi

Líbrea

Negritos

Bahía de
Sechura

DESIERTO DE
SECHURA

Olmos

Salas

Chachapoyas

Lamas
Tarapoto

Bellavista

Huallaga

Juruá

Purus

Pauini

PUNTA NEGRA

Ferreñafe
Lambayeque
Chiclayo

Cutervo

Cajamarca

Juanjuí

Cruzeiro do Sul

Tonantins

Iruri

Chepén
Pacasmayo
Puerto Chicama
CHAN CHAN
Trujillo
Salaverry

CORDILLERA CENTRAL

ACRE

Feijó

Tayabamba

© Rand McNally
A-101694-1

0   50   100   150   200   250   300 Miles
0 50 100 150 200 250 300 350 400 450 500 Kilometers

Lambert Azimuthal Equal Area Projection
Scale 1:10,000,000
One inch to 160 miles
One cm to 100 km

ATLANTIC OCEAN

ST. VINCENT
Kingstown
BARBADOS
Bridgetown
ST. VINCENT
AND THE
GRENADINES
GRENADA
St. George's
TOBAGO
Scarborough
TRINIDAD
AND
TOBAGO
Port of Spain
Arima
TRINIDAD
San Fernando

ISLA DE
MARGARITA
La Asunción
Porlamar
Carúpano
PENÍNSULA DE PARIA
Güiria
Irapa
Pedernales
Cumaná
Caripito
Maturin
DELTA DEL ORINOCO
Juseplin
El Tigre
Temblador
San José de Guanipa
Tucupita
Barrancas
Soledad
Orinoco
Ciudad Guayana
Morawhanna
Ciudad Bolívar
Upata
Mabaruma
Ciudad Piar
Cerro Bolívar
2631 ft.
802 m
El Callao
La Paragua
Tumeremo
Guasipati
Marlborough
El Dorado
Suddie
Georgetown
Bartica
Hyde Park
Angel Falls
(Salto Ángel)
Auyán Tepuy
9678 ft.
2950 m
LA GRAN
SABANA
Luepa
Issano
Rockstone
Linden
New Amsterdam
GUYANA
Paramaribo
Groningen
Nieuw
Nickerie
Onverwacht
Moengo
Iracoubo
Sinnamary
Kourou
Cayenne
Rémiré
Mt. Roraima
9432 ft.
2875 m
Tumatumari
Corriverton
Brokopondo
W.J. van
Blommestein
Meer
Saint-Laurent
du Maroni
Saint-Élie
SURINAME
FRENCH
GUIANA
(France)
Saül
CABO ORANGE
Saint-Georges
Oiapoque
PAKARAIMA MTS
Conceição
do Maú
Uraricoera
Lethem
WILHELMINA GEBERGTE
Juliana Top
4035 ft.
1230 m
Vila Velha
Boa Vista
Dadanawa
ACARAI MOUNTAINS
Cunani
Calçoene
ILHA DE MARACÁ
Isherton
TUMUC-HUMAC MOUNTAINS
Amapá
CABO NORTE
Sucuriju
RORAIMA
São José
de Anauá
Serra do Navio
AMAPÁ
Aporema
Ferreira Gomes
Porto Grande
ILHA JANAUCU
Caracaraí
ILHA CAVIANA DE FORA
ILHA MEXIANA
Macapá
Porto Santana
Mazagão
CABO
MAGUARI
Boiaçu
ILHA GRANDE
DO GURUPÁ
Roça do Jari
Itatupa
Anajás
Soure
Salinópolis
Muralá
Maracanã
Bragança
Carvoeiro
Moura
Gurupá
São Miguel
dos Macacos
Muaná
Belém
Igarapé-Açu
Capanema
Novo Airão
Oriximiná
Óbidos
Alenquer
Monte
Alegre
Prainha
Carrazedo
Porto de Moz
Breves
Curralinho
São Domingos
do Capim
Irituia
Represa
Balbina
Terra Santa
Veiros
Portel
Cametá
Acará
Itamataré
MANAUS
Itacoatiara
Faro
Juriti
Santarém
Baião
Juaba
Carapajó
Tomé-Açu
Manacapuru
Careiro
Itapiranga
Parintins
Vitória
Xingu
Tucuruí
Anamã
Barreirinha
Ariaú
Altamira
Maués
Jacundá
Nova Olinda
do Norte
PARÁ
Coari
Anori
Axinim
Canumã
Itaituba
Represa
de Tucuruí
Abufari
Tapauá
Novo
Aripuanã
Borba
São Félix do Xingu
Açailândia
MARANHÃO
Amarante do
Maranhão
Manicoré
Itupiranga
Marabá
Imperatriz
BRAZIL
Araguatins
Santa Isabel do Araguaia
Sítio
Novo
Montes Altos
SERRA DOS CARAJÁS
Carajás
Xambioá
Tocantinópolis
Humaitá
Prainha
Nova
Gradaús
Araguaína
Babaçulândia
Riachão
MATO
GROSSO
SERRA DO CACHIMBO
Conceição do Araguaia
TOCANTINS
Carolina

0   50   100   150   200   250   300 Miles
0   50   100 150 200 250 300 350 400 450 500 Kilometers

© Rand McNally A-101695-1

Lambert Azimuthal Equal Area Projection
Scale 1:10,000,000
One inch to 160 miles
One cm to 100 km

A T L A N T I C   O C E A N

AMAPÁ

Macapá

ILHA GRANDE DO GURUPÁ

PARÁ

Belém

Z I L

MARANHÃO

CEARÁ

Fortaleza

Maracanaú

Teresina

São Luís

RIO GRANDE DO NORTE

Natal

PIAUÍ

PARAÍBA

João Pessoa

Campina Grande

Olinda

PERNAMBUCO

RECIFE

ALAGOAS

Maceió

TOCANTINS

Palmas

SERGIPE

Aracaju

BAHIA

Feira de Santana

SALVADOR

GOIÁS

BRASÍLIA

DISTRITO FEDERAL

GOIÂNIA

Rio Verde

Uberlândia

MINAS GERAIS

Montes Claros

ESPÍRITO SANTO

Governador Valadares

Lambert Azimuthal Equal Area Projection
Scale 1:10,000,000
One inch to 160 miles
One cm to 100 km

Primavera do Leste
Poxoréu
General Carneiro
Barra do Garças
Canavieiras
Una
Itapetinga
BRASÍLIA
Guiratinga
Aragarças
Jussara
Anápolis
**DISTRITO
FEDERAL**
Luziânia
Formosa
Cabeceiras
São Francisco
Januária
Monte Azul
São João do Paraíso
Belmonte
Salto da Divisa
Rondonópolis
Baliza
Piranhas
Íporá
GOIÁNIA
Silvânia
Unaí
Paracatu
Pirapora
São Romão
Coronel
Murta
Itabim
Jequitinhonha
Porto Seguro
GOIÁS
BAHIA
Alto Araguaia
Mineiros
Caiapônia
Pontalina
Campo Alegre
de Goiás
Bocaiúva
Coração
Capelinha
Itamaraju
BRAZIL
Pres. Epitácio
**SÃO
PAULO**
BELO HORIZONTE
**ESPÍRITO
SANTO**
Vitória
Vila Velha
**RIO DE
JANEIRO**
RIO DE JANEIRO
Niterói
Tropic of Capricorn
Santos

**BRAZIL
BASIN**

ATLANTIC OCEAN

CURITIBA
Paranaguá

SANTA CATARINA
Florianópolis

RIO GRANDE DO SUL
PORTO ALEGRE

Lagoa
dos
Patos

Pelotas
Rio Grande

Inset map a
Lambert Conformal Conic Projection
Scale 1:1,000,000
One inch to 16 miles
One cm to 10 km

Zárate
Campana
**DELTA DEL
PARANÁ**
COLONIA
PUNTA
MARTÍN CHICO
PUNTA PEREYRA
Belén de
Escobar
Tigre
San Fernando
San Isidro
Vicente López
Río de la Plata
**URUGUAY
ARGENTINA**
Pilar
**San
Miguel**
José C. Paz
General San Martín
Colonia del
Sacramento
**BUENOS
AIRES**
Hurlingham
Caseros
**DISTRITO
FEDERAL**
BUENOS AIRES
Moreno
Morón
Avellaneda
Merlo
San Justo
Lanús
Quilmes
Lomas de
Zamora
Berazategui
Esteban Echeverría
Ezeiza
**Almirante
Brown**
**Florencio
Varela**
Ensenada
Berisso
La Plata

© Rand McNally
A-101696-1

© Rand McNally
A-101697-1

PERU and ECUADOR

COLOMBIA

VEN.

ECUADOR

QUITO

GUAYAQUIL

AMAZONAS

A N D E S

PACIFIC OCEAN

BRAZIL

S E L V A S

PERU

C O R D I L L E R A   O R I E N T A L

C O R D I L L E R A   C E N T R A L

C O R D I L L E R A   O C C I D E N T A L

Lima

ACRE

Rio Branco

BOLIVIA

CHILE

A N D E S

MACHU PICCHU

Cusco

ALTIPLANO

La Paz

El Alto

DESIERTO DE ATACAMA

PERU-CHILE TRENCH

© Rand McNally
A-101698-1

a

PACIFIC OCEAN

ARCHIPIÉLAGO DE COLÓN
(GALAPAGOS ISLANDS)
(Ecuador)

ISLA DARWIN
ISLA WOLF
ISLA PINTA
ISLA MARCHENA
ISLA GENOVESA
ISLA ISABELA
Volcán Wolf
5400 ft.
1646 m
Equator
Volcán La Cumbre
4800 ft.
1463 m
ISLA FERNANDINA
ISLA SANTIAGO
ISLA BALTRA
ISLA SANTA CRUZ
Volcán Santo Tomás
4888 ft.
1490 m
Cerro Azul
5541 ft.
1689 m
ISLA SANTA FE
ISLA SAN CRISTÓBAL
Puerto Villamil
Puerto Ayora
Puerto Baquerizo Moreno
ISLA SANTA MARÍA
ISLA ESPAÑOLA

© Rand McNally
A-101699-1

Inset map a
Lambert Conformal Conic Projection
Scale 1:6,000,000
One inch to 96 miles
One cm to 60 km

0   50   100   150   200   250   300 Miles
0   50 100 150 200 250 300 350 400 450 500 Kilometers

Lambert Azimuthal Equal Area Projection
Scale 1:10,000,000
One inch to 160 miles
One cm to 100 km

PACIFIC
OCEAN

ATLANTIC
OCEAN

URUGUAY

ARGENTINA

CHILE

MENDOZA

SAN LUIS

CÓRDOBA

SANTA FE

ENTRE RÍOS

BUENOS AIRES

LA PAMPA

NEUQUÉN

RÍO NEGRO

CHUBUT

SANTA CRUZ

TIERRA DEL FUEGO

PATAGONIA

SANTIAGO
Valparaíso
Viña del Mar

MONTEVIDEO

BUENOS AIRES
La Plata

Mar del Plata

Bahía Blanca

Comodoro Rivadavia

Río Gallegos

Punta Arenas

Ushuaia

FALKLAND ISLANDS
(U.K.; claimed by Argentina)

WEST FALKLAND

EAST FALKLAND

Stanley
Mt. Usborne
2313 ft.
705 m

CAPE HORN
(CABO DE HORNOS)

ANTÁRTIDA E ISLAS
DEL ATLÁNTICO SUR
TIERRA DEL FUEGO

Lambert Azimuthal Equal Area Projection
Scale 1:10,000,000
One inch to 160 miles
One cm to 100 km

0   50   100   150   200   250   300 Miles
0 50 100 150 200 250 300 350 400 450 500 Kilometers

© Rand McNally
A-101700-1

ATLANTIC OCEAN

© Rand McNally
A-101701-1

a Franco da Rocha

b

© Rand McNally
A-101702-1

© Rand McNally
A-101703-1

| 0 | 30 | 60 | 90 | 120 | 150 | 180 Miles |
| 0 | 30 | 60 | 90 | 120 | 150 | 180 | 210 | 240 | 270 | 300 Kilometers |

Lambert Conformal Conic Projection
Scale 1:6,000,000
One inch to 96 miles
One cm to 60 km

Inset maps a, b
Lambert Conformal Conic Projection
Scale 1:1,000,000
One inch to 16 miles
One cm to 10 km

SANTIAGO DEL ESTERO

GRAN CHACO

CHACO

PARAGUAY

MISIONES

SANTA CATARINA

CORRIENTES

BRAZIL

RIO GRANDE DO SUL

Resistencia
Corrientes

Posadas
Encarnación

SANTA FE

MESOPOTAMIA

CÓRDOBA

Santa Fe
Paraná

ENTRE RÍOS

URUGUAY

CORDILLERA DE SANTA ANA

CUCHILLA GRANDE

CUCHILLA DE HAEDO

Rosario

San Nicolás de los Arroyos

BUENOS AIRES
Avellaneda
La Plata

MONTEVIDEO
Maldonado

ARGENTINA

BUENOS AIRES

LA PAMPA

Mar del Plata

RÍO NEGRO

Bahía Blanca

ATLANTIC OCEAN

△ Cerro Tres Picos
4065 ft.
1239 m

© Rand McNally
A-101704-1

Lambert Conformal Conic Projection
Scale 1:6,000,000
One inch to 96 miles
One cm to 60 km

0   30   60   90   120   150   180 Miles
0 30 60 90 120 150 180 210 240 270 300 Kilometers

ICELAND

NORWEGIAN SEA

Arctic Circle

NORDKAPP

Hammerfest

Severomorsk
Murmansk
Monchegorsk
Kandalaksha

Tromsø
Narvik
Kiruna
Kebnekaise
6926 ft.
2111 m

FINLAND

Rovaniemi

Bodø

Oulu

FAROE
ISLANDS
(Denmark)
Tórshavn

SWEDEN
Umeå
Sundsvall
Gävle

NORWAY
Trondheim
Ålesund
Galdhøpiggen
8100 ft.
2469 m
Bergen
Stavanger
Kristiansand
Oslo
Örebro
Uppsala
Stockholm

Tampere
Jyväskylä
Vaasa
Turku
Lahti
Helsinki
Tallinn

ESTONIA
Tartu
Pskov

ATLANTIC
OCEAN

SHETLAND
ISLANDS
ORKNEY
ISLANDS
HEBRIDES
ISLE OF
LEWIS
ISLAND
OF SKYE
Loch
Ness
KINNAIRD HEAD
THE NAZE
Skagerrak
Göteborg
Jönköping
BALTIC
SEA
GOTLAND
ÖLAND
BORNHOLM
Gulf of
Riga
LATVIA
Jelgava
Riga
Liepāja
Klaipėda
Šiauliai
Daugavpils
LITHUANIA
Kaunas
Vilnius
Barysaw

IRELAND
Sligo
Galway
Limerick
Waterford
Cork
MIZEN HEAD
LAND'S END
Belfast
Dublin

ISLE
OF MAN
(U.K.)
Glasgow
Dundee
Aberdeen
Edinburgh
Newcastle
upon Tyne

UNITED
KINGDOM
Leeds
Manchester
Liverpool
Sheffield
Birmingham
Kingston
upon Hull
Cardiff
GREAT
BRITAIN
LONDON
Bristol
Southampton
Plymouth
Dover

NORTH
SEA

DENMARK
Aalborg
Århus
Copenhagen
(København)
FYN
Malmö
SJAELLAND
Kiel
Lübeck

HAMBURG
Bremen
Hannover
BERLIN

GERMANY
Essen
Düsseldorf
Cologne
Halle
Leipzig
Dresden
Chemnitz
Frankfurt
am Main
Mannheim
Karlsruhe
Stuttgart
Nürnberg
Augsburg
MUNICH

Kaliningrad
RUSSIA
Gdynia
Gdańsk
Szczecin
Bydgoszcz
Poznań
POLAND
Łódź
WARSAW
Białystok
Hrodna
Baranavichy

MINSK
BELARUS
Brest
Pinsk
Prypyats'

Wrocław
Radom
Lublin
Czestochowa
Katowice
Kraków
PRAGUE
CZECH
REPUBLIC
Plzeň
Ostrava
Brno
Gerlachovský Štít
8711 ft.
2655 m
L'viv
Khmel'nyts'kyi
Rivne
Luts'k
Ivano-Frankivs'k
Chernivtsi
CARPATH

NETHERLANDS
Amsterdam
The Hague
('s-Gravenhage)
Rotterdam
Utrecht
Antwerp
Brussels
BELGIUM
Liège
LUXEMBOURG
Lille

ENGLISH CHANNEL
GUERNSEY
(U.K.)
JERSEY
(U.K.)
Cherbourg
Brest
Le Havre
Rouen

FRANCE
PARIS
Rennes
Nantes
La Rochelle
Orléans
Tours
Dijon
Clermont-Ferrand
Saint-Étienne
Lyon
Grenoble
Bordeaux
Reims
Strasbourg
Basel
Karlsruhe

SWITZERLAND
Bern
Geneva
Lausanne
Zürich
LIECHTENSTEIN
Innsbruck
Mont Blanc
15,771 ft.
4807 m

AUSTRIA
Linz
VIENNA
(WIEN)
Graz
BUDAPEST
HUNGARY
Debrecen
Szeged
Pécs

SLOVAKIA
Bratislava
Košice
Miskolc
Oradea
Cluj-Napoca
ROMANIA
Timişoara
Braşov
Iaşi

SLOVENIA
Ljubljana
Zagreb
CROATIA
Trieste
Venice
Banja Luka
Novi Sad
BELGRADE
(BEOGRAD)
SERBIA

BOSNIA AND
HERZEGOVINA
Sarajevo
Split
MONTENEGRO
Podgorica
Kragujevac
Niš

Bay of
Biscay

A Coruña
CABO DE
FISTERRA
Vigo
Porto
Braga
PORTUGAL
Coimbra
Lisbon
(Lisboa)
CABO DE
SÃO VICENTE
Faro

Gijón
Oviedo
Bilbao
Donostia-
San Sebastián
Pamplona
Burgos
Valladolid
Salamanca
Duero
SPAIN
MADRID
Toledo
Zaragoza
Aneto
11,168 ft.
3404 m
ANDORRA
PYRENEES
Tagus
Jucar
Valencia
Albacete
Murcia
Córdoba
Sevilla
Granada
Mulhacén
11,424 ft.
3482 m
Almería

Toulouse
Montpellier
Marseille
Nice
MONACO
Toulon
BARCELONA
Palma de
Mallorca
MALLORCA
MENORCA
EIVISSA
CAP DE
LA NAO
BALEARIC ISLANDS

Cádiz
Málaga
Tanger
Gibraltar
Ceuta (Sp.)
Strait of Gibraltar
Melilla
Oran

RABAT
CASABLANCA
Fès
MOROCCO

ALGIERS
(ALGER)
Constantine

ALGERIA
Chott
Melrhir

TUNISIA

MEDITERRANEAN

Nantes
Genoa
Turin
MILAN
Verona
Bologna
Florence
Pisa
SAN MARINO
Perugia
ITALY
ROME
(ROMA)
NAPLES
(NAPOLI)
Vesuvius
4203 ft.
1281 m
Bari
Taranto
CORSICA
(Fr.)
Ajaccio
ISOLA
D'ELBA
SARDINIA
(Italy)
Sassari
Cagliari
Palermo
SICILY
(Italy)
Monte Etna
10,902 ft.
3323 m
Catania
Messina
CAPO PASSERO
MALTA
Valletta
ISOLA DI
LAMPEDUSA
(Italy)

ADRIATIC SEA
APENNINES
TYRRHENIAN
SEA
IONIAN
SEA

BULGARIA
SOFIA
Stara
Zagora
Plovdiv
Skopje
MACEDONIA
Tirane
Durrës
ALBANIA
Thessaloniki
Mt. Olympus
9570 ft.
2917 m
Ioánnina
Lárisa
Vólos
GREECE
Athens
(Athina)
Pátra
CYCLADES
KÝTHIRA
CRETE
Irákleio

AEGEAN
SEA
LÉSVOS
CHIOS
ÉVVOIA
LIMNOS

IONIAN
ISLANDS

BUCHAREST
Craiova
Danube
Ploieşti

© Rand McNally
A-101710-1

| 0 | 80 | 160 | 240 | 320 | 400 | 480 Miles |

| 0 | 80 | 160 | 240 | 320 | 400 | 480 | 560 | 640 | 720 | 800 Kilometers |

Lambert Conformal Conic Projection
Scale 1:16,000,000
One inch to 256 miles
One cm to 160 km

0   80   160   240   320   400   480 Miles

0   80   160   240   320   400   480   560   640   720   800 Kilometers

Lambert Conformal Conic Projection
Scale 1:16,000,000
One inch to 256 miles
One cm to 160 km

MYS KANIN
NOS
MYS SVYATOY
NOS
OSTROV
KOLGUYEV
Naryan-Mar
Gora Narodnaya
6214 ft.
1894m
Usa

KOL'SKIY
POLUOSTROV
Ponoy

WHITE SEA

Arkhangel'sk

TIMANSKIY KRYAZH

Pechora

URAL MOUNTAINS

Ob'

WEST SIBERIAN PLAIN
(ZAPADNO-SIBIRSKAYA RAVNINA)

Severnaya Sos'va

S I B E R I A

Novosibirsk
Ob'

Lake
Ladoga
Lake
Onega
Ozero
Beloye

Syktyvkar

Konzhakovskiy Kamen
5148 ft.
1569 m

Irtysh

Demyanka
Konda

Om

SEVERNYYE UVALY

Kirov

R U S S I A

Yekaterinburg

Tura

Tobol

Omsk

Ozero
Chany

Ozero
Kulundinskoye

Rybinskoye
Vodokhranilishche

Kama

Gora Yamantau
5381 ft.
1640 m

Ishim

Astana
(Aqmola)

Nizhne-Kamskoye
Vodokhranilishche

Ufa

Belaya

Nura

Moscow

Volga

Kazan'

Kuybyshevskoye
Vodokhranilishche

Demo

KAZAKH HILLS

Smolensk

SREDNERUSSKAYA VOZVYSHENNOST'

Saratovskoye
Vodokhranilishche

Samara

Elek

Torghay

Tengiz
köli

Lake Balkhash
(Balqash köli)

Dnieper

PRIVOLZHSKAYA VOZVYSHENNOST'

K A Z A K H S T A N

Zhem

Sarysu

Shu

Kiev
(Kyïv)

Volgogradskoye
Vodokhranilishche

Syr Darya

Tashkent

UKRAINE

Kremenchuts'ke
vodoskhovyshche

Don

Volgograd

Ural Depression

Aral Sea

QIZILQUM

Kakhovs'ke
vodoskhovyshche

CASPIAN DEPRESSION

UST-URT PLATEAU

UZBEKISTAN

Aydar Köl

MOLDOVA

Odesa

SEA OF
AZOV

Astrahan'

Volga

Kuban'

Northern Donets

Donets'k

Ozero
Manych-
Gudilo

Manych

Kuma

Sarygamysh
köli

Amu Darya

Kara-Bogaz-
Gol Gulf

K A R A

TURKMENISTAN

Kara-Kum Canal

CRIMEAN
PENINSULA

Gora El'brus
18 510 ft.
5642 m

Gora Kazbek
16 558 ft.
5047 m

CASPIAN
SEA

K U M

KOPPEH DAGH

Atrak

BLACK
SEA

CAUCASUS MOUNTAINS

Terek

Baku
(Bakı)

AFGHANISTAN

INCE
BURUN

GEORGIA

Tbilisi

Mingechaur
Reservoir

AZERBAIJAN

Kür

ELBURZ MOUNTAINS

ARMENIA

Sevan
Lich

AZER.

Daryächeh-ye
Orümiyeh

Koh-e Damavand
18 386 ft.
5604 m

DASHT-E KAVIR

Bosporus

Mt. Ararat
16 854 ft.
5137 m

Murat

Tehrān

Istanbul

SEA OF
MARMARA

Ankara

Sakarya

T U R K E Y

Kızılırmak

Van
Gölü

Tigris

Ozarı Nval

I R A N

DASHT-E LUT

Tuz
Gölü

Erciyes Dağı
12 851 ft.
3917 m

Daryächeh-ye
Namak

Gediz

Büyükmenderes

Beyşehir
Gölü

TAURUS MOUNTAINS

ZAGROS MOUNTAINS

Zard Koh
14 918 ft.
4547 m

Daryächeh-ye
Tashk

SAMOS

RODOS

DODECANESE

KARPATHOS

CYPRUS

Ólimbos
6401 ft.
1951 m

Qurnat as
Sawda
10 115 ft.
3083 m

LEBANON

SYRIA

IRAQ

SYRIAN
DESERT

Euphrates

Baghdād

Bahr
al-Milḥ

Tigris

Kārūn

Zohreh

Daryächeh-ye
Bakhtegān

ATLANTIC
OCEAN

NORWEGIAN SEA

Arctic Circle

FAROE
ISLANDS

SHETLAND
ISLANDS

HEBRIDES

ORKNEY
ISLANDS

Trondheim

Gulf of Bothnia

Helsinki

Oslo

Gulf of Finland

St. Petersburg

Glasgow

Stockholm

BALTIC

Göteborg

SAAREMAA

Dublin

IRISH SEA

Leeds

GOTLAND

Manchester

Riga

NORTH
SEA

ÖLAND

SEA

Western Dvina

Birmingham

Copenhagen

BORNHOLM

London

Hamburg

Minsk

Amsterdam

Berlin

Elbe

Warsaw

English Channel

Brussels

Essen

Rhine

Łódź

Bug

Frankfurt
am Main

Prague

Katowice

Oder

Seine

Paris

Mannheim

CARPATHIAN MOUNTAINS

Loire

Stuttgart

Dniester

Danube

Munich

Bay of
Biscay

Bordeaux

MASSIF
CENTRAL

Lyon

Vienna

A   L   P   S

Danube

Budapest

Rhône

CORDILLERA CANTÁBRICA

Turin

Milan

Porto

PYRENEES

Ebro

TRANSYLVANIAN ALPS

Marseille

LIGURIAN
SEA

A
P
E
N
N
I
N
E
S

Belgrade

Bucharest

Madrid

Tagus

Danube

Lisbon

Barcelona

CORSICA

ADRIATIC SEA

Sofia

SIERRA MORENA

València

Rome

Sevilla

SARDINIA

Naples

Pindos Óros

AEGEAN
SEA

BALEARIC ISLANDS

TYRRHENIAN
SEA

IONIAN
ISLANDS

Strait of Gibraltar

M E D I T E R R A N E A N

SICILY

IONIAN
SEA

Athens

CYCLADES

MALTA

S E A

SEA OF CRETE

CRETE

| 0 | 80 | 160 | 240 | 320 | 400 | 480 Miles |

| 0 | 80 | 160 | 240 | 320 | 400 | 480 | 560 | 640 | 720 | 800 Kilometers |

Lambert Conformal Conic Projection
Scale 1:16,000,000
One inch to 256 miles
One cm to 160 km

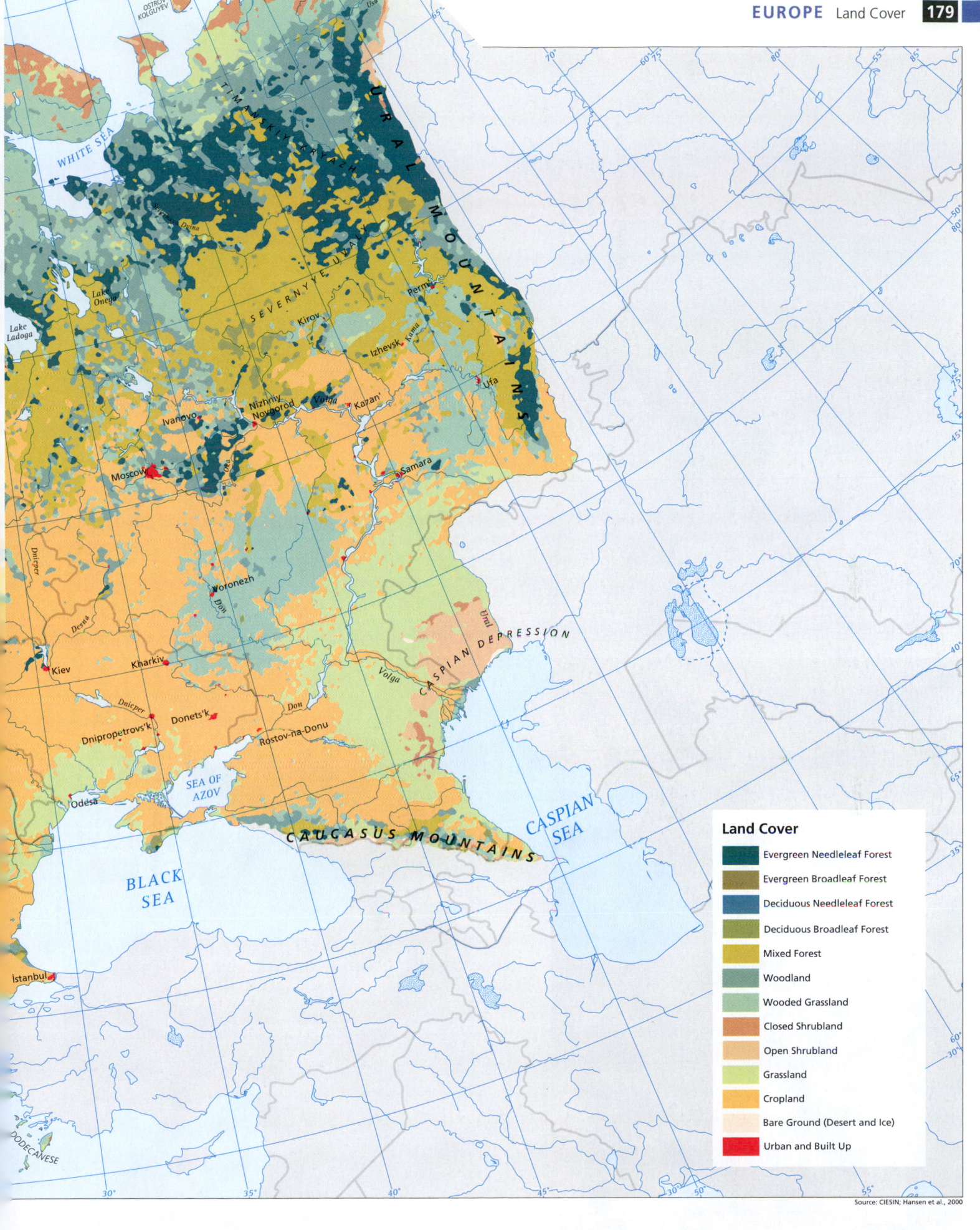

Land Cover

- Evergreen Needleleaf Forest
- Evergreen Broadleaf Forest
- Deciduous Needleleaf Forest
- Deciduous Broadleaf Forest
- Mixed Forest
- Woodland
- Wooded Grassland
- Closed Shrubland
- Open Shrubland
- Grassland
- Cropland
- Bare Ground (Desert and Ice)
- Urban and Built Up

Source: CIESIN; Hansen et al., 2000

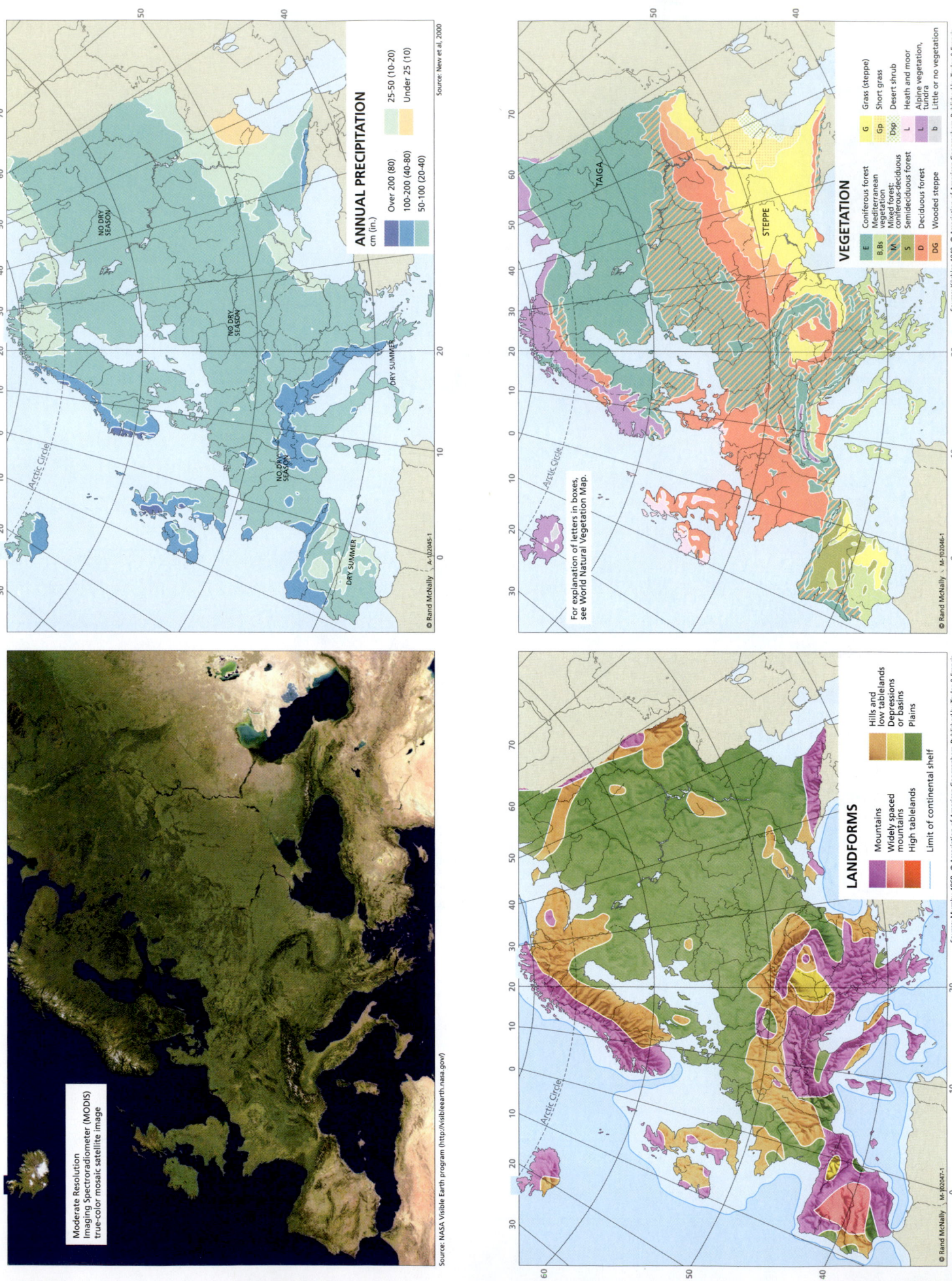

ANNUAL PRECIPITATION

cm (in.)

- Over 200 (80)
- 100-200 (40-80)
- 50-100 (20-40)
- 25-50 (10-20)
- Under 25 (10)

Source: New et al., 2000

© Rand McNally   A-102045-1

VEGETATION

- E — Coniferous forest
- B, Bs — Mediterranean vegetation
- M — Mixed forest; coniferous-deciduous
- S — Semideciduous forest
- D — Deciduous forest
- DG — Wooded steppe
- G — Grass (steppe)
- Gp — Short grass
- Dsp — Desert shrub
- L — Heath and moor
- L — Alpine vegetation, tundra
- b — Little or no vegetation

For explanation of letters in boxes, see World Natural Vegetation Map.

Source: Küchler, 1949. © Association of American Geographers. Published by Taylor & Francis. Adapted with permission of the Association of American Geographers.

© Rand McNally   M-102046-1

Moderate Resolution Imaging Spectroradiometer (MODIS) true-color mosaic satellite image

Source: NASA Visible Earth program (http://visibleearth.nasa.gov/)

LANDFORMS

- Mountains
- Widely spaced mountains
- High tablelands
- Hills and low tablelands
- Depressions or basins
- Plains
- Limit of continental shelf

Source: Murphy, 1968. © Association of American Geographers. Published by Taylor & Francis. Adapted with permission of the Association of American Geographers.

© Rand McNally   M-102047-1

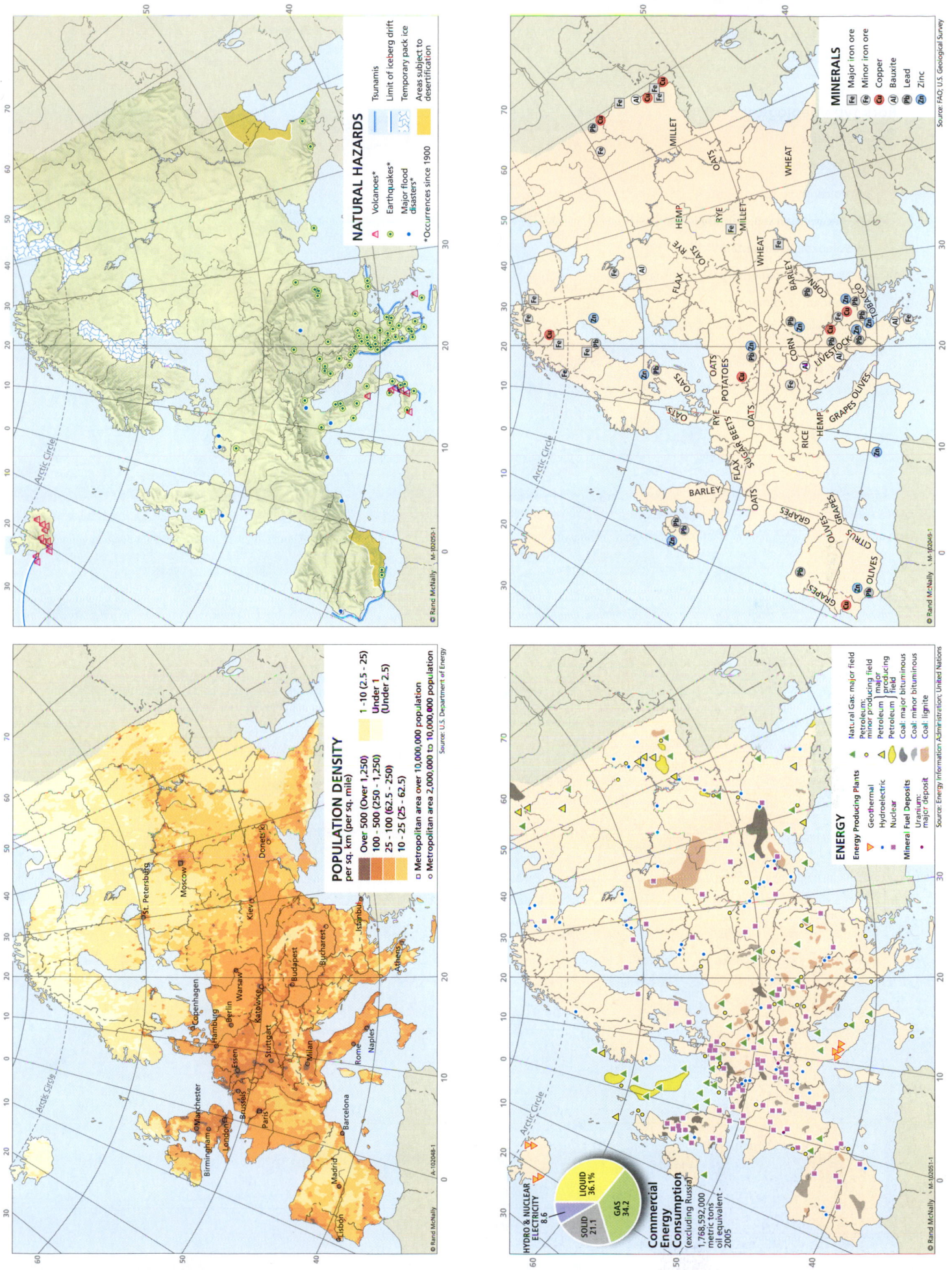

NATURAL HAZARDS

- ◁ Volcanoes*
- ◉ Earthquakes*
- ● Major flood disasters*
- ─── Tsunamis
- ─── Limit of iceberg drift
- ～～ Temporary pack ice
- ▨ Areas subject to desertification

*Occurrences since 1900

© Rand McNally   M-102050-1

MINERALS

- Fe Major iron ore
- Fe Minor iron ore
- Cu Copper
- Al Bauxite
- Pb Lead
- Zn Zinc

Source: FAO; U.S. Geological Survey

© Rand McNally   M-102049-1

POPULATION DENSITY
per sq. km (per sq. mile)

- Over 500 (Over 1,250)
- 100 - 500 (250 - 1,250)
- 25 - 100 (62.5 - 250)
- 10 - 25 (25 - 62.5)
- 1 -10 (2.5 - 25)
- Under 1 (Under 2.5)

□ Metropolitan area over 10,000,000 population
○ Metropolitan area 2,000,000 to 10,000,000 population

Source: U.S. Department of Energy

© Rand McNally   A-102048-1

ENERGY

Energy Producing Plants
- ◁ Geothermal
- ◁ Hydroelectric
- ■ Nuclear

Mineral Fuel Deposits
- ● Uranium: major deposit
- ▼ Natural Gas: major field
- ▼ Petroleum: minor producing field
- ○ Petroleum: major producing field
- ○ Petroleum: field
- ▬ Coal: major bituminous
- ▬ Coal: minor bituminous
- ▬ Coal: lignite

Source: Energy Information Administration; United Nations

Commercial Energy Consumption (excluding Russia) 1,768,592,000 metric tons oil equivalent - 2005

- LIQUID 36.1%
- GAS 34.2
- SOLID 21.1
- HYDRO & NUCLEAR ELECTRICITY 8.6

© Rand McNally   M-102051-1

Geology

Rock type/geological era

- Intrusive
- Metamorphic
- Volcanic, tectonic
- Precambrian sedimentary
- Paleozoic sedimentary
- Mesozoic sedimentary
- Cenozoic sedimentary

Note: Areas classified as sedimentary also include some sedimentary/volcanic areas.

Source: Chorlton, 2007

The geological information on this map is highly generalized, and is intended for use at scales of 1:10,000,000 or smaller.

ATLANTIC OCEAN

NORWEGIAN SEA

Arctic Circle

Reykjavík

FAROE ISLANDS

SHETLAND ISLANDS

HEBRIDES

ORKNEY ISLANDS

NORTH SEA

Trondheim

Gulf of Bothnia

Oslo

Stockholm

Göteborg

Helsinki

Gulf of Finland

St. Petersburg

Lake Peipus

BALTIC SEA

SAAREMAA

GOTLAND

ÖLAND

Rīga

Western Dvina

BORNHOLM

Copenhagen

Glasgow

Dublin

IRISH SEA

Leeds

Manchester

Birmingham

London

Hamburg

Amsterdam

Elbe

Berlin

Minsk

Brussels

Essen

Warsaw

Bug

Łódź

English Channel

Seine

Paris

Rhine

Frankfurt am Main

Mannheim

Prague

Katowice

Oder

Vistula

Bay of Biscay

Loire

Stuttgart

Danube

Munich

Vienna

CARPATHIAN MOUNTAINS

Dniester

Bordeaux

Lyon

Dordogne

Rhône

MASSIF CENTRAL

A L P S

Turin

Milan

Po

Danube

Budapest

Drava

Sava

Belgrade

TRANSYLVANIAN ALPS

Bucharest

Danube

Porto

CORDILLERA CANTABRICA

PYRENEES

Marseille

LIGURIAN SEA

A P E N N I N E S

ADRIATIC SEA

Lisbon

Madrid

Tagus

Duero

Ebro

Barcelona

CORSICA

Rome

Sofia

PINDOS OROS

Sevilla

SIERRA MORENA

València

SARDINIA

Naples

BALEARIC ISLANDS

TYRRHENIAN SEA

IONIAN ISLANDS

AEGEAN SEA

Strait of Gibraltar

MEDITERRANEAN SEA

Algiers

SICILY

IONIAN SEA

Athens

CYCLADES

Casablanca

MALTA

SEA OF CRETE

ATLAS MOUNTAINS

CRETE

0 80 160 240 320 400 480 Miles

0 80 160 240 320 400 480 560 640 720 800 Kilometers

Lambert Conformal Conic Projection
Scale 1:16,000,000
One inch to 256 miles
One cm to 160 km

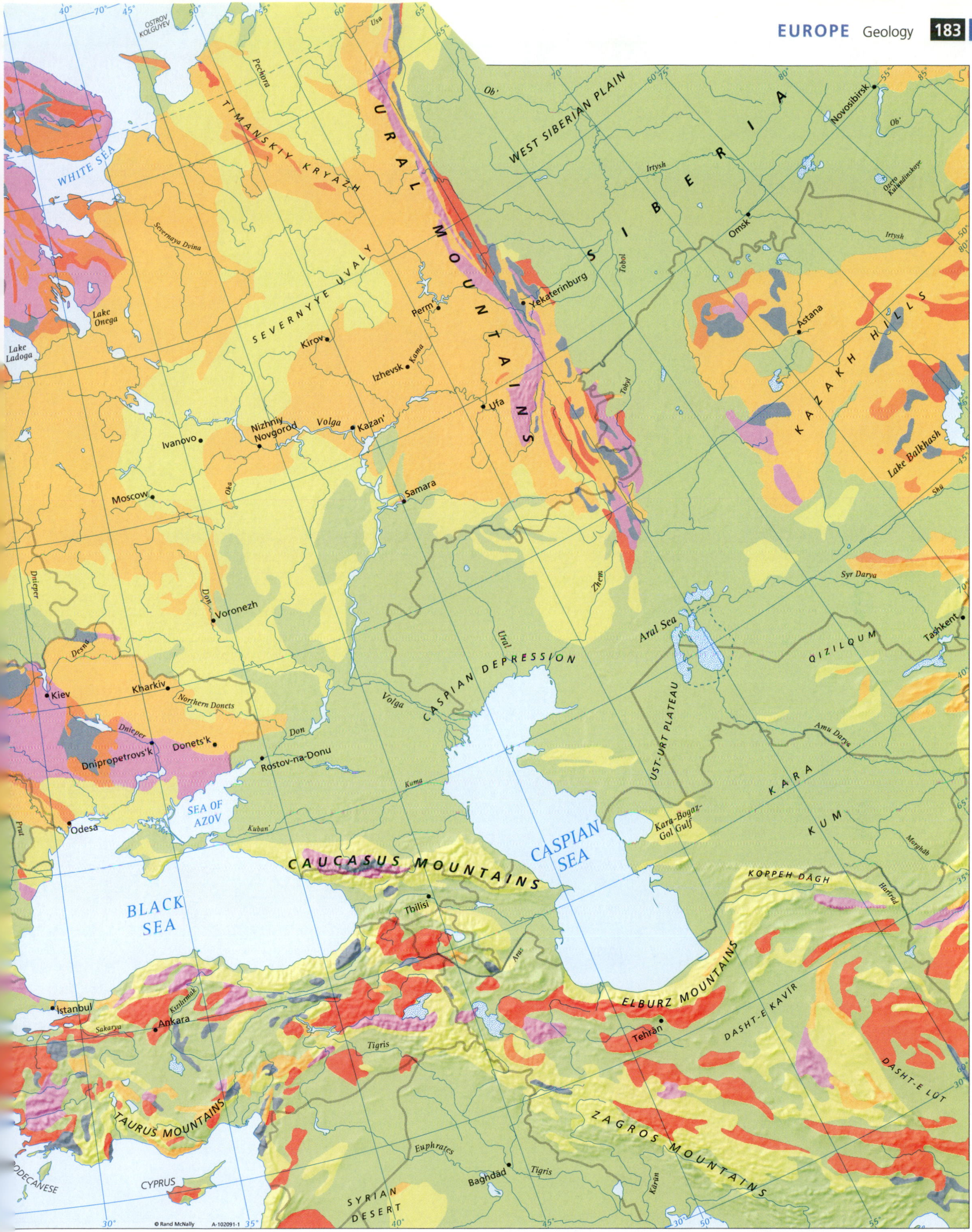

Map Labels

OSTROV
KOLGUYEV

WHITE SEA

Pechora

Usa

Ob'

WEST SIBERIAN PLAIN

S I B E R I A

Novosibirsk

Ob'

Severnaya Dvina

T I M A N S K I Y   K R Y A Z H

U R A L   M O U N T A I N S

Irtysh

Omsk

Irtysh

Ozero
Kulundinskoye

Lake
Onega

Lake
Ladoga

S E V E R N Y Y E   U V A L Y

Kirov

Perm

Yekaterinburg

Tobol

Astana

K A Z A K H   H I L L S

Izhevsk

Kama

Ufa

Ivanovo

Nizhniy
Novgorod

Volga

Kazan'

Oka

Tobyl

Lake Balkhash

Moscow

Samara

Zhem

Shu

Dnieper

Desna

Don

Voronezh

Ural

Syr Darya

Aral Sea

QIZILQUM

Tashkent

Kiev

Kharkiv

Northern Donets

CASPIAN DEPRESSION

UST-URT PLATEAU

Dnieper

Donets'k

Don

Amu Darya

Dnipropetrovs'k

Rostov-na-Donu

Volga

K A R A

Odesa

SEA OF
AZOV

Kuma

Kuban'

CASPIAN
SEA

Kara-Bogaz-
Gol Gulf

K U M

Murghab

BLACK
SEA

CAUCASUS MOUNTAINS

Tbilisi

Aras

KOPPEH DAGH

Hari Rud

Istanbul

Kizilirmak

ELBURZ MOUNTAINS

Ankara

Sakarya

Tehran

DASHT-E KAVIR

DASHT-E LUT

Tigris

TAURUS MOUNTAINS

ZAGROS MOUNTAINS

Euphrates

Baghdad

Tigris

Karun

CYPRUS

DODECANESE

SYRIAN
DESERT

© Rand McNally   A-102091-1

BARENTS SEA

RUSSIA

FINLAND

Murmansk

Helsinki

ESTONIA
Tallinn
Tartu

LATVIA
Riga

LITHUANIA
Vilnius

RUSSIA

POLAND

BELARUS

Gulf of Bothnia

SWEDEN

Stockholm

Uppsala

BALTIC SEA

GOTLAND

Göteborg

ÖLAND

Kaliningrad
Gdynia
Gdańsk

Oslo

NORWAY

Bergen
Stavanger

DENMARK
Copenhagen
(København)
Aalborg
Århus

Kiel
HAMBURG
Rostock
Lübeck

NORTH SEA

Trondheim

Ålesund

Egersund

NORWEGIAN SEA

Arctic Circle

FAROE ISLANDS
(Den.)
EYSTUROY
STREYMOY
VÁGAR
SUÐUROY

SHETLAND ISLANDS
MAINLAND
Lerwick

ORKNEY ISLANDS
MAINLAND
Kirkwall

UNITED KINGDOM

Aberdeen
Dundee
SCOTLAND
Edinburgh
Glasgow

Newcastle upon Tyne
Sunderland
Middlesbrough
Scarborough
Kingston upon Hull
York
Leeds
Manchester
Liverpool
Blackpool

GREAT BRITAIN

ISLE OF MAN

NORTHERN IRELAND
Belfast
Londonderry

IRELAND
Dublin
Galway

HEBRIDES

ISLE OF LEWIS
NORTH UIST
SOUTH UIST
ISLAND OF SKYE
ISLAND OF MULL
ISLAY

IRISH SEA

North Channel

ATLANTIC OCEAN

GREENLAND SEA

ICELAND
Reykjavík
Keflavík

| 0 | 50 | 100 | 150 | 200 | 250 | 300 Miles |

| 0 | 50 | 100 | 150 | 200 | 250 | 300 | 350 | 400 | 450 | 500 Kilometers |

Lambert Azimuthal Equal Area Projection
Scale 1:10,000,000
One inch to 160 miles
One cm to 100 km

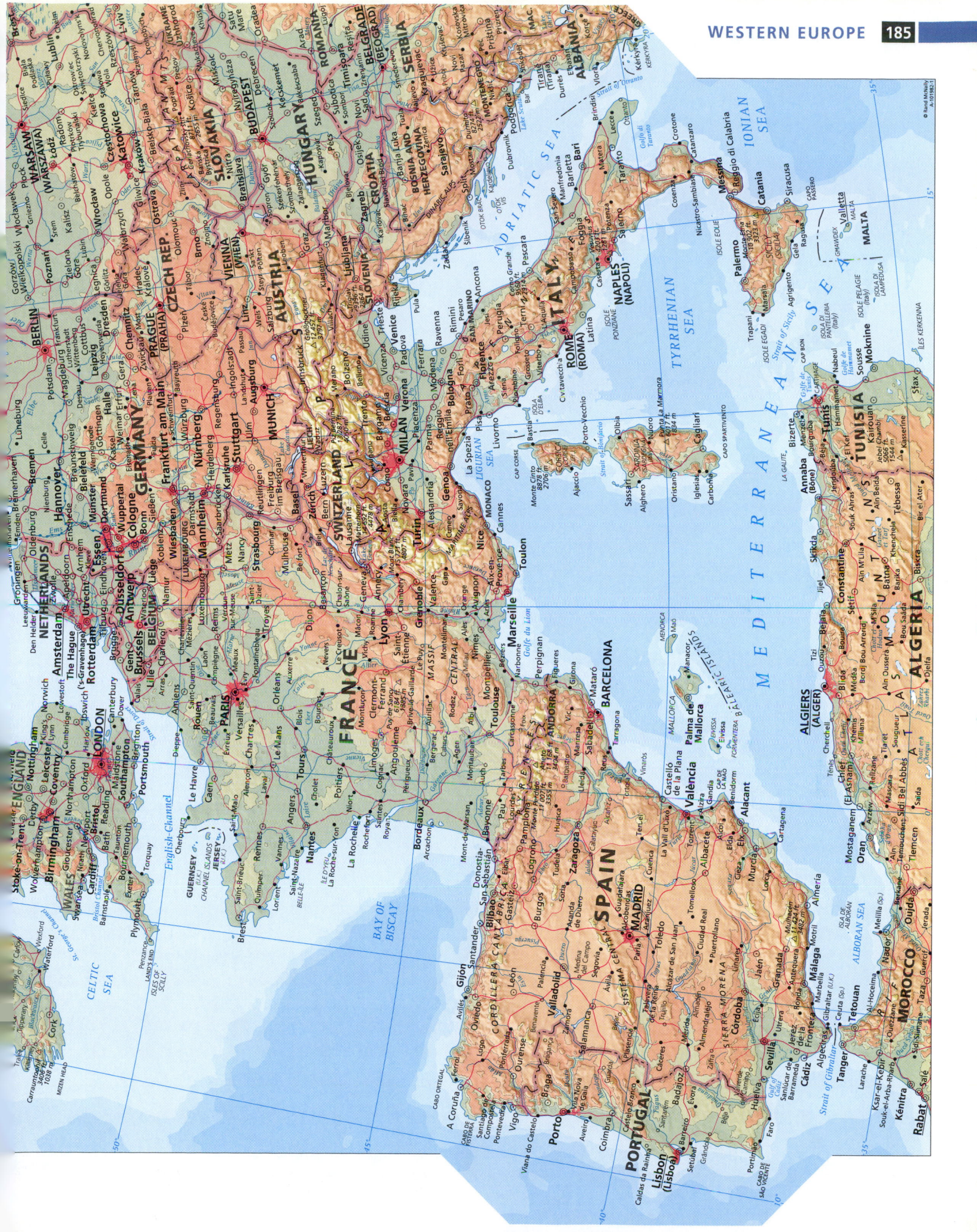

KARA SEA

BARENTS SEA

PECHORSKOYE MORE

NOVAYA ZEMLYA

WHITE SEA

URAL MTS.

KOMI

TIMANSKIY KRYAZH

RUSSIA

PERM
UFA
BASHKORTOSTAN
SAMARA
TATARSTAN
KAZAN'
UDMURTIYA
Izhevsk
Tol'yatti
CHUVASHIYA
Cheboksary
MARIY-EL
Yoshkar-Ola
NIZHNIY NOVGOROD (GORKY)
MORDOVIYA
Saransk
Penza
Ul'yanovsk
PRIVOLZHSKAYA
SREDNERUSSKAYA

Kirov
Vologda
Cherepovets
Kostroma
Yaroslavl'
Ivanovo
Vladimir
MOSCOW
Ryazan'
Tula
Kaluga
Smolensk
Bryansk

Arkhangel'sk (Archangel)
Severodvinsk
Plesetsk

KOL'SKIY POLUOSTROV
Murmansk
Monchegorsk

KARELIYA
Petrozavodsk
ST. PETERSBURG (LENINGRAD)
Novgorod
Pskov
Velikiye Luki

FINLAND
Helsinki
Tampere
Turku

ESTONIA
Tallinn
Tartu

LATVIA
Riga
Daugavpils

LITHUANIA
Vilnius
Kaunas
Šiauliai
Panevėžys
Klaipėda

BELARUS
MINSK
Vicebsk
Mahilëŭ
Babruysk
Barysaw
Baranavichy

RUSSIA
Kaliningrad

POLAND
WARSAW (WARSZAWA)
Białystok

NORWAY
NORWEGIAN SEA

SWEDEN
Stockholm
Uppsala

LAPLAND

Gulf of Bothnia

BALTIC SEA
Gulf of Finland
Gulf of Riga
GOTLAND
ÖLAND

Lake Ladoga (Ladozhskoye Oz.)
Lake Onega (Onezhskoye Oz.)

Lambert Azimuthal Equal Area Projection
Scale 1:10,000,000
One inch to 160 miles
One cm to 100 km

0 50 100 150 200 250 300 Miles
0 50 100 150 200 250 300 350 400 450 500 Kilometers

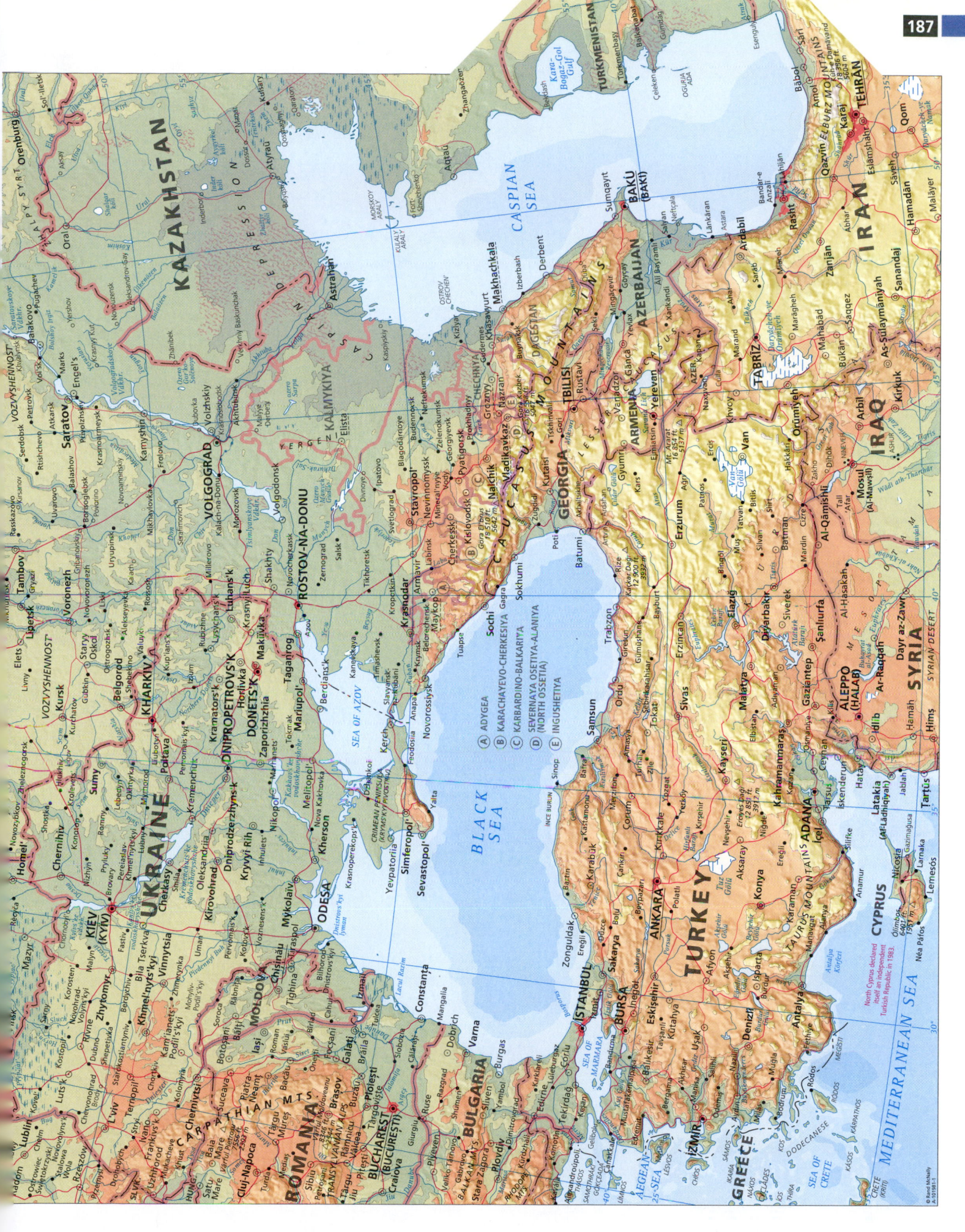

ATLANTIC OCEAN

BAY OF BISCAY

FRANCE

GERMANY

BELGIUM

LUXEMBOURG

CZECH

AUSTRIA

SWITZERLAND

SLOVENIA

PORTUGAL

SPAIN

ANDORRA

ITALY

SAN MARINO

MONACO

LIGURIAN SEA

ADRIATIC SEA

TYRRHENIAN SEA

MEDITERRANEAN

MOROCCO

ALGERIA

TUNISIA

ATLAS MOUNTAINS

HAUT ATLAS

MOYEN ATLAS

GRAND ERG OCCIDENTAL

GRAND ERG ORIENTAL

TRIPOLITANIA

SAHARA

ALBORAN SEA

BALEARIC ISLANDS

SARDINIA (SARDEGNA)

CORSICA (CORSE)

SICILY (SICILIA)

MALTA

Lisbon (Lisboa)

MADRID

BARCELONA

Porto

Sevilla

VALÈNCIA

ALGIERS (ALGER)

Tunis

ROME (ROMA)

NAPLES (NAPOLI)

PARIS

Lyon

MILAN

Munich

PRAGUE (PRAHA)

Tripoli (Tarābulus)

CASABLANCA

Rabat

0   50   100 150 200 250   300 Miles

0 50 100 150 200 250 300 350 400 450 500 Kilometers

Lambert Azimuthal Equal Area Projection
Scale 1:10,000,000
One inch to 160 miles
One cm to 100 km

a

GREENLAND SEA

Denmark Strait

Arctic Circle

HORN   GRÍMSEY   RIFSTANGI   Raufarhöfn   FONTUR

Kópasker

Ísafjarðardjúp   Þistilfjörður

Flateyri   Siglufjörður   Þórshöfn   Bakkaflói
Dyrafjörður   Ólafsfjörður   Bakkafjörður
Vatneyri   Skagaströnd   Dalvík   Húsavík   Vopnafjörður
Hólmavík   Sauðárkrókur   Akureyri   Grímsstaðir   Vopnafjörður   Héraðsflói
HÚNAFLÓI   Mývatn   Borgarfjörður
BJARGTANGAR   Blönduós   Egilsstaðir   Seyðisfjörður
Breiðafjörður   Herðubreið   Neskaupstaður
Stykkishólmur   5518 ft.   Eskifjörður
1682 m
Búðardalur   Askja   ICELAND   Búðir   Snæfell
Borðeyri   4954 ft.   6014 ft.
SNÆFELLSNESS   1510 m   Kverkfjöll   1833 m
FAXAFLÓI   Hofsjökull   6299 ft.
1920 m
Borgarnes   Djúpivogur
Langjökull   Hvítárvatn
Akranes   Vatnajökull   Höfn
Þingvellir   Grímsvötn
Reykjavík   5640 ft.   STOKKSNES
Hafnarfjörður   Kópavogur   1719 m
Keflavík   Skarð   Hekla   Hvannadalshnúkur
REYKJANES   4892 ft.   6952 ft.
Grindavík   Þorlákshöfn   Selfoss   1491 m   2119 m
Eyrarbakki   Öræfajökull   Fagurhólsmýri
Hvolsvöllur   Kirkjubæjarklaustur
Mýrdalsjökull
Vestmannaeyjar   HEIMAEY
SURTSEY

ATLANTIC OCEAN

© Rand McNally
A-101769-1

b

NORWEGIAN SEA

Slættaratindur
2894 ft.   VIÐOY
882 m   FUGLOY
STREYMOY   SVÍNOY
VÁGAR   BORÐOY
MYKINES   EYSTUROY
NÓLSOY
SANDOY   Tórshavn
SKÚVOY   Húsavík
SUÐUROY
FAROE
ISLANDS
(Denmark)

ATLANTIC OCEAN

© Rand McNally
A-101763-1

c

SHETLAND
ISLANDS   UNST
(U.K.)   FETLAR
YELL
ATLANTIC   St. Magnus Bay   WHALSAY
Melby House   MAINLAND
Lerwick
FOULA   BRESSAY

OCEAN   SUMBURGH HEAD

FAIR ISLE

NORTH
RONALDSAY
WESTRAY   North   SANDAY
Sound
ROUSAY   STRONSAY
MAINLAND   SHAPINSAY
Stromness   Kirkwall   ORKNEY
HOY   ISLANDS
Burwick   SOUTH RONALDSAY   (U.K.)
Pentland Firth
Thurso   DUNCANSBY HEAD   NORTH
Castletown   SEA

© Rand McNally
A-101764-1

Carloway   ISLE OF
Stornoway   LEWIS
SCARP   TARANSAY   Tarbert
HEBRIDES   St. KILDA   PABBAY
NORTH   RAASAY
UIST   ISLAND
BENBECULA   Uig   OF SKYE   Torridon
SOUTH   Plockton
UIST   Lochboisdale
ERISKAY   CANNA   Kyle of Lochalsh
BARRA   SANDRAY   RUM   EIGG   Mallaig
MINGULAY   SEA OF
THE HEBRIDES   COLL   Tobermory
TIREE   IONA   MULL
COLONSAY   SCARBA   Lochgilphead
Sound of Jura
ISLAY   JURA
Port Askaig
Port Ellen   ISLAND
OF
Campbeltown   ARRAN

MALIN
HEAD   RATHLIN
ISLAND
Gaoth   Moville   Coleraine   Larne
Dobhair   Buncrana   Londonderry   Ballycastle
An Earagail   Letterkenny   Ballymena   North
2467 ft.   Strabane   Antrim   Channel
ARAINN   752 m   Lifford   NORTHERN   Newtownabbey
MHÓR   Killybegs   Omagh   IRELAND   Belfast   Bangor
CEANN ROS   Donegal   Lough Neagh   Lisburn   Strangford
EOGHAIN   Ballybofey   Dungannon   Lurgan   Lough
Béal an   Donegal Bay   Enniskillen   Armagh   Banbridge   Downpatrick
Mhuirthead   Bundoran   Monaghan   Newry   Newcastle
Killala   Sligo   Lower   MOURNE
ACHILL   Ballina   Lough Erne   Cavan   MTS.
ISLAND   Castleblayney   Dundalk
Swinford   Boyle   Carrick-on-   Dundalk Bay
CLARE ISLAND   Castlebar   Shannon   Ballieborough
INISHTURK   Westport   Claremorris   Castlerea   Cavan   Ardee   Drogheda
INISHBOFIN   Ballinrobe   Roscommon   Longford   Kells   Navan   Balbriggan
CONNEMARA   Tuam   Mullingar   Swords   Dublin
Clifden   Lough   Athlone   Edenderry   Maynooth   (Baile Átha Cliath)
GARUMNA   Corrib   Lough Ree   Grand Canal   Naas   Dún Laoghaire
Galway   Ballinasloe   Tullamore   Droichead Nua   Bray
INIS MÓR   Galway Bay   Loughrea   Birr   Portlaoise
INIS MEÁIN   Ennis   Roscrea   Athy   Lugnaquilla
Nenagh   Carlow   Mountain   Wicklow
IRELAND   Thurles   3031 ft.
LOOP   Limerick   924 m   Arklow
HEAD   Kilrush   Tipperary   Kilkenny   Gorey
Listowel   Cashel   Enniscorthy
Newcastle   Carrick-   New
An Daingean   West   Cahir   on-Suir   Ross   Wexford
Tralee   Castleisland   Clonmel   Rosslare
AN BLASCAOD MÓR   Carrauntoohil   Mallow   Mitchelstown   Waterford   CARNSORE
Dingle Bay   3406 ft.   Fermoy   Dungarvan   POINT
VALENCIA ISLAND   1038 m   Killarney   Blackwater   Tramore
Cahersiveen   Macroom   Cork   Youghal
Kenmare   Passage   Cobh
DURSEY   West   Kinsale   Cork
ISLAND   Bantry   Clonakilty   Harbour
MIZEN   Bantry Bay   OLD HEAD   CLEAR
HEAD   Skibbereen   OF KINSALE   ISLAND

© Rand McNally
A-101759-1

ATLANTIC

OCEAN

CELTIC
SEA

St. George's Channel
Fishguard
ST. DAVID'S
HEAD   St. David's
Haverfordwest
Milford Haven
Pembroke

Truro
Camborne
Penzance   Falmouth
LAND'S END   ISLES OF
SCILLY   LIZARD
POINT

0   20   40   60   80   100   120 Miles
0   20   40   60   80   100   120   140   160   180   200 Kilometers

Lambert Conformal Conic Projection
Scale 1:4,000,000
One inch to 64 miles
One cm to 40 km

Inset map d
Lambert Conformal Conic Projection
Scale 1:1,000,000
One inch to 16 miles
One cm to 10 km

NORWAY

SWEDEN

DENMARK

GERMANY

POLAND

Gulf

North Sea

Baltic

Skagerrak

Kattegat

Bergen

Stavanger

Oslo

Stockholm

Uppsala

Göteborg

Göteborg

Copenhagen
(København)

Malmö

Hamburg

Gdańsk
(Danzig)

Gdynia

BORNHOLM
(Denmark)

GOTLAND

ÖLAND

Lambert Conformal Conic Projection
Scale 1:4,000,000
One inch to 64 miles
One cm to 40 km

0 20 40 60 80 100 120 Miles

0 20 40 60 80 100 120 140 160 180 200 Kilometers

0   20   40   60   80   100   120 Miles

0   20   40   60   80   100   120   140   160   180   200 Kilometers

Lambert Conformal Conic Projection
Scale 1:4,000,000
One inch to 64 miles
One cm to 40 km

Lambert Conformal Conic Projection
Scale 1:4,000,000
One inch to 64 miles
One cm to 40 km

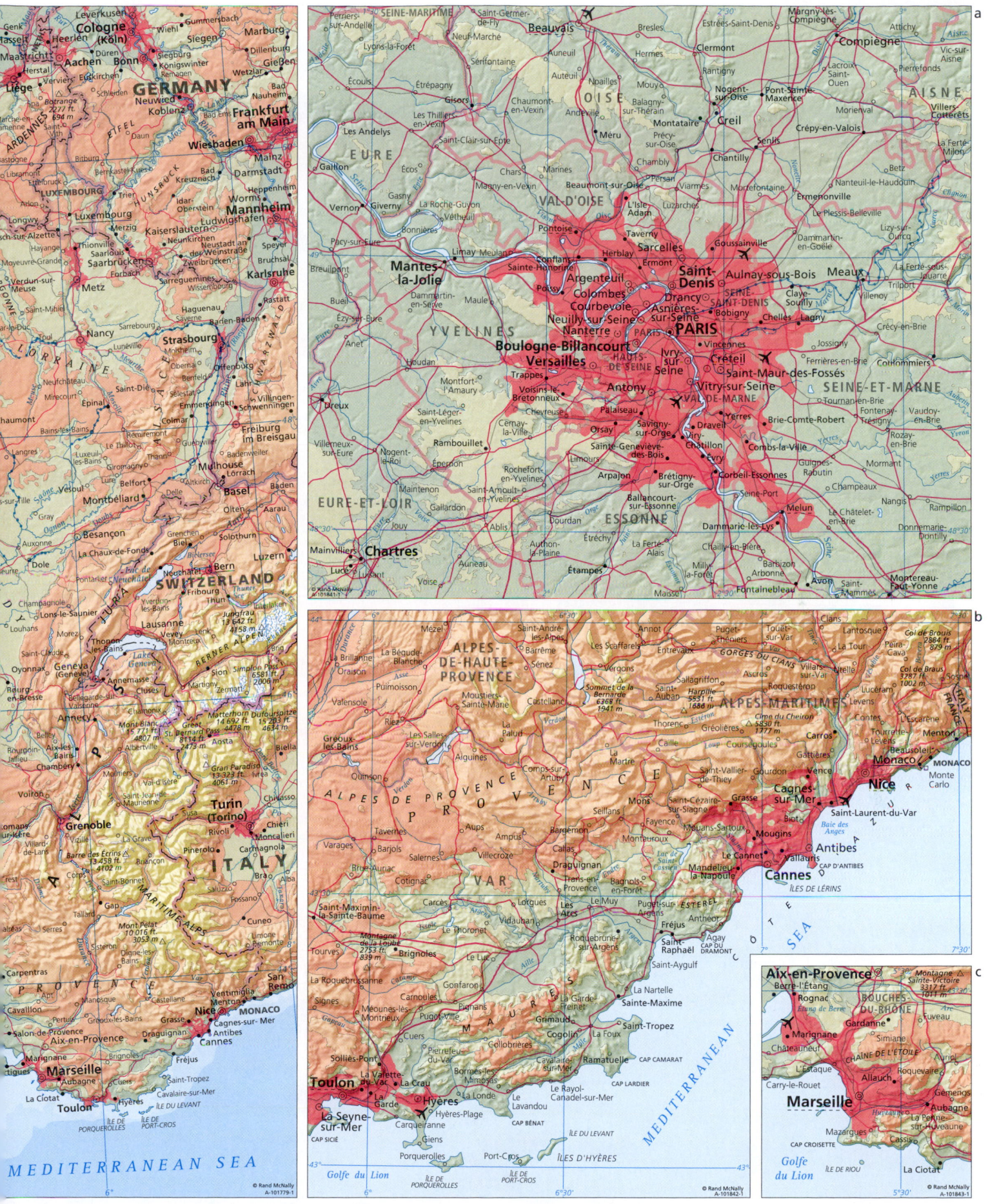

a

b

c

Inset maps a - c
Lambert Conformal Conic Projection
Scale 1:1,000,000
One inch to 16 miles
One cm to 10 km

Main Map (France, Spain, Mediterranean, Algeria)

FRANCE

Mont-de-Marsan • Aire-sur-l'Adour • Pau • Oloron-Sainte-Marie • Lourdes • Tarbes • Bagnères-de-Bigorre • Saint-Gaudens • Saint-Girons • Gaillac • Albi • Graulhet • Castres • Mazamet • Colomiers • Toulouse • Muret • Pamiers • Foix • Lavelanet • Ax-les-Thermes • Limoux • Carcassonne • Castelnaudary • Narbonne • Béziers • Pézenas • Lodève • Lunel • Montpellier • Le Grau-du-Roi • Sète • Agde • Arles • Salon-de-Provence • Martigues

P Y R E N E E S

Monte Perdido 11 007 ft 3355 m • Aneto 11 168 ft 3404 m

ANDORRA • Andorra la Vella • La Seu d'Urgell • Puigcerdà • Jaca • Sabiñánigo • Huesca • Barbastro • Monzón • Balaguer • Lleida • Tàrrega • Cervera • Manresa • Berga • Ripoll • Olot • Banyoles • Figueres • Llançà • CAP DE CREUS • CAP DE BEGUR • Girona • Palamós • Sant Feliu de Guixols • Vic • Granollers • Blanes • Calella • Mataró • Badalona • BARCELONA • L'Hospitalet de Llobregat • Sabadell • Terrassa • Igualada • Vilafranca del Penedès • Molins de Rei • Gavà • El Vendrell • Vilanova i la Geltrú • Reus • Tarragona • Cambrils

CATALUNYA

Embalse de Mequinenza • Fraga • Caspe • Alcañiz • Tortosa • Amposta • CAP DE TORTOSA • Sant Carles de la Ràpita • Morella • Vinarós • Benicarló • Alcanar

SIERRA DE GUDAR

Torreblanca • Onda • Castelló de la Plana • Almassora • Borriana • La Vall d'Uixó • Sagunt • Burjassot • VALÈNCIA • Torrent • Algemesí • Sueca • Cullera • L'Albufera • Alzira • Xàtiva • Tavernes de la Valldigna • Oliva • Gandia • Dénia • CAP DE LA NAO • Ontinyent • Alcoi • Serra d'Aitana 5112 ft 1558 m • Benidorm • La Vila Joiosa • Elda • Novelda • Alacant • Elx • Torrevella • Mar Menor • CABO DE PALOS • La Unión

Golf de Sant Jordi

BALEARIC ISLANDS (ILLES BALEARS)

Ciutadella de Menorca • Alaior • Maó • MENORCA (MINORCA) • CAP DE FORMENTOR • Puig Major 4741 ft 1445 m • Alcúdia • Badia d'Alcúdia • Sa Pobla • Artà • Inca • MALLORCA (MAJORCA) • Palma de Mallorca • Manacor • Llucmajor • Felanitx • Badia de Palma • CAP DE SES SALINES • ILLA DE CABRERA

Golf de València

EIVISSA (IBIZA) • Sant Antoni de Portmany • Sant Joan de Labritja • Santa Eulària del Riu • Eivissa • FORMENTERA

M E D I T E R R A N E A N   S E A

ALGIERS (ALGER) • Aïn Benian • Cherchell • Bou Ismail • Boudouaou • Boufarik • Blida • El Affroun • Khemis Miliana • Aïn Defla • Oued Fodda • Chlef (El Asnam) • Médéa • Sour el Ghozlane • Bouira • Dellys • Tizi Ouzou • Bordj Menaiel • Lakhdaria • Sidi Aissa • Ksar el-Boukhari • Theniet el Had • Aïn el Hadjel

A T L A S   M O U N T A I N S

Mostaganem • Arzew • CAP FERRAT • Golfe d'Arzew • Mers el Kebir • Oran (Ouahran) • Gdyel • Sig • Mascara • Mohammadia • Sebkha d'Oran • Sfizef • Sidi Bel Abbès • Ben Badis • Tighenif • Tiaret • Relizane • Zemmora • Oued Rhiou • Idioula • Aïn Tedeles • Sidi Ali • Kadir • Tissemsilt • Tiaret • Mehdia • Ksar Chellala • Sougueur • Aïn Oussera • Zahrez Chergui • ALGERIA

DAHRA ATLAS

TELL ATLAS

Lambert Conformal Conic Projection
Scale 1:4,000,000
One inch to 64 miles
One cm to 40 km

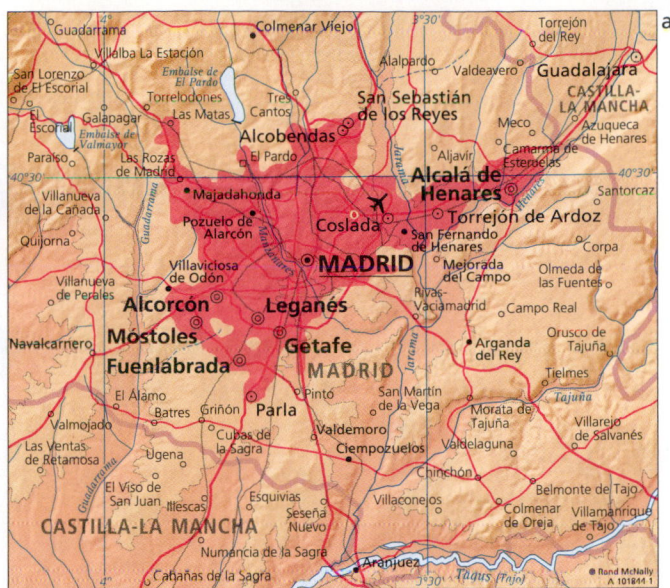

a

Guadarrama • Colmenar Viejo • Torrejón del Rey • San Lorenzo de El Escorial • Villalba La Estación • El Escorial • Galapagar • Torrelodones • Las Matas • Alalpardo • Valdeavero • GUADALAJARA • CASTILLA-LA MANCHA • Paracuellos • Las Rozas de Madrid • Majadahonda • Tres Cantos • San Sebastián de los Reyes • Meco • Camarma de Esteruelas • Azuqueca de Henares • Alcobendas • Villanueva de la Cañada • Pozuelo de Alarcón • Coslada • ALCALÁ DE HENARES • Aljavir • Santorcaz • Torrejón de Ardoz • San Fernando de Henares • Mejorada del Campo • Olmeda de las Fuentes • Villaviciosa de Odón • MADRID • Rivas-Vaciamadrid • Corpa • Alcorcón • Leganés • Getafe • MADRID • San Martín de la Vega • Arganda del Rey • Orusco de Tajuña • Móstoles • Fuenlabrada • Navalcarnero • El Álamo • Batres • Griñón • Parla • Pinto • Valdemoro • Morata de Tajuña • Villarejo de Salvanés • Las Ventas de Retamosa • Ugena • Cubas de la Sagra • Seseña Nuevo • Ciempozuelos • Valdelaguna • Chinchón • Belmonte de Tajo • El Viso de San Juan • Illescas • Esquivias • Villaconejos • Colmenar de Oreja • Villamanrique de Tajo • CASTILLA-LA MANCHA • Numancia de la Sagra • Cabañas de la Sagra • Aranjuez

b

Ericeira • Arruda dos Vinhos • Benavente • Mafra • Vila Franca de Xira • Porto Alto • SANTARÉM • Melveira • Bucelas • Alverca do Ribatejo • Infantado • LISBOA • Loures • Sacavém • CABO DA ROCA • Algueirão-Mem Martins • Agualva-Cacém • Sintra • Mosqueide • Canha • CABO RASO • Alcabideche • Queluz • Amadora • Lisbon (Lisboa) • Alcochete • SETÚBAL • Estoril • Carnaxide • Almada • Montijo • Cascais • Oeiras • Laranjeiro • Barreiro • Pinhal Novo • Costa de Caparica • Moita • ÉVORA • Seixal • Palmela • A T L A N T I C   O C E A N • Coina • Setúbal • Sesimbra • Tróia • Palma • CABO ESPICHEL • Baía de Setúbal • Comporta

c

CORVO • FLORES • AZORES (AÇORES) (Port.) • GRACIOSA • TERCEIRA • FAIAL • Horta • SÃO JORGE • Angra do Heroísmo • Ponta do Pico 7713 ft 2351 m • PICO • Ponta Delgada • SÃO MIGUEL • A T L A N T I C   O C E A N • SANTA MARIA

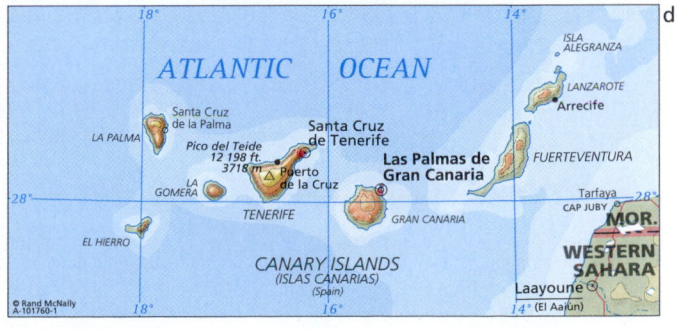

d

A T L A N T I C   O C E A N • ISLA ALEGRANZA • LANZAROTE • Arrecife • Santa Cruz de la Palma • Santa Cruz de Tenerife • LA PALMA • Pico del Teide 12 198 ft 3718 m • Puerto de la Cruz • Las Palmas de Gran Canaria • FUERTEVENTURA • LA GOMERA • TENERIFE • GRAN CANARIA • Tarfaya • CAP JUBY • EL HIERRO • CANARY ISLANDS (ISLAS CANARIAS) (Spain) • MOR. • WESTERN SAHARA • Laayoune (El Aaiun)

Inset maps a, b
Lambert Conformal Conic Projection
Scale 1:1,000,000
One inch to 16 miles
One cm to 10 km

Inset maps c, d
Lambert Conformal Conic Projection
Scale 1:8,000,000
One inch to 128 miles
One cm to 80 km

0 20 40 60 80 100 120 Miles
0 20 40 60 80 100 120 140 160 180 200 Kilometers

Lambert Conformal Conic Projection
Scale 1:4,500,000
One inch to 71 miles
One cm to 45 km

Inset map b
Lambert Conformal Conic Projection
Scale 1:2,000,000
One inch to 32 miles
One cm to 20 km

A Kosovo unilaterally declared its
   independence from Serbia in 2008.

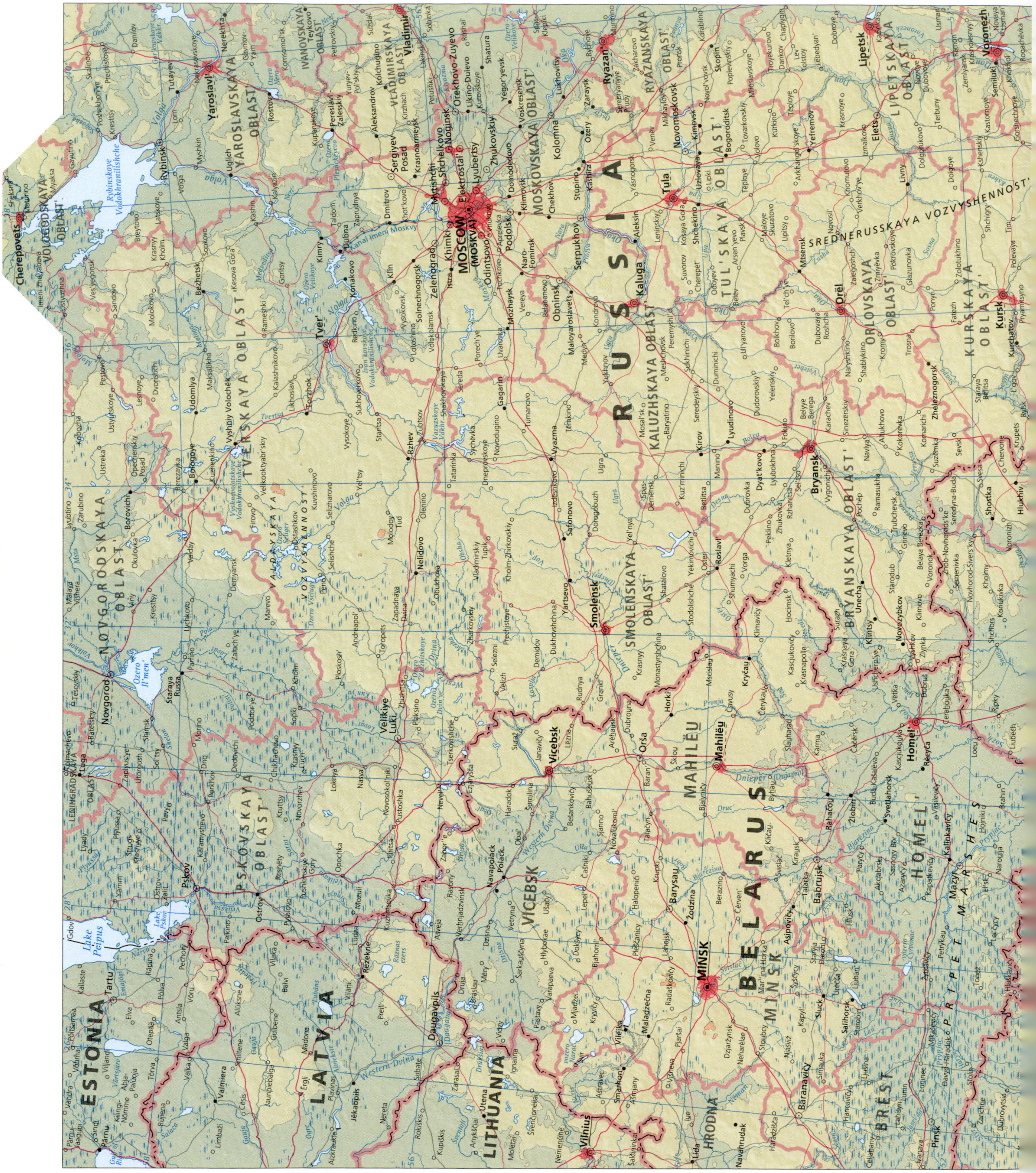

RUSSIA

BELARUS

ESTONIA

LATVIA

LITHUANIA

MOSCOW (MOSKVA)

MINSK

VILNIUS

Yaroslavl'

Cherepovets

Rybinsk

Vladimir

Ryazan'

Lipetsk

Voronezh

Tula

Kaluga

Orël

Kursk

Bryansk

Smolensk

Tver'

Novgorod

Pskov

Vicebsk

Mahilëŭ

Homel'

Vilnius

Daugavpils

Tartu

Pärnu

YAROSLAVSKAYA OBLAST'

IVANOVSKAYA OBLAST'

VLADIMIRSKAYA OBLAST'

MOSKOVSKAYA OBLAST'

RYAZANSKAYA OBLAST'

LIPETSKAYA OBLAST'

TUL'SKAYA OBLAST'

KALUZHSKAYA OBLAST'

ORLOVSKAYA OBLAST'

KURSKAYA OBLAST'

BRYANSKAYA OBLAST'

SMOLENSKAYA OBLAST'

TVERSKAYA OBLAST'

NOVGORODSKAYA OBLAST'

PSKOVSKAYA OBLAST'

LENINGRADSKAYA OBLAST'

VOLOGODSKAYA OBLAST'

VICEBSK

MAHILËŬ

MINSK

HOMEL'

HRODNA

BREST

VALDAYSKAYA VOZVYSHENNOST'

SREDNERUSSKAYA VOZVYSHENNOST'

P R Y P E T   M A R S H E S

Lake Peipus

Ozero Il'men'

Rybinskoye Vodokhranilishche

Lake Pskov

Dnieper [Dnjapro]

Western Dvina

Volga

0   20   40   60   80   100   120 Miles
0 20 40 60 80 100 120 140 160 180 200 Kilometers

Lambert Conformal Conic Projection
Scale 1:4,000,000
One inch to 64 miles
One cm to 40 km

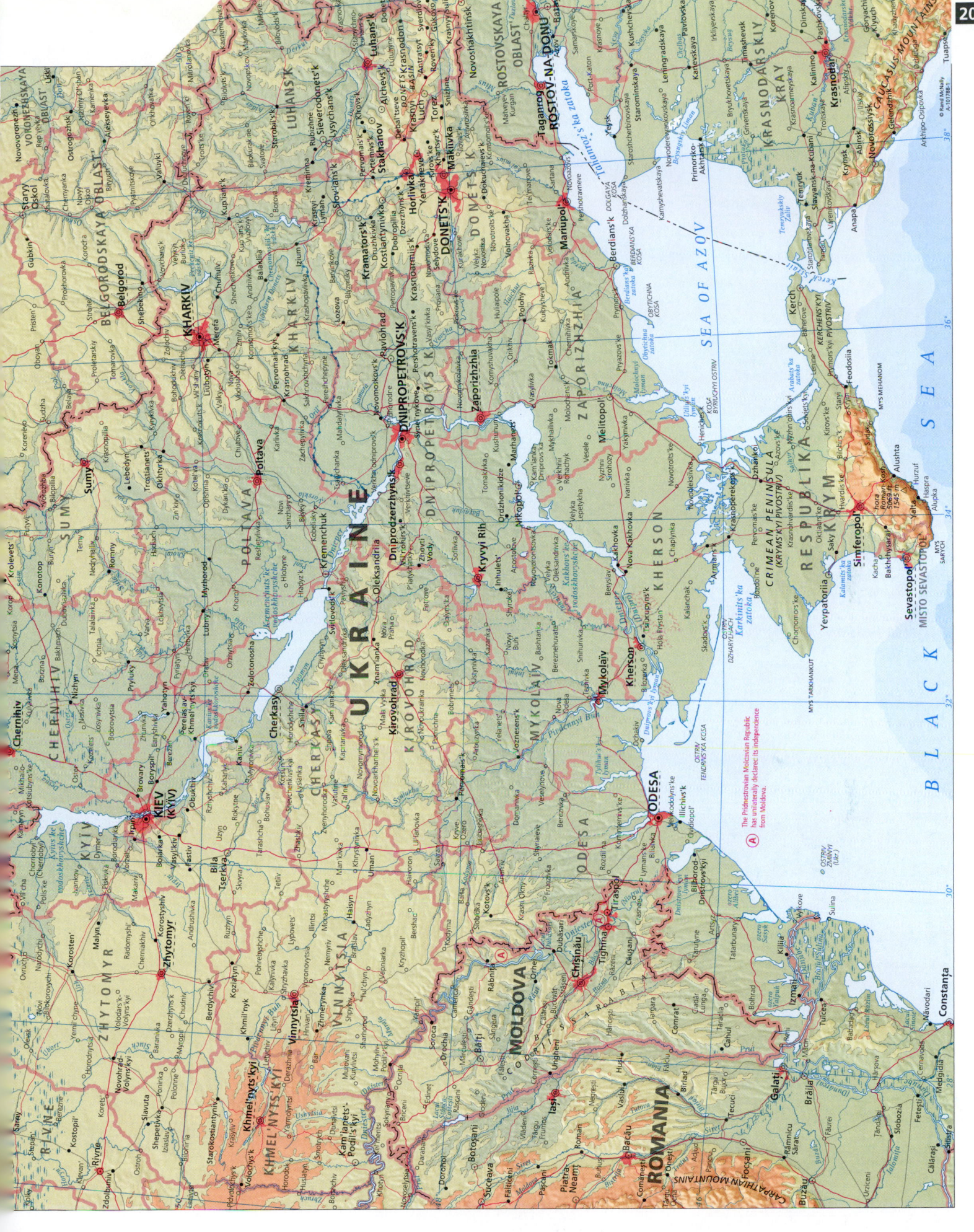

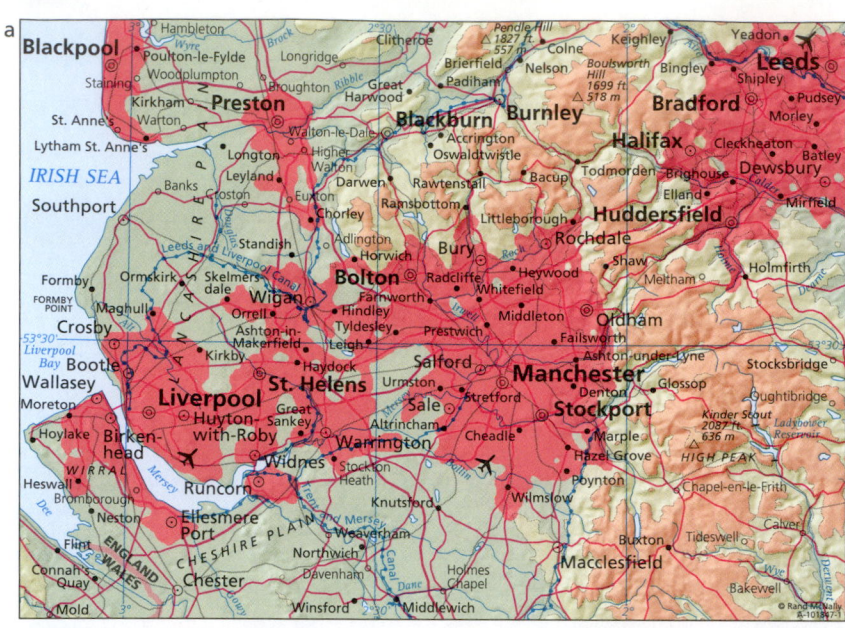

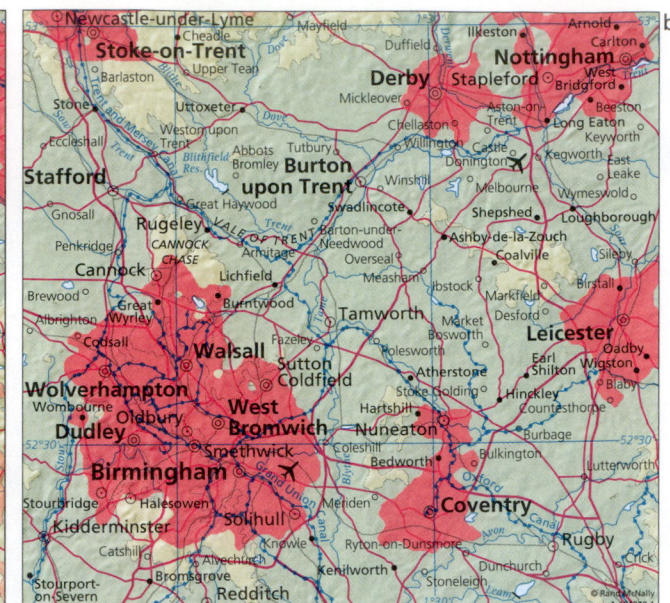

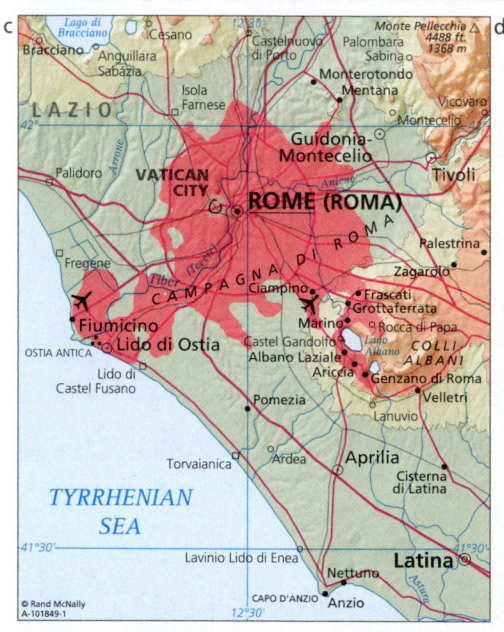

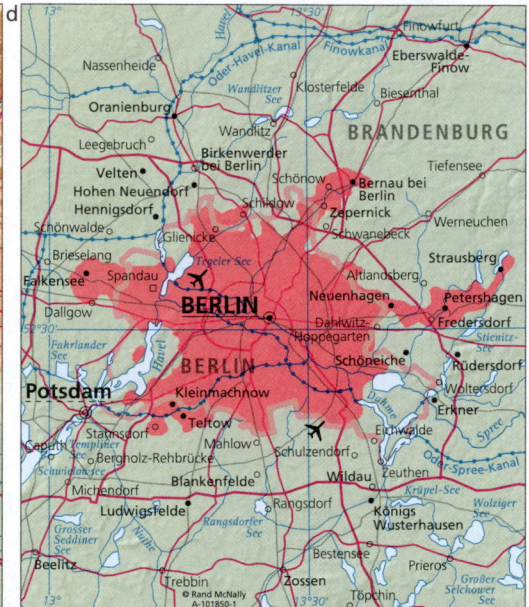

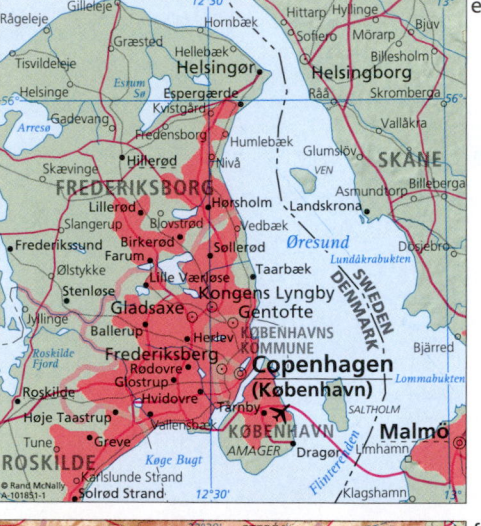

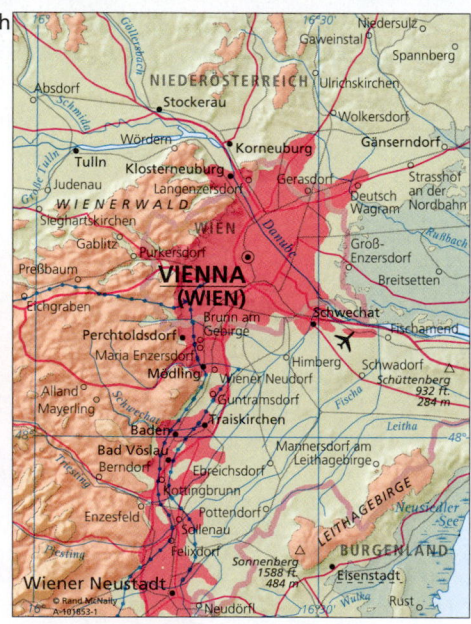

Lambert Conformal Conic Projection
Scale 1:1,000,000
One inch to 16 miles
One cm to 10 km

| 0 | 5 | 10 | 15 | 20 | 25 | 30 Miles |
| 0 | 5 | 10 | 15 | 20 | 25 | 30 | 35 | 40 | 45 | 50 Kilometers |

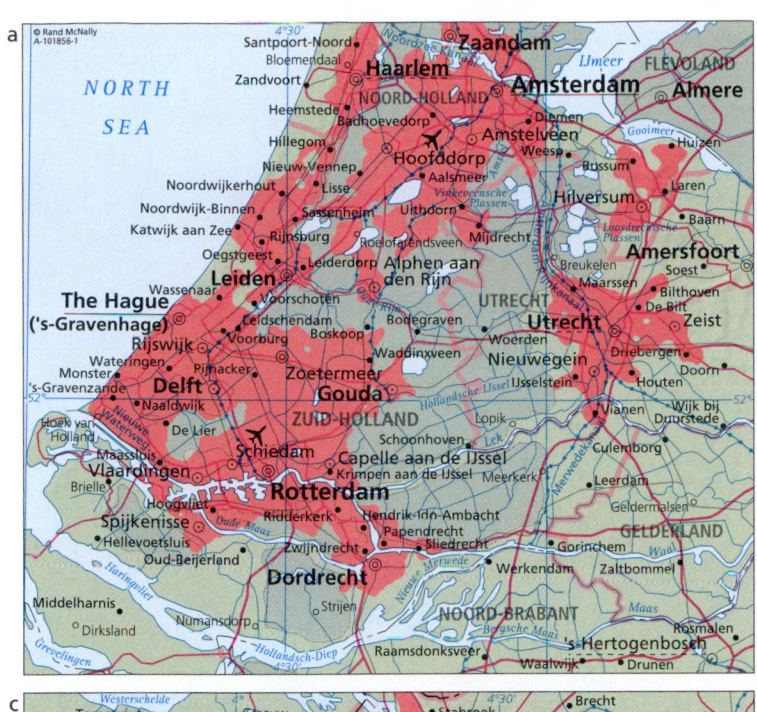

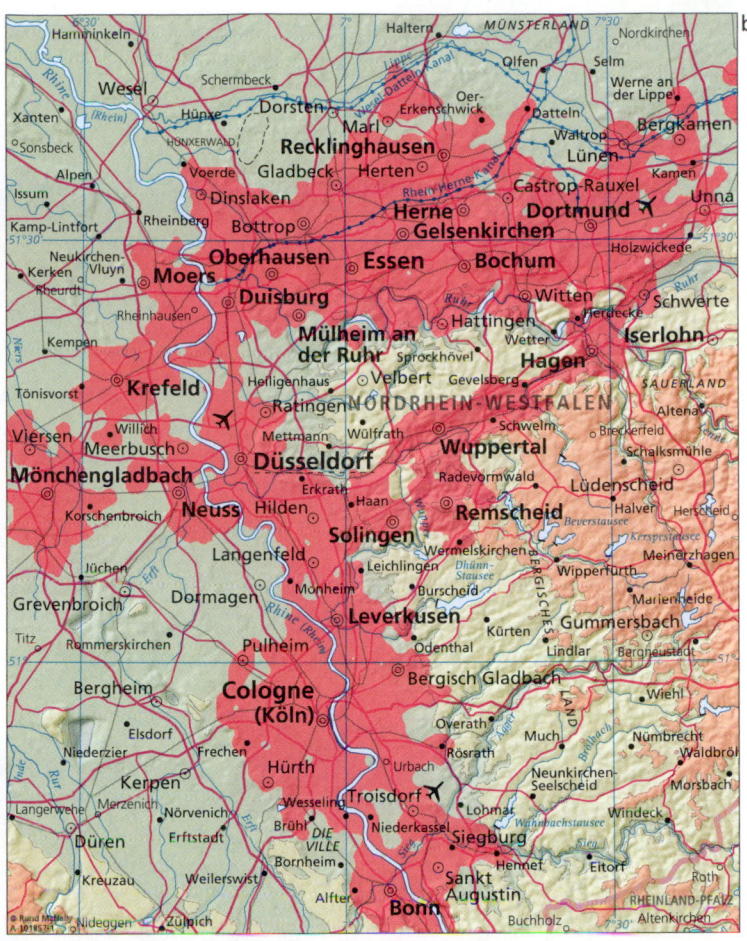

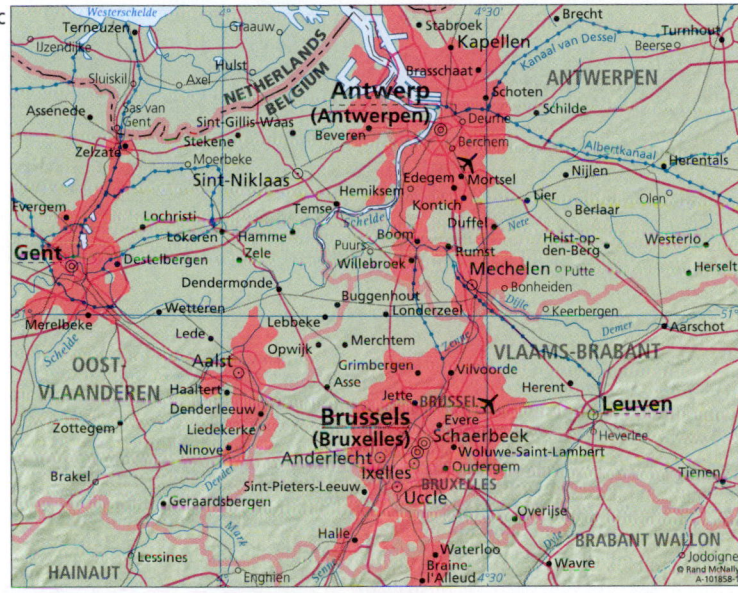

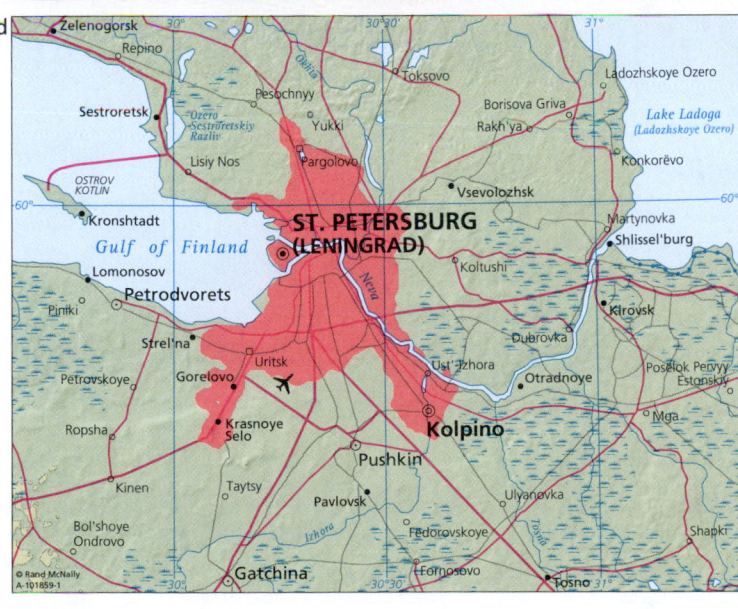

0   5   10   15   20   25   30 Miles
0 5 10 15 20 25 30 35 40 45 50 Kilometers

Lambert Conformal Conic Projection
Scale 1:1,000,000
One inch to 16 miles
One cm to 10 km

UNITED STATES

ASIA

LAPTEV
SEA

EAST
SIBERIAN
SEA

NEW SIBERIAN
ISLANDS

OSTROV
VRANGELYA

MYS DEZHNEVA

ST. LAWRENCE
ISLAND

ST. MATTHEW
ISLAND

BERING
SEA

ALEUTIAN ISLANDS

Arctic Circle

Tiksi

Zhigansk

Gora Pobeda
10 325 ft.
3147 m

Cherskiy

Anadyr'

CAPE
OLYUTORSKIY

Yakutsk

Lensk

Aldan

Magadan

Kolyma

Indigirka

Lena

Vilyuy

Nizhnyaya Tunguska

Tunguska

Lake
Baikal

Irkutsk

Ulan-
Ude

Chita

Argun

Kerulen

MONGOLIA

Ulaanbaatar

GOBI DESERT

Klyuchevskaya
Sopka
15 584 ft.
4750 m

Vulkan

Petropavlovsk-
Kamchatskiy

MYS
LOPATKA

SEA OF
OKHOTSK

Nikolayevsk-
na-Amure

Komsomol'sk-
na-Amure

Khabarovsk

Amur

Ussuri

SAKHALIN

Yuzhno-
Sakhalinsk

KURIL ISLANDS

Vladivostok

QIQIHAR

HARBIN

CHANGCHUN

SHENYANG

SAPPORO

HOKKAIDŌ

SEA OF
JAPAN

NORTH
KOREA

P'YŎNGYANG

Sendai

HONSHŪ

PACIFIC OCEAN

MIDWAY ISLANDS
(U.S.)

Tropic of Cancer

BEIJING

TIANJIN

SEOUL

SOUTH
KOREA

Fujisan
12 388 ft.
3776 m

TŌKYŌ

Yinchuan

TAIYUAN

JINAN

QINGDAO

PUSAN

ŌSAKA

NAGOYA

JAPAN

Huang

LANZHOU

XI'AN

ZHENGZHOU

NANJING

SHANGHAI

SHIKOKU

KYŪSHŪ

Kagoshima

EAST
CHINA
SEA

RYUKYU
ISLANDS

BONIN ISLANDS
(Japan)

VOLCANO ISLANDS
(Japan)

WAKE ISLAND
(U.S.)

CHINA

Yalong

CHENGDU

WUHAN

Yangtze

CHONGQING

CHANGSHA

NANCHANG

Gan

GUIYANG

FUZHOU

T'AIPEI

Naha

OKINAWA-
JIMA

KUNMING

GUANGZHOU

HONG
KONG

TAIWAN

PHILIPPINE
SEA

MARIANA TRENCH

NORTHERN
MARIANA
ISLANDS
(U.S.)

MICRONESIA

MARSHALL
ISLANDS

Mandalay

Ha Noi

Haikou

HAINAN DAO

ESCARPADA
POINT

TINIAN
SAIPAN

MYANMAR
(BURMA)

LAOS

Vientiane

Da Nang

LUZON

PHILIPPINES

GUAM
(U.S.)

YANGON

Mekong

VIETNAM

MANILA

MINDORO

SAMAR

CAROLINE ISLANDS

POHNPEI

THAILAND

BANGKOK

CAMBODIA

SOUTH

CHINA

Cebu

NEGROS

MINDANAO

PALAU

KOSRAE

KIRIBATI

ANDAMAN
ISLANDS
(India)

ANDAMAN SEA

Phnom Penh

HO CHI
MINH CITY
(SAIGON)

SEA

MUI CA MAU

Davao

SULU
SEA

FEDERATED STATES
OF MICRONESIA

NAURU

NICOBAR
ISLANDS
(India)

Gunong Kinabalu
13 455 ft.
4101 m

Bandar Seri Begawan

BRUNEI

CELEBES
SEA

MALAYSIA

KUALA LUMPUR

MALAYSIA

Manado

NEW IRELAND

MELANESIA

MEDAN

SINGAPORE

SINGAPORE

BORNEO

Balikpapan

TANJUNG
D'URVILLE

Jayapura

BISMARCK
SEA

BOUGAINVILLE

NEW
BRITAIN

CHOISEUL

SANTA
ISABEL

MALAITA

Padang

SUMATRA

PALEMBANG

Banjarmasin

CELEBES

MOLUCCAS

Puncak Jaya
16 503 ft.
5030 m

NEW GUINEA

Gunung Kerinci
12 467 ft.
3800 m

JAKARTA

SURABAYA

JAVA

MAKASSAR

BALI

BANDA SEA

FLORES SEA

Dili

FLORES

EAST
TIMOR

TIMOR

INDONESIA

JAVA SEA

PAPUA NEW
GUINEA

SOLOMON
SEA

SAN CRISTOBAL

SANTA
CRUZ IS.

SOLOMON ISLANDS

Port
Moresby

TANJUNG VALS

MELVILLE
ISLAND

ARAFURA SEA

AUSTRALIA

CHRISTMAS ISLAND
(Austl.)

SUMBAWA

SUMBA

TIMOR SEA

© Rand McNally
A-101711-1

Equator

```
0    200   400   600   800   1000  1200 Miles
0  200 400 600 800 1000 1200 1400 1600 1800  2000 Kilometers
```

Lambert Azimuthal Equal Area Projection
Scale 1:40,000,000
One inch to 640 miles
One cm to 400 km

LAPTEV SEA

EAST SIBERIAN SEA

NEW SIBERIAN ISLANDS

BERING SEA

UNITED STATES

ALEUTIAN ISLANDS

ALEUTIAN TRENCH

CHERSKIY MTS.

VERKHOYANSK MTS.

KAMCHATKA PENINSULA

Anadyr

Gulf of Anadyr

MYS NAVARIN

KOMANDORSKI ISLANDS

CAPE WRANGELL

SIBERIA

ASIA

Yakutsk

Nizhnyaya

STANOVOY RANGE

STANOVOY MTS.

Lake Baikal

DZHUGDZHUR RANGE

Magadan

Klyuchevskaya Vulkan Sopka 15 584 ft. 4750 m

Petropavlovsk-Kamchatskiy

SEA OF OKHOTSK

MYS YELIZAVETY

MYS TERPENIYA

SAKHALIN

MYS LOPATKA

KURIL ISLANDS

KURIL TRENCH

JAPAN TRENCH

PACIFIC OCEAN

MIDWAY ISLANDS

HAWAI'IAN ISLANDS

NECKER RIDGE

Komsomol'sk-na-Amure

Irkutsk

MONGOLIA

Ulaanbaatar

Hovsgol Nuur

GREATER KHINGAN RANGE

SIKHOTE-ALIN'

Tatar Strait

Sapporo

HOKKAIDO

SEA OF JAPAN

Harbin

Lake Khanka

NORTH KOREA

HONSHU

Tokyo

JAPAN

Fuji-san 12 388 ft. 3776 m

GOBI DESERT

Beijing

Seoul

SOUTH KOREA

SHIKOKU

IZU-SHOTO

WAKE ISLAND (U.S.)

CHENGSHAN JIAO

YELLOW SEA

KYUSHU

EAST CHINA SEA

CHEJU-DO

Qinghai Hu

CHINA

Xi'an

QIN LING

Shanghai

RYUKYU ISLANDS

OKINAWA-JIMA

BONIN IS. (Japan)

VOLCANO ISLANDS (Japan)

MARIANA TRENCH

Tropic of Cancer

Three Gorges Reservoir

Chongqing

T'aipei

TAIWAN

Yu Shan 13 114 ft. 3997 m

RYUKYU TRENCH

PHILIPPINE SEA

MARIANA ISLANDS

NORTHERN MARIANA ISLANDS (U.S.)

MICRONESIA

BIKINI

ENEWETAK

KWAJALEIN

MARSHALL ISLANDS

MAJURO

MYANMAR (BURMA)

Hong Kong

Gulf of Tonkin

HAINAN DAO

Taiwan Strait

Luzon Strait

SAIPAN

TINIAN

GUAM (U.S.)

LAOS

Yangon

THAILAND

Bangkok

CAMBODIA

Tonle Sap

Gulf of Thailand

VIETNAM

ESCARPADA POINT

LUZON

SOUTH CHINA SEA

PHILIPPINES

Manila

MINDORO

SAMAR

PHILIPPINE TRENCH

YAP TRENCH

YAP

CAROLINE ISLANDS

CHUUK

POHNPEI

KOSRAE

KIRIBATI

TARAWA

ANDAMAN ISLANDS (India)

ANDAMAN SEA

Ho Chi Minh City (Saigon)

MUI CA MAU

PALAWAN

PANAY

NEGROS

Gunong Kinabalu 13 455 ft. 4101 m

SULU SEA

Mt. Apo 9692 ft. 2954 m

MINDANAO

TINACA POINT

PALAU

FEDERATED STATES OF MICRONESIA

NAURU

NICOBAR ISLANDS (India)

MALAY PENINSULA

MALAYSIA

Strait of Malacca

SINGAPORE

Singapore

BRUNEI

MALAYSIA

CROCKER MTS.

BORNEO

Kapuas

CELEBES SEA

HALMAHERA

MOLUCCA SEA

PULAU WAIGEO

MELANESIA

MANUS ISLAND

NEW HANOVER

NEW IRELAND

Equator

PULAU SIMEULUE

PULAU NIAS

PULAU SIBERUT

SUMATRA

Gunung Kerinci 12 467 ft. 3800 m

Bukit Raya 7474 ft. 2278 m

GREATER SUNDA ISLANDS

TANJUNG PUTING

CELEBES

MAKASSAR STRAIT

TANJUNG SELATAN

Makassar

BURU

CERAM

MOLUCCAS

PULAU BUTON

BANDA SEA

PULAU YAPEN

Jayapura

NEW GUINEA

Puncak Jaya 16 503 ft. 5030 m

Sepik

BIAK

TANJUNG D'URVILLE

BISMARCK SEA

NEW BRITAIN

NEW BRITAIN TRENCH

BOUGAINVILLE

CHOISEUL

SANTA ISABEL

SOLOMON ISLANDS

MALAITA

INDONESIA

Jakarta

JAVA

Gunung Semeru 12 060 ft. 3676 m

JAVA SEA

FLORES SEA

BALI

LOMBOK

SUMBAWA

LESSER SUNDA ISLANDS

FLORES

SUMBA

TIMOR

EAST TIMOR

PULAU WETAR

PULAU YAMDENA

TANJUNG VALS

ARAFURA SEA

KEPULAUAN ARU

Mt. Wilhelm 14 793 ft. 4509 m

PAPUA NEW GUINEA

NEW GEORGIA

GUADALCANAL

SOLOMON SEA

SAN CRISTOBAL

RENNELL

SAN CRISTOBAL TRENCH

SANTA CRUZ IS.

JAVA TRENCH

CHRISTMAS ISLAND (Aust.)

TIMOR SEA

MELVILLE ISLAND

CAPE YORK

AUSTRALIA

CAPE ARNHEM

© Rand McNally A-101712-1

ARCTIC OCEAN

ATLANTIC OCEAN

BARENTS SEA

SEVERNAYA ZEMLYA

KARA SEA

U R A L   M O U N T A I N S

WEST SIBERIAN PLAIN

Yekaterinburg

Chelyabinsk

Ural

CENT

SAYAN

ALTAY MTS.

KAZAKH HILLS

Lake Balkhash

Irtysh

Yenisey

MEDITERRANEAN SEA

BLACK SEA

CASPIAN SEA

Aral Sea

CAUCASUS MTS.

Istanbul

Ankara

UST-URT PLAT.

QIZILQUM

Syr Darya

Almaty

TIEN SHAN

Tashkent

KARA KUM

Tabriz

Tel Aviv-Yafo

Damascus

Euphrates

Tigris

Tehrān

Mashhad

Dushanbe

Amu Darya

PAMIRS

TARIM PENDI

ALTUN SHAN

Tropic of Cancer

'Ammān

Baghdād

ZAGROS MTS.

Eşfahān

DASHT-E KAVIR

HINDU KUSH

KUNLUN SHAN

PLATEAU OF TIBET

AN-NAFŪD

DASHT-E LUT

Islāmābād

Lāhore

H   I   M   A   L   A   Y

Brahmaputra

AL HIJAZ

RED SEA

Riyadh

Persian Gulf

Gulf of Oman

Indus

GREAT INDIAN DESERT

Delhi

Hyderābād

Kānpur

Kathmandu

Ganges

Dhaka

Jiddah

Mecca

Karāchi

Ahmadābād

Indore

Kolkata

'ASIR

RUB' AL-KHALI

D E C C A N

Mumbai

Hyderābād

WESTERN GHATS

EASTERN GHATS

BAY OF BENGAL

Sanaa

ARABIAN SEA

Gulf of Aden

Bengalūru

Chennai

Cochin

Colombo

Equator

INDIAN   OCEAN

A-102095-1
© Rand McNally

0   200   400   600   800   1000   1200 Miles

0   200   400   600   800   1000   1200   1400   1600   1800   2000 Kilometers

Lambert Azimuthal Equal Area Projection
Scale 1:40,000,000
One inch to 640 miles
One cm to 400 km

Land Cover

- Evergreen Needleleaf Forest
- Evergreen Broadleaf Forest
- Deciduous Needleleaf Forest
- Deciduous Broadleaf Forest
- Mixed Forest
- Woodland
- Wooded Grassland
- Closed Shrubland
- Open Shrubland
- Grassland
- Cropland
- Bare Ground (Desert and Ice)
- Urban and Built Up

LAPTEV SEA
EAST SIBERIAN SEA
NEW SIBERIAN ISLANDS
OSTROV VRANGELYA
BERING SEA
SEA OF OKHOTSK
CHERSKIY MTS.
VERKHOYANSK MTS.
Kolyma
Lena
CENTRAL SIBERIAN PLATEAU
SIBERIA
STANOVOY RANGE
STANOVOY MTS.
DZHUGDZHUR RANGE
Lake Baikal
MTS.
Indigirka
Aldan
SREDINNYY KHREBET
SAKHALIN
KURIL ISLANDS
SIKHOTE-ALIN
Amur
Harbin
Changchun
Shenyang
GREATER KHINGAN RANGE
HOKKAIDO
Sapporo
SEA OF JAPAN
HONSHŪ
Beijing
Baotou
Tianjin
Taiyuan
Jinan
Qingdao
GOBI DESERT
Huang
Huang
Seoul
Tōkyō
Osaka
Nagoya
Fukuoka
SHIKOKU
KYŪSHŪ
Xi'an
QIN LING
Nanjing
Shanghai
YELLOW SEA
EAST CHINA SEA
RYUKYU ISLANDS
Chengdu
Chongqing
Guiyang
Nanchang
Fuzhou
Yangtze
T'aipei
Taiwan Strait
TROPIC OF CANCER
Guangzhou
Xi
Hong Kong
PHILIPPINE SEA
MARIANA ISLANDS
MICRONESIA
Ha Noi
HAINAN DAO
LUZON
Manila
SOUTH CHINA SEA
CAROLINE ISLANDS
Salween
Mekong
Bangkok
ANDAMAN ISLANDS
Gulf of Thailand
ANDAMAN SEA
NICOBAR ISLANDS
Ho Chi Minh City
MINDORO
PALAWAN
NEGROS
SAMAR
MINDANAO
SULU SEA
CELEBES SEA
Medan
Kuala Lumpur
Singapore
SUMATRA
BORNEO
IRAN MTS.
Palu
CELEBES
MOLUCCAS
NEW GUINEA
PEGUNUNGAN MAOKE
BANDA SEA
Palembang
GREATER SUNDA ISLANDS
Bandar Lampung
JAVA SEA
Jakarta
Semarang
Surabaya
Makassar
FLORES SEA
LESSER SUNDA ISLANDS
ARAFURA SEA
JAVA
Denpasar
TIMOR SEA

PACIFIC OCEAN

Equator

Arctic Circle

Source: CIESIN; Hansen et al., 2000

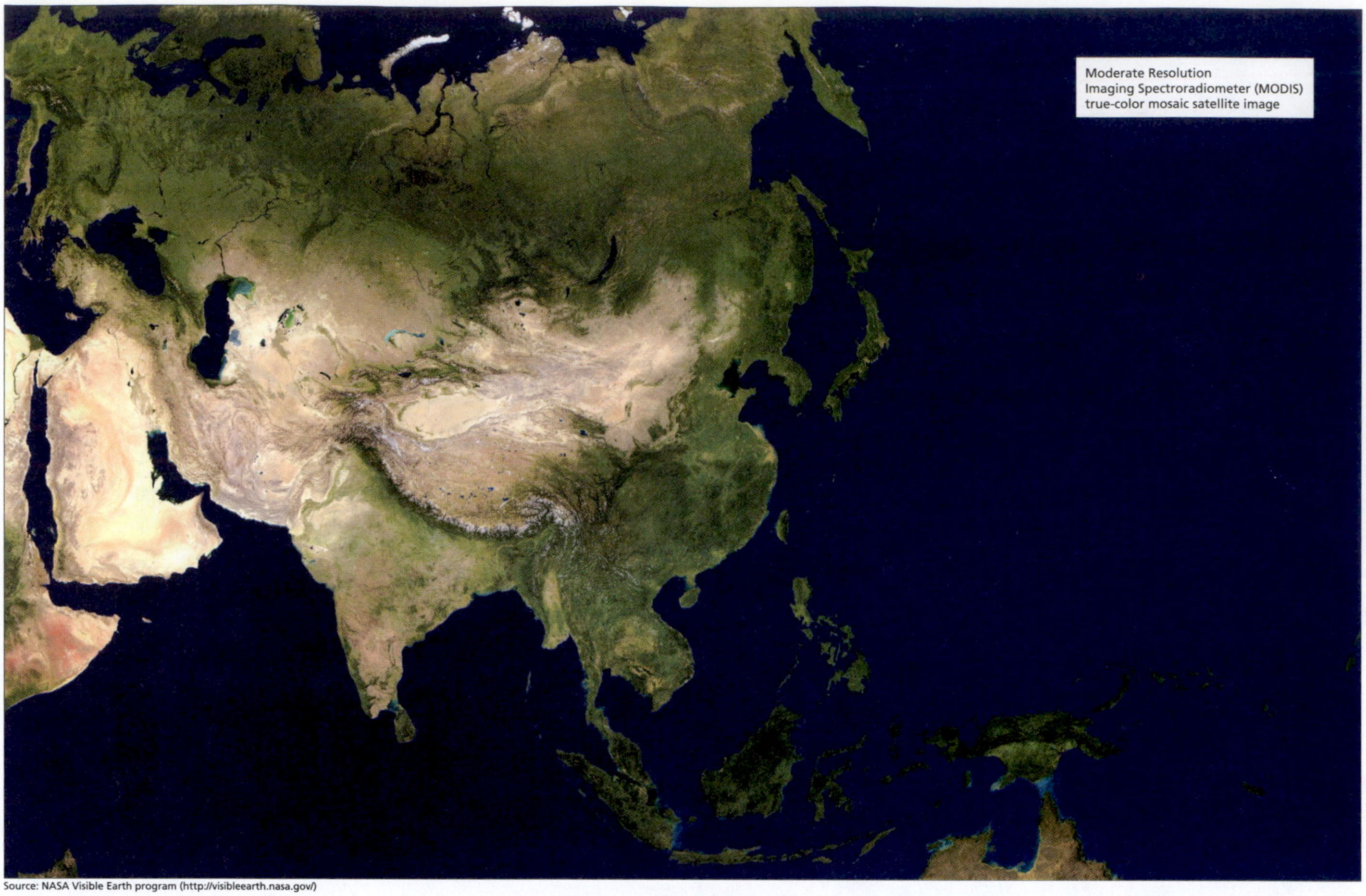
Moderate Resolution
Imaging Spectroradiometer (MODIS)
true-color mosaic satellite image

Source: NASA Visible Earth program (http://visibleearth.nasa.gov/)

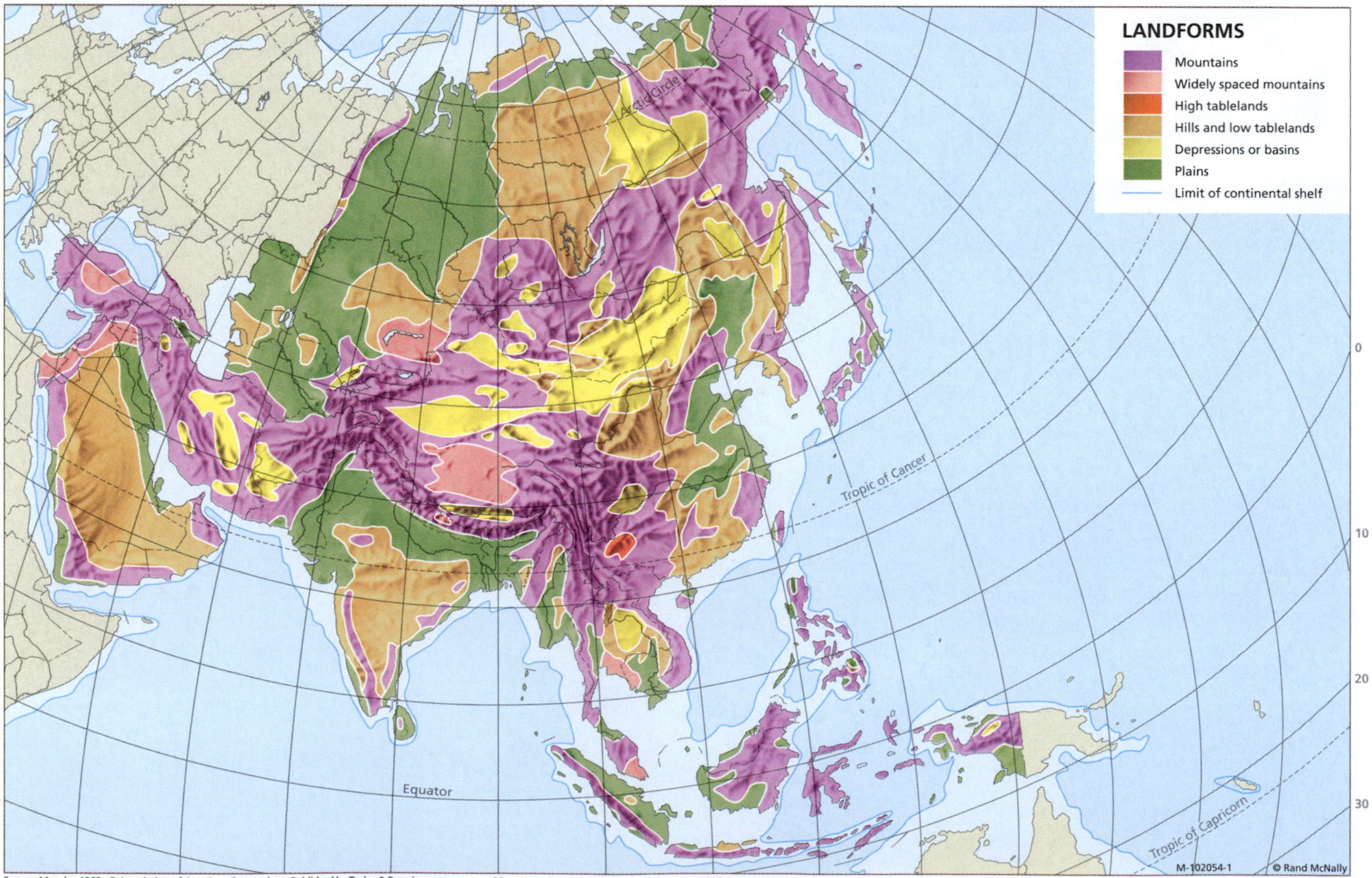
LANDFORMS
Mountains
Widely spaced mountains
High tablelands
Hills and low tablelands
Depressions or basins
Plains
Limit of continental shelf
Arctic Circle
Tropic of Cancer
Equator
Tropic of Capricorn
40
30
20
10
0
10
0
10
20
30
90
100
110
120
130
140
150
160
170
M-102054-1
© Rand McNally

Source: Murphy, 1968. © Association of American Geographers. Published by Taylor & Francis.
Adapted with permission of the Association of American Geographers.

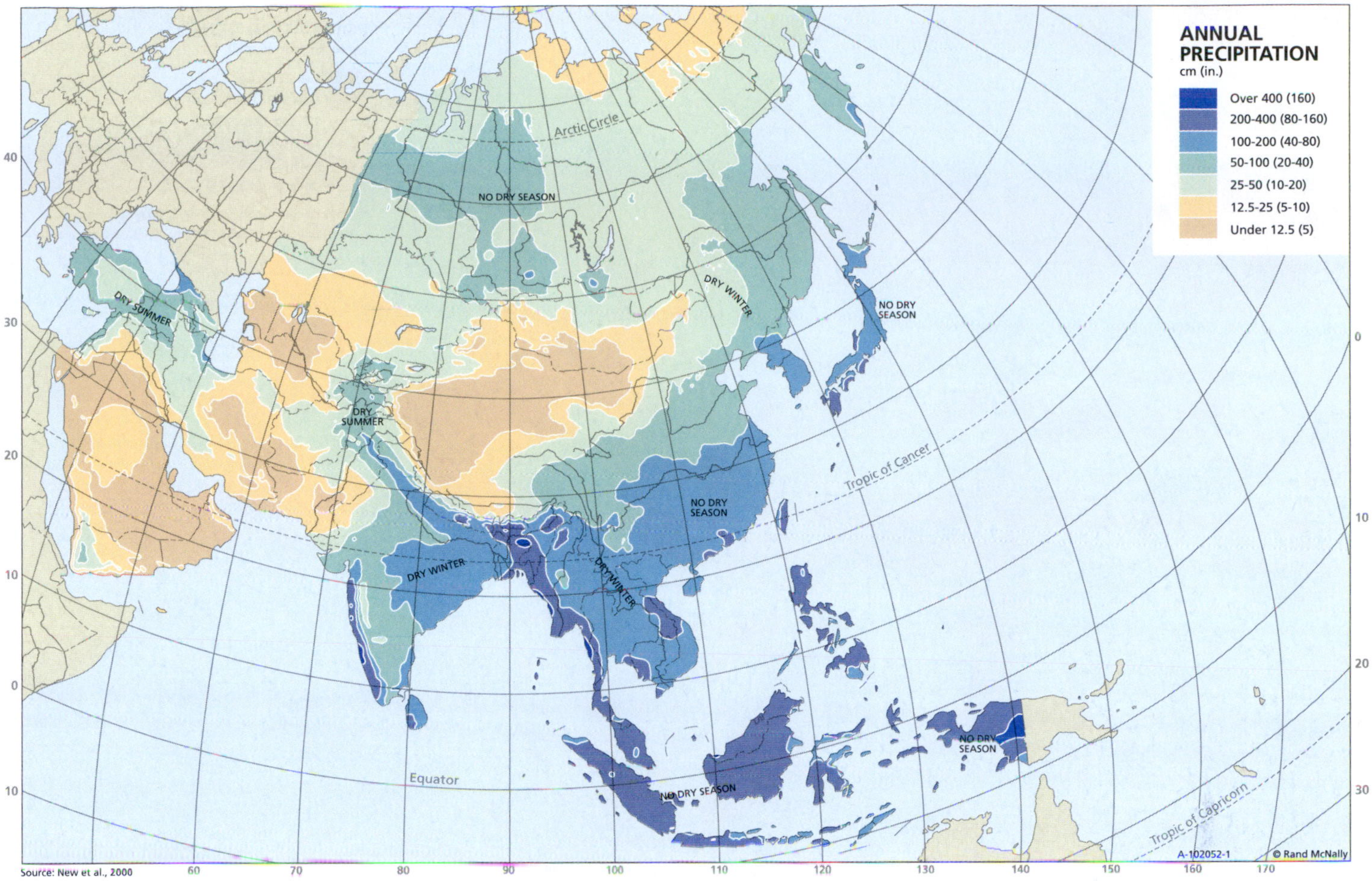

ANNUAL PRECIPITATION
cm (in.)

- Over 400 (160)
- 200-400 (80-160)
- 100-200 (40-80)
- 50-100 (20-40)
- 25-50 (10-20)
- 12.5-25 (5-10)
- Under 12.5 (5)

ARCTIC CIRCLE

NO DRY SEASON

DRY WINTER

NO DRY SEASON

DRY SUMMER

DRY SUMMER

DRY WINTER

NO DRY SEASON

DRY WINTER

DRY WINTER

Tropic of Cancer

NO DRY SEASON

NO DRY SEASON

Equator

NO DRY SEASON

Tropic of Capricorn

Source: New et al., 2000

A-102052-1   © Rand McNally

VEGETATION

B	Tropical rain forest
B	Subtropical rain forest
B,Bs	Mediterranean vegetation
S	Semideciduous mixed forest
DBs, D,Di	Tropical dry deciduous forest
ND-D	Temperate deciduous forest
M,(SE)	Temperate mixed forest
Ep,E,N	Coniferous forest
DsG,GBp, GSp	Savanna (locally wooded)
DG	Wooded steppe
G	Grass (steppe)
Gp	Short grass
Dzp, Dzp	Desert shrub
L	Tundra, alpine vegetation
b	Little or no vegetation

For explanation of letters in boxes, see World Natural Vegetation Map.

ARCTIC CIRCLE

TAIGA

TAKLA MAKAN

GOBI

Tropic of Cancer

Equator

Tropic of Capricorn

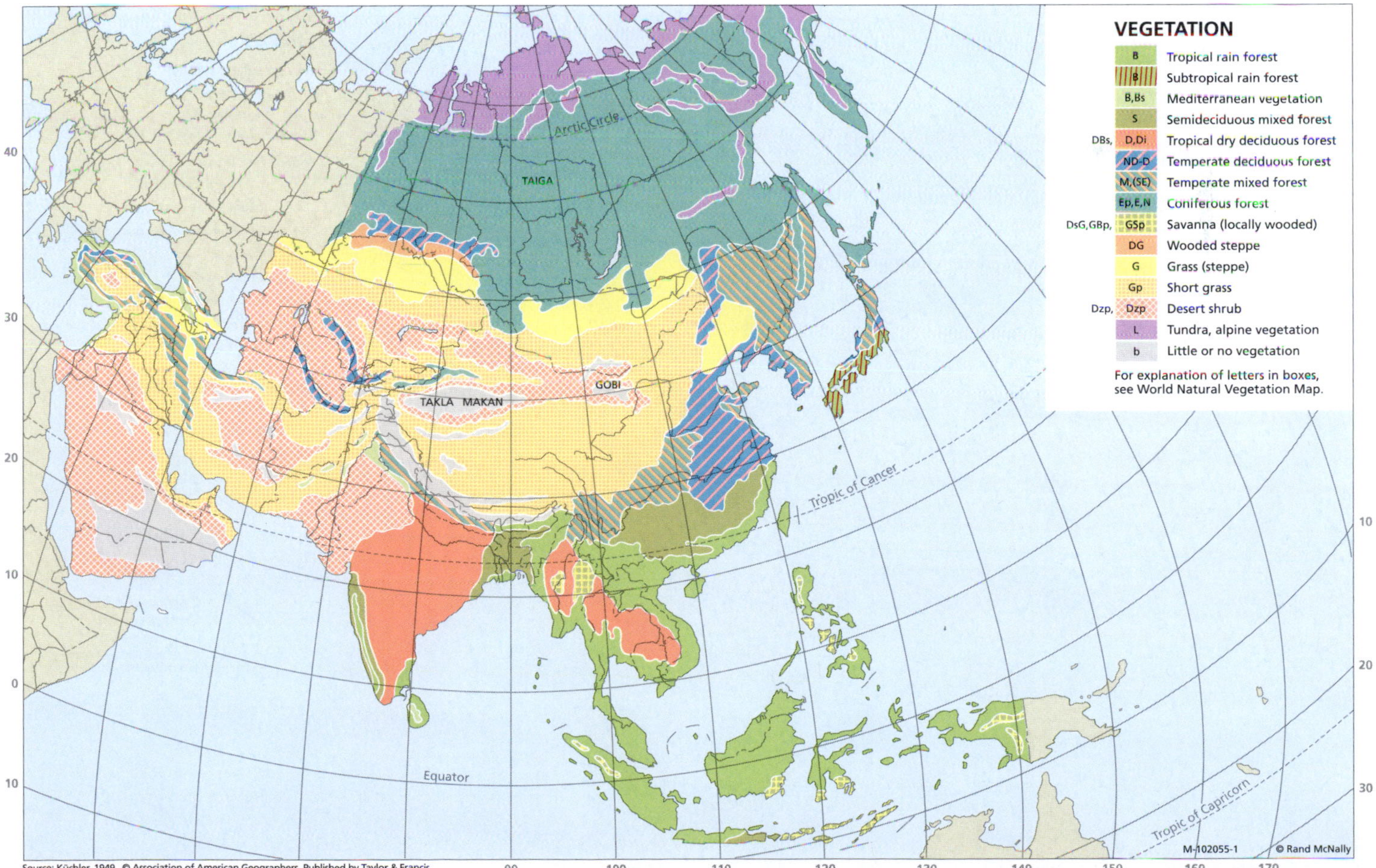

Source: Küchler, 1949. © Association of American Geographers. Published by Taylor & Francis.
Adapted with permission of the Association of American Geographers.

M-102055-1   © Rand McNally

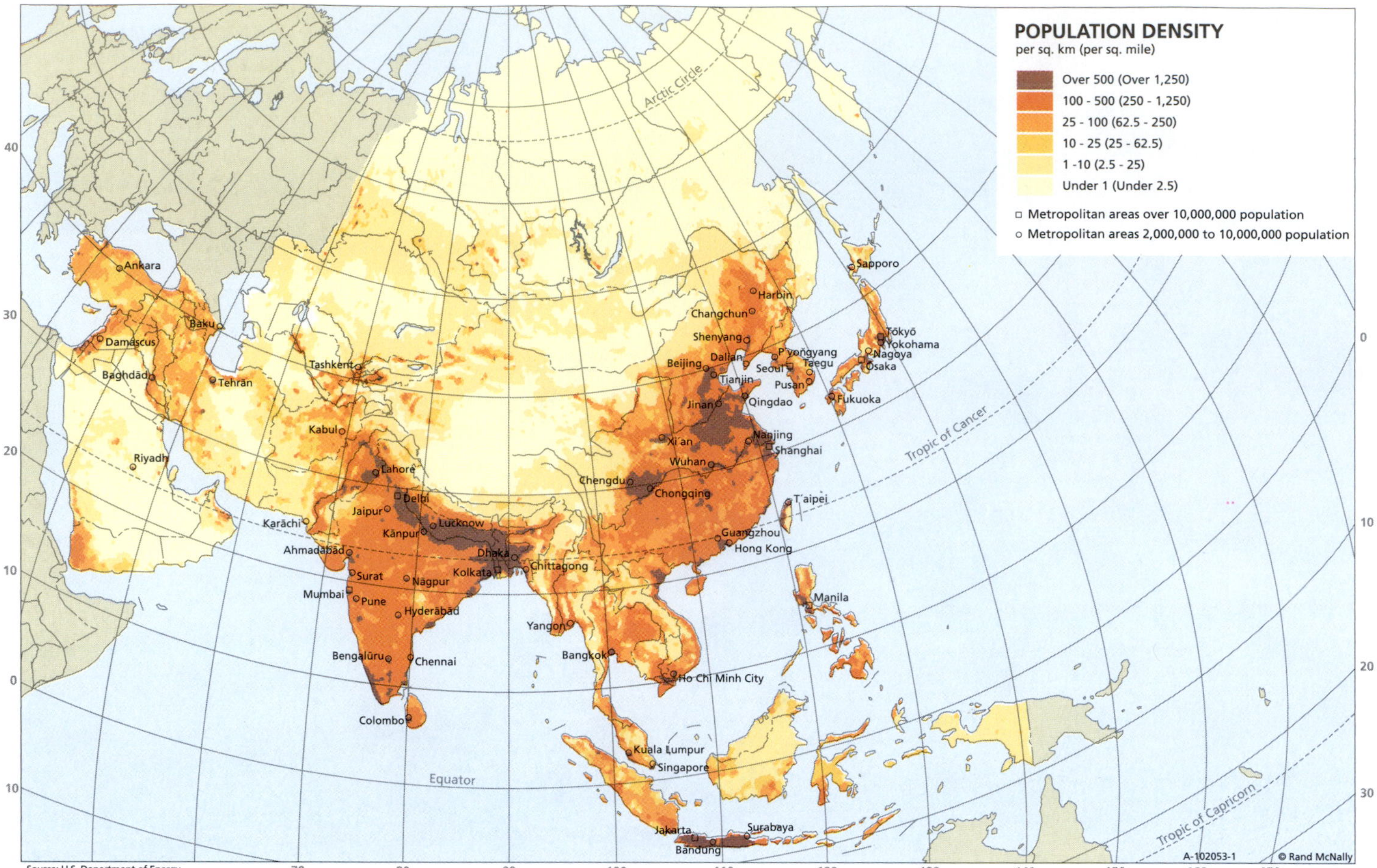
POPULATION DENSITY
per sq. km (per sq. mile)
Over 500 (Over 1,250)
100 - 500 (250 - 1,250)
25 - 100 (62.5 - 250)
10 - 25 (25 - 62.5)
1 -10 (2.5 - 25)
Under 1 (Under 2.5)
Metropolitan areas over 10,000,000 population
Metropolitan areas 2,000,000 to 10,000,000 population
Arctic Circle
Tropic of Cancer
Equator
Tropic of Capricorn
Ankara
Baku
Damascus
Baghdād
Tehrān
Tashkent
Riyadh
Kabul
Lahore
Karāchi
Delhi
Jaipur
Lucknow
Kanpur
Ahmadābād
Surat
Nagpur
Kolkata
Dhaka
Chittagong
Mumbai
Pune
Hyderābād
Bengalūru
Chennai
Colombo
Harbin
Changchun
Shenyang
Beijing
Dalian
Tianjin
P'yongyang
Seoul
Taegu
Pusan
Qingdao
Jinan
Xi'an
Nanjing
Shanghai
Wuhan
Chengdu
Chongqing
T'aipei
Guangzhou
Hong Kong
Sapporo
Tōkyō
Yokohama
Nagoya
Ōsaka
Fukuoka
Manila
Yangon
Bangkok
Ho Chi Minh City
Kuala Lumpur
Singapore
Jakarta
Bandung
Surabaya
A-102053-1
© Rand McNally

Source: U.S. Department of Energy

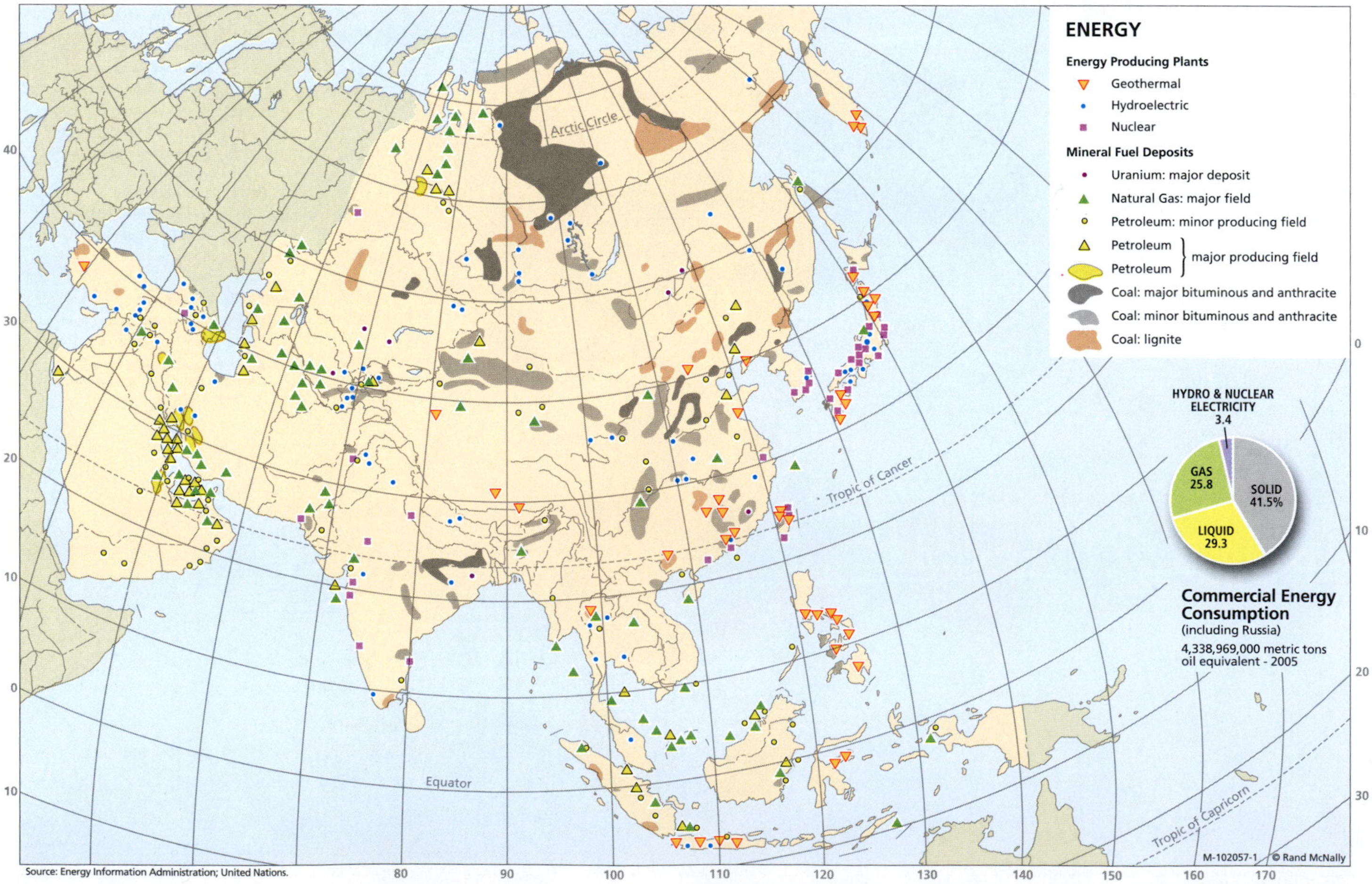
ENERGY
Energy Producing Plants
Geothermal
Hydroelectric
Nuclear
Mineral Fuel Deposits
Uranium: major deposit
Natural Gas: major field
Petroleum: minor producing field
Petroleum
Petroleum
major producing field
Coal: major bituminous and anthracite
Coal: minor bituminous and anthracite
Coal: lignite
HYDRO & NUCLEAR ELECTRICITY 3.4
GAS 25.8
SOLID 41.5%
LIQUID 29.3
Commercial Energy Consumption
(including Russia)
4,338,969,000 metric tons oil equivalent - 2005
Arctic Circle
Tropic of Cancer
Equator
Tropic of Capricorn
M-102057-1
© Rand McNally

Source: Energy Information Administration; United Nations.

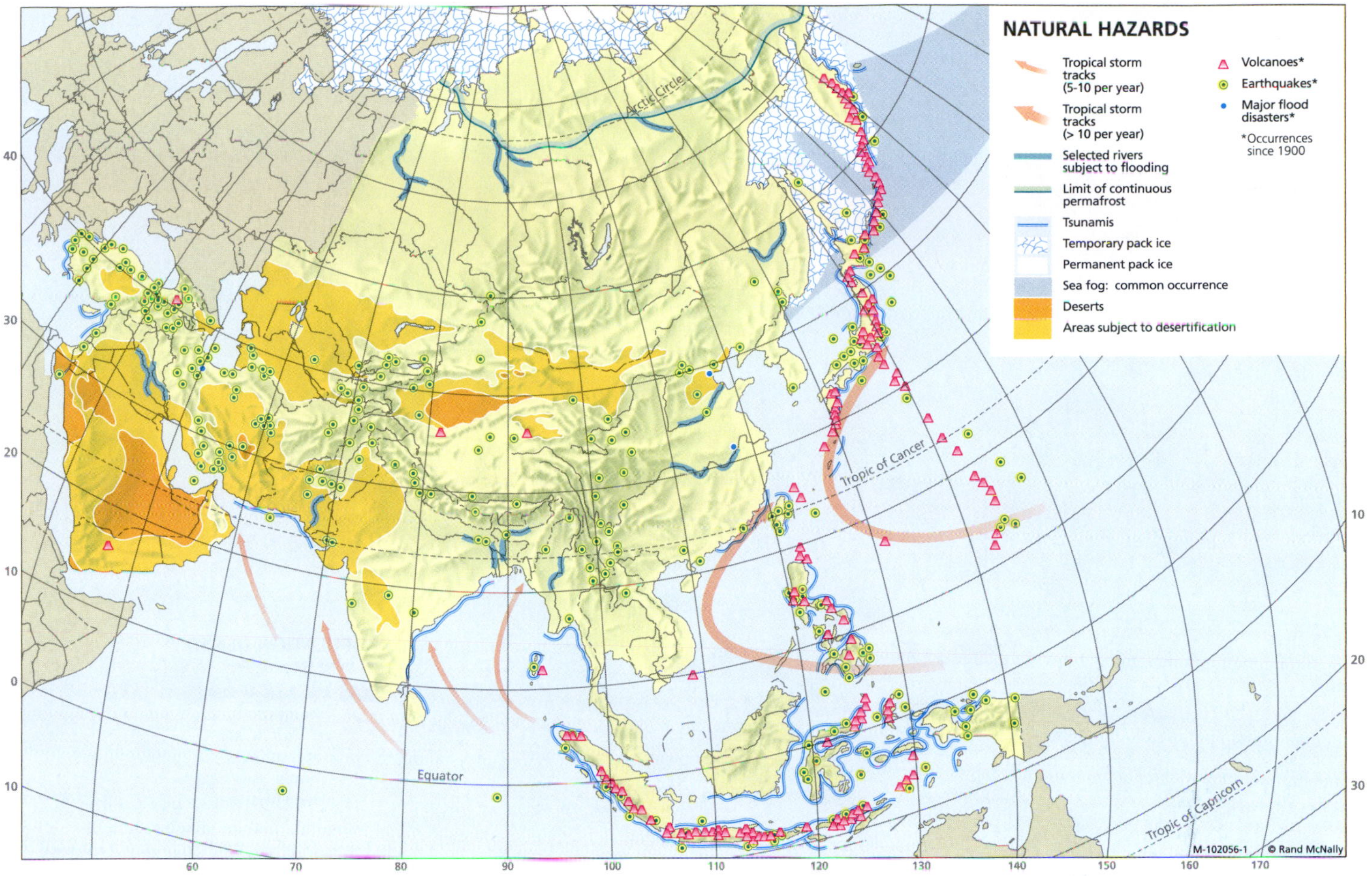

NATURAL HAZARDS

- Tropical storm tracks (5–10 per year)
- Tropical storm tracks (> 10 per year)
- Selected rivers subject to flooding
- Limit of continuous permafrost
- Tsunamis
- Temporary pack ice
- Permanent pack ice
- Sea fog: common occurrence
- Deserts
- Areas subject to desertification
- Volcanoes*
- Earthquakes*
- Major flood disasters*

*Occurrences since 1900

Arctic Circle
Tropic of Cancer
Equator
Tropic of Capricorn

M-102056-1 © Rand McNally

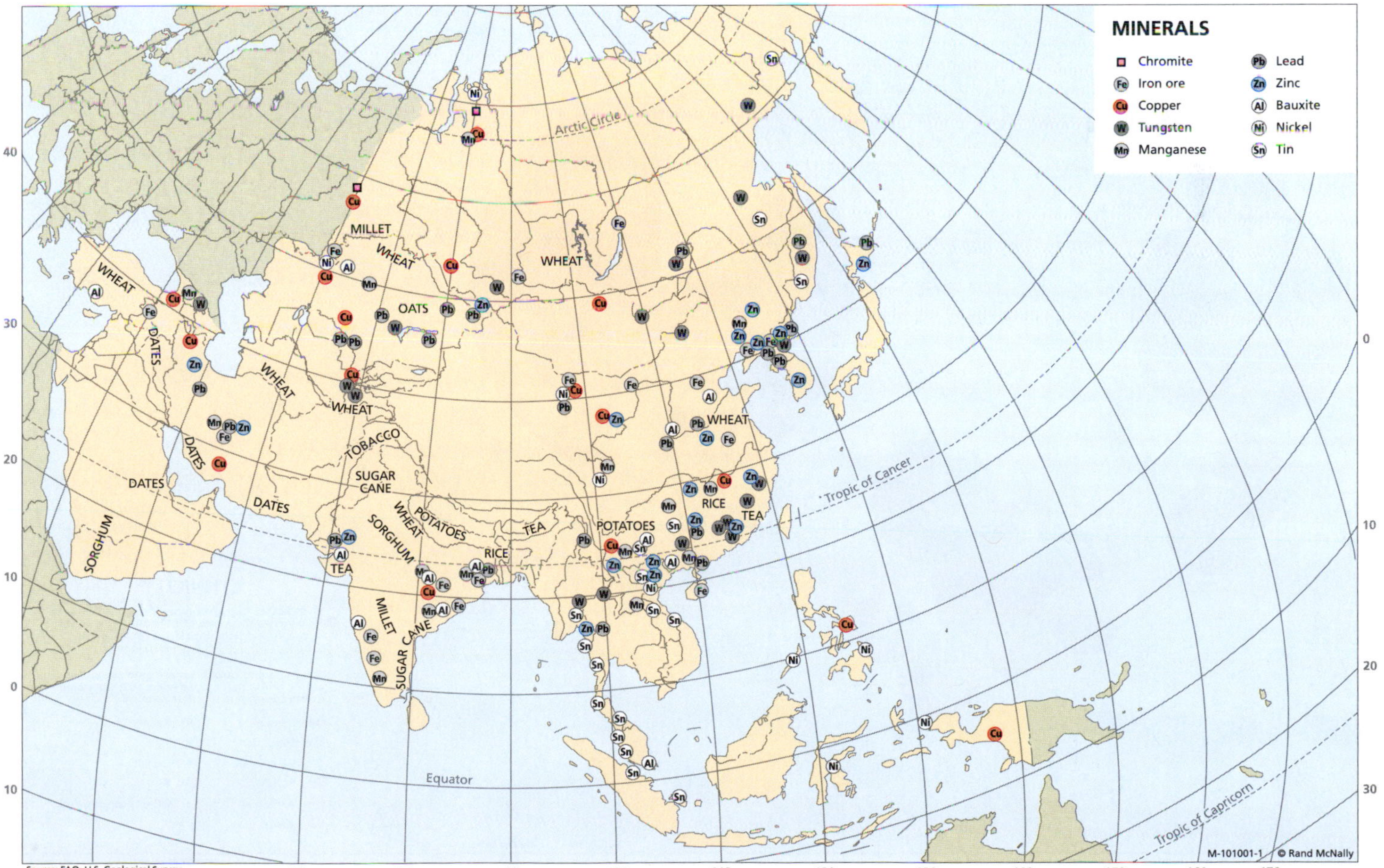

MINERALS

- Chromite
- Fe Iron ore
- Cu Copper
- W Tungsten
- Mn Manganese
- Pb Lead
- Zn Zinc
- Al Bauxite
- Ni Nickel
- Sn Tin

Arctic Circle
Tropic of Cancer
Equator
Tropic of Capricorn

MILLET, WHEAT, OATS, RICE, TEA, DATES, SORGHUM, TOBACCO, SUGAR CANE, POTATOES

Source: FAO; U.S. Geological Survey

M-101001-1 © Rand McNally

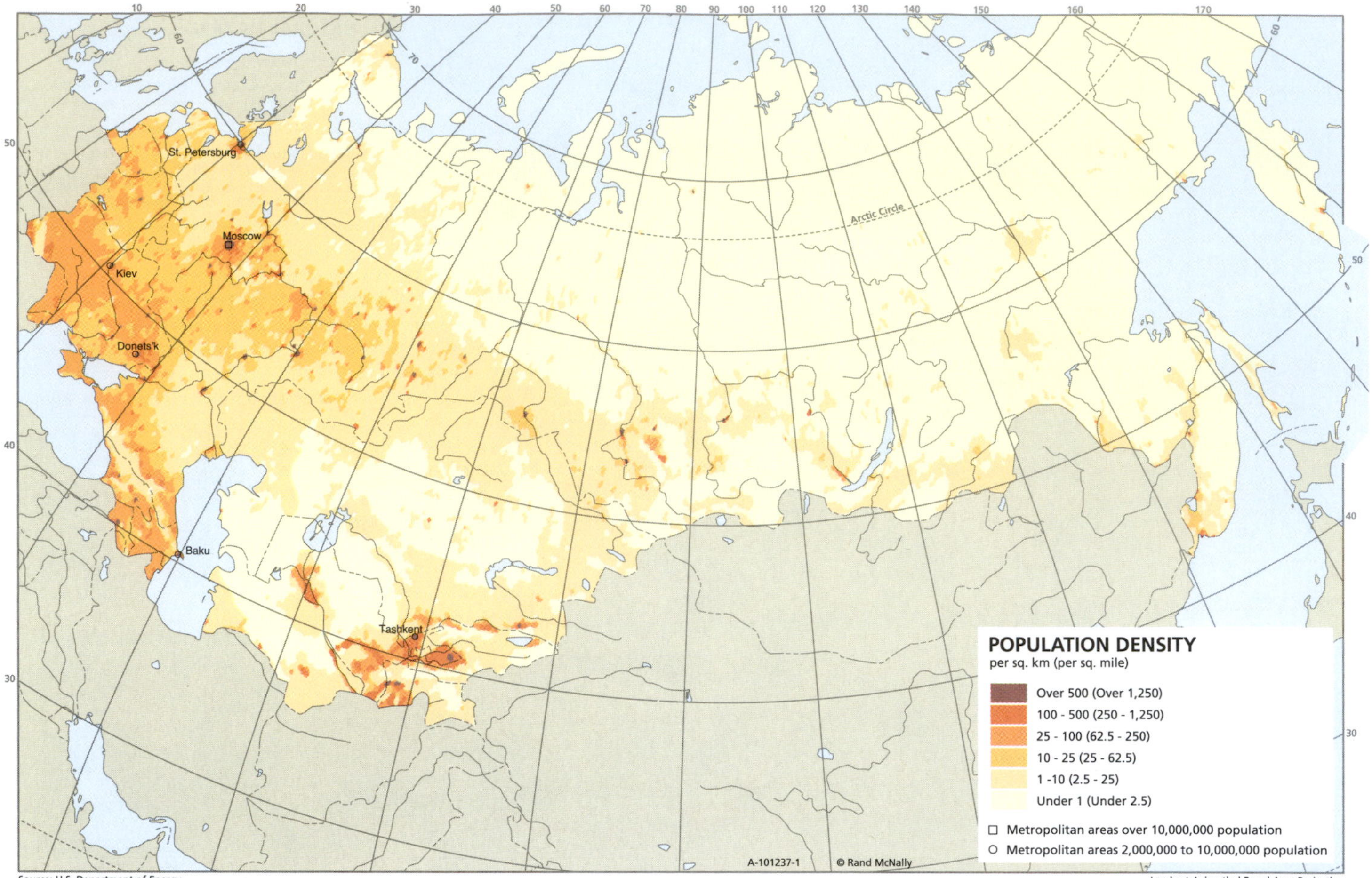

POPULATION DENSITY
per sq. km (per sq. mile)

Over 500 (Over 1,250)
100 - 500 (250 - 1,250)
25 - 100 (62.5 - 250)
10 - 25 (25 - 62.5)
1 - 10 (2.5 - 25)
Under 1 (Under 2.5)

□ Metropolitan areas over 10,000,000 population
○ Metropolitan areas 2,000,000 to 10,000,000 population

Source: U.S. Department of Energy

A-101237-1   © Rand McNally

Lambert Azimuthal Equal Area Projection
Scale 1:45,000,000

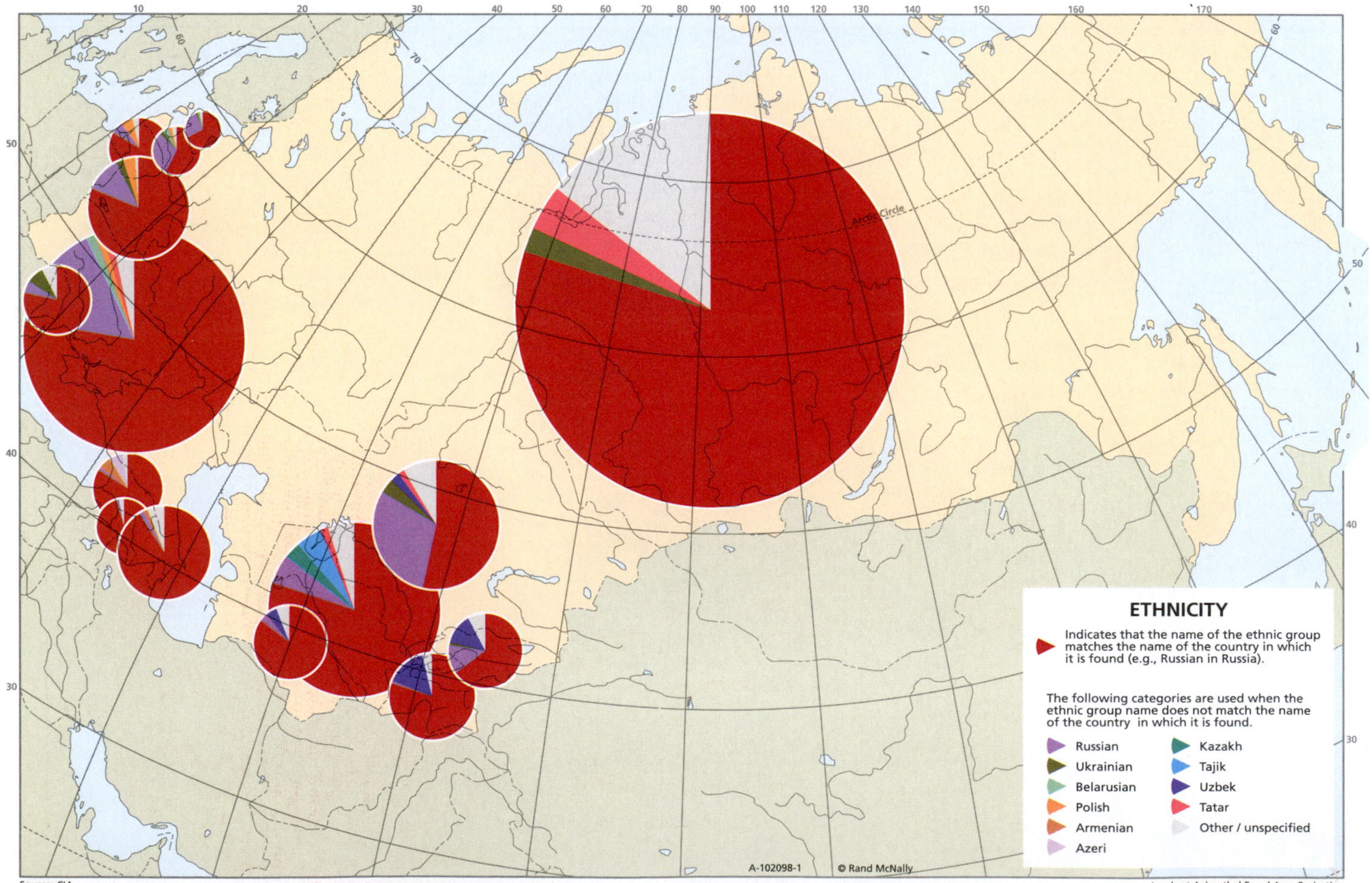

ETHNICITY

▶ Indicates that the name of the ethnic group matches the name of the country in which it is found (e.g., Russian in Russia).

The following categories are used when the ethnic group name does not match the name of the country in which it is found.

▶ Russian   ▶ Kazakh
▶ Ukrainian   ▶ Tajik
▶ Belarusian   ▶ Uzbek
▶ Polish   ▶ Tatar
▶ Armenian   ▶ Other / unspecified
▶ Azeri

Source: CIA

A-102098-1   © Rand McNally

Lambert Azimuthal Equal Area Projection
Scale 1:45,000,000

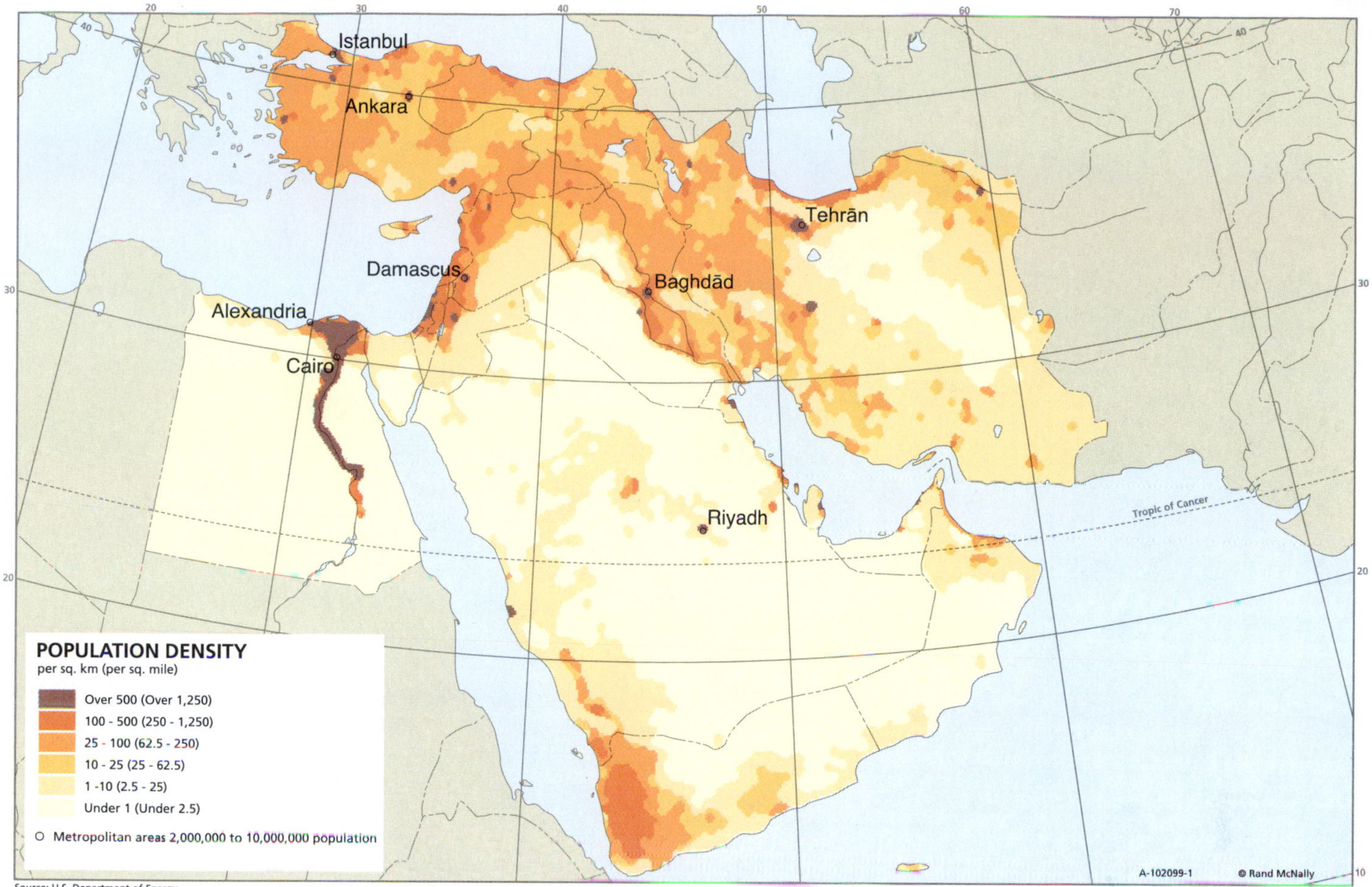

Istanbul
Ankara
Tehrān
Damascus
Baghdād
Alexandria
Cairo
Riyadh

Tropic of Cancer

POPULATION DENSITY
per sq. km (per sq. mile)

Over 500 (Over 1,250)
100 - 500 (250 - 1,250)
25 - 100 (62.5 - 250)
10 - 25 (25 - 62.5)
1 - 10 (2.5 - 25)
Under 1 (Under 2.5)

O Metropolitan areas 2,000,000 to 10,000,000 population

Source: U.S. Department of Energy

A-102099-1   © Rand McNally

Lambert Conformal Conic Projection
Scale 1:29,000,000

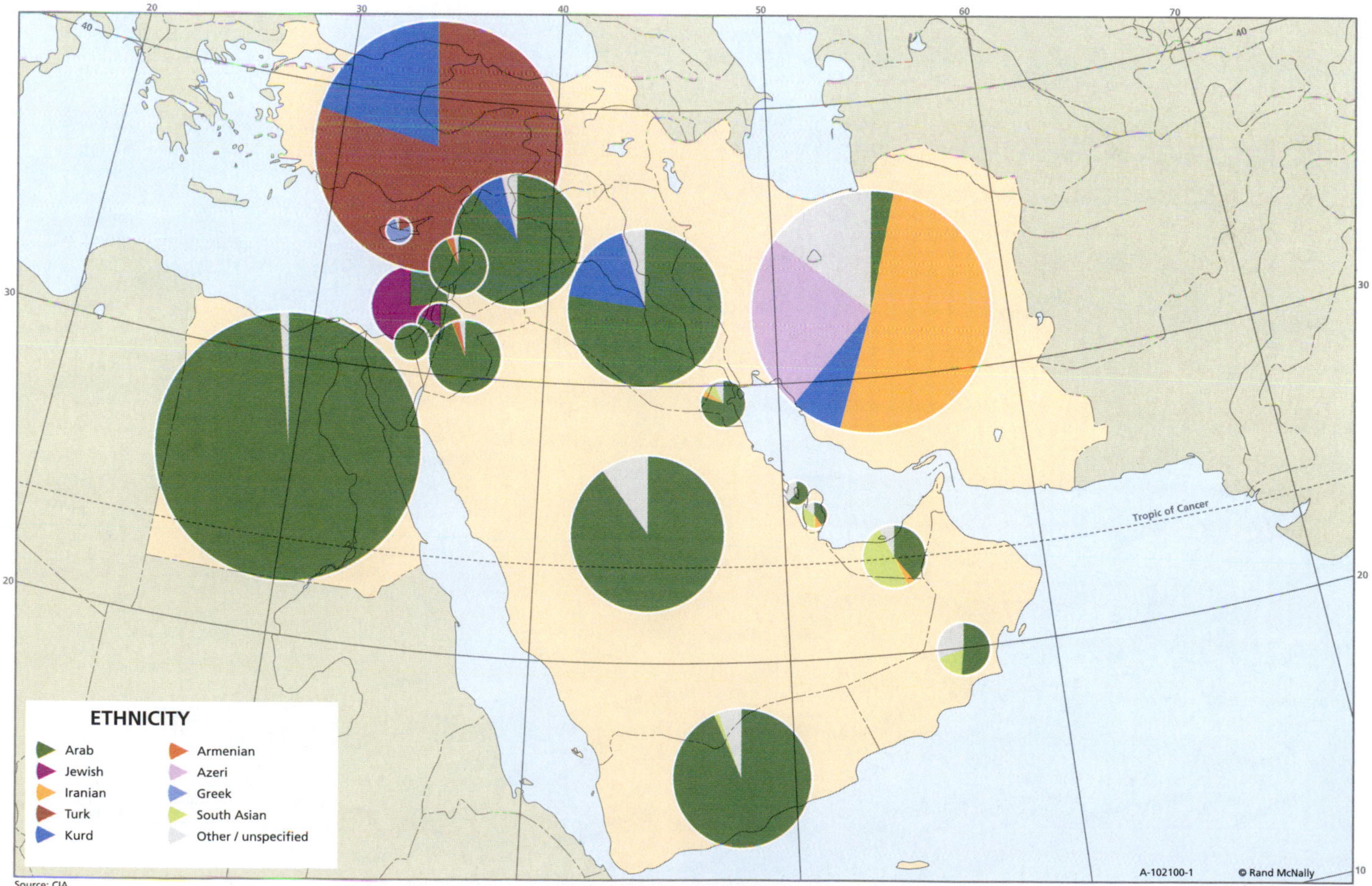

Tropic of Cancer

ETHNICITY

Arab
Jewish
Iranian
Turk
Kurd
Armenian
Azeri
Greek
South Asian
Other / unspecified

Source: CIA

A-102100-1   © Rand McNally

Lambert Conformal Conic Projection
Scale 1:29,000,000

O C E A N

CHUKCHI SEA

Bering Strait

EAST SIBERIAN SEA

LAPTEV SEA

NEW SIBERIAN ISLANDS (NOVOSIBIRSKIYE OSTROVA)

CHUKCHI PENINSULA

Gulf of Anadyr

ST. LAWRENCE ISLAND (U.S.)

ST. MATTHEW ISLAND (U.S.)

KORYAKSKOYE NAGOR'YE

BERING BASIN

BERING SEA

ALEUTIAN SEA

KHREBET CHERSKOGO

SEVERO-SIBIRSKAYA NIZMENNOST'

POLUOSTROV TAYMYR

GORY PUTORANA

R U S S I A

S I B E R I A

YAKUTSK

ALDANSKOYE NAGORYE

STANOVOY KHREBET

STANOVOYE NAGOR'YE

Bratsk

Krasnoyarsk

SAYAN MTS.

Irkutsk

Lake Baikal

Ulan-Ude

Chita

Darhan

Ulaanbaatar

M O N G O L I A

GOBI DESERT

ALTAYN NURUU

HANGAYN NURUU

Hami

BAOTOU

Datong

BEIJING

TIANJIN

TANGSHAN

C H I N A

GREATER KHINGAN RANGE (DA HINGGAN LING)

QIQIHAR

Hailar

Zalantun

Ulanhot

CHANGCHUN

JILIN

SHENYANG

ANSHAN

FUSHUN

HARBIN

Mudanjiang

Jiamusi

Hegang

Shuangyashan

Jixi

Khabarovsk

Komsomol'sk-na-Amure

KHREBET DZHUGDZHUR

SEA OF OKHOTSK

OKHOTSK BASIN

SAKHALIN

Yuzhno-Sakhalinsk

KAMCHATKA PENINSULA

Petropavlovsk-Kamchatskiy

SREDINNYY KHREBET

KURIL ISLANDS

HOKKAIDO

SAPPORO

Hakodate

Aomori

Akita

Morioka

Sendai

HONSHU

NORTH KOREA

P'YONGYANG

SOUTH KOREA

SEOUL (SOUL)

PUSAN

Vladivostok

SEA OF JAPAN

J A P A N

NAGOYA

TOKYO

YOKOHAMA

KYOTO

OSAKA

KOBE

HIROSHIMA

FUKUOKA

KYUSHU

SHIKOKU

PACIFIC OCEAN

YELLOW SEA

Korea Bay

Bo Hai

DALIAN

0 100 200 300 400 500 600 Miles
0 100 200 300 400 500 600 700 800 900 1000 Kilometers

Lambert Azimuthal Equal Area Projection
Scale 1:20,000,000
One inch to 320 miles
One cm to 200 km

© Rand McNally
A-101754-R

MEDITERRANEAN SEA

CASPIAN SEA

TURKEY

Antalya Isparta Aksaray Kayseri
Konya Kahramanmaraş Malatya Elazığ Muş Ağrı Ararat 16,854 ft 5137 m Yevlax Yerevan ARMENIA AZERBAIJAN Sumqayıt
Karaman ADANA Gaziantep Siverek Diyarbakır Bitlis Van Gölü Van Orūmīyeh Xankändi AZER. BAKU (BAKI) Türkmenbaşy Urganch UZBEKI
Alanya İçel Hatay İskenderun Şanlıurfa Mardin Al-Hasakah Mosul Orūmīyeh TABRĪZ Ardabīl Navoiy Buxoro
Nicosia (Al-Ladhiqiyah) CYPRUS Lemesós Latakia Tartūs (Tarābulus) Hamāh az-Zawr Dayr Kirkuk Arbil As-Sulaymānīyah Sanandaj Mahābād Saqqez Zanjān Rasht Āmol Sārī Gorgān TURKMENISTAN Gyzylarbat Gomdag Balkanabat Gonbad-e Kāvūs Shāhrūd Quchān Bäherden Aşgabat Türkmenabat Mary Bayram-Ali Atamyrat
LEBANON Beirut Him Tripoli SYRIA Hamāh Tikrit Sāmarrā Ba'qubah Kermānshāh Hamadān Qazvīn Karaj TEHRĀN Kūh-e Damāvand 18,386 ft 5604 m ELBURZ MOUNTAINS Sabzevār Neyshābūr MASHHAD Meymaneh
Haifa Tel Aviv-Yafo ISRAEL Jerusalem Gaza Port Said Tanta Ismailia DAMASCUS (DIMASHQ) Az-Zarqā' Amman Irbid Ar-Ramādī BAGHDAD Karbalā' Al-Hillah Al-Kūt Borūjerd Khorramābād ARĀK Qom Kāshān ESFAHĀN Gonābād Torbat-e Heydarīyeh SELSELEH-YE SAFĪD Herāt AFGHA
CAIRO (EL-QĀHIRA) Suez JORDAN Ma'ān An-Najaf Ad-Dīwānīyah Dezfūl Najafābād DASHT-E KAVĪR Tabas Qā'en Farāh
SINAI PENINSULA Elat Al-'Aqabah Ar'ar Sakākah As-Samāwah An Nāşirīyah Al-'Amārah Masjed-e Soleymān Qomsheh Yazd
EGYPT Hurghada Jabal al-Lawz 2884 ft 2403 m Tabūk Al-Jawf Rafhā' Basra Ābādān Ahvāz Behbahān Zard Kūh 14,547 ft 4547 m Rafsanjān Kermān Bam DASHT-E LŪT HĀMŪN Zābol RĪGESTĀN
Qena El-Uqsor Edfu Kom Ombo AN-NAFŪD Hā'il Kāzerūn SHĪRĀZ Jahrom Lār ZĀHEDĀN Hāmūn-i-Mashkel Hāmūn-i-Lora
Aswān Lake Nasser Umm Lajj KUWAIT Kuwait (Al-Kuwayt) BŪBIYĀN Būshehr Darvācheh-ye Bakhtegān Bandar Abbās Īrānshahr
Quseir Buraydah Az-Zilfi 'Unayzah Al-Majma'ah Ad-Dammām Al-Jubayl JAZĪREH-YE LĀVĀN JAZĪREH-YE KĪSH Strait of Hormuz JAZĪREH-YE QESHM Bandar Beheshtī Gwādar
Yanbu'al-Bahr Medina (Al-Madīnah) Ad-Dawādimī RIYADH (AR-RIYĀD) Al-Khubar Al-Hufūf BAHRAIN Al-Manāmah QATAR Doha DUBAI Ash-Shāriqah Gwātar Bay Turbat
'Afif JABAL TUWAYQ Ad-Dilam Abu Dhabi OMAN Ash-Shām Şuhār Adam Matrah Muscat RA'S AL-HADD Tropic of Cancer
Rābigh Halā'ib SAUDI ARABIA AD-DAHNĀ UNITED ARAB EMIRATES Al-'Ayn Jabal ash-Shām 9957 ft 3035 m Al-Khābūrah Şūr
NUBIAN DESERT Mecca (Makkah) At-Tā'if Qal'at Bishah ARABIAN PENINSULA Wādī ad-Dawāsir
Būr Sūdān JIDDAH ASĪR RUB' AL-KHALI MAŞĪRAH Khalīj Maşīrah
SUDAN Sawākin Sinkāt Tawkar Khamīs Mushayt Abha OMAN
Kassala ERITREA Keren Akordat Jīzān Abū 'Arīsh Sa'dah Najrān Salālah JUZUR AL-HALLĀNĪYAH ARABIAN
Al-Qadārif Kassala Barentu Teseney DAHLAK ARCHIPELAGO Massawa Asmara Hajjah Şa'dah Şan'ā' Shibām Saywūn Al-Ghaydah 'ABD AL-KŪRI (Yemen) Ghubbat al-Qamar Ghubbat al-Qamar ARABIAN
Aksum Adīgrat Jabāl an-Nabī Shu'ayb 12,008 ft 3660 m SANAA (ŞAN'Ā') HADRAMAWT RA'S FARTAK SOCOTRA (Yemen)
Mek'elē Al-Hudaydah Dhamār Ridā' Ibb Al-Mukallā Ash-Shihr
Ras Dejen 15,158 ft 4620 m Gonder Zabīd Ta'izz YEMEN Al-Hawrah RAAS XAAFUUN
Bahir Dar Mot'a Desē Al-Mukhā Aseb Bab el-Mandeb Aden ('Adan) Gulf of Aden Caluula GEES GWARDAFUY Qandala
Debre Mark'os Tald 14,178 ft 4413 m DJIBOUTI Djibouti Boosaaso Ceerigaabo RAAS XAAFUUN
ADDIS ABABA (ĀDĪS ĀBEBA) Nek'emtē Lake Ālī Sabieh Saylac Berbera Shimbiris 7897 ft 2407 m Burco Hargeysa
Jima Hosa'ina Dirē Dawa Hārer Jijiga Degeh Bur SOMALIA
Arba Minch' ETHIOPIA OGADEN Werdēr Laascaanood SOMALI BASIN
Negēlē Goba K'ebrī Dehar Gaalkacyo Eyl CARLSBERG RIDGE

RED SEA

Persian Gulf

Gulf of Oman

IRAN

Gurgān
Sārī
Shāhrūd
Semnān

Lambert Azimuthal Equal Area Projection
Scale 1:16,000,000
One inch to 256 miles
One cm to 160 km

0   80   160   240   320   400   480 Miles
0   80   160   240   320 400 480 560 640 720 800 Kilometers

0 80 160 240 320 400 480 Miles

0 80 160 240 320 400 480 560 640 720 800 Kilometers

Lambert Azimuthal Equal Area Projection
Scale 1:16,000,000
One inch to 256 miles
One cm to 160 km

RUSSIA

MANCHURIA

GREATER KHINGAN RANGE (DA HINGGAN LING)

LESSER KHINGAN RANGE

SIKHOTE-ALIN

SEA OF OKHOTSK

KURIL ISLANDS

The islands known in Japan as the Northern Territories and in Russia as the Southern Kuril Islands are occupied by Russia and claimed by Japan.

HOKKAIDO

SAPPORO

Asahikawa

Hakodate

SEA OF JAPAN

HONSHU

TŌKYŌ
YOKOHAMA

KYŌTO NAGOYA
KŌBE OSAKA
HIROSHIMA

JAPAN

SHIKOKU

KYUSHU

FUKUOKA
Nagasaki

Both North Korea and South Korea claim to be the sole legitimate government of Korea.

NORTH KOREA

P'YŎNGYANG

SOUTH KOREA

SEOUL (SŎUL)
INCH'ŎN
PUSAN

YELLOW SEA

EAST CHINA SEA

DESERT

MONGOL

GOBI DESERT

BAOTOU
BEIJING
TIANJIN
TANGSHAN

HEBEI

SHANXI
TAIYUAN

SHAANXI
XI'AN

QIN LING

HENAN
ZHENGZHOU

SHANDONG
JINAN
QINGDAO

JIANGSU
NANJING
SHANGHAI

ANHUI
HEFEI

HUBEI
WUHAN

HUNAN
CHANGSHA

JIANGXI
NANCHANG

ZHEJIANG
HANGZHOU
NINGBO

FUJIAN
FUZHOU

China and many other countries do not recognize the existence of Taiwan as a separate country.

TAIWAN
T'AIPEI
KAOHSIUNG

GUANGDONG
GUANGZHOU
HONG KONG (XIANGGANG)
Macau (Aomen)

GUANGXI
Nanning

HAINAN
Haikou

SOUTH CHINA SEA

PHILIPPINE SEA

PHILIPPINE BASIN

RYUKYU ISLANDS (NANSEI-SHOTŌ)

Tropic of Cancer

PHILIPPINES
LUZON

Gulf of Tonkin

© Rand McNally
A-101749-1

Tonghai
Tropic of Cancer
YUNNAN
Gejiu
Bose
Nanning
CHINA
Jinghong
Fan Si Pan
10,312 ft.
3143 m
Cao Bang
Thai
Nguyen
GUANGXI
Jiangmen
Shenzhen
Macau
(Aomen)
HONG KONG
(XIANGGANG)
KAOHSIUNG
TAIWAN
MT. VICTORIA
10,016 ft.
Paletwa 3053 m
Maymyo
Mandalay
Keng
Tung
Yen Bai
Ha Noi
GUANGDONG
Beihai
Zhanjiang
Macau
Bashi Channel
OLUAN PI
BATAN
ISLANDS
Meiktila
Myingyan
Chiang
Rai
Louangphrabang
Hoa
Binh
Hai Phong
LEIZHOU
BANDAO
Haikou
PRATAS
ISLAND
(Occupied by Taiwan; claimed by China)
Luzon Strait
BABUYAN ISLANDS
Yenangyaung
Prome
Pyinmana
LAOS
Muang
Xaignabouri
Chiang
Mai
Nam Ngum
Reservoir
Nam Dinh
Gulf of
Tonkin
HAINAN DAO
Dongfang
HAINAN
Wuzhi Shan
6125 ft.
1867 m
Balintang Channel
MYANMAR
(BURMA)
Sittwe
Lampang
Vientiane
(Viangchan)
Vinh
Sanya
Baoting
CAPE BOJEADOR
Laoag
ESCARPADA
POINT
Tuguegarao
City
RAMREE
ISLAND
Henzada
Bago
Pha-an
Phitsanulok
Khon
Kaen
Udon
Thani
Thanh
Hoa
CHEDUBA
ISLAND
Pathein
YANGON
(RANGOON)
Mawlamyine
THAILAND
Nakhon
Sawan
Phra Nakhon
Si Ayutthaya
Savannakhét
Dong Hoi
Hue
Da Nang
Vigan
Mt. Pulog
9626 ft.
2934 m
Baguio
LUZON
ARAKAN YOMA
Dawei
Nakhon
Ratchasima
Ubon
Ratchathani
Pakxé
INDOCHINA
VIETNAM
Dagupan
Cabanatuan
Gulf of
Martaban
Ye
Nakhon
Pathom
Chon
Buri
Play Ku
Quy Nhon
Angeles
San Fernando
Quezon
City
MANILA
PREPARIS
ISLAND
BANGKOK
(KRUNG THEP)
Bàtdâmbâng
Siĕmréab
Stoeng Treng
Kâmpông
Thum
Krâchéh
Da Lat
Nha Trang
Calapan
Lucena
Naga
COCO IS.
Chanthaburi
Tonle
Sap
MINDORO
TABLAS
ISLAND
MASBATE
Dawei
KO CHANG
CAMBODIA
Phnom Penh
Bien
Hoa
SIBUYAN
SEA
NORTH
ANDAMAN
KO KUT
HO CHI MINH CITY
(SAIGON)
Phan Thiet
BUSUANGA
ISLAND
Roxas
Iloilo
MIDDLE
ANDAMAN
ANDAMAN
SEA
Chumphon
Kâmpóng Saôm
Kâmpôt
Vung Tau
CULION
ISLAND
PANAY
Bacolod
Port Blair
MERGUI
ARCHIPELAGO
ISTHMUS
OF KRA
Rach
Gia
Can Tho
CUYO
ISLANDS
SOUTH
ANDAMAN
Kawthaung
DAO PHU
QUOC
Bac Lieu
CON SON
SOUTH CHINA BASIN
NAMYIT
ISLAND
NANSHAN
ISLAND
PALAWAN
NEGROS
Dumaguete
LITTLE
ANDAMAN
KO SAMUI
Surat Thani
MUI
CA MAU
Puerto
Princesa
SULU SEA
Ten Degree
Channel
ANDAMAN
AND NICOBAR
ISLANDS
(India)
Nakhon Si
Thammarat
Gulf of
Thailand
SPRATLY
ISLANDS
(Claimed by China,
Malaysia, the
Philippines,
Taiwan and Vietnam)
Pagadian
CAR NICOBAR
ISLAND
KO
PHUKET
Trang
Songkhla
Thale Sap
Songkhla
DUMARAN
ISLAND
BALABAC
ISLAND
Balabac Strait
PULAU
BANGGI
Zamboanga
Jolo
Moro
Gulf
KATCHALL ISLAND
Hat Yai
Yala
Kota
Bharu
JOLO
ISLAND
LITTLE
NICOBAR
Banda
Aceh
Alor Setar
George Town
Kuala Terengganu
Kudat
CAGAYAN
SULU IS.
NICOBAR ISLANDS
GREAT
NICOBAR
PULAU LANGKAWI
PULAU PINANG
Kota
Kinabalu
Gunung
Kinabalu
13,455 ft.
4101 m
Sandakan
TAWITAWI
ISLAND
CELEBES BASIN
Lhokseumawe
Taiping
Ipoh
Gunong Tahan
7175 ft.
2187 m
PULAU
LAUT
Bandar Seri Begawan
Lahad
Datu
Langsa
MEDAN
MALAYSIA
SUNDA SHELF
NATUNA
BESAR
BRUNEI
Miri
Tawau
CELEBES
SEA
Binjai
KUALA
LUMPUR
PULAU
TIOMAN
KEPULAUAN
ANAMBAS
Gunong
Murud
7946 ft.
2422 m
Tebingtinggi
Klang
Melaka
Batu Pahat
Bintulu
Tarakan
PULAU
SIMEULUE
Pematangsiantar
Dumai
KEPULAUAN
NATUNA
TANJUNG DATU
MALAYSIA
Sibu
RANAU
Sibolga
KEPULAUAN
BANYAK
PULAU
NIAS
Johor Bahru
SINGAPORE
SINGAPORE
Singkawang
KEPULAUAN
RIAU
Kuching
UPPER KAPUAS MTS.
TANJUNG
MANGKALIHAT
Tolitoli
Pekanbaru
Strait of Malacca
Pulau
Batam
PULAU
LINGGA
Pontianak
Sintang
KLINGKANG MTS.
IRAN MTS.
Bontang
Bukittinggi
Tembilahan
KEPULAUAN
LINGGA
BORNEO
(KALIMANTAN)
Samarinda
Palu
Teluk Tomini
Padang
Gunung Kerinci
12,467 ft.
3800 m
Jambi
Indragiri
PULAU
SINGKEP
KEPULAUAN
KARIMATA
PEG. MULLER
Bukit Raya
7474 ft.
2278 m
Balikpapan
CELEBES
(SULAWESI)
PULAU
PELENG
PULAU
SIBERUT
Hari
PULAU
BANGKA
Ketapang
PEG. SCHWANER
Makassar Strait
(Selat Makasar)
Luwuk
KEPULAUAN
MENTAWAI
Musi
Tanjungpandan
BELITUNG
Barito
Palangkaraya
Majene
Bulu Rantekombola
11,335 ft.
3455 m
Teluk
Tolo
PULAU PAGAI UTARA
SUMATRA
(SUMATERA)
PALEMBANG
Selat Karimata
TANJUNG
PUTING
Banjarmasin
Banjarbaru
INDONESIA
PULAU
TOGIAN
PULAU PAGAI SELATAN
Bengkulu
Gunung Dempo
10,364 ft.
3159 m
Petabumulih
GREATER
SUNDA
ISLANDS
PULAU
LAUT
Parepare
Palopo
Kotabumi
TANJUNG
SELATAN
Watampone
PULAU
MUNA
Kendari
PULAU
BUTON
BUKIT BARISAN
PULAU
ENGGANO
Bandar Lampung
JAVA SEA
(LAUT JAWA)
KEPULAUAN
MASALEMBU BESAR
MAKASSAR
(UJUNGPANDANG)
Teluk
Bone
PULAU
KABAENA
Equator
KEPULAUAN
BATU
TANJUNG
CINA
KEPULAUAN
KARIMUNJAWA
PULAU BAWEAN
KEPULAUAN
KANGEAN
PULAU
SELAYAR
FLORES SEA
JAKARTA
Cirebon
SEMARANG
MADURA
Sumenep
Selat Sunda
Bogor
Gunung
Slamet
11,247 ft.
3428 m
SURABAYA
BANDUNG
Sukabumi
Surakarta
Pasuruan
Gunung Rinjani
12,224 ft.
3726 m
Singaraja
Raba
PULAU
KALAO
INDIAN OCEAN
JAVA
(JAWA)
Kediri
Malang
Yogyakarta
Gunung
Semeru
12,060 ft.
3676 m
Denpasar
SUMBAWA
BESAR
SUMBAWA
Ende
FLORES
Larantuka
JAVA TRENCH
Jember
LOMBOK
Mataram
Waikabubak
SUMBA
LESSER SUNDA ISLANDS
SAVU SEA
Kupang
PULAU
SAWU
PULAU
ROTI
SOUTH
CHINA
SEA
PARACEL
ISLANDS
(Occupied by China;
claimed by Taiwan and Vietnam)
CHRISTMAS
ISLAND
(Austl.)
COCOS
ISLANDS
(Austl.)
ASHMORE
AND CARTIER
ISLANDS
(Austl.)

© Rand McNally
A-101748-1

0 80 160 240 320 400 480 Miles
0 80 160 240 320 400 480 560 640 720 800 Kilometers

Lambert Azimuthal Equal Area Projection
Scale 1:16,000,000
One inch to 256 miles
One cm to 160 km

a

EAST
CHINA SEA

PHILIPPINE
SEA

CHINA

FUZHOU

FUJIAN

Quanzhou

Xiamen

TAIWAN

Tanshui
Chilung
T'AIPEI
Taoyüan
Chungli
Hsintien
Hsinchu
Lotung
Chutung
Suao
Miaoli
Fengyüan
T'aichung
Lukang
Changhua
Yüanlin
Nant'ou
Huwei
Touliu
Peikang
Chiai
YÜ SHAN
13 114 ft
3997 m
Chiali
Kuan Shan
12 188 ft
3715 m
T'ainan
Kangshan
P'ingtung
KAOHSIUNG
Fangshan

Hualien

Fengpin

T'aitung

PHILIPPINE
SEA

China and many other countries do not recognize
the existence of Taiwan as a separate country.

Taiwan Strait

Tropic of Cancer

P'ENGHU
CH'ÜNTAO
Makung

SOUTH
CHINA SEA

Bashi Channel

© Rand McNally
A-101808-1

PHILIPPINES

PHILIPPINE BASIN

Legaspi
Sorsogon

Samar
Catbalogan
Tacloban
Cebu
Tagbilaran
Butuan
Cagayan de Oro
Iligan
MINDANAO
Cotabato
Davao
Mt. Apo
9692 ft
2954 m
General Santos

PHILIPPINE
TRENCH

PALAU

Manado
Bitung

MOLUCCA
SEA

MOLUCCAS
(MALUKU)

CERAM SEA

Ambon

BANDA SEA
(LAUT BANDA)

EAST TIMOR

Dili

TIMOR SEA

Darwin

AUSTRALIA

WEST CAROLINE
BASIN

Equator

Sorong
Manokwari

JAZIRAH
DOBERAI

Jayapura

PEGUNUNGAN MAOKE

Puncak Jaya
16 503 ft
5030 m
Puncak Trikora
15 584 ft
4750 m
Puncak Mandala
15 617 ft
4760 m

NEW GUINEA

ARAFURA SEA

Merauke

Port
Moresby

EAST CAROLINE
BASIN

BISMARCK
BISMARCK SEA
ARCHIPELAGO

Rabaul

NEW
IRELAND

Madang

PAPUA
NEW GUINEA

Mt. Wilhelm
14 793 ft
4509 m

Mt. Giluwe
14 331 ft
4368 m

SOLOMON SEA

Mt. Bangeta
13 520 ft
4121 m

NEW BRITAIN

Mt. Ulawun
7657 ft
2334 m

Lae

Gulf of
Papua

Mt. Victoria
13 238 ft
4035 m

CORAL SEA

Inset map a
Lambert Conformal Conic Projection
Scale 1:4,000,000
One inch to 64 miles
One cm to 40 km

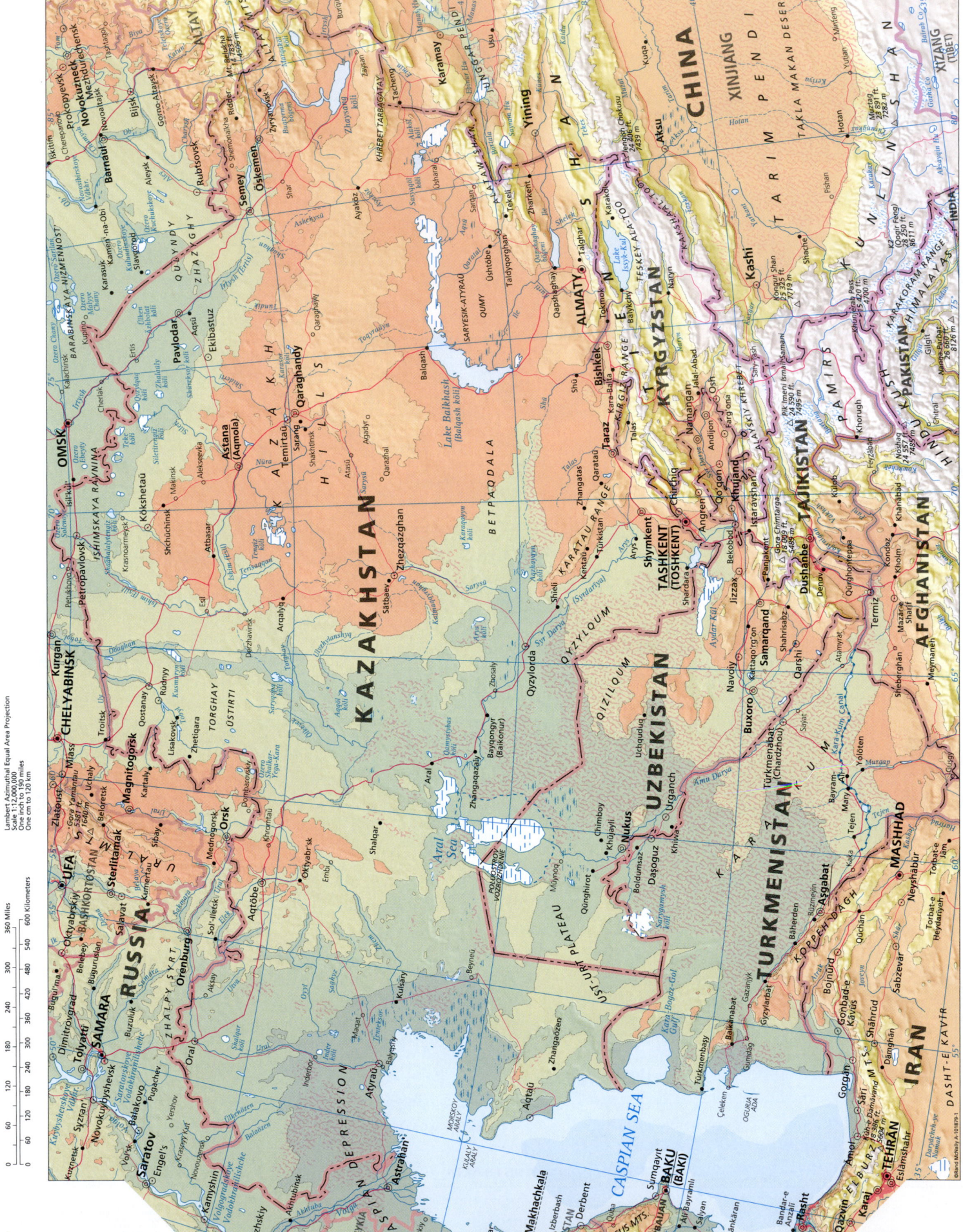

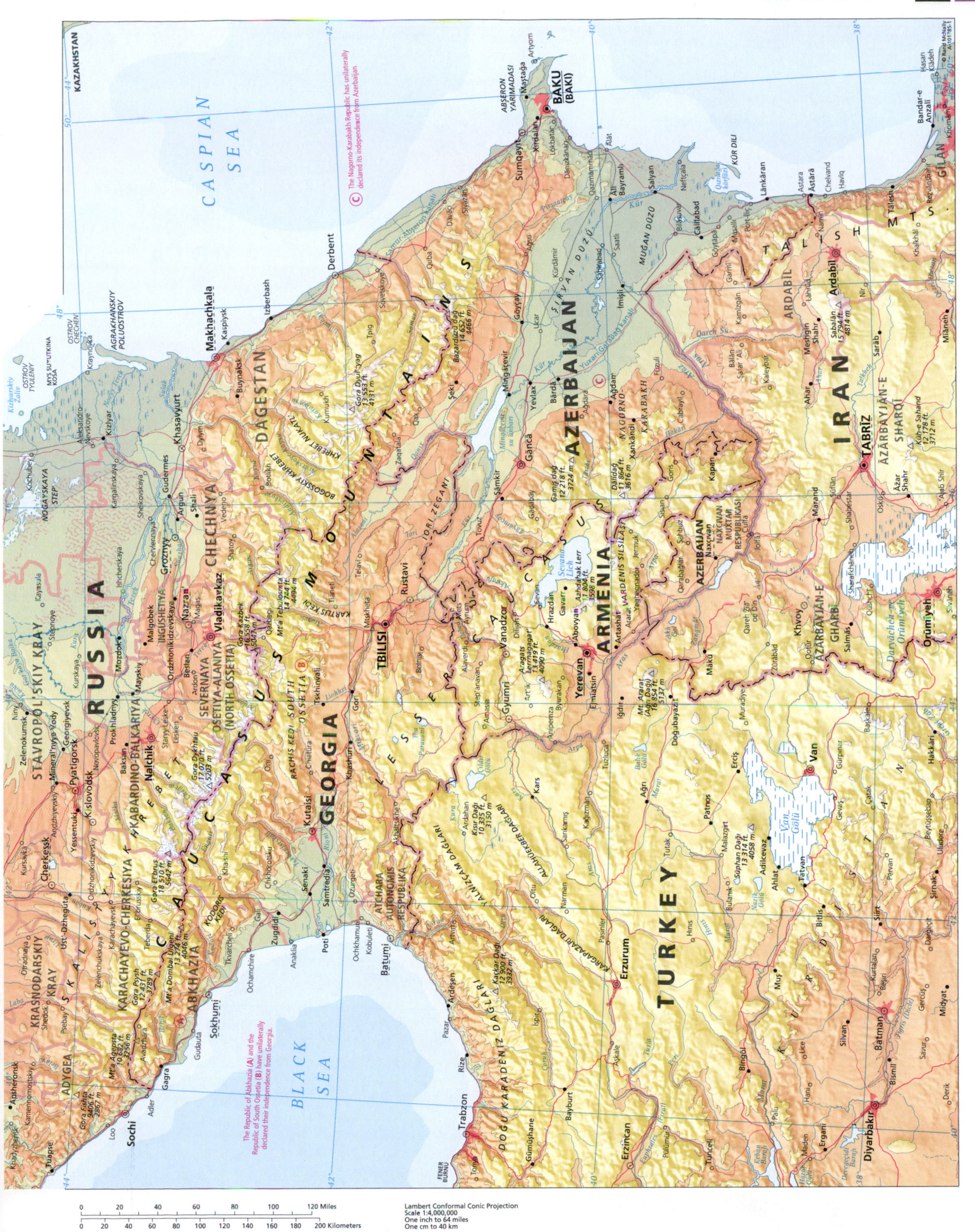

TURKEY

Şanlıurfa • Viranşehir • Derik

TAURUS MOUNTAINS

Alanya • Gazipaşa • Anamur • Silifke • Mut • Erdemli • İçel • Tarsus • ADANA • İskenderun • Gaziantep • Nizip • Birecik • Sürüç • Ceylanpınar • Ra's al-'Ayn • Tall Tamir

Antalya Körfezi

Kuzucubelen • Emenlik • Gülnar • Seyhan • Dörtyol • Kırıkhan • Oğuzeli • Kilis • Jarābulus • Salūq • 'Atīq • Dulq Maghār

İNCEKUM BURNU • ANAMUR BURNU • Hatay • Reyhanlı • Afrin • Al-Bāb • Manbij • A'zāz • Al-'Atay

CYPRUS

North Cyprus declared itself an independent Turkish Republic in 1983.

KORUÇAM BURNU • Dipkarpaz • ZAFER BURNU • Ziyamet • İskele • Girne • Güzelyurt • Nicosia • Strovolos • Gazimağusa • Larnaka

Kólpos Khrisokhoús • Güzelyurt Körfezi • Kólpos Lárnakos • Gazimağusa Körfezi

Polis • Olimbos 6401 ft. 1951 m • Néa Páfos • Lemesós • Yermasóyia • AKROTÍRION PIDÁLION

Akrotíri • Akrotíri GÁTAS

Samandağı • Al-Haffah • As-Safirah • Maskanah • Buhayrat al-Asad • Ar-Raqqah • Suwaydah • Euphrates

Jisr ash-Shughūr • Arīhā • Ma'arrat an-Nu'mān • As-Saqlabīyah

Idlib

Latakia (Al-Lādhiqīyah) • Jablah • Bāniyās • Shūrān • Al-Ghāb

SYRIA

Dayr az-Zawr

RA'S AL-BASĪT

Al-Kawm • At-Tayyibah • Al-Mayādīn • Dablān • Busayrah

Hamāh • Salamīyah • As-Sukhnah

Ṭarṭūs • Tall Kalakh • Buhayrat Qaṭṭīnah • Shinshār • Furqlus

MEDITERRANEAN SEA

Tripoli (Tarābulus) • Al-Batrūn • Al-Hirmil • Al-Qusayr • Tudmur • PALMYRA • Al-Qaryatayn

Qurnat as-Sawdā' 10 115 ft. 3083 m

LEBANON • Jubayl • BYBLOS • Bsharrī

Beirut (Bayrūt) • Jūnīyah • B'abdā • Zahlah • Ba'labakk • BAALBEK • An-Nabk • Sab 'Ābār • Akāshāt

BEKAA VALLEY

Şaydā • Az-Zabadānī • Al-Qutayfah • Khān Abū Shāmāt

DAMASCUS (DIMASHQ) • Dūmā • Jaramānah • Darayya • Al-Kiswah • At-Tanf

Mt. Hermon 9232 ft. 2814 m • Qatanā • Jdaydat • Ar-Ruṭbah

Tyre (Sūr) • Iwaytā • Qiryat Shemona • Al-Qunaytirah • Al-Mismīyah • Lāhithah • As-Suwaydā' • Jabal ad-Durūz 5909 ft. 1801 m

Nahariyya • Har Meron 3963 ft. 1208 m • Zefat • GOLAN HEIGHTS

SYRIAN DESERT

Haifa (Hefa) • Akko • Teverya • Sea of Galilee • Fiq • Dar'ā • Jabal 'Unayzah 3084 ft. 940 m

Tirat Karmel • Nazareth (Nazerat) • Irbid • Ar-Rutbah

AL-HAMĀD

'Afula • Bet She'an • Ar-Ramthā • Ajlūn • Jarash • Al-Mafraq • Mahattat al-Hafif • Azraq ash-Shishan

Hadera • Tūlkarm • Tubas • As-Salt

ISRAEL • Netanya • Nābulus • Az-Zarqā' • Ar-Ruṣayfah • Amman • Al-Hadīthah • Kāf • Al-'Īsāwīyah

Herzliyya • Qalqiliya • WEST BANK • Rām Allāh • Arīhā (Jericho)

Tel Aviv-Yafo • Petah Tiqwa • Madabā • Al-Jīzah • Turayf

Rishon LeZiyyon • Rehovot • Jerusalem (Yerushalayim) • Al-Khalīl • Dhībān • Al-Hadīthah

Ashdod • Bethlehem (Bayt Laḥm) • Qiryat Gat • Dead Sea • Al-Karak • Al-Qaṭrānah

Ashqelon • GAZA STRIP (A) • Qiryat Gat • Yattah • Al-Mazra'ah • Sabkhat Hazawzā'

Port Said (Būr Sa'īd) • Gaza (Ghazzah) • Be'er Sheva • MASADA • Arad • WADI AS-SIRHĀN

Būr Fu'ād • Khān Yūnis • Dimona • Al-'Īsāwīyah

Khalīg el-Tína • Rafah • Yeroham • Al-Ghinah

El-Arish • HOLOT HALUZA • Nizzana • Mizpé Ramon • Wādī al-Ghinah

El-Qantara • Romani • Gebel Yi'allaq 3589 ft. 1094 m • At-Tafilah • Ash-Shawbak

Ismailia • NEGEV • Wādī al-Hasah • Al-Hadrū'

Sabkhet el-Baraawil

EGYPT • El-Quseima • Ash-Shawbak • Al-Jafr • QĀ'AL-JAFR

Suez (El-Suweis) • Nakhl • Ra's an-Naqb • Ma'ān

Bur Taufiq • GEBEL EL-TÎH • El-Kuntilla • PETRA

Great Bitter Lake • SINAI PENINSULA • Makhfar al-Quwayrah • JORDAN

Gulf of Suez (Khalig el-Suweis)

Gebel El-Igma • Elat • Jabal Ramm 5755 ft. 1754 m • Al-Jafr

Abu Zenima • Rás el-Gineina 5335 ft. 1626 m • Al-'Aqabah • Al-Mudawwarah

Mt. Sinai (Gebel Mûsa) 7497 ft. 2285 m • Jabal al-Lawz 7884 ft. 2403 m • Al-Bi'r

SAUDI

AT-TAWĪL

AL-BUSAYTĀ' • Sakākah • Al-Jawf • Qārah

AL-'URAYQ

Gulf of Aqaba • Haql • Nuweiba • Dabah • Al-Qalībah • Wādī Fajr

Gebel Abu Khashaba 4797 ft. 1462 m • El-Tûr • Maqna • Al-Bad' • Tabūk

MIDYAN

Nabq • Sharm el-Sheikh • Aynūnah • Ash-Sharmah • Ra's Mohammed

Madiq Tiran

RED SEA

SANĀFIR

AL-HUFRAH

Lambert Conformal Conic Projection
Scale 1:4,000,000
One inch to 64 miles
One cm to 40 km

0 20 40 60 80 100 120 Miles
0 20 40 60 80 100 120 140 160 180 200 Kilometers

A Gaza Strip is administered by the Palestinian Authority following unilateral withdrawal by Israel in 2005.

B West Bank is controlled by Israel and parts are administered by the Palestinian Authority.

C Golan Heights has been unilaterally annexed by Israel.

Lambert Conformal Conic Projection
Scale 1:4,000,000
One inch to 64 miles
One cm to 40 km

IRAN

Anār
Shahr-e Bābak
Rafsanjān
Zarand
Ravar
Lakar Küh
9764 ft.
2976 m
Bāghīn
Kermān
Küh-e Palvär
13 888 ft.
4233 m
Mashīz
Golbāf
KERMĀN
Sirjān
Küh-e Lāleh Zār
14 357 ft.
4376 m
Rāyen
Küh-e Hazār
14 649 ft.
4465 m
Bāft
Küh-e Khabīr
12 612 ft.
3844 m
Bam
Fahraj
Esfandaqeh
Dārāb
Jīroft
Rīgān
Küh-e
Qashqeh
9190 ft.
2801 m
Fürg
Kol
Do Sāri
Dowlatābād
Sarā-ye
Ahmadī
Golāshkerd
Bizhanābād
Küh-e Bazmān
11 453 ft.
3491 m
Bazmān
LARISTĀN
Kahnūj
Manūjān
Hāmün-e
Jaz Müriän
Bampür
Īrānshahr
Bampür
SĪSTĀN VA BĀLŪCHESTĀN
Shamil
Qal'eh-ye
Deh-e Bārez
Bandar
'Abbās
Mīnāb
Remeshk
Maskūtān
Sarbāz
JAZĪREH-YE
HORMOZ
Küh-e Büniken
7169 ft.
2185 m
Bāsa'īdū
Qeshm
JAZĪREH-YE
LĀRAK
Angohrān
Bent
Nīkshahr
Qasr-e
Qand
Rāsk
Bandar-e
Lengeh
JAZĪREH-YE
QESHM
JAZĪREH-YE
HENGAM
Strait of Hormuz
RA'S
SHARĪTAH
Gevān
Gur Küh
6270 ft.
1911 m
Gābrik
Sūrak
Karkandar
ABŪ
MÜSĀ
MÚSANDAM
PENINSULA
Kumzār
Khasab
Jāsk
PAKISTAN

OMAN
Ra's al-Khaymah
Jabal al-Harīm
6847 ft.
2087 m
Hümedān
RA'S-E
KÜH LAB
Bandar
Beheshti
Umm al-Qaywayn
Dadnah
MAKRĀN COAST
Ash-Shāriqah
'Ajmān
OMAN
Al-Fujayrah
DUBAI
(DUBAYY)
Kalbā'
Shinās
Gulf of Oman
Al-Buraymī
Al-Buraymī
Şuḥār
ARABIAN
SEA
Al-'Ayn
Al-Ghurayfah
Al-Khābūrah
As-Suwayq
Jabal Ḥafīt
3806 ft.
1160 m
Al-Qābil
Dank
As-Sīb
Matraḥ
Muscat
(Masqaṭ)
Tropic of Cancer
Maskin
Bawshar
Al-Amrat
Ar-Rustāq
Sarūr
Quryyāt
RA'S ABŪ DĀ'ŪD
'Ibrī
Jabal ash-Shām
9957 ft.
3035 m
Samā'il
Tan'am
Bahlā'
Nizwā
Izkī
OMAN
Ibrā
Fins
Tiwi
Al-Muḍaybī
Şūr
RA'S AL-HADD
Al-Hadd

© Rand McNally
A-101797-1

0   40   80   120   160   200   240 Miles

0   40   80   120   160   200   240   280   320   360   400 Kilometers

Lambert Azimuthal Equal Area Projection
Scale 1:8,000,000
One inch to 128 miles
One cm to 80 km

KAZAKHSTAN

UZBEKISTAN

KYRGYZSTAN

TASHKENT (TOSHKENT)

TAJIKISTAN

CHINA

XINJIANG

TARIM PENDI

KUNLUN SHAN

PAMIRS

HINDU KUSH

KARAKORAM RANGE

HIMALAYAS

NORTHERN AREAS

JAMMU AND KASHMIR

HIMACHAL PRADESH

NORTH-WEST FRONTIER

AZAD KASHMIR

FEDERALLY ADMINISTERED TRIBAL AREAS

AFGHANISTAN

SELSELEH-YE SAFID KOH

Kabul (Kābol)

Peshāwar

Islāmābād

RĀWALPINDI

Srinagar

Jammu

Sialkot

PUNJAB

LAHORE

Amritsar

LUDHIĀNA

Chandigarh

DELHI

New Delhi

HARYĀNA

FAISALĀBĀD

Gujrānwāla

Sargodha

MULTĀN

PAKISTAN

Kandahar

Quetta

BALUCHISTAN

RĪGESTĀN

DASHT-E MĀRGOW

TOBA KAKAR RANGE

CENTRAL MAKRĀN RANGE

KIRTHAR RANGE

SULAIMĀN RANGE

SIND

HYDERĀBĀD

KARĀCHI

MAKRĀN COAST

ARABIAN SEA

RANN OF KUTCH

GUJARĀT

AHMADĀBĀD

INDIA

RĀJASTHĀN

Jaipur

Jodhpur

Bīkāner

THAR DESERT

GREAT INDIAN DESERT

MADHYA PRADESH

INDORE

Hāmūn-e Sāberī

Herāt

Zābol

Tropic of Cancer

TAJIKISTAN

Taxkorgan Tajik
Zizhixian

TURK...

AFGHANISTAN

HINDU KUSH

KARAKORAM RANGE

KUN

NORTHERN AREAS

K2 (Qogir Feng)
28 250 ft.
8611 m

Nanga Parbat
26 660 ft.
8126 m

KASHMIR

NORTH-WEST
FRONTIER

JAMMU AND
KASHMIR

Kabul
(Kābol)

Peshāwar

Islāmābād

Srinagar

RĀWALPINDI

AZAD
KASHMIR

HIMĀCHAL

FEDERALLY
ADMINISTERED
TRIBAL AREAS

Gujrāt
Siālkot
Jammu

PRADESH

HIM

Gujrānwāla

Amritsar

FAISALĀBĀD

LAHORE

PUNJAB

Jalandhar

PUNJAB

LUDHIĀNA

Shimla

Chandīgarh

Dehra Dūn

PAKISTAN

MULTĀN

Bahāwalpur

Patiāla

Sahāranpur
UTTARANCHAL

Haridwār

BALUCHISTAN

THAR DESERT

HARYĀNA

MEERUT

Quetta

DELHI

New Delhi

RĀMPUR

Bareilly

GREAT INDIAN DESERT

Bīkāner

SHĀHJAHĀNPUR

Sukkur

SIND

RĀJASTHĀN

JAIPUR

ĀGRA

UTTAR PRADESH

LUCKNOW

Jodhpur

Ajmer

KĀNPUR

HYDERABAD

Gwalior

Jhānsi

KARACHI

Kota

I N D

Udaipur

RANN OF KUTCH

Tropic of Cancer

ARAVALLI RANGE

VINDHYA

MĀDHYA

BHOPĀL

PRADESH

GUJARĀT

AHMADĀBĀD

INDORE

Jabalpur

Jamnagar

Rājkot

Vadodara

KĀTHIĀWAR PENINSULA

Bhāvnagar

NARMADA

ARABIAN

SEA

SŪRAT

MAHĀRĀSHTRA

NĀGPUR

Nāshik

© Rand McNally
A-101821-1

0   40   80   120   160   200   240 Miles
0 40 80 120 160 200 240 280 320 360 400 Kilometers

Lambert Azimuthal Equal Area Projection
Scale 1:8,000,000
One inch to 128 miles
One cm to 80 km

GUJARAT
Talaja
Mahuva
SURAT
Gulf of Khambhát
Navsari
DAMAN AND DIU
Bilimora
Bulsar
Daman
Silvassa
DADRA AND NAGAR HAVELI
Vasai
NASHIK
Deolali
Igatpuri
Kalyán
Thane
Ulhásnagar
Panvel
MUMBAI (BOMBAY)
Lonávale
Pune
Bárámati
Nandurbar
Shirpur
Navápur
Dhule
Chopda
Amalner
Málkápur
Chálisgaon
Kopargaon
Srirampur
Sangamner
Deolali
Daund
Phaltan
Wai
Satara
Chiplun
Ratnágiri
Mahad
Pandharpur
Sángola
Karád
Sháháda
Nepa Nagar
Burhánpur
Bhusáwal
Jálgaon
Manmád
Chikhli
Aurangábád
Jálna
Hingoli
Pusad
Ádilábád
MAHARASHTRA
Warud
Achalpur
Anjangaon
Amrávati
Pulgaon
Wardha
Yavatmál
Wáshim
Digras
Wani
Chandrapur
Ballálpur
Káránja
Akola
Shegaon
Buldána
Basmat
Bhaisa
Koratla
Nirmal
Belampalli
Mancheriál
Gondia
NAGPUR
Umred
Hinganghát
Dongargarh
Kátol
Kámthi
Bhandára
Tumsar
Durg
Bhilai
Raipur
Raj Nandgaon
Dalli Rájhara
Kánker
Baloda Bázar
Saraipáli
Mahásamund
Dhamtari
Bargarh
Sambalpur
Balángir
Sonepur
Titilágarh
Anugul
Talcher
Dhenkánal
Bhuban
Cuttack
Bhubaneshwar
ORISSA
Khámmam
Kondagaon
Jagdalpur
Nowrangapur
Ráyagada
Jaypur
Koráput
Párvatipuram
Parlákimidi
Salúr
Bobbili
Srikákulam
Vizianagaram
Narasannapeta
Anakápalle
Narsipatnam
Tuni
Vishákhapatnam
Pithápuram
Kákináda
Rájahmundry
Yanam
PONDICHERRY
Amalápuram
Narasápur
Machilipatnam
Vijayawáda
Eluru
Tádepallegúdem
Gudivada
Tenáli
Guntúr
Bápatla
Chirála
Ongole
Kandukúr
FALSE DIVI POINT
Nellore
Gúdúr
Kávali
Sullurpet
Tirupati
Chittoor
CHENNAI (MADRAS)
Támbaram
Kanchipuram
Vellore
Arcot
Ámbúr
Vániyambádi
PONDICHERRY
Tindivanam
Cuddalore
Pondicherry
Chidambaram
Neyveli
Máyúram
Karaikál
Nágappattinam
Thanjávúr
Tiruchchiráppalli
Pattukkottai
Vedáranniyam
POINT CALIMERE
Karáikkudi
Pudukkottai
Devakottai
Rámeswaram
PÁMBAN ISLAND
MANNAR ISLAND
Jaffna
Jaffna Lagoon
Kilinochchi
Vavuniya
Trincomalee
Anurádhapura
Puttalam
SRI LANKA
Polonnaruwa
Batticaloa
Chilaw
Kurunegala
Matale
Kandy
Amparai
Negombo
Colombo
Pidurutalagala 8281 ft. 2524 m
Dehiwala-Mount Lavinia
Moratuwa
Kalutara
Sri Jayewardenepura Kotte
Badulla
Ratnapura
Ambalangoda
Galle
Tangalla
Hambantota
Matara
DONDRA HEAD

ARABIAN SEA

BAY OF BENGAL

INDIA

DECCAN

HYDERABAD
Tándúr
Medak
Siddipet
Jangaon
Warangal
Nalgonda
Mahbúbnagar
Náráyanpet
Yádgir
Raichúr
Gadwal
Kurnool
ANDHRA PRADESH
Nandyál
Gooty
Guntakal
Tádpatri
Anantapur
Dharmávaram
Cuddapah
Kadiri
Rájampet
Rayachoti
WESTERN GHATS
EASTERN GHATS

KARNATAKA
Bijápur
Gulbarga
Sháhábád
Bidar
Basavakalyán
Homnábád
Aland
Indi
Solápur
Akalkot
Bágalkot
Gokák
Belgaum
GOA
Panaji
Marmagao
Madgaon
Dandeli
Hubli-Dhárwár
Gadag
Gajendragarh
Gangávati
Hospet
HAMPI
Bellary
Ráyadrug
Challakere
Chitradurga
Hiriyúr
Sira
Davangere
Harihar
Shimoga
Bhadrávati
Tarikere
Kádúr
Chikmagalúr
Hassan
BENGALÚRU (BANGALORE)
Rámanagaram
Mandya
Kolár
Hosúr
Hosúr
Kanakapura
Málavalli
Krishnagiri
Dharmapuri
Mysore
Kollegal
Nanjangúd
Gundlupet
Badagara
Kozhikode
Beypore
Manjeri
Tirúr
Ponnáni
Chávakkád
Thrissur
KERALA
Cochin
Shertallai
Alappuzha
Kottayam
Káyankulam
Kollam
Varkkallai
Thiruvananthapuram
Neyyáttinkara
Nágercoil
CAPE COMORIN
TAMIL NADU
Salem
Attúr
Mettúr
Idáppadi
Erode
Namakkal
Kumbakónam
Karúr
Dindigul
Palani
Madurai
Virudunagar
Aruppukkottai
Rámanáthapuram
Kovilpatti
Tenkási
Tuticorin
Tirunelveli
Tiruchchendúr
Gulf of Mannar
Palk Strait
Palk Bay
Mannar
Mangalore
Kásaragod
Taliparamba
Cannanore
Mahe
PONDICHERRY
Udagamandalam
Coonoor
Tiruppur
Coimbatore
Pollachi
Válparai
Pálghát

BITRA ISLAND
CHETLATT ISLAND
KILTÁN ISLAND
KADAMATT ISLAND
AGATTI ISLAND
ÁNDROTT ISLAND
PITTI ISLAND
Kavaratti
KAVARATTI ISLAND
KALPENI ISLAND
LAKSHADWEEP (LACCADIVE ISLANDS)
KELTAN ISLAND
MINICOY ISLAND

Nine Degree Channel
Eight Degree Channel

LAKSHADWEEP SEA

KANDUFURI
MULADU
NAGURI
HANIMADU
MAKUNUDU
NUMARA
KANDUTE
FARUKOLU
WADU
KENDIKOLU
WATARU
DIFURI
MALDIVES
MALE ATOLL
Male

INDIAN OCEAN

© Rand McNally
A-101815-1

0 40 80 120 160 200 240 Miles
0 40 80 120 160 200 240 280 320 360 400 Kilometers

Lambert Azimuthal Equal Area Projection
Scale 1:8,000,000
One inch to 128 miles
One cm to 80 km

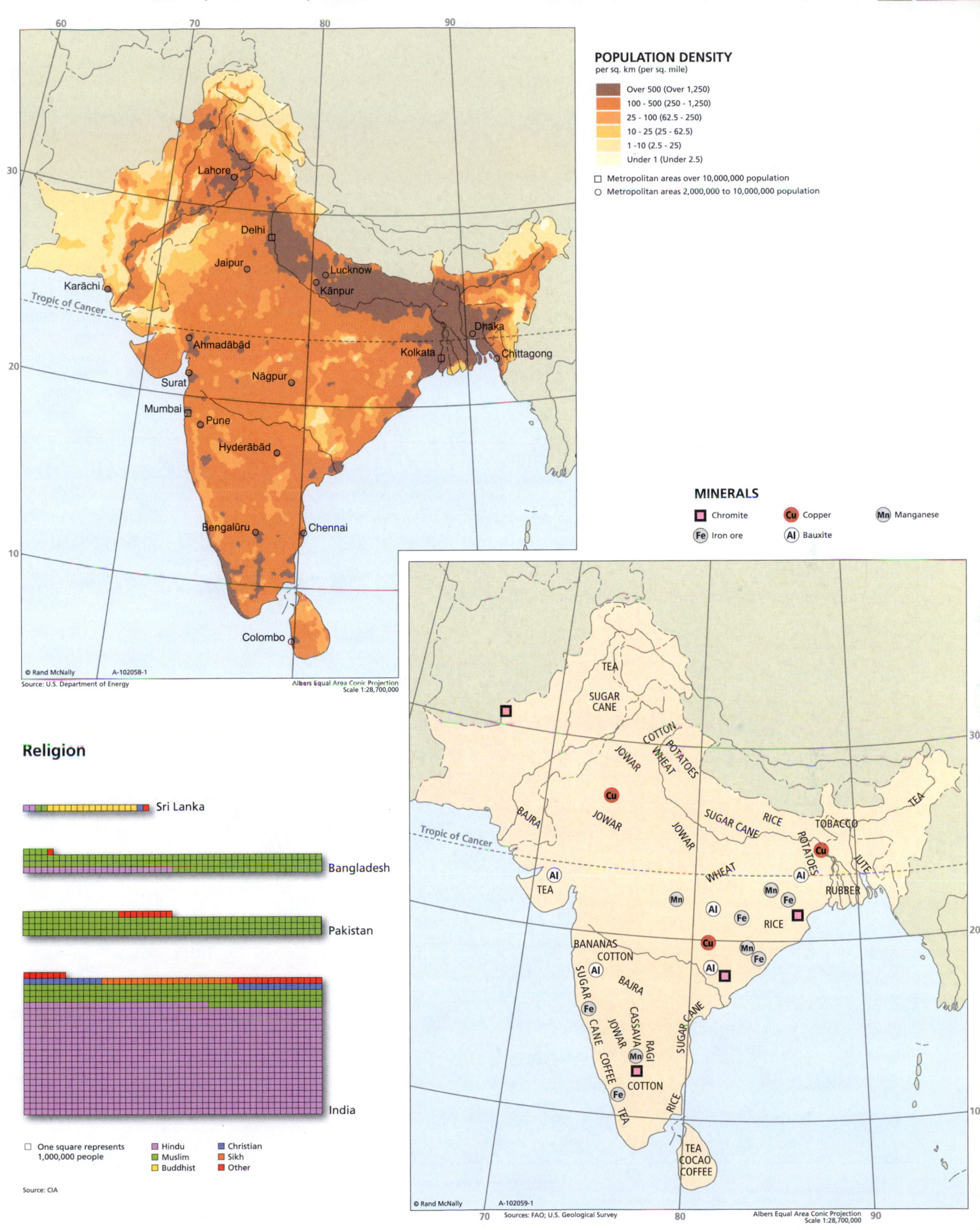

POPULATION DENSITY
per sq. km (per sq. mile)

- Over 500 (Over 1,250)
- 100 - 500 (250 - 1,250)
- 25 - 100 (62.5 - 250)
- 10 - 25 (25 - 62.5)
- 1 - 10 (2.5 - 25)
- Under 1 (Under 2.5)

□ Metropolitan areas over 10,000,000 population
○ Metropolitan areas 2,000,000 to 10,000,000 population

© Rand McNally A-102058-1

Source: U.S. Department of Energy

Albers Equal Area Conic Projection
Scale 1:28,700,000

MINERALS

■ Chromite   ● Cu Copper   Mn Manganese
Fe Iron ore   Al Bauxite

Religion

Sri Lanka
Bangladesh
Pakistan
India

□ One square represents 1,000,000 people

- Hindu
- Muslim
- Buddhist
- Christian
- Sikh
- Other

Source: CIA

© Rand McNally A-102059-1   Sources: FAO; U.S. Geological Survey   Albers Equal Area Conic Projection
Scale 1:28,700,000

0   40   80   120   160   200   240 Miles
0   40 80 120 160 200 240 280 320 360 400 Kilometers

Lambert Azimuthal Equal Area Projection
Scale 1:8,000,000
One inch to 128 miles
One cm to 80 km

0   40   80   120   160   200   240 Miles

0 40 80 120 160 200 240 280 320 360 400 Kilometers

Lambert Azimuthal Equal Area Projection
Scale 1:8,000,000
One inch to 128 miles
One cm to 80 km

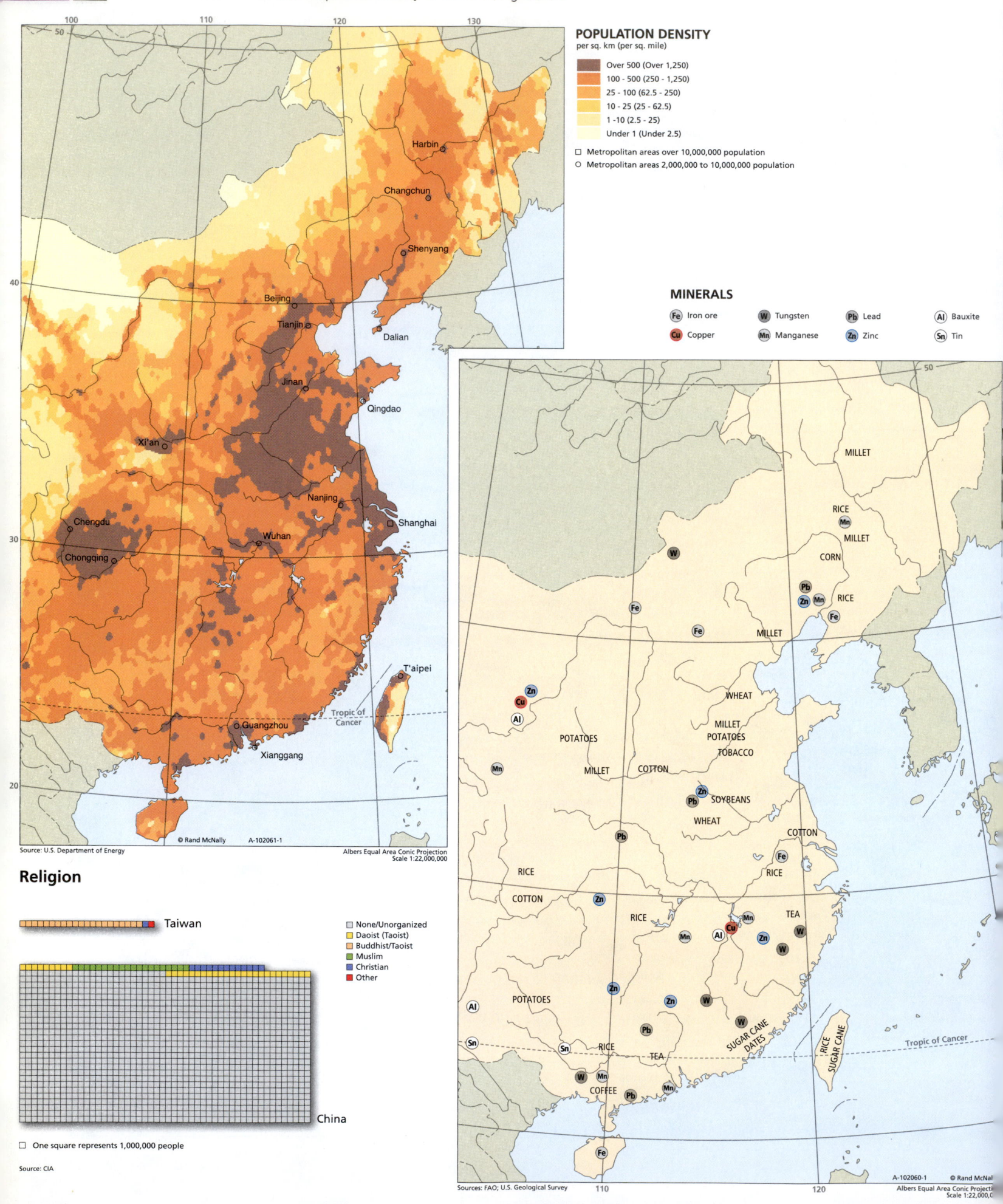

CHINA

LIAONING

JILIN

NORTH KOREA

HAMGYÕNG-BUKTO

YANGGANG-DO

CHAGANG-DO

HAMGYÕNG-NAMDO

P'YÕNGAN-BUKTO

P'YÕNGAN-NAMDO

P'YÕNGYANG

P'YÕNGYANG-SI

NAMP'O-SI

KANGWÕN-DO

HWANGHAE-BUKTO

HWANGHAE-NAMDO

KAESÕNG-SI

SEOUL (SÕUL)

INCH'ÕN

INCH'ÕN-GWANGYÕKSI

KYÕNGGI-DO

KANGWÕN-DO

SOUTH KOREA

CH'UNGCH'ÕNG-BUKTO

CH'UNGCH'ÕNG-NAMDO

KYÕNGSANG-BUKTO

CHÕLLA-BUKTO

KYÕNGSANG-NAMDO

KWANGJU-GWANGYÕKSI

CHÕLLA-NAMDO

PUSAN

PUSAN-GWANGYÕKSI

TAEGU-GWANGYÕKSI

ULSAN-GWANGYÕKSI

TAEJÕN-GWANGYÕKSI

RUSSIA

NAJIN SÕNBONG-SI

KOREA BAY

YELLOW SEA

SEA OF JAPAN

Korea Strait

JAPAN

HONSHU

YAMAGUCHI

Both North Korea and South Korea claim to be the sole legitimate government of Korea.

Lambert Conformal Conic Projection
Scale 1:4,000,000
One inch to 64 miles
One cm to 40 km

0   20   40   60   80   100   120 Miles
0   20   40   60   80   100   120   140   160   180   200 Kilometers

© Rand McNally
A-101809-1

MANCHURIA

HEILONGJIANG

CHINA

Jiamusi
Tangyuan
Youyi
Baoqing
Raohe
Bikin
Svetlaya

RUSSIA

Kholmsk
Pravda
Yuzhno-Sakhalinsk
Nevel'sk
Gornozavodsk
SAKHALIN
Korsakov

Tatar Strait
OSTROV MONERON
Zaliv Aniva
Aniva

SEA OF OKHOTSK

Shuangyashan
Jixian
Boli
Huanan
Qitaihe
Mishan

La Perouse Strait

The islands known in Japan as the Northern Territories and in Russia as the Southern Kuril Islands are occupied by Russia and claimed by Japan.

Mudanjiang
Hailin
Ning'an
Muling
Suifenhe
REBUN-TŌ
RISHIRI-TŌ
Wakkanai

OSTROV KUNASHIR (KUNASHIRI-TŌ) (Rus.)

Dunhua

JILIN

Yanji
Yanji (Longjing)
Tumen
Helong
Hoeryŏng-up
Musan-ŭp
Najin

HOKKAIDŌ

Nayoro
Mombetsu
SHIRETOKO-MISAKI
OSTROVA ZELENYY

Rumoi
Fukagawa
Asahikawa
Kitami
Abashiri
Takikawa
Bibai
Furano
Obihiro
Nemuro

Ch'ŏngjin

Asahi-dake
7513 ft.
2290 m

Kyŏngsŏng-ŭp
SAPPORO
Otaru
Ebetsu
Eniwa
Chitose
Kushiro
Akkeshi

Hyesan
Kapsan-ŭp

Esashi
Ō-SHIMA
Hakodate

NORTH KOREA

Tanch'ŏn-ŭp

Tsugaru-kaikyō
Mutsu

Sinch'ang-ŭp

Goshogawara
Aomori
Misawa
Hirosaki
Hachinohe
Odate
Towada
Kuji

SEA OF JAPAN

Noshiro
Oga
Akita
Morioka
Miyako
Honjō
Yokote
Kitakami
Kamaishi

JAPAN

Ryōtsu
SADO

Sakata
Tsuruoka
Shinjō
Furukawa
Tendō
Ishinomaki

PACIFIC OCEAN

Yamagata
Murakami
Sendai
Natori

Niigata
Niitsu
Shibata
Yonezawa
Fukushima
Haramachi

Sanjō
Aizu-wakamatsu
Kōriyama
Iwaki
Kitaibaraki
Hitachi

Wajima
Kashiwazaki
Joetsu
Nagaoka
Tōkamachi
Sukagawa
Kuroiso
Otawara

NOTO-HANTŌ
Nanao
Itoigawa
Nagano
Utsunomiya
Hitachinaka

Himi
Uozu
Takaoka
Toyama
Maebashi
Takasaki
Ashikaga
Mito
Tsukuba

Kanazawa
Kaga
Komatsu
Matsumoto
Takayama
Shiojiri
Chino
Kumagaya

Fukui
Takefu
Wakasa-wan
Tsuruga

SOUTH KOREA

Chumunjin
Kangnŭng
Tonghae
Samch'ŏk
ULLŬNG-DO (S. Kor.)
Ulchin

Yŏngdŏk
P'ohang
Kyŏngju
Ulsan

OKI-SHOTŌ

Matsue
Tottori
Izumo
Yonago

SAITAMA
KAWASAKI
TOKYO
Chiba
YOKOHAMA
Yokosuka

Hamada
Tsuyama
Fukuchiyama
Maizuru
Ōgaki
Gifu
NAGOYA
Iida
Fuji-san
12,388 ft.
3776 m

PUSAN
Korea Strait

Hikone
Otsu
Fuji
Chōshi

KAMINO-SHIMA
TSUSHIMA
SHIMONO-SHIMA
Izuhara

Miyoshi
Hiroshima
Fukuyama
Kurashiki
Okayama
KYOTO
KOBE
ŌSAKA
Toyohashi
Shizuoka
Numazu

Masuda
Yamaguchi
Iwakuni
Kure
Akashi
Sakai
Tsu
Ise-wan
Shimizu
Tateyama
Ō-SHIMA

Shimonoseki
Tokuyama
Ube
Iizuka
Usa
Takamatsu
Kishiwada
Ise
Hamamatsu
Fujieda

Munakata
FUKUOKA
Kitakyūshū
Matsuyama
Niihama
Wakayama
Enshū-nada

IKI
HIRADO-SHIMA
Saga
Hita
Beppu
Ōita
Tokushima

Kurume
Kumamoto
Kōchi
Anan
Tanabe
Gobō
Shingū

GOTŌ-RETTŌ
Fukue
Sasebo
Ōmuta
Kujū-san
5869 ft
1787 m
SHIKOKU
Uwajima
Muroto
Tosa-wan

FUKUE-JIMA
Nagasaki
AMAKUSA-SHIMO-SHIMA
Yatsushiro
Hitoyoshi
Nobeoka
Hyūga

EAST CHINA SEA

Sendai
Miyazaki
Miyakonojō
Bungo-suidō
Saiki
Nakamura
SHIONO-MISAKI
Kumano-nada

Kagoshima
Kanoya
Nichinan
HACHIJŌ-JIMA

SATA-MISAKI
ŌSUMI-SHOTŌ
Nishinoomote
TANEGA-SHIMA
Ōsumi-kaikyō

PHILIPPINE SEA

YAKU-SHIMA
RYUKYU ISLANDS (NANSEI-SHOTŌ)

NAKANO-SHIMA
SUWANOSE-JIMA

AOGA-SHIMA
KŌZU-SHIMA
NII-JIMA
MIYAKE-JIMA
MIKURA-JIMA

IZU-SHOTŌ
TORI SIMA
SŌHU GAN

© Rand McNally
A-101814-1

Lambert Conformal Conic Projection
Scale 1:8,000,000
One inch to 128 miles
One cm to 80 km

0 40 80 120 160 200 240 Miles
0 40 80 120 160 200 240 280 320 360 400 Kilometers

Inset map (a)

EAST CHINA SEA

AMAMI-Ō-SHIMA
Naze
KIKAI-SHIMA
Setouchi

RYUKYU ISLANDS (NANSEI-SHOTŌ) (Japan)
AMAMI-SHOTŌ

TOKUNO-SHIMA
OKINO-ERABU-SHIMA
YORON-JIMA

OKINAWA-SHOTŌ
Nago
Ishikawa
OKINAWA-JIMA

Okinawa
Naha
Ginowan
Itoman

PHILIPPINE SEA

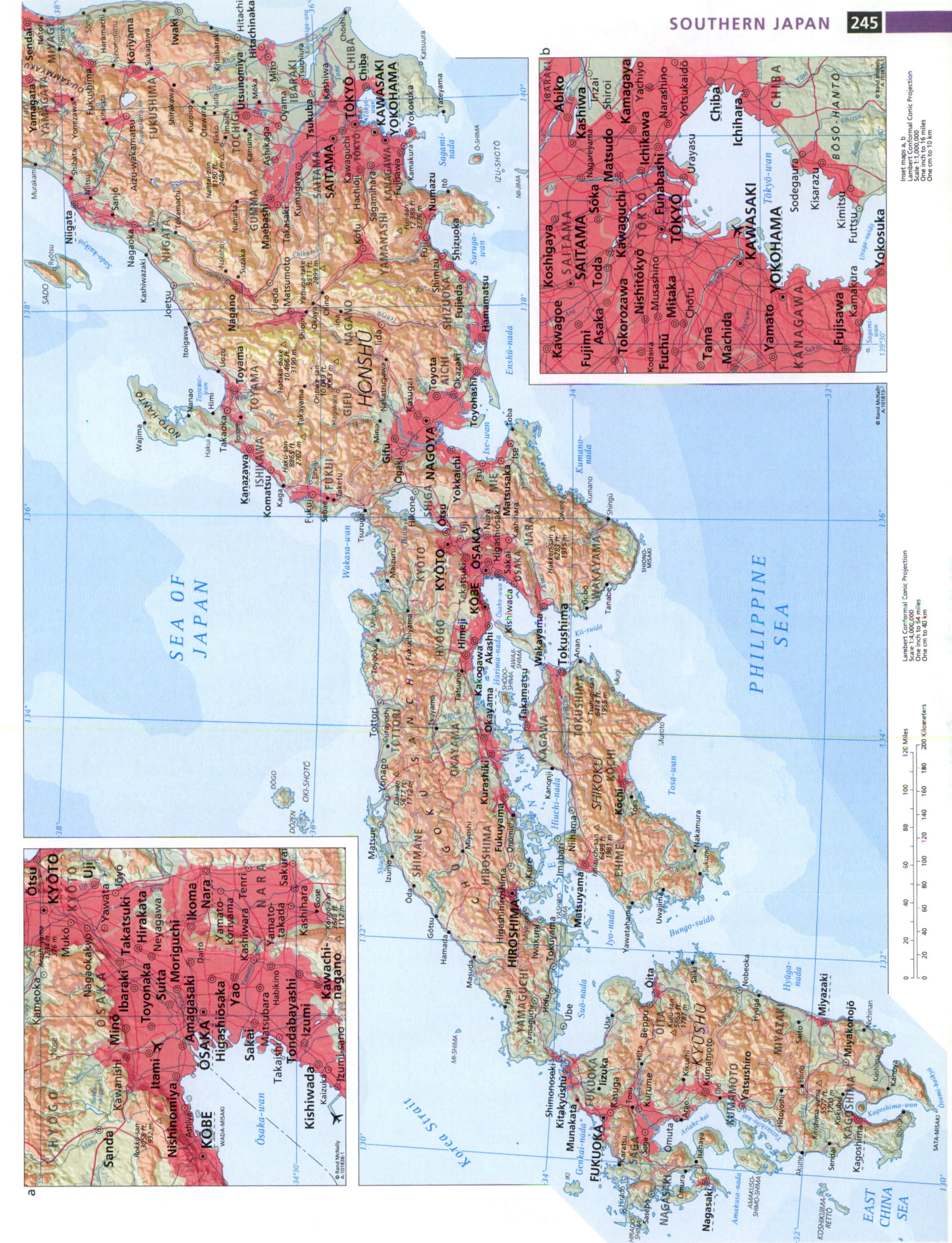

SEA OF JAPAN

PHILIPPINE SEA

EAST CHINA SEA

Korea Strait

HONSHU

SHIKOKU

KYUSHU

TOKYO

YOKOHAMA

KAWASAKI

CHIBA

SAITAMA

OSAKA

KOBE

KYOTO

NAGOYA

HIROSHIMA

FUKUOKA

NAGASAKI

KUMAMOTO

KAGOSHIMA

MIYAZAKI

Inset maps a, b
Lambert Conformal Conic Projection
Scale 1:1,000,000
One inch to 16 miles
One cm to 10 km

Lambert Conformal Conic Projection
Scale 1:4,000,000
One inch to 54 miles
One cm to 40 km

© Rand McNally
A-101813-1

Lambert Azimuthal Equal Area Projection
Scale 1:8,000,000
One inch to 128 miles
One cm to 80 km

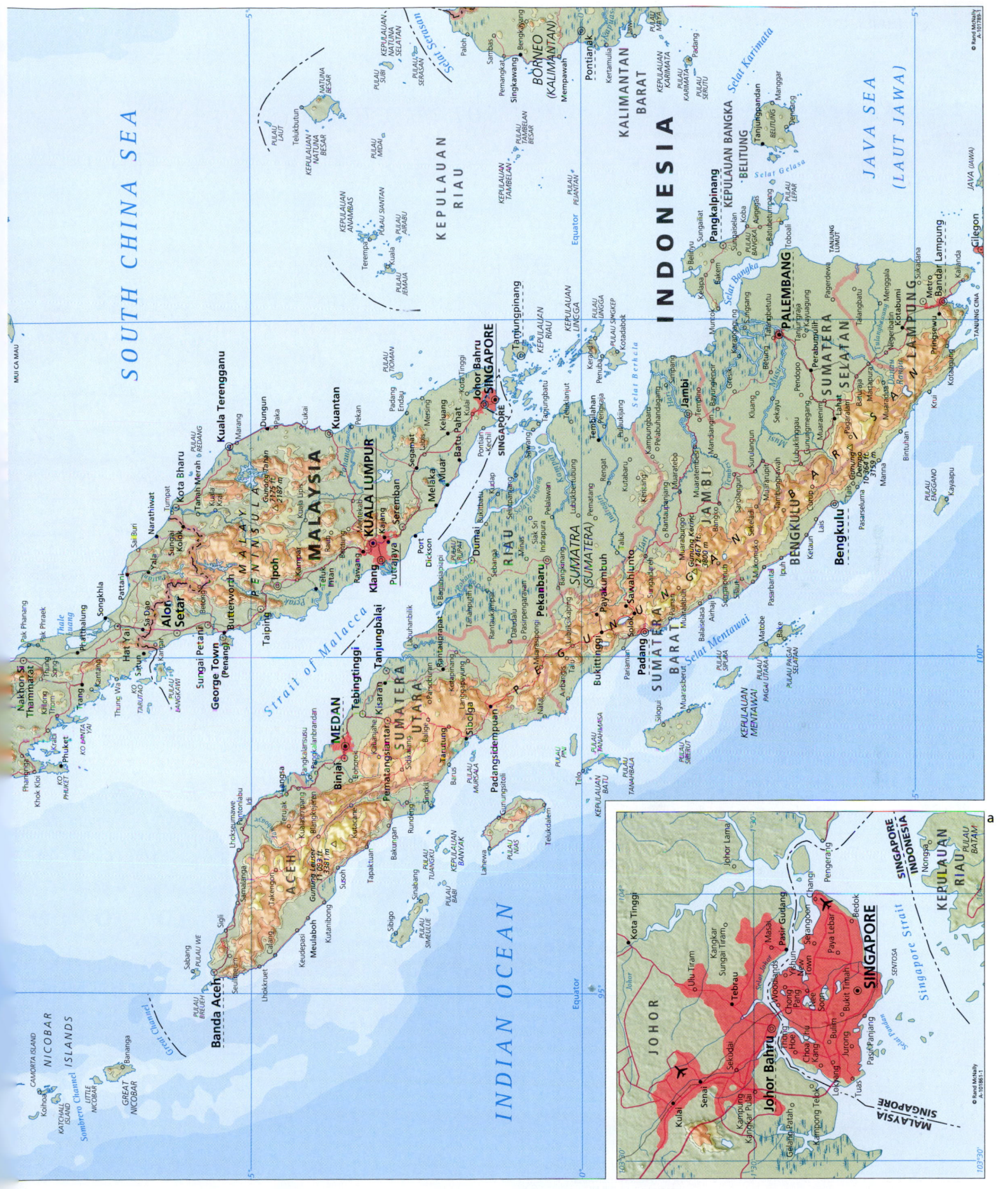

SOUTH CHINA SEA

INDONESIA

JAVA SEA
(LAUT JAWA)

KALIMANTAN
BARAT

BORNEO
(KALIMANTAN)

KEPULAUAN
RIAU

KEPULAUAN BANGKA
BELITUNG

MALAYSIA

Kuala Terengganu

Kuantan

KUALA LUMPUR

SINGAPORE
Johor Bahru

SUMATERA
(SUMATERA)

SUMATERA
UTARA

RIAU

JAMBI

PALEMBANG

SUMATERA
SELATAN

LAMPUNG

Bandar Lampung

MEDAN

George Town
(Penang)

Strait of Malacca

BENGKULU

Bengkulu

ACEH

Banda Aceh

INDIAN OCEAN

NICOBAR
ISLANDS

Equator

Inset map a
Lambert Conformal Conic Projection
Scale 1:1,000,000
One inch to 16 miles
One cm to 10 km

a

JOHOR

SINGAPORE
INDONESIA

KEPULAUAN
RIAU

PULAU
BATAM

SINGAPORE

Johor Bahru

MALAYSIA
SINGAPORE

Singapore Strait

THAILAND

SOUTH CHINA SEA

Hat Yai
Pattani
Sai Buri
Narathiwat
Tumpat
Kota Bharu

PULAU
REDANG

Alor
Setar
Sungai
Kolok
Tanah
Merah
Kuala Krai

Kuala Terengganu

George
Town
(Penang)
Butterworth
Kuala Lipis
Marang

MALAY
PENINSULA

Taiping
Ipoh
Gunong Tahan
7175 ft
2187 m
Dungun
Paka
Cukai

Kampar

MALAYSIA
Kuantan

Raub
Bentong
Pekan

Rawang
Mentekab

Klang
KUALA LUMPUR
Kajang
Putrajaya
Seremban

Tanjungbalai
Port
Dickson
Segamat
Labis
Mersing

Melaka
Muar
Batu Pahat
Keluang

Rantauprapat
Kotapinang
Bagansiapiapi
Pontian
Kechil
Kulai
Kota Tinggi

SUMATERA
UTARA

Labuhanbilik
Bukitbatu
Johor Bahru
SINGAPORE

Dumai
Kudap
SINGAPORE

Daludalu
Sebanga
Selatpanjang
Tanjungpinang

RIAU
Siak Sri
Indrapura

Minas

Pekanbaru

KEPULAUAN
RIAU

KEPULAUAN
ANAMBAS

Terempa
PULAU SIANTAN

KEPULAUAN
NATUNA
BESAR

Telukbutun
NATUNA
BESAR

PULAU
LAUT

Miri
Niah

Bintulu
Lutong

Mukah
Igan
Balingian

SARAWAK

Sibu
MALAYSIA

Kapit
Belaga

Sematan
Sri Aman
Betong

UPPER KAPUAS MTS

Kuching
Tanjong Datu
Selat Serasan

Paloh
Bau
Simunjan
Sanggau
Sintang

KALIMANTAN
BARAT

Singkawang
Bengkayang
Ngabang
Mempawah
Pontianak

PEGUNUNGAN MULLER

Gunung Niut
5581 ft
1701 m

KALIMANTAN
TENGAH

Palangkaraya

INDIAN OCEAN

JAVA SEA
(LAUT JAWA)

GREATER SUNDA-

I N D O N

CHRISTMAS
ISLAND
(Austl.)
Settlement

JAKARTA
BANDUNG
SURABAYA
SEMARANG

JAVA
(JAWA)

0   40   80   120   160   200   240 Miles
0 40 80 120 160 200 240 280 320 360 400 Kilometers

Lambert Azimuthal Equal Area Projection
Scale 1:8,000,000
One inch to 128 miles
One cm to 80 km

PHILIPPINES

SOUTH CHINA SEA

PHILIPPINE SEA

SULU SEA

CELEBES SEA

LUZON

MINDORO

PANAY

NEGROS

CEBU

BOHOL

SAMAR

LEYTE

PALAWAN

MINDANAO

MALAYSIA

BORNEO

a

SOUTH CHINA SEA

Bashi Channel
AMIANAN ISLAND
ITBAYAT ISLAND   BATAN ISLANDS
Basco
BATAN ISLAND

Luzon   Strait

BABUYAN ISLANDS
CALAYAN ISLAND
Calayan
DALUPIRI ISLAND   BABUYAN ISLAND
FUGA ISLAND   CAMIGUIN ISLAND

PHILIPPINE SEA

Pagudpud   Babuyan Channel   PALAUI ISLAND
CAPE BOJEADOR   ESCARPADA POINT
Laoag   Aparri
San Nicolas   Gonzaga
Batac
LUZON
Mt. Sicapoo
7329 ft.
2234 m

© Rand McNally   A-101808-1

Lambert Conformal Conic Projection
Scale 1:6,000,000
One inch to 96 miles
One cm to 60 km

0   30   60   90   120   150   180 Miles
0   30   60   90   120 150 180 210 240 270 300 Kilometers

© Rand McNally   A-101807-1

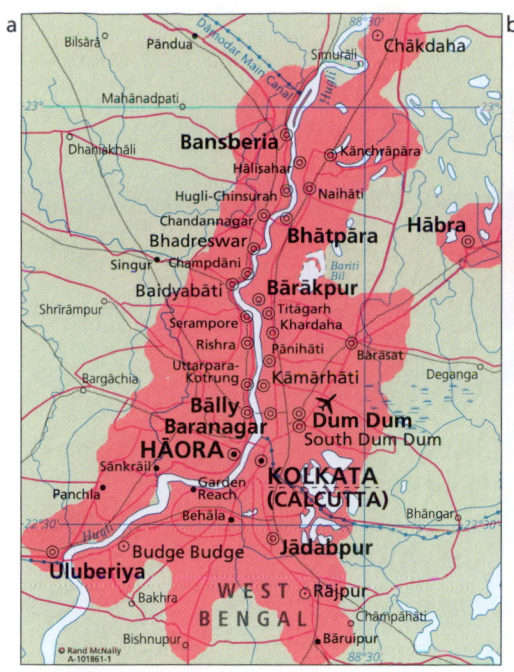

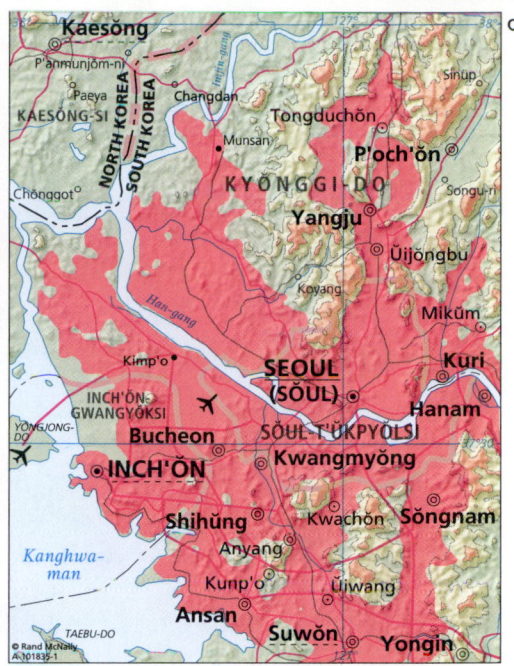
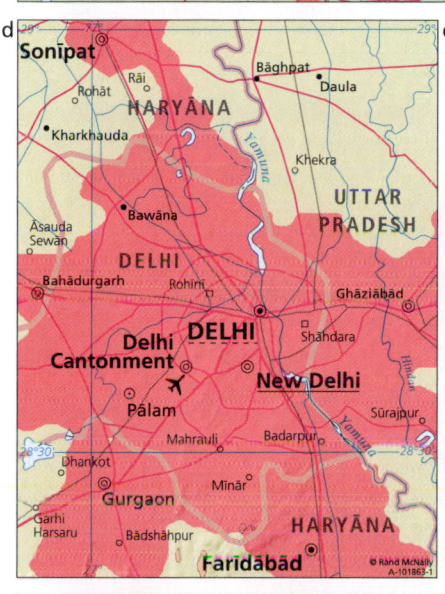

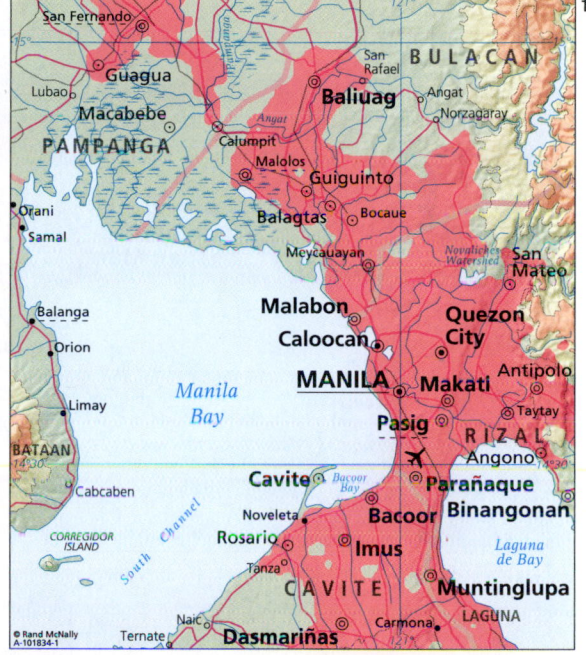
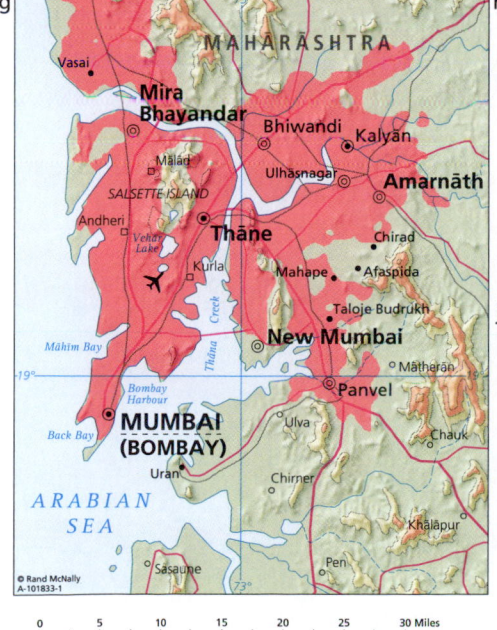
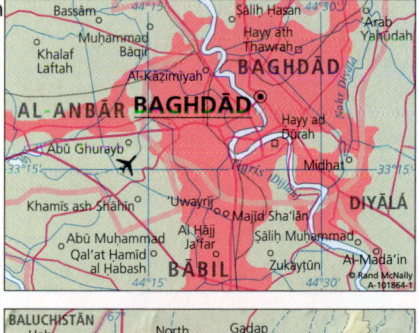
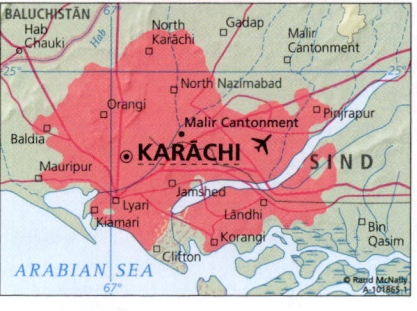
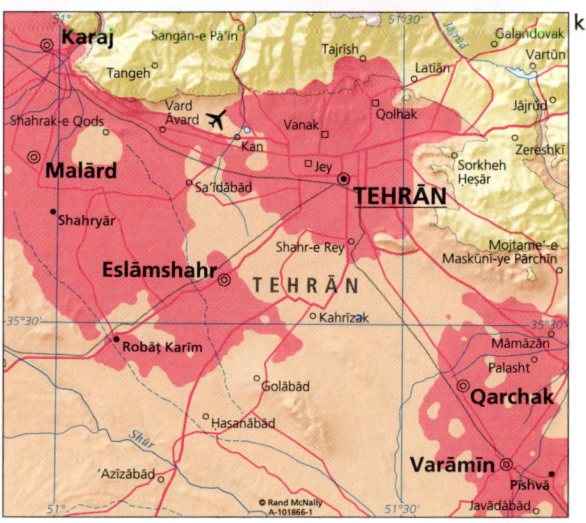

Lambert Conformal Conic Projection
Scale 1:1,000,000
One inch to 16 miles
One cm to 10 km

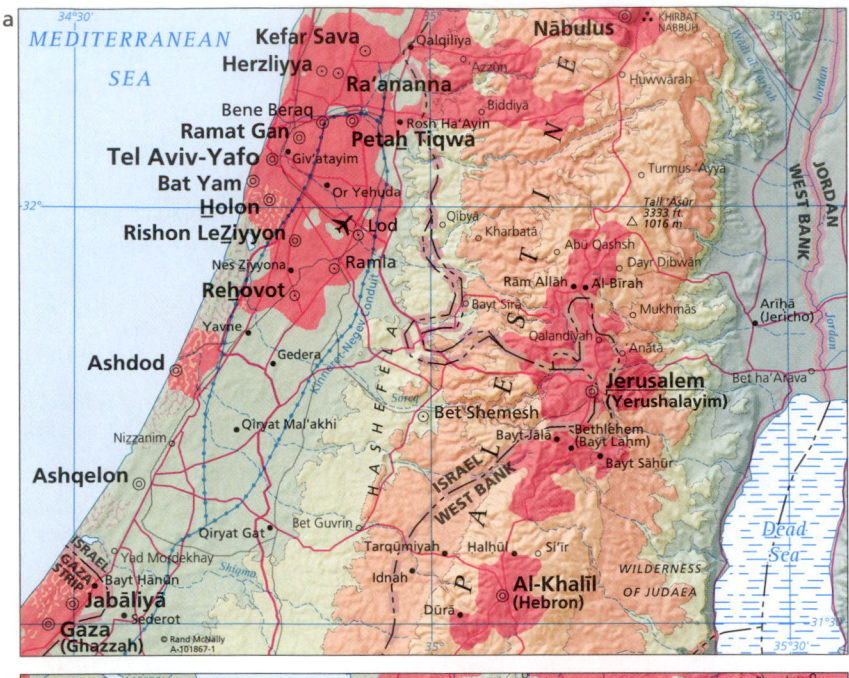

a

MEDITERRANEAN SEA

Kefar Sava
Herzliyya
Ra'ananna
Bene Beraq
Ramat Gan
Tel Aviv-Yafo
Bat Yam
Holon
Rishon LeZiyyon
Rehovot
Ashdod
Nizzanim
Ashqelon
GAZA STRIP
Jabāliyā
Gaza (Ghazzah)
Sederot
Bayt Hānūn

Qalqiliya
Azzun
Biddiya
Petah Tiqwa
Or Yehuda
Lod
Ramla
Nes Ziyyona
Yavne
Gedera
Qiryat Mal'akhi
Yad Mordekhay
Qiryat Gat
Bet Guvrin
Idnah
Dūrā

Nābulus
CHIRBAT NABBŪH
Huwwāran
Turmus 'Ayya
Abu Qashsh
Dayr Dibwān
Rām Allāh
Al-Bīrah
Qalandiyah
Mukhmās
'Anāta
Jerusalem (Yerushalayim)
Bet Shemesh
Bayt-Jālā
Bethlehem (Bayt Lahm)
Bayt Sāhūr
Al-Khalīl (Hebron)
Halhūl
Tarqūmiyah
Si'īr

WEST BANK
JORDAN
Tall 'Āsūr 3333 ft. 1016 m
Bet ha'Arava
Arīḥā (Jericho)
Dead Sea
WILDERNESS OF JUDAEA

ISRAEL
PALESTINE
HASHEFELA

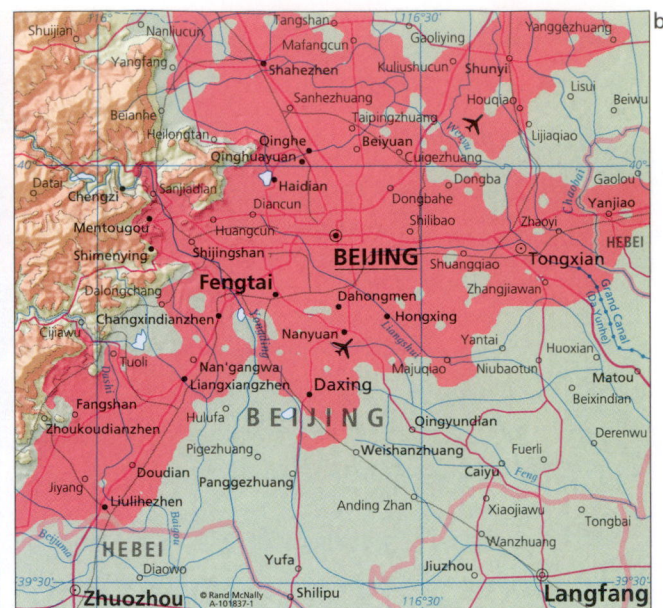

b

Shuijian
Nankucun
Tangshan
Gaoliying
Yanggezhuang
Yangfang
Mafangcun
Kuliushucun
Shunyi
Houjia
Lisu
Beiwu
Beianhe
Heilongtan
Shahezhen
Sanhezhuang
Taipingzhuang
Beiyuan
Lijiaqiao
Datou
Chengzi
Qinghe
Haidian
Cuigezhuang
Dongba
Yanjiao
Gaolou
Mentougou
Huangcun
Diancun
Shilibao
Dongbahe
Zhaoyi
Zhangjiawan
HEBEI
Shimenying
Shijingtai
BEIJING
Tongxian
Changxindianzhen
Dalongzhang
Dahongmen
Hongxing
Yantai
Huoxian
Matou
Tuoli
Nanyuan
Hongliang
Niubaotun
Beixindian
Fangshan
Nan'gangwa
Majuqiao
Derenzhu
Huluja
Liangxiangzhen
BEIJING
Daxing
Qingyundian
Zhoukoudianzhen
Pigezhuang
Doudian
Panggezhuang
Fuerli
Jiyang
Liulihezhen
Weishanzhuang
Caiyu
Xiaojiawu
Anding Zhan
Tongbai
HEBEI
Diaowo
Yufa
Jiuzhou
Wanzhuang
Zhuozhou
Shilipu
Langfang

c

Gangkou
Longhua
Fuyong
Pingshan
GUANGDONG
Buji
Zhangjiablan
Xin'an
Shenzhen
Dahuan
Nantou
Kuichong
Nanlang
Shekou
Yantian
Zhongshan
Zhujiang Kou
Hau-Hoi Wan
Sheung Shui
Tai Pang Wan
GUANGDONG
Yúen Long
Tai Po
Tuen Mun
XIANGGANG
XINJIULONG
Sha Tin
Me On Shan
Pinglan
Tangjia
Tsing Yi
Jiulong (Kowloon)
Port Shelter
Tseung Kwan O
Zhuhai
Tung Chung
Aberdeen
HONG KONG (XIANGGANG)
Sanxiang
Tai O
LANTAU ISLAND
West Lamma Channel
East Lamma Channel
Macau (Aomen)
AOMEN
Taipa
SANZAO DAO
DAHENGQIN DAO
Luhuan
SOUTH CHINA SEA

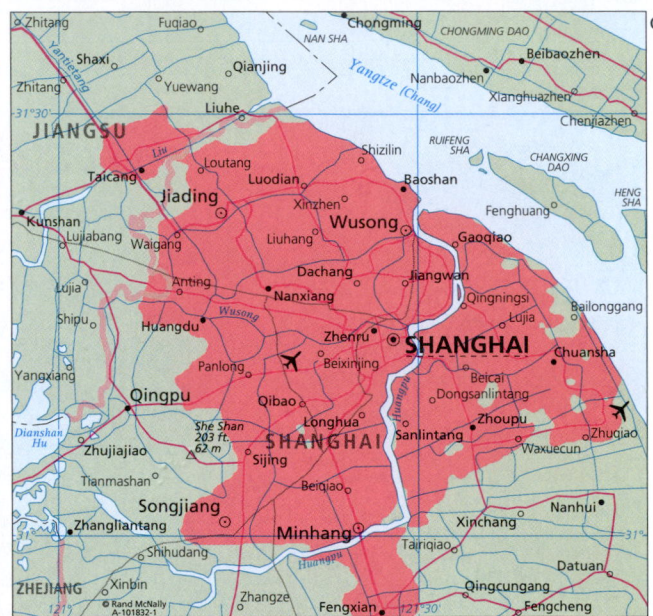

d

Zhitang
Chongming
CHONGMING DAO
Beibaozhen
Shaxi
Fuqiao
NAN SHA
Zhitang
Qianjing
Yuewang
Liuhe
Nanbaozhen
Xianghuazhen
Chenjiazhen
JIANGSU
Taicang
Shizilin
RUIFENG SHA
Loutang
Luodian
Baoshan
Kunshan
Jiading
Xinzhen
Wusong
CHANGXING DAO
Lujiabang
Waigang
Liuhang
Jiangwan
Gaoqiao
HENG SHA
Anting
Dachang
Lujia
Shipu
Huangdu
Nanxiang
Qingningsi
Bailonggang
Yangxiang
Zhenru
Beixinjing
SHANGHAI
Qingpu
Panlong
Qibao
Beical
Chuansha
Dianshan Hu
Zhujiajiao
She Shan 203 ft. 62 m
Sijing
SHANGHAI
Dongsanlintang
Zhoupu
Tianmashan
Beijiao
Waxuecun
Zhujiao
Songjiang
Xinchang
Nanhui
Zhangliantang
Minhang
Tairiqiao
Qingcungang
ZHEJIANG
Shihudang
Xinbin
Zhangze
Fengxian
Fengcheng
Datuan

e

Kāsimpur
Jaydebpur
Pākrajanj
Bhudi
Dhīrāsrām
Pubāil
Dhāmrai
Narsinghdi
Tongi
Kāliganj
Dānga
Sābhār
Gulshan
Rupganj
Bīraba
Ajihāzar
Mīrpur
Bānchhārāmpur
Ayubnagar
Fatulla
DHAKA
Baidyer Bāzār
Rohitpur
Srinagar
Nārāyanganj
DHAKA
Daudkandi
Nāyāgaon
Munshiganj
Bāghia
Ganges (Padma)
Rājābāri
Naria
Kedarpur
Mohanpur
CHITTAGONG
Matlab Bāzār
Tropic of Cancer

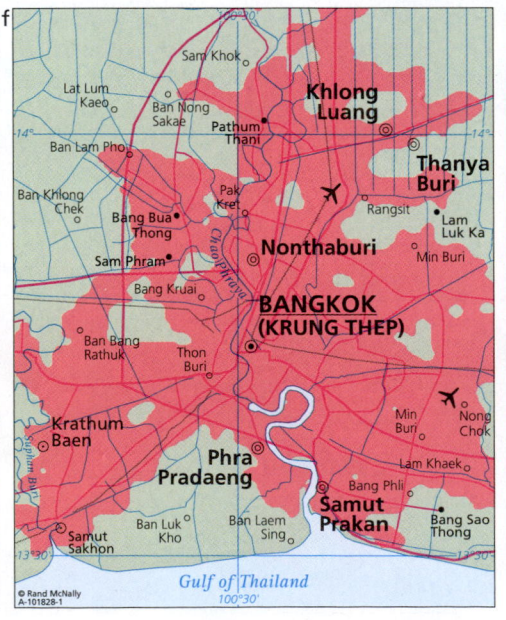

f

Sam Khok
Lat Lum Kaeo
Ban Nong Sakae
Pathum Thani
Khlong Luang
Ban Lam Pho
Thanya Buri
Ban Khlong Chek
Pak Kret
Rangsit
Lam Luk Ka
Bang Bua Thong
Min Buri
Sam Phram
Nonthaburi
Bang Kruai
BANGKOK (KRUNG THEP)
Bang Bang Rathuk
Thon Buri
Min Buri
Nong Chok
Krathum Baen
Lam Khaek
Bang Phli
Phra Pradaeng
Bang Sao Thong
Ban Luk Kho
Samut Prakan
Samut Sakhon
Ban Laem Sing
Gulf of Thailand

g

Teluknaga
Kedaung
Teluk Jakarta
Utankrmat
Sundakelapa
Kosambi
Cengkareng
Babelan
Sepatan
JAKARTA
TANGERANG
JAKARTA RAYA
BEKASI
Dukuhatas
Cibitung
BANTEN
Selangcau
Serpong
Taman Mina
Tambun
Ciputat
Cijantung
BEKASI
Cileungsir
DEPOK
Parung
Cibarusa
Rumpin
Cibinong
Jonggol
JAWA BARAT
Kedungmanggu
Leuwiliang
Gunung Salak 7254 ft. 2211 m
Bogor
Ciawi
Cisarua

0 5 10 15 20 25 30 Miles
0 5 10 15 20 25 30 35 40 45 50 Kilometers

Lambert Conformal Conic Projection
Scale 1:1,000,000
One inch to 16 miles
One cm to 10 km

Lambert Azimuthal Equal Area Projection
Scale 1:40,000,000
One inch to 640 miles
One cm to 400 km

| 0 | 200 | 400 | 600 | 800 | 1000 | 1200 Miles |

| 0 | 200 | 400 | 600 | 800 | 1000 | 1200 | 1400 | 1600 | 1800 | 2000 Kilometers |

Lambert Azimuthal Equal Area Projection
Scale 1:40,000,000
One inch to 640 miles
One cm to 400 km

| 0 | 200 | 400 | 600 | 800 | 1000 | 1200 Miles |

| 0 | 200 | 400 | 600 | 800 | 1000 | 1200 | 1400 | 1600 | 1800 | 2000 Kilometers |

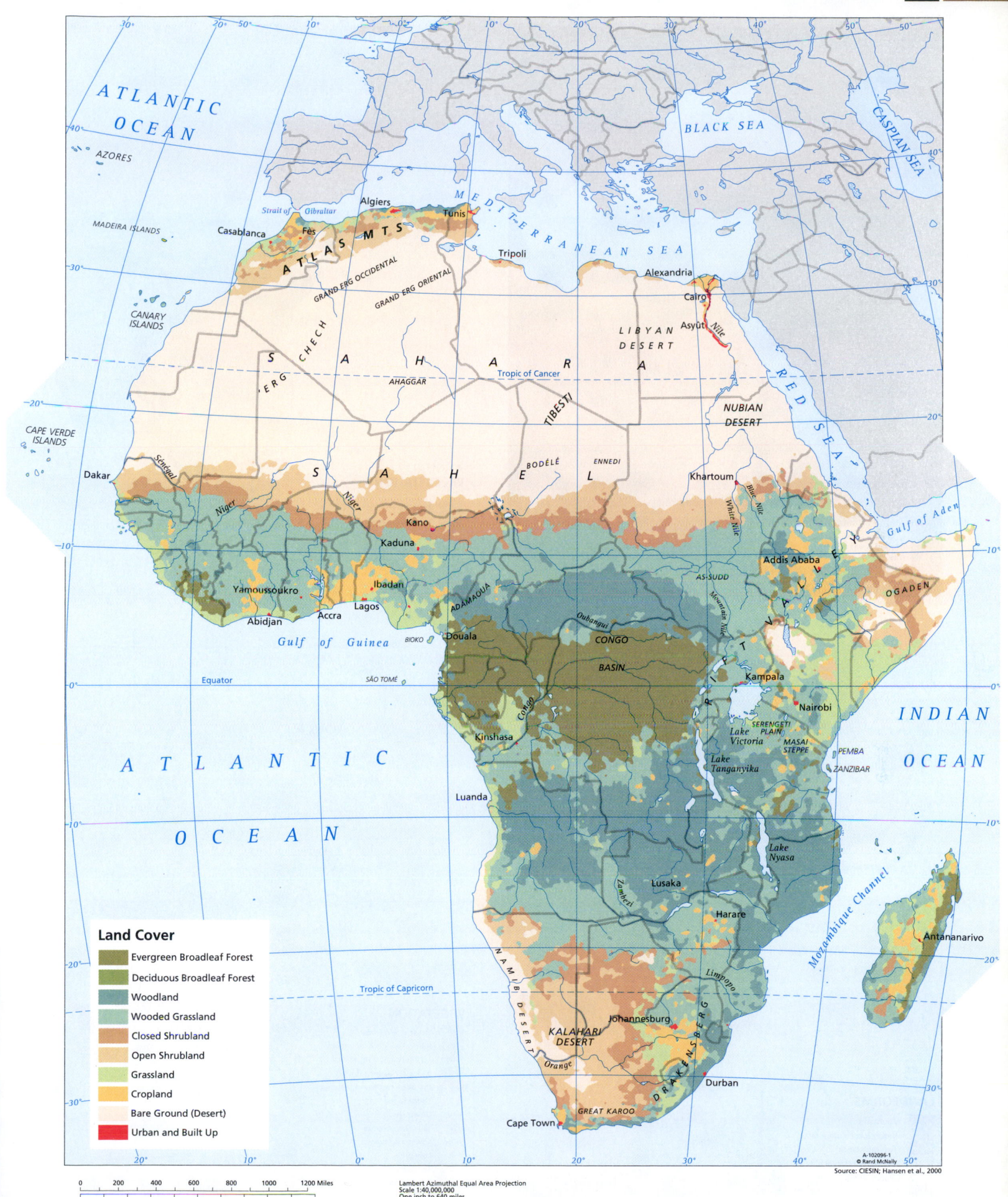

ATLANTIC OCEAN

AZORES

MADEIRA ISLANDS

CANARY ISLANDS

CAPE VERDE ISLANDS

BLACK SEA

CASPIAN SEA

MEDITERRANEAN SEA

Strait of Gibraltar
Algiers
Tunis
Casablanca
Fès
ATLAS MTS
Tripoli
Alexandria
Cairo
Asyût
Nile
LIBYAN DESERT
NUBIAN DESERT
RED SEA
Gulf of Aden

GRAND ERG OCCIDENTAL
GRAND ERG ORIENTAL
S A H A R A
Tropic of Cancer
ERG CHECH
ERG
AHAGGAR
TIBESTI
BODÉLÉ
ENNEDI

S A H E L
Dakar
Senegal
Niger
Niger
Kano
Kaduna
Khartoum
White Nile
Blue Nile
Addis Ababa
OGADEN

Yamoussoukro
Ibadan
Lagos
Accra
Abidjan
ADAMAOUA
Douala
BIOKO
CONGO BASIN
Oubangui
AS-SUDD
Mountain Nile
RIFT VALLEY
Kampala
Nairobi

Gulf of Guinea
SÃO TOMÉ
Equator
Congo
Kinshasa
SERENGETI PLAIN
Lake Victoria
MASAI STEPPE
PEMBA
ZANZIBAR

ATLANTIC OCEAN
Luanda
Lake Tanganyika

INDIAN OCEAN

Lake Nyasa
Zambezi
Lusaka
Harare
Mozambique Channel

Antananarivo

NAMIB DESERT
Tropic of Capricorn
Limpopo
KALAHARI DESERT
Johannesburg
DRAKENSBERG
Durban
Orange
GREAT KAROO
Cape Town

Land Cover

- Evergreen Broadleaf Forest
- Deciduous Broadleaf Forest
- Woodland
- Wooded Grassland
- Closed Shrubland
- Open Shrubland
- Grassland
- Cropland
- Bare Ground (Desert)
- Urban and Built Up

0 200 400 600 800 1000 1200 Miles
0 200 400 600 800 1000 1200 1400 1600 1800 2000 Kilometers

Lambert Azimuthal Equal Area Projection
Scale 1:40,000,000
One inch to 640 miles
One cm to 400 km

A-102096-1
© Rand McNally

Source: CIESIN; Hansen et al., 2000

Moderate Resolution
Imaging Spectroradiometer (MODIS)
true-color mosaic satellite image

Source: NASA Visible Earth program (http://visibleearth.nasa.gov/)

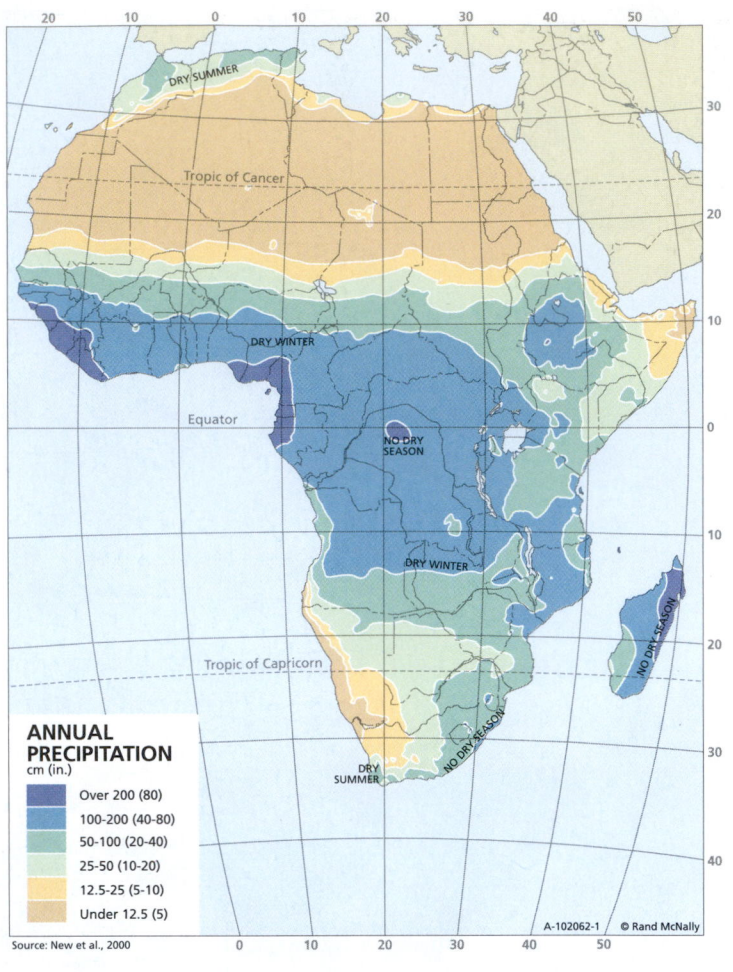

ANNUAL PRECIPITATION
cm (in.)

- Over 200 (80)
- 100–200 (40–80)
- 50–100 (20–40)
- 25–50 (10–20)
- 12.5–25 (5–10)
- Under 12.5 (5)

Source: New et al., 2000

A-102062-1 © Rand McNally

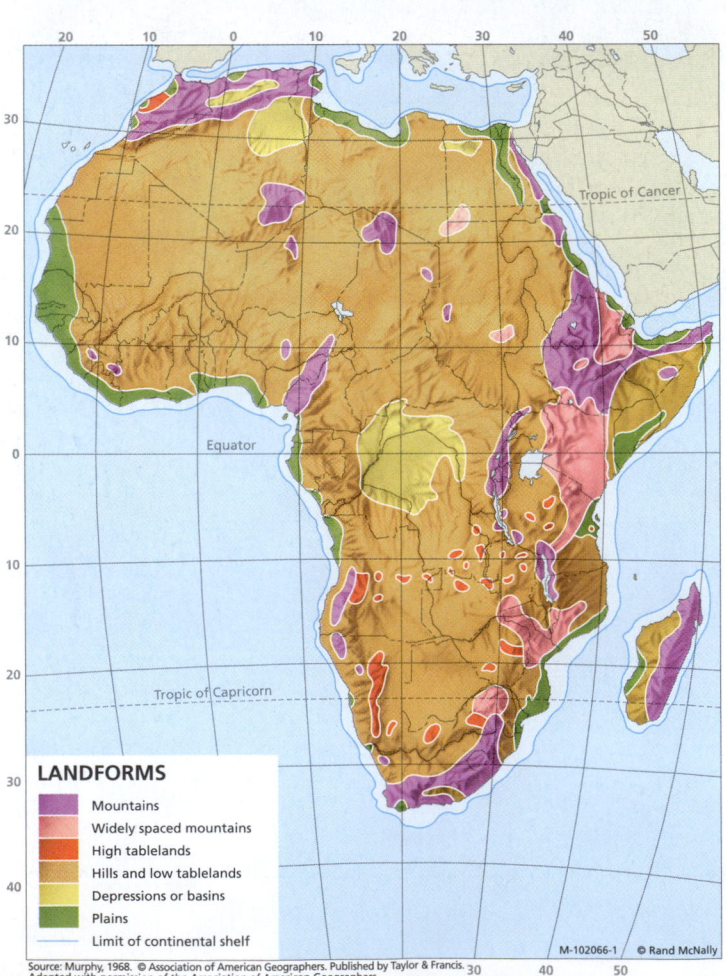

LANDFORMS

- Mountains
- Widely spaced mountains
- High tablelands
- Hills and low tablelands
- Depressions or basins
- Plains
- Limit of continental shelf

Source: Murphy, 1968. © Association of American Geographers. Published by Taylor & Francis.
Adapted with permission of the Association of American Geographers.

M-102066-1 © Rand McNally

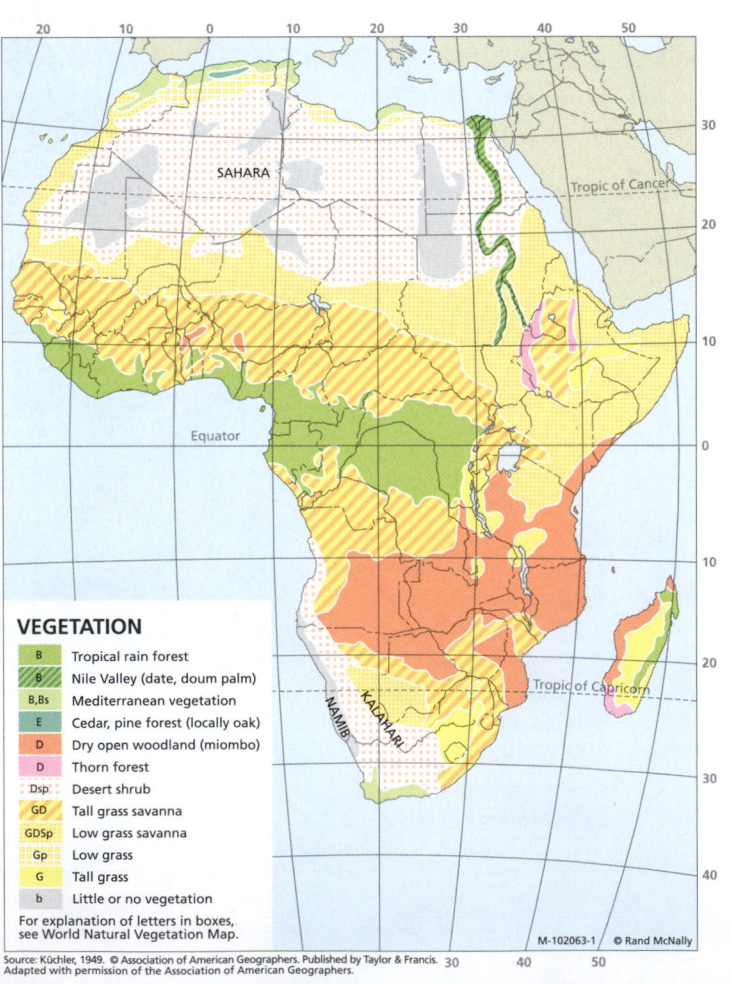

VEGETATION

B	Tropical rain forest
B	Nile Valley (date, doum palm)
B,Bs	Mediterranean vegetation
E	Cedar, pine forest (locally oak)
D	Dry open woodland (miombo)
D	Thorn forest
Dsp	Desert shrub
GD	Tall grass savanna
GDSp	Low grass savanna
Gp	Low grass
G	Tall grass
b	Little or no vegetation

For explanation of letters in boxes,
see World Natural Vegetation Map.

Source: Küchler, 1949. © Association of American Geographers. Published by Taylor & Francis.
Adapted with permission of the Association of American Geographers.

M-102063-1 © Rand McNally

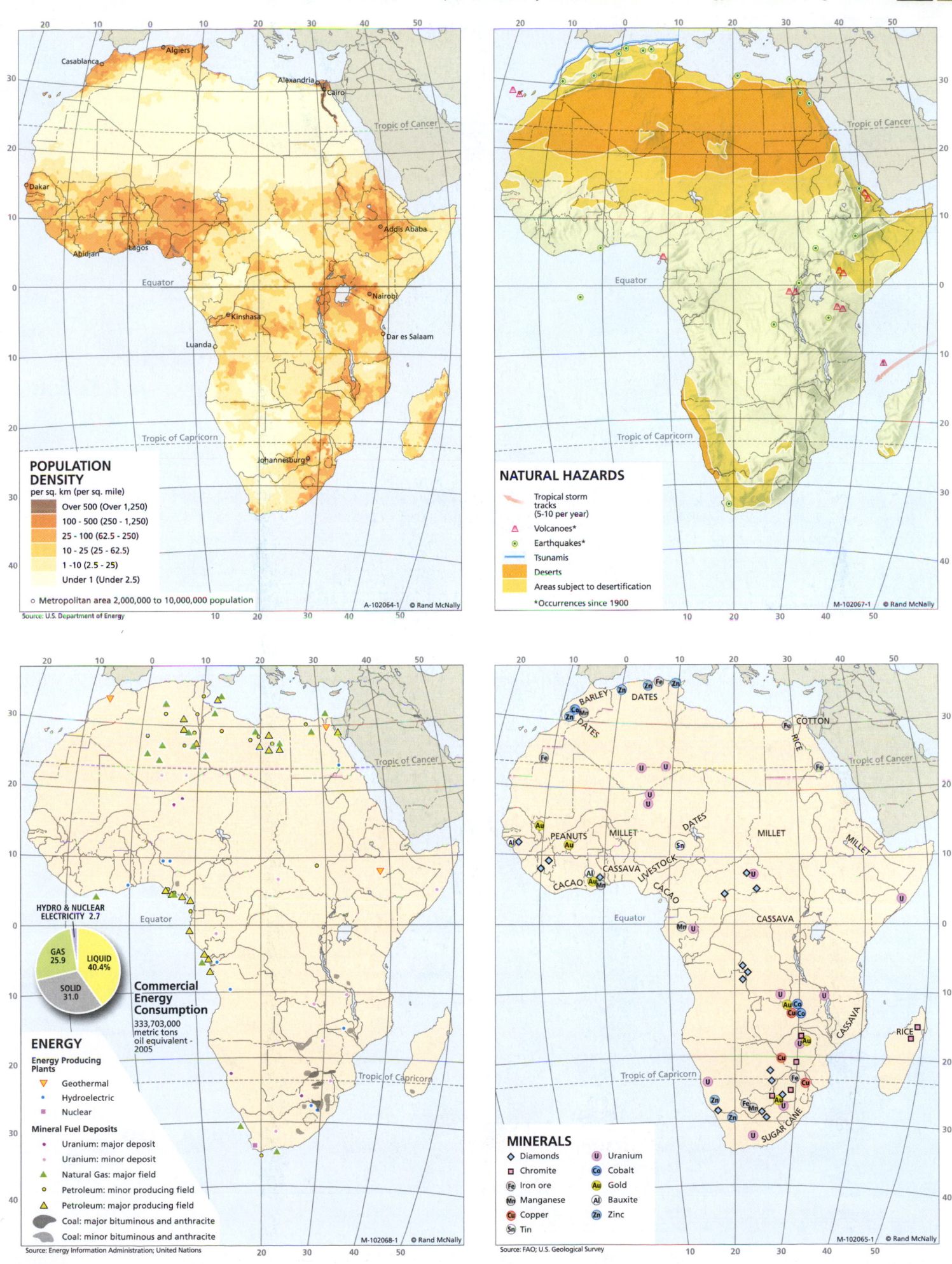

POPULATION DENSITY
per sq. km (per sq. mile)

- Over 500 (Over 1,250)
- 100 - 500 (250 - 1,250)
- 25 - 100 (62.5 - 250)
- 10 - 25 (25 - 62.5)
- 1 - 10 (2.5 - 25)
- Under 1 (Under 2.5)

○ Metropolitan area 2,000,000 to 10,000,000 population

Source: U.S. Department of Energy

A-102064-1 © Rand McNally

NATURAL HAZARDS

- Tropical storm tracks (5-10 per year)
- ▲ Volcanoes*
- ⊙ Earthquakes*
- Tsunamis
- Deserts
- Areas subject to desertification

*Occurrences since 1900

M-102067-1 © Rand McNally

ENERGY

Energy Producing Plants
- ▽ Geothermal
- • Hydroelectric
- ■ Nuclear

Mineral Fuel Deposits
- • Uranium: major deposit
- • Uranium: minor deposit
- ▲ Natural Gas: major field
- ○ Petroleum: minor producing field
- △ Petroleum: major producing field
- Coal: major bituminous and anthracite
- Coal: minor bituminous and anthracite

HYDRO & NUCLEAR ELECTRICITY 2.7

GAS 25.9
LIQUID 40.4%
SOLID 31.0

Commercial Energy Consumption
333,703,000 metric tons oil equivalent - 2005

Source: Energy Information Administration; United Nations

M-102068-1 © Rand McNally

MINERALS

- ◆ Diamonds
- ⬛ Chromite
- Ⓕ Iron ore
- Ⓜ Manganese
- Ⓒu Copper
- Ⓢn Tin
- Ⓤ Uranium
- Ⓒo Cobalt
- Ⓐu Gold
- Ⓐl Bauxite
- Ⓩn Zinc

Source: FAO; U.S. Geological Survey

M-102065-1 © Rand McNally

PORTUGAL

SPAIN

CABO DE SÃO VICENTE
Faro
Huelva
Sevilla
Jaén
Mulhacén
11 424 ft
3482 m
Granada
Cartagena
ALGIERS
(ALGER)

Cádiz
Gulf of
Cadiz
Málaga
Almería
Mostaganem
Oued Cheliff
Médéa

Strait of Gibraltar
Gibraltar (U.K.)
ISLA DE
ALBORÁN
Chlef
(El Asnam)

Tanger
Ceuta (Sp.)
Al-Hoceima
Melilla (Sp.)
Oran
Sidi Bel Abbès
Zahrez Rharbi
Djelfa

Tetouan
Larache
R I F
Berkane
Taza
Oujda

CASABLANCA
Rabat
Salé
Oued Sebou
Laghouat

Meknès
Fès
Chott ech
Chergui

El-Jadida
MOYEN ATLAS
Oued Moulouya
Ain
Sefra

Khouribga
A T L A S
Djebel Aïssa
7333 ft
2235 m
Figuig

Safi
Beni-Mellal
Irhil M'Goun
13 356 ft
4071 m
Er-Rachidia
Béchar
Ghardaïa

Youssoufia
H A U T
GRAND ERG OCCIDENTAL
El Golea

Essaouira
Marrakech
MOROCCO
Ouarzazate
Oued Guir

Jebel Toubkal
13 665 ft
4165 m
A N T I - A T L A S
Agadir

Tiznit
HAMADA DU DRÂA
Adrar

CAP RHIR
Tan-Tan
Oued Draâ
Oued Saoura
Aoulef
I-n-Salah

A L G E R I A

Sebkha de
Timimoun

PLATEAU
DU TADEMAÏT

CANARY ISLANDS
(ISLAS CANARIAS)
(Spain)
LANZAROTE
Arrecife
Tarfaya
As Saquia al Hamra
Laâyoune (El Aaiún)
Semara

LA PALMA
TENERIFE
Santa Cruz
de Tenerife
FUERTEVENTURA
CAP JUBY
Tindouf

Pico del Teide
12 198 ft
3718 m
GRAN
CANARIA
Las Palmas
de Gran Canaria
CAP BOJADOR

EL HIERRO

MADEIRA ISLANDS
(ARQUIPÉLAGO DA MADEIRA)
(Portugal)
PORTO
SANTO

Funchal
MADEIRA

A T L A N T I C   O C E A N

Western Sahara has been
unilaterally annexed by Morocco.

Tropic of Cancer
Dakhla
Blr
Mogrein
Sebkhet Oumm
ed Droûs Telli
Sebkhet Oumm
ed Droûs Guebli

WESTERN
SAHARA
Sabkhat
Aghzoumal

E L   H A N K
E R G S   C H E C H

CAP BARBAS
Zouérat
Oued Tamanrasset

Khatt Atoui
ADRAR
I J Â F E N E
ADRAR DES IFÔGHAS
Oued Tilemsi

Nouâdhibou
RÂS NOUÂDHIBOU
OUARÂNE
Tessalit

Atar

ET TÎDRA
RÂS TIMIRIST
Sebkhet
Chemchâm

M A U R I T A N I A
M A L I

Sebkhet
ti-n-Dghâmcha
Tidjikja
Tichît
Kidal

Nouakchott
AOUKÂR

Boutilimit
Lac
Faguibine
Niger
Vallée du Tilemsi
Ménaka

Rosso
Bogué
Kiffa
Lac
Débo
Goundam
Tombouctou
(Timbuktu)
Gao
Ansongo

Saint-Louis
Kaédi
Hamoud
KUMBI SALEH
Boû Gâdoûm
'Adel Bagrou
Niger

Louga
Vallée du Ferlo
Nioro
Lac
Niangay

DAKAR
Thiès
S E N E G A L
Kayes
PARC NATIONAL
DE LA BOUCLE
DU BAOULÉ
Mopti

Mbour
Kaolack
Séngégal
Djenné
Ségou

Banjul (Bathurst)
THE GAMBIA
Tambacounda
Kita
San
Niamey

Ziguinchor
Kolda
Kédougou
PARC NATIONAL
DU NIOKOLO KOBA
Kati
Bamako
Koutiala

Cacheu
GUINEA-
Bissau
Bafatá
Koumbia
Mali
BURKINA FASO

ARQUIPÉLAGO
DOS BIJAGÓS
BISSAU
Labé
Siguiri
Sikasso
Koudougou
Ouagadougou
Fada-
Ngourma

G U I N E A
Ouahigouya
White Volta
BENIN

© Rand McNally
A-101816-1

0   60   120   180   240   300   360 Miles
0 60 120 180 240 300 360 420 480 540 600 Kilometers

Lambert Azimuthal Equal Area Projection
Scale 1:12,000,000
One inch to 190 miles
One cm to 120 km

MEDITERRANEAN SEA

GREECE

ITALY
SICILY
Catania
Agrigento
Siracusa
CAPO PASSERO
CYCLADES
MILOS 25
ÍOS
DODECANESE
RÓDOS
KÁRPATHOS
RÓDOS
ÁKRA TAÍNARO
KÍTHIRA
SEA OF CRETE
Irákleio
GÁVDOS
CRETE
(KRÍTI)
KALAMÁTA
THÍRA
KÁRPATHOS
35°

Annaba
(Bône)
Bizerte
Golfe de
Tunis
CAP BON
CARTHAGE
Tunis
ISOLA DI
PANTELLERIA
Gela
Valletta
MALTA
ISOLE
PELAGIE
Golfe de
Hammamet
Sousse
Moknine
Strait of Sicily
El Kef
Sétif
Constantine
Batna
Kasserine
Jebel Chambi
5066 ft.
1544 m
Biskra
Bejaïa
AINS
Chott el
Hodna
Chott
Melrhir
Chott el
Gharsa
Gafsa
Chott
el Jerid
Sfax
ÎLES KERKENNA
Golfe de Gabès
ÎLE DE JERBA
Tozeur
Gabès
Chott
Merouane
Ouargla
Sebkhet Safioune
El Oued
Tataouine
Chott
Jerid
GRAND ERG
ORIENTAL
TUNISIA
Az-
Zāwiyah
Al-
Khums
Tripoli (Ṭarābulus)
Gharyān
Miṣrātah
Nālūt
Mizdah
TRIPOLITANIA
Bi'r 'Allāq
Surt
Khalīj Surt
Al-Baydā'
Darnah
Al-Marj
Banghāzī
Ṭubruq (Tobruk)
Salūm
Sīdī Barrānī
Mersa Matruh
El-Alamein
CYRENAICA
Abyār
al-Ḥakīm
Ajdābiyā
Marsá al-
Burayqah
Sabkhat al-
Qunayyin
Sabkhat
Ghuzayyil
'Awjilah
Siwa
QAŢŢĀRA DEPRESSION
30°
Ghadāmis
HAMADA DE
TINRHERT
HAMÁDAT
TINGHERT
Sūknah
Al-Jufrah
Zillah
LIBYA
WESTERN
DESERT
EGYPT
Bawiti
Adīrī
Wādī ash-Shāṭi'
Wādī Bayy al-Kabīr
Wādī Zamzam
Sabhā
Burayk
Murzuq
FEZZAN
Ghāt
Al-Birkah
TASSILI-N-AJJER
IDHĀN MURZŪQ
Ilizi
SAHARA
LIBYAN (AS-ṢAḤRĀ' AL-LĪBIYAH) DESERT
Bi'r al-
Ḥarash
Al-Jawf
Al-Jawf
Tropic of Cancer
Jabal al-'Uwaynāt
6345 ft.
1934 m
Oued Ighurghar
HAGGAR
Tahat
9541 ft.
2908 m
Tamanrasset
Oued Tafassasset
SARĪR TIBASTI
Pic Toussidé
10 876 ft.
3315 m
Bardaï
TIBESTI
Emi Koussi
11 204 ft.
3415 m
TASSILI OUA-N-AHAGGAR
I-n-Guezzâm
Gréboun
6378 ft.
1944 m
TÉNÉRÉ
Bilma
GRAND ERG DE BILMA
Arlit
MASSIF DE
L'AÏR
Idoûkâl-en-Taghès
6634 ft.
2022 m
Ighazer oua-n-Agadès
Agadez
Faya-Largeau
Fada
ENNEDI
Ouadi Chili
Jabal al-'Uwaynāt
BODÉLÉ
NIGER
HEL
LEL
CHAD
Tanout
SUDAN
Tahoua
Birnin
Konni
Nguigmi
Mao
Biltine
Abéché
Al-Junaynah
Al-Fāshir
Zinder
Tessaoua
Maradi
Massakory
Moussoro
Ati
Oum-Hadjer
Jabal Marrah
10 072 ft.
3070 m
Sokoto
Birnin-Kebbi
Gusau
Katsina
Nguru
Gashua
Lake Chad
(Lac Tchad)
Massakory
Lac Fitri
Zalingei
Nyala
DĀRFŪR
NIGERIA
Kano
Fúntua
Azare
Damaturu
Maiduguri
N'Djamena
(Fort-Lamy)
Kousséri
Bama
CAMEROON
Mongo
Abou-Deïa
Melfi
Am Timan
Ad-Du'ayn
20°
5°
10°
20°
25°
35°
30°
25°
20°
15°

S

MAURITANIA

AOUKÂR

MALI

CAPE
VERDE

SENEGAL

DAKAR

THE GAMBIA

GUINEA-
BISSAU

GUINEA

Conakry

SIERRA
LEONE

Freetown

COTE D'IVOIRE
(IVORY COAST)

LIBERIA

Monrovia

ABIDJAN

a

BENIN

NIGERIA

Bight of Benin

NIGER
DELTA

CAMEROON

Gulf of Guinea

Bight of Biafra

© Rand McNally
A-101799-1

Inset map a
Lambert Conformal Conic Projection
Scale 1:4,000,000
One inch to 64 miles
One cm to 40 km

0   60   120   180   240   300   360 Miles

0   60   120 180 240 300 360 420 480 540 600 Kilometers

Lambert Azimuthal Equal Area Projection
Scale 1:12,000,000
One inch to 190 miles
One cm to 120 km

0   60   120   180   240   300   360 Miles

0   60   120   180 240 300 360 420 480 540 600 Kilometers

Lambert Azimuthal Equal Area Projection
Scale 1:12,000,000
One inch to 190 miles
One cm to 120 km

SUDAN

ERITREA

YEMEN

Al-Ubayyiḍ
Ad-Duwaym
Wad Madanī
Khashm al-Qirbah
Barentu
Teseney
Adigrat
Al-Hudaydah
RED SEA
Bajil
Ash-Shiḥr
Al-Mukallā

Al-Qaḑārif
Aksum
Adwa
Mek'elē
Ras Dejen
15 158 ft.
4620 m
Zabid
Dhamār
Rida'
Ibb
Ta'izz
HADRAMAWT
Al-Hawrah
RA'S AL-KALB

Ad-Duwaym
Kusti
Sinjah
Al-Qadārif
Gonder
T'ana Hāyk'
Bahir Dar
Guna Terara
4231 m
Tisisat Falls
Mot'a
Dese
Desē
Al-Mukhā
Aden ('Adan)

DANAKIL
Aseb
Bab el Mandeb
Gulf of Aden
Caluula
GEES GWARDAFUY

Dilling
Kāduqli
Malakāl
Umm Ruwābah
Ar-Rusayris
Kurmuk
Blue Nile
Debre Mark'os
Talo
14 478 ft.
4413 m
DJIBOUTI
Djibouti
Dikhil
As Sabieh
Saylac
Berbera
Boosaaso
Qandala
Ceengaabo
Dhud
RAAS XAAFUUN

Tulu Welel
10 833 ft.
3302 m
ADDIS ABABA
(ĀDĪS ĀBEBA)
Nek'emte
Giyon
Nazrēt
Dirē Dawa
Hārer
Jijiga
Hargeysa
Burco
Laascaanood
Shimbiris
7897 ft.
2407 m
Eyl

SOMALILAND The Republic of Somaliland unilaterally declared its independence from Somalia in 1991.

Dembi Dolo
Agaro
Guragē
12 208 ft.
3721 m
Āsela
Lake Ziway
AHMAR MTS.
Gara Muleta
3405 m
Degeh Bur
Dator
Werdēr
Gaalkacyo
Eyl

Jima
Hosa'ina
Sodo
Awasa
Batu
14 131 ft.
4307 m
Goba
OGADEN
K'ebri
Dehar

Maji
Guge
13 780 ft.
4200 m
Arba Minch
Dila
Kibre Mengist
Genalē

ETHIOPIA

SOMALIA

Ch'ew Bahir
(Lake Stefanie)
Gamud
8156 ft.
2486 m
Negēlē
Dawa
Mandera
Baydhabo

Kinyeti
10 456 ft.
3187 m
Moyale
Lagh Kulala

Lake Rudolf
CHALBI DESERT
Marsabit
Lak Bor
Jawhar
Mogadishu (Muqdisho)

Lodwar
Ng'iro
2752 m
Wajir
Marka

Arua
Gulu
Moroto
10 118 ft.
3084 m
Kitale
Lake Baringo
Maralal
Ewaso Ng'iro
Lagh Dera
Kismaayo

UGANDA
Lira
Mt. Elgon
14 177 ft.
4321 m
KENYA

Mbale
Eldoret
Meru
Garissa

Margherita Peak
16 763 ft.
5109 m
KAMPALA
Entebbe
Jinja
Nakuru
Nyeri
Mt. Kenya
(Kirinyaga)
17 058 ft.
5199 m
Tana
Hola
Lamu
PATE ISLAND
MANDA ISLAND

Kisumu
Kisii
Lake Naivasha
Thika
NAIROBI
Machakos

RWANDA
KIGALI
Gitarama
Bukoba
Lake Victoria
Mwanza
Lake Natron
Mt. Meru
14 977 ft.
4565 m
Arusha
Moshi
Kilimanjaro
19 340 ft.
5895 m
TSAVO EAST NATL. PARK
Voi
Malindi

BURUNDI
BUJUMBURA
SERENGETI PLAIN
Lake Eyasi
Lake Manyara
MASAI STEPPE
TSAVO WEST NATL. PARK
Mombasa

TANZANIA
Shinyanga
Singida
Hanang
11 211 ft.
3417 m
Tanga
PEMBA

INDIAN OCEAN

Kigoma
Ujiji
Tabora
Manyoni
Dodoma
Morogoro
ZANZIBAR
Zanzibar
DAR ES SALAAM

ZAMBIA
Mbeya
Iringa
MAFIA ISLAND

MALAWI
Lake Nyasa
Songea
Mtwara
MOZAMBIQUE
SEYCHELLES

0   60   120   180   240   300   360 Miles
0 60 120 180 240 300 360 420 480 540 600 Kilometers

Lambert Azimuthal Equal Area Projection
Scale 1:12,000,000
One inch to 190 miles
One cm to 120 km

Mbeya
Mbala
Kasama
Chambeshi
Chinsali
Mpika
Bangweulu
Swamps
Luangwa
Kasungu
Chipata
MALAWI
Lilongwe
Mangochi
Ulónguè
Zomba
Blantyre
Tete
Nsanje
Mocuba
Chinhoyi
HARARE
(SALISBURY)
Chitungwiza
Marondera
Rusape
BWE
Mutare
Chimoio
Dondo
Beira
Masvingo
Zvishavane
Chiredzi
GONAREZHOU
NATIONAL PARK
Beitbridge
GREAT LIMPOPO
TRANSFRONTIER PARK
PARQUE
NACIONAL
DO LIMPOPO
Tzaneen
KRUGER
NATIONAL
PARK
Chókwe
Chibuto
Xai-Xai
Nelspruit
Matola
Mbabane
Maputo
(Lourenço Marques)
SWAZILAND
Ermelo
Lobamba
Pondolo
Vryheid
ZULULAND
Richards Bay
Pietermaritzburg
Durban
Port Shepstone

TANZANIA
Songea
Lindi
Mtwara
CABO DELGADO
Mocímboa da Praia
Mueda
Montepuez
Pemba
Nampula
Nacala
MOZAMBIQUE
Quelimane
ILHA DO BAZARUTO
PONTA SÃO SEBASTIÃO
Vilankulu
PONTA DA BARRA FALSA
Massinga
Maxixe
PONTA DA BARRA

Mozambique Channel

SEYCHELLES
GROUPE
D'ALDABRA
ASSOMPTION
ATOLL DE COSMOLEDO
ST. PIERRE
ASTOVE
ATOLL DE PROVIDENCE
ATOLL DE
FARQUHAR

COMOROS
Moroni
NJAZIDJA
NZWANI
Mutsamudu
MWALI
Mamoudzou
MAYOTTE
(France; claimed by Comoros)

ÎLES GLORIEUSES
(France; claimed by Madagascar)

TANJONA BOBAOMBY
Antsiranana
(Diego-Suarez)
TANJONA ANORONTANY
NOSY MITSIO
NOSY BE
Ambanja
Maromokotro
9436 ft.
2876 m
Sambava
Antalaha
TANJONA ANGONTSY
SAIKANOSY
MASOALA
Mahajanga
Marovoay
Mananara
Avaratra
NOSY SAINTE
MARIE
Soanierana
Ivongo
Toamasina
ANTANANARIVO
Mahanoro
Nosy-Varika
MADAGASCAR
Fianarantsoa
Manakara
Farafangana
Vangaindrano
Toliara
Tôlañaro
(Faradofay)
Ambovombe
TANJONA
VOHIMENA

INDIAN
OCEAN

INDIAN OCEAN

REUNION
(France)
Le Port
Saint-Denis
Saint-André
Saint-Paul
Saint-Benoît
Piton des Neiges
10 072 ft.
3070 m
Saint-
Pierre
Piton de la Fournaise
8635 ft.
2632 m
Saint-Louis
Saint-Joseph

POINTE L'HORTAL
Triolet
Rivière du Rempart
Port Louis
Rose Hill
Curepipe
MAURITIUS
Mahébourg

MASCARENE ISLANDS

© Rand McNally
A-101782-1

Inset map a
Lambert Conformal Conic Projection
Scale 1:4,000,000
One inch to 64 miles
One cm to 40 km

0   60   120   180   240   300   360 Miles
0 60 120 180 240 300 360 420 480 540 600 Kilometers

Lambert Azimuthal Equal Area Projection
Scale 1:12,000,000
One inch to 190 miles
One cm to 120 km

Lambert Conformal Conic Projection
Scale 1:6,000,000
One inch to 96 miles
One cm to 60 km

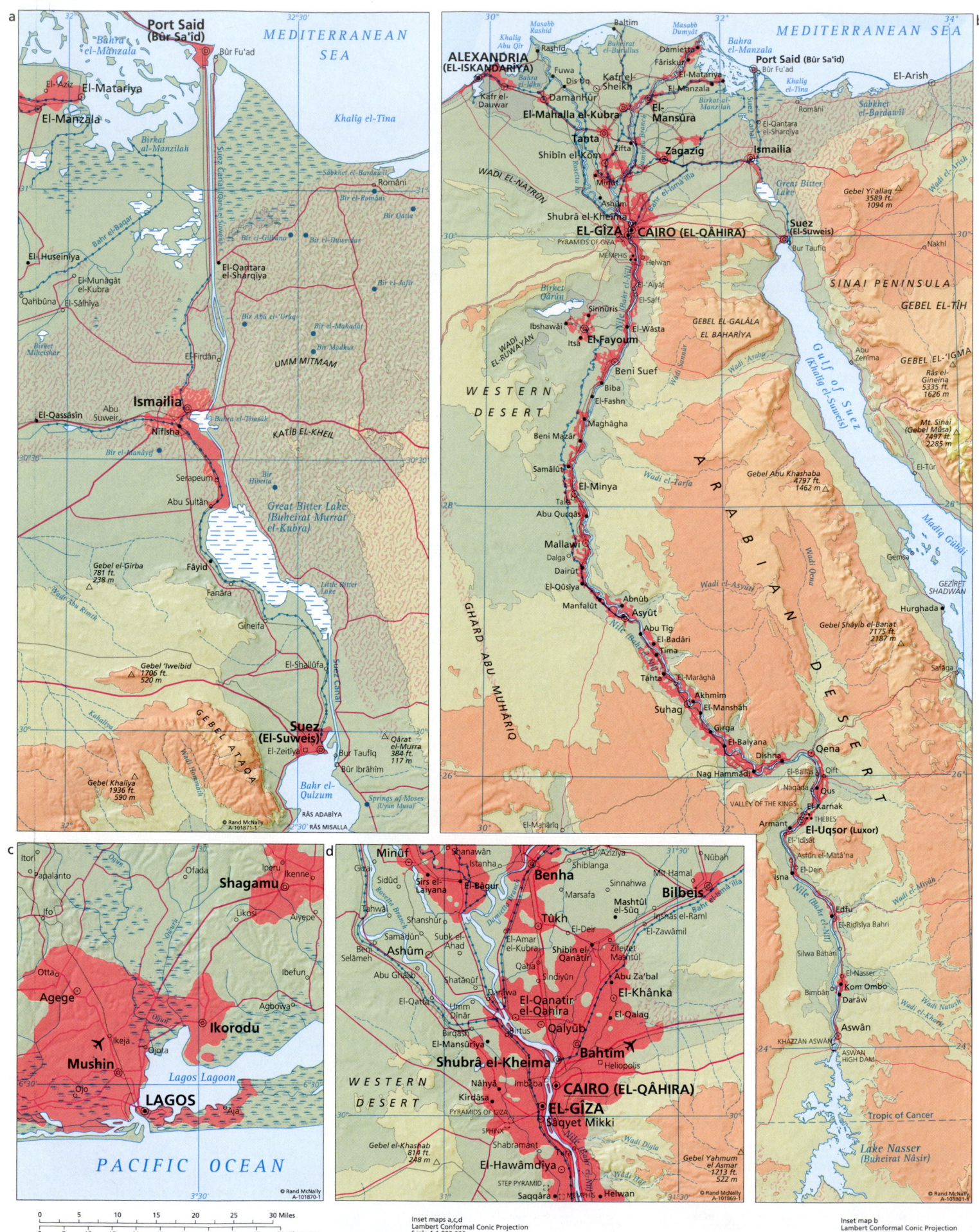

Inset maps a,c,d
Lambert Conformal Conic Projection
Scale 1:1,000,000
One inch to 16 miles
One cm to 10 km

Inset map b
Lambert Conformal Conic Projection
Scale 1:4,000,000
One inch to 64 miles
One cm to 40 km

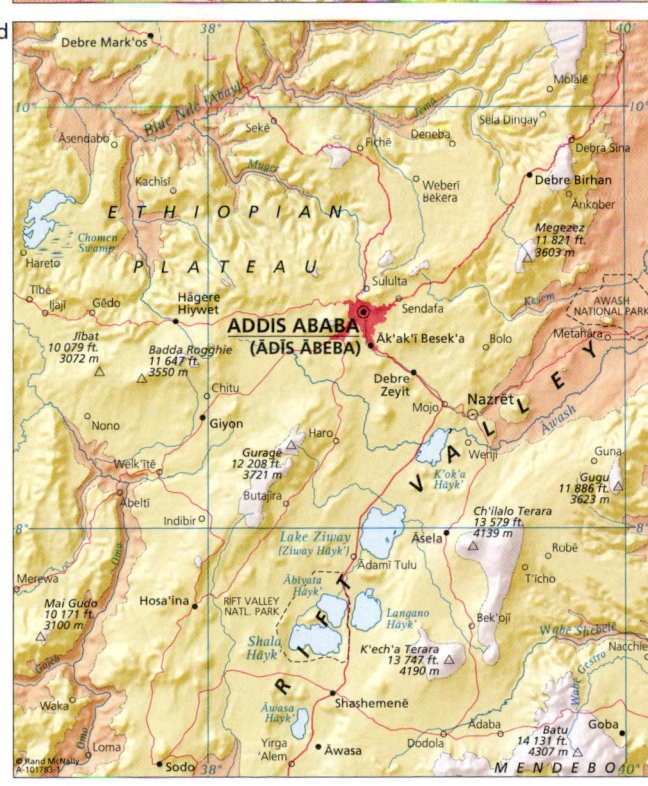

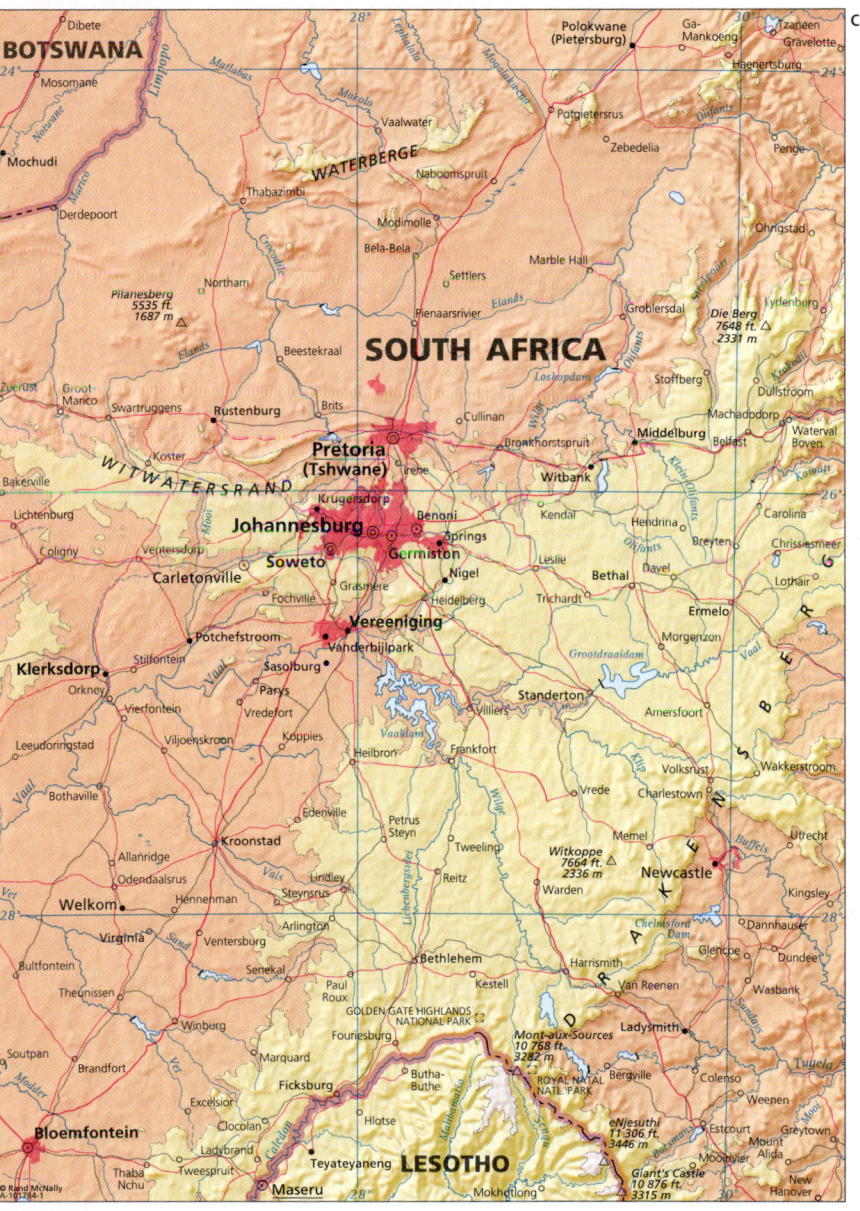

a (Map — Spain / Morocco)

SPAIN
Cádiz
San Fernando
Chiclana de la Frontera
CABO TRAFALGAR
Barbate
Algeciras
Tarifa
Strait of Gibraltar
CAP SPARTEL
Tanger
Asilah
Larache
Ksar-el-Kebir
Souk-el-Arba-Rharb
Mechra-Belqsiri
Kénitra
Rabat Salé
Temara
Tiflet
Khemisset Meknès
Mohammedia
CASABLANCA
Azemmour
El-Jadida
Berrechid
Settat
Sidi-Smail
Sidi-Bennour
Benahmed
MOROCCO
Khouribga
Oued-Zem Boujad
Kasba-Tadla
Fqih-ben-Salah
Souk-Sebt-des-Oulad-Nemaa
Béni-Mellal
El-Borouj
Youssoufia
Benguerir
El-Kelaa-Srahna
Tameleit
Tamelelt
Marrakech
Demnate
Azilal
Aït-Ourir
Tinerhir
ATLANTIC OCEAN
MOYEN ATLAS
ATLAS MOUNTAINS
HAUT ATLAS
Massif de Kousser 10 157 ft. 3096 m
Ibel Ghat 12 549 ft. 3825 m
Irhil M'Goun 13 356 ft. 4071 m

Estepona
Marbella
La Línea de la Concepción
Gibraltar (U.K.)
PUNTA DE ALMINA
Ceuta (Sp.)
Fnideq
Smir-Restinga
Tetouan
Dar Chaoui
Chechaouen
Bab-Taza
Ouezzane
RIF
Karia-ba-Mohammed
Sidi-Slimane
Sidi-Kacem
Moulay-Idriss VOLUBILIS
Fès
El-Hajeb
Ifrane
Azrou
Ben-Slimane
Rommani
Jemaa-de-Mritt
Khenifra
Ifrane
ATLAS

© Rand McNally A-101787-1

d (Map — Ethiopia)

Debre Mark'os
ETHIOPIAN PLATEAU
Blue Nile (Abay)
Asendabo
Kachisi
Fitche
Seke
Sela Dingay
Deneba
Debre Sina
Debre Birhan
Ankober
Weberi
Bekera
Megezez 11 821 ft. 3603 m
Hareto
Chomen Swamp
Tibe
Gedo
Welk'ite
Hägere Hiywet
Jibat 10 079 ft. 3072 m
Badda Rogghie 11 647 ft. 3550 m
Giyon
Sululta
Sendafa
ADDIS ABABA (ADIS ABEBA)
Ak'ak'i Besek'a
Chitu
Debre Zeyit
Mojo
Nazrét
AWASH NATIONAL PARK
Metahara
Nono
Gurage 12 208 ft. 3721 m
Haro
Wenji
Abelti
Indibir
Butajira
RIFT VALLEY
Gugu 11 886 ft. 3623 m
Guna
Merewa
Mai Gudo 10 171 ft. 3100 m
Hosa'ina
Lake Ziway (Ziway Häyk')
Adami Tulu
Abijata Häyk'
Langano Häyk'
Shala Häyk'
Ch'ilalo Terara 13 579 ft. 4139 m
Asela
Robe
T'icho
K'ech'a Terara 13 747 ft. 4190 m
Bek'oji
Wabe Shebele
Waka
Awasa Häyk'
Loma
Sodo
Shashemene
Awasa
Yirga Alem
Dodola
Adaba
Batu 14 131 ft. 4307 m
Goba
Nachele
MENDEBO

© Rand McNally A-101783-1

0 20 40 60 80 100 120 Miles
0 20 40 60 80 100 120 140 160 180 200 Kilometer

b (Map — Algeria)

MEDITERRANEAN SEA
CAP BOUGAROUN
ALGIERS (ALGER)
'Aïn Benian
Bou Ismaïl
Cherchell
El Affroun
Miliana
Khemis Miliana
Dellys
Azeffoun
CAP SIGLI
Tizi Ouzou
Zaouga
Bejaïa
Golfe de Bejaïa
Jijel
El Milia
Collo
Skikda
Boudouaou
Bordj Menaiel
Boufarik
Lakhdaria
Blida
Médéa
Sour el Ghozlane
Akbou
Bougaa
Bordj Bou Arreridj
Kherrata
Sétif
El Eulma
Mila
Constantine
Chelghoum el Aïd
Aïn M'Lila
Ksar el-Boukhari
Oued el Ham
Sidi Aïssa
Aïn Oussera
Aïn el Hadjel
M'Sila
Bou Saâda
Djebel Refaa 7119 ft. 2170 m
Chott Reda
Aïn Yagout
Batna
TIMGAD
Aïn Touta
Barika
Chott el Hodna
Djebel Chelia 7638 ft. 2328 m
AURÈS
ATLAS TELLIEN
Ksar Chellala
HAUTS PLATEAUX
Zahrez Rharbi
Zahrez Chergui
ATLAS MOUNTAINS
El Idrissia
Djelfa
Biskra
Sidi Okba
Tolga
Ouled Djellal
El Idrissia
Oued Djedi
Chott Melrhir

© Rand McNally A-101790-1

c (Map — South Africa)

BOTSWANA
Dibete
Mosomane
Mochudi
Derdepoort
WATERBERGE
Thabazimbi
Polokwane (Pietersburg)
Ga-Mankoeng
Gravelotte
Hoenertsburg
Tzaneen
Vaalwater
Potgietersrus
Zebedelia
Penge
Naboomspruit
Modimolle
Bela-Bela
Marble Hall
Ohrigstad
Northam
Pilanesberg 5535 ft. 1687 m
Settlers
Die Berg 7648 ft. 2331 m
Lydenburg
Zeerust
Swartruggens
Rustenburg
Brits
Beestekraal
Renaarsrivier
Groblersdal
Stoffberg
Machadodorp
Dullstroom
Waterval Boven
Koster
Krugersdorp
Pretoria (Tshwane)
Irene
Cullinan
Bronkhorstspruit
Middelburg
Belfast
SOUTH AFRICA
WITWATERSRAND
Johannesburg
Benoni
Springs
Germiston
Soweto
Nigel
Witbank
Kendal
Hendrina
Carolina
Carletonville
Vereeniging
Heidelberg
Leslie
Bethal
Davel
Breyten
Chrissiesmeer
Lothair
Vanderbijlpark
Sasolburg
Standerton
Amersfoort
Ermelo
Morgenzon
Klerksdorp
Stilfontein
Orkney
Parys
Vredefort
Viljoenskroon
Koppies
Heilbron
Frankfort
Villiers
Volksrust
Charlestown
Utrecht
Vierfontein
Leeudoringstad
Odendaalsrus
Allanridge
Bothaville
Edenville
Vrede
Memel
Wakkerstroom
Welkom
Virginia
Hennenman
Arlington
Lindley
Reitz
Warden
Witkoppe 7664 ft. 2336 m
Newcastle
Kingsley
Dannhauser
Kroonstad
Petrus Steyn
Tweeling
Steynsrus
Senekal
Winburg
Ventersburg
Theunissen
Bultfontein
Brandfort
Soutpan
Marquard
Paul Roux
Bethlehem
Kestell
Harrismith
Van Reenen
Glencoe
Dundee
Wasbank
Ladysmith
Bloemfontein
Excelsior
Clocolan
Ladybrand
Ficksburg
Fouriesburg
GOLDEN GATE HIGHLANDS NATIONAL PARK
Mont-aux-Sources 10 768 ft. 3282 m
ROYAL NATAL NATL. PARK
Bergville
Colenso
Weenen
Greytown
New Hanover
Butha-Buthe
eNjesuthi 11 306 ft. 3446 m
Estcourt
Mooirivier
Thaba Nchu
Maseru
Teyateyaneng
LESOTHO
Mokhotlong
Giant's Castle 10 876 ft. 3315 m
DRAKENSBERG
Tugela

© Rand McNally A-101784-1

Lambert Azimuthal Equal Area Projection
Scale 1:4,000,000
One inch to 64 miles
One cm to 40 km

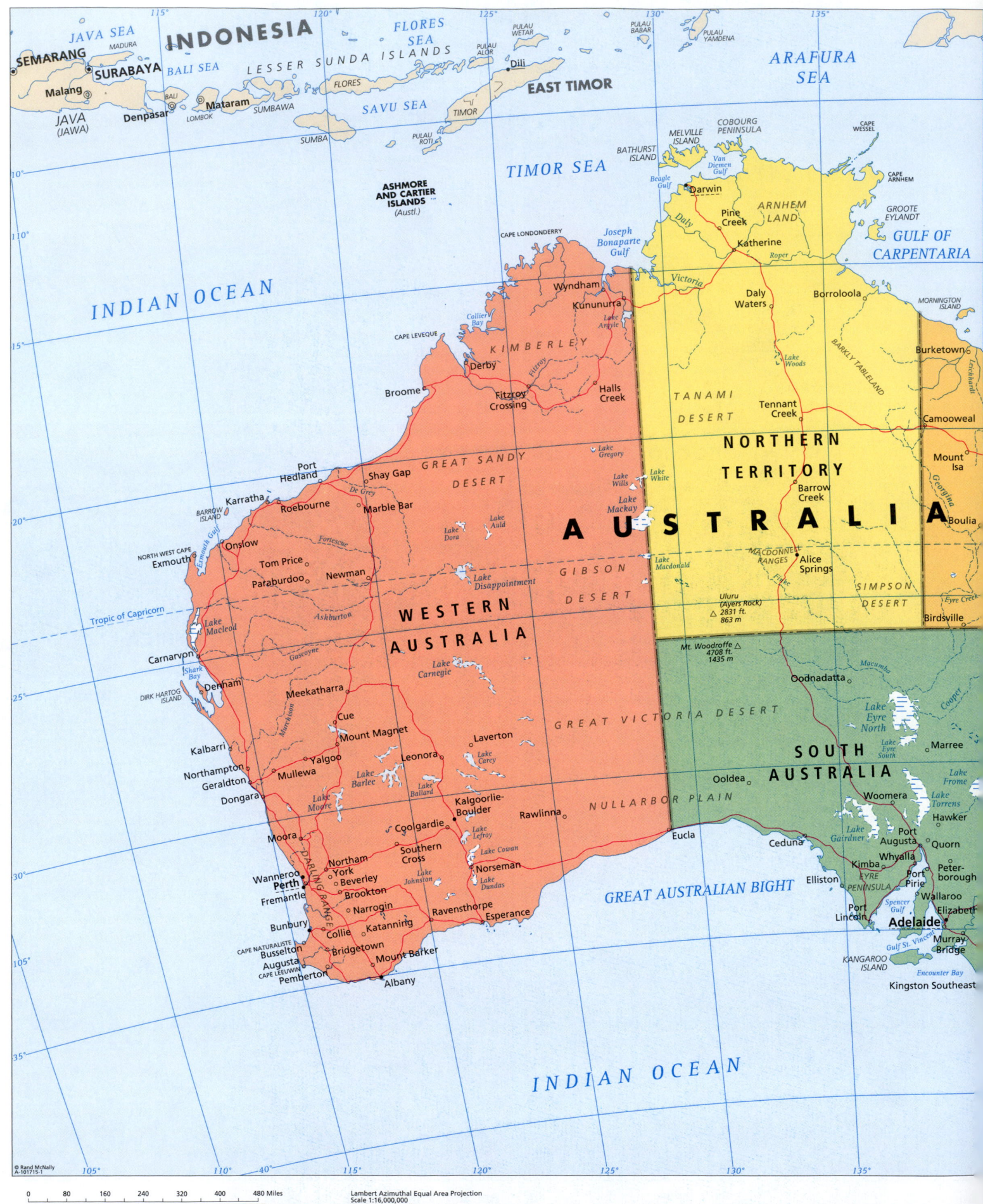

INDONESIA

JAVA SEA

SEMARANG
SURABAYA
Malang
Denpasar
Mataram
Madura
Bali
Lombok
Sumbawa
Java (Jawa)
Sumba
Pulau Roti

BALI SEA

LESSER SUNDA ISLANDS

FLORES SEA

FLORES
Savu Sea
Timor

SUMBA

Pulau Alor
Pulau Wetar
Dili

EAST TIMOR

ARAFURA SEA

TIMOR SEA

Pulau Babar
Pulau Yamdena

ASHMORE AND CARTIER ISLANDS (Austl.)

MELVILLE ISLAND
COBOURG PENINSULA
BATHURST ISLAND
Van Diemen Gulf
Beagle Gulf
Darwin

CAPE WESSEL
GROOTE EYLANDT
CAPE ARNHEM

GULF OF CARPENTARIA

MORNINGTON ISLAND

INDIAN OCEAN

CAPE LONDONDERRY
Joseph Bonaparte Gulf

Wyndham
Kununurra
Lake Argyle

Collier Bay
KIMBERLEY
Derby
Fitzroy
Halls Creek
Broome
Fitzroy Crossing

CAPE LEVEQUE

Pine Creek
Katherine
Roper

ARNHEM LAND

Daly Waters
Borroloola

Lake Woods

Burketown

BARKLY TABLELAND

NORTHERN TERRITORY

TANAMI DESERT

Tennant Creek

Camooweal

GREAT SANDY DESERT

Port Hedland
Shay Gap
De Grey
Karratha
Roebourne
Marble Bar
BARROW ISLAND
NORTH WEST CAPE
Exmouth
Onslow
Fortescue
Tom Price
Paraburdoo
Newman
Ashburton

Lake Dora
Lake Auld

Lake Disappointment

Lake Gregory
Lake Wills
Lake White
Lake Mackay

AUSTRALIA

Barrow Creek

Mount Isa
Boulia

GIBSON DESERT

Lake Macdonald

MACDONNELL RANGES
Alice Springs

SIMPSON DESERT

Georgina

Birdsville

Eyre Creek

Tropic of Capricorn

Lake Macleod
Carnarvon
Shark Bay
DIRK HARTOG ISLAND
Denham

Gascoyne

WESTERN AUSTRALIA

Uluru (Ayers Rock) △ 2831 ft. 863 m

Mt. Woodroffe △ 4708 ft. 1435 m

Oodnadatta

Macumba
Cooper

Lake Eyre North

Marree

Meekatharra

Murchison
Cue

Mount Magnet

Laverton
Lake Carey

Lake Carnegie

GREAT VICTORIA DESERT

SOUTH AUSTRALIA

Lake Eyre South

Lake Frome

Woomera
Hawker

Kalbarri
Northampton
Geraldton
Dongara
Yalgoo
Mullewa
Lake Moore
Lake Barlee
Lake Ballard

Leonora

Lake Carcy

Ooldea

Lake Gairdner

Lake Torrens

Kimba
Whyalla
Quorn
Port Augusta
Peterborough

Moora
Kalgoorlie-Boulder
Coolgardie
Lake Lefroy
Lake Cowan

Rawlinna

NULLARBOR PLAIN

Eucla

Ceduna

Elliston

EYRE PENINSULA

Port Pirie

Wallaroo
Elizabeth

Wanneroo
Perth
Fremantle
Northam
York
Beverley
Brookton
Narrogin
Bunbury
Collie
Katanning
Bridgetown
Southern Cross
Lake Johnston
Norseman
Lake Dundas
Ravensthorpe
Esperance

DARLING RANGE

Port Lincoln

Spencer Gulf

Adelaide

Gulf St. Vincent

Murray Bridge

CAPE NATURALISTE
Busselton
Augusta
CAPE LEEUWIN
Pemberton
Mount Barker
Albany

GREAT AUSTRALIAN BIGHT

KANGAROO ISLAND
Encounter Bay

Kingston Southeast

INDIAN OCEAN

© Rand McNally
A-101715-1

0 80 160 240 320 400 480 Miles
0 80 160 240 320 400 480 560 640 720 800 Kilometers

Lambert Azimuthal Equal Area Projection
Scale 1:16,000,000
One inch to 256 miles
One cm to 160 km

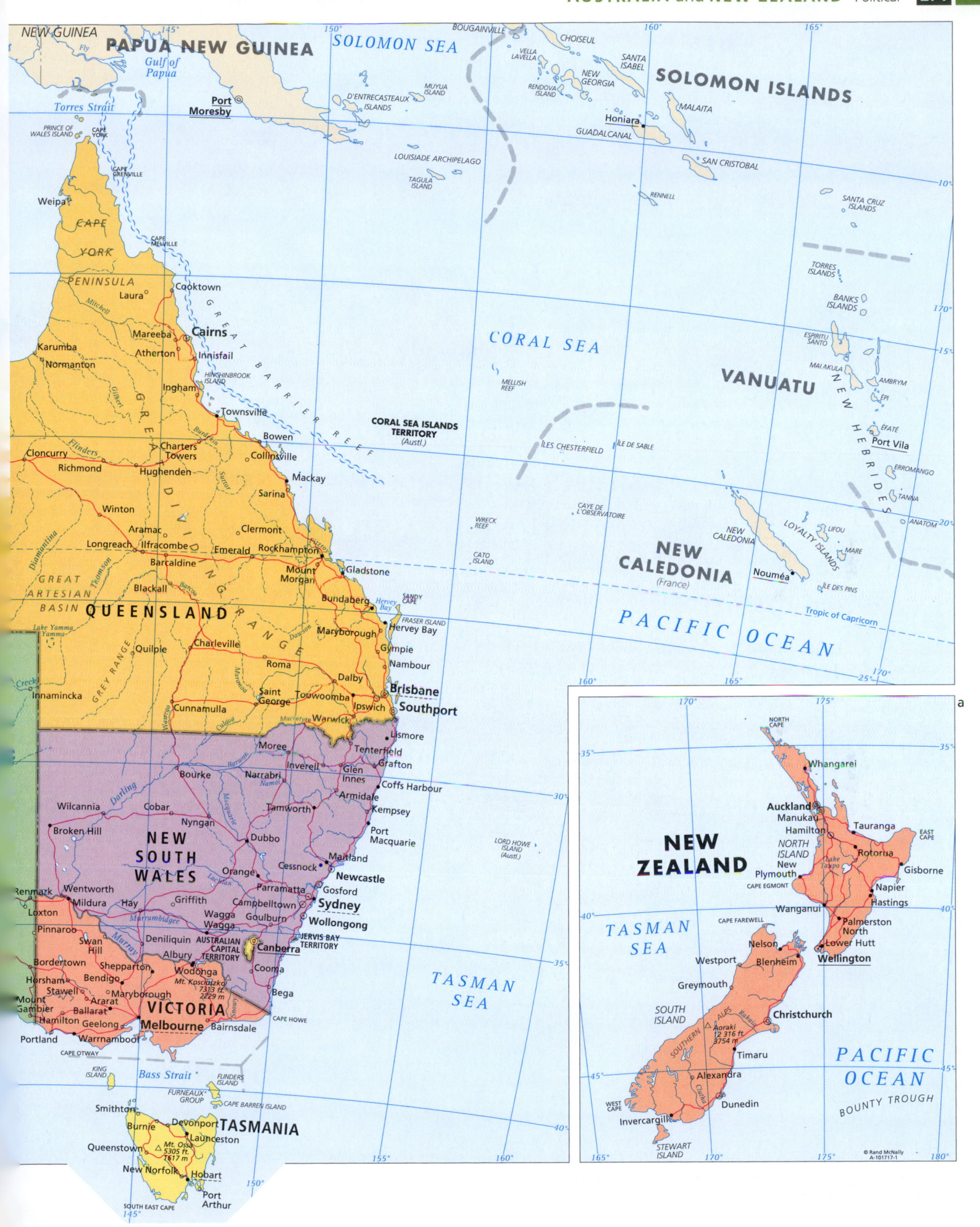

NEW GUINEA
Fly

PAPUA NEW GUINEA

Gulf of Papua

Torres Strait

PRINCE OF WALES ISLAND
CAPE YORK

Port Moresby

CAPE GRENVILLE

SOLOMON SEA

BOUGAINVILLE

D'ENTRECASTEAUX ISLANDS

MUYUA ISLAND

CHOISEUL

VELLA LAVELLA

NEW GEORGIA

RENDOVA ISLAND

SANTA ISABEL

SOLOMON ISLANDS

MALAITA

Honiara

GUADALCANAL

SAN CRISTOBAL

LOUISIADE ARCHIPELAGO

TAGULA ISLAND

RENNELL

TORRES ISLANDS

BANKS ISLANDS

SANTA CRUZ ISLANDS

CAPE YORK PENINSULA

Weipa

CAPE MELVILLE

Cooktown

Laura

Mareeba
Atherton

Cairns

Innisfail

HINCHINBROOK ISLAND

CORAL SEA

MELLISH REEF

VANUATU

ESPÍRITU SANTO

MALAKULA

AMBRYM

EPI

ÉFATÉ

Port Vila

NEW HEBRIDES

Karumba

Normanton

Ingham

Townsville

Bowen

Collinsville

Mackay

Sarina

ÎLES CHESTERFIELD

ÎLE DE SABLE

ERROMANGO

TANNA

ANATOM

Cloncurry

Richmond

Hughenden

Charters Towers

GREAT DIVIDING RANGE

Winton

Aramac

Longreach
Ilfracombe

Clermont

Emerald

Rockhampton

Mount Morgan

Gladstone

CORAL SEA ISLANDS TERRITORY (Austl.)

WRECK REEF

CAYE DE L'OBSERVATOIRE

CATO ISLAND

NEW CALEDONIA

LOYALTY ISLANDS

LIFOU

MARÉ

Barcaldine

Blackall

QUEENSLAND

Diamantina

GREAT ARTESIAN BASIN

Lake Yamma Yamma

Quilpie

Charleville

Roma

Dalby

Bundaberg

Hervey Bay

SANDY CAPE

FRASER ISLAND

Maryborough

Gympie

Nambour

Toowoomba

Brisbane

NEW CALEDONIA
(France)

Nouméa

ÎLE DES PINS

Tropic of Capricorn

PACIFIC OCEAN

Creek

Innamincka

Cunnamulla

Saint George

Ipswich

Southport

Warwick

Lismore

Tenterfield

Grafton

Glen Innes

Coffs Harbour

Moree

Inverell

Bourke

Narrabri

Armidale

Kempsey

Port Macquarie

LORD HOWE ISLAND (Austl.)

Wilcannia

Cobar

Nyngan

Tamworth

Broken Hill

NEW SOUTH WALES

Dubbo

Maitland

Cessnock

Newcastle

Gosford

Sydney

Darling

Orange

Parramatta

Campbelltown

Wollongong

Renmark
Wentworth

Hay

Griffith

Wagga Wagga

Goulburn

JERVIS BAY TERRITORY

Loxton
Mildura

Pinnaroo

Swan Hill

Deniliquin

AUSTRALIAN CAPITAL TERRITORY

Canberra

Bordertown

Shepparton

Albury

Wodonga

Mt. Kosciuszko 7313 ft. 2229 m

Cooma

Horsham
Stawell

Bendigo

Maryborough

Bega

Mount Gambier

Ararat

Ballarat

VICTORIA

Geelong

Melbourne

Bairnsdale

CAPE HOWE

Portland

Hamilton

Warrnambool

CAPE OTWAY

KING ISLAND

Bass Strait

FLINDERS ISLAND

TASMAN SEA

Smithton

Burnie
Devonport

TASMANIA

Launceston

FURNEAUX GROUP

CAPE BARREN ISLAND

Queenstown

Mt. Ossa 5305 ft. 1617 m

New Norfolk

Hobart

Port Arthur

SOUTH EAST CAPE

New Zealand inset

a

NORTH CAPE

Whangarei

Auckland

Manukau

Hamilton

Tauranga

EAST CAPE

NEW ZEALAND

NORTH ISLAND

New Plymouth

CAPE EGMONT

Lake Taupo

Rotorua

Gisborne

Napier

Hastings

Wanganui

Palmerston North

TASMAN SEA

CAPE FAREWELL

Nelson

Lower Hutt

Wellington

Westport

Blenheim

Greymouth

SOUTH ISLAND

SOUTHERN ALPS

Rakaia

Aoraki 12 316 ft. 3754 m

Christchurch

Timaru

WEST CAPE

Alexandra

Clutha

PACIFIC OCEAN

BOUNTY TROUGH

Invercargill

Dunedin

STEWART ISLAND

© Rand McNally
A-101717-1

INDONESIA

JAVA SEA

PULAU
BAWEAN

MADURA

Surabaya

BALI SEA

BALI

LOMBOK

SUMBAWA

JAVA
(JAWA)

SUMBA

PULAU KALAO

PULAU TANAHJAMPEA

FLORES
SEA

LESSER SUNDA ISLANDS

FLORES

PULAU
LOMBLEN

PULAU
PANTAR

PULAU
ALOR

SAVU SEA

PULAU
ROTI

PULAU
SAWU

TIMOR

PULAU WETAR

Dili

EAST TIMOR

PULAU
MOA

PULAU
DAMAR

PULAU
ROMANG

PULAU BABAR

PULAU
YAMDENA

PULAU
SELARU

ARAFURA
SEA

TANJUNG
VALS

ASHMORE
AND CARTIER
ISLANDS
(Austl.)

TIMOR SEA

MELVILLE
ISLAND

BATHURST
ISLAND

Beagle
Gulf

Clarence Str.

Van
Diemen
Gulf

COBOURG
PENINSULA

CROKER ISLAND

CAPE
WESSEL

Darwin

ARNHEM
LAND

GROOTE
EYLANDT

CAPE
ARNHEM

GULF OF
CARPENTARIA

CAPE LONDONDERRY

BROWSE
ISLAND

BIGGE
ISLAND

Joseph
Bonaparte
Gulf

Daly

Katherine

Roper

VANDERLIN
ISLAND

INDIAN OCEAN

AUGUSTUS
ISLAND

ADÈLE
ISLAND

Collier
Bay

CAPE LEVEQUE

KIMBERLEY

Fitzroy

Ord

Lake
Argyle

Victoria

Lake
Woods

BARKLY TABLELAND

MORNINGTON
ISLAND

Nicholson

Leichhardt

Broome

CAPE LATOUCHE
TREVILLE

De Grey

GREAT SANDY

DESERT

Lake
Gregory

TANAMI

DESERT

Mount
Isa

NORTHERN

BARROW
ISLAND

NORTH WEST CAPE

HAMERSLEY RANGE

Mt. Bruce
4052 ft.
1235 m

Fortescue

Ashburton

Lake
Dora

Lake
Auld

Lake
Disappointment

Lake
Mackay

Lake
Wills

Lake
White

Lake
Macdonald

TERRITORY

AUSTRALIA

GIBSON

MACDONNELL
RANGES

Alice
Springs

SIMPSON

Esperance Creek

Exmouth Gulf

Tropic of Capricorn

Lake
Macleod

BERNIER
ISLAND

DORRE ISLAND

Carnarvon

Shark
Bay

DIRK HARTOG
ISLAND

Lyons

Gascoyne

Wooramel

Murchison

WESTERN

AUSTRALIA

Savory Creek

DESERT

Lake
Carnegie

Lake
Wells

Yeo Lake

GREAT VICTORIA DESERT

Uluru
(Ayers Rock)
2831 ft.
863 m

Mt. Woodroffe
4708 ft.
1435 m

Lake
Neale

Finke

Alberga Creek

Warburton Creek

Macumba

Cooper

DESERT

Eyre Creek

Georgina

Marshall

SOUTH

Lake
Eyre
North

Lake
Eyre
South

Lake
Blanche

Lake
Frome

Lake
Austin

Lake
Barlee

Lake
Moore

Lake
Ballard

Lake
Deborah
West

Lake
Seabrook

Lake
Carey

Lake
Minigwal

Lake
Cowan

Kalgoorlie-
Boulder

Lake
Lefroy

Lake
Johnston

Lake
Dundas

NULLARBOR PLAIN

AUSTRALIA

Lake
Harris

Lake
Everard

Lake
Gairdner

Lake
Torrens

EYRE
PENINSULA

Spencer
Gulf

YORKE PEN.

Lake
Gregory

ST. PETER
ISLAND

PERTH BASIN

Perth

DARLING RANGE

Geographe
Bay

CAPE NATURALISTE

CAPE LEEUWIN

POINT D'ENTRECASTEAUX

WEST CAPE
HOWE

GREAT AUSTRALIAN BIGHT

WEST
POINT

Gulf St. Vincent

KANGAROO
ISLAND

Adelaide

Encounter Bay

INDIAN OCEAN

SOUTH AUSTRALIAN BASIN

© Rand McNally
A-101729-1

0   80   160   240   320   400   480 Miles

0 80 160 240 320 400 480 560 640 720 800 Kilometers

Lambert Azimuthal Equal Area Projection
Scale 1:16,000,000
One inch to 256 miles
One cm to 160 km

NEW GUINEA

PAPUA NEW GUINEA

Gulf of
Papua

Huon Gulf

SOLOMON SEA

BOUGAINVILLE

CHOISEUL

SOLOMON ISLANDS

KIRIWINA
ISLANDS

VELLA
LAVELLA
KOLOMBANGARA
Island

NEW
GEORGIA

SANTA
ISABEL

BOIGU ISLAND

SAIBAI ISLAND

Torres Strait

MOA
ISLAND

PRINCE OF
WALES ISLAND

CAPE
YORK

Port
Moresby

OWEN STANLEY RANGE

D'ENTRECASTEAUX
ISLANDS

MUYUA
ISLAND

RENDOVA
ISLAND

VANGUNU
ISLAND

MALAITA

Honiara

MARAMASIKE

GUADALCANAL

SAN CRISTOBAL

RENNELL

NENDO

SANTA CRUZ
ISLANDS

VANIKOLO

MISIMA
ISLAND

LOUISIADE ARCHIPELAGO

CAPE
KEER-WEER

CAPE

YORK

CAPE
GRENVILLE

PENINSULA

Coleman

CAPE
MELVILLE

CORAL SEA BASIN

TAGULA
ISLAND

YELA
ISLAND

CHILCOTT
ISLET

CORAL SEA

MELLISH
REEF

TORRES
ISLANDS

NORTH FIJI BASIN

VANUA
LAVA

BANKS
ISLANDS

SANTA
MARIA

ESPIRITU
SANTO

AOBA

MAEWO

MAI AKULA

PENTECOST
ISLAND

AMBRYM

ÉPI

ÉFATÉ

VANUATU

NEW
HEBRIDES

Weipa

Mitchell

Staaten

Cairns

Bartle Frere
5322 ft.
1622 m

GREAT BARRIER REEF

HINCHINBROOK
ISLAND

MAGNETIC
ISLAND

Townsville

GREAT

Gilbert

Norman

**SELWYN
RANGE**

Flinders

DIVIDING

CUMBERLAND
ISLANDS

TOWNSHEND
ISLAND

WRECK
REEF

CORAL SEA ISLANDS
TERRITORY
(Austl.)

ÎLES CHESTERFIELD

ÎLE DE SABLE

CAYE DE
L'OBSERVATOIRE

NEW
CALEDONIA

LOYALTY ISLANDS

OUVEA

LIFOU

MARE

ERROMANGO

TANNA

ANATOM

20°

Diamantina

**GREAT
ARTESIAN
BASIN**

Thomson

QUEENSLAND

RANGE

Rockhampton

CURTIS
ISLAND

SANDY
CAPE

HERVEY
BAY

FRASER
ISLAND

**NEW
CALEDONIA**
(France)

Nouméa

ÎLE DES PINS

Tropic of Capricorn

PACIFIC OCEAN

Lake Yamma
Yamma

Barcoo

Cooper

GREY RANGE

**STURT
STONY
DESERT**

Warrego

Condamine

Brisbane

MORETON
ISLAND

NORTH STRADBROKE
ISLAND

Creek

Strzelecki Creek

Darling

Balonne

Namoi

Round Mountain
5203 ft.
1586 m

Macleay

LORD HOWE
ISLAND
(Austl.)

**NEW
ZEALAND**

NORTH
CAPE

GREAT
BARRIER
ISLAND

Auckland

Bay of
Plenty

EAST
CAPE

**NEW
SOUTH
WALES**

DIVIDING

Macintyre

Barwon

Gwydir

Castlereagh

Lachlan

Murrumbidgee

Lake
Victoria

Murray

Lake
Hume

GREAT

RANGE

Sydney

JERVIS BAY
TERRITORY

Canberra

**AUSTRALIAN CAPITAL
TERRITORY**

Mt. Kosciuszko
7313 ft.
2229 m

**NORTH
ISLAND**

CAPE EGMONT

Mt. Ruapehu
9177 ft.
2797 m

Hawke
Bay

**TASMAN
SEA**

CAPE FAREWELL

D'URVILLE
ISLAND

Tasman
Bay

Wellington

CAPE PALLISER

VICTORIA

DIVIDING RANGE

Melbourne

Port Phillip
Bay

CAPE
NELSON

CAPE OTWAY

WILSONS
PROMONTORY

CAPE HOWE

**TASMAN

SEA**

35°

**SOUTH
ISLAND**

SOUTHERN ALPS

Aoraki
12,316 ft.
3754 m

Christchurch

Canterbury
Bight

**PACIFIC
OCEAN**

KING
ISLAND

FURNEAUX
GROUP

FLINDERS
ISLAND

CAPE BARREN ISLAND

Bass Strait

TASMAN BASIN

40°

WEST
CAPE

Lake

Dunedin

BOUNTY TROUGH

HUNTER ISLAND

CAPE GRIM

TASMANIA

Mt. Ossa
5305 ft.
1617 m

Hobart

SCHOUTEN
ISLAND

SOUTH BRUNY
ISLAND

SOUTH EAST CAPE

STEWART
ISLAND

45°

Land Cover

- Evergreen Broadleaf Forest
- Mixed Forest
- Woodland
- Wooded Grassland
- Closed Shrubland
- Open Shrubland
- Grassland
- Cropland
- Bare Ground (Desert)
- Urban and Built Up

PACIFIC OCEAN

Equator

NEW GUINEA

NEW BRITAIN

SOLOMON SEA

SOLOMON ISLANDS

ARAFURA SEA

TIMOR SEA

INDIAN OCEAN

ARNHEM LAND

Gulf of Carpentaria

CORAL SEA

NEW HEBRIDES

KIMBERLEY

TANAMI DESERT

BARKLY TABLELAND

GREAT SANDY DESERT

GREAT DIVIDING RANGE

NEW CALEDONIA

Tropic of Capricorn

GIBSON DESERT

SIMPSON DESERT

GREAT ARTESIAN BASIN

Brisbane

GREAT VICTORIA DESERT

STURT STONY DESERT

Lake Eyre North

NULLARBOR PLAIN

Darling

Sydney

DARLING RA.

Perth

GREAT AUSTRALIAN BIGHT

Adelaide

Murray

Melbourne

TASMAN SEA

NORTH ISLAND

Auckland

INDIAN OCEAN

TASMANIA

SOUTH ISLAND

SOUTHERN ALPS

Source: CIESIN; Hansen et al., 2000

A-102089-1   © Rand McNally

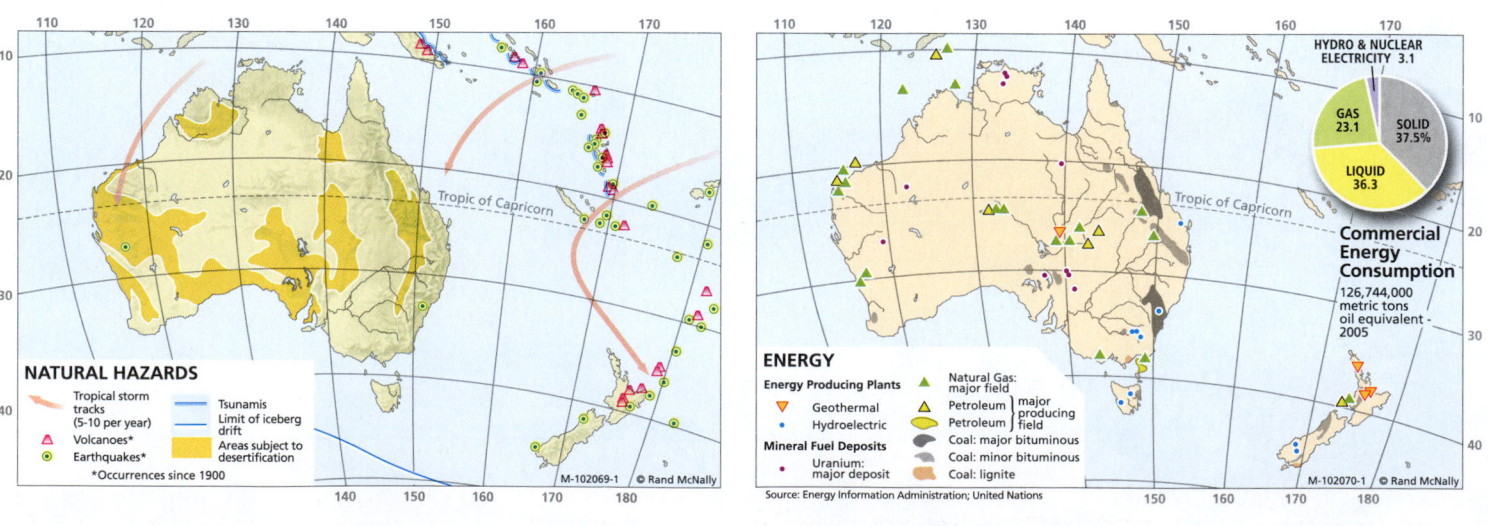

NATURAL HAZARDS

- Tropical storm tracks (5-10 per year)
- Volcanoes*
- Earthquakes*
- Tsunamis
- Limit of iceberg drift
- Areas subject to desertification

Tropic of Capricorn

*Occurrences since 1900

M-102069-1   © Rand McNally

ENERGY

Energy Producing Plants
- Geothermal
- Hydroelectric
- Natural Gas: major field
- Petroleum: major producing field
- Petroleum

Mineral Fuel Deposits
- Uranium: major deposit
- Coal: major bituminous
- Coal: minor bituminous
- Coal: lignite

Tropic of Capricorn

HYDRO & NUCLEAR ELECTRICITY 3.1

GAS 23.1

SOLID 37.5%

LIQUID 36.3

Commercial Energy Consumption
126,744,000 metric tons oil equivalent - 2005

Source: Energy Information Administration; United Nations

M-102070-1   © Rand McNally

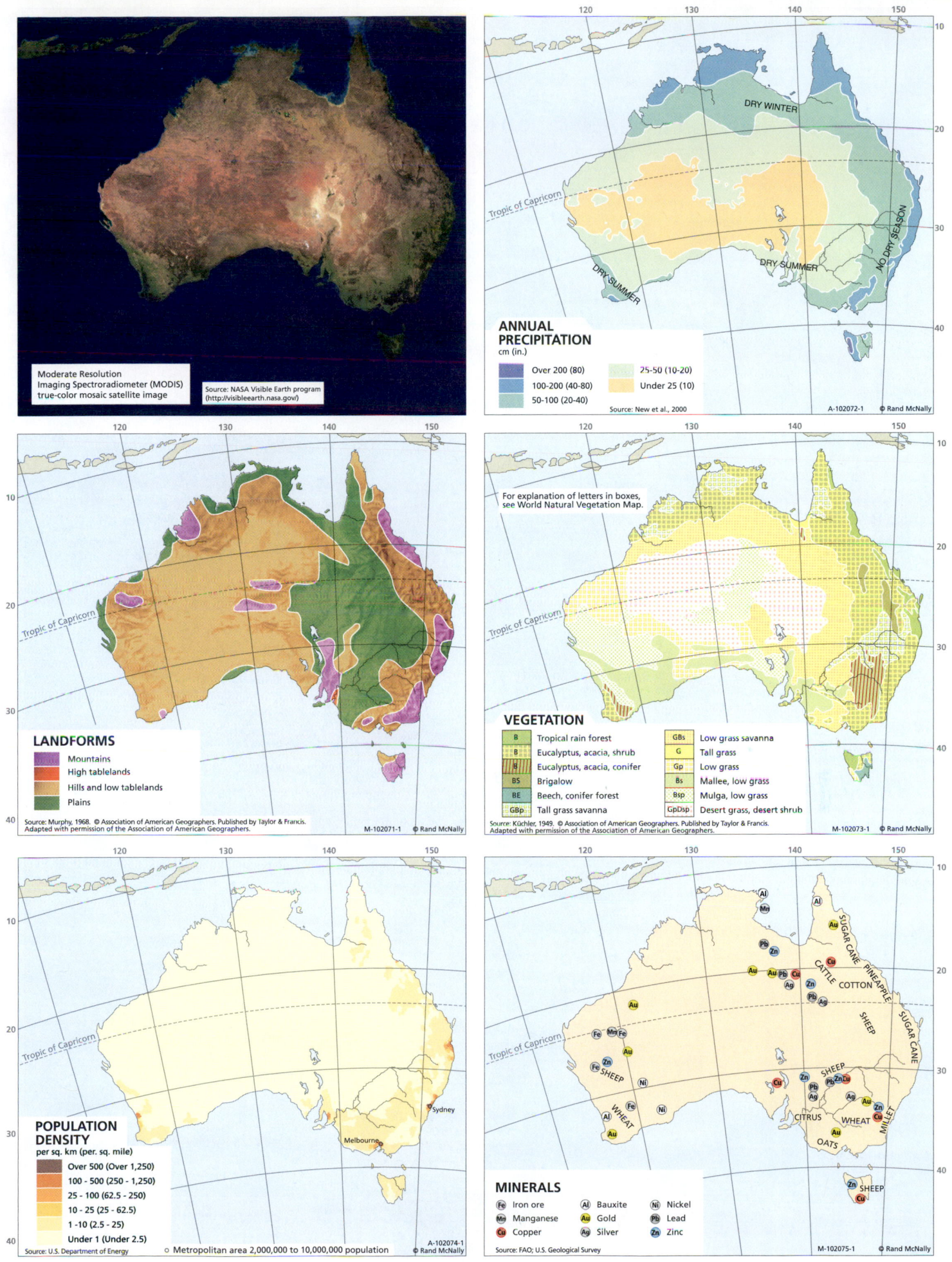

Moderate Resolution
Imaging Spectroradiometer (MODIS)
true-color mosaic satellite image

Source: NASA Visible Earth program
(http://visibleearth.nasa.gov/)

ANNUAL PRECIPITATION
cm (in.)

- Over 200 (80)
- 100–200 (40–80)
- 50–100 (20–40)
- 25–50 (10–20)
- Under 25 (10)

Source: New et al., 2000   A-102072-1   © Rand McNally

DRY WINTER

DRY SUMMER

DRY SUMMER

NO DRY SEASON

Tropic of Capricorn

LANDFORMS

- Mountains
- High tablelands
- Hills and low tablelands
- Plains

Source: Murphy, 1968. © Association of American Geographers. Published by Taylor & Francis.
Adapted with permission of the Association of American Geographers.   M-102071-1   © Rand McNally

Tropic of Capricorn

VEGETATION

For explanation of letters in boxes,
see World Natural Vegetation Map.

B	Tropical rain forest
B	Eucalyptus, acacia, shrub
B	Eucalyptus, acacia, conifer
BS	Brigalow
BE	Beech, conifer forest
GBp	Tall grass savanna
GBs	Low grass savanna
G	Tall grass
Gp	Low grass
Bs	Mallee, low grass
Bsp	Mulga, low grass
GpDsp	Desert grass, desert shrub

Source: Küchler, 1949. © Association of American Geographers. Published by Taylor & Francis.
Adapted with permission of the Association of American Geographers.   M-102073-1   © Rand McNally

Tropic of Capricorn

POPULATION DENSITY
per sq. km (per. sq. mile)

- Over 500 (Over 1,250)
- 100 – 500 (250 – 1,250)
- 25 – 100 (62.5 – 250)
- 10 – 25 (25 – 62.5)
- 1 – 10 (2.5 – 25)
- Under 1 (Under 2.5)

Sydney

Melbourne

Source: U.S. Department of Energy   ○ Metropolitan area 2,000,000 to 10,000,000 population   A-102074-1   © Rand McNally

Tropic of Capricorn

SUGAR CANE

PINEAPPLE

CATTLE

COTTON

SHEEP

SUGAR CANE

SHEEP

SHEEP

CITRUS

WHEAT

MILLET

OATS

WHEAT

SHEEP

MINERALS

Fe	Iron ore	Al	Bauxite	Ni	Nickel
Mn	Manganese	Au	Gold	Pb	Lead
Cu	Copper	Ag	Silver	Zn	Zinc

Source: FAO; U.S. Geological Survey   M-102075-1   © Rand McNally

SIMPSON DESERT NATL PARK
Birdsville
Haddon Downs
Cordillo Downs
Innamincka
STRZELECKI DESERT
Cowarie

GREAT ARTESIAN BASIN
Morney
Windorah
Betoota
Mount Howitt
Eromanga
Thylungra
Adavale

QUEENSLAND
Quilpie
Cooladdi
Charleville
Augathella
CHESTERTON RANGE
Injune
Taroom
Dawson
Eidsvold
Childers
Isis
Hervey Bay
FRASER ISLAND
Maryborough
Gayndah
Murgon
Wondai
Kingaroy
Nanango
Mt. Kiangarow 3760 ft. 1146 m
Dalby
Chinchilla
Miles
Wandoan
Moonie
GREAT SANDY NATIONAL PARK
Gympie
Tewantin-Noosa
Caloundra
MORETON ISLAND
Nambour
Caboolture
Redcliffe
Ipswich
Brisbane
Logan
Southport
Boonah

Lake Eyre North
Lake Eyre South
LAKE EYRE NATIONAL PARK
Cowarie
Etadunna
Marree
Muloorina

STURT STONY DESERT
Mt. Sturt 961 ft. 293 m
Tibooburra
Hungerford

DARLING DOWNS
Toowoomba
Warwick
Stanthorpe
Tenterfield
Mt. Bajimba 475 ft. 1446 m
Murwillumbah
Lismore
Casino
Ballina
CAPE BYRON

Lake Torrens
NORTH FLINDERS RANGE
Copley
Balcanoona
Lake Frome

NEW SOUTH WALES

GREAT DIVIDING RANGE
NEW ENGLAND RANGE
Glen Innes
Grafton
Maclean

SOUTH AUSTRALIA
St. Mary Peak 3832 ft. 1168 m
Hawker
Quorn
Port Augusta

BARRIER RANGE
Broken Hill

Round Mountain 5203 ft. 1586 m
Coffs Harbour

Whyalla
Iron Knob
EYRE PENINSULA
Kimba

MOUNT LOFTY RANGES

RIVERINA

VICTORIA

TASMANIA

INDIAN OCEAN

TASMAN SEA

BASS STRAIT

Scale 1:8,000,000
One inch to 128 miles
One cm to 80 km
Lambert Azimuthal Equal Area Projection

© Rand McNally
A-101780-1

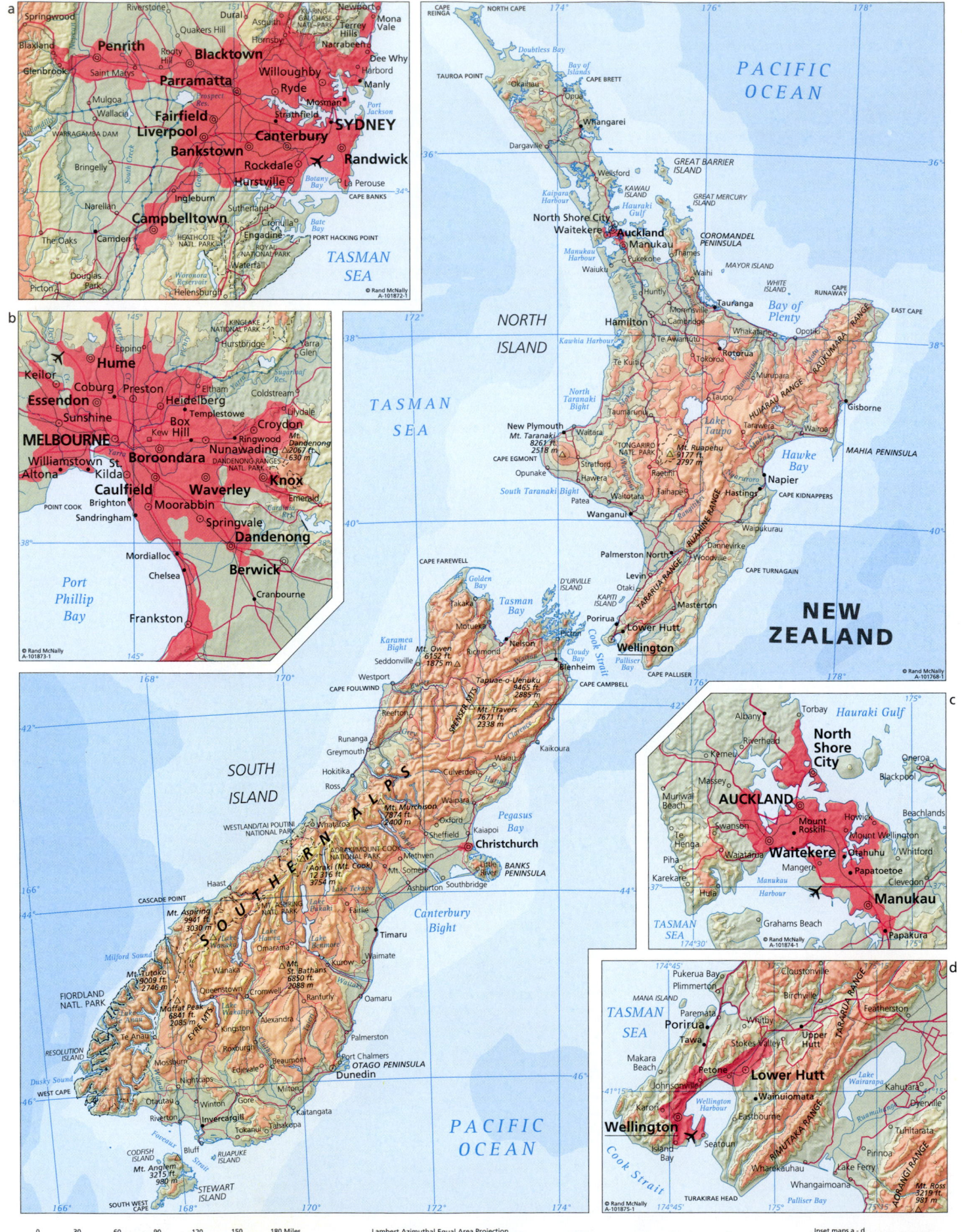

a

Springwood · Riverstone · Dural
Blaxland · Quakers Hill · Asquith · KU-RING-GAI CHASE NATL. PARK · Newport · Mona Vale
Glenbrook · **Penrith** · Rooty Hill · Hornsby · Terrey Hills · Dee Why
· Saint Marys · **Blacktown** · **Willoughby** · Harbord
Mulgoa · Wallacia · **Parramatta** · **Ryde** · Mosman · Manly
WARRAGAMBA DAM · **Fairfield** · Strathfield · Port Jackson
Bringelly · **Liverpool** · **Canterbury** · **SYDNEY**
· **Bankstown** · **Rockdale** · **Randwick**
Campbelltown · **Hurstville** · La Perouse
The Oaks · Camden · Ingleburn · Sutherland · Botany Bay · CAPE BANKS
Narellan · Cronulla · Bate Bay
HEATHCOTE NATL. PARK · Engadine · PORT HACKING POINT
Picton · Douglas Park · Waterfall · ROYAL NATIONAL PARK
Woronora Reservoir · Helensburgh
TASMAN SEA
© Rand McNally A-101872-1

b

KINGLAKE NATIONAL PARK
Epping · Hurstbridge · Yarra Glen
Keilor · **Hume** · Eltham · Coldstream
Essendon · **Coburg** · **Preston** · Heidelberg · Lilydale
Sunshine · Box Hill · Templestowe · Ringwood · **Croydon**
MELBOURNE · Kew · **Nunawading** · Mt. Dandenong 2067 ft. 630 m
Williamstown · St. Kilda · **Boroondara** · DANDENONG RANGES NATL. PARK
Altona · **Caulfield** · **Waverley** · **Knox** · Emerald
POINT COOK · Brighton · Moorabbin
Sandringham · **Springvale** · **Dandenong**
Port Phillip Bay · Mordialloc · Chelsea · **Berwick**
· Cranbourne
Frankston
© Rand McNally A-101873-1

NORTH ISLAND

CAPE REINGA · NORTH CAPE
TAUROA POINT · Doubtless Bay · CAPE BRETT
Okaihau · Bay of Islands · Opua
PACIFIC OCEAN
Whangarei
Dargaville · GREAT BARRIER ISLAND
Wellsford · KAWAU ISLAND · GREAT MERCURY ISLAND
Kaipara Harbour · Hauraki Gulf · MAYOR ISLAND
North Shore City · COROMANDEL PENINSULA
Waitekere · **Auckland** · WHITE ISLAND · CAPE RUNAWAY
Manukau Harbour · **Manukau** · Thames · EAST CAPE
Pukekohe · Bay of Plenty
Waiuku · Waihi
Huntly · Tauranga
Kawhia Harbour · Morrinsville · Cambridge · Whakatane · Opotiki
Hamilton · RAUKUMARA RANGE
Te Awamutu · Whakatane
Te Kuiti · Tokoroa · Rotorua
North Taranaki Bight · Taumarunu · Murupara · Gisborne
New Plymouth · Mt. Taranaki 8261 ft. 2518 m · Lake Taupo · Tarawera · Wairoa
Mt. Egmont · TONGARIRO NATL. PARK · Taupo · HUIARAU RANGE
CAPE EGMONT · Stratford · Mt. Ruapehu 9177 ft. 2797 m · MAHIA PENINSULA
Opunake · Hawera · Raetihi · Taihape · RUAHINE RANGE · Hawke Bay
South Taranaki Bight · Patea · Hastings · Napier
Waitotara · Waipukurau · CAPE KIDNAPPERS
Wanganui · Dannevirke
Palmerston North · Woodville · CAPE TURNAGAIN
CAPE FAREWELL · D'URVILLE ISLAND · Levin
Golden Bay · Takaka · KAPITI ISLAND · Otaki · Masterton
Tasman Bay · Motueka · TARARUA RANGE · Porirua · Lower Hutt
Karamea Bight · Richmond · Nelson · Picton · **Wellington**
Mt. Owen 6152 ft. 1875 m · Cook Strait · Blenheim · Cloudy Bay · Palliser Bay
NEW ZEALAND
Seddonville · CAPE CAMPBELL · CAPE PALLISER
Westport · Tapuae-o-Uenuku 9465 ft. 2885 m
CAPE FOULWIND · Mt. Travers 7671 ft. 2338 m
Reefton · SPENSER MTS. · Clarence
Runanga · Waiau
Greymouth · Kaikoura
SOUTH ISLAND · Hokitika · Culverden
Ross · Waipara
WESTLAND/TAI POUTINI NATIONAL PARK · Oxford · Pegasus Bay
Whataroa · Mt. Murchison 7874 ft. 2400 m · Sheffield · Kaiapoi
SOUTHERN ALPS · Aoraki/Mount Cook National Park · Methven · **Christchurch**
Aoraki (Mt. Cook) 12,316 ft. 3754 m · Mt. Somers · Little River
Haast · MT. ASPIRING NATL. PARK · Ashburton · Southbridge · BANKS PENINSULA
CASCADE POINT · Mt. Aspiring 9941 ft. 3030 m · Lake Tekapo · Canterbury Bight
Faithe · Timaru
Mt. Tutoko 9009 ft. 2746 m · Lake Pukaki · Mt. St. Bathans 6850 ft. 2088 m · Kurow · Waimate
FIORDLAND NATL. PARK · Moffat Peak 6841 ft. 2085 m · Wanaka · Omarama · Waitaki
Milford Sound · EYRE MTS. · Queenstown · Cromwell · Oamaru
RESOLUTION ISLAND · Lake Wakatipu · Alexandra · Palmerston
Te Anau · Kingston · Ranfurly
Dusky Sound · Mossburn · Roxburgh · Beaumont · Port Chalmers
WEST CAPE · Nightcaps · Edievale · OTAGO PENINSULA
Otautau · Winton · Gore · Milton · **Dunedin**
CODFISH ISLAND · Riverton · Invercargill · Kaitangata
Mt. Anglem 3215 ft. 980 m · Tokanui · Tahakopa
SOUTH WEST CAPE · Bluff · RUAPUKE ISLAND · Foveaux Strait
STEWART ISLAND
PACIFIC OCEAN
© Rand McNally A-101768-1

c

Torbay · Hauraki Gulf
Albany · Kermeu · Riverhead · Oneroa
Massey · **North Shore City** · Blackpool
Muriwai Beach · Swanson · Mount Roskill · Howick · Beachlands
Te Henga · **Auckland** · Mount Wellington · Whitford
Piha · **Waitekere** · Otahuhu
Karekare · Mangere · Papatoetoe · Clevedon
Hula · Manukau Harbour · **Manukau** · Grahams Beach
TASMAN SEA · **Papakura**
© Rand McNally A-101874-1

d

Cloustonville
Pukerua Bay · Plimmerton · Birchville
MANA ISLAND · Paremata · TARARUA RANGE · Featherston
TASMAN SEA · Whitby · Upper Hutt
Porirua · Tawa · Stokes Valley
Makara Beach · Petone · Lake Wairarapa
Lower Hutt · Kahutara
Karori · Johnsonville · Wainuiomata · RIMUTAKA RANGE · Gladstone
Wellington · Wellington Harbour · Eastbourne · Tuhitarata
Island Bay · Seatoun · Pirinoa · Lake Ferry
Cook Strait · Whangaimoana · AORANGI RANGE
TURAKIRAE HEAD · Wharekauhau · Mt. Ross 3219 ft. 981 m
Palliser Bay
© Rand McNally A-101875-1

0 30 60 90 120 150 180 Miles
0 30 60 90 120 150 180 210 240 270 300 Kilometers

Lambert Azimuthal Equal Area Projection
Scale 1:6,000,000
One inch to 96 miles
One cm to 60 km

Inset maps a – d
Lambert Conformal Conic Projection
Scale 1:1,000,000
One inch to 16 miles
One cm to 10 km

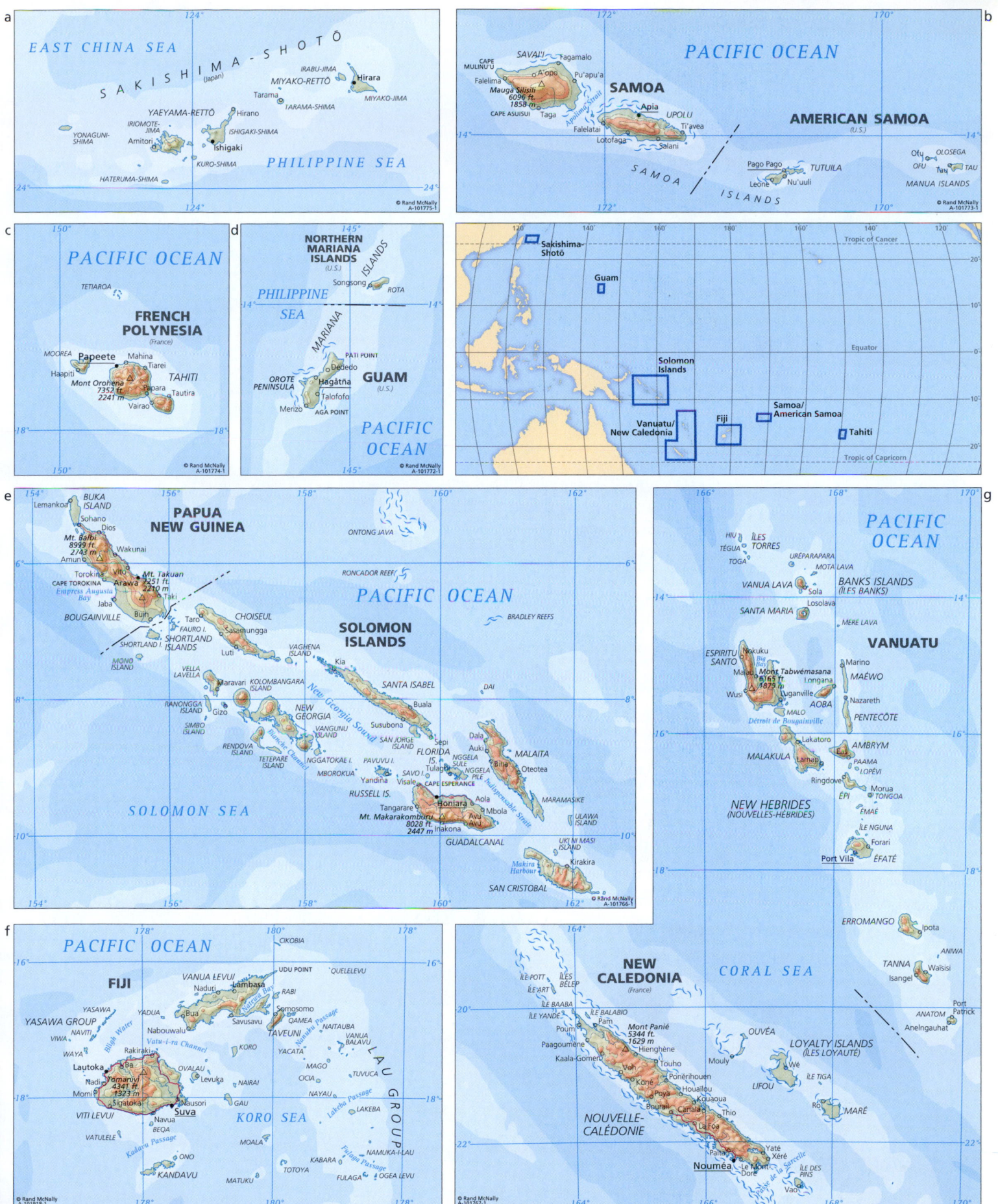

a

EAST CHINA SEA

SAKISHIMA-SHOTŌ (Japan)

MIYAKO-RETTŌ

Hirara

Irabu-Jima
Tarama
TARAMA-SHIMA
MIYAKO-JIMA

YAEYAMA-RETTŌ
Hirano
IRIOMOTE-JIMA
Amitori
ISHIGAKI-SHIMA
Ishigaki

YONAGUNI-SHIMA

HATERUMA-SHIMA

PHILIPPINE SEA

© Rand McNally
A-101775-1

b

PACIFIC OCEAN

CAPE MULINU'U
SAVAI'I
Fagamalo
Falelima
Pu'apu'a
A'opo
Mauga Silisili
6096 ft.
1858 m
SAMOA
Apia
Taga
UPOLU
CAPE ASUISUI
Falelatai
Ti'avea
Lotofaga
Salani
Apolima Strait

AMERICAN SAMOA
(U.S.)

Ofu
OLOSEGA
OFU
TAU
Pago Pago
Leone
TUTUILA
Nu'uuli
MANUA ISLANDS

SAMOA

ISLANDS

© Rand McNally
A-101773-1

c

PACIFIC OCEAN

TETIAROA

FRENCH POLYNESIA
(France)

MOOREA
Papeete
Mahina
Haapiti
Tiarei
TAHITI
Mont Orohena
7352 ft
2241 m
Papara
Tautira
Vairao

© Rand McNally
A-101774-1

d

NORTHERN MARIANA ISLANDS (U.S.)

Songsong
ROTA

PHILIPPINE SEA

MARIANA ISLANDS

PATI POINT
OROTE PENINSULA
Dededo
Hagåtña
GUAM
(U.S.)
Talofofo
Merizo
AGA POINT

PACIFIC OCEAN

© Rand McNally
A-101772-1

Tropic of Cancer

Sakishima-Shotō

Guam

Solomon Islands

Vanuatu/
New Caledonia
Fiji
Samoa/
American Samoa
Tahiti

Equator

Tropic of Capricorn

e

BUKA ISLAND
Lemankoa
Sohano
Dios
PAPUA NEW GUINEA
Mt. Balbi
8999 ft.
2743 m
Wakunai
Amun
Torokina
Vito
Mt. Takuan
7251 ft.
2210 m
CAPE TOROKINA
Arawa
Empress Augusta Bay
Jaba
Buin
Taki
BOUGAINVILLE

ONTONG JAVA

RONCADOR REEF

PACIFIC OCEAN

BRADLEY REEFS

Taro
FAURO I.
SHORTLAND ISLANDS
SHORTLAND I.
MONO ISLAND

CHOISEUL
Sasamungga
Luti
VAGHENA ISLAND
Kia

SANTA ISABEL

DAI

SOLOMON ISLANDS

VELLA LAVELLA
Maravari
KOLOMBANGARA ISLAND
RANONGGA ISLAND
Gizo
NEW GEORGIA
New Georgia Sound
Buala
Susubona
SIMBO ISLAND
RENDOVA ISLAND
VANGUNU ISLAND
SAN JORGE ISLAND
TETEPARE ISLAND
NGGATOKAE I.
PAVUVU I.
Sepi
Dala
Auki
FLORIDA IS.
NGGELA SULE
MALAITA
MBOROKUA
SAVO I.
Tulaghi
NGGELA PILE
Oteotea
RUSSELL IS.
Yandina
Visale
CAPE ESPERANCE
Aola
MARAMASIKE
Tangarare
Honiara
Avu Avu
ULAWA ISLAND
Mt. Makarakomburu
8028 ft.
2447 m
Inakona
Mbola
UKI NI MASI ISLAND
SOLOMON SEA
GUADALCANAL
Kirakira
Makira Harbour
SAN CRISTOBAL

© Rand McNally
A-101766-1

g

PACIFIC OCEAN

HIU
ÎLES TORRES
TÉGUA
 URÉPARAPARA
TOGA
MOTA LAVA
VANUA LAVA
Sola
BANKS ISLANDS
(ÎLES BANKS)
SANTA MARIA
Losolava

MERE LAVA

ESPIRITU SANTO
Nokuku
Big Bay
Malao
Mont Tabwémasana
6165 ft.
1879 m
Longana
Marino
VANUATU
MAÉWO
Wusi
Luganville
AOBA
Nazareth
MALO
Détroit de Bougainville
PENTECÔTE
Lakatoro
AMBRYM
MALAKULA
Lamap
Lili
PAAMA
LOPÉVI
Ringdove
Morua
ÉPI
TONGOA
NEW HEBRIDES
(NOUVELLES-HÉBRIDES)
ÉMAE
ÎLE NGUNA
Forari
Port Vila
ÉFATÉ

f

PACIFIC OCEAN

CIKOBIA

FIJI

VANUA LEVU
UDU POINT
QUELELEVU
Naduri
Labasa
RABI
YASAWA GROUP
YASAWA
YADUA
Bua
Somosomo
NAVITI
Nabouwalu
Savusavu
TAVEUNI
QAMEA
NAITAUBA
VIWA
Rakiraki
KORO
NANUKU PASSAGE
VANUA BALAVU
WAYA
Vatu-i-ra Channel
YACATA
MAGO
Lautoka
Ba
OVALAU
Levuka
NAIRAI
CICIA
TUVUCA
Nadi
Tomaniivi
4341 ft.
1323 m
Sigatoka
Nausori
GAU
NAYAU
LAKEBA
Momi
Suva
BEQA
MOALA
LAU GROUP
VITI LEVU
Navua
Lakeba Passage
KOBARA
VATULELE
KORO SEA
ONO
TOTOYA
NAMUKA-I-LAU
Kadavu Passage
KANDAVU
MATUKU
Fulaga Passage
OGEA LEVU
FULAGA

© Rand McNally
A-101918-1

ERROMANGO
Ipota

NEW CALEDONIA
(France)

ÎLE POTT
ÎLES BÉLEP
ÎLE ART
ÎLE BAABA
ÎLE YANDÉ
ÎLE BALABIO
Poum
Pam
TANNA
Isangel
Waisisi
ANIWA
CORAL SEA
Port Patrick
ANATOM
Anelngauhat

Paagoumene
Kaala-Gomen
Mont Panié
5344 ft.
1629 m
Hienghène
Touho
OUVÉA
Voh
Ponérihouen
Koné
Mouly
Poya
Houailou
LOYALTY ISLANDS
(ÎLES LOYAUTÉ)
Bourail
Kouaoua
LIFOU
ÎLE TIGA
Carala
Thio
Nouméa
La Foa
NOUVELLE-CALÉDONIE
Paita
Yaté
Xépé
Dore
ÎLE DES PINS
Le Mont-Dore
Passe de la Sarcelle
Vao

© Rand McNally
A-101767-1

Inset maps a - d
Lambert Azimuthal Equal Area Projection
Scale 1:4,000,000
One inch to 64 miles
One cm to 40 km

Inset maps e - g
Lambert Azimuthal Equal Area Projection
Scale 1:8,000,000
One inch to 128 miles
One cm to 80 km

MINAMI-DAITŌ-JIMA (Jpn.)
HAHAJIMA-RETTO (Jpn.)
OKINO-DAITŌ-JIMA (Jpn.)
OGASAWARA-SHOTŌ (Jpn.)
KITA-IŌ-JIMA (Jpn.)
KAZAN-RETTO
IWO JIMA
MINAMI-IŌ-JIMA (Jpn.)
Tropic of Cancer

MARCUS ISLAND (Jpn.)

PHILIPPINE BASIN

OKINO-TORI-SHIMA (Jpn.)
FARALLON DE PAJAROS

PHILIPPINE SEA

ASUNCION ISLAND
AGRIHAN
PAGAN
ALAMAGAN
GUGUAN
ANATAHAN
SARIGAN
FARALLON DE MEDINILLA
SAIPAN
TINIAN
ROTA

NORTHERN MARIANA ISLANDS (U.S.)

EAST MARIANA BASIN

MID-PACIFIC MOUNTAINS

WAKE ISLAND (U.S.)

MICRO

TAONGI

MARSHALL ISLANDS

ENEWETAK
BIKINI
RONGELAP
UTRIK
BIKAR

CENT

Hagåtña
GUAM (U.S.)

Challenger Deep
-35 810 ft.
-10 915 m

M
A
R
I
A
N
A
T
R
E
N
C
H

YAP
ULITHI

GAFERUT

HALL ISLANDS

WOLEAI
EAURIPIK
LAMOTREK
CHUUK (TRUK ISLANDS)
LOSAP ATOLL
OROLUK
NAMOLOK ATOLL
SENYAVIN ISLANDS
Palikir
Pohnpei
MWOKIL
MORTLOCK ISLANDS
PINGELAP
KOSRAE

UJELANG

WOTHO

KWAJALEIN
LIB

WOTJE
MALOELAP
MAJURO
MILI

KILI
EBON

PACI

BAS

BABELDAOB
Melekeok
BELILIOU

PALAU

SONSOROL ISLANDS
PULO ANNA
MERIR
HELEN ISLAND
TOBI

WEST CAROLINE BASIN

CAROLINE ISLANDS

NUKUORO

FEDERATED STATES OF MICRONESIA

EAST CAROLINE BASIN

KAPINGAMARANGI

BUTARITARI

TARAWA
KURIA
ABEMAMA

K
I
R
I
B
A
T
I

KEPULAUAN MAPIA

PULAU WAIGEO
Equator

Sorong
JAZIRAH DOBERAI
Manokwari
BIAK
TANJUNG D'URVILLE
PULAU YAPEN

NINIGO GROUP
WUVULU ISLAND

MUSSAU ISLAND

MANUS ISLAND
ADMIRALTY ISLANDS
NEW HANOVER
Kavieng
NEW IRELAND
TABAR ISLANDS
LIHIR GROUP

NAURU

BANABA

BERU
NONOUTI
NIKUNAU
ARORAE

Fakfak
CERAM

Jayapura
Aitape
Wewak

PEGUNUNGAN VAN REES

BISMARCK SEA
WITU ISLANDS
Rabaul
BUKA ISLAND

M
E
L
A

MELANESIA

KEPULAUAN KAI
KEPULAUAN ARU

PEGUNUNGAN MAOKE
Puncak Jaya
16 503 ft.
5030 m

NEW GUINEA

Mt. Wilhelm
14 793 ft.
4509 m
Madang

BISMARCK ARCHIPELAGO
NEW BRITAIN
Mt. Ulawun
7657 ft.
2334 m

BOUGAINVILLE

NANUMEA
NIUTAO

BANDA SEA

Mt. Giluwe
14 331 ft.
4368 m

PAPUA NEW GUINEA
Lae

SOLOMON SEA

VELLA LAVELLA
KIRIWINA ISLANDS
NEW GEORGIA

CHOISEUL

Santa Isabel

SOLOMON ISLANDS

MALAITA

TUVALU

NIU
VAITUPU

FUNAFUTI

INDONESIA
KEPULAUAN TANIMBAR

TANJUNG VALS

Digul

Merauke

Fly

Owen Stanley Range

Popondetta
Samarai

MUYUA ISLAND
VANGUNU I.

D'ENTRECASTEAUX ISLANDS
MISIMA ISLAND
LOUISIADE ARCHIPELAGO
TAGULA ISLAND
YELA ISLAND

GUADALCANAL
Honiara

SAN CRISTOBAL
RENNELL

NENDO
SANTA CRUZ ISLANDS
VANIKOLO

NIULAKITA

ROTUMA

ARAFURA SEA

Gulf of Papua

Torres Strait

Port Moresby

CAPE YORK

CORAL SEA BASIN

TORRES ISLANDS
VANUA LAVA
SANTA MARIA
BANKS ISLANDS

MELVILLE ISLAND
COBOURG PENINSULA
CAPE WESSEL

CAPE ARNHEM

CAPE GRENVILLE

CHILCOTT ISLET

ESPIRITU SANTO
MAÉWO
PENTECÔTE
AMBRYM

NORTH FIJI BASIN

VANUA LEVU

Darwin
ARNHEM LAND
Katherine
Roper

GROOTE EYLANDT

Weipa
CAPE YORK PENINSULA
Cooktown

Gulf of Carpentaria
WELLESLEY ISLANDS

CORAL SEA

MELLISH REEF

MALAKULA
ÉPI
ÉFATÉ
Port Vila
VANUATU

FIJI

VITI LEVU
Suva

Birdum

Mitchell

Normanton

ÎLES CHESTERFIELD

ÎLE DE SABLE

ERROMANGO
TANNA

KANDAVU

TANAMI DESERT

BARKLY TABLELAND
Tennant Creek

Cairns
Bartle Frere
5322 ft.
1622 m
Charters Towers

CAYE DE L'OBSERVATOIRE

ANATOM

Mount Isa

Flinders

Townsville
Bowen

Mackay

NOUVELLE-CALÉDONIE
OUVÉA
LOYALTY ISLANDS
LIFOU

NEW HEBRIDES

Alice Springs
SIMPSON DESERT
Birdsville

AUSTRALIA

GIBSON DESERT

Lake Mackay

Tropic of Capricorn

GREAT ARTESIAN BASIN
Longreach
Emerald
Rockhampton
Gladstone
SANDY CAPE

NEW CALEDONIA
Nouméa
ÎLE DES PINS

SOUTH FIJI BASIN

Eyre Cr.

Charleville
Toowoomba

Diamantina

Barcoo

GREY RANGE

Warrego

FRASER ISLAND
Harvey Bay

CATO ISLAND

GREAT VICTORIA DESERT

Mt. Woodroffe
4708 ft.
1435 m

Lake Eyre

Macumba

Cooper Cr.

Charleville

Moree

Brisbane
Southport
Lismore

Coffs Harbour

NORFOLK ISLAND (Austl.)

GREAT DIVIDING RANGE

GREAT ARTESIAN BASIN

0   150   300   450   600   750 Miles
0 150 300 450 600 750 900 1,050 Kilometers

Lambert Azimuthal Equal Area Projection
Scale 1:27,000,000
One inch to 426 miles
One cm to 270 km

KURE
MIDWAY
ISLANDS
(U.S.)
LISIANSKI
ISLAND
LAYSAN
ISLAND
MARO
REEF
H A W A I I A N   I S L A N D S
NECKER
ISLAND
FRENCH
FRIGATE
SHOALS
NIHOA
KAUA'I
NI'IHAU
O'AHU
MOLOKA'I
MAUI
LĀNA'I
UNITED
STATES
Honolulu
Mauna Kea Hilo
13 796 ft
4205 m
HAWAI'I
KALAE

Tropic of Cancer

CLARION FRACTURE ZONE

P A C I F I C   O C E A N

JOHNSTON
ATOLL
(U.S.)

SCHJETMAN
REEF

RA L

F I C

I N

CLIPPERTON FRACTURE ZONE

KINGMAN
REEF
PALMYRA
ATOLL
(U.S.)
TERAINA
TABUAERAN
KIRIMATI
(CHRISTMAS
ISLAND)
C H R I S T M A S   R I D G E
L I N E   I S L A N D S

JARVIS
ISLAND
(U.S.)
Equator

HOWLAND ISLAND
(U.S.)
BAKER ISLAND
(U.S.)
WINSLOW
REEF
P
CANTON
BIRNIE
ENDERBURY
RAWAKI
NIKUMARORO
PHOENIX ISLANDS
ORONA
MANRA
MALDEN

K I R I B A T I
STARBUCK

ATAFU
TOKELAU
(N.Z.)
FAKAOFO
SWAINS
ISLANDS
NASSAU
ISLAND
PENRHYN
MANIHIKI
NORTHERN
COOK ISLANDS
SUWARROW
VOSTOK
CAROLINE
FLINT
EIAO
NUKU HIVA
UA POU
HIVA OA
MARQUESAS ISLANDS
FATU
HIVA

WALLIS
AND
FUTUNA
(Fr.)
ÎLE FUTUNA
ÎLES WALLIS
SAMOA
Matā'utu
Apia
SAVAI'I
UPOLU
AMERICAN
SAMOA
(U.S.)
SAMOA ISLANDS
TUTUILA
Pago
Pago
MANUA
ISLANDS
MATAIVA
ÎLES DU
ROI GEORGES
ÎLES DU
DÉSAPPOINTEMENT
ÎLE TIKEI
TAFAHI
TONGA
VAVA'U
NIUE
(N.Z.)
COOK
ISLANDS
(N.Z.)
PALMERSTON
AITUTAKI
SOUTHERN
COOK ISLANDS
MITIARO
ATIU
MAUKE
RAROTONGA
MANGAIA
ÎLES MARIA
MAKATEA
MANUAE
BORA-
BORA
RAIATEA
SOCIETY ISLANDS
MOOREA
Papeete
TAHITI
ANAA
RARAKA
RAROÏA
MARUTEA NORD
ÎLES TUAMOTU
PUKARUA
REAO
FRENCH
POLYNESIA
(Fr.)
AHUNUI
TUREIA
MURUROA
MARUTEA
SUD
ÎLES GAMBIER
LAU
GROUP
ONO-I-LAU
TONGA ISLANDS
TONGATAPU
Nuku'alofa
EUA
RIMATARA
RURUTU
TUBUAI
ÎLES TUBUAI
RAIVAVAE
Tropic of Capricorn

SOUTHWEST PACIFIC
BASIN
INTERNATIONAL DATE LINE

KERMADEC TRENCH
RAOUL
KERMADEC
ISLANDS
(N.Z.)
RAPA
ÎLES MAROTIRI
OENO
ATOLL
PITCAIRN
ISLAND
HENDERSON
ISLAND
PITCAIRN
ISLANDS
(U.K.)

© Rand McNally
A-101776-1

0   300   600   900   1200   1500 Miles

0   300   600   900   1200   1500   1800   2100 Kilometers

Mollweide Projection
Scale 1:55,000,000
One inch to 868 miles
One cm to 550 km

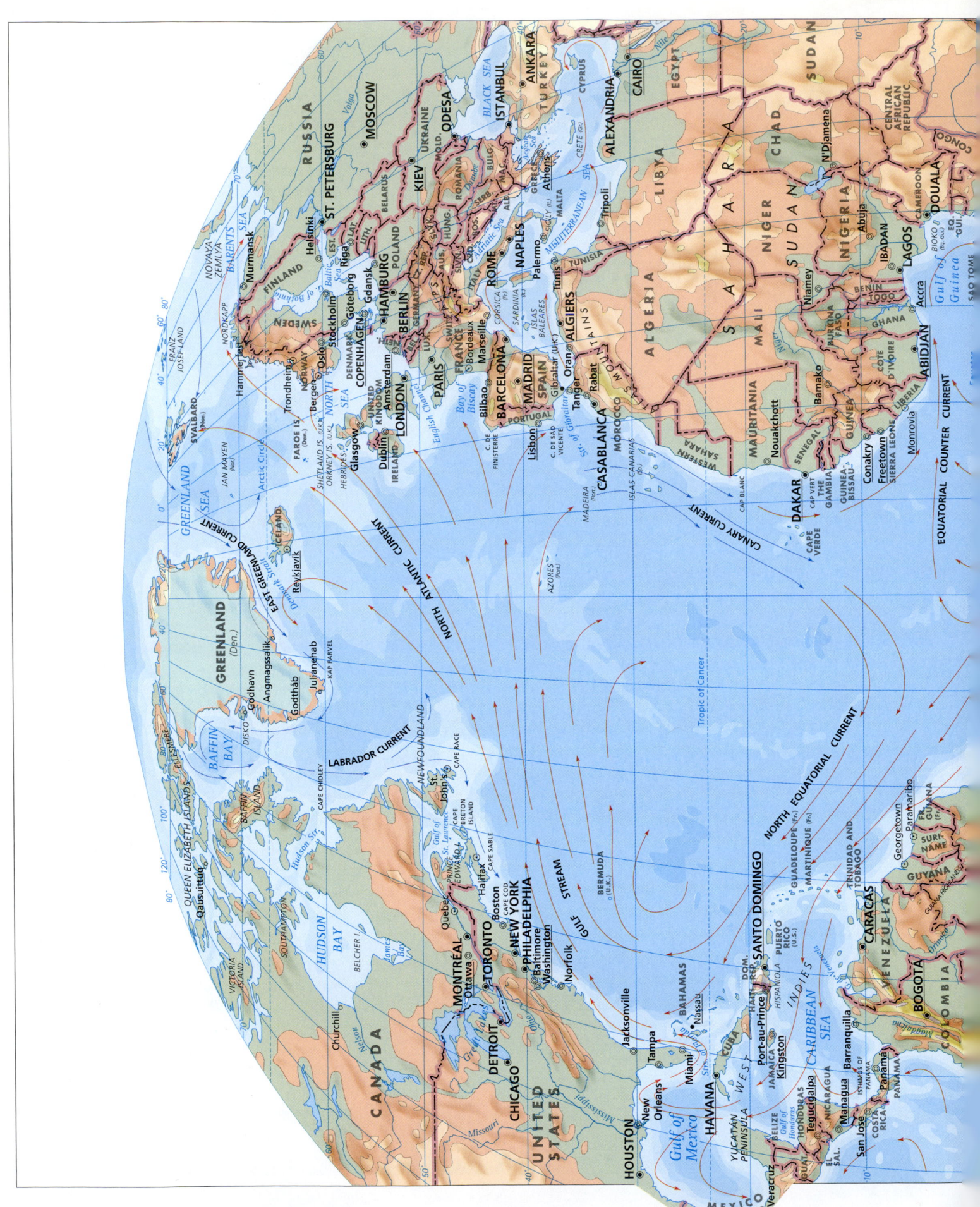

CONGO BASIN
DEM. REP. OF THE CONGO (ZAIRE)
ZAMBIA
ZIMBABWE
20°
BOTSWANA
KALAHARI DESERT
SWAZILAND
LESOTHO
30°
Durban
40°
50°
60°
CAPE ANN
© Rand McNally
M-100302-1

GABON
& PRINCIPE
CAP LOPEZ
Brazzaville
KINSHASA
LUANDA
ANGOLA
Benguela
NAMIBIA
Walvis Bay
NAMIB DESERT
Orange
SOUTH AFRICA
CAPE OF GOOD HOPE
Port Elizabeth
CAPE AGULHAS
CAPE TOWN

BENGUELA CURRENT

70°

ST. HELENA
(U.K.)

80°

Tropic of Capricorn

SOUTHERN OCEAN

60°

QUEEN MAUD LAND

ASCENSION
(St. Hel.)

GOUGH
(St. Hel.)

BOUVETØYA
(Nor.)

40°

ARQUIPÉLAGO FERNANDO DE NORONHA (Braz.)

20°

0°

TRISTAN DA CUNHA
(St. Hel.)

COATS LAND

CABO DE SAO ROQUE

IS. MARTIN
VAZ (Braz.)

WESTWIND DRIFT

20°

ANTARCTICA

RECIFE
Fortaleza
BRAZIL
SALVADOR
BRAZILIAN HIGHLANDS
São Francisco
BRAZIL CURRENT

SOUTH GEORGIA AND THE SOUTH SANDWICH ISLANDS (U.K.)

SOUTH SANDWICH ISLANDS

WEDDELL SEA

40°

Belém
Manaus
Amazon
Madeira
RIO DE JANEIRO
CABO FRIO
PORTO ALEGRE
SOUTH GEORGIA
SOUTH ORKNEY IS. (U.K.)
BERKNER I.

60°

SÃO PAULO
Brasília
Rio de la Plata
MONTEVIDEO
URUGUAY
FALKLAND IS. (U.K.)
SOUTH SHETLAND IS. (U.K.)
ANTARCTIC PEN.

PARAGUAY
Paraná
GRAN CHACO
Rosario
PAMPAS
BUENOS AIRES
Bahía Blanca
Golfo San Matías
Estrecho de Magallanes
TIERRA DEL FUEGO
CABO DE HORNOS
ALEXANDER
BELLINGHAUSEN SEA
ADELAIDE

BOLIVIA
Sucre
ARGENTINA
Golfo San Jorge
Punta Arenas
WELLINGTON
ELLSWORTH LAND

80°

Manaus
LA PAZ
CHILE
ANDES
Cerro Aconcagua 22 831 ft 6959 m
Valparaíso
SANTIAGO
Concepción
ISLA GRANDE DE CHILOÉ
ARCHIPIÉLAGO DE LOS CHONOS
THURSTON SEA

100°

PERU
Antofagasta
SAN AMBROSIO (Chile)
SAN FELIX (Chile)
IS. DE JUAN FERNÁNDEZ (Chile)

120°

GUAYAQUIL
ECUADOR
Trujillo
LIMA

PACIFIC OCEAN

70°

60°

50°

40°

30°

20°

10°

Antarctic Circle

Warm ocean currents
Cold ocean currents

Mollweide Projection
Scale 1:50,000,000
One inch to 790 miles
One cm to 500 km

Miles
Kilometers
0   200   400   600   800   1000
0   400   800   1200 1600

Mollweide Projection
Scale 1:50,000,000
One inch to 790 miles
One cm to 500 km

→ Warm ocean currents

→ Cold ocean currents

0 200 400 600 800 1000 Miles
0 400 800 1200 1600 Kilometers

© Rand McNally
M-180301-1

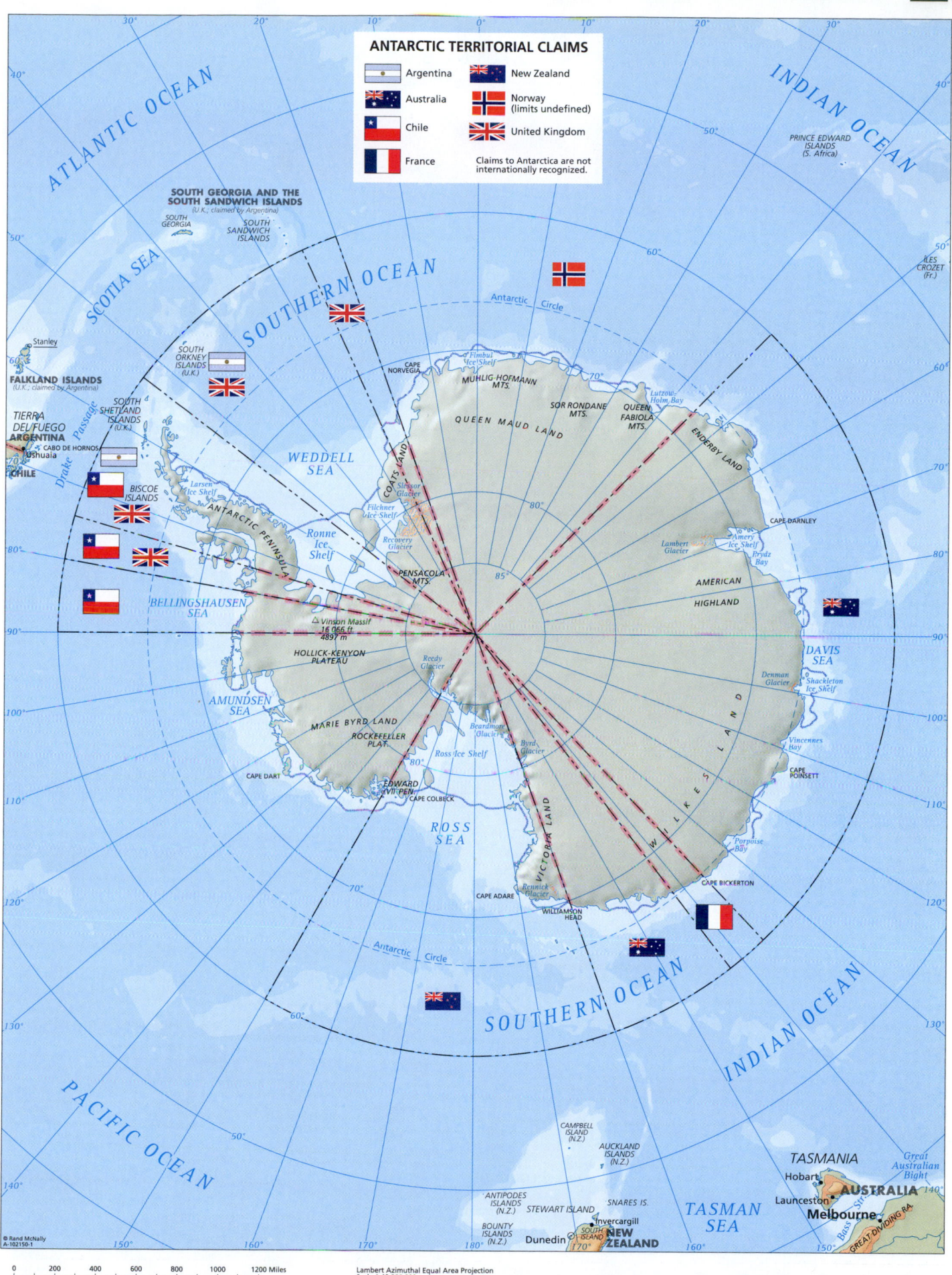

ATLANTIC OCEAN

INDIAN OCEAN

ANTARCTIC TERRITORIAL CLAIMS

Argentina

Australia

Chile

France

New Zealand

Norway
(limits undefined)

United Kingdom

Claims to Antarctica are not
internationally recognized.

PRINCE EDWARD
ISLANDS
(S. Africa)

SOUTH GEORGIA AND THE
SOUTH SANDWICH ISLANDS
(U.K.; claimed by Argentina)

SOUTH
GEORGIA

SOUTH
SANDWICH
ISLANDS

ÎLES
CROZET
(Fr.)

SCOTIA SEA

SOUTHERN OCEAN

Antarctic Circle

CAPE
NORVEGIA

Fimbul
Ice Shelf

MUHLIG HOFMANN
MTS.

SOR RONDANE
MTS.

QUEEN
FABIOLA
MTS.

Lutzow-
Holm Bay

ENDERBY LAND

Stanley

SOUTH ORKNEY
ISLANDS
(U.K.)

QUEEN MAUD LAND

FALKLAND ISLANDS
(U.K.; claimed by Argentina)

SOUTH
SHETLAND
ISLANDS
(U.K.)

TIERRA
DEL FUEGO
ARGENTINA

CABO DE HORNOS
Ushuaia

CHILE

Drake Passage

WEDDELL
SEA

COATS LAND

Slessor
Glacier

CAPE DARNLEY

BISCOE
ISLANDS

ANTARCTIC PENINSULA

Larsen
Ice Shelf

Ronne
Ice
Shelf

Filchner
Ice Shelf

Recovery
Glacier

Amery
Ice Shelf

Lambert
Glacier

Brydz
Bay

Ronne
Ice
Shelf

PENSACOLA
MTS.

AMERICAN

HIGHLAND

BELLINGSHAUSEN
SEA

△ Vinson Massif
16,066 ft
4897 m

HOLLICK-KENYON
PLATEAU

Reedy
Glacier

DAVIS
SEA

Denman
Glacier

Shackleton
Ice Shelf

AMUNDSEN
SEA

MARIE BYRD LAND

ROCKEFELLER
PLAT.

Beardmore
Glacier

Byrd
Glacier

Ross Ice Shelf

Vincennes
Bay

CAPE
POINSETT

CAPE DART

EDWARD
VII PEN.

CAPE COLBECK

ROSS
SEA

VICTORIA LAND

WILKES LAND

Porpoise
Bay

CAPE BICKERTON

CAPE ADARE

Rennick
Glacier

WILLIAMSON
HEAD

Antarctic Circle

SOUTHERN OCEAN

PACIFIC OCEAN

INDIAN OCEAN

CAMPBELL
ISLAND
(N.Z.)

AUCKLAND
ISLANDS
(N.Z.)

TASMANIA

Great
Australian
Bight

ANTIPODES
ISLANDS
(N.Z.)

STEWART ISLAND

SNARES IS.

TASMAN
SEA

Hobart

AUSTRALIA

BOUNTY
ISLANDS
(N.Z.)

SOUTH
ISLAND

Invercargill
NEW
ZEALAND

Launceston

Melbourne

Dunedin

GREAT DIVIDING RA.

© Rand McNally
A-102150-1

0   200   400   600   800   1000   1200 Miles

0   200 400 600 800 1000 1200 1400 1600 1800 2000 Kilometer

Lambert Azimuthal Equal Area Projection
Scale 1:40,000,000
One inch to 640 miles
One cm to 400 km

PACIFIC OCEAN

HONSHŪ
HOKKAIDŌ
JAPAN
SAPPORO
KURIL ISLANDS
SEA OF JAPAN
SIKHOTE-ALIN'
ALEUTIAN ISLANDS
KOMANDORSKI ISLANDS
SEA OF OKHOTSK
SAKHALIN
Khabarovsk
BERING SEA
KAMCHATKA PENINSULA
CAPE OLYUTORSKI
Petropavlovsk-Kamchatskiy
CHINA
KODIAK ISLAND
Bristol Bay
NUNIVAK ISLAND
ST. LAWRENCE ISLAND
MYS NAVARIN
Gulf of Anadyr
STANOVOY RANGE
STANOVOY MTS.
ALASKA PEN.
Gulf of Alaska
Mt. McKinley 20 320 ft. 6194 m
Nome
Cherskiy
CHERSKIY MOUNTAINS
Yakutsk
Aldan
Anchorage
A.R.
ALASKA
Fairbanks
CHUKCHI SEA
VERKHOYANSK MTS.
Zhigansk
Lensk
QUEEN CHARLOTTE ISLANDS
VANCOUVER ISLAND
COAST MTS.
Prince Rupert
Whitehorse
BROOKS RANGE
Arctic Circle
POINT BARROW
OSTROV VRANGELYA
EAST SIBERIAN SEA
Tiksi
Lena
CENTRAL SIBERIAN PLATEAU
Vancouver
ROCKY MTS.
MACKENZIE MTS.
Mackenzie
BEAUFORT SEA
NEW SIBERIAN ISLANDS
LAPTEV SEA
Edmonton
Great Slave Lake
Great Bear Lake
Amundsen Gulf
BANKS ISLAND
PRINCE PATRICK ISLAND
TAYMYR PENINSULA
Khatanga
RUSSIA
Yellowknife
Kugluktuk
CANADA
VICTORIA ISLAND
QUEEN ELIZABETH ISLANDS
ELLEF RINGNES ISLAND
North Magnetic Pole
SEVERNAYA ZEMLYA
Noril'sk
Arviat
Nelson
PRINCE OF WALES ISLAND
SOMERSET ISLAND
Resolute
ELLESMERE ISLAND
ARCTIC OCEAN
FRANZ JOSEF LAND
KARA SEA
WEST SIBERIAN PLAIN
SOUTHAMPTON ISLAND
HUDSON BAY
COATS ISLAND
Foxe Basin
DEVON ISLAND
KAP MORRIS JESUP
NOVAYA ZEMLYA
YAMAL PEN.
Ob
OMSK
MANSEL ISLAND
Thule
NORDOSTRUNDINGEN
YENISEY
PÉNINSULE D'UNGAVA
BAFFIN ISLAND
BAFFIN BAY
SVALBARD (Nor.)
BARENTS SEA
OSTROV KOLGUYEV
URAL
Churchill
Iqaluit
SPITSBERGEN
KANIN NOS
YEKATERINBURG
GREENLAND (Den.)
NOVAYA ZEMLYA
KAZAKH.
Davis Strait
BJØRNØYA
MYS
CHELYABINSK
MTS.
Godthåb
NORDKAPP
Murmansk
LABRADOR SEA
GREENLAND SEA
Arctic Circle
Julianehåb
KAP BREWSTER
JAN MAYEN (Nor.)
Arkhangel'sk
KAZAKHSTAN
CAPE BAULD
CAPE FAREWELL
Denmark Strait
NORWEGIAN SEA
NEWFOUNDLAND
HORN
FINLAND
ST. PETERSBURG
Volga
ICELAND
FONTUR
NORWAY
SWEDEN
Volga
MOSCOW
Reykjavík
LATVIA
FAROE ISLANDS (Den.)
ESTONIA
Stockholm
Gora El'brus 18 510 ft. 5642 m
TBILISI
SHETLAND IS.
Bergen
BALTIC SEA
LITH.
BELARUS
KIEV
GEOR.
ATLANTIC OCEAN
HEBRIDES
ORKNEY IS.
Oslo
RUSSIA
UKRAINE
BLACK SEA
NORTH SEA
DENMARK
POLAND
IRELAND
UNITED KINGDOM
NETH.
BERLIN
Danube
BUDAPEST
ROMANIA
BUCHAREST
TURKEY
ANKARA
MIZEN HEAD
LONDON
BELG.
GERMANY
CZ. REP.
SLVK.
CARPATHIAN MTS.
HUNG.
BULGARIA
SERBIA
AZORES (Port.)
PARIS
LUX.
AUS.
SLVN.
CRO.
BOS.
ISTANBUL
SYRIA
FRANCE
SWITZ.
ITALY
MOLD.
Bay of Biscay

0 200 400 600 800 1000 1200 Miles
0 200 400 600 800 1000 1200 1400 1600 1800 2000 Kilometers

Lambert Azimuthal Equal Area Projection
Scale 1:40,000,000
One inch to 640 miles
One cm to 400 km

© Rand McNally
A-102149-1

This table gives the area, population, population density, political status, capital, and predominant languages for every country in the world. The political units listed are categorized by political status in the 'Form of Government and Ruling Power' column of the table, as follows:

A independent countries;

B internally independent political entities which are under the protection of another country in matters of defense and foreign affairs;

C colonies and other dependent political units;

D the major administrative subdivisions of Australia, Canada, China, the United Kingdom, and the United States.

For comparison, the table also includes the continents and the world. All footnotes appear at the end of the table.

The populations are estimates for January 1, 2009, made by Rand McNally on the basis of official data, United States Census Bureau estimates, and other available information. Area figures include inland water.

Region or political division	Est. Pop. 1/1/09	Area sq. km.	Area sq. mi.	Pop. per sq. km.	Pop. per sq. mi.	Form of Government and Ruling Power	Political Status	Capital	Predominant Languages
Afars and Issas *see Djibouti*									
† Afghanistan	33,170,000	652,090	251,773	51	132	Transitional	A	Kabul (Kābol)	Dari, Pashto, Uzbek, Turkmen
Africa	985,490,000	30,300,000	11,700,000	33	84				
Alabama	4,685,000	135,765	52,419	35	89	State (U.S.)	D	Montgomery	English
Alaska	690,000	1,717,854	663,267	0.4	1.0	State (U.S.)	D	Juneau	English, indigenous
† Albania	3,630,000	28,748	11,100	126	327	Republic	A	Tiranë	Albanian, Greek
Alberta	3,570,000	661,848	255,541	5.4	14	Province (Canada)	D	Edmonton	English
† Algeria	33,975,000	2,381,741	919,595	14	37	Republic	A	Algiers (Alger)	Arabic, Berber dialects, French
American Samoa	65,000	199	77	327	844	Unincorporated territory (U.S.)	C	Pago Pago	Samoan, English
† Andorra	83,000	468	181	177	459	Parliamentary co-principality (Spanish and French)	B	Andorra la Vella	Catalan, Spanish (Castilian), French
† Angola	12,665,000	1,246,700	481,354	10	26	Republic	A	Luanda	Portuguese, indigenous
Anguilla	14,000	96	37	146	378	Overseas territory (U.K. protection)	B	The Valley	English
Anhui	61,865,000	139,000	53,668	445	1,153	Province (China)	D	Hefei	Chinese (Mandarin)
Antarctica	(1)	14,000,000	5,400,000						
† Antigua and Barbuda	85,000	442	171	192	497	Parliamentary state	A	St. John's	English, local dialects
Aomen *see Macau*									
† Argentina	40,700,000	2,780,400	1,073,519	15	38	Republic	A	Buenos Aires	Spanish, English, Italian, German, French
Arizona	6,535,000	295,254	113,998	22	57	State (U.S.)	D	Phoenix	English
Arkansas	2,870,000	137,732	53,179	21	54	State (U.S.)	D	Little Rock	English
† Armenia	2,965,000	29,800	11,506	99	258	Republic	A	Yerevan	Armenian, Russian
Aruba	100,000	193	75	518	1,333	Self-governing territory (Netherlands protection)	B	Oranjestad	Dutch, Papiamento, English, Spanish
Ascension	1,000	88	34	11	29	Dependency (St. Helena)	C	Georgetown	English
Asia	4,078,790,000	44,900,000	17,300,000	91	236				
† Australia	21,135,000	7,692,030	2,969,910	2.7	7.1	Federal parliamentary state	A	Canberra	English, indigenous
Australian Capital Territory	340,000	2,360	911	144	373	Territory (Australia)	D	Canberra	English
† Austria	8,210,000	83,858	32,378	98	254	Federal republic	A	Vienna (Wien)	German
† Azerbaijan	8,205,000	86,600	33,437	95	245	Republic	A	Baku (Baki)	Azeri, Russian, Armenian
† Bahamas	310,000	13,939	5,382	22	58	Parliamentary State	A	Nassau	English, Creole
† Bahrain	725,000	691	267	1,049	2,715	Monarchy	A	Manama (Al-Manāmah)	Arabic, English, Farsi, Urdu
† Bangladesh	155,045,000	143,998	55,598	1,077	2,789	Republic	A	Dhaka	Bangla, English
† Barbados	285,000	430	166	663	1,717	Parliamentary state	A	Bridgetown	English
Beijing (Peking)	16,010,000	16,800	6,487	953	2,468	Autonomous city (China)	D	Beijing	Chinese (Mandarin)
† Belarus	9,665,000	207,600	80,155	47	121	Republic	A	Minsk	Belarussian, Russian
Belau *see Palau*									
† Belgium	10,410,000	30,528	11,787	341	883	Constitutional monarchy	A	Brussels (Bruxelles)	Dutch (Flemish), French, German
† Belize	305,000	22,966	8,867	13	34	Parliamentary state	A	Belmopan	English, Spanish, Mayan, Garifuna
† Benin	8,660,000	112,622	43,484	77	199	Republic	A	Porto-Novo and Cotonou	French, Fon, Yoruba, indigenous
Bermuda	68,000	54	21	1,259	3,238	Overseas territory (U.K.)	C	Hamilton	English
† Bhutan	685,000	46,500	17,954	15	38	Monarchy (Indian protection)	B	Thimphu	Dzongkha, Tibetan and Nepalese dialects
† Bolivia	9,690,000	1,098,581	424,165	8.8	23	Republic	A	La Paz and Sucre	Aymara, Quechua, Spanish
† Bosnia and Herzegovina	4,605,000	51,197	19,767	90	233	Republic	A	Sarajevo	Bosnian, Croatian, Serbian
† Botswana	1,970,000	581,730	224,607	3.4	8.8	Republic	A	Gaborone	English, Tswana
† Brazil	197,550,000	8,547,404	3,300,172	23	60	Federal republic	A	Brasília	Portuguese, Spanish, English, French
British Columbia	4,380,000	944,735	364,764	4.6	12	Province (Canada)	D	Victoria	English
British Indian Ocean Territory	(1)	60	23			Overseas territory (U.K.)	C		English
British Virgin Islands	24,000	151	58	159	414	Overseas territory (U.K.)	C	Road Town	English
† Brunei	385,000	5,765	2,226	67	173	Monarchy	A	Bandar Seri Begawan	Malay, English, Chinese
† Bulgaria	7,235,000	110,994	42,855	65	169	Republic	A	Sofia (Sofiya)	Bulgarian, Turkish
† Burkina Faso	15,500,000	274,200	105,869	57	146	Republic	A	Ouagadougou	French, indigenous
Burma *see Myanmar*									
† Burundi	8,840,000	27,830	10,745	318	823	Republic	A	Bujumbura	French, Kirundi, Swahili
California	36,955,000	423,970	163,696	87	226	State (U.S.)	D	Sacramento	English
† Cambodia	14,365,000	181,035	69,898	79	206	Constitutional monarchy	A	Phnom Penh (Phnum Pénh)	Khmer, French
† Cameroon	18,670,000	475,440	183,568	39	102	Republic	A	Yaoundé	English, French, indigenous
† Canada	33,350,000	9,984,670	3,855,103	3.3	8.7	Federal parliamentary state	A	Ottawa	English, French
† Cape Verde	430,000	4,033	1,557	107	276	Republic	A	Praia	Portuguese, Crioulo
Cayman Islands	48,000	264	102	182	471	Overseas territory (U.K.)	C	George Town	English
† Central African Republic	4,480,000	622,984	240,536	7.2	19	Republic	A	Bangui	French, Sango, Arabic, indigenous
Ceylon *see Sri Lanka*									
† Chad	10,220,000	1,284,000	495,755	8.0	21	Republic	A	N'Djamena (Fort-Lamy)	Arabic, French, indigenous
Channel Islands	155,000	194	75	799	2,067	Two crown dependencies (U.K. protection)			English, French
† Chile	16,530,000	756,096	291,930	22	57	Republic	A	Santiago	Spanish
† China (incl. Hong Kong and Macau) (2)	1,341,820,000	9,557,172	3,690,045	140	364	Socialist republic	A	Beijing	Chinese dialects
Chongqing	28,430,000	82,400	31,815	345	894	Autonomous city (China)	D	Chongqing	Chinese (Mandarin)
Christmas Island	1,500	135	52	11	29	External territory (Australia)	D	Settlement	English, Chinese, Malay
Cocos (Keeling) Islands	600	14	5.4	43	111	External territory (Australia)	C	West Island	English, Cocos-Malay, Malay
† Colombia	45,330,000	1,138,914	439,737	40	103	Republic	A	Bogotá	Spanish
Colorado	4,965,000	269,601	104,094	18	48	State (U.S.)	D	Denver	English
† Comoros (excl. Mayotte)	740,000	2,235	863	331	857	Federal Islamic republic	A	Moroni	Arabic, French, Comoran
† Congo	3,960,000	342,000	132,047	12	30	Republic	A	Brazzaville	French, Lingala, Kikongo, indigenous
† Congo, Democratic Republic of the (Zaire)	67,590,000	2,345,095	905,446	29	75	Republic	A	Kinshasa (Léopoldville)	French, Kikongo, Lingala, Swahili, Tshiluba, Kingwana

Region or political division	Est. Pop. 1/1/09	Area sq. km.	Area sq. mi.	Pop. per sq. km.	Pop. per sq. mi.	Form of Government and Ruling Power	Political Status	Capital	Predominant Languages
Connecticut	3,520,000	14,357	5,543	245	635	State (U.S.)	D	Hartford	English
Cook Islands	12,000	236	91	51	132	Self-governing territory (New Zealand protection)	B	Avarua	English, Maori
† Costa Rica	4,225,000	51,100	19,730	83	214	Republic	A	San José	Spanish
† Cote d'Ivoire (Ivory Coast)	20,395,000	322,463	124,504	63	164	Republic	A	Abidjan and Yamoussoukro	French, Dioula and other indigenous
† Croatia	4,490,000	56,538	21,829	79	206	Republic	A	Zagreb	Croatian
† Cuba	11,440,000	110,861	42,804	103	267	Socialist republic	A	Havana (La Habana)	Spanish
† Cyprus	795,000	9,251	3,572	86	223	Republic	A	Nicosia	Greek, Turkish, English
† Czech Republic	10,215,000	78,866	30,450	130	335	Republic	A	Prague (Praha)	Czech, Slovak
Delaware	880,000	6,447	2,489	136	354	State (U.S.)	D	Dover	English
† Denmark	5,495,000	43,096	16,640	128	330	Constitutional monarchy	A	Copenhagen (København)	Danish
District of Columbia	595,000	177	68	3,362	8,750	Federal district (U.S.)	D	Washington	English
† Djibouti	510,000	23,200	8,958	22	57	Republic	A	Djibouti	French, Arabic, Somali, Afar
† Dominica	73,000	751	290	97	252	Republic	A	Roseau	English, French
† Dominican Republic	9,580,000	48,511	18,730	197	511	Republic	A	Santo Domingo	Spanish
† East Timor (Timor-Leste)	1,120,000	14,874	5,743	75	195	Republic	A	Dili	Portuguese, Tetum, Bahasa Indonesia (Malay)
† Ecuador	14,465,000	283,561	109,484	51	132	Republic	A	Quito	Spanish, Quechua, indigenous
† Egypt	82,400,000	1,001,449	386,662	82	213	Socialist republic	A	Cairo (El Qâhira)	Arabic
Ellice Islands *see* Tuvalu									
† El Salvador	7,125,000	21,041	8,124	339	877	Republic	A	San Salvador	Spanish, Nahua
England	51,135,000	130,422	50,356	392	1,015	Administrative division (U.K.)	D	London	English
† Equatorial Guinea	625,000	28,051	10,831	22	58	Republic	A	Malabo	Spanish, indigenous, English
† Eritrea	5,575,000	117,600	45,406	47	123	Republic	A	Asmera	Tigre, Kunama, Cushitic dialects, Nora Bana, Arabic
† Estonia	1,305,000	45,227	17,462	29	75	Republic	A	Tallinn	Estonian, Latvian, Lithuanian, Russian
† Ethiopia	83,870,000	1,104,300	426,373	76	197	Federal republic	A	Addis Ababa (Ādīs Ābeba)	Amharic, Tigrinya, Orominga, Guaraginga, Somali, Arabic
Europe	728,420,000	9,900,000	3,800,000	74	192				
Falkland Islands (3)	3,000	12,173	4,700	0.2	0.6	Overseas territory (U.K.)	C	Stanley	English
Faroe Islands	49,000	1,399	540	35	91	Self-governing territory (Danish protection)	B	Tórshavn	Danish, Faroese
† Fiji	940,000	18,274	7,056	51	133	Republic	A	Suva	English, Fijian, Hindustani
† Finland	5,250,000	338,145	130,559	16	40	Republic	A	Helsinki	Finnish, Swedish, Lapp, Russian
Florida	18,430,000	170,304	65,755	108	280	State (U.S.)	D	Tallahassee	English
† France (excl. Overseas Departments)	62,260,000	539,965	208,482	115	299	Republic	A	Paris	French
French Guiana	210,000	83,534	32,253	2.5	6.5	Overseas department (France)	C	Cayenne	French
French Polynesia	285,000	4,000	1,544	71	185	Overseas territory (France)	C	Papeete	French, Tahitian
Fujian	36,025,000	120,000	46,332	300	778	Province (China)	D	Fuzhou	Chinese dialects
† Gabon	1,500,000	267,668	103,347	5.6	15	Republic	A	Libreville	French, Fang, indigenous
† Gambia, The	1,760,000	10,689	4,127	165	426	Republic	A	Banjul (Bathurst)	English, Malinke, Wolof, Fula, indigenous
Gansu	26,385,000	450,000	173,746	59	152	Province (China)	D	Lanzhou	Chinese (Mandarin), Mongolian, Tibetan dialects
Gaza Strip	1,525,000	360	139	4,236	10,971	Israeli territory with limited self-government			Arabic
Georgia	9,740,000	153,910	59,425	63	164	State (U.S.)	D	Atlanta	English
† Georgia	4,625,000	69,700	26,911	66	172	Republic	A	Tbilisi	Georgian, Russian, Armenian, Azeri
† Germany	82,350,000	357,022	137,847	231	597	Federal republic	A	Berlin	German
† Ghana	23,610,000	238,533	92,098	99	256	Republic	A	Accra	English, Akan and other indigenous
Gibraltar	28,000	6.0	2.3	4,667	12,174	Overseas territory (U.K.)	C	Gibraltar	English, Spanish, Italian, Portuguese
Gilbert Islands *see* Kiribati									
Golan Heights	41,000	1,176	454	35	90	Occupied by Israel			Arabic, Hebrew
Great Britain *see* United Kingdom									
† Greece	10,730,000	131,957	50,949	81	211	Republic	A	Athens (Athína)	Greek, English, French
Greenland	58,000	2,166,086	836,331	0.03	0.07	Self-governing territory (Danish protection)	B	Godthåb	Danish, Greenlandic, Inuit dialects
† Grenada	91,000	344	133	265	684	Parliamentary state	A	St. George's	English, French
Guadeloupe (incl. St. Barthelemy and St. Martin)	465,000	1,780	687	261	677	Overseas department (France)	C	Basse-Terre	French, Creole
Guam	175,000	549	212	319	825	Unincorporated territory (U.S.)	C	Hagåtña	English, Chamorro, Japanese
Guangdong	94,205,000	177,800	68,649	530	1,372	Province (China)	D	Guangzhou (Canton)	Chinese dialects, Miao-Yao
Guangxi Zhuangzu	47,780,000	236,300	91,236	202	524	Autonomous region (China)	D	Nanning	Chinese dialects, Thai, Miao-Yao
† Guatemala	13,140,000	108,889	42,042	121	313	Republic	A	Guatemala	Spanish, Amerindian
Guernsey (incl. Dependencies)	66,000	78	30	846	2,200	Crown dependency (U.K. protection)	B	St. Peter Port	English, French
† Guinea	9,930,000	245,857	94,926	40	105	Republic	A	Conakry	French, indigenous
† Guinea-Bissau	1,520,000	36,125	13,948	42	109	Republic	A	Bissau	Portuguese, Crioulo, indigenous
Guizhou	38,040,000	170,000	65,637	224	580	Province (China)	D	Guiyang	Chinese (Mandarin), Thai, Miao-Yao
† Guyana	770,000	214,969	83,000	3.6	9.3	Republic	A	Georgetown	English, indigenous
Hainan	8,465,000	34,200	13,205	248	641	Province (China)	D	Haikou	Chinese, Min, Tai
† Haiti	8,955,000	27,750	10,714	323	836	Republic	A	Port-au-Prince	Creole, French
Hawaii	1,295,000	28,311	10,931	46	118	State (U.S.)	D	Honolulu	English, Hawaiian, Japanese
Hebei	69,845,000	190,000	73,359	368	952	Province (China)	D	Shijiazhuang	Chinese (Mandarin)
Heilongjiang	38,710,000	469,000	181,082	83	214	Province (China)	D	Harbin	Chinese dialects, Mongolian, Tungus
Henan	95,095,000	167,000	64,479	569	1,475	Province (China)	D	Zhengzhou	Chinese (Mandarin)
Holland *see* Netherlands									
† Honduras	7,715,000	112,088	43,277	69	178	Republic	A	Tegucigalpa	Spanish, indigenous
Hong Kong (Xianggang)	7,035,000	1,100	425	6,395	16,553	Special administrative region (China)	C	Hong Kong (Xianggang)	Chinese (Cantonese), English, Putonghua
Hubei	57,645,000	187,400	72,356	308	797	Province (China)	D	Wuhan	Chinese dialects
Hunan	64,215,000	210,000	81,082	306	792	Province (China)	D	Changsha	Chinese dialects, Miao-Yao
† Hungary	9,920,000	93,030	35,919	107	276	Republic	A	Budapest	Hungarian
† Iceland	305,000	103,000	39,769	3.0	7.7	Republic	A	Reykjavík	Icelandic
Idaho	1,530,000	216,446	83,570	7.1	18	State (U.S.)	D	Boise	English
Illinois	12,970,000	149,998	57,914	86	224	State (U.S.)	D	Springfield	English
† India (incl. part of Jammu and Kashmir)	1,157,055,000	3,166,285	1,222,510	365	946	Federal republic	A	New Delhi	English, Hindi, Telugu, Bengali, indigenous
Indiana	6,410,000	94,321	36,418	68	176	State (U.S.)	D	Indianapolis	English
† Indonesia	238,910,000	1,904,443	735,310	125	325	Republic	A	Jakarta	Bahasa Indonesia (Malay), English, Dutch, indigenous
Iowa	3,020,000	145,743	56,272	21	54	State (U.S.)	D	Des Moines	English

Region or political division	Est. Pop. 1/1/09	Area sq. km.	Area sq. mi.	Pop. per sq. km.	Pop. per sq. mi.	Form of Government and Ruling Power	Political Status	Capital	Predominant Languages
† **Iran**	66,135,000	1,648,195	636,372	40	104	Islamic republic	A	Tehrān	Farsi, Turkish dialects, Kurdish
† **Iraq**	28,585,000	438,317	169,235	65	169	Republic	A	Baghdād	Arabic, Kurdish, Assyrian, Armenian
† **Ireland**	4,180,000	70,273	27,133	59	154	Republic	A	Dublin (Baile Átha Cliath)	English, Irish Gaelic
Isle of Man	76,000	572	221	133	344	Crown dependency (U.K. protection)	B	Douglas	English, Manx Gaelic
† **Israel (excl. Occupied Areas)**	7,175,000	20,770	8,019	345	895	Republic	A	Jerusalem (Yerushalayim)	Hebrew, Arabic
† **Italy**	58,140,000	301,323	116,342	193	500	Republic	A	Rome (Roma)	Italian, German, French, Slovene
Ivory Coast *see Cote d'Ivoire*		...	...	...	...	...		...	...
† **Jamaica**	2,815,000	10,991	4,244	256	663	Parliamentary state	A	Kingston	English, Creole
† **Japan**	127,200,000	377,750	145,850	337	872	Constitutional monarchy	A	Tōkyō	Japanese
Jersey	92,000	116	45	793	2,044	Crown dependency (U.K. protection)	B	St. Helier	English, French
Jiangsu	76,445,000	102,600	39,614	745	1,930	Province (China)	D	Nanjing	Chinese dialects
Jiangxi	43,935,000	166,600	64,325	264	683	Province (China)	D	Nanchang	Chinese dialects
Jilin	27,570,000	187,000	72,201	147	382	Province (China)	D	Changchun	Chinese (Mandarin), Mongolian, Korean
† **Jordan**	6,270,000	89,342	34,495	70	182	Constitutional monarchy	A	'Ammān	Arabic
Kansas	2,815,000	213,096	82,277	13	34	State (U.S.)	D	Topeka	English
† **Kazakhstan**	15,370,000	2,717,300	1,049,156	5.7	15	Republic	A	Astana (Aqmola)	Kazakh, Russian
Kentucky	4,290,000	104,659	40,409	41	106	State (U.S.)	D	Frankfort	English
† **Kenya**	38,475,000	582,646	224,961	66	171	Republic	A	Nairobi	English, Swahili, indigenous
† **Kiribati**	110,000	811	313	136	351	Republic	A	Bairiki	English, Gilbertese
† **Korea, North**	22,620,000	120,538	46,540	188	486	Socialist republic	A	P'yŏngyang	Korean
† **Korea, South**	48,445,000	99,268	38,328	488	1,264	Republic	A	Seoul (Sŏul)	Korean
Kosovo *(4)*	1,800,000	10,887	4,203	165	428	Republic	A	Priština	Albanian, Serbian
† **Kuwait**	2,645,000	17,818	6,880	148	384	Constitutional monarchy	A	Kuwait (Al-Kuwayt)	Arabic, English
† **Kyrgyzstan**	5,395,000	199,900	77,182	27	70	Republic	A	Bishkek	Kirghiz, Russian
† **Laos**	6,755,000	236,800	91,429	29	74	Socialist republic	A	Vientiane (Viangchan)	Lao, French, English
† **Latvia**	2,240,000	64,600	24,942	35	90	Republic	A	Rīga	Latvian, Russian, Lithuanian
† **Lebanon**	3,995,000	10,400	4,016	384	995	Republic	A	Beirut (Bayrūt)	Arabic, French, Armenian, English
† **Lesotho**	2,130,000	30,355	11,720	70	182	Constitutional monarchy	A	Maseru	English, Sesotho, Zulu, Xhosa
Liaoning	43,245,000	145,700	56,255	297	769	Province (China)	D	Shenyang	Chinese (Mandarin), Mongolian
† **Liberia**	3,395,000	111,369	43,000	30	79	Republic	A	Monrovia	English, indigenous
† **Libya**	6,240,000	1,759,540	679,362	3.5	9.2	Socialist republic	A	Tripoli (Ṭarābulus)	Arabic
† **Liechtenstein**	35,000	160	62	219	565	Constitutional monarchy	A	Vaduz	German
† **Lithuania**	3,560,000	65,300	25,213	55	141	Republic	A	Vilnius	Lithuanian, Polish, Russian
Louisiana	4,435,000	134,264	51,840	33	86	State (U.S.)	D	Baton Rouge	English
† **Luxembourg**	490,000	2,586	999	189	490	Constitutional monarchy	A	Luxembourg	French, Luxembourgish, German
Macau (Aomen)	555,000	18	6.9	30,833	80,435	Special administrative region (China)	C	Macau (Aomen)	Chinese (Cantonese), Portuguese
† **Macedonia**	2,065,000	25,713	9,928	80	208	Republic	A	Skopje	Macedonian, Albanian
† **Madagascar**	20,345,000	587,041	226,658	35	90	Republic	A	Antananarivo	Malagasy, French
Maine	1,325,000	91,646	35,385	14	37	State (U.S.)	D	Augusta	English
† **Malawi**	14,100,000	118,484	45,747	119	308	Republic	A	Lilongwe	Chichewa, English
† **Malaysia**	25,495,000	329,758	127,320	77	200	Federal constitutional monarchy	A	Kuala Lumpur and Putrajaya	Malay, Chinese dialects, English, Tamil
† **Maldives**	395,000	298	115	1,326	3,435	Republic	A	Male'	Divehi
† **Mali**	12,490,000	1,240,192	478,841	10	26	Republic	A	Bamako	French, Bambara, indigenous
† **Malta**	405,000	316	122	1,282	3,320	Republic	A	Valletta	English, Maltese
Manitoba	1,210,000	647,797	250,116	1.9	4.8	Province (Canada)	D	Winnipeg	English
† **Marshall Islands**	64,000	181	70	354	914	Republic (U.S. protection)	A	Majuro (island)	English, indigenous, Japanese
Martinique	445,000	1,100	425	405	1,047	Overseas department (France)	C	Fort-de-France	French, Creole
Maryland	5,665,000	32,133	12,407	176	457	State (U.S.)	D	Annapolis	English
Massachusetts	6,535,000	27,336	10,555	239	619	State (U.S.)	D	Boston	English
† **Mauritania**	3,090,000	1,030,700	397,956	3.0	7.8	Republic	A	Nouakchott	Arabic, Pular, Soninke, Wolof
† **Mauritius (incl. Dependencies)**	1,280,000	2,040	788	627	1,624	Republic	A	Port Louis	English, Creole, Bhojpuri, French, Hindi, Tamil, others
Mayotte *(5)*	220,000	374	144	588	1,528	Territorial collectivity (France)	C	Mamoudzou	French, Swahili (Mahorian)
† **Mexico**	110,585,000	1,964,382	758,452	56	146	Federal republic	A	Mexico City (Ciudad de México)	Spanish, indigenous
Michigan	10,060,000	250,494	96,716	40	104	State (U.S.)	D	Lansing	English
† **Micronesia, Federated States of**	110,000	702	271	157	406	Republic (U.S. protection)	A	Palikir	English, indigenous
Midway Islands	*(1)*	5.2	2.0	...	...	Unincorporated territory (U.S.)	C	...	English
Minnesota	5,250,000	225,171	86,939	23	60	State (U.S.)	D	St. Paul	English
Mississippi	2,955,000	125,434	48,430	24	61	State (U.S.)	D	Jackson	English
Missouri	5,945,000	180,533	69,704	33	85	State (U.S.)	D	Jefferson City	English
† **Moldova**	4,320,000	33,851	13,070	128	331	Republic	A	Chişinău	Romanian (Moldovan), Russian
† **Monaco**	33,000	2.0	0.8	16,500	41,250	Constitutional monarchy	A	Monaco	French, English, Italian, Monegasque
† **Mongolia**	3,020,000	1,566,500	604,829	1.9	5.0	Republic	A	Ulaanbaatar	Khalkha Mongol, Turkish dialects, Russian, Chinese
Montana	970,000	380,838	147,042	2.5	6.6	State (U.S.)	D	Helena	English
† **Montenegro**	675,000	13,812	5,333	49	127	Republic	A	Podgorica	Serbian, Albanian
Montserrat	5,000	102	39	49	128	Overseas territory (U.K.)	C	Plymouth (abandoned)	English
† **Morocco (excl. Western Sahara)**	34,600,000	446,550	172,414	77	201	Constitutional monarchy	A	Rabat	Arabic, Berber dialects, French
† **Mozambique**	21,475,000	801,590	309,496	27	69	Republic	A	Maputo (Lourenço Marques)	Portuguese, indigenous
† **Myanmar (Burma)**	47,950,000	676,578	261,228	71	184	Provisional military government	A	Yangon (Rangoon) and Nay Pyi Taw	Burmese, indigenous
† **Namibia**	2,100,000	823,144	317,818	2.6	6.6	Republic	A	Windhoek	English, Afrikaans, German, indigenous
† **Nauru**	14,000	21	8.1	667	1,728	Republic	A	Yaren District	Nauruan, English
Nebraska	1,795,000	200,345	77,354	9.0	23	State (U.S.)	D	Lincoln	English
Nei Mongol (Inner Mongolia)	24,270,000	1,183,000	456,759	21	53	Autonomous region (China)	D	Hohhot	Mongolian
† **Nepal**	28,380,000	147,181	56,827	193	499	Federal republic	A	Kathmandu (Kāṭhmāṇḍāu)	Nepali, Maithali, Bhojpuri, other indigenous
† **Netherlands**	16,680,000	41,864	16,164	398	1,032	Constitutional monarchy	A	Amsterdam and The Hague ('s-Gravenhage)	Dutch
Netherlands Antilles	225,000	800	309	281	728	Self-governing territory (Netherlands protection)	B	Willemstad	Dutch, Papiamento, English
Nevada	2,615,000	286,351	110,561	9.1	24	State (U.S.)	D	Carson City	English
New Brunswick	750,000	72,908	28,150	10	27	Province (Canada)	D	Fredericton	English, French
New Caledonia	225,000	18,575	7,172	12	31	Overseas territory (France)	C	Nouméa	French, indigenous
New Hampshire	1,325,000	24,216	9,350	55	142	State (U.S.)	D	Concord	English
New Hebrides *see Vanuatu*		...	...	...	...	...		...	...
New Jersey	8,730,000	22,588	8,721	386	1,001	State (U.S.)	D	Trenton	English
New Mexico	1,995,000	314,915	121,590	6.3	16	State (U.S.)	D	Santa Fe	English, Spanish

Region or political division	Est. Pop. 1/1/09	Area sq. km.	Area sq. mi.	Pop. per sq. km.	Pop. per sq. mi.	Form of Government and Ruling Power	Political Status	Capital	Predominant Languages
New South Wales	6,960,000	800,640	309,129	8.7	23	State (Australia)	D	Sydney	English
New York	19,595,000	141,299	54,556	139	359	State (U.S.)	D	Albany	English
† New Zealand	4,195,000	270,534	104,454	16	40	Parliamentary state	A	Wellington	English, Maori
Newfoundland and Labrador	510,000	405,212	156,453	1.3	3.3	Province (Canada)	D	St. John's	English
† Nicaragua	5,840,000	129,640	50,054	45	117	Republic	A	Managua	Spanish, English, indigenous
† Niger	15,025,000	1,267,000	489,192	12	31	Provisional military government	A	Niamey	French, Hausa, Djerma, indigenous
† Nigeria	147,735,000	923,768	356,669	160	414	Transitional military government	A	Abuja	English, Hausa, Fulani, Yorbua, Ibo, indigenous
Ningxia Huizu	6,115,000	66,400	25,637	92	239	Autonomous region (China)	D	Yinchuan	Chinese (Mandarin)
Niue	1,500	259	100	5.8	15	Self-governing territory (New Zealand protection)	B	Alofi	English, indigenous
Norfolk Island	2,000	36	14	56	143	External territory (Australia)	C	Kingston	English, Norfolk
North America	531,180,000	24,700,000	9,500,000	22	56	....			
North Carolina	9,270,000	139,389	53,819	67	172	State (U.S.)	D	Raleigh	English
North Dakota	645,000	183,112	70,700	3.5	9.1	State (U.S.)	D	Bismarck	English
Northern Ireland	1,760,000	13,576	5,242	130	336	Administrative division (U.K.)	D	Belfast	English
Northern Mariana Islands	88,000	464	179	190	492	Commonwealth (U.S. protection)	B	Saipan (island)	English, Chamorro, Carolinian
Northern Territory	215,000	1,349,130	520,902	0.2	0.4	Territory (Australia)	D	Darwin	English, indigenous
Northwest Territories	43,000	1,346,106	519,735	0.03	0.08	Territory (Canada)	D	Yellowknife	English, indigenous
† Norway (incl. Jan Mayen and Svalbard)	4,655,000	323,877	125,050	14	37	Constitutional monarchy	A	Oslo	Norwegian, Lapp, Finnish
Nova Scotia	945,000	55,284	21,345	17	44	Province (Canada)	D	Halifax	English
Nunavut	30,000	2,093,190	808,185	0.01	0.04	Territory (Canada)	D	Iqaluit	English, indigenous
Oceania (incl. Australia)	34,605,000	8,500,000	3,300,000	4.1	10	....			
Ohio	11,550,000	116,096	44,825	99	258	State (U.S.)	D	Columbus	English
Oklahoma	3,660,000	181,036	69,898	20	52	State (U.S.)	D	Oklahoma City	English
† Oman	3,365,000	309,500	119,499	11	28	Monarchy	A	Muscat (Masqat)	Arabic, English, Baluchi, Urdu, Indian dialects
Ontario	12,950,000	1,076,395	415,599	12	31	Province (Canada)	D	Toronto	English
Oregon	3,810,000	254,805	98,381	15	39	State (U.S.)	D	Salem	English
† Pakistan (incl. part of Jammu and Kashmir)	174,525,000	879,902	339,732	198	514	Federal Islamic republic	A	Islāmābād	English, Urdu, Punjabi, Sindhi, Pashto
† Palau (Belau)	21,000	487	188	43	112	Republic	A	Melekeok	Angaur, English, Japanese, Palauan, Sonsorolese, Tobi
† Panama	3,335,000	75,517	29,157	44	114	Republic	A	Panamá	Spanish, English
† Papua New Guinea	5,995,000	462,840	178,704	13	34	Parliamentary state	A	Port Moresby	English, Motu, Pidgin, indigenous
† Paraguay	6,915,000	406,752	157,048	17	44	Republic	A	Asunción	Spanish, Guarani
Pennsylvania	12,515,000	119,282	46,055	105	272	State (U.S.)	D	Harrisburg	English
Peru	29,365,000	1,285,216	496,225	23	59	Republic	A	Lima	Quechua, Spanish, Aymara
† Philippines	97,020,000	300,000	115,831	323	838	Republic	A	Manila	English, Pilipino, Tagalog
Pitcairn Islands (incl. Dependencies)	100	49	19	2.0	5.3	Overseas territory (U.K.)	C	Adamstown	English, Tahitian
† Poland	38,490,000	312,685	120,728	123	319	Republic	A	Warsaw (Warszawa)	Polish
† Portugal	10,695,000	91,985	35,516	116	301	Republic	A	Lisbon (Lisboa)	Portuguese
Prince Edward Island	140,000	5,660	2,185	25	64	Province (Canada)	D	Charlottetown	English
Puerto Rico	3,965,000	9,104	3,515	436	1,128	Commonwealth (U.S. protection)	B	San Juan	Spanish, English
† Qatar	830,000	11,427	4,412	73	188	Monarchy	A	Doha (Ad-Dawḥah)	Arabic, English
Qinghai	5,550,000	720,000	277,994	7.7	20	Province (China)	D	Xining	Tibetan dialects, Mongolian, Turkish dialects, Chinese (Mandarin)
Quebec	7,775,000	1,542,056	595,391	5.0	13	Province (Canada)	D	Québec	French, English
Queensland	4,180,000	1,730,650	668,208	2.4	6.3	State (Australia)	D	Brisbane	English
Reunion	815,000	2,510	969	325	841	Overseas department (France)	C	Saint-Denis	French, Creole
Rhode Island	1,055,000	4,002	1,545	264	683	State (U.S.)	D	Providence	English
Rhodesia see Zimbabwe	....	....	....	......	......				
† Romania	22,230,000	237,500	91,699	94	242	Republic	A	Bucharest (Bucureşti)	Romanian, Hungarian, German
† Russia	140,370,000	17,075,400	6,592,849	8.2	21	Federal republic	A	Moscow (Moskva)	Russian, Tatar, Ukrainian
† Rwanda	10,330,000	26,338	10,169	392	1,016	Republic	A	Kigali	French, Kinyarwanda, Kiswahili
St. Helena (incl. Dependencies)	7,500	314	121	24	62	Overseas territory (U.K.)	C	Jamestown	English
† St. Kitts and Nevis	40,000	261	101	153	396	Parliamentary state	A	Basseterre	English
† St. Lucia	160,000	616	238	260	672	Parliamentary state	A	Castries	English, French
St. Pierre and Miquelon	7,000	242	93	29	75	Territorial collectivity (France)	C	Saint-Pierre	French
† St. Vincent and the Grenadines	105,000	388	150	271	700	Parliamentary state	A	Kingstown	English, French
† Samoa	220,000	2,831	1,093	78	201	Constitutional monarchy	A	Apia	English, Samoan
† San Marino	30,000	61	24	492	1,250	Republic	A	San Marino	Italian
† Sao Tome and Principe	210,000	964	372	218	565	Republic	A	São Tomé	Portuguese, Fang
Saskatchewan	1,015,000	651,036	251,366	1.6	4.0	Province (Canada)	D	Regina	English
† Saudi Arabia	28,420,000	2,149,690	830,000	13	34	Monarchy	A	Riyadh (Ar-Riyāḍ)	Arabic
Scotland	5,150,000	78,133	30,167	66	171	Administrative division (U.K.)	D	Edinburgh	English, Scots Gaelic
† Senegal	13,525,000	196,712	75,951	69	178	Republic	A	Dakar	French, Wolof, Fulani, Serer, indigenous
† Serbia (excl. Kosovo)	7,395,000	77,474	29,913	95	247	Republic	A	Belgrade (Beograd)	Serbian
† Seychelles	87,000	455	176	191	494	Republic	A	Victoria	English, French, Creole
Shaanxi	37,815,000	205,000	79,151	184	478	Province (China)	D	Xi'an	Chinese (Mandarin)
Shandong	94,255,000	153,000	59,074	616	1,596	Province (China)	D	Jinan	Chinese (Mandarin)
Shanghai	18,375,000	6,200	2,394	2,964	7,675	Autonomous city (China)	D	Shanghai	Chinese (Wu)
Shanxi	34,170,000	156,000	60,232	219	567	Province (China)	D	Taiyuan	Chinese (Mandarin)
Sichuan	82,710,000	487,600	188,263	170	439	Province (China)	D	Chengdu	Chinese (Mandarin), Tibetan dialects, Miao-Yao
† Sierra Leone	6,365,000	71,740	27,699	89	230	Transitional military government	A	Freetown	English, Krio, Mende, Temne, indigenous
† Singapore	4,635,000	683	264	6,786	17,557	Republic	A	Singapore	Chinese (Mandarin), English, Malay, Tamil
† Slovakia	5,460,000	49,012	18,924	111	289	Republic	A	Bratislava	Slovak, Hungarian
† Slovenia	2,005,000	20,256	7,821	99	256	Republic	A	Ljubljana	Slovenian
† Solomon Islands	590,000	28,370	10,954	21	54	Parliamentary state	A	Honiara	English, indigenous
† Somalia	9,695,000	637,657	246,201	15	39	None	A	Mogadishu (Muqdisho)	Arabic, Somali, English, Italian
† South Africa	48,985,000	1,219,090	470,693	40	104	Republic	A	Pretoria (Tshwane), Cape Town and Bloemfontein	Afrikaans, English, Xhosa, Zulu, other indigenous
South America	391,890,000	17,800,000	6,900,000	22	57	....			
South Australia	1,600,000	983,480	379,724	1.6	4.2	State (Australia)	D	Adelaide	English
South Carolina	4,505,000	82,932	32,020	54	141	State (U.S.)	D	Columbia	English
South Dakota	810,000	199,731	77,117	4.1	11	State (U.S.)	D	Pierre	English
South Georgia and the South Sandwich Islands (3)	(1)	3,755	1,450	......	......	Overseas territory (U.K.)	C	Grytviken Harbour	English

Region or political division	Est. Pop. 1/1/09	Area sq. km.	Area sq. mi.	Pop. per sq. km.	Pop. per sq. mi.	Form of Government and Ruling Power	Political Status	Capital	Predominant Languages
South West Africa *see Namibia*	...	...	...	...	...	...		...	...
† **Spain**	40,510,000	504,750	194,885	80	208	Constitutional monarchy	A	Madrid	Spanish (Castilian), Catalan, Galician, Basque
Spanish North Africa *(6)*	150,000	32	12	4,688	12,500	Five possessions (Spain)	C	...	Spanish, Arabic, Berber dialects
Spanish Sahara *see Western Sahara*	...	...	...	...	...	...		...	...
† **Sri Lanka**	21,230,000	65,610	25,332	324	838	Socialist republic	A	Colombo and Sri Jayewardenepura Kotte	English, Sinhala, Tamil
† **Sudan**	40,650,000	2,505,813	967,500	16	42	Provisional military government	A	Khartoum (Al-Kharṭūm)	Arabic, Nubian and other indigenous, English
† **Suriname**	480,000	163,265	63,037	2.9	7.6	Republic	A	Paramaribo	Dutch, Sranan Tongo, English, Hindustani, Javanese
† **Swaziland**	1,125,000	17,364	6,704	65	168	Monarchy	A	Mbabane and Lobamba	English, siSwati
† **Sweden**	9,050,000	449,964	173,732	20	52	Constitutional monarchy	A	Stockholm	Swedish, Lapp, Finnish
† **Switzerland**	7,595,000	41,293	15,943	184	476	Federal republic	A	Bern	German, French, Italian, Romansch
† **Syria**	19,965,000	185,180	71,498	108	279	Socialist republic	A	Damascus (Dimashq)	Arabic, Kurdish, Armenian, Aramaic, Circassian
Taiwan	22,950,000	36,002	13,901	637	1,651	Republic	A	T'aipei	Chinese (Mandarin), Taiwanese (Min), Hakka
† **Tajikistan**	7,280,000	143,100	55,251	51	132	Republic	A	Dushanbe	Tajik, Uzbek, Russian
† **Tanzania**	40,630,000	945,087	364,900	43	111	Republic	A	Dar es Salaam and Dodoma	English, Swahili, indigenous
Tasmania	500,000	68,400	26,409	7.3	19	State (Australia)	D	Hobart	English
Tennessee	6,250,000	109,151	42,143	57	148	State (U.S.)	D	Nashville	English
Texas	24,460,000	695,621	268,581	35	91	State (U.S.)	D	Austin	English, Spanish
† **Thailand**	65,705,000	513,115	198,115	128	332	Constitutional monarchy	A	Bangkok (Krung Thep)	Thai, indigenous
Tianjin (Tientsin)	10,885,000	11,300	4,363	963	2,495	Autonomous city (China)	D	Tianjin	Chinese (Mandarin)
Timor-Leste *see East Timor*	...	...	...	...	...	...		...	...
† **Togo**	5,940,000	56,785	21,925	105	271	Provisional military government	A	Lomé	French, Ewe, Mina, Kabye, Dagomba
Tokelau	1,500	12	4.6	125	326	Island territory (New Zealand)	C	...	English, Tokelauan
† **Tonga**	120,000	650	251	185	478	Constitutional monarchy	A	Nuku'alofa	Tongan, English
† **Trinidad and Tobago**	1,230,000	5,128	1,980	240	621	Republic	A	Port of Spain	English, Hindi, French, Spanish
Tristan da Cunha	300	104	40	2.9	7.5	Dependency (St. Helena)	C	Edinburgh	English
† **Tunisia**	10,435,000	163,610	63,170	64	165	Republic	A	Tunis	Arabic, French
† **Turkey**	76,300,000	783,577	302,541	97	252	Republic	A	Ankara	Turkish, Kurdish, Arabic
† **Turkmenistan**	4,855,000	488,100	188,457	9.9	26	Republic	A	Aşgabat	Turkmen, Russian, Uzbek
Turks and Caicos Islands	23,000	430	166	53	139	Overseas territory (U.K.)	C	Grand Turk	English
† **Tuvalu**	12,000	26	10	462	1,200	Parliamentary state	A	Funafuti	Tuvaluan, English
† **Uganda**	31,935,000	241,038	93,065	132	343	Republic	A	Kampala	English, Luganda, Swahili, indigenous
† **Ukraine**	45,845,000	603,700	233,090	76	197	Republic	A	Kiev (Kyiv)	Ukrainian, Russian, Romanian, Polish
† **United Arab Emirates**	4,710,000	83,600	32,278	56	146	Federation of monarchs	A	Abu Dhabi (Abū Ẓaby)	Arabic, Farsi, English, Hindi, Urdu
† **United Kingdom**	61,030,000	242,910	93,788	251	651	Parliamentary monarchy	A	London	English, Welsh, Scots Gaelic
† **United States**	305,710,000	9,826,630	3,794,083	31	81	Federal republic	A	Washington	English, Spanish
Upper Volta *see Burkina Faso*	...	...	...	...	...	...		...	...
† **Uruguay**	3,485,000	175,016	67,574	20	52	Republic	A	Montevideo	Spanish
Utah	2,750,000	219,887	84,899	13	32	State (U.S.)	D	Salt Lake City	English
† **Uzbekistan**	27,475,000	447,400	172,742	61	159	Republic	A	Tashkent (Toshkent)	Uzbek, Russian
† **Vanuatu**	215,000	12,190	4,707	18	46	Republic	A	Port Vila	Bislama, English, French
Vatican City	800	0.4	0.2	2,000	4,000	Monarchical-sacerdotal state	A	Vatican City	Italian, Latin, other
† **Venezuela**	26,615,000	912,050	352,145	29	76	Federal republic	A	Caracas	Spanish, Amerindian
Vermont	625,000	24,901	9,614	25	65	State (U.S.)	D	Montpelier	English
Victoria	5,235,000	227,420	87,807	23	60	State (Australia)	D	Melbourne	English
† **Vietnam**	86,545,000	331,689	128,066	261	676	Socialist republic	A	Ha Noi	Vietnamese, French, Chinese, English, Khmer, indigenous
Virginia	7,810,000	110,785	42,774	70	183	State (U.S.)	D	Richmond	English
Virgin Islands (U.S.)	110,000	347	134	317	821	Unincorporated territory (U.S.)	C	Charlotte Amalie	English, Spanish, Creole
Wake Island	*(1)*	7.8	3.0	...	...	Unincorporated territory (U.S.)	C	...	English
Wales	2,985,000	20,779	8,023	144	372	Administrative division (U.K.)	D	Cardiff	English, Welsh Gaelic
Wallis and Futuna	15,000	255	99	59	152	Overseas territory (France)	C	Matā'utu	French, Wallisian
Washington	6,585,000	184,665	71,300	36	92	State (U.S.)	D	Olympia	English
West Bank (incl. East Jerusalem)	2,435,000	5,860	2,263	416	1,076	Israeli territory with limited self-government		...	Arabic, Hebrew
Western Australia	2,105,000	2,529,880	976,792	0.8	2.2	State (Australia)	D	Perth	English
Western Sahara	400,000	266,000	102,703	1.5	3.9	Occupied by Morocco		...	Arabic
West Virginia	1,825,000	62,755	24,230	29	75	State (U.S.)	D	Charleston	English
Wisconsin	5,660,000	169,639	65,498	33	86	State (U.S.)	D	Madison	English
Wyoming	535,000	253,336	97,814	2.1	5.5	State (U.S.)	D	Cheyenne	English
Xianggang *see Hong Kong*	...	...	...	...	...	...		...	...
Xinjiang Uygur (Sinkiang)	20,755,000	1,600,000	617,764	13	34	Autonomous region (China)	D	Ürümqi	Turkish dialects, Mongolian, Tungus, English
Xizang (Tibet)	2,845,000	1,220,000	471,045	2.3	6.0	Autonomous region (China)	D	Lhasa	Tibetan dialects
† **Yemen**	23,410,000	527,968	203,850	44	115	Republic	A	Sanaa (Ṣan'ā')	Arabic
Yugoslavia *see Serbia*	...	...	...	...	...	...		...	...
Yukon	32,000	482,443	186,272	0.07	0.2	Territory (Canada)	D	Whitehorse	English, Inuktitut, indigenous
Yunnan	45,390,000	394,000	152,124	115	298	Province (China)	D	Kunming	Chinese (Mandarin), Tibetan dialects, Khmer, Miao-Yao
Zaire *see Congo, Democratic Republic of the*	...	...	...	...	...	...		...	...
† **Zambia**	11,765,000	752,614	290,586	16	40	Republic	A	Lusaka	English, Tonga, Lozi, other indigenous
Zhejiang	50,425,000	101,800	39,305	495	1,283	Province (China)	D	Hangzhou	Chinese dialects
† **Zimbabwe**	11,305,000	390,759	150,873	29	75	Republic	A	Harare (Salisbury)	English, Shona, Sindebele
WORLD	6,750,375,000	150,100,000	57,900,000	45	117	...		...	...

(1) No Permanent Population.
(2) Population estimate includes 26,760,000 people not included in any province.
(3) Claimed by Argentina.
(4) Kosovo unilaterally declared its independence from Serbia in 2008.
(5) Claimed by Comoros.
(6) Comprises Ceuta, Melilla and several small islands.

† Member of the United Nations (2008)
... None, or not applicable.

General Information

Equatorial diameter of Earth 12,756 km (7,926 mi.)
Polar diameter of Earth 12,713 km (7,900 mi.)
Mean diameter of Earth 12,742 km (7,918 mi.)
Equatorial circumference of Earth 40,075 km (24,901 mi.)
Mean distance from Earth to Sun 149,598,000 km (92,955,900 mi.)
Mean distance from Earth to Moon 384,403 km (238,857 mi.)
Total area of Earth 510,100,000 sq. km (197,000,000 sq. mi.)
Highest elevation on Earth's surface, Mt. Everest, Asia 8,848 m (29,028 ft.)
Lowest elevation on Earth's land surface, shores of the Dead Sea, Asia 408 m (1,339 ft.) below sea level
Greatest known depth of the ocean, southwest of Guam, Pacific Ocean 10,924 m (35,840 ft.)
Total land area of Earth (incl. inland water and Antarctica) 150,100,000 sq. km (57,900,000 sq. mi.)
Area of Africa 30,300,000 sq. km (11,700,000 sq. mi.)
Area of Antarctica 14,000,000 sq. km (5,400,000 sq. mi.)
Area of Australia and Oceania 8,500,000 sq. km (3,300,000 sq. mi.)
Area of Asia 44,900,000 sq. km (17,300,000 sq. mi.)
Area of Europe 9,900,000 sq. km (3,800,000 sq. mi.)
Area of North America 24,700,000 sq. km (9,500,000 sq. mi.)
Area of South America 17,800,000 sq. km (6,900,000 sq. mi.)
World Population (est. 1/1/09), 6,750,375,000

Principal Islands Area in sq. km (sq. mi.)

Baffin I., Nu., Can. 507,451 (195,928)
Banks I., N.T., Can. 70,028 (27,038)
Borneo, Asia 748,168 (288,869)
Bougainville, Pap. N. Gui. 9,317 (3,597)
Cape Breton I., N.S., Can. 10,311 (3,981)
Celebes, Indon. 180,680 (69,761)
Ceram, Indon. 17,454 (6,739)
Corsica, Fr. 8,741 (3,375)
Crete, Grc. 8,349 (3,224)
Cuba, Cuba 105,805 (40,852)
Cyprus, Cyp. 9,234 (3,565)
Devon I., Nu., Can. 55,247 (21,331)
Ellesmere I., Nu., Can. 196,236 (75,767)
Flores, Indon. 14,154 (5,465)
Great Britain, U.K. 226,000 (87,259)
Greenland, Green. 2,166,086 (836,330)
Guadalcanal, Sol. Is. 5,352 (2,066)
Hainan Dao, China 33,209 (12,822)
Hawai' i, Hi., U.S. 10,500 (4,054)
Hispaniola, N.A. 73,929 (28,544)
Hokkaidō, Japan 78,719 (30,394)
Honshū, Japan 225,800 (87,182)
Iceland, Ice. 101,826 (39,315)
Ireland, Ire.-U.K. 81,638 (31,521)
Jamaica, Jam. 11,189 (4,320)
Java, Indon. 138,793 (53,588)
Kodiak I., Ak., U.S. 9,578 (3,698)
Kyūshū, Japan 37,437 (14,455)
Leyte, Phil. 7,367 (2,844)
Long I., N.Y., U.S. 3,502 (1,352)
Luzon, Phil. 109,964 (42,457)
Madagascar, Madag. 587,713 (226,917)
Melville I., Can. 42,149 (16,274)
Mindanao, Phil. 97,530 (37,657)
Mindoro, Phil. 10,571 (4,081)
Negros, Phil. 13,074 (5,048)
New Britain, Pap. N. Gui. 35,144 (13,569)
New Caledonia, N. Cal. 16,648 (6,428)
Newfoundland, Nf., Can. 108,860 (42,031)
New Guinea, Asia-Oc. 785,753 (303,381)
North East Land, Nor. 14,247 (5,501)
North I., N.Z. 111,582 (43,082)
Palawan, Phil. 12,188 (4,706)
Panay, Phil. 12,011 (4,637)
Prince of Wales I., Nu., Can. 33,339 (12,872)
Puerto Rico, P.R. 8,733 (3,372)
Sakhalin, Russia 72,492 (27,989)
Samar, Phil. 12,849 (4,961)
Sardinia, Italy 23,949 (9,247)
Shikoku, Japan 18,544 (7,160)
Sicily, Italy 25,662 (9,908)
Southampton I., Nu., Can. 41,214 (15,913)
South I., N.Z. 145,836 (56,308)
Spitsbergen, Nor. 38,980 (15,050)
Sri Lanka, Sri L. 67,654 (26,121)
Sumatra, Indon. 443,065 (171,068)
Taiwan, Tai. 34,506 (13,323)
Tasmania, Austl. 65,519 (25,297)
Tierra del Fuego, S.A. 47,401 (18,302)
Timor, Asia 28,418 (10,972)
Vancouver I., B.C., Can. 31,285 (12,079)
Victoria I., Can. 217,291 (83,896)
Vrangelya, Ostrov (Wrangel I.), Russia 7,865 (3,037)

Principal Lakes, Oceans and Seas Area in sq. km (sq. mi.)

Arabian Sea, Afr.-Asia 3,864,264 (1,492,000)
Aral Sea, Kaz.-Uzb. 17,158 (6,625)
Arctic Ocean 14,056,000 (5,400,000)
Athabasca, L., Can. 7,935 (3,064)
Atlantic Ocean 76,762,000 (29,600,000)
Baikal, L., Russia 31,500 (12,162)
Balkhash, L., Kaz. 18,200 (7,027)
Baltic Sea, Eur. 422,168 (163,000)
Bering Sea, Asia-N.A. 2,291,900 (884,900)
Black Sea, Eur.-N.A. 461,018 (178,000)
Caribbean Sea, N.A.-S.A. 2,754,000 (1,063,000)
Caspian Sea, Asia-Eur. 371,000 (143,244)
Chad, L., Afr. 1,540 (595)
Erie, L., Can.-U.S. 25,667 (9,910)
Eyre, L., Austl. 9,500 (3,668)
Great Bear Lake, Can.-U.S. 31,328 (12,096)
Great Salt Lake, U.S. 5,483 (2,117)
Great Slave Lake, Can. 28,568 (11,030)
Hudson Bay, Can. 1,230,245 (475,000)
Huron, L., Can.-U.S. 59,570 (23,000)
Indian Ocean 68,556,000 (26,500,000)
Japan, Sea of, Asia 1,007,800 (389,100)
Kok Nor (Qinghai Hu), China 4,460 (1,722)
Ladoga, L., Russia 18,135 (7,002)
Manitoba, L., Can. 4,623 (1,785)
Maracaibo, L., Ven. 13,010 (5,023)
Mediterranean Sea 2,500,000 (965,000)
Mexico, Gulf of, N.A. 1,500,000 (600,000)
Michigan, L., U.S. 57,757 (22,300)
Nicaragua, Lago de, Nicaragua 8,150 (3,147)
North Sea, Eur. 574,978 (222,000)
Nyasa, L., Afr. 30,900 (11,931)
Onega, L., Russia 9,890 (3,819)
Ontario, L., Can.-U.S. 18,960 (7,320)
Pacific Ocean 15,555,700 (6,000,000)
Red Sea, Afr.-Asia 437,708 (169,000)
Rudolf, L., Eth.-Kenya 6,750 (2,606)
Southern Ocean 20,327,000 (7,800,000)
Superior, L., Can.-U.S. 82,100 (31,700)
Tanganyika. L., Afr. 32,000 (12,355)
Titicaca, Lago, Bol.-Peru 8,372 (3,232)
Torrens, L., Austl. 5,745 (2,218)
Vänern (L.), Swe. 5,648 (2,181)
Van Gölü (L.), Tur. 3,740 (1,444)
Victoria, L., Afr. 68,800 (26,564)
Winnipeg, L., Can. 24,387 (9,416)
Winnipegosis, L., Can. 5,374 (2,075)
Yellow Sea, Asia 1,243,195 (480,000)

Principal Mountains Elevation in m (ft.)

Aconcagua, Cerro, Arg. 6,959 (22,831)
Annapūrṇa, Nepal 8,091 (26,545)
Aoraki (Mt. Cook), N.Z. 3,754 (12,316)
Apo, Mt., Phil. 2,954 (9,692)
Ararat, Mt., Tur. 5,137 (16,854)
Barú, Volcán, Pan. 3,475 (11,401)
Belukha, Mt., Asia 4,506 (14,783)
Bia, Phou, Laos 2,820 (9,252)
Blanc, Mont, Eur. 4,807 (15,771)
Blanca Pk., Co., U.S. 4,372 (14,345)
Bolívar, Pico, Ven. 5,007 (16,427)
Bonete Grande, Cerro, Arg. 6,872 (22,546)
Borah Pk., Id., U.S. 3,859 (12,662)
Boundary Pk., Nv., U.S. 4,006 (13,143)
Cameroon Mtn., Camrn. 4,100 (13,451)
Carrauntoohil, Ire. 1,038 (3,406)
Chaltel, Cerro, S.A. 3,340 (10,958)
Chimborazo, Ec. 6,310 (20,702)
Chirripó, Cerro, C.R. 3,819 (12,530)
Colima, Nevado de, Mex. 4,240 (13,911)
Cotopaxi, Ec. 5,897 (19,347)
Cristóbal Colón, Pico, Col. 5,775 (18,947)
Damāvand, Kūh-e, Iran 5,604 (18,386)
Dhawalāgiri, Nepal 8,167 (26,795)
Duarte, Pico, Dom. Rep. 3,175 (10,417)
Dufourspitze, Eur. 4,634 (15,203)
Elbert, Mt., Co., U.S. 4,399 (14,433)
El'brus, Gora, Russia 5,642 (18,510)
Elgon, Mt., Afr. 4,321 (14,177)
Erciyes Dağı, Tur. 3,917 (12,851)
Etna, Monte, Italy 3,323 (10,902)
Everest, Mt., Asia 8,848 (29,028)
Fairweather, Mt., N.A. 4,663 (15,300)
Folādī, Koh-e, Afg. 5,135 (16,847)
Fuji-san, Japan 3,776 (12,388)
Galdhøpiggen, Nor. 2,469 (8,100)
Gannett Pk., Wy., U.S. 4,207 (13,804)
Gerlachovský štít, Slvk. 2,655 (8,711)
Giluwe, Mt., Pap. N. Gui. 4,368 (14,331)
Gongga Shan, China 7,590 (24,902)
Grand Teton, Wy., U.S. 4,197 (13,770)
Großglockner, Aus. 3,797 (12,457)
Gunnbjørn Fjeld, Green. 3,700 (12,139)
Hekla, Ice. 1,491 (4,892)
Hkakabo Razi, Mya. 5,881 (19,295)
Hood, Mt., Or., U.S. 3,426 (11,239)
Huascarán, Nevado, Peru 6,746 (22,133)
Huila, Nevado del, Col. 5,750 (18,865)
Hvannadalshnúkur, Ice. 2,119 (6,952)
Illampu, Nevado, Bol. 6,421 (21,066)
Illimani, Nevado de, Bol. 6,457 (21,184)
Imeni Ismail Samani, Pik (Communism Pk.), Taj. 7,495 (24,590)
Inthanon, Doi, Thai. 2,600 (8,530)
Jaya, Puncak, Indon. 5,030 (16,503)
Jungfrau, Switz. 4,158 (13,642)
K2 (Qogir Feng), Asia 8,611 (28,250)
Kāmet, Asia 7,756 (25,446)
Kānchenjunga, Asia 8,598 (28,208)
Karisimbi, Volcan, Afr. 4,507 (14,787)
Kebnekaise, Swe. 2,111 (6,926)
Kenya,Mt.,(Kirinyaga), Kenya 5,199 (17,058)
Kerinci, Gunung, Indon. 3,800 (12,467)
Kilimanjaro, Tan. 5,895 (19,340)
Kinabalu, Gunong, Malay. 4,101 (13,455)
Kinyeti, Sudan 3,187 (10,456)
Klyuchevskaya Sopka, Vulkan, Russia 4,750 (15,584)
Kosciuszko, Mt., Austl. 2,229 (7,313)
Koussi, Emi, Chad 3,415 (11,204)
Kula Kangri, Bhu. 7,554 (24,784)
La Selle, Morne, Haiti 2,674 (8,773)
Lassen Pk., Ca., U.S. 3,187 (10,457)
Llullaillaco, Volcán, S.A. 6,739 (22,110)
Logan, Mt., Yk., Can. 5,959 (19,551)
Longs Pk., Co., U.S. 4,345 (14,255)
Margherita Pk., Afr. 5,109 (16,763)
Maromokotro, Madag. 2,876 (9,436)
Massive, Mt., Co., U.S. 4,396 (14,421)
Matterhorn, Eur. 4,478 (14,692)
Mauna Kea, Hi., U.S. 4,205 (13,796)
Mauna Loa, Hi., U.S. 4,169 (13,677)
Mayon Volcano, Phil. 2,462 (8,077)
McKinley, Mt. (Denali), Ak., U.S. 6,194 (20,320)
Meru, Mt., Tan. 4,565 (14,977)
Misti, Volcán, Peru 5,822 (19,101)
Mitchell, Mt., N.C., U.S. 2,037 (6,684)
Môco, Morro de, Ang. 2,620 (8,596)
Moldoveanu, Vârful, Rom. 2,544 (8,346)
Mulhacén, Spain 3,482 (11,424)
Musala, Blg. 2,925 (9,596)
Muztag, China 7,723 (25,338)
Namjagbarwa Feng, China 7,755 (25,443)
Nanda Devi, India 7,817 (25,645)
Nanga Parbat, Pak. 8,126 (26,660)
Nevis, Ben, Scot., U.K. 1,343 (4,406)
Ojos del Salado, Nevado, S.A. 6,893 (22,615)
Olympus, Mt., Grc. 2,917 (9,570)
Paektu-san, Asia 2,744 (9,003)
Paricutín, Mex. 2,800 (9,186)
Parnassós, Grc. 2,457 (8,061)
Pelée, Montagne, Mart. 1,397 (4,583)
Pico de Orizaba, Volcán, Mex. 5,610 (18,406)
Pidurutalagala, Sri L. 2,524 (8,281)
Pikes Pk., Co., U.S. 4,301 (14,110)
Pinatubo, Mt., Phil. 1,780 (5,840)
Pobeda, Gora Russia 3,147 (10,325)
Popocatépetl, Volcán, Mex. 5,465 (17,930)
Pulog, Mt., Phil. 2,934 (9,626)
Rainier, Mt., Wa., U.S. 4,392 (14,411)
Ramm, Jabal, Jord. 1,754 (5,755)
Ras Dejen, Eth. 4,620 (15,158)
Rinjani, Gunung, Indon. 3,726 (12,224)
Robson, Mt., B.C., Can. 3,954 (12,972)
Roraima, Mt., S.A. 2,875 (9,432)
Ruapehu, Mt., N.Z. 2,797 (9,177)
Ruiz, Nevado del, Col. 5,400 (17,717)
Saint Elias, Mt., N.A. 5,489 (18,009)
Saint Helens, Mt., Wa., U.S. 2,549 (8,364)
Sajama, Nevado, Bol. 6,542 (21,463)
Semeru, Gunung, Indon. 3,676 (12,060)
Shām, Jabal ash-, Oman 3,035 (9,957)
Shasta, Mt., Ca., U.S. 4,317 (14,162)
Snowdon, Wales, U.K. 1,085 (3,560)
Tahat, Alg. 2,908 (9,541)
Tajumulco, Volcán, Guat. 4,220 (13,845)
Tirich Mīr, Pak. 7,690 (25,230)
Toubkal, Jebel, Mor. 4,165 (13,665)
Triglav, Slvn. 2,864 (9,396)
Trikora, Puncak (Wilhelmina Pk.), Indon. 4,750 (15,584)
Tupungato, Cerro, S.A. 6,750 (22,146)
Turquino, Pico, Cuba 1,972 (6,470)
Uluru (Ayers Rock), Austl. 863 (2,831)
Uncompahgre Pk., Co., U.S. 4,361 (14,309)
Vesuvius, Italy 1,281 (4,203)
Vinson Massif, Ant. 4,897 (16,066)
Waddington, Mt., B.C., Can. 4,015 (13,173)
Washington, Mt., N.H., U.S. 1,917 (6,288)
Whitney, Mt.,, Ca., U.S. 4,418 (14,494)
Wilhelm, Mt., Pap. N. Gui. 4,509 (14,793)
Yü Shan, Tai. 3,997 (13,114)
Zugspitze, Eur. 2,962 (9,718)

Principal Rivers Length in km (mi.)

Albany, N.A. 982 (610)
Aldan, Asia 2,209 (1,373)
Amazonas-Ucayali, S.A. 6,280 (3,902)
Amu Darya, Asia 1,687 (1,048)
Amur, Asia 2,820 (1,752)
Araguaia, S.A. 1,969 (1,223)
Arkansas, N.A. 2,350 (1,460)
Atchafalaya-Red, N.A. 2,285 (1,420)
Athabasca, N.A. 1,231 (765)
Ayeyarwady, Asia 1,573 (977)
Brahmaputra, Asia 2,897 (1,800)
Brazos, N.A. 2,060 (1,280)
Canadian, N.A. 1,458 (906)
Churchill, N.A. 1,609 (1,000)
Colorado, N.A. (U.S.-Mex.) 2,334 (1,450)
Colorado, N.A. (TX) 1,387 (862)
Columbia, N.A. 2,000 (1,243)
Congo, Afr. 4,370 (2,715)
Danube, Eur. 2,860 (1,777)
Darling, Austl. 1,472 (915)
Dnieper, Eur. 2,285 (1,420)
Don, Eur. 1,907 (1,185)
Elbe, Eur. 1,091 (678)
Essequibo, S.A. 970 (603)
Euphrates, Asia 2,412 (1,499)
Fraser, N.A. 1,370 (851)
Ganges, Asia 3,000 (1,864)
Gila, N.A. 1,044 (649)
Godāvari, Asia 1,500 (932)
Huang (Yellow), Asia 4,667 (2,900)
Indigirka, Asia 1,726 (1,072)
Indus, Asia 3,180 (1,976)
Juruá, S.A. 2,758 (1,714)
Kama, Eur. 1,685 (1,047)
Kasai, Afr. 1,968 (1,223)
Kolyma, Asia 2,130 (1,324)
Lena, Asia 4,400 (2,734)
Limpopo, Afr. 1,212 (753)
Loire, Eur. 1,110 (690)
Mackenzie, N.A. 4,241 (2,635)
Madeira, S.A. 3,381 (2,101)
Magdalena, S.A. 1,530 (951)
Marañón, S.A. 1,546 (961)
Mekong, Asia 4,500 (2,796)
Mississippi, N.A. 3,766 (2,340)
Mississippi-Missouri, N.A. 6,420, (3,989)
Missouri, N.A. 4,088 (2,540)
Murray-Darling, Austl. 2,844 (1,767)
Negro, S.A. 1,341 (833)
Nelson, N.A. 2,575 (1,600)
Niger, Afr. 4,160 (2,585)
Nile, Afr. 6,650 (4,132)
Ob', Asia 3,650 (2,268)
Oder, Eur. 906 (563)
Ohio, N.A. 2,108 (1,310)
Oka, Eur. 1,304 (810)
Orange, Afr. 2,300 (1,429)
Orinoco, S.A. 2,740 (1,703)
Ottawa, N.A. 1,271 (790)
Paraguay, S.A. 2,297 (1,427)
Paranaíba, S.A. 1,450 (901)
Peace, N.A. 1,923 (1,192)
Pechora, Eur. 1,810 (1,125)
Pecos, N.A. 1,490 (926)
Plata-Paraná, S.A. 4,700 (2,920)
Platte, N.A. 1,593 (990)
Purús, S.A. 2,588 (1,608)
Red, N.A. 2,076 (1,290)
Rhine, Eur. 1,320 (820)
Rhône, Eur. 810 (503)
Rio Grande, N.A. 3,058 (1,900)
St. Lawrence, N.A. 3,058 (1,900)
Salado, S.A. 1,800 (1,118)
São Francisco, S.A. 2,800 (1,740)
Saskatchewan-Bow, N.A. 2,036 (1,265)
Severnaya Dvina (N. Dvina), Eur. 711 (442)
Snake, N.A. 1,674 (1,040)
Songhua (Sungari), Asia 872 (542)
Syr Darya, Asia 1,590 (988)
Tagus, Eur. 1,100 (684)
Tarim, Asia 964 (599)
Tennessee, N.A. 1,426 (886)
Tigris, Asia 1,752 (1,089)
Tisa, Eur. 881 (547)
Tocantins, S.A. 2,124 (1,320)
Ucayali, S.A. 1,484 (922)
Ural, Asia 2,102 (1,306)
Uruguay, S.A. 1,616 (1,004)
Vilyuy, Asia 2,446 (1,520)
Volga, Eur. 3,360 (2,088)
Volta, Afr. 1,600 (994)
Xiang, Asia 934 (580)
Xingu, S.A. 1,883 (1,170)
Yangtze (Chang), Asia 6,301 (3,915)
Yellowstone, N.A. 1,114 (692)
Yenisey, Asia 3,490 (2,169)
Yukon, N.A. 3,187 (1,980)
Zambezi, Afr. 2,660 (1,653)

Abidjan, Cote d'Ivoire ... 1,929,079
Abu Dhabi (Abū Ẓaby), United Arab Emirates ... 552,000
Accra, Ghana (1,390,000) ... 949,113
Ad-Dammām, Saudi Arabia (1,250,000) ... 525,000
Addis Ababa (Ādīs Ābeba), Ethiopia (2,200,000) ... 2,084,588
Ahmadābād, India (4,519,278) ... 3,515,361
Aleppo (Ḥalab), Syria (1,640,000) ... 1,591,400
Alexandria (El-Iskandarîya), Egypt (3,350,000) ... 2,926,859
Algiers (Alger), Algeria (2,547,983) ... 1,507,241
Almaty, Kazakhstan (1,190,000) ... 1,156,200
'Ammān, Jordan (1,500,000) ... 963,490
Amsterdam, Netherlands (1,121,303) ... 727,053
Ankara, Turkey (2,650,000) ... 2,559,471
Antananarivo, Madagascar ... 1,103,304
Antwerp (Antwerpen), Belgium (1,135,000) ... 453,030
Aşgabat, Turkmenistan ... 557,600
Asunción, Paraguay (700,000) ... 502,426
Athens (Athína), Greece (3,150,000) ... 772,072
Atlanta, United States (4,112,198) ... 416,474
Auckland, New Zealand (1,129,800) ... 380,154
Baghdād, Iraq ... 3,841,268
Baku (Bakı), Azerbaijan (2,020,000) ... 1,080,500
Bamako, Mali ... 658,275
Bandung, Indonesia (2,300,000) ... 2,136,260
Banghāzī, Libya (472,000) ... 446,250
Bangkok (Krung Thep), Thailand (7,360,000) ... 6,355,144
Bangui, Central African Republic ... 451,690
Barcelona, Spain (4,000,000) ... 1,496,266
Barranquilla, Colombia (1,260,000) ... 990,547
Beijing, China (7,320,000) ... 6,690,000
Beirut (Bayrūt), Lebanon (1,675,000) ... 509,000
Belfast, United Kingdom (730,000) ... 296,700
Belgrade (Beograd), Serbia (1,554,826) ... 1,136,786
Belo Horizonte, Brazil (4,055,000) ... 1,366,301
Bengalūru (Bangalore), India (5,686,844) ... 4,292,223
Berlin, Germany (4,220,000) ... 3,425,759
Birmingham, United Kingdom (2,705,000) ... 965,928
Bishkek, Kyrgyzstan ... 631,300
Bogotá, Colombia (5,290,000) ... 4,931,796
Bonn, Germany (600,000) ... 304,841
Boston, United States (5,819,100) ... 589,141
Brasília, Brazil ... 1,947,133
Brazzaville, Congo ... 1,050,000
Brisbane, Australia (1,627,535) ... 888,449
Brussels (Bruxelles), Belgium (2,390,000) ... 133,845
Bucharest (București), Romania (2,300,000) ... 2,067,545
Budapest, Hungary (2,450,000) ... 1,906,798
Buenos Aires, Argentina (11,460,575) ... 2,776,138
Bulawayo, Zimbabwe ... 621,742
Cairo (El-Qâhira), Egypt (9,300,000) ... 6,068,695
Calgary, Canada (1,079,310) ... 987,969
Cali, Colombia (1,735,000) ... 1,641,498
Cape Town, South Africa (1,900,000) ... 854,616
Caracas, Venezuela (4,000,000) ... 1,822,465
Cardiff, United Kingdom (645,000) ... 272,129
Casablanca, Morocco (3,200,000) ... 2,761,975
Changchun, China ... 2,470,000
Chelyabinsk, Russia (1,310,000) ... 1,077,174
Chengdu, China ... 2,760,000
Chennai (Madras), India (6,424,624) ... 4,216,268
Chicago, United States (9,157,540) ... 2,896,016
Chișinău, Moldova ... 676,700
Chittagong, Bangladesh (2,342,662) ... 1,566,070
Chongqing, China ... 3,870,000
Cincinnati, United States (1,979,202) ... 331,285
Cleveland, United States (2,945,831) ... 478,403
Cologne (Köln), Germany (1,830,000) ... 964,311
Colombo, Sri Lanka (2,250,000) ... 642,163
Conakry, Guinea ... 950,000
Copenhagen (København), Denmark (2,030,000) ... 499,148
Córdoba, Argentina (1,368,301) ... 1,267,521
Cotonou, Benin (605,000) ... 536,827
Curitiba, Brazil (2,595,000) ... 1,586,848
Dakar, Senegal ... 1,490,450
Dalian, China ... 2,400,000
Dallas, United States (5,221,801) ... 1,188,580
Damascus (Dimashq), Syria (2,230,000) ... 1,549,932
Dar es Salaam, Tanzania ... 2,497,940
Delhi, India (12,791,458) ... 9,817,439
Denver, United States (2,581,506) ... 554,636
Detroit, United States (5,456,428) ... 951,270
Dhaka, Bangladesh (6,537,308) ... 3,637,892
Dnipropetrovs'k, Ukraine (1,590,000) ... 1,147,000
Donets'k, Ukraine (2,090,000) ... 1,088,000
Douala, Cameroon ... 712,251
Dubai (Dubayy), United Arab Emirates ... 1,171,000
Dublin (Baile Átha Cliath), Ireland (1,175,000) ... 481,854
Durban, South Africa (1,740,000) ... 715,669
Dushanbe, Tajikistan (800,000) ... 562,000
Düsseldorf, Germany (1,200,000) ... 529,062
Edinburgh, United Kingdom (640,000) ... 401,910
Edmonton, Canada (1,034,945) ... 730,372
El-Gîza, Egypt ... 1,883,189
Eşfahān, Iran (1,525,000) ... 1,266,072
Essen, Germany (5,040,000) ... 608,732
Faisalābād, Pakistan ... 2,008,861
Fortaleza, Brazil (2,780,000) ... 788,956
Frankfurt am Main, Germany (1,960,000) ... 643,469
Freetown, Sierra Leone (525,000) ... 469,776
Fukuoka, Japan (2,200,000) ... 1,302,454
Glasgow, United Kingdom (1,870,000) ... 662,954
Goiânia, Brazil ... 1,075,761
Guadalajara, Mexico (4,095,853) ... 1,600,894
Guangzhou (Canton), China ... 3,750,000
Guatemala, Guatemala (1,500,000) ... 823,301
Guayaquil, Ecuador ... 1,985,379
Hamburg, Germany (2,460,000) ... 1,704,731
Hannover, Germany (1,015,000) ... 520,670
Ha Noi, Vietnam (1,275,000) ... 905,939
Harare (Salisbury), Zimbabwe (1,470,000) ... 1,189,103
Harbin, China ... 3,120,000
Havana (La Habana), Cuba (2,285,000) ... 2,189,716
Helsinki, Finland (1,075,000) ... 512,686
Hiroshima, Japan (1,700,000) ... 1,113,786
Ho Chi Minh City (Saigon), Vietnam (3,300,000) ... 2,796,229
Hong Kong (Xianggang), China (4,770,000) ... 1,250,993
Honolulu, United States (876,156) ... 371,657
Houston, United States (4,669,571) ... 1,953,631
Hyderābād, India (5,533,640) ... 3,449,878
Ibadan, Nigeria ... 1,144,000
Islāmābād, Pakistan ... 529,180
İstanbul, Turkey (7,550,000) ... 6,620,241
İzmir, Turkey (1,900,000) ... 1,757,414
Jaipur, India ... 2,324,319
Jakarta, Indonesia (11,500,000) ... 8,347,083
Jerusalem (Yerushalayim), Israel (740,000) ... 680,500
Jiddah, Saudi Arabia ... 2,200,000
Jinan, China ... 2,150,000
Johannesburg, South Africa (4,000,000) ... 712,507
Kabul (Kābol), Afghanistan ... 1,424,400
Kampala, Uganda ... 1,208,544
Kānpur, India (2,690,486) ... 2,540,069
Kaohsiung, Taiwan (2,400,000) ... 1,509,510
Karāchi, Pakistan ... 9,339,023
Kathmandu (Kāṭhmāṇḍāũ), Nepal (1,150,000) ... 671,846
Katowice, Poland (2,755,000) ... 327,032
Kharkiv, Ukraine (1,950,000) ... 1,555,000
Khartoum (Al-Kharṭūm), Sudan (2,950,000) ... 947,483
Kiev (Kyïv), Ukraine (3,250,000) ... 2,630,000
Kigali, Rwanda ... 603,049
Kingston, Jamaica (830,000) ... 516,500
Kinshasa (Léopoldville), Congo, Dem. Rep. of the ... 3,000,000
Kolkata (Calcutta), India (13,216,546) ... 4,580,544
Kuala Lumpur, Malaysia (2,500,000) ... 1,297,526
Kuwait (Al-Kuwayt), Kuwait (1,126,000) ... 28,747
Lagos, Nigeria (3,800,000) ... 1,213,000
Lahore, Pakistan ... 5,143,495
La Paz, Bolivia (1,487,854) ... 789,585
Leeds, United Kingdom (1,530,000) ... 424,194
León, Mexico (1,425,210) ... 1,137,465
Lilongwe, Malawi ... 435,964
Lima, Peru (6,321,173) ... 340,422
Lisbon (Lisboa), Portugal (2,350,000) ... 663,394
Liverpool, United Kingdom (1,515,000) ... 481,786
Lomé, Togo ... 450,000
London, United Kingdom (12,000,000) ... 7,650,944
Los Angeles, United States (16,373,645) ... 3,694,820
Luanda, Angola ... 1,459,900
Lucknow, India (2,266,933) ... 2,207,340
Lusaka, Zambia ... 1,084,703
Lyon, France (1,648,216) ... 445,452
Madrid, Spain (4,690,000) ... 2,882,860
Managua, Nicaragua ... 864,201
Manaus, Brazil ... 1,394,724
Manchester, United Kingdom (2,760,000) ... 402,889
Manila, Philippines (11,200,000) ... 1,654,761
Mannheim, Germany (1,525,000) ... 310,475
Maputo (Lourenço Marques), Mozambique ... 966,837
Maracaibo, Venezuela ... 1,249,670
Marrakech, Morocco (760,000) ... 672,506
Marseille, France (1,516,340) ... 798,430
Mashhad, Iran ... 1,887,405
Mecca (Makkah), Saudi Arabia ... 1,025,000
Medan, Indonesia ... 1,904,273
Medellín, Colombia (2,290,000) ... 1,551,160
Melbourne, Australia (3,366,542) ... 67,784
Mexico City (Ciudad de México), Mexico (19,231,829) ... 8,720,916
Miami, United States (3,876,380) ... 362,470
Milan (Milano), Italy (3,790,000) ... 1,305,591
Milwaukee, United States (1,689,572) ... 596,974
Minneapolis, United States (2,968,806) ... 382,618
Minsk, Belarus (1,722,000) ... 1,661,000
Mogadishu (Muqdisho), Somalia ... 600,000
Mombasa, Kenya ... 665,018
Monrovia, Liberia ... 465,000
Monterrey, Mexico (3,664,331) ... 1,133,070
Montevideo, Uruguay (1,610,000) ... 1,269,552
Montréal, Canada (3,635,571) ... 1,620,693
Moscow (Moskva), Russia (13,500,000) ... 10,126,424
Mumbai (Bombay), India (16,368,084) ... 11,914,398
Munich (München), Germany (1,930,000) ... 1,205,923
Nagoya, Japan (5,280,000) ... 2,109,681
Nāgpur, India (2,122,965) ... 2,051,320
Nairobi, Kenya ... 2,143,254
Nanjing, China ... 2,490,000
Naples (Napoli), Italy (3,150,000) ... 1,046,987
N'Djamena (Fort-Lamy), Chad ... 546,572
Newcastle upon Tyne, United Kingdom (1,350,000) ... 189,150
New Delhi, India ... 294,783
New York, United States (21,199,865) ... 8,008,278
Nizhniy Novgorod (Gorky), Russia (1,900,000) ... 1,311,252
Nouakchott, Mauritania ... 558,195
Novosibirsk, Russia (1,530,000) ... 1,425,508
Nürnberg, Germany (1,065,000) ... 489,758
Odesa, Ukraine (1,150,000) ... 1,046,000
Omdurman (Umm Durmān), Sudan ... 1,271,403
Omsk, Russia (1,175,000) ... 1,134,016
Oran (Ouahran), Algeria ... 628,558
Ōsaka, Japan (16,500,000) ... 2,484,326
Oslo, Norway (773,498) ... 504,040
Ottawa, Canada (1,130,761) ... 648,480
Ouagadougou, Burkina Faso ... 709,700
Palembang, Indonesia ... 1,430,627
Panamá, Panama (995,000) ... 415,964
Paris, France (11,174,743) ... 2,125,246
Perm', Russia (1,100,000) ... 1,001,653
Perth, Australia (1,333,993) ... 13,463
Philadelphia, United States (6,188,463) ... 1,517,550
Phnom Penh (Phnum Pénh), Cambodia ... 570,155
Phoenix, United States (3,251,876) ... 1,321,045
Port-au-Prince, Haiti (1,425,594) ... 846,247
Portland, United States (2,265,223) ... 529,121
Port Louis, Mauritius (500,000) ... 144,303
Port Moresby, Papua New Guinea ... 246,664
Porto, Portugal (1,230,000) ... 302,472
Porto Alegre, Brazil (3,375,000) ... 1,304,998
Prague (Praha), Czech Republic (1,328,000) ... 1,214,174
Pretoria (Tshwane), South Africa (1,100,000) ... 525,583
Puebla de Zaragoza, Mexico (2,109,049) ... 1,399,519
Pune, India (3,755,525) ... 2,540,069
Pusan, Korea, South ... 3,797,566
P'yŏngyang, Korea, North ... 2,741,260
Qingdao, China ... 2,300,000
Québec, Canada (715,515) ... 490,614
Quezon City, Philippines ... 1,989,419
Quito, Ecuador (1,650,000) ... 1,399,378
Rabat, Morocco (1,210,000) ... 623,457
Recife, Brazil (3,160,000) ... 1,421,993
Rīga, Latvia (1,000,000) ... 874,200
Rio de Janeiro, Brazil (10,465,000) ... 5,851,914
Riyadh (Ar-Riyāḍ), Saudi Arabia ... 2,950,000
Rome (Roma), Italy (3,235,000) ... 2,649,765
Rosario, Argentina (1,161,188) ... 908,163
Rostov-na-Donu, Russia (1,220,000) ... 1,068,267
Rotterdam, Netherlands (1,089,979) ... 539,000
Sacramento, United States (1,796,857) ... 407,018
St. Louis, United States (2,603,607) ... 348,189
St. Petersburg (Leningrad), Russia (5,950,000) ... 4,661,219
Salvador, Brazil (2,855,000) ... 2,439,823
Samara, Russia (1,440,000) ... 1,157,880
San Diego, United States (2,813,833) ... 1,223,400
San Francisco, United States (7,039,362) ... 776,733
San José, Costa Rica (996,194) ... 309,672
San Juan, Puerto Rico (2,450,292) ... 421,958
San Salvador, El Salvador (1,250,000) ... 415,346
Santiago, Chile (4,740,000) ... 4,295,593
Santo Domingo, Dominican Republic (2,005,000) ... 913,540
São Paulo, Brazil (17,380,000) ... 9,713,692
Sapporo, Japan (2,200,000) ... 1,822,992
Saratov, Russia (1,130,000) ... 873,055
Seattle, United States (3,554,760) ... 563,374
Seoul (Sŏul), Korea, South (15,850,000) ... 10,627,790
Shanghai, China (11,010,000) ... 8,930,000
Shenyang, China ... 4,050,000
Singapore, Singapore (4,800,000) ... 4,185,200
Sofia (Sofiya), Bulgaria (1,280,000) ... 1,190,126
Stockholm, Sweden (1,491,726) ... 674,452
Stuttgart, Germany (2,020,000) ... 585,274
Surabaya, Indonesia ... 2,599,796
Sūrat, India (2,811,466) ... 2,433,787
Sydney, Australia (3,997,321) ... 47,204
Tabrīz, Iran ... 1,191,043
T'aipei, Taiwan (6,800,000) ... 2,641,856
Tallinn, Estonia ... 403,981
Tashkent (Toshkent), Uzbekistan (2,325,000) ... 2,113,300
Tbilisi, Georgia (1,350,000) ... 1,081,678
Tegucigalpa, Honduras ... 769,061
Tehrān, Iran (8,800,000) ... 6,758,845
Tel Aviv-Yafo, Israel (2,000,000) ... 360,500
Tianjin, China ... 5,000,000
Tijuana, Mexico (1,483,992) ... 1,286,187
Tōkyō, Japan (32,000,000) ... 8,025,508
Toronto, Canada (5,113,149) ... 2,503,281
Tripoli (Ṭarābulus), Libya (960,000) ... 591,062
Tunis, Tunisia (1,350,000) ... 702,330
Turin (Torino), Italy (1,550,000) ... 921,485
Ufa, Russia (1,110,000) ... 1,042,437
Ulaanbaatar, Mongolia ... 649,797
Ürümqi, China ... 1,130,000
València, Spain (1,340,000) ... 739,014
Vancouver, Canada (2,116,581) ... 578,041
Vienna (Wien), Austria (1,950,000) ... 1,609,631
Vientiane (Viangchan), Laos ... 464,000
Vilnius, Lithuania ... 578,639
Volgograd, Russia (1,375,000) ... 1,011,417
Warsaw (Warszawa), Poland (2,400,000) ... 1,707,147
Washington, United States (7,608,070) ... 572,059
Winnipeg, Canada (694,668) ... 631,774
Wuhan, China ... 3,870,000
Xi'an, China ... 2,410,000
Yangon (Rangoon), Myanmar (2,800,000) ... 2,705,039
Yekaterinburg, Russia (1,550,000) ... 1,293,537
Yerevan, Armenia (1,320,000) ... 1,103,488
Yokohama, Japan ... 3,433,612
Zagreb, Croatia ... 867,865
Zürich, Switzerland (870,000) ... 365,043

Values are latest available city populations or recent estimates.
Metropolitan area populations are shown in parentheses.

Annam ... Annamese
Arab ... Arabic
Bantu ... Bantu
Bur ... Burmese
Camb ... Cambodian
Celt ... Celtic
Chn ... Chinese
Czech ... Czech
Dan ... Danish
Du ... Dutch
Fin ... Finnish
Fr ... French
Ger ... German
Gr ... Greek
Hung ... Hungarian
Ice ... Icelandic
India ... India
Indian ... American Indian
In don ... Indonesian
It ... Italian
Jap ... Japanese
Kor ... Korean
Mal ... Malayan
Mong ... Mongolian
Nor ... Norwegian
Per ... Persian
Pol ... Polish
Port ... Portuguese
Rom ... Romanian
Rus ... Russian
Serb ... Serbian
Siam ... Siamese
So. Slav ... Southern Slavonic
Sp ... Spanish
Swe ... Swedish
Tib ... Tibetan
Tur ... Turkish

å, Nor., Swe. ... brook, river
aa, Dan., Nor ... brook
āb, Per ... water, river
abad, India, Per ... town, city
ada, Tur ... island
adrar, Berber ... mountain
ákra, Gr ... cape
älf, Swe ... river
alp, Ger ... mountain
altipiano, It ... plateau
alto, Sp ... height
archipel, Fr ... archipelago
archipiélago, Sp ... archipelago
arquipélago, Port ... archipelago
arroyo, Sp ... brook, stream
as, Nor., Swe ... ridge
austral, Sp ... southern
baai, Du ... bay
bab, Arab ... gate, port
bach, Ger ... brook, stream
backe, Swe ... Hill
bad, Ger ... bath, spa
bahía, Sp ... bay, gulf
bahr, Arab ... river, sea, lake
baia, It ... bay, gulf
baía, Port ... bay
baie, Fr ... bay, gulf
bajo, Sp ... depression
bak, Indon ... stream
bakke, Dan., Nor ... hill
balkan, Tur ... mountain range
bana, Jap ... point, cape
banco, Sp ... bank
bandao, Chn ... peninsula
bandar, Mal., Per .. town, port, harbor
bang, Siam ... village
bassin, Fr ... basin
batang, Indon., Mal ... river
bei, Chn ... north
ben, Celtic ... mountain, summit
bender, Arab ... harbor, port
bereg, Rus ... coast, shore
berg, Du., Ger., Nor., Swe ... mountain, hill
bir, Arab ... well
birkat, Arab ... lake, pond, pool
bit, Arab ... house
bjaerg, Dan., Nor ... mountain
bocche, It ... mouth
boğazı, Tur ... strait
bois, Fr ... forest, wood
bolsón, Sp ... flat-floored desert valley
boreal, Sp ... northern
borg, Dan., Nor., Swe ... castle, town
borgo, It ... town, suburb
bosch, Du ... forest, wood
bouche, Fr ... river mouth
bourg, Fr ... town, borough
bro, Dan., Nor., Swe ... bridge
brücke, Ger ... bridge
bucht, Ger ... bay, bight
bugt, Dan., Nor., Swe ... bay, gulf
bulu, Indon ... mountain
burg, Du., Ger ... castle, town
buri, Siam ... town
burun, burnu, Tur ... cape
by, Dan., Nor., Swe ... village
caatinga, Port. (Brazil) ... open brushland
cabezo, Sp ... summit
cabo, Port., Sp ... cape
campo, It., Port., Sp ... plain, field
campos, Port. (Brazil) ... plains
cañón, Sp ... canyon
cap, Fr ... cape
capo, It ... cape
casa, It., Port., Sp ... house
castello, It., Port ... castle, fort
castillo, Sp ... castle
càte, Fr ... hill
çay, Tur ... stream, river
cayo, Sp ... rock, shoal, islet
cerro, Sp ... mountain, hill
champ, Fr ... field
château, Fr ... castle
chott, Arab ... salt lake
chu, Tib ... water, stream
cidade, Port ... town, city
cima, Sp ... summit, peak
città, It ... town, city
ciudad, Sp ... town, city
cochilha, Port ... ridge
col, Fr ... pass
colina, Sp ... hill
cordillera, Sp ... mountain chain
costa, It., Port., Sp ... coast
côte, Fr ... coast
cuchilla, Sp ... mountain ridge
dağ, Tur ... mountain(s)
dake, Jap ... peak, summit
dal, Dan., Du., Nor., Swe ... valley
dan, Kor ... point, cape
danau, Indon ... lake
dao, Chn ... island
dar, Arab ... house, abode, country
darya, Per ... river, sea
dasht, Per ... plain, desert
deniz, Tur ... sea
désert, Fr ... desert
deserto, It ... desert
desierto, Sp ... desert
détroit, Fr ... strait
dijk, Du ... dam, dike
djebel, Arab ... mountain
do, Kor ... island
dong, Chn ... east
dorf, Ger ... village
dorp, Du ... village
duin, Du ... dune
dzong, Tib . fort, administrative capital
eau, Fr ... water
ecuador, Sp ... equator
eiland, Du ... island
elv, Dan., Nor ... river, stream
embalse, Sp ... reservoir
erg, Arab ... dune, sandy desert
est, Fr., It ... east
estado, Sp ... state
este, Port., Sp ... east
estrecho, Sp ... strait
étang, Fr ... pond, lake
état, Fr ... state
eyjar, Ice ... islands
feld, Ger ... field, plain
festung, Ger ... fortress
fiume, It ... river
fjäll, Swe ... mountain
fjärd, Swe ... bay, inlet
fjeld, Nor ... mountain, hill
fjord, Dan., Nor ... fiord, inlet
fjördur, Ice ... fiord, inlet
fleuve, Fr ... river
flod, Dan., Swe ... river
flói, Ice ... bay, marshland
fluss, Ger ... river
foce, It ... river mouth
fontein, Du ... a spring
forêt, Fr ... forest
fors, Swe ... waterfall
forst, Ger ... forest
fos, Dan., Nor ... waterfall
fu, Chn ... town, residence
fuente, Sp ... spring, fountain
fuerte, Sp ... fort
furt, Ger ... ford
gang, Kor ... stream, river
gangri, Tib ... mountain
gat, Dan., Nor ... channel
gàve, Fr ... stream
gawa, Jap ... river
gebergte, Du ... mountain range
gebiet, Ger ... district, territory
gebirge, Ger ... mountains
ghat, India ... pass, mountain range
gobi, Mong ... desert
gol, Mong ... river
göl, gölü, Tur ... lake
golfe, Fr ... gulf, bay
golfo, It., Port., Sp ... gulf, bay
gomba, gompa, Tib ... monastery
gora, Rus., So. Slav ... mountain
góra, Pol ... mountain
gorod, Rus ... town
grad, Rus., So. Slav ... town
guba, Rus ... bay, gulf
gundung, Indon ... mountain
guntō, Jap ... archipelago
gunung, Mal ... mountain
haf, Swe ... sea, ocean
hafen, Ger ... port, harbor
haff, Ger ... gulf, inland sea
hai, Chn ... sea, lake
hama, Jap ... beach, shore
hamada, Arab ... rocky plateau
hamn, Swe ... harbor
hāmūn, Per ... swampy lake, plain
hantō, Jap ... peninsula
hassi, Arab ... well, spring
haus, Ger ... house
haut, Fr ... summit, top
hav, Dan., Nor ... sea, ocean
havn, Dan., Nor ... harbor, port
havre, Fr ... harbor, port
háza, Hung ... house, dwelling of
heim, Ger ... hamlet, home
hem, Swe ... hamlet, home
higashi, Jap ... east
hisar, Tur ... fortress
hissar, Arab ... fort
ho, Chn ... river
hoek, Du ... cape
hof, Ger ... court, farmhouse
höfn, Ice ... harbor
hoku, Jap ... north
holm, Dan., Nor., Swe ... island
hora, Czech ... mountain
horn, Ger ... peak
hoved, Dan., Nor ... cape
hu, Chn ... lake
huang, Chn ... yellow
hügel, Ger ... hill
huk, Dan., Swe ... point
hus, Dan., Nor., Swe ... house
île, Fr ... island
ilha, Port ... island
indsö, Dan., Nor ... lake
insel, Ger ... island
insjö, Swe ... lake
irmak, irmagi, Tur ... river
isla, Sp ... island
isola, It ... island
istmo, It., Sp ... isthmus
jarvi, jaur, Fin ... lake
jebel, Arab ... mountain
jiang, Chn ... river
jima, Jap ... island
jökel, Nor ... glacier
joki, Fin ... river
jökull, Ice ... glacier
kaap, Du ... cape
kai, Jap ... bay, gulf, sea
kaikyō, Jap ... channel, strait
kalat, Per ... castle, fortress
kale, Tur ... fort
kali, Mal ... creek, river
kand, Per ... village
kap, Dan., Ger ... cape
kapp, Nor, Swe ... cape
kasr, Arab ... fort, castle
kawa, Jap ... river
kefr, Arab ... village
kei, Jap ... creek, river
ken, Jap ... prefecture
khor, Arab ... bay, inlet
khrebet, Rus ... mountain range
kita, Jap ... north
ko, Jap ... lake
köbstad, Dan ... market-town
kol, Mong ... lake
kólpos, Gr ... gulf
kong, Chn ... river
kopf, Ger ... head, summit, peak
köpstad, Swe ... market town
körfezi, Tur ... gulf
kosa, Rus ... spit
kou, Chn ... river mouth
köy, Tur ... village
kraal, Du. (Africa) ... native village
ksar, Arab ... fortified village
kuala, Mal ... bay, river mouth
kuh, Per ... mountain
kum, Tur ... sand
kuppe, Ger ... summit
küste, Ger ... coast
kyo, Jap ... town, capital
la, Tib ... mountain pass
labuan, Mal ... anchorage, port
lac, Fr ... lake
lago, It., Port., Sp ... lake
lagoa, Port ... lake, bay
laguna, It., Port., Sp ... lagoon, lake
lahti, Fin ... bay, gulf
lan, Swe ... county
landsby, Dan., Nor ... village
liman, Tur ... bay, port
ling, Chn ... pass, ridge, mountain
llanos, Sp ... plains
loch, Celt. (Scotland) ... lake, bay
loma, Sp ... long, low hill
lough, Celt. (Ireland) ... lake, bay
machi, Jap ... town
man, Kor ... bay
mar, Port., Sp ... sea
mare, It., Rom ... sea
marisma, Sp ... marsh, swamp
mark, Ger ... boundary limit
massif, Fr ... block of mountains
mato, Port ... forest, thicket
me, Siam ... river
meer, Du., Ger ... lake, sea
mer, Fr ... sea
mesa, Sp ... flat-topped mountain
meseta, Sp ... plateau
mina, Port., Sp ... mine
minami, Jap ... south
minato, Japan ... harbor, haven
misaki, Jap ... cape, headland
mont, Fr ... mount, mountain
montagna, It ... mountain
montagne, Fr ... mountain
montaña, Sp ... mountain
monte, It., Port., Sp .. mount, mountain
more, Rus., So. Slav ... sea
morro, Port., Sp ... hill, bluff
mühle, Ger ... mill
mund, Ger ... mouth, opening
mündung, Ger ... river mouth
mura, Jap ... township
myit, Bur ... river
mys, Rus ... cape
nada, Jap ... sea
nadi, India ... river, creek
naes, Dan., Nor ... cape
nafud, Arab ... desert of sand dunes
nagar, India ... town, city
nahr, Arab ... river
nam, Siam ... river, water
nan, Chn., Jap ... south
näs, Nor., Swe ... cape
nez, Fr ... point, cape
nishi, nisi, Jap ... west
njarga, Fin ... peninsula
nong, Siam ... marsh
noord, Du ... north
nor, Mong ... lake
nord, Dan., Fr., Ger., It., Nor., Swe .. north
norte, Port., Sp ... north
nos, Rus ... cape
nyasa, Bantu ... lake
ö, Dan., Nor., Swe ... island
occidental, Sp ... western
ocna, Rom ... salt mine
odde, Dan., Nor ... point, cape
oeste, Port., Sp ... west
oka, Jap ... hill
oost, Du ... east
oriental, Sp ... eastern
óros, Gr ... mountain
ost, Ger., Swe ... east
öster, Dan., Nor., Swe ... eastern
ostrov, Rus ... island
oued, Arab ... river, stream
ouest, Fr ... west
ozero, Rus ... lake
pää, Fin ... mountain
padang, Mal ... plain, field
pampas, Sp. (Argentina) ... grassy plains
pará, Indian (Brazil) ... river
pas, Fr ... channel, passage
paso, Sp ... mountain pass, passage
passo, It., Port ... mountain pass, passage, strait
patam, India ... city, town
pélagos, Gr ... open sea
pegunungan, Indon ... mountains
peña, Sp ... rock
pendi, Chn ... basin
pertuis, Fr ... strait
pic, Fr ... mountain peak
pico, Port., Sp ... mountain peak
piedra, Sp ... stone, rock
ping, Chn ... plain, flat
planalto, Port ... plateau
planina, Serb ... mountains
playa, Sp ... shore, beach
ploskogor'ye, Rus ... mountains
pnom, Camb ... mountain
pointe, Fr ... point
polder, Du., Ger ... reclaimed marsh
polje, So. Slav ... plain, field
poluostrov, Rus ... peninsula
pont, Fr ... bridge
ponta, Port ... point, headland
ponte, It., Port ... bridge
pore, India ... city, town
porthmós, Gr ... strait
porto, It., Port ... port, harbor
potamós, Gr ... river
prado, Sp ... field, meadow
presqu'île, Fr ... peninsula
proliv, Rus ... strait
pueblo, Sp ... town, village
puerto, Sp ... port, harbor
pulau, Indon ... island
punkt, Ger ... point
punt, Du ... point
punta, It., Sp ... point
pur, India ... city, town
puy, Fr ... peak
qal'a, qal'at, Arab ... fort, village
qasr, Arab ... fort, castle
rann, India ... wasteland
ra's, Arab ... cape, head
reka, Rus., So. Slav ... river
represa, Port ... reservoir
rettō, Jap ... island chain
ría, Sp ... estuary
ribeira, Port ... stream
riberão, Port ... river
rio, It., Port ... stream, river
río, Sp ... river
rivière, Fr ... river
roca, Sp ... rock
rt, Serb ... cape
rūd, Per ... river
saari, Fin ... island
sable, Fr ... sand
sahara, Arab ... desert, plain
saki, Jap ... cape
sal, Sp ... salt
salar, Sp ... salt flat, salt lake
salto, Sp ... waterfall
san, Jap., Kor ... mountain, hill
sat, satul, Rom ... village
schloss, Ger ... castle
sebkha, Arab ... salt marsh
see, Ger ... lake, sea
şehir, Tur ... town, city
selat, Indon ... strait
selvas, Port., (Brazil) . tropical rain forests
seno, Sp ... bay
serra, Port ... mountain chain
serrania, Sp ... mountain ridge
seto, Jap ... strait
severnaya, Rus ... northern
shahr, Per ... town, city
shamo, Chn ... desert
shan, Chn ... mountain, hill, island
shatt, Arab ... river
shi, Jap, Chn ... city
shima, Jap ... island
shōtō, Jap ... archipelago
sierra, Sp ... mountain range
sjö, Nor., Swe ... lake, sea
sö, Dan., Nor ... lake, sea
söder, södra, Swe ... south
song, Annam ... river
sopka, Rus ... peak, volcano
source, Fr ... a spring
spitze, Ger ... summit, point
staat, Ger ... state
stad, Dan., Du., Nor., Swe ... city, town
stadt, Ger ... city, town
stato, It ... state
step', Rus ... treeless plain, steppe
straat, Du ... strait
strand, Dan., Du., Ger., Nor., Swe ... shore, beach
stretto, It ... strait
strom, Ger ... river, stream
ström, Dan., Nor., Swe .. stream, river
stroom, Du ... stream, river
su, suyu, Tur ... water, river
sud, Fr., Sp ... south
süd, Ger ... south
suidō, Jap ... channel
sul, Port ... south
sund, Dan., Nor., Swe ... sound
sungai, sungei, Indon., Mal ... river
sur, Sp ... south
syd, Dan., Nor., Swe ... south
tafelland, Ger ... plateau
take, Jap ... peak, summit
tal, Ger ... valley
tanjung, tanjong, Mal ... cape
târg, târgul, Rom ... market, town
tell, Arab ... hill
teluk, Indon ... bay, gulf
terra, It ... land
terre, Fr ... earth, land
thal, Ger ... valley
tierra, Sp ... earth, land
tō, Jap ... east; island
tonle, Camb ... river, lake
top, Du ... peak
torp, Swe ... hamlet, cottage
tsangpo, Tib ... river
tso, Tib ... lake
tsu, Jap ... harbor, port
tundra, Rus ... treeless arctic plains
tuz, Tur ... salt
udde, Swe ... cape
ufer, Ger ... shore, riverbank
ujung, Indon ... point, cape
umi, Jap ... sea, gulf
ura, Jap ... bay, coast, creek
ust'ye, Rus ... river mouth
valle, It., Port., Sp ... valley
vallée, Fr ... valley
valli, It ... lake
vár, Hung ... fortress
város, Hung ... town
varoš, So. Slav ... town
veld, Du ... open plain, field
verkh, Rus ... top, summit
ves, Czech ... village
vest, Dan., Nor., Swe ... west
vik, Swe ... cove, bay
vila, Port ... town
villa, Sp ... town
villar, Sp ... village, hamlet
ville, Fr ... town, city
vodokhranilishche, Rus ... reservoir
vostok, Rus ... east
wad, wādī, Arab . intermittent stream
wald, Ger ... forest, woodland
wan, Chn., Jap ... bay, gulf
weiler, Ger ... hamlet, village
westersch, Ger ... western
wüste, Ger ... desert
xi, Chn ... west, western
yama, Jap ... mountain
yarimada, Tur ... peninsula
yug, Rus ... south
zaki, Jap ... cape
zaliv, Rus ... bay, gulf
zapad, Rus ... west
zee, Du ... sea
zemlya, Rus ... land
zuid, Du ... south

Abbreviations of Geographic Names and Terms

Ab., Can.	Alberta, Can.
Afg.	Afghanistan
Afr.	Africa
Ak., U.S.	Alaska, U.S.
Al., U.S.	Alabama, U.S.
Alb.	Albania
Alg.	Algeria
Am. Sam.	American Samoa
And.	Andorra
Ang.	Angola
Ant.	Antarctica
Antig.	Antigua and Barbuda
Ar., U.S.	Arkansas, U.S.
Arg.	Argentina
Arm.	Armenia
Aus.	Austria
Austl.	Australia
Az., U.S.	Arizona, U.S.
Azer.	Azerbaijan
b.	Bay, Gulf, Inlet, Lagoon
Bah.	Bahamas
Bahr.	Bahrain
Barb.	Barbados
bas.	Basin
B.C.	British Columbia, Can.
Bdi.	Burundi
Bel.	Belgium
Bela.	Belarus
Ber.	Bermuda
Bhu.	Bhutan
B.I.O.T.	British Indian Ocean Territory
Blg.	Bulgaria
Bngl.	Bangladesh
Bol.	Bolivia
Bos.	Bosnia and Herzegovina
Bots.	Botswana
Braz.	Brazil
Bru.	Brunei
Br. Vir. Is.	British Virgin Islands
Burkina	Burkina Faso
c.	Cape, Point
Ca., U.S.	California, U.S.
Camb.	Cambodia
Camrn.	Cameroon
can.	Canal
Can.	Canada
C.A.R.	Central African Republic
Cay. Is.	Cayman Islands
C. Iv.	Cote d'Ivoire
clf.	Cliff, Escarpment
co.	County, Parish
Co., U.S.	Colorado, U.S.
Col.	Colombia
Com.	Comoros
cont.	Continent
Cook Is.	Cook Islands
C.R.	Costa Rica
Cro.	Croatia
cst.	Coast, Beach
Ct., U.S.	Connecticut, U.S.
C.V.	Cape Verde
Cyp.	Cyprus
Czech Rep.	Czech Republic
d.	Dam
D.C., U.S.	District of Columbia, U.S.
De., U.S.	Delaware, U.S.
del.	Delta
Den.	Denmark
dep.	Dependency, Colony
depr.	Depression
des.	Desert
Dji.	Djibouti
Dom.	Dominica
Dom. Rep.	Dominican Republic
D.R.C.	Democratic Republic of the Congo
Ec.	Ecuador
El Sal.	El Salvador
Eng., U.K.	England, U.K.
Eq. Gui.	Equatorial Guinea
Erit.	Eritrea
Est.	Estonia
est.	Estuary
Eth.	Ethiopia
E. Timor	East Timor
Eur.	Europe
Falk. Is.	Falkland Islands
Far. Is.	Faroe Islands
Fin.	Finland
Fl., U.S.	Florida, U.S.
for.	Forest, Moor
Fr.	France
Fr. Gu.	French Guiana
Fr. Poly.	French Polynesia
Ga., U.S.	Georgia, U.S.
Gam.	The Gambia
Gaza	Gaza Strip
Geor.	Georgia
Ger.	Germany
Gib.	Gibraltar
Grc.	Greece
Green.	Greenland
Gren.	Grenada
Guad.	Guadeloupe
Guat.	Guatemala
Guern.	Guernsey
Gui.	Guinea
Gui.-B.	Guinea-Bissau
Guy.	Guyana
Hi., U.S.	Hawaii, U.S.
hist.	Historic Site, Ruins
hist. reg.	Historic Region
Hond.	Honduras
Hung.	Hungary
i.	Island
Ia., U.S.	Iowa, U.S.
ice	Ice Feature, Glacier
Ice.	Iceland
Id., U.S.	Idaho, U.S.
Il., U.S.	Illinois, U.S.
In., U.S.	Indiana, U.S.
Indon.	Indonesia
ind. res.	Indian Reservation
I. of Man	Isle of Man
Ire.	Ireland
is.	Islands
Isr.	Israel
isth.	Isthmus
Jam.	Jamaica
Jord.	Jordan
Kaz.	Kazakhstan
Kir.	Kiribati
Kor., N.	Korea, North
Kor., S.	Korea, South
Ks., U.S.	Kansas, U.S.
Kuw.	Kuwait
Ky., U.S.	Kentucky, U.S.
Kyrg.	Kyrgyzstan
La., U.S.	Louisiana, U.S.
Lat.	Latvia
Leb.	Lebanon
Leso.	Lesotho
Lib.	Liberia
Liech.	Liechtenstein
Lith.	Lithuania
lk.	Lake
Lux.	Luxembourg
Ma., U.S.	Massachusetts, U.S.
Mac.	Macedonia
Madag.	Madagascar
Malay.	Malaysia
Mald.	Maldives
Marsh. Is.	Marshall Islands
Mart.	Martinique
Maur.	Mauritania
May.	Mayotte
Mb., Can.	Manitoba, Can.
Md., U.S.	Maryland, U.S.
Me., U.S.	Maine, U.S.
Mex.	Mexico
Mi., U.S.	Michigan, U.S.
Micron.	Micronesia, Federated States of
Mn., U.S.	Minnesota, U.S.
Mo., U.S.	Missouri, U.S.
Mol.	Moldova
Mong.	Mongolia
Mont.	Montenegro
Mor.	Morocco
Moz.	Mozambique
Ms., U.S.	Mississippi, U.S.
Mt., U.S.	Montana, U.S.
mth.	River Mouth or Channel
mtn.	Mountain
mts.	Mountains
Mya.	Myanmar
N.A.	North America
nat. cap.	National Capital
N.B., Can.	New Brunswick, Can.
N.C., U.S.	North Carolina, U.S.
N. Cal.	New Caledonia
N.D., U.S.	North Dakota, U.S.
Ne., U.S.	Nebraska, U.S.
Neth.	Netherlands
Neth. Ant.	Netherlands Antilles
Nf., Can.	Newfoundland, Can.
N.H., U.S.	New Hampshire, U.S.
Nic.	Nicaragua
Nig.	Nigeria
N. Ire., U.K.	Northern Ireland, U.K.
N.J., U.S.	New Jersey, U.S.
N.M., U.S.	New Mexico, U.S.
N. Mar. Is.	Northern Mariana Islands
Nmb.	Namibia
Nor.	Norway
n.p.	National Park or Monument
N.S., Can.	Nova Scotia, Can.
N.T., Can.	Northwest Territories, Can.
Nu., Can.	Nunavut, Can.
Nv., U.S.	Nevada, U.S.
N.Y., U.S.	New York, U.S.
N.Z.	New Zealand
oc.	Ocean
Oc.	Australia and Oceania
Oh., U.S.	Ohio, U.S.
Ok., U.S.	Oklahoma, U.S.
On., Can.	Ontario, Can.
Or., U.S.	Oregon, U.S.
p.	Pass
Pa., U.S.	Pennsylvania, U.S.
Pak.	Pakistan
Pan.	Panama
Pap. N. Gui.	Papua New Guinea
P.E., Can.	Prince Edward I., Can.
Para.	Paraguay
pen.	Peninsula
Phil.	Philippines
Pit.	Pitcairn
pk.	Park, Reserve
pl.	Plain, Flat
plat.	Plateau, Highland
p.o.i.	Point of Interest
Pol.	Poland
Port.	Portugal
P.R.	Puerto Rico
Qc., Can.	Québec, Can.
r.	Rock
rec.	Recreational Site, Park
reg.	Physical Region
res.	Reservoir
Reu.	Reunion
rf.	Reef, Shoal
R.I., U.S.	Rhode Island, U.S.
Rom.	Romania
Rw.	Rwanda
s.	Sea
S.A.	South America
S. Afr.	South Africa
Sau. Ar.	Saudi Arabia
S.C., U.S.	South Carolina, U.S.
Scot., U.K.	Scotland, U.K.
S.D., U.S.	South Dakota, U.S.
Sen.	Senegal
Serb.	Serbia
Sey.	Seychelles
S. Geor.	South Georgia
Sing.	Singapore
Sk., Can.	Saskatchewan, Can.
S.L.	Sierra Leone
Slvk.	Slovakia
Slvn.	Slovenia
S. Mar.	San Marino
Sol. Is.	Solomon Islands
Som.	Somalia
Sp. N. Afr.	Spanish North Africa
Sri L.	Sri Lanka
state	State, Province, Department, Region, etc.
St. Hel.	St. Helena
St. K./N.	St. Kitts and Nevis
St. Luc.	St. Lucia
stm.	River, Creek, Stream
St. P./M.	St. Pierre and Miquelon
S. Tom./P.	Sao Tome and Principe
strt.	Strait, Channel, Sound
St. Vin.	St. Vincent and the Grenadines
Sur.	Suriname
sw.	Swamp, Marsh
Swaz.	Swaziland
Swe.	Sweden
Switz.	Switzerland
Tai.	Taiwan
Taj.	Tajikistan
Tan.	Tanzania
T./C. Is.	Turks and Caicos Islands
Thai.	Thailand
Tn., U.S.	Tennessee, U.S.
Tok.	Tokelau
Trin.	Trinidad and Tobago
Tun.	Tunisia
Tur.	Turkey
Turkmen.	Turkmenistan
Tx., U.S.	Texas, U.S.
U.A.E.	United Arab Emirates
Ug.	Uganda
U.K.	United Kingdom
Ukr.	Ukraine
Ur.	Uruguay
U.S.	United States
Ut., U.S.	Utah, U.S.
Uzb.	Uzbekistan
Va., U.S.	Virginia, U.S.
val.	Valley, Watercourse
Ven.	Venezuela
Viet.	Vietnam
V.I.U.S.	Virgin Islands (U.S.)
vol.	Volcano
Vt., U.S.	Vermont, U.S.
Wa., U.S.	Washington, U.S.
Wal./F.	Wallis and Futuna
W.B.	West Bank
Wi., U.S.	Wisconsin, U.S.
W. Sah.	Western Sahara
wtfl.	Waterfall
W.V., U.S.	West Virginia, U.S.
Wy., U.S.	Wyoming, U.S.
Yk., Can.	Yukon, Can.
Zam.	Zambia
Zimb.	Zimbabwe

Pronunciation of Geographic Names

Key to the sound values of letters and symbols used in the index to indicate pronunciation

ă	ăt; băttle
ă	fin*ă*l; appe*ă*l
ā	rāte; elāte
å	senåte; inanimåte
ä	ärm; cälm
ȧ	ȧsk; bȧth
ȧ	sof*ȧ*; m*ȧ*rine (short neutral or indeterminate sound)
â	fâre; prepâre
ch	choose; church
dh	as th in other; either
ē	bē; ēve
e̊	e̊vent; cre̊ate
ĕ	bĕt; ĕnd
ĕ	rec*ĕ*nt (short neutral or indeterminate sound)
ẽ	cratẽr; cindẽr
g	gō; gāme
gh	guttural g
ĭ	bĭt; wĭll
ĭ	(short neutral or indeterminate sound)
ī	rīde; bīte
ᴋ	gutteral k as *ch* n German *ich*
ng	sing
ŋ	baŋk; liŋger
ɴ	indicates nasalized
ŏ	nŏd; ŏdd
ŏ	c*ŏ*mmit; c*ŏ*nnect
ō	ōld; bōld
o̊	o̊bey; ho̊tel
ô	ôrder; lông
oi	boil
o͞o	fo͞od; ro͞ot
ȯ	as oo in foot; wood
ou	out; thou
s	soft; so; sane
sh	dish; finish
th	thin; thick
ū	pūre; cūre
ů	ůnite; ůsůrp
û	ûrn; fûr
ŭ	stŭd; ŭp
ŭ	circ*ŭ*s; s*ŭ*bmit
ü	as in French tu
zh	as z in azure
'	indeterminate vowel sound

In many cases the spelling of foreign geographical names does not even remotely indicate the pronunciation to an American, e.g., Słupsk in Poland is pronounced swȯpsk; Jujuy in Argentina is pronounced ho͞ohwē; La Spezia in Italy is lä-spĕ'zyä.

This condition is hardly surprising, however, when we consider that in our own language Worcester, Massachusetts, is pronounced wȯs'tẽr; Sioux City, Iowa, so͞o sĭ'tē; Schuylkill Haven, Pennsylvania, sko͞ol'kĭl hā-vĕn; Poughkeepsie, New York, pŏ-kĭp'sē.

The indication of pronunciation of geographic names presents several peculiar problems:

1. Many foreign languages use sounds that are not present in the English language and which an American cannot normally articulate. Thus, though the nearest English equivalent sound has been indicated, only approximate results are possible.

2. There are several dialects in each foreign language that cause variation in the local pronunciation of names. This also occurs in identical names in the various divisions of a great language group.

3. Within the United States there are marked differences in pronunciation, not only of local geographic names, but also of common words, indicating that the sound and tone values for letters as well as the placing of the emphasis vary considerably from one part of the country to another.

4. A number of different letters and diacritical combinations could be used to indicate essentially the same or approximate pronunciations.

Some variation in pronunciation other than that indicated in this index may be encountered, but such a difference does not necessarily indicate that either is in error, and in many cases it is a matter of individual choice as to which is preferred. In fact, an exact indication of pronunciation of many foreign names using English letters and diacritical marks is extremely diffiicult and sometimes impossible.

The following sources have been consulted during the process of creating and updating the thematic maps and statistics for the 22nd Edition.

Andreassen, L., M. Beedle, E. Berthier, F. Cawkwell, N. Dickmann, E. Dolgova, A. Fountain, N. Glasser, E. Hansson, U. Haritashya, G. Hartman, C. Helm, L. Iacovelli, H. Jiskoot, G. Kapustin, T. Khromova, J. Kincaid, S. Kutuzov, I. Lavrentiev, X. Li, L. Mabileau, J. Meyer, P. Mool, A. Muravyev, G. Nosenko, F. Paul, A. Racoviteanu, F. Rau, A. Rivera, M. Schnirch, Y. Seliverstov, O. Sigurdsson, S. Taschner, P. Zenteno, and N. Zheltyhina. (2001-2008). *GLIMS Glacier Database*. National Snow and Ice Data Center/World Data Center for Glaciology.

American Wind Energy Association (AWEA). (http://www.awea.org/)

Brohan, P., J.J. Kennedy, I. Harris, S.F.B. Tett, and P.D. Jones. (2006). Uncertainty estimates in regional and global observed temperature changes: A new dataset from 1850. *Journal of Geophysical Research*, 111, D12106, doi:10.1029/2005JD006548. (http://www.cru.uea.ac.uk/cru/data/temperature)

Brown, J., O.J. Ferrians, Jr., J.A. Heginbottom, and E.S. Melnikov. (1998). *Circum-Arctic Map of Permafrost and Ground Ice Conditions*. National Snow and Ice Data Center/World Data Center for Glaciology.

Census of Canada. *Population Counts, for Canada, Provinces and Territories, and Census Divisions by Urban and Rural, 2001 Census*.

Center for International Earth Science Information Network (CIESIN), Columbia University; International Food Policy Research Institute (IFPRI); The World Bank; and Centro Internacional de Agricultural Tropical (CIAT). (2005). *Global Rural-Urban Mapping Project (GRUMP), Alpha Version*. Socioeconomic Data and Applications Center (SEDAC), Columbia University. (http://sedac.ciesin.columbia.edu/gpw/)

Center for Systemic Peace. *Major Episodes of Political Violence 1946-2007*.

Central Intelligence Agency (CIA). *World Factbook*. (https://www.cia.gov/library/publications/the-world-factbook/)

Chorlton, L B. (2007). *Generalized Geology of the World: Bedrock Domains and Major Faults in GIS Format: A Small-Scale World Geology Map with an Extended Geological Attribute Database*. Geological Survey of Canada, Open File 5529.

Coastal Services Center, National Oceanic and Atmospheric Administration. (http://www.csc.noaa.gov/)

Energy Information Administration (EIA), United States Department of Energy. *Coal Production and Number of Mines by State and Mine Type, 2007-2008*.

Energy Information Administration (EIA), United States Department of Energy. *International Energy Annual*.

Energy Information Administration (EIA), United States Department of Energy. *Natural Gas Annual 2006*.

Energy Information Administration (EIA), United States Department of Energy. *Petroleum Supply Annual 2006*.

Energy Information Administration (EIA), United States Department of Energy. *World Anthracite Coal Production, Most Recent Annual Estimates, 1980-2006*.

Energy Information Administration (EIA), United States Department of Energy. *World Bituminous Coal Production, Most Recent Annual Estimates, 1980-2006*.

Energy Information Administration (EIA), United States Department of Energy. *World Coal Production, Most Recent Annual Estimates, 1980-2007*.

Energy Information Administration (EIA), United States Department of Energy. *World Crude Oil Reserves, January 1, 1980 - January 1, 2008 Estimates*.

Energy Information Administration (EIA), United States Department of Energy. *World Dry Natural Gas Production, Most Recent Annual Estimates, 1980-2007*.

Energy Information Administration (EIA), United States Department of Energy. *World Production of Crude Oil, NGPL, and Other Liquids, and Refinery Processing Gain, Most Recent Annual Estimates, 1980-2007*.

Energy Information Administration (EIA), United States Department of Energy. *World Proved Natural Gas Reserves, January 1, 1980 - January 1, 2008 Estimates*.

Farr, T.G., P.A. Rosen, E. Caro, R. Crippen, R. Duren, S. Hensley, M. Kobrick, M. Paller, E. Rodriguez, L. Roth, D. Seal, S. Shaffer, J. Shimada, J. Umland, M. Werner, M. Oskin, D. Burbank, and D. Alsdorf. (2007). The Shuttle Radar Topography Mission. *Reviews of Geophysics*, 45, RG2004, doi:10.1029/2005RG000183.

Federal Aviation Administration (FAA). *CY 2007 Passenger Boarding and All-Cargo Data*.

Federation of American Scientists. *Status of World Nuclear Forces 2009*.

Fetterer, F. and K. Knowles. (2002). *Sea Ice Index*. National Snow and Ice Data Center.

Food and Agriculture Organization of the United Nations (FAO). *FAOSTAT*.

Global Volcanism Program, Smithsonian Institution. *Volcanoes of the World*.

Halpern, B.S., S. Walbridge, K.A. Selkoe, C.V. Kappel, F. Micheli, C. D'Agrosa, J.F. Bruno, K.S. Casey, C. Ebert, H.E. Fox, R. Fujita, D. Heinemann, H.S. Lenihan, E.M. P. Madin, M.T. Perry, E.R. Selig, M. Spalding, R. Steneck, and R. Watson. (2008). A global map of human impact on marine ecosystems. *Science*, 319(5865), pp. 948-952. doi: 10.1126/science.1149345.

Hansen, M., R. DeFries, J.R.G. Townshend, and R. Sohlberg. (2000). Global land cover classification at 1km resolution using a decision tree classifier. *International Journal of Remote Sensing*, 21, pp. 1331-1365.

Hansen, M.C., S.V. Stehman, P.V. Potapov, T.R. Loveland, J.R.G. Townshend, R.S. DeFries, K.W. Pittman, F. Stolle, M.K. Steininger, M. Carroll, and C. Dimiceli. (2008). Humid tropical forest clearing from 2000 to 2005 quantified using multi-temporal and multi-resolution remotely sensed data. *PNAS*, 105(27), pp. 9439-9444.

Heidelberg Institute for International Conflict Research. *Conflict Barometer*.

Heinrich J. , C. Klinke, and C.B. Schmidt. (1994). The Hop Atlas: *The History and Geography of the Cultivated Plant*. Nuremberg, Germany: Jon. Barth & Sohn.

Hulme, M. (1998). *Global Land Precipitation Dataset, Version 1.0*. Climatic Research Unit, University of East Anglia.

International Center for Prison Studies. (2009). *World Prison Population List, 8th Edition*. King's College, London.

International Lake Environment Committee. *World Lakes Database*.

International Water Power & Dam Construction. *Yearbook 2008*.

Inter-Parliamentary Union. *Women in National Parliaments*.

Inter-Parliamentary Union. *Women's Suffrage: A World Chronology of the Recognition of Women's Rights to Vote and to Stand for Election*.

Keeling, C.D., S.C. Piper, R.B. Bacastow, M. Wahlen, T.P. Whorf, M. Heimann, and H.A. Meijer. (2001). Exchanges of atmospheric CO_2 and $13CO_2$ with the terrestrial biosphere and oceans from 1978 to 2000. *I. Global Aspects, SIO Reference Series, No. 01-06*. Scripps Institution of Oceanography.

Kelly, T.D. and M.D. Fenton. (2003). *Iron and Steel Statistics*. United States Geological Survey.

Küchler, A.W. (1949). A physiognomic classification of vegetation. *Annals of the Association of American Geographers*, 39(3), pp. 201-210.

Laboratory for Satellite Altimetry, Satellite Oceanography and Climatology Division, National Oceanic and Atmospheric Administration. *Altimetry Data*. (http://ibis.grdl.noaa.gov/)

LakeNet Global Lake Database.

Mackay, J., M. Eriksen, and O. Shafey. (2006). *The Tobacco Atlas, 2nd Edition*. American Cancer Society.

McDaniel, P. (2008). *The Twelve Soil Orders*. (http://soils.ag.uidaho.edu/soilorders/index.htm/)

Murphy, R.E. (1968). Annals map supplement number 9. Landforms of the world. *Annals of the Association of American Geographers*, 58(1), pp. 198-200.

National Aeronautics and Space Administration (NASA), Atmospheric Science Data Center. (http://eosweb.larc.nasa.gov/)

National Aeronautics and Space Administration (NASA). (http://www.nasa.gov/)

National Oceanic and Atmospheric Administration (NOAA). (http://www.noaa.gov/)

National Snow and Ice Data Center. (http://nsidc.org/)

National Weather Service, National Oceanic and Atmospheric Administration. (http://www.spc.noaa.gov/)

Natural Resources Canada. *The Atlas of Canada.*

New, M., D. Lister, M. Hulme, and I. Makin. (2000). A high-resolution data set of surface climate over global land areas. *Climate Research,* 21, pp. 1-25.

Olson, D.M., E. Dinerstein, E.D. Wikramanayake, N.D. Burgess, G.V.N. Powell, E.C. Underwood, J.A. D'Amico, I. Itoua, H.E. Strand, J.C. Morrison, C.J. Loucks, T.F. Allnutt, T.H. Ricketts, Y. Kura, J.F. Lamoreux, W.W. Wettengel, P. Hedao, and K.R. Kassem. (2001). Terrestrial ecoregions of the world: A new map of life on earth. *BioScience,* 51(11), pp. 933-938.

Rand McNally. *The Rand McNally Road Atlas 2009.*

Statistics Canada. *Air Carrier Traffic at Canadian Airports.*

Stockholm International Peace Research Institute. *The Financial Value of National Arms Exports, 1998-2006.*

Tapley, B., J. Ries, S. Bettadpur, D. Chambers, M. Cheng, F. Condi, B. Gunter, Z. Kang, P.Nagel, R. Pastor, T. Pekker, S.Poole, and F. Wang, (2005). GGM02 - An improved Earth gravity field model from GRACE. *Journal of Geodesy,* doi 10.1007/s00190-005-0480-z. (http://www.csr.utexas.edu/grace/gravity/)

TeleGeography Research. (http://www.telegeography.com/)

The Canadian Wind Energy Association (CanWEA). (http://www.canwea.ca/)

Thornthwaite, C.W. (1944). Report of committee on transpiration and evaporation. *American Geophysical Union Transactions,* 25(5), pp. 683-693.

Transport Canada. *Transportation in Canada 2007.*

Trewartha, G.T. (1968). *An Introduction to Climate, 4th Edition.* New York: McGraw-Hill Book Company.

United Nations (UN). *Comtrade Database, SITC Rev.3. 2006.*

United Nations (UN). *Human Development Reports 2007/2008.*

United Nations (UN). *World Contraceptive Use 2007.*

United Nations (UN). *World Population Prospects Database: The 2006 Revision.*

United Nations Children's Fund (UNICEF). *Report on the Global AIDS Epidemic.*

United Nations Educational, Scientific and Cultural Organization (UNESCO), Institute for Statistics Data Centre. *Public Reports.*

United Nations Educational, Scientific and Cultural Organization (UNESCO), International Hydrological Programme. *World Water Resources and Their Use.*

United Nations Environment Program. *Global Resource Information Database.*

United Nations Environment Program. *Islands Directory.*

United Nations High Commissioner for Refugees (UNHCR). *2007 Global Trends: Refugees, Asylum-Seekers, Returnees, Internally Displaced and Stateless Persons.*

United Nations Peacekeeping. *List of Operations 1948-2008.*

United Nations, Department of Economic and Social Affairs. *2005 UN Energy Statistics Yearbook.*

United Nations, Department of Economic and Social Affairs. *World Urbanization Prospects, 2007 Revision.*

United Nations, Office on Drugs and Crime. *2008 World Drug Report.*

United Nations, Organization for Economic Co-operation and Development (OECD). *Uranium 2007: Resources, Production and Demand.*

United States Bureau of Labor Statistics. *Quarterly Census of Employment and Wages.*

United States Census Bureau. American FactFinder. *2006 Annual Survey of Manufactures.*

United States Census Bureau. *Census 2000 Summary Files.*

United States Census Bureau. *International Database.*

United States Census Bureau. *Statistical Abstract of the United States, 2008 Edition.*

United States Census Bureau. *Statistical Abstract of the United States, 2009 Edition.*

United States Department of Agriculture (USDA), Economic Research Service. *Sugar and Sweeteners Outlook, 2008.*

United States Department of Agriculture (USDA), Natural Resource Conservation Service. *Soil Taxonomy: A Basic System of Soil Classification for Making and Interpreting Soil Surveys.*

United States Department of Agriculture (USDA). *Chickens and Eggs-2007 Summary.*

United States Department of Agriculture (USDA). *Feed Grains Database.*

United States Department of Agriculture (USDA). *Poultry-Production and Value-2007 Summary.*

United States Department of Energy. *Landscan 2001 High Resolution Global Population Data Set.* © 2003 UT-Battelle, LLC. All rights reserved. Notice: These data were produced by UT-Battelle, LLC under Contract No. DE-AC05-00OR22725 with the Department of Energy. The Government has certain rigths in this data. Neither UT-Battelle, LLC nor the United States Department of Energy, nor any of their employees, makes any warranty, express or implied, or assumes any legal liability or responsibility for the accuracy, completeness, or usefulness of any data, apparatus, product, or process disclosed, or represents that its use would not infringe privately owned rights.

United States Environmental Protection Agency (EPA). (http://www.epa.gov/)

United States Environmental Protection Agency (EPA). *Great Lakes Factsheet No. 1.*

United States Geological Survey (USGS). *Lengths of Major Rivers.*

United States Geological Survey (USGS). *Mineral Commodity Summaries.*

United States Geological Survey (USGS). *Mineral Resources Data System (MRDS).*

United States Geological Survey (USGS). *Minerals Yearbook 2006.*

United States Geological Survey (USGS). *National Atlas of the United States.* (http://www.nationalatlas.gov/)

United States Geological Survey (USGS). *Significant Earthquakes of the World.*

Woodworth, P.L. and R. Player. (2003). The Permanent Service for Mean Sea Level: An update to the 21st century. *Journal of Coastal Research,* 19, pp. 287-295. (http://www.pol.ac.uk/psmsl/)

World Energy Council. *2007 Survey of Energy Resources.*

World Health Organization (WHO). *Global Atlas of the Health Workforce.*

World Health Organization (WHO). *Global Information System on Alcohol and Health.*

World Health Organization (WHO). *Global Status Report on Alcohol 2004.*

World Health Organization (WHO). *Statistical Information System (WHOSIS).* (http://www.who.int/whosis/)

World Health Organization (WHO). *World Malaria Report 2008.*

World Wind Energy Association. *Worldwide Wind Energy Installation Figures per Continent.*

The editor wishes to thank the individual scientists, research units, and organizations that made their datasets and research available for this edition of Goode's World Atlas.

Listed below are page references for major topics covered by the thematic maps and graphs, the introductory text, and the tables.

This universal index includes in a single alphabetical list the names of selected features that appear on the reference maps. Each name is followed by a page number and geographical coordinates.

Abbreviation and Capitalization. Abbreviations of names on the maps have been standardized as much as possible. Names that are abbreviated on the maps are generally spelled out in full in the index.

Most initial letters of names are capitalized, except for a few Dutch names such as "s-Gravenhage". Capitalization of non-initial words in a name generally follows local practice.

Alphabetization. Names are alphabetized in the order of the letters of the English alphabet. Spanish *ll* and *ch*, for example, are not treated as separate letters. Furthermore, diacritical marks are disregarded in alphabetization – German or Scandinavian *ä* or *ö* are treated as *a* or *o*.

The names of physical features may appear inverted, since they are always alphabetized under the proper, not the generic, part of the name, thus: "Gibraltar, Strait of", not "Strait of Gibraltar". In this case "Gibraltar" is the proper part of the name and "Strait of" is the generic. Otherwise every entry, whether consisting of one word or more, is alphabetized as a single continuous entity on the basis of the proper part of the name. "Lakeland", for example, appears after "Lake Havasu City" and before "La Luz".

In the case of identical names, towns are listed first, then political divisions, then physical features.

Generic Terms. Except for cities, the names of all features are followed by terms that represent broad classes of features, for example, "Mississippi, stm." or "Alabama, state". A list of all abbreviations used in the index is on page 297.

Country names and the names of features that extend beyond the boundaries of one country are followed by the name of the continent in which each is located. Country designations follow the names of all other places in the index. The locations of places in the United States, Canada and the United Kingdom are further defined by abbreviations that include the state or political division in which each is located.

Pronunciations. Pronunciations are included for many of the names listed. An explanation of the pronunciation system used appears on page 297.

Page References and Geographical Coordinates. The page references and geographical coordinates are found in the last columns of each entry.

If a page contains several maps or insets, a lowercase letter identifies the specific map or inset.

Latitude and longitude coordinates for point features, such as cities and mountain peaks, indicate the location of the symbols. For extensive areal features, such as countries or mountain ranges, the locations are for the approximate center of the feature. For rivers, locations are given for the mouth.

Feature (Pronunciation)	Page	Lat.	Long.
A			
Aachen, Ger. (ä´kĕn) 194-95		50°46´N	6°06´E
Aalborg, Den. (ôl´bôr) 192-93		57°02´N	9°55´E
Aalen, Ger. (ä´lĕn) 194-95		48°50´N	10°06´E
Aali, Sadd el-, d., Egypt			
see Aswan High Dam 268b		23°59´N	32°53´E
Aarau, Switz. (ä´rŏu) 194-95		47°24´N	8°03´E
Aba, China 238-39		33°06´N	101°59´E
Aba, Nig. .260a		5°07´N	7°22´E
Abacaxis, stm., Braz. 166-67		3°54´S	58°46´W
Abaco, i., Bah. 142-43		26°28´N	77°05´W
Ābādān, Iran (äb´ē-dän´) 228-29		30°21´N	48°17´E
Abadla, Alg. 188-89		31°01´N	2°41´W
Abaetetuba, Braz. (ä´bå-ĕ-tĕ-tōō´bå) 166-67		1°44´S	48°53´W
Abagnar Qi, China *see* Xilinhot 240-41		43°56´N	116°03´E
Abag Qi, China. 240-41		43°43´N	114°39´E
Abakan, Russia (ŭ-bá-kän´) 218-19		53°43´N	91°27´E
Abancay, Peru (ä-bän-kä´ē) 170		13°37´S	72°53´W
Abashiri, Japan (ä-bä-shē´rē) 244		44°01´N	144°16´E
Abasolo, Mex. (ä-bä-sō´lō) 146-47		24°04´N	98°22´W
Abay, stm., Afr. *see* Blue Nile 254		15°38´N	32°30´E
Ābaya Hāyk´, lk., Eth. (ä-bä´yá) 262-63		6°18´N	37°52´E
Abbé, Lac, lk., Afr. *see* Abe, Lake 262-63		11°10´N	41°48´E
Abbeville, Fr. (áb-vēl´) 196-97		50°07´N	1°50´E
Abbeville, Al., U.S. (ăb´ē-vĭl) 124-25		31°34´N	85°15´W
Abbeville, Ga., U.S. (ăb´ē-vĭl) 124-25		31°60´N	83°18´W
Abbeville, La., U.S. (ăb´ē-vĭl) 122-23		29°58´N	92°08´W
Abbeville, S.C., U.S. (ăb´ē-vĭl) 124-25		34°11´N	82°23´W
Abbotsford, B.C., Can. (ăb´ŭts-fĕrd) . . .132-33		49°03´N	122°17´W
Abbottābād, Pak. 232-33		34°09´N	73°13´E
'Abd al-Kūrī, i., Yemen (ăbd-ĕl-kô´rē) . . .220-21		12°12´N	52°13´E
Abdulino, Russia (äb-dò-lē´nō) 186-87		53°41´N	53°40´E
Abe, Lake, lk., Afr. 262-63		11°10´N	41°48´E
Abéché, Chad 258-59		13°50´N	20°50´E
Abemama, at., Kir. 280-81		0°26´N	173°54´E
Abengourou, C. Iv. 260-61		6°44´N	3°29´W
Abeokuta, Nig. (ä-bå-ô-kōō´tä) 260a		7°09´N	3°21´E
Aberdare, Wales, U.K. 190-91		51°43´N	3°28´W
Aberdare National Park, n.p., Kenya . . .267		0°30´S	36°45´E
Aberdeen, Scot., U.K. (ăb-ĕr-dēn´) 190-91		57°09´N	2°06´W
Aberdeen, Id., U.S. (ăb-ĕr-dēn´) 112-13		42°57´N	112°51´W
Aberdeen, Md., U.S. 116-17		39°31´N	76°10´W
Aberdeen, Ms., U.S. (ăb-ĕr-dēn´) 124-25		33°50´N	88°33´W
Aberdeen, S.D., U.S. (ăb-ĕr-dēn´) . . .114-15		45°28´N	98°29´W
Aberdeen, Wa., U.S. (ăb-ĕr-dēn´) 112-13		46°59´N	123°49´W
Aberdeen Lake, lk., Nu., Can. 130-31		64°27´N	99°00´W
Aberystwyth, Wales, U.K.			
(ă-bĕr-ĭst´wĭth) 190-91		52°25´N	4°05´W
Abez', Russia 186-87		66°32´N	61°44´E
Abhā, Sau. Ar. 266		18°13´N	42°30´E
Abhé Bad, lk., Afr. *see* Abe, Lake 262-63		11°10´N	41°48´E
Ābhē Bid Hāyk´, lk., Afr.			
see Abe, Lake 262-63		11°10´N	41°48´E
Abidjan, nat. cap., C. Iv. (ä-bēd-zhän´) . . .260-61		5°20´N	4°01´W
Abilene, Ks., U.S. (ăb´ĭ-lēn) 120-21		38°55´N	97°13´W
Abilene, Tx., U.S. (ăb´ĭ-lēn) 120-21		32°27´N	99°44´W
Abingdon, Il., U.S. (ăb´ĭng-dŭn) 114-15		40°48´N	90°23´W
Abingdon, Va., U.S. (ăb´ĭng-dŭn) 124-25		36°43´N	81°59´W
Abitibi, stm., On., Can. 130-31		51°03´N	80°55´W
Abitibi, Lac, lk., Can. (lăk äb-ĭ-tĭb´ĭ)			
see Abitibi, Lake 136-37		48°41´N	79°35´W
Abitibi, Lake, lk., Can. (lăk äb-ĭ-tĭb´ĭ) . . .136-37		48°41´N	79°35´W
Ābīyata Hāyk´, lk., Eth. 269d		7°36´N	38°36´E
Abkhazeti Autonomis Respublika,			
state, Geor. *see* Abkhazia. 227		43°10´N	41°00´E
Abkhazia, state, Geor. 227		43°10´N	41°00´E
Åbo, Fin. *see* Turku 192-93		60°27´N	22°16´E
Abou-Deïa, Chad. 258-59		11°27´N	19°17´E
Abou Simbel, hist., Egypt			
see Abu Simbel 266		22°22´N	31°38´E
Abovyan, Arm. 227		40°15´N	44°35´E
Abrantes, Port. (á-brän´tĕs) 198-99		39°28´N	8°12´W
Abra Pampa, Arg. 168-69		22°43´S	65°42´W
Abruka saar, i., Est. (á-brò´ká-sä´ár) . . .192-93		58°09´N	22°31´E
Abū ʿAlī, i., Sau. Ar. 230-31		27°19´N	49°35´E
Abū ʿArīsh, Sau. Ar. (ä-bōō á-rēsh´) 266		16°58´N	42°50´E
Abu Dhabi, nat. cap., U.A.E.			
(ä-bōō dä´bē) 230-31		24°28´N	54°22´E
Abuja, nat. cap., Nig. (ä-bū´já) 260-61		9°12´N	7°11´E
Abū Kamāl, Syria 228-29		34°27´N	40°56´E
Abū Mūsā, i., Asia 230-31		25°52´N	55°00´E
Abū Mūsā, Jazīreh-ye, i., Asia			
see Abū Mūsā 230-31		25°52´N	55°02´E
Abunã, Braz. 166-67		9°41´S	65°22´W
Abuná, stm., S.A. 166-67		9°40´S	65°26´W
Abuná, stm., S.A. (á-bōō-nä´) 166-67		9°40´S	65°26´W
Ābu Road, India (á´bōō rōd) 234-35		24°30´N	72°49´E
Abū Shajarah, Ra's, c., Sudan 266		21°05´N	37°13´E
Abu Simbel, hist., Egypt 266		22°22´N	31°38´E
Abū Sunbul, hist., Egypt *see* Abu Simbel. . .266		22°22´N	31°38´E
Abū Zaby, nat. cap., U.A.E.			
see Abu Dhabi 230-31		24°28´N	54°22´E
Abyad, Al-Bahr al-, stm., Sudan			
see White Nile 254		15°38´N	32°31´E
Abyssinia, nation, Afr. *see* Ethiopia . . .253		9°0´N	39°00´E
Acacías, Col. (á-kä-sē´äs) 163c		4°00´N	73°45´W
Acadia National Park, n.p., Me., U.S.			
(ä-kā´dĭ-á näsh´ŭn-ăl pärk) 117a		44°20´N	68°14´W
Acajutla, El Sal. (ä-kä-hōōt´lä) 148		13°35´N	89°50´W
Acámbaro, Mex. (ä-kämˊbä-rō) 146-47		20°03´N	100°43´W
Acaponeta, Mex. (ä-kä-pō-nä´tá) 146-47		22°29´N	105°22´W
Acaponeta, stm., Mex. (ä-kä-pō-nä´tá) . . .146-47		22°23´N	105°38´W
Acapulco de Juárez, Mex. 146-47		16°51´N	99°54´W
Acaraí, Serra, mts., S.A.			
see Acarai Mountains 164-65		1°30´N	58°15´W
Acarai Mountains, mts., S.A. 164-65		1°30´N	58°15´W
Acaraú, Braz. 166-67		2°53´S	40°07´W
Acarigua, Ven. (ä-kä-rē´gwä) 164-65		9°34´N	69°12´W
Acatlán de Osorio, Mex.			
(ä-kät-län´dä ô-sō´rē-ō) 146-47		18°13´N	98°03´W
Acayucan, Mex. (ä-kä-yōō´kän) 146-47		17°57´N	94°54´W
Accra, nat. cap., Ghana (ä´krá) 260-61		5°34´N	0°12´W
Acerra, Italy (ä-chĕ´r-rä). 200-01		40°57´N	14°22´E
Achacachi, Bol. (ä-chä-kä´chē) 168-69		16°02´S	68°41´W
Achalpur, India. 234-35		21°18´N	77°31´E
Acheng, China 240-41		45°32´N	126°59´E
Achinsk, Russia (á-chĕnsk´) 218-19		56°16´N	90°30´E
Acireale, Italy (ä-chē-rä-ä´lä) 200-01		37°37´N	15°10´E
Acklins, i., Bah. (ăk´lĭns) 142-43		22°26´N	73°58´W
Acklins, Bight of, b., Bah.			
(bīt ŭv ăk´lĭns) 142-43		22°32´N	74°08´W
Aconcagua, Cerro, mtn., Arg.			
(sĕ´r-rō ä-kŏn-kä´gwä) 163e		32°39´S	70°02´W

n-sing; ŋ-bank; N-nasalized n; nŏd; cŏmmit; ōld; ŏbey; ôrder; oi-boil; fōͦd; ȯ-as oo in foot; ou-out; s-soft; sh-dish; th-thin; p̄ure; ŭnite; ûrn; stŭd; circŭs; ü-as in French tu; ´-indeterminate vowel.

302 Açores – Alayskiy khrebet PRONOUNCING INDEX

Feature (Pronunciation)	Page	Lat.	Long.
Açores, is., Port. (ä-zô´rĕs) see Azores	199c	38°30'N	28°00'W
A Coruña, Spain	198-99	43°22'N	8°25'W
Acoyapa, Nic. (ä-kō-yä´pä)	149	11°58'N	85°11'W
Acre, Isr. see 'Akko	228-29	32°55'N	35°06'E
Acre, state, Braz. (ä´krā)	166-67	9°0'S	70°00'W
Acre, stm., S.A. (ä´krā)	170	8°45'S	67°24'W
Actopan, Mex. (äk-tô-pän´)	146-47	20°16'N	98°57'W
Ada, Mn., U.S. (ā´dū)	114-15	47°18'N	96°31'W
Ada, Oh., U.S. (ā´dū)	116-17	40°46'N	83°49'W
Ada, Ok., U.S. (ā´dū)	120-21	34°47'N	96°41'W
Adak Island, i., Ak., U.S. (ă-dăk´ ī´lănd)	126a	51°43'N	176°43'W
Adam, Oman	220-21	22°23'N	57°31'E
Adama, Eth. see Nazrēt	269d	8°32'N	39°16'E
Adamaoua, mts., Afr.	260-61	7°0'N	12°00'E
Adamawa, mts., Afr. see Adamaoua	260-61	7°0'N	12°00'E
Adams, Ma., U.S. (ăd´ămz)	116-17	42°38'N	73°07'W
Adams, Wi., U.S. (ăd´ămz)	116-17	43°57'N	89°49'W
Adams, stm., B.C., Can. (ăd´ămz)	132-33	50°54'N	119°33'W
Adams, Mount, vol., Wa., U.S.	112-13	46°13'N	121°29'W
Adams Lake, lk., B.C., Can.	132-33	51°13'N	119°33'W
'Adan, Yemen see Aden	266	12°49'N	45°02'E
Adana, Tur. (ä´dä-nä)	228-29	37°00'N	35°20'E
Adapazarı, Tur. (ä-dä-pä-zä´rē) see Sakarya	186-87	40°47'N	30°24'E
Adare, Cape, c., Ant.	287	71°20'S	170°08'E
Adavale, Austl.	276	25°55'S	144°36'E
Ad-Dahnā', des., Sau. Ar.	220-21	24°30'N	48°10'E
Ad-Dammām, Sau. Ar.	230-31	26°26'N	50°07'E
Ad-Dawādimī, Sau. Ar.	266	24°28'N	44°18'E
Ad-Dawḥah, nat. cap., Qatar see Doha	230-31	25°17'N	51°32'E
Ad-Dilam, Sau. Ar.	230-31	23°56'N	47°06'E
Addis Ababa, nat. cap., Eth. (ä´dĭs ä´bä-bä)	269d	9°02'N	38°45'E
Ad-Dīwānīyah, Iraq	228-29	31°59'N	44°55'E
Addo Elephant National Park, n.p., S. Afr.	264-65	33°29'S	25°46'E
Ad-Du'ayn, Sudan	266	11°26'N	26°10'E
Ad-Duwaym, Sudan (ad-dò-ām´)	266	13°59'N	32°18'E
Adel, Ga., U.S. (ā-dĕl´)	124-25	31°08'N	83°25'W
Adel, Ia., U.S. (ā-dĕl´)	114-15	41°37'N	94°01'W
Adelaide, Austl. (ăd´ē-lād)	276	34°55'S	138°35'E
Adelaide Peninsula, pen., Nu., Can.	130-31	68°09'N	97°45'W
Aden, Yemen (ä´dĕn)	266	12°49'N	45°02'E
Aden, Gulf of, b., (gŭlf ŭv ä´dĕn)	220-21	12°40'N	48°07'E
Ādīgrat, Eth.	266	14°17'N	39°27'E
Ādilābād, India (ŭ-dĭl-ä-băd´)	234-35	19°41'N	78°33'E
Adīrī, Libya	258-59	27°32'N	13°13'E
Adirondack Mountains, mts., N.Y., U.S. (ăd-ĭ-rŏn´dăk moun´tĭnz)	116-17	44°0'N	74°00'W
Ādīs Ābeba, nat. cap., Eth. (ä-dēs´ ä´bä-bä) see Addis Ababa	269d	9°02'N	38°45'E
Adjud, Rom. (äd´zhòd)	202-03	46°06'N	27°11'E
Adjuntas, Presa de las, res., Mex. see Vicente Guerrero, Presa	146-47	23°57'N	98°46'W
Admiralty Island National Monument, n.p., U.S. (ăd´mĭ-răl-tē ī´lănd năsh´ŭn-ăl mŏn´ū-mĕnt)	126	57°40'N	134°16'W
Admiralty Islands, is., Pap. N. Gui. (ăd´mĭ-răl-tē ī´lăndz)	277	2°10'S	147°00'E
Adolfo Gonzales Chaves, Arg.	173	38°01'S	60°08'W
Adonara, Pulau, i., Indon.	248-49	8°20'S	123°10'E
Ādoni, India	236	15°38'N	77°16'E
Adra, Spain (ä´drä)	198-99	36°45'N	3°01'W
Adrano, Italy (ä-drä´nō)	200-01	37°40'N	14°50'E
Adrar, Alg.	258-59	27°52'N	0°18'W
Adrâr, reg., Maur.	258-59	20°26'N	12°46'W
Adria, Italy (ä´drē-ä)	200-01	45°03'N	12°04'E
Adrian, Mi., U.S. (ā´drĭ-ăn)	116-17	41°53'N	84°02'W
Adrian, Mn., U.S. (ā´drĭ-ăn)	114-15	43°38'N	95°56'W
Adrianople, Tur. see Edirne	200-01	41°41'N	26°34'E
Adriatico, Mare, s., Eur. see Adriatic Sea	200-01	42°30'N	16°00'E
Adriatic Sea, s., Eur. (ā-drē-ă´tĭc sē)	200-01	42°30'N	16°00'E
Adriatik, Deti, s., Eur. see Adriatic Sea	200-01	42°30'N	16°00'E
Ādwa, Eth.	266	14°11'N	38°53'E
Adycha, stm., Russia (ä´dĭ-chå)	218-19	68°13'N	134°48'E
Adygea, state, Russia see Adygheya	186-87	45°0'N	40°00'E
Adygheya, state, Russia	186-87	45°0'N	40°00'E
Adz'va, stm., Russia (ädz´vå)	186-87	66°36'N	59°24'E
Aegean Sea, s., (ē-jē´ăn sē)	200-01	38°30'N	25°00'E
Afars and Issas, nation, Afr. see Djibouti	253	11°30'N	43°00'E
Affon, stm., Benin see Ouémé	260a	6°27'N	2°33'E
Afghānestān, nation, Asia see Afghanistan	206-07	33°0'N	65°00'E
Afghanistan, nation, Asia (ăf-găn-ĭ-stăn´)	206-07	33°0'N	65°00'E
'Afīf, Sau. Ar.	266	23°55'N	42°56'E
Afikpo, Nig.	260a	5°55'N	7°55'E
Aflou, Alg. (ä-flōō´)	188-89	34°07'N	2°06'E
Afognak Island, i., Ak., U.S. (ä-fŏg-nåk´ ī´lănd)	126	58°14'N	152°39'W
Africa, cont., (ăf´rĭ-kă)	254	10°0'N	22°00'E
Afton, Ok., U.S. (ăf´tŭn)	120-21	36°42'N	94°58'W
Afton, Wy., U.S. (ăf´tŭn)	112-13	42°43'N	110°56'W
'Afula, Isr. (ä-fò´là)	228-29	32°36'N	35°18'E
Afyon, Tur. (ä-fē-ōn)	186-87	38°46'N	30°33'E
Afyonkarahisar, Tur. see Afyon	186-87	38°46'N	30°33'E
Agadez, Niger (ä´gȧ-dĕs)	258-59	16°58'N	7°59'E
Agadir, Mor. (ä-gȧ-dēr)	258-59	30°28'N	9°39'W
Agadyr, Kaz.	226	48°16'N	72°53'E
Agana, nat. cap., Guam see Hagåtña	279c	13°28'N	144°45'E
Āgaro, Eth.	262-63	7°50'N	36°40'E
Agartala, India	234-35	23°50'N	91°16'E
Agate Fossil Beds National Monument, n.p., Ne., U.S.	114-15	42°25'N	103°43'W
Ağdam, Azer. (äg´dăm)	227	39°59'N	46°56'E
Agde, Fr. (ägd)	196-97	43°19'N	3°28'E
Agen, Fr. (å-zhäN´)	196-97	44°12'N	0°38'E
Āghā Jārī, Iran	230-31	30°42'N	49°50'E
Agno, Phil. (äg´nō)	250	16°07'N	119°48'E
Agno, stm., Phil. (äg´nō)	250	16°02'N	120°09'E
Āgra, India (ä´grä)	234-35	27°11'N	78°00'E
Ağrı, Tur.	227	39°43'N	43°04'E
Ağrı Dağı, vol., Tur. see Ararat, Mount	227	39°42'N	44°18'E
Agrigento, Italy	200-01	37°18'N	13°35'E
Agrihan, i., N. Mar. Is.	280-81	18°46'N	145°40'E
Agryz, Russia	186-87	56°31'N	53°01'E
Aguadas, Col. (ä-gwä´dás)	163c	5°38'N	75°27'W
Aguadilla, P.R. (ä-gwä-dēl´yä)	142a	18°26'N	67°09'W
Aguadulce, Pan. (ä-gwä-dōōl´sā)	150	8°15'N	80°31'W
Aguán, stm., Hond. (ä-gwá´n)	149	15°58'N	85°44'W
Aguanaval, stm., Mex. (á-guä-nä-väl´)	144-45	25°25'N	102°49'W
Aguanish, stm., Qc., Can.	138-39	50°15'N	62°07'W
Agua Prieta, Mex.	144-45	31°19'N	109°33'W
Aguarico, stm., S.A.	170	0°58'S	75°11'W
Aguascalientes, Mex.	146-47	21°53'N	102°18'W
Aguascalientes, state, Mex. (ä´gwäs-käl-yĕn´tās)	146-47	22°0'N	102°30'W
Água Vermelha, Represa de, res., Braz.	168-69	20°0'S	50°00'W
Águilas, Spain (ä´-gē-läs)	198-99	37°25'N	1°35'W
Aguililla, Mex. (ä-gē-lēl-yä)	146-47	18°44'N	102°44'W
Agulhas, c., S. Afr. (ä-gōōl´yäs)	264-65	34°49'S	20°03'E
Agusan, stm., Phil. (ä-gōō´sän)	250	9°01'N	125°31'E
Ahaggar, mts., Alg. (á-hå-gär´)	258-59	23°0'N	6°30'E
Ahaggar, Tassili oua-n-, plat., Alg.	258-59	21°0'N	6°00'E
Ahar, Iran	227	38°28'N	47°04'E
Ahlen, Ger. (ä´lĕn)	194-95	51°46'N	7°54'E
Ahmadābād, India (ŭ-mĕd-ä-băd´)	234-35	23°02'N	72°35'E
Ahmadnagar, India (ä´mûd-nû-gûr)	236	19°05'N	74°45'E
Aḥmar, Al-Baḥr al-, s., see Red Sea	266	20°0'N	38°00'E
Ahmar Mountains, mts., Eth.	262-63	9°14'N	41°25'E
Ahoskie, N.C., U.S. (ä-hŏs´kē)	124-25	36°17'N	76°59'W
Ahuacatlán, Mex. (ä-wä-kät-län´)	146-47	21°05'N	104°29'W
Ahumada, Mex.	144-45	30°37'N	106°31'W
Ahunui, at., Fr. Poly.	280-81	19°39'S	140°25'W
Åhus, Swe. (ô´hòs)	192-93	55°55'N	14°18'E
Ahvāz, Iran	228-29	31°19'N	48°42'E
Ahvenanmaa, is., Fin. (ä´vĕ-nán-mô) see Aland Islands	192-93	60°14'N	19°46'E
Aidar, stm., Eur.	202-03	48°44'N	39°16'E
Aigaíon Pélagos, s., see Aegean Sea	200-01	38°30'N	25°00'E
Aiken, S.C., U.S. (ā´kĕn)	124-25	33°33'N	81°43'W
Ailao Shan, mts., China	238-39	24°13'N	101°20'E
Aimorés, Braz.	172	19°30'S	41°05'W
Aïn Beni Mathar, Mor.	188-89	34°01'N	2°01'W
Aïn Sefra, Alg.	188-89	32°46'N	0°34'W
Ainsworth, Ne., U.S. (ānz´wûrth)	114-15	42°33'N	99°52'W
'Aïn Temouchent, Alg. (ä´ēntĕ-mōō-shaN´)	198-99	35°18'N	1°09'W
Aipe, Col. (ī´pĕ)	163c	3°13'N	75°14'W
Aïr, Massif de l', mts., Niger	258-59	18°0'N	8°30'E
Air Force Island, i., Nu., Can.	130-31	67°55'N	74°10'W
Aïssa, Djebel, mtn., Alg.	258-59	32°51'N	0°30'W
Aitape, Pap. N. Gui. (ä-ē-tä´pä)	277	3°09'S	142°20'E
Aitkin, Mn., U.S. (āt´kĭn)	114-15	46°32'N	93°43'W
Aitutaki, at., Cook Is. (ī-tōō-tä´kē)	280-81	18°52'S	159°45'W
Aiud, Rom. (ä´ē-òd)	194-95	46°19'N	23°44'E
Aix-en-Provence, Fr. (ĕks-prō-väNs)	196-97	43°32'N	5°27'E
Aix-la-Chapelle, Ger. see Aachen	194-95	50°46'N	6°06'E
Aix-les-Bains, Fr. (ĕks´-lā-băN´)	196-97	45°42'N	5°55'E
Āīzawl, India	234-35	23°44'N	92°43'E
Aizu-wakamatsu, Japan	245	37°30'N	139°56'E
Ajaccio, Fr. (ä-yät´chō)	184-85	41°56'N	8°44'E
Ajdābiyā, Libya	188-89	30°45'N	20°14'E
Ajjer, Tassili-n-, plat., Alg.	258-59	25°41'N	7°29'E
'Ajmān, U.A.E.	230-31	25°24'N	55°28'E
Ajmer, India (ŭj-mēr´)	234-35	26°27'N	74°38'E
Ajo, Az., U.S. (ä´hō)	118-19	32°23'N	112°52'W
Akagera, stm., Afr. see Kagera	267	0°56'S	31°47'E
Akan-kokuritsu-kōen, n.p., Japan	244	43°30'N	144°15'E
Akashi, Japan (ä´kä-shē)	245	34°39'N	134°59'E
Akdeniz, s., see Mediterranean Sea	188-89	35°0'N	20°00'E
Aketi, D.R.C. (ä-kå-tē)	262-63	2°45'N	23°46'E
Akhaltsikhe, Geor. (äkå´l-tsĭ-kĕ)	227	41°38'N	42°59'E
Akhisar, Tur. (äk-hĭs-sär´)	200-01	38°56'N	27°50'E
Akhtuba, stm., Russia	186-87	46°40'N	48°08'E
Akhtubinsk, Russia	186-87	48°16'N	46°10'E
Akimiski Island, i., Nu., Can. (ä-kĭ-mĭ´skĭ ī´lănd)	130-31	53°0'N	81°20'W
Akita, Japan (ä´kē-tä)	244	39°43'N	140°07'E
Akkerman, Ukr. see Bilhorod-Dnistrovs'kyi	202-03	46°12'N	30°18'E
'Akko, Isr.	228-29	32°55'N	35°06'E
Aklavik, N.T., Can. (äk´lä-vĭk)	128-29	68°15'N	135°06'W
Ākobo, stm., Afr.	262-63	7°47'N	33°03'E
Akola, India (á-kō´lä)	234-35	20°43'N	77°00'E
Akordat, Erit.	266	15°32'N	37°53'E
Akpatok Island, i., Nu., Can. (ăk´pá-tŏk iī´lănd))	130-31	60°25'N	67°60'W
Akron, Co., U.S. (ăk´rŭn)	120-21	40°10'N	103°13'W
Akron, Oh., U.S. (ăk´rŭn)	116-17	41°05'N	81°31'W
Aksaray, Tur. (äk-så-rī´)	186-87	38°23'N	34°03'E
Akşehir, Tur. (äk´shå-hēr)	186-87	38°21'N	31°25'E
Akşehir Gölü, lk., Tur. (äk´shå-hēr)	186-87	38°32'N	31°27'E
Aksu, China (ä-kŭ-sōō)	226	41°08'N	80°15'E
Āksum, Eth.	266	14°08'N	38°43'E
Aktyubinsk, Kaz. see Aqtöbe	226	50°18'N	57°10'E
Akūbū, stm., Afr.	262-63	7°47'N	33°03'E
Akune, Japan (ä´kò-nå)	245	32°01'N	130°12'E
Akure, Nig.	260a	7°15'N	5°11'E
Akureyri, Ice. (ä-kò-rå´rē)	190a	65°39'N	18°07'W
Akyab, Mya. see Sittwe	246-47	20°09'N	92°54'E
Al-'Amārah, Iraq	228-29	31°50'N	47°09'E
Al-'Aqabah, Jord.	228-29	29°32'N	35°01'E
Al-'Arabīyah as-Su'ūdīyah, nation, Asia see Saudi Arabia	206-07	25°0'N	45°00'E
Al-'Ayn, U.A.E.	230-31	24°13'N	55°45'E
Al-'Azīzīyah, Libya	188-89	32°32'N	13°01'E
Al-'Īrāq, nation, Asia see Iraq	206-07	33°0'N	44°00'E
Al-'Uqaylah, Libya	188-89	30°15'N	19°12'E
Alabama, state, U.S. (ăl-ȧ-băm´ȧ)	108-09	32°50'N	87°00'W
Alabama, stm., Al., U.S. (ăl-ȧ-băm´ȧ)	124-25	31°08'N	87°57'W
Alabat Island, i., Phil. (ä-lä-bät´ ī´lănd)	250	14°07'N	122°03'E
Alacant, Spain	198-99	38°21'N	0°30'W
Alagoa Grande, Braz.	163d	7°03'S	35°38'W
Alagoas, state, Braz. (ä-lä-gō´äzh)	163d	9°0'S	36°00'W
Alagoinhas, Braz. (ä-lä-gō-ēn´yäzh)	166-67	12°08'S	38°25'W
Alagón, stm., Spain (ä-lä-gōn´)	198-99	39°45'N	6°52'W
Alajuela, C.R. (ä-lä-hwa´lä)	149	10°01'N	84°13'W
Alajuela, Lago, res., Pan. (lä´gô-ä-lä-hwa´lä)	150	9°15'N	79°35'W
Alaköl köli, lk., Kaz.	226	46°10'N	81°45'E
Alamagan, i., N. Mar. Is.	280-81	17°36'N	145°50'E
Alamein, Egypt see El-Alamein	188-89	30°49'N	28°58'E
Alamo, Nv., U.S. (ä´lȧ-mō)	118-19	37°22'N	115°10'W
Alamogordo, N.M., U.S. (ăl-ȧ-mȧ-gôr´dō)	120-21	32°54'N	105°57'W
Alamosa, Co., U.S. (ăl-ȧ-mō´sȧ)	118-19	37°28'N	105°52'W
Aland Islands, is., Fin. (ô´lănd ī´lăndz)	192-93	60°14'N	19°46'E
Alanya, Tur.	228-29	36°33'N	32°01'E
Alaotra, Farihy, lk., Madag. (ä-lä-ō´trȧ)	264-65	17°25'S	48°33'E
Alappuzha, India	236	9°29'N	76°20'E
Alashanyouqi, China	240-41	40°04'N	103°33'E
Alaska, state, U.S. (ȧ-lăs´kȧ)	108-09	65°0'N	153°00'W
Alaska, Gulf of, b., Ak., U.S. (gŭlf ŭv ȧ-lăs´kȧ)	126	58°0'N	146°00'W
Alaska Peninsula, pen., Ak., U.S. (ȧ-lăs´kȧ pĕ-nĭn´sūlȧ)	126	57°0'N	158°00'W
Alaska Range, mts., Ak., U.S. (ȧ-lăs´kȧ rānj)	126	63°26'N	149°07'W
Alataw Shan, mts., Asia	226	45°0'N	81°00'E
Alatyr', Russia (ä´lä-tür)	186-87	54°51'N	46°34'E
Alausí, Ec.	170	2°13'S	78°51'W
Alayskiy khrebet, mts., Kyrg.	226	39°51'N	72°07'E

ăt; finăl; rāte; senåte; ärm; åsk; sofȧ; fâre; ch-choose; dh-as th in other; bē; ēvent; bĕt; recĕnt; cratēr; g-gō; gh-guttural g; bĭt; ĭ-short neutral; rīde; K-guttural k as ch in German ich;

PRONOUNCING INDEX

Alazeya – Altavista 303

Feature (Pronunciation)	Page	Lat.	Long.
Alazeya, stm., Russia	218-19	70°51′N	153°39′E
Alba, Italy (äl′bä)	200-01	44°42′N	8°02′E
Albacete, Spain (äl-bä-thā′tā)	198-99	38°59′N	1°52′W
Al-Baḥrayn, nation, Asia *see* Bahrain	230-31	26°0′N	50°30′E
Albania, nation, Eur. (ăl-bā′nĭ-*ȧ*)	174-75	41°0′N	20°00′E
Albano Laziale, Italy (äl-bä′nō lät-zē-ä′lā)	200-01	41°44′N	12°39′E
Albany, Austl. (ôl′b*ȧ*-nĭ)	270-71	35°01′S	117°53′E
Albany, Ga., U.S. (ôl′b*ȧ*-nĭ)	124-25	31°34′N	84°09′W
Albany, Ky., U.S. (ôl′b*ȧ*-nĭ)	124-25	36°41′N	85°08′W
Albany, Mo., U.S. (ôl′b*ȧ*-nĭ)	120-21	40°15′N	94°20′W
Albany, N.Y., U.S. (ôl′b*ȧ*-nĭ)	116-17	42°40′N	73°47′W
Albany, Or., U.S. (ôl′b*ȧ*-nĭ)	112-13	44°38′N	123°05′W
Albany, Tx., U.S. (ôl′b*ȧ*-nĭ)	120-21	32°43′N	99°17′W
Albany, stm., On., Can. (ôl′b*ȧ*-nĭ)	130-31	52°17′N	81°32′W
Al-Baṣrah, Iraq *see* Basra	228-29	30°30′N	47°48′E
Al-Batrūn, Leb. (äl-bä-trōōn′)	228-29	34°15′N	35°40′E
Al-Bayḍā', Libya	188-89	32°45′N	21°37′E
Albemarle, N.C., U.S. (ăl′bē-märl)	124-25	35°14′N	80°12′W
Albemarle Island, i., Ec. *see* Isabela, Isla	170a	0°30′S	91°06′W
Albemarle Sound, strt., N.C., U.S. (ăl′bē-märl sound)	124-25	36°03′N	76°12′W
Albenga, Italy (äl-bĕŋ′gä)	200-01	44°03′N	8°13′E
Alberga Creek, stm., Austl. (ăl-bŭr′g*ȧ* krēk)	272-73	27°07′S	135°30′E
Albert, Fr. (ál-bâr′)	196-97	49°60′N	2°39′E
Albert, Lac, lk., Afr. (läk ál-bâr′) *see* Albert, Lake	267	1°40′N	31°00′E
Albert, Lake, lk., Afr. (läk *ă*l′bērt)	267	1°40′N	31°00′E
Alberta, state, Can. (ăl-bûr′t*ȧ*)	128-29	54°0′N	113°00′W
Alberta, Mount, mtn., Ab., Can. (mount ăl-bûr′t*ȧ*)	132-33	52°18′N	117°28′W
Albert Edward, Mount, mtn., Pap. N. Gui. (mount ăl′bērt ĕd′wērd)	277	8°24′S	147°22′E
Albert Lea, Mn., U.S. (ăl′bērt lē′)	114-15	43°39′N	93°22′W
Albert Nile, stm., Ug. (ăl-bērt nīl)	267	3°36′N	32°02′E
Alberton, P.E., Can. (ăl′bēr-t*ŭ*n)	138-39	46°49′N	64°04′W
Albertville, D.R.C. *see* Kalemie	267	5°55′S	29°11′E
Albertville, Fr. (ál-bâr-vēl′)	196-97	45°40′N	6°23′E
Albertville, Al., U.S. (ăl′bērt-vĭl)	124-25	34°16′N	86°13′W
Albi, Fr. (äl-bē′)	196-97	43°55′N	2°08′E
Albia, Ia., U.S. (ăl-bĭ-*ȧ*)	114-15	41°02′N	92°48′W
Albion, Il., U.S. (ăl′bĭ-*ŭ*n)	116-17	38°22′N	88°04′W
Albion, In., U.S. (ăl′bĭ-*ŭ*n)	116-17	41°23′N	85°24′W
Albion, Mi., U.S. (ăl′bĭ-*ŭ*n)	116-17	42°15′N	84°45′W
Albion, Ne., U.S. (ăl′bĭ-*ŭ*n)	114-15	41°41′N	98°00′W
Al-Birkah, Libya	258-59	24°52′N	10°12′E
Alborán, Isla de, i., Spain (ē′s-lä-däl-äl-bō-rä′n)	198-99	35°57′N	3°02′W
Alborz, Reshteh-ye Kūhhā-ye, mts., Iran *see* Elburz Mountains	232-33	36°0′N	53°00′E
Albuquerque, N.M., U.S. (ăl-b*ŭ*-kûr′kē)	118-19	35°05′N	106°38′W
Albury, Austl. (ôl′bēr-ē)	276	36°04′S	146°56′E
Alcalá de Henares, Spain (äl-kä-lä′ dā ā-na′räs)	198-99	40°29′N	3°22′W
Alcalá la Real, Spain (äl-kä-lä′lä rā-äl′)	198-99	37°28′N	3°56′W
Alcamo, Italy (äl′kä-mō)	200-01	37°59′N	12°58′E
Alcanar, Spain (äl-kä-när′)	198-99	40°33′N	0°29′E
Alcañiz, Spain (äl-kän-yēth′)	198-99	41°03′N	0°08′W
Alcântara, Braz. (äl-kän′tá-rá)	166-67	2°24′S	44°24′W
Alcázar de San Juan, Spain (äl-kä′thär dā sän hwän′)	198-99	39°23′N	3°12′W
Alcazarquivir, Mor. *see* Er-Rachidia	188-89	31°57′N	4°26′W
Alcazarquivir, Mor. *see* Ksar-el-Kebir	269a	35°01′N	5°54′W
Alcira, Spain (ä-thē′rä) *see* Alzira	198-99	39°09′N	0°26′W
Alcobaça, Braz.	172	17°31′S	39°13′W
Alcobendas, Spain (äl-kō-bĕn′däs)	198-99	40°33′N	3°38′W
Alcoi, Spain	198-99	38°42′N	0°28′W
Alcoy, Spain *see* Alcoi	198-99	38°42′N	0°28′W
Aldabra, Groupe d', is., Sey. (grūp-däl-dä′brä)	264-65	9°24′S	46°27′E
Aldama, Mex. (äl-dä′mä)	146-47	22°55′N	98°04′W
Aldama, Mex. (äl-dä′mä)	122-23	28°51′N	105°54′W
Aldan, Russia	218-19	58°36′N	125°24′E
Aldan, stm., Russia	218-19	63°26′N	129°26′E
Aldan Plateau, plat., Russia (ŭl-dän′) *see* Aldanskoye Nagor'ye	218-19	57°0′N	127°00′E
Aldanskoye Nagor'ye, plat., Russia	218-19	57°0′N	127°00′E
Alderney, i., Guern. (ôl′dēr-nĭ)	196-97	49°43′N	2°13′W
Aldershot, Eng., U.K. (ôl′dēr-shŏt)	190-91	51°15′N	0°46′W
Aledo, Il., U.S. (*ȧ*-lē′dō)	114-15	41°12′N	90°45′W
Alegranza, Isla, i., Spain	199d	29°24′N	13°30′W
Alegrete, Braz. (ä-lå-grā′tā)	173	29°47′S	55°47′W
Aleksandrov, Russia (ä-lyĕk-sän′ drôf)	202-03	56°24′N	38°43′E
Aleksandrov-Gay, Russia	186-87	50°08′N	48°34′E
Aleksandrovsk-Sakhalinskiy, Russia	218-19	50°54′N	142°10′E
Aleksandrów Kujawski, Pol. (ä-lĕk-säh′drōōv kōō-yav′skē)	194-95	52°52′N	18°43′E
Alekseevka, Kaz.	226	52°00′N	70°57′E
Alekseyevka, Russia (ä-lyĕk-sā-yĕf′k*ȧ*)	202-03	50°38′N	38°41′E
Aleksin, Russia (ăb′ĭng-t*ŭ*n)	202-03	54°30′N	37°05′E
Além Paraíba, Braz. (äl-lĕ′m-pá-rāē′bá)	172	21°52′S	42°40′W
Alençon, Fr. (á-län-sôN′)	196-97	48°26′N	0°05′E
Alenquer, Braz. (ä-lĕŋ-kĕr′)	166-67	1°56′S	54°46′W
Alep, Syria *see* Aleppo	228-29	36°13′N	37°10′E
Aleppo, Syria (*ȧ*-lĕp-ō)	228-29	36°13′N	37°10′E
Alès, Fr. (ä-lĕs′)	196-97	44°08′N	4°05′E
Alessandria, Italy (ä-lĕs-sän′drē-ä)	200-01	44°55′N	8°37′E
Ålesund, Nor. (ô′lĕ-sŏn′)	184-85	62°28′N	6°10′E
Aleutian Islands, is., Ak., U.S. (*ȧ*-lu′sh*ă*n ī′l*ă*ndz)	126a	52°0′N	176°00′W
Alexander City, Al., U.S. (ăl-ĕg-zăn′dēr sĭ′tē)	124-25	32°57′N	85°57′W
Alexandra, N.Z.	278	45°15′S	169°23′E
Alexandretta, Tur. *see* İskenderun	228-29	36°35′N	36°11′E
Alexandretta, Gulf of, b., Tur. *see* İskenderun Körfezi	228-29	36°30′N	35°40′E
Alexandria, On., Can. (ăl-ĕg-zăn′drĭ-*ȧ*)	136-37	45°18′N	74°38′W
Alexandria, Egypt (ăl-ĕg-zăn′drĭ-*ȧ*)	268b	31°11′N	29°54′E
Alexandria, Rom. (ăl-ĕg-zăn′drĭ-*ȧ*)	200-01	43°59′N	25°21′E
Alexandria, In., U.S. (ăl-ĕg-zăn′drĭ-*ȧ*)	116-17	40°15′N	85°40′W
Alexandria, La., U.S. (ăl-ĕg-zăn′drĭ-*ȧ*)	122-23	31°18′N	92°27′W
Alexandria, Mn., U.S. (ăl-ĕg-zăn′drĭ-*ȧ*)	114-15	45°53′N	95°23′W
Alexandria, S.D., U.S. (ăl-ĕg-zăn′drĭ-*ȧ*)	114-15	43°39′N	97°47′W
Alexandria, Va., U.S. (ăl-ĕg-zăn′drĭ-*ȧ*)	116-17	38°48′N	77°03′W
Alexandria Bay, N.Y., U.S. (ăl-ĕg-zăn′drĭ-*ȧ* bā)	116-17	44°20′N	75°55′W
Alexandrina, Lake, lk., Austl.	276	35°26′S	139°10′E
Alexandroúpoli, Grc.	200-01	40°52′N	25°53′E
Aleysk, Russia	226	52°29′N	82°46′E
Alfaro, Spain (äl-färō)	198-99	42°11′N	1°45′W
Al-Fāshir, Sudan (äl-fä′shēr)	266	13°38′N	25°21′E
Alfenas, Braz. (äl-fĕ′näs)	172	21°27′S	45°57′W
Al-Furāt, stm., Asia *see* Euphrates	208-09	30°60′N	47°27′E
Algeciras, Spain (äl-hä-thē′räs)	198-99	36°08′N	5°27′W
Alger, nat. cap., Alg. *see* Algiers	269b	36°46′N	3°03′E
Algeria, nation, Afr. (ăl-gē′rĭ-*ȧ*)	253	28°0′N	3°00′E
Algérie, nation, Afr. *see* Algeria	253	28°0′N	3°00′E
Al-Ghayḍah, Yemen	220-21	16°13′N	52°12′E
Alghero, Italy (äl-gâ′rō)	200-01	40°34′N	8°19′E
Algiers, nat. cap., Alg. (ăl-jērs)	269b	36°46′N	3°03′E
Al-Ḥamād, pl., Sau. Ar.	228-29	32°0′N	39°30′E
Al-Ḥasakah, Syria	228-29	36°30′N	40°46′E
Al-Ḥawrah, Yemen	220-21	13°50′N	47°34′E
Al-Ḥayy, Iraq	228-29	32°10′N	46°03′E
Al-Ḥijāz, reg., Sau. Ar.	266	24°30′N	38°30′E
Al-Ḥillah, Iraq	228-29	32°29′N	44°26′E
Al-Hoceima, Mor.	198-99	35°15′N	3°56′W
Al-Ḥudaydah, Yemen	266	14°48′N	42°57′E
Al-Hufūf, Sau. Ar.	230-31	25°22′N	49°34′E
Alicante, Spain *see* Alacant	198-99	38°21′N	0°30′W
Alice, Tx., U.S. (ăl′ĭs)	122-23	27°45′N	98°05′W
Alice Springs, Austl. (ăl′ĭs sprĭngz)	270-71	23°42′S	133°52′E
Alīgarh, India (ä-lē-gŭr′)	234-35	27°54′N	78°04′E
Alima, stm., Congo	262-63	1°31′S	16°40′E
Al-Imārāt al-'Arabīyah al-Muttaḥidah, nation, Asia *see* United Arab Emirates	206-07	24°0′N	54°00′E
Alingsås, Swe. (á′lĭŋ-sôs)	192-93	57°56′N	12°32′E
'Ali Sabieh, Dji.	266	11°08′N	42°42′E
Aliwal North, S. Afr. (ä-lē-wäl′ nôrth)	264-65	30°42′S	26°43′E
Al-Jawf, Libya	258-59	24°12′N	23°17′E
Al-Jawf, Sau. Ar.	228-29	29°48′N	39°52′E
Al-Jazaïr, nat. cap., Alg. *see* Algiers	269b	36°46′N	3°03′E
Al-Jazīrah, reg., Sudan	266	14°17′N	32°53′E
Aljezur, Port. (äl-zhā-zōōr′)	198-99	37°18′N	8°48′W
Al-Jubayl, Sau. Ar.	230-31	27°01′N	49°40′E
Al-Jufrah, well, Libya	258-59	29°06′N	15°57′E
Al-Junaynah, Sudan	262-63	13°27′N	22°27′E
Al-Karak, Jord. (äl-kĕ-räk′)	228-29	31°11′N	35°42′E
Al-Khābūrah, Oman	230-31	23°58′N	57°06′E
Al-Khalīl, W.B. *see* Hebron	228-29	31°32′N	35°06′E
Al-Kharṭūm, nat. cap., Sudan *see* Khartoum	266	15°35′N	32°32′E
Al-Khaṣab, Oman	230-31	26°12′N	56°15′E
Al-Khubar, Sau. Ar.	230-31	26°17′N	50°12′E
Al-Khums, Libya	188-89	32°39′N	14°16′E
Alkmaar, Neth. (älk-mär′)	190-91	52°38′N	4°45′E
Al-Kūt, Iraq	228-29	32°30′N	45°49′E
Al-Kuwayt, nation, Asia *see* Kuwait	206-07	29°30′N	47°45′E
Al-Kuwayt, nat. cap., Kuw. (äl-kōō-wit) *see* Kuwait	228-29	29°19′N	47°60′E
Al-Lādhiqīyah, Syria *see* Latakia	228-29	35°31′N	35°48′E
Allahābād, India (ŭl-ŭ-hä-bäd′)	234-35	25°26′N	81°51′E
Allakaket, Ak., U.S.	126	66°33′N	152°38′W
'Allāq, Bi'r, well, Libya	258-59	31°05′N	11°58′E
Allegan, Mi., U.S. (ăl′ĕ-găn)	116-17	42°32′N	85°51′W
Allegheny Plateau, plat., U.S. (ăl-ē-gā′nĭ plă-tō′)	116-17	41°30′N	78°00′W
Allendale, S.C., U.S. (ăl′ĕn-dāl)	124-25	33°00′N	81°19′W
Allende, Mex. (äl-yĕn′då)	122-23	28°20′N	100°50′W
Allende, Mex. (äl-yĕn′då)	122-23	25°17′N	100°01′W
Allenstein, Pol. *see* Olsztyn	194-95	53°47′N	20°29′E
Allentown, Pa., U.S.	116-17	40°37′N	75°29′W
Alleppey, India (á-lĕp′ē) *see* Alappuzha	236	9°29′N	76°20′E
Aller, stm., Ger. (äl′ĕr)	194-95	52°57′N	9°11′E
Alliance, Ne., U.S. (*ȧ*-lī′*ă*ns)	114-15	42°06′N	102°52′W
Alliance, Oh., U.S. (*ȧ*-lī′*ă*ns)	116-17	40°55′N	81°06′W
Allier, stm., Fr. (á-lyā′)	196-97	46°58′N	3°04′E
Allinge, Den. (äl′ĭŋ-*ĕ*)	194-95	55°16′N	14°48′E
Al-Lubnān, nation, Asia *see* Lebanon	206-07	34°0′N	36°00′E
Alma, N.B., Can. (ăl′m*ȧ*)	138-39	45°36′N	64°57′W
Alma, Qc., Can. (ăl′m*ȧ*)	136-37	48°33′N	71°39′W
Alma, Ga., U.S. (ăl′m*ȧ*)	124-25	31°33′N	82°28′W
Alma, Mi., U.S. (ăl′m*ȧ*)	116-17	43°23′N	84°39′W
Alma, Ne., U.S. (ăl′m*ȧ*)	120-21	40°06′N	99°21′W
Alma, Wi., U.S. (ăl′m*ȧ*)	114-15	44°20′N	91°54′W
Almadén, Spain (ál-má-dhān)	198-99	38°46′N	4°50′W
Al-Madīnah, Sau. Ar. *see* Medina	266	24°28′N	39°37′E
Al-Maghrib, nation, Afr. *see* Morocco	253	32°0′N	5°00′W
Almagro, Spain (äl-mä′grō)	198-99	38°53′N	3°43′W
Al-Majma'ah, Sau. Ar.	232-33	25°55′N	45°21′E
Al-Makhā', Yemen *see* Mocha	266	13°19′N	43°15′E
Al-Manāmah, nat. cap., Bahr. (äl-mă-nä′m*ȧ*)	230-31	26°13′N	50°35′E
Almansa, Spain (äl-män′sä)	198-99	38°52′N	1°06′W
Al-Marj, Libya	188-89	32°30′N	20°53′E
Almas, Pico das, mtn., Braz.	166-67	13°33′S	41°56′W
Almaty, Kaz.	226	43°17′N	76°56′E
Al-Mawṣil, Iraq *see* Mosul	228-29	36°20′N	43°08′E
Almazán, Spain (äl-mä-thän′)	198-99	41°29′N	2°32′W
Almelo, Neth. (äl′mē-lō)	190-91	52°22′N	6°39′E
Almenara, Braz.	168-69	16°12′S	40°41′W
Almendralejo, Spain (äl-män-drä-lā′hō)	198-99	38°41′N	6°24′W
Almería, Spain (äl-mā-rē′ä)	198-99	36°51′N	2°27′W
Almería, Golfo de, b., Spain (gôl-fô-dĕ-äl-māī-rēN′)	198-99	36°46′N	2°30′W
Al'met'yevsk, Russia	186-87	54°54′N	52°19′E
Älmhult, Swe. (ĕlm′hōōlt)	192-93	56°33′N	14°09′E
Almirante, Pan. (äl-mē-rän′tä)	150	9°17′N	82°24′W
Almonte, On., Can. (ăl-mŏn′tē)	136-37	45°13′N	76°11′W
Almora, India	234-35	29°36′N	79°40′E
Al-Mubarraz, Sau. Ar.	230-31	25°25′N	49°35′E
Al-Muḥarraq, Bahr.	230-31	26°16′N	50°37′E
Al-Mukallā, Yemen	220-21	14°32′N	49°08′E
Almuñécar, Spain (äl-mōōn-yā′kär)	198-99	36°45′N	3°41′W
Alnön, i., Swe.	192-93	62°25′N	17°26′E
Alor, Pulau, i., Indon. (pōō-lou ä′lôr)	248-49	8°15′S	124°45′E
Alor Setar, Malay. (ä′lôr stär)	246-47	6°07′N	100°23′E
Alpen, mts., Eur. *see* Alps	184-85	46°25′N	10°00′E
Alpena, Mi., U.S. (ăl-pē′n*ȧ*)	116-17	45°03′N	83°26′W
Alpes, mts., Eur. *see* Alps	184-85	46°25′N	10°00′E
Alpi, mts., Eur. *see* Alps	184-85	46°25′N	10°00′E
Alpine, Az., U.S. (ăl′pīn)	118-19	33°50′N	109°08′W
Alpine, Tx., U.S. (ăl′pīn)	122-23	30°21′N	103°40′W
Alpine National Park, n.p., Austl.	276	36°57′S	147°12′E
Alps, mts., Eur. (ălps)	194-95	46°25′N	10°00′E
Al-Qaḍārif, Sudan	266	14°02′N	35°23′E
Al-Qaṭīf, Sau. Ar.	230-31	26°33′N	50°00′E
Al-Quds, nat. cap., Isr. *see* Jerusalem	228-29	31°47′N	35°14′E
Als, i., Den. (äls)	194-95	54°59′N	9°55′E
Alsace, hist. reg., Fr. (ál-sá′s)	196-97	48°30′N	7°30′E
Alta Gracia, Arg. (äl′tä grä′sē-ä)	173	31°40′S	64°26′W
Altagracia, Ven.	164-65	10°43′N	71°30′W
Altamaha, stm., Ga., U.S. (ôl-tá-má-hô′)	124-25	31°19′N	81°18′W
Altamira, Braz. (äl-tä-mē′rä)	166-67	3°11′S	52°14′W
Altamira, Chile	168-69	25°48′S	69°51′W
Altamura, Italy (äl-tä-mōō′rä)	200-01	40°50′N	16°33′E
Altavista, Va., U.S. (äl-tä-vĭs′tá)	124-25	37°07′N	79°18′W

n-sing; ŋ-baŋk; N-nasalized n; nŏd; c*ŏ*mmit; ōld; ôbey; ôrder; oi-boil; fōōd; ŏ-as oo in foot; ou-out; s-soft; sh-dish; th-thin; pūre; ûnite; ûrn; stŭd; circ*ŭ*s; ü-as in French tu; ′-indeterminate vowel.

Feature (Pronunciation)	Page	Lat.	Long.
Altay, Mong.	240-41	46°24'N	96°15'E
Altay, Mong.	240-41	49°42'N	96°24'E
Altay, state, Russia	226	51°0'N	86°00'E
Altay, mts., Asia see Altay Mountains	222-23	48°0'N	90°00'E
Altay Mountains, mts., Asia (äl´tī´ moun´tĭnz)	222-23	48°0'N	90°00'E
Altay Shan, mts., Asia see Altay Mountains	222-23	48°0'N	90°00'E
Altenburg, Ger. (äl-tĕn-bŏŏrgh)	194-95	50°59'N	12°26'E
Altiplano, plat., S.A. (äl-tē-plä´nō)	168-69	18°0'S	68°00'W
Alto Araguaia, Braz.	168-69	17°19'S	53°13'W
Alton, Il., U.S. (ôl´tŭn)	120-21	38°55'N	90°12'W
Altona, Mb., Can.	134-35	49°06'N	97°35'W
Altoona, Ia., U.S. (ăl-tōō´nȧ)	114-15	41°38'N	93°28'W
Altoona, Pa., U.S. (ăl-tōō´nȧ)	116-17	40°29'N	78°24'W
Altoona, Wi., U.S. (ăl-tōō´nȧ)	114-15	44°48'N	91°26'W
Alto Parnaíba, Braz.	166-67	9°07'S	45°57'W
Alto Río Senguer, Arg.	171	45°03'S	70°51'W
Altun Shan, mts., China (äl-tòn shän)	222-23	38°0'N	88°00'E
Alturas, Ca., U.S. (ăl-tōō´rȧs)	112-13	41°30'N	120°32'W
Altus, Ok., U.S. (ăl´tŭs)	120-21	34°38'N	99°20'W
Alu, i., Sol. Is. see Shortland Island	279e	7°04'S	155°43'E
Al-Ubayyiḍ, Sudan	266	13°11'N	30°13'E
Alūksne, Lat. (ä´lòks-nĕ)	192-93	57°25'N	27°04'E
Alula, Som. see Caluula	262-63	11°57'N	50°46'E
Al-Urdun, nation, Asia see Jordan	206-07	31°0'N	36°00'E
Al-Urdunn, stm., Asia see Jordan	228-29	31°46'N	35°34'E
Alushta, Ukr. (ä´lshò-tȧ)	202-03	44°41'N	34°24'E
Alva, Ok., U.S. (ăl´vȧ)	120-21	36°48'N	98°40'W
Alvarado, Mex. (äl-vä-rä´dhō)	146-47	18°46'N	95°46'W
Älvdalen, Swe. (ĕlv´dä-lĕn)	192-93	61°14'N	14°02'E
Alvear, Arg.	173	29°03'S	56°33'W
Alvesta, Swe. (äl-vĕs´tä)	192-93	56°54'N	14°33'E
Alwar, India (ŭl´wŭr)	234-35	27°34'N	76°37'E
Alxa Zuoqi, China	240-41	38°49'N	105°35'E
Al-Yaman, nation, Asia see Yemen	206-07	15°0'N	44°00'E
Alytus, Lith. (ä´lē-tòs)	194-95	54°24'N	24°04'E
Alzira, Spain	198-99	39°09'N	0°26'W
Amadjuak Lake, lk., Nu., Can. (ä-mädj´wäk läk)	130-31	65°0'N	71°00'W
Amahai, Indon.	248-49	3°20'S	128°56'E
Amakuso-Shimo-shima, i., Japan (ämä-kōō´sä shē-mō shē´mä)	245	32°20'N	130°05'E
Åmål, Swe. (ô´môl)	192-93	59°03'N	12°42'E
Amalfi, Col. (ä-mà´l-fē)	164-65	6°55'N	75°05'W
Amambaí, Braz.	168-69	23°07'S	55°13'W
Amami-Ō-shima, i., Japan	244a	28°15'N	129°20'E
Amami-shotō, is., Japan	244a	27°58'N	129°02'E
Amapá, Braz.	166-67	2°02'N	50°46'W
Amapá, state, Braz.	166-67	1°0'N	52°00'W
Amarante, Braz. (ä-mä-rän´tä)	166-67	6°14'S	42°50'W
Amarillo, Tx., U.S. (ăm-ȧ-rĭl´ō)	120-21	35°13'N	101°50'W
Amarkantak, India	234-35	22°40'N	81°46'E
Amaro, Monte, mtn., Italy (môn-tĕ ä-mä´rō)	200-01	42°05'N	14°06'E
Amasya, Tur. (ä-mä´sē-ȧ)	186-87	40°39'N	35°50'E
Amazon, stm., S.A. (ă´mȧ-zŏn)	164-65	0°04'S	49°15'W
Amazonas, state, Braz. (ä-mä-thō´näs)	166-67	5°0'S	63°00'W
Amazonas, stm., S.A. (ä-mä-thō´näs) see Amazon	164-65	0°04'S	49°15'W
Ambāla, India (ŭm-bä´lŭ)	234-35	30°21'N	76°49'E
Ambanja, Madag.	264-65	13°41'S	48°27'E
Ambargasta, Salinas de, pl., Arg.	168-69	29°15'S	64°30'W
Ambato, Ec. (äm-bä´tō)	170	1°15'S	78°37'W
Ambatondrazaka, Madag.	264-65	17°52'S	48°24'E
Ambelau, Pulau, i., Indon.	248-49	3°51'S	127°12'E
Amberg, Ger. (äm´bĕrgh)	194-95	49°27'N	11°52'E
Ambergris Cay, i., Belize (ăm´bēr-grēs kā)	148	18°03'N	87°55'W
Ambert, Fr. (äɴ-bĕr´)	196-97	45°33'N	3°45'E
Ambikāpur, India	234-35	23°07'N	83°12'E
Amboina, Indon. see Ambon	248-49	3°44'S	128°11'E
Amboise, Fr. (äɴ-bwăz´)	196-97	47°24'N	0°60'E
Ambon, Indon.	248-49	3°44'S	128°11'E
Ambon, Pulau, i., Indon.	248-49	3°40'S	128°05'E
Amboseli National Park, n.p., Kenya	267	2°36'S	37°12'E
Ambositra, Madag. (äɴ-bô-sē´trä)	264-65	20°32'S	47°15'E
Ambovombe, Madag.	264-65	25°11'S	46°05'E
Amboy, Il., U.S. (ăm´boi)	116-17	41°43'N	89°20'W
Ambre, Cap d', c., Madag. see Bobaomby, Tanjona	264-65	11°58'S	49°15'E
Ambridge, Pa., U.S. (ăm´brĭdj)	116-17	40°36'N	80°13'W
Ambriz, Ang.	262-63	7°51'S	13°10'E
Ambrym, i., Vanuatu	279g	16°15'S	168°10'E
Amchitka Pass, strt., Ak., U.S. (ăm-chĭt´kȧ păs)	126a	51°30'N	179°30'W
Amderma, Russia	186-87	69°45'N	61°39'E
Amdo, China	234-35	32°17'N	91°44'E
Ameca, Mex. (ä-mĕ´kä)	146-47	20°33'N	104°02'W
Amecameca de Juárez, Mex.	146-47	19°07'N	98°46'W
Ameland, i., Neth.	190-91	53°27'N	5°45'E
Amelia Island, i., Fl., U.S.	124-25	30°37'N	81°27'W
American Falls, Id., U.S. (ȧ-mĕr´ĭ-kăn fôlz)	112-13	42°47'N	112°51'W
American Falls Reservoir, res., Id., U.S. (ȧ-mĕr´ĭ-kăn fôlz rĕ´sēr-vwär)	112-13	42°57'N	112°44'W
American Fork, Ut., U.S. (ȧ-mĕr´ĭ-kăn fôrk)	118-19	40°24'N	111°48'W
American Highland, plat., Ant. (ȧ-mĕr´ĭ-kăn)	287	72°30'S	78°00'E
Americanos, Barra de los, i., Mex.	122-23	24°53'N	97°35'W
American Samoa, dep., Oc. (ȧ-mĕr´ĭ-kăn sȧ-mō´ȧ)	279b	14°20'S	170°00'W
Americus, Ga., U.S. (ȧ-mĕr´ĭ-kŭs)	124-25	32°05'N	84°14'W
Amerika Samoa, dep., Oc. see American Samoa	279b	14°20'S	170°00'W
Amersfoort, Neth. (ä´mĕrz-fōrt)	190-91	52°10'N	5°24'E
Ames, Ia., U.S. (āmz)	114-15	42°01'N	93°37'W
Amesbury, Ma., U.S. (āmz´bēr-ē)	116-17	42°52'N	70°56'W
Ámfissa, Grc. (ȧm-fī´sȧ)	200-01	38°32'N	22°23'E
Amga, Russia (ŭm-gä´)	218-19	60°54'N	131°58'E
Amga, stm., Russia (ŭm-gä´)	218-19	62°35'N	135°04'E
Amgun, stm., Russia	218-19	52°56'N	139°41'E
Amherst, N.S., Can. (ăm´hērst)	138-39	45°50'N	64°12'W
Amherst, Ma., U.S. (ăm´hērst)	116-17	42°23'N	72°31'W
Amherst, N.Y., U.S. (ăm´hērst)	116-17	42°58'N	78°47'W
Amherst, Va., U.S. (ăm´hērst)	116-17	37°35'N	79°04'W
Amiens, Fr. (ä-myăɴ´)	196-97	49°54'N	2°18'E
Amistad, Presa de la, res., N.A. see Amistad Reservoir	122-23	29°28'N	101°07'W
Amistad Reservoir, res., N.A.	122-23	29°28'N	101°07'W
Amite, La., U.S. (ă-mēt´)	124-25	30°43'N	90°31'W
Amite, stm., La., U.S. (ă-mēt´)	124-25	30°13'N	90°36'W
Amlia Island, i., Ak., U.S. (ȧ´mlēȧ ī´lȧnd)	126a	52°07'N	173°34'W
'Ammān, nat. cap., Jord. (äm´mȧn)	228-29	31°57'N	35°56'E
Amnok-kang, stm., Asia see Yalu	243	39°57'N	124°22'E
Āmol, Iran	232-33	36°28'N	52°21'E
Amorgós, i., Grc. (ä-môr´gōs)	200-01	36°52'N	25°56'E
Amory, Ms., U.S. (āmô-rē)	124-25	33°59'N	88°29'W
Amos, Qc., Can. (ā´mŭs)	136-37	48°34'N	78°08'W
Amoy, China see Xiamen	225a	24°27'N	118°07'E
Amposta, Spain (äm-pōs´tä)	198-99	40°44'N	0°35'E
Amraoti, India see Amrāvati	234-35	20°56'N	77°46'E
Amrāvati, India	234-35	20°56'N	77°46'E
Amreli, India	234-35	21°36'N	71°13'E
Amritsar, India (ŭm-rĭt´sŭr)	234-35	31°38'N	74°52'E
Amroha, India	234-35	28°54'N	78°28'E
Amsterdam, N.Y., U.S. (ăm´stēr-dăm)	116-17	42°57'N	74°11'W
Amsterdam, nat. cap., Neth. (äm-stēr-däm´)	190-91	52°22'N	4°54'E
Amstetten, Aus. (äm´stĕt-ĕn)	194-95	48°07'N	14°52'E
Am Timan, Chad (äm´tē-män´)	258-59	11°02'N	20°17'E
Amu Darya, stm., Asia (ä-mò-dä´rēä)	226	44°14'N	59°41'E
Āmū Daryā, stm., Asia see Amu Darya	226	44°14'N	59°41'E
Amukta Pass, strt., Ak., U.S. (ä-mōōk´tȧ păs)	126a	52°26'N	171°51'W
Amundsen Gulf, b., Can. (ä´mŭn-sĕn-gŭlf´)	86	71°0'N	124°00'W
Amundsen Sea, s., Ant. (ä´mŭn-sĕn sē)	287	72°30'S	112°00'W
Amuntai, Indon.	248-49	2°25'S	115°15'E
Amur, stm., Asia (ä-mōōr´)	218-19	52°57'N	141°10'E
Anaa, at., Fr. Poly.	280-81	17°26'S	145°31'W
Anabar, stm., Russia (ăn-ȧ-bär´)	218-19	73°13'N	113°32'E
Anaco, Ven. (ä-nȧ´kô)	163b	9°25'N	64°28'W
Anaconda, Mt., U.S. (ăn-ȧ-kŏn´dȧ)	112-13	46°08'N	112°58'W
Anacortes, Wa., U.S. (ăn-ȧ-kôr´tĕz)	112-13	48°30'N	122°37'W
Anadarko, Ok., U.S. (ăn-ȧ-där´kō)	120-21	35°04'N	98°15'W
Anadyr', Russia (ŭ-nȧ-dĭr´)	218-19	64°44'N	177°30'E
Anadyr', stm., Russia (ŭ-nȧ-dĭr´)	218-19	64°52'N	176°15'E
Anadyr, Gulf of, b., Russia (gŭlf ŭv ä-nă-dyĭr´)	218-19	64°0'N	179°00'W
Anadyr Mountains, plat., Russia (ä-nă-dyĭr´ moun´tĭnz) see Anadyrskoye Ploskogor'ye	218-19	67°0'N	174°00'E
Anadyrskiy Zaliv, b., Russia see Anadyr, Gulf of	218-19	64°0'N	179°00'W
Anadyrskoye Ploskogor'ye, plat., Russia	218-19	67°0'N	174°00'E
Anaheim, Ca., U.S. (ăn´ȧ-hīm)	118-19	33°50'N	117°55'W
Ānai Mudi, mtn., India	236	10°10'N	77°04'E
Anaktuvuk Pass, Ak., U.S.	126	68°09'N	151°43'W
Anambas, Kepulauan, is., Indon. (ä-näm-bäs)	246-47	3°0'N	106°00'E
Anamosa, Ia., U.S. (ăn-ȧ-mō´sȧ)	114-15	42°06'N	91°16'W
Anamur, Tur.	228-29	36°04'N	32°50'E
Anantapur, India	236	14°41'N	77°36'E
Anantnāg, India	234-35	33°45'N	75°08'E
Anapa, Russia (á-nä´pä)	202-03	44°54'N	37°20'E
Anápolis, Braz. (ä-nȧ´pō-lēs)	168-69	16°21'S	48°57'W
Anatahan, i., N. Mar. Is.	280-81	16°22'N	145°40'E
Anatom, i., Vanuatu	279g	20°12'S	169°48'E
Añatuya, Arg. (á-nyä-tōō´yȧ)	173	28°27'S	62°49'W
Anauá, stm., Braz.	166-67	0°58'N	61°22'W
Anbanjing, China	238-39	23°57'N	100°54'E
Anchiang, China see Qianyang	238-39	27°11'N	110°02'E
Anchorage, Ak., U.S. (ăŋ´kēr-āj)	126	61°12'N	149°53'W
Ancona, Italy (än-kō´nä)	200-01	43°37'N	13°31'E
Ancud, Chile (äŋ-kōōdh´)	171	41°53'S	73°49'W
Ancud, Golfo de, b., Chile (gôl-fô-dĕ-äŋ-kōōdh´)	171	42°05'S	73°00'W
Anda, China	240-41	46°24'N	125°19'E
Andalgalá, Arg.	168-69	27°35'S	66°19'W
Andalucía, hist. reg., Spain (än-dä-lōō-sē´ä)	198-99	37°15'N	4°30'W
Andalusia, Al., U.S. (ăn-dȧ-lōō´zhĭȧ)	124-25	31°19'N	86°29'W
Andaman and Nicobar Islands, state, India	246-47	11°0'N	93°00'E
Andaman Islands, is., India (ăn-dȧ-măn´ ī´lăndz)	246-47	12°0'N	92°45'E
Andaman Sea, s., Asia (ăn-dȧ-măn´ sē)	246-47	10°0'N	95°00'E
Anderson, Ca., U.S. (ăn´dēr-sŭn)	112-13	40°29'N	122°22'W
Anderson, In., U.S. (ăn´dēr-sŭn)	116-17	40°05'N	85°41'W
Anderson, S.C., U.S. (ăn´dēr-sŭn)	124-25	34°30'N	82°39'W
Anderson, stm., N.T., Can. (ăn´dēr-sŭn)	130-31	69°42'N	128°54'W
Andes, mts., S.A. (ăn´dēz) (än´dās)	159	20°0'S	67°00'W
Andhra Pradesh, state, India	236	16°0'N	79°00'E
Andijon, Uzb.	232-33	40°47'N	72°21'E
Andkhvoy, Afg.	232-33	36°55'N	65°07'E
Andong, Kor., S. (än´dŭng´)	243	36°34'N	128°43'E
Andorra, nation, Eur. (än-dôr´rä)	196-97	42°30'N	1°30'E
Andorra la Vella, nat. cap., And.	198-99	42°30'N	1°31'E
Andover, Mn., U.S. (ăn´dō-vēr)	114-15	45°14'N	93°17'W
Andøya, i., Nor. (änd-ûē)	184-85	69°08'N	15°54'E
Andradina, Braz.	168-69	20°55'S	51°23'W
Andrews, N.C., U.S. (ăn´drōōz)	124-25	35°12'N	83°49'W
Andrews, S.C., U.S. (ăn´drōōz)	124-25	33°27'N	79°34'W
Andrews, Tx., U.S. (ăn´drōōz)	120-21	32°19'N	102°33'W
Andria, Italy (än´drē-ä)	200-01	41°13'N	16°17'E
Andros, i., Bah. (ăn´drōs)	142-43	24°26'N	77°57'W
Ándros, i., Grc. (àn´drōs)	200-01	37°50'N	24°53'E
Anegada, i., Br. Vir. Is.	143b	18°45'N	64°20'W
Aneto, mtn., Spain (ä-nĕ´tō)	198-99	42°38'N	0°40'E
Angamos, Punta, c., Chile	168-69	23°02'S	70°31'W
Ang'angxi, China (äŋ-äŋ-shyē)	240-41	47°09'N	123°48'E
Angara, stm., Russia	218-19	58°06'N	93°02'E
Angarsk, Russia	222-23	52°35'N	103°55'E
Ángel, Salto, wtfl., Ven. (säl´tō-á´n-hĕl) see Angel Falls	164-65	6°01'N	62°28'W
Ángel de la Guarda, Isla, i., Mex. (ĕ´s-lä-á´n-hĕl-dĕ-lä-gwä´r-dä)	144-45	29°22'N	113°28'W
Angeles, Phil. (än´hā-lās)	250	15°08'N	120°36'E
Angel Falls, wtfl., Ven. (ān´jĕl fôlz)	164-65	6°01'N	62°28'W
Ängelholm, Swe. (ĕng´ĕl-hôlm)	192-93	56°15'N	12°53'E
Angers, Fr.	196-97	47°28'N	0°33'W
Angicos, Braz.	163d	5°40'S	36°36'W
Angijak Island, i., Nu., Can.	130-31	65°40'N	62°15'W
Angkor Wat, hist., Camb. (äng´kôr)	246-47	13°26'N	103°52'E
Anglesey, i., Wales, U.K. (ăŋ´g'l-sē)	190-91	53°17'N	4°22'W
Angleton, Tx., U.S. (aŋ´g'l-tŭn)	122-23	29°10'N	95°26'W
Angmagssalik, Green. (àŋ-má´sá-lĭk)	284-85	65°35'N	37°50'W
Angoche, Moz.	264-65	16°14'S	39°55'E
Angoche, Ilha, i., Moz. (ē´lä-ăn-gō´chå)	264-65	16°21'S	39°51'E
Angol, Chile (aŋ-gōl´)	171	37°48'S	72°43'W
Angola, In., U.S. (ăŋ-gō´lȧ)	116-17	41°38'N	84°59'W
Angola, nation, Afr. (ăŋ-gō´lȧ)	253	12°30'S	18°30'E
Angontsy, Tanjona, c., Madag.	264-65	15°13'S	50°27'E
Angora, nat. cap., Tur. see Ankara	186-87	39°56'N	32°53'E
Angostura, Ven. see Ciudad Bolívar	164-65	8°07'N	63°33'W
Angostura, Presa de la, res., Mex.	144-45	16°02'N	92°22'W
Angoulême, Fr. (äŋ-gōō-lâm´)	196-97	45°39'N	0°09'E
Angra dos Reis, Braz. (aŋ´grä dōs rā´ēs)	172	23°01'S	44°19'W
Angren, Uzb.	232-33	41°01'N	70°08'E
Anguilla, dep., N.A. (ăŋ-gwĭl´ȧ)	140-41	18°15'N	63°05'W

ăt; finăl; rāte; senāte; ärm; ȧsk; sofȧ; fâre; ch-choose; dh-as th in other; bē; ēvent; bĕt; recĕnt; cratẽr; g-gō; gh-guttural g; bĭt; ĭ-short neutral; rīde; ĸ-guttural k as ch in German ich;

PRONOUNCING INDEX

Anguilla Cays – Ardahan 305

Feature (Pronunciation)	Page	Lat.	Long.
Anguilla Cays, is., Bah. (ăŋ-gwĭl'ȧ kēs)	142-43	23°31'N	79°33'W
Anguille, Cape, c., Nf., Can. (kăp'-ăŋ-gē'yĕ)	138-39	47°55'N	59°24'W
Anholt, i., Den. (än'hŏlt)	192-93	56°42'N	11°34'E
Anhui, state, China (än-hwā)	238-39	32°0'N	117°00'E
Anhwei, state, China *see* Anhui	238-39	32°0'N	117°00'E
Aniak, Ak., U.S. (ä-nyȧ'k)	126	61°35'N	159°33'W
Anina, Rom. (ä-nē'nä)	200-01	45°05'N	21°51'E
Anita, Pa., U.S. (ȧ-nē'ȧ)	116-17	41°0'N	78°58'W
Aniva, Zaliv, b., Russia (zä'lĭf ȧ-nē'vȧ)	244	46°16'N	142°48'E
Anjār, India	234-35	23°07'N	70°02'E
Anjouan, i., Com. *see* Nzwani	264-65	12°15'S	44°25'E
Anju-ŭp, Kor., N.	243	39°37'N	125°40'E
Ankaboa, Tanjona, c., Madag.	264-65	21°55'S	43°18'E
Ankang, China (än-κäŋ)	238-39	32°41'N	109°01'E
Ankara, nat. cap., Tur. (än'kȧ-rȧ)	186-87	39°56'N	32°53'E
Ankazoabo, Madag.	264-65	22°18'S	44°31'E
Ānkober, Eth.	269d	9°35'N	39°44'E
Anlong, China (än-loŋ)	238-39	25°07'N	105°28'E
Anlu, China (än'lōō')	238-39	31°16'N	113°41'E
Anmyŏn-do, i., Kor., S.	243	36°30'N	126°22'E
Anna, Il., U.S. (ăn'ȧ)	116-17	37°27'N	89°14'W
Annaba, Alg.	184-85	36°54'N	7°46'E
An-Nafūd, des., Sau. Ar.	228-29	28°30'N	41°00'E
An-Najaf, Iraq (än nä-jäf')	228-29	32°00'N	44°20'E
Annamitique, Chaîne, mts., Asia	246-47	17°0'N	106°00'E
Annapolis, Md., U.S. (ă-năp'ô-lĭs)	116-17	38°58'N	76°31'W
Annapūrṇa, mtn., Nepal	234-35	28°34'N	83°50'E
Ann Arbor, Mi., U.S. (ăn är'bĕr)	116-17	42°16'N	83°43'W
An-Nāṣirīyah, Iraq	228-29	31°03'N	46°15'E
An-Nawfalīyah, Libya	188-89	30°46'N	17°50'E
Annecy, Fr. (ȧn sē')	196-97	45°54'N	6°07'E
Annemasse, Fr. (än'mäs')	196-97	46°12'N	6°14'E
An Nhon, Viet.	246-47	13°54'N	109°05'E
Anniston, Al., U.S. (ăn'ĭs-tŭn)	124-25	33°39'N	85°50'W
Annobón, i., Eq. Gui.	260-61	1°26'S	5°37'E
Annonay, Fr. (ȧn'ĭs-tsiŭn)	196-97	45°15'N	4°40'E
An-Nuhūd, Sudan	266	12°42'N	28°26'E
Anori, Braz.	166-67	3°45'S	61°42'W
Anorontany, Tanjona, c., Madag.	264-65	12°26'S	48°45'E
Anpu, China (än-pōō)	238-39	21°27'N	110°01'E
Anqing, China	238-39	30°30'N	117°02'E
Ansbach, Ger. (äns'bäk)	194-95	49°18'N	10°35'E
Anse-d'Hainault, Haiti (äɴs'dĕnō)	142-43	18°30'N	74°26'W
Anserma, Col. (á'n-sĕ'r-mȧ)	163c	5°14'N	75°48'W
Anshan, China	243	41°08'N	122°60'E
Anshun, China (än-shōōn')	238-39	26°15'N	105°56'E
Anson, Tx., U.S. (ăn'sŭn)	120-21	32°44'N	99°53'W
Ansongo, Mali	258-59	15°40'N	0°30'E
Antakya, Tur. *see* Antioch	228-29	36°12'N	36°10'E
Antalaha, Madag.	264-65	14°55'S	50°17'E
Antalya, Tur. (än-tä'lē-ä) (ä-dä'lē-ä)	186-87	36°54'N	30°42'E
Antalya, Gulf of, b., Tur. *see* Antalya Körfezi	186-87	36°30'N	30°60'E
Antalya Körfezi, b., Tur.	186-87	36°30'N	30°60'E
Antananarivo, nat. cap., Madag. (än-tä'nä-nä-rēv)	264-65	18°55'S	47°32'E
An tAonach, Ire. *see* Nenagh	190-91	52°52'N	8°12'W
Antarctica, cont., (ănt-ärk'tĭ-kȧ)	287	87°0'S	60°00'E
Antarctic Peninsula, pen., Ant.	287	70°15'S	65°55'W
Antequera, Spain (än-tĕ-kĕ'rä)	198-99	37°01'N	4°33'W
Anthony, Tx., U.S. (ăn'thô-nē)	118-19	31°60'N	106°36'W
Anti-Atlas, mts., Mor.	258-59	30°0'N	8°30'W
Antibes, Fr. (äɴ-tēb')	196-97	43°35'N	7°07'E
Anticosti, Île d', i., Qc., Can. (ăn-tĭ-kŏs'tē)	138-39	49°30'N	63°00'W
Antigo, Wi., U.S. (ăn'tĭ-gō)	116-17	45°08'N	89°08'W
Antigonish, N.S., Can. (ăn-tĭ-gô-nēsh')	138-39	45°37'N	61°60'W
Antigua, i., Antig.	143b	17°05'N	61°49'W
Antigua and Barbuda, nation, N.A. (ăn-tē'gwä ănd bär-bōō'dȧ)	140-41	17°03'N	61°48'W
Antigua Guatemala, Guat.	148	14°33'N	90°44'W
Antillas, Archipiélago de las, is., *see* West Indies	140-41	19°0'N	70°00'W
Antillas, Mar de las, s., *see* Caribbean Sea	140-41	15°0'N	73°00'W
Antillas Mayores, is., N.A. *see* Greater Antilles	142-43	20°0'N	74°00'W
Antillen, Nederlandse, dep., N.A. *see* Netherlands Antilles	140-41	12°15'N	68°45'W
Antilles, Grandes, is., N.A. *see* Greater Antilles	142-43	20°0'N	74°00'W
Antilles, Mer des, s., *see* Caribbean Sea	140-41	15°0'N	73°00'W
Antilles, Petites, is., *see* Lesser Antilles	143b	15°0'N	61°00'W
Antioch, Tur.	228-29	36°12'N	36°10'E
Antioch, Il., U.S. (ăn'tĭ-ŏk)	116-17	42°29'N	88°06'W
Antioquia, Col. (än-tē-ō'kēä)	163c	6°34'N	75°49'W
Antipodes Islands, is., N.Z.	287	49°40'S	178°47'E
Antlers, Ok., U.S. (ănt'lērz)	120-21	34°13'N	95°37'W
Antofagasta, Chile (än-tô-fä-gäs'tä)	168-69	23°39'S	70°23'W
Antón, Pan. (än-tōn')	150	8°24'N	80°14'W
Antongila, Helodrano, b., Madag.	264-65	15°45'S	49°50'E
António Enes, Moz. (ăn-to'nyō ĕn'ĕs) *see* Angoche	264-65	16°14'S	39°55'E
Antsirabe, Madag. (änt-sē-rä'bā)	264-65	19°52'S	47°02'E
Antsirañana, Madag.	264-65	12°17'S	49°17'E
Antsirane, Madag. *see* Antsirañana	264-65	12°17'S	49°17'E
Antsla, Est. (änt'slȧ)	192-93	57°50'N	26°32'E
Antsohihy, Madag.	264-65	14°49'S	48°03'E
Antung, China *see* Dandong	243	40°07'N	124°21'E
Antwerp, Bel. (ăn'twûrp)	190-91	51°13'N	4°25'E
Antwerpen, Bel. *see* Antwerp	190-91	51°13'N	4°25'E
Anugul, India	234-35	20°51'N	85°06'E
Anūpgarh, India (ŭ-nòp'gŭr)	234-35	29°11'N	73°13'E
Anuradhapura, Sri L. (ŭ-nōō'rä-dŭ-pōō'rŭ)	236	8°21'N	80°24'E
Anvers, Bel. *see* Antwerp	190-91	51°13'N	4°25'E
Anvers Island, i., Ant.	287	64°33'S	63°35'W
Anxi, China (än-shyē)	225a	25°04'N	118°11'E
Anxi, China (än-shyē)	240-41	40°29'N	95°47'E
Anyang, China (än'yäng)	240-41	36°06'N	114°20'E
Anykščiai, Lith. (anīksh-chä'ē)	192-93	55°32'N	25°07'E
Anyuanyi, China *see* Tianzhu	240-41	36°60'N	103°07'E
Anzhero-Sudzhensk, Russia (än'zhâ-rô-sōd'zhĕnsk)	218-19	56°05'N	86°01'E
Anzio, Italy (änt'zē-ō)	200-01	41°27'N	12°37'E
Aoba, i., Vanuatu	279g	15°25'S	167°50'E
Aoga-shima, i., Japan	244	32°28'N	139°46'E
Aomen, China	238-39	22°13'N	113°33'E
Aomori, Japan (äô-mō'rē)	244	40°49'N	140°45'E
Aoraki/Mount Cook National Park, n.p., N.Z.	278	43°35'S	170°15'E
Aoraki, mtn., N.Z.	278	43°36'S	170°10'E
Aôral, Phnum, mtn., Camb.	246-47	12°02'N	104°10'E
Aouk, Bahr, stm., Afr. (bär ä-ōk')	262-63	8°51'N	18°52'E
Aoukâr, reg., Maur.	258-59	18°0'N	9°30'W
Aoulef, Alg.	258-59	26°58'N	1°04'E
Apalachicola, Fl., U.S. (ăp-ȧ-lăch-ĭ-kō'lȧ)	124-25	29°44'N	84°60'W
Apalachicola, stm., Fl., U.S. (ăpȧ-lăch'ĭ-cōlä)	124-25	29°44'N	84°59'W
Apaporis, stm., S.A. (ä-pä-pô'rĭs)	170	1°21'S	69°25'W
Aparri, Phil. (ä-pär'rē)	250	18°20'N	121°40'E
Apatin, Serb. (ŏ'pŏ-tĭn)	200-01	45°40'N	18°59'E
Apatity, Russia	184-85	67°34'N	33°23'E
Apeldoorn, Neth. (ä'pĕl-dōōrn)	190-91	52°13'N	5°58'E
Apennines, mts., Italy (ă'pȧ-nīnz)	200-01	43°0'N	13°00'E
Apía, Col. (ȧ-pē'ä)	163c	5°06'N	75°58'W
Apia, nat. cap., Samoa (ä'-pē-ȧ) (ä-pē'-ȧ)	279b	13°50'S	171°45'W
Apiacás, Serra dos, plat., Braz.	166-67	10°15'S	57°15'W
Apizaco, Mex. (ä-pē-zä'kō)	146-47	19°25'N	98°08'W
Apo, Mount, mtn., Phil. (mount ä'pō)	250	6°59'N	125°16'E
Apolo, Bol.	166-67	14°43'S	68°31'W
Aporé, stm., Braz.	168-69	19°28'S	50°56'W
Apostle Islands, is., Wi., U.S. (ă-pŏs'l ī'lăndz)	114-15	46°50'N	90°30'W
Apóstoles, Arg.	173	27°55'S	55°48'W
Apostolove, Ukr.	202-03	47°39'N	33°43'E
Appalaches, Les, mts., N.A. *see* Appalachian Mountains	110-11	41°0'N	77°00'W
Appalachia, Va., U.S. (ăpȧ-lăch'ĭ-ȧ)	124-25	36°54'N	82°48'W
Appalachian Mountains, mts., N.A. (ăp-ȧ-lăch'ĭ-ăn moun'tĭnz)	110-11	41°0'N	77°00'W
Appennino, mts., Italy (äp-pĕn-nē'nô) *see* Apennines	200-01	43°0'N	13°00'E
Appleton, Mn., U.S. (ăp'l-tŭn)	114-15	45°12'N	96°01'W
Appleton, Wi., U.S. (ăp'l-tŭn)	116-17	44°15'N	88°25'W
Appleton City, Mo., U.S. (ăp'l-tŭn sĭ'tē)	120-21	38°11'N	94°02'W
Apt, Fr. (äpt)	196-97	43°52'N	5°24'E
Apucarana, Braz.	168-69	23°33'S	51°27'W
Apure, stm., Ven. (ä-pōō'rä)	164-65	7°37'N	66°23'W
Apurímac, stm., Peru (ä-pōō-rē-mäk')	170	11°52'S	73°57'W
Aqaba, Gulf of, b., (gŭlf ŭv ä'kȧ-bȧ)	228-29	29°05'N	34°44'E
Aqmola, nat. cap., Kaz. *see* Astana	226	51°12'N	71°27'E
Aqtaū, Kaz.	186-87	43°38'N	51°11'E
Aqtöbe, Kaz.	226	50°18'N	57°10'E
Aquidauana, Braz. (ä-kē-däwä'nä)	168-69	20°29'S	55°48'W
Aquila, Italy *see* L'Aquila	200-01	42°21'N	13°24'E
Aquin, Haiti (ä-kăn')	142-43	18°17'N	73°24'W
Ar'ar, Sau. Ar.	228-29	30°56'N	41°04'E
Ara, India	234-35	25°34'N	84°40'E
Ara, stm., Japan (ä-rä)	245	35°40'N	139°51'E
Ara, stm., Japan (ä-rä)	245	38°09'N	139°25'E
'Arab, Baḥr al-, stm., Sudan	262-63	9°02'N	29°28'E
'Arab, Shaṭṭ al-, stm., Asia	228-29	29°57'N	48°33'E
Arabian Desert, des., Egypt (ȧ-rā'bĭ-ăn dĕs'ērt)	266	28°0'N	32°00'E
Arabian Gulf, b., Asia *see* Persian Gulf	230-31	27°0'N	51°00'E
Arabian Peninsula, pen., Asia (ȧ-rā'bĭ-ăn pĕ-nĭn'sūlȧ)	220-21	25°0'N	45°00'E
Arabian Sea, s., (ȧ-rā'bĭ-ăn sē)	220-21	15°0'N	65°00'E
Aracaju, Braz. (ä-rä'kä-zhōō')	163d	10°54'S	37°04'W
Aracati, Braz. (ä-rä'kä-tē')	166-67	4°34'S	37°46'W
Araçatuba, Braz. (ä-rä-sȧ-tōō'bä)	168-69	21°12'S	50°27'W
Aracruz, Braz. (ä-rä-krōō's)	172	19°49'S	40°16'W
Araçuaí, Braz.	168-69	16°53'S	42°04'W
Arad, Rom. (ŏ'rŏd)	194-95	46°11'N	21°19'E
Arafura, Laut, s., *see* Arafura Sea	224-25	9°0'S	133°00'E
Arafura Sea, s., (ä-rä-fōō'rä sē)	224-25	9°0'S	133°00'E
Aragarças, Braz.	168-69	15°55'S	52°15'W
Aragón, hist. reg., Spain (ä-rä-gōn')	198-99	41°30'N	1°00'W
Araguacema, Braz.	166-67	8°50'S	49°34'W
Aragua de Barcelona, Ven.	163b	9°27'N	64°50'W
Araguaia, stm., Braz. (ä-rä-gwä'yä)	166-67	5°20'S	48°42'W
Araguari, Braz. (ä-rä-gwä'rē)	172	18°39'S	48°12'W
Araguari, stm., Braz.	166-67	1°13'N	50°02'W
Araguatins, Braz. (ä-rä-gwä-tēns)	166-67	5°39'S	48°06'W
Arāk, Iran	232-33	34°05'N	49°41'E
Aral, Kaz.	226	46°48'N	61°40'E
Aral Sea, lk., Asia (ă'-rŭl sē)	226	45°0'N	60°00'E
Aral Tengizi, lk., Asia *see* Aral Sea	226	45°0'N	60°00'E
Aramac, Austl.	277	22°58'S	145°15'E
Aramberri, Mex. (ä-rȧm-bĕr-rē')	146-47	24°06'N	99°49'W
Aranda de Duero, Spain (ä-rän'dä dā dwā'rō)	198-99	41°41'N	3°41'W
Arandas, Mex. (ä-rän'däs)	146-47	20°43'N	102°20'W
Aranjuez, Spain (ä-rän-hwāth')	198-99	40°02'N	3°37'W
Aransas Pass, Tx., U.S. (ȧ-răn'sȧs pȧs)	122-23	27°54'N	97°09'W
Aranyaprathet, Thai.	246-47	13°41'N	102°31'E
Arapiraca, Braz.	163d	9°45'S	36°39'W
Araranguá, Braz.	172	28°56'S	49°29'W
Araraquara, Braz. (ä-rä-rä-kwä'rä)	172	21°47'S	48°10'W
Ararat, Austl. (ăr'ărăt)	276	37°17'S	142°56'E
Ararat, Mount, vol., Tur. (mount ăr'ȧrăt)	227	39°42'N	44°18'E
Araripe, Chapada do, plat., Braz. (shä-pä'dä-dô-ä-rä-rē'pĕ)	166-67	7°23'S	39°49'W
Araruama, Lagoa de, b., Braz. (lȧ-gô'ä-ä-rä-rōō-ä'mä)	172	22°53'S	42°12'W
Aras, stm., Asia (ȧ-räs)	227	40°01'N	48°28'E
Arauca, Col. (ä-rou'kä)	164-65	7°04'N	70°45'W
Arauca, stm., S.A. (ä-rou'kä)	164-65	7°25'N	66°31'W
Arāvalli Range, mts., India (ä-rä'vŭ-lē rănj)	234-35	24°42'N	73°19'E
Araxá, Braz.	172	19°36'S	46°55'W
Araya, Punta de, c., Ven. (pŭn'tȧ-dĕ-ä-rä'yä)	163b	10°38'N	64°17'W
Araz, stm., Asia.	227	40°01'N	48°28'E
Ārba Minch', Eth.	262-63	6°01'N	37°34'E
Arbīl, Iraq	228-29	36°11'N	44°01'E
Arboga, Swe. (är-bō'gä)	192-93	59°24'N	15°51'E
Arboréa, Italy (är-bō-rĕ'ä)	200-01	39°46'N	8°35'E
Arbroath, Scot., U.K. (är-brōth')	190-91	56°34'N	2°36'W
Arcachon, Fr. (är-κä-shôɴ')	196-97	44°40'N	1°10'W
Arcadia, Fl., U.S. (är-kā'dĭ-ȧ)	125a	27°13'N	81°51'W
Arcadia, La., U.S. (är-kā'dĭ-ȧ)	120-21	32°34'N	92°56'W
Arcadia, Wi., U.S. (är-kā'dĭ-ȧ)	114-15	44°15'N	91°29'W
Arcata, Ca., U.S. (är-kȧ'tȧ)	112-13	40°53'N	124°05'W
Arc Dome, mtn., Nv., U.S. (ärk dōm)	118-19	38°50'N	117°21'W
Arcelia, Mex. (är-sā'lē-ä)	146-47	18°18'N	100°17'W
Archangel, Russia *see* Arkhangel'sk	186-87	64°32'N	40°25'E
Archbald, Pa., U.S. (ärch'bôld)	116-17	41°30'N	75°33'W
Archer Bend National Park, n.p., Austl. *see* Mungkan Kandju National Park	277	13°32'S	142°37'E
Arches National Park, n.p., Ut., U.S. (är'ches năsh'ŭn-ăl pärk)	118-19	38°43'N	109°36'W
Arco, Id., U.S. (är'kô)	112-13	43°39'N	113°18'W
Arcoverde, Braz.	163d	8°25'S	37°04'W
Arctic Ocean, oc., (ärk'tĭk ōshŭn)	288	85°0'N	170°00'E
Arctic Red, stm., N.T., Can.	130-31	67°27'N	133°45'W
Arctic Village, Ak., U.S.	126	68°05'N	145°31'W
Ardabīl, Iran	227	38°15'N	48°18'E
Ardahan, Tur. (är-dȧ-hän')	227	41°06'N	42°43'E

Feature (Pronunciation)	Page	Lat.	Long.
Ardebil, Iran *see* Ardabīl	227	38°15'N	48°18'E
Ardennen, reg., Eur. *see* Ardennes	190-91	50°10'N	5°45'E
Ardennes, reg., Eur. (ȧr-dĕn')	190-91	50°10'N	5°45'E
Ardila, stm., Eur. (är-dē'lȧ)	198-99	38°10'N	7°29'W
Ardmore, Ok., U.S. (ärd'mōr)	120-21	34°10'N	97°09'W
Arecibo, P.R. (ä-rå-sē'bō)	142a	18°28'N	66°43'W
Areia Branca, Braz. (ä-rĕ'yä-brà'n-kă)	163d	4°56'S	37°07'W
Arena, Point, c., Ca., U.S. (point ä-rā'nȧ)	118-19	38°57'N	123°44'W
Arena, Punta, c., Mex.	144-45	23°34'N	109°28'W
Arendal, Nor. (ä'rĕn-däl)	192-93	58°27'N	8°48'E
Arequipa, Peru (ä-rå-kē'pä)	170	16°24'S	71°32'W
Arezzo, Italy (ä-rĕt'sō)	200-01	43°28'N	11°53'E
Argentan, Fr. (ȧr-zhäN-täN')	196-97	48°45'N	0°01'W
Argenteuil, Fr. (är-zhäN-tû'y')	196-97	48°57'N	2°14'E
Argentina, nation, S.A. (är-jĕn-tē'nȧ)	158	34°0'S	64°00'W
Argentino, Lago, lk., Arg. (lä'gō är-кĕn-tē'nō)	171	50°14'S	72°26'W
Argenton-sur-Creuse, Fr. (är-zhäN'tôN-sür-krôs)	196-97	46°35'N	1°31'E
Arghandāb, stm., Afg.	232-33	31°27'N	64°23'E
Argonne, reg., Fr. (ä'r-gôn)	196-97	49°07'N	5°14'E
Árgos, Grc. (är'gŏs)	200-01	37°38'N	22°44'E
Arguello, Point, c., Ca., U.S. (point är-gwāl'yō)	118-19	34°35'N	120°38'W
Argun', stm., Asia (ȧr-gōōn')	218-19	53°19'N	121°27'E
Århus, Den. (ôr'hōōs)	192-93	56°09'N	10°13'E
Ariake-kai, b., Japan (ä'rē-ä'kä)	245	33°0'N	130°20'E
Arica, Chile (ä-rē'kä)	168-69	18°29'S	70°19'W
Arica, Col.	164-65	2°07'S	71°44'W
Arīḥā, W.B. *see* Jericho	228-29	31°52'N	35°27'E
Arima, Trin.	143b	10°37'N	61°17'W
Arinos, stm., Braz. (ä-rē'nôzh)	166-67	10°26'S	58°20'W
Aripuanã, stm., Braz. (ȧ-rē-pwän'yȧ)	166-67	5°07'S	60°23'W
Ariquemes, Braz.	166-67	9°54'S	63°05'W
Aristazabal Island, i., B.C., Can.	132-33	52°38'N	129°07'W
Arizona, Arg.	171	35°43'S	65°19'W
Arizona, state, U.S. (ăr-ĭ-zō'nȧ)	108-09	34°0'N	112°00'W
Arkadelphia, Ar., U.S. (är-kȧ-dĕl'fĭ-ȧ)	120-21	34°07'N	93°04'W
Arkansas, state, U.S. (är'kăn-sô) (är-kăn'sȧs)	108-09	34°50'N	92°30'W
Arkansas, stm., U.S. (är'kăn-sô) (är-kăn'sȧs)	110-11	33°47'N	91°04'W
Arkansas City, Ks., U.S.	120-21	37°04'N	97°02'W
Arkhangel'sk, Russia (ȧr-кän'gĕlsk)	186-87	64°32'N	40°25'E
Arkhangel'skoye, Russia (är-kän-gĕl'skô-yĕ)	202-03	53°16'N	37°42'E
Arles, Fr. (ärl)	196-97	43°41'N	4°38'E
Arlington, S.D., U.S. (är'lĕng-tŭn)	114-15	44°22'N	97°08'W
Arlington, Tx., U.S. (ȧr'lĭng-tŭn)	120-21	32°45'N	97°07'W
Arlington, Va., U.S. (ȧr'lĭng-tŭn)	116-17	38°52'N	77°07'W
Arlington, Vt., U.S. (ȧr'lĭng-tŭn)	116-17	43°04'N	73°09'W
Arlington Heights, Il., U.S. (är'lĕng-tŭn hīts)	116-17	42°05'N	87°59'W
Arlit, Niger	258-59	18°45'N	7°21'E
Armant, Egypt (är-mänt')	268b	25°37'N	32°32'E
Armavir, Russia (ȧr-mȧ-vĭr')	186-87	44°59'N	41°07'E
Armenia, Col. (ȧr-mĕ'nēȧ)	163c	4°31'N	75°42'W
Armenia, nation, Asia (är-mē'nē-ȧ)	227	40°0'N	45°00'E
Armeniya, nation, Asia *see* Armenia	227	40°0'N	45°00'E
Armentières, Fr. (ȧr-mäN-tyâr')	196-97	50°41'N	2°53'E
Armidale, Austl. (är'mĭ-dāl)	276	30°31'S	151°40'E
Armour, S.D., U.S. (är'mẽr)	114-15	43°19'N	98°21'W
Armstrong, On., Can.	134-35	50°18'N	89°04'W
Arnaud, stm., Qc., Can.	130-31	59°58'N	69°58'W
Arnedo, Spain (är-nā'dō)	198-99	42°14'N	2°07'W
Arnhem, Neth. (ärn'hĕm)	190-91	51°59'N	5°55'E
Arnhem, Cape, c., Austl. (käp ärn'hĕm)	272-73	12°22'S	136°57'E
Arnhem Land, reg., Austl. (ärn'hĕm-lănd)	272-73	13°13'S	133°50'E
Arnold, Mn., U.S. (är'nŭld)	114-15	46°53'N	92°05'W
Arnprior, On., Can. (ärn-prī'ẽr)	136-37	45°26'N	76°21'W
Arnsberg, Ger. (ärns'bĕrgh)	194-95	51°24'N	8°04'E
Arnstadt, Ger. (ärn'shtät)	194-95	50°50'N	10°57'E
Aroma, Sudan	266	15°48'N	36°08'E
Aroostook, stm., N.A.	138-39	46°49'N	67°43'W
Arop Island, i., Pap. N. Gui.	277	5°20'S	147°05'E
Arorae, i., Kir.	280-81	2°38'S	176°49'E
Arqalyq, Kaz.	226	50°15'N	66°53'E
Arraias, Braz.	166-67	12°58'S	46°55'W
Ar-Ramādī, Iraq	228-29	33°26'N	43°19'E
Arran, Island of, i., Scot., U.K. (ĭ'lȧnd ŏv ă'răn)	190-91	55°35'N	5°15'W
Arras, Fr. (ȧ-räs')	196-97	50°17'N	2°47'E
Ar-Rass, Sau. Ar.	266	25°52'N	43°30'E
Arrecife, Spain	199d	28°57'N	13°33'W
Arrecifes, Arg. (är-rå-sē'fäs)	173	34°04'S	60°06'W
Arriaga, Mex. (är-rêä'gä)	146-47	16°14'N	93°53'W
Ar-Riyāḍ, nat. cap., Sau. Ar. *see* Riyadh	230-31	24°38'N	46°43'E
Ar-Rub'al-Khālī, des., Asia *see* Rub'al-Khali	220-21	20°0'N	51°00'E
Ar-Ruṣayriṣ, Sudan	266	11°48'N	34°22'E
Ar-Ruṭbah, Iraq	228-29	33°02'N	40°17'E
Arsen'yev, Russia	244	44°09'N	133°17'E
Art, Île, i., N. Cal.	279g	19°43'S	163°39'E
Árta, Grc. (är'tā)	200-01	39°09'N	20°59'E
Arteaga, Mex. (är-tā-ä'gä)	146-47	18°20'N	102°18'W
Arteaga, Mex. (är-tā-ä'gä)	122-23	25°28'N	100°51'W
Artëm, Russia (ȧr-tyôm')	244	43°21'N	132°11'E
Artemisa, Cuba (är-tå-mē'sä)	142-43	22°49'N	82°46'W
Artesia, N.M., U.S. (är-tē'sĭ-ȧ)	120-21	32°51'N	104°24'W
Artibonite, stm., Haiti (är-tē-bō-nē'tā)	142-43	19°15'N	72°46'W
Artigas, Ur.	173	30°24'S	56°28'W
Artillery Lake, lk., N.T., Can.	130-31	63°09'N	107°52'W
Artvin, Tur.	227	41°10'N	41°50'E
Artyk, Russia	218-19	64°09'N	145°12'E
Aru, Kepulauan, is., Indon.	224-25	6°0'S	134°30'E
Aru, Tanjung, c., Indon.	248-49	2°11'S	116°35'E
Arua, Ug. (ä'rōō-ä)	267	3°01'N	30°55'E
Aruanã, Braz.	166-67	14°54'S	51°05'W
Aruba, dep., N.A. (ä-rōō'bȧ)	140-41	12°30'N	69°58'W
Arunāchal Pradesh, state, India	234-35	28°30'N	95°00'E
Aruppukkottai, India	236	9°31'N	78°06'E
Arusha, Tan. (ȧ-rōō'shä)	267	3°22'S	36°41'E
Aruwimi, stm., D.R.C.	262-63	1°13'N	23°36'E
Arvayheer, Mong.	240-41	46°15'N	102°48'E
Arviat, Nu., Can.	128-29	61°08'N	94°07'W
Arvidsjaur, Swe.	184-85	65°36'N	19°07'E
Arvika, Swe. (är-vē'kȧ)	192-93	59°40'N	12°38'E
Arxan, China	240-41	47°11'N	119°57'E
Arys, Kaz.	226	42°26'N	68°48'E
Arzamas, Russia (är-zä-mäs')	186-87	55°23'N	43°50'E
Aš, Czech Rep. (äsh')	194-95	50°13'N	12°12'E
Asad, Buḥayrat al-, res., Syria	228-29	36°00'N	38°10'E
Asahi-dake, vol., Japan	244	43°40'N	142°51'E
Asahigawa, Japan *see* Asahikawa	244	43°46'N	142°22'E
Asahikawa, Japan	244	43°46'N	142°22'E
Āsānsol, India	234-35	23°41'N	86°59'E
Asbestos, Qc., Can. (ăs-bĕs'tŏs)	136-37	45°46'N	71°57'W
Asbury Park, N.J., U.S. (ăz'bĕr-ĭ pärk)	116-17	40°13'N	74°01'W
Ascensión, Mex. (äs-sĕn-sê-ōn')	144-45	31°06'N	107°60'W
Ascension, i., St. Hel. (ȧ-sĕn'shŭn)	254	7°57'S	14°22'W
Aschaffenburg, Ger. (ä-shäf'ĕn-bōrgh)	194-95	49°59'N	9°09'E
Aschersleben, Ger. (äsh'ĕrs-lā-bĕn)	194-95	51°46'N	11°28'E
Ascoli Piceno, Italy (äs'kō-lēpē-chā'nō)	200-01	42°52'N	13°35'E
Aseb, Erit.	266	12°58'N	42°42'E
Āsela, Eth.	269d	7°58'N	39°08'E
Åsele, Swe.	184-85	64°10'N	17°21'E
Aşgabat, nat. cap., Turkmen.	232-33	37°57'N	58°23'E
Asha, Russia (ä'shä)	186-87	55°00'N	57°16'E
Ashburn, Ga., U.S. (ăsh'bŭrn)	124-25	31°42'N	83°39'W
Ashburton, stm., Austl. (ăsh'bûr-tŭn)	272-73	21°42'S	114°55'E
Ashdown, Ar., U.S. (ăsh'doun)	120-21	33°41'N	94°08'W
Asheboro, N.C., U.S. (ăsh'bŭr-ō)	124-25	35°42'N	79°49'W
Asheville, N.C., U.S. (ăsh'vĭl)	124-25	35°36'N	82°34'W
Ashgabat, nat. cap., Turkmen. *see* Aşgabat	232-33	37°57'N	58°23'E
Ashikaga, Japan (ä'shē-kä'gȧ)	245	36°20'N	139°27'E
Ashkhabad, nat. cap., Turkmen. *see* Aşgabat	232-33	37°57'N	58°23'E
Ashland, Ky., U.S. (ăsh'lȧnd)	116-17	38°28'N	82°39'W
Ashland, Me., U.S. (ăsh'lȧnd)	117a	46°38'N	68°28'W
Ashland, Ne., U.S. (ăsh'lȧnd)	114-15	41°02'N	96°22'W
Ashland, Oh., U.S. (ăsh'lȧnd)	116-17	40°52'N	82°18'W
Ashland, Or., U.S. (ăsh'lȧnd)	112-13	42°12'N	122°42'W
Ashland, Va., U.S. (ăsh'lȧnd)	116-17	37°45'N	77°29'W
Ashland, Wi., U.S. (ăsh'lȧnd)	114-15	46°36'N	90°53'W
Ashley, N.D., U.S. (ăsh'lē)	114-15	46°02'N	99°22'W
Ashmore and Cartier Islands, dep., Oc.	224-25	12°25'S	123°20'E
Ashqelon, Isr. (äsh'kĕ-lōn)	228-29	31°40'N	34°35'E
Ash-Shāriqah, U.A.E. *see* Sharjah	230-31	25°22'N	55°24'E
Ash-Shiḥr, Yemen	220-21	14°46'N	49°37'E
Ashtabula, Oh., U.S. (ăsh-tȧ-bū'lȧ)	116-17	41°51'N	80°48'W
Ashton, Id., U.S. (ăsh'tŭn)	112-13	44°05'N	111°27'W
Ashur, hist., Iraq	228-29	35°30'N	43°16'E
Asia, cont., (ā'zhȧ)	208-09	50°0'N	100°00'E
Asinara, Golfo dell', b., Italy (gôl'fō-dĕl-ä-sē-nä'rä)	200-01	41°0'N	8°32'E
Asinara, Isola, i., Italy	200-01	41°04'N	8°16'E
Asino, Russia	218-19	56°60'N	86°08'E
'Asīr, reg., Sau. Ar. (ä-sēr')	220-21	19°0'N	42°00'E
Askersund, Swe. (äs'kĕr-sōnd)	192-93	58°53'N	14°54'E
Asmara, nat. cap., Erit. (äz-mä'-rȧ)	266	15°20'N	38°55'E
Asmera, nat. cap., Erit. (äs-mä'rä) *see* Asmara	266	15°20'N	38°55'E
Asotin, Wa., U.S. (ȧ-sō'tĭn)	112-13	46°20'N	117°03'W
Aspen, Co., U.S. (ăs'pĕn)	118-19	39°12'N	106°49'W
Aspiring, Mount, mtn., N.Z.	278	44°23'S	168°44'E
Assab, Erit. *see* Aseb	266	12°58'N	42°42'E
Assam, state, India (ăs-săm')	234-35	26°0'N	93°00'E
As-Samāwah, Iraq	228-29	31°19'N	45°17'E
Assateague Island, i., U.S.	116-17	38°05'N	75°12'W
Assens, Den. (äs'sĕns)	192-93	55°16'N	9°55'E
Assiniboia, Sk., Can.	134-35	49°38'N	105°59'W
Assiniboine, stm., Can. (ă-sĭn'ĭ-boin)	134-35	49°53'N	97°08'W
Assiniboine, Mount, mtn., Can. (mount ă-sĭn'ĭ-boin)	132-33	50°52'N	115°39'W
Assis, Braz. (ä-sê's)	168-69	22°40'S	50°26'W
Assomption, i., Sey.	264-65	9°44'S	46°30'E
As-Sūdān, nation, Afr. *see* Sudan	253	15°0'N	30°00'E
As-Sudd, reg., Sudan	262-63	8°0'N	31°00'E
As-Sulaymānīyah, Iraq	228-29	35°34'N	45°27'E
As-Sūrīyah, nation, Asia *see* Syria	206-07	35°0'N	38°00'E
As-Suwaydā', Syria	228-29	32°42'N	36°34'E
Astana, nat. cap., Kaz. (ä'stä-nä')	226	51°12'N	71°27'E
Astara, Azer.	227	38°28'N	48°52'E
Asterābād, Iran *see* Gorgān	232-33	36°51'N	54°26'E
Asti, Italy (äs'tē)	200-01	44°55'N	8°13'E
Astorga, Spain (äs-tôr'gä)	198-99	42°28'N	6°03'W
Astoria, Or., U.S. (ăs-tō'rĭ-ȧ)	112-13	46°11'N	123°50'W
Astove, i., Sey.	264-65	10°06'S	47°45'E
Astrakhan', Russia (äs-trȧ-kän')	186-87	46°21'N	48°02'E
Asunción, nat. cap., Para. (ä-sōōn-syōn')	168-69	25°16'S	57°39'W
Asuncion Island, i., N. Mar. Is.	280-81	19°42'N	145°24'E
Aswân, Egypt	268b	24°05'N	32°55'E
Aswan High Dam, d., Egypt	268b	23°59'N	32°53'E
Asyût, Egypt	268b	27°11'N	31°11'E
Atacama, Desierto de, des., Chile (dĕ-syĕ'r-tô-dĕ-ä-tä-kȧ'mä)	168-69	20°08'S	69°53'W
Atacama, Puna de, plat., S.A. (pōō'nä-dĕ-ä-tä-kȧ'mä)	168-69	23°46'S	67°45'W
Atacama, Salar de, pl., Chile (sȧ-lȧr'dĕ-ätä-kȧ'mä)	168-69	23°33'S	68°14'W
Atacama Desert, des., Chile (ä-tä-kȧ'mä) *see* Atacama, Desierto de	168-69	20°08'S	69°53'W
Ataco, Col. (ä-tá'kō)	163c	3°35'N	75°23'W
Atafu, at., Tok.	280-81	8°33'S	172°30'W
Atakpamé, Togo	260-61	7°32'N	1°09'E
Atamyrat, Turkmen.	232-33	37°50'N	65°13'E
Aṭar, Maur. (ä-tär')	258-59	20°32'N	13°02'W
Atascadero, Ca., U.S. (ăt-ăs-kȧ-dâ'rō)	118-19	35°30'N	120°39'W
Atasū, Kaz.	226	48°41'N	71°39'E
Atbara, stm., Afr. *see* 'Aṭbarah	266	17°40'N	33°58'E
'Aṭbarah, Sudan (ät'bȧ-rä)	266	17°42'N	33°59'E
'Aṭbarah, stm., Afr.	266	17°40'N	33°58'E
Atbasar, Kaz. (ät'bä-sär')	226	51°48'N	68°21'E
Atchafalaya, stm., La., U.S. (ăch-ȧ-fȧ-lī'ȧ)	124-25	29°28'N	91°16'W
Atchafalaya Bay, b., La., U.S. (ăch-ȧ-fȧ-lī'ȧ bă)	124-25	29°27'N	91°23'W
Atchara Autonomis Respublika, state, Geor.	227	41°40'N	42°00'E
Atchison, Ks., U.S. (ăch'ĭ-sŭn)	120-21	39°34'N	95°07'W
Athabasca, Ab., Can. (ăth-ȧ-băs'kȧ)	132-33	54°42'N	113°17'W
Athabasca, stm., Ab., Can. (ăth-ȧ-băs'kȧ)	130-31	58°40'N	110°55'W
Athabasca, Lake, lk., Can. (lāk ăth-ȧ-băs'kȧ)	130-31	59°07'N	109°59'W
Athens, Al., U.S. (ăth'ĕnz)	124-25	34°48'N	86°58'W
Athens, Ga., U.S. (ăth'ĕnz)	124-25	33°57'N	83°22'W
Athens, Oh., U.S. (ăth'ĕnz)	116-17	39°20'N	82°06'W
Athens, Tn., U.S. (ăth'ĕnz)	124-25	35°27'N	84°36'W
Athens, Tx., U.S. (ăth'ĕnz)	122-23	32°13'N	95°51'W
Athens, nat. cap., Grc. (ăth'ĕnz)	200-01	37°59'N	23°44'E
Atherton, Austl.	277	17°16'S	145°30'E
Athi, stm., Kenya (ä'tē)	262-63	2°58'S	38°31'E
Athína, nat. cap., Grc. (ä-thē'nĕ) *see* Athens	200-01	37°59'N	23°44'E
Athos, Mount, mtn., Grc.	200-01	40°09'N	24°19'E
Athy, Ire. (ȧ-thī)	190-91	52°60'N	6°59'W
Ati, Chad	258-59	13°12'N	18°19'E

PRONOUNCING INDEX

Atikokan – Bahía Blanca 307

Feature (Pronunciation)	Page	Lat.	Long.
Atikokan, On., Can.	136-37	48°45'N	91°37'W
Atikonak Lake, lk., Nf., Can.	130-31	52°38'N	64°30'W
Atiu, i., Cook Is.	280-81	20°02'S	158°07'W
Atka, Russia	218-19	60°45'N	151°46'E
Atka Island, i., Ak., U.S. (ăt'kȧ ī'lănd)	126a	52°15'N	174°08'W
Atkarsk, Russia (ăt-kärsk')	186-87	51°53'N	45°00'E
Atkinson, Ne., U.S. (ăt'kĭn-sŭn)	114-15	42°32'N	98°59'W
Atlanta, Ga., U.S. (ăt-lăn'tȧ)	124-25	33°46'N	84°25'W
Atlanta, Il., U.S. (ăt-lăn'tȧ)	116-17	40°16'N	89°14'W
Atlanta, Tx., U.S. (ăt-lăn'tȧ)	120-21	33°07'N	94°11'W
Atlantic, Ia., U.S. (ăt-lăn'tĭk)	114-15	41°24'N	95°01'W
Atlantic City, N.J., U.S. (ăt-lăn'tĭk sĭ'tē)	116-17	39°21'N	74°26'W
Atlantic Ocean, oc., (ăt-lăn'tĭk ōshŭn)	20-21	5°0'S	25°00'W
Atlantis, S. Afr.	264-65	33°32'S	18°29'E
Atlas Mountains, mts., Afr. (ăt'lăs moun'tĭnz)	258-59	33°0'N	2°00'W
Atlin, B.C., Can.	128-29	59°34'N	133°41'W
Atmore, Al., U.S. (ăt'mōr)	124-25	31°01'N	87°30'W
Atoka, Ok., U.S. (ȧ-tō'kȧ)	120-21	34°23'N	96°08'W
Atoui, Khaṭṭ, stm., Afr. (ȧ-tōō-ē')	258-59	20°03'N	15°58'W
Atoyac, stm., Mex. (ä-tō-yäk')	146-47	18°07'N	98°44'W
Atoyac de Álvarez, Mex. (ä-tō-yäk'dā äl'vä-rāz)	146-47	17°11'N	100°25'W
Atrak, stm., Asia	232-33	37°26'N	53°53'E
Atrato, stm., Col. (ä-trä'tō)	164-65	8°11'N	76°56'W
Atrek, stm., Asia *see* Atrak	232-33	37°26'N	53°53'E
Aṭ-Ṭā'if, Sau. Ar.	266	21°16'N	40°25'E
Attapu, Laos	246-47	14°48'N	106°51'E
Attawapiskat, On., Can.	128-29	52°56'N	82°25'W
Attawapiskat, stm., On., Can. (ăt'ȧ-wȧ-pĭs'kăt)	130-31	52°57'N	82°18'W
Attawapiskat Lake, lk., On., Can.	134-35	52°17'N	87°55'W
Attica, N.Y., U.S. (ăt'ĭ-kȧ)	116-17	42°52'N	78°17'W
Attleboro, Ma., U.S. (ăt''l-bŭr-ō)	116-17	41°57'N	71°17'W
Attu Island, i., Ak., U.S. (ăt-tōō' ī'lănd)	126a	52°55'N	173°00'E
Atuel, stm., Arg.	171	36°16'S	66°51'W
Åtvidaberg, Swe. (ôt-vē'dȧ-bĕrgh)	192-93	58°12'N	16°00'E
Atyraū, Kaz.	186-87	47°07'N	51°55'E
Aubagne, Fr. (ō-bän'y')	196-97	43°17'N	5°34'E
Aubry Lake, lk., N.T., Can.	130-31	67°22'N	126°27'W
Auburn, Al., U.S. (ô'bŭrn)	124-25	32°37'N	85°29'W
Auburn, Il., U.S. (ô'bŭrn)	120-21	39°35'N	89°45'W
Auburn, In., U.S. (ô'bŭrn)	116-17	41°22'N	85°03'W
Auburn, Ma., U.S. (ô'bŭrn)	116-17	42°12'N	71°50'W
Auburn, Ne., U.S. (ô'bŭrn)	120-21	40°23'N	95°51'W
Auburn, N.Y., U.S.	116-17	42°56'N	76°34'W
Auburn, Wa., U.S. (ô'bŭrn)	112-13	47°19'N	122°12'W
Aubusson, Fr. (ō-bü-sôn')	196-97	45°57'N	2°10'E
Auch, Fr. (ōsh)	196-97	43°39'N	0°35'E
Auckland, N.Z. (ôk'lănd)	278	36°51'S	174°45'E
Auckland Islands, is., N.Z. (ôk'lănd ī'lăndz)	287	50°46'S	166°12'E
Audubon, Ia., U.S. (ô'dō-bŏn)	114-15	41°43'N	94°56'W
Augathella, Austl. (ôr'gȧ'thĕ-lȧ)	276	25°48'S	146°34'E
Augrabies Falls National Park, n.p., S. Afr.	264-65	28°35'S	20°19'E
Augsburg, Ger. (ouks'bōrgh)	194-95	48°23'N	10°53'E
Augusta, Austl.	270-71	34°19'S	115°10'E
Augusta, Ar., U.S. (ô-gŭs'tȧ)	124-25	35°17'N	91°22'W
Augusta, Ga., U.S. (ô-gŭs'tȧ)	124-25	33°28'N	81°59'W
Augusta, Ky., U.S. (ô-gŭs'tȧ)	116-17	38°46'N	84°00'W
Augusta, Me., U.S.	117a	44°19'N	69°47'W
Augusta, Wi., U.S. (ô-gŭs'tȧ)	114-15	44°41'N	91°07'W
Augustus Island, i., Austl.	272-73	15°21'S	124°31'E
Auob, stm., Afr. (ä'wŏb)	264-65	26°26'S	20°37'E
Aurangābād, India (ou-rŭŋ-gä-bäd')	234-35	19°53'N	75°20'E
Aurillac, Fr. (ō-rē-yȧk')	196-97	44°55'N	2°26'E
Aurora, On., Can. (ô-rō'rȧ)	136-37	43°59'N	79°28'W
Aurora, Co., U.S. (ô-rō'rȧ)	120-21	39°44'N	104°52'W
Aurora, Il., U.S. (ô-rō'rȧ)	116-17	41°45'N	88°20'W
Aurora, In., U.S. (ô-rō'rȧ)	116-17	39°03'N	84°55'W
Aurora, Mn., U.S. (ô-rō'rȧ)	114-15	47°32'N	92°14'W
Aurora, Mo., U.S. (ô-rō'rȧ)	120-21	36°58'N	93°43'W
Aurora, Ne., U.S. (ô-rō'rȧ)	114-15	40°52'N	98°01'W
Au Sable, stm., Mi., U.S. (ô-sä'b'l)	116-17	44°24'N	83°19'W
Aussig, Czech Rep. *see* Ústí nad Labem	194-95	50°40'N	14°02'E
Austin, Mn., U.S. (ôs'tĭn)	114-15	43°40'N	92°58'W
Austin, Nv., U.S. (ôs'tĭn)	118-19	39°31'N	117°07'W
Austin, Tx., U.S. (ôs'tĭn)	122-23	30°16'N	97°42'W
Austin, Lake, lk., Austl.	272-73	27°40'S	118°00'E
Australia, nation, Oc. (ôs-trā'lĭ-ȧ)	270-71	25°0'S	135°00'E
Australian Capital Territory, state, Austl. (ôs-trā'lĭ-ăn)	276	35°30'S	149°00'E
Austral Islands, is., Fr. Poly. *see* Tubuaï, Îles	280-81	23°0'S	150°00'W
Austria, nation, Eur. (ôs'trĭ-ȧ)	174-75	47°20'N	13°20'E
Austvågøya, i., Nor.	184-85	68°21'N	14°38'E
Autlán de Navarro, Mex.	146-47	19°47'N	104°22'W
Autun, Fr. (ō-tŭn')	196-97	46°57'N	4°18'E
Auxerre, Fr. (ō-sâr')	196-97	47°48'N	3°34'E
Auyán Tepuy, mtn., Ven.	164-65	5°51'N	62°25'W
Auzangate, Nevado, mtn., Peru	170	13°48'S	71°14'W
Ava, Mo., U.S. (ā'vȧ)	120-21	36°57'N	92°40'W
Avallon, Fr. (ȧ-vȧ-lôn')	196-97	47°30'N	3°54'E
Avalon, Ca., U.S. (ăv'ȧ-lŏn)	118-19	33°20'N	118°19'W
Avaré, Braz.	172	23°07'S	48°55'W
Aveiro, Port. (ä-vā'rō)	198-99	40°38'N	8°39'W
Avellaneda, Arg. (ä-vĕl-yä-nä'dhä)	173	29°07'S	59°40'W
Avellaneda, Arg. (ä-vĕl-yä-nä'dhä)	173	34°40'S	58°23'W
Avellino, Italy (ä-vĕl-lē'nō)	200-01	40°55'N	14°47'E
Avesta, Swe. (ä-vĕs'tä)	192-93	60°09'N	16°11'E
Avezzano, Italy (ä-vät-sä'nō)	200-01	42°02'N	13°25'E
Avignon, Fr. (ȧ-vē-nyôn')	196-97	43°57'N	4°49'E
Ávila, Spain (ä-vē-lä)	198-99	40°40'N	4°42'W
Avilés, Spain (ä-vē-lās')	198-99	43°34'N	5°54'W
Avon, Ct., U.S. (ā'vŏn)	116-17	41°49'N	72°50'W
Avon, stm., Eng., U.K. (ā'vŭn)	190-91	50°44'N	1°47'W
Avon, stm., Eng., U.K. (ā'vŭn)	190-91	51°59'N	2°11'W
Avon Park, Fl., U.S. (ā'vŏn pärk')	125a	27°36'N	81°30'W
Avranches, Fr. (ȧ-vränsh')	196-97	48°41'N	1°22'W
Awaji-shima, i., Japan	245	34°21'N	134°51'E
Āwasa, Eth.	269d	6°56'N	38°32'E
Āwash, stm., Eth.	262-63	11°09'N	41°41'E
Awjilah, Libya	188-89	29°08'N	21°18'E
Axiós, stm., Eur.	200-01	40°31'N	22°43'E
Ax-les-Thermes, Fr. (äks'lā tĕrm')	196-97	42°43'N	1°51'E
Ayacucho, Arg. (ä-yä-kōō'chō)	173	37°09'S	58°29'W
Ayacucho, Peru	170	13°08'S	74°14'W
Ayaköz, Kaz.	226	47°57'N	80°26'E
Ayamonte, Spain (ä-yä-mō'n-tĕ)	198-99	37°13'N	7°24'W
Ayan, Russia (ȧ-yän')	218-19	56°26'N	138°13'E
Ayan, stm., Russia	218-19	70°10'N	95°47'E
Ayapel, Col.	164-65	8°19'N	75°09'W
Ayaviri, Peru (ä-yä-vē'rē)	170	14°53'S	70°35'W
Aydar, stm., Eur. (ī-där') *see* Aidar	202-03	48°44'N	39°16'E
Aydar Kŭl, lk., Uzb.	232-33	40°49'N	67°20'E
Ayden, N.C., U.S. (ā'dĕn)	124-25	35°28'N	77°25'W
Aydın, Tur. (āīy-dĕn)	200-01	37°51'N	27°50'E
Ayers Rock, mtn., Austl. *see* Uluru	272-73	25°20'S	130°60'E
Ayeyarwady, stm., Mya.	220-21	15°51'N	95°05'E
Aylesbury, Eng., U.K. (ālz'bĕr-ĭ)	190-91	51°49'N	0°50'W
Aylmer Lake, lk., N.T., Can. (āl'mēr lăk)	130-31	64°05'N	108°30'W
Ayon, Ostrov, i., Russia (ōs-trôf' ī-ôn')	218-19	69°47'N	168°41'E
Ayr, Austl.	277	19°34'S	147°24'E
Ayr, Scot., U.K. (âr)	190-91	55°28'N	4°38'W
Ayvalık, Tur. (āīy-wä-lĭk)	200-01	39°20'N	26°42'E
Azaouagh, stm., Afr.	258-59	15°30'N	3°18'E
Azärbaycan, nation, Asia *see* Azerbaijan	227	40°30'N	47°30'E
Azare, Nig.	260-61	11°41'N	10°11'E
Azemmour, Mor. (ȧ-zē-mōōr')	269a	33°18'N	8°21'W
Azerbaidzhan, nation, Asia *see* Azerbaijan	227	40°30'N	47°30'E
Azerbaijan, nation, Asia (ä'zĕr-bä-ē-jän')	227	40°30'N	47°30'E
Azogues, Ec. (ä-sō'gās)	170	2°44'S	78°50'W
Azores, is., Port. (ȧ'zōrz) (ȧ-zō'rĕz')	199c	38°30'N	28°00'W
Azov, Russia (ȧ-zôf') (ä-zôf)	202-03	47°07'N	39°26'E
Azov, Sea of, s., Eur. (sē ŭv ä-zôf')	202-03	46°0'N	36°00'E
Azovs'ke more, s., Eur. (ȧ-zôf'skō-yĕ mō'rĕ) *see* Azov, Sea of	202-03	46°0'N	36°00'E
Azovskoye More, s., Eur. *see* Azov, Sea of	202-03	46°0'N	36°00'E
Azraq, Al-Baḥr al-, stm., Afr. *see* Blue Nile	254	15°38'N	32°30'E
Azrou, Mor.	269a	33°26'N	5°12'W
Aztec, N.M., U.S. (ăz'tĕk)	118-19	36°49'N	108°00'W
Azua, Dom. Rep. (ä'swä)	142-43	18°27'N	70°44'W
Azuaga, Spain (ä-thwä'gä)	198-99	38°15'N	5°40'W
Azuero, Península de, pen., Pan.	150	7°40'N	80°35'W
Azul, Arg. (ä-sōōl')	173	36°47'S	59°52'W
Az-Zahrān, Sau. Ar. *see* Dhahran	230-31	26°18'N	50°08'E
Az-Zarqā', Jord.	228-29	32°03'N	36°05'E
Az-Zāwiyah, Libya	188-89	32°47'N	12°44'E
Az-Zilfī, Sau. Ar.	266	26°18'N	44°49'E
B			
Ba'qūbah, Iraq	228-29	33°45'N	44°40'E
Baaba, Île, i., N. Cal.	279g	20°03'S	163°58'E
Babadaýhan, Turkmen.	232-33	37°42'N	60°24'E
Babaeski, Tur. (bä'bä-ĕs'kĭ)	200-01	41°26'N	27°06'E
Babahoyo, Ec. (bä-bä-ō'yō)	170	1°48'S	79°32'W
Babar, Pulau, i., Indon. (pōō-lou bä'bár)	224-25	7°55'S	129°45'E
Babeldaob, i., Palau	280-81	7°30'N	134°35'E
Bab el Mandeb, strt.,	266	12°44'N	43°21'E
Babelthuap, i., Palau *see* Babeldaob	280-81	7°30'N	134°35'E
Babi, Pulau, i., Indon.	246-47	2°05'N	96°39'E
Babine Lake, lk., B.C., Can. (băb'ēn lăk)	132-33	54°45'N	126°00'W
Bābol, Iran	232-33	36°33'N	52°41'E
Babrujsk, Bela.	202-03	53°08'N	29°14'E
Babuyan Island, i., Phil.	250a	19°32'N	121°57'E
Babuyan Islands, is., Phil. (bä-bōō-yän' ī'lăndz)	250a	19°15'N	121°40'E
Bacabal, Braz.	166-67	4°14'S	44°47'W
Bacan, Pulau, i., Indon.	248-49	0°35'S	127°30'E
Bacău, Rom.	202-03	46°34'N	26°55'E
Bac Bo, Vinh, b., Asia *see* Tonkin, Gulf of	246-47	20°0'N	108°00'E
Back, stm., Nu., Can. (băk)	130-31	67°09'N	95°21'W
Bačka Palanka, Serb. (băch'kä pälän-kä)	200-01	45°15'N	19°24'E
Bac Lieu, Viet.	246-47	9°17'N	105°43'E
Bac Ninh, Viet. (băk'nĕn')	246-47	21°12'N	106°05'E
Baco, Mount, mtn., Phil. (mount bä'kō)	250	12°49'N	121°10'E
Bacolod, Phil. (bä-kō'lŏd)	250	10°40'N	122°57'E
Badajoz, Spain (bȧ-dhä-hōth')	198-99	38°53'N	6°58'W
Badalona, Spain (bä-dhä-lō'nä)	198-99	41°28'N	2°16'E
Bad Axe, Mi., U.S. (băd' ăks)	116-17	43°48'N	82°59'W
Baden-Baden, Ger. (bä'dĕn-bä'dĕn)	194-95	48°46'N	8°14'E
Bad Hersfeld, Ger. (bät hĕrsh'fĕlt)	194-95	50°52'N	9°42'E
Bad Kissingen, Ger. (bät kĭs'ĭng-ĕn)	194-95	50°12'N	10°05'E
Badlands, hills, U.S. (băd' lănds)	114-15	46°14'N	103°37'W
Badlands National Park, n.p., S.D., U.S. (băd' lănds năsh'ŭn-ăl pärk)	114-15	43°50'N	102°21'W
Bad Reichenhall, Ger. (bät rī'kĕn-häl)	194-95	47°44'N	12°53'E
Bad River Indian Reservation, ind. res., Wi., U.S. (băd rĭv'ĕr ĭn'dĭ-ăn rĕ-sĕr-vā'shĕn)	114-15	46°33'N	90°40'W
Bad Tölz, Ger. (bät tûltz)	194-95	47°45'N	11°35'E
Badu Island, i., Austl.	277	10°07'S	142°08'E
Baena, Spain (bä-ā'nä)	198-99	37°37'N	4°19'W
Bafatá, Gui.-B.	260-61	12°10'N	14°41'W
Baffin Bay, b., N.A. (băf'ĭn bā)	86	73°0'N	66°00'W
Baffin Bugt, b., N.A. *see* Baffin Bay	86	73°0'N	66°00'W
Baffin Island, i., Nu., Can. (băf'ĭn ī'lănd)	86	68°0'N	70°00'W
Bafia, Camrn.	260-61	4°45'N	11°16'E
Bafing, stm., Afr.	260-61	13°47'N	10°50'W
Bafoussam, Camrn.	260-61	5°29'N	10°25'E
Bāfq, Iran (bäfk)	232-33	31°35'N	55°24'E
Bafra, Tur. (bäf'rä)	186-87	41°34'N	35°53'E
Bafwasende, D.R.C.	262-63	1°06'N	27°16'E
Bagan, hist., Mya.	246-47	21°13'N	94°54'E
Bagansiapiapi, Indon.	246-47	2°09'N	100°48'E
Bagata, D.R.C.	262-63	3°44'S	17°59'E
Bagdad, nat. cap., Iraq *see* Baghdād	228-29	33°21'N	44°25'E
Bagé, Braz.	173	31°19'S	54°06'W
Baghdād, nat. cap., Iraq (bágh-däd') (băg'dăd)	228-29	33°21'N	44°25'E
Bagheria, Italy (bä-gȧ-rē'ä)	200-01	38°05'N	13°30'E
Baghlān, Afg.	232-33	36°08'N	68°42'E
Bagley, Mn., U.S. (băg'lē)	114-15	47°30'N	95°23'W
Bagnères-de-Bigorre, Fr. (băn-yâr'dē-bē-gor')	196-97	43°04'N	0°09'E
Bago, Mya.	246-47	17°20'N	96°29'E
Bagoé, stm., Afr. (bȧ-gō'ā)	260-61	12°35'N	6°34'W
Baguio, Phil. (bä-gē-ō')	250	16°25'N	120°36'E
Bahama, Canal Viejo de, strt., N.A. *see* Old Bahama Channel	142-43	22°40'N	78°41'W
Bahama Islands, is., Bah.	20-21	24°15'N	76°00'W
Bahamas, nation, N.A. (bȧ-hā'mȧs)	140-41	24°15'N	76°00'W
Baharampur, India	234-35	24°06'N	88°15'E
Bahāwalpur, Pak. (bŭ-hä'wŭl-pōōr)	232-33	29°23'N	71°40'E
Bäherden, Turkmen.	232-33	38°26'N	57°26'E
Bahia, Braz. (bä-ē'ä) *see* Salvador	166-67	12°59'S	38°30'W
Bahia, state, Braz.	166-67	12°0'S	42°00'W
Bahía, Islas de la, is., Hond. (ē's-läs-dĕ-lä-bä-ē'ä)	149	16°20'N	86°30'W
Bahía Blanca, Arg. (bä-ē'ä blăŋ'kä)	173	38°43'S	62°17'W

n-sing; ŋ-baŋk; N-nasalized n; nŏd; cŏmmit; ōld; ôbey; ôrder; oi-boil; fōōd; ô-as oo in foot; ou-out; s-soft; sh-dish; th-thin; pūre; ûnite; ûrn; stŭd; circŭs; ü-as in French tu; '-indeterminate vowel.

308 **Bahía de Caráquez – Baños** PRONOUNCING INDEX

Feature (Pronunciation)	Page	Lat.	Long.
Bahía de Caráquez, Ec. (bä-e'ä dä kä-rä'kĕz)	170	0°37'S	80°26'W
Bahir Dar, Eth.	266	11°35'N	37°24'E
Bahraich, India	234-35	27°35'N	81°36'E
Bahrain, nation, Asia (bä-rān')	230-31	26°0'N	50°30'E
Baḥrānī, Ḥālat al-, i., U.A.E.	230-31	24°28'N	54°21'E
Baia Mare, Rom. (bä'yä mä'rā)	194-95	47°39'N	23°35'E
Baicheng, China	240-41	45°37'N	122°51'E
Baidoa, Som.	262-63	3°07'N	43°39'E
Baie-Comeau, Qc., Can.	138-39	49°13'N	68°10'W
Baie-Saint-Paul, Qc., Can. (bā'săn'-pôl')	138-39	47°27'N	70°30'W
Baikal, Lake, lk., Russia (lăk bī-käl')	218-19	53°0'N	107°40'E
Baile Átha Cliath, nat. cap., Ire. *see* Dublin	190-91	53°21'N	6°15'W
Bailén, Spain (bä-ê-lān')	198-99	38°06'N	3°46'W
Băileşti, Rom. (bă-ī-lĕsh'tê)	200-01	44°02'N	23°21'E
Bailong, stm., China	238-39	32°21'N	105°43'E
Bainbridge, Ga., U.S. (bān'brĭj)	124-25	30°54'N	84°34'W
Bainbridge, Oh., U.S. (bān'brĭj)	116-17	39°14'N	83°16'W
Baiquan, China (bī-chyuän)	240-41	47°36'N	126°05'E
Baird, Tx., U.S. (bârd)	120-21	32°24'N	99°23'W
Bairin Zuoqi, China	240-41	43°59'N	119°23'E
Bairnsdale, Austl. (bârnz'dāl)	276	37°50'S	147°37'E
Baishuijiang, China	238-39	33°29'N	106°02'E
Baitou Shan, mtn., Asia *see* Paektu-san	243	41°59'N	128°07'E
Baiyin, China	240-41	36°33'N	104°12'E
Baja, Hung. (bŏ'yŏ)	194-95	46°11'N	18°57'E
Baja California, state, Mex. (bä-hä käl-ĭ-fôr'nĭ-á)	144-45	30°0'N	115°00'W
Baja California, pen., Mex. (bä-hä käl-ĭ-fôr'nĭ-á)	144-45	27°53'N	113°28'W
Baja California Norte, state, Mex. *see* Baja California	144-45	30°0'N	115°00'W
Baja California Sur, state, Mex. (bä-hä käl-ĭ-fôr'nĭ-á sōōr')	144-45	26°0'N	112°00'W
Bajestān, Iran	232-33	34°31'N	58°11'E
Bājil, Yemen	266	15°04'N	43°17'E
Bajo Boquete, Pan.	150	8°47'N	82°26'W
Baker, Ca., U.S. (bā'kẽr)	118-19	35°16'N	116°04'W
Baker, La., U.S. (bā'kẽr)	124-25	30°35'N	91°10'W
Baker, Mt., U.S. (bā'kẽr)	112-13	46°22'N	104°17'W
Baker, Or., U.S. (bā'kẽr)	112-13	44°47'N	117°50'W
Baker, Mount, vol., Wa., U.S. (mount bā'kẽr)	112-13	48°47'N	121°49'W
Baker Island, dep., Oc. (bā'kẽr ī'lǎnd)	280-81	0°15'N	176°27'W
Baker Island, i., Oc.	280-81	0°12'N	176°29'W
Baker Lake, Nu., Can.	128-29	64°18'N	95°55'W
Baker Lake, lk., Nu., Can. (bā'kẽr lăk)	130-31	64°10'N	95°30'W
Bakersfield, Ca., U.S. (bā'kẽrz-fēld)	118-19	35°22'N	119°01'W
Bakhmach, Ukr. (bak-mäch')	202-03	51°11'N	32°50'E
Bākhtarān, Iran *see* Kermānshāh	228-29	34°18'N	47°04'E
Bakhtegān, Daryācheh-ye, lk., Iran	230-31	29°20'N	54°05'E
Bakı, nat. cap., Azer. *see* Baku	227	40°23'N	49°51'E
Bakony, mts., Hung. (bá-kōn'y')	194-95	47°01'N	17°45'E
Bakoy, stm., Afr. (bá-kô'ê)	258-59	13°48'N	10°49'W
Baku, nat. cap., Azer. (bá-kōō')	227	40°23'N	49°51'E
Bakwanga, D.R.C. *see* Mbuji-Mayi	262-63	6°08'S	23°39'E
Balabac, Selat, strt., Asia *see* Balabac Strait	250	7°35'N	117°00'E
Balabac Island, i., Phil. (bä'lä-bäk ī'lǎnd)	250	7°57'N	117°01'E
Balabac Strait, strt., Asia (bä'lä-bäk strāt)	250	7°35'N	117°00'E
Balabanovo, Russia (bá-lá-bä'nô-vô)	202-03	55°11'N	36°40'E
Balabio, Île, i., N. Cal.	279g	20°07'S	164°11'E
Bālāghāt, India	234-35	21°49'N	80°11'E
Balaguer, Spain (bä-lä-gĕr')	198-99	41°48'N	0°49'E
Balakovo, Russia (bá'lá-kô'vô)	186-87	52°01'N	47°47'E
Balambangan, Pulau, i., Malay.	248-49	7°16'N	116°55'E
Balāngīr, India	234-35	20°43'N	83°30'E
Balaözen, stm., Eur.	186-87	48°58'N	49°38'E
Balashov, Russia (bá'lá-shôf)	186-87	51°32'N	43°10'E
Balasore, India (bä-lá-sōr') *see* Bāleshwar	234-35	21°29'N	86°57'E
Balassagyarmat, Hung. (bô'lôsh-shô-dyôr'môt)	194-95	48°04'N	19°19'E
Balaton, lk., Hung. (bô'lô-tôn)	194-95	46°50'N	17°45'E
Balayan, Phil. (bä-lä-yän')	250	13°57'N	120°44'E
Balbina, Represa, res., Braz.	166-67	1°20'S	59°40'W
Balcarce, Arg. (bäl-kär'sā)	173	37°51'S	58°15'W
Baldock Lake, lk., Mb., Can.	134-35	56°33'N	97°57'W
Baldwinsville, N.Y., U.S. (bôld'wĭns-vĭl)	116-17	43°10'N	76°20'W
Baldy Peak, mtn., Az., U.S. (bôl'dê pēk)	118-19	33°55'N	109°35'W
Bâle, Switz. *see* Basel	194-95	47°33'N	7°36'E
Baleares, Islas, is., Spain *see* Balearic Islands	198-99	39°29'N	3°01'E
Balearic Islands, is., Spain (băl-ē-ă'-rĭk ī'lǎndz)	198-99	39°29'N	3°01'E
Balears, Illes, is., Spain *see* Balearic Islands	198-99	39°29'N	3°01'E
Baler, Phil. (bä-lar')	250	15°46'N	121°34'E
Bāleshwar, India	234-35	21°29'N	86°57'E
Baley, Russia (bál-yā')	222-23	51°34'N	116°38'E
Bali, i., Indon. (bä'lê)	248-49	8°20'S	115°00'E
Bali, Laut, s., Indon. *see* Bali Sea	248-49	7°45'S	115°30'E
Balıkesir, Tur. (balĭk'ĭysĭr)	200-01	39°39'N	27°53'E
Balikpapan, Indon. (bä'lêk-pä'pän)	248-49	1°16'S	116°50'E
Balimo, Pap. N. Gui.	277	8°03'S	142°56'E
Balin, China	240-41	48°19'N	122°19'E
Balintang Channel, strt., Phil. (bä-lĭn-täng' chăn'ĕl)	250a	19°59'N	121°51'E
Bali Sea, s., Indon. (bä'lê sē)	248-49	7°45'S	115°30'E
Balkanabat, Turkmen	232-33	39°31'N	54°23'E
Balkan Peninsula, pen., Eur. (bôl'kǎn pĕ-nĭn'sūlă)	200-01	44°0'N	23°00'E
Balkaria, state, Russia	227	43°30'N	43°30'E
Balkh, Afg. (bälk)	232-33	36°45'N	66°54'E
Balkh, stm., Afg.	232-33	36°38'N	66°56'E
Balkhash, Kaz. *see* Balqash	226	46°51'N	74°58'E
Balkhash, Lake, lk., Kaz. (lăk bal-käsh')	226	46°0'N	74°00'E
Ballarat, Austl. (băl'á-răt)	276	37°34'S	143°51'E
Ballard, Lake, lk., Austl. (lăk băl'árd)	272-73	29°27'S	120°55'E
Ballia, India	234-35	25°45'N	84°09'E
Ballina, Austl. (băl-ĭ-nä')	276	28°52'S	153°33'E
Ballinasloe, Ire. (băl'ĭ-ná-slō')	190-91	53°20'N	8°14'W
Ballinger, Tx., U.S. (băl'ĭn-jẽr)	122-23	31°44'N	99°57'W
Ballston Spa, N.Y., U.S. (bôls'tǔn spä')	116-17	43°00'N	73°51'W
Balonne, stm., Austl. (băl-ōn')	276	28°37'S	148°10'E
Balqash, Kaz.	226	46°51'N	74°58'E
Balqash köli, lk., Kaz. *see* Balkhash, Lake	226	46°0'N	74°00'E
Balranald, Austl. (băl'-rán-ăld)	276	34°38'S	143°33'E
Balsas, Braz. (bäl'säs)	166-67	7°33'S	46°04'W
Balsas, stm., Braz.	166-67	7°14'S	44°34'W
Balsas, stm., Mex.	146-47	17°54'N	102°11'W
Balta, Ukr. (bál'tá)	202-03	47°56'N	29°40'E
Baltasar Brum, Ur.	173	30°42'S	57°19'W
Bălţi, Mol.	202-03	47°46'N	27°55'E
Baltic Sea, s., Eur. (bôl'tĭk sē)	192-93	57°0'N	19°00'E
Baltijas jūra, s., Eur. *see* Baltic Sea	192-93	57°0'N	19°00'E
Baltijos jūra, s., Eur. *see* Baltic Sea	192-93	57°0'N	19°00'E
Baltim, Egypt (bál-tēm')	268b	31°34'N	31°05'E
Baltimore, Md., U.S. (bôl'tĭ-môr)	116-17	39°17'N	76°37'W
Baltiysk, Russia (bál-tēysk')	194-95	54°39'N	19°55'E
Baltiyskoye More, s., Eur. *see* Baltic Sea	192-93	57°0'N	19°00'E
Bałtyckie, Morze, s., Eur. *see* Baltic Sea	192-93	57°0'N	19°00'E
Balūchestān, hist. reg., Asia *see* Baluchistan	232-33	28°0'N	63°00'E
Baluchistan, hist. reg., Asia	232-33	28°0'N	63°00'E
Baluchistān, hist. reg., Asia (bá-lò-chĭ-stän') *see* Baluchistan	232-33	28°0'N	63°00'E
Balykchy, Kyrg.	226	42°28'N	76°12'E
Balyqshy, Kaz.	186-87	47°05'N	51°54'E
Bam, Iran	230-31	29°07'N	58°21'E
Bama, Nig.	260-61	11°32'N	13°41'E
Bamako, nat. cap., Mali (bä-mä-kō')	258-59	12°39'N	7°60'W
Bambari, C.A.R. (bäm-bá-rē)	262-63	5°46'N	20°39'E
Bamberg, Ger. (bäm'bĕrgh)	194-95	49°54'N	10°54'E
Bamberg, S.C., U.S. (băm'bûrg)	124-25	33°18'N	81°02'W
Bamenda, Camrn.	260-61	5°58'N	10°09'E
Bāmīān, Afg.	232-33	34°50'N	67°49'E
Bamingui, stm., C.A.R.	262-63	8°34'N	19°04'E
Bamingui-Bangoran, Parc National du, n.p., C.A.R.	262-63	7°54'N	19°42'E
Bampūr, Iran (bŭm-pōōr')	230-31	27°11'N	60°26'E
Banaba, i., Kir.	280-81	0°52'S	169°33'E
Banaras, India *see* Vārānasi	234-35	25°20'N	82°59'E
Banās, stm., India (băn-äs')	234-35	25°55'N	76°44'E
Banâs, Râs, c., Egypt	266	23°54'N	35°47'E
Ban Bat, Viet.	246-47	13°13'N	108°40'E
Bancroft, On., Can. (băn'krŏft)	136-37	45°03'N	77°51'W
Bānda, India (bän'dä)	234-35	25°29'N	80°20'E
Banda, Laut, s., Indon. *see* Banda Sea	224-25	5°0'S	128°00'E
Banda Aceh, Indon.	246-47	5°33'N	95°19'E
Bandama, stm., C. Iv.	260-61	5°08'N	4°60'W
Bandar, India *see* Machilīpatnam	236	16°11'N	81°09'E
Bandar 'Abbās, Iran	230-31	27°11'N	56°16'E
Bandar Beheshtī, Iran	230-31	25°18'N	60°38'E
Bandar-e Anzalī, Iran	227	37°28'N	49°28'E
Bandar-e Khomeynī, Iran	228-29	30°26'N	49°06'E
Bandar-e Lengeh, Iran	230-31	26°34'N	54°53'E
Bandar-e Pahlavī, Iran *see* Bandar-e Anzalī	227	37°28'N	49°28'E
Bandar-e Shāhpūr, Iran *see* Bandar-e Khomeynī	228-29	30°26'N	49°06'E
Bandar-e Torkeman, Iran	232-33	36°54'N	54°04'E
Bandar Lampung, Indon.	246-47	5°26'S	105°16'E
Bandar Maharani, Malay. (bän-där' mä-hä-rä'nê) *see* Muar	246-47	2°02'N	102°34'E
Bandar Penggaram, Malay. *see* Batu Pahat	246-47	1°51'N	102°56'E
Bandar Seri Begawan, nat. cap., Bru. (bän'där sĕr'ē bŭ'gä-wän)	248-49	4°56'N	114°56'E
Banda Sea, s., Indon. (bän'-dä sē) (băn'-dä sē)	224-25	5°0'S	128°00'E
Bandeira, Pico da, mtn., Braz. (pē'kô dä bän dā'rä)	172	20°26'S	41°47'W
Bandelier National Monument, n.p., N.M., U.S. (băn-dĕ-lēr' năsh'ŭn-ăl mŏn'ŭ-mĕnt)	118-19	35°45'N	106°20'W
Bandera, Arg.	173	28°53'S	62°16'W
Banderas, Bahía de, b., Mex. (bä-ē'ä dĕ băn-dĕ'räs)	146-47	20°38'N	105°27'W
Bandiantaolehai, China	240-41	41°47'N	104°05'E
Bandırma, Tur. (bän-dĭr'má)	200-01	40°22'N	27°59'E
Ban Don, Thai. *see* Surat Thani	246-47	9°06'N	99°18'E
Bandon, Or., U.S. (băn'dŭn)	112-13	43°07'N	124°23'W
Bandundu, D.R.C.	262-63	3°16'S	17°21'E
Bandung, Indon.	248-49	6°54'S	107°36'E
Banes, Cuba (bä'nās)	142-43	20°58'N	75°42'W
Banff, Ab., Can. (bănf)	132-33	51°10'N	115°36'W
Banff National Park, n.p., Ab., Can. (bănf năsh'ŭn-ăl pärk)	132-33	51°38'N	116°22'W
Banfora, Burkina	260-61	10°39'N	4°45'W
Bangalore, India (băŋ'gá'lôr) *see* Bengalūru	236	12°59'N	77°36'E
Bangassou, C.A.R. (bäN-gá-sōō')	262-63	4°44'N	22°49'E
Banggai, Indon.	248-49	1°35'S	123°30'E
Banggai, Kepulauan, is., Indon. (bäng-gī')	248-49	1°30'S	123°15'E
Banggai, Pulau, i., Indon.	248-49	1°37'S	123°33'E
Banggi, Pulau, i., Malay.	248-49	7°16'N	117°10'E
Banggong Co, lk., Asia (bäŋ-gôŋ tswo) *see* Pangong Tso	234-35	33°45'N	78°42'E
Banghāzī, Libya (bĕn-gä'zē)	258-59	32°07'N	20°04'E
Bangka, Pulau, i., Indon. (pōō-lou bäŋ'ká)	246-47	2°15'S	106°00'E
Bangka, Selat, strt., Indon.	246-47	2°20'S	105°45'E
Bangkalan, Indon. (bäng-kà-län')	248-49	7°02'S	112°45'E
Bangkok, nat. cap., Thai. (băN'kŏk)	246-47	13°45'N	100°31'E
Bangkulu, Pulau, i., Indon.	248-49	1°50'S	123°06'E
Bangladesh, nation, Asia (bän'-glă-dĕsh')	206-07	24°0'N	90°00'E
Bangor, N. Ire., U.K. (băŋ'ŏr)	190-91	54°39'N	5°41'W
Bangor, Wales, U.K. (băŋ'ŏr)	190-91	53°14'N	4°09'W
Bangor, Me., U.S.	117a	44°48'N	68°47'W
Bangor, Mi., U.S. (băn'gẽr)	116-17	42°19'N	86°06'W
Bangor, Pa., U.S. (băn'gẽr)	116-17	40°51'N	75°13'W
Bangued, Phil. (bän-gād')	250	17°36'N	120°37'E
Bangui, nat. cap., C.A.R. (bäN-gē')	262-63	4°22'N	18°33'E
Bangweulu, Lake, lk., Zam. (lăk băng-wê-ōō'lōō)	264-65	11°04'S	29°53'E
Ban Hat Yai, Thai. *see* Hat Yai	246-47	7°01'N	100°28'E
Ban Houayxay, Laos	246-47	20°15'N	100°24'E
Baní, Dom. Rep. (bä'-nê)	142-43	18°17'N	70°19'W
Banifing, stm., Mali	260-61	14°29'N	4°13'W
Banja Luka, Bos. (bän-yä-lōō'kä)	200-01	44°46'N	17°12'E
Banjarbaru, Indon.	248-49	3°24'S	114°50'E
Banjarmasin, Indon. (bän-jẽr-mä'sĕn)	248-49	3°20'S	114°36'E
Banjul, nat. cap., Gam. (bôn-jōōl')	260-61	13°27'N	16°36'W
Banks, Îles, is., Vanuatu *see* Banks Islands	279g	13°25'S	167°42'E
Banks Island, i., B.C., Can. (bănks ī'lǎnd)	132-33	53°25'N	130°10'W
Banks Island, i., N.T., Can. (bănks ī'lǎnd)	86	73°15'N	121°30'W
Banks Islands, is., Vanuatu	279g	13°25'S	167°42'E
Banks Peninsula, pen., N.Z. (bănks pĕ-nĭn'sūlă)	278	43°45'S	173°00'E
Banks Strait, strt., Austl. (bănks strāt)	276	40°40'S	148°07'E
Banningville, D.R.C. *see* Bandundu	262-63	3°16'S	17°21'E
Bannu, Pak.	232-33	32°59'N	70°37'E
Baños, Ec. (bä'-nyōs)	170	1°24'S	78°25'W

ăt; finăl; rāte; senâte; ärm; ȧsk; sofá; fâre; ch-choose; dh-as th in other; bē; ėvent; bĕt; recĕnt; cratẽr; g-gō; gh-guttural g; bĭt; ĭ-short neutral; rīde; K-guttural k as ch in German ich;

PRONOUNCING INDEX
Bānswāra – Bayonne 309

Feature (Pronunciation)	Page	Lat.	Long.
Bānswāra, India	234-35	23°33'N	74°27'E
Bantaeng, Indon.	248-49	5°32'S	119°56'E
Bantayan Island, i., Phil.	250	11°13'N	123°44'E
Bantry, Ire. (băn'trĭ)	190-91	51°41'N	9°27'W
Banyak, Kepulauan, is., Indon.	246-47	2°10'N	97°15'E
Banyuwangi, Indon. (bän-jo̤-wäŋ'gē)	248-49	8°12'S	114°21'E
Baode, China	240-41	39°01'N	111°05'E
Baoding, China (bou-dĭŋ)	240-41	38°51'N	115°29'E
Baoji, China (bou-jyē)	238-39	34°23'N	107°09'E
Bao Lac, Viet.	246-47	11°33'N	107°47'E
Baoshan, China (bou-shän)	238-39	25°07'N	99°10'E
Baoting, China	238-39	18°38'N	109°47'E
Baotou, China (bou-tō)	240-41	40°35'N	109°58'E
Baoying, China (bou-yĭŋ)	238-39	33°14'N	119°19'E
Baquedano, Chile	168-69	23°20'S	69°50'W
Bar, Mont.	200-01	42°05'N	19°06'E
Baraboo, Wi., U.S. (bâr'ȧ-bōō)	116-17	43°28'N	89°44'W
Baracoa, Cuba (bä-rä-kō'ä)	142-43	20°21'N	74°30'W
Baradero, Arg. (bä-rä-dĕ'ō)	173	33°48'S	59°31'W
Baragaon, India *see* Nālanda	234-35	25°08'N	85°24'E
Barahona, Dom. Rep. (bä-rä-ō'nä)	142-43	18°12'N	71°06'W
Baranavičy, Bela.	194-95	53°08'N	26°01'E
Baranof Island, i., Ak., U.S. (bä-rä'nôf ī'lănd)	126	57°0'N	135°00'W
Barão de Melgaço, Braz. (bä-rouɴ-dĕ-mĕl-gä'sō)	168-69	16°13'S	55°58'W
Barat Daya, Kepulauan, is., Indon.	248-49	7°25'S	128°00'E
Baraya, Col. (bä-rà'yä)	163c	3°10'N	75°04'W
Barbacena, Braz. (bär-bä-sā'nȧ)	172	21°13'S	43°45'W
Barbacoas, Col. (bär-bä-kō'äs)	164-65	1°41'N	78°09'W
Barbados, nation, N.A. (bär-bā'dōz)	140-41	13°10'N	59°32'W
Barbas, Cap, c., W. Sah.	258-59	22°18'N	16°40'W
Barbastro, Spain (bär-bäs'trō)	198-99	42°02'N	0°08'E
Barberton, Oh., U.S. (bär'bēr-tŭn)	116-17	41°02'N	81°36'W
Barbosa, Col. (bär-bô'-sȧ)	163c	6°26'N	75°20'W
Barboursville, W.V., U.S. (bär'bērs-vĭl)	116-17	38°25'N	82°18'W
Barbuda, i., Antig. (bär-bōō'dȧ)	143b	17°38'N	61°48'W
Barcaldine, Austl. (bär'kôl-dīn)	277	23°34'S	145°18'E
Barce, Libya *see* Al-Marj	188-89	32°30'N	20°53'E
Barcelona, Spain (bär-thȧ-lō'nä)	198-99	41°24'N	2°10'E
Barcelona, Ven. (bär-sȧ-lō'nä)	163b	10°08'N	64°41'W
Barcelos, Braz. (bär-sĕ'lôs)	166-67	0°59'S	62°54'W
Barcelos, Port. (bär-thȧ'lōs)	198-99	41°32'N	8°37'W
Barcoo, stm., Austl.	277	25°12'S	142°50'E
Bardaï, Chad	258-59	21°22'N	16°59'E
Barddhamān, India	234-35	23°14'N	87°52'E
Bardsey Island, i., Wales, U.K. (bärd'sē ī'lănd)	190-91	52°46'N	4°48'W
Bardstown, Ky., U.S. (bärds'toun)	116-17	37°49'N	85°28'W
Bardwell, Ky., U.S. (bärd'wĕl)	124-25	36°52'N	89°01'W
Bareilly, India	234-35	28°21'N	79°25'E
Barentsevo More, s., Eur. *see* Barents Sea	218-19	74°0'N	36°00'E
Barentshavet, s., Eur. *see* Barents Sea	218-19	74°0'N	36°00'E
Barents Sea, s., Eur. (bä'rĕnts sē)	218-19	74°0'N	36°00'E
Barentu, Erit. (bä-rĕn'tōō)	266	15°07'N	37°35'E
Barfleur, Pointe de, c., Fr. (pwăɴt' dĕ bȧr-flûr')	196-97	49°42'N	1°16'W
Barguzin, stm., Russia	218-19	53°25'N	108°59'E
Bar Harbor, Me., U.S. (bär här'bēr)	117a	44°23'N	68°13'W
Bari, Italy (bä'rē)	200-01	41°07'N	16°52'E
Bariloche, Arg. *see* San Carlos de Bariloche	171	41°09'S	71°18'W
Barinas, Ven. (bä-rē'näs)	164-65	8°38'N	70°13'W
Baring, Cape, c., N.T., Can. (kāp bâr'ĭng)	130-31	70°03'N	117°16'W
Bāripada, India	234-35	21°56'N	86°43'E
Barisāl, Bngl.	234-35	22°42'N	90°22'E
Barito, stm., Indon. (bä-rē'tō)	248-49	3°20'S	114°32'E
Barkley, Lake, res., U.S.	124-25	36°44'N	87°57'W
Barkley Sound, strt., B.C., Can.	132-33	48°53'N	125°20'W
Barkly Tableland, plat., Austl. (bär'klē tā'-bĕl-lănd)	272-73	18°0'S	136°00'E
Barkol, China (bär-kûl)	240-41	43°33'N	93°02'E
Bar-le-Duc, Fr. (bär-lē-dük')	196-97	48°47'N	5°10'E
Barlee, Lake, lk., Austl. (lăk bär-lē')	272-73	29°10'S	119°30'E
Barletta, Italy (bär-lĕt'tä)	200-01	41°19'N	16°17'E
Bārmer, India	234-35	25°44'N	71°24'E
Barnaul, Russia (bär-nä-ōl')	218-19	53°22'N	83°45'E
Barnesville, Ga., U.S. (bärnz'vĭl)	124-25	33°03'N	84°10'W
Barnesville, Mn., U.S. (bärnz'vĭl)	114-15	46°39'N	96°25'W
Barnsley, Eng., U.K. (bärnz'lĭ)	190-91	53°34'N	1°29'W
Barnstaple, Eng., U.K. (bärn'stȧ-p'l)	190-91	51°05'N	4°03'W
Barnwell, S.C., U.S. (bärn'wĕl)	124-25	33°14'N	81°22'W
Baro, stm., Afr.	262-63	8°26'N	33°13'E
Baroda, India (bär-rō'dä) *see* Vadodara	234-35	22°18'N	73°11'E
Barpeta, India	234-35	26°19'N	91°00'E
Barqah, hist. reg., Libya *see* Cyrenaica	258-59	31°0'N	22°30'E
Barquisimeto, Ven. (bär-kē-sē-mā'tō)	164-65	10°05'N	69°19'W
Barra, Braz. (bär'rä)	166-67	11°05'S	43°09'W
Barra, Ponta da, c., Moz.	264-65	23°48'S	35°31'E
Barra do Corda, Braz. (bär'rä do̤ cōr-dä)	166-67	5°31'S	45°15'W
Barra Falsa, Ponta da, c., Moz.	264-65	22°54'S	35°34'E
Barra Mansa, Braz. (bär'rä män'sä)	172	22°33'S	44°10'W
Barranca, Peru	170	10°45'S	77°46'W
Barrancabermeja, Col. (bär-räŋ'kä-bēr-mā'hä)	164-65	7°04'N	73°51'W
Barrancas, Ven.	164-65	8°44'N	62°11'W
Barranquilla, Col. (bär-rän-kēl'yä)	164-65	10°59'N	74°48'W
Barras, Braz. (bȧ'r-räs)	166-67	4°15'S	42°18'W
Barre, Vt., U.S. (băr'ē)	116-17	44°12'N	72°30'W
Barreiras, Braz. (bär-rā'räs)	166-67	12°09'S	45°01'W
Barreiro, Port. (bär-rĕ'ê-ro̤)	198-99	38°39'N	9°04'W
Barreiros, Braz.	163d	8°49'S	35°12'W
Barren, Nosy, is., Madag.	264-65	18°30'S	43°53'E
Barretos, Braz. (bär-rā'tōs)	172	20°34'S	48°34'W
Barrhead, Ab., Can. (băr'hĕd)	132-33	54°07'N	114°24'W
Barrie, On., Can. (băr'ĭ)	136-37	44°23'N	79°41'W
Barrington Tops, mtn., Austl. (bă-rĕng-tŏn tŏps)	276	32°0'S	151°28'E
Barron, Wi., U.S. (băr'ŭn)	114-15	45°24'N	91°51'W
Barrow, Ak., U.S. (băr'ō)	126	71°18'N	156°38'W
Barrow, stm., Ire. (bȧ-rȧ)	190-91	52°17'N	7°00'W
Barrow, Point, c., Ak., U.S. (point băr'ō)	126	71°23'N	156°29'W
Barrow Creek, Austl.	270-71	21°31'S	133°55'E
Barrow Island, i., Austl.	272-73	20°48'S	115°23'E
Bārsi, India	236	18°14'N	75°42'E
Barstow, Ca., U.S. (bär'stō)	118-19	34°54'N	117°01'W
Bartica, Guy. (bär'tĭ-kȧ)	164-65	6°24'N	58°37'W
Bartın, Tur. (bär'tĭn)	186-87	41°38'N	32°21'E
Bartle Frere, mtn., Austl. (bärt''l frēr')	277	17°23'S	145°49'E
Bartlesville, Ok., U.S. (bär'tlz-vĭl)	120-21	36°45'N	95°59'W
Bartlett, Tn., U.S. (bärt'lĕt)	124-25	35°13'N	89°52'W
Bartlett, Tx., U.S. (bärt'lĕt)	122-23	30°48'N	97°26'W
Bartoszyce, Pol. (bär-tô-shĭ'tsȧ)	194-95	54°15'N	20°49'E
Bartow, Fl., U.S. (bär'tō)	125a	27°54'N	81°50'W
Bārū, stm., Afr. *see* Baro	262-63	8°26'N	33°13'E
Barú, Volcán, vol., Pan.	150	8°48'N	82°33'W
Baruun-Urt, Mong.	240-41	46°41'N	113°17'E
Barwon, stm., Austl. (bär'wŭn)	276	30°08'S	147°23'E
Barycz, stm., Pol. (bä'rĭch)	194-95	51°41'N	16°15'E
Barysau, Bela.	192-93	54°14'N	28°31'E
Barysh, Russia	186-87	53°39'N	47°07'E
Basankusu, D.R.C. (bä-sän-kōō'sōō)	262-63	1°13'N	19°48'E
Basarabia, hist. reg., Eur. *see* Bessarabia	202-03	46°53'N	28°44'E
Basco, Phil.	250a	20°27'N	121°58'E
Bascuñán, Cabo, c., Chile	168-69	28°52'S	71°29'W
Basel, Switz. (bä'z'l)	194-95	47°33'N	7°36'E
Basey, Phil.	250	11°18'N	125°04'E
Bashi Channel, strt., Asia (bäsh'ē chăn'ĕl)	222-23	22°0'N	121°00'E
Bashkortostan, state, Russia	186-87	54°0'N	56°00'E
Bashtanka, Ukr. (bȧsh-tän'kȧ)	202-03	47°24'N	32°27'E
Basilaki Island, i., Pap. N. Gui.	277	10°37'S	150°60'E
Basilan, Phil. *see* Isabela	250	6°41'N	121°58'E
Basilan Island, i., Phil.	250	6°34'N	122°03'E
Basin, Wy., U.S. (bā's'n)	112-13	44°23'N	108°03'W
Basingstoke, Eng., U.K. (bā'zĭng-stōk)	190-91	51°16'N	1°07'W
Başkale, Tur. (bäsh-kä'lĕ)	227	38°03'N	44°01'E
Baskatong, Réservoir, res., Qc., Can.	136-37	46°46'N	75°50'W
Basoko, D.R.C. (bȧ-sō'kō)	262-63	1°14'N	23°36'E
Bas Qafqaz Silsilasi, mts., *see* Caucasus Mountains	227	42°38'N	45°00'E
Basra, Iraq (bäs'-rä)	228-29	30°30'N	47°48'E
Bassano, Ab., Can. (bäs-sän'ō)	132-33	50°47'N	112°27'W
Bassein, Mya. *see* Pathein	246-47	16°46'N	94°44'E
Basse-Terre, i., Guad. (bäs' târ')	143b	16°10'N	61°40'W
Basse-Terre, nat. cap., Guad. (bäs' târ')	143b	16°00'N	61°43'W
Basseterre, nat. cap., St. K./N.	143b	17°18'N	62°44'W
Bassett, Ne., U.S. (băs'sĕt)	114-15	42°35'N	99°32'W
Bassett, Va., U.S. (băs'sĕt)	124-25	36°46'N	79°59'W
Bass Strait, strt., Austl. (băs strāt)	276	39°20'S	145°30'E
Båstad, Swe. (bô'stät)	192-93	56°25'N	12°52'E
Bastia, Fr. (bäs'tē-ä)	184-85	42°42'N	9°27'E
Bastrop, La., U.S. (băs'trŭp)	120-21	32°47'N	91°55'W
Bastrop, Tx., U.S. (băs'trŭp)	122-23	30°06'N	97°18'W
Basutoland, nation, Afr. *see* Lesotho	253	29°30'S	28°30'E
Bata, Eq. Gui. (bä'tä)	260-61	1°52'N	9°46'E
Batabanó, Golfo de, b., Cuba (gôl-fô-dĕ-bä-tä-bȧ'nô)	142-43	22°15'N	82°30'W
Batagay, Russia	218-19	67°40'N	134°40'E
Batagay-Alyta, Russia	218-19	67°48'N	130°25'E
Batala, India	234-35	31°49'N	75°13'E
Batang, China (bä-täŋ)	238-39	30°02'N	99°11'E
Batangafo, C.A.R.	262-63	7°19'N	18°18'E
Batangas, Phil. (bä-tän'gäs)	250	13°46'N	121°04'E
Batan Island, i., Phil.	250	13°15'N	124°00'E
Batan Island, i., Phil.	250a	20°27'N	121°59'E
Batan Islands, is., Phil. (bä-tän' ī'lăndz)	250a	20°30'N	121°50'E
Batanta, Pulau, i., Indon.	224-25	0°52'S	130°39'E
Batavia, Il., U.S. (bȧ-tā'vĭ-ȧ)	116-17	41°51'N	88°19'W
Batavia, Oh., U.S. (bȧ-tā'vĭ-ȧ)	116-17	39°05'N	84°11'W
Batavia, nat. cap., Indon. *see* Jakarta	248-49	6°11'S	106°50'E
Bataysk, Russia (bȧ-tīsk')	202-03	47°08'N	39°46'E
Bătdâmbâng, Camb. (bát-tȧm-bāng')	246-47	13°06'N	103°12'E
Batesville, Ar., U.S. (bāts'vĭl)	124-25	35°47'N	91°39'W
Batesville, In., U.S. (bāts'vĭl)	116-17	39°18'N	85°13'W
Batesville, Ms., U.S. (bāts'vĭl)	124-25	34°19'N	89°57'W
Bath, N.B., Can. (bȧth)	138-39	46°31'N	67°35'W
Bath, Eng., U.K. (bȧth)	190-91	51°23'N	2°22'W
Bathurst, Austl. (bȧth'ŭrst)	276	33°25'S	149°35'E
Bathurst, N.B., Can.	138-39	47°36'N	65°39'W
Bathurst, nat. cap., Gam. *see* Banjul	260-61	13°27'N	16°36'W
Bathurst, Cape, c., N.T., Can. (kāp bath'-ûrst)	130-31	70°35'N	128°00'W
Bathurst Island, i., Austl. (bȧth'ŭrst ī'lănd)	272-73	11°37'S	130°17'E
Batna, Alg. (bät'nä)	269b	35°34'N	6°11'E
Baton Rouge, La., U.S. (băt'ŭn rōōzh')	124-25	30°27'N	91°08'W
Battambang, Camb. *see* Bătdâmbâng	246-47	13°06'N	103°12'E
Batticaloa, Sri L.	236	7°43'N	81°42'E
Battle, stm., Can.	130-31	52°42'N	108°15'W
Battle Creek, Mi., U.S. (băt''l krēk')	116-17	42°19'N	85°11'W
Battle Creek, Ne., U.S. (băt''l krēk')	114-15	42°00'N	97°36'W
Battle Harbour, Nf., Can. (băt''l här'bēr)	128-29	52°16'N	55°35'W
Battle Mountain, Nv., U.S. (băt''l moun'tĭn)	112-13	40°39'N	116°55'W
Batu, mtn., Eth.	269d	6°55'N	39°46'E
Batu, Kepulauan, is., Indon. (bä'tōō)	246-47	0°18'S	98°28'E
Batuata, Pulau, i., Indon.	248-49	6°12'S	122°42'E
Batumi, Geor. (bŭ-tōō'mē)	227	41°39'N	41°39'E
Batu Pahat, Malay.	246-47	1°51'N	102°56'E
Baturaja, Indon.	246-47	4°08'S	104°09'E
Baturité, Braz.	166-67	4°20'S	38°53'W
Baubau, Indon.	248-49	5°28'S	122°37'E
Bauchi, Nig. (bȧ-ōō'chē)	260-61	10°19'N	9°50'E
Bauld, Cape, c., Nf., Can.	138-39	51°38'N	55°26'W
Bauru, Braz. (bou-rōō')	172	22°19'S	49°04'W
Bauska, Lat. (bou'skȧ)	192-93	56°24'N	24°14'E
Bautzen, Ger. (bout'sĕn)	194-95	51°11'N	14°26'E
Bavaria, hist. reg., Ger. (bȧ-vâ-rĭ-ȧ)	194-95	48°30'N	11°30'E
Bawdwin, Mya.	246-47	23°07'N	97°15'E
Bawean, Pulau, i., Indon. (pōō-lou bä'vē-än)	248-49	5°46'S	112°40'E
Bawiti, Egypt	188-89	28°21'N	28°52'E
Bawku, Ghana	260-61	11°04'N	0°15'W
Baxley, Ga., U.S. (băks'lĭ)	124-25	31°47'N	82°21'W
Bay, Laguna de, lk., Phil. (lä-gōō'nä dȧ bä'ē)	250	14°23'N	121°15'E
Bayamo, Cuba (bä-yä'mō)	142-43	20°23'N	76°38'W
Bayan Har Shan, mts., China	238-39	33°47'N	97°54'E
Bayanhongor, Mong.	240-41	46°10'N	100°42'E
Bayano, Lago, res., Pan.	150	9°12'N	78°44'W
Bayan Obo, China	240-41	41°59'N	110°08'E
Bayard, Ne., U.S. (bā'ērd)	114-15	41°46'N	103°20'W
Bayard, N.M., U.S. (bā'ērd)	118-19	32°46'N	108°08'W
Bayburt, Tur. (bä'ĭ-bo̤rt)	227	40°16'N	40°14'E
Bay City, Mi., U.S. (bā sĭ'tē)	116-17	43°36'N	83°53'W
Bay City, Tx., U.S. (bā sĭ'tĭ)	122-23	28°59'N	95°58'W
Baydhabo, Som. *see* Baidoa	262-63	3°07'N	43°39'E
Baydrag, stm., Mong.	240-41	45°37'N	99°15'E
Bayern, hist. reg., Ger. (bī'ĕrn) *see* Bavaria	194-95	48°30'N	11°30'E
Bayeux, Fr. (bȧ-yû')	196-97	49°17'N	0°42'W
Baykal, Ozero, lk., Russia *see* Baikal, Lake	218-19	53°0'N	107°40'E
Baykit, Russia (bī-kēt')	218-19	61°41'N	96°25'E
Baykonur, Kaz. *see* Bayqongyr	226	45°38'N	63°18'E
Bay Minette, Al., U.S. (bā'mĭn-ĕt')	124-25	30°53'N	87°47'W
Bayombong, Phil. (bä-yōm-bŏng')	250	16°29'N	121°09'E
Bayonne, Fr. (bȧ-yŏn')	196-97	43°30'N	1°29'W
Bayonne, N.J., U.S. (bā-yōn')	116-17	40°40'N	74°07'W

n-sing; ŋ-baŋk; ɴ-nasalized n; nŏd; cŏmmit; ōld; ôbey; ôrder; oi-boil; fōōd; ŏŏ-as oo in foot; ou-out; s-soft; sh-dish; th-thin; pūre; ûnite; ûrn; stŭd; circŭs; ü-as in French tu; '-indeterminate vowel.

310 Bayou Bodcau Reservoir – Berdigestyakh PRONOUNCING INDEX

Feature (Pronunciation)	Page	Lat.	Long.
Bayou Bodcau Reservoir, res., La., U.S. (bī′yōō bŏd′kō rĕ′sẽr-vwär)	120-21	32°48′N	93°27′W
Bayqongyr, Kaz.	226	45°38′N	63°18′E
Bayram-Ali, Turkmen.	232-33	37°37′N	62°10′E
Bayreuth, Ger. (bī-roit′)	194-95	49°57′N	11°34′E
Bay Roberts, Nf., Can. (bā rŏb′ẽrts)	138-39	47°35′N	53°18′W
Bayrūt, nat. cap., Leb. *see* Beirut	228-29	33°53′N	35°30′E
Bays, Lake of, lk., On., Can. (lāk ŭv bās)	136-37	45°15′N	78°60′W
Bay Saint Louis, Ms., U.S. (bā′ sānt lōō′ĭs)	124-25	30°19′N	89°20′W
Bayt Laḥm, W.B. *see* Bethlehem	228-29	31°43′N	35°12′E
Baytown, Tx., U.S. (bā′town)	122-23	29°44′N	94°59′W
Baza, Spain (bä′thä)	198-99	37°29′N	2°46′W
Bazaruto, Ilha do, i., Moz. (ē′lä-dô-bä-zä-rōō′tō)	264-65	21°41′S	35°28′E
Be, Nosy, i., Madag.	264-65	13°20′S	48°15′E
Beach, N.D., U.S. (bēch)	114-15	46°55′N	104°00′W
Beachy Head, c., Eng., U.K. (bēchē hĕd)	190-91	50°45′N	0°15′E
Beacon, N.Y., U.S. (bē′kŭn)	116-17	41°31′N	73°58′W
Beagle Gulf, b., Austl.	272-73	12°0′S	130°20′E
Beardmore, On., Can.	134-35	49°36′N	87°58′W
Beardstown, Il., U.S. (bērds′toun)	120-21	40°01′N	90°26′W
Bear Island, i., Nor. (bâr ī′lănd) *see* Bjørnøya	218-19	74°27′N	19°02′E
Bear Lake, lk., Mb., Can. (bâr lāk)	134-35	55°08′N	96°00′W
Bear Lake, lk., U.S. (bâr lāk)	112-13	42°0′N	111°20′W
Bear River Range, mts., U.S. (bâr rĭv′ẽr rānj)	112-13	41°29′N	111°41′W
Beata, Cabo, c., Dom. Rep. (kä′bô-bĕ-ä′tä)	142-43	17°37′N	71°25′W
Beata, Isla, i., Dom. Rep.	142-43	17°35′N	71°31′W
Beatrice, Ne., U.S. (bē′ă-trĭs)	120-21	40°16′N	96°45′W
Beatton, stm., B.C., Can.	132-33	56°05′N	120°22′W
Beatty, Nv., U.S. (bēt′ē)	118-19	36°55′N	116°45′W
Beattyville, Ky., U.S. (bēt′ē-vĭl)	116-17	37°34′N	83°43′W
Beaucaire, Fr. (bō-kâr′)	196-97	43°48′N	4°39′E
Beaufort, Malay.	248-49	5°22′N	115°44′E
Beaufort, N.C., U.S. (bō′fōrt)	124-25	34°43′N	76°40′W
Beaufort, S.C., U.S. (bō′fōrt)	124-25	32°24′N	80°44′W
Beaufort Sea, s., N.A. (bō′fōrt sē)	86	73°0′N	140°00′W
Beaufort West, S. Afr.	264-65	32°21′S	22°35′E
Beaumont, Tx., U.S. (bō′mŏnt)	122-23	30°05′N	94°08′W
Beaune, Fr. (bōn)	196-97	47°01′N	4°50′E
Beauport, Qc., Can. (bō-pôr′)	136-37	46°52′N	71°10′W
Beaupré, Qc., Can.	138-39	47°03′N	70°54′W
Beausejour, Mb., Can.	134-35	50°04′N	96°31′W
Beauvais, Fr. (bō-vĕ′)	196-97	49°26′N	2°05′E
Beaver, Ok., U.S. (bē′vẽr)	120-21	36°49′N	100°31′W
Beaver, Ut., U.S. (bē′vẽr)	118-19	38°17′N	112°38′W
Beaver, stm., Can.	130-31	55°26′N	107°47′W
Beaver Dam, Wi., U.S. (bē′vẽr dăm)	116-17	43°27′N	88°50′W
Beaverhead Mountains, mts., U.S. (bē′vẽr-hĕd moun′tĭnz)	112-13	44°58′N	113°26′W
Beaver Island, i., Mi., U.S. (bē′vẽr ī′lănd)	116-17	45°40′N	85°32′W
Beaverton, Or., U.S. (bē′vẽr-tŭn)	112-13	45°29′N	122°49′W
Beāwar, India	234-35	26°06′N	74°19′E
Bečej, Serb. (bĕc′chā)	200-01	45°37′N	20°03′E
Béchar, Alg.	258-59	31°37′N	2°14′W
Bechuanaland, nation, Afr. *see* Botswana	253	22°0′S	24°00′E
Beckley, W.V., U.S. (bĕk′lĭ)	116-17	37°48′N	81°11′W
Bedford, Qc., Can. (bĕd′fẽrd)	136-37	45°07′N	72°59′W
Bedford, In., U.S. (bĕd′fẽrd)	116-17	38°51′N	86°29′W
Bedford, Va., U.S. (bĕd′fẽrd)	124-25	37°20′N	79°31′W
Beebe, Ar., U.S. (bē′bē)	124-25	35°04′N	91°53′W
Beecroft Head, c., Austl. (bē′krŭft hĕd)	276	35°00′S	150°51′E
Beersheba, Isr.	228-29	31°14′N	34°48′E
Be'er Sheva', Isr. (bẽr-shē′bȧ) *see* Beersheba	228-29	31°14′N	34°48′E
Beeville, Tx., U.S. (bē′vĭl)	122-23	28°24′N	97°45′W
Bega, Austl. (bā′gă)	276	36°41′S	149°51′E
Beggs, Ok., U.S. (bĕgz)	120-21	35°45′N	96°05′W
Behbahān, Iran	230-31	30°35′N	50°14′E
Bei, stm., China (bā)	238-39	23°09′N	112°49′E
Bei'an, China (bā-än)	240-41	48°14′N	126°31′E
Beibu Wan, b., Asia *see* Tonkin, Gulf of	246-47	20°0′N	108°00′E
Beida, Libya *see* Al-Bayḍā'	188-89	32°45′N	21°37′E
Beihai, China (bā-hī)	238-39	21°27′N	109°05′E
Beijing, state, China	240-41	40°15′N	116°30′E
Beijing, nat. cap., China (bā-jyĭŋ)	240-41	39°55′N	116°22′E
Beipan, stm., China	238-39	25°01′N	106°04′E
Beipiao, China	240-41	41°48′N	120°46′E
Beira, Moz. (bā′rȧ)	264-65	19°50′S	34°50′E
Beirut, nat. cap., Leb. (bā-rōōt′)	228-29	33°53′N	35°30′E
Beitbridge, Zimb.	264-65	22°12′S	30°01′E
Beja, Port. (bā′zhä)	198-99	38°01′N	7°52′W
Béja, Tun.	184-85	36°44′N	9°11′E
Bejaïa, Alg.	269b	36°45′N	5°04′E
Bejuco, Pan. (bĕ-κōō′kō)	150	8°36′N	79°53′W
Bekdash, Turkmen. *see* Karabogaz	186-87	41°32′N	52°35′E
Békés, Hung. (bā′kāsh)	194-95	46°46′N	21°08′E
Békéscsaba, Hung. (bā′kāsh-chô′bô)	194-95	46°40′N	21°05′E
Bekobod, Uzb.	232-33	40°13′N	69°11′E
Bela, Pak.	232-33	26°13′N	66°18′E
Bela-Bela, S. Afr.	269c	24°53′S	28°19′E
Bela Crkva, Serb. (bĕ′lä tsĕrk′vä)	200-01	44°54′N	21°26′E
Belaga, Malay.	248-49	2°43′N	113°47′E
Belarus, nation, Eur. (byĭ-lă-rōōs′) (bĕ-lă-rōōs′)	174-75	53°50′N	28°00′E
Belau, nation, Oc. *see* Palau	280-81	5°0′N	137°00′E
Bela Vista, Braz.	168-69	22°06′S	56°32′W
Belaya, stm., Russia (byĕ′lá-yȧ)	227	45°06′N	39°29′E
Belaya, stm., Russia (byĕ′lá-yȧ)	186-87	55°47′N	54°04′E
Belaya Tserkov, Ukr. *see* Bila Tserkva	202-03	49°48′N	30°08′E
Belcher Islands, is., Nu., Can. (bĕl′chẽr ī′lăndz)	130-31	56°20′N	79°30′W
Belding, Mi., U.S. (bĕl′dĭng)	116-17	43°06′N	85°13′W
Belebey, Russia (byĕ′lĕ-bā′ĭ)	186-87	54°06′N	54°08′E
Belém, Braz. (bĕ-lĕɴ)	166-67	1°27′S	48°29′W
Belén, Para. (bā-lān′)	168-69	23°28′S	57°15′W
Belen, N.M., U.S. (bĕ-lăn′)	118-19	34°40′N	106°46′W
Belëv, Russia (byĕl′yĕf)	202-03	53°48′N	36°09′E
Belfast, S. Afr.	269c	25°43′S	30°04′E
Belfast, N. Ire., U.K. (bĕl′făst)	190-91	54°36′N	5°56′W
Belfort, Fr. (bā-fôr′)	196-97	47°38′N	6°51′E
Belgaum, India	236	15°51′N	74°31′E
België, nation, Eur. *see* Belgium	174-75	50°50′N	4°00′E
Belgique, nation, Eur. *see* Belgium	174-75	50°50′N	4°00′E
Belgium, nation, Eur. (bĕl′jĭ-ŭm)	174-75	50°50′N	4°00′E
Belgorod, Russia (byĕl′gŭ-rŭt)	202-03	50°37′N	36°35′E
Belgrade, nat. cap., Serb. (bĕl′grād)	200-01	44°50′N	20°28′E
Belhaven, N.C., U.S. (bĕl′hā-vĕn)	124-25	35°32′N	76°37′W
Beliliou, i., Palau	280-81	7°00′N	134°15′E
Belitung, i., Indon.	246-47	2°50′S	107°55′E
Belize, nation, N.A. (bĕ-lēz′)	85	17°15′N	88°45′W
Belize, stm., Belize (bĕ-lēz′)	148	17°30′N	88°11′W
Belize City, Belize (bĕ-lēz′ sĭ′tē)	148	17°30′N	88°11′W
Bel'kovskiy, Ostrov, i., Russia (ôs-trôf′ byĕl-kôf′skĭ)	218-19	75°32′N	135°44′E
Bella Bella, B.C., Can.	132-33	52°09′N	128°07′W
Bella Coola, B.C., Can.	132-33	52°21′N	126°46′W
Bellary, India (bĕl-lä′rē)	236	15°09′N	76°55′E
Bella Unión, Ur. (bĕ′l-yä-ōō-nyô′n)	173	30°15′S	57°35′W
Bella Vista, Arg. (bā′lyȧ vēs′tȧ)	168-69	27°02′S	65°18′W
Bella Vista, Arg. (bā′lyȧ vēs′tȧ)	173	28°30′S	59°02′W
Bellavista, Peru	170	7°04′S	76°35′W
Belle Bay, b., Nf., Can. (bĕl bā)	138-39	47°36′N	55°18′W
Bellefontaine, Oh., U.S. (bel-fŏn′tăn)	116-17	40°21′N	83°45′W
Belle Fourche, S.D., U.S. (bĕl′ fōōrsh′)	114-15	44°40′N	103°51′W
Belle Glade, Fl., U.S. (bĕl glād)	125a	26°42′N	80°40′W
Belle Isle, Strait of, strt., Nf., Can.	130-31	51°36′N	56°28′W
Belle Plaine, Ia., U.S. (bĕl plān′)	114-15	41°54′N	92°17′W
Belleville, On., Can. (bĕl′vĭl)	136-37	44°10′N	77°23′W
Belleville, Il., U.S. (bĕl′vĭl)	120-21	38°31′N	89°59′W
Belleville, Ks., U.S. (bĕl′vĭl)	120-21	39°49′N	97°38′W
Bellevue, Ia., U.S. (bĕl′vū)	114-15	42°15′N	90°25′W
Bellevue, Id., U.S. (bĕl′vū)	112-13	43°28′N	114°16′W
Bellevue, Ne., U.S. (bĕl′vū)	114-15	41°09′N	95°55′W
Bellevue, Oh., U.S. (bĕl′vū)	116-17	41°16′N	82°50′W
Bellevue, Wa., U.S. (bĕl′vū)	112-13	47°37′N	122°12′W
Belley, Fr. (bĕ-lē′)	196-97	45°46′N	5°41′E
Bellingham, Wa., U.S. (bĕl′ĭng-hăm)	112-13	48°46′N	122°29′W
Bellingshausen Sea, s., Ant. (bĕl′ĭngz houz′n sē)	287	71°0′S	85°00′W
Bellinzona, Switz. (bĕl-ĭn-tsō′nä)	194-95	46°11′N	9°01′E
Bell Island, i., Nf., Can. (bĕl ī′lănd)	138-39	50°44′N	55°35′W
Bello, Col. (bĕ′l-yō)	163c	6°20′N	75°34′W
Bell Peninsula, pen., Nu., Can. (bĕl pĕ-nĭn′sūlă)	130-31	63°50′N	81°60′W
Belluno, Italy (bĕl-lōō′nō)	200-01	46°09′N	12°13′E
Bell Ville, Arg. (bĕl vēl′)	173	32°39′S	62°41′W
Belmond, Ia., U.S. (bĕl′mŏnd)	114-15	42°51′N	93°37′W
Belmonte, Braz. (bĕl-mōn′tȧ)	168-69	15°54′S	38°53′W
Belmopan, nat. cap., Belize (bĕl-mō-pän′)	148	17°14′N	88°47′W
Belogorsk, Russia	222-23	50°54′N	128°30′E
Belo Horizonte, Braz. (bĕ′lôre-sô′n-tĕ)	172	19°55′S	43°56′W
Beloit, Ks., U.S. (bĕ-loit′)	120-21	39°27′N	98°06′W
Beloit, Wi., U.S. (bĕ-loit′)	116-17	42°31′N	89°02′W
Belomorsk, Russia (byĕl-ô-môrsk′)	186-87	64°32′N	34°45′E
Belorechensk, Russia	186-87	44°46′N	39°52′E
Beloretsk, Russia (byĕ′lō-rĕtsk)	226	53°58′N	58°24′E
Belorussia, nation, Eur. *see* Belarus	174-75	53°50′N	28°00′E
Belorussiya, nation, Eur. *see* Belarus	174-75	53°50′N	28°00′E
Belo Tsiribihina, Madag.	264-65	19°42′S	44°33′E
Belovo, Russia (bvĕ′lŭ-vŭ)	218-19	54°25′N	86°19′E
Beloye, Ozero, lk., Russia	186-87	60°11′N	37°37′E
Beloye More, s., Russia *see* White Sea	186-87	65°37′N	37°52′E
Beloz'orsk, Russia	186-87	60°02′N	37°48′E
Belton, Mo., U.S. (bĕl′tŭn)	120-21	38°48′N	94°32′W
Belton, Tx., U.S. (bĕl′tŭn)	122-23	31°03′N	97°27′W
Belts, Mol. *see* Bălţi	202-03	47°46′N	27°55′E
Beltsy, Mol. *see* Bălţi	202-03	47°46′N	27°55′E
Belukha, Gora, mtn., Asia *see* Belukha, Mount	226	49°51′N	86°29′E
Belukha, Mount, mtn., Asia (mount byĭ-lōō′-khŭ)	226	49°51′N	86°29′E
Belvidere, Il., U.S. (bĕl-vĕ-dēr′)	116-17	42°15′N	88°49′W
Belzoni, Ms., U.S. (bĕl-zō′nē)	124-25	33°11′N	90°29′W
Bembézar, stm., Spain (bĕm-bā-thär′)	198-99	37°45′N	5°12′W
Bemidji, Mn., U.S. (bĕ-mĭj′ĭ)	114-15	47°29′N	94°54′W
Benalla, Austl. (bĕn-ăl′ȧ)	276	36°33′S	145°59′E
Benares, India *see* Vārānasi	234-35	25°20′N	82°59′E
Benavente, Spain (bā-nä-vĕn′tā)	198-99	42°00′N	5°40′W
Bend, Or., U.S. (bĕnd)	112-13	44°04′N	121°18′W
Bender, Mol. *see* Tighina	202-03	46°50′N	29°29′E
Bender Cassim, Som.	262-63	11°17′N	49°11′E
Bendery, Mol. *see* Tighina	202-03	46°50′N	29°29′E
Bendigo, Austl. (bĕn′dĭ-gō)	276	36°46′S	144°17′E
Benedito Leite, Braz.	166-67	7°13′S	44°34′W
Benešov, Czech Rep. (bĕn′ĕ-shôf)	194-95	49°47′N	14°43′E
Benevento, Italy (bā-nā-vĕn′tō)	200-01	41°08′N	14°46′E
Bengal, Bay of, b., Asia (bā ŭv bĕn-gôl′)	220-21	15°0′N	90°00′E
Bengalūru, India	236	12°59′N	77°36′E
Bengbu, China (bŭŋ-bōō)	238-39	32°57′N	117°21′E
Bengkulu, Indon.	246-47	3°48′S	102°16′E
Benguela, Ang. (bĕn-gĕl′ȧ)	264-65	12°35′S	13°25′E
Beni, D.R.C.	267	0°30′N	29°28′E
Beni, stm., Bol. (bā′nē)	166-67	10°59′S	66°07′W
Beni Abbes, Alg.	188-89	30°08′N	2°10′W
Beni Mazâr, Egypt	268b	28°29′N	30°48′E
Beni-Mellal, Mor.	269a	32°21′N	6°22′W
Benin, nation, Afr. (bĕn-ēn′)	253	9°30′N	2°15′E
Benin, stm., Nig. (bĕn-ēn′)	260a	5°45′N	5°04′E
Benin, Bight of, b., Afr. (bĭt ŭv bĕn-ēn′)	260-61	5°30′N	3°00′E
Bénin, Golfe de, b., Afr. *see* Benin, Bight of	260-61	5°30′N	3°00′E
Benin City, Nig. (bĕn-ēn′ sĭ′tē)	260a	6°20′N	5°38′E
Beni Saf, Alg. (bā′nē sāf′)	198-99	35°18′N	1°23′W
Beni Suef, Egypt	268b	29°04′N	31°06′E
Benito Juárez, Arg.	173	37°41′S	59°48′W
Benjamín, Isla, i., Chile	171	44°40′S	74°08′W
Benjamin Constant, Braz.	166-67	4°28′S	70°01′W
Benkelman, Ne., U.S. (bĕn-kĕl-măn)	120-21	40°03′N	101°32′W
Bennetta, Ostrov, i., Russia	218-19	76°41′N	149°06′E
Bennettsville, S.C., U.S. (bĕn′ĕts vĭl)	124-25	34°37′N	79°41′W
Benoni, S. Afr. (bĕ-nō′nī)	269c	26°11′S	28°19′E
Bénoué, stm., Afr.	260-61	7°48′N	6°46′E
Benson, Az., U.S. (bĕn-sŭn)	118-19	31°58′N	110°18′W
Benson, Mn., U.S. (bĕn-sŭn)	114-15	45°19′N	95°36′W
Bentinck Island, i., Austl.	277	17°04′S	139°30′E
Benton, Ar., U.S. (bĕn′tŭn)	120-21	34°34′N	92°36′W
Benton, Il., U.S. (bĕn′tŭn)	116-17	37°60′N	88°55′W
Benton, Ky., U.S. (bĕn′tŭn)	124-25	36°52′N	88°21′W
Benton, La., U.S. (bĕn′tŭn)	120-21	32°42′N	93°45′W
Benton Harbor, Mi., U.S. (bĕn′tŭn här′bẽr)	116-17	42°06′N	86°28′W
Bentonville, Ar., U.S. (bĕn′tŭn-vĭl)	120-21	36°22′N	94°12′W
Benue, stm., Afr. (bā′nōō-â)	260-61	7°48′N	6°46′E
Benxi, China (bŭn-shyē)	243	41°18′N	123°45′E
Beograd, nat. cap., Serb. (bĕ-ō′gräd) *see* Belgrade	200-01	44°50′N	20°28′E
Beppu, Japan (bĕ′pōō)	245	33°17′N	131°30′E
Bequia, i., St. Vin. (bĕk-ē′ä)	143b	13°02′N	61°13′W
Berau, Teluk, b., Indon.	224-25	2°30′S	132°30′E
Berbera, Som. (bûr′bûr-ȧ)	262-63	10°26′N	45°01′E
Berbérati, C.A.R.	262-63	4°14′N	15°48′E
Berbice, stm., Guy.	164-65	6°15′N	57°32′W
Berck, Fr. (bĕrk)	196-97	50°25′N	1°35′E
Berdians'k, Ukr.	202-03	46°45′N	36°49′E
Berdigestyakh, Russia	218-19	62°06′N	126°41′E

ăt; finăl; rāte; senâte; ärm; ȧsk; sofȧ; fâre; ch-choose; dh-as th in other; bē; ēvent; bĕt; recĕnt; cratẽr; g-gō; gh-guttural g; bĭt; ĭ-short neutral; rīde; κ-guttural k as ch in German ich;

n-sing; ŋ-baŋk; ɴ-nasalized n; nŏd; cŏmmit; ōld; ôbey; ôrder; oi-boil; fōōd; ò-as oo in foot; ou-out; s-soft; sh-dish; th-thin; pūre; ūnite; ûrn; stŭd; circŭs; ü-as in French tu; ′-indeterminate vowel.

312 Bissau – Boonville PRONOUNCING INDEX

Feature (Pronunciation)	Page	Lat.	Long.
Bissau, nat. cap., Gui.-B. (bė-sa'o͞o)	260-61	11°52'N	15°36'W
Bissett, Mb., Can.	134-35	51°02'N	95°40'W
Bistcho Lake, lk., Ab., Can.	130-31	59°44'N	118°46'W
Bistineau, Lake, res., La., U.S. (lăk bĭs-tĭ-nō')	120-21	32°25'N	93°22'W
Bistrița, Rom. (bĭs-trĭt-sȧ)	194-95	47°08'N	24°30'E
Bistrița, stm., Rom. (bĭs-trĭt-sȧ)	188-89	46°28'N	26°57'E
Bitlis, Tur. (bĭt-lēs')	227	38°22'N	42°06'E
Bitola, Mac. (bė'tô-lä) (mô'nä-stêr)	200-01	41°02'N	21°20'E
Bitolj, Mac. *see* Bitola	200-01	41°02'N	21°20'E
Bitonto, Italy (bė-tôn'tō)	200-01	41°06'N	16°42'E
Bitra Island, i., India	236	11°36'N	72°11'E
Bitterfeld, Ger. (bĭt'ēr-fĕlt)	194-95	51°37'N	12°19'E
Bitterroot Range, mts., U.S. (bĭt'ēr-o͞ot rānj)	110-11	47°06'N	115°10'W
Bitung, Indon.	248-49	1°26'N	125°08'E
Bityug, stm., Russia (bĭt'yo͞og)	186-87	50°38'N	39°56'E
Biwa-ko, lk., Japan (bė-wä'kō)	245	35°15'N	136°05'E
Biya, stm., Russia (bĭ'yȧ)	218-19	52°26'N	85°00'E
Biysk, Russia (bēsk)	226	52°34'N	85°15'E
Bizerte, Tun. (bė-zĕrt')	184-85	37°16'N	9°52'E
Bjarèzina, stm., Bela. (bĕr-yĕ'zē-nȧ)	202-03	52°33'N	30°14'E
Bjelovar, Cro. (byĕ-lō'vär)	200-01	45°54'N	16°50'E
Björneborg, Fin. *see* Pori	192-93	61°29'N	21°47'E
Bjørnøya, i., Nor.	218-19	74°27'N	19°02'E
Black, stm., Asia (blăk)	246-47	21°15'N	105°21'E
Black, stm., Ar., U.S. (blăk)	120-21	35°38'N	91°19'W
Blackall, Austl. (blăk'ŭl)	277	24°26'S	145°28'E
Black Bay, b., On., Can. (blăk bā)	136-37	48°34'N	88°32'W
Blackburn, Eng., U.K. (blăk'bûrn)	190-91	53°45'N	2°29'W
Black Canyon of the Gunnison National Park, n.p., Co., U.S.	118-19	38°34'N	107°44'W
Blackduck, Mn., U.S. (blăk'dŭk)	114-15	47°43'N	94°32'W
Blackfeet Indian Reservation, ind. res., Mt., U.S. (blăk'fēt ĭn'dĭ-ăn rĕ-sēr-vā'shĕn)	112-13	48°40'N	113°00'W
Blackfoot, Id., U.S. (blăk'fŏt)	112-13	43°12'N	112°21'W
Black Forest, mts., Ger. *see* Schwarzwald	194-95	48°21'N	8°11'E
Black Hills, mts., U.S. (blăk hĭlz)	114-15	44°0'N	104°00'W
Black Lake, Qc., Can. (blăk lāk)	136-37	46°03'N	71°22'W
Blackpool, Eng., U.K. (blăk'po͞ol)	190-91	53°50'N	3°02'W
Black Range, mts., N.M., U.S. (blăk rānj)	118-19	33°20'N	107°50'W
Black River Falls, Wi., U.S. (blăk rĭv'ēr fôlz)	114-15	44°18'N	90°50'W
Black Rock Desert, des., Nv., U.S. (blăk rŏk dĕs'ērt)	112-13	41°06'N	118°51'W
Blacksburg, Va., U.S. (blăks'bûrg)	124-25	37°14'N	80°25'W
Black Sea, s., (blăk sē)	186-87	43°0'N	35°00'E
Blackshear, Ga., U.S. (blăk'shĭr)	124-25	31°18'N	82°15'W
Blackstone, Va., U.S. (blăk'stŏn)	124-25	37°05'N	77°60'W
Blacktown, Austl. (blăk'toun)	276	33°46'S	150°54'E
Black Volta, stm., Afr. (blăk vôl'tȧ)	260-61	8°41'N	0°60'W
Blackwell, Ok., U.S. (blăk'wĕl)	120-21	36°48'N	97°18'W
Blagodarnoye, Russia (blä'gô-där-nō'yĕ)	186-87	45°06'N	43°25'E
Blagoveshchensk, Russia	240-41	50°17'N	127°33'E
Blaine, Mn., U.S. (blān)	114-15	45°11'N	93°15'W
Blaine, Wa., U.S. (blān)	112-13	48°60'N	122°45'W
Blair, Ne., U.S. (blâr)	114-15	41°33'N	96°08'W
Blairsville, Pa., U.S. (blârs'vĭl)	116-17	40°26'N	79°16'W
Blakely, Ga., U.S. (blāk'lė)	124-25	31°23'N	84°56'W
Blanc, Cap, c., Afr. *see* Nouâdhibou, Râs	258-59	20°47'N	17°03'W
Blanc, Mont, mtn., Eur. (môɴ bläɴ)	196-97	45°50'N	6°52'E
Blanca, Bahía, b., Arg. (bä-ē'ä-blán'kä)	173	38°55'S	62°10'W
Blanca Peak, mtn., Co., U.S. (blăŋ'kȧ pēk)	120-21	37°35'N	105°29'W
Blanche, Lake, lk., Austl. (lăk blănch)	276	29°15'S	139°39'E
Blanco, Cabo, c., C.R. (kȧ'bô-bläŋ'kō)	149	9°34'N	85°07'W
Blanco, Cape, c., Or., U.S. (kāp blăn'kō)	112-13	42°50'N	124°33'W
Blanquilla, Isla, i., Ven.	164-65	11°51'N	64°37'W
Blantyre, Malawi (blăn-tīyr)	264-65	15°47'S	35°01'E
Blenheim, N.Z.	278	41°31'S	173°58'E
Bleus, Monts, mts., D.R.C.	267	1°37'N	30°28'E
Blida, Alg.	269b	36°29'N	2°49'E
Blind River, On., Can. (blīnd rĭv'ēr)	136-37	46°11'N	82°56'W
Blissfield, Mi., U.S. (blĭs-fēld)	116-17	41°50'N	83°52'W
Blitar, Indon.	248-49	8°06'S	112°10'E
Bloemfontein, S. Afr.	269c	29°07'S	26°12'E
Blois, Fr. (blwä)	196-97	47°35'N	1°20'E
Bloodvein, stm., Can.	134-35	51°48'N	96°53'W
Bloomer, Wi., U.S. (blo͞om'ēr)	114-15	45°06'N	91°29'W
Bloomfield, Ia., U.S. (blo͞om'fēld)	114-15	40°46'N	92°25'W
Bloomfield, In., U.S. (blo͞om'fēld)	116-17	39°01'N	86°56'W
Bloomfield, Mo., U.S. (blo͞om'fēld)	124-25	36°53'N	89°56'W
Bloomfield, Ne., U.S. (blo͞om'fēld)	114-15	42°36'N	97°39'W
Blooming Prairie, Mn., U.S. (blo͞om'ĭng prā'rĭ)	114-15	43°52'N	93°03'W
Bloomington, Il., U.S. (blo͞om'ĭng-tŭn)	116-17	40°29'N	88°60'W
Bloomington, In., U.S. (blo͞om'ĭng-tŭn)	116-17	39°09'N	86°32'W
Bloomington, Mn., U.S. (blo͞om'ĭng-tŭn)	114-15	44°50'N	93°19'W
Bloomsburg, Pa., U.S. (blo͞omz'bûrg)	116-17	40°60'N	76°27'W
Blossburg, Pa., U.S. (blŏs'bûrg)	116-17	41°41'N	77°05'W
Blountstown, Fl., U.S. (blŭnts'tun)	124-25	30°27'N	85°03'W
Bludenz, Aus. (blo͞o-dĕnts')	194-95	47°09'N	9°50'E
Blue Earth, Mn., U.S. (blo͞o ûrth)	114-15	43°38'N	94°06'W
Bluefield, W.V., U.S. (blo͞o'fēld)	124-25	37°15'N	81°14'W
Bluefields, Nic. (blo͞o'fēldz)	149	12°01'N	83°46'W
Blue Mountain, mtn., Nf., Can. (blo͞o moun'tĭn)	138-39	50°24'N	57°10'W
Blue Mountain Peak, mtn., Jam.	142-43	18°03'N	76°35'W
Blue Mountains, mts., Austl. (blo͞o moun'tĭnz)	276	33°37'S	150°17'E
Blue Mountains, mts., U.S. (blo͞o moun'tĭnz)	112-13	45°16'N	118°42'W
Blue Mountains National Park, n.p., Austl.	276	33°47'S	150°23'E
Blue Nile, stm., Afr. (blo͞o nīl)	254	15°38'N	32°30'E
Bluenose Lake, lk., Nu., Can.	130-31	68°25'N	119°45'W
Blue Ridge, mts., U.S. (blo͞o rĭj)	124-25	37°0'N	82°00'W
Blue River, B.C., Can. (blo͞o rĭv'ēr)	132-33	52°06'N	119°20'W
Bluff, Ut., U.S. (blŭf)	118-19	37°17'N	109°33'W
Bluffton, In., U.S. (blŭf-tŭn)	116-17	40°44'N	85°10'W
Blumenau, Braz. (blo͞o'mĕn-ou)	172	26°56'S	49°05'W
Blyth, Eng., U.K. (blīth)	190-91	55°08'N	1°31'W
Blytheville, Ar., U.S. (blīth'vĭl)	124-25	35°56'N	89°55'W
Bo, S.L.	260-61	7°59'N	11°44'W
Boaco, Nic. (bô-ä'kō)	149	12°29'N	85°39'W
Bo'ai, China (bwo-ī)	240-41	35°10'N	113°04'E
Boano, Pulau, i., Indon.	248-49	2°58'S	127°56'E
Boa Vista, i., C.V. (bō-ä-vēsh'tȧ)	260-61	16°05'N	22°50'W
Bobaomby, Tanjona, c., Madag.	264-65	11°58'S	49°15'E
Bobbili, India	236	18°35'N	83°22'E
Bobo-Dioulasso, Burkina (bō'bō-dyo͞o-lȧs-sō')	260-61	11°11'N	4°18'W
Bobruysk, Bela. *see* Babrujsk	202-03	53°08'N	29°14'E
Boby, mtn., Madag.	264-65	22°13'S	46°55'E
Boca do Acre, Braz.	166-67	8°45'S	67°23'W
Bocas del Toro, Pan. (bō'käs dĕl tō'rō)	150	9°20'N	82°15'W
Bochnia, Pol. (bôĸ'nyä)	194-95	49°58'N	20°25'E
Bocholt, Ger. (bō'ĸōlt)	194-95	51°50'N	6°37'E
Bodaybo, Russia (bō-dī'bō)	218-19	57°51'N	114°11'E
Bodélé, reg., Chad (bō-dȧ-lā')	258-59	16°30'N	16°30'E
Boden, Swe.	184-85	65°50'N	21°43'E
Bodh Gaya, India	234-35	24°42'N	84°58'E
Bodmin, Eng., U.K. (bŏd'mĭn)	190-91	50°29'N	4°43'W
Bodø, Nor.	184-85	67°17'N	14°24'E
Bodrum, Tur.	200-01	37°02'N	27°26'E
Boende, D.R.C. (bō-ĕn'dȧ)	262-63	0°14'S	20°52'E
Boerne, Tx., U.S. (bō'ērn)	122-23	29°47'N	98°43'W
Bōfu, Japan (bō'fo͞o) *see* Hōfu	245	34°03'N	131°35'E
Bogal, Lagh, stm., Kenya	262-63	0°40'N	40°50'E
Bogale, Mya.	246-47	16°17'N	95°24'E
Bogalusa, La., U.S. (bō-gȧ-lo͞o'sȧ)	124-25	30°47'N	89°51'W
Bogan, stm., Austl. (bô'gĕn)	276	29°58'S	146°20'E
Bogo, Phil.	250	11°02'N	124°01'E
Bogong, Mount, mtn., Austl.	276	36°44'S	147°18'E
Bogor, Indon.	248-49	6°35'S	106°47'E
Bogoroditsk, Russia (bŏ-gŏ'rō-dĭtsk)	202-03	53°47'N	38°08'E
Bogotá, nat. cap., Col. (bō-gō-tä')	163c	4°37'N	74°06'W
Bogra, Bngl.	234-35	24°50'N	89°22'E
Boguchany, Russia	218-19	58°23'N	97°29'E
Bogué, Maur.	258-59	16°35'N	14°16'W
Bo Hai, b., China	240-41	38°30'N	120°02'E
Bohai Haixia, strt., China (bwo-hī hī-shyä)	240-41	38°15'N	121°00'E
Bohain-en-Vermandois, Fr. (bō-ăɴ-ŏɴ-vâr-mäɴ-dwä')	196-97	49°59'N	3°27'E
Bohea Hills, mts., China *see* Wuyi Shan	238-39	27°42'N	117°09'E
Bohemia, hist. reg., Czech Rep.	194-95	49°50'N	14°00'E
Bohol, i., Phil. (bō-hōl')	250	9°55'N	123°44'E
Bohol Sea, s., Phil.	250	9°10'N	124°25'E
Boipeba, Ilha de, i., Braz.	166-67	13°38'S	38°56'W
Bois, Lac des, lk., N.T., Can.	130-31	66°46'N	125°08'W
Boise, Id., U.S. (boi'zē)	112-13	43°37'N	116°13'W
Boise City, Ok., U.S. (boi'zē sĭ'tė)	120-21	36°44'N	102°30'W
Boissevain, Mb., Can. (bois'vān)	134-35	49°14'N	100°03'W
Bojeador, Cape, c., Phil.	250	18°30'N	120°35'E
Bojnūrd, Iran	232-33	37°29'N	57°20'E
Boksitogorsk, Russia	186-87	59°28'N	33°52'E
Bokurdak, Turkmen.	232-33	38°46'N	58°29'E
Bolbec, Fr. (bôl-bĕk')	196-97	49°34'N	0°29'E
Bolgatanga, Ghana	260-61	10°48'N	0°51'W
Boli, China (bwo-lē)	244	45°45'N	130°34'E
Bolívar, Col.	163c	4°21'N	76°10'W
Bolivar, Mo., U.S. (bŏl'ĭ-vȧr)	120-21	37°37'N	93°25'W
Bolivar, Tn., U.S. (bŏl'ĭ-vȧr)	124-25	35°16'N	88°59'W
Bolívar, Cerro, mtn., Ven.	164-65	7°28'N	63°25'W
Bolívar, Pico, mtn., Ven.	164-65	8°33'N	71°01'W
Bolivar Peninsula, pen., Tx., U.S. (bŏl'ĭ-vȧr pĕ-nĭn'sūlȧ)	122-23	29°27'N	94°39'W
Bolivia, nation, S.A. (bō-lĭv'ĭ-ȧ)	158	17°0'S	65°00'W
Bolkhov, Russia (bŏl-ĸôf')	202-03	53°27'N	36°00'E
Bollnäs, Swe. (bôl'nĕs)	192-93	61°21'N	16°24'E
Bolmen, lk., Swe. (bôl'mĕn)	192-93	56°55'N	13°40'E
Bolobo, D.R.C. (bō'lô-bō)	262-63	2°11'S	16°15'E
Bologna, Italy (bō-lōn'yä)	200-01	44°30'N	11°20'E
Bologoye, Russia (bŏ-lŏ-gô'yĕ)	202-03	57°54'N	34°03'E
Bol'shevik, Ostrov, i., Russia	218-19	78°40'N	102°30'E
Bol'shezemel'skaya Tundra, reg., Russia	186-87	67°30'N	55°60'E
Bol'shoy Begichëv, Ostrov, i., Russia	218-19	74°20'N	112°30'E
Bol'shoy Kavkaz, mts., *see* Caucasus Mountains	227	42°38'N	45°00'E
Bol'shoy Lyakhovskiy, Ostrov, i., Russia	218-19	73°35'N	142°00'E
Bol'shoy Uzen', stm., Eur. *see* Ülkenözen	186-87	48°60'N	49°59'E
Bol'shoy Yenisey, stm., Russia	218-19	51°44'N	94°28'E
Bolu, Tur. (bō'lò)	186-87	40°44'N	31°36'E
Bolzano, Italy (bôl-tsä'nō)	200-01	46°30'N	11°21'E
Boma, D.R.C. (bō'mä)	262-63	5°51'S	13°04'E
Bombala, Austl. (bŭm-bä'lă)	276	36°55'S	149°14'E
Bombay, India *see* Mumbai	236	18°57'N	72°50'E
Bom Jesus da Lapa, Braz.	166-67	13°15'S	43°25'W
Bømlo, i., Nor. (bûmlô)	192-93	59°47'N	5°12'E
Bomokandi, stm., D.R.C.	262-63	3°39'N	26°08'E
Bomu, stm., Afr.	262-63	4°09'N	22°29'E
Bon, Cap, c., Tun. (kăp bôɴ)	258-59	37°05'N	11°03'E
Bonaire, i., Neth. Ant. (bō-nâr')	140a	12°10'N	68°15'W
Bonaventure, Qc., Can.	138-39	48°02'N	65°30'W
Bonavista, Nf., Can. (bŏ-nȧ-vĭs'tȧ)	138-39	48°39'N	53°07'W
Bonavista Bay, b., Nf., Can. (bŏ-nȧ-vĭs'tȧ bā)	138-39	48°50'N	53°21'W
Bondo, D.R.C. (bôn'dô)	262-63	3°49'N	23°41'E
Bondoc Peninsula, pen., Phil. (bôn-dŏk' pĕ-nĭn'sūlȧ)	250	13°30'N	122°30'E
Bondoukou, C. Iv. (bŏn-do͞o'ko͞o)	260-61	8°02'N	2°48'W
Bône, Alg. *see* Annaba	184-85	36°54'N	7°46'E
Bone, Indon. *see* Watampone	248-49	4°32'S	120°19'E
Bone, Teluk, b., Indon.	248-49	4°0'S	120°40'E
Bonerate, Pulau, i., Indon.	248-49	7°21'S	121°07'E
Bonete Grande, Cerro, mtn., Arg. (sĕ'r-rô bô'nĕtĕh grän'dĕ)	168-69	27°57'S	68°45'W
Bongo, Massif des, mts., C.A.R.	262-63	8°36'N	22°50'E
Bonham, Tx., U.S. (bŏn'ăm)	120-21	33°35'N	96°11'W
Bonifacio, Bouches de, strt., Eur. *see* Bonifacio, Strait of	200-01	41°18'N	9°15'E
Bonifacio, Strait of, strt., Eur. (strāt ŭv bō-nė-fä'chō)	200-01	41°18'N	9°15'E
Bonifay, Fl., U.S. (bŏn-ĭ-fā')	124-25	30°47'N	85°41'W
Bonin Islands, is., Japan (bō'nĭn ī'lăndz)	282-83	26°58'N	142°14'E
Bonn, Ger. (bŏn)	194-95	50°44'N	7°05'E
Bonners Ferry, Id., U.S. (bonẽrz fĕr'ė)	112-13	48°41'N	116°19'W
Bonne Terre, Mo., U.S. (bŏn târ')	120-21	37°55'N	90°33'W
Bonny, Nig. (bŏn'ė)	260a	4°26'N	7°10'E
Bonnyville, Ab., Can. (bŏnė-vĭl)	132-33	54°16'N	110°44'W
Bontang, Indon.	248-49	0°08'N	117°30'E
Bontoc, Phil. (bôn-tŏk')	250	17°05'N	120°60'E
Boodjamulla National Park, n.p., Austl.	277	18°45'S	138°27'E
Booker T. Washington National Monument, n.p., Va., U.S. (bŏk'ẽr tē wŏsh'ĭng-tŭn năsh'ŭn-ăl mŏn'ū-mĕnt)	124-25	37°01'N	79°45'W
Boonah, Austl.	276	28°00'S	152°41'E
Boone, Ia., U.S. (bo͞on)	114-15	42°04'N	93°53'W
Boone, N.C., U.S. (bo͞on)	124-25	36°13'N	81°41'W
Booneville, Ar., U.S. (bo͞on'vĭl)	120-21	35°08'N	93°56'W
Booneville, Ms., U.S. (bo͞on'vĭl)	124-25	34°39'N	88°34'W
Boonville, In., U.S. (bo͞on'vĭl)	116-17	38°03'N	87°17'W
Boonville, Mo., U.S. (bo͞on'vĭl)	120-21	38°58'N	92°45'W

PRONOUNCING INDEX

Boorama – Bristol 313

Feature (Pronunciation)	Page	Lat.	Long.
Boorama, Som.	262-63	9°58'N	43°09'E
Boosaaso, Som. *see* Bender Cassim	262-63	11°17'N	49°11'E
Boothbay Harbor, Me., U.S. (bōōth'bā här'bẽr)	117a	43°51'N	69°38'W
Boothia, Gulf of, b., Nu., Can. (gŭlf ŭv bōō'thĭ-ȧ)	86	71°0'N	91°00'W
Boothia Peninsula, pen., Nu., Can.	130-31	70°30'N	95°00'W
Booué, Gabon	260-61	0°06'S	11°57'E
Borđoy, i., Far. Is.	190b	62°17'N	6°33'W
Bora-Bora, i., Fr. Poly.	280-81	16°30'S	151°45'W
Borah Peak, mtn., Id., U.S. (bō'rä pēk)	112-13	44°08'N	113°48'W
Borås, Swe. (bô'rōs)	192-93	57°44'N	12°57'E
Borāzjān, Iran (bō-räz-jän')	230-31	29°16'N	51°12'E
Borba, Braz. (bôr'bä)	166-67	4°23'S	59°35'W
Bordeaux, Fr. (bôr-dō')	196-97	44°50'N	0°34'W
Bordentown, N.J., U.S. (bôr'dĕn-toun)	116-17	40°08'N	74°44'W
Bordertown, Austl.	276	36°19'S	140°46'E
Bordj Bou Arreridj, Alg. (bôrj-bōō-ȧ-rä-rēj')	269b	36°04'N	4°46'E
Borgå, Fin. *see* Porvoo	192-93	60°24'N	25°40'E
Borgarnes, Ice.	190a	64°34'N	21°55'W
Borger, Tx., U.S. (bôr'gẽr)	120-21	35°40'N	101°24'W
Borgholm, Swe. (bôrg-hŏlm')	192-93	56°52'N	16°40'E
Borgne, Lake, b., La., U.S. (läk bôrn'y')	124-25	30°05'N	89°35'W
Borgomanero, Italy (bôr'gō-mä-nâ'rō)	200-01	45°42'N	8°28'E
Borgo Val di Taro, Italy (bô'r-zhō-väl-dē-tá'rō)	200-01	44°29'N	9°46'E
Borisoglebsk, Russia (bŏ-rē sō-glyĕpsk')	186-87	51°22'N	42°06'E
Borken, Ger. (bōr'kĕn)	194-95	51°51'N	6°52'E
Borkum, i., Ger. (bōr'kōōm)	194-95	53°36'N	6°42'E
Borlänge, Swe. (bôr-lĕŋ'gĕ)	192-93	60°29'N	15°27'E
Borneo, i., Asia (bôr'-nē-ō)	248-49	0°30'N	114°00'E
Bornholm, i., Den. (bôrn-hôlm)	192-93	55°09'N	14°55'E
Boro, stm., Sudan	262-63	8°51'N	26°11'E
Borogontsy, Russia	218-19	62°41'N	131°09'E
Borovichi, Russia (bŏ-rô-vē'chē)	202-03	58°23'N	33°55'E
Borroloola, Austl. (bŏr-rō-lōō'lȧ)	270-71	16°05'S	136°17'E
Borūjerd, Iran	228-29	33°53'N	48°45'E
Borzna, Ukr. (bôrz'ná)	202-03	51°15'N	32°26'E
Borzya, Russia (bôrz'yá)	240-41	50°22'N	116°31'E
Bosa, Italy (bō'sä)	200-01	40°18'N	8°30'E
Bosanska Gradiška, Bos. (bō'sän-skä grä-dĭsh'kä)	200-01	45°09'N	17°15'E
Bosanski Novi, Bos. (bō's sän-skĭ nō'vē)	200-01	45°04'N	16°23'E
Boscobel, Wi., U.S. (bŏs'kō-bĕl)	114-15	43°08'N	90°42'W
Bose, China (bwo-sŭ)	238-39	23°55'N	106°38'E
Boshan, China (bwo-shan)	240-41	36°29'N	117°51'E
Bosna, stm., Bos.	200-01	45°04'N	18°28'E
Bosna i Hercegovina, nation, Eur. *see* Bosnia and Herzegovina	174-75	44°15'N	17°50'E
Bosnia and Hercegovina, nation, Eur. *see* Bosnia and Herzegovina	174-75	44°15'N	17°50'E
Bosnia and Herzegovina, nation, Eur. (bŏs'nĭ-ȧ ănd hĕr-tsĕ-gô'vē-nȧ)	174-75	44°15'N	17°50'E
Bosporus, strt., Tur. (bŏs'pȧ-rŭs)	200-01	41°06'N	29°04'E
Bossembélé, C.A.R.	262-63	5°16'N	17°39'E
Bossier City, La., U.S. (bŏsh'ẽr sĭ'tĭ)	120-21	32°31'N	93°44'W
Bosso, Dallol, stm., Niger	258-59	12°24'N	2°52'E
Bosten Hu, lk., China (bwo-stŭn hōō)	222-23	42°0'N	87°00'E
Boston, Ma., U.S. (bôs'tŭn)	116-17	42°22'N	71°03'W
Boston Mountains, mts., Ar., U.S. (bôs'tŭn moun'tĭnz)	120-21	35°50'N	93°20'W
Boteti, stm., Bots.	264-65	20°09'S	23°23'E
Bothaville, S. Afr. (bō'tā-vĭl)	269c	27°24'S	26°37'E
Bothnia, Gulf of, b., Eur. (gŭlf ŭv bŏth'nĭ-ȧ)	184-85	63°0'N	20°00'E
Botoşani, Rom. (bô-tô-shán'ĭ)	194-95	47°45'N	26°40'E
Botswana, nation, Afr. (bŏtswănă)	253	22°0'S	24°00'E
Bottineau, N.D., U.S. (bŏt-ĭ-nō')	114-15	48°49'N	100°27'W
Bottniska Viken, b., Eur. *see* Bothnia, Gulf of	184-85	63°0'N	20°00'E
Botucatu, Braz.	172	22°52'S	48°27'W
Botwood, Nf., Can. (bŏt'wŏd)	138-39	49°09'N	55°22'W
Bouaké, C. Iv.	260-61	7°42'N	5°02'W
Bouar, C.A.R. (bōō-är)	262-63	5°57'N	15°36'E
Boufarik, Alg. (bōō-fá-rēk')	269b	36°35'N	2°54'E
Bougainville, i., Pap. N. Gui. (bōō-găn-vēl')	279e	6°0'S	155°00'E
Bougie, Alg. *see* Bejaïa	269b	36°45'N	5°04'E
Bouira, Alg. (boo-ē'rá)	269b	36°23'N	3°54'E
Boujdour, Cap, c., W. Sah.	258-59	26°08'N	14°29'W
Boulder, Co., U.S. (bōl'dẽr)	118-19	40°02'N	105°15'W
Boulder, Mt., U.S. (bōld'ẽr)	112-13	46°14'N	112°08'W
Boulder, stm., Mt., U.S. (bōld'ẽr)	112-13	45°52'N	111°57'W
Boulder City, Nv., U.S. (bōl'dẽr sĭ'tê)	118-19	35°59'N	114°50'W
Boulia, Austl.	277	22°55'S	139°55'E
Boulogne-Billancourt, Fr. (bōō-lôn'y'-bē-yän-kōōr')	196-97	48°51'N	2°15'E
Boulogne-sur-Mer, Fr. (bōō-lôn'y-sür-mâr')	196-97	50°43'N	1°36'E
Boundary Peak, mtn., Nv., U.S.	118-19	37°51'N	118°21'W
Bountiful, Ut., U.S. (boun'tĭ-fŏl)	112-13	40°53'N	111°53'W
Bounty Islands, is., N.Z.	287	47°42'S	179°04'E
Bourg-en-Bresse, Fr. (bōōr-gĕn-brĕs')	196-97	46°13'N	5°13'E
Bourges, Fr. (bōōrzh)	196-97	47°05'N	2°24'E
Bourke, Austl. (bŭrk)	276	30°06'S	145°56'E
Bournemouth, Eng., U.K. (bôrn'mŭth)	190-91	50°44'N	1°52'W
Bou Saâda, Alg. (bōō-sä'dä)	269b	35°13'N	4°11'E
Boutilimit, Maur.	258-59	17°33'N	14°42'W
Bouvetøya, i., Afr.	284-85	54°26'S	3°24'E
Bow, stm., Ab., Can. (bō)	132-33	49°56'N	111°42'W
Bowbells, N.D., U.S. (bō'bĕls)	114-15	48°48'N	102°15'W
Bowen, Austl. (bō'ĕn)	277	20°01'S	148°14'E
Bowie, Md., U.S. (bōō'ĭ) (bō'ê)	116-17	39°00'N	76°46'W
Bowie, Tx., U.S. (bōō'ĭ) (bō'ê)	120-21	33°34'N	97°51'W
Bowling Green, Ky., U.S. (bōlĭng grēn)	124-25	36°59'N	86°27'W
Bowling Green, Mo., U.S. (bōlĭng grēn)	120-21	39°21'N	91°12'W
Bowling Green, Oh., U.S. (bōlĭng grēn)	116-17	41°22'N	83°39'W
Bowling Green, Va., U.S. (bōlĭng grēn)	116-17	38°03'N	77°21'W
Bowman, N.D., U.S. (bō'măn)	114-15	46°11'N	103°24'W
Bowral, Austl.	276	34°28'S	150°26'E
Bowron, stm., B.C., Can. (bō'rŭn)	132-33	54°03'N	121°50'W
Boxing, China (bwo-shyĭŋ)	240-41	37°08'N	118°07'E
Boyang, China (bwo-yäŋ)	238-39	28°60'N	116°40'E
Boyle, Ire. (boil)	190-91	53°59'N	8°18'W
Boyoma Falls, wtfl., D.R.C. *see* Stanley Falls	262-63	0°29'N	25°13'E
Boysun, Uzb.	232-33	38°12'N	67°12'E
Bozeman, Mt., U.S. (bōz'măn)	112-13	45°41'N	111°03'W
Bozen, Italy *see* Bolzano	200-01	46°30'N	11°21'E
Bozhen, China (bwo-jŭn)	240-41	38°05'N	116°33'E
Bozhou, China	238-39	33°52'N	115°46'E
Bra, Italy (brä)	200-01	44°41'N	7°51'E
Bracebridge, On., Can. (brās'brĭj)	136-37	45°02'N	79°18'W
Brackettville, Tx., U.S. (brăk'ĕt-vĭl)	122-23	29°18'N	100°25'W
Bradano, stm., Italy (brä-dä'nō)	200-01	40°23'N	16°51'E
Bradenton, Fl., U.S. (brā'dĕn-tŭn)	125a	27°30'N	82°33'W
Bradford, Eng., U.K. (brăd'fẽrd)	190-91	53°48'N	1°45'W
Bradley, Il., U.S. (brăd'lĭ)	116-17	41°08'N	87°51'W
Brady, Tx., U.S. (brā'dĭ)	122-23	31°08'N	99°20'W
Braga, Port. (brä'gä)	198-99	41°33'N	8°26'W
Bragado, Arg. (brä-gä'dō)	173	35°08'S	60°30'W
Bragança, Braz. (brä-gän'sä)	166-67	1°03'S	46°46'W
Bragança, Port.	198-99	41°49'N	6°45'W
Brāhmanbāria, Bngl.	234-35	23°59'N	91°07'E
Brāhmani, stm., India	234-35	20°47'N	87°01'E
Brahmapur, India	236	19°18'N	84°49'E
Brahmaputra, stm., Asia (brä'mȧ-pōō'trȧ)	234-35	24°02'N	91°00'E
Braidwood, Il., U.S. (brād'wŏd)	116-17	41°16'N	88°12'W
Brăila, Rom. (brē'ēlȧ)	202-03	45°16'N	27°58'E
Brainerd, Mn., U.S. (brān'ẽrd)	114-15	46°21'N	94°12'W
Brampton, On., Can. (brămp'tŭn)	136-37	43°42'N	79°45'W
Branco, stm., Braz. (brăŋ'kō)	164-65	1°24'S	61°52'W
Brandberg, mtn., Nmb.	264-65	21°10'S	14°33'E
Brandenburg, Ger. (brän'dĕn-bŏrgh)	194-95	52°25'N	12°33'E
Brandfort, S. Afr. (brăn'd-fôrt)	269c	28°42'S	26°28'E
Brandon, Mb., Can. (brăn'dŭn)	134-35	49°50'N	99°58'W
Brandon, Ms., U.S. (brăn'dŭn)	124-25	32°16'N	89°59'W
Brandon, S.D., U.S. (brăn'dŭn)	114-15	43°36'N	96°34'W
Brandon, Vt., U.S. (brăn'dŭn)	116-17	43°48'N	73°05'W
Braniewo, Pol. (brä-nyĕ'vô)	194-95	54°23'N	19°50'E
Brantford, On., Can. (brănt'fẽrd)	136-37	43°09'N	80°15'W
Bras d'Or Lake, lk., N.S., Can. (brä-dôr' lăk)	138-39	45°52'N	60°50'W
Brasil, nation, S.A. *see* Brazil	158	10°0'S	55°00'W
Brasiléia, Braz.	166-67	10°60'S	68°45'W
Brasília, nat. cap., Braz. (brä-sē'lvä)	168-69	15°48'S	47°53'W
Braşov, Rom.	194-95	45°39'N	25°37'E
Brass, Nig. (brăs)	260a	4°19'N	6°15'E
Brassó, Rom. *see* Braşov	194-95	45°39'N	25°37'E
Bratislava, nat. cap., Slvk. (brä'tĭs-lä-vä)	194-95	48°09'N	17°07'E
Bratsk, Russia (brätsk)	218-19	56°08'N	101°39'E
Bratskoye Vodokhranilishche, res., Russia	218-19	55°57'N	101°52'E
Bratsk Reservoir, res., Russia (brätsk rĕ'sẽr-vwär) *see* Bratskoye Vodokhranilishche	218-19	55°57'N	101°52'E
Bratslav, Ukr. (brät'sláf)	202-03	48°49'N	28°57'E
Brattleboro, Vt., U.S. (brăt''l-bŭr-ô)	116-17	42°51'N	72°34'W
Braunschweig, Ger. (broun'shvīgh)	194-95	52°16'N	10°31'E
Brava, i., C.V.	260-61	14°52'N	24°43'W
Bravo, stm., N.A. *see* Rio Grande	110-11	25°57'N	97°09'W
Bravo del Norte, stm., N.A. *see* Rio Grande	110-11	25°57'N	97°09'W
Brawley, Ca., U.S. (brô'lĭ)	118-19	32°59'N	115°33'W
Brazeau, stm., Ab., Can.	132-33	52°55'N	115°14'W
Brazeau, Mount, mtn., Ab., Can. (mount bră-zō')	132-33	52°33'N	117°21'W
Brazil, In., U.S. (brȧ-zĭl')	116-17	39°31'N	87°07'W
Brazil, nation, S.A. (brȧ-zĭl')	158	10°0'S	55°00'W
Brazos, stm., Tx., U.S. (brä'zōs)	122-23	33°15'N	100°00'W
Brazos, Salt Fork, stm., U.S. (sôlt fôrk)	120-21	33°16'N	100°01'W
Brazzaville, nat. cap., Congo (brȧ-zȧ-vēl')	262-63	4°16'S	15°17'E
Brčko, Bos. (bĕrch'kô)	200-01	44°52'N	18°49'E
Breckenridge, Mn., U.S. (brĕk'ĕn-rĭj)	114-15	46°15'N	96°34'W
Breckenridge, Tx., U.S. (brĕk'ĕn-rĭj)	120-21	32°45'N	98°55'W
Břeclav, Czech Rep. (brzhĕl'láf)	194-95	48°46'N	16°54'E
Breda, Neth. (brā-dä')	190-91	51°35'N	4°46'E
Bregenz, Aus. (brā'gĕnts)	194-95	47°30'N	9°46'E
Bregovo, Blg. (brĕ'gô-vô)	200-01	44°10'N	22°39'E
Breidafjördur, b., Ice.	190a	65°15'N	23°15'W
Brejo, Braz. (brå'zhò)	166-67	3°41'S	42°47'W
Bremen, Ger. (brā-mĕn)	194-95	53°04'N	8°51'E
Bremen, Ga., U.S. (brē'mĕn)	124-25	33°43'N	85°09'W
Bremen, In., U.S. (brē'mĕn)	116-17	41°27'N	86°08'W
Bremerhaven, Ger. (brām-ẽr-hä'fĕn)	194-95	53°32'N	8°36'E
Bremerton, Wa., U.S. (brĕm'ẽr-tŭn)	112-13	47°34'N	122°39'W
Brenham, Tx., U.S. (brĕn'ăm)	122-23	30°10'N	96°24'W
Brentwood, N.Y., U.S. (brĕnt'wŏd)	116-17	40°47'N	73°15'W
Brentwood, Tn., U.S. (brĕnt'wŏd)	124-25	36°02'N	86°47'W
Brescia, Italy (brā'shä)	200-01	45°33'N	10°13'E
Breslau, Pol. *see* Wrocław	194-95	51°07'N	17°02'E
Bressanone, Italy (brĕs-sä-nō'nā)	200-01	46°43'N	11°39'E
Bressuire, Fr. (grĕ-swēr')	196-97	46°50'N	0°29'W
Brèst, Bela.	194-95	52°07'N	23°42'E
Brest, Fr. (brĕst)	196-97	48°24'N	4°30'W
Bretagne, hist. reg., Fr. (brĕ-tän'yĕ) *see* Brittany	196-97	48°0'N	3°00'W
Breton Sound, strt., La., U.S. (brĕt'ŭn sound)	124-25	29°34'N	89°16'W
Brevard, N.C., U.S. (brĕ-värd')	124-25	35°14'N	82°44'W
Breves, Braz. (brā'vĕzh)	166-67	1°40'S	50°29'W
Brewarrina, Austl. (brōō-ẽr-rē'nȧ)	276	29°57'S	146°52'E
Brewster, Wa., U.S. (brōō'stẽr)	112-13	48°06'N	119°47'W
Brewster, Kap, c., Green.	86	70°09'N	22°06'W
Brewton, Al., U.S. (brōō'tŭn)	124-25	31°07'N	87°05'W
Brezhnev, Russia *see* Naberezhnye Chelny	186-87	55°42'N	52°19'E
Bria, C.A.R.	262-63	6°33'N	21°58'E
Briançon, Fr. (brē-än-sôN')	196-97	44°54'N	6°37'E
Bridgeport, Al., U.S. (brĭj'pôrt)	124-25	34°57'N	85°43'W
Bridgeport, Ca., U.S. (brĭj'pôrt)	118-19	38°16'N	119°14'W
Bridgeport, Ct., U.S. (brĭj'pôrt)	116-17	41°11'N	73°14'W
Bridgeport, Il., U.S. (brĭj'pôrt)	116-17	38°42'N	87°46'W
Bridgeport, Ne., U.S. (brĭj'pôrt)	114-15	41°40'N	103°05'W
Bridgeport, Tx., U.S. (brĭj'pôrt)	120-21	33°13'N	97°46'W
Bridgetown, Austl.	270-71	33°58'S	116°08'E
Bridgetown, N.S., Can. (brĭj' toun)	138-39	44°52'N	65°16'W
Bridgetown, nat. cap., Barb. (brĭj' toun)	143b	13°06'N	59°37'W
Bridgewater, N.S., Can.	138-39	44°22'N	64°31'W
Bridgton, Me., U.S. (brĭj'tŭn)	116-17	44°04'N	70°42'W
Bridlington, Eng., U.K. (brĭd'lĭng-tŭn)	190-91	54°05'N	0°12'W
Brig, Switz. (brēg)	194-95	46°19'N	8°00'E
Brigham City, Ut., U.S. (brĭg'ăm sĭ'tê)	112-13	41°31'N	112°01'W
Bright, Austl. (brīt)	276	36°44'S	146°58'E
Brighton, Eng., U.K. (brīt'ŭn)	190-91	50°50'N	0°08'W
Brighton, Co., U.S. (brīt'ŭn)	120-21	39°59'N	104°49'W
Brighton, N.Y., U.S. (brīt'ŭn)	116-17	43°09'N	77°33'W
Brindisi, Italy (brēn'dē-zē)	200-01	40°38'N	17°56'E
Brinkley, Ar., U.S. (brĭŋk'lĭ)	124-25	34°54'N	91°11'W
Brioude, Fr. (brē-ōōd')	196-97	45°18'N	3°23'E
Brisbane, Austl. (brĭz'bân)	276	27°28'S	153°02'E
Bristol, Eng., U.K.	190-91	51°27'N	2°36'W
Bristol, Ct., U.S. (brĭs'tŭl)	116-17	41°41'N	72°57'W
Bristol, R.I., U.S. (brĭs'tŭl)	116-17	41°40'N	71°16'W

n-sing; ŋ-baŋk; N-nasalized n; nŏd; cŏmmit; ōld; ôbey; ôrder; oi-boil; fōōd; ō-as oo in foot; ou-out; s-soft; sh-dish; th-thin; pūre; ûnite; ûrn; stŭd; circŭs; ü-as in French tu; '-indeterminate vowel.

314 Bristol – Buyr nuur

PRONOUNCING INDEX

Feature (Pronunciation)	Page	Lat.	Long.
Bristol, Tn., U.S. (brĭs′tŭl)	124-25	36°35′N	82°11′W
Bristol, Va., U.S. (brĭs′tŭl)	124-25	36°36′N	82°11′W
Bristol Bay, b., Ak., U.S. (brĭs′tŭl bā)	126	58°0′N	159°00′W
Bristol Channel, strt., U.K.	190-91	51°23′N	4°01′W
Bristow, Ok., U.S. (brĭs′tō)	120-21	35°50′N	96°24′W
British Columbia, state, Can. (brĭt′ĭsh kŏl′ŭm-bĭ-*a*)	128-29	54°0′N	125°00′W
British Guiana, nation, S.A. *see* Guyana	158	5°0′N	59°00′W
British Honduras, nation, N.A. *see* Belize	85	17°15′N	88°45′W
British Indian Ocean Territory, dep., Afr.	206-07	7°0′S	72°00′E
British Solomon Islands, nation, Oc. *see* Solomon Islands	279e	8°0′S	159°00′E
British Virgin Islands, dep., N.A.	140-41	18°30′N	64°30′W
Britt, Ia., U.S. (brĭt)	114-15	43°06′N	93°49′W
Brittany, hist. reg., Fr.	196-97	48°0′N	3°00′W
Britton, S.D., U.S. (brĭt′*ŭ*n)	114-15	45°48′N	97°45′W
Brive-la-Gaillarde, Fr. (brēv-lä-gī-yärd′*ĕ*)	196-97	45°09′N	1°32′E
Brixen, Italy *see* Bressanone	200-01	46°43′N	11°39′E
Brno, Czech Rep. (b′r′nô)	194-95	49°12′N	16°37′E
Brockport, N.Y., U.S. (brŏk′pōrt)	116-17	43°13′N	77°56′W
Brockton, Ma., U.S. (brŏk′t*ŭ*n)	116-17	42°05′N	71°01′W
Brockville, On., Can. (brŏk′vĭl)	136-37	44°36′N	75°41′W
Brodnica, Pol. (brôd′nĭt-sȧ)	194-95	53°15′N	19°24′E
Brody, Ukr. (brô′dĭ)	194-95	50°05′N	25°10′E
Broken Arrow, Ok., U.S. (brō′k*ĕ*n ăr′ō)	120-21	36°03′N	95°47′W
Broken Bow, Ne., U.S. (brō′k*ĕ*n bō)	114-15	41°24′N	99°39′W
Broken Bow, Ok., U.S. (brō′k*ĕ*n bō)	120-21	34°02′N	94°44′W
Broken Hill, Austl. (brōk′*ĕ*n hĭl)	276	31°58′S	141°27′E
Broken Hill, Zam. *see* Kabwe	264-65	14°27′S	28°27′E
Brokopondo, Sur.	164-65	5°04′N	54°59′W
Brokopondo Stuwmeer, res., Sur. *see* W.J. van Blommestein Meer	164-65	4°49′N	55°04′W
Bromberg, Pol. *see* Bydgoszcz	194-95	53°07′N	18°01′E
Bronlund Peak, mtn., B.C., Can.	130-31	57°26′N	126°38′W
Brookfield, Mo., U.S. (brŏok′fēld)	120-21	39°48′N	93°05′W
Brookfield, Wi., U.S. (brŏok′fēld)	116-17	43°04′N	88°07′W
Brookhaven, Ms., U.S. (brŏok′hāv′n)	124-25	31°34′N	90°27′W
Brookings, Or., U.S. (brŏok′ĭngs)	112-13	42°04′N	124°17′W
Brookings, S.D., U.S. (brŏok′ĭngs)	114-15	44°19′N	96°48′W
Brooklyn Park, Mn., U.S. (brŏok′lĭn pärk)	114-15	45°07′N	93°20′W
Brooks, Ab., Can. (brŏoks)	132-33	50°34′N	111°54′W
Brooks Range, mts., Ak., U.S. (brŏoks rānj)	126	68°0′N	154°00′W
Brooksville, Fl., U.S. (brŏoks′vĭl)	125a	28°33′N	82°24′W
Brookton, Austl.	270-71	32°22′S	117°01′E
Broome, Austl. (bro͞om)	270-71	17°58′S	122°14′E
Brownfield, Tx., U.S. (broun′fēld)	120-21	33°11′N	102°16′W
Browning, Mt., U.S. (broun′ĭng)	112-13	48°33′N	112°60′W
Brownstown, In., U.S. (brounz′toun)	116-17	38°53′N	86°03′W
Brownsville, Tn., U.S. (brounz′vĭl)	124-25	35°36′N	89°16′W
Brownsville, Tx., U.S. (brounz′vĭl)	122-23	25°56′N	97°29′W
Brownwood, Tx., U.S. (broun′wŏod)	122-23	31°43′N	98°59′W
Bruce, Mount, mtn., Austl. (mount bro͞os)	272-73	22°35′S	118°08′E
Bruchsal, Ger. (brŏok′zäl)	194-95	49°08′N	8°36′E
Bruit, Pulau, i., Malay.	248-49	2°35′N	111°20′E
Bruneau, stm., U.S. (bro͞o-nō′)	112-13	42°57′N	115°57′W
Brunei, nation, Asia (brŏo-nī′)	206-07	4°30′N	114°40′E
Brunei, nat. cap., Bru. *see* Bandar Seri Begawan	248-49	4°56′N	114°56′E
Brünn, Czech Rep. *see* Brno	194-95	49°12′N	16°37′E
Brunswick, Ger. *see* Braunschweig	194-95	52°16′N	10°31′E
Brunswick, Ga., U.S. (brŭnz′wĭk)	124-25	31°11′N	81°30′W
Brunswick, Md., U.S. (brŭnz′wĭk)	116-17	39°19′N	77°38′W
Brunswick, Me., U.S. (brŭnz′wĭk)	117a	43°55′N	69°58′W
Brunswick, Península, pen., Chile	171	53°11′S	71°11′W
Brush, Co., U.S. (brŭsh)	120-21	40°15′N	103°38′W
Brusque, Braz. (bro͞o′s-ko͞oĕ)	172	27°07′S	48°56′W
Brussel, nat. cap., Bel. *see* Brussels	190-91	50°50′N	4°22′E
Brussels, nat. cap., Bel. (brŭs′*ĕ*ls)	190-91	50°50′N	4°22′E
Brüx, Czech Rep. *see* Most	194-95	50°31′N	13°39′E
Bruxelles, nat. cap., Bel. (brü-sĕl′) *see* Brussels	190-91	50°50′N	4°22′E
Bryan, Oh., U.S. (brī′*ă*n)	116-17	41°28′N	84°33′W
Bryan, Tx., U.S. (brī′*ă*n)	122-23	30°41′N	96°23′W
Bryansk, Russia	202-03	53°14′N	34°22′E
Bryce Canyon National Park, n.p., Ut., U.S. (brīs kăn′y*ŭ*n năsh′ŭn-*ă*l pärk)	118-19	37°29′N	112°15′W
Bryson City, N.C., U.S. (brīs′*ŭ*n sĭ′tē)	124-25	35°26′N	83°27′W
Bryukhovetskaya, Russia (b′ryŭk′ô-vyĕt-skä′yä)	202-03	45°49′N	39°00′E
Bua Yai, Thai.	246-47	15°35′N	102°26′E
Būbiyān, i., Kuw.	230-31	29°45′N	48°15′E
Bucaramanga, Col. (bo͞o-kä′rä-mäŋ′gä)	164-65	7°03′N	73°05′W
Buchach, Ukr. (bŏ′chȧch)	194-95	49°04′N	25°25′E
Buchanan, Lib. (bû-kăn′*ă*n)	260-61	5°53′N	10°02′W
Buchanan, Mi., U.S. (bû-kăn′*ă*n)	116-17	41°49′N	86°22′W
Buchanan, Va., U.S. (bû-kăn′*ă*n)	116-17	37°31′N	79°41′W
Buchanan, Lake, lk., Tx., U.S. (lāk bû-kăn′*ă*n)	122-23	30°48′N	98°25′W
Buchans, Nf., Can.	138-39	48°49′N	56°52′W
Bucharest, nat. cap., Rom. (bo͞o-kȧ-rĕst′)	200-01	44°26′N	26°06′E
Buckhannon, W.V., U.S. (bŭk-hăn′*ŭ*n)	116-17	38°59′N	80°14′W
Buckhaven, Scot., U.K. (bŭk-hā′v′n)	190-91	56°11′N	3°03′W
Buckie, Scot., U.K. (bŭk′ĭ)	190-91	57°40′N	2°59′W
Bucksport, Me., U.S. (bŭks′pôrt)	117a	44°34′N	68°48′W
București, nat. cap., Rom. (bo͞o-kŏ-rĕsh′tĭ) *see* Bucharest	200-01	44°26′N	26°06′E
Bucyrus, Oh., U.S. (bû-sī′r*ŭ*s)	116-17	40°48′N	82°58′W
Budapest, nat. cap., Hung. (bo͞o′dȧ-pĕsht′)	194-95	47°30′N	19°05′E
Budaun, India	234-35	28°02′N	79°08′E
Budennovsk, Russia	186-87	44°47′N	44°09′E
Budweis, Czech Rep. *see* České Budějovice	194-95	48°59′N	14°28′E
Buena Esperanza, Arg.	171	34°45′S	65°16′W
Buenaventura, Col. (bwä′nä-vĕn-to͞o′rȧ)	163c	3°53′N	77°04′W
Buenaventura, Mex.	144-45	29°51′N	107°28′W
Buena Vista, Bol.	168-69	17°27′S	63°40′W
Buena Vista, Co., U.S. (bū′n*ȧ* vĭs′t*ȧ*)	118-19	38°50′N	106°09′W
Buena Vista, Va., U.S. (bū′n*ȧ* vĭs′t*ȧ*)	116-17	37°44′N	79°21′W
Buenos Aires, state, Arg. (bwā′nōs ī′rās)	173	36°0′S	60°00′W
Buenos Aires, nat. cap., Arg. (bwā′nōs ī′rās)	173	34°37′S	58°23′W
Buenos Aires, Lago, lk., S.A. (lä′gô-bwā′nōs ī′rās)	171	46°26′S	71°40′W
Buffalo, Mn., U.S. (buf′*ȧ*-lō)	114-15	45°11′N	93°53′W
Buffalo, Mo., U.S. (buf′*ȧ*-lō)	120-21	37°39′N	93°06′W
Buffalo, N.Y., U.S. (buf′*ȧ*-lō)	116-17	42°53′N	78°52′W
Buffalo, Ok., U.S. (buf′*ȧ*-lō)	120-21	36°50′N	99°38′W
Buffalo, Tx., U.S. (buf′*ȧ*-lō)	122-23	31°27′N	96°04′W
Buffalo, Wy., U.S. (buf′*ȧ*-lō)	112-13	44°22′N	106°42′W
Buffalo, stm., Tn., U.S. (buf′*ȧ*-lō)	124-25	35°60′N	87°50′W
Buffalo Lake, lk., N.T., Can.	130-31	60°10′N	115°30′W
Buford, Ga., U.S. (bū′fērd)	124-25	34°07′N	84°00′W
Buga, Col. (bo͞o′gä)	163c	3°54′N	76°18′W
Bugojno, Bos. (bŏ-gō′ĭ nô)	200-01	44°03′N	17°27′E
Bugsuk Island, i., Phil.	250	8°15′N	117°18′E
Bugt, China	240-41	48°46′N	121°54′E
Bugul'ma, Russia (bŏ-gŏl′mȧ)	186-87	54°31′N	52°47′E
Buguma, Nig.	260a	4°43′N	6°53′E
Buguruslan, Russia (bŏ-gŏ-rŏs-lȧn′)	186-87	53°39′N	52°27′E
Buhl, Id., U.S. (būl)	112-13	42°37′N	114°46′W
Buin, Chile (bŏ-ēn′)	163e	33°42′S	70°43′W
Buir Nur, lk., Asia (bo͞o-ēr no͞or)	240-41	47°48′N	117°42′E
Buitenzorg, Indon. *see* Bogor	248-49	6°35′S	106°47′E
Bujumbura, nat. cap., Bdi. (bo͞o-jŭm-bo͞o′rȧ)	267	3°23′S	29°22′E
Buka Island, i., Pap. N. Gui.	279e	5°15′S	154°35′E
Bukama, D.R.C. (bo͞o-kä′mä)	262-63	9°12′S	25°51′E
Bukavu, D.R.C.	267	2°30′S	28°51′E
Bukhara, Uzb. (bŏ-kä′rä) *see* Buxoro	232-33	39°46′N	64°26′E
Bukittinggi, Indon.	246-47	0°18′S	100°22′E
Bukoba, Tan.	267	1°19′S	31°48′E
Bulan, Phil.	250	12°40′N	123°53′E
Bulawayo, Zimb. (bo͞o-lȧ-wä′yō)	264-65	20°10′S	28°35′E
Bulgan, Mong.	240-41	48°49′N	103°33′E
Bulgaria, nation, Eur. (bŏl-gā′rĭ-ă)	174-75	43°0′N	25°00′E
Bŭlgariya, nation, Eur. *see* Bulgaria	174-75	43°0′N	25°00′E
Bulkley Ranges, mts., B.C., Can. (bŭlk′lē rānj*ĕ*z)	132-33	54°30′N	127°30′W
Bulloo, stm., Austl.	272-73	28°40′S	142°31′E
Bull Shoals Lake, res., U.S. (bŏl shōlz lāk)	120-21	36°29′N	92°47′W
Bultfontein, S. Afr. (bŏlt′fŏn-tān′)	269c	28°17′S	26°09′E
Bulungu, D.R.C. (bo͞o-lŏŋ′go͞o)	262-63	6°03′S	21°53′E
Bumba, D.R.C. (bŏm′bȧ)	262-63	2°11′N	22°28′E
Bumbire Island, i., Tan.	267	1°39′S	31°53′E
Bunbury, Austl. (bŭn′b*ŭ*rĭ)	270-71	33°19′S	115°38′E
Bundaberg, Austl. (bŭn′d*ȧ*-bûrg)	277	24°52′S	152°20′E
Būndi, India	234-35	25°27′N	75°38′E
Bungo-suidō, strt., Japan	245	33°0′N	132°13′E
Bunia, D.R.C.	267	1°32′N	30°15′E
Bunkie, La., U.S. (bŭŋ′kĭ)	124-25	30°57′N	92°11′W
Buntok, Indon.	248-49	1°44′S	114°50′E
Buon Ma Thuot, Viet.	246-47	12°40′N	108°03′E
Buqayq, Sau. Ar.	230-31	25°56′N	49°40′E
Burang, China	234-35	30°14′N	81°11′E
Buraydah, Sau. Ar.	266	26°19′N	43°59′E
Burayk, Libya	258-59	26°37′N	13°07′E
Burbank, Ca., U.S. (bûr′bănk)	118-19	34°11′N	118°19′W
Burco, Som.	262-63	9°32′N	45°33′E
Burdur, Tur. (bo͞or-dŏr′)	186-87	37°43′N	30°17′E
Bureya, stm., Russia (bŏ-rā′yä)	240-41	49°25′N	129°32′E
Burgas, Blg. (bŏr-gäs′)	200-01	42°31′N	27°28′E
Burgaw, N.C., U.S. (bûr′gô)	124-25	34°33′N	77°56′W
Burgos, Spain (bo͞o′r-gōs)	198-99	42°21′N	3°42′W
Burgsvik, Swe. (bŏrgs′vĭk)	192-93	57°02′N	18°18′E
Burhānpur, India (bŏr′hȧn-po͞or)	234-35	21°18′N	76°14′E
Burias Island, i., Phil. (bo͞o′rē-äs ī′l*ă*nd)	250	12°57′N	123°08′E
Burica, Punta, c., N.A. (po͞o′n-tä-bo͞o′rē-kä)	150	8°03′N	82°52′W
Burin, Nf., Can. (bûr′ĭn)	138-39	47°02′N	55°11′W
Burkburnett, Tx., U.S. (bûrk-bûr′nĕt)	120-21	34°06′N	98°34′W
Burke, stm., Austl.	277	23°12′S	139°34′E
Burketown, Austl. (bûrk′toun)	277	17°44′S	139°33′E
Burkina Faso, nation, Afr. (bo͞or-kē′-nȧ fä′sō)	253	13°0′N	1°30′W
Burley, Id., U.S. (bûr′lĭ)	112-13	42°33′N	113°47′W
Burlington, On., Can. (bûr′lĭng-t*ŭ*n)	136-37	43°19′N	79°48′W
Burlington, Co., U.S. (bûr′lĭng-t*ŭ*n)	120-21	39°18′N	102°16′W
Burlington, Ia., U.S. (bûr′lĭng-t*ŭ*n)	114-15	40°48′N	91°06′W
Burlington, N.C., U.S. (bûr′lĭng-t*ŭ*n)	124-25	36°06′N	79°26′W
Burlington, N.D., U.S. (bûr′lĭng-t*ŭ*n)	114-15	48°16′N	101°25′W
Burlington, Vt., U.S.	116-17	44°29′N	73°12′W
Burlington, Wi., U.S. (bûr′lĭng-t*ŭ*n)	116-17	42°41′N	88°16′W
Burma, nation, Asia *see* Bhutan	206-07	22°0′N	98°00′E
Burnie, Austl. (bûr′nē)	276	41°04′S	145°54′E
Burnley, Eng., U.K. (bûrn′lē)	190-91	53°48′N	2°15′W
Burns, Or., U.S. (bûrnz)	112-13	43°36′N	119°03′W
Burnside, stm., Nu., Can.	130-31	66°51′N	108°12′W
Burns Lake, B.C., Can. (bûrnz lāk)	132-33	54°14′N	125°46′W
Burntwood, stm., Mb., Can.	134-35	56°08′N	96°20′W
Burqin, China	226	47°43′N	86°54′E
Burra, Austl.	276	33°40′S	138°55′E
Bursa, Tur. (bo͞or′sȧ)	200-01	40°12′N	29°04′E
Bûr Sa'îd, Egypt *see* Port Said	268b	31°16′N	32°18′E
Būr Sūdān, Sudan *see* Port Sudan	266	19°37′N	37°13′E
Burton, Mi., U.S. (bûr′t*ŭ*n)	116-17	43°00′N	83°35′W
Burton upon Trent, Eng., U.K. (bŭr′t*ŭ*n-ŭp′-ŏn-trĕnt)	190-91	52°49′N	1°38′W
Buru, i., Indon.	248-49	3°24′S	126°40′E
Burundi, nation, Afr. (bū-rūn′-dē)	253	3°15′S	30°00′E
Burun-Shibertuy, Gora, mtn., Russia	240-41	49°42′N	109°58′E
Burwell, Ne., U.S. (bûr′w*ĕ*l)	114-15	41°46′N	99°08′W
Buryatia, state, Russia	222-23	53°0′N	109°00′E
Buryatiya, state, Russia *see* Buryatia	222-23	53°0′N	109°00′E
Bury Saint Edmunds, Eng., U.K. (bĕr′ĭ-sānt ĕd′m*ŭ*ndz)	190-91	52°15′N	0°42′E
Busan, Kor., S. *see* Pusan	243	35°05′N	129°03′E
Būshehr, Iran	230-31	28°58′N	50°51′E
Bushire, Iran *see* Būshehr	230-31	28°58′N	50°51′E
Bushnell, Il., U.S. (bŏsh′nĕl)	120-21	40°33′N	90°30′W
Businga, D.R.C. (bŏ-sĭŋ′gȧ)	262-63	3°20′N	20°53′E
Busselton, Austl. (bŭs′l-t*ŭ*n)	270-71	33°39′S	115°21′E
Busto Arsizio, Italy (bo͞os′tō är-sēd′zē-ō)	200-01	45°37′N	8°51′E
Busuanga Island, i., Phil. (bo͞o-swäŋ′gä ī′l*ă*nd)	250	12°05′N	120°05′E
Buta, D.R.C. (bo͞o′tȧ)	262-63	2°49′N	24°45′E
Butare, Rw.	267	2°36′S	29°44′E
Butaritari, at., Kir.	280-81	3°06′N	172°50′E
Bute Inlet, b., B.C., Can.	132-33	50°37′N	124°53′W
Butembo, D.R.C.	267	0°08′N	29°18′E
Butere, Kenya	267	0°13′N	34°30′E
Butha-Buthe, Leso. (bo͞o-thȧ-bo͞o′thȧ)	269c	28°45′S	28°16′E
Butha Qi, China *see* Zalantun	240-41	47°60′N	122°45′E
Butler, In., U.S. (bŭt′lēr)	116-17	41°25′N	84°52′W
Butler, Mo., U.S. (bŭt′lēr)	120-21	38°15′N	94°20′W
Butler, Pa., U.S.	116-17	40°51′N	79°54′W
Buton, Pulau, i., Indon.	248-49	5°02′S	122°53′E
Butte, Mt., U.S. (būt)	112-13	45°60′N	112°32′W
Butterworth, Malay.	246-47	5°24′N	100°23′E
Butuan, Phil. (bo͞o-to͞o′än)	250	8°57′N	125°32′E
Butwal, Nepal	234-35	27°43′N	83°28′E
Buxoro, Uzb.	232-33	39°46′N	64°26′E
Buy, Russia (bwē)	186-87	58°29′N	41°33′E
Buyant-Uhaa, Mong.	240-41	44°55′N	110°09′E
Buynaksk, Russia	227	42°50′N	47°06′E
Buyr nuur, lk., Asia *see* Buir Nur	240-41	47°48′N	117°42′E

ăt; fin*ă*l; rāte; senåte; ärm; ȧsk; sof*ȧ*; fâre; ch-choose; dh-as th in other; bē; ēvent; bĕt; recĕnt; cratẽr; g-gō; gh-guttural g; bĭt; ĭ-short neutral; rīde; ĸ-guttural k as ch in German ich;

PRONOUNCING INDEX

Büyük Ağrı Dağı – Canaveral, Cape 315

Feature (Pronunciation)	Page	Lat.	Long.
Büyük Ağrı Dağı, vol., Tur. see Ararat, Mount	227	39°42'N	44°18'E
Buzău, Rom. (bōō-zĕ'ŏ)	202-03	45°09'N	26°50'E
Búzi, stm., Moz.	264-65	19°53'S	34°45'E
Buzuluk, Russia (bŏ-zŏ-lŏk')	186-87	52°47'N	52°15'E
Byala Slatina, Blg. (byä'la slä'tēnä)	200-01	43°28'N	23°58'E
Byblos, Leb. see Jubayl	228-29	34°08'N	35°40'E
Bydgoszcz, Pol. (bĭd'gôshch)	194-95	53°07'N	18°01'E
Byelorussia, nation, Eur. see Belarus	174-75	53°50'N	28°00'E
Bytantay, stm., Russia (byän'täy)	218-19	68°45'N	134°27'E
Bytom, Pol. (bĭ'tŭm)	194-95	50°21'N	18°55'E
Byumba, Rw.	267	1°36'S	30°04'E
Byzantium, Tur. see İstanbul	200-01	41°02'N	28°59'E
C			
Ca, stm., Asia	246-47	18°44'N	105°45'E
Caacupé, Para.	168-69	25°22'S	57°08'W
Caála, Ang.	264-65	12°51'S	15°33'E
Caazapá, Para.	168-69	26°11'S	56°22'W
Cabanatuan, Phil. (kä-bä-nä-twän')	250	15°29'N	120°59'E
Cabano, Qc., Can. (kä-bä-nō')	138-39	47°41'N	68°53'W
Cabedelo, Braz. (kä-bē-dā'lŏ)	163d	6°58'S	34°50'W
Cabeza del Buey, Spain (kȧ-bā'thä dĕl bwā')	198-99	38°43'N	5°13'W
Cabimas, Ven. (kä-bē'mäs)	164-65	10°24'N	71°26'W
Cabinda, Ang. (kä-bĭn'dȧ)	260-61	5°33'S	12°12'E
Cabinet Mountains, mts., U.S. (kăb'ĭ-nĕt moun'tĭnz)	112-13	48°19'N	116°12'W
Cabo, Braz.	163d	8°17'S	35°02'W
Cabo Frio, Braz. (kä'bō-frē'ŏ)	172	22°53'S	42°02'W
Cabonga, Réservoir, res., Qc., Can.	136-37	47°17'N	76°33'W
Caborca, Mex.	144-45	30°43'N	112°09'W
Cabot Strait, strt., Can. (kăb'ŭt strāt)	138-39	47°20'N	59°30'W
Cabo Verde, nation, Afr. see Cape Verde	253	16°0'N	24°00'W
Cabra, Spain (käb'rä)	198-99	37°29'N	4°27'W
Cabrera, Illa de, i., Spain	198-99	39°09'N	2°57'E
Cabrera, Isla de, i., Spain see Cabrera, Illa de	198-99	39°09'N	2°57'E
Cabriel, stm., Spain (kä-brē-ĕl')	198-99	39°14'N	1°03'W
Caçador, Braz.	168-69	26°47'S	51°01'W
Čačak, Serb. (chä'chȧk)	200-01	43°54'N	20°21'E
Cáceres, Braz. (kà'sĕ-rĕs)	168-69	16°04'S	57°42'W
Cáceres, Spain (kà'thå-räs)	198-99	39°28'N	6°22'W
Cache, stm., Ar., U.S. (kăsh)	124-25	34°42'N	91°20'W
Cache Creek, B.C., Can. (kăsh krēk)	132-33	50°49'N	121°19'W
Cachimbo, Serra do, mts., Braz.	166-67	8°25'S	55°45'W
Cachoeira do Sul, Braz. (kä-shô-ā'rä-dō-sōō'l)	173	30°02'S	52°54'W
Cachoeiras de Macacu, Braz. (kä-shô-ā'räs-dĕ-mä-kà'kōō)	172	22°28'S	42°39'W
Cachoeiro de Itapemirim, Braz.	172	20°51'S	41°08'W
Cadereyta Jiménez, Mex. (kä-dä-rā'tä hē-mā'nāz)	122-23	25°35'N	99°60'W
Cadillac, Mi., U.S. (kăd'ĭ-lăk)	116-17	44°15'N	85°24'W
Cádiz, Spain (kȧ'dēz)	198-99	36°31'N	6°17'W
Cadiz, Ky., U.S. (kā'dĭz)	124-25	36°52'N	87°50'W
Cadiz, Oh., U.S. (kā'dĭz)	116-17	40°16'N	80°60'W
Cádiz, Golfo de, b., Eur. (gôl-fô-dĕ-kà'dēz) see Cadiz, Gulf of	198-99	36°50'N	7°10'W
Cadiz, Gulf of, b., Eur. (gŭlf ŭv kā'dĭz)	198-99	36°50'N	7°10'W
Caen, Fr. (kän)	196-97	49°11'N	0°21'W
Caetité, Braz.	166-67	14°04'S	42°29'W
Cafayate, Arg.	168-69	26°04'S	65°59'W
Cagayan, stm., Phil.	250	18°22'N	121°37'E
Cagayan de Oro, Phil.	250	8°29'N	124°38'E
Cagayan Islands, is., Phil.	250	9°40'N	121°16'E
Cagayan Sulu Island, i., Phil.	250	7°01'N	118°30'E
Cagliari, Italy (käl'yä-rē)	200-01	39°14'N	9°07'E
Cagliari, Golfo di, b., Italy (gôl-fô-dē-käl'yä-rē)	200-01	39°08'N	9°11'E
Cagua, Ven. (kä'gwä)	163b	10°12'N	67°26'W
Caguas, P.R. (kä'gwäs)	142a	18°14'N	66°02'W
Cahaba, stm., Al., U.S. (kȧ hä-bä)	124-25	32°20'N	87°06'W
Cahors, Fr. (kȧ-ôr')	196-97	44°27'N	1°26'E
Cahul, Mol.	202-03	45°55'N	28°12'E
Caibarién, Cuba (kī-bä-rē-ĕn')	142-43	22°31'N	79°28'W
Caicedonia, Col. (kī-sĕ-dô-nêä)	163c	4°19'N	75°48'W
Caicó, Braz.	163d	6°27'S	37°06'W
Caicos Islands, is., T./C. Is. (kī'kōs ī'lȧndz)	142-43	21°42'N	71°54'W
Caicos Passage, strt., N.A. (kī'kōs pàs'ĭj)	142-43	22°00'N	72°30'W
Caimanera, Cuba (kī-mä-nā'rä)	142-43	19°59'N	75°10'W
Cairns, Austl. (kârnz)	277	16°56'S	145°45'E
Cairo, Ga., U.S. (kā'rō)	124-25	30°53'N	84°13'W
Cairo, Il., U.S. (kā'rō)	124-25	37°00'N	89°11'W
Cairo, nat. cap., Egypt (kī'rô)	268b	30°03'N	31°14'E
Cajamarca, Peru (kä-hä-mär'kä)	170	7°10'S	78°31'W
Cajazeiras, Braz.	166-67	6°54'S	38°34'W
Čakovec, Cro. (chà'kō-vĕts)	200-01	46°23'N	16°26'E
Calabar, Nig. (kăl-ȧ-bär')	260a	4°58'N	8°19'E
Calabozo, Ven. (kä-lä-bō'zō)	163b	8°55'N	67°26'W
Calafat, Rom. (kȧ-lȧ-fàt')	200-01	43°59'N	22°57'E
Calagua Islands, is., Phil. (kä-gä-yän ī'lȧndz)	250	14°27'N	122°55'E
Calahorra, Spain (kä-lä-ôr'rä)	198-99	42°18'N	1°58'W
Calais, Fr. (kȧ-lĕ')	196-97	50°58'N	1°51'E
Calais, Me., U.S.	117a	45°11'N	67°16'W
Calais, Pas de, strt., Eur. see Dover, Strait of	190-91	50°59'N	1°31'E
Calama, Chile (kä-lä'mä)	168-69	22°27'S	68°55'W
Calamar, Col. (kä-lä-mär')	164-65	1°58'N	72°42'W
Calamian Group, is., Phil. (kä-lä-myän' grōōp)	250	12°0'N	120°00'E
Calapan, Phil. (kä-lä-pän')	250	13°24'N	121°11'E
Călărași, Rom. (kŭ-lŭ-rȧsh'ĭ)	202-03	44°13'N	27°19'E
Calatayud, Spain (kä-lä-tä-yōōdh')	198-99	41°21'N	1°38'W
Calayan Island, i., Phil.	250a	19°20'N	121°27'E
Calbayog, Phil.	250	12°04'N	124°34'E
Calcasieu, stm., La., U.S. (kăl'kȧ-shū)	122-23	30°03'N	93°19'W
Calcasieu Lake, lk., La., U.S. (kăl'kȧ-shū lāk)	122-23	29°56'N	93°16'W
Calçoene, Braz.	166-67	2°30'N	50°57'W
Calcutta, India (kăl-kŭt'ȧ) see Kolkata	234-35	22°32'N	88°22'E
Caldas, Col. (kà'l-däs)	163c	6°04'N	75°38'W
Caldas da Rainha, Port. (käl'däs dä rīn'yȧ)	198-99	39°24'N	9°08'W
Caldera, Chile (käl-dā'rä)	168-69	27°04'S	70°50'W
Caldwell, Id., U.S. (kôld'wĕl)	112-13	43°40'N	116°41'W
Caldwell, Oh., U.S. (kôld'wĕl)	116-17	39°44'N	81°31'W
Caldwell, Tx., U.S. (kôld'wĕl)	122-23	30°31'N	96°42'W
Caledonia, Mn., U.S. (kăl-ē-dō'nĭ-ȧ)	114-15	43°39'N	91°31'W
Calella, Spain (kä-lĕl'yä)	198-99	41°37'N	2°40'E
Calexico, Ca., U.S. (kȧ-lĕk'sĭ-kō)	118-19	32°41'N	115°30'W
Calgary, Ab., Can. (kăl'gȧ-rĭ)	132-33	51°03'N	114°05'W
Calhoun, Ga., U.S. (kăl-hōōn')	124-25	34°30'N	84°58'W
Calhoun, Ky., U.S. (kăl-hōōn')	116-17	37°32'N	87°15'W
Cali, Col. (kä'lē)	164-65	3°27'N	76°31'W
Calicut, India see Kozhikode	236	11°16'N	75°47'E
California, Mo., U.S. (kăl-ĭ-fôr'nĭ-ȧ)	120-21	38°38'N	92°34'W
California, state, U.S. (kăl-ĭ-fôr'nĭ-ȧ)	108-09	37°30'N	119°30'W
California, Golfo de, b., Mex. (gôl-fô-dĕ-kä-lē-fôr-nyä)	144-45	28°0'N	112°00'W
California, Gulf of, b., Mex. (gŭlf ŭv kăl-ĭ-fôr'nĭ-ȧ) see California, Golfo de	144-45	28°0'N	112°00'W
Calimere, Point, c., India	236	10°17'N	79°52'E
Calipatria, Ca., U.S. (kăl-ĭ-pàt'rĭ-ȧ)	118-19	33°08'N	115°31'W
Calkiní, Mex. (käl-kē-nē')	148	20°23'N	90°02'W
Callabonna, Lake, lk., Austl. (lăk călă'bŏnȧ)	276	29°41'S	140°03'E
Callao, Peru (käl-yä'ô)	163a	12°04'S	77°08'W
Calling Lake, lk., Ab., Can. (kôl'ĭng lāk)	132-33	55°13'N	113°15'W
Calmar, Swe. see Kalmar	192-93	56°40'N	16°22'E
Caloosahatchee, stm., Fl., U.S. (kȧ-loo-sȧ-hăch'ē)	125a	26°32'N	82°01'W
Caltagirone, Italy (käl-tä-jē-rō'nå)	200-01	37°14'N	14°31'E
Caltanissetta, Italy (käl-tä-nē-sĕt'tä)	200-01	37°29'N	14°04'E
Caluula, Som.	262-63	11°57'N	50°46'E
Calvert Island, i., B.C., Can.	132-33	51°33'N	128°02'W
Calvillo, Mex. (käl-vēl'yō)	146-47	21°51'N	102°43'W
Calvinia, S. Afr. (kăl-vĭn'ĭ-ȧ)	264-65	31°28'S	19°46'E
Camacupa, Ang.	264-65	12°01'S	17°28'E
Camagüey, Cuba (kä-mä-gwā')	142-43	21°22'N	77°55'W
Camagüey, state, Cuba (kä-mä-gwā')	142-43	21°30'N	78°00'W
Camaná, Peru	170	16°37'S	72°42'W
Camaquã, Braz.	168-69	30°51'S	51°49'W
Camará, Braz.	166-67	3°55'S	62°44'W
Camarón, Cabo, c., Hond. (kà'bô-kä-mä-rōn')	149	15°59'N	85°02'W
Camarones, Arg.	171	44°48'S	65°43'W
Camas, Wa., U.S. (kăm'ȧs)	112-13	45°35'N	122°24'W
Ca Mau, Viet.	246-47	9°11'N	105°09'E
Ca Mau, Mui, c., Viet.	246-47	8°37'N	104°43'E
Cambodia, nation, Asia (kăm-bō'dē-ȧ)	206-07	13°0'N	105°00'E
Camborne, Eng., U.K. (kăm'bôrn)	190-91	50°13'N	5°18'W
Cambrai, Fr. (käN-brĕ')	196-97	50°11'N	3°15'E
Cambrian Mountains, mts., Wales, U.K. (kăm'brĭ-ăn moun'tĭnz)	190-91	52°35'N	3°35'W
Cambridge, On., Can. (kām'brĭj)	136-37	43°21'N	80°18'W
Cambridge, Eng., U.K. (kām'brĭj)	190-91	52°13'N	0°08'E
Cambridge, Il., U.S. (kām'brĭj)	114-15	41°18'N	90°11'W
Cambridge, Ma., U.S.	116-17	42°22'N	71°06'W
Cambridge, Md., U.S.	116-17	38°33'N	76°04'W
Cambridge, Mn., U.S. (kām'brĭj)	114-15	45°34'N	93°13'W
Cambridge, Ne., U.S. (kām'brĭj)	120-21	40°17'N	100°10'W
Cambridge, Oh., U.S. (kām'brĭj)	116-17	40°02'N	81°35'W
Cambridge Bay, Nu., Can.	128-29	69°07'N	105°04'W
Cambridge City, In., U.S. (kām'brĭj sĭ'tē)	116-17	39°49'N	85°11'W
Camden, Al., U.S. (kăm'dĕn)	124-25	31°59'N	87°17'W
Camden, Ar., U.S. (kăm'dĕn)	120-21	33°36'N	92°50'W
Camden, Me., U.S. (kăm'dĕn)	117a	44°13'N	69°05'W
Camden, N.J., U.S.	116-17	39°56'N	75°07'W
Camden, S.C., U.S. (kăm'dĕn)	124-25	34°15'N	80°36'W
Cameron, Mo., U.S. (kăm'ēr-ŭn)	120-21	39°44'N	94°14'W
Cameron, Tx., U.S. (kăm'ēr-ŭn)	122-23	30°51'N	96°59'W
Cameron, Wi., U.S. (kăm'ēr-ŭn)	114-15	45°25'N	91°45'W
Cameroon, nation, Afr. (kă'mȧ-rōōn')	253	6°0'N	12°00'E
Cameroon Mountain, vol., Camrn.	260-61	4°12'N	9°11'E
Cameroun, nation, Afr. see Cameroon	253	6°0'N	12°00'E
Cametá, Braz.	166-67	2°15'S	49°31'W
Camiguin Island, i., Phil.	250a	18°56'N	121°55'E
Camiling, Phil. (kä-mē-lĭng')	250	15°41'N	120°25'E
Camilla, Ga., U.S. (kȧ-mĭl'ȧ)	124-25	31°14'N	84°12'W
Caminha, Port. (kä-mĭn'yȧ)	198-99	41°52'N	8°49'W
Camiranga, Braz.	166-67	1°49'S	46°16'W
Camiri, Bol.	168-69	20°03'S	63°31'W
Camocim, Braz. (kä-mô-sēN')	166-67	2°54'S	40°51'W
Camooweal, Austl.	277	19°55'S	138°08'E
Campana, Arg. (käm-pä'nä)	173	34°10'S	58°57'W
Campana, Isla, i., Chile (ē's-lä-käm-pän'yä)	171	48°20'S	75°15'W
Campbell Island, i., N.Z.	287	52°33'S	169°08'E
Campbell River, B.C., Can.	132-33	50°01'N	125°15'W
Campbellsville, Ky., U.S. (kăm'bĕlz-vĭl)	124-25	37°21'N	85°21'W
Campbellton, N.B., Can. (kăm'bĕl-tŭn)	138-39	47°60'N	66°41'W
Campbelltown, Austl. (kăm'bĕl-toun)	276	34°04'S	150°49'E
Campeche, Mex. (käm-pā'chå)	148	19°50'N	90°31'W
Campeche, state, Mex. (käm-pā'chå)	148	19°0'N	90°30'W
Campechuela, Cuba (käm-pȧ-chwā'lä)	142-43	20°14'N	77°17'W
Cam Pha, Viet.	246-47	21°02'N	107°21'E
Campina Grande, Braz. (käm-pē'nä grän'dĕ)	163d	7°13'S	35°53'W
Campinas, Braz. (käm-pē'näzh)	172	22°55'S	47°05'W
Campo Alegre de Goiás, Braz.	172	17°38'S	47°46'W
Campobasso, Italy (käm'pô-bäs'sō)	200-01	41°34'N	14°40'E
Campo Belo, Braz.	172	20°54'S	45°16'W
Campo de Criptana, Spain (käm'pō dā krēp-tä'nä)	198-99	39°24'N	3°07'W
Campo Gallo, Arg.	173	26°34'S	62°50'W
Campo Grande, Braz. (käm-pŏ grän'dĕ)	168-69	20°28'S	54°38'W
Campo Maior, Braz. (käm-pŏ mä-yôr')	166-67	4°49'S	42°10'W
Campo Mourão, Braz.	168-69	24°02'S	52°24'W
Campos, Braz. (kä'm-pôs)	172	21°45'S	41°21'W
Camrose, Ab., Can. (kăm-rōz)	132-33	53°01'N	112°50'W
Canada, nation, N.A. (kăn'ȧ-dȧ)	85	60°0'N	95°00'W
Cañada de Gómez, Arg. (kä-nyä'dä-dĕ-gô'mĕz)	173	32°49'S	61°24'W
Canadian, Tx., U.S. (kȧ-nā'dĭ-ăn)	120-21	35°55'N	100°23'W
Canadian, stm., U.S. (kȧ-nā'dĭ-ăn)	110-11	35°27'N	95°05'W
Canajoharie, N.Y., U.S. (kăn-ȧ-jō-hăr'ē)	116-17	42°54'N	74°35'W
Çanakkale, Tur. (chä-näk-kä'lĕ)	200-01	40°09'N	26°25'E
Çanakkale Boğazı, strt., Tur. see Dardanelles	200-01	40°17'N	26°33'E
Canandaigua, N.Y., U.S. (kăn-ăn-dā'gwȧ)	116-17	42°53'N	77°17'W
Cananea, Mex. (kä-nä-nĕ'ä)	144-45	30°59'N	110°18'W
Canarias, Islas, is., Spain (ē's-läs-kä-nä'ryäs) see Canary Islands	199d	28°01'N	15°35'W
Canary Islands, is., Spain (kȧ-nâ'-rē ī'lȧndz)	199d	28°01'N	15°35'W
Cañas, C.R. (kä'-nyäs)	149	10°25'N	85°06'W
Canastota, N.Y., U.S. (kăn-ȧs-tō'tȧ)	116-17	43°05'N	75°46'W
Canatlán, Mex. (kä-nät-län')	146-47	24°31'N	104°46'W
Canaveral, Cape, c., Fl., U.S.	125a	28°27'N	80°32'W

n-sing; ŋ-baŋk; N-nasalized n; nŏd; cŏmmit; ōld; ôbey; ôrder; oi-boil; fōōd; ŏ-as oo in foot; ou-out; s-soft; sh-dish; th-thin; pūre; ûnite; ûrn; stŭd; circŭs; ü-as in French tu; '-indeterminate vowel.

316 Canavieiras – Casey PRONOUNCING INDEX

Feature (Pronunciation)	Page	Lat.	Long.
Canavieiras, Braz. (kä-nȧ-vē-ā´räs)	168-69	15°39´s	38°57´w
Canberra, nat. cap., Austl. (kăn´bĕr-*ȧ*)	276	35°17´s	149°08´e
Canby, Mn., U.S. (kăn´bī)	114-15	44°43´n	96°17´w
Cancún, Mex.	148	21°08´n	86°51´w
Candala, Som. *see* Qandala	262-63	11°28´n	49°52´e
Candeias, Braz.	166-67	12°40´s	38°32´w
Candelaria, Cuba (kän-dĕ-lä´ryä)	142-43	22°45´n	82°58´w
Candelaria, stm., Mex. (kän-dĕ-lä-ryä)	148	18°38´n	91°17´w
Cando, N.D., U.S. (kăn´dō)	114-15	48°29´n	99°13´w
Candon, Phil. (kän-dōn´)	250	17°11´n	120°27´e
Canea, Grc. *see* Chaniá	200a	35°31´n	24°01´e
Canelones, Ur. (kä-nĕ-lô-nĕs)	173	34°32´s	56°17´w
Cangas, Spain (kän´gäs)	198-99	42°16´n	8°47´w
Cangas de Narcea, Spain (kä´n-gäs-dĕ-när-sĕ-ä)	198-99	43°11´n	6°33´w
Cangkuang, Tanjung, c., Indon.	248-49	6°50´s	105°15´e
Canguçu, Braz.	173	31°21´s	52°37´w
Cangzhou, China (tsäŋ-jō)	240-41	38°18´n	116°52´e
Caniapiscau, stm., Qc., Can.	130-31	57°41´n	69°29´w
Caniapiscau, Réservoir de, res., Qc., Can. *see* Caniapiscau, Lac	130-31	0°0´	0°00´
Caniapiscau, Lac, res., Qc., Can.	130-31	54°09´n	69°51´w
Canicattì, Italy (kä-nē-kät´tē)	200-01	37°21´n	13°51´e
Çankırı, Tur.	186-87	40°36´n	33°37´e
Cannanore, India	236	11°52´n	75°22´e
Cannelton, In., U.S. (kăn´*ĕl*-t*ŭ*n)	116-17	37°55´n	86°45´w
Cannes, Fr. (kȧn)	196-97	43°33´n	7°01´e
Canning, N.S., Can. (kăn´ĭng)	138-39	45°09´n	64°25´w
Canoas, stm., Braz.	168-69	27°37´s	51°26´w
Canon City, Co., U.S. (kăn´y*ŭ*n sĭ´tē)	120-21	38°27´n	105°15´w
Canonsburg, Pa., U.S. (kăn´*ŭ*nz-bûrg)	116-17	40°16´n	80°11´w
Canora, Sk., Can. (k*ȧ*-nōr*ȧ*)	134-35	51°37´n	102°26´w
Canouan, i., St. Vin.	143b	12°43´n	61°20´w
Canso, N.S., Can. (kăn´sō)	138-39	45°20´n	61°00´w
Cantabrian Mountains, mts., Spain (kăn-tā´brē-*ă*n moun´tĭnz) *see* Cantábrica, Cordillera	198-99	43°0´n	5°00´w
Cantábrica, Cordillera, mts., Spain	198-99	43°0´n	5°00´w
Cantandica, Moz.	264-65	18°02´s	33°08´e
Cantanhede, Port. (kän-tän-yä´dȧ)	198-99	40°21´n	8°36´w
Cantaura, Ven.	163b	9°18´n	64°21´w
Canterbury, Eng., U.K. (kăn´tēr-bĕr-ē)	190-91	51°17´n	1°05´e
Canterbury Bight, b., N.Z.	278	44°15´s	171°38´e
Can Tho, Viet.	246-47	10°02´n	105°47´e
Canton, China *see* Guangzhou	238-39	23°08´n	113°16´e
Canton, Ms., U.S.	124-25	32°37´n	90°02´w
Canton, Oh., U.S.	116-17	40°48´n	81°23´w
Canton, i., Kir.	280-81	2°49´s	171°41´w
Cañuelas, Arg. (kä-nyoĕ´-läs)	173	35°03´s	58°45´w
Canutama, Braz.	166-67	6°31´s	64°21´w
Canyon, Tx., U.S. (kăn´y*ŭ*n)	120-21	34°59´n	101°55´w
Canyon de Chelly National Monument, n.p., Az., U.S.	118-19	36°07´n	109°27´w
Canyonlands National Park, n.p., Ut., U.S. (kăn´y*ŭ*n-lăndz năsh´ŭn-*ă*l pärk)	118-19	38°10´n	110°00´w
Cao Bang, Viet.	246-47	22°40´n	106°15´e
Capanaparo, stm., S.A.	164-65	7°03´n	67°04´w
Cap aux Meules, Île du, i., Qc., Can.	138-39	47°23´n	61°55´w
Cap-Chat, Qc., Can. (kȧp-shä´)	138-39	49°05´n	66°41´w
Cap-de-la-Madeleine, Qc., Can. (kȧp dē lȧ mȧ-d´lĕn´)	136-37	46°22´n	72°31´w
Cape Barren Island, i., Austl.	276	40°25´s	148°12´e
Cape Breton Highlands National Park, n.p., N.S., Can.	138-39	46°45´n	60°45´w
Cape Breton Island, i., N.S., Can. (kāp brĕt´*ŭ*n ī´l*ȧ*nd)	138-39	46°04´n	60°30´w
Cape Charles, Va., U.S. (kāp chärlz)	124-25	37°16´n	76°01´w
Cape Coast, Ghana	260-61	5°07´n	1°16´w
Cape Dorset, Nu., Can.	128-29	64°14´n	76°33´w
Cape Fear, stm., N.C., U.S. (kāp fēr)	124-25	33°53´n	78°01´w
Cape Girardeau, Mo., U.S. (kāp jē-rär-dō´)	120-21	37°18´n	89°32´w
Cape May, N.J., U.S. (kāp mā)	116-17	38°56´n	74°56´w
Cape Town, nat. cap., S. Afr. (kāp toun)	264-65	33°55´s	18°30´e
Cape Verde, nation, Afr. (kāp vērd´) (kāp vĕr´dē)	253	16°0´n	24°00´w
Cape York Peninsula, pen., Austl. (kāp yôrk pē-nĭn´sūl*ȧ*)	277	14°0´s	142°30´e
Cap-Haïtien, Haiti (kȧp ȧ-ē-syăn´)	142-43	19°45´n	72°12´w
Capim, stm., Braz.	166-67	1°41´s	47°47´w
Capitol Reef National Park, n.p., Ut., U.S. (kăp´ĭ-tŏl rēf năsh´ŭn-*ă*l pärk)	118-19	38°15´n	111°10´w
Capiz, Phil. *see* Roxas	250	11°35´n	122°45´e
Caprara, Punta, c., Italy (pōō´n-tä-kä-prä´rä)	200-01	41°07´n	8°19´e
Capreol, On., Can.	136-37	46°42´n	80°55´w
Capri, Isola di, i., Italy (ē´-sō-lä-dē-kä´prē)	200-01	40°33´n	14°13´e
Caprivi Strip, hist. reg., Nmb.	264-65	17°59´s	23°00´e
Cap Saint Jacques, Viet. *see* Vung Tau	246-47	10°21´n	107°05´e
Capulin Volcano National Monument, n.p., N.M., U.S. (kȧ-pū´lĭn vŏl-kā´nō năsh´ŭn-*ă*l mŏn´*ŭ*-m*ĕ*nt)	120-21	36°47´n	103°56´w
Caquetá, stm., S.A.	166-67	3°08´s	64°46´w
Caracal, Rom. (kȧ-rȧ-kăl´)	200-01	44°07´n	24°22´e
Caracaraí, Braz.	166-67	1°50´n	61°08´w
Caracas, nat. cap., Ven. (kä-rä´käs)	164-65	10°30´n	66°56´w
Caraguatatuba, Braz. (kä-rä-gwä-tä-tōō´bä)	172	23°37´s	45°25´w
Caraïbes, Îles des, is., *see* West Indies	140-41	19°0´n	70°00´w
Caraïbes, Mer des, s., *see* Caribbean Sea	140-41	15°0´n	73°00´w
Carajás, Braz.	166-67	6°06´s	50°23´w
Carajás, Serra dos, hills, Braz. (sĕ´r-rä-dôs-kä-rä-zhà´s)	166-67	6°16´s	51°21´w
Carangola, Braz. (kä-rän´gō´lä)	172	20°43´s	42°02´w
Caraquet, N.B., Can. (kȧ-rȧ-kĕt´)	138-39	47°47´n	64°57´w
Caratasca, Laguna de, b., Hond. (lä-gō´nä-dĕ-kä-rä-täs´kä)	149	15°24´n	83°54´w
Caratinga, Braz.	172	19°47´s	42°09´w
Carauari, Braz.	166-67	4°52´s	66°52´w
Caravelas, Braz. (kȧ-rä-vĕl´äzh)	172	17°44´s	39°15´w
Carazinho, Braz. (kä-rȧ´zē-ny*ō*)	168-69	28°17´s	52°46´w
Carballo, Spain (kär-bäl´yō)	198-99	43°13´n	8°41´w
Carberry, Mb., Can.	134-35	49°52´n	99°21´w
Carbonara, Capo, c., Italy (kä´pō är-bō-nä´rä)	200-01	39°06´n	9°31´e
Carbondale, Il., U.S. (kär´bŏn-dāl)	116-17	37°43´n	89°13´w
Carbondale, Pa., U.S. (kär´bŏn-dāl)	116-17	41°35´n	75°30´w
Carbonear, Nf., Can. (kär-bō-nēr´)	138-39	47°45´n	53°14´w
Carbon Hill, Al., U.S. (kär´bŏn hĭl)	124-25	33°54´n	87°32´w
Carcassonne, Fr. (kȧr-kȧ-sôn´)	196-97	43°13´n	2°21´e
Carcross, Yk., Can. (kär´krôs)	128-29	60°11´n	134°42´w
Cárdenas, Cuba (kär´dȧ-näs)	142-43	23°02´n	81°12´w
Cárdenas, Mex. (kȧ´r-dĕ-näs)	146-47	18°00´n	93°22´w
Cárdenas, Mex. (kȧ´r-dĕ-näs)	146-47	21°60´n	99°39´w
Cardiel, Lago, lk., Arg.	171	48°55´s	71°15´w
Cardiff, Wales, U.K. (kär´dĭf)	190-91	51°29´n	3°11´w
Cardigan, Wales, U.K. (kär´dĭ-g*ă*n)	190-91	52°05´n	4°39´w
Cardston, Ab., Can. (kärds´tŭn)	132-33	49°12´n	113°18´w
Carei, Rom. (kä-rĕ´)	194-95	47°41´n	22°28´e
Careiro, Braz.	166-67	3°14´s	59°46´w
Careiro, Ilha do, i., Braz.	166-67	3°09´s	59°48´w
Carey, Oh., U.S. (kā´rē)	116-17	40°57´n	83°23´w
Carey, Lake, lk., Austl. (lāk kâr´ē)	272-73	29°04´s	122°19´e
Caribbean Sea, s., (kăr-ĭ-bē´*ă*n sē)	140-41	15°0´n	73°00´w
Caribe, Mar, s., *see* Caribbean Sea	140-41	15°0´n	73°00´w
Caribische Zee, s., *see* Caribbean Sea	140-41	15°0´n	73°00´w
Cariboo Mountains, mts., B.C., Can. (kă´rĭ-bōō moun´tĭnz)	132-33	53°0´n	121°00´w
Caribou, Me., U.S.	117a	46°51´n	68°00´w
Caribou Mountains, mts., Ab., Can.	130-31	59°06´n	115°10´w
Caricyn, Russia *see* Volgograd	186-87	48°44´n	44°25´e
Carinhanha, Braz. (kä-rĭ-nyän´yä)	166-67	14°19´s	43°48´w
Caripito, Ven.	164-65	10°06´n	63°06´w
Carleton, Mount, mtn., N.B., Can.	138-39	47°23´n	66°53´w
Carleton Place, On., Can. (kärl´tŭn plās)	136-37	45°09´n	76°09´w
Carletonville, S. Afr.	269c	26°21´s	27°24´e
Carlinville, Il., U.S. (kär´lĭn-vĭl)	120-21	39°16´n	89°53´w
Carlisle, Eng., U.K. (kär-līl´)	190-91	54°54´n	2°56´w
Carlos Casares, Arg. (kär-lôs-kä-sä´rĕs)	173	35°38´s	61°21´w
Carlow, Ire. (kär´lō)	190-91	52°50´n	6°55´w
Carlsbad, Czech Rep. *see* Karlovy Vary	194-95	50°14´n	12°53´e
Carlsbad, Ca., U.S. (kärlz´băd)	118-19	33°09´n	117°20´w
Carlsbad, N.M., U.S. (kärlz´băd)	120-21	32°25´n	104°14´w
Carlsbad Caverns National Park, n.p., N.M., U.S. (kärlz´băd kăv´ērnz năsh´ŭn-*ă*l pärk)	120-21	32°08´n	104°35´w
Carlyle, Il., U.S. (kärlīl´)	116-17	38°36´n	89°22´w
Carmacks, Yk., Can.	128-29	62°05´n	136°15´w
Carman, Mb., Can. (kär´mȧn)	134-35	49°31´n	97°59´w
Carmarthen, Wales, U.K. (kär-mär´th*ĕ*n)	190-91	51°52´n	4°19´w
Carmaux, Fr. (kȧr-mō´)	196-97	44°03´n	2°10´e
Carmel, In., U.S. (kär´m*ĕ*l)	116-17	39°58´n	86°07´w
Carmelo, Ur. (kär-mĕ´lo)	173	33°60´s	58°17´w
Carmen, Mex. *see* Ciudad del Carmen	148	18°39´n	91°49´w
Carmen, Isla, i., Mex.	144-45	26°00´n	111°08´w
Carmen, Isla del, i., Mex. (ē´s-lä-dĕl-kȧ´r-mĕn)	148	18°43´n	91°40´w
Carmen de Areco, Arg. (kär´mĕn´ dā ä-rā´kō)	173	34°23´s	59°50´w
Carmi, Il., U.S. (kär´mī)	116-17	38°05´n	88°10´w
Carnarvon, Austl. (kär-när´v*ŭ*n)	270-71	24°52´s	113°40´e
Carnarvon, S. Afr.	264-65	30°58´s	22°08´e
Carnarvon National Park, n.p., Austl.	277	24°42´s	147°55´e
Carnegie, Ok., U.S. (kär-nĕg´ĭ)	120-21	35°07´n	98°35´w
Carnegie, Lake, lk., Austl.	272-73	26°11´s	122°31´e
Carnot, C.A.R.	262-63	4°56´n	15°53´e
Carnsore Point, c., Ire. (kärn´sôr point)	190-91	52°11´n	6°22´w
Caro, Mi., U.S. (kâ´rō)	116-17	43°29´n	83°23´w
Carolina, Braz. (kä-rō-lē´nä)	166-67	7°21´s	47°25´w
Carolina, S. Afr. (kăr-ô-lī´n*ȧ*)	269c	26°04´s	30°08´e
Caroline, at., Kir.	280-81	9°58´s	150°13´w
Caroline Islands, is., Oc. (kă´-rô-līn´ ī´l*ă*ndz)	280-81	8°0´n	147°00´e
Caroní, stm., Ven. (kä-rō´nē)	164-65	8°21´n	62°48´w
Carora, Ven. (kä-rō´rä)	164-65	10°10´n	70°05´w
Carpathian Mountains, mts., Eur. (kär-pā´thĭ-*ă*n moun´tĭnz)	186-87	48°0´n	24°00´e
Carpaţii, mts., Eur. *see* Carpathian Mountains	186-87	48°0´n	24°00´e
Carpaţii Meridionali, mts., Rom. *see* Transylvanian Alps	200-01	45°25´n	23°33´e
Carpentaria, Gulf of, b., Austl. (gŭlf ŭv kär-pĕn-târ´ĭ*ȧ*)	272-73	14°0´s	139°00´e
Carpentras, Fr. (kär-päɴ-träs´)	196-97	44°04´n	5°03´e
Carranza, Cabo, c., Chile	171	35°36´s	72°38´w
Carrara, Italy (kä-rä´rä)	200-01	44°05´n	10°06´e
Carrauntoohil, mtn., Ire.	190-91	51°59´n	9°45´w
Carreta, Punta, c., Peru (pōō´n-tä-kär-rĕ´tĕ´rȧ)	170	14°11´s	76°17´w
Carriacou, i., Gren.	143b	12°30´n	61°26´w
Carrington, N.D., U.S. (kăr´ĭng-t*ŭ*n)	114-15	47°27´n	99°07´w
Carrizal Bajo, Chile	168-69	28°06´s	71°09´w
Carrizozo, N.M., U.S. (kär-rē-zō´zō)	120-21	33°39´n	105°53´w
Carroll, Ia., U.S. (kăr´*ŭ*l)	114-15	42°04´n	94°52´w
Carrollton, Ga., U.S. (kăr-*ŭ*l-t*ŭ*n)	124-25	33°35´n	85°05´w
Carrollton, Il., U.S. (kăr-*ŭ*l-t*ŭ*n)	120-21	39°18´n	90°24´w
Carrollton, Ky., U.S. (kăr-*ŭ*l-t*ŭ*n)	116-17	38°41´n	85°11´w
Carrollton, Mi., U.S. (kăr-*ŭ*l-t*ŭ*n)	116-17	43°27´n	83°57´w
Carrollton, Mo., U.S. (kăr-*ŭ*l-t*ŭ*n)	120-21	39°22´n	93°30´w
Carrollton, Tx., U.S. (kăr-*ŭ*l-t*ŭ*n)	120-21	32°58´n	96°53´w
Carrot, stm., Can.	134-35	53°50´n	101°19´w
Carson City, Nv., U.S.	118-19	39°10´n	119°46´w
Cartagena, Col. (kär-tä-hä´nä)	164-65	10°25´n	75°30´w
Cartagena, Spain (kär-tä-ĸĕ´nä)	198-99	37°37´n	0°59´w
Cartago, Col. (kär-tä´gō)	163c	4°45´n	75°55´w
Cartago, C.R.	149	9°51´n	83°55´w
Cartersville, Ga., U.S. (kär´tērs-vĭl)	124-25	34°10´n	84°48´w
Carthage, Il., U.S. (kär´thâj)	120-21	40°25´n	91°08´w
Carthage, Mo., U.S. (kär´thâj)	120-21	37°11´n	94°19´w
Carthage, Ms., U.S. (kär´thâj)	124-25	32°44´n	89°32´w
Carthage, N.Y., U.S. (kär´thâj)	116-17	43°59´n	75°37´w
Carthage, Tx., U.S. (kär´thâj)	122-23	32°09´n	94°22´w
Cartwright, Nf., Can. (kärt´rīt)	128-29	53°41´n	56°60´w
Caruaru, Braz. (kä-rò-ȧ-rōō´)	163d	8°17´s	35°58´w
Carúpano, Ven. (kä-rōō´pä-nō)	164-65	10°40´n	63°15´w
Carutapera, Braz.	166-67	1°13´s	46°00´w
Caruthersville, Mo., U.S. (k*ȧ*-rŭdh´ērz-vĭl)	124-25	36°11´n	89°40´w
Carvoeiro, Braz.	166-67	1°26´s	61°60´w
Carvoeiro, Cabo, c., Port. (kȧ´bō-kär-vô-ĕ´y-rō)	198-99	39°21´n	9°24´w
Cary, N.C., U.S. (kă´rē)	124-25	35°47´n	78°47´w
Casablanca, Mor. (kä-sä-bläŋ´kä)	269a	33°36´n	7°36´w
Casa Branca, Braz. (kȧ´sä-brȧ´ɴ-kä)	172	21°48´s	47°04´w
Casa Grande, Az., U.S. (kä´sä grän´dā)	118-19	32°53´n	111°45´w
Casa Grande Ruins National Monument, n.p., Az., U.S.	118-19	32°59´n	111°32´w
Casamance, stm., Sen. (kä-sä-mäɴs´)	260-61	12°33´n	16°45´w
Casanare, stm., Col.	164-65	6°02´n	69°51´w
Cascade Mountains, mts., N.A. (kăs-kād´ moun´tĭnz)	110-11	45°14´n	121°56´w
Cascade Point, c., N.Z. (kăs-kād´ point)	278	44°00´s	168°22´e
Cascade Range, mts., N.A. (kăs-kād´ rānj) *see* Cascade Range	110-11	45°14´n	121°56´w
Cascais, Port. (käs-k*ȧ*-ēzh)	198-99	38°42´n	9°25´w
Cascavel, Braz.	168-69	24°58´s	53°27´w
Caserta, Italy (kä-zĕr´tä)	200-01	41°05´n	14°19´e
Casey, Il., U.S. (kā´sĭ)	116-17	39°18´n	87°60´w

n-sing; ŋ-bank; ɴ-nasalized n; nŏd; cŏmmit; ōld; ôbey; ôrder; oi-boil; fōōd; ò-as oo in foot; ou-out; s-soft; sh-dish; th-thin; pūre; ûnite; ûrn; stŭd; circŭs; ü-as in French tu; ′-indeterminate vowel.

318 Changane – Chicago PRONOUNCING INDEX

Feature (Pronunciation)	Page	Lat.	Long.
Changane, stm., Moz.	264-65	24°44'S	33°32'E
Changbaek-sanjulgi, mts., Asia *see* Changbai Shan	243	41°53'N	128°02'E
Changbai Shan, mts., Asia	243	41°53'N	128°02'E
Chang Cheng, p.o.i., China *see* Great Wall	240-41	40°0'N	112°30'E
Changchun, China (chäŋ-chòn)	240-41	43°53'N	125°19'E
Changde, China (chäŋ-dŭ)	238-39	29°02'N	111°41'E
Changhua, Tai. (chäng'hwä')	225a	24°04'N	120°30'E
Changji, China	222-23	44°01'N	87°18'E
Changjiang, China	238-39	19°16'N	109°02'E
Changkiakow, China *see* Zhangjiakou	240-41	40°49'N	114°53'E
Changli, China (chäŋ-lē)	240-41	39°42'N	119°10'E
Changmar, China	234-35	34°16'N	79°57'E
Changning, China (chäŋ-nĭŋ)	238-39	24°58'N	99°43'E
Changning, China (chäŋ-nĭŋ)	238-39	26°19'N	112°21'E
Changning, China (chäŋ-nĭŋ)	238-39	28°21'N	104°53'E
Changqing, China (chäŋ-chyĭŋ)	240-41	36°33'N	116°44'E
Changsha, China	238-39	28°12'N	112°58'E
Changshu, China (chäŋ-shōō)	238-39	31°38'N	120°44'E
Changting, China	238-39	25°50'N	116°21'E
Changyi, China (chäŋ-yē)	240-41	36°52'N	119°24'E
Changzhi, China (chäŋ-jr)	240-41	36°11'N	113°07'E
Changzhou, China (chäŋ-jō)	238-39	31°47'N	119°57'E
Chaniá, Grc.	200a	35°31'N	24°01'E
Chankiang, China *see* Zhanjiang	238-39	21°12'N	110°23'E
Channel Islands, is. Eur (chăn'ĕl ī'lăndz)	196-197	49°20'N	2°20'W
Channel Islands, is., Ca., U.S. (chăn'ĕl ī'lăndz)	118-19	34°0'N	120°00'W
Channel Islands National Park, n.p., Ca., U.S.	118-19	33°28'N	119°02'W
Channel-Port aux Basques, Nf., Can.	138-39	47°35'N	59°10'W
Chanthaburi, Thai.	246-47	12°37'N	102°07'E
Chantilly, Fr. (shäN-tē-yē')	196-97	49°12'N	2°28'E
Chanute, Ks., U.S. (shă-nōōt')	120-21	37°41'N	95°27'W
Chany, Ozero, lk., Russia (ô'zĕ-rô chä'nê)	226	54°50'N	77°30'E
Chao'an, China (chou-än)	238-39	23°40'N	116°39'E
Chao Hu, lk., China	238-39	31°31'N	117°33'E
Chao Phraya, stm., Thai.	246-47	13°32'N	100°36'E
Chaor, stm., China (chou-r)	240-41	46°48'N	123°35'E
Chaoxian, China (chou shyĕn)	238-39	31°35'N	117°51'E
Chaoyang, China (chou-yäŋ)	238-39	23°16'N	116°35'E
Chaoyang, China (chou-yäŋ)	240-41	41°35'N	120°28'E
Chapala, Mex. (chä-pä'lä)	146-47	20°17'N	103°11'W
Chapala, Laguna de, lk., Mex. (lä-ŏ'nä-dĕ-chä-pä'lä)	146-47	20°15'N	103°00'W
Chaparral, Col. (chä-pär-rá'l)	163c	3°44'N	75°28'W
Chapayevsk, Russia (châ-pī'ĕfsk)	186-87	52°58'N	49°42'E
Chapecó, Braz.	168-69	27°06'S	52°38'W
Chapel Hill, N.C., U.S. (chăp''l hĭl)	124-25	35°55'N	79°04'W
Chapleau, On., Can. (chăp-lō')	136-37	47°51'N	83°25'W
Chapman, Mount, mtn., B.C., Can. (mount chăp'măn)	132-33	51°50'N	118°20'W
Chappell, Ne., U.S. (chă-pĕl')	114-15	41°06'N	102°28'W
Charadai, Arg.	173	27°39'S	59°52'W
Chār Borjak, Afg.	230-31	30°18'N	62°01'E
Charcas, Mex. (chär'käs)	146-47	23°08'N	101°08'W
Chärdjew, Turkmen. *see* Türkmenabat	232-33	39°05'N	63°35'E
Chardzhou, Turkmen. *see* Türkmenabat	232-33	39°05'N	63°35'E
Chari, stm., Afr. (shä-rē')	262-63	12°56'N	14°34'E
Chārīkār, Afg.	232-33	35°01'N	69°10'E
Chariton, Ia., U.S. (châr'ĭ-tŭn)	114-15	41°01'N	93°19'W
Charkhlik, China *see* Ruoqiang	220-21	39°01'N	88°11'E
Charleroi, Bel. (shár-lē-rwä')	190-91	50°25'N	4°26'E
Charleroi, Pa., U.S. (shär'lē-roi)	116-17	40°08'N	79°54'W
Charles, Cape, c., Va., U.S. (kāp chärlz)	124-25	37°08'N	75°58'W
Charles City, Ia., U.S. (chärlz sĭ'tê)	114-15	43°04'N	92°41'W
Charleston, Il., U.S. (chärlz'tŭn)	116-17	39°29'N	88°11'W
Charleston, Mo., U.S. (chärlz'tŭn)	124-25	36°55'N	89°21'W
Charleston, S.C., U.S. (chärlz'tŭn)	124-25	32°47'N	79°56'W
Charleston, W.V., U.S. (chärlz'tŭn)	116-17	38°21'N	81°38'W
Charlestown, In., U.S. (chärlz'toun)	116-17	38°27'N	85°40'W
Charleville, Austl. (chär'lê-vĭl)	276	26°24'S	146°14'E
Charlevoix, Mi., U.S. (shär'lē-voi)	116-17	45°18'N	85°15'W
Charlotte, Mi., U.S. (shär'lŏt)	116-17	42°33'N	84°50'W
Charlotte, N.C., U.S. (shär'lŏt)	124-25	35°14'N	80°51'W
Charlotte Amalie, nat. cap., V.I.U.S. (shär-lŏt'ĕ ä-mä'lĭ-å)	143b	18°21'N	64°56'W
Charlotte Harbor, b., Fl., U.S. (shär'lŏt här'bĕr)	125a	26°45'N	82°11'W
Charlottenberg, Swe. (shär-lŭt'ĕn-bĕrg)	192-93	59°54'N	12°18'E
Charlottesville, Va., U.S. (shär'lŏtz-vĭl)	116-17	38°02'N	78°29'W
Charlottetown, P.E., Can.	138-39	46°14'N	63°08'W
Charlton Island, i., Nu., Can.	130-31	52°0'N	79°30'W
Chārsadda, Pak. (chŭr-sä'dä)	232-33	34°09'N	71°44'E
Charters Towers, Austl.	277	20°04'S	146°16'E
Chartres, Fr. (shärt'r')	196-97	48°27'N	1°29'E
Chascomús, Arg. (chäs-kō-mōōs')	173	35°35'S	58°01'W
Chase City, Va., U.S. (chās sĭ'tĭ)	124-25	36°47'N	78°28'W
Châteaudun, Fr. (shä-tō-dăN')	196-97	48°04'N	1°20'E
Château-Gontier, Fr. (chå-tō'gôN'tyā')	196-97	47°50'N	0°42'W
Châteauguay, Qc., Can. (chå-tō-gā)	136-37	45°23'N	73°44'W
Châteauroux, Fr. (shå-tō-rōō')	196-97	46°48'N	1°42'E
Château-Thierry, Fr. (shå-tō'ty-ĕr-rē')	196-97	49°03'N	3°24'E
Châtellerault, Fr. (shä-tĕl-rō')	196-97	46°49'N	0°33'E
Chatham, On., Can. (chăt'ăm)	136-37	42°24'N	82°11'W
Chatham, Il., U.S. (chăt'ăm)	116-17	39°40'N	89°42'W
Chatham, i., Ec. *see* San Cristóbal, Isla	170a	0°50'S	89°26'W
Chatham, Isla, i., Chile	171	50°38'S	74°27'W
Chatham Sound, strt., B.C., Can. (chăt'ăm sound)	132-33	54°32'N	130°35'W
Chatham Strait, strt., Ak., U.S. (chăt'ăm strāt)	126	57°30'N	134°45'W
Chatrapur, India	236	19°21'N	84°60'E
Chattahoochee, Fl., U.S. (chăt-tå-hōō' cheē)	124-25	30°42'N	84°51'W
Chattahoochee, stm., U.S. (chăt-tå-hōō' cheē)	110-11	30°46'N	84°52'W
Chattanooga, Tn., U.S. (chăt-ă-nōō'gă)	124-25	35°03'N	85°18'W
Chaudière, stm., Qc., Can. (shō-dyĕr')	138-39	46°45'N	71°17'W
Chauk, Mya.	246-47	20°54'N	94°49'E
Chaumont, Fr. (shō-môN')	196-97	48°06'N	5°08'E
Chauny, Fr. (shō-nē')	196-97	49°37'N	3°13'E
Chaves, Port. (chä'vĕzh)	198-99	41°44'N	7°28'W
Chavin, hist., Peru	170	9°37'S	77°14'W
Chavin de Huantar, hist., Peru *see* Chavin	170	9°37'S	77°14'W
Chaykovskij, Russia	186-87	56°46'N	54°06'E
Cheb, Czech Rep. (κĕb)	194-95	50°05'N	12°22'E
Cheboksary, Russia (chyĕ-bôk-sä'rê)	186-87	56°08'N	47°15'E
Cheboygan, Mi., U.S. (shê-boi'găn)	116-17	45°38'N	84°29'W
Chech, 'Erg, des., Afr.	258-59	24°43'N	2°31'W
Chechen', Ostrov, i., Russia (ôs-trôf' chyĕch'ĕn)	227	43°59'N	47°41'E
Chechnya, state, Russia	227	43°20'N	45°45'E
Checotah, Ok., U.S. (chê-kō'tă)	120-21	35°29'N	95°31'W
Chedabucto Bay, b., N.S., Can. (chĕd-ă-bŭk-tō bā)	138-39	45°23'N	61°10'W
Cheduba Island, i., Mya.	246-47	18°48'N	93°38'E
Cheektowaga, N.Y., U.S. (chēk-tŏ-wä'gă)	116-17	42°54'N	78°45'W
Chefoo, China *see* Yantai	240-41	37°32'N	121°21'E
Chegdomyn, Russia	218-19	51°08'N	133°05'E
Chehalis, Wa., U.S. (chê-hā'lĭs)	112-13	46°40'N	122°58'W
Cheju, Kor., S. (chĕ'jōō')	240-41	33°30'N	126°32'E
Cheju-do, i., Kor., S. (chĕ'jōō')	240-41	33°22'N	126°30'E
Chekiang, state, China *see* Zhejiang	238-39	29°0'N	120°00'E
Chelan, Wa., U.S. (chê-lăn')	112-13	47°50'N	120°00'W
Chelif, Oued, stm., Alg. (wĕd shä-lēf)	198-99	36°03'N	0°08'E
Chełm, Pol. (κĕlm)	194-95	51°08'N	23°30'E
Chełmno, Pol. (κĕlm'nō)	194-95	53°21'N	18°27'E
Chelmsford, Eng., U.K. (chĕlm's-fērd)	190-91	51°44'N	0°28'E
Chelsea, Mi., U.S. (chĕl'sê)	116-17	42°19'N	84°01'W
Chelsea, Ok., U.S. (chĕl'sê)	120-21	36°32'N	95°26'W
Cheltenham, Eng., U.K. (chĕlt'năm)	190-91	51°54'N	2°04'W
Chelyabinsk, Russia (chĕl-yä-bênsk')	226	55°10'N	61°26'E
Chelyuskin, Mys, c., Russia (mĭs chĕl-yòs'-kĭn)	218-19	77°45'N	104°20'E
Chemnitz, Ger.	194-95	50°50'N	12°56'E
Chemulpo, Kor., S. *see* Inch'ŏn	243	37°28'N	126°38'E
Chenāb, stm., Asia (chê-näb)	232-33	29°21'N	71°02'E
Cheney, Wa., U.S. (chē'nå)	112-13	47°29'N	117°35'W
Chengchow, China *see* Zhengzhou	238-39	34°46'N	113°39'E
Chengde, China (chŭŋ-dŭ)	240-41	40°58'N	117°56'E
Chengdu, China (chŭŋ-dōō)	238-39	30°39'N	104°04'E
Chengshan Jiao, c., China (jyou chŭŋ-shän)	240-41	37°23'N	122°42'E
Chennai, India	236	13°06'N	80°15'E
Chenyang, China *see* Shenyang	243	41°48'N	123°24'E
Chenzhou, China	238-39	25°48'N	112°59'E
Chepén, Peru (chĕ-pĕ'n)	170	7°14'S	79°25'W
Chepo, Pan. (chā'pō)	150	9°10'N	79°06'W
Cheraw, S.C., U.S. (chē'rô)	124-25	34°42'N	79°54'W
Cherbourg, Fr. (shăr-bòr')	196-97	49°39'N	1°38'W
Cheremkhovo, Russia (chĕr'yĕm-kô-vō)	218-19	53°09'N	103°04'E
Cherepanovo, Russia (chĕr'yĕ pä-nô'vō)	226	54°13'N	83°21'E
Cherepovets, Russia (chĕr-yĕ-pô'vyĕtz)	202-03	59°08'N	37°55'E
Chergui, Chott ech, lk., Alg. (chĕr-gē)	258-59	34°13'N	0°26'E
Cherkassy, Ukr. *see* Cherkasy	202-03	49°26'N	32°05'E
Cherkasy, Ukr.	202-03	49°26'N	32°05'E
Cherkessia, state, Russia	227	44°0'N	42°00'E
Cherkessk, Russia	227	44°13'N	42°04'E
Cherlak, Russia (chĭr-läk')	226	54°09'N	74°49'E
Chermoz, Russia (chĕr-môz')	186-87	58°47'N	56°09'E
Chernigov, Ukr. *see* Chernihiv	202-03	51°30'N	31°17'E
Chernihiv, Ukr.	202-03	51°30'N	31°17'E
Chernivtsi, Ukr.	194-95	48°17'N	25°58'E
Chernobyl, *see* Chornobyl', Ukr.	202-203	51°17'N	30°14'E
Cherno More, s., *see* Black Sea	186-87	43°0'N	35°00'E
Chernovtsy, Ukr. *see* Chernivtsi	194-95	48°17'N	25°58'E
Chernoye More, s., *see* Black Sea	186-87	43°0'N	35°00'E
Chernyakhovsk, Russia	194-95	54°38'N	21°49'E
Chernyanka, Russia (chĕrn-yäŋ'kä)	202-03	50°56'N	37°49'E
Cherokee, Ia., U.S. (chĕr-ô-kē')	114-15	42°45'N	95°33'W
Cherokee, Ok., U.S. (chĕr-ô-kē')	120-21	36°45'N	98°21'W
Cherrapunji, India	234-35	25°13'N	91°42'E
Cherryville, N.C., U.S. (chĕr'ĭ-vĭl)	124-25	35°23'N	81°23'W
Cherskiy, Russia	218-19	68°46'N	161°24'E
Cherskiy Mountains, mts., Russia (chĕr'skē moun'tĭnz) *see* Cherskogo, Khrebet	218-19	65°0'N	144°00'E
Cherskogo, Khrebet, mts., Russia	218-19	65°0'N	144°00'E
Cherson, Ukr. *see* Kherson	202-03	46°38'N	32°35'E
Chervonohrad, Ukr.	194-95	50°23'N	24°14'E
Chesaning, Mi., U.S. (chĕs'ă-nĭng)	116-17	43°11'N	84°07'W
Chesapeake, Va., U.S. (chĕs'å-pēk)	124-25	36°48'N	76°16'W
Chesapeake Bay, b., U.S. (chĕs'å-pēk bā)	116-17	38°38'N	76°27'W
Chester, Eng., U.K. (chĕs'tēr)	190-91	53°12'N	2°54'W
Chester, Il., U.S. (chĕs'tēr)	120-21	37°55'N	89°49'W
Chester, Mt., U.S. (chĕs'tēr)	112-13	48°32'N	110°57'W
Chester, Pa., U.S. (chĕs'tēr)	116-17	39°51'N	75°21'W
Chester, S.C., U.S. (chĕs'tēr)	124-25	34°42'N	81°13'W
Chester, Va., U.S. (chĕs'tēr)	116-17	37°21'N	77°26'W
Chester, W.V., U.S. (chĕs'tēr)	116-17	40°36'N	80°33'W
Chesterfield, Eng., U.K. (chĕs'tēr-fēld)	190-91	53°14'N	1°26'W
Chesterfield, Îles, is., N. Cal.	280-81	19°30'S	158°00'E
Chesterfield, Nosy, i., Madag.	264-65	16°20'S	43°58'E
Chesterfield Inlet, Nu., Can.	128-29	63°21'N	90°43'W
Chetek, Wi., U.S. (chĕ'tĕk)	114-15	45°19'N	91°39'W
Chettlatt Island, i., India	236	11°41'N	72°42'E
Chetumal, Mex.	148	18°30'N	88°18'W
Chetumal, Bahía, b., N.A. (bă-ē-ă-chĕt-ōō-mäl')	148	18°39'N	88°06'W
Chevak, Ak., U.S.	126	61°39'N	165°17'W
Cheviot, Oh., U.S. (shĕv'ĭ-ŭt)	116-17	39°09'N	84°37'W
Ch'ew Bahir, lk., Afr.	267	4°40'N	36°50'E
Chewelah, Wa., U.S. (chē-wē'lä)	112-13	48°17'N	117°43'W
Cheyenne, Wy., U.S. (shī-ĕn')	114-15	41°10'N	104°48'W
Cheyenne, stm., U.S. (shī-ĕn')	110-11	44°47'N	100°44'W
Cheyenne River Indian Reservation, ind. res., S.D., U.S. (shī-ĕn' rĭv'ĕr ĭn'dĭ-ăn rĕ-sĕr-vā'shĕn)	114-15	45°0'N	100°40'W
Cheyenne Wells, Co., U.S. (shī-ĕn' wĕls)	120-21	38°49'N	102°21'W
Chhapra, India	234-35	25°47'N	84°45'E
Chhatarpur, India	234-35	24°55'N	79°36'E
Chhattisgarh, state, India	234-35	21°30'N	82°00'E
Chhindwāra, India	234-35	22°03'N	78°57'E
Chi, stm., Thai.	246-47	15°11'N	104°43'E
Chiai, Tai. (chī'ī')	225a	23°29'N	120°27'E
Chiang Mai, Thai.	246-47	18°48'N	99°00'E
Chiang Rai, Thai.	246-47	19°55'N	99°50'E
Chiapa de Corzo, Mex. (chê-ä'pä dā kŏr'zō)	146-47	16°41'N	92°60'W
Chiapas, state, Mex. (chê-ä'päs)	146-47	16°30'N	92°30'W
Chiavari, Italy (kyä-vä'rē)	200-01	44°20'N	9°20'E
Chiba, Japan (chē'bá)	245	35°36'N	140°08'E
Chiba, state, Japan (chē'bá)	245	35°30'N	140°20'E
Chibougamau, Qc., Can. (chē-bōō'gä-mou)	138-39	49°55'N	74°22'W
Chibougamau, Lac, lk., Qc., Can. (läk chē-bōō'gä-mou)	138-39	49°50'N	74°15'W
Chibuto, Moz.	264-65	24°42'S	33°34'E
Chicago, Il., U.S. (shĭ-kô-gō) (chĭ-kä'gō)	116-17	41°52'N	87°38'W

n-sing; ŋ-bank; N-nasalized n; nŏd; cŏmmit; ōld; ôbey; ôrder; oi-boil; fōōd; ȯ-as oo in foot; ou-out; s-soft; sh-dish; th-thin; pūre; ûnite; ûrn; stŭd; circŭs; ü-as in French tu; ´-indeterminate vowel.

320 Cinto, Monte – Colmar PRONOUNCING INDEX

Feature (Pronunciation)	Page	Lat.	Long.
Cinto, Monte, mtn., Fr. (môɴ chēn´tō)	184-85	42°23´N	8°56´E
Cipolletti, Arg.	171	38°56´S	67°59´W
Circleville, Oh., U.S. (sûr´k'l-vĭl)	116-17	39°36´N	82°57´W
Circleville, Ut., U.S. (sûr´k'lvĭl)	118-19	38°10´N	112°16´W
Cirebon, Indon.	248-49	6°45´S	108°34´E
Cisco, Tx., U.S. (sĭs´kō)	120-21	32°24´N	98°59´W
Cisneros, Col. (sēs-nĕ´rôs)	163c	6°33´N	75°04´W
Cisterna di Latina, Italy (chēs-tĕ´r-nä-dē-lä-tē´nä)	200-01	41°36´N	12°49´E
Citlaltépetl, Volcán, vol., Mex. *see* Pico de Orizaba, Volcán	146-47	19°01´N	97°16´W
Citronelle, Al., U.S. (cĭt-rō´nĕl)	124-25	31°06´N	88°14´W
Città di Castello, Italy (chēt-tä´dē käs-tĕl´lō)	200-01	43°28´N	12°15´E
Ciudad Acuña, Mex.	122-23	29°19´N	100°56´W
Ciudad Altamirano, Mex. (syōō-dä´d-äl-tä-mē-rä´nô)	146-47	18°21´N	100°39´W
Ciudad Bolívar, Ven. (syōō-dhädh´ bô-lē´vär)	164-65	8°07´N	63°33´W
Ciudad Camargo, Mex.	122-23	27°42´N	105°10´W
Ciudad Cortés, C.R.	149	8°58´N	83°32´W
Ciudad Darío, Nic. (syōō-dhädh´dä´rē-ō)	149	12°43´N	86°07´W
Ciudad del Carmen, Mex. (syōō-dä´d-dĕl-kȧ´r-mĕn)	148	18°39´N	91°49´W
Ciudad del Maíz, Mex. (syōō-dhädh´del mä-ēz´)	146-47	22°24´N	99°36´W
Ciudad de México, nat. cap., Mex. *see* Mexico City	146-47	19°24´N	99°09´W
Ciudad de Nutrias, Ven.	164-65	8°05´N	69°17´W
Ciudad Guayana, Ven.	164-65	8°21´N	62°39´W
Ciudad Hidalgo, Mex. (syōō-dä´d-ē-dä´l-gô)	146-47	19°41´N	100°34´W
Ciudad Jiménez, Mex. *see* Jiménez	122-23	27°08´N	104°56´W
Ciudad Juárez, Mex. (syōō-dhädh hwä´räz)	122-23	31°45´N	106°28´W
Ciudad Lerdo, Mex. *see* Lerdo	122-23	25°32´N	103°31´W
Ciudad Madero, Mex. (syōō-dä´d-mä-dĕ´rô)	146-47	22°16´N	97°50´W
Ciudad Mante, Mex. (syōō-dä´d-mȧn´tĕ)	146-47	22°44´N	98°58´W
Ciudad Netzahualcóyotl, Mex.	146-47	19°27´N	99°03´W
Ciudad Obregón, Mex. (syōō-dhädh-ô-brĕ-gô´n)	144-45	27°29´N	109°57´W
Ciudad Ojeda, Ven.	164-65	10°13´N	71°19´W
Ciudad Real, Spain (thyōō-dhädh´rā-äl´)	198-99	38°59´N	3°55´W
Ciudad Rodrigo, Spain (thyōō-dhädh´rô-drē´gō)	198-99	40°36´N	6°32´W
Ciudad Valles, Mex.	146-47	21°59´N	99°00´W
Ciudad Victoria, Mex. (syōō-dhädh´vĕk-tō´rē-ä)	146-47	23°44´N	99°08´W
Civitavecchia, Italy (chē´vē-tä-vĕk´kyä)	200-01	42°06´N	11°48´E
Clairton, Pa., U.S. (klâr´tŭn)	116-17	40°18´N	79°53´W
Clanton, Al., U.S. (klăn´tŭn)	124-25	32°51´N	86°38´W
Clanwilliam, S. Afr.	264-65	32°10´S	18°54´E
Clare, Mi., U.S. (klâr)	116-17	43°49´N	84°45´W
Claremont, N.H., U.S. (klâr´mŏnt)	116-17	43°22´N	72°20´W
Claremore, Ok., U.S. (klâr´mōr)	120-21	36°19´N	95°37´W
Claremorris, Ire. (klâr-mŏr´ĭs)	190-91	53°43´N	8°60´W
Clarence, Isla, i., Chile	171	54°11´S	71°49´W
Clarence Island, i., Ant.	287	61°11´S	54°03´W
Clarence Strait, strt., Austl. (klăr´ĕns strāt)	272-73	12°0´S	131°00´E
Clarendon, Tx., U.S. (klâr´ĕn-dŭn)	120-21	34°56´N	100°54´W
Claresholm, Ab., Can. (klâr´ĕs-hōlm)	132-33	50°01´N	113°35´W
Clarinda, Ia., U.S. (klȧ-rĭn´dȧ)	120-21	40°44´N	95°02´W
Clarines, Ven. (klä-rē´nĕs)	163b	9°58´N	65°09´W
Clarion, Ia., U.S. (klăr´ĭ-ŭn)	114-15	42°44´N	93°44´W
Clarion, Pa., U.S. (klăr´ĭ-ŭn)	116-17	41°13´N	79°23´W
Clarión, Isla, i., Mex.	144-45	18°22´N	114°44´W
Clark, S.D., U.S. (klärk)	114-15	44°53´N	97°44´W
Clarke Island, i., Austl.	276	40°33´S	148°10´E
Clarksburg, W.V., U.S. (klärkz´bûrg)	116-17	39°16´N	80°20´W
Clarksdale, Ms., U.S. (klärks-dāl)	124-25	34°12´N	90°34´W
Clark's Harbour, N.S., Can. (klärks här´bẽr)	138-39	43°28´N	65°38´W
Clarks Hill Lake, res., U.S. (klärks hĭl lăk) *see* J. Strom Thurmond Reservoir	124-25	33°45´N	82°16´W
Clarkston, Wa., U.S. (klärks´tŭn)	112-13	46°25´N	117°04´W
Clarksville, Ar., U.S. (klärks-vĭl)	120-21	35°28´N	93°28´W
Clarksville, Tn., U.S. (klärks-vĭl)	124-25	36°31´N	87°21´W
Clarksville, Tx., U.S. (klärks-vĭl)	120-21	33°37´N	95°04´W
Claxton, Ga., U.S. (klăks´tŭn)	124-25	32°10´N	81°54´W
Clay Center, Ks., U.S. (klā sĕn´tẽr)	120-21	39°23´N	97°07´W
Clay City, Ky., U.S. (klā sĭ´tĭ)	116-17	37°52´N	83°57´W
Clayton, Ga., U.S. (klā´tŭn)	124-25	34°53´N	83°23´W
Clayton, N.C., U.S. (klā´tŭn)	124-25	35°39´N	78°28´W
Clayton, N.M., U.S. (klā´tŭn)	120-21	36°27´N	103°11´W
Clearfield, Ut., U.S. (klēr-fēld)	112-13	41°07´N	112°01´W
Clear Lake, Ia., U.S. (klēr lāk)	114-15	43°08´N	93°23´W
Clear Lake, S.D., U.S. (klēr lāk)	114-15	44°45´N	96°42´W
Clear Lake, lk., Ca., U.S. (klēr lāk)	118-19	39°02´N	122°50´W
Clearwater, Fl., U.S. (klēr-wô´tẽr)	125a	27°58´N	82°47´W
Clearwater, stm., Can. (klēr-wô´tẽr)	134-35	56°45´N	111°23´W
Clearwater, stm., Ab., Can. (klēr-wô´tẽr)	132-33	52°22´N	114°57´W
Clearwater Mountains, mts., Id., U.S. (klēr-wô´tẽr moun´tĭnz)	112-13	46°00´N	115°30´W
Cleburne, Tx., U.S. (klē´bŭrn)	120-21	32°22´N	97°24´W
Cle Elum, Wa., U.S. (klē ĕl´ŭm)	112-13	47°12´N	120°56´W
Clermont, Austl. (klēr´mŏnt)	277	22°49´S	147°40´E
Clermont-Ferrand, Fr. (klĕr-môn´fĕr-rän´)	196-97	45°47´N	3°06´E
Cleveland, Ms., U.S. (klēv´lănd)	124-25	33°45´N	90°43´W
Cleveland, Oh., U.S. (klēv´lănd)	116-17	41°29´N	81°42´W
Cleveland, Ok., U.S. (klēv´lănd)	120-21	36°19´N	96°28´W
Cleveland, Tn., U.S. (klēv´lănd)	124-25	35°10´N	84°52´W
Cleveland, Tx., U.S. (klēv´lănd)	122-23	30°21´N	95°05´W
Cleveland, Cape, c., Austl.	277	19°13´S	147°02´E
Cleveland Heights, Oh., U.S. (klēv´lănd hīts)	116-17	41°30´N	81°36´W
Cleves, Ger. *see* Kleve	194-95	51°47´N	6°09´E
Clewiston, Fl., U.S. (klē´wis-tŭn)	125a	26°45´N	80°54´W
Clifden, Ire. (klĭf´dĕn)	190-91	53°29´N	10°01´W
Clifton, Az., U.S. (klĭf´tŭn)	118-19	33°04´N	109°18´W
Clifton, Il., U.S. (klĭf´tŭn)	116-17	40°56´N	87°56´W
Clifton, N.J., U.S. (klĭf´tŭn)	116-17	40°53´N	74°10´W
Clifton, Tx., U.S. (klĭf´tŭn)	122-23	31°46´N	97°35´W
Clifton Forge, Va., U.S. (klĭf´tŭn fôrj)	116-17	37°49´N	79°50´W
Clinch, stm., U.S. (klĭnch)	124-25	35°53´N	84°30´W
Clingmans Dome, mtn., U.S. (klĭng´măns dōm)	124-25	35°35´N	83°30´W
Clinton, B.C., Can. (klĭn´tŭn)	132-33	51°05´N	121°37´W
Clinton, On., Can. (klĭn-´tŭn)	136-37	43°37´N	81°32´W
Clinton, Ar., U.S. (klĭn-´tŭn)	120-21	35°36´N	92°28´W
Clinton, Ia., U.S. (klĭn-´tŭn)	114-15	41°51´N	90°12´W
Clinton, Il., U.S. (klĭn-´tŭn)	116-17	40°09´N	88°57´W
Clinton, In., U.S. (klĭn-´tŭn)	116-17	39°39´N	87°24´W
Clinton, Ky., U.S. (klĭn-´tŭn)	124-25	36°40´N	89°00´W
Clinton, Mo., U.S. (klĭn-´tŭn)	120-21	38°22´N	93°46´W
Clinton, Ms., U.S. (klĭn-´tŭn)	124-25	32°21´N	90°19´W
Clinton, N.C., U.S. (klĭn-´tŭn)	124-25	34°59´N	78°19´W
Clinton, Ok., U.S. (klĭn-´tŭn)	120-21	35°31´N	98°58´W
Clinton, S.C., U.S. (klĭn-´tŭn)	124-25	34°28´N	81°53´W
Clinton, Tn., U.S. (klĭn-´tŭn)	124-25	36°06´N	84°08´W
Clintonville, Wi., U.S. (klĭn´tŭn-vĭl)	116-17	44°36´N	88°46´W
Clio, Mi., U.S. (klē´ō)	116-17	43°10´N	83°44´W
Clipperton, Île, at., Oc.	140-41	10°18´N	109°13´W
Clipperton Island, at., Oc. *see* Clipperton, Île	140-41	10°18´N	109°13´W
Clodomira, Arg.	173	27°33´S	64°07´W
Cloncurry, Austl. (klŏn-kŭr´ē)	277	20°43´S	140°30´E
Cloquet, Mn., U.S. (klô-kā´)	114-15	46°43´N	92°28´W
Cloud Peak, mtn., Wy., U.S. (kloud pēk)	112-13	44°25´N	107°10´W
Clover, S.C., U.S. (klō´vẽr)	124-25	35°07´N	81°14´W
Cloverdale, Ca., U.S. (klō´vẽr-dāl)	118-19	38°48´N	123°01´W
Clovis, Ca., U.S. (klō´vĭs)	118-19	36°50´N	119°42´W
Clovis, N.M., U.S. (klō´vĭs)	120-21	34°24´N	103°13´W
Cluj-Napoca, Rom.	194-95	46°47´N	23°36´E
Cluny, Fr. (klü-nē´)	196-97	46°26´N	4°39´E
Clyde, Oh., U.S. (klīd)	116-17	41°18´N	82°58´W
Clyde, Tx., U.S. (klīd)	120-21	32°25´N	99°29´W
Cnossus, hist., Grc. *see* Knossos	200a	35°17´N	25°12´E
Côa, stm., Port. (kô´ä)	198-99	41°05´N	7°06´W
Coahuila, state, Mex. (kō-ä-wē´lȧ)	122-23	27°20´N	102°00´W
Coalcomán de Matamoros, Mex.	146-47	18°47´N	103°09´W
Coaldale, Ab., Can. (kōl´dāl)	132-33	49°44´N	112°37´W
Coalgate, Ok., U.S. (kōl´gāt)	120-21	34°32´N	96°14´W
Coalinga, Ca., U.S. (kō-ȧ-lĭn´gȧ)	118-19	36°09´N	120°22´W
Coari, Braz. (kō-är´ē)	166-67	4°06´S	63°07´W
Coari, stm., Braz.	166-67	4°27´S	63°29´W
Coast Mountains, mts., N.A. (kōst moun´tĭnz)	130-31	55°0´N	129°00´W
Coast Ranges, mts., U.S. (kōst rānjĕz)	110-11	40°46´N	123°38´W
Coatesville, Pa., U.S. (kōts´vĭl)	116-17	39°59´N	75°49´W
Coaticook, Qc., Can. (kō´tĭ-kŏŏk)	136-37	45°08´N	71°48´W
Coats Island, i., Nu., Can. (kōts ī´lănd)	130-31	62°30´N	82°60´W
Coats Land, reg., Ant. (kōts lănd)	287	77°0´S	28°00´W
Coatzacoalcos, Mex.	146-47	18°08´N	94°26´W
Cobá, hist., Mex. (kô´bä)	148	20°36´N	87°35´W
Cobalt, On., Can. (kō´bôlt)	136-37	47°24´N	79°41´W
Cobán, Guat. (kō-bän´)	148	15°28´N	90°22´W
Cobar, Austl.	276	31°30´S	145°50´E
Cobija, Bol. (kô-bē´hä)	166-67	11°02´S	68°44´W
Coblenz, Ger. *see* Koblenz	194-95	50°21´N	7°35´E
Cobourg, On., Can. (kō´bŏŏrgh)	136-37	43°58´N	78°09´W
Cobourg Peninsula, pen., Austl.	272-73	11°22´S	132°17´E
Coburg, Ger. (kō´bōōrg)	194-95	50°16´N	10°58´E
Cocanada, India *see* Kākināda	236	16°57´N	82°15´E
Cochabamba, Bol.	168-69	17°23´S	66°10´W
Cochin, India	236	9°56´N	76°15´E
Cochran, Ga., U.S. (kŏk´răn)	124-25	32°23´N	83°21´W
Cochrane, Ab., Can. (kŏk´răn)	132-33	51°11´N	114°29´W
Cochrane, On., Can. (kŏk´răn)	136-37	49°04´N	81°02´W
Cochrane, Lago, lk., S.A.	171	47°21´S	71°56´W
Cockburn Island, i., On., Can. (kŏk-bûrn ī´lănd)	136-37	45°55´N	83°22´W
Cockburn Town, nat. cap., T./C. Is. *see* Grand Turk	142-43	21°27´N	71°08´W
Coco, stm., N.A. (kô-kô)	149	14°59´N	83°11´W
Coco, Cayo, i., Cuba (kä´-yō-kô´kô)	142-43	22°29´N	78°28´W
Coco, Isla del, i., C.R. (ē´s-lä-dĕl-kô-kô)	86	5°32´N	87°04´W
Cocoa, Fl., U.S. (kō´kō)	125a	28°22´N	80°44´W
Cocoa Beach, Fl., U.S. (kō´kō bēch)	125a	28°19´N	80°37´W
Coco Channel, strt., Asia	246-47	13°45´N	93°01´E
Coco Islands, is., Mya.	246-47	14°09´N	93°25´E
Cocos Islands, dep., Oc. (kō´kôs ī´lăndz)	224-25	12°10´S	96°55´E
Cocula, Mex. (kō-kōō´lä)	146-47	20°23´N	103°50´W
Cod, Cape, pen., Ma., U.S. (kāp kŏd)	116-17	41°42´N	70°15´W
Codajás, Braz. (kō-dä-hàzh´)	166-67	3°49´S	62°05´W
Codera, Cabo, c., Ven. (kȧ´bô-kô-dĕ´rä)	163b	10°34´N	66°03´W
Codó, Braz.	166-67	4°29´S	43°53´W
Cody, Wy., U.S. (kō´dĭ)	112-13	44°32´N	109°03´W
Coeur d'Alene, Id., U.S. (kûr dȧ-lān´)	112-13	47°41´N	116°47´W
Coeur d'Alene Indian Reservation, ind. res., Id., U.S. (kûr dȧ-lān´ ĭn´dĭ-ăn rĕ-sẽr-vā´shĕn)	112-13	47°18´N	116°45´W
Coffeyville, Ks., U.S. (kŏf´ĭ-vĭl)	120-21	37°02´N	95°37´W
Coffs Harbour, Austl.	276	30°19´S	153°08´E
Cognac, Fr. (kôn-yak´)	196-97	45°42´N	0°20´W
Cohoes, N.Y., U.S. (kô-hōz´)	116-17	42°47´N	73°42´W
Coiba, Isla de, i., Pan.	150	7°27´N	81°45´W
Coig, stm., Arg. (kô´ĕk)	171	50°57´S	69°09´W
Coihaique, Chile	171	45°34´S	72°04´W
Coimbatore, India (kô-ēm-bȧ-tôr´)	236	10°60´N	76°58´E
Coimbra, Port. (kô-ēm´brä)	198-99	40°13´N	8°25´W
Coín, Spain (kô-ēn´)	198-99	36°40´N	4°46´W
Coire, Switz. *see* Chur	194-95	46°51´N	9°31´E
Cojutepeque, El Sal. (kô-hò-tĕ-pā´kå)	148	13°43´N	88°56´W
Cokato, Mn., U.S. (kô-kā´tō)	114-15	45°04´N	94°12´W
Colac, Austl. (kŏ´lȧc)	276	38°21´S	143°35´E
Colatina, Braz. (kô-lä-tē´nä)	172	19°32´S	40°39´W
Colbeck, Cape, c., Ant.	287	77°25´S	157°33´W
Colby, Ks., U.S. (kōl´bĭ)	120-21	39°24´N	101°03´W
Colchester, Eng., U.K. (kōl´chĕs-tẽr)	190-91	51°53´N	0°54´E
Cold Lake, Ab., Can.	132-33	54°27´N	110°10´W
Cold Lake, lk., Can. (kōld lāk)	132-33	54°33´N	110°05´W
Coldwater, Mi., U.S. (kōld´wô-tẽr)	116-17	41°57´N	85°00´W
Coleman, Tx., U.S. (kōl´măn)	122-23	31°50´N	99°25´W
Colenso, S. Afr. (kŏ-lĕnz´ô)	269c	28°45´S	29°50´E
Coleraine, Mn., U.S. (kōl-rān´)	114-15	47°17´N	93°26´W
Colesberg, S. Afr.	264-65	30°43´S	25°06´E
Colfax, Ia., U.S. (kōl´făks)	114-15	41°41´N	93°15´W
Colfax, La., U.S. (kōl´făks)	122-23	31°31´N	92°42´W
Colfax, Wa., U.S. (kōl´făks)	112-13	46°53´N	117°22´W
Colhué Huapi, Lago, lk., Arg. (lä´gô kôl-wā´ōȧ´pē)	171	45°32´S	68°46´W
Colima, Mex.	146-47	19°14´N	103°44´W
Colima, state, Mex. (kōlē´mä)	146-47	19°10´N	104°00´W
Colima, Nevado de, vol., Mex. (nĕ-vä´dô-dĕ-kô-lē´mä)	146-47	19°33´N	103°38´W
Colinas, Braz.	166-67	6°02´S	44°14´W
Coll, i., Scot., U.K. (kōl)	190-91	56°38´N	6°34´W
College, Ak., U.S. (kŏl´ĕj)	126	64°51´N	147°46´W
College Park, Ga., U.S. (kŏl´ĕj pärk)	124-25	33°39´N	84°27´W
Collie, Austl. (kŏl´ē)	270-71	33°21´S	116°09´E
Collier Bay, b., Austl. (kŏl-yẽr bā)	272-73	16°10´S	124°15´E
Collingwood, On., Can. (kŏl´ĭng-wŏŏd)	136-37	44°29´N	80°12´W
Collins, Ms., U.S. (kŏl´ĭns)	124-25	31°38´N	89°34´W
Collinsville, Austl.	277	20°34´S	147°51´E
Collinsville, Il., U.S. (kŏl´ĭnz-vĭl)	120-21	38°41´N	89°58´W
Collinsville, Ok., U.S. (kŏl´ĭnz-vĭl)	120-21	36°22´N	95°50´W
Collipulli, Chile	171	37°57´S	72°26´W
Colmar, Fr. (kôl´mär)	196-97	48°05´N	7°22´E

PRONOUNCING INDEX
Colmenar Viejo – Corpus Christi Bay 321

Feature (Pronunciation)	Page	Lat.	Long.
Colmenar Viejo, Spain (kôl-mā-när´vyā´hō)	198-99	40°40'N	3°46'W
Cologne, Ger. (kŭ-lōn´)	194-95	50°56'N	6°57'E
Colomb-Béchar, Alg. see Béchar	258-59	31°37'N	2°14'W
Colombia, Col. (kô-lôm´bē-ä)	163c	3°24'N	74°48'W
Colombia, nation, S.A. (kô-lôm´bē-ä)	158	4°0'N	72°00'W
Colombo, nat. cap., Sri L. (kô-lôm´bō)	236	6°55'N	79°52'E
Colón, Arg. (kō-lōn´)	173	32°16'S	58°08'W
Colón, Arg. (kō-lōn´)	173	33°55'S	61°04'W
Colón, Cuba (kô-lô´n)	142-43	22°43'N	80°54'W
Colón, Pan. (kō-lô´n)	150	9°22'N	79°54'W
Colón, Archipiélago de, is., Ec.	170a	0°43'N	91°30'W
Colonia Alvear Norte, Arg. see General Alvear	171	34°59'S	67°42'W
Colonia del Sacramento, Ur.	173	34°29'S	57°50'W
Colonia Dora, Arg.	173	28°37'S	62°57'W
Colonia Suiza, Ur. (kô-lô´nēä-soē´zä)	173	34°18'S	57°14'W
Colorado, state, U.S. (kŏl-ô-rä´dō)	108-09	39°0'N	105°30'W
Colorado, stm., Arg.	171	39°52'S	62°09'W
Colorado, stm., N.A. (kŏl-ô-rä´dō)	110-11	31°55'N	114°58'W
Colorado, stm., Tx., U.S. (kŏl-ô-rä´dō)	122-23	28°36'N	95°59'W
Colorado City, Tx., U.S. (kŏl-ô-rä´dō sĭ´tĭ)	120-21	32°23'N	100°52'W
Colorado National Monument, n.p., Co., U.S. (kŏl-ô-rä´dō năsh´ŭn-ăl mŏn´ū-mĕnt)	118-19	39°03'N	108°41'W
Colorado Plateau, plat., U.S. (kŏl-ô-rä´dō plä-tō´)	118-19	38°0'N	109°00'W
Colorado Springs, Co., U.S. (kŏl-ô-rä´dō sprĭngz)	120-21	38°50'N	104°49'W
Colotepec, stm., Mex. (kô-lô´tĕ-pĕk)	146-47	15°48'N	97°01'W
Colotlán, Mex. (kô-lô-tlän´)	146-47	22°06'N	103°15'W
Colquechaca, Bol. (kôl-kä-chä´kä)	168-69	18°41'S	66°02'W
Colstrip, Mt., U.S. (kōl´strip)	112-13	45°53'N	106°39'W
Columbia, Il., U.S. (kô-lŭm´bĭ-ȧ)	120-21	38°26'N	90°11'W
Columbia, Ky., U.S. (kô-lŭm´bĭ-ȧ)	124-25	37°06'N	85°18'W
Columbia, Md., U.S. (kô-lŭm´bĭ-ȧ)	116-17	39°14'N	76°50'W
Columbia, Mo., U.S. (kô-lŭm´bĭ-ȧ)	120-21	38°57'N	92°21'W
Columbia, Ms., U.S. (kô-lŭm´bĭ-ȧ)	124-25	31°15'N	89°50'W
Columbia, S.C., U.S. (kô-lŭm´bĭ-ȧ)	124-25	34°00'N	81°02'W
Columbia, Tn., U.S. (kô-lŭm´bĭ-ȧ)	124-25	35°37'N	87°02'W
Columbia, stm., N.A. (kô-lŭm´bĭ-ȧ)	130-31	46°14'N	124°06'W
Columbia, Mount, mtn., Ab., Can. (mount kô-lŭm´bĭ-ȧ)	132-33	52°09'N	117°25'W
Columbia City, In., U.S. (kô-lŭm´bĭ-ȧ sĭ´tē)	116-17	41°09'N	85°28'W
Columbia Icefield, ice, Can. (kô-lŭm´bĭ-ȧ ī´fēld)	132-33	52°08'N	117°27'W
Columbia Mountains, mts., N.A. (kô-lŭm´bĭ-ȧ moun´tĭnz)	130-31	52°0'N	119°00'W
Columbiana, Al., U.S. (kô-ŭm-bĭ-ă´nȧ)	124-25	33°11'N	86°36'W
Columbus, Ga., U.S. (kô-lŭm´bŭs)	124-25	32°28'N	84°58'W
Columbus, In., U.S. (kô-lŭm´bŭs)	116-17	39°12'N	85°55'W
Columbus, Ms., U.S. (kô-lŭm´bŭs)	124-25	33°29'N	88°25'W
Columbus, Mt., U.S. (kô-lŭm´bŭs)	112-13	45°39'N	109°16'W
Columbus, Ne., U.S. (kô-lŭm´bŭs)	114-15	41°26'N	97°22'W
Columbus, N.M., U.S. (kô-lŭm´bŭs)	118-19	31°50'N	107°38'W
Columbus, Oh., U.S.	116-17	39°58'N	82°60'W
Columbus, Tx., U.S. (kô-lŭm´bŭs)	122-23	29°42'N	96°32'W
Columbus, Wi., U.S. (kô-lŭm´bŭs)	116-17	43°21'N	89°01'W
Colusa, Ca., U.S. (kô-lū´sȧ)	118-19	39°12'N	122°01'W
Colville, Wa., U.S. (kōl´vĭl)	112-13	48°33'N	117°54'W
Colville, stm., Ak., U.S. (kōl´vĭl)	126	70°27'N	150°18'W
Colville Indian Reservation, ind. res., Wa., U.S. (kōl´vĭl ĭn´dĭ-ăn rĕ-sĕr-vā´shĕn)	112-13	48°15'N	119°00'W
Comacchio, Italy (kô-mäk´kyō)	200-01	44°43'N	12°11'E
Comala, Mex. (kō-mä-lä´)	146-47	19°19'N	103°45'W
Comalcalco, Mex. (kō-mäl-käl´kō)	146-47	18°16'N	93°12'W
Comanche, Ok., U.S. (kō-măn´chē)	120-21	34°21'N	97°58'W
Comanche, Tx., U.S. (kō-măn´chē)	122-23	31°54'N	98°36'W
Comandante Fontana, Arg.	168-69	25°19'S	59°40'W
Comayagua, Hond. (kō-mä-yä´gwä)	149	14°27'N	87°39'W
Combarbalá, Chile	168-69	31°11'S	71°03'W
Comilla, Bngl. (kō-mĭl´ä)	234-35	23°27'N	91°11'E
Comino, Capo, c., Italy (kä´pō kō-mē´nō)	200-01	40°32'N	9°49'E
Comitán de Domínguez, Mex.	148	16°15'N	92°07'W
Commentry, Fr. (kô-mäɴ-trē´)	196-97	46°17'N	2°44'E
Commerce, Ga., U.S. (kŏm´ẽrs)	124-25	34°12'N	83°27'W
Commerce, Ok., U.S. (kŏm´ẽrs)	120-21	36°56'N	94°52'W
Commerce, Tx., U.S. (kŏm´ẽrs)	120-21	33°16'N	95°54'W
Committee Bay, b., Nu., Can.	130-31	68°30'N	86°30'W
Communism Peak, mtn., Taj. see Imeni Ismail Samani, Pik	226	38°57'N	72°01'E
Como, Italy (kō´mō)	200-01	45°47'N	9°05'E
Comodoro Rivadavia, Arg.	171	45°52'S	67°30'W
Comoé, Parc National de la, n.p., C. Iv.	260-61	9°0'N	3°30'W
Comores, nation, Afr. see Comoros	264-65	12°10'S	44°15'E
Comores, Archipel des, is., Afr.	264-65	12°07'S	44°03'E
Comorin, Cape, c., India (kāp kŏ´mô-rĭn)	236	8°05'N	77°34'E
Comoros, nation, Afr. (kŏm´ō-rōz) (kȧ-mō´-rōz)	264-65	12°10'S	44°15'E
Comox, B.C., Can. (kō´mŏks)	132-33	49°41'N	124°56'W
Compiègne, Fr. (kôɴ-pyĕn´y')	196-97	49°25'N	2°49'E
Compostela, Mex. (kōm-pô-stä´lä)	146-47	21°14'N	104°53'W
Conakry, nat. cap., Gui. (kô-nȧ-krē´)	260-61	9°31'N	13°43'W
Concarneau, Fr. (kôɴ-kär-nō´)	196-97	47°52'N	3°55'W
Conceição do Araguaia, Braz.	166-67	8°15'S	49°19'W
Concepción, Bol. (kôn-sĕp´syōn´)	166-67	11°29'S	66°36'W
Concepción, Bol. (kôn-sĕp´syōn´)	168-69	16°15'S	62°04'W
Concepción, Chile	171	36°49'S	73°05'W
Concepción, Para.	168-69	23°24'S	57°25'W
Concepción del Oro, Mex. (kôn-sĕp-syōn´ dĕl ō´rō)	146-47	24°37'N	101°24'W
Concepción del Uruguay, Arg. (kôn-sĕp-syō´n-dĕl-ōō-rōō-gwī´)	173	32°29'S	58°14'W
Conception Bay, b., Nf., Can. (kŏn-sĕp´shŭn bā)	138-39	47°44'N	52°59'W
Conchos, stm., Mex. (kōn´chōs)	144-45	24°56'N	97°38'W
Conchos, stm., Mex. (kōn´chōs)	144-45	29°34'N	104°24'W
Concord, Ca., U.S. (kŏŋ´kŏrd)	118-19	37°59'N	122°02'W
Concord, N.C., U.S. (kŏŋ´kŏrd)	124-25	35°24'N	80°36'W
Concord, N.H., U.S.	116-17	43°12'N	71°32'W
Concordia, Arg. (kōn-kôr´dĭ-ä)	173	31°23'S	58°01'W
Concórdia, Braz.	168-69	27°14'S	52°02'W
Concordia, Mex. (kôn-kô´r-dyä)	146-47	23°16'N	106°04'W
Concordia, Ks., U.S. (kôn-kô´r-dyä)	120-21	39°34'N	97°40'W
Condega, Nic. (kŏn-dĕ´gä)	149	13°22'N	86°24'W
Condobolin, Austl.	276	33°05'S	147°09'E
Condoto, Col.	163c	5°05'N	76°38'W
Conegliano, Italy (kō-nāl-yä´nō)	200-01	45°53'N	12°18'E
Conghua, China (tsôŋ-hwä)	238-39	23°33'N	113°35'E
Congo, nation, Afr. (kŏn´gō)	253	1°0'S	15°00'E
Congo, stm., Afr. (kŏn´gō)	262-63	5°58'S	12°44'E
Congo, Democratic Republic of the, nation, Afr. (dĕ-mō-krā´tĭc rē-pŭb´lĭk ŭv thȧ kŏn´gō)	253	4°0'S	25°00'E
Congo, République démocratique du, nation, Afr. see Congo, Democratic Republic of the	253	4°0'S	25°00'E
Conjeeveram, India see Kānchipuram	236	12°50'N	79°43'E
Conneaut, Oh., U.S. (kŏn-ē-ôt´)	116-17	41°57'N	80°34'W
Connecticut, state, U.S. (kŏ-nĕt´ĭ-kŭt)	108-09	41°45'N	72°45'W
Connecticut, stm., U.S.	110-11	41°16'N	72°20'W
Connellsville, Pa., U.S. (kŏn´nĕlz-vĭl)	116-17	40°01'N	79°36'W
Connersville, In., U.S. (kŏn´ẽrz-vĭl)	116-17	39°39'N	85°08'W
Connors Range, mts., Austl. (kŏn´nŏrs rānj)	277	21°40'S	149°10'E
Conrad, Mt., U.S. (kŏn´răd)	112-13	48°10'N	111°56'W
Conroe, Tx., U.S. (kŏn´rō)	122-23	30°19'N	95°28'W
Conselheiro Lafaiete, Braz.	172	20°40'S	43°47'W
Conshohocken, Pa., U.S. (kŏn-shô-hŏk´ĕn)	116-17	40°05'N	75°18'W
Constance, Ger. see Konstanz	194-95	47°40'N	9°10'E
Constance, Lake, lk., Eur. (lāk kŏn´stăns)	194-95	47°39'N	8°54'E
Constanța, Rom. (kōn-stán´tsá)	202-03	44°11'N	28°38'E
Constantine, Alg. (kôn-stän´tēn´)	269b	36°22'N	6°37'E
Constantine, Mi., U.S. (kŏn´stăn-tēn)	116-17	41°50'N	85°39'W
Constantinople, Tur. see İstanbul	200-01	41°02'N	28°59'E
Constitución, Chile (kōn´stĭ-tōō-syōn´)	171	35°19'S	72°25'W
Contreras, Isla, i., Chile	171	51°52'S	74°57'W
Contwoyto Lake, lk., Can.	130-31	65°42'N	110°50'W
Converse, Tx., U.S. (kŏn´vĕrs)	122-23	29°31'N	98°18'W
Conway, Ar., U.S. (kŏn´wā)	120-21	35°05'N	92°27'W
Conway, N.H., U.S. (kŏn´wā)	116-17	43°59'N	71°07'W
Conway, S.C., U.S. (kŏn´wā)	124-25	33°50'N	79°03'W
Cook, Cape, c., B.C., Can. (kāp kŏŏk)	132-33	50°07'N	127°54'W
Cook, Mount, mtn., N.Z. (mount kŏŏk) see Aoraki	278	43°36'S	170°10'E
Cookeville, Tn., U.S. (kŏŏk´vĭl)	124-25	36°10'N	85°31'W
Cook Inlet, b., Ak., U.S. (kŏŏk ĭn´lĕt)	126	60°32'N	151°40'W
Cook Islands, dep., Oc. (kŏŏk ī´lăndz)	280-81	20°0'S	158°00'W
Cook Strait, strt., N.Z. (kŏŏk strāt)	278	41°15'S	174°30'E
Cooktown, Austl. (kŏŏk´toun)	277	15°29'S	145°15'E
Coolgardie, Austl. (kōōl-gär´dē)	270-71	30°57'S	121°10'E
Cooma, Austl. (kōō´mȧ)	276	36°14'S	149°08'E
Coonabarabran, Austl.	276	31°16'S	149°17'E
Coonamble, Austl. (kōō-năm´b'l)	276	30°58'S	148°23'E
Coonoor, India	236	11°20'N	76°48'E
Coon Rapids, Mn., U.S. (kōōn răp´ĭdz)	114-15	45°10'N	93°20'W
Cooper, Tx., U.S. (kōōp´ẽr)	120-21	33°23'N	95°41'W
Cooper Creek, stm., Austl.	276	28°18'S	137°29'E
Cooperstown, N.D., U.S. (kōōp´ẽrs-toun)	114-15	47°27'N	98°07'W
Coosa, stm., U.S. (kōō´sȧ)	124-25	32°30'N	86°16'W
Coos Bay, Or., U.S. (kōōs bā)	112-13	43°22'N	124°13'W
Cootamundra, Austl. (kŏŏtȧ-mŭnd´rȧ)	276	34°39'S	148°01'E
Copan, hist., Hond.	149	14°50'N	89°09'W
Copenhagen, nat. cap., Den. (kō´pĕn-hā´gĕn)	192-93	55°41'N	12°34'E
Copiapó, Chile (kō-pyä-pō´)	168-69	27°22'S	70°20'W
Copley, Austl.	276	30°33'S	138°26'E
Copper, stm., Ak., U.S. (kŏp´ẽr)	126	60°33'N	144°52'W
Copper Harbor, Mi., U.S. (kŏp´ẽr här´bẽr)	114-15	47°28'N	87°55'W
Coppermine, Nu., Can. see Kugluktuk	128-29	67°47'N	115°11'W
Coppermine, stm., Can. (kŏp´ẽr mīn)	130-31	67°48'N	115°08'W
Coquilhatville, D.R.C. see Mbandaka	262-63	0°02'N	18°15'E
Coquimbo, Chile (kō-kēm´bō)	168-69	29°58'S	71°20'W
Corabia, Rom. (kô-rä´bĭ-ȧ)	200-01	43°47'N	24°31'E
Corail, Mer de, s., Oc. see Coral Sea	272-73	20°0'S	158°00'E
Coral Harbour, Nu., Can.	128-29	64°08'N	83°12'W
Coral Sea, s., Oc. (kŏr´ăl sē)	272-73	20°0'S	158°00'E
Corangamite, Lake, lk., Austl. (lăk cŏr-ăŋg´á-mīt)	276	38°10'S	143°25'E
Corato, Italy (kō´rä-tô)	200-01	41°09'N	16°25'E
Corbin, Ky., U.S. (kôr´bĭn)	124-25	36°57'N	84°06'W
Corby, Eng., U.K. (kôr´bĭ)	190-91	52°29'N	0°40'W
Corcaigh, Ire. see Cork	190-91	51°54'N	8°28'W
Corcovado, Golfo, b., Chile (gôl-fô-kôr-kô-vä´dhō)	171	43°30'S	73°30'W
Corcovado, Volcán, vol., Chile	171	43°12'S	72°48'W
Cordele, Ga., U.S. (kôr-dēl´)	124-25	31°58'N	83°47'W
Cordell, Ok., U.S. (kôr-dĕl´)	120-21	35°18'N	98°59'W
Córdoba, Arg. (kôr´dô-vä)	173	31°24'S	64°12'W
Córdoba, Mex. (kô´r-dô-bä)	146-47	18°53'N	96°56'W
Córdoba, Spain (kô´r-dô-bä)	198-99	37°54'N	4°47'W
Córdoba, state, Arg. (kôr´dô-vä)	173	32°0'S	64°00'W
Cordova, Spain see Córdoba	198-99	37°54'N	4°47'W
Cordova, Ak., U.S. (kôr´dô-vä)	126	60°33'N	145°45'W
Cordova, Al., U.S. (kôr´dô-ȧ)	124-25	33°46'N	87°11'W
Corfu, i., Grc. see Kérkyra	200-01	39°40'N	19°45'E
Corinth, Grc.	200-01	37°56'N	22°58'E
Corinth, Ms., U.S. (kŏr´ĭnth)	124-25	34°56'N	88°31'W
Corinto, Braz. (kô-rē´n-tō)	172	18°23'S	44°27'W
Cork, Ire. (kôrk)	190-91	51°54'N	8°28'W
Corleone, Italy (kôr-lā-ô´nā)	200-01	37°49'N	13°18'E
Cornelia, Ga., U.S. (kôr-nē´lyȧ)	124-25	34°31'N	83°32'W
Cornell, Wi., U.S. (kôr-nĕl´)	114-15	45°10'N	91°09'W
Corner Brook, Nf., Can. (kôr´nẽr brŏŏk)	138-39	48°57'N	57°58'W
Corning, Ar., U.S. (kôr´nĭng)	124-25	36°25'N	90°35'W
Corning, Ia., U.S. (kôr´nĭng)	114-15	40°60'N	94°45'W
Corning, N.Y., U.S. (kôr´nĭng)	116-17	42°09'N	77°03'W
Corno Grande, mtn., Italy (kôr´nō grän´dĕ)	200-01	42°28'N	13°34'E
Cornwall, On., Can. (kôrn´wôl)	136-37	45°02'N	74°44'W
Coro, Ven. (kō´rô)	164-65	11°27'N	69°40'W
Corocoro, Bol. (kō-rô-kō´rô)	168-69	17°11'S	68°27'W
Coromandel Coast, cst., India (kŏr-ô-man´dĕl kōst)	236	13°30'N	80°30'E
Coronado, Ca., U.S. (kŏr-ô-nä´dō)	118-19	32°41'N	117°11'W
Coronado, Bahía de, b., C.R. (bä-ē´ä-dĕ-kô-rô-nä´dō)	149	9°0'N	83°50'W
Coronation Gulf, b., Nu., Can. (kŏr-ô-nā´shŭn gŭlf)	130-31	68°24'N	109°56'W
Coronel, Chile (kō-rō-nĕl´)	171	37°01'S	73°08'W
Coronel Dorrego, Arg. (kŏ-rô-nĕl-dôr-rĕ´gô)	173	38°43'S	61°17'W
Coronel Fabriciano, Braz.	172	19°31'S	42°39'W
Coronel Oviedo, Para. (kŏ-rô-nĕl-ô-vēĕ´dô)	168-69	25°27'S	56°26'W
Coronel Pringles, Arg. (kŏ-rô-nĕl-prēn´glĕs)	173	37°59'S	61°22'W
Coronel Suárez, Arg. (kŏ-rô-nĕl-swä´rās)	173	37°27'S	61°56'W
Coropuna, Nevado, vol., Peru (nĕ-vä-dô-kō-rō-pōō´nä)	170	15°31'S	72°42'W
Corozal, Belize (cŏr-ŏth-äl´)	148	18°24'N	88°24'W
Corpus Christi, Tx., U.S. (kôr´pŭs krĭstē)	122-23	27°48'N	97°24'W
Corpus Christi, Lake, res., Tx., U.S. (lăk kôr´pŭs krĭstē)	122-23	28°10'N	97°55'W
Corpus Christi Bay, b., Tx., U.S. (kôr´pŭs krĭstē bā)	122-23	27°48'N	97°20'W

322 Corral – Curtis Island
PRONOUNCING INDEX

Feature (Pronunciation)	Page	Lat.	Long.
Corral, Chile (kô-räl′)	171	39°53′S	73°28′W
Corral de Almaguer, Spain (kô-räl′dä äl-mä-gâr′)	198-99	39°45′N	3°10′W
Corrente, stm., Braz.	166-67	13°08′S	43°28′W
Correntina, Braz. (kô-rĕn-tē-nȧ)	166-67	13°21′S	44°39′W
Corrientes, Arg. (kō-ryĕn′täs)	173	27°29′S	58°50′W
Corrientes, state, Arg. (kō-ryĕn′täs)	173	29°0′S	58°00′W
Corrientes, stm., S.A.	170	3°44′S	74°33′W
Corrientes, Cabo, c., Col. (kä′bô-kō-ryĕn′täs)	163c	5°30′N	77°32′W
Corrientes, Cabo, c., Cuba (kä′bô-kôr-rē-ĕn′tĕs)	142-43	21°46′N	84°31′W
Corrientes, Cabo, c., Mex.	146-47	20°24′N	105°41′W
Corriverton, Guy.	164-65	5°53′N	57°09′W
Corry, Pa., U.S. (kŏr′ĭ)	116-17	41°55′N	79°38′W
Corse, i., Fr. *see* Corsica	184-85	42°0′N	9°00′E
Corse, Cap, c., Fr. (kȧp kôrs)	184-85	43°01′N	9°25′E
Corsica, i., Fr. (kô′r-sē-kä)	184-85	42°0′N	9°00′E
Corsicana, Tx., U.S. (kôr-sĭ-kăn′ȧ)	122-23	32°06′N	96°29′W
Cortazar, Mex. (kôr-tä-zär)	146-47	20°29′N	100°56′W
Cortés, Mar de, b., Mex. *see* California, Golfo de	144-45	28°0′N	112°00′W
Cortez, Co., U.S.	118-19	37°21′N	108°35′W
Cortez, Sea of, b., Mex. *see* California, Golfo de	144-45	28°0′N	112°00′W
Corubal, stm., Afr.	258-59	11°57′N	15°03′W
Coruche, Port. (kô-rōō′she)	198-99	38°58′N	8°31′W
Çorum, Tur. (chô-rōōm′)	186-87	40°33′N	34°57′E
Corumbá, Braz.	168-69	19°01′S	57°39′W
Corumbá, stm., Braz.	168-69	18°19′S	48°54′W
Corunna, Spain *see* A Coruña	198-99	43°22′N	8°25′W
Corunna, Mi., U.S. (kô-rŭn′ȧ)	116-17	42°59′N	84°07′W
Coruripe, Braz. (kō-rò-rē′pĭ)	163d	10°09′S	36°10′W
Corvallis, Or., U.S. (kŏr-văl′ĭs)	112-13	44°35′N	123°16′W
Corvo, i., Port.	199c	39°42′N	31°06′W
Corydon, In., U.S. (kŏr′ĭ-dŭn)	116-17	38°13′N	86°07′W
Cos, i., Grc. *see* Kos	200-01	36°50′N	27°10′E
Cosenza, Italy (kô-zĕnt′sä)	200-01	39°17′N	16°15′E
Coshocton, Oh., U.S. (kô-shŏk′tŭn)	116-17	40°16′N	81°51′W
Cosmoledo, Atoll de, at., Sey. (kŏs-mô-lā′dō)	264-65	9°42′S	47°31′E
Cosne-sur-Loire, Fr. (kōn-sür-lwär′)	196-97	47°24′N	2°56′E
Costa Rica, nation, N.A. (kŏs′tȧ rē′kȧ)	85	10°0′N	84°00′W
Costermansville, D.R.C. *see* Bukavu	267	2°30′S	28°51′E
Cotabato, Phil. (kō-tä-bä′tō)	250	7°12′N	124°14′E
Cote d'Ivoire, nation, Afr. (kōt-dē-vwär)	253	8°0′N	5°00′W
Cotija de la Paz, Mex. (kô-tē′-ĸä-dĕ-lä-pȧ′z)	146-47	19°49′N	102°43′W
Cotonou, nat. cap., Benin (kô-tô-nōō′)	260a	6°22′N	2°26′E
Cotopaxi, vol., Ec. (kō-tō-păk′sê)	170	0°41′S	78°27′W
Cotswold Hills, hills, Eng., U.K. (kŭtz′wōld hĭlz)	190-91	51°49′N	1°57′W
Cottage Grove, Or., U.S. (kŏt′āj grōv)	112-13	43°48′N	123°03′W
Cottbus, Ger. (kŏtt′bōōs)	194-95	51°45′N	14°19′E
Cotulla, Tx., U.S. (kŏ-tŭl′lȧ)	122-23	28°26′N	99°14′W
Coudersport, Pa., U.S. (kou′dērz-pōrt)	116-17	41°46′N	78°01′W
Coudres, Île aux, i., Qc., Can.	138-39	47°24′N	70°23′W
Coulommiers, Fr. (kōō-lô-myā′)	196-97	48°49′N	3°05′E
Council Bluffs, Ia., U.S. (koun′sĭl blŭfs)	114-15	41°16′N	95°51′W
Courtenay, B.C., Can. (cōōrt-nā′)	132-33	49°41′N	124°60′W
Coushatta, La., U.S. (kou-shăt′ȧ)	122-23	32°01′N	93°21′W
Couture, Lac, lk., Qc., Can.	130-31	60°07′N	75°20′W
Coventry, Eng., U.K. (kŭv′ĕn-trĭ)	190-91	52°25′N	1°30′W
Covington, Ga., U.S. (kŭv′ĭng-tŭn)	124-25	33°36′N	83°51′W
Covington, In., U.S. (kŭv′ĭng-tŭn)	116-17	40°08′N	87°23′W
Covington, Ky., U.S. (kŭv′ĭng-tŭn)	116-17	39°05′N	84°31′W
Covington, La., U.S. (kŭv′ĭng-tŭn)	124-25	30°28′N	90°06′W
Covington, Tn., U.S. (kŭv′ĭng-tŭn)	124-25	35°34′N	89°39′W
Covington, Va., U.S. (kŭv′ĭng-tŭn)	116-17	37°48′N	79°60′W
Cowan, Lake, lk., Austl. (läk kou′ȧn)	272-73	31°50′S	121°50′E
Cowes, Eng., U.K. (kouz)	190-91	50°46′N	1°18′W
Cowra, Austl. (kou′rȧ)	276	33°50′S	148°41′E
Coxim, Braz. (kō-shēN′)	168-69	18°30′S	54°45′W
Cox's Bāzār, Bngl.	246-47	21°26′N	91°58′E
Coyame, Mex. (kō-yä′mä)	122-23	29°28′N	105°07′W
Coyle, stm., Arg. *see* Coig	171	50°57′S	69°09′W
Coyuca de Benítez, Mex. (kō-yōō′kä dā bā-nē′täz)	146-47	17°01′N	100°05′W
Coyuca de Catalán, Mex. (kō-yōō′kä dā kä-tä-län′)	146-47	18°19′N	100°42′W
Cozad, Ne., U.S. (kō′zăd)	114-15	40°52′N	99°59′W
Cozumel, Mex. (kŏ-zōō-mĕ′l)	148	20°31′N	86°55′W
Cozumel, Isla, i., Mex. (ē′s-lä-kŏ-zōō-mĕ′l)	148	20°25′N	86°55′W
Cracow, Pol. *see* Kraków	194-95	50°04′N	19°58′E
Cradock, S. Afr. (krā′dŭk)	264-65	32°10′S	25°37′E
Craig, Ak., U.S. (krāg)	126	55°28′N	133°06′W
Craig, Co., U.S. (krāg)	112-13	40°31′N	107°32′W
Craiova, Rom. (krȧ-yō′vȧ)	200-01	44°19′N	23°48′E
Cranbrook, B.C., Can. (krăn′brŏŏk)	132-33	49°31′N	115°46′W
Crandon, Wi., U.S. (krăn′dŭn)	116-17	45°34′N	88°54′W
Cranston, R.I., U.S. (krăns′tŭn)	116-17	41°48′N	71°26′W
Crater Lake, lk., Or., U.S. (krā′tẽr lăk)	112-13	42°56′N	122°06′W
Crater Lake National Park, n.p., Or., U.S. (krā′tẽr lăk năsh′ŭn-ăl pärk)	112-13	42°52′N	122°10′W
Craters of the Moon National Monument and Preserve, n.p., Id., U.S. (krā′tẽrz ŭv thȧ mōōn năsh′ŭn-ăl mŏn′ū-mĕnt ănd prĭ-zûrv)	112-13	43°25′N	113°33′W
Crateús, Braz. (krä-tå-ōōzh′)	166-67	5°10′S	40°40′W
Crato, Braz. (krä′tò)	166-67	7°14′S	39°23′W
Crawford, Ne., U.S. (krô′fẽrd)	114-15	42°41′N	103°25′W
Crawfordsville, In., U.S. (krô′fẽrdz-vĭl)	116-17	40°02′N	86°54′W
Crazy Mountains, mts., Mt., U.S. (krā′zĭ moun′tĭnz)	112-13	46°08′N	110°20′W
Cree, stm., Sk., Can.	130-31	58°55′N	105°46′W
Cree Lake, lk., Sk., Can. (krē lăk)	130-31	57°30′N	106°30′W
Creil, Fr. (krĕ′y′)	196-97	49°16′N	2°29′E
Crema, Italy (krā′mä)	200-01	45°22′N	9°42′E
Cremona, Italy (krā-mō′nä)	200-01	45°09′N	10°01′E
Crépy-en-Valois, Fr. (krā-pē′ĕN-vä-lwä′)	196-97	49°14′N	2°54′E
Crescent City, Ca., U.S.	112-13	41°46′N	124°12′W
Cresco, Ia., U.S. (krĕs′kō)	114-15	43°22′N	92°07′W
Crestline, Oh., U.S. (krĕst-līn)	116-17	40°47′N	82°44′W
Creston, B.C., Can. (krĕs′tŭn)	132-33	49°06′N	116°31′W
Creston, Ia., U.S. (krĕs′tŭn)	114-15	41°04′N	94°22′W
Crestview, Fl., U.S. (krĕst′vū)	124-25	30°46′N	86°34′W
Crestwood, Ky., U.S. (krĕst′wŏŏd)	116-17	38°19′N	85°28′W
Crete, Ne., U.S. (krēt)	120-21	40°37′N	96°58′W
Crete, i., Grc. (krēt)	200a	35°13′N	25°00′E
Crete, Sea of, s., Grc. (sē ŭv krēt)	188-89	35°54′N	25°01′E
Crewe, Eng., U.K. (krōō)	190-91	53°06′N	2°27′W
Criciúma, Braz.	172	28°41′S	49°24′W
Crimea, pen., Ukr. *see* Crimean Peninsula	202-03	45°0′N	34°00′E
Crimean Peninsula, pen., Ukr.	202-03	45°0′N	34°00′E
Cripple Creek, Co., U.S. (krĭp′'l krēk)	120-21	38°45′N	105°11′W
Crisfield, Md., U.S. (krĭs-fēld)	116-17	37°59′N	75°51′W
Cristalândia, Braz.	166-67	10°36′S	49°12′W
Cristóbal Colón, Pico, mtn., Col. (pē′kô-krēs-tô′bäl-kō-lôn′)	164-65	10°50′N	73°41′W
Crna Gora, nation, Eur. *see* Montenegro	174-75	42°30′N	19°18′E
Croatia, nation, Eur. (krō-ā′-shȧ)	174-75	45°10′N	15°30′E
Crockett, Tx., U.S. (krŏk′ĕt)	122-23	31°18′N	95°28′W
Crocodile, stm., S. Afr.	269c	24°11′S	26°53′E
Crooked, stm., B.C., Can. (krŏŏk′ĕd)	132-33	54°50′N	122°53′W
Crooked Island, i., Bah.	142-43	22°45′N	74°13′W
Crooked Island Passage, strt., Bah. (krŏŏk′ĕd ī′lȧnd păs′ĭj)	142-43	22°43′N	74°35′W
Crookston, Mn., U.S. (krŏŏks′tŭn)	114-15	47°47′N	96°37′W
Crosby, Mn., U.S. (krôz′bĭ)	114-15	46°29′N	93°58′W
Crosby, N.D., U.S. (krôz′bĭ)	114-15	48°55′N	103°18′W
Cross, stm., Afr. (krôs)	260a	4°49′N	8°15′E
Cross City, Fl., U.S. (krôs sĭ′tĭ)	124-25	29°38′N	83°07′W
Crossett, Ar., U.S. (krôs′ĕt)	120-21	33°08′N	91°58′W
Cross Lake, res., Mb., Can.	134-35	54°45′N	97°30′W
Cross Sound, strt., Ak., U.S. (krŏs sound)	126	58°10′N	136°30′W
Crotone, Italy (krō-tô′nĕ)	200-01	39°05′N	17°07′E
Crow Creek Indian Reservation, ind. res., S.D., U.S. (krō krēk ĭn′dĭ-ăn rĕ-sẽr-vā′shĕn)	114-15	44°11′N	99°30′W
Crow Indian Reservation, ind. res., Mt., U.S. (krō ĭn′dĭ-ăn rĕ-sẽr-vā′shĕn)	112-13	45°27′N	108°00′W
Crowley, La., U.S. (krou′lē)	122-23	30°13′N	92°23′W
Crown Point, N.Y., U.S. (kroun point′)	116-17	43°57′N	73°26′W
Crowsnest Pass, Ab., Can.	132-33	49°37′N	114°25′W
Crozet, Archipel, is., Afr. *see* Crozet, Îles	287	46°0′S	52°00′E
Crozet, Îles, is., Afr. (ēl-krō-zĕ′)	287	46°0′S	52°00′E
Cruz, Cabo, c., Cuba (kä′-bô-krōōz)	142-43	19°51′N	77°44′W
Cruz Alta, Braz. (krōōz äl′tä)	173	28°37′S	53°36′W
Cruz del Eje, Arg. (krōō′s-dĕl-ĕ-kĕ)	168-69	30°43′S	64°49′W
Cruzeiro, Braz. (krōō-zā′rò)	172	22°35′S	44°58′W
Cruzeiro do Sul, Braz. (krōō-zā′rò dò sōōl)	170	7°39′S	72°41′W
Crystal City, Tx., U.S. (krĭs′tăl sĭ′tĭ)	122-23	28°41′N	99°50′W
Crystal Falls, Mi., U.S. (krĭs′tăl fôlz)	114-15	46°06′N	88°19′W
Crystal Lake, Il., U.S. (krĭs′tăl lăk lăk)	116-17	42°14′N	88°17′W
Crystal Springs, Ms., U.S. (krĭs′tăl sprĭngz)	124-25	31°59′N	90°22′W
Csongrád, Hung. (chôn′gräd)	194-95	46°43′N	20°09′E
Cúa, Ven. (kōō′ä)	163b	10°09′N	66°53′W
Cua Lo, Viet.	246-47	18°49′N	105°43′E
Cuamba, Moz.	264-65	14°47′S	36°32′E
Cuando, stm., Afr.	264-65	18°30′S	23°36′E
Cuango, stm., Afr.	262-63	3°13′S	17°23′E
Cuanza, stm., Ang. (kwän′zä)	264-65	9°21′S	13°09′E
Cuatrociénegas, Mex. (kwä′trō syā′nȧ-gäs)	122-23	26°60′N	102°04′W
Cuauhtémoc, Mex. (kwä-ōō-tĕ-mŏk′)	146-47	22°33′N	98°09′W
Cuauhtémoc, Mex. (kwä-ōō-tĕ-mŏk′)	144-45	28°25′N	106°52′W
Cuautitlán, Mex. (kwä-ōō-tĕt-län′)	146-47	19°27′N	104°21′W
Cuautla, Mex. (kwä-ōō′tlä)	146-47	18°49′N	98°57′W
Cuba, nation, N.A. (kū′bȧ)	140-41	21°30′N	80°00′W
Cubagua, Isla, i., Ven. (ē′s-lä-kōō-bä′gwä)	163b	10°49′N	64°11′W
Cubal, Ang.	264-65	13°03′S	14°17′E
Cubango, stm., Afr. (kōō-bäŋ′gō)	264-65	18°57′S	22°25′E
Cubia, Ang.	264-65	16°01′S	21°43′E
Cúcuta, Col. (kōō′kōō-tä)	164-65	7°53′N	72°29′W
Cuddalore, India (kŭd ȧ-lōr′)	236	11°45′N	79°46′E
Cuddapah, India (kŭd′ȧ-pä)	236	14°28′N	78°49′E
Cue, Austl. (kū)	270-71	27°26′S	117°54′E
Cuenca, Ec. (kwĕn′kä)	170	2°53′S	79°00′W
Cuenca, Spain	198-99	40°05′N	2°08′W
Cuencamé de Ceniceros, Mex.	122-23	24°52′N	103°42′W
Cuernavaca, Mex. (kwĕr-nä-vä′kä)	146-47	18°55′N	99°14′W
Cuero, Tx., U.S. (kwā′rō)	122-23	29°06′N	97°17′W
Cuiabá, Braz.	168-69	15°36′S	56°05′W
Cuiabá, stm., Braz.	166-67	17°54′S	57°28′W
Cuicatlán, Mex. (kwē-kä-tlän′)	146-47	17°46′N	96°58′W
Cuilapa, Guat. (kò-ē-lä′pä)	148	14°17′N	90°18′W
Cuilo, stm., Afr.	262-63	5°53′S	16°35′E
Cuilo, stm., Afr.	260-61	3°23′S	17°23′E
Cuíto, stm., Ang. (kōō-ē-′tō)	264-65	18°01′S	20°47′E
Cuitzeo, Lago de, lk., Mex. (lä′gô-dĕ-kwēt′zä-ō)	146-47	19°55′N	101°05′W
Culebra, Isla de, i., P.R. (ē′s-lä-dĕ-kōō-lā′brä)	142a	18°19′N	65°17′W
Culfa, Azer.	227	38°58′N	45°38′E
Culgoa, stm., Austl. (kŭl-gō′ȧ)	276	29°59′S	146°07′E
Culiacán, Mex. (kōō-lyä-kä′n)	146-47	24°04′N	107°05′W
Culiacán, Mex.	144-45	24°49′N	107°24′W
Culion Island, i., Phil.	250	11°51′N	119°57′E
Cullera, Spain (kōō-lyā′rä)	198-99	39°10′N	0°14′W
Cullinan, S. Afr. (kò′lĭ-năn)	269c	25°40′S	28°33′E
Cullman, Al., U.S. (kŭl′măn)	124-25	34°10′N	86°51′W
Culpeper, Va., U.S. (kŭl′pĕp-ẽr)	116-17	38°27′N	77°60′W
Culuene, stm., Braz.	166-67	12°56′S	52°50′W
Culver, In., U.S. (kŭl′vẽr)	116-17	41°13′N	86°25′W
Cumaná, Ven.	163b	10°27′N	64°11′W
Cumbal, Nevado, vol., Col.	164-65	0°57′N	77°52′W
Cumberland, Md., U.S.	116-17	39°39′N	78°46′W
Cumberland, Wi., U.S. (kŭm′bẽr-lănd)	114-15	45°32′N	92°01′W
Cumberland, stm., U.S. (kŭm′bẽr-lănd)	110-11	37°08′N	88°25′W
Cumberland, Lake, res., Ky., U.S. (lăk kŭm′bẽr-lănd)	124-25	36°57′N	84°55′W
Cumberland Peninsula, pen., Nu., Can. (kŭm′bẽr-lănd pĕ-nĭn′sūlȧ)	130-31	66°32′N	64°13′W
Cumberland Plateau, plat., U.S. (kŭm′bẽr-lănd plă-tō′)	124-25	36°0′N	85°00′W
Cumberland Sound, strt., Nu., Can. (kŭm′bẽr-lănd sound)	130-31	65°10′N	65°30′W
Cumbres de Monterrey, Parque Nacional, n.p., Mex.	122-23	25°30′N	100°25′W
Cunani, Braz.	164-65	2°52′N	51°06′W
Cunco, Chile	171	38°56′S	72°02′W
Cunene, stm., Afr.	264-65	17°15′S	11°45′E
Cunnamulla, Austl. (kŭn-ȧ-mŭl-ȧ)	276	28°04′S	145°41′E
Curaçao, i., Neth. Ant. (kōō-rä-sä′ō)	140a	12°11′N	69°00′W
Curacautín, Chile (kä-rä-käōō-tē′n)	171	38°25′S	71°56′W
Curacó, stm., Arg. *see* Salado	171	38°49′S	64°59′W
Curanilahue, Chile	171	37°28′S	73°21′W
Curaray, stm., S.A.	170	2°26′S	74°04′W
Curepipe, Mauritius	265a	20°19′S	57°31′E
Curicó, Chile	171	34°59′S	71°14′W
Curitiba, Braz. (kōō-rē-tē′bȧ)	172	25°26′S	49°16′W
Currais Novos, Braz. (kōōr-rä′ēs nŏ-vōs)	163d	6°15′S	36°31′W
Curralinho, Braz.	166-67	1°48′S	49°47′W
Current, stm., U.S. (kûr′ĕnt)	120-21	36°15′N	90°55′W
Curtis Island, i., Austl.	277	23°38′S	151°09′E

ăt; finăl; rāte; senāte; ärm; àsk; sofȧ; fâre; ch-choose; dh-as th in other; bē; ēvent; bĕt; recĕnt; craterẽ; g-gō; gh-guttural g; bĭt; ĭ-short neutral; rīde; ĸ-guttural k as ch in German ich;

Feature (Pronunciation)	Page	Lat.	Long.
Decatur, In., U.S. (dē-kā′tŭr)	**116-17**	40°50′N	84°55′W
Decatur, Mi., U.S. (dē-kā′tŭr)	**116-17**	42°06′N	85°58′W
Decatur, Tx., U.S. (dē-kā′tŭr)	**120-21**	33°14′N	97°35′W
Decazeville, Fr. (dē-käz′vēl′)	**196-97**	44°34′N	2°15′E
Deccan, plat., India (dĕk′ăn)	**236**	17°0′N	78°00′E
Deception Lake, lk., Sk., Can. (dē-sĕp′shŭn lāk)	**134-35**	56°33′N	104°10′W
Decorah, Ia., U.S. (dē-kō′rȧ)	**114-15**	43°18′N	91°47′W
Dee, stm., Scot., U.K. (dē)	**190-91**	57°08′N	2°05′W
Deep River, On., Can. (dēp rĭv′ẽr)	**136-37**	46°06′N	77°30′W
Deerfield, Ma., U.S. (dēr′fēld)	**116-17**	42°33′N	72°36′W
Deer Lake, Nf., Can. (dēr lāk)	**138-39**	49°11′N	57°26′W
Deer Lake, lk., On., Can. (dēr lāk)	**134-35**	52°39′N	94°29′W
Deer Lodge, Mt., U.S. (dēr lŏj)	**112-13**	46°24′N	112°44′W
Deer Park, Wa., U.S. (dēr pärk)	**112-13**	47°57′N	117°28′W
Deer River, Mn., U.S. (dēr rĭv′ẽr)	**114-15**	47°19′N	93°48′W
Defiance, Oh., U.S. (dē-fī′ăns)	**116-17**	41°16′N	84°22′W
Defuniak Springs, Fl., U.S. (dē fū′nĭ-ăk sprĭngz)	**124-25**	30°43′N	86°07′W
Dêgê, China	**238-39**	31°50′N	98°40′E
Degeh Bur, Eth.	**262-63**	8°13′N	43°33′E
Deggendorf, Ger. (dĕ′ghĕn-dôrf)	**194-95**	48°51′N	12°58′E
Dehalak' Desēt, i., Erit.	**266**	15°40′N	40°06′E
Dehiwala-Mount Lavinia, Sri L.	**236**	6°52′N	79°52′E
Dehra Dūn, India (dā′rŭ dōōn)	**234-35**	30°19′N	78°02′E
Dehri, India	**234-35**	24°54′N	84°11′E
Dehua, China (dŭ-hwä)	**225a**	25°30′N	118°14′E
Dehui, China	**240-41**	44°32′N	125°43′E
Dej, Rom. (dāzh)	**194-95**	47°09′N	23°53′E
De Kalb, Il., U.S. (dē kălb′)	**116-17**	41°56′N	88°45′W
DeLand, Fl., U.S. (dē lănd′)	**124-25**	29°02′N	81°18′W
Delano, Ca., U.S. (dĕl′ȧ-nō)	**118-19**	35°47′N	119°15′W
Delavan, Wi., U.S. (dĕl′ȧ-văn)	**116-17**	42°38′N	88°39′W
Delaware, Oh., U.S. (dĕl′ȧ-wâr)	**116-17**	40°18′N	83°04′W
Delaware, state, U.S. (dĕl′ȧ-wâr)	**108-09**	39°10′N	75°30′W
Delaware, stm., Ks., U.S. (dĕl′ȧ-wâr)	**120-21**	39°04′N	95°25′W
Delaware, stm., U.S.	**116-117**	39°20′N	75°25′E
Delaware Bay, b., U.S. (dĕl′ȧ-wâr bā)	**116-17**	39°05′N	75°15′W
De Leon, Tx., U.S. (dē lē-ŏn′)	**122-23**	32°07′N	98°33′W
Delft, Neth. (dĕlft)	**190-91**	52°01′N	4°22′E
Delgado, Cabo, c., Moz. (kȧ′bô-dĕl-gä′dō)	**264-65**	10°41′S	40°38′E
Delger, stm., Mong.	**240-41**	49°17′N	100°42′E
Delhi, India (dĕl′hī)	**234-35**	28°40′N	77°14′E
Delhi, La., U.S. (dĕl′hī)	**124-25**	32°28′N	91°30′W
Delhi, state, India (dĕl′hī)	**234-35**	28°37′N	77°10′E
Delicias, Mex.	**122-23**	28°12′N	105°29′W
Déline, N.T., Can.	**128-29**	65°11′N	123°25′W
Delingha, China	**240-41**	37°15′N	97°11′E
Dell Rapids, S.D., U.S. (dĕl răp′ĭdz)	**114-15**	43°49′N	96°43′W
Delmarva Peninsula, pen., U.S.	**116-17**	38°30′N	75°30′W
Delmenhorst, Ger. (dĕl′mĕn-hôrst)	**194-95**	53°04′N	8°38′E
De Long Mountains, mts., Ak., U.S. (dē′lŏng moun′tĭnz)	**126**	68°20′N	162°00′W
Delphi, In., U.S. (dĕl′fī)	**116-17**	40°35′N	86°40′W
Delphos, Oh., U.S. (dĕl′fŏs)	**116-17**	40°51′N	84°21′W
Del Rio, Tx., U.S. (dĕl rē′ō)	**122-23**	29°22′N	100°54′W
Delta Junction, Ak., U.S.	**126**	64°02′N	145°44′W
Dëma, stm., Russia (dyĕm′ä)	**176-77**	54°44′N	55°54′E
Dembī Dolo, Eth.	**262-63**	8°32′N	34°48′E
Demidov, Russia (dzyě′mê-dô′f)	**192-93**	55°16′N	31°32′E
Deming, N.M., U.S. (dĕm′ĭng)	**118-19**	32°16′N	107°45′W
Demini, stm., Braz.	**166-67**	0°46′S	62°56′W
Demopolis, Al., U.S. (dē-mŏp′ô-lĭs)	**124-25**	32°31′N	87°50′W
Dempo, Gunung, vol., Indon. (gōō-nōng dĕm′pô)	**246-47**	4°00′S	103°09′E
Demyanka, stm., Russia (dyĕm-yän′kä)	**218-19**	59°31′N	69°05′E
Demyansk, Russia (dyĕm-yänsk′)	**192-93**	57°38′N	32°28′E
Denakil, reg., Afr. *see* Danakil	**266**	13°0′N	41°00′E
Denali, mtn., Ak., U.S. *see* McKinley, Mount	**126**	63°04′N	151°00′W
Denali National Park and Preserve, n.p., Ak., U.S.	**126**	63°15′N	150°30′W
Dêngqên, China	**238-39**	31°27′N	95°27′E
Denham, Austl.	**270-71**	25°55′S	113°33′E
Denham, Mount, mtn., Jam.	**142-43**	18°13′N	77°32′W
Denham Range, mts., Austl.	**277**	21°41′S	147°55′E
Deniliquin, Austl. (dĕ-nĭl′ĭ-kwĭn)	**276**	35°32′S	144°58′E
Denison, Ia., U.S. (dĕn′ĭ-sŭn)	**114-15**	42°01′N	95°22′W
Denison, Tx., U.S. (dĕn′ĭ-sŭn)	**120-21**	33°45′N	96°33′W
Denizli, Tur. (dĕn-ĭz-lē′)	**200-01**	37°47′N	29°05′E
Denmark, S.C., U.S. (dĕn′märk)	**124-25**	33°20′N	81°09′W
Denmark, nation, Eur. (dĕn′märk)	**174-75**	56°0′N	10°00′E
Denmark Strait, strt., (dĕn′märk strāt)	**86**	67°0′N	25°00′W
Denov, Uzb.	**232-33**	38°16′N	67°54′E
Denpasar, Indon.	**248-49**	8°39′S	115°13′E
Denton, Tx., U.S. (dĕn′tŭn)	**120-21**	33°14′N	97°08′W
D'Entrecasteaux Islands, is., Pap. N. Gui. (dăɴ-tr'-kȧs-tō′ ī′lȧndz)	**277**	9°27′S	150°32′E
Denver, Co., U.S. (dĕn′vẽr)	**120-21**	39°44′N	104°58′W
Deolāli, India	**234-35**	19°57′N	73°50′E
De Pere, Wi., U.S. (dē pēr′)	**116-17**	44°26′N	88°03′W
Dêqên, China	**238-39**	28°38′N	98°52′E
De Queen, Ar., U.S. (dē kwēn′)	**120-21**	34°03′N	94°21′W
De Quincy, La., U.S. (dē kwĭn′sĭ)	**122-23**	30°27′N	93°26′W
Dera, Lach, stm., Afr. (dā′rä)	**262-63**	0°13′N	42°18′E
Dera Ghāzi Khān, Pak. (dā′rŭ gä-zē′ ĸan′)	**232-33**	30°03′N	70°38′E
Dera Ismāīl Khān, Pak. (dā′rŭ ĭs-mä-ēl′ ĸăn′)	**232-33**	31°49′N	70°55′E
Derbent, Russia (dĕr-bĕnt′)	**227**	42°03′N	48°17′E
Derby, Austl. (där′bē) (dûr′bē)	**270-71**	17°20′S	123°38′E
Derby, Eng., U.K. (där′bē)	**190-91**	52°55′N	1°29′W
Derby, Ks., U.S. (dûr′bē)	**120-21**	37°32′N	97°15′W
De Ridder, La., U.S. (dē rĭd′ẽr)	**122-23**	30°51′N	93°18′W
Dermott, Ar., U.S. (dûr′mŏt)	**124-25**	33°32′N	91°26′W
Derry, N. Ire., U.K. *see* Londonderry	**190-91**	54°59′N	7°20′W
Derry, N.H., U.S. (dâr′ĭ)	**116-17**	42°53′N	71°20′W
Derventa, Bos. (dĕr′ven-tȧ)	**200-01**	44°59′N	17°54′E
Derzhavinsk, Kaz.	**226**	51°06′N	66°19′E
Desaguadero, stm., S.A.	**170**	18°04′S	67°06′W
Désappointement, Îles du, is., Fr. Poly.	**280-81**	14°10′S	141°20′W
Deschambault Lake, lk., Sk., Can.	**134-35**	54°40′N	103°35′W
Deschutes, stm., Or., U.S. (dā-shōōt′)	**112-13**	45°39′N	120°55′W
Desē, Eth.	**266**	11°09′N	39°38′E
Deseado, stm., Arg. (dā-sā-ä′dhō)	**171**	47°46′S	65°53′W
Desengaño, Punta, c., Arg.	**171**	49°15′S	67°37′W
De Smet, S.D., U.S. (dē smĕt′)	**114-15**	44°23′N	97°33′W
Des Moines, Ia., U.S. (dē moin′)	**114-15**	41°34′N	93°36′W
Des Moines, stm., U.S. (dē moin′)	**110-11**	40°22′N	91°26′W
Desna, stm., Eur. (dyĕs-ná′)	**202-03**	50°33′N	30°34′E
Desolación, Isla, i., Chile (ĕ′s-lä-dĕ-sô-lä-syô′n)	**171**	53°00′S	74°09′W
De Soto, Mo., U.S. (dē sō′tō)	**120-21**	38°08′N	90°34′W
Dessau, Ger. (dĕsou)	**194-95**	51°50′N	12°14′E
Destruction Bay, Yk., Can.	**128-29**	61°14′N	138°50′W
Detmold, Ger. (dĕt′mōld)	**194-95**	51°56′N	8°53′E
Detroit, Mi., U.S. (dē-troit′)	**116-17**	42°21′N	83°04′W
Detroit Lakes, Mn., U.S. (dē-troit′ lākz)	**114-15**	46°49′N	95°51′W
Detva, Slvk. (dyĕt′vȧ)	**194-95**	48°32′N	19°29′E
Deutschland, nation, Eur. *see* Germany	**174-75**	51°0′N	10°00′E
Deva, Rom. (dā′vä)	**194-95**	45°53′N	22°55′E
Deventer, Neth. (dĕv′ĕn-tẽr)	**190-91**	52°16′N	6°10′E
Devils, stm., Tx., U.S. (dĕv′'lz)	**122-23**	29°32′N	100°59′W
Devils Lake, N.D., U.S. (dĕv′'lz lāk)	**114-15**	48°07′N	98°52′W
Devils Postpile National Monument, n.p., Ca., U.S. (dĕv′'lz pōst-pīl năsh′ŭn-ăl mŏn′ū-mĕnt)	**118-19**	37°37′N	119°05′W
Devils Tower National Monument, n.p., Wy., U.S. (dĕv′'lz tou′ẽr năsh′ŭn-ăl mŏn′ū-mĕnt)	**112-13**	44°36′N	104°43′W
Devon Island, i., Nu., Can.	**86**	75°0′N	87°00′W
Devonport, Austl. (dĕv′ŭn-pôrt)	**276**	41°11′S	146°21′E
Dewās, India	**234-35**	22°58′N	76°03′E
Dewey, Ok., U.S. (dū′ĭ)	**120-21**	36°48′N	95°56′W
De Witt, Ar., U.S. (dē wĭt′)	**124-25**	34°18′N	91°20′W
De Witt, Ia., U.S. (dē wĭt′)	**114-15**	41°49′N	90°32′W
Dexter, Me., U.S. (dĕks′tẽr)	**117a**	45°02′N	69°17′W
Dexter, Mo., U.S. (dĕks′tẽr)	**124-25**	36°48′N	89°58′W
Dexter, N.M., U.S. (dĕks′tẽr)	**120-21**	33°12′N	104°22′W
Dezfūl, Iran	**228-29**	32°23′N	48°24′E
Dezhnëva, Mys, c., Russia (mĭs dyĕzh′nyĭf)	**126**	66°08′N	169°41′W
Dezhou, China (dŭ-jō)	**240-41**	37°27′N	116°17′E
Dhahran, Sau. Ar.	**230-31**	26°18′N	50°08′E
Dhaka, nat. cap., Bngl. (dä′kä) (dăk′ȧ)	**234-35**	23°43′N	90°25′E
Dhamār, Yemen	**266**	14°33′N	44°24′E
Dhanbād, India	**234-35**	23°48′N	86°26′E
Dhār, India	**234-35**	22°36′N	75°18′E
Dhawalāgiri, mtn., Nepal	**234-35**	28°42′N	83°30′E
Dhuburi, India	**234-35**	26°01′N	89°59′E
Dhule, India	**234-35**	20°54′N	74°46′E
Diablo, Pico del, mtn., Mex.	**144-45**	30°59′N	115°45′W
Diablo Range, mts., Ca., U.S. (dyä′blō rānj)	**118-19**	37°0′N	121°20′W
Diamante, Arg.	**173**	32°04′S	60°39′W
Diamantina, Braz.	**172**	18°15′S	43°37′W
Diamantina, stm., Austl. (dī′man-tē′nȧ)	**277**	26°58′S	138°49′E
Diamantina National Park, n.p., Austl.	**277**	23°43′S	141°11′E
Diamantino, Braz. (dā-ȧ-män-tē′no)	**166-67**	14°25′S	56°27′W
Dian Chi, lk., China (dĭĕn chē)	**238-39**	24°50′N	102°42′E
Dianópolis, Braz.	**166-67**	11°38′S	46°50′W
D' Iberville, Mont, mtn., Can. *see* Caubvick, Mount	**130-31**	58°53′N	63°43′W
Dibrugarh, India	**234-35**	27°29′N	94°55′E
Dickinson, N.D., U.S. (dĭk′ĭn-sŭn)	**114-15**	46°53′N	102°47′W
Dickson, Tn., U.S. (dĭk′sŭn)	**124-25**	36°04′N	87°22′W
Dickson City, Pa., U.S. (dĭk′sŭn sĭ′tē)	**116-17**	41°28′N	75°37′W
Dicle, stm., Asia *see* Tigris	**208-09**	30°60′N	47°27′E
Diego de Almagro, Isla, i., Chile	**171**	51°28′S	75°11′W
Diégo-Suarez, Madag. *see* Antsirañana	**264-65**	12°17′S	49°17′E
Dien Bien, Viet.	**246-47**	21°23′N	103°01′E
Dien Bien Phu, Viet. *see* Dien Bien	**246-47**	21°23′N	103°01′E
Dieppe, N.B., Can. (dē-ĕp′)	**138-39**	46°06′N	64°44′W
Dieppe, Fr.	**196-97**	49°56′N	1°05′E
Difuri, i., Mald.	**236**	5°24′N	73°38′E
Digboi, India	**234-35**	27°23′N	95°38′E
Digby, N.S., Can. (dĭg′bĭ)	**138-39**	44°37′N	65°46′W
Digul, stm., Indon.	**277**	7°10′S	138°41′E
Dijlah, stm., Asia *see* Tigris	**208-09**	30°60′N	47°27′E
Dijon, Fr. (dē-zhŏɴ′)	**196-97**	47°19′N	5°02′E
Dikhil, Dji.	**266**	11°06′N	42°22′E
Dikson, Russia (dĭk′sŏn)	**218-19**	73°30′N	80°33′E
Dīla, Eth.	**262-63**	6°19′N	38°14′E
Dili, nat. cap., E. Timor (dĭl′ē)	**248-49**	8°35′S	125°35′E
Dilling, Sudan	**266**	12°02′N	29°40′E
Dillingham, Ak., U.S. (dĭl′ĕng-hăm)	**126**	59°03′N	158°28′W
Dillon, Mt., U.S. (dĭl′ŭn)	**112-13**	45°13′N	112°38′W
Dillon, S.C., U.S. (dĭl′ŭn)	**124-25**	34°25′N	79°22′W
Dilolo, D.R.C. (dē-lō′lō)	**262-63**	10°42′S	22°21′E
Dimāpur, India	**234-35**	25°55′N	93°44′E
Dimashq, nat. cap., Syria *see* Damascus	**228-29**	33°31′N	36°18′E
Dimitrovgrad, Blg.	**200-01**	42°03′N	25°37′E
Dimitrovgrad, Russia	**186-87**	54°13′N	49°36′E
Dimlang, mtn., Nig.	**260-61**	8°24′N	11°47′E
Dinagat Island, i., Phil.	**250**	10°12′N	125°35′E
Dinājpur, Bngl.	**234-35**	25°38′N	88°38′E
Dinan, Fr. (dē-näɴ′)	**196-97**	48°28′N	2°03′W
Dinant, Bel. (dē-näɴ′)	**190-91**	50°16′N	4°55′E
Dinara Planina, mts., Eur. (dē′nä-rä plä′nē-na) *see* Dinaric Alps	**200-01**	43°55′N	16°38′E
Dinaric Alps, mts., Eur.	**200-01**	43°55′N	16°38′E
Dinariche, Alpi, mts., Eur. *see* Dinaric Alps	**200-01**	43°55′N	16°38′E
Dindigul, India	**236**	10°22′N	77°59′E
Dingalan Bay, b., Phil. (dĭŋ-gä′län bā)	**250**	15°18′N	121°25′E
Dinggyê, China	**234-35**	28°35′N	86°37′E
Dinghai, China	**238-39**	30°01′N	122°06′E
Dingwall, Scot., U.K. (dĭng′wôl)	**190-91**	57°36′N	4°26′W
Dingxi, China	**240-41**	35°33′N	104°32′E
Dingxian, China (dĭŋ shyĕn)	**240-41**	38°31′N	114°60′E
Dingyuan, China (diŋ-yûän)	**238-39**	32°32′N	117°40′E
Dinosaur National Monument, n.p., U.S. (dī′nô-sôr năsh′ŭn-ăl mŏn′ū-mĕnt)	**112-13**	40°32′N	108°58′W
Dipolog, Phil.	**250**	8°35′N	123°21′E
Dirē Dawa, Eth.	**262-63**	9°35′N	41°52′E
Diriamba, Nic. (dēr-yäm′bä)	**149**	11°51′N	86°15′W
Dirj, Libya	**188-89**	30°10′N	10°28′E
Dirranbandi, Austl. (dĭ-rȧ-băn′dē)	**276**	28°35′S	148°14′E
Disappointment Islands, is., Fr. Poly. (dĭs′ȧ-point′ment ī′lȧndz) *see* Désappointement, Îles du	**280-81**	14°10′S	141°20′W
Dispur, India	**234-35**	26°08′N	91°48′E
Disraëli, Qc., Can. (dĭs-rā′lĭ)	**136-37**	45°54′N	71°21′W
District of Columbia, state, U.S.	**108-09**	38°54′N	77°01′W
Distrito Federal, state, Braz. (dēs-trē′tô-fĕ-dĕ-rä′l)	**168-69**	15°45′S	47°45′W
Distrito Federal, state, Mex.	**146-47**	19°15′N	99°10′W
Dis ûq, Egypt	**268b**	31°08′N	30°39′E
Diu, India (dē′ōō)	**234-35**	20°43′N	70°59′E
Divinópolis, Braz. (dē-vē-nô′pō-lēs)	**172**	20°09′S	44°53′W
Divnoye, Russia	**186-87**	45°55′N	43°22′E
Divo, C. Iv.	**260-61**	5°50′N	5°22′W
Dixon, Il., U.S. (dĭks′ŭn)	**116-17**	41°50′N	89°29′W
Dixon Entrance, strt., N.A.	**126**	54°25′N	132°30′W
Diyarbakır, Tur. (dē-yär-bĕk′ĭr)	**227**	37°55′N	40°14′E
Dja, stm., Afr.	**260-61**	2°02′N	15°12′E
Djajapura, Indon. *see* Jayapura	**277**	2°32′S	140°43′E
Djakarta, nat. cap., Indon. *see* Jakarta	**248-49**	6°11′S	106°50′E
Djambala, Congo	**262-63**	2°33′S	14°46′E
Djedi, Oued, stm., Alg.	**258-59**	34°28′N	6°06′E
Djelfa, Alg.	**269b**	34°41′N	3°15′E

ăt; finăl; rāte; senâte; ärm; ȧsk; sofȧ; fâre; ch-choose; dh-as th in other; bē; ēvent; bĕt; recĕnt; cratẽr; g-gō; gh-guttural g; bĭt; ĭ-short neutral; rīde; ĸ-guttural k as ch in German ich;

PRONOUNCING INDEX

Djenné – Dunkirk 325

Feature (Pronunciation)	Page	Lat.	Long.
Djenné, Mali	258-59	13°54'N	4°33'W
Djérem, stm., Camrn.	260-61	5°19'N	13°24'E
Djibouti, nation, Afr. (jē-bōō-tē´)	253	11°30'N	43°00'E
Djibouti, nat. cap., Dji. (jē-bōō-tē´)	266	11°34'N	43°09'E
Djokjakarta, Indon. *see* Yogyakarta	248-49	7°48'S	110°22'E
Djougou, Benin	260-61	9°42'N	1°40'E
Djugu, D.R.C.	267	1°58'N	30°30'E
Dmitrov, Russia (d'mē´trôf)	202-03	56°21'N	37°31'E
Dnepr, stm., Eur. *see* Dnieper	202-03	46°31'N	32°22'E
Dneprodzerzhinsk, Ukr. *see* Dniprodzerzhyns'k	202-03	48°29'N	34°41'E
Dnestr, stm., Eur. *see* Dniester	188-89	46°19'N	30°17'E
Dnieper, stm., Eur. (nē´pûr)	202-03	46°31'N	32°22'E
Dniester, stm., Eur. (nēs´-tēr)	188-89	46°19'N	30°17'E
Dnipro, stm., Eur. *see* Dnieper	202-03	46°31'N	32°22'E
Dniprodzerzhyns'k, Ukr.	202-03	48°29'N	34°41'E
Dnipropetrovs'k, Ukr.	202-03	48°28'N	34°58'E
Dnister, stm., Eur. *see* Dniester	188-89	46°19'N	30°17'E
Dnjapro, stm., Eur. *see* Dnieper	202-03	46°31'N	32°22'E
Dno, Russia (d'nô´)	192-93	57°49'N	29°59'E
Doba, Chad	262-63	8°39'N	16°51'E
Doberai, Jazirah, pen., Indon.	224-25	1°30'S	132°30'E
Doboj, Bos. (dō´boi)	200-01	44°44'N	18°06'E
Dobrich, Blg.	200-01	43°35'N	27°50'E
Dobryanka, Russia (dôb-ryän´kȧ)	186-87	58°28'N	56°25'E
Doce, stm., Braz. (dō´sȧ)	172	19°39'S	39°49'W
Doctor Arroyo, Mex. (dōk-tōr´ är-rō´yō)	146-47	23°42'N	100°11'W
Dodecanese, is., Grc. (dō´dĕ-cȧ-nēs´)	200-01	36°30'N	27°00'E
Dodekanisoy, is., Grc. *see* Dodecanese	200-01	36°30'N	27°00'E
Dodge City, Ks., U.S. (dŏj sĭ´tē)	120-21	37°45'N	100°01'W
Dodgeville, Wi., U.S. (dŏj´vĭl)	116-17	42°58'N	90°08'W
Dodola, Eth.	269d	7°00'N	39°07'E
Dodoma, nat. cap., Tan. (dō´dō-mȧ)	267	6°11'S	35°45'E
Dogai Coring, lk., China	234-35	34°35'N	88°59'E
Dog Island, i., Anguilla	143b	18°17'N	63°15'W
Dog Lake, lk., On., Can. (dŏg lāk)	136-37	48°46'N	89°33'W
Dōgo, i., Japan	245	36°15'N	133°16'E
Doğu Karadeniz Dağları, mts., Tur.	227	40°30'N	40°30'E
Doha, nat. cap., Qatar (dō´hȧ)	230-31	25°17'N	51°32'E
Dolbeau-Mistassini, Qc., Can.	136-37	48°53'N	72°13'W
Dole, Fr. (dōl)	196-97	47°06'N	5°29'E
Dolgaya Kosa, spit, Russia (dôl-gä´yȧ kô´sȧ)	202-03	46°41'N	37°43'E
Dolinsk, Russia (dȧ-lēnsk´)	222-23	47°20'N	142°48'E
Dolisie, Congo *see* Loubomo	262-63	4°11'S	12°40'E
Dolores, Arg. (dō-lō´rĕs)	173	36°20'S	57°41'W
Dolores, Ur.	173	33°32'S	58°12'W
Dolores Hidalgo, Mex. (dō-lō´rĕs-ē-däl´gō)	146-47	21°09'N	100°56'W
Domažlice, Czech Rep. (dō´mäzh-lē-tsĕ)	194-95	49°27'N	12°56'E
Dombarovskiy, Russia	226	50°46'N	59°32'E
Dombås, Nor.	192-93	62°05'N	9°08'E
Dombóvár, Hung. (dŏm´bō-vär)	194-95	46°22'N	18°08'E
Domeyko, Chile	168-69	28°57'S	70°54'W
Domeyko, Cordillera, mts., Chile (kôr-dēl-yĕ´rä-dō-mā´kō)	168-69	24°45'S	69°09'W
Dominica, nation, N.A. (dō-mĭ-nē´kȧ)	140-41	15°30'N	61°20'W
Dominican Republic, nation, N.A. (dō-mĭn´ĭ-kăn rē-pŭb´lĭk)	140-41	19°0'N	70°40'W
Dominion, Cape, c., Nu., Can.	130-31	66°09'N	74°27'W
Dominique, Canal de la, strt., N.A. *see* Martinique Passage	143b	15°10'N	61°15'W
Domodedovo, Russia (dō-mō-dyĕ´do-vô)	202-03	55°26'N	37°47'E
Dom Pedrito, Braz.	173	30°59'S	54°40'W
Domuyo, Volcán, vol., Arg.	171	36°38'S	70°26'W
Don, stm., Russia (dŏn)	186-87	47°05'N	39°15'E
Don, stm., Scot., U.K. (dŏn)	190-91	57°11'N	2°06'W
Donaldsonville, La., U.S. (dŏn´ăld-sŭn-vĭl)	124-25	30°06'N	90°60'W
Donau, stm., Eur. *see* Danube	188-89	45°23'N	29°36'E
Don Benito, Spain (dōn´bå-nē´tō)	198-99	38°57'N	5°52'W
Doncaster, Eng., U.K. (doŋ´kăs-tēr)	190-91	53°32'N	1°08'W
Dondo, Moz.	264-65	19°35'S	34°44'E
Dondra Head, c., Sri L.	236	5°55'N	80°35'E
Donegal, Ire. (dŏn-ē-gôl´)	190-91	54°39'N	8°07'W
Donegal Bay, b., Ire. (dŏn-ē-gôl´ bā)	190-91	54°30'N	8°30'W
Donets'k, Ukr.	202-03	47°60'N	37°48'E
Dong, stm., China (dôŋ)	238-39	23°05'N	113°60'E
Dong, stm., China (dôŋ)	240-41	42°17'N	101°06'E
Dongara, Austl. (dôn-gä´rȧ)	270-71	29°15'S	114°58'E
Dongfang, China (dôŋ-fäŋ)	238-39	19°05'N	108°38'E
Donggala, Indon. (dôn-gä´lä)	248-49	0°41'S	119°44'E
Dongguan, China (dôŋ-gůän)	238-39	23°03'N	113°44'E
Dong Hai, s., Asia *see* East China Sea	222-23	30°0'N	126°00'E
Donghai Dao, i., China	238-39	21°02'N	110°25'E
Dong Hoi, Viet. (dông-hô-ē´)	246-47	17°29'N	106°37'E
Dong Nai, stm., Viet.	246-47	10°44'N	106°46'E
Dongola, Sudan *see* Dunqulah	266	19°11'N	30°28'E
Dong San Shen, hist. reg., China *see* Manchuria	240-41	47°0'N	125°00'E
Dongting Hu, lk., China (dôŋ-tĭŋ hōō)	238-39	29°20'N	112°54'E
Dongyang, China	238-39	29°16'N	120°14'E
Dongzhi, China	238-39	30°07'N	117°01'E
Doniphan, Mo., U.S. (dŏn´ĭ-făn)	124-25	36°37'N	90°50'W
Doniphan, Ne., U.S. (dŏn´ĭ-făn)	114-15	40°46'N	98°23'W
Donostia, Spain *see* Donostia-San Sebastián	198-99	43°19'N	1°60'W
Donostia-San Sebastián, Spain	198-99	43°19'N	1°60'W
Door Peninsula, pen., Wi., U.S. (dōr pĕ-nĭn´sŭlȧ)	116-17	44°55'N	87°20'W
Dorchester, Eng., U.K. (dôr´chĕs-tēr)	190-91	50°43'N	2°27'W
Dorchester, Cape, c., Nu., Can.	130-31	65°27'N	77°26'W
Dordogne, stm., Fr. (dôr-dôn´yĕ)	196-97	45°02'N	0°35'W
Dore Lake, lk., Sk., Can.	134-35	54°46'N	107°17'W
Dores do Indaiá, Braz.	172	19°28'S	45°36'W
Dori, Burkina	260-61	14°02'N	0°02'W
Dornbirn, Aus. (dôrn´bērn)	194-95	47°25'N	9°45'E
Dorogobuzh, Russia (dôrôgô´-bōō´zh)	202-03	54°55'N	33°18'E
Dorohoi, Rom. (dō-rô-hoi´)	194-95	47°57'N	26°24'E
Dorpat, Est. *see* Tartu	192-93	58°23'N	26°43'E
Dorre Island, i., Austl. (dôr ī´lȧnd)	272-73	25°07'S	113°06'E
Dortmund, Ger. (dôrt´mònt)	194-95	51°31'N	7°28'E
Dörtyol, Tur. (dûrt´yōl)	228-29	36°52'N	36°13'E
Dosatuy, Russia	240-41	50°22'N	118°34'E
Dos Bahías, Cabo, c., Arg. (kȧ´bô-dôs-bä-ē´äs)	171	44°56'S	65°33'W
Dos Hermanas, Spain (dōsĕr-mä´näs)	198-99	37°17'N	5°55'W
Dosso, Niger (dôs-ō´)	258-59	13°03'N	3°12'E
Dossor, Kaz.	186-87	47°32'N	52°59'E
Dothan, Al., U.S. (dō´thăn)	124-25	31°13'N	85°24'W
Douai, Fr. (dōō-å´)	196-97	50°22'N	3°05'E
Douala, Camrn. (dōō-ä´lä)	260-61	4°03'N	9°42'E
Douarnenez, Fr. (dōō-ȧr nē-nĕs´)	196-97	48°06'N	4°20'W
Douglas, Az., U.S. (dŭg´lăs)	118-19	31°20'N	109°34'W
Douglas, Ga., U.S. (dŭg´lăs)	124-25	31°30'N	82°51'W
Douglas, Mi., U.S. (dŭg´lăs)	116-17	42°39'N	86°12'W
Douglas, Wy., U.S. (dŭg´lăs)	112-13	42°45'N	105°23'W
Douglas, nat. cap., I. of Man (dŭg´lăs)	190-91	54°10'N	4°29'W
Douglas Channel, strt., B.C., Can. (dŭg´lăs chăn´ĕl)	132-33	53°30'N	129°12'W
Douglasville, Ga., U.S. (dŭg´lăs-vĭl)	124-25	33°45'N	84°45'W
Dourada, Serra, plat., Braz. (sĕ´r-rä-dōōō-rȧ´dä)	166-67	13°10'S	48°34'W
Dourados, Braz.	168-69	22°13'S	54°49'W
Douro, stm., Eur. (dô´ō-rō)	198-99	41°09'N	8°41'W
Dover, Eng., U.K. (dō vēr)	190-91	51°08'N	1°18'E
Dover, De., U.S.	116-17	39°09'N	75°31'W
Dover, N.H., U.S.	116-17	43°12'N	70°53'W
Dover, N.J., U.S. (dō vēr)	116-17	40°54'N	74°32'W
Dover, Oh., U.S. (dō vēr)	116-17	40°31'N	81°28'W
Dover, Strait of, strt., Eur. (strāt ŭv dō vēr)	190-91	50°59'N	1°31'E
Dover-Foxcroft, Me., U.S. (dō´vēr fôks´krôft)	117a	45°11'N	69°14'W
Dovrefjell, mts., Nor. (dōv´rĕ fyĕl´)	192-93	62°06'N	9°25'E
Dowagiac, Mi., U.S. (dô wô´jăk)	116-17	41°59'N	86°06'W
Drâa, Hamada du, des., Alg.	258-59	29°0'N	6°45'W
Drâa, Oued, stm., Afr. (wĕd drä)	258-59	28°41'N	11°07'W
Drăgăşani, Rom. (drä-gȧ-shän´ĭ)	200-01	44°40'N	24°16'E
Draguignan, Fr. (drä-gēn-yän´)	196-97	43°33'N	6°28'E
Drake, Pasaje de, strt., *see* Drake Passage	287	58°0'S	70°00'W
Drakensberg, mts., Afr. (drä´kĕnz-bĕrgh)	264-65	27°0'S	30°00'E
Drake Passage, strt. (drāk păs´ĭj)	287	58°0'S	70°00'W
Dráma, Grc. (drä´mä)	200-01	41°09'N	24°09'E
Drammen, Nor. (dräm´ĕn)	192-93	59°45'N	10°13'E
Drau, stm., Eur. (drou) *see* Drava	200-01	45°33'N	18°56'E
Drava, stm., Eur. (drä´vä)	200-01	45°33'N	18°56'E
Drayton Valley, Ab., Can. (drā´tŭn văl´ē)	132-33	53°14'N	114°59'W
Dresden, Ger. (drās´dĕn)	194-95	51°03'N	13°44'E
Dreux, Fr. (drû)	196-97	48°44'N	1°22'E
Drin, stm., Alb. (drēn)	200-01	41°45'N	19°35'E
Drina, stm., Eur. (drē´nä)	200-01	44°54'N	19°21'E
Drøbak, Nor. (drû´bäk)	192-93	59°39'N	10°39'E
Drohobych, Ukr.	194-95	49°21'N	23°31'E
Druc', stm., Bela. (drōōt)	202-03	53°04'N	30°02'E
Druk-Yul, nation, Asia *see* Bhutan	206-07	27°30'N	90°30'E
Drumheller, Ab., Can. (drŭm-hĕl-ēr)	132-33	51°28'N	112°42'W
Drummond Island, i., Mi., U.S. (drŭm´ŭnd ī´lănd)	116-17	46°0'N	83°40'W
Drummondville, Qc., Can. (drŭm´ŭnd-vĭl)	136-37	45°53'N	72°30'W
Drumright, Ok., U.S. (drŭm´rīt)	120-21	35°60'N	96°36'W
Drwęca, stm., Pol. (d'r-văn´tsȧ)	194-95	52°60'N	18°41'E
Dryden, On., Can. (drī-dĕn)	134-35	49°47'N	92°51'W
Dry Tortugas, is., Fl., U.S. (drī tôr-tōō´gäz)	125a	24°38'N	82°55'W
Dry Tortugas National Park, n.p., Fl., U.S. (drī tôr-tōō´gäz năsh´ŭn-ăl pärk)	125a	24°37'N	82°54'W
Duala, Camrn. *see* Douala	260-61	4°03'N	9°42'E
Duarte, Pico, mtn., Dom. Rep. (pēcô dŭü´ärtĕh)	142-43	19°02'N	70°59'W
Dubai, U.A.E.	230-31	25°16'N	55°19'E
Dubawnt, stm., Can. (dōō-bônt´)	130-31	64°31'N	100°05'W
Dubawnt Lake, lk., Can. (dōō-bônt´ lāk)	130-31	63°08'N	101°30'W
Dubayy, U.A.E. *see* Dubai	230-31	25°16'N	55°19'E
Dubbo, Austl. (dŭb´ō)	276	32°15'S	148°36'E
Dublin, Ga., U.S. (dŭb´lĭn)	124-25	32°32'N	82°54'W
Dublin, Oh., U.S. (dŭb´lĭn)	116-17	40°06'N	83°07'W
Dublin, Tx., U.S. (dŭb´lĭn)	122-23	32°05'N	98°20'W
Dublin, nat. cap., Ire. (dŭb´lĭn)	190-91	53°21'N	6°15'W
Dubno, Ukr. (dōō´b-nô)	194-95	50°24'N	25°45'E
Du Bois, Pa., U.S. (dò-bois´)	116-17	41°07'N	78°46'W
Dubovka, Russia (dò-bôf´kȧ)	186-87	49°04'N	44°49'E
Dubrovka, Russia (dōō-brôf´kȧ)	202-03	53°42'N	33°31'E
Dubrovnik, Cro. (dò´brôv-nĕk)	200-01	42°39'N	18°06'E
Dubuque, Ia., U.S. (dò-bŭk´)	114-15	42°30'N	90°41'W
Duchesne, Ut., U.S. (dò-shān´)	118-19	40°10'N	110°24'W
Duck Lake, Sk., Can. (dŭk lāk)	134-35	52°49'N	106°14'W
Duck Valley Indian Reservation, ind. res., U.S. (dŭk văl´ē ĭn´dĭ-ăn rĕ-sĕr-vā´shĕn)	112-13	42°00'N	116°10'W
Dudinka, Russia (dōō-dĭn´kȧ)	218-19	69°24'N	86°11'E
Dudley, Eng., U.K. (dŭd´lĭ)	190-91	52°30'N	2°05'W
Duero, stm., Eur.	198-99	41°09'N	8°41'W
Dufourspitze, mtn., Eur.	194-95	45°55'N	7°52'E
Dugi Otok, i., Cro. (dōō´gē o´tôk)	200-01	43°59'N	15°04'E
Duisburg, Ger. (dōō´ĭs-bòrgh)	194-95	51°26'N	6°47'E
Duitama, Col.	164-65	5°50'N	73°02'W
Dukhān, Qatar	230-31	25°25'N	50°48'E
Dukhovshchina, Russia (dōō-kôfsh-´chēnȧ)	202-03	55°12'N	32°25'E
Dulan, China	240-41	36°10'N	98°22'E
Dulce, Golfo, b., C.R. (gōl´fô dōōl´sä)	149	8°32'N	83°14'W
Duluth, Mn., U.S. (dò-lōōth´)	114-15	46°46'N	92°09'W
Dumaguete, Phil.	250	9°18'N	123°18'E
Dumai, Indon.	246-47	1°40'N	101°27'E
Dumali Point, c., Phil. (dōō-mä´lē point)	250	13°07'N	121°33'E
Dumaran Island, i., Phil.	250	10°33'N	119°51'E
Dumaring, Indon.	248-49	1°32'N	118°13'E
Dumfries, Scot., U.K. (dŭm-frēs´)	190-91	55°04'N	3°37'W
Duna, stm., Eur. *see* Danube	188-89	45°23'N	29°36'E
Dünaburg, Lat. *see* Daugavpils	192-93	55°53'N	26°32'E
Dunai, stm., Eur. *see* Danube	188-89	45°23'N	29°36'E
Dunaj, stm., Eur. *see* Danube	188-89	45°23'N	29°36'E
Dunărea, stm., Eur. *see* Danube	188-89	45°23'N	29°36'E
Dunav, stm., Eur. *see* Danube	188-89	45°23'N	29°36'E
Duncan, B.C., Can. (dŭŋ´kăn)	132-33	48°47'N	123°42'W
Duncan, Ok., U.S. (dŭn´kăn)	120-21	34°30'N	97°57'W
Duncan, stm., B.C., Can. (dŭŋ´kăn)	132-33	50°11'N	116°57'W
Duncansby Head, c., Scot., U.K. (dŭn´kănz-bĭ hĕd)	190-91	58°39'N	3°02'W
Dundalk, Ire. (dŭn´kôk)	190-91	54°01'N	6°24'W
Dundas, Lake, lk., Austl. (lāk dŭn-dăs)	272-73	32°35'S	121°50'E
Dundas Island, i., B.C., Can. (dŭn-dăs´ ī´lănd)	132-33	54°33'N	130°55'W
Dún Dealgan, Ire. *see* Dundalk	190-91	54°01'N	6°24'W
Dundee, S. Afr.	269c	28°09'S	30°15'E
Dundee, Scot., U.K.	190-91	56°29'N	2°59'W
Dund-Us, Mong.	240-41	47°60'N	91°38'E
Dunedin, N.Z.	278	45°52'S	170°29'E
Dunfermline, Scot., U.K. (dŭn-fĕrm´lĭn)	190-91	56°04'N	3°29'W
Dūngarpur, India	234-35	23°50'N	73°43'E
Dungarvan, Ire. (dŭn-gàr´văn)	190-91	52°06'N	7°38'W
Dungu, D.R.C.	267	3°37'N	28°34'E
Dunhua, China (dòn-hwä)	244	43°22'N	128°14'E
Dunhuang, China	240-41	40°08'N	94°40'E
Dunkerque, Fr. (dŭn-kĕrk´)	196-97	51°03'N	2°23'E
Dunkirk, Fr. *see* Dunkerque	196-97	51°03'N	2°23'E
Dunkirk, In., U.S. (dŭn´kûrk)	116-17	40°22'N	85°12'W

n-sing; ŋ-baŋk; ɴ-nasalized n; nŏd; cŏmmit; ōld; ôbey; ôrder; oi-boil; fōōd; ò-as oo in foot; ou-out; s-soft; sh-dish; th-thin; pūre; ůnite; ûrn; stŭd; circŭs; ü-as in French tu; ´-indeterminate vowel.

326 Dunkirk – Elektrostal'

PRONOUNCING INDEX

Feature (Pronunciation)	Page	Lat.	Long.
Dunkirk, N.Y., U.S. (dŭn′kûrk)	116-17	42°29′N	79°19′W
Dún Laoghaire, Ire. (dūn-lâ′rĕ)	190-91	53°17′N	6°08′W
Dunlap, Ia., U.S. (dŭn′lăp)	114-15	41°51′N	95°36′W
Dunlap, Tn., U.S. (dŭn′lăp)	124-25	35°22′N	85°23′W
Dunleary, Ire. *see* Dún Laoghaire	190-91	53°17′N	6°08′W
Dunmore, Pa., U.S. (dŭn′mōr)	116-17	41°27′N	75°38′W
Dunn, N.C., U.S. (dŭn)	124-25	35°18′N	78°37′W
Dunqulah, Sudan	266	19°11′N	30°28′E
Dunsmuir, Ca., U.S. (dŭnz′mūr)	112-13	41°13′N	122°17′W
Duolun, China (dwô-lōōn)	240-41	42°12′N	116°28′E
Duomula, China	234-35	34°07′N	82°30′E
Duque de York, Isla, i., Chile	171	50°40′S	75°20′W
Duquesne, Pa., U.S. (do̤-kān′)	116-17	40°22′N	79°51′W
Du Quoin, Il., U.S. (do̤-kwoin′)	116-17	38°01′N	89°15′W
Durand, Mi., U.S. (dů-rănd′)	116-17	42°55′N	83°59′W
Durand, Wi., U.S. (dů-rănd′)	114-15	44°37′N	91°57′W
Durango, Mex. (dōō-rä′n-gô)	146-47	24°02′N	104°41′W
Durango, Co., U.S. (do̤-răŋ′gō)	118-19	37°17′N	107°52′W
Durango, state, Mex. (dōō-rä′n-gô)	122-23	24°50′N	104°50′W
Durant, Ms., U.S. (dů-rănt′)	124-25	33°05′N	89°52′W
Durant, Ok., U.S. (dů-rănt′)	120-21	33°60′N	96°23′W
Durazno, Ur. (dōō-räz′nō)	173	33°25′S	56°30′W
Durazzo, Alb. *see* Durrës	200-01	41°19′N	19°27′E
Durban, S. Afr. (dûr′băn)	264-65	29°55′S	30°56′E
Durbe, Lat. (do̤or′bĕ)	192-93	56°35′N	21°21′E
Düren, Ger. (dü′rĕn)	194-95	50°48′N	6°29′E
Durg, India	234-35	21°11′N	81°17′E
Durham, Eng., U.K. (dûr′ăm)	190-91	54°47′N	1°34′W
Durham, N.C., U.S.	124-25	35°60′N	78°54′W
Durmitor, mtn., Mont.	200-01	43°08′N	19°01′E
Durrës, Alb. (do̤r′ĕs)	200-01	41°19′N	19°27′E
Durrësi, Alb. *see* Durrës	200-01	41°19′N	19°27′E
D'Urville, Tanjung, c., Indon.	277	1°28′S	137°54′E
D'Urville Island, i., N.Z.	278	40°50′S	173°52′E
Dushan, China (dōō-shän)	238-39	25°50′N	107°32′E
Dushanbe, nat. cap., Taj. (dū-shän′-bȧ) (dū-shän-bă′)	232-33	38°34′N	68°47′E
Düsseldorf, Ger. (düs′ĕl-dôrf)	194-95	51°14′N	6°48′E
Duyfken Point, c., Austl.	277	12°34′S	141°38′E
Duyun, China (dōō-yòn)	238-39	26°16′N	107°30′E
Dwārka, India	234-35	22°14′N	68°59′E
Dwight, Il., U.S. (dwīt)	116-17	41°05′N	88°25′W
Dyat'kovo, Russia (dyät′kō-vō)	202-03	53°35′N	34°21′E
Dyersburg, Tn., U.S. (dī′ērz-bûrg)	124-25	36°02′N	89°23′W
Dyersville, Ia., U.S. (dī′ērz-vĭl)	114-15	42°29′N	91°07′W
Dzavhan, stm., Mong.	240-41	48°53′N	93°26′E
Dzerzhinsk, Russia	186-87	56°15′N	43°24′E
Dzhambul, Kaz. *see* Taraz	226	42°54′N	71°21′E
Dzhankoi, Ukr.	202-03	45°43′N	34°23′E
Dzharylhach, ostriv, i., Ukr.	202-03	46°02′N	32°55′E
Dzhebariki-Khaya, Russia	218-19	62°11′N	135°46′E
Dzhezkazgan, Kaz. *see* Zhezqazghan	226	47°47′N	67°41′E
Dzhugdzhur, Khrebet, mts., Russia	218-19	58°0′N	136°00′E
Dzhugdzhur Range, mts., Russia (jo̤og-jo̤or′ rānj) *see* Dzhugdzhur, Khrebet	218-19	58°0′N	136°00′E
Dzhungarian Alatau Mountains, mts., Asia *see* Alataw Shan	226	45°0′N	81°00′E
Dzibalchén, Mex. (zē-bäl-chĕ′n)	148	19°28′N	89°44′W
Dzilam González, Mex. (zē-lä′m-gôn-zä′lĕz)	148	21°17′N	88°56′W
Dzitás, Mex. (zē-tá′s)	148	20°51′N	88°31′W
Dzuunmod, Mong.	240-41	47°43′N	106°57′E

E

Feature (Pronunciation)	Page	Lat.	Long.
Eagle, Id., U.S. (ē′g'l)	112-13	43°41′N	116°19′W
Eagle Grove, Ia., U.S. (ē′g'l grōv)	114-15	42°40′N	93°54′W
Eagle Lake, Me., U.S. (ē′g'l lāk)	117a	47°02′N	68°36′W
Eagle Lake, Tx., U.S. (ē′g'l lāk)	122-23	29°35′N	96°20′W
Eagle Pass, Tx., U.S. (ē′g'l pås)	122-23	28°42′N	100°29′W
Earle, Ar., U.S. (ûrl)	124-25	35°16′N	90°28′W
Earlington, Ky., U.S. (ûr′lĭng-tŭn)	124-25	37°16′N	87°31′W
Easley, S.C., U.S. (ēz′lĭ)	124-25	34°50′N	82°35′W
East Angus, Qc., Can. (ēst ăŋ′gŭs)	136-37	45°29′N	71°40′W
Eastbourne, Eng., U.K. (ēst′bôrn)	190-91	50°46′N	0°17′E
East Caicos, i., T./C. Is. (ēst kī′kōs)	142-43	21°42′N	71°29′W
East Cape, c., N.Z.	278	37°41′S	178°33′E
East Chicago, In., U.S. (ēst shĭ-kô′gō)	116-17	41°39′N	87°26′W
East China Sea, s., Asia (ēst chī′nȧ sē)	222-23	30°0′N	126°00′E
East Detroit, Mi., U.S. (ēst dē-troit′) *see* Eastpointe	116-17	42°28′N	82°57′W
Easter Island, i., Chile (ēs′tēr ī′lănd) *see* Pascua, Isla de	282-83	27°07′S	109°22′W
Eastern Desert, des., Egypt *see* Arabian Desert	266	28°0′N	32°00′E
Eastern Ghāts, mts., India (ē′stērn ghäts) (ē′stērn ghôts)	236	14°0′N	78°50′E
East Falkland, i., Falk. Is.	171	51°53′S	59°11′W
East Grand Forks, Mn., U.S. (ēst grănd fôrks)	114-15	47°55′N	97°00′W
East Helena, Mt., U.S. (ēst hĕ-hē′nȧ)	112-13	46°35′N	111°55′W
East Jordan, Mi., U.S. (ēst jôr′dăn)	116-17	45°09′N	85°07′W
Eastland, Tx., U.S. (ēst′lănd)	120-21	32°24′N	98°49′W
East Lansing, Mi., U.S. (ēst lăn′sĭng)	116-17	42°44′N	84°29′W
East Liverpool, Oh., U.S. (ēst lĭv′ēr-pōōl)	116-17	40°38′N	80°35′W
East London, S. Afr. (ēst ŭn′dŭn)	264-65	32°60′S	27°54′E
Eastmain, Qc., Can.	128-29	52°13′N	78°33′W
Eastmain, stm., Qc., Can. (ēst′mān)	130-31	52°15′N	78°35′W
Eastmain-Opinaca, Réservoir, res., Qc., Can.	130-31	52°23′N	76°35′W
Eastman, Ga., U.S. (ēst′măn)	124-25	32°12′N	83°10′W
East Moline, Il., U.S. (ēst mô-lēn′)	114-15	41°32′N	90°25′W
East Nishnabotna, stm., Ia., U.S. (ēst nĭsh-nȧ-bŏt′nȧ)	120-21	40°39′N	95°38′W
East Orange, N.J., U.S. (ēst ŏr′ĕnj)	116-17	40°46′N	74°12′W
East Pakistan, nation, Asia *see* Bangladesh	206-07	24°0′N	90°00′E
East Peoria, Il., U.S. (ēst pē-ō′rĭ-ȧ)	116-17	40°40′N	89°35′W
Eastpointe, Mi., U.S.	116-17	42°28′N	82°57′W
Eastport, Me., U.S. (ēst′pōrt)	117a	44°54′N	66°60′W
East Providence, R.I., U.S. (ēst prŏv′ĭ-dĕns)	116-17	41°49′N	71°23′W
East Saint Louis, Il., U.S.	120-21	38°37′N	90°09′W
East Sea, s., Asia *see* Japan, Sea of	222-23	40°0′N	135°00′E
East Siberian Sea, s., Russia (ēst sī-bĭr′y′n sē)	218-19	74°0′N	166°00′E
East Stroudsburg, Pa., U.S. (ēst stroudz′bûrg)	116-17	41°00′N	75°11′W
East Tawas, Mi., U.S. (ēst tô′wȧs)	116-17	44°17′N	83°28′W
East Timor, nation, Asia (ēst tē-mōr′)	248-49	8°35′S	126°00′E
Eaton, Oh., U.S. (ē′tŭn)	116-17	39°45′N	84°38′W
Eaton Rapids, Mi., U.S. (ē′tŭn răp′ĭdz)	116-17	42°30′N	84°39′W
Eatonton, Ga., U.S. (ē′tŭn-tŭn)	124-25	33°20′N	83°23′W
Eau Claire, Wi., U.S. (ō klâr′)	114-15	44°49′N	91°30′W
Eau Claire, Lac à l', lk., Qc., Can.	130-31	56°11′N	74°26′W
Eauripik, at., Micron.	280-81	6°41′N	143°03′E
Ebinur Hu, lk., China	226	44°56′N	82°52′E
Eboli, Italy (ĕb′ô-lē)	200-01	40°38′N	15°04′E
Ebolowa, Camrn.	260-61	2°55′N	11°09′E
Echoing, stm., Can. (ĕk′ō-ĭng)	134-35	55°51′N	92°04′W
Echuca, Austl. (ē-cho̤′kȧ)	276	36°08′S	144°45′E
Écija, Spain (ā′thē-hä)	198-99	37°32′N	5°05′W
Ecuador, nation, S.A. (ĕk′wȧ-dôr)	158	2°0′S	77°30′W
Eddyville, Ia., U.S. (ĕd′ĭ-vĭl)	114-15	41°09′N	92°38′W
Eddyville, Ky., U.S. (ĕd′ĭ-vĭl)	124-25	37°06′N	88°05′W
Ede, Nig.	260a	7°44′N	4°25′E
Edéa, Camrn. (ĕ-dā′ä)	260-61	3°48′N	10°08′E
Eden, Austl.	276	37°04′S	149°54′E
Eden, N.C., U.S. (ē′dĕn)	124-25	36°29′N	79°46′W
Eden, Tx., U.S. (ē′dĕn)	122-23	31°13′N	99°51′W
Eden Prairie, Mn., U.S. (ē′dĕn prâr′ĭ)	114-15	44°51′N	93°28′W
Edenton, N.C., U.S. (ē′dĕn-tŭn)	124-25	36°04′N	76°36′W
Edenville, S. Afr. (ē′d'n-vĭl)	269c	27°34′S	27°41′E
Edfu, Egypt	268b	24°58′N	32°52′E
Edgefield, S.C., U.S. (ĕj′fēld)	124-25	33°47′N	81°56′W
Edgeley, N.D., U.S. (ĕj′lĭ)	114-15	46°21′N	98°43′W
Edgemont, S.D., U.S. (ĕj′mŏnt)	114-15	43°18′N	103°48′W
Edgerton, Wi., U.S. (ĕj′ēr-tŭn)	116-17	42°50′N	89°04′W
Edinburg, Tx., U.S. (ĕd′'n-bûrg)	122-23	26°18′N	98°10′W
Edinburgh, Scot., U.K. (ĕd′'n-bŭr-ô)	190-91	55°57′N	3°13′W
Edirne, Tur.	200-01	41°41′N	26°34′E
Edmond, Ok., U.S. (ĕd′mŭnd)	120-21	35°39′N	97°29′W
Edmonton, Ab., Can. (ĕd′mŭn-tŭn)	132-33	53°33′N	113°30′W
Edmundston, N.B., Can. (ĕd′mŭn-stŭn)	138-39	47°22′N	68°19′W
Edna, Tx., U.S. (ĕd′nȧ)	122-23	28°59′N	96°39′W
Édouard, Lac, lk., Afr. *see* Edward, Lake	267	0°23′S	29°36′E
Edremit, Tur. (ĕd-rĕ-mēt′)	200-01	39°36′N	27°01′E
Edson, Ab., Can. (ĕd′sŭn)	132-33	53°35′N	116°26′W
Eduardo Castex, Arg.	173	35°55′S	64°18′W
Edward, Lake, lk., Afr. (lāk ĕd′wērd)	267	0°23′S	29°36′E
Edwards Plateau, plat., Tx., U.S.	122-23	30°46′N	100°47′W
Edwardsville, Il., U.S. (ĕd′wērdz-vĭl)	120-21	38°48′N	89°57′W
Edward VII Peninsula, pen., Ant.	287	77°40′S	154°60′W
Eel, stm., Ca., U.S. (ēl)	110-11	40°38′N	124°20′W
Eesti, nation, Eur. *see* Estonia	174-75	59°0′N	26°00′E
Éfaté, i., Vanuatu (å-fä′tā)	279g	17°40′S	168°25′E
Effigy Mounds National Monument, n.p., Ia., U.S. (ĕf′ĭ-jŭ mounds năsh′ŭn-ăl mŏn′ŭ-mĕnt)	114-15	43°06′N	91°13′W
Effingham, Il., U.S. (ĕf′ĭng-hăm)	116-17	39°07′N	88°33′W
Eg, stm., Mong.	240-41	49°23′N	103°38′E
Egadi, Isole, is., Italy (ĕ′sō-lĕ-ĕ′gä-dē)	200-01	37°58′N	12°16′E
Ege Denizi, s., *see* Aegean Sea	200-01	38°30′N	25°00′E
Eger, Czech Rep. *see* Cheb	194-95	50°05′N	12°22′E
Eger, Hung. (ĕ gĕr)	194-95	47°54′N	20°23′E
Egersund, Nor. (ĕ′ghĕr-sȯn′)	192-93	58°27′N	6°00′E
Egmont, Cape, c., N.Z. (kāp ĕg′mŏnt)	278	39°17′S	173°45′E
Eğridir Gölü, lk., Tur.	186-87	38°02′N	30°53′E
Egum Atoll, at., Pap. N. Gui.	277	9°25′S	151°55′E
Egvekinot, Russia	218-19	66°18′N	179°11′W
Egypt, nation, Afr. (ē′jĭpt)	253	27°0′N	30°00′E
Eichstätt, Ger. (īk′shtät)	194-95	48°54′N	11°11′E
Eidfjord, Nor. (ĕĭd′fyōr)	192-93	60°28′N	7°05′E
Eidsvoll, Nor. (ĭdhs′vôl)	192-93	60°19′N	11°14′E
Eifel, mts., Ger. (ī′fĕl)	194-95	50°14′N	6°42′E
Eight Degree Channel, strt., Asia	236	8°0′N	73°00′E
Einbeck, Ger. (īn′bĕk)	194-95	51°49′N	9°52′E
Eindhoven, Neth. (īnd′hō-vĕn)	190-91	51°26′N	5°29′E
Éire, nation, Eur. *see* Ireland	174-75	53°0′N	8°00′W
Eirunepé, Braz.	166-67	6°39′S	69°52′W
Eisenach, Ger. (ī′zĕn-äĸ)	194-95	50°59′N	10°19′E
Eivissa, Spain	198-99	38°55′N	1°25′E
Eivissa, i., Spain	198-99	39°0′N	1°25′E
Ejin Qi, China	240-41	41°52′N	100°56′E
Ejmiatsin, Arm.	227	40°10′N	44°18′E
Ejutla de Crespo, Mex. (å-ho̤t′lä dā krās′pō)	146-47	16°34′N	96°44′W
Ekenäs, Fin. (ĕ′kĕ-nâs)	192-93	59°58′N	23°26′E
Ekibastuz, Kaz.	226	51°43′N	75°20′E
Ekimchan, Russia	218-19	53°04′N	132°57′E
Eko, Nig. *see* Lagos	260a	6°27′N	3°24′E
Ekwan, stm., On., Can.	130-31	53°12′N	82°14′W
El Aaiún, nat. cap., W. Sah. *see* Laayoune	258-59	27°10′N	13°12′W
El Abiodh Sidi Cheikh, Alg.	188-89	32°53′N	0°32′E
El Affroun, Alg. (ĕl åf-froun′)	269b	36°28′N	2°37′E
El-Agheila, Libya *see* Al-'Uqaylah	188-89	30°15′N	19°12′E
El-Alamein, Egypt	188-89	30°49′N	28°58′E
Elands, stm., S. Afr. (ĕlånds)	269c	25°17′S	27°32′E
El-Arish, Egypt	268b	31°08′N	33°50′E
El Asnam, Alg. *see* Chlef	198-99	36°10′N	1°20′E
Elat, Isr.	228-29	29°33′N	34°57′E
Elat, Gulf of, b., *see* Aqaba, Gulf of	228-29	29°05′N	34°44′E
Elath, Isr. *see* Elat	228-29	29°33′N	34°57′E
Elazığ, Tur. (ĕl-ä′zĕz)	186-87	38°41′N	39°15′E
Elba, Al., U.S. (ĕl′bȧ)	124-25	31°25′N	86°04′W
Elba, Isola d', i., Italy (ē-sō lä-d-ĕl′bȧ)	200-01	42°46′N	10°17′E
El Banco, Col. (ĕl băn′cȯ)	164-65	9°01′N	73°58′W
Elbe, stm., Eur. (ĕl′bĕ)	194-95	53°53′N	9°01′E
Elbert, Mount, mtn., Co., U.S. (mount ĕl′bērt)	118-19	39°07′N	106°27′W
Elberton, Ga., U.S. (ĕl′bēr-tŭn)	124-25	34°07′N	82°51′W
Elbeuf, Fr. (ĕl-bûf′)	196-97	49°17′N	1°01′E
Elbing, Pol. *see* Elbląg	194-95	54°10′N	19°24′E
Elbistan, Tur. (ĕl-bē-stän′)	186-87	38°13′N	37°12′E
Elbląg, Pol. (ĕl′blăng)	194-95	54°10′N	19°24′E
El Bonillo, Spain (ĕl bō-nēl′yō)	198-99	38°57′N	2°33′W
Elbow Lake, Mn., U.S. (ĕl′bō lāk)	114-15	45°60′N	95°59′W
El'brus, Gora, mtn., Russia (gȧ-rä′ĕl′brȯs′)	227	43°21′N	42°26′E
Elburz Mountains, mts., Iran (ĕl′bȯrz′ moun′tĭnz)	232-33	36°0′N	53°00′E
El Cajon, Ca., U.S.	118-19	32°48′N	116°57′W
El Calafate, Arg.	171	50°21′S	72°17′W
El Campo, Tx., U.S. (ĕl-kăm′pō)	122-23	29°11′N	96°16′W
El Carmen de Bolívar, Col.	164-65	9°43′N	75°07′W
El Centro, Ca., U.S. (ĕl-sĕn′trō)	118-19	32°48′N	115°33′W
Elche, Spain *see* Elx	198-99	38°15′N	0°42′W
Elda, Spain (ĕl′dä)	198-99	38°29′N	0°47′W
El'dikan, Russia	218-19	60°46′N	135°09′E
El Djazaïr, nation, Afr. *see* Algeria	253	28°0′N	3°00′E
El Djazaïr, nat. cap., Alg. *see* Algiers	269b	36°46′N	3°03′E
Eldon, Mo., U.S. (ĕl-dŭn)	120-21	38°21′N	92°35′W
Eldora, Ia., U.S. (ĕl-dō′rȧ)	114-15	42°22′N	93°06′W
Eldorado, Arg.	173	26°24′S	54°38′W
El Dorado, Ar., U.S. (ĕl dō-rä′dō)	120-21	33°12′N	92°41′W
El Dorado, Ks., U.S. (ĕl dō-rä′dō)	120-21	37°49′N	96°51′W
Eldoret, Kenya (ĕl-dō-rĕt′)	267	0°31′N	35°17′E
Electra, Tx., U.S. (ē-lĕk′trȧ)	120-21	34°03′N	98°55′W
Elek, stm., Asia	186-87	51°30′N	53°20′E
Elektrostal', Russia (ĕl-yĕk′trō-stál)	202-03	55°47′N	38°28′E

PRONOUNCING INDEX

El Encanto – Esquel 327

Feature (Pronunciation)	Page	Lat.	Long.
El Encanto, Col.	164-65	1°42'S	73°14'W
Elephant Butte Reservoir, res., N.M., U.S. (ĕl′ē-fănt būt rē′sēr-vwär)	118-19	33°17'N	107°10'W
Elets, Russia	202-03	52°37'N	38°30'E
Eleuthera, i., Bah. (ē-lū′thēr-ȧ)	142-43	25°11'N	76°13'W
El-Fayoum, Egypt	268b	29°19'N	30°50'E
El Ferrol del Caudillo, Spain see Ferrol	198-99	43°29'N	8°14'W
El Galpón, Arg.	168-69	25°24'S	64°38'W
Elgin, Scot., U.K. (ĕl′jĭn)	190-91	57°39'N	3°19'W
Elgin, Il., U.S. (ĕl′jĭn)	116-17	42°02'N	88°17'W
Elgin, Or., U.S. (ĕl′jĭn)	112-13	45°34'N	117°55'W
Elgin, Tx., U.S. (ĕl′jĭn)	122-23	30°21'N	97°22'W
El-Gîza, Egypt see Giza	268b	30°01'N	31°13'E
El Golea, Alg.	188-89	30°33'N	2°54'E
Elgon, Mount, mtn., Afr. (mount ĕl′gŏn)	267	1°08'N	34°33'E
El Guapo, Ven. (ĕl-gwá′pō)	163b	10°09'N	65°58'W
El Ḩank, clf., Afr.	258-59	24°23'N	6°36'W
El Hierro, i., Spain	199d	27°45'N	18°00'W
Elila, stm., D.R.C. (ĕ-lē′lá)	262-63	2°44'S	25°53'E
Élisabethville, D.R.C. see Lubumbashi	262-63	11°41'S	27°28'E
Elisenvaara, Russia (ā-lē′sĕn-vä′rá)	192-93	61°24'N	29°46'E
El-Iskandariya, Egypt see Alexandria	268b	31°11'N	29°54'E
Elista, Russia	186-87	46°19'N	44°16'E
Elizabeth, Austl.	276	34°43'S	138°40'E
Elizabeth City, N.C., U.S. (ē-lĭz′ȧ-bĕth sĭ′tĭ)	124-25	36°18'N	76°13'W
Elizabethton, Tn., U.S. (ē-lĭz-á-bĕth′tŭn)	124-25	36°21'N	82°14'W
Elizabethtown, Ky., U.S. (ē-lĭz′ȧ-bĕth-toun)	116-17	37°42'N	85°52'W
Elizabethtown, Pa., U.S. (ē-lĭz′ȧ-bĕth-toun)	116-17	40°09'N	76°37'W
El-Jadida, Mor.	269a	33°15'N	8°31'W
Elk, stm., B.C., Can. (ĕlk)	132-33	49°10'N	115°14'W
Elk City, Ok., U.S. (ĕlk sĭ′tē)	120-21	35°25'N	99°25'W
El Kef, Tun. (ĕl-xĕf′)	184-85	36°11'N	8°43'E
El-Khârga, Egypt	266	25°27'N	30°33'E
Elkhart, In., U.S. (ĕlk′härt)	116-17	41°42'N	85°57'W
Elkhorn, Wi., U.S. (ĕlk′hôrn)	116-17	42°40'N	88°33'W
Elkin, N.C., U.S. (ĕl′kĭn)	124-25	36°15'N	80°51'W
Elk Island National Park, n.p., Ab., Can. (ĕlk ī′lȧnd năsh′ŭn-ăl pärk)	132-33	53°36'N	112°54'W
Elko, Nv., U.S. (ĕl′kō)	112-13	40°50'N	115°46'W
Elk Point, S.D., U.S. (ĕlk point)	114-15	42°41'N	96°41'W
Elk Rapids, Mi., U.S. (ĕlk răp′ĭdz)	116-17	44°53'N	85°24'W
Elk River, Mn., U.S. (ĕlk rĭv′ēr)	114-15	45°18'N	93°35'W
Elkton, Ky., U.S. (ĕlk′tŭn)	124-25	36°49'N	87°09'W
Elkton, S.D., U.S. (ĕlk′tŭn)	114-15	44°14'N	96°29'W
Ellás, nation, Eur. see Greece	174-75	39°0'N	22°00'E
Ellendale, N.D., U.S. (ĕl′ĕn-dāl)	114-15	46°00'N	98°32'W
Ellensburg, Wa., U.S. (ĕl′ĕnz-bûrg)	112-13	46°60'N	120°32'W
Ellesmere Island, i., Nu., Can. (ĕlz′mēr ī′lȧnd)	86	81°0'N	80°00'W
Ellice Islands, nation, Oc. see Tuvalu	280-81	8°0'S	178°00'E
Elliot Lake, On., Can.	136-37	46°23'N	82°39'W
Elliston, Austl.	270-71	33°39'S	134°54'E
Ellisville, Ms., U.S. (ĕl′ĭs-vĭl)	124-25	31°36'N	89°12'W
Ellore, India see Elūru	236	16°43'N	81°07'E
Ellsworth, Ks., U.S. (ĕlz′wûrth)	120-21	38°44'N	98°13'W
Elma, Wa., U.S. (ĕl′må)	112-13	47°00'N	123°24'W
El-Mahalla el-Kubra, Egypt	268b	30°58'N	31°10'E
El-Mansûra, Egypt	268b	31°02'N	31°23'E
Elmhurst, Il., U.S. (ĕlm′hûrst)	116-17	41°53'N	87°57'W
El-Minya, Egypt	268b	28°06'N	30°45'E
Elmira, N.Y., U.S.	116-17	42°05'N	76°48'W
Elmira Heights, N.Y., U.S. (ĕl-mī′rȧ hīts)	116-17	42°09'N	76°50'W
El Nevado, Cerro, mtn., Arg. see Nevado, Cerro	171	35°34'S	68°28'W
El-Obeid, Sudan see Al-Ubayyiḍ	266	13°11'N	30°13'E
El Oued, Alg.	188-89	33°21'N	6°53'E
El Pao, Ven. (ĕl pá′ō)	163b	9°38'N	68°08'W
El Paso, Tx., U.S. (ĕl-pas′ō)	118-19	31°48'N	106°27'W
El Paso de Robles, Ca., U.S. see Paso Robles	118-19	35°38'N	120°41'W
El Pital, Cerro, mtn., N.A.	148	14°23'N	89°08'W
El Porvenir, Pan. (ĕl-pôr-vä-nēr′)	150	9°33'N	78°59'W
El-Qâhira, nat. cap., Egypt see Cairo	268b	30°03'N	31°14'E
El Reno, Ok., U.S. (ĕl-rē′nō)	120-21	35°32'N	97°57'W
El Salto, Mex. (ĕl-säl′tō)	146-47	23°46'N	105°21'W
El Salvador, nation, N.A. (ĕl säl′vä-dôr)	85	13°50'N	88°55'W
Elsaß, hist. reg., Fr. see Alsace	196-97	48°30'N	7°30'E
Elsberry, Mo., U.S. (ĕlz′bĕr-ĭ)	120-21	39°10'N	90°48'W
Elsinore, Den. see Helsingør	192-93	56°02'N	12°37'E
El-Suweis, Egypt see Suez	268b	29°58'N	32°33'E
El Tajín, hist., Mex.	146-47	20°27'N	97°23'W
El Tigre, Ven. (ĕl-tē′grĕ)	163b	8°54'N	64°15'W
El-Uqsor, Egypt see Luxor	268b	25°42'N	32°39'E
Elūru, India	236	16°43'N	81°07'E
Elvas, Port. (ĕl′väzh)	198-99	38°53'N	7°10'W
Elverum, Nor. (ĕl′vĕ-rôm)	192-93	60°53'N	11°34'E
El Viejo, Nic. (ĕl-vyĕ′ĸō)	149	12°40'N	87°10'W
Elwood, In., U.S. (ĕ′wòd)	116-17	40°16'N	85°50'W
Elx, Spain	198-99	38°15'N	0°42'W
Ely, Mn., U.S. (ē′lĭ)	114-15	47°54'N	91°52'W
Ely, Nv., U.S.	118-19	39°15'N	114°53'W
Elyria, Oh., U.S. (ē-lĭr′ĭ-ȧ)	116-17	41°22'N	82°06'W
Émaé, i., Vanuatu	279g	17°04'S	168°22'E
Emāmshahr, Iran see Shāhrūd	232-33	36°25'N	54°58'E
Embi, Kaz.	226	48°50'N	58°09'E
Embira, stm., Braz. see Envira	166-67	6°42'S	69°48'W
Embu, Kenya	267	0°32'S	37°27'E
Emden, Ger. (ĕm′dĕn)	194-95	53°22'N	7°12'E
Emerald, Austl.	277	23°31'S	148°10'E
Emiliano Zapata, Mex. (ĕ-mē-lyá′nô-zä-pá′tá)	148	17°45'N	91°46'W
Emiliano Zapata, Mex. (ĕ-mē-lyá′nô-zä-pá′tá)	146-47	18°51'N	99°11'W
Eminence, Ky., U.S. (ĕm′ĭ-nĕns)	116-17	38°22'N	85°11'W
Emmen, Neth. (ĕm′ĕn)	190-91	52°47'N	6°54'E
Emmetsburg, Ia., U.S. (ĕm′ĕts-bûrg)	114-15	43°07'N	94°41'W
Emmett, Id., U.S. (ĕm′ĕt)	112-13	43°53'N	116°30'W
Emory Peak, mtn., Tx., U.S. (ĕ′mŏ-rē pēk)	122-23	29°14'N	103°19'W
Empalme, Mex.	144-45	27°58'N	110°49'W
Empedrado, Arg.	173	27°57'S	58°48'W
Empoli, Italy (ām′pô-lē)	200-01	43°43'N	10°57'E
Emporia, Ks., U.S. (ĕm-pō′rĭ-ȧ)	120-21	38°24'N	96°11'W
Emporia, Va., U.S. (ĕm-pō′rĭ-ȧ)	124-25	36°42'N	77°33'W
Emporium, Pa., U.S. (ĕm-pō′rĭ-ŭm)	116-17	41°30'N	78°15'W
Empty Quarter, des., Asia see Rub'al-Khali	220-21	20°0'N	51°00'E
En, stm., Eur. see Inn	194-95	48°34'N	13°28'E
Encarnación, Para. (ĕn-kär-nä-syōn′)	173	27°20'S	55°52'W
Encinal, Tx., U.S. (ĕn′sĭ-nôl)	122-23	28°02'N	99°21'W
Encontrados, Ven. (ĕn-kōn-trä′dōs)	164-65	9°03'N	72°14'W
Encounter Bay, b., Austl. (ĕn-koun′tēr bā)	276	35°35'S	138°44'E
Ende, Indon.	248-49	8°50'S	121°40'E
Enderbury, at., Kir. (ĕn′dēr-bûrĭ)	280-81	3°08'S	171°05'W
Enderby Land, reg., Ant. (ĕn′dēr-bĭ lănd)	287	68°05'S	52°53'E
Enderlin, N.D., U.S. (ĕn′dēr-lĭn)	114-15	46°37'N	97°36'W
Endicott, N.Y., U.S. (ĕn′dĭ-kŏt)	116-17	42°07'N	76°04'W
Ene, stm., Peru	170	11°10'S	74°15'W
Enewetak, at., Marsh. Is.	280-81	11°39'N	162°17'E
Enfield, N.C., U.S. (ĕn′fēld)	124-25	36°11'N	77°40'W
Engaño, Cabo, c., Dom. Rep. (kȧ′-bô- ĕn-gä-nô)	142-43	18°37'N	68°20'W
Engel's, Russia (ĕn′gĕls)	186-87	51°29'N	46°08'E
Enggano, Pulau, i., Indon. (pōō-lou ĕng-gä′nō)	246-47	5°24'S	102°16'E
England, Ar., U.S. (ĭŋ′glȧnd)	124-25	34°33'N	91°58'W
England, state, U.K. (ĭŋ′glȧnd)	190-91	52°30'N	1°30'W
Englehart, On., Can.	136-37	47°49'N	79°52'W
Englewood, Co., U.S. (ĕn′g′l-wòd)	120-21	39°39'N	104°59'W
English, stm., On., Can. (ĭn′glĭsh)	134-35	50°11'N	95°03'W
English Bāzār, India see Ingrāj Bāzār	234-35	24°60'N	88°09'E
English Channel, strt., Eur. (ĭn′glĭsh chăn′ĕl)	190-91	50°13'N	2°20'W
Enguri, stm., Geor. (ĕn-gôr′)	227	42°24'N	41°33'E
Enid, Ok., U.S. (ē′nĭd)	120-21	36°24'N	97°52'W
Eniwetok, at., Marsh. Is. see Enewetak	280-81	11°39'N	162°17'E
eNjesuthi, mtn., Afr.	269c	29°09'S	29°23'E
Enköping, Swe. (ĕn′kû-pĭng)	192-93	59°38'N	17°05'E
Ennedi, plat., Chad (ĕn-nĕd′ē)	258-59	17°15'N	22°00'E
Enniskillen, N. Ire., U.K. (ĕn-ĭs-kĭl′ĕn)	190-91	54°21'N	7°38'W
Enriquillo, Dom. Rep. (ĕn-rē-kē′l-yō)	142-43	17°53'N	71°16'W
Enriquillo, Lago, lk., Dom. Rep. (lä′gô-ĕn-rē-kē′l-yō)	142-43	18°29'N	71°38'W
Enschede, Neth. (ĕns′kȧ-dĕ)	190-91	52°13'N	6°54'E
Ensenada, Mex. (ĕn-sĕ-nä′dä)	144-45	31°52'N	116°37'W
Enshi, China (ŭn-shr)	238-39	30°14'N	109°27'E
Entebbe, Ug.	267	0°04'N	32°28'E
Enterprise, Or., U.S. (ĕn′tēr-prīz)	112-13	45°26'N	117°17'W
Enugu, Nig. (ĕ-nōō′gōō)	260a	6°27'N	7°27'E
Enumclaw, Wa., U.S. (ĕn′ŭm-klô)	112-13	47°12'N	121°59'W
Enurmino, Russia	126	66°55'N	171°48'W
Envigado, Col. (ĕn-vē-gá′dō)	163c	6°10'N	75°35'W
Envira, stm., Braz.	166-67	6°42'S	69°48'W
Épernay, Fr. (ā-pĕr-nĕ′)	196-97	49°03'N	3°58'E
Ephraim, Ut., U.S. (ē′frå-ĭm)	118-19	39°22'N	111°35'W
Ephrata, Pa., U.S. (ĕfrȧ′tȧ)	116-17	40°11'N	76°11'W
Ephrata, Wa., U.S. (ĕfrȧ′tȧ)	112-13	47°19'N	119°33'W
Épi, i., Vanuatu	279g	16°43'S	168°16'E
Épinal, Fr. (ā-pē-nál′)	196-97	48°11'N	6°26'E
Equatorial Guinea, nation, Afr. (ē-kwä-tō′rĭ-ăl gĭn′ē)	253	2°0'N	9°00'E
Erciyes Daği, vol., Tur.	186-87	38°32'N	35°28'E
Erdenebulgan, Mong.	240-41	50°06'N	101°35'E
Erding, Ger. (ĕr′dēng)	194-95	48°18'N	11°55'E
Erechim, Braz. (ĕ-rĕ-shē′ɴ)	168-69	27°38'S	52°17'W
Ereğli, Tur. (ĕ-rā′ĭ-le)	186-87	37°31'N	34°04'E
Ereğli, Tur. (ĕ-rā′ĭ-le)	186-87	41°17'N	31°26'E
Erenhot, China	240-41	43°39'N	111°60'E
Erfoud, Mor.	188-89	31°26'N	4°14'W
Erfurt, Ger. (ĕr′fòrt)	194-95	50°58'N	11°01'E
Erguig, Bahr, stm., Chad	260-61	11°21'N	15°24'E
Ergun, stm., Asia	240-41	53°19'N	121°27'E
Er Hai, lk., China	238-39	25°48'N	100°11'E
Erick, Ok., U.S. (âr′ĭk)	120-21	35°14'N	99°52'W
Erie, Pa., U.S.	116-17	42°07'N	80°03'W
Erie, Lake, lk., N.A. (lāk ē′rĭ)	116-17	42°15'N	80°60'W
Erimo-misaki, c., Japan (ā′rē-mō mē′sä-kē)	244	41°55'N	143°15'E
Eritrea, nation, Afr. (ā-rē-trā′á)	266	15°20'N	39°00'E
Erlangen, Ger. (ĕr′läng-ĕn)	194-95	49°36'N	11°01'E
Ermelo, S. Afr.	269c	26°31'S	29°59'E
Erne, Lower Lough, lk., N. Ire., U.K. (lō′ēr lŏk ûrn)	190-91	54°28'N	7°45'W
Erode, India	236	11°21'N	77°44'E
Eromanga, Austl.	276	26°40'S	143°16'E
Er-Rachidia, Mor.	188-89	31°57'N	4°26'W
Erromango, i., Vanuatu	279g	18°45'S	169°05'E
Ertis, Kaz.	226	53°20'N	75°28'E
Ertis, stm., Asia see Irtysh	218-19	61°05'N	68°47'E
Ertix, stm., Asia see Irtysh	218-19	61°05'N	68°47'E
Ērtra, nation, Afr. see Eritrea	266	15°20'N	39°00'E
Erwin, Tn., U.S. (ûr′wĭn)	124-25	36°08'N	82°25'W
Erzin, Russia	240-41	50°15'N	95°09'E
Erzincan, Tur. (ĕr-zĭn-jän′)	227	39°44'N	39°31'E
Erzurum, Tur. (ĕrz′rōōm′)	227	39°54'N	41°17'E
Esashi, Japan (ĕs′ä-shē)	244	41°52'N	140°10'E
Esbjerg, Den. (ĕs′byĕrgh)	192-93	55°28'N	8°27'E
Escalante, Ut., U.S. (ĕs-kȧ-lăn′tē)	118-19	37°46'N	111°36'W
Escambia, stm., Fl., U.S. (ĕs-kăm′bĭ-ȧ)	124-25	30°32'N	87°11'W
Escanaba, Mi., U.S. (ĕs-kȧ-nô′bȧ)	116-17	45°45'N	87°04'W
Escarpada Point, c., Phil.	250	18°31'N	122°13'E
Escondido, Ca., U.S. (ĕs-kŏn-dē′dō)	118-19	33°07'N	117°05'W
Escuinapa de Hidalgo, Mex.	146-47	22°51'N	105°48'W
Escuintla, Guat. (ĕs-kwēn′tlä)	148	14°18'N	90°47'W
Esenguly, Turkmen.	232-33	37°27'N	54°01'E
Eşfahān, Iran	232-33	32°39'N	51°40'E
Esh-Sham, nat. cap., Syria see Damascus	228-29	33°31'N	36°18'E
Esil, Kaz.	226	51°57'N	66°24'E
Esil, stm., Asia see Ishim	218-19	57°43'N	71°12'E
Eskifjördur, Ice. (ĕs′kē-fyûr′dōōr)	190a	65°04'N	13°57'W
Eskilstuna, Swe. (å′shĕl-stü-na)	192-93	59°22'N	16°31'E
Eskimo Point, Nu., Can. see Arviat	128-29	61°08'N	94°07'W
Eskişehir, Tur. (ĕs-kĕ-shĕ′h'r)	186-87	39°47'N	30°31'E
Esla, stm., Spain (ĕs-lä)	198-99	41°29'N	6°03'W
Eslāmshahr, Iran	232-33	35°33'N	51°14'E
Eslöv, Swe. (ĕs′lûv)	192-93	55°50'N	13°19'E
Esmeralda, Isla, i., Chile	171	48°57'S	75°25'W
Esmeraldas, Ec. (ĕs-má-rál′dás)	170	0°57'N	79°39'W
España, nation, Eur. see Spain	174-75	40°0'N	4°00'W
Espanola, On., Can. (ĕs-pȧ-nō′lȧ)	136-37	46°16'N	81°47'W
Española, Isla, i., Ec.	170a	1°23'S	89°42'W
Esperance, Austl. (ĕs′pē-rȧns)	270-71	33°51'S	121°53'E
Esperanza, Arg.	173	31°27'S	60°56'W
Espichel, Cabo, c., Port. (ká′bō-ĕs-pē-shĕl′)	198-99	38°25'N	9°13'W
Espinal, Col. (ĕs-pē-näl′)	163c	4°09'N	74°53'W
Espinhaço, Serra do, mts., Braz. (sĕ′r-rä-dô-ĕs-pē-ná-sô)	172	17°25'S	43°40'W
Espírito Santo, Braz. (ĕs-pē′rē-tô-sán′tô) see Vila Velha	172	20°20'S	40°17'W
Espírito Santo, state, Braz. (ĕs-pē′rē-tô-sán′tô)	172	19°30'S	40°30'W
Espiritu Santo, i., Vanuatu (ĕs-pē′rē-tōō sän′tô)	279g	15°15'S	166°50'E
Espíritu Santo, Isla del, i., Mex.	144-45	24°29'N	110°21'W
Espita, Mex. (ĕs-pē′tä)	148	21°02'N	88°18'W
Esposende, Port. (ĕs-pō-zĕn′dä)	198-99	41°32'N	8°47'W
Esquel, Arg. (ĕs-kĕ′l)	171	42°54'S	71°19'W

n-sing; ŋ-baŋk; ɴ-nasalized n; nŏd; cŏmmit; ōld; ôbey; ôrder; oi-boil; fōōd; ȯ-as oo in foot; ou-out; s-soft; sh-dish; th-thin; pūre; ûnite; ûrn; stŭd; circŭs; ü-as in French tu; ′-indeterminate vowel.

328 Esquimalt – Feijó PRONOUNCING INDEX

Feature (Pronunciation)	Page	Lat.	Long.
Esquimalt, B.C., Can. (ĕs-kwī´mŏlt)	132-33	48°26′N	123°24′W
Esquina, Arg.	173	30°01′S	59°32′W
Essaouira, Mor.	258-59	31°30′N	9°45′W
Essen, Ger. (ĕs´sĕn)	194-95	51°28′N	7°01′E
Essequibo, stm., Guy. (ĕs-ā-kē´bō)	164-65	7°04′N	58°26′W
Essex, Md., U.S. (ĕs´ĕks)	116-17	39°19′N	76°29′W
Essexville, Mi., U.S. (ĕs´ĕks-vĭl)	116-17	43°37′N	83°50′W
Est, Pointe de l', c., Qc., Can.	138-39	49°08′N	61°41′W
Estación Colonia Alvear Norte, Arg. *see* General Alvear	171	34°59′S	67°42′W
Estación Foguista J. F. Juárez, Arg. *see* El Galpón	168-69	25°24′S	64°38′W
Estación Gobernador Vera, Arg. *see* Vera	173	29°28′S	60°13′W
Estación J. J. Castelli, Arg. *see* Castelli	168-69	25°57′S	60°37′W
Estados, Isla de los, i., Arg.	171	54°48′S	64°33′W
Estância, Braz. (ĕs-tän´sĭ-ä)	166-67	11°16′S	37°26′W
Estarreja, Port. (ĕ-tär-rā´zhä)	198-99	40°45′N	8°34′W
Estcourt, S. Afr. (ĕst-coort)	269c	29°00′S	29°53′E
Estelí, Nic.	149	13°05′N	86°22′W
Estepona, Spain (ĕs-tâ-pō´nä)	198-99	36°26′N	5°08′W
Esterhazy, Sk., Can. (ĕs´tẽr-hā-zē)	134-35	50°39′N	102°05′W
Estevan, Sk., Can. (ĕ-stē´văn)	134-35	49°08′N	103°00′W
Estherville, Ia., U.S. (ĕs´tẽr-vĭl)	114-15	43°25′N	94°50′W
Estill, S.C., U.S. (ĕs´tĭl)	124-25	32°45′N	81°14′W
Eston, Sk., Can.	134-35	51°10′N	108°46′W
Estonia, nation, Eur. (ĕs-tō´nĭ-ȧ)	174-75	59°0′N	26°00′E
Estrela, mtn., Port. (ĕs-trā´lȧ)	198-99	40°19′N	7°37′W
Estremoz, Port. (ĕs-trā-mōzh´)	198-99	38°51′N	7°35′W
Estrondo, Serra do, plat., Braz. (sĕr´-rȧ dò ĕs-trôn´-dò)	166-67	9°0′S	48°45′W
Esumba, Île, i., D.R.C.	262-63	2°0′N	21°12′E
Eszék, Cro. *see* Osijek	200-01	45°33′N	18°42′E
Étampes, Fr. (ā-täɴp´)	196-97	48°26′N	2°10′E
Étaples, Fr. (ā-täp´l')	196-97	50°31′N	1°38′E
Etāwah, India	234-35	26°46′N	79°01′E
Ethiopia, nation, Afr. (ē-thē-ō´pē-ȧ)	253	9°0′N	39°00′E
Etna, Monte, vol., Italy (mōn-tå ĕt´nȧ)	200-01	37°45′N	15°00′E
Etolin Strait, strt., Ak., U.S. (ĕt ō lĭn strāt)	126	60°20′N	165°15′W
Etorofu-tō, i., Russia *see* Iturup, Ostrov	218-19	44°51′N	147°27′E
Etosha National Park, n.p., Nmb.	264-65	18°60′S	15°07′E
Etosha Pan, pl., Nmb. (ětō´shä)	264-65	18°45′S	16°15′E
Etowah, Tn., U.S. (ĕt´ô-wä)	124-25	35°19′N	84°32′W
Et Tîdra, i., Maur.	258-59	19°44′N	16°24′W
Eua, i., Tonga	280-81	21°22′S	174°56′W
Euboea, i., Grc. *see* Évvoia	200-01	38°34′N	23°50′E
Eucla, Austl. (ū´klȧ)	270-71	31°42′S	128°54′E
Euclid, Oh., U.S. (ū´klĭd)	116-17	41°35′N	81°31′W
Eufaula, Al., U.S. (ů-fô´lȧ)	124-25	31°54′N	85°09′W
Eufaula, Ok., U.S. (ů-fô´lȧ)	120-21	35°16′N	95°36′W
Eugene, Or., U.S. (ů-jēn´)	112-13	44°03′N	123°05′W
Eugenia, Punta, c., Mex.	144-45	27°51′N	115°05′W
Eunice, La., U.S. (ū´nĭs)	122-23	30°30′N	92°25′W
Eunice, N.M., U.S. (ū´nĭs)	120-21	32°26′N	103°10′W
Euphrates, stm., Asia (ů-frā´tēz)	208-09	30°60′N	47°27′E
Eureka, Ca., U.S.	112-13	40°47′N	124°09′W
Eureka, Il., U.S. (û-rē´kȧ)	116-17	40°43′N	89°16′W
Eureka, Ks., U.S. (û-rē´kȧ)	120-21	37°50′N	96°18′W
Eureka, Mt., U.S. (û-rē´kȧ)	112-13	48°53′N	115°03′W
Eureka, S.D., U.S. (û-rē´kȧ)	114-15	45°46′N	99°38′W
Eureka Springs, Ar., U.S. (û-rē´kȧ sprĭngz)	120-21	36°24′N	93°45′W
Europa, Île, i., Reu.	264-65	22°20′S	40°21′E
Europa Island, i., Reu. *see* Europa, Île	264-65	22°20′S	40°21′E
Europe, cont., (ū´rŭp)	20-21	50°0′N	28°00′E
Eustis, Fl., U.S. (ūs´tĭs)	124-25	28°51′N	81°41′W
Eutaw, Al., U.S. (ū-tȧ)	124-25	32°50′N	87°53′W
Eutsuk Lake, lk., B.C., Can. (ōōt´sŭk lăk)	132-33	53°19′N	126°44′W
Evans, Lac, lk., Qc., Can.	130-31	50°55′N	77°00′W
Evanston, Il., U.S. (ĕv´ăn-stŭn)	116-17	42°01′N	87°41′W
Evanston, Wy., U.S. (ĕv´ăn-stŭn)	112-13	41°17′N	110°58′W
Evansville, In., U.S. (ĕv´ănz-vĭl)	116-17	37°59′N	87°35′W
Evansville, Wi., U.S. (ĕv´ănz-vĭl)	116-17	42°47′N	89°17′W
Evansville, Wy., U.S. (ĕv´ănz-vĭl)	112-13	42°50′N	106°15′W
Eva Perón, Arg. *see* La Plata	173	34°55′S	57°57′W
Eveleth, Mn., U.S. (ĕv´ê-lĕth)	114-15	47°28′N	92°32′W
Evensk, Russia	218-19	61°57′N	159°15′E
Everard, Lake, lk., Austl. (lăk ĕv´ẽr-ărd)	272-73	31°25′S	135°06′E
Everest, Mount, mtn., Asia (mount ĕv´ẽr-ĕst)	234-35	27°59′N	86°56′E
Everett, Wa., U.S. (ĕv´ẽr-ĕt)	112-13	47°58′N	122°12′W
Everglades, The, sw., Fl., U.S. (thȧ ĕv´ẽr-glădz swŏmp)	125a	26°0′N	80°40′W
Everglades National Park, n.p., Fl., U.S. (ĕv´ẽr-glādz năsh´ŭn-ăl pärk)	125a	25°27′N	80°53′W
Evergreen, Al., U.S. (ĕv´ẽr-grēn)	124-25	31°26′N	86°57′W
Evergreen, Co., U.S. (ĕv´ẽr-grēn)	118-19	39°38′N	105°19′W
Evergreen, Mt., U.S. (ĕv´ẽr-grēn)	112-13	48°13′N	114°17′W
Évora, Port. (ĕv´ô-rä)	198-99	38°34′N	7°54′W
Evpatoria, Ukr. *see* Yevpatoriia	202-03	45°12′N	33°22′E
Évreux, Fr. (ā-vrû´)	196-97	49°01′N	1°09′E
Évvoia, i., Grc.	200-01	38°34′N	23°50′E
Exe, stm., Eng., U.K. (ĕks)	190-91	50°42′N	3°29′W
Exeter, Eng., U.K. (ĕk´sê-tẽr)	190-91	50°43′N	3°32′W
Exmoor, plat., Eng., U.K. (ĕks´mōr)	190-91	51°09′N	3°44′W
Exmouth, Austl.	270-71	21°56′S	114°07′E
Exmouth, Eng., U.K. (ĕks´mŭth)	190-91	50°38′N	3°24′W
Exmouth Gulf, b., Austl.	272-73	22°0′S	114°20′E
Exploits, stm., Nf., Can. (ĕks-ploits´)	138-39	49°05′N	55°18′W
Exuma Sound, strt., Bah. (ĕk-sōō´mä sound)	142-43	24°12′N	76°01′W
Eyasi, Lake, lk., Tan. (lāk å-yä´sê)	267	3°40′S	35°05′E
Eyl, Som.	262-63	7°59′N	49°49′E
Eyre Creek, stm., Austl.	277	26°38′S	138°59′E
Eyre North, Lake, lk., Austl. (lăk âr nôrth)	272-73	28°33′S	137°15′E
Eyre Peninsula, pen., Austl.	272-73	33°15′S	135°48′E
Eyre South, Lake, lk., Austl. (lăk âr south)	276	29°18′S	137°26′E
Eysturoy, i., Far. Is.	190b	62°12′N	6°55′W
Ezequiel Ramos Mexía, Embalse, res., Arg.	171	39°27′S	69°01′W
Ezine, Tur. (â´zĭ-nå)	200-01	39°47′N	26°20′E

F

Feature (Pronunciation)	Page	Lat.	Long.
Faaborg, Den. (fô´bôrg)	194-95	55°06′N	10°15′E
Fabriano, Italy (fä-brē-ä´nō)	200-01	43°21′N	12°54′E
Fada, Chad (fä´dä)	258-59	17°12′N	21°35′E
Fada-Ngourma, Burkina (fä´dä´'n gōōr´mä)	260-61	12°03′N	0°22′E
Faddeyevskiy, Ostrov, i., Russia (ôs-trôf´ fȧd-yä´skĭ)	218-19	75°27′N	144°20′E
Faenza, Italy (fä-ĕnd´zä)	200-01	44°17′N	11°53′E
Færøerne, dep., Eur. *see* Faroe Islands	174-75	62°0′N	7°00′W
Fafen, stm., Eth.	262-63	5°39′N	44°08′E
Făgăraș, Rom. (fă-gă´răsh)	194-95	45°50′N	24°59′E
Fagernes, Nor.	192-93	60°59′N	9°15′E
Fagnano, Lago, lk., S.A. (lä´gô fäk-nä´nô)	171	54°34′S	67°58′W
Faguibine, Lac, lk., Mali	258-59	16°49′N	3°50′W
Faial, i., Port. (fä-yä´l)	199c	38°34′N	28°42′W
Fairbanks, Ak., U.S. (fâr´bănks)	126	64°51′N	147°42′W
Fairbury, Ne., U.S. (fâr´bĕr-ĭ)	120-21	40°09′N	97°11′W
Fairfax, Mn., U.S. (fâr´făks)	114-15	44°31′N	94°43′W
Fairfax, S.C., U.S. (fâr´făks)	124-25	32°57′N	81°14′W
Fairfield, Ia., U.S. (fâr´fēld)	114-15	41°01′N	91°58′W
Fairfield, Il., U.S. (fâr´fēld)	116-17	38°22′N	88°22′W
Fairfield, Oh., U.S. (fâr´fēld)	116-17	39°21′N	84°34′W
Fairfield, Tx., U.S. (fâr´fēld)	122-23	31°43′N	96°10′W
Fair Haven, Vt., U.S. (fâr ā´vĕn)	116-17	43°36′N	73°16′W
Fair Isle, i., Scot., U.K. (fâr īl)	190c	59°32′N	1°39′W
Fairmont, Mn., U.S. (fâr´mŏnt)	114-15	43°40′N	94°28′W
Fairmont, W.V., U.S. (fâr´mŏnt)	116-17	39°29′N	80°08′W
Fair Ness, c., Nu., Can.	130-31	63°25′N	72°02′W
Fairview, Ok., U.S. (fâr´vū)	120-21	36°16′N	98°29′W
Fairweather, Mount, mtn., N.A. (mount fâr-wĕdh´ẽr)	126	58°54′N	137°32′W
Fairweather Mountain, mtn., N.A. *see* Fairweather, Mount	126	58°54′N	137°32′W
Faisalābād, Pak.	232-33	31°25′N	73°05′E
Faith, S.D., U.S. (fāth)	114-15	45°01′N	102°01′W
Faiyum, Egypt *see* El-Fayoum	268b	29°19′N	30°50′E
Faizābād, India	234-35	26°47′N	82°08′E
Fakaofo, at., Tok.	280-81	9°22′S	171°14′W
Fakfak, Indon.	224-25	2°56′S	132°18′E
Faku, China (fä-kōō)	243	42°30′N	123°25′E
Falam, Mya.	246-47	22°54′N	93°41′E
Falémé, stm., Afr.	258-59	14°46′N	12°15′W
Falfurrias, Tx., U.S. (făl´fōō-rē´ås)	122-23	27°14′N	98°09′W
Falher, Ab., Can. (făl´ẽr)	132-33	55°44′N	117°13′W
Falkenberg, Swe. (fäl´kĕn-bĕrgh)	192-93	56°54′N	12°29′E
Falkensee, Ger. (fäl´kĕn-zā)	194-95	52°34′N	13°04′E
Falkirk, Scot., U.K. (fôl´kûrk)	190-91	56°00′N	3°47′W
Falkland Islands, dep., S.A. (fôk´lănd ī´lăndz)	158	51°45′S	59°00′W
Falkland Islands, is., Falk. Is. (fôk´lănd ī´lăndz)	171	51°41′S	59°08′W
Falkland Sound, strt., Falk. Is.	171	51°45′S	59°25′W
Falköping, Swe. (fäl´chûp-ĭng)	192-93	58°10′N	13°32′E
Fall River, Ma., U.S. (fôl rĭv´ẽr)	116-17	41°42′N	71°10′W
Falls City, Ne., U.S. (fôlz sĭ´tê)	120-21	40°04′N	95°37′W
Falmouth, Jam. (făl´mŭth)	142-43	18°29′N	77°39′W
Falmouth, Eng., U.K. (făl´mŭth)	190-91	50°09′N	5°03′W
Falmouth, Ky., U.S. (făl´mŭth)	116-17	38°41′N	84°20′W
False Divi Point, c., India	236	15°43′N	80°50′E
Falster, i., Den. (fäls´tẽr)	192-93	54°48′N	11°58′E
Fălticeni, Rom. (fŭl-tê-chân´y')	194-95	47°28′N	26°19′E
Falun, Swe. (fä-lōōn´)	192-93	60°36′N	15°38′E
Famagusta, Cyp. *see* Gazimağusa	228-29	35°07′N	33°57′E
Fanch'eng, China *see* Xiangfan	238-39	32°02′N	112°09′E
Fangxian, China (fäŋ-shyĕn)	238-39	32°03′N	110°44′E
Fanning Island, at., Kir. *see* Tabuaeran	280-81	3°51′N	159°18′W
Fano, Italy (fä´nō)	200-01	43°51′N	13°01′E
Fanø, i., Den. (fän´û)	192-93	55°25′N	8°25′E
Fan Si Pan, mtn., Viet.	246-47	22°15′N	103°46′E
Faradofay, Madag. *see* Tôlañaro	264-65	25°02′S	47°00′E
Farafangana, Madag. (fä-rä-fäŋ-gä´nä)	264-65	22°49′S	47°50′E
Farāh, Afg. (fä-rä´)	232-33	32°22′N	62°04′E
Farāh, stm., Afg.	232-33	31°27′N	61°27′E
Farallon de Medinilla, i., N. Mar. Is.	280-81	16°01′N	146°04′E
Farallon de Pajaros, i., N. Mar. Is.	280-81	20°32′N	144°54′E
Farasān, Jazā'ir, is., Sau. Ar.	266	16°48′N	41°54′E
Farewell, Cape, c., Green.	86	59°46′N	43°60′W
Farewell, Cape, c., N.Z. (kāp fâr-wĕl´)	278	40°30′S	172°41′E
Farg'ona, Uzb.	232-33	40°23′N	71°48′E
Fargo, N.D., U.S. (fär´gō)	114-15	46°52′N	96°49′W
Faribault, Mn., U.S. (fâ´rĭ-bō)	114-15	44°18′N	93°17′W
Farīdpur, Bngl.	234-35	23°36′N	89°51′E
Farmersburg, In., U.S. (fär´mẽrz-bûrg)	116-17	39°15′N	87°23′W
Farmersville, Tx., U.S. (fär´mẽrz-vĭl)	120-21	33°10′N	96°22′W
Farmington, Il., U.S. (färm-ĭng-tŭn)	114-15	40°42′N	90°00′W
Farmington, Mo., U.S. (färm-ĭng-tŭn)	120-21	37°47′N	90°25′W
Farmington, N.M., U.S. (färm-ĭng-tŭn)	118-19	36°44′N	108°12′W
Farmville, N.C., U.S. (färm-vĭl)	124-25	35°35′N	77°36′W
Farmville, Va., U.S. (färm-vĭl)	124-25	37°18′N	78°24′W
Farnham, Qc., Can. (fär´năm)	136-37	45°17′N	72°59′W
Faro, Braz. (fä´rò)	166-67	2°10′S	56°45′W
Faro, Port. (fä´rò)	198-99	37°01′N	7°56′W
Faro, stm., Afr.	260-61	9°20′N	12°54′E
Faroe Islands, dep., Eur. (fâr´ō ī´lăndz)	174-75	62°0′N	7°00′W
Fårön, i., Swe.	192-93	57°56′N	19°08′E
Farquhar, Atoll de, at., Sey.	264-65	10°10′S	51°10′E
Farrukhābād, India (fŭ-ròk-hä-bäd´)	234-35	27°24′N	79°35′E
Farsund, Nor. (fär´sòn)	192-93	58°05′N	6°48′E
Fartak, Ra's, c., Yemen	220-21	15°39′N	52°12′E
Farukolu, i., Mald.	236	6°12′N	73°16′E
Farvel, Kap, c., Green. *see* Farewell, Cape	86	59°46′N	43°60′W
Farwell, Tx., U.S. (fär´wĕl)	120-21	34°24′N	103°01′W
Fasano, Italy (fä-zä´nō)	200-01	40°50′N	17°21′E
Fatehpur Sīkri, India	234-35	27°06′N	77°40′E
Fauro Island, i., Sol. Is.	279e	6°55′S	156°04′E
Fauske, Nor.	184-85	67°16′N	15°24′E
Fawn, stm., On., Can.	134-35	55°22′N	88°20′W
Faxaflói, b., Ice.	190a	64°25′N	23°00′W
Faya-Largeau, Chad	258-59	17°56′N	19°07′E
Fayette, Al., U.S. (få-yĕt´)	124-25	33°41′N	87°50′W
Fayette, Mo., U.S. (få-yĕt´)	120-21	39°09′N	92°41′W
Fayette, Ms., U.S. (få-yĕt´)	124-25	31°43′N	91°04′W
Fayetteville, Ar., U.S. (få-yĕt´vĭl)	120-21	36°05′N	94°10′W
Fayetteville, N.C., U.S. (få-yĕt´vĭl)	124-25	35°03′N	78°53′W
Fayetteville, Tn., U.S. (få-yĕt´vĭl)	124-25	35°09′N	86°34′W
Fayetteville, W.V., U.S. (få-yĕt´vĭl)	116-17	38°03′N	81°06′W
Faylakah, i., Kuw.	230-31	29°26′N	48°20′E
Fayyum, Egypt *see* El-Fayoum	268b	29°19′N	30°50′E
Fazzān, hist. reg., Libya *see* Fezzan	258-59	26°0′N	14°00′E
Fear, Cape, c., N.C., U.S. (kāp fēr)	124-25	33°57′N	77°56′W
Fécamp, Fr. (fā-käɴ´)	196-97	49°46′N	0°23′E
Fedala, Mor. *see* Mohammedia	269a	33°42′N	7°23′W
Federal, Arg.	173	30°57′S	58°47′W
Federated States of Micronesia, nation, Oc. *see* Micronesia, Federated States of	280-81	5°0′N	152°00′E
Feia, Lagoa, b., Braz. (lä´gō-å fĕ´yä)	172	22°0′S	41°20′W
Feijó, Braz.	166-67	8°11′S	70°24′W

ăt; finăl; rāte; senâte; ärm; åsk; sofȧ; fâre; ch-choose; dh-as th in other; bē; ēvent; bĕt; recĕnt; cratẽr; g-gō; gh-guttural g; bĭt; ĭ-short neutral; rīde; ĸ-guttural k as ch in German ich;

PRONOUNCING INDEX
Feira de Santana – Fort Myers 329

Feature (Pronunciation)	Page	Lat.	Long.
Feira de Santana, Braz. (fē′á-rä dä sänt-än′ä)	166-67	12°15′S	38°58′W
Feixian, China (fā-shyěn)	240-41	35°16′N	117°58′E
Fejaj, Chott, lk., Tun.	258-59	33°53′N	9°10′E
Felanitx, Spain (fā-lä-nēch′)	198-99	39°29′N	3°09′E
Feldkirch, Aus. (fĕlt′kĭrk)	194-95	47°14′N	9°36′E
Felipe Carrillo Puerto, Mex.	148	19°35′N	88°02′W
Felix, Cape, c., Nu., Can.	130-31	69°53′N	97°57′W
Feltre, Italy (fĕl′trā)	200-01	46°01′N	11°54′E
Fen, stm., China	240-41	35°28′N	110°34′E
Fengcheng, China (fŭŋ-chŭŋ)	238-39	28°10′N	115°46′E
Fengcheng, China (fŭŋ-chŭŋ)	243	40°27′N	124°04′E
Fengdu, China (fŭŋ-dōō)	238-39	29°58′N	107°46′E
Fengfeng, China	240-41	36°29′N	114°14′E
Fengtien, China *see* Shenyang	243	41°48′N	123°24′E
Fengxian, China (fŭŋ-shyĕn)	238-39	33°57′N	106°40′E
Fengyang, China (fŭng′yäng′)	238-39	32°52′N	117°33′E
Fengzhen, China (fŭŋ-jŭn)	240-41	40°26′N	113°09′E
Feni Islands, is., Pap. N. Gui.	277	4°04′S	153°38′E
Fenton, Mi., U.S. (fĕn-tŭn)	116-17	42°48′N	83°42′W
Fenyang, China	240-41	37°16′N	111°47′E
Feodosiia, Ukr.	202-03	45°02′N	35°22′E
Ferdows, Iran	232-33	34°01′N	58°10′E
Fergus Falls, Mn., U.S. (fûr′gŭs fôlz)	114-15	46°17′N	96°05′W
Fergusson Island, i., Pap. N. Gui.	277	9°31′S	150°39′E
Ferlo, Vallée du, stm., Sen.	260-61	15°50′N	15°43′W
Fermo, Italy (fĕr′mō)	200-01	43°10′N	13°43′E
Fermoy, Ire. (fûr-moi′)	190-91	52°08′N	8°17′W
Fernandina, Isla, i., Ec.	170a	0°26′S	91°30′W
Fernandina Beach, Fl., U.S. (fûr-năn-dē′nȧ bēch)	124-25	30°40′N	81°27′W
Fernando de Noronha, Ilha, i., Braz.	159	3°51′S	32°25′W
Fernandópolis, Braz.	168-69	20°16′S	50°15′W
Fernando Póo, i., Eq. Gui. *see* Bioko	260-61	3°30′N	8°40′E
Fernie, B.C., Can. (fûr′nĭ)	132-33	49°30′N	115°03′W
Ferrara, Italy (fĕr-rä′rä)	200-01	44°51′N	11°36′E
Ferrat, Cap, c., Alg. (kăp fĕr-rät)	198-99	35°55′N	0°23′W
Ferreñafe, Peru (fĕr-rĕn-yá′fĕ)	170	6°38′S	79°47′W
Ferriday, La., U.S. (fĕr′ĭ-dā)	124-25	31°38′N	91°33′W
Ferro, i., Spain *see* El Hierro	199d	27°45′N	18°00′W
Ferrol, Spain	198-99	43°29′N	8°14′W
Fès, Mor. (fĕs)	269a	34°03′N	5°00′W
Fessenden, N.D., U.S. (fĕs′ĕn-dĕn)	114-15	47°39′N	99°38′W
Festus, Mo., U.S. (fĕst′ŭs)	120-21	38°14′N	90°24′W
Fethiye, Tur. (fĕt-hē′yĕ)	200-01	36°37′N	29°08′E
Feuilles, stm., Qc., Can.	130-31	58°39′N	70°25′W
Feyzābād, Afg.	232-33	37°08′N	70°34′E
Fez, Mor. *see* Fès	269a	34°03′N	5°00′W
Fezzan, hist. reg., Libya	258-59	26°0′N	14°00′E
Fianarantsoa, Madag. (fyȧ-nä′rän-tsō′ȧ)	264-65	21°25′S	47°07′E
Fianga, Chad	262-63	9°55′N	15°09′E
Ficksburg, S. Afr. (fĭks′bûrg)	269c	28°52′S	27°53′E
Fife Ness, c., Scot., U.K. (fīf′nes′)	190-91	56°17′N	2°36′W
Figeac, Fr. (fē-zhák′)	196-97	44°37′N	2°02′E
Figueira da Foz, Port. (fē-gwĕy-rä-dá-fô′z)	198-99	40°09′N	8°51′W
Figuig, Mor.	188-89	32°08′N	1°13′W
Fiji, nation, Oc. (fē′jē)	279f	18°0′S	178°00′E
Fiji, nation, Oc. (fē′jē)	279f	18°0′S	178°00′E
Filicudi, Isola, i., Italy (ē′-sō-lä fē′le-kōō′dē)	200-01	38°34′N	14°34′E
Fillmore, Ut., U.S. (fĭl′môr)	118-19	38°58′N	112°20′W
Fimi, stm., D.R.C.	262-63	3°02′S	16°56′E
Findlay, Oh., U.S. (fĭnd′lȧ)	116-17	41°02′N	83°38′W
Finisterre, Cabo de, c., Spain *see* Fisterra, Cabo de	198-99	42°53′N	9°16′W
Finland, nation, Eur. (fĭn′lănd)	174-75	64°0′N	26°00′E
Finland, Gulf of, b., Eur. (gŭlf ŭv fĭn′lănd)	192-93	60°0′N	27°00′E
Finskiy Zaliv, b., Eur. *see* Finland, Gulf of	192-93	60°0′N	27°00′E
Fiordland National Park, n.p., N.Z.	278	45°30′S	167°20′E
Firat, stm., Asia *see* Euphrates	208-09	30°60′N	47°27′E
Firenze, Italy *see* Florence	200-01	43°47′N	11°14′E
Fīrozābād, India	234-35	27°09′N	78°24′E
Fīrozpur, India	234-35	30°55′N	74°37′E
Fisterra, Cabo de, c., Spain	198-99	42°53′N	9°16′W
Fitchburg, Ma., U.S. (fĭch′bûrg)	116-17	42°35′N	71°48′W
Fitzgerald, Ga., U.S. (fĭts-jĕr′ăld)	124-25	31°43′N	83°15′W
Fitz Roy, Arg.	171	47°03′S	67°14′W
Fitz Roy, Monte, mtn., S.A.	171	49°17′S	73°05′W
Fitzroy Crossing, Austl.	270-71	18°12′S	125°34′E
Fiume, Cro. *see* Rijeka	200-01	45°20′N	14°27′E
Fizi, D.R.C.	267	4°19′S	28°56′E
Flagstaff, Az., U.S. (flăg-stáf)	118-19	35°11′N	111°39′W
Flaherty Island, i., Nu., Can.	130-31	56°14′N	79°17′W
Flåm, Nor. (flôm)	192-93	60°51′N	7°07′E
Flaming Gorge Reservoir, res., U.S. (flā′mĭng gôrj rĕ′sĕr-vwär)	112-13	41°14′N	109°35′W
Flandreau, S.D., U.S. (flăn′drō)	114-15	44°03′N	96°36′W
Flathead Indian Reservation, ind. res., Mt., U.S. (flăt′hĕd ĭn′dĭ-ăn rĕ-sĕr-vā′shĕn)	112-13	47°30′N	114°25′W
Flathead Lake, lk., Mt., U.S. (flăt′hĕd lāk)	112-13	47°52′N	114°08′W
Flat Rock, Mi., U.S. (flăt rŏk)	116-17	42°06′N	83°17′W
Flattery, Cape, c., Wa., U.S. (kāp flăt′ēr-ĭ)	112-13	48°23′N	124°43′W
Flekkefjord, Nor. (fläk′kē-fyôr)	192-93	58°18′N	6°41′E
Flemingsburg, Ky., U.S. (flĕm′ĭngz-bûrg)	116-17	38°25′N	83°45′W
Flensburg, Ger. (flĕns′bórgh)	194-95	54°47′N	9°26′E
Flers, Fr. (flĕr)	196-97	48°45′N	0°34′W
Flinders, stm., Austl. (flĭn′dẽrz)	277	17°36′S	140°36′E
Flinders Chase National Park, n.p., Austl.	276	35°58′S	136°44′E
Flinders Island, i., Austl. (flĭn′dẽrz ī′lănd)	276	40°0′S	148°00′E
Flin Flon, Mb., Can. (flĭn flŏn)	134-35	54°46′N	101°53′W
Flint, Mi., U.S. (flĭnt)	116-17	43°00′N	83°41′W
Flint, i., Kir.	280-81	11°25′S	151°48′W
Flint, stm., Ga., U.S. (flĭnt)	124-25	30°46′N	84°48′W
Flora, Il., U.S. (flō′rȧ)	116-17	38°40′N	88°29′W
Florala, Al., U.S. (flŏr-ăl′ȧ)	124-25	31°00′N	86°20′W
Florence, Italy (flŏr′ĕns)	200-01	43°47′N	11°14′E
Florence, Al., U.S. (flŏr′ĕns)	124-25	34°48′N	87°41′W
Florence, Az., U.S. (flŏr′ĕns)	118-19	33°02′N	111°23′W
Florence, Ky., U.S. (flŏr′ĕns)	116-17	38°60′N	84°38′W
Florence, Or., U.S. (flŏr′ĕns)	112-13	43°59′N	124°06′W
Florence, S.C., U.S. (flŏr′ĕns)	124-25	34°11′N	79°46′W
Florencia, Col. (flō-rĕn′sē-ȧ)	164-65	1°36′N	75°36′W
Flores, i., Indon. (flō′rĕs)	248-49	8°38′S	120°56′E
Flores, i., Port.	199c	39°26′N	31°13′W
Flores, Laut, s., Indon. *see* Flores Sea	248-49	8°0′S	120°00′E
Flores Island, i., B.C., Can.	132-33	49°20′N	126°10′W
Flores Sea, s., Indon. (flō′rĕs sē)	248-49	8°0′S	120°00′E
Floresville, Tx., U.S. (flō′rĕs-vĭl)	122-23	29°08′N	98°09′W
Floriano, Braz. (flō-rá-ä′nō)	166-67	6°47′S	43°01′W
Florianópolis, Braz. (flō-rē-ä-nō′pō-lēs)	172	27°35′S	48°32′W
Florida, Col. (flō-rē′dä)	163c	3°21′N	76°15′W
Florida, Ur. (flô-rē-dhä)	173	34°06′S	56°12′W
Florida, state, U.S. (flŏr′ĭ-dȧ)	108-09	28°0′N	82°00′W
Florida, Estrecho de la, strt., N.A. *see* Florida, Straits of	142-43	24°59′N	79°45′W
Florida, Straits of, strt., N.A. (strāts ŭv flŏr′ĭ-dȧ)	142-43	24°59′N	79°45′W
Florida Bay, b., Fl., U.S. (flŏr′ĭ-dȧ bā)	125a	24°58′N	80°48′W
Florida Keys, is., Fl., U.S. (flŏr′ĭ-dȧ kēz)	125a	24°47′N	81°06′W
Florido, stm., Mex. (flō-rē′dō)	144-45	27°43′N	105°11′W
Flórina, Grc. (flō-rē′nä)	200-01	40°47′N	21°24′E
Florissant, Mo., U.S. (flŏr′ĭ-sănt)	120-21	38°48′N	90°20′W
Florø, Nor.	192-93	61°35′N	5°01′E
Floydada, Tx., U.S. (floi-dā′dȧ)	120-21	33°59′N	101°20′W
Flushing, Mi., U.S. (flŭsh′ĭng)	116-17	43°04′N	83°50′W
Fly, stm., (flī)	277	8°14′S	142°09′E
Foča, Bos. (fō′chä)	200-01	43°30′N	18°47′E
Fochville, S. Afr. (fŏk′vĭl)	269c	26°29′S	27°31′E
Focșani, Rom. (fōk-shä′nė)	202-03	45°42′N	27°12′E
Fogang, China (fwo-găŋ)	238-39	23°52′N	113°32′E
Foggia, Italy (fōd′jä)	200-01	41°28′N	15°32′E
Fogo, Nf., Can. (fō′gō)	138-39	49°43′N	54°18′W
Fogo, i., C.V.	260-61	14°54′N	24°23′W
Fogo Island, i., Nf., Can. (fō′gō ī′lănd)	138-39	49°39′N	54°11′W
Foguista J. F. Juárez, Arg. *see* El Galpón	168-69	25°24′S	64°38′W
Foix, Fr. (fwä)	196-97	42°58′N	1°37′E
Fokino, Russia	202-03	53°26′N	34°26′E
Folādī, Koh-e, mtn., Afg.	232-33	34°38′N	67°32′E
Foley Island, i., Nu., Can.	130-31	68°32′N	75°07′W
Foligno, Italy (fō-lēn′yō)	200-01	42°58′N	12°42′E
Fond-du-Lac, Sk., Can.	128-29	59°20′N	107°10′W
Fond du Lac, Wi., U.S. (fŏn dū lăk′)	116-17	43°46′N	88°27′W
Fond du Lac Indian Reservation, ind. res., Mn., U.S. (fŏn dū lăk′ ĭn′dĭ-ăn rĕ-sĕr-vā′shĕn)	114-15	46°45′N	92°37′W
Fondi, Italy (fōn′dē)	200-01	41°22′N	13°26′E
Fonseca, Golfo de, b., N.A. (gôl-fô-dĕ-fōn-sā′kä)	149	13°10′N	87°40′W
Fontainebleau, Fr. (fôn-tĕn-blō′)	196-97	48°24′N	2°42′E
Fontana, Ca., U.S. (fŏn-tă′ná)	118-19	34°06′N	117°26′W
Fonte Boa, Braz. (fōn′tȧ bō′ȧ)	166-67	2°32′S	66°01′W
Fontenay-le-Comte, Fr. (fônt-nĕ′lē-kônt′)	196-97	46°28′N	0°48′W
Fontur, c., Ice.	190a	66°22′N	14°35′W
Foochow, China *see* Fuzhou	225a	26°06′N	119°17′E
Forbach, Fr. (fôr′bäk)	196-97	49°12′N	6°54′E
Forbes, Austl. (fôrbz)	276	33°23′S	148°00′E
Forchheim, Ger. (fôrk′hīm)	194-95	49°43′N	11°04′E
Fordyce, Ar., U.S. (fôr′dīs)	120-21	33°49′N	92°25′W
Forest, Ms., U.S. (fŏr′ĕst)	124-25	32°22′N	89°28′W
Forest City, Ia., U.S. (fŏr′ĕst sĭ′tē)	114-15	43°16′N	93°39′W
Forest City, N.C., U.S. (fŏr′ĕst sĭ′tĭ)	124-25	35°20′N	81°52′W
Forest City, Pa., U.S. (fŏr′ĕst sĭ′tē)	116-17	41°39′N	75°28′W
Forestville, Qc., Can. (fŏr′ĕst-vĭl)	138-39	48°45′N	69°06′W
Forfar, Scot., U.K. (fôr′fȧr)	190-91	56°38′N	2°54′W
Forlì, Italy (fôr-lē′)	200-01	44°13′N	12°03′E
Formentera, i., Spain (fôr-mĕn-tā′rä)	198-99	38°42′N	1°28′E
Formiga, Braz. (fôr-mē′gȧ)	172	20°28′S	45°26′W
Formosa, Arg. (fôr-mō′sä)	168-69	26°10′S	58°12′W
Formosa, Braz.	168-69	15°32′S	47°20′W
Formosa, nation, Asia (fôr-mō′sȧ) *see* Taiwan	206-07	23°30′N	121°00′E
Formosa, state, Arg. (fôr-mō′sä)	168-69	25°0′S	60°00′W
Formosa, Serra, plat., Braz. (sĕ′r-rä fôr-mō′sä)	166-67	12°0′S	55°00′W
Formosa Strait, strt., Asia *see* Taiwan Strait	225a	24°0′N	119°00′E
Føroyar, dep., Eur. *see* Faroe Islands	174-75	62°0′N	7°00′W
Forrest City, Ar., U.S. (for′ĕst sĭ′tĭ)	124-25	35°00′N	90°48′W
Forsyth, Ga., U.S. (fôr-sīth′)	124-25	33°02′N	83°57′W
Forsyth, Mt., U.S. (fôr-sīth′)	112-13	46°16′N	106°41′W
Fort Albany, On., Can. (fôrt ôl′bȧ nĭ)	128-29	52°13′N	81°40′W
Fortaleza, Braz. (fôr′tä-lā′zȧ)	166-67	3°44′S	38°30′W
Fort-Archambault, Chad *see* Sarh	262-63	9°09′N	18°23′E
Fort Atkinson, Wi., U.S. (fôrt ăt′kĭn-sŭn)	116-17	42°55′N	88°51′W
Fort Bayard, China *see* Zhanjiang	238-39	21°12′N	110°23′E
Fort Benton, Mt., U.S. (fôrt bĕn′tŭn)	112-13	47°49′N	110°41′W
Fort Berthold Indian Reservation, ind. res., N.D., U.S. (fôrt bĕrth′ôld ĭn′dĭ-ăn rĕ-sĕr-vā′shĕn)	114-15	47°40′N	102°25′W
Fort Bragg, Ca., U.S.	118-19	39°27′N	123°48′W
Fort Branch, In., U.S. (fôrt brănch)	116-17	38°15′N	87°35′W
Fort Chipewyan, Ab., Can.	128-29	58°43′N	111°10′W
Fort Collins, Co., U.S. (fôrt kŏl′ĭns)	120-21	40°35′N	105°05′W
Fort-Dauphin, Madag. *see* Tôlañaro	264-65	25°02′S	47°00′E
Fort-de-France, nat. cap., Mart. (dē frăns)	143b	14°36′N	61°04′W
Fort Dodge, Ia., U.S. (fôrt dŏj)	114-15	42°30′N	94°11′W
Fort Edward, N.Y., U.S. (fôrt wẽrd)	116-17	43°16′N	73°35′W
Fortescue, stm., Austl. (fôr′tĕs-kū)	272-73	21°00′S	116°06′E
Fort-Foureau, Camrn. *see* Kousséri	260-61	12°05′N	15°02′E
Fort Frances, On., Can. (fôrt frăn′sĕs)	134-35	48°37′N	93°24′W
Fort Franklin, N.T., Can. *see* Déline	128-29	65°11′N	123°25′W
Fort Frederica National Monument, n.p., Ga., U.S. (fôrt frĕd′ē-rĭ-kȧ năsh′ŭn-ăl mŏn′ū-mĕnt)	124-25	31°12′N	81°26′W
Fort-George, Qc., Can. *see* Chisasibi	128-29	53°48′N	79°02′W
Fort Gibson, Ok., U.S. (fôrt gĭb′sŭn)	120-21	35°49′N	95°15′W
Fort Good Hope, N.T., Can. (fôrt gŏŏd hōp)	128-29	66°15′N	128°37′W
Forth, Firth of, b., Scot., U.K. (fûrth ŏv fôrth)	190-91	56°07′N	2°58′W
Fort Johnston, Malawi *see* Mangochi	264-65	14°28′S	35°15′E
Fort Kent, Me., U.S. (fôrt kĕnt)	117a	47°15′N	68°35′W
Fort-Lamy, nat. cap., Chad *see* N'Djamena	258-59	12°07′N	15°03′E
Fort Lauderdale, Fl., U.S. (fôrt lô′dẽr-dāl)	125a	26°07′N	80°09′W
Fort Liard, N.T., Can.	128-29	60°14′N	123°27′W
Fort Lupton, Co., U.S. (fôrt lŭp′tŭn)	120-21	40°05′N	104°49′W
Fort Macleod, Ab., Can. (fôrt mȧ-kloud′)	132-33	49°43′N	113°25′W
Fort Madison, Ia., U.S. (fôrt măd′ĭ-sŭn)	120-21	40°38′N	91°19′W
Fort McMurray, Ab., Can. (fôrt mȧk-mŭr′ĭ)	134-35	56°44′N	111°25′W
Fort McPherson, N.T., Can. (fôrt mȧk-fŭr′s′n)	128-29	67°25′N	134°52′W
Fort Meade, Fl., U.S. (fôrt mēd)	125a	27°46′N	81°48′W
Fort Mill, S.C., U.S. (fôrt mĭl)	124-25	35°00′N	80°57′W
Fort Mojave Indian Reservation, ind. res., Az., U.S. (fôrt mô-hä′vâ ĭn′dĭ-ăn rĕ-sĕr-vā′shĕn)	118-19	34°55′N	114°35′W
Fort Morgan, Co., U.S. (fôrt môr′găn)	120-21	40°15′N	103°48′W
Fort Myers, Fl., U.S. (fôrt mī′ẽrz)	125a	26°38′N	81°52′W

n-sing; ŋ-baŋk; ɴ-nasalized n; nŏd; cŏmmit; ōld; ôbey; ôrder; oi-boil; fōōd; ŏŏ-as oo in foot; ou-out; s-soft; sh-dish; th-thin; pūre; ûnite; ûrn; stŭd; circŭs; ü-as in French tu; ′-indeterminate vowel.

330 Fort Nelson – Gabès, Golfe de
PRONOUNCING INDEX

Feature (Pronunciation)	Page	Lat.	Long.
Fort Nelson, B.C., Can. (fôrt nĕl´sŭn)	128-29	58°49'N	122°41'W
Fort Nelson, stm., B.C., Can. (fôrt nĕl´sŭn)	130-31	59°31'N	124°03'W
Fort Norman, N.T., Can. *see* Tulita	128-29	64°54'N	125°34'W
Fort Payne, Al., U.S. (fôrt pān)	124-25	34°27'N	85°43'W
Fort Peck Indian Reservation, ind. res., Mt., U.S. (fôrt pĕk ĭn´dĭ-ăn rĕ-sẽr-vā´shĕn)	112-13	48°22'N	105°40'W
Fort Peck Lake, res., Mt., U.S. (fôrt pĕk lāk)	112-13	47°45'N	106°45'W
Fort Pierce, Fl., U.S. (fôrt pērs)	125a	27°27'N	80°20'W
Fort Portal, Ug. (fôrt pôr´tăl)	267	0°40'N	30°17'E
Fort Providence, N.T., Can. (fôrt prŏv´ĭ-dĕns)	128-29	61°21'N	117°35'W
Fort Pulaski National Monument, n.p., Ga., U.S. (fôrt pu-lăs´kĭ năsh´ŭn-ăl mŏn´ū-mĕnt)	124-25	32°01'N	80°55'W
Fort Qu'Appelle, Sk., Can.	134-35	50°46'N	103°48'W
Fort Resolution, N.T., Can. (fôrt rĕz´ō-lū´shŭn)	128-29	61°10'N	113°38'W
Fort Rosebery, Zam. *see* Mansa	264-65	11°12'S	28°53'E
Fort Saint James, B.C., Can. (fôrt sånt jāmz)	132-33	54°28'N	124°16'W
Fort Saint John, B.C., Can. (fôrt sånt jŏn)	132-33	56°17'N	120°54'W
Fort Saskatchewan, Ab., Can. (fôrt săs-kăt´chōō-ån)	132-33	53°43'N	113°14'W
Fort Severn, On., Can. (fôrt sĕv´ẽrn)	134-35	55°60'N	87°38'W
Fort-Shevchenko, Kaz. (fôrt shĕv-chĕn´kô)	186-87	44°30'N	50°16'E
Fort Simpson, N.T., Can. (fôrt sĭmp´sŭn)	128-29	61°51'N	121°22'W
Fort Smith, N.T., Can. (fôrt smĭth)	128-29	60°01'N	111°54'W
Fort Smith, Ar., U.S. (fôrt smĭth)	120-21	35°23'N	94°25'W
Fort Stockton, Tx., U.S. (fôrt stŏk´tŭn)	122-23	30°54'N	102°53'W
Fort Sumner, N.M., U.S. (fôrt sŭm´nẽr)	120-21	34°29'N	104°14'W
Fort Sumter National Monument, n.p., S.C., U.S. (fôrt sŭm´tẽr năsh´ŭn-ăl mŏn´ū-mĕnt)	124-25	32°45'N	79°52'W
Fortuna, Ca., U.S. (fôr-tū´nȧ)	112-13	40°36'N	124°09'W
Fortune, Nf., Can. (fôr´tŭn)	138-39	47°04'N	55°50'W
Fortune Bay, b., Nf., Can. (fôr´tŭn bā)	138-39	47°25'N	55°25'W
Fort Union National Monument, n.p., N.M., U.S. (fôrt ūn´yŭn năsh´ŭn-ăl mŏn´ū-mĕnt)	120-21	35°56'N	105°03'W
Fort Valley, Ga., U.S. (fôrt văl´ê)	124-25	32°33'N	83°53'W
Fort Vermilion, Ab., Can. (fôrt vẽr-mĭl´yŭn)	128-29	58°23'N	116°02'W
Fort Walton Beach, Fl., U.S.	124-25	30°25'N	86°36'W
Fort Wayne, In., U.S. (fôrt wān)	116-17	41°04'N	85°07'W
Fort William, Scot., U.K. (fôrt wĭl´yŭm)	190-91	56°49'N	5°06'W
Fort Worth, Tx., U.S. (fôrt wûrth)	120-21	32°45'N	97°21'W
Fort Yukon, Ak., U.S. (fôrt yōō´kŏn)	126	66°34'N	145°15'W
Forūr, Jazīreh-ye, i., Iran	230-31	26°17'N	54°31'E
Foshan, China	238-39	23°03'N	113°07'E
Fossano, Italy (fôs-sä´nō)	200-01	44°33'N	7°44'E
Fossil Butte National Monument, n.p., Wy., U.S.	112-13	41°50'N	110°40'W
Fosston, Mn., U.S. (fôs´tŭn)	114-15	47°34'N	95°45'W
Foster, Austl.	276	38°39'S	146°12'E
Foster, stm., Sk., Can.	134-35	55°47'N	105°48'W
Fostoria, Oh., U.S. (fŏs-tō´rĭ-ȧ)	116-17	41°10'N	83°24'W
Fougères, Fr. (fōō-zhâr´)	196-97	48°21'N	1°12'W
Foulwind, Cape, c., N.Z. (kāp foul´wĭnd)	278	41°45'S	171°28'E
Fouriesburg, S. Afr. (fō´rēz-bûrg)	269c	28°37'S	28°13'E
Fourmies, Fr. (fōōr-mē´)	196-97	50°01'N	4°03'E
Foveaux Strait, strt., N.Z. (fô-vō´ strāt)	278	46°35'S	168°00'E
Fowler, In., U.S. (foul´ẽr)	116-17	40°37'N	87°19'W
Foxe Basin, b., Nu., Can. (fŏks bā´s'n)	130-31	68°25'N	76°60'W
Foxe Peninsula, pen., Nu., Can. (fŏks pĕ-nĭn´sūlă)	130-31	65°0'N	76°00'W
Foz do Iguaçu, Braz.	168-69	25°33'S	54°35'W
Fraga, Spain (frä´gä)	198-99	41°32'N	0°21'E
Franca, Braz. (frä´n-kä)	172	20°32'S	47°24'W
France, nation, Eur. (fråns)	174-75	46°0'N	2°00'E
Francés Viejo, Cabo, c., Dom. Rep. (kå´bô-frän´sås vyā´hô)	142-43	19°39'N	69°55'W
Franceville, Gabon (fräns-vēl´)	260-61	1°38'S	13°35'E
Francis Case, Lake, res., S.D., U.S. (lāk från´sĭs kās)	114-15	43°15'N	98°57'W
Francistown, Bots. (från´sis-toun)	264-65	21°10'S	27°30'E
Francois Lake, lk., B.C., Can.	132-33	54°02'N	125°43'W
Francs Peak, mtn., Wy., U.S.	112-13	43°58'N	109°20'W
Frankfort, S. Afr. (frănk´fŏrt)	269c	27°17'S	28°31'E
Frankfort, In., U.S. (frăŋk´fŭrt)	116-17	40°17'N	86°30'W
Frankfort, Ky., U.S.	116-17	38°12'N	84°50'W
Frankfort, Mi., U.S. (frăŋk´fŭrt)	116-17	44°38'N	86°14'W
Frankfurt, Ger.	194-95	52°21'N	14°32'E
Frankfurt am Main, Ger.	194-95	50°07'N	8°40'E
Franklin, In., U.S. (frănk´lĭn)	116-17	39°28'N	86°03'W
Franklin, Ky., U.S. (frănk´lĭn)	124-25	36°43'N	86°35'W
Franklin, La., U.S. (frănk´lĭn)	124-25	29°47'N	91°30'W
Franklin, N.C., U.S. (frănk´lĭn)	124-25	35°11'N	83°23'W
Franklin, N.H., U.S. (frănk´lĭn)	116-17	43°27'N	71°40'W
Franklin, Tx., U.S. (frănk´lĭn)	122-23	31°01'N	96°29'W
Franklin, Va., U.S. (frănk´lĭn)	124-25	36°41'N	76°56'W
Franklin, Wi., U.S. (frănk´lĭn)	116-17	42°52'N	87°60'W
Franklin, W.V., U.S. (frănk´lĭn)	116-17	38°39'N	79°21'W
Franklin Mountains, mts., N.T., Can. (frănk´lĭn moun´tĭnz)	130-31	62°59'N	123°43'W
Franklinton, La., U.S. (frăŋk´lĭn-tŭn)	124-25	30°51'N	90°09'W
Frantsa-Iosifa, Zemlya, is., Russia *see* Franz Josef Land	218-19	81°0'N	55°00'E
Franz Josef Land, is., Russia	218-19	81°0'N	55°00'E
Frascati, Italy (fräs-kä´tē)	200-01	41°48'N	12°41'E
Fraser, stm., B.C., Can.	132-33	49°06'N	123°11'W
Fraserburgh, Scot., U.K. (frā´zẽr-bûrg)	190-91	57°42'N	2°01'W
Fraser Island, i., Austl.	276	25°15'S	153°10'E
Fraser Plateau, plat., B.C., Can.	132-33	52°0'N	123°00'W
Fray Bentos, Ur.	173	33°08'S	58°18'W
Frazee, Mn., U.S. (frā-zē´)	114-15	46°44'N	95°42'W
Fredericia, Den. (frĕdh-ĕ-rē´tsē-à)	192-93	55°35'N	9°46'E
Frederick, Ok., U.S. (frĕd´ẽr-ĭk)	120-21	34°23'N	99°01'W
Fredericksburg, Tx., U.S. (frĕd´ẽr-ĭkz-bûrg)	122-23	30°16'N	98°52'W
Fredericksburg, Va., U.S. (frĕd´ẽr-ĭkz-bûrg)	116-17	38°18'N	77°28'W
Fredericktown, Mo., U.S. (frĕd´ẽr-ĭk-toun)	120-21	37°34'N	90°18'W
Fredericton, N.B., Can. (frĕd´-ẽr-ĭk-tŭn)	138-39	45°57'N	66°39'W
Frederikshavn, Den. (frĕdh´ĕ-rĕks-houn)	192-93	57°26'N	10°32'E
Fredonia, Col. (frĕ-dō´nyà)	163c	5°56'N	75°40'W
Fredonia, N.Y., U.S. (frê-dō´nĭ-ȧ)	116-17	42°26'N	79°20'W
Fredrikstad, Nor. (frådh´rĕks-ståd)	192-93	59°12'N	10°56'E
Freels, Cape, c., Nf., Can. (kāp frēlz)	138-39	49°15'N	53°28'W
Freeport, Bah. (frē´pōrt)	142-43	26°31'N	78°39'W
Freeport, Il., U.S. (frē´pōrt)	116-17	42°18'N	89°37'W
Freeport, N.Y., U.S. (frē´pōrt)	116-17	40°39'N	73°35'W
Freeport, Tx., U.S. (frē´pōrt)	122-23	28°57'N	95°22'W
Freetown, nat. cap., S.L. (frē´toun)	260-61	8°29'N	13°13'W
Freiberg, Ger. (frī´bĕrgh)	194-95	50°55'N	13°21'E
Freirina, Chile (frå-ĭ-rē´nä)	168-69	28°30'S	71°06'W
Freising, Ger. (frī´zĭng)	194-95	48°24'N	11°44'E
Fréjus, Fr. (frā-zhüs´)	196-97	43°26'N	6°45'E
Fremantle, Austl. (frē´măn-t'l)	270-71	32°03'S	115°45'E
Fremont, Ca., U.S. (frê-mŏnt´)	118-19	37°33'N	121°59'W
Fremont, Mi., U.S. (frê´-mŏnt)	116-17	43°28'N	85°57'W
Fremont, Ne., U.S. (frê´-mŏnt)	114-15	41°27'N	96°30'W
Fremont, Oh., U.S. (frê´-mŏnt)	116-17	41°21'N	83°07'W
French Guiana, dep., S.A. (frĕnch gē-ä´nä)	158	4°0'N	53°00'W
French Lick, In., U.S. (frĕnch lĭk)	116-17	38°33'N	86°37'W
French Polynesia, dep., Oc. (frĕnch pŏl-ĭ-nē´zhȧ)	280-81	15°0'S	140°00'W
French Somaliland, nation, Afr. *see* Djibouti	253	11°30'N	43°00'E
Fresco, stm., Braz.	166-67	6°40'S	52°00'W
Freshfield, Mount, mtn., Can. (mount frĕsh´fēld)	132-33	51°44'N	116°57'W
Fresnillo, Mex. (frås-nēl´yô)	146-47	23°10'N	102°52'W
Fresno, Col. (frĕs´nô)	163c	5°09'N	75°01'W
Fresno, Ca., U.S.	118-19	36°45'N	119°46'W
Fria, Cape, c., Nmb. (kāp frīȧ)	264-65	18°29'S	12°02'E
Frías, Arg. (frē´äs)	168-69	28°38'S	65°07'W
Friedberg, Ger. (frēd´bĕrgh)	194-95	48°22'N	10°59'E
Friedrichshafen, Ger. (frē-drĕks-häf´ĕn)	194-95	47°40'N	9°29'E
Friend, Ne., U.S. (frĕnd)	120-21	40°39'N	97°17'W
Friesische Inseln, is., Eur. *see* Frisian Islands	190-91	53°27'N	5°50'E
Frio, Cabo, c., Braz. (kå´bō-frê´ō)	172	22°53'S	42°00'W
Frisian Islands, is., Eur. (frē´zhăn ī´lȧndz)	190-91	53°27'N	5°50'E
Frobisher Bay, Nu., Can. *see* Iqaluit	128-29	63°44'N	68°28'W
Frobisher Bay, b., Nu., Can. (frŏb´ĭsh´ẽr bā)	130-31	62°30'N	65°60'W
Frobisher Lake, lk., Sk., Can. (frŏb´ĭsh´ẽr lāk)	134-35	56°22'N	108°17'W
Frolovo, Russia	186-87	49°47'N	43°39'E
Frome, Lake, lk., Austl. (lāk frōōm)	276	30°42'S	139°48'E
Frontera, Mex. (frôn-tā´rä)	146-47	18°32'N	92°38'W
Frontera, Mex. (frôn-tā´rä)	122-23	26°56'N	101°27'W
Front Royal, Va., U.S. (frŭnt roi´ăl)	116-17	38°55'N	78°12'W
Frosinone, Italy (frō-zê-nō´nå)	200-01	41°39'N	13°21'E
Frostburg, Md., U.S. (frôst´bûrg)	116-17	39°39'N	78°55'W
Frøya, i., Nor.	184-85	63°43'N	8°42'E
Fruita, Co., U.S. (frōōt-ȧ)	118-19	39°10'N	108°44'W
Fuchun, stm., China (fōō-chòn)	238-39	30°06'N	120°10'E
Fuego, Volcán de, vol., Guat. (vôl-kå´n-dĕ-fwā´gō)	148	14°29'N	90°53'W
Fuente de Cantos, Spain (fwĕn´tå dā kän´tōs)	198-99	38°15'N	6°18'W
Fuerte, stm., Mex. (fōō-ĕ´r-tĕ)	144-45	25°51'N	109°25'W
Fuerte Olimpo, Para. (fwĕr´tå ō-lēm-pō)	168-69	21°05'S	57°52'W
Fuerteventura, i., Spain (fwĕr´tå-vĕn-tōō´rä)	199d	28°20'N	14°00'W
Fuga Island, i., Phil.	250a	18°52'N	121°22'E
Fuji, Japan (fōō´jê)	245	35°09'N	138°40'E
Fuji, stm., Japan (fōō´jê)	245	35°07'N	138°39'E
Fujian, state, China (fōō-jyĕn)	225a	26°0'N	118°00'E
Fujin, China (fōō-jyĭn)	240-41	47°15'N	132°02'E
Fuji-san, vol., Japan (fōō´jê-sän)	245	35°22'N	138°44'E
Fujiyama, vol., Japan *see* Fuji-san	245	35°22'N	138°44'E
Fukien, state, China *see* Fujian	225a	26°0'N	118°00'E
Fukuchiyama, Japan (fōō´kò-chê-yä´ma)	245	35°18'N	135°07'E
Fukue-jima, i., Japan (fò-kōō´ä jē´mȧ)	244	32°40'N	128°45'E
Fukui, Japan (fōō´kōō-ê)	245	36°04'N	136°13'E
Fukuoka, Japan	245	33°35'N	130°25'E
Fukushima, Japan (fōō´kò-shē´mà)	245	37°45'N	140°28'E
Fulaga, i., Fiji	279f	19°09'S	178°36'W
Fulaga Passage, strt., Fiji	279f	18°56'S	178°36'W
Fulda, Ger. (fòl´dä)	194-95	50°33'N	9°41'E
Fuling, China (fōō-lĭŋ)	238-39	29°42'N	107°25'E
Fullerton, Ne., U.S. (fòl´ẽr-tŭn)	114-15	41°22'N	97°58'W
Fulton, Il., U.S. (fŭl´tŭn)	114-15	41°52'N	90°10'W
Fulton, Ky., U.S. (fŭl´tŭn)	124-25	36°31'N	88°53'W
Fulton, Mo., U.S. (fŭl´tŭn)	120-21	38°51'N	91°57'W
Fulton, Ms., U.S. (fŭl´tŭn)	124-25	34°14'N	88°24'W
Fulton, N.Y., U.S. (fŭl´tŭn)	116-17	43°19'N	76°25'W
Funafuti, at., Tuvalu	280-81	8°29'S	179°11'E
Funan, China *see* Fushun	243	41°52'N	123°54'E
Funchal, Port. (fòn-shäl´)	258-59	32°39'N	16°54'W
Fundación, Col. (fōōn-dä-syō´n)	164-65	10°31'N	74°11'W
Fundy, Bay of, b., Can. (bā ŭv fŭn´dĭ)	138-39	45°0'N	66°00'W
Fundy National Park, n.p., N.B., Can. (fŭn´dĭ năsh´ŭn-ăl pärk)	138-39	45°38'N	65°00'W
Fünfkirchen, Hung. *see* Pécs	194-95	46°04'N	18°13'E
Funing, China (fōō-nĭŋ)	238-39	23°34'N	105°37'E
Furnas, Represa de, res., Braz.	172	21°12'S	45°57'W
Furneaux Group, is., Austl. (fûr´nō grōōp)	276	40°10'S	148°05'E
Fürstenwalde, Ger. (für´stĕn-väl-dĕ)	194-95	52°21'N	14°04'E
Fürth, Ger. (fürt)	194-95	49°28'N	10°59'E
Fusan, Kor., S. *see* Pusan	243	35°05'N	129°03'E
Fushun, China (fōō´shōōn´)	243	41°52'N	123°54'E
Fusong, China (fōō-sòŋ)	243	42°20'N	127°17'E
Fusui, China	238-39	22°38'N	107°55'E
Futuna, Île, i., Wal./F.	280-81	14°18'S	178°09'W
Fuxian, China (fōō shyĕn)	240-41	36°02'N	109°22'E
Fuxian, China (fōō shyĕn) *see* Wafangdian	240-41	39°37'N	122°01'E
Fuxian Hu, lk., China	238-39	24°29'N	102°53'E
Fuxin, China (fōō-shyĭn)	240-41	42°08'N	121°45'E
Fuyang, China (fōō-yäŋ)	238-39	32°54'N	115°49'E
Fuyang, stm., China (fōō-yäŋ)	240-41	38°11'N	116°04'E
Fuyu, China (fōō-yōō)	240-41	45°10'N	124°49'E
Fuyu, China (fōō-yōō)	240-41	47°49'N	124°28'E
Fuzhou, China	225a	26°06'N	119°17'E
Fuzhou, China (fōō-jō)	238-39	28°01'N	116°20'E
Fyn, i., Den. (fü´n)	192-93	55°20'N	10°30'E

G

Feature (Pronunciation)	Page	Lat.	Long.
Gaalkacyo, Som.	262-63	6°46'N	47°26'E
Gabela, Ang.	264-65	10°51'S	14°22'E
Gaberones, nat. cap., Bots. *see* Gaborone	264-65	24°40'S	25°56'E
Gabès, Tun. (gä´bĕs)	188-89	33°54'N	10°06'E
Gabès, Golfe de, b., Tun. (gôlf-dĕ-gä´bĕs)	258-59	34°14'N	10°30'E

ăt; finăl; rāte; senåte; ärm; åsk; sofȧ; fâre; ch-choose; dh-as th in other; bē; êvent; bĕt; recĕnt; cratẽr; g-gō; gh-guttural g; bĭt; ĭ-short neutral; rīde; κ-guttural k as ch in German ich;

PRONOUNCING INDEX

Gabon – Geographe Bay 331

Feature (Pronunciation)	Page	Lat.	Long.
Gabon, nation, Afr. (gȧ-bôɴ′)	253	1°0′S	11°45′E
Gaborone, nat. cap., Bots. (gä-bō-rō′-nä) (gä′bô-rōō-nä)	264-65	24°40′S	25°56′E
Gabrovo, Blg. (gäb′rô-vō)	200-01	42°51′N	25°19′E
Gachsārān, Iran	230-31	30°12′N	50°47′E
Gacko, Bos. (gäts′kô)	200-01	43°10′N	18°32′E
Gadag, India	236	15°25′N	75°37′E
Gadsden, Al., U.S. (gădz′dĕn)	124-25	34°00′N	86°01′W
Găeşti, Rom. (gä-yĕsh′tê)	200-01	44°43′N	25°20′E
Gaeta, Italy (gä-å′tä)	200-01	41°13′N	13°34′E
Gaferut, i., Micron.	280-81	9°12′N	145°23′E
Gaffney, S.C., U.S. (găf′nĭ)	124-25	35°04′N	81°39′W
Gafsa, Tun. (găf′sä)	188-89	34°24′N	8°49′E
Gagnoa, C. Iv.	260-61	6°07′N	5°56′W
Gagra, Geor.	227	43°20′N	40°15′E
Gaillimh, Ire. see Galway	190-91	53°16′N	9°03′W
Gainesville, Fl., U.S. (gānz′vĭl)	124-25	29°39′N	82°18′W
Gainesville, Ga., U.S. (gānz′vĭl)	124-25	34°18′N	83°49′W
Gainesville, Tx., U.S. (gānz′vĭl)	120-21	33°38′N	97°09′W
Gainesville, Va., U.S. (gānz′vĭl)	116-17	38°47′N	77°38′W
Gairdner, Lake, lk., Austl. (lāk gȧrd′nẽr)	272-73	31°33′S	135°57′E
Gaithersburg, Md., U.S. (gā′thẽrs′bûrg)	116-17	39°08′N	77°12′W
Gaixian, China (gī-shyĕn)	240-41	40°24′N	122°22′E
Galán, Cerro, mtn., Arg.	168-69	25°57′S	66°54′W
Galana, stm., Kenya	262-63	3°09′S	40°08′E
Galapagos Islands, is., Ec. (gä-lä′-pä-gōs ī′lȧndz) see Colón, Archipiélago de	170a	0°43′N	91°30′W
Galashiels, Scot., U.K. (găl-ȧ-shēlz)	190-91	55°38′N	2°50′W
Galați, Rom.	202-03	45°26′N	28°03′E
Galatina, Italy (gä-lä-tē′nä)	200-01	40°10′N	18°10′E
Galatz, Rom. see Galați	202-03	45°26′N	28°03′E
Galdhøpiggen, mtn., Nor.	192-93	61°37′N	8°17′E
Galeana, Mex. (gä-lå-ä′nä)	122-23	24°50′N	100°04′W
Galela, Indon.	248-49	1°50′N	127°50′E
Galena, Ak., U.S. (gȧ-lē′nȧ)	126	64°44′N	156°57′W
Galena, Il., U.S. (gȧ-lē′nȧ)	114-15	42°25′N	90°25′W
Galera, Punta, c., Chile	171	39°58′S	73°40′W
Galera, Punta, c., Ec.	170	0°49′N	80°03′W
Galesburg, Il., U.S. (gālz′bûrg)	114-15	40°57′N	90°22′W
Galeton, Pa., U.S. (gāl′tŭn)	116-17	41°44′N	77°39′W
Galich, Russia (gȧl′ĭch)	186-87	58°23′N	42°22′E
Galicia, hist. reg., Eur. (gȧ-lĭsh′ĭ-ȧ)	194-95	49°0′N	22°00′E
Galicja, hist. reg., Eur. see Galicia	194-95	49°0′N	22°00′E
Galilee, Sea of, lk., Isr. (sē ŭv găl′ĭ-lē)	228-29	32°48′N	35°35′E
Galion, Oh., U.S. (găl′ĭ-ŭn)	116-17	40°44′N	82°47′W
Galkynyş, Turkmen.	232-33	39°16′N	63°11′E
Gallatin, Mo., U.S. (găl′ȧ-tĭn)	120-21	39°55′N	93°58′W
Gallatin, Tn., U.S. (găl′ȧ-tĭn)	124-25	36°24′N	86°27′W
Galle, Sri L. (gäl)	236	6°02′N	80°13′E
Gallinas, Punta, c., Col. (pōō′n-tä-gä-lyē′näs)	164-65	12°28′N	71°40′W
Gallipoli, Italy (gäl-lē′pô-lē)	200-01	40°03′N	17°59′E
Gallipoli, Tur.	200-01	40°26′N	26°41′E
Gallipoli Peninsula, pen., Tur. (gäl-lē′pô-lē pĕ-nĭn′sūlȧ)	200-01	40°20′N	26°30′E
Gallipolis, Oh., U.S. (găl-ĭ-pô-lēs)	116-17	38°49′N	82°12′W
Gällivare, Swe. (yĕl-ĭ-vär′ĕ)	184-85	67°08′N	20°41′E
Gallup, N.M., U.S. (găl′ŭp)	118-19	35°32′N	108°45′W
Galva, Il., U.S. (găl′vȧ)	114-15	41°10′N	90°02′W
Galveston, Tx., U.S. (găl′vĕs-tŭn)	122-23	29°18′N	94°48′W
Galveston Bay, b., Tx., U.S. (găl′vĕs-tŭn bā)	122-23	29°36′N	94°57′W
Galveston Island, i., Tx., U.S. (găl′vĕs-tŭn ī′lȧnd)	122-23	29°13′N	94°55′W
Gálvez, Arg.	173	32°02′S	61°13′W
Galway, Ire. (gôl′wā)	190-91	53°16′N	9°03′W
Gamba, China (gäm-bä)	234-35	28°17′N	88°31′E
Gambell, Ak., U.S.	126	63°47′N	171°44′W
Gambia, The, nation, Afr. (thȧ găm′bē-ȧ)	253	13°30′N	15°30′W
Gambier, Îles, is., Fr. Poly.	280-81	23°08′S	134°57′W
Gamboma, Congo (gäm-bō′mä)	262-63	1°53′S	15°51′E
Gamlakarleby, Fin. see Kokkola	184-85	63°50′N	23°09′E
Gamleby, Swe. (gäm′lĕ-bü)	192-93	57°55′N	16°23′E
Gan, stm., China (gän)	222-23	49°11′N	125°10′E
Gananoque, On., Can.	136-37	44°20′N	76°10′W
Gäncä, Azer.	227	40°41′N	46°21′E
Ganda, Ang.	264-65	13°02′S	14°39′E
Gandajika, D.R.C.	262-63	6°44′S	23°57′E
Gander, Nf., Can. (găn′dẽr)	138-39	48°57′N	54°35′W
Gander, stm., Nf., Can. (găn′dẽr)	138-39	49°29′N	54°24′W
Gander Lake, lk., Nf., Can. (găn′dẽr lāk)	138-39	48°57′N	54°39′W
Gāndhinagar, India	234-35	23°13′N	72°40′E
Gandia, Spain	198-99	38°58′N	0°11′W
Ganga, stm., Asia see Ganges	234-35	21°58′N	90°57′E
Gangānagar, India	234-35	29°55′N	73°52′E
Gangaw, Mya.	246-47	22°11′N	94°09′E
Gangdisê Shan, mts., China	234-35	31°0′N	82°00′E
Ganges, stm., Asia (găn′jēz)	234-35	21°58′N	90°57′E
Ganges, Mouths of the, mth., Asia (mouthz ŭv thȧ găn′jēz)	234-35	22°0′N	89°00′E
Gangneung, Kor., S. see Kangnŭng	243	37°46′N	128°54′E
Gangotri, India	234-35	30°60′N	78°59′E
Gangtok, India	234-35	27°19′N	88°38′E
Gangu, China	238-39	34°45′N	105°20′E
Gannan, China (gän-nän)	240-41	47°56′N	123°30′E
Gannett Peak, mtn., Wy., U.S. (găn′ĕt pēk)	112-13	43°11′N	109°39′W
Gansu, state, China (gän-sōō)	240-41	37°0′N	103°00′E
Ganzê, China	238-39	31°38′N	100°01′E
Ganzhou, China (gän-jō)	238-39	25°53′N	114°55′E
Gao, Mali (gä′ō)	258-59	16°16′N	0°02′W
Gao'an, China (gou-än)	238-39	28°26′N	115°23′E
Gaoyi, China (gou-yē)	240-41	37°37′N	114°36′E
Gaoyou, China (gou-yō)	238-39	32°47′N	119°26′E
Gaoyou Hu, lk., China (kä′ō-yōō′hōō)	238-39	32°50′N	119°20′E
Gap, Fr. (gȧp)	196-97	44°34′N	6°05′E
Garabogazköl Aylagy, b., Turkmen. see Kara-Bogaz-Gol Gulf	232-33	41°15′N	53°24′E
Garagum, des., Turkmen. see Kara Kum	226	39°0′N	60°00′E
Garagum Kanaly, can., Turkmen. see Kara-Kum Canal	232-33	37°34′N	65°41′E
Garanhuns, Braz. (gä-rän-yōɴsh′)	163d	8°54′S	36°29′W
Garber, Ok., U.S. (gȧr′bẽr)	120-21	36°26′N	97°35′W
Garden City, Ga., U.S. (gär′d′n sĭ′tē)	124-25	32°07′N	81°09′W
Garden City, Ks., U.S. (gär′d′n sĭ′tē)	120-21	37°58′N	100°52′W
Gardeyz, Afg.	232-33	33°36′N	69°13′E
Gardiner, Mt., U.S. (gärd′nẽr)	112-13	45°02′N	110°42′W
Gardner, Ks., U.S. (gärd′nẽr)	120-21	38°49′N	94°56′W
Gardner, Ma., U.S. (gärd′nẽr)	116-17	42°35′N	71°60′W
Gardner Canal, b., B.C., Can. (gärd′nẽr kȧ′nȧl)	132-33	53°28′N	128°18′W
Gardner Pinnacles, r., Hi., U.S. (gärd′nẽr pĭn′ȧ-k′lz)	127	25°0′N	167°55′W
Gargždai, Lith. (gärgzh′dī)	192-93	55°43′N	21°24′E
Garibaldi, Mount, vol., B.C., Can. (mount gâr-ĭ-băl′dê)	132-33	49°51′N	122°59′W
Garissa, Kenya	262-63	0°27′S	39°39′E
Garland, Tx., U.S. (gär′lănd)	120-21	32°56′N	96°38′W
Garmisch-Partenkirchen, Ger. (gär′mēsh pär′tĕn-kēr′kĕn)	194-95	47°30′N	11°06′E
Garnett, Ks., U.S. (gär′nĕt)	120-21	38°17′N	95°14′W
Garoua, Camn. (gär′wä)	260-61	9°19′N	13°23′E
Garqu Yan, China	238-39	33°54′N	92°19′E
Garrett, In., U.S. (găr′ĕt)	116-17	41°21′N	85°07′W
Garrison, N.D., U.S. (găr′ĭ-sŭn)	114-15	47°39′N	101°25′W
Garry Lake, lk., Nu., Can. (găr′ĭ lāk)	130-31	66°0′N	100°00′W
Garut, Indon.	248-49	7°12′S	107°54′E
Garwolin, Pol. (gär-vō′lĕn)	194-95	51°54′N	21°38′E
Gary, In., U.S. (gā′rĭ)	116-17	41°36′N	87°21′W
Garyarsa, China	234-35	31°43′N	80°20′E
Garzón, Col. (gär-thōn′)	164-65	2°12′N	75°38′W
Gas City, In., U.S. (găs sĭ′tĕ)	116-17	40°29′N	85°37′W
Gascogne, Golfe de, b., Eur. see Biscay, Bay of	196-97	44°0′N	4°00′W
Gash, stm., Afr.	266	16°45′N	35°54′E
Gaspé, Qc., Can.	138-39	48°49′N	64°29′W
Gasteiz, Spain	198-99	42°51′N	2°40′W
Gastonia, N.C., U.S. (găs-tô′nĭ-ȧ)	124-25	35°16′N	81°11′W
Gastre, Arg. (gäs-trĕ)	171	42°17′S	69°14′W
Gata, Cabo de, c., Spain (kȧ′bô-dĕ-gȧ′tä)	198-99	36°44′N	2°11′W
Gata, Sierra de, mts., Spain (syĕr′rȧ dā gȧ′tä)	198-99	40°16′N	6°44′W
Gatchina, Russia (gä-chē′nȧ)	192-93	59°33′N	30°08′E
Gates of the Arctic National Park and Preserve, n.p., Ak., U.S.	126	67°45′N	153°30′W
Gatesville, Tx., U.S. (gāts′vĭl)	122-23	31°25′N	97°44′W
Gatineau, Qc., Can. (gȧ′tē-nō)	136-37	45°29′N	75°38′W
Gatineau, stm., Qc., Can. (gȧ′tē-nō)	136-37	45°27′N	75°42′W
Gauer Lake, lk., Mb., Can.	134-35	57°0′N	97°50′W
Gauja, stm., Eur. (gȧ′ô-yä)	192-93	57°09′N	24°17′E
Gaustatoppen, mtn., Nor.	192-93	59°50′N	8°35′E
Gávdos, i., Grc. (gäv′dôs)	200a	34°50′N	24°06′E
Gävle, Swe. (yĕv′lĕ)	192-93	60°40′N	17°10′E
Gavrilov-Yam, Russia (gȧ′vrê-lôf yäm′)	202-03	57°18′N	39°52′E
Gaxun Nur, lk., China	240-41	42°22′N	100°34′E
Gaya, India (gŭ′yä)(gī′ȧ)	234-35	24°48′N	85°00′E
Gaylord, Mi., U.S. (gā′lôrd)	116-17	45°02′N	84°40′W
Gaylord, Mn., U.S. (gā′lôrd)	114-15	44°33′N	94°14′W
Gayndah, Austl. (gān′dăh)	276	25°38′S	151°36′E
Gayny, Russia	186-87	60°18′N	54°19′E
Gaza, Gaza (gä′zȧ) (gă′zȧ)	228-29	31°30′N	34°28′E
Gazanjyk, Turkmen.	232-33	39°15′N	55°32′E
Gaziantep, Tur. (gä-zē-än′tĕp)	228-29	37°04′N	37°23′E
Gazimağusa, Cyp.	228-29	35°07′N	33°57′E
Gbadolite, D.R.C.	262-63	4°15′N	21°00′E
Gbanga, Lib.	260-61	7°00′N	9°29′W
Gboko, Nig.	260-61	7°20′N	8°60′E
Gdańsk, Pol. (g′dänsk)	194-95	54°21′N	18°38′E
Gdov, Russia (g′dôf′)	192-93	58°45′N	27°49′E
Gdynia, Pol. (g′dĕn′yȧ)	194-95	54°32′N	18°31′E
Geary, Ok., U.S. (gē′rĭ)	120-21	35°38′N	98°19′W
Gediz, stm., Tur.	200-01	38°36′N	26°48′E
Geelong, Austl. (jē-lông′)	276	38°08′S	144°21′E
Geeveston, Austl.	276	43°10′S	146°55′E
Gefle, Swe. see Gävle	192-93	60°40′N	17°10′E
Geita, Tan.	267	2°52′S	32°10′E
Gejiu, China (gŭ-jĭo)	238-39	23°22′N	103°09′E
Gela, Italy	200-01	37°04′N	14°15′E
Gelasa, Selat, strt., Indon.	246-47	2°55′S	107°13′E
Gelibolu, Tur. (gĕ-lĭb′ô-lò) see Gallipoli	200-01	40°26′N	26°41′E
Gelibolu Yarımadası, pen., Tur. see Gallipoli Peninsula	200-01	40°20′N	26°30′E
Gemena, D.R.C.	262-63	3°14′N	19°47′E
Gemlik, Tur. (gĕm′lĭk)	200-01	40°26′N	29°09′E
Gemsbok National Park, n.p., Bots.	264-65	25°15′S	21°10′E
Gen, stm., China	240-41	50°15′N	119°21′E
Genalē, stm., Afr.	262-63	0°15′S	42°39′E
General Acha, Arg.	173	37°23′S	64°36′W
General Alvear, Arg. (hĕ-nĕ-räl′ äl-vĕ-ä′r)	171	34°59′S	67°42′W
General Alvear, Arg. (hĕ-nĕ-räl′ äl-vĕ-ä′r)	173	36°01′S	60°01′W
General Belgrano, Arg. (hĕ-nĕ-räl′ bĕl-grá′nô)	173	35°46′S	58°29′W
General Carrera, Lago, lk., S.A.	171	46°26′S	71°40′W
General Cepeda, Mex. (hĕ-nĕ-räl′ sĕ-pĕ′dä)	122-23	25°23′N	101°28′W
General Conesa, Arg. (hĕ-nĕ-räl′ kô-nĕ′sä)	171	40°07′S	64°26′W
General Eugenio A. Garay, Para.	168-69	20°30′S	62°11′W
General Guido, Arg. (hĕ-nĕ-räl′ gē′dô)	173	36°40′S	57°48′W
General Juan Madariaga, Arg.	173	37°00′S	57°09′W
General La Madrid, Arg.	173	37°15′S	61°17′W
General Lavalle, Arg. (hĕ-nĕ-räl′ lä-vá′l-yĕ)	173	36°25′S	56°57′W
General Levalle, Arg.	173	34°01′S	63°55′W
General Manuel Belgrano, Cerro, mtn., Arg.	168-69	29°01′S	67°50′W
General Pico, Arg. (hĕ-nĕ-räl′ pē′kô)	173	35°40′S	63°46′W
General Pinedo, Arg.	173	27°19′S	61°17′W
General Roca, Arg. (hĕ-nĕ-räl′ rô-kä)	171	39°01′S	67°35′W
General San Martín, Arg. (hĕ-nĕ-räl′ sän-mär-tē′n)	173	34°34′S	58°33′W
General Santos, Phil.	250	6°07′N	125°10′E
General Viamonte, Arg. (hĕ-nĕ-räl′ vēȧ′môn-tĕ)	173	34°60′S	61°02′W
General Villegas, Arg.	173	35°02′S	63°01′W
Geneseo, Il., U.S. (jĕ-nĕsêō)	114-15	41°27′N	90°09′W
Geneva, Switz. (jĕ-nē′vȧ)	194-95	46°12′N	6°09′E
Geneva, Al., U.S. (jĕ-nē′vȧ)	124-25	31°02′N	85°52′W
Geneva, In., U.S. (jĕ-nē′vȧ)	116-17	40°35′N	84°57′W
Geneva, Ne., U.S. (jĕ-nē′vȧ)	120-21	40°32′N	97°36′W
Geneva, N.Y., U.S. (jĕ-nē′vȧ)	116-17	42°52′N	76°59′W
Geneva, Oh., U.S. (jĕ-nē′vȧ)	116-17	41°48′N	80°56′W
Geneva, Lake, lk., Eur. (lāk jĕ-nē′vȧ)	194-95	46°24′N	6°22′E
Genève, Switz. see Geneva	194-95	46°12′N	6°09′E
Genève, Lac de, lk., Eur. see Geneva, Lake	194-95	46°24′N	6°22′E
Genf, Switz. see Geneva	194-95	46°12′N	6°09′E
Genil, stm., Spain (hå-nēl′)	198-99	37°42′N	5°19′W
Genoa, Italy (jen′ô-ȧ)	200-01	44°25′N	8°57′E
Genova, Italy see Genoa	200-01	44°25′N	8°57′E
Genova, Golfo di, b., Italy (gôl-fô-dē-jĕn′ō-vä)	200-01	44°10′N	8°55′E
Genovesa, Isla, i., Ec. (ĕ′s-lä-gĕ-nō-vĕ-sä)	170a	0°20′N	89°57′W
Gensan, Kor., N. see Wŏnsan	243	39°09′N	127°26′E
Geographe Bay, b., Austl. (jē-ô-graf′ bā)	272-73	33°35′S	115°15′E

n-sing; ŋ-baŋk; ɴ-nasalized n; nŏd; cŏmmit; ōld; ōbey; ôrder; oi-boil; fōōd; ò-as oo in foot; ou-out; s-soft; sh-dish; th-thin; pūre; ûnite; ûrn; stŭd; circŭs; ü-as in French tu; ′-indeterminate vowel.

332 George – Gorgona, Isla PRONOUNCING INDEX

Feature (Pronunciation)	Page	Lat.	Long.
George, S. Afr.	**264-65**	33°58'S	22°27'E
George, stm., Qc., Can.	**130-31**	58°46'N	66°08'W
George, Lake, lk., Ug. (lăk jôrg)	**267**	0°02'N	30°12'E
George, Lake, lk., Fl., U.S. (lăk jôr-ĭj)	**124-25**	29°17'N	81°36'W
Georgetown, On., Can. (jôr-ĭj-toun)	**136-37**	43°39'N	79°55'W
Georgetown, P.E., Can. (jôr-ĭj-toun)	**138-39**	46°11'N	62°32'W
Georgetown, Gam.	**260-61**	13°33'N	14°46'W
George Town, Malay.	**246-47**	5°25'N	100°20'E
Georgetown, De., U.S. (jôrg-toun)	**116-17**	38°41'N	75°23'W
Georgetown, Il., U.S. (jôrg-toun)	**116-17**	39°58'N	87°38'W
Georgetown, Ky., U.S. (jôrg-toun)	**116-17**	38°12'N	84°34'W
Georgetown, Oh., U.S. (jôrg-toun)	**116-17**	38°51'N	83°52'W
Georgetown, S.C., U.S. (jôr-ĭj-toun)	**124-25**	33°23'N	79°18'W
Georgetown, Tx., U.S. (jôrg-toun)	**122-23**	30°38'N	97°41'W
George Town, nat. cap., Cay. Is. (jôr-ĭj-toun)	**142-43**	19°18'N	81°22'W
Georgetown, nat. cap., Guy. (jôrj'toun)	**164-65**	6°48'N	58°09'W
George Washington Birthplace National Monument, n.p., Va., U.S. (jôrj wŏsh'ĭng-tŭn bûrth'plās năsh'ŭn-ăl mŏn'ū-mĕnt)	**116-17**	38°11'N	76°56'W
George Washington Carver National Monument, n.p., Mo., U.S. (jôrg wăsh-ĭng-tŭn kär'vēr năsh'ŭn-ăl mŏn'ū-mĕnt)	**120-21**	37°00'N	94°21'W
George West, Tx., U.S. (jôrg wĕst)	**122-23**	28°20'N	98°07'W
Georgia, nation, Asia (jôr'ji-ă)	**227**	42°0'N	44°00'E
Georgia, state, U.S. (jôr'ji-ă)	**108-09**	32°50'N	83°15'W
Georgiana, Al., U.S. (jôr-jē-ăn'ă)	**124-25**	31°38'N	86°45'W
Georgian Bay, b., On., Can.	**136-37**	45°15'N	80°50'W
Georgiyevsk, Russia (gyôr-gyĕfsk')	**227**	44°09'N	43°29'E
Gera, Ger. (gā'rä)	**194-95**	50°52'N	12°05'E
Geral, Serra, mts., Braz. (sĕr'rá zhâ-räl')	**168-69**	26°30'S	50°30'W
Geraldton, Austl. (jĕr'ăld-tŭn)	**270-71**	28°46'S	114°37'E
Geraldton, On., Can.	**128-29**	49°41'N	86°60'W
Gereshk, Afg.	**232-33**	31°49'N	64°34'E
Gering, Ne., U.S. (gē'rĭng)	**114-15**	41°48'N	103°40'W
Gerlachovský štít, mtn., Slvk.	**194-95**	49°11'N	20°09'E
Germantown, Tn., U.S. (jûr'măn-toun)	**124-25**	35°06'N	89°49'W
Germantown, Wi., U.S. (jûr'măn-toun)	**116-17**	43°14'N	88°07'W
Germany, nation, Eur. (jûr'mȧ-nĭ)	**174-75**	51°0'N	10°00'E
Germiston, S. Afr. (jûr'mĭs-tŭn)	**269c**	26°13'S	28°11'E
Gerona, Spain *see* Girona	**198-99**	41°59'N	2°49'E
Getafe, Spain (hä-tä'fā)	**198-99**	40°19'N	3°44'W
Gettysburg, S.D., U.S. (gĕt'ĭs-bûrg)	**114-15**	45°01'N	99°57'W
Ghaapplato, plat., S. Afr.	**264-65**	27°29'S	24°19'E
Ghadāmis, Libya	**188-89**	30°12'N	9°33'E
Ghāghara, stm., Asia	**234-35**	25°45'N	84°48'E
Ghâghra, stm., Asia *see* Ghāghara	**234-35**	25°45'N	84°48'E
Ghana, nation, Afr. (găn'ä)	**253**	8°0'N	1°00'W
Ghanzi, Bots. (găn'zē)	**264-65**	21°42'S	21°39'E
Ghardaïa, Alg. (gär-dä'ē-ä)	**258-59**	32°33'N	3°40'E
Gharm, Taj.	**232-33**	39°02'N	70°23'E
Gharyān, Libya	**188-89**	32°10'N	13°01'E
Ghāt, Libya	**258-59**	24°56'N	10°12'E
Ghawdex, i., Malta *see* Gozo	**200b**	36°03'N	14°15'E
Ghazal, Bahr el, stm., Chad (bär ĕl ghä-zäl')	**258-59**	13°05'N	15°20'E
Ghāziābād, India	**234-35**	28°40'N	77°26'E
Ghaznī, Afg.	**232-33**	33°33'N	68°25'E
Ghazzah, Gaza (gä'ziä) *see* Gaza	**228-29**	31°30'N	34°28'E
Ghijduwon, Uzb.	**232-33**	40°06'N	64°41'E
Ghorīān, Afg.	**232-33**	34°21'N	61°29'E
Gibara, Cuba (hē-bä'rä)	**142-43**	21°07'N	76°08'W
Gibraleón, Spain (hē-brä-lå-ōn')	**198-99**	37°23'N	6°58'W
Gibraltar, dep., Eur. (gĭ-bräl-tă'r)	**174-75**	36°08'N	5°21'W
Gibraltar, nat. cap., Gib. (gĭ-bräl-tă'r)	**198-99**	36°08'N	5°21'W
Gibraltar, Estrecho de, strt., *see* Gibraltar, Strait of	**198-99**	35°57'N	5°36'W
Gibraltar, Strait of, strt., (stāt ŭv gĭ-bräl-tă'r)	**198-99**	35°57'N	5°36'W
Gibson City, Il., U.S. (gĭb'sŭn sĭ'tē)	**116-17**	40°28'N	88°22'W
Gibson Desert, des., Austl. (gĭb'sŭn dĕs'ērt)	**272-73**	24°30'S	126°00'E
Giddings, Tx., U.S. (gĭd'ĭngz)	**122-23**	30°11'N	96°56'W
Gien, Fr. (zhē-ăn')	**196-97**	47°41'N	2°38'E
Gießen, Ger. (gēs'sĕn)	**194-95**	50°35'N	8°40'E
Gifu, Japan (gē'fōō)	**245**	35°25'N	136°45'E
Gijón, Spain (hē-hōn')	**198-99**	43°32'N	5°40'W
Gila, stm., U.S. (hē'lȧ)	**110-11**	32°43'N	114°33'W
Gila Bend, Az., U.S. (hē'lȧ bĕnd)	**118-19**	32°57'N	112°43'W
Gila Cliff Dwellings National Monument, n.p., N.M., U.S. (hē'lȧ klĭf dwĕl'ĭngz năsh'ŭn-ăl mŏn'ū-mĕnt)	**118-19**	33°02'N	108°16'W
Gilbert, Mn., U.S. (gĭl'bērt)	**114-15**	47°29'N	92°28'W
Gilbert, Mount, mtn., B.C., Can. (mount gĭl-bērt)	**132-33**	50°54'N	124°17'W
Gilbert Islands, nation, Oc. *see* Kiribati	**280-81**	5°0'S	170°00'W
Gilbert Islands, is., Kir. (gĭl-bērt ī'lăndz) *see* Kiribati	**280-81**	0°30'S	174°00'E
Gilbués, Braz.	**166-67**	9°50'S	45°21'W
Gilford Island, i., B.C., Can. (gĭl'fērd ī'lănd)	**132-33**	50°45'N	126°20'W
Gilgandra, Austl.	**276**	31°43'S	148°40'E
Gilgit, Pak. (gĭl'gĭt)	**232-33**	35°53'N	74°21'E
Gilgit, stm., Pak.	**232-33**	35°42'N	74°38'E
Gil Island, i., B.C., Can. (gĭl ī'lănd)	**132-33**	53°11'N	129°15'W
Gillam, Mb., Can.	**134-35**	56°21'N	94°43'W
Gillette, Wy., U.S. (jĭ-lĕt')	**112-13**	44°18'N	105°30'W
Gillingham, Eng., U.K. (gĭl'ĭng ăm)	**190-91**	51°23'N	0°34'E
Gilman, Il., U.S. (gĭl'măn)	**116-17**	40°46'N	87°59'W
Gilmer, Tx., U.S. (gĭl'mēr)	**120-21**	32°44'N	94°57'W
Gīlo, stm., Eth.	**262-63**	8°07'N	33°11'E
Gilroy, Ca., U.S. (gĭl-roi')	**118-19**	37°01'N	121°34'W
Giluwe, Mount, mtn., Pap. N. Gui.	**277**	6°02'S	143°51'E
Gilyuy, stm., Russia	**218-19**	53°59'N	127°27'E
Gimcheon, Kor., S. *see* Kimch'ŏn	**243**	36°07'N	128°07'E
Gimli, Mb., Can. (gĭm'lē)	**134-35**	50°38'N	96°59'W
Gioia del Colle, Italy (jô'yä dĕl kôl'lā)	**200-01**	40°48'N	16°55'E
Girardot, Col. (hē-rär-dōt')	**163c**	4°18'N	74°47'W
Giresun, Tur. (ghĕr'ĕ-sòn')	**186-87**	40°55'N	38°24'E
Girga, Egypt	**268b**	26°20'N	31°53'E
Girīdīh, India (jē-rē-dē)	**234-35**	24°11'N	86°18'E
Girona, Spain	**198-99**	41°59'N	2°49'E
Girvan, Scot., U.K. (gûr'văn)	**190-91**	55°15'N	4°52'W
Gisborne, N.Z. (gĭz'bŭrn)	**278**	38°40'S	178°01'E
Gisenyi, Rw.	**267**	1°42'S	29°16'E
Gisors, Fr. (zhē-zôr')	**196-97**	49°17'N	1°47'E
Gitarama, Rw.	**267**	2°04'S	29°44'E
Gitega, Bdi.	**267**	3°21'S	29°54'E
Giurgiu, Rom. (jòr'jò)	**200-01**	43°54'N	25°58'E
Givet, Fr. (zhē-vĕ')	**196-97**	50°08'N	4°50'E
Giyon, Eth.	**269d**	8°32'N	37°59'E
Giza, Egypt	**268b**	30°01'N	31°13'E
Gizo, Sol. Is.	**279e**	8°06'S	156°50'E
Giżycko, Pol. (gĭ'zhĭ-ko)	**194-95**	54°02'N	21°46'E
Gjoa Haven, Nu., Can.	**128-29**	68°39'N	95°55'W
Gjøvik, Nor. (gyû'vĕk)	**192-93**	60°48'N	10°41'E
Glace Bay, N.S., Can. (gläs bā)	**138-39**	46°13'N	59°58'W
Glacier Bay National Park and Preserve, n.p., Ak., U.S.	**126**	59°04'N	136°36'W
Glacier National Park, n.p., B.C., Can. (glā'shēr năsh'ŭn-ăl pärk)	**132-33**	51°15'N	117°35'W
Glacier National Park, n.p., Mt., U.S.	**112-13**	48°35'N	113°40'W
Glacier Peak, vol., Wa., U.S. (glā'shēr pēk) (glā'shēr pēk)	**112-13**	48°07'N	121°07'W
Gladstone, Austl. (glăd'stōn)	**277**	23°51'S	151°15'E
Gladstone, Austl. (glăd'stōn)	**276**	33°17'S	138°21'E
Gladstone, Mi., U.S. (glăd'stōn)	**116-17**	45°51'N	87°01'W
Gladstone, Mo., U.S. (glăd'stōn)	**120-21**	39°14'N	94°35'W
Gladwin, Mi., U.S. (glăd'wĭn)	**116-17**	43°59'N	84°29'W
Glåma, stm., Nor. *see* Glomma	**184-85**	59°11'N	10°58'E
Glasgow, Scot., U.K. (glås'gō)	**190-91**	55°53'N	4°15'W
Glasgow, Ky., U.S.	**124-25**	37°00'N	85°55'W
Glasgow, Mt., U.S.	**112-13**	48°12'N	106°38'W
Glauchau, Ger. (glou'kou)	**194-95**	50°49'N	12°33'E
Glazov, Russia (glä'zôf)	**186-87**	58°08'N	52°39'E
Gleiwitz, Pol. *see* Gliwice	**194-95**	50°17'N	18°40'E
Glen Canyon, val., U.S. (glĕn kăn'yŭn)	**118-19**	37°10'N	110°50'W
Glencoe, S. Afr. (glĕn-cô)	**269c**	28°12'S	30°06'E
Glendale, Az., U.S. (glĕn'dāl)	**118-19**	33°32'N	112°12'W
Glendale, Ca., U.S. (glĕn'dāl)	**118-19**	34°08'N	118°14'W
Glendive, Mt., U.S. (glĕn'dīv)	**112-13**	47°06'N	104°43'W
Glen Innes, Austl. (glĕn ĭn'ĕs)	**276**	29°44'S	151°44'E
Glenns Ferry, Id., U.S. (glĕns fĕr'ē)	**112-13**	42°58'N	115°18'W
Glenrock, Wy., U.S. (glĕn'rŏk)	**112-13**	42°52'N	105°53'W
Glens Falls, N.Y., U.S. (glĕnz fôlz)	**116-17**	43°19'N	73°39'W
Glittertinden, mtn., Nor.	**192-93**	61°39'N	8°33'E
Gliwice, Pol. (gwĭ-wĭt'sĕ)	**194-95**	50°17'N	18°40'E
Globe, Az., U.S. (glōb)	**118-19**	33°24'N	110°47'W
Glomma, stm., Nor.	**184-85**	59°11'N	10°58'E
Glorieuses, Îles, is., Reu.	**264-65**	11°30'S	47°20'E
Glorioso Islands, is., Reu. *see* Glorieuses, Îles	**264-65**	11°30'S	47°20'E
Gloucester, Eng., U.K. (glŏs'tēr)	**190-91**	51°53'N	2°14'W
Gloversville, N.Y., U.S. (glŭv'ērz-vĭl)	**116-17**	43°03'N	74°21'W
Glovertown, Nf., Can. (glŭv'ēr-toun)	**138-39**	48°40'N	54°03'W
Glückstadt, Ger. (glük-shtät)	**194-95**	53°47'N	9°26'E
Gmunden, Aus. (g'mòn'dĕn)	**194-95**	47°55'N	13°47'E
Gnesen, Pol. *see* Gniezno	**194-95**	52°32'N	17°37'E
Gniezno, Pol. (g'nyăz'nô)	**194-95**	52°32'N	17°37'E
Gnjilane, Serb. (gnyē'lä-nĕ)	**200-01**	42°28'N	21°29'E
Goa, state, India (gō'ă)	**236**	15°20'N	74°00'E
Goālpāra, India	**234-35**	26°10'N	90°37'E
Goba, Eth. (gō'bä)	**269d**	7°00'N	39°59'E
Gobabis, Nmb. (gō-bä'bĭs)	**264-65**	22°27'S	18°58'E
Gobernador Gregores, Arg.	**171**	48°46'S	70°15'W
Gobernador Vera, Arg. *see* Vera	**173**	29°28'S	60°13'W
Gobi Desert, des., Asia (gō'be dĕs'ērt)	**240-41**	43°0'N	105°00'E
Goch, Ger. (gôk)	**194-95**	51°41'N	6°09'E
Godāvari, stm., India (gô-dä'vŭ-rē)	**236**	16°59'N	81°47'E
Goderich, On., Can. (gōd'rĭch)	**136-37**	43°45'N	81°42'W
Godfrey, Il., U.S. (gŏd'frē)	**120-21**	38°57'N	90°11'W
Godhavn, Green. (gōdh'håvn)	**284-85**	69°15'N	53°33'W
Godhra, India	**234-35**	22°46'N	73°37'E
Godoy Cruz, Arg.	**163e**	32°55'S	68°50'W
Gods, stm., Mb., Can. (gŏdz)	**134-35**	56°23'N	92°51'W
Gods Lake, lk., Mb., Can.	**134-35**	54°43'N	94°14'W
Godthåb, nat. cap., Green. (gŏt'hòb)	**284-85**	64°11'N	51°44'W
Godwin Austen, mtn., Asia *see* K2	**232-33**	35°53'N	76°30'E
Goeie Hoop, Kaap die, c., S. Afr. *see* Good Hope, Cape of	**264-65**	34°21'S	18°28'E
Goiana, Braz.	**163d**	7°33'S	34°59'W
Goiânia, Braz. (gô-yá'nyä)	**168-69**	16°40'S	49°16'W
Goiás, Braz. (gô-yá's)	**168-69**	15°55'S	50°07'W
Goiás, state, Braz. (gô-yá's)	**166-67**	16°0'S	50°00'W
Gökçeada, i., Tur.	**200-01**	40°10'N	25°50'E
Gökova Körfezi, b., Tur.	**200-01**	36°54'N	27°51'E
Göksu, stm., Tur. (gûk'sōō')	**228-29**	36°19'N	34°03'E
Gol, Nor. (gûl)	**192-93**	60°42'N	8°57'E
Gold Coast, Austl. *see* Southport	**276**	27°58'S	153°25'E
Golden, B.C., Can. (gōl'dĕn)	**132-33**	51°18'N	116°58'W
Golden, Co., U.S. (gōl'dĕn)	**118-19**	39°45'N	105°13'W
Goldendale, Wa., U.S. (gōl'dĕn-dāl)	**112-13**	45°49'N	120°50'W
Golden Hinde, mtn., B.C., Can. (gōl'dĕn hīnd)	**132-33**	49°40'N	125°45'W
Goldsboro, N.C., U.S. (gōldz-bûr'ô)	**124-25**	35°23'N	77°60'W
Goldthwaite, Tx., U.S. (gōld'thwāt)	**122-23**	31°27'N	98°34'W
Golfito, C.R. (gôl-fē'tō)	**149**	8°38'N	83°10'W
Goliad, Tx., U.S. (gō-lĭ-ăd')	**122-23**	28°40'N	97°23'W
Golmud, China	**240-41**	36°25'N	94°54'E
Goma, D.R.C.	**267**	1°41'S	29°13'E
Gombe, Nig.	**260-61**	10°17'N	11°10'E
Gomel', Bela. *see* Homel'	**202-03**	52°26'N	30°59'E
Gómez Palacio, Mex. (gô'mĕz pä-lä'syō)	**122-23**	25°35'N	103°30'W
Gonābād, Iran	**232-33**	34°21'N	58°41'E
Gonaïves, Haiti (gō-nà-ēv')	**142-43**	19°27'N	72°41'W
Gonam, stm., Russia	**218-19**	57°19'N	131°15'E
Gonarezhou National Park, n.p., Zimb.	**264-65**	21°34'S	31°56'E
Gonâve, Île de la, i., Haiti (ēl-dē-lá-gô-náv')	**142-43**	18°51'N	73°03'W
Gonbad-e Kāvūs, Iran	**232-33**	37°15'N	55°10'E
Gonda, India	**234-35**	27°08'N	81°58'E
Gondar, Eth. *see* Gonder	**266**	12°37'N	37°28'E
Gonder, Eth.	**266**	12°37'N	37°28'E
Gondia, India	**234-35**	21°28'N	80°12'E
Gongbo'gyamda, China	**238-39**	29°55'N	93°26'E
Gongga Shan, mtn., China (gôŋ-gä shän)	**238-39**	29°35'N	101°51'E
Gongola, stm., Nig.	**260-61**	9°29'N	12°03'E
Gongxian, China	**240-41**	34°48'N	113°03'E
Gongzhuling, China	**240-41**	43°30'N	124°49'E
Gonzales, La., U.S. (gŏn-zä'lĕz)	**124-25**	30°14'N	90°55'W
Gonzales, Tx., U.S. (gŏn-zä'lĕz)	**122-23**	29°30'N	97°27'W
Goodenough Island, i., Pap. N. Gui.	**277**	9°20'S	150°15'E
Good Hope, Cape of, c., S. Afr. (kāp ŏv gōōd hōp)	**264-65**	34°21'S	18°28'E
Good Hope Mountain, mtn., B.C., Can. (gōōd hōp moun'tĭn)	**132-33**	51°09'N	124°10'W
Gooding, Id., U.S. (gòd'ĭng)	**112-13**	42°57'N	114°43'W
Goodland, Ks., U.S. (gòd'lănd)	**120-21**	39°20'N	101°43'W
Goole, Eng., U.K. (gōōl)	**190-91**	53°42'N	0°53'W
Goondiwindi, Austl.	**276**	28°32'S	150°19'E
Goose Lake, lk., U.S. (gōōs lāk)	**112-13**	41°57'N	120°25'W
Goqên, China	**238-39**	29°09'N	97°14'E
Gorakhpur, India (gō'rŭk-pōōr)	**234-35**	26°46'N	83°22'E
Gorda, Punta, c., Cuba (pōō'n-tä-gôr-dä)	**142-43**	22°23'N	82°09'W
Gorgān, Iran	**232-33**	36°51'N	54°26'E
Gorgona, Isla, i., Col.	**164-65**	2°58'N	78°11'W

PRONOUNCING INDEX

Gorgona, Isola di – Great Pee Dee 333

Feature (Pronunciation)	Page	Lat.	Long.
Gorgona, Isola di, i., Italy (gôr-gō´nä)	200-01	43°26'N	9°54'E
Gori, Geor. (gō´rē)	227	41°59'N	44°06'E
Gorica, Italy *see* Gorizia	200-01	45°57'N	13°38'E
Gorinchem, Neth. (gō´rĭn-kĕm)	190-91	51°50'N	5°01'E
Gorizia, Italy (gô-rē´tsē-yä)	200-01	45°57'N	13°38'E
Gorkhā, Nepal	234-35	28°0'N	84°37'E
Gorky, Russia *see* Nizhniy Novgorod	186-87	56°19'N	44°01'E
Gorki Reservoir, res., Russia (gôr´kē rĕ´sĕr-vwär) *see* Gor'kovskoye Vodokhranilishche	186-87	57°02'N	43°10'E
Gor'kovskoye Vodokhranilishche, res., Russia	186-87	57°02'N	43°10'E
Gorlice, Pol. (gôr-lē´tsĕ)	194-95	49°39'N	21°10'E
Görlitz, Ger. (gûr´lĭts)	194-95	51°09'N	14°59'E
Gorlovka, Ukr. *see* Horlivka	202-03	48°20'N	38°03'E
Gorna Oryakhovitsa, Blg. (gôr´nä-ôr-yĕk´ô-vē-tsá)	200-01	43°08'N	25°42'E
Gornji Milanovac, Serb. (gôrn´yē-mē´la-nô-väts)	200-01	44°01'N	20°27'E
Gorno-Altaysk, Russia (gôr´nŭ´ŭl-tīsk´)	226	51°58'N	85°51'E
Gornozavodsk, Russia	244	46°33'N	141°51'E
Gorodets, Russia	186-87	56°39'N	43°28'E
Goroka, Pap. N. Gui.	277	6°05'S	145°24'E
Gorontalo, Indon. (gō-rōn-tä´lō)	248-49	0°32'N	123°04'E
Görz, Italy *see* Gorizia	200-01	45°57'N	13°38'E
Gorzów Wielkopolski, Pol. (gō-zhōōv´vyĕl-ko-pōl´skē)	194-95	52°44'N	15°14'E
Gosford, Austl.	276	33°25'S	151°21'E
Goshen, In., U.S. (gō´shĕn)	116-17	41°35'N	85°49'W
Goslar, Ger. (gôs´lär)	194-95	51°55'N	10°26'E
Gostivar, Mac. (gos´tē-vär)	200-01	41°48'N	20°55'E
Gostynin, Pol. (gôs-tē´nĭn)	194-95	52°26'N	19°28'E
Göta, stm., Swe. (gōĕtä)	192-93	57°41'N	11°53'E
Göteborg, Swe.	192-93	57°43'N	11°58'E
Gotha, Ger. (gō´tá)	194-95	50°57'N	10°42'E
Gothenburg, Swe. *see* Göteborg	192-93	57°43'N	11°58'E
Gothenburg, Ne., U.S. (gŏth´ĕn-bûrg)	114-15	40°56'N	100°10'W
Gotland, i., Swe.	192-93	57°30'N	18°33'E
Gotō-rettō, is., Japan	244	32°50'N	129°00'E
Gotska Sandön, i., Swe.	192-93	58°22'N	19°16'E
Göttingen, Ger. (gût´ĭng-ĕn)	194-95	51°32'N	9°56'E
Gouda, Neth. (gou´dä)	190-91	52°01'N	4°42'E
Gouin, Réservoir, res., Qc., Can.	136-37	48°37'N	74°55'W
Goulburn, Austl. (gōl´bŭrn)	276	34°45'S	149°43'E
Goundam, Mali (gōōn-däɴ´)	258-59	16°25'N	3°40'W
Gouverneur, N.Y., U.S. (gŭv-ĕr-nōōr´)	116-17	44°20'N	75°28'W
Governador Valadares, Braz. (gô-vĕr-nä-dō-´r vä-lä-dä´rĕs)	172	18°53'S	41°58'W
Goya, Arg. (gō´yä)	173	29°09'S	59°15'W
Goyania, Braz. *see* Goiânia	168-69	16°40'S	49°16'W
Göyçay, Azer. (gĕ-ôk´chī)	227	40°39'N	47°45'E
Gozo, i., Malta	200b	36°03'N	14°15'E
Graaff-Reinet, S. Afr. (gräf´rī´nĕt)	264-65	32°16'S	24°33'E
Gračac, Cro. (grä´chäts)	200-01	44°18'N	15°50'E
Graceville, Fl., U.S. (grās´vĭl)	124-25	30°57'N	85°31'W
Gracias a Dios, Cabo, c., N.A.	149	14°60'N	83°10'W
Graciosa, i., Port. (grä-syō´sä)	199c	39°04'N	28°00'W
Gradačac, Bos. (gra-dä´chats)	200-01	44°53'N	18°26'E
Gradaús, Braz.	166-67	7°43'S	51°10'W
Grænlandshav, s., *see* Greenland Sea	288	77°0'N	1°00'W
Grænlandssund, strt., *see* Denmark Strait	86	67°0'N	25°00'W
Grafton, Austl. (graf´tŭn)	276	29°42'S	152°56'E
Grafton, N.D., U.S. (graf´tŭn)	114-15	48°25'N	97°25'W
Grafton, W.V., U.S. (graf´tŭn)	116-17	39°20'N	80°01'W
Grafton, Cape, c., Austl.	277	16°53'S	145°56'E
Graham, N.C., U.S. (grā´ăm)	124-25	36°04'N	79°24'W
Graham, Tx., U.S. (grā´ăm)	120-21	33°07'N	98°35'W
Graham Island, i., B.C., Can. (grā´ăm ī´lănd)	132-33	53°47'N	132°34'W
Grahamstad, S. Afr. *see* Grahamstown	264-65	33°18'S	26°31'E
Grahamstown, S. Afr. (grā´ăms´toun)	264-65	33°18'S	26°31'E
Grajaú, Braz.	166-67	5°47'S	46°07'W
Grajaú, stm., Braz.	166-67	3°41'S	44°49'W
Grajewo, Pol. (grä-yä´vo)	194-95	53°39'N	22°28'E
Grampian Mountains, mts., Scot., U.K. (grăm´pĭ-ăn moun´tĭnz)	190-91	56°55'N	4°00'W
Grampians National Park, n.p., Austl.	276	37°15'S	142°25'E
Granada, Nic. (grä-nä´dhä)	149	11°56'N	85°58'W
Granada, Spain (grä-nä´dä)	198-99	37°11'N	3°36'W
Granbury, Tx., U.S. (grăn´bĕr-ĭ)	120-21	32°27'N	97°48'W
Granby, Qc., Can. (grăn´bĭ)	136-37	45°24'N	72°43'W
Granby, Co., U.S. (grăn´bĭ)	118-19	40°06'N	105°57'W
Granby, Mo., U.S. (grăn´bĭ)	120-21	36°55'N	94°15'W
Gran Canaria, i., Spain (grän´kä-nä´rē-ä)	199d	27°52'N	15°37'W
Gran Chaco, reg., S.A. (grán´chá´kō)	168-69	23°0'S	60°00'W
Grand, stm., On., Can. (grănd)	136-37	42°52'N	79°34'W
Grand, stm., Mi., U.S. (grănd)	116-17	43°04'N	86°14'W
Grand Bahama, i., Bah. (grănd bȧ-hā´mȧ)	142-43	26°38'N	78°25'W
Grand Bank, Nf., Can. (grănd băngk)	138-39	47°06'N	55°45'W
Grand-Bassam, C. Iv. (grän bȧ-säɴ´)	260-61	5°13'N	3°45'W
Grand-Bourg, Guad. (gräɴ bōōr´)	143b	15°54'N	61°19'W
Grand Canal, can., China (grănd kȧ´năl)	240-41	32°11'N	119°33'E
Grand Canyon, Az., U.S. (grănd kăn´yŭn)	118-19	36°02'N	112°10'W
Grand Canyon, val., Az., U.S. (grănd kăn´yŭn)	118-19	36°22'N	112°30'W
Grand Canyon National Park, n.p., Az., U.S. (grănd kăn´yŭn năsh´ŭn-ăl pärk)	118-19	36°20'N	112°53'W
Grand Canyon-Parashant National Monument, n.p., Az., U.S.	118-19	36°20'N	113°44'W
Grand Cayman, i., Cay. Is. (grănd kā´măn) (grănd kī-măn´)	142-43	19°20'N	81°15'W
Grand Coulee Dam, d., Wa., U.S. (grănd kōō´lē dăm)	112-13	47°57'N	119°01'W
Grande, stm., Bol. (grän´dĕ)	168-69	15°50'S	64°47'W
Grande, stm., Braz. (grän´dĕ)	166-67	11°05'S	43°09'W
Grande, stm., Braz. (grän´dĕ)	168-69	20°08'S	51°00'W
Grande, Bahía, b., Arg. (bä-ē´ä-grán´dĕ)	171	51°15'S	68°31'W
Grande, Cuchilla, mts., Ur. (kōō-chē´l-yä grän´dĕ)	173	33°25'S	55°06'W
Grande, Ilha, i., Braz. (ē´lä-grän´dĕ)	172	23°09'S	44°14'W
Grande, Rio, stm., N.A. (rē´ō grăn´dā) *see* Rio Grande	110-11	25°57'N	97°09'W
Grande Cayemite, i., Haiti	142-43	18°37'N	73°45'W
Grande Comore, i., Com. *see* Njazidja	264-65	11°35'S	43°20'E
Grande de Santiago, stm., Mex. (grä´n-dĕ-dĕ-sän-tyá´gô)	146-47	21°37'N	105°28'W
Grande do Gurupá, Ilha, i., Braz.	166-67	1°0'S	51°30'W
Grande Prairie, Ab., Can. (grănd prâr´ĭ)	132-33	55°10'N	118°48'W
Grand Erg de Bilma, des., Niger	258-59	18°30'N	14°00'E
Grand Erg Occidental, des., Alg.	258-59	30°56'N	1°35'E
Grand Erg Oriental, des., Alg.	258-59	30°30'N	7°00'E
Grandes, Salinas, pl., Arg.	168-69	30°06'S	65°14'W
Grandes Antillas, Islas, is., N.A. *see* Greater Antilles	142-43	20°0'N	74°00'W
Grande-Terre, i., Guad.	143b	16°19'N	61°22'W
Grand Falls, N.B., Can. (grănd fôlz)	138-39	47°03'N	67°44'W
Grand Falls-Windsor, Nf., Can.	138-39	48°56'N	55°39'W
Grandfather Mountain, mtn., N.C., U.S. (grănd-fä-thēr moun´tĭn)	124-25	36°07'N	81°48'W
Grandfield, Ok., U.S. (grănd´fēld)	120-21	34°14'N	98°41'W
Grand Forks, B.C., Can. (grănd fôrks)	132-33	49°02'N	118°27'W
Grand Forks, N.D., U.S. (grănd fôrks)	114-15	47°55'N	97°03'W
Grand Haven, Mi., U.S. (grănd hā´v'n)	116-17	43°04'N	86°13'W
Grand Island, Ne., U.S. (grănd ī´lănd)	114-15	40°55'N	98°21'W
Grand Island, i., Mi., U.S. (grănd ī´lănd)	114-15	46°30'N	86°40'W
Grand Junction, Co., U.S. (grănd jŭngk´shŭn)	118-19	39°04'N	108°34'W
Grand Lake, lk., N.B., Can. (grănd lāk)	138-39	45°53'N	66°03'W
Grand Lake, lk., Nf., Can. (grănd lāk)	138-39	48°59'N	57°22'W
Grand Lake, lk., La., U.S. (grănd lāk)	122-23	29°53'N	92°45'W
Grand Ledge, Mi., U.S. (grănd lĕj)	116-17	42°45'N	84°44'W
Grand Manan Island, i., N.B., Can. (grănd mȧ-năn ī´lănd)	138-39	44°43'N	66°49'W
Grand-Mère, Qc., Can. (gräɴ mâr´)	136-37	46°37'N	72°42'W
Grândola, Port. (grăɴ´dô-lȧ)	198-99	38°10'N	8°34'W
Grand Portage Indian Reservation, ind. res., Mn., U.S. (grănd pōr´tĭj ĭn´dĭ-ăn rĕ-sĕr-vā´shĕn)	114-15	47°58'N	89°47'W
Grand Rapids, Mb., Can. (grănd răp´ĭdz)	134-35	53°12'N	99°17'W
Grand Rapids, Mi., U.S. (grănd răp´ĭdz)	116-17	42°58'N	85°40'W
Grand Rapids, Mn., U.S. (grănd răp´ĭdz)	114-15	47°14'N	93°31'W
Grand-Sault, N.B., Can. *see* Grand Falls	138-39	47°03'N	67°44'W
Grand Staircase-Escalante National Monument, n.p., Ut., U.S.	118-19	37°30'N	111°30'W
Grand Teton, mtn., Wy., U.S. (grănd tē´tŏn)	112-13	43°44'N	110°48'W
Grand Teton National Park, n.p., Wy., U.S. (grănd tē´tŏn năsh´ŭn-ăl pärk)	112-13	43°56'N	110°46'W
Grand Traverse Bay, b., Mi., U.S. (grănd trăv´ērs bā)	116-17	45°02'N	85°30'W
Grand Turk, nat. cap., T./C. Is. (grănd tûrk)	142-43	21°27'N	71°08'W
Grandview, Mb., Can.	134-35	51°10'N	100°42'W
Grandview, Wa., U.S. (grănd´vyōō)	112-13	46°15'N	119°54'W
Grangeville, Id., U.S. (grānj´vĭl)	112-13	45°56'N	116°07'W
Granite City, Il., U.S. (grăn´ĭt sĭ´tē)	120-21	38°42'N	90°09'W
Granite Falls, Mn., U.S. (grăn´ĭt fôlz)	114-15	44°49'N	95°33'W
Granite Falls, N.C., U.S. (grăn´ĭt fôlz)	124-25	35°48'N	81°26'W
Granite Peak, mtn., Mt., U.S.	112-13	45°10'N	109°48'W
Gränna, Swe. (grĕn´á)	192-93	58°00'N	14°28'E
Granollers, Spain (grä-nôl-yĕrs´)	198-99	41°37'N	2°17'E
Grantham, Eng., U.K. (grăn´tăm)	190-91	52°55'N	0°39'W
Grants, N.M., U.S.	118-19	35°10'N	107°51'W
Grants Pass, Or., U.S. (grȧnts pȧs)	112-13	42°26'N	123°19'W
Granville, Fr. (grän-vēl´)	196-97	48°51'N	1°35'W
Granville, N.Y., U.S. (grăn´vĭl)	116-17	43°24'N	73°16'W
Granville Lake, lk., Mb., Can.	134-35	56°17'N	100°30'W
Gräsö, i., Swe.	192-93	60°24'N	18°25'E
Grasse, Fr. (gräs)	196-97	43°40'N	6°55'E
Grasslands National Park, n.p., Sk., Can.	134-35	49°04'N	106°58'W
Grates Point, c., Nf., Can. (grāts point)	138-39	48°10'N	52°57'W
Graudenz, Pol. *see* Grudziądz	194-95	53°29'N	18°44'E
Gravatá, Braz.	163d	8°12'S	35°34'W
Gravelbourg, Sk., Can. (grăv´ĕl-bôrg)	134-35	49°52'N	106°34'W
Gravenhage, 's-, nat. cap., Neth. *see* Hague, The	190-91	52°06'N	4°18'E
Gray, Fr. (grå)	196-97	47°26'N	5°35'E
Grayling, Mi., U.S. (grā´lĭng)	116-17	44°40'N	84°42'W
Grays Peak, mtn., Co., U.S. (grāz pēk)	118-19	39°37'N	105°45'W
Graz, Aus. (gräts)	194-95	47°05'N	15°27'E
Great Artesian Basin, bas., Austl. (grāt är-tēzh-ăn bā´s'n)	272-73	25°0'S	143°00'E
Great Australian Bight, b., Austl. (grāt ôs-trā´lĭ-ăn bīt)	272-73	35°0'S	130°00'E
Great Barrier Island, i., N.Z. (grāt băr´ĭ-ēr ī´lănd)	278	36°10'S	175°25'E
Great Barrier Reef, rf., Austl.	277	18°0'S	146°50'E
Great Barrier Reef Marine Park, n.p., Austl.	277	18°0'S	146°50'E
Great Basin, bas., U.S. (grāt bā´s'n)	110-11	40°0'N	117°00'W
Great Basin National Park, n.p., Nv., U.S.	118-19	38°55'N	114°14'W
Great Bear Lake, lk., N.T., Can. (grāt bâr lāk)	130-31	66°0'N	120°00'W
Great Bend, Ks., U.S. (grāt bĕnd)	120-21	38°22'N	98°45'W
Great Britain, nation, Eur. *see* United Kingdom	174-75	54°0'N	2°00'W
Great Britain, i., U.K. (grāt brĭt´'n)	190-91	54°0'N	2°00'W
Great Channel, strt., Asia	246-47	6°25'N	94°20'E
Great Dismal Swamp, sw., U.S. (grāt dĭz´măl swŏmp)	124-25	36°28'N	76°28'W
Great Divide Basin, bas., Wy., U.S. (grāt dĭ-vīd´ bā´s'n)	112-13	42°0'N	108°10'W
Great Dividing Range, mts., Austl. (grāt dĭ-vī-dĭng rānj)	270-71	25°0'S	147°00'E
Greater Antilles, is., N.A. (grāt´ēr ăn-tĭ´lēz)	142-43	20°0'N	74°00'W
Greater Khingan Range, mts., China (grāt´ēr hĭŋ-gän rānj)	222-23	49°0'N	122°00'E
Greater Sunda Islands, is., Asia (grāt´ēr sōōn´dă ī´lăndz)	248-49	2°0'S	110°00'E
Great Exuma, i., Bah. (grāt ĕk-sōō´mä)	142-43	23°32'N	75°50'W
Great Falls, Mt., U.S. (grāt fôlz)	112-13	47°30'N	111°18'W
Great Falls, S.C., U.S. (grāt fôlz)	124-25	34°34'N	80°54'W
Great Grimsby, Eng., U.K. *see* Grimsby	190-91	53°35'N	0°05'W
Grimsby, Eng., U.K.	190-91	53°35'N	0°05'W
Great Guana Cay, i., Bah. (grāt gwä´nä kē)	142-43	24°0'N	76°20'W
Great Inagua, i., Bah. (grāt ē-nä´gwä)	142-43	21°05'N	73°18'W
Great Indian Desert, des., Asia (grāt ĭn´dĭ-ăn dĕs´ērt)	232-33	27°0'N	71°00'E
Great Karoo, plat., S. Afr.	264-65	32°47'S	22°32'E
Great Limpopo Transfrontier Park, n.p., Afr.	264-65	23°0'S	31°30'E
Great Namaqualand, hist. reg., Nmb.	264-65	25°0'S	17°00'E
Great Nicobar, i., India (grāt nĭk-ô-bär´)	246-47	7°0'N	93°50'E
Great Palm Island, i., Austl.	277	18°43'S	146°37'E
Great Pee Dee, stm., S.C., U.S. (grāt pē-dē´)	124-25	33°18'N	79°17'W

n-sing; ŋ-baŋk; ɴ-nasalized n; nŏd; cŏmmit; ōld; ôbey; ôrder; oi-boil; fōōd; ŏŏ-as oo in foot; ou-out; s-soft; sh-dish; th-thin; pūre; ûnite; ûrn; stŭd; circŭs; ü-as in French tu; ´-indeterminate vowel.

334 Great Plains – Güines
PRONOUNCING INDEX

Feature (Pronunciation)	Page	Lat.	Long.
Great Plains, pl., U.S. (grāt plānz)	**110-11**	42°0'N	100°00'W
Great Ruaha, stm., Tan.	**267**	7°56'S	37°48'E
Great Salt Lake, lk., Ut., U.S. (grāt sôlt lāk)	**112-13**	41°10'N	112°30'W
Great Salt Lake Desert, des., Ut., U.S. (grāt sôlt lāk dĕs'ērt)	**110-11**	40°40'N	113°30'W
Great Sand Dunes National Park and Preserve, n.p., Co., U.S.	**118-19**	37°46'N	105°33'W
Great Sandy Desert, des., Austl. (grāt săn'dē dĕs'ērt)	**272-73**	21°30'S	125°00'E
Great Sandy National Park, n.p., Austl.	**277**	24°55'S	153°16'E
Great Slave Lake, lk., N.T., Can. (grāt slāv lāk)	**130-31**	61°30'N	114°00'W
Great Smoky Mountains National Park, n.p., U.S. (grāt smōk-ê moun'tĭnz năsh'ŭn-ăl pärk)	**124-25**	35°39'N	83°30'W
Great Victoria Desert, des., Austl. (grāt vĭk-tō'rĭ-á dĕs'ērt)	**272-73**	28°30'S	127°45'E
Great Wall, p.o.i., China	**240-41**	40°0'N	112°30'E
Gréboun, mtn., Niger	**258-59**	20°0'N	8°35'E
Gredos, Sierra de, mts., Spain (syĕr'rä dā grā'dōs)	**198-99**	40°20'N	4°51'W
Greece, nation, Eur. (grēs)	**174-75**	39°0'N	22°00'E
Greeley, Co., U.S. (grē'lĭ)	**114-15**	40°24'N	104°41'W
Greeley, Ne., U.S. (grē'lĭ)	**114-15**	41°33'N	98°32'W
Green, stm., U.S. (grēn)	**110-11**	38°11'N	109°53'W
Green, stm., Ky., U.S. (grēn)	**116-17**	37°54'N	87°31'W
Green Bay, Wi., U.S. (grēn bā)	**116-17**	44°30'N	87°60'W
Green Bay, b., U.S. (grēn bā)	**116-17**	44°58'N	87°35'W
Greencastle, In., U.S. (grēn-kås''l)	**116-17**	39°38'N	86°51'W
Green Cove Springs, Fl., U.S. (grēn kōv sprĭngz)	**124-25**	29°60'N	81°42'W
Greenfield, Ca., U.S. (grēn'fēld)	**118-19**	36°19'N	121°15'W
Greenfield, Ia., U.S. (grēn'fēld)	**114-15**	41°18'N	94°28'W
Greenfield, In., U.S. (grēn'fēld)	**116-17**	39°47'N	85°46'W
Greenfield, Oh., U.S. (grēn'fēld)	**116-17**	39°20'N	83°23'W
Greenfield, Tn., U.S. (grēn'fēld)	**124-25**	36°09'N	88°48'W
Greenfield, Wi., U.S. (grēn'fēld)	**116-17**	42°57'N	88°01'W
Green Islands, is., Pap. N. Gui.	**277**	4°30'S	154°10'E
Greenland, dep., N.A. (grēn'lănd)	**85**	70°0'N	40°00'W
Greenland, i., Green. (grēn'lănd)	**86**	70°0'N	40°00'W
Greenland Sea, s., (grēn'lănd sē)	**288**	77°0'N	1°00'W
Green Mountains, mts., N.A. (grēn moun'tĭnz)	**116-17**	43°45'N	72°45'W
Greenock, Scot., U.K. (grēn'ŭk)	**190-91**	55°57'N	4°45'W
Green River, Ut., U.S. (grēn rĭv'ēr)	**118-19**	38°60'N	110°09'W
Green River, Wy., U.S. (grēn rĭv'ēr)	**112-13**	41°32'N	109°28'W
Greensboro, Al., U.S. (grēnz'bŭro)	**124-25**	32°42'N	87°36'W
Greensboro, Ga., U.S. (grēns-bûr'ô)	**124-25**	33°35'N	83°11'W
Greensboro, N.C., U.S. (grēns-bûr'ô)	**124-25**	36°04'N	79°48'W
Greensburg, In., U.S. (grēnz'bûrg)	**116-17**	39°20'N	85°29'W
Greensburg, Ky., U.S. (grēns-bûrg)	**124-25**	37°16'N	85°30'W
Greenville, Lib. (grēn'vĭl)	**260-61**	5°02'N	9°03'W
Greenville, Al., U.S. (grēn'vĭl)	**124-25**	31°50'N	86°37'W
Greenville, Il., U.S. (grēn'vĭl)	**116-17**	38°53'N	89°25'W
Greenville, Ky., U.S. (grēn'vĭl)	**124-25**	37°12'N	87°11'W
Greenville, Me., U.S. (grēn'vĭl)	**117a**	45°27'N	69°34'W
Greenville, Mi., U.S. (grēn'vĭl)	**116-17**	43°11'N	85°15'W
Greenville, Ms., U.S. (grēn'vĭl)	**124-25**	33°25'N	91°03'W
Greenville, N.C., U.S. (grēn'vĭl)	**124-25**	35°37'N	77°22'W
Greenville, Oh., U.S. (grēn'vĭl)	**116-17**	40°06'N	84°38'W
Greenville, Pa., U.S. (grēn'vĭl)	**116-17**	41°24'N	80°23'W
Greenville, S.C., U.S. (grēn'vĭl)	**124-25**	34°51'N	82°24'W
Greenville, Tx., U.S. (grēn'vĭl)	**120-21**	33°09'N	96°07'W
Greenwood, Ar., U.S. (grēn-wŏŏd)	**120-21**	35°12'N	94°16'W
Greenwood, In., U.S. (grēn-wŏŏd)	**116-17**	39°36'N	86°05'W
Greenwood, La., U.S. (grēn-wŏŏd)	**120-21**	32°27'N	93°58'W
Greenwood, Ms., U.S. (grēn-wŏŏd)	**124-25**	33°31'N	90°11'W
Greenwood, S.C., U.S. (grēn-wŏŏd)	**124-25**	34°12'N	82°09'W
Greer, S.C., U.S. (grēr)	**124-25**	34°56'N	82°14'W
Gregory, S.D., U.S. (grĕg'ô-rĭ)	**114-15**	43°14'N	99°26'W
Gregory, Lake, lk., Austl. (lāk grĕg'ô-rê)	**276**	28°55'S	139°00'E
Gregory Range, mts., Austl.	**277**	19°0'S	143°05'E
Greifswald, Ger. (grīfs'vält)	**194-95**	54°05'N	13°23'E
Greiz, Ger. (grīts)	**194-95**	50°39'N	12°13'E
Gremyachinsk, Russia (grâ'myá-chĭnsk)	**186-87**	58°35'N	57°51'E
Grenada, Ms., U.S. (grê-nā'da)	**124-25**	33°46'N	89°49'W
Grenada, nation, N.A. (grĕ-nā'dá)	**140-41**	12°07'N	61°40'W
Grenadines, is., N.A. (grĕn'á-dēnz)	**143b**	12°40'N	61°15'W
Grenoble, Fr. (grē-nô'bl')	**196-97**	45°11'N	5°42'E
Grenville, Cape, c., Austl.	**277**	11°58'S	143°14'E
Gresham, Or., U.S. (grĕsh'ăm)	**112-13**	45°29'N	122°26'W
Gresik, Indon.	**248-49**	7°10'S	112°39'E
Gretna, La., U.S. (grĕt'ná)	**124-25**	29°55'N	90°04'W
Gretna, Ne., U.S. (grĕt'ná)	**114-15**	41°08'N	96°15'W
Grey, stm., Nf., Can. (grā)	**138-39**	47°33'N	57°08'W
Greybull, Wy., U.S. (grā'bŏŏl)	**112-13**	44°30'N	108°03'W
Grey Islands, is., Nf., Can.	**138-39**	50°50'N	55°37'W
Greymouth, N.Z. (grā'mouth)	**278**	42°28'S	171°13'E
Grey Range, mts., Austl. (grā rānj)	**276**	27°0'S	143°35'E
Greytown, S. Afr. (grā'toun)	**269c**	29°04'S	30°35'E
Gribanovskiy, Russia	**186-87**	51°27'N	41°58'E
Gribbel Island, i., B.C., Can.	**132-33**	53°25'N	129°00'W
Griffin, Ga., U.S. (grĭf'ĭn)	**124-25**	33°15'N	84°16'W
Griffith, Austl. (grĭf-ĭth)	**276**	34°17'S	146°03'E
Grim, Cape, c., Austl. (kāp grĭm)	**276**	40°39'S	144°43'E
Grímsey, i., Ice. (grĭms'å)	**190a**	66°33'N	18°01'W
Grimstad, Nor. (grĭm-städh)	**192-93**	58°20'N	8°36'E
Groesbeck, Tx., U.S. (grōs'bĕk)	**122-23**	31°31'N	96°32'W
Gronau, Ger. (grō'nou)	**194-95**	52°13'N	7°01'E
Groningen, Neth. (grō'nĭng-ĕn)	**190-91**	53°13'N	6°34'E
Grønland, dep., N.A. *see* Greenland	**85**	70°0'N	40°00'W
Grønland, i., Green. *see* Greenland	**86**	70°0'N	40°00'W
Grønlandshavet, s., *see* Greenland Sea	**288**	77°0'N	1°00'W
Groote Eylandt, i., Austl. (grō'tē ī'lănt)	**272-73**	13°60'S	136°38'E
Grootfontein, Nmb. (grōt'fōn-tān')	**264-65**	19°34'S	18°06'E
Groot Karroo, plat., S. Afr. *see* Great Karoo	**264-65**	32°47'S	22°32'E
Groot Namaland, hist. reg., Nmb. *see* Great Namaqualand	**264-65**	25°0'S	17°00'E
Gros Morne, mtn., Nf., Can. (grō môrn')	**138-39**	49°36'N	57°48'W
Gros Morne National Park, n.p., Nf., Can. (grō môrn' năsh'ŭn-ăl pärk)	**138-39**	49°40'N	57°45'W
Grosseto, Italy (grôs-sā'tō)	**200-01**	42°46'N	11°07'E
Großglockner, mtn., Aus.	**194-95**	47°04'N	12°42'E
Grosswardein, Rom. *see* Oradea	**194-95**	47°04'N	21°56'E
Groton, Ct., U.S. (grŏt'ŭn)	**116-17**	41°21'N	72°05'W
Groton, S.D., U.S. (grŏt'ŭn)	**114-15**	45°27'N	98°06'W
Grouard Mission, Ab., Can.	**132-33**	55°32'N	116°09'W
Groveton, N.H., U.S. (grōv'tŭn)	**116-17**	44°36'N	71°31'W
Growa Point, c., Lib.	**260-61**	4°21'N	7°36'W
Groznyy, Russia (grŏz'nĭ)	**227**	43°19'N	45°41'E
Grudziądz, Pol. (gró'jyŏnts)	**194-95**	53°29'N	18°44'E
Grünberg, Pol. *see* Zielona Góra	**194-95**	51°56'N	15°31'E
Grundy Center, Ia., U.S. (grŭn'dĭ sĕn'tēr)	**114-15**	42°21'N	92°47'W
Gruziya, nation, Asia *see* Georgia	**227**	42°0'N	44°00'E
Gryazi, Russia (gryä'zĭ)	**186-87**	52°29'N	39°57'E
Gryazovets, Russia (gryä'zô-vĕts)	**186-87**	58°53'N	40°15'E
Gryfice, Pol. (grĭ'fĭ-tsĕ)	**194-95**	53°55'N	15°12'E
Guacanayabo, Golfo de, b., Cuba (gôl-fô-dĕ-gwä-kä-nä-yä'bō)	**142-43**	20°28'N	77°30'W
Guacara, Ven. (gwä'kä-rä)	**163b**	10°14'N	67°53'W
Guadalajara, Mex. (gwä-dhä-lä-hä'rä)	**146-47**	20°40'N	103°20'W
Guadalajara, Spain (gwä-dä-lä-kä'rä)	**198-99**	40°38'N	3°10'W
Guadalcanal, i., Sol. Is. (gwä-dhäl-kä-näl')	**279e**	9°32'S	160°12'E
Guadalquivir, stm., Spain (gwä-dhäl-kê-vēr')	**198-99**	36°47'N	6°24'W
Guadalupe, Mex.	**122-23**	25°41'N	100°15'W
Guadalupe, stm., Tx., U.S. (gwä-dhä-lōō'på)	**122-23**	28°27'N	96°49'W
Guadalupe, Isla, i., Mex.	**140-41**	29°03'N	118°21'W
Guadalupe, Sierra de, mts., Spain (syĕr'rä dā gwä-dhä-lōō'pä)	**198-99**	39°29'N	5°28'W
Guadalupe Mountains, mts., U.S. (gwä-dhä-lōō'på moun'tĭnz)	**122-23**	32°24'N	105°04'W
Guadalupe Mountains National Park, n.p., Tx., U.S.	**122-23**	31°55'N	104°55'W
Guadalupe Peak, mtn., Tx., U.S. (gwä-dhä-lōō'på pēk)	**122-23**	31°50'N	104°52'W
Guadarrama, Sierra de, mts., Spain (syĕr'rä dā gwä-dhär-rä'mä)	**198-99**	40°51'N	4°01'W
Guadeloupe, dep., N.A. (gwä-dē-lōōp)	**140-41**	16°15'N	61°35'W
Guadiana, stm., Eur. (gwä-dvä'nä)	**198-99**	37°10'N	7°24'W
Guadix, Spain (gwä-dēsh')	**198-99**	37°18'N	3°08'W
Guafo, Isla, i., Chile	**171**	43°36'S	74°43'W
Guaíra, Braz. (gwä-ē-rä)	**172**	20°19'S	48°18'W
Guaíra, Braz. (gwä-ē-rä)	**168-69**	24°06'S	54°15'W
Guajaba, Cayo, i., Cuba (kä'yō-gwä-hä'bä)	**142-43**	21°50'N	77°30'W
Guajará-Mirim, Braz. (gwä-zhä-rä'mē-rēɴ')	**166-67**	10°48'S	65°22'W
Gualeguay, Arg. (gwä-lĕ-gwä'y)	**173**	33°09'S	59°20'W
Gualeguay, stm., Arg. (gwä-lĕ-gwä'y)	**173**	33°19'S	59°39'W
Gualeguaychú, Arg.	**173**	33°01'S	58°31'W
Guam, dep., Oc. (gwäm)	**279c**	13°28'N	144°47'E
Guam, i., Guam (gwäm)	**279c**	13°28'N	144°47'E
Guaminí, Arg.	**173**	37°01'S	62°25'W
Guamo, Col. (gwá'mō)	**163c**	4°02'N	74°58'W
Guanaja, Isla de, i., Hond.	**149**	16°29'N	85°53'W
Guanajuato, Mex. (gwä-nä-hwä'tō)	**146-47**	21°01'N	101°16'W
Guanajuato, state, Mex. (gwä-nä-hwä'tō)	**146-47**	21°0'N	101°00'W
Guanambi, Braz.	**166-67**	14°14'S	42°47'W
Guanare, Ven. (gwä-nä'rå)	**164-65**	9°03'N	69°46'W
Guandacol, Arg.	**168-69**	29°31'S	68°32'W
Guane, Cuba (gwä'nå)	**142-43**	22°12'N	84°05'W
Guang'an, China	**238-39**	30°28'N	106°38'E
Guangchang, China (gůäŋ-chäŋ)	**238-39**	26°51'N	116°19'E
Guangdong, state, China (gůäŋ-dôŋ)	**287**	23°0'N	113°00'E
Guanghua, China *see* Laohekou	**238-39**	32°25'N	111°36'E
Guangnan, China	**238-39**	24°10'N	105°06'E
Guangxi, state, China	**238-39**	24°0'N	109°00'E
Guangyuan, China	**238-39**	32°25'N	105°49'E
Guangzhou, China	**238-39**	23°08'N	113°16'E
Guanta, Ven. (gwän'tä)	**163b**	10°14'N	64°36'W
Guantánamo, Cuba (gwän-tä'nä-mô)	**142-43**	20°08'N	75°13'W
Guantánamo, state, Cuba (gwän-tä'nä-mô)	**142-43**	20°20'N	75°00'W
Guanxian, China (gůän-shyĕn)	**238-39**	31°00'N	103°36'E
Guanxian, China (gůän-shyĕn)	**240-41**	36°28'N	115°26'E
Guapí, Col.	**164-65**	2°36'N	77°54'W
Guápiles, C.R. (gwä-pē-lĕs)	**149**	10°12'N	83°47'W
Guaporé, stm., S.A. (gwä-pô-rā')	**166-67**	11°55'S	65°00'W
Guarabira, Braz. (gwä-rä-bē'rá)	**163d**	6°51'S	35°29'W
Guaranda, Ec. (gwä-rän'dä)	**170**	1°36'S	78°60'W
Guarapari, Braz. (gwä-rä-pä'rê)	**172**	20°40'S	40°30'W
Guarapuava, Braz. (gwä-rä-pwä'vá)	**168-69**	25°23'S	51°29'W
Guarda, Port. (gwär'dä)	**198-99**	40°33'N	7°15'W
Guarulhos, Braz. (gwá-rò'l-yôs)	**172**	23°29'S	46°32'W
Guasave, Mex.	**144-45**	25°34'N	108°28'W
Guasdualito, Ven.	**164-65**	7°15'N	70°45'W
Guasipati, Ven. (gwä-sê-pä'tē)	**164-65**	7°29'N	61°53'W
Guastalla, Italy (gwäs-täl'lä)	**200-01**	44°55'N	10°39'E
Guatemala, nation, N.A. (guä-tå-mä'lä)	**85**	15°30'N	90°15'W
Guatemala, nat. cap., Guat. (guä-tå-mä'lä)	**148**	14°38'N	90°32'W
Guaviare, stm., Col.	**164-65**	4°04'N	67°43'W
Guaxupé, Braz.	**172**	21°18'S	46°42'W
Guayama, P.R. (gwä-yä'mä)	**142a**	17°59'N	66°07'W
Guayana, Ven. *see* Ciudad Guayana	**164-65**	8°21'N	62°39'W
Guayana, nation, S.A. *see* Guyana	**158**	5°0'N	59°00'W
Guayaquil, Ec. (gwī-ä-kēl')	**170**	2°12'S	79°54'W
Guayaquil, Golfo de, b., S.A. (gôl-fô-dĕ gwī-ä-kēl')	**170**	2°57'S	80°36'W
Guaymas, Mex. (gwá'y-mäs)	**144-45**	27°55'N	110°55'W
Gûbâl, Madîq, strt., Egypt	**268b**	27°40'N	33°55'E
Gubakha, Russia (gōō-bä'kå)	**186-87**	58°52'N	57°33'E
Gubbio, Italy (gōōb'byô)	**200-01**	43°21'N	12°34'E
Gubkin, Russia	**202-03**	51°17'N	37°33'E
Gucheng, China (gōō-chŭŋ)	**238-39**	32°18'N	111°35'E
Gudermes, Russia	**227**	43°21'N	46°06'E
Guebwiller, Fr. (gĕb-vê-lâr')	**196-97**	47°55'N	7°12'E
Guelph, On., Can. (gwĕlf)	**136-37**	43°33'N	80°15'W
Guercif, Mor.	**184-85**	34°14'N	3°20'W
Guéret, Fr. (gā-rē')	**196-97**	46°10'N	1°52'E
Guernesey, dep., Eur. *see* Guernsey	**196-97**	49°28'N	2°35'W
Guernsey, dep., Eur. (gûrn'zĭ)	**196-97**	49°28'N	2°35'W
Guerrero, Mex. (gĕr-rā'rō)	**144-45**	28°33'N	107°30'W
Guerrero, state, Mex. (gĕr-rā'rō)	**146-47**	17°40'N	100°00'W
Gugē, mtn., Eth.	**262-63**	6°11'N	37°24'E
Guguan, i., N. Mar. Is.	**280-81**	17°19'N	145°51'E
Guide, China	**240-41**	36°01'N	101°27'E
Guilin, China (gwä-lĭn)	**238-39**	25°17'N	110°17'E
Guimarães, Port. (gē-mä-răɴsh')	**198-99**	41°27'N	8°18'W
Guimaras Island, i., Phil.	**250**	10°35'N	122°37'E
Guiné, Golfo da, b., Afr. *see* Guinea, Gulf of	**260-61**	2°0'N	2°30'E
Guinea, nation, Afr. (gĭn'ê)	**253**	11°0'N	10°00'W
Guinea, Golfo de, b., Afr. *see* Guinea, Gulf of	**260-61**	2°0'N	2°30'E
Guinea, Gulf of, b., Afr. (gŭlf ŭv gĭn'ê)	**260-61**	2°0'N	2°30'E
Guinea-Bissau, nation, Afr. (gĭn'ê bê-sa'ōō)	**253**	12°0'N	15°00'W
Guinea Ecuatorial, nation, Afr. *see* Equatorial Guinea	**253**	2°0'N	9°00'E
Guiné-Bissau, nation, Afr. *see* Guinea-Bissau	**253**	12°0'N	15°00'W
Guinée, nation, Afr. *see* Guinea	**253**	11°0'N	10°00'W
Guinée, Golfe de, b., Afr. *see* Guinea, Gulf of	**260-61**	2°0'N	2°30'E
Güines, Cuba	**142-43**	22°51'N	82°02'W

PRONOUNCING INDEX
Guingamp – Hanzhong 335

Feature (Pronunciation)	Page	Lat.	Long.
Guingamp, Fr. (găn-gän´)	196-97	48°34'N	3°09'W
Guiping, China	238-39	23°23'N	110°04'E
Güira de Melena, Cuba (gwē´rä dĕ må-lā´nä)	142-43	22°48'N	82°30'W
Guiratinga, Braz.	168-69	16°21'S	53°45'W
Güiria, Ven. (gwê-rē´ä)	143b	10°35'N	62°18'W
Guiuan, Phil.	250	11°02'N	125°44'E
Guixian, China	238-39	23°06'N	109°39'E
Guiyang, China	238-39	26°35'N	106°43'E
Guizhou, state, China (gwā-jō)	238-39	27°0'N	107°00'E
Gujarāt, state, India	234-35	22°0'N	72°00'E
Gujrānwāla, Pak.	232-33	32°09'N	74°11'E
Gujrāt, Pak.	232-33	32°34'N	74°05'E
Gulbarga, India (gòl-bûr´gȧ)	236	17°20'N	76°50'E
Gulbene, Lat. (gòl-bā´nĕ)	192-93	57°10'N	26°46'E
Gulfport, Ms., U.S. (gŭlf´pōrt)	124-25	30°22'N	89°06'W
Gulian, China	222-23	52°56'N	122°19'E
Guliston, Uzb.	232-33	40°30'N	68°46'E
Gulja, China *see* Yining	226	43°55'N	81°18'E
Gull Lake, Sk., Can. (gŭl lāk)	134-35	50°08'N	108°27'W
Gull Lake, lk., Ab., Can. (gŭl lāk)	132-33	52°33'N	114°02'W
Gulu, Ug.	267	2°47'N	32°18'E
Gumaca, Phil. (gōō-mä-kä´)	250	13°55'N	122°06'E
Gumdag, Turkmen.	232-33	39°12'N	54°36'E
Gummersbach, Ger. (gòm´ĕrs-bäk)	194-95	51°02'N	7°34'E
Gumti, stm., India	234-35	25°31'N	83°10'E
Gümüşhane, Tur.	227	40°28'N	39°28'E
Guna, India	234-35	24°39'N	77°18'E
Gundagai, Austl.	276	35°04'S	148°06'E
Gunisao, stm., Mb., Can. (gŭn-*i*-sā´ō)	134-35	53°53'N	97°60'W
Gunisao Lake, lk., Mb., Can. (gŭn-*i*-sā´ō lāk)	134-35	53°33'N	96°15'W
Gunnbjørn Fjeld, mtn., Green.	86	68°53'N	30°00'W
Gunnedah, Austl. (gŭ´nē-dä)	276	30°59'S	150°15'E
Gunnison, Co., U.S. (gŭn´ĭ-s*ŭ*n)	118-19	38°33'N	106°55'W
Gunnison, Ut., U.S. (gŭn´ĭ-s*ŭ*n)	118-19	39°09'N	111°49'W
Gunsan, Kor., S. *see* Kunsan	243	35°59'N	126°43'E
Guntersville, Al., U.S. (gŭn´tĕrz-vĭl)	124-25	34°22'N	86°18'W
Guntūr, India (gòn´tōōr)	236	16°18'N	80°27'E
Gunungsitoli, Indon.	246-47	1°15'N	97°37'E
Guoyang, China (gwô-yäŋ)	238-39	33°30'N	116°12'E
Gurara, stm., Nig.	260-61	8°11'N	6°42'E
Gurdon, Ar., U.S. (gûr´d*ŭ*n)	120-21	33°55'N	93°10'W
Guri, Embalse de, res., Ven.	164-65	7°30'N	62°50'W
Gurnee, Il., U.S. (gûr´nē)	116-17	42°22'N	87°54'W
Gurué, Moz.	264-65	15°27'S	36°59'E
Gurupá, Braz.	166-67	1°25'S	51°39'W
Gurupi, Braz.	166-67	11°43'S	49°02'W
Gurupi, stm., Braz.	166-67	1°16'S	46°09'W
Guryev, Kaz. *see* Atyrau	186-87	47°07'N	51°55'E
Gusau, Nig. (gōō-zä´ōō)	260-61	12°10'N	6°40'E
Guşgy, Turkmen.	232-33	35°16'N	62°21'E
Gushi, China (gōō-shr)	238-39	32°11'N	115°41'E
Gusinoozërsk, Russia	240-41	51°17'N	106°31'E
Gus'-Khrustal'nyy, Russia (gōōs-krōō-stäl'ny')	186-87	55°37'N	40°40'E
Gütersloh, Ger. (gü´tĕrs-lō)	194-95	51°54'N	8°23'E
Guthrie, Ok., U.S. (gŭth´rĭ)	120-21	35°53'N	97°26'W
Gutian, China	238-39	26°36'N	118°46'E
Gutiérrez Zamora, Mex. (gōō-tē-âr´räz zä-mō´rä)	146-47	20°27'N	97°05'W
Guttenberg, Ia., U.S. (gŭt´ĕn-bûrg)	114-15	42°47'N	91°06'W
Guwāhāti, India	234-35	26°11'N	91°44'E
Guyana, nation, S.A. (gūy´ănä)	158	5°0'N	59°00'W
Guyane, dep., S.A. *see* French Guiana	158	4°0'N	53°00'W
Guyang, China (gōō-yäŋ)	240-41	41°02'N	110°04'E
Guymon, Ok., U.S. (gī´mŏn)	120-21	36°41'N	101°29'W
Guyuan, China	240-41	35°59'N	106°18'E
Guzhen, China (gōō-jŭn)	238-39	33°19'N	117°19'E
Guzmán, Mex.	146-47	19°42'N	103°28'W
G'uzor, Uzb.	232-33	38°36'N	66°15'E
Gvardeysk, Russia (gvár-dĕysk´)	194-95	54°39'N	21°05'E
Gwādar, Pak. (gwä´dŭr)	230-31	25°08'N	62°20'E
Gwalior, India	234-35	26°13'N	78°09'E
Gwangju, Kor., S. *see* Kwangju	243	35°09'N	126°54'E
Gwardafuy, Gees, c., Som.	262-63	11°50'N	51°17'E
Gweru, Zimb.	264-65	19°27'S	29°49'E
Gwinn, Mi., U.S. (gwĭn)	114-15	46°17'N	87°25'W
Gyandzha, Azer. *see* Gäncä	227	40°41'N	46°21'E
Gyangzê, China	234-35	28°56'N	89°34'E
Gyaring Co, lk., China	234-35	31°05'N	88°24'E
Gyaring Hu, lk., China	240-41	34°54'N	97°15'E
Gyeongju, Kor., S. *see* Kyŏngju	243	35°51'N	129°13'E
Gympie, Austl. (gĭm´pē)	276	26°12'S	152°40'E
Gyöngyös, Hung. (dyûn´dyûsh)	194-95	47°47'N	19°56'E
Győr, Hung. (dyûr)	194-95	47°41'N	17°39'E
Gyula, Hung. (dyò´lä)	194-95	46°39'N	21°20'E
Gyumri, Arm.	227	40°47'N	43°51'E
Gyzylarbat, Turkmen.	232-33	38°59'N	56°16'E
Gyzyletrek, Turkmen.	232-33	37°36'N	54°47'E

H

Feature (Pronunciation)	Page	Lat.	Long.
Haapamäki, Fin. (häp´ä-mĕ-kē)	192-93	62°15'N	24°27'E
Haapsalu, Est. (häp´sä-lò)	192-93	58°56'N	23°33'E
Haar, Ger. (här)	194-95	48°06'N	11°44'E
Haarlem, Neth. (här´lĕm)	190-91	52°23'N	4°38'E
Hachijō-jima, i., Japan	244	33°05'N	139°48'E
Hachinohe, Japan (hä´chē-nō´hå)	244	40°30'N	141°29'E
Ḩadd, Ra's al-, c., Oman	230-31	22°32'N	59°48'E
Hadejia, stm., Nig.	260-61	12°50'N	10°51'E
Ḩadera, Isr. (ĸå-dĕ´rå)	228-29	32°27'N	34°55'E
Haderslev, Den. (hä´dhĕrs-lĕv)	192-93	55°15'N	9°30'E
Hadībū, Yemen	220-21	12°39'N	54°02'E
Ḩadīthah, Iraq	228-29	34°02'N	42°22'E
Ḩaḑramawt, reg., Yemen	220-21	15°0'N	50°00'E
Hadyai, Thai. *see* Hat Yai	246-47	7°01'N	100°28'E
Haeju, Kor., N. (hä´ĕ-jŭ)	243	38°03'N	125°43'E
Haft Gel, Iran	232-33	31°26'N	49°32'E
Hagåtña, nat. cap., Guam	279c	13°28'N	144°45'E
Hagen, Ger. (hä´gĕn)	194-95	51°22'N	7°28'E
Hagerstown, Md., U.S. (hā´gẽrz-toun)	116-17	39°39'N	77°43'W
Haggin, Mount, mtn., Mt., U.S.	112-13	46°05'N	113°05'W
Hagi, Japan (hä´gĭ)	245	34°24'N	131°24'E
Hague, Cap de la, c., Fr. (kåp dē lå äg´)	196-97	49°43'N	1°56'W
Hague, The, nat. cap., Neth.	190-91	52°06'N	4°18'E
Haguenau, Fr. (åg'nō´)	196-97	48°49'N	7°47'E
Hahajima-rettō, is., Japan	280-81	26°37'N	142°10'E
Haicheng, China (hī-chŭŋ)	240-41	40°51'N	122°46'E
Haifa, Isr. (hä´ē-fȧ)	228-29	32°49'N	35°00'E
Haifeng, China (hä´ē-fĕng´)	238-39	22°58'N	115°20'E
Haikang, China	238-39	20°55'N	110°05'E
Haikou, China	238-39	20°03'N	110°22'E
Ḩā'il, Sau. Ar.	266	27°31'N	41°42'E
Hailar, China	240-41	49°11'N	119°44'E
Hailar, stm., China	240-41	49°30'N	117°51'E
Hailey, Id., U.S. (hā´lĭ)	112-13	43°32'N	114°19'W
Hailun, China (hä´ē-lōōn´)	240-41	47°27'N	126°58'E
Hailuoto, i., Fin.	184-85	65°02'N	24°42'E
Hainan, state, China (hī´-nän´)	238-39	19°0'N	109°30'E
Hainan Dao, i., China (hī-nän dou)	238-39	19°0'N	109°30'E
Hainan Strait, strt., China (hī´-nän´ strŭt) *see* Qiongzhou Haixia	238-39	20°10'N	110°15'E
Haines, Ak., U.S. (hānz)	126	59°14'N	135°27'W
Haines City, Fl., U.S. (hānz sĭ´tĭ)	125a	28°07'N	81°38'W
Haines Junction, Yk., Can.	128-29	60°45'N	137°28'W
Hai Ninh, Viet.	246-47	21°32'N	107°56'E
Hai Phong, Viet. (hī´fŏng´)(hä´ēp-hŏng)	246-47	20°52'N	106°41'E
Haiti, nation, N.A. (hā´tĭ)	140-41	19°0'N	72°25'W
Haïti, i., N.A. *see* Hispaniola	142-43	19°0'N	71°00'W
Haizhou, China	238-39	34°35'N	119°08'E
Hajdúböszörmény, Hung. (hôl´dò-bû´sûr-män')	194-95	47°40'N	21°31'E
Hajdúnánás, Hung. (hô´ĭ-dò-nä´näsh)	194-95	47°50'N	21°27'E
Ḩajjah, Yemen	266	15°42'N	43°36'E
Ḩakīm, Abyār al-, well, Libya	258-59	31°36'N	23°29'E
Hakodate, Japan (hä-kō-dä´t å)	244	41°45'N	140°43'E
Haku-san, vol., Japan (hä´kōō-sän´)	245	36°09'N	136°46'E
Ḩalab, Syria *see* Aleppo	228-29	36°13'N	37°10'E
Ḩalā'ib, Sudan	266	22°13'N	36°38'E
Halberstadt, Ger. (häl´bĕr-shtät)	194-95	51°53'N	11°03'E
Halcon, Mount, mtn., Phil. (mount häl-kōn´)	250	13°16'N	121°00'E
Halden, Nor. (häl´dĕn)	192-93	59°08'N	11°23'E
Haleakalā National Park, n.p., Hi., U.S. (hä´lä-ä´kä-lä näsh´ŭn-*ă*l pärk)	127a	20°44'N	156°13'W
Haleyville, Al., U.S. (hā´lĭ-vĭl)	124-25	34°14'N	87°38'W
Halfway, stm., B.C., Can.	132-33	56°13'N	121°26'W
Halifax, N.S., Can. (hăl´ĭ-făks)	138-39	44°39'N	63°36'W
Halifax Bay, b., Austl. (hăl´ĭ-făx bā)	277	18°50'S	146°30'E
Halla-san, mtn., Kor., S. (häl´lå-sän´)	240-41	33°22'N	126°32'E
Halle, Ger.	194-95	51°29'N	11°58'E
Hallettsville, Tx., U.S. (hăl´ĕts-vĭl)	122-23	29°27'N	96°56'W
Hall Islands, is., Micron.	280-81	8°35'N	151°59'E
Hallock, Mn., U.S. (hăl´*ŭ*k)	114-15	48°46'N	96°57'W
Hall Peninsula, pen., Nu., Can. (hôl pĕ-nĭn´sūl*ă*)	130-31	63°30'N	66°00'W
Hallsberg, Swe. (häls´bĕrgh)	192-93	59°05'N	15°08'E
Halls Creek, Austl. (hôlz krēk)	270-71	18°15'S	127°40'E
Halmahera, i., Indon. (häl-mä-hā´rä)	248-49	1°0'N	128°00'E
Halmahera, Laut, s., Indon. *see* Halmahera Sea	224-25	1°0'S	129°00'E
Halmahera Sea, s., Indon. (häl-mä-hā´rä sē)	224-25	1°0'S	129°00'E
Halmstad, Swe. (hälm´städ)	192-93	56°40'N	12°53'E
Hälsingborg, Swe. *see* Helsingborg	192-93	56°03'N	12°42'E
Haltern, Ger. (häl´tĕrn)	194-95	51°45'N	7°11'E
Haltiatunturi, mtn., Eur.	184-85	69°18'N	21°16'E
Halton Hills, On., Can. *see* Georgetown	136-37	43°39'N	79°55'W
Halys, stm., Tur. *see* Kızılırmak	186-87	41°44'N	35°58'E
Hamada, Japan	245	34°53'N	132°05'E
Hamadān, Iran (hŭ-mŭ-dän´)	228-29	34°48'N	48°31'E
Ḩamāh, Syria (hä´mä)	228-29	35°08'N	36°45'E
Hamamatsu, Japan (hä´mä-mät´sò)	245	34°43'N	137°42'E
Hamar, Nor. (hä´mär)	192-93	60°48'N	11°05'E
Hamburg, Ger. (häm´bōōrgh)	194-95	53°33'N	9°59'E
Hamburg, Ar., U.S. (hăm´bûrg)	124-25	33°14'N	91°48'W
Hamburg, N.Y., U.S. (hăm´bûrg)	116-17	42°43'N	78°50'W
Hamden, Ct., U.S. (hăm´dĕn)	116-17	41°24'N	72°54'W
Hämeenlinna, Fin. (hĕ´mån-lĭn-nȧ)	192-93	60°58'N	24°31'E
HaMelaḩ, Yam, lk., Asia *see* Dead Sea	228-29	31°30'N	35°30'E
Hameln, Ger. (hä´m*ĕ*ln)	194-95	52°06'N	9°22'E
Hamersley Range, mts., Austl. (hăm´ẽrz-lē rānj)	272-73	22°24'S	117°34'E
Hamhŭng, Kor., N. (häm´hòng´)	243	39°55'N	127°32'E
Hami, China (hä-mē)	240-41	42°50'N	93°31'E
Hamilton, Austl. (hăm´ĭl-t*ŭ*n)	276	37°45'S	142°01'E
Hamilton, On., Can. (hăm´ĭl-t*ŭ*n)	136-37	43°15'N	79°51'W
Hamilton, N.Z. (hăm´ĭl-t*ŭ*n)	278	37°47'S	175°17'E
Hamilton, Al., U.S. (hăm´ĭl-t*ŭ*n)	124-25	34°08'N	87°59'W
Hamilton, Mo., U.S. (hăm´ĭl-t*ŭ*n)	120-21	39°45'N	94°00'W
Hamilton, Mt., U.S. (hăm´ĭl-t*ŭ*n)	112-13	46°14'N	114°10'W
Hamilton, Oh., U.S. (hăm´ĭl-t*ŭ*n)	116-17	39°24'N	84°34'W
Hamilton, Tx., U.S. (hăm´ĭl-t*ŭ*n)	122-23	31°41'N	98°08'W
Hamilton, nat. cap., Ber. (hăm´ĭl-t*ŭ*n)	140-41	32°18'N	64°48'W
Hamina, Fin. (hȧ´mē-nȧ)	192-93	60°34'N	27°19'E
Hamlet, N.C., U.S. (hăm´lĕt)	124-25	34°54'N	79°42'W
Hamlin, Tx., U.S. (hăm´lĭn)	120-21	32°53'N	100°08'W
Hamm, Ger. (häm)	194-95	51°41'N	7°49'E
Hammamet, Tun.	184-85	36°24'N	10°37'E
Hammamet, Golfe de, b., Tun.	258-59	36°05'N	10°40'E
Hammerfest, Nor. (hä´mĕr-fĕst)	184-85	70°40'N	23°42'E
Hammond, In., U.S. (hăm´*ŭ*nd)	116-17	41°35'N	87°30'W
Hammond, La., U.S. (hăm´*ŭ*nd)	124-25	30°30'N	90°28'W
Hammonton, N.J., U.S. (hăm´ŭn-t*ŭ*n)	116-17	39°38'N	74°48'W
Hampton, N.B., Can. (hămp´t*ŭ*n)	138-39	45°32'N	65°51'W
Hampton, Ia., U.S. (hămp´t*ŭ*n)	114-15	42°45'N	93°12'W
Hampton, S.C., U.S. (hămp´t*ŭ*n)	124-25	32°52'N	81°07'W
Hampton, Va., U.S. (hămp´t*ŭ*n)	124-25	37°02'N	76°21'W
Ḩamrā', Al-Ḩamādah al-, des., Libya	188-89	30°0'N	12°00'E
Hāmūn, Daryācheh-ye, lk., Iran	230-31	30°43'N	61°07'E
Han, stm., China (hän)	238-39	23°41'N	116°38'E
Han, stm., China (hän)	238-39	30°34'N	114°17'E
Hāna, Hi., U.S. (hä´nä)	127a	20°45'N	155°59'W
Hancheng, China	240-41	35°29'N	110°25'E
Hancock, Mi., U.S. (hăn´kŏk)	114-15	47°08'N	88°36'W
Handan, China (hän-dän)	240-41	36°37'N	114°28'E
Hanford, Ca., U.S. (hăn´fẽrd)	118-19	36°20'N	119°38'W
Hangayn nuruu, mts., Mong.	240-41	47°32'N	98°42'E
Hangchow, China *see* Hangzhou	238-39	30°15'N	120°10'E
Hanggin Houqi, China	240-41	40°57'N	107°14'E
Hanggin Qi, China	240-41	39°55'N	108°52'E
Hangö, Fin. (häŋ´gû) *see* Hanko	192-93	59°50'N	22°58'E
Hangzhou, China (hăng´chō´)	238-39	30°15'N	120°10'E
Hanjiang, China	225a	25°30'N	119°06'E
Hankinson, N.D., U.S. (häŋ´kĭn-s*ŭ*n)	114-15	46°04'N	96°55'W
Hanko, Fin.	192-93	59°50'N	22°58'E
Hankow, China *see* Wuhan	238-39	30°34'N	114°17'E
Hanna, Ab., Can. (hăn´ȧ)	132-33	51°39'N	111°56'W
Hannibal, Mo., U.S. (hăn´ĭ b*ă*l)	120-21	39°42'N	91°22'W
Hannover, Ger. (hän-ō´vĕr)	194-95	52°24'N	9°44'E
Ha Noi, nat. cap., Viet. (hä-noi´)	246-47	21°02'N	105°50'E
Hanover, On., Can. (hăn´ô-vẽr)	136-37	44°09'N	81°01'W
Hanover, Ger. *see* Hannover	194-95	52°24'N	9°44'E
Hanover, N.H., U.S. (hăn´ô-vẽr)	116-17	43°42'N	72°17'W
Hanover, Pa., U.S. (hăn´ô-vẽr)	116-17	39°48'N	76°59'W
Hanover, Va., U.S. (hăn´ô-vẽr)	116-17	37°46'N	77°23'W
Hanover, Isla, i., Chile	171	50°58'S	74°45'W
Hantsport, N.S., Can. (hănts´pōrt)	138-39	45°04'N	64°12'W
Hanuy, stm., Mong.	240-41	49°21'N	102°22'E
Hanzhong, China (hän-jōŋ)	238-39	33°04'N	107°02'E

n-sing; ŋ-baŋk; ɴ-nasalized n; nŏd; c*ŏ*mmit; ōld; ôbey; ôrder; oi-boil; fōōd; ȯ-as oo in foot; ou-out; s-soft; sh-dish; th-thin; pūre; ûnite; ûrn; stŭd; circ*ŭ*s; ü-as in French tu; ´-indeterminate vowel.

336 Hāora – Hermansville PRONOUNCING INDEX

Feature (Pronunciation)	Page	Lat.	Long.
Hāora, India	234-35	22°35′N	88°20′E
Haparanda, Swe. (hä-pa-rän′dä)	184-85	65°50′N	24°06′E
Happy Valley-Goose Bay, Nf., Can.	128-29	53°20′N	60°25′W
Hāpur, India	234-35	28°44′N	77°47′E
Harare, nat. cap., Zimb. (hä-rä′-rē)	264-65	17°50′S	31°03′E
Ḥarash, Bi'r al-, well, Libya	258-59	25°39′N	22°08′E
Harbin, China	240-41	45°45′N	126°38′E
Harbor Beach, Mi., U.S. (här′bẽr bēch)	116-17	43°51′N	82°39′W
Harbour Breton, Nf., Can. (här′bẽr brĕt′ŭn) (brē-tôn′)	138-39	47°30′N	55°49′W
Harbour Grace, Nf., Can. (här′bẽr grās)	138-39	47°44′N	53°15′W
Hardangerfjorden, b., Nor.	192-93	60°10′N	6°00′E
Hardin, Mt., U.S. (här′dĭn)	112-13	45°44′N	107°37′W
Hardoi, India	234-35	27°23′N	80°09′E
Hare Bay, b., Nf., Can. (hâr bā)	138-39	51°16′N	55°51′W
Hareidlandet, i., Nor.	184-85	62°21′N	5°57′E
Hārer, Eth.	262-63	9°18′N	42°08′E
Hargeysa, Som. (här-gā′ê-sȧ)	262-63	9°34′N	44°04′E
Har Horin, hist., Mong. see Karakorum	240-41	47°14′N	102°50′E
Har Hu, lk., China	240-41	38°15′N	97°40′E
Hari, stm., Indon.	246-47	1°04′S	104°12′E
Haridwār, India	234-35	29°56′N	78°07′E
Harīrūd, stm., Asia	232-33	37°24′N	60°31′E
Harlan, Ia., U.S. (här′lăn)	114-15	41°39′N	95°20′W
Harlan, Ky., U.S. (här′lăn)	124-25	36°51′N	83°19′W
Harlem, Mt., U.S. (hár′lĕm)	112-13	48°32′N	108°47′W
Harlingen, Neth. (här′lĭng-ĕn)	190-91	53°10′N	5°26′E
Harlingen, Tx., U.S. (här′lĭng-ĕn)	122-23	26°12′N	97°42′W
Harlow, Eng., U.K. (här′lō)	190-91	51°47′N	0°07′E
Harlowton, Mt., U.S. (hár′lō-tun)	112-13	46°26′N	109°50′W
Harney Basin, bas., Or., U.S. (här′nĭ bā′s′n)	112-13	43°15′N	119°00′W
Harney Peak, mtn., S.D., U.S. (här′nĭ pēk)	114-15	43°52′N	103°32′W
Härnösand, Swe. (hĕr-nû-sănd)	184-85	62°38′N	17°56′E
Haro, Spain (ä′rō)	198-99	42°36′N	2°52′W
Hārot, stm., Afg.	232-33	31°29′N	61°16′E
Harper, Lib. (här′pẽr)	260-61	4°23′N	7°43′W
Harpers Ferry, W.V., U.S. (här′pẽrz fĕr′ē)	116-17	39°19′N	77°45′W
Harricana, stm., Can.	130-31	51°10′N	79°47′W
Harriman, Tn., U.S. (hăr′ĭ-măn)	124-25	35°56′N	84°33′W
Harrington, De., U.S. (hăr′ĭng-tŭn)	116-17	38°56′N	75°34′W
Harris, Lake, lk., Austl.	272-73	31°06′S	135°11′E
Harrisburg, Il., U.S. (hăr′ĭs-bûrg)	116-17	37°44′N	88°32′W
Harrisburg, Pa., U.S.	116-17	40°16′N	76°54′W
Harrismith, S. Afr. (hă-rĭs′mĭth)	269c	28°17′S	29°08′E
Harrison, Ar., U.S. (hăr′ĭ-sŭn)	120-21	36°14′N	93°07′W
Harrison, Mi., U.S. (hăr′ĭ-sŭn)	116-17	44°01′N	84°48′W
Harrison, Cape, c., Nf., Can.	130-31	54°55′N	57°56′W
Harrisonburg, Va., U.S. (hăr′ĭ-sŭn-bûrg)	116-17	38°27′N	78°52′W
Harrison Lake, lk., B.C., Can. (hăr′ĭ-sŭn lāk)	132-33	49°33′N	121°52′W
Harrisonville, Mo., U.S. (hăr-ĭ-sŭn-vĭl)	120-21	38°39′N	94°21′W
Harrisville, Mi., U.S. (hăr′ĭs-vĭl)	116-17	44°39′N	83°18′W
Harrisville, W.V., U.S. (hăr′ĭs-vĭl)	116-17	39°13′N	81°03′W
Harrodsburg, Ky., U.S. (hăr′ŭdz-bûrg)	116-17	37°46′N	84°51′W
Harstad, Nor. (här′städh)	184-85	68°47′N	16°34′E
Hart, Mi., U.S. (härt)	116-17	43°42′N	86°22′W
Hartford, Ct., U.S. (härt′fẽrd)	116-17	41°46′N	72°41′W
Hartford, Ky., U.S. (härt′fẽrd)	116-17	37°27′N	86°54′W
Hartford, Mi., U.S. (härt′fẽrd)	116-17	42°12′N	86°10′W
Hartford, S.D., U.S. (härt′fẽrd)	114-15	43°38′N	96°58′W
Hartford City, In., U.S. (härt′fẽrd sĭ′tĕ)	116-17	40°27′N	85°22′W
Hartlepool, Eng., U.K. (här′t′l-pōōl)	190-91	54°42′N	1°12′W
Hart Mountain, mtn., Mb., Can. (härt moun′tĭn)	134-35	52°29′N	101°25′W
Harts, stm., S. Afr.	264-65	28°24′S	24°17′E
Hartselle, Al., U.S. (härt′sĕl)	124-25	34°27′N	86°56′W
Hartshorne, Ok., U.S. (härts′hôrn)	120-21	34°51′N	95°34′W
Hartsville, S.C., U.S. (härts′vĭl)	124-25	34°22′N	80°05′W
Hartwell, Ga., U.S. (härt′wĕl)	124-25	34°21′N	82°55′W
Hartwell Lake, res., U.S. (härt′wĕl lāk)	124-25	34°28′N	82°51′W
Har Us nuur, lk., Mong.	240-41	48°0′N	92°10′E
Harvard, Il., U.S. (här′vȧrd)	116-17	42°25′N	88°37′W
Harvey, N.D., U.S.	114-15	47°46′N	99°55′W
Harwich, Eng., U.K. (här′wĭch)	190-91	51°57′N	1°17′E
Haryāna, state, India	234-35	29°20′N	76°20′E
Harz, mts., Ger. (härts)	194-95	51°45′N	10°30′E
Haskell, Tx., U.S. (hăs′kĕl)	120-21	33°09′N	99°44′W
Hassan, India	236	12°60′N	76°06′E
Hassi Messaoud, Alg.	188-89	31°41′N	6°04′E
Hässleholm, Swe. (häs′lĕ-hōlm)	192-93	56°09′N	13°46′E
Hastings, N.Z. (hās′tĭngz)	278	39°38′S	176°51′E
Hastings, Eng., U.K. (hās′tĭngz)	190-91	50°52′N	0°35′E
Hastings, Mi., U.S. (hās′tĭngz)	116-17	42°39′N	85°17′W
Hastings, Mn., U.S. (hās′tĭngz)	114-15	44°44′N	92°51′W
Hastings, Ne., U.S. (hās′tĭngz)	120-21	40°35′N	98°24′W
Hatay, Tur. see Antioch	228-29	36°12′N	36°10′E
Haţeg, Rom. (kät-säg′)	200-01	45°36′N	22°57′E
Hāthras, India	234-35	27°36′N	78°03′E
Ha Tinh, Viet.	246-47	18°20′N	105°54′E
Hatteras, Cape, c., N.C., U.S. (kāp hăt′ẽr-ȧs)	124-25	35°13′N	75°32′W
Hatteras Island, i., N.C., U.S.	124-25	35°25′N	75°29′W
Hattiesburg, Ms., U.S. (hăt′ĭz-bûrg)	124-25	31°20′N	89°17′W
Hatvan, Hung. (hôt′vôn)	194-95	47°40′N	19°41′E
Hat Yai, Thai.	246-47	7°01′N	100°28′E
Haugesund, Nor. (hou′gē-soon′)	192-93	59°25′N	5°18′E
Hauraki Gulf, b., N.Z. (hä-ōō-rä′kē gŭlf)	278	36°35′S	175°05′E
Haut Atlas, mts., Mor.	258-59	31°47′N	6°04′W
Haute-Volta, nation, Afr. see Burkina Faso	253	13°0′N	1°30′W
Havana, Il., U.S. (hȧ-vă′nȧ)	120-21	40°18′N	90°03′W
Havana, nat. cap., Cuba (hȧ-vă′nȧ)	142-43	23°06′N	82°27′W
Havel, stm., Ger. (hä′fĕl)	194-95	52°53′N	12°01′E
Haverhill, Ma., U.S. (hā′vẽr-hĭl)	116-17	42°47′N	71°05′W
Havre, Fr. see Le Havre	196-97	49°29′N	0°08′E
Havre, Mt., U.S. (hăv′ẽr)	112-13	48°33′N	109°41′W
Havre Aubert, Île du, i., Qc., Can.	138-39	47°14′N	61°57′W
Havre de Grace, Md., U.S. (hăv′ẽr dē grȧs′)	116-17	39°33′N	76°06′W
Havre-Saint-Pierre, Qc., Can.	138-39	50°15′N	63°36′W
Hawai'i, i., Hi., U.S. (hä-wī′ē)	127a	19°29′N	155°30′W
Hawai'ian Islands, is., Hi., U.S. (hä-wī′ȧn ī′lȧndz)	127	24°0′N	157°00′W
Hawai'i Volcanoes National Park, n.p., Hi., U.S.	127a	19°23′N	155°17′W
Hawaii, state, U.S. (häw wī′ē)	108-09	20°0′N	157°45′W
Hawi, Hi., U.S. (hä′wē)	127a	20°15′N	155°50′W
Hawick, Scot., U.K. (hô′ĭk)	190-91	55°25′N	2°47′W
Hawke Bay, b., N.Z. (hôk bā)	278	39°20′S	177°30′E
Hawker, Austl. (hô′kẽr)	276	31°53′S	138°25′E
Hawkesbury, On., Can. (hôks′bẽr-ĭ)	136-37	45°37′N	74°36′W
Hawkesbury Island, i., B.C., Can.	132-33	53°38′N	129°00′W
Hawkinsville, Ga., U.S. (hô′kĭnz-vĭl)	124-25	32°17′N	83°28′W
Hawley, Mn., U.S. (hô′lĭ)	114-15	46°53′N	96°19′W
Hawthorne, Nv., U.S.	118-19	38°32′N	118°37′W
Haxtun, Co., U.S. (hăks′tŭn)	114-15	40°38′N	102°38′W
Hay, Austl.	276	34°31′S	144°50′E
Hay, stm., Can. (hā)	130-31	60°52′N	115°44′W
HaYarden, stm., Asia see Jordan	228-29	31°46′N	35°34′E
Hayastan, nation, Asia see Armenia	227	40°0′N	45°00′E
Hayden, Id., U.S. (hā′dĕn)	112-13	47°46′N	116°47′W
Hayes, stm., Mb., Can. (hāz)	134-35	57°03′N	92°14′W
Hayes, Mount, mtn., Ak., U.S. (mount hāz)	126	63°37′N	146°43′W
Haynesville, La., U.S. (hānz′vĭl)	120-21	32°58′N	93°08′W
Hay River, N.T., Can. (hā rĭv′ẽr)	128-29	60°49′N	115°48′W
Hays, Ks., U.S. (hāz)	120-21	38°52′N	99°18′W
Hazard, Ky., U.S. (hăz′ȧrd)	124-25	37°15′N	83°12′W
Hazārībāg, India	234-35	23°60′N	85°22′E
Hazelton, B.C., Can. (hā′z′l-tŭn)	132-33	55°15′N	127°42′W
Hazelton Mountains, mts., B.C., Can. (hā′z′l-tŭn moun′tĭnz)	132-33	54°51′N	128°00′W
Hazleton, Pa., U.S. (hā′z′l-tŭn)	116-17	40°57′N	75°59′W
Headland, Al., U.S. (hĕd′lȧnd)	124-25	31°21′N	85°21′W
Healdsburg, Ca., U.S. (hēldz′bûrg)	118-19	38°37′N	122°52′W
Healdton, Ok., U.S. (hēld′tŭn)	120-21	34°14′N	97°29′W
Heard and McDonald Islands, dep., Oc.	282-83	53°05′S	73°00′E
Heard Island, i., Austl. (hûrd ī′lȧnd)	286	53°06′S	73°30′E
Hearne, Tx., U.S. (hûrn)	122-23	30°53′N	96°36′W
Hearst, On., Can. (hûrst)	128-29	49°41′N	83°42′W
Heavener, Ok., U.S. (hēv′nẽr)	120-21	34°54′N	94°36′W
Hebbronville, Tx., U.S. (hē′brŭn-vĭl)	122-23	27°18′N	98°41′W
Hebei, state, China (hŭ-bā)	240-41	38°0′N	116°00′E
Heber City, Ut., U.S. (hē′bẽr sĭ′tĕ)	118-19	40°31′N	111°25′W
Heber Springs, Ar., U.S. (hē′bẽr sprĭngz)	124-25	35°29′N	92°02′W
Hebi, China	240-41	35°58′N	114°09′E
Hebrides, is., Scot., U.K.	190-91	57°0′N	6°30′W
Hebron, Nf., Can. (hĕb′rŭn)	128-29	58°12′N	62°38′W
Hebron, N.D., U.S. (hĕb′rŭn)	114-15	46°54′N	102°03′W
Hebron, Ne., U.S. (hĕb′rŭn)	120-21	40°09′N	97°35′W
Hebron, W.B.	228-29	31°32′N	35°06′E
Hecate Strait, strt., B.C., Can. (hĕk′ȧ-tē strāt)	132-33	53°0′N	131°00′W
Hecelchakán, Mex. (ā-sĕl-chä-kän′)	148	20°10′N	90°08′W
Hechi, China (hŭ-chr)	238-39	24°42′N	108°02′E
Hechuan, China (hŭ-chyuän)	238-39	29°60′N	106°16′E
Hedemora, Swe. (hĭ-dĕ-mō′rä)	192-93	60°17′N	15°59′E
Hefa, Isr. see Haifa	228-29	32°49′N	35°00′E
Hefei, China (hŭ-fā)	238-39	31°51′N	117°17′E
Heflin, Al., U.S. (hĕf′lĭn)	124-25	33°39′N	85°35′W
Hegang, China	240-41	47°19′N	130°16′E
Heho, Mya.	246-47	20°43′N	96°49′E
Heidelberg, Ger. (hīdĕl-bĕrgh)	194-95	49°25′N	8°42′E
Heihe, China	240-41	50°14′N	127°30′E
Heijō, nat. cap., Kor., N. see P'yŏngyang	243	39°01′N	125°44′E
Heilbron, S. Afr. (hĭl′brōn)	269c	27°17′S	27°59′E
Heilbronn, Ger. (hīl′brōn)	194-95	49°08′N	9°12′E
Heilong, stm., Asia see Amur	218-19	52°57′N	141°10′E
Heilongjiang, state, China (hā-lôŋ-jyäŋ)	240-41	48°0′N	128°00′E
Heilongjiang, stm., Asia see Amur	218-19	52°57′N	141°10′E
Heilungkiang, state, China see Heilongjiang	240-41	48°0′N	128°00′E
Heinola, Fin. (hå-nō′lä)	192-93	61°12′N	26°03′E
Hejaz, reg., Sau. Ar. (hĕ-jäz′) (hē-jăz′) see Al-Ḥijāz	266	24°30′N	38°30′E
Hejian, China (hŭ-jyĕn)	240-41	38°26′N	116°05′E
Hekla, vol., Ice.	190a	64°0′N	19°39′W
Hel, Pol. (hāl)	194-95	54°37′N	18°48′E
Helagsfjället, mtn., Swe.	184-85	62°55′N	12°27′E
Helena, Ar., U.S. (hē-lē′nȧ)	124-25	34°32′N	90°36′W
Helena, Mt., U.S.	112-13	46°36′N	112°02′W
Helen Island, i., Palau	280-81	2°58′N	131°49′E
Helgoland, i., Ger. (hĕl′gō-lănd)	194-95	54°11′N	7°52′E
Hellín, Spain (ĕl-yĕn′)	198-99	38°30′N	1°42′W
Hells Canyon, val., U.S. (hĕls kăn′yŭn)	112-13	45°17′N	116°40′W
Helmand, stm., Asia (hĕl′mŭnd)	232-33	31°19′N	61°29′E
Helmond, Neth. (hĕl′mōnt) (ĕl′môn′)	190-91	51°29′N	5°40′E
Helmstedt, Ger. (hĕlm′shtĕt)	194-95	52°13′N	11°01′E
Helsingborg, Swe. (hĕl′sĭng-bôrgh)	192-93	56°03′N	12°42′E
Helsingfors, nat. cap., Fin. see Helsinki	192-93	60°10′N	24°57′E
Helsingør, Den. (hĕl-sĭng-ûr′)	192-93	56°02′N	12°37′E
Helsinki, nat. cap., Fin. (hĕl′sên-kê)	192-93	60°10′N	24°57′E
Helvetia, nation, Eur. see Switzerland	174-75	47°0′N	8°00′E
Hemingford, Ne., U.S. (hĕm′ĭng-fẽrd)	114-15	42°19′N	103°05′W
Hempstead, N.Y., U.S. (hĕmp′stĕd)	116-17	40°42′N	73°41′W
Hempstead, Tx., U.S. (hĕmp′stĕd)	122-23	30°05′N	96°05′W
Hemse, Swe. (hĕm′sē)	192-93	57°14′N	18°23′E
Henan, state, China (hŭ-nän)	238-39	34°0′N	114°00′E
Henderson, Ky., U.S. (hĕn′dẽr-sŭn)	116-17	37°50′N	87°35′W
Henderson, N.C., U.S. (hĕn′dẽr-sŭn)	124-25	36°20′N	78°24′W
Henderson, Nv., U.S. (hĕn′dẽr-sŭn)	118-19	36°02′N	114°59′W
Henderson, Tn., U.S. (hĕn′dẽr-sŭn)	124-25	35°26′N	88°38′W
Henderson, Tx., U.S. (hĕn′dẽr-sŭn)	122-23	32°09′N	94°48′W
Henderson Island, i., Pit.	280-81	24°22′S	128°19′W
Hendersonville, N.C., U.S. (hĕn′dẽr-sŭn-vĭl)	124-25	35°19′N	82°28′W
Hendersonville, Tn., U.S. (hĕn′dẽr-sŭn-vĭl)	124-25	36°18′N	86°37′W
Hendorābī, Jazīreh-ye, i., Iran	230-31	26°41′N	53°38′E
Hendrina, S. Afr. (hĕn-drē′nȧ)	269c	26°10′S	29°44′E
Hendū Kosh, mts., Asia see Hindu Kush	232-33	36°0′N	71°30′E
Hengām, Jazīreh-ye, i., Iran	230-31	26°39′N	55°53′E
Hengelo, Neth. (hĕngĕ-lō)	190-91	52°16′N	6°48′E
Hengshan, China (hĕng′shän′)	238-39	27°15′N	112°51′E
Hengshan, China (hĕng′shän′)	240-41	37°57′N	109°18′E
Hengshui, China (hĕng′shōō-ē′)	240-41	37°44′N	115°42′E
Hengxian, China (hŭŋ shyĕn)	238-39	22°41′N	109°12′E
Hengyang, China	238-39	26°54′N	112°36′E
Henlopen, Cape, c., De., U.S. (kāp hĕn-lō′pĕn)	116-17	38°47′N	75°06′W
Hennebont, Fr. (ĕn-bôn′)	196-97	47°48′N	3°16′W
Hennessey, Ok., U.S. (hĕn′ĕ-sĭ)	120-21	36°07′N	97°54′W
Henrietta, Tx., U.S. (hen-rĭ-ĕ′tȧ)	120-21	33°49′N	98°12′W
Henrietta Maria, Cape, c., On., Can. (kăp hĕn-rĭ-ĕt′ȧ mȧ-rē′ȧ)	130-31	55°08′N	82°20′W
Henzada, Mya.	246-47	17°38′N	95°28′E
Hepu, China (hŭ-pōō)	238-39	21°41′N	109°11′E
Herāt, Afg. (hĕ-rät′)	232-33	34°21′N	62°12′E
Heredia, C.R. (ā-rā′dhē-ä)	149	9°59′N	84°07′W
Hereford, Eng., U.K. (hĕrĕ′fẽrd)	190-91	52°04′N	2°43′W
Hereford, Tx., U.S. (hĕr′ĕ-fẽrd)	120-21	34°50′N	102°24′W
Herford, Ger. (hĕr′fōrt)	194-95	52°07′N	8°40′E
Herkimer, N.Y., U.S. (hûr′kĭ-mẽr)	116-17	43°02′N	74°58′W
Herlen, stm., Asia see Kerulen	240-41	48°44′N	117°03′E
Hermannstadt, Rom. see Sibiu	194-95	45°47′N	24°09′E
Hermansville, Mi., U.S. (hûr′mănz-vĭl)	116-17	45°42′N	87°36′W

ăt; finăl; rāte; senāte; ärm; åsk; sofȧ; fâre; ch-choose; dh-as th in other; bē; ēvent; bĕt; recĕnt; cratẽr; g-gō; gh-guttural g; bĭt; ĭ-short neutral; rīde; ĸ-guttural k as ch in German ich;

PRONOUNCING INDEX

Hermit Islands – Houma 337

Feature (Pronunciation)	Page	Lat.	Long.
Hermit Islands, is., Pap. N. Gui. (hûr´mĭt ī´lăndz)	277	1°30'S	145°05'E
Hermon, Mount, mtn., Asia	228-29	33°25'N	35°51'E
Hermosillo, Mex. (ĕr-mô-sē´l-yō)	144-45	29°05'N	110°58'W
Hermus, stm., Tur. see Gediz	200-01	38°36'N	26°48'E
Herning, Den. (hĕr´nĭng)	192-93	56°08'N	8°59'E
Herrin, Il., U.S. (hĕr´ĭn)	116-17	37°48'N	89°02'W
Herstal, Bel. (hĕr´stäl)	190-91	50°40'N	5°38'E
Hertford, N.C., U.S. (hûrt´fērd)	124-25	36°11'N	76°29'W
Hervey Bay, Austl.	276	25°17'S	152°50'E
Hervey Bay, b., Austl.	272-73	25°0'S	153°00'E
Hessen, hist. reg., Ger. (hĕs´ĕn)	194-95	50°30'N	9°15'E
Hettinger, N.D., U.S. (hĕt´ĭn-jēr)	114-15	46°00'N	102°38'W
Hexian, China (hŭ shyĕn)	238-39	24°18'N	111°39'E
Heyuan, China (hŭ-yūän)	238-39	23°43'N	114°42'E
Heze, China (hŭ-dzŭ)	240-41	35°15'N	115°27'E
Hialeah, Fl., U.S. (hī-ȧ-lē´ăh)	125a	25°51'N	80°17'W
Hiawatha, Ia., U.S. (hī-ȧ-wô´thȧ)	114-15	42°02'N	91°41'W
Hibbing, Mn., U.S. (hĭb´ĭng)	114-15	47°25'N	92°56'W
Hickman, Ky., U.S. (hĭk´măn)	124-25	36°34'N	89°11'W
Hickory, N.C., U.S. (hĭk´ô-rĭ)	124-25	35°44'N	81°21'W
Hicks, Point, c., Austl.	276	37°48'S	149°16'E
Hidalgo, Mex. (ē-dhäl´gō)	146-47	24°15'N	99°26'W
Hidalgo, Mex. (ē-dhäl´gō)	122-23	25°58'N	100°27'W
Hidalgo, state, Mex. (ē-dhäl´gō)	146-47	20°30'N	99°00'W
Hidalgo del Parral, Mex. (ē-dä´l-gō-dĕl-pär-rä´l)	122-23	26°57'N	105°40'W
Higasi Sina Kai, s., Asia see East China Sea	222-23	30°0'N	126°00'E
Higginsville, Mo., U.S. (hĭg´ĭnz-vĭl)	120-21	39°05'N	93°43'W
Highland, Il., U.S. (hī´lănd)	120-21	38°44'N	89°41'W
Highland Park, Il., U.S. (hī´lănd pärk)	116-17	42°11'N	87°48'W
Highland Park, Mi., U.S. (hī´lănd pärk)	116-17	42°24'N	83°07'W
High Level, Ab., Can.	128-29	58°31'N	117°08'W
Highmore, S.D., U.S. (hī´mōr)	114-15	44°31'N	99°26'W
High Point, N.C., U.S. (hī point)	124-25	35°57'N	80°01'W
High Prairie, Ab., Can. (hī prâ´rĭ)	132-33	55°26'N	116°29'W
High River, Ab., Can. (hī rĭv´ēr)	132-33	50°35'N	113°52'W
Hightstown, N.J., U.S. (hīts-toun)	116-17	40°17'N	74°32'W
High Wycombe, Eng., U.K. (hī wĭ-kŭm)	190-91	51°38'N	0°45'W
Higüey, Dom. Rep. (ē-gwĕ´y)	142-43	18°37'N	68°43'W
Hiiumaa, i., Est. (hē´ŏm-ô)	192-93	58°55'N	22°38'E
Hikone, Japan (hē´kô-nĕ)	245	35°15'N	136°15'E
Hildesheim, Ger. (hĭl´dĕs-hīm)	194-95	52°09'N	9°57'E
Hilla, Iraq see Al-Ḥillah	228-29	32°29'N	44°26'E
Hillaby, Mount, mtn., Barb. (mount hĭl´ȧ-bĭ)	143b	13°12'N	59°35'W
Hillerød, Den. (hē´lĕ-rûdh hĭl)	192-93	55°56'N	12°19'E
Hillsboro, Il., U.S. (hĭlz´bŭr-ō)	116-17	39°09'N	89°29'W
Hillsboro, N.D., U.S. (hĭlz´bŭr-ō)	114-15	47°24'N	97°04'W
Hillsboro, Oh., U.S. (hĭlz´bŭr-ō)	116-17	39°12'N	83°37'W
Hillsboro, Or., U.S. (hĭlz´bŭr-ō)	112-13	45°31'N	122°59'W
Hillsboro, Tx., U.S. (hĭlz´bŭr-ō)	122-23	32°01'N	97°08'W
Hillsboro, W.V., U.S. (hĭlz´bŭr-ō)	116-17	38°08'N	80°13'W
Hillsdale, Mi., U.S. (hĭls-dāl hĭlz)	116-17	41°55'N	84°38'W
Hillston, Austl.	276	33°29'S	145°33'E
Hilo, Hi., U.S. (hē´lō)	127a	19°43'N	155°05'W
Himāchal Pradesh, state, India	234-35	32°0'N	77°00'E
Himalayas, mts., Asia (hĭ-mä´lȧ-yȧz) (hĭ-mȧ-lā´-yȧz)	234-35	28°0'N	84°00'E
Himalaya Shan, mts., Asia see Himalayas	234-35	28°0'N	84°00'E
Himatnagar, India	234-35	23°35'N	72°58'E
Himeji, Japan (hē´mȧ-jē)	245	34°50'N	134°42'E
Ḥimṣ, Syria	228-29	34°45'N	36°44'E
Hinche, Haiti (hēn´chȧ) (ănsh)	142-43	19°09'N	72°00'W
Hinchinbrook Island, i., Austl. (hĭn-chĭn-brŏŏk ī´lănd)	277	18°23'S	146°17'E
Hindenburg, Pol. see Zabrze	194-95	50°18'N	18°46'E
Hindu Kush, mts., Asia (hĭn´dōō kōōsh´)	232-33	36°0'N	71°30'E
Hindupur, India (hĭn´dōō-pōōr)	236	13°49'N	77°30'E
Hinnøya, i., Nor.	184-85	68°32'N	15°59'E
Hinton, Ab., Can. (hĭn´tŭn)	132-33	53°25'N	117°34'W
Hinton, W.V., U.S. (hĭn´tŭn)	116-17	37°40'N	80°53'W
Hirado-shima, i., Japan (hē´rä-dō shē´mä)	245	33°20'N	129°30'E
Hirara, Japan	279a	24°47'N	125°17'E
Hīrmand, stm., Asia see Helmand	232-33	31°19'N	61°29'E
Hirosaki, Japan (hē´rô-sä´kē)	244	40°36'N	140°29'E
Hiroshima, Japan (hē-rô-shē´mȧ)	245	34°24'N	132°28'E
Hirosima, Japan see Hiroshima	245	34°24'N	132°28'E
Hirschberg, Pol. see Jelenia Góra	194-95	50°54'N	15°44'E
Hirson, Fr. (ēr-sôN´)	196-97	49°56'N	4°05'E
Hisār, India	234-35	29°09'N	75°44'E
Hispaniola, i., N.A. (hĭs´spăn-ĭ-ō-lȧ)	142-43	19°0'N	71°00'W
Hitachi, Japan (hē-tä´chē)	245	36°36'N	140°39'E
Hitoyoshi, Japan (hē´tô-yō´shē)	245	32°12'N	130°46'E
Hitra, i., Nor. (hĭträ)	184-85	63°33'N	8°45'E
Hiu, i., Vanuatu	279g	13°08'S	166°33'E
Hiva Oa, i., Fr. Poly.	280-81	9°45'S	139°00'W
Hjo, Swe. (yō)	192-93	58°18'N	14°17'E
Hjørring, Den. (jûr´ĭng)	192-93	57°28'N	9°59'E
Hkakabo Razi, mtn., Mya.	238-39	28°17'N	97°46'E
Hlohovec, Slvk. (hlō´ho-vĕts)	194-95	48°26'N	17°48'E
Ho, Ghana	260-61	6°36'N	0°28'E
Hoa Binh, Viet.	246-47	20°50'N	105°20'E
Hobart, Austl. (hō´bȧrt)	276	42°52'S	147°18'E
Hobart, Ok., U.S. (hō´bȧrt)	120-21	35°02'N	99°06'W
Hobbs, N.M., U.S. (hŏbs)	120-21	32°42'N	103°08'W
Hobro, Den. (hô-brō´)	192-93	56°38'N	9°48'E
Ho Chi Minh City, Viet. (hō-chē-mĭn sĭ´tē)	246-47	10°45'N	106°40'E
Hodeida, Yemen see Al-Ḥudaydah	266	14°48'N	42°57'E
Hodgenville, Ky., U.S. (hŏj´ĕn-vĭl)	116-17	37°34'N	85°44'W
Hódmezővásárhely, Hung. (hōd´mĕ-zû-vô´shôr-hĕl-y´)	194-95	46°25'N	20°20'E
Hodna, Chott el, lk., Alg.	269b	35°25'N	4°45'E
Hodonín, Czech Rep. (hē´dô-nēn)	194-95	48°51'N	17°08'E
Hoei, Bel. see Huy	190-91	50°31'N	5°14'E
Hof, Ger. (hōf)	194-95	50°18'N	11°55'E
Hofsjökull, ice, Ice. (hôfs´yü´kōōl)	190a	64°50'N	18°54'W
Hōfu, Japan	245	34°03'N	131°35'E
Hofuf, Sau. Ar. see Al-Hufūf	230-31	25°22'N	49°34'E
Hogansville, Ga., U.S. (hō´gănz-vĭl)	124-25	33°11'N	84°55'W
Hoggar, mts., Alg. see Ahaggar	258-59	23°0'N	6°30'E
Hohensalza, Pol. see Inowrocław	194-95	52°48'N	18°15'E
Hohe Tauern, mts., Aus. (hō´ĕ tou´ērn)	194-95	47°06'N	12°56'E
Hohhot, China (hŭ-hōō-tŭ)	240-41	40°49'N	111°39'E
Hoihow, China see Haikou	238-39	20°03'N	110°22'E
Hoisington, Ks., U.S. (hoi´zĭng-tŭn)	120-21	38°31'N	98°46'W
Hokitika, N.Z. (hō-kĭ-tē´kä)	278	42°44'S	170°58'E
Hokkaidō, i., Japan (hŏk´kĭ-dō)	244	44°0'N	143°00'E
Hola, Kenya	262-63	1°30'S	40°01'E
Holbrook, Az., U.S. (hōl´brŏŏk)	118-19	34°54'N	110°10'W
Holden, Mo., U.S. (hōl´dĕn)	120-21	38°43'N	93°60'W
Holden, W.V., U.S. (hōl´dĕn)	116-17	37°49'N	82°04'W
Holdenville, Ok., U.S. (hōl´dĕn-vĭl)	120-21	35°05'N	96°24'W
Holdrege, Ne., U.S. (hōl´drĕj)	120-21	40°27'N	99°22'W
Holguín, Cuba (ōl-gēn´)	142-43	20°53'N	76°15'W
Holguín, state, Cuba (ōl-gēn´)	142-43	20°55'N	75°50'W
Holland, Mi., U.S. (hŏl´ănd)	116-17	42°47'N	86°06'W
Holland, nation, Eur. see Netherlands	174-75	52°15'N	5°30'E
Hollandia, Indon. see Jayapura	277	2°32'S	140°43'E
Hollandsbird Island, i., Nmb.	264-65	24°39'S	14°32'E
Hollick-Kenyon Plateau, plat., Ant.	287	79°0'S	97°00'W
Hollis, Ok., U.S. (hŏl´ĭs)	120-21	34°41'N	99°55'W
Hollister, Mo., U.S. (hŏl´ĭs-tēr)	120-21	36°37'N	93°13'W
Holly Springs, Ms., U.S. (hŏl´ĭ sprĭngz)	124-25	34°46'N	89°27'W
Hollywood, Fl., U.S. (hŏl´ē-wŏŏd)	125a	26°01'N	80°09'W
Holmestrand, Nor. (hôl´mĕ-strän)	192-93	59°29'N	10°18'E
Holstebro, Den. (hôl´stĕ-brô)	192-93	56°22'N	8°38'E
Holyhead, Wales, U.K. (hŏl´ē-hĕd)	190-91	53°19'N	4°38'W
Holyoke, Co., U.S. (hōl´yōk)	114-15	40°35'N	102°18'W
Holyoke, Ma., U.S. (hōl´yōk)	116-17	42°12'N	72°37'W
Homa Bay, Kenya	267	0°31'S	34°27'E
Homalin, Mya.	238-39	24°51'N	94°56'E
Homel', Bela.	202-03	52°26'N	30°59'E
Homer, Ak., U.S. (hō´mēr)	126	59°39'N	151°31'W
Homer, La., U.S. (hō´mēr)	120-21	32°48'N	93°04'W
Homestead, Fl., U.S. (hōm´stĕd)	125a	25°29'N	80°28'W
Homestead National Monument of America, n.p., Ne., U.S. (hōm´stĕd)	120-21	40°16'N	96°48'W
Homewood, Al., U.S. (hōm´wŏŏd)	124-25	33°28'N	86°48'W
Hominy, Ok., U.S. (hŏm´ĭ-nĭ)	120-21	36°25'N	96°24'W
Homs, Libya see Al-Khums	188-89	32°39'N	14°16'E
Homs, Syria see Ḥimṣ	228-29	34°45'N	36°44'E
Honan, state, China see Henan	238-39	34°0'N	114°00'E
Honda, Col. (hōn´dȧ)	163c	5°13'N	74°45'W
Hondo, stm., N.A. (hon-dō´)	148	18°29'N	88°18'W
Honduras, nation, N.A. (hŏn-dōō´rȧs)	85	15°0'N	86°30'W
Honduras, Golfo de, b., N.A. see Honduras, Gulf of	148	16°05'N	87°58'W
Honduras, Gulf of, b., N.A. (gŭlf ŭv hŏn-dōō´rȧs)	148	16°05'N	87°58'W
Hønefoss, Nor. (hē´nĕ-fōs)	192-93	60°11'N	10°15'E
Honesdale, Pa., U.S. (hōnz´dāl)	116-17	41°34'N	75°16'W
Honfleur, Fr. (ôN-flûr´)	196-97	49°25'N	0°14'E
Hong, Song, stm., Asia see Red	238-39	20°18'N	106°32'E
Hon Gai, Viet.	246-47	21°03'N	107°04'E
Hongjiang, China	238-39	27°04'N	109°58'E
Hong Kong, China (hông kông)	238-39	22°16'N	114°10'E
Hongliuyuan, China	240-41	41°02'N	95°25'E
Hongshui, stm., China (hôŋ-shwā)	238-39	23°48'N	109°32'E
Hongtong, China	240-41	36°17'N	111°40'E
Honguedo, Détroit d', strt., Qc., Can.	138-39	49°15'N	64°00'W
Hongze Hu, lk., China	238-39	33°16'N	118°34'E
Honiara, nat. cap., Sol. Is. (hō-nē-ä´-rä)	279e	9°26'S	159°57'E
Honiton, Eng., U.K. (hŏn´ĭ-tŏn)	190-91	50°48'N	3°12'W
Honolulu, Hi., U.S. (hŏn-ô-lōō´lōō)	127a	21°19'N	157°52'W
Honshū, i., Japan (hŏn´-shōō)	244	36°0'N	138°00'E
Hood, i., Ec. see Española, Isla	170a	1°23'S	89°42'W
Hood, Mount, vol., Or., U.S. (mount hŏŏd)	112-13	45°23'N	121°42'W
Hood River, Or., U.S. (hŏŏd rĭv´ēr)	112-13	45°42'N	121°31'W
Hooker, Ok., U.S. (hŏŏk´ēr)	120-21	36°52'N	101°13'W
Hook Island, i., Austl.	277	20°08'S	148°55'E
Hoonah, Ak., U.S. (hōō´nā)	126	58°07'N	135°26'W
Hooper Bay, Ak., U.S. (hŏŏp´ēr bā)	126	61°31'N	166°06'W
Hoopeston, Il., U.S. (hōōps´tŭn)	116-17	40°28'N	87°39'W
Hoosick Falls, N.Y., U.S. (hōō´sĭk fôlz)	116-17	42°54'N	73°21'W
Hoover Dam, d., U.S. (hōō´vēr dăm)	118-19	36°02'N	114°43'W
Hope, B.C., Can.	132-33	49°23'N	121°26'W
Hope, Ar., U.S. (hōp)	120-21	33°40'N	93°35'W
Hope, Ben, mtn., Scot., U.K. (bĕn hōp)	190-91	58°24'N	4°37'W
Hopedale, Nf., Can. (hōp´dāl)	128-29	55°28'N	60°13'W
Hopeh, state, China see Hebei	240-41	38°0'N	116°00'E
Hopelchén, Mex. (o-pĕl-chĕ´n)	148	19°46'N	89°51'W
Hopes Advance, Cap, c., Qc., Can. (kȧp hōps ăd-vans´)	130-31	61°04'N	69°34'W
Hopetoun, Austl. (hōp´toun)	276	35°44'S	142°22'E
Hopetown, S. Afr. (hōp´toun)	264-65	29°35'S	24°04'E
Hopewell, Va., U.S. (hōp´wĕl)	124-25	37°18'N	77°17'W
Hopi Indian Reservation, ind. res., Az., U.S. (hō´pē ĭn´dĭ-ăn rĕ-sēr-vā´shĕn)	118-19	35°45'N	110°35'W
Hopkinsville, Ky., U.S. (hŏp´kĭns-vĭl)	124-25	36°52'N	87°29'W
Hoquiam, Wa., U.S. (hō´kwĭ-ăm)	112-13	46°59'N	123°53'W
Horicon, Wi., U.S. (hŏr´ĭ-kŏn)	116-17	43°27'N	88°37'W
Horlivka, Ukr.	202-03	48°20'N	38°03'E
Hormoz, Jazīreh-ye, i., Iran	230-31	27°04'N	56°28'E
Hormuz, Strait of, strt., Asia (strāt ŭv hôr´mŭz´)	230-31	26°34'N	56°15'E
Horn, c., Ice.	190a	66°28'N	22°28'W
Horn, Cape, c., Chile (kāp hôrn)	171	55°59'S	67°16'W
Hornavan, lk., Swe.	184-85	66°10'N	17°46'E
Hornell, N.Y., U.S. (hôr-nĕl´)	116-17	42°20'N	77°39'W
Hornepayne, On., Can.	136-37	49°12'N	84°47'W
Horn Island, i., Ms., U.S.	124-25	30°15'N	88°43'W
Hornos, Cabo de, c., Chile see Horn, Cape	171	55°59'S	67°16'W
Horn Plateau, plat., N.T., Can.	130-31	62°08'N	120°16'W
Horqin Youyi Qianqi, China see Ulanhot	240-41	46°04'N	122°04'E
Horqueta, Para. (ŏr-kĕ´tä)	168-69	23°20'S	57°03'W
Horse Islands, is., Nf., Can. (hôrs ī´lăndz)	138-39	50°13'N	55°45'W
Horsens, Den. (hôrs´ĕns)	192-93	55°52'N	9°52'E
Horsham, Austl. (hôr´shăm) (hôrs´ăm)	276	36°43'S	142°12'E
Horten, Nor. (hôr´tĕn)	192-93	59°25'N	10°29'E
Horton, stm., N.T., Can.	130-31	69°55'N	127°02'W
Hosa'ina, Eth.	269d	7°37'N	37°56'E
Hoséré Vokré, mtn., Camrn.	260-61	8°20'N	13°15'E
Hoshangābād, India	234-35	22°45'N	77°43'E
Hoshiārpur, India	234-35	31°32'N	75°55'E
Hospet, India	236	15°16'N	76°23'E
Hoste, Isla, i., Chile (ĕ´s-lä-ôs´tā)	171	55°05'S	69°15'W
Hotan, China (hwô-tän)	226	37°07'N	79°55'E
Hotan, stm., China (hwô-tän)	226	40°30'N	80°56'E
Hot Springs, Ar., U.S. (hŏt sprĭngz)	120-21	34°30'N	93°04'W
Hot Springs, N.M., U.S. (hŏt sprĭngz) see Truth or Consequences	118-19	33°08'N	107°15'W
Hot Springs, S.D., U.S. (hŏt sprĭngz)	114-15	43°26'N	103°29'W
Hot Springs, Va., U.S. (hŏt sprĭngz)	116-17	37°60'N	79°49'W
Hot Springs National Park, n.p., Ar., U.S. (hŏt sprĭngz năsh´ŭn-ăl pärk)	120-21	34°31'N	93°02'W
Hottah Lake, lk., N.T., Can.	130-31	65°04'N	118°29'W
Houghton, Mi., U.S. (hō´tŭn)	114-15	47°06'N	88°36'W
Houghton Lake, lk., Mi., U.S. (hō´tŭn lāk)	116-17	44°20'N	84°45'W
Houlton, Me., U.S. (hōl´tŭn)	117a	46°08'N	67°50'W
Houma, China	240-41	35°37'N	111°21'E
Houma, La., U.S. (hōō´mȧ)	124-25	29°35'N	90°43'W

n-sing; ŋ-baŋk; N-nasalized n; nŏd; cŏmmit; ōld; ôbey; ôrder; oi-boil; fōōd; ŏŏ-as oo in foot; ou-out; s-soft; sh-dish; th-thin; pūre; ûnite; ûrn; stŭd; circŭs; ü-as in French tu; ´-indeterminate vowel.

338 Houston – Iguassu Falls PRONOUNCING INDEX

Feature (Pronunciation)	Page	Lat.	Long.
Houston, Ms., U.S. (hūs′tŭn)	124-25	33°54′N	88°60′W
Houston, Tx., U.S. (hūs′tŭn)	122-23	29°45′N	95°22′W
Hovd, Mong. *see* Dund-Us	240-41	47°60′N	91°38′E
Hovd, stm., Mong.	218-19	48°05′N	92°13′E
Hövsgöl nuur, lk., Mong.	240-41	51°0′N	100°30′E
Howard, S.D., U.S. (hou′ard)	114-15	44°00′N	97°32′W
Howe, Cape, c., Austl. (kāp hou)	276	37°30′S	149°58′E
Howell, Mi., U.S. (hou′ĕl)	116-17	42°36′N	83°56′W
Howe Sound, strt., B.C., Can. (hou sound)	132-33	49°22′N	123°18′W
Howland Island, dep., Oc. (hou′lănd ī′lănd)	280-81	0°51′N	176°38′W
Howland Island, i., Oc. (hou′lănd ī′lănd)	280-81	0°48′N	176°38′W
Hoxie, Ar., U.S. (kŏh′sĭ)	124-25	36°03′N	90°59′W
Hradec Králové, Czech Rep.	194-95	50°12′N	15°50′E
Hranice, Czech Rep. (hrän′yĕ-tsĕ)	194-95	49°33′N	17°45′E
Hrodna, Bela.	194-95	53°41′N	23°50′E
Hrubieszów, Pol. (hrōō-byā′shōōf)	194-95	50°49′N	23°56′E
Hrvatska, nation, Eur. (hr-väts′kä) *see* Croatia	174-75	45°10′N	15°30′E
Hsinchu, Tai. (hsĭn′chōō′)	225a	24°48′N	120°58′E
Hsinhailien, China *see* Lianyungang	238-39	34°37′N	119°11′E
Hsipaw, Mya.	246-47	22°37′N	97°18′E
Huacho, Peru	170	11°08′S	77°37′W
Huadian, China (hwä-dĭĕn)	240-41	42°58′N	126°45′E
Hua Hin, Thai.	246-47	12°35′N	99°57′E
Huai'an, China (hwī-än)	238-39	33°31′N	119°08′E
Huai'an, China (hwī-än)	240-41	40°40′N	114°25′E
Huaicheng, China *see* Huai'an	238-39	33°31′N	119°08′E
Huaide, China *see* Gongzhuling	240-41	43°30′N	124°49′E
Huailai, China	240-41	40°23′N	115°34′E
Huainan, China	238-39	32°40′N	117°01′E
Huaiyang, China (hōōāī′yang)	238-39	33°44′N	114°53′E
Huajuapan de León, Mex. (wäj-wä′päm dā lā-ōn′)	146-47	17°49′N	97°45′W
Hualfín, Arg.	168-69	27°14′S	66°50′W
Hualien, Tai. (hwä′lyĕn′)	225a	23°58′N	121°35′E
Huallaga, stm., Peru (wäl-yä′gä)	170	5°06′S	75°36′W
Huallanca, Peru	170	8°49′S	77°52′W
Huambo, Ang.	264-65	12°46′S	15°44′E
Huancavelica, Peru (wän′kä-vä-lē′kä)	163a	12°47′S	75°01′W
Huancayo, Peru (wän-kä′yō)	163a	12°05′S	75°13′W
Huang, stm., China (hůäŋ)	222-23	37°49′N	118°53′E
Huangchuan, China (hůäŋ-chůän)	238-39	32°08′N	115°03′E
Huang Hai, s., Asia *see* Yellow Sea	222-23	36°0′N	123°00′E
Huangho, stm., China *see* Huang	222-23	37°49′N	118°53′E
Huanghua, China (hůäŋ-hwä)	240-41	38°22′N	117°21′E
Huangshan, China	238-39	29°45′N	118°18′E
Huangshi, China	238-39	30°13′N	115°05′E
Huangyuan, China (hůäŋ-yůän)	240-41	36°41′N	101°16′E
Huanren, China (hůän-rŭn)	243	41°13′N	125°20′E
Huánuco, Peru (wä-nōō′kō)	170	9°56′S	76°15′W
Huanuni, Bol. (wä-nōō′nē)	168-69	18°17′S	66°50′W
Huaral, Peru (wä-rä'l)	163a	11°30′S	77°12′W
Huaraz, Peru	170	9°32′S	77°33′W
Huascarán, Nevado, mtn., Peru (nĕ-vä′dō wäs-kä-rän′)	170	9°07′S	77°37′W
Huasco, Chile (wäs′kō)	168-69	28°28′S	71°15′W
Huatabampo, Mex.	144-45	26°50′N	109°38′W
Huauchinango, Mex. (wä-ōō-chē-näŋ′gō)	146-47	20°11′N	98°03′W
Huautla, Mex. (wä-ōō′tlä)	146-47	18°08′N	96°50′W
Huaxian, China (hwä shyĕn)	238-39	23°23′N	113°12′E
Huaynamota, stm., Mex. (wäy-nä-mō′tä)	146-47	21°57′N	104°32′W
Hubbard, Tx., U.S. (hŭb′ẽrd)	122-23	31°50′N	96°48′W
Hubbard Creek Reservoir, lk., Tx., U.S. (hŭb′ẽrd krēk rĕ′sẽr-vwär)	120-21	32°48′N	99°01′W
Hubei, state, China (hōō-bā)	238-39	31°0′N	112°00′E
Hubli-Dhārwār, India	236	15°21′N	75°09′E
Huddersfield, Eng., U.K. (hŭd′ẽrz-fēld)	190-91	53°39′N	1°47′W
Hudiksvall, Swe. (hōō′dĭks-väl)	192-93	61°44′N	17°07′E
Hudson, Mi., U.S. (hŭd′sŭn)	116-17	41°51′N	84°21′W
Hudson, Wi., U.S. (hŭd′sŭn)	114-15	44°59′N	92°45′W
Hudson, stm., U.S. (hŭd′sŭn)	110-11	40°41′N	74°02′W
Hudson, Détroit d', strt., Can. *see* Hudson Strait	130-31	62°30′N	71°60′W
Hudson Bay, Sk., Can. (hŭd′sŭn bā)	134-35	52°52′N	102°23′W
Hudson Bay, b., Can. (hŭd′sŭn bā)	130-31	60°0′N	86°00′W
Hudson Falls, N.Y., U.S. (hŭd′sŭn fôlz)	116-17	43°19′N	73°35′W
Hudson Strait, strt., Can. (hŭd′sŭn strāt)	130-31	62°30′N	71°60′W
Hue, Viet. (ü-ā′)	246-47	16°28′N	107°35′E
Huehuetenango, Guat. (wā-wå-tå-näŋ′gō)	148	15°21′N	91°27′W
Huejuquilla El Alto, Mex. (wā-hōō-kēl′yä ĕl äl′tō)	146-47	22°38′N	103°54′W
Huelva, Spain (wĕl′vä)	198-99	37°16′N	6°57′W
Huesca, Spain (wĕs-kä)	198-99	42°08′N	0°25′W
Huéscar, Spain (wās′kär)	198-99	37°48′N	2°33′W
Huetamo de Núñez, Mex.	146-47	18°35′N	100°53′W
Hughenden, Austl. (hū′ĕn-dĕn)	277	20°51′S	144°13′E
Hugli, stm., India (hōōg′lĭ)	234-35	21°36′N	87°60′E
Hugo, Ok., U.S. (hū′gō)	120-21	34°01′N	95°31′W
Hugoton, Ks., U.S. (hū′gō-tŭn)	120-21	37°11′N	101°21′W
Huhehot, China *see* Hohhot	240-41	40°49′N	111°39′E
Huichapan, Mex. (wē-chä-pän′)	146-47	20°22′N	99°40′W
Hŭich'ŏn, Kor., N.	243	40°10′N	126°17′E
Huila, Nevado del, vol., Col. (nĕ-vä-dō-del-wē′lä)	163c	2°59′N	75°58′W
Huili, China	238-39	26°40′N	102°14′E
Huimin, China (hōōī mĭn)	240-41	37°29′N	117°32′E
Huinan, China	243	42°41′N	126°02′E
Huixtla, Mex.	148	15°08′N	92°27′W
Huize, China	238-39	26°25′N	103°18′E
Huizhou, China	238-39	23°05′N	114°24′E
Hujirt, Mong.	240-41	48°53′N	101°14′E
Hukuoka, Japan *see* Fukuoka	245	33°35′N	130°25′E
Hulan, China (hōō′län′)	240-41	45°59′N	126°36′E
Hulan Ergi, China	240-41	47°12′N	123°38′E
Hulin, China (hōō′lĭn′)	244	45°46′N	132°59′E
Hulun, China *see* Hailar	240-41	49°11′N	119°44′E
Hulun Nur, lk., China (hōō-lōn nòr)	240-41	49°01′N	117°32′E
Humacao, P.R. (ōō-mä-kä′ō)	142a	18°09′N	65°49′W
Humahuaca, Arg.	168-69	23°12′S	65°21′W
Humaitá, Braz.	166-67	7°30′S	63°02′W
Humaitá, Para.	173	27°05′S	58°32′W
Humble, Tx., U.S. (hŭm′b'l)	122-23	29°59′N	95°16′W
Humboldt, Sk., Can. (hŭm′bōlt)	134-35	52°11′N	105°07′W
Humboldt, Ia., U.S. (hŭm′bōlt)	114-15	42°43′N	94°13′W
Humboldt, Tn., U.S. (hŭm′bōlt)	124-25	35°50′N	88°55′W
Humboldt, stm., Nv., U.S. (hŭm′bōlt)	110-11	40°01′N	118°33′W
Hume, Lake, res., Austl.	276	36°08′S	147°02′E
Humphreys Peak, mtn., Az., U.S. (hŭm′frĭs pēk)	118-19	35°20′N	111°40′W
Húnaflói, b., Ice. (hōō′nä-flō′ĭ)	190a	65°50′N	20°50′W
Hunan, state, China (hōō′nän′)	238-39	28°0′N	111°00′E
Hunchun, China (hòn-chůn)	243	42°52′N	130°22′E
Hunedoara, Rom. (κōō′nĕd-wä′rà)	200-01	45°46′N	22°55′E
Hungary, nation, Eur. (hŭŋ′gȧ-rĭ)	174-75	47°0′N	20°00′E
Hŭngdŏki-dong, Kor., N.	243	39°50′N	127°38′E
Hungerford, Austl. (hŭn′gẽr-fẽrd)	276	28°59′S	144°24′E
Hŭngnam, Kor., N. *see* Hŭngdŏki-dong	243	39°50′N	127°38′E
Hunjiang, China	243	41°57′N	126°28′E
Hunsrück, mts., Ger. (hōōns′rûk)	194-95	49°46′N	7°08′E
Hunter, Île, i., N. Cal.	280-81	22°24′S	172°06′E
Hunter Island, i., Austl.	276	40°32′S	144°45′E
Hunter Island, i., B.C., Can.	132-33	51°54′N	128°03′W
Huntingburg, In., U.S. (hŭnt′ĭng-bûrg)	116-17	38°18′N	86°57′W
Huntingdon, Qc., Can. (hŭnt′ĭng-dŭn)	136-37	45°06′N	74°10′W
Huntingdon, Tn., U.S. (hŭnt′ĭng-dŭn)	124-25	36°00′N	88°26′W
Huntington, In., U.S. (hŭnt′ĭng-tŭn)	116-17	40°52′N	85°28′W
Huntington, Ut., U.S. (hŭnt′ĭng-tŭn)	118-19	39°20′N	110°58′W
Huntington, W.V., U.S. (hŭnt′ĭng-tŭn)	116-17	38°25′N	82°26′W
Huntington Beach, Ca., U.S. (hŭnt′ĭng-tŭn bēch)	118-19	33°39′N	117°59′W
Huntsville, On., Can. (hŭnts′vĭl)	136-37	45°19′N	79°12′W
Huntsville, Al., U.S. (hŭnts′vĭl)	124-25	34°43′N	86°36′W
Huntsville, Mo., U.S. (hŭnts′vĭl)	120-21	39°26′N	92°33′W
Huntsville, Tx., U.S. (hŭnts′vĭl)	122-23	30°43′N	95°33′W
Hunucmá, Mex.	148	21°01′N	89°52′W
Hunyuan, China	240-41	39°42′N	113°41′E
Huong Thuy, Viet.	246-47	16°25′N	107°40′E
Huon Gulf, b., Pap. N. Gui.	277	7°10′S	147°25′E
Huonville, Austl.	276	43°01′S	147°02′E
Huoqiu, China (hwŏ-chyō)	238-39	32°20′N	116°16′E
Huoshan, China (hwŏ-shän)	238-39	31°24′N	116°20′E
Hurd, Cape, c., On., Can. (kāp hûrd)	136-37	45°14′N	81°42′W
Hurghada, Egypt	268b	27°14′N	33°50′E
Hurley, Wi., U.S. (hûr′lĭ)	114-15	46°27′N	90°11′W
Huron, S.D., U.S. (hū′rŏn)	114-15	44°22′N	98°13′W
Huron, Lake, lk., N.A. (lāk hū′rŏn)	116-17	44°30′N	82°15′W
Hurricane, Ut., U.S. (hŭr′ĭ-kān)	118-19	37°11′N	113°17′W
Húsavík, Ice.	190a	66°03′N	17°19′W
Huşi, Rom. (kòsh')	202-03	46°41′N	28°04′E
Husum, Ger. (hōō′zòm)	194-95	54°28′N	9°04′E
Hutchinson, Ks., U.S. (hŭch′ĭn-sŭn)	120-21	38°03′N	97°55′W
Hutchinson, Mn., U.S. (hŭch′ĭn-sŭn)	114-15	44°53′N	94°23′W
Huy, Bel. (û-ē′) (hû′ē)	190-91	50°31′N	5°14′E
Huzhou, China	238-39	30°52′N	120°06′E
Hvannadalshnúkur, mtn., Ice.	190a	64°01′N	16°41′W
Hvar, Otok, i., Cro. (ŏ′tŏk кhvär)	200-01	43°09′N	16°45′E
Hwaining, China *see* Anqing	238-39	30°30′N	117°02′E
Hwange, Zimb.	264-65	18°22′S	26°30′E
Hwange National Park, n.p., Zimb.	264-65	19°0′S	26°35′E
Hwang-hae, s., Asia *see* Yellow Sea	222-23	36°0′N	123°00′E
Hyargas nuur, lk., Mong.	240-41	49°12′N	93°24′E
Hyde Park, Guy.	164-65	6°30′N	58°16′W
Hyde Park, N.Y., U.S. (hīd pärk)	116-17	41°47′N	73°56′W
Hyderābād, India (hī-dẽr-å-băd′)	236	17°23′N	78°29′E
Hyderābād, Pak. (hī-dẽr-å-băd′)	232-33	25°23′N	68°21′E
Hyères, Fr. (ē-år′)	196-97	43°08′N	6°08′E
Hyesan, Kor., N.	243	41°24′N	128°10′E
Hyndman Peak, mtn., Id., U.S. (hīnd′măn pēk)	112-13	43°45′N	114°08′W
Hyōgo, state, Japan (hĭyō′gō)	245	35°0′N	135°00′E

I

Feature (Pronunciation)	Page	Lat.	Long.
Iaco, stm., S.A.	170	9°02′S	68°35′W
Iaşi, Rom. (yä′shē)	202-03	47°10′N	27°36′E
Iba, Phil. (ē′bä)	250	15°20′N	119°58′E
Ibadan, Nig. (ē-bä′dän)	260a	7°23′N	3°54′E
Ibagué, Col.	163c	4°27′N	75°15′W
Iban, Pegunungan, mts., Asia *see* Iran Mountains	248-49	2°05′N	114°55′E
Ibarra, Ec. (ē-bär′rä)	170	0°22′N	78°08′W
Ibb, Yemen	266	13°58′N	44°11′E
Iberian Peninsula, pen., Eur. (ī-bẽr′ĕ-ăn pĕ-nĭn′sūlă)	176-77	40°0′N	5°00′W
Ibérica, Península, pen., Eur. *see* Iberian Peninsula	176-77	40°0′N	5°00′W
Iberville, Qc., Can. (ē-bår-vēl′) (ī′bẽr-vĭl)	136-37	45°19′N	73°14′W
Ibiá, Braz.	172	19°29′S	46°32′W
Ibicaraí, Braz.	166-67	14°51′S	39°37′W
Ibicuí, stm., Braz.	173	29°25′S	56°47′W
Ibiza, Spain *see* Eivissa	198-99	38°55′N	1°25′E
Ibiza, i., Spain (ē-bē′thä) *see* Eivissa	198-99	39°0′N	1°25′E
Ica, Peru (ē′kä)	170	14°04′S	75°45′W
Içá, stm., S.A.	170	3°07′S	67°56′W
Içana, Braz. (ē-sä′nä)	166-67	0°21′N	67°19′W
İçel, Tur.	228-29	36°49′N	34°38′E
Iceland, nation, Eur. (īs′lănd)	174-75	65°0′N	18°00′W
Ichalkaranji, India	236	16°41′N	74°28′E
Ichilo, stm., Bol.	168-69	15°50′S	64°47′W
Icó, Braz.	166-67	6°24′S	38°51′W
Idabel, Ok., U.S. (ī′dȧ-bĕl)	120-21	33°53′N	94°49′W
Ida Grove, Ia., U.S. (ī′dȧ-grōv)	114-15	42°21′N	95°28′W
Idah, Nig. (ē′dä)	260a	7°07′N	6°45′E
Idaho, state, U.S. (ī′dȧ-hō)	108-09	45°0′N	115°00′W
Idaho Falls, Id., U.S. (ī′dȧ-hō fôlz)	112-13	43°30′N	112°03′W
Idaho Springs, Co., U.S. (ī′dȧ-hō sprĭngz)	118-19	39°44′N	105°31′W
Ider, stm., Mong.	240-41	49°16′N	100°41′E
Idi, Indon. (ē′dē)	246-47	4°57′N	97°46′E
Idi Amin Dada, Lac, lk., Afr. *see* Edward, Lake	267	0°23′S	29°36′E
Idiofa, D.R.C.	262-63	5°01′S	19°35′E
Ídi Óros, mtn., Grc.	200a	35°18′N	24°43′E
Idlib, Syria	228-29	35°56′N	36°39′E
Idoûkâl-en-Taghès, mtn., Niger	258-59	17°43′N	8°45′E
Iesi, Italy (yā′sē) *see* Jesi	200-01	43°31′N	13°14′E
Ife, Nig.	260a	7°28′N	4°33′E
Ifôghas, Adrar des, mts., Afr.	258-59	20°0′N	2°00′E
Igarka, Russia (ē-gär′kȧ)	218-19	67°28′N	86°38′E
Iglesias, Italy (ē-lĕ′syōs)	200-01	39°19′N	8°32′E
Igloolik, Nu., Can.	128-29	69°23′N	81°48′W
Igluligaarjuk, Nu., Can. *see* Chesterfield Inlet	128-29	63°21′N	90°43′W
Iglulik, Nu., Can. *see* Igloolik	128-29	69°23′N	81°48′W
Igombe, stm., Tan.	267	4°43′S	31°23′E
Iguaçu, stm., S.A. (ē-gwä-sōō′)	168-69	25°36′S	54°36′W
Iguaçu, Cataratas do, wtfl., S.A. *see* Iguassu Falls	168-69	25°42′S	54°27′W
Iguaçu, Saltos do, wtfl., S.A. *see* Iguassu Falls	168-69	25°42′S	54°27′W
Iguala, Mex. (ē-gwä′lä)	146-47	18°21′N	99°32′W
Igualada, Spain (ē-gwä-lä′dä)	198-99	41°35′N	1°39′E
Iguape, Braz.	172	24°43′S	47°34′W
Iguassu Falls, wtfl., S.A. (ē-gwä-sōō′ fôlz)	168-69	25°42′S	54°27′W

ăt; fināl; rāte; senåte; ärm; ȧsk; sofȧ; fâre; ch-choose; dh-as th in other; bē; ēvent; bĕt; recĕnt; cratẽr; g-gō; gh-guttural g; bĭt; ĭ-short neutral; rīde; κ-guttural k as ch in German ich;

n-sing; ŋ-bank; ɴ-nasalized n; nŏd; cŏmmit; ōld; ōbey; ôrder; oi-boil; fōōd; ȯ-as oo in foot; ou-out; s-soft; sh-dish; th-thin; pūre; ûnite; ûrn; stŭd; circŭs; ü-as in French tu; ′-indeterminate vowel.

340 İskenderun Körfezi – Jaú

PRONOUNCING INDEX

Feature (Pronunciation)	Page	Lat.	Long.
İskenderun Körfezi, b., Tur.	228-29	36°30'N	35°40'E
Iskitim, Russia	226	54°39'N	83°18'E
Iskŭr, stm., Blg. (ĭs'k'r)	200-01	43°45'N	24°26'E
Isla Cristina, Spain (ī'lä-krē-stē'nä)	198-99	37°12'N	7°19'W
Islāmābād, nat. cap., Pak. (ĭs'lä-mä-bäd') (ĭs-lä'-mä-bäd')	232-33	33°39'N	73°05'E
Isla Mujeres, Mex. (ē's-lä-mōō-kĕ'rĕs)	148	21°12'N	86°43'W
Ísland, nation, Eur. *see* Iceland	174-75	65°0'N	18°00'W
Island Lake, lk., Mb., Can. (ī'lănd lăk ī'lănd)	134-35	53°47'N	94°25'W
Islands, Bay of, b., Nf., Can. (bā ŭv ī'lăndz)	138-39	49°10'N	58°15'W
Íslandshaf, s., Eur. *see* Norwegian Sea	184-85	70°0'N	2°00'E
Islay, i., Scot., U.K. (ī'lā)	190-91	55°49'N	6°17'W
Isle of Man, dep., Eur. (īl ŭv măn)	190-91	54°15'N	4°30'W
Isle Royale National Park, n.p., Mi., U.S. (īl'roi-ăl' năsh'ŭn-ăl pärk)	114-15	47°58'N	88°55'W
Ismailia, Egypt (ĭs-mä-ēl'ēȧ)	268b	30°36'N	32°16'E
Isparta, Tur. (ē-spär'tȧ)	186-87	37°46'N	30°33'E
Israel, nation, Asia (ĭz'rē-ĕl)	206-07	31°30'N	34°45'E
Isrā'īl, nation, Asia *see* Israel	206-07	31°30'N	34°45'E
Issoire, Fr. (ē-swär')	196-97	45°33'N	3°15'E
Issoudun, Fr. (ē-sōō-dăN')	196-97	46°57'N	2°00'E
Issyk-Kul, Lake, lk., Kyrg. (lăk ē'-sĭk-kōōl')	226	42°25'N	77°15'E
İstanbul, Tur. (ē-stän-bōōl')	200-01	41°02'N	28°59'E
İstanbul Boğazı, strt., Tur. *see* Bosporus	200-01	41°06'N	29°04'E
Istaravshan, Taj.	232-33	39°54'N	69°00'E
Istiaía, Grc. (ĭs-tyī'yä)	200-01	38°57'N	23°09'E
Istmina, Col. (ēst-mē'nä)	163c	5°09'N	76°41'W
Istra, pen., Eur. (ē-strä)	200-01	45°17'N	13°57'E
Istria, pen., Eur. *see* Istra	200-01	45°17'N	13°57'E
Itabaiana, Braz. (ē-tä-bä-yȧ-nä)	163d	7°20'S	35°20'W
Itabaiana, Braz. (ē-tä-bä-yȧ-nä)	166-67	10°41'S	37°26'W
Itabapoana, Braz. (ē-tä'-bä-pôȧ'nä)	172	21°18'S	40°59'W
Itaberaí, Braz.	168-69	16°01'S	49°48'W
Itabira, Braz.	172	19°38'S	43°14'W
Itabuna, Braz. (ē-tä-bōō'nȧ)	166-67	14°47'S	39°17'W
Itacoatiara, Braz. (ē-tȧ-kwȧ-tyä'rȧ)	166-67	3°08'S	58°26'W
Itagüí, Col. (ē-tä'gwē)	163c	6°10'N	75°38'W
Itaipu, Represa de, res., S.A.	168-69	24°56'S	54°26'W
Itaipu Reservoir, res., S.A. (ē-tī'pōō rĕ'sĕr-vwär) *see* Itaipu, Represa de	168-69	24°56'S	54°26'W
Itaituba, Braz. (ē-tä'ī-tōō'bȧ)	166-67	4°15'S	55°59'W
Itajaí, Braz. (ē-tä-zhī')	172	26°54'S	48°40'W
Itajubá, Braz.	172	22°26'S	45°27'W
Italia, nation, Eur. *see* Italy	174-75	43°0'N	13°00'E
Italy, nation, Eur. (ĭt'ȧ-lē)	174-75	43°0'N	13°00'E
Itämeri, s., Eur. *see* Baltic Sea	192-93	57°0'N	19°00'E
Itānagar, India	234-35	27°09'N	93°33'E
Itaparica, Ilha de, i., Braz.	166-67	13°0'S	38°42'W
Itapecuru-Mirim, Braz. (ē-tä-pĕ'kōō-rōō-mē-rēN')	166-67	3°24'S	44°20'W
Itapemirim, Braz.	172	21°01'S	40°49'W
Itaperuna, Braz. (ē-tȧ'pâ-rōō'nä)	172	21°12'S	41°54'W
Itapetinga, Braz.	168-69	15°15'S	40°16'W
Itapetininga, Braz. (ē-tä-pĕ-tē-nē'N-gä)	172	23°35'S	48°02'W
Itapicuru, stm., Braz.	166-67	2°51'S	44°12'W
Itapicuru, stm., Braz.	166-67	11°45'S	37°31'W
Itaquari, Braz.	172	20°20'S	40°23'W
Itaqui, Braz.	173	29°08'S	56°32'W
Itararé, Braz.	172	24°07'S	49°21'W
Itārsi, India	234-35	22°36'N	77°46'E
Itasca, Tx., U.S. (ī-tăs'kȧ)	122-23	32°10'N	97°09'W
Itaúna, Braz. (ē-tä-ōō'nä)	172	20°04'S	44°34'W
Itbayat Island, i., Phil.	250a	20°46'N	121°50'E
Itenes, stm., S.A. *see* Iténez	166-67	11°55'S	65°00'W
Iténez, stm., S.A.	166-67	11°55'S	65°00'W
Ithaca, Mi., U.S. (ĭth'ȧ-kȧ)	116-17	43°17'N	84°36'W
Ithaca, N.Y., U.S. (ĭth'ȧ-kȧ)	116-17	42°26'N	76°30'W
Itu, Braz. (ē-tōō')	172	23°16'S	47°18'W
Ituango, Col. (ē-twäŋ'gō)	164-65	7°06'N	75°44'W
Ituí, stm., Braz.	164-65	4°39'S	70°15'W
Ituiutaba, Braz. (ē-tōō-ēōō-tä'bä)	168-69	18°58'S	49°27'W
Itumbiara, Braz.	172	18°25'S	49°12'W
Iturbide, Mex. (ē'tōōr-bē'dhā)	148	19°38'N	89°36'W
Ituri, stm., D.R.C.	262-63	1°40'N	27°02'E
Iturup, Ostrov, i., Russia (ôs-trôf' ē-tōō-rōōp')	218-19	44°51'N	147°27'E
Ituxi, stm., Braz.	166-67	7°18'S	64°51'W
Ituzaingó, Arg. (ē-tōō-zä-ē'n-gô)	173	27°36'S	56°40'W
Ītyop'iya, nation, Afr. *see* Ethiopia	253	9°0'N	39°00'E
Iuka, Ms., U.S. (ī-ū'kȧ)	124-25	34°49'N	88°11'W
Iul'tin, Russia	218-19	67°43'N	178°51'W
Ivaí, stm., Braz.	168-69	23°18'S	53°44'W
Ivalo, Fin.	184-85	68°40'N	27°32'E
Ivanhoe, Austl. (īv'ăn-hō)	276	32°55'S	144°19'E
Ivano-Frankivs'k, Ukr.	194-95	48°55'N	24°44'E
Ivanovo, Russia (ē-vä'nô-vō)	186-87	57°01'N	40°59'E
Ivanovo-Voznesensk, Russia *see* Ivanovo	186-87	57°01'N	40°59'E
Ivdel', Russia (ĭv'dyĕl)	186-87	60°41'N	60°27'E
Iviza, Spain *see* Eivissa	198-99	38°55'N	1°25'E
Ivory Coast, nation, Afr. *see* Cote d'Ivoire	253	8°0'N	5°00'W
Ivrea, Italy (ē-vrĕ'ä)	200-01	45°28'N	7°53'E
Ivujivik, Qc., Can.	128-29	62°23'N	77°55'W
Iwaki, Japan	245	37°03'N	140°55'E
Iwo, Nig.	260a	7°38'N	4°11'E
Iwo Jima, i., Japan (ē'wō jē'mȧ)	280-81	24°47'N	141°20'E
Ixmiquilpan, Mex. (ēs-mē-kēl'pän)	146-47	20°29'N	99°13'W
Ixtepec, Mex. (ēks-tĕ'pĕk)	146-47	16°32'N	95°05'W
Ixtlán de Juárez, Mex. (ēs-tlän' dā hwä'rāz)	146-47	17°20'N	96°30'W
Ixtlán del Río, Mex. (ēs-tlän'dĕl rē'ō)	146-47	21°02'N	104°22'W
Iyo-nada, s., Japan (ē'yō nä-dä)	245	33°40'N	132°20'E
Izabal, Lago de, lk., Guat. (lä'gô-dĕ-ē'zä-bäl')	148	15°30'N	89°10'W
Izamal, Mex. (ē-zä-mä'l)	148	20°56'N	89°01'W
Izberbash, Russia	227	42°33'N	47°52'E
Izhevsk, Russia (ē-zhyĕfsk')	186-87	56°50'N	53°12'E
Izhma, stm., Russia	186-87	65°19'N	52°55'E
Izium, Ukr.	202-03	49°13'N	37°17'E
Izmaïl, Ukr.	200-01	45°21'N	28°50'E
İzmir, Tur. (ĭz-mēr')	200-01	38°26'N	27°09'E
İzmit, Tur. (ĭz-mēt')	200-01	40°47'N	29°57'E
Izuhara, Japan (ē'zōō-hä'rä)	243	34°12'N	129°17'E
Izumo, Japan (ē'zōō-mō)	245	35°22'N	132°46'E
Izu-shotō, is., Japan	244	32°0'N	140°00'E

J

Feature (Pronunciation)	Page	Lat.	Long.
Jabal, Baḥr al-, stm., Sudan *see* Mountain Nile	262-63	9°30'N	30°30'E
Jabalpur, India	234-35	23°10'N	79°56'E
Jaboatão, Braz. (zhä-bô-ȧ-touN)	163d	8°07'S	35°01'W
Jaca, Spain (hä'kä)	198-99	42°35'N	0°34'W
Jacala, Mex. (hä-kä'lä)	146-47	21°01'N	99°11'W
Jacaltenango, Guat. (hä-käl-tĕ-näŋ'gō)	148	15°40'N	91°44'W
Jacareí, Braz.	172	23°19'S	45°58'W
Jacarezinho, Braz. (zhä-kä-rĕ'zē-nyô)	168-69	23°10'S	49°59'W
Jacksboro, Tx., U.S. (jăks'bŭr-ô)	120-21	33°13'N	98°09'W
Jackson, Al., U.S. (jăk'sŭn)	124-25	31°31'N	87°54'W
Jackson, Ga., U.S. (jăk'sŭn)	124-25	33°18'N	83°58'W
Jackson, Ky., U.S. (jăk'sŭn)	116-17	37°33'N	83°24'W
Jackson, La., U.S. (jăk'sŭn)	124-25	30°50'N	91°13'W
Jackson, Mi., U.S. (jăk'sŭn)	116-17	42°15'N	84°24'W
Jackson, Mn., U.S. (jăk'sŭn)	114-15	43°37'N	94°59'W
Jackson, Mo., U.S. (jăk'sŭn)	120-21	37°23'N	89°40'W
Jackson, Ms., U.S. (jăk'sŭn)	124-25	32°19'N	90°11'W
Jackson, Oh., U.S. (jăk'sŭn)	116-17	39°03'N	82°39'W
Jackson, Tn., U.S. (jăk'sŭn)	124-25	35°37'N	88°49'W
Jackson, Wy., U.S. (jăk'sŭn)	112-13	43°29'N	110°45'W
Jackson Lake, lk., Wy., U.S. (jăk'sŭn lăk)	112-13	43°55'N	110°40'W
Jacksonville, Al., U.S. (jăk'sŭn-vĭl)	124-25	33°49'N	85°46'W
Jacksonville, Ar., U.S. (jăk'sŭn-vĭl)	120-21	34°52'N	92°07'W
Jacksonville, Fl., U.S. (jăk'sŭn-vĭl)	124-25	30°21'N	81°39'W
Jacksonville, Il., U.S. (jăk'sŭn-vĭl)	120-21	39°44'N	90°14'W
Jacksonville, N.C., U.S. (jăk'sŭn-vĭl)	124-25	34°45'N	77°25'W
Jacksonville, Tx., U.S. (jăk'sŭn-vĭl)	122-23	31°58'N	95°16'W
Jacksonville Beach, Fl., U.S. (jăk'sŭn-vĭl bēch)	124-25	30°17'N	81°24'W
Jacmel, Haiti (zhȧk-mĕl')	142-43	18°14'N	72°32'W
Jacobābād, Pak.	232-33	28°17'N	68°26'E
Jacobina, Braz. (zhä-kô-bē'nȧ)	166-67	11°11'S	40°31'W
Jacques-Cartier, Détroit de, strt., Qc., Can.	138-39	49°53'N	62°45'W
Jacques-Cartier, Mont, mtn., Qc., Can.	138-39	48°59'N	65°57'W
Jacquet River, N.B., Can. (zhȧ-kĕ' rĭv'ēr) (jăk'ĕt rĭv'ēr)	138-39	47°55'N	66°01'W
Jacuí, stm., Braz.	168-69	30°02'S	51°15'W
Jadotville, D.R.C. *see* Likasi	262-63	10°59'S	26°43'E
Jadransko more, s., Eur. *see* Adriatic Sea	200-01	42°30'N	16°00'E
Jadransko morje, s., Eur. *see* Adriatic Sea	200-01	42°30'N	16°00'E
Jaén, Peru (kä-ĕ'n)	170	5°43'S	78°47'W
Jaén, Spain	198-99	37°46'N	3°48'W
Jaffa, Cape, c., Austl. (kăp jăf'ȧ)	276	36°58'S	139°40'E
Jaffna, Sri L. (jăf'nȧ)	236	9°40'N	80°01'E
Jagādhri, India	234-35	30°10'N	77°18'E
Jagdalpur, India	236	19°05'N	82°02'E
Jägerndorf, Czech Rep. *see* Krnov	194-95	50°05'N	17°42'E
Jaguarão, Braz.	173	32°34'S	53°23'W
Jaguariaíva, Braz.	168-69	24°15'S	49°42'W
Jaguaribe, stm., Braz.	166-67	4°25'S	37°46'W
Jagüey Grande, Cuba (hä'gwā grän'dā)	142-43	22°32'N	81°08'W
Jahrom, Iran	230-31	28°29'N	53°33'E
Jaipur, India	234-35	26°55'N	75°48'E
Jaisalmer, India	234-35	26°55'N	70°55'E
Jajce, Bos. (yī'tsĕ)	200-01	44°20'N	17°17'E
Jājpur, India	234-35	20°51'N	86°20'E
Jakarta, nat. cap., Indon. (yä-kär'tä)	248-49	6°11'S	106°50'E
Jakobstad, Fin. (yȧ'kôb-stȧdh)	184-85	63°41'N	22°43'E
Jalālābād, Afg. (jŭ-lä-lȧ-bäd)	232-33	34°26'N	70°27'E
Jalal-Abad, Kyrg.	226	40°56'N	73°00'E
Jalandhar, India	234-35	31°19'N	75°35'E
Jalapa, Guat. (hä-lä'pȧ)	148	14°38'N	89°59'W
Jalapa, Mex. *see* Xalapa	146-47	19°32'N	96°55'W
Jālgaon, India	234-35	21°01'N	75°34'E
Jalisco, state, Mex. (hä-lēs'kō)	146-47	20°20'N	103°40'W
Jālna, India	234-35	19°51'N	75°54'E
Jalón, stm., Spain (hä-lōn')	198-99	41°47'N	1°03'W
Jālor, India	234-35	25°21'N	72°37'E
Jalostotitlán, Mex. (hä-lōs-tē-tlȧn')	146-47	21°11'N	102°27'W
Jalpa, Mex. (häl'pä)	146-47	21°38'N	102°60'W
Jalpāiguri, India	234-35	26°31'N	88°42'E
Jamaame, Som.	262-63	0°01'N	42°42'E
Jamaica, nation, N.A. (jȧ-mā'kȧ)	140-41	18°15'N	77°30'W
Jamanxim, stm., Braz.	166-67	4°45'S	56°27'W
Jambi, Indon. (mäm'bē)	246-47	1°37'S	103°36'E
Jambongan, Pulau, i., Malay.	248-49	6°40'N	117°27'E
James, stm., U.S. (jāmz)	110-11	42°52'N	97°19'W
James, stm., Va., U.S. (jāmz)	116-17	36°56'N	76°26'W
James Bay, b., Can. (jāmz bā)	130-31	53°30'N	80°30'W
Jamestown, Austl.	276	33°12'S	138°36'E
Jamestown, Ky., U.S. (jāmz'toun)	124-25	36°59'N	85°04'W
Jamestown, N.D., U.S. (jāmz'toun)	114-15	46°54'N	98°42'W
Jamestown, N.Y., U.S. (jāmz'toun)	116-17	42°06'N	79°14'W
Jammu, India (jŭm'ōō)	234-35	32°43'N	74°51'E
Jammu and Kashmir, state, India (jŭm'ōō ănd kȧsh-mēr')	234-35	34°0'N	76°00'E
Jammu and Kashmir, hist. reg., Asia	234-35	34°0'N	76°00'E
Jamnagar, India (jäm-nû'gŭr)	234-35	22°28'N	70°04'E
Jamshedpur, India (jäm'shād-pōōr)	234-35	22°48'N	86°11'E
Jamuna, stm., Bngl.	234-35	23°43'N	89°49'E
Janaucu, Ilha, i., Braz.	166-67	0°30'N	50°10'W
Janesville, Ca., U.S. (jānz'vĭl)	118-19	40°18'N	120°32'W
Janesville, Wi., U.S. (jānz'vĭl)	116-17	42°41'N	89°02'W
Jangīpur, India	234-35	24°28'N	88°04'E
Jan Mayen, dep., Eur. (yän mī'ĕn)	288	71°02'N	8°19'W
Jan Mayen, i., Nor. (yän mī'ĕn)	288	71°03'N	8°19'W
Januária, Braz. (zhä-nwä'rē-ä)	168-69	15°29'S	44°22'W
Japan, nation, Asia (jȧ-păn')	206-07	36°0'N	138°00'E
Japan, Sea of, s., Asia (sē ŭv jȧ-păn')	222-23	40°0'N	135°00'E
Japurá, stm., S.A.	166-67	3°08'S	64°46'W
Jaraguá do Sul, Braz.	172	26°29'S	49°05'W
Jarama, stm., Spain (hä-rä'mä)	198-99	40°02'N	3°39'W
Jari, stm., Braz. (zhä-rē)	166-67	1°09'S	51°53'W
Jarkand, China *see* Shache	226	38°25'N	77°15'E
Jarocin, Pol. (yä-rō'tsyēn)	194-95	51°58'N	17°30'E
Jarosław, Pol. (yȧ-rôs-wȧf)	194-95	50°01'N	22°41'E
Jarud Qi, China (jya-lōō-tŭ shyē)	240-41	44°34'N	120°54'E
Jarvis Island, dep., Oc.	280-81	0°19'S	160°01'W
Jarvis Island, i., Oc.	280-81	0°23'S	160°01'W
Jāsk, Iran (jäsk)	230-31	25°39'N	57°47'E
Jasło, Pol. (yäs'wō)	194-95	49°45'N	21°28'E
Jason Islands, is., Falk. Is.	171	51°09'S	60°54'W
Jasper, Ab., Can. (jăs'pēr)	132-33	52°52'N	118°05'W
Jasper, Al., U.S. (jăs'pēr)	124-25	33°50'N	87°17'W
Jasper, Fl., U.S. (jăs'pēr)	124-25	30°31'N	82°57'W
Jasper, Ga., U.S. (jăs'pēr)	124-25	34°28'N	84°25'W
Jasper, In., U.S. (jăs'pēr)	116-17	38°23'N	86°56'W
Jasper, Tx., U.S. (jăs'pēr)	122-23	30°54'N	94°00'W
Jasper National Park, n.p., Ab., Can. (jăs'pēr năsh'ŭn-ăl pärk)	132-33	52°53'N	118°03'W
Jassy, Rom. *see* Iași	202-03	47°10'N	27°36'E
Jataí, Braz.	168-69	17°53'S	51°45'W
Jaú, Braz.	172	22°18'S	48°33'W

ăt; finăl; rāte; senāte; ärm; ȧsk; sofȧ; fâre; ch-choose; dh-as th in other; bē; ēvent; bĕt; recĕnt; cratēr; g-gō; gh-guttural g; bĭt; ĭ-short neutral; rīde; K-guttural k as ch in German ich;

PRONOUNCING INDEX

Jauja – Julesburg 341

Feature (Pronunciation)	Page	Lat.	Long.
Jauja, Peru (kä-ō´κ)	163a	11°47'S	75°29'W
Jaumave, Mex. (hou-mä´vå)	146-47	23°25'N	99°23'W
Jaunpur, India	234-35	25°44'N	82°41'E
Java, i., Indon. (jä´vŭ)	248-49	7°30'S	109°59'E
Javari, stm., S.A. (κå-vä-rē)	170	4°21'S	70°02'W
Java Sea, s., Indon. (jä´vŭ sē)	248-49	5°0'S	110°00'E
Javhlant, Mong. see Uliastay	240-41	47°44'N	96°51'E
Jawa, i., Indon. see Java	248-49	7°30'S	109°59'E
Jawa, Laut, s., Indon. see Java Sea	248-49	5°0'S	110°00'E
Jawhar, Som.	262-63	2°47'N	45°31'E
Jaworzno, Pol. (yä-vôzh´nô)	194-95	50°12'N	19°15'E
Jaya, Puncak, mtn., Indon.	224-25	4°05'S	137°11'E
Jayapura, Indon.	277	2°32'S	140°43'E
Jaz Mūrīān, Hāmūn-e, lk., Iran	230-31	27°14'N	58°49'E
Jeanerette, La., U.S. (jĕn-ēr-et´) (zhän-rĕt´)	124-25	29°55'N	91°40'W
Jeddah, Sau. Ar. see Jiddah	266	21°30'N	39°12'E
Jędrzejów, Pol. (yăɴ-dzhā´yôf)	194-95	50°39'N	20°19'E
Jefferson, Ia., U.S. (jĕf´ēr-sŭn)	114-15	42°01'N	94°23'W
Jefferson, Oh., U.S. (jĕf´ēr-sŭn)	116-17	41°44'N	80°46'W
Jefferson, Tx., U.S. (jĕf´ēr-sŭn)	120-21	32°45'N	94°21'W
Jefferson, Wi., U.S. (jĕf´ēr-sŭn)	116-17	43°00'N	88°48'W
Jefferson, Mount, mtn., Nv., U.S. (mount jĕf´ēr-sŭn)	118-19	38°46'N	116°55'W
Jefferson City, Mo., U.S.	120-21	38°33'N	92°10'W
Jefferson City, Tn., U.S. (jĕf´ēr-sŭn sĭ´tė)	124-25	36°07'N	83°30'W
Jeffersontown, Ky., U.S. (jĕf´ēr-sŭn-toun)	116-17	38°13'N	85°35'W
Jeffersonville, In., U.S. (jĕf´ēr-sŭn-vĭl)	116-17	38°17'N	85°44'W
Jeju, Kor., S. see Cheju	240-41	33°30'N	126°32'E
Jēkabpils, Lat. (yĕk´ăb-pĭls)	192-93	56°30'N	25°52'E
Jelenia Góra, Pol. (yĕ-lĕn´yá gó´rá)	194-95	50°54'N	15°44'E
Jelgava, Lat.	192-93	56°39'N	23°44'E
Jellico, Tn., U.S. (jĕl´ĭ-kō)	124-25	36°35'N	84°08'W
Jemaja, Pulau, i., Indon.	246-47	2°55'N	105°45'E
Jember, Indon.	248-49	8°10'S	113°42'E
Jena, Ger. (yā´nä)	194-95	50°56'N	11°35'E
Jengish Chokusu, mtn., Asia	226	42°02'N	80°05'E
Jenkins, Ky., U.S. (jĕŋ´kĭnz)	124-25	37°10'N	82°39'W
Jennings, La., U.S. (jĕn´ĭngz)	122-23	30°13'N	92°39'W
Jeonju, Kor., S. see Chŏnju	243	35°49'N	127°09'E
Jequié, Braz.	166-67	13°52'S	40°05'W
Jequitinhonha, stm., Braz. (zhĕ-kē-tēŋ-ō´n-yä)	168-69	15°51'S	38°53'W
Jerada, Mor.	184-85	34°19'N	2°10'W
Jerba, Île de, i., Tun.	258-59	33°48'N	10°54'E
Jérémie, Haiti (zhā-rå-mē´)	142-43	18°39'N	74°07'W
Jeremoabo, Braz. (zhĕ-rā-mō-á´bō)	166-67	10°06'S	38°19'W
Jerevan, nat. cap., Arm. see Yerevan	227	40°11'N	44°30'E
Jerez de la Frontera, Spain	198-99	36°42'N	6°08'W
Jericho, W.B.	228-29	31°52'N	35°27'E
Jerid, Chott, lk., Tun. (shôt jĕr´ĭd)	258-59	33°42'N	8°26'E
Jerome, Id., U.S. (jĕ-rōm´)	112-13	42°44'N	114°31'W
Jersey, dep., Eur. (jûr´zĭ)	196-97	49°15'N	2°10'W
Jersey City, N.J., U.S. (jûr´zĭ sĭ´tė)	116-17	40°44'N	74°04'W
Jersey Shore, Pa., U.S. (jûr´zĭ shōr)	116-17	41°12'N	77°15'W
Jerseyville, Il., U.S. (jĕr´zė-vĭl)	120-21	39°07'N	90°20'W
Jerusalem, nat. cap., Isr. (jĕ-rōō´sá-lĕm)	228-29	31°47'N	35°14'E
Jesi, Italy	200-01	43°31'N	13°14'E
Jesselton, Malay. see Kota Kinabalu	248-49	5°58'N	116°05'E
Jessore, Bngl.	234-35	23°10'N	89°13'E
Jesup, Ga., U.S. (jĕs´ŭp)	124-25	31°36'N	81°53'W
Jesús Carranza, Mex. (hĕ-sōō´s-kär-rá´n-zä)	146-47	17°24'N	95°02'W
Jesús María, Arg.	173	30°59'S	64°05'W
Jewel Cave National Monument, n.p., S.D., U.S. (jū´ĕl kāv)	114-15	43°45'N	103°51'W
Jhālāwār, India	234-35	24°36'N	76°10'E
Jhang Sadar, Pak.	232-33	31°16'N	72°19'E
Jhānsi, India (jän´sė)	234-35	25°27'N	78°35'E
Jharkhand, state, India	234-35	23°30'N	85°00'E
Jhelum, Pak.	232-33	32°56'N	73°43'E
Jhelum, stm., Asia (jā´lŭm)	232-33	31°12'N	72°08'E
Jhunjhunūn, India	234-35	28°08'N	75°24'E
Jiading, China (jyä-dĭŋ)	238-39	31°23'N	121°14'E
Jiali, China	238-39	30°45'N	93°20'E
Jialing, China see Guangyuan	238-39	32°25'N	105°49'E
Jialing, stm., China (jyä-lĭŋ)	238-39	29°34'N	106°35'E
Jiamusi, China	244	46°48'N	130°22'E
Ji'an, China (jyē-än)	238-39	27°07'N	114°59'E
Ji'an, China (jyē-än)	243	41°06'N	126°10'E
Jianchuan, China	238-39	26°34'N	99°53'E
Jiangjin, China	238-39	29°17'N	106°15'E
Jiangkou, China	238-39	23°35'N	110°11'E
Jiangling, China (jyäŋ-lĭŋ)	238-39	30°19'N	112°12'E
Jiangmen, China	238-39	22°34'N	113°05'E
Jiangsu, state, China (jyäŋ-sōō)	238-39	33°0'N	120°00'E
Jiangxi, state, China (jyäŋ-shyē)	238-39	28°0'N	116°00'E
Jiangyin, China (jyäŋ-yĭn)	238-39	31°54'N	120°15'E
Jianli, China (jyĕn-lē)	238-39	29°49'N	112°54'E
Jianning, China (jyĕn-nĭŋ)	238-39	26°50'N	116°49'E
Jian'ou, China (jyĕn-ō)	238-39	27°02'N	118°19'E
Jianshi, China (jyĕn-shr)	238-39	30°36'N	109°44'E
Jianshui, China	238-39	23°37'N	102°49'E
Jiaohe, China (jyou-hŭ)	240-41	43°43'N	127°20'E
Jiaoxian, China (jyou shyĕn)	240-41	36°17'N	119°60'E
Jiaozuo, China (jyou-dzwô)	240-41	35°15'N	113°14'E
Jiashan, China (jyä-shän)	238-39	32°46'N	117°59'E
Jiashun Hu, lk., China	234-35	34°24'N	85°47'E
Jiaxing, China (jyä-shyĭŋ)	238-39	30°46'N	120°45'E
Jiayu, China (jyä-yōō)	238-39	29°58'N	113°55'E
Jibuti, nat. cap., Dji. see Djibouti	266	11°34'N	43°09'E
Jicarilla Apache Indian Reservation, ind. res., N.M., U.S. (kē-kå-rēl´yå ĭn´dĭ-ăn rĕ-sĕr-vā´shĕn)	118-19	36°40'N	107°00'W
Jicarón, Isla, i., Pan. (ĕ´s-lä-κē-kä-rōn´)	150	7°16'N	81°49'W
Jiddah, Sau. Ar.	266	21°30'N	39°12'E
Jieyang, China (jyĕ-yäŋ)	238-39	23°33'N	116°21'E
Jiguaní, Cuba (κē-gwä-nē´)	142-43	20°22'N	76°25'W
Jijiga, Eth.	262-63	9°21'N	42°48'E
Jilin, China (jyē-lĭn)	240-41	43°51'N	126°33'E
Jilin, state, China	240-41	44°0'N	126°00'E
Jīma, Eth.	262-63	7°38'N	36°50'E
Jiménez, Mex. (κė-mā´nåz)	122-23	27°08'N	104°56'W
Jiménez, Mex. (κė-mā´nåz)	122-23	29°02'N	100°41'W
Jiménez del Téul, Mex. (κē-mā´nåz dĕl tē-ōō´l)	146-47	23°14'N	103°49'W
Jimeta, Nig.	260-61	9°16'N	12°26'E
Jim Thorpe, Pa., U.S. (jĭm´ thôrp´)	116-17	40°52'N	75°44'W
Jinan, China (jyē-nän)	240-41	36°40'N	116°59'E
Jincheng, China (jyĭn-chŭŋ)	240-41	35°30'N	112°50'E
Jindřichuv Hradec, Czech Rep. (yĕn´d'r-zhĭ-kōōf hrä´dĕts)	194-95	49°09'N	15°01'E
Jing, stm., China (jyĭŋ)	238-39	34°28'N	109°05'E
Jingdezhen, China (jyĭŋ-dŭ-jŭn)	238-39	29°17'N	117°12'E
Jinggangshan, China	238-39	26°36'N	114°05'E
Jinghong, China	238-39	21°59'N	100°49'E
Jingning, China (jyĭŋ-nĭŋ)	240-41	35°32'N	105°44'E
Jingxian, China (jyĭŋ shyĕn)	238-39	26°40'N	109°25'E
Jingxian, China (jyĭŋ shyĕn)	238-39	30°41'N	118°24'E
Jingxian, China (jyĭŋ shyĕn)	240-41	37°41'N	116°16'E
Jinhae, Kor., S. see Chinhae	243	35°08'N	128°40'E
Jinhua, China (jyĭn-hwä)	238-39	29°07'N	119°39'E
Jining, China (jyē-nĭŋ)	240-41	35°24'N	116°34'E
Jining, China (jyē-nĭŋ)	240-41	41°02'N	113°06'E
Jinja, Ug. (jĭn´jä)	267	0°26'N	33°13'E
Jinju, Kor., S. see Chinju	243	35°10'N	128°05'E
Jinmu Jiao, c., China	238-39	18°11'N	109°35'E
Jinning, China	238-39	24°40'N	102°35'E
Jinotega, Nic. (κē-nō-tā´gä)	149	13°05'N	85°60'W
Jinotepe, Nic. (κē-nō-tā´på)	149	11°51'N	86°12'W
Jinsen, Kor., S. see Inch'ŏn	243	37°28'N	126°38'E
Jinsha, stm., China see Yangtze	238-39	31°24'N	121°54'E
Jinshi, China	238-39	29°38'N	111°52'E
Jinta, China (jyĭn-tä)	240-41	40°00'N	98°53'E
Jinxi, China	240-41	40°45'N	120°50'E
Jinyun, China (jyĭn-yön)	238-39	28°40'N	120°03'E
Jinzhai, China (jyĭn-jī)	238-39	31°45'N	115°55'E
Jinzhou, China (jyĭn-jō)	240-41	39°06'N	121°43'E
Jinzhou, China (jyĭn-jō)	240-41	41°07'N	121°08'E
Ji-Paraná, Braz.	166-67	10°52'S	61°57'W
Jiparaná, stm., Braz. see Machado	166-67	8°02'S	62°53'W
Jipijapa, Ec. (κē-pė-hä´pä)	170	1°21'S	80°35'W
Jiujiang, China (jyô-jyän)	238-39	29°43'N	115°59'E
Jiulian Shan, mts., China	238-39	24°17'N	114°36'E
Jiuling Shan, mts., China	238-39	28°46'N	114°45'E
Jiuquan, China (jyô-chyän)	240-41	39°45'N	98°30'E
Jiutai, China	240-41	44°09'N	125°50'E
Jixi, China	244	45°17'N	130°58'E
Jixian, China (jyē shyĕn)	244	46°43'N	131°08'E
Jixian, China (jyē shyĕn)	240-41	35°25'N	114°04'E
Jixian, China (jyē shyĕn)	240-41	40°02'N	117°24'E
Jīzān, Sau. Ar.	266	16°54'N	42°36'E
Jizzax, Uzb.	232-33	40°08'N	67°51'E
J. J. Castelli, Arg. see Castelli	168-69	25°57'S	60°37'W
João Belo, Moz. see Xai-Xai	264-65	25°03'S	33°39'E
João Pessoa, Braz.	163d	7°07'S	34°52'W
Joaquín V. González, Arg.	168-69	25°05'S	64°09'W
Jódar, Spain (hō´där)	198-99	37°50'N	3°21'W
Jodhpur, India (hōd´pōōr)	234-35	26°17'N	73°01'E
Joensuu, Fin. (yô-ĕn´sōō)	184-85	62°36'N	29°47'E
Joetsu, Japan	245	37°09'N	138°15'E
Joffre, Mount, mtn., Can. (mount jŏ´f'r)	132-33	50°32'N	115°13'W
Jõgeva, Est. (yû´gĕ-vå)	192-93	58°45'N	26°24'E
Jogjakarta, Indon. see Yogyakarta	248-49	7°48'S	110°22'E
Johannesburg, S. Afr. (yô-hän´ĕs-bôrgh)	269c	26°12'S	28°05'E
John Day, stm., Or., U.S. (jŏn´ dā)	112-13	45°44'N	120°39'W
Johnsonburg, Pa., U.S. (jŏn´sŭn-bûrg)	116-17	41°29'N	78°41'W
Johnson City, N.Y., U.S. (jŏn´sŭn sĭ´tė)	116-17	42°07'N	75°58'W
Johnson City, Tn., U.S. (jŏn´sŭn sĭ´tė)	124-25	36°19'N	82°22'W
Johnson City, Tx., U.S. (jŏn´sŭn sĭ´tė)	122-23	30°16'N	98°24'W
Johnston, Lake, lk., Austl.	272-73	32°18'S	120°46'E
Johnston Atoll, dep., Oc.	280-81	16°45'N	169°32'W
Johnston Atoll, at., Oc. (jŏn´stŭn ă´tŏl)	280-81	16°45'N	169°32'W
Johnstown, Pa., U.S. (jonz´toun)	116-17	40°19'N	78°55'W
Johor Bahru, Malay.	246-47	1°28'N	103°45'E
Joigny, Fr. (zhwån-yē´)	196-97	47°59'N	3°24'E
Joinville, Braz.	172	26°18'S	48°50'W
Jokkmokk, Swe.	184-85	66°37'N	19°50'E
Joliet, Il., U.S. (jō-lĭ-ĕt´)	116-17	41°31'N	88°04'W
Joliette, Qc., Can. (zhō-lyĕt´)	136-37	46°02'N	73°25'W
Jolo, Phil. (hō-lō)	250	6°02'N	120°60'E
Jolo Group, is., Phil.	250	6°01'N	121°18'E
Jolo Island, i., Phil. (hō-lō ī´lănd)	250	5°58'N	121°06'E
Jomda, China	238-39	31°27'N	98°15'E
Jon, Deti, s., Eur. see Ionian Sea	200-01	39°0'N	19°00'E
Jonava, Lith. (yō-nä´vå)	192-93	55°05'N	24°17'E
Jonesboro, Ar., U.S. (jōnz´bûrō)	124-25	35°51'N	90°42'W
Jonesboro, La., U.S. (jōnz´bûrō)	120-21	32°14'N	92°43'W
Jonesville, La., U.S. (jōnz´vĭl)	124-25	31°37'N	91°49'W
Joniškis, Lith. (yô´nĭsh-kĭs)	192-93	56°14'N	23°38'E
Jönköping, Swe. (yûn´chû-pĭng)	192-93	57°47'N	14°11'E
Jonquière, Qc., Can. (zhôɴ-kyâr´)	136-37	48°26'N	71°11'W
Jonuta, Mex. (hô-nōō´tä)	148	18°06'N	92°07'W
Joplin, Mo., U.S. (jŏp´lĭn)	120-21	37°05'N	94°31'W
Jordan, Mt., U.S.	112-13	47°20'N	106°57'W
Jordan, nation, Asia (jôr´dăn)	206-07	31°0'N	36°00'E
Jordan, stm., Asia (jôr´dăn)	228-29	31°46'N	35°34'E
Jorhāt, India (jôr-hät´)	234-35	26°46'N	94°13'E
Jos, Nig.	260-61	9°56'N	8°53'E
José Batlle y Ordóñez, Ur.	173	33°29'S	55°08'W
José de San Martín, Arg.	171	44°02'S	70°29'W
Joseph Bonaparte Gulf, b., Austl. (jō´sĕf bō´ná-pärt gŭlf)	272-73	14°15'S	128°30'E
Joshua Tree National Park, n.p., Ca., U.S. (jō´shū-á trē năsh´ŭn-ăl pärk)	118-19	33°55'N	116°00'W
Jostedalsbreen, ice, Nor.	192-93	61°40'N	7°00'E
Jovellanos, Cuba (hō-vĕl-yä´nōs)	142-43	22°48'N	81°11'W
J. Strom Thurmond Reservoir, res., U.S.	124-25	33°45'N	82°16'W
Juan Aldama, Mex. (kōá´n-äl-dá´mä)	146-47	24°19'N	103°19'W
Juan de Fuca, Strait of, strt., N.A. (strāt ŭv hwän´ dā fōō´kä)	112-13	48°18'N	124°00'W
Juan de Fuca Strait, strt., N.A. see Juan de Fuca, Strait of	112-13	48°18'N	124°00'W
Juan Fernández, Archipiélago, is., Chile	159	33°0'S	80°00'W
Juanjuí, Peru	170	7°10'S	76°45'W
Juárez, Arg. (hōōá´rĕz) see Benito Juárez	173	37°41'S	59°48'W
Juazeiro, Braz. (zhōōá´zā´rō)	166-67	9°25'S	40°30'W
Juazeiro do Norte, Braz. (zhōōá´zā´rō-dō-nôr-tĕ)	166-67	7°12'S	39°20'W
Juba, Sudan	267	4°51'N	31°37'E
Jubal, Strait of, strt., Egypt see Gûbâl, Madîq	268b	27°40'N	33°55'E
Jubayl, Leb. (jōō-bīl´)	228-29	34°08'N	35°40'E
Jubba, stm., Afr.	262-63	0°15'S	42°39'E
Juby, Cap, c., Mor. (kăp yōō´bė)	258-59	27°57'N	12°55'W
Júcaro, Cuba (hōō´kå-rō)	142-43	21°38'N	78°51'W
Juchipila, Mex. (hōō-chė-pē´lä)	146-47	21°24'N	103°07'W
Juchitán de Zaragoza, Mex.	146-47	16°26'N	95°01'W
Juchitlán, Mex. (hōō-chē-tlän)	146-47	20°05'N	104°06'W
Juddah, Sau. Ar. see Jiddah	266	21°30'N	39°12'E
Juidongshan, China	238-39	23°44'N	117°30'E
Juigalpa, Nic. (hwē-gäl´pä)	149	12°06'N	85°22'W
Juiz de Fora, Braz. (zhō-ēzh´ dā fō´rä)	172	21°45'S	43°22'W
Jujuy, Arg. (hōō-hwē´) see San Salvador de Jujuy	168-69	24°12'S	65°18'W
Jujuy, state, Arg. (hōō-hwē´)	168-69	23°0'S	66°00'W
Julesburg, Co., U.S. (jōōlz´bûrg)	114-15	40°59'N	102°17'W

n-sing; ŋ-baŋk; ɴ-nasalized n; nŏd; cŏmmit; ōld; ôbey; ôrder; oi-boil; fōōd; ȯ-as oo in foot; ou-out; s-soft; sh-dish; th-thin; pūre; ûnite; ûrn; stŭd; circŭs; ü-as in French tu; ´-indeterminate vowel.

342 Juliaca – Kangaroo Island PRONOUNCING INDEX

Feature (Pronunciation)	Page	Lat.	Long.
Juliaca, Peru (hōō-lē-ä′kä)	170	15°30′S	70°08′W
Juliana Top, mtn., Sur.	164-65	3°39′N	56°32′W
Julianehåb, Green.	284-85	60°44′N	46°02′W
Jumentos Cays, is., Bah. (hōō-mĕn′tōs kēs)	142-43	22°42′N	75°55′W
Jumilla, Spain (hōō-mēl′yä)	198-99	38°28′N	1°20′W
Jūnāgadh, India (jŏ-nä′gŭd)	234-35	21°31′N	70°27′E
Junction, Tx., U.S. (jŭngk′shŭn)	122-23	30°29′N	99°47′W
Junction City, Ks., U.S. (jŭngk′shŭn sĭ′tē)	120-21	39°02′N	96°50′W
Junction City, Or., U.S. (jŭngk′shŭn sĭ′tē)	112-13	44°14′N	123°11′W
Jundiaí, Braz.	172	23°11′S	46°53′W
Juneau, Ak., U.S. (jōō′nō)	126	58°20′N	134°25′W
Junee, Austl.	276	34°52′S	147°35′E
Jungar Qi, China	240-41	39°49′N	111°10′E
Jungfrau, mtn., Switz. (yŏng′frou)	194-95	46°32′N	7°58′E
Junín, Arg. (hōō-nē′n)	173	34°36′S	60°58′W
Junín de los Andes, Arg.	171	39°55′S	71°05′W
Jūniyah, Leb. (jōō-nē′ĕ)	228-29	33°60′N	35°39′E
Junxian, China	238-39	32°32′N	111°31′E
Juquiá, Braz.	172	24°19′S	47°38′W
Jur, stm., Sudan (jŏr)	262-63	8°39′N	29°17′E
Jura, i., Scot., U.K. (jōō′rå)	190-91	56°01′N	5°56′W
Jura, mts., Eur. (zhü-rà′)	194-95	47°06′N	6°50′E
Jurbarkas, Lith. (yōōr-bär′käs)	192-93	55°05′N	22°47′E
Jūrmala, Lat.	192-93	56°58′N	23°42′E
Juruá, stm., S.A.	166-67	2°35′S	65°47′W
Juruena, stm., Braz. (zhōō-rōōĕ′nä)	166-67	7°21′S	58°09′W
Justo Daract, Arg.	171	33°52′S	65°11′W
Jutaí, stm., Braz.	166-67	2°44′S	66°48′W
Jutiapa, Guat. (hōō-tē-ä′pä)	148	14°18′N	89°54′W
Juticalpa, Hond. (hōō-tē-käl′pä)	149	14°40′N	86°13′W
Jutland, reg., Den. *see* Jylland	192-93	56°0′N	9°15′E
Juventud, Isla de la, i., Cuba	142-43	21°40′N	82°50′W
Jyekundo, China *see* Yushu	238-39	33°00′N	97°00′E
Jylland, reg., Den.	192-93	56°0′N	9°15′E
Jyväskylä, Fin.	192-93	62°15′N	25°45′E

K

Feature (Pronunciation)	Page	Lat.	Long.
K2, mtn., Asia (kä-tōō)	232-33	35°53′N	76°30′E
Ka'ena Point, c., Hi., U.S. (kä′ā-nä point)	127a	21°35′N	158°17′W
Kaapstad, nat. cap., S. Afr. *see* Cape Town	264-65	33°55′S	18°30′E
Kaarlela, Fin. *see* Kokkola	184-85	63°50′N	23°09′E
Kaba, stm., Afr. *see* Little Scarcies	260-61	8°51′N	13°07′W
Kabaena, Pulau, i., Indon. (pōō-lou kä-bà-ā′nà)	248-49	5°15′S	121°55′E
Kabala, S.L. (kà-bà′là)	260-61	9°35′N	11°33′W
Kabale, Ug.	267	1°11′S	29°56′E
Kabalega Falls, wtfl., Ug.	267	2°17′N	31°42′E
Kabalo, D.R.C. (kä-bä′lō)	262-63	6°03′S	26°55′E
Kabara, i., Fiji	279f	18°57′S	178°57′W
Kabardin-Balkaria, state, Russia *see* Balkaria	227	43°30′N	43°30′E
Kabardino-Balkariya, state, Russia *see* Balkaria	227	43°30′N	43°30′E
Kabīr Kūh, mts., Iran	228-29	33°36′N	46°12′E
Kābol, nat. cap., Afg. (kä′bōōl) *see* Kabul	232-33	34°32′N	69°10′E
Kābol, stm., Asia	232-33	33°55′N	72°14′E
Kabompo, stm., Zam. (kà-bôm′pō)	264-65	14°12′S	23°11′E
Kabul, nat. cap., Afg. (kä′bōōl)	232-33	34°32′N	69°10′E
Kabul, stm., Asia (kä′bŏl) *see* Kābol	232-33	33°55′N	72°14′E
Kaburuang, Pulau, i., Indon.	248-49	3°48′N	126°48′E
Kabwe, Zam.	264-65	14°27′S	28°27′E
Kachchh, Gulf of, b., India	234-35	22°37′N	69°30′E
Kachchh, Rann of, reg., Asia *see* Kutch, Rann of	234-35	24°15′N	70°46′E
Kachul, Mol. *see* Cahul	202-03	45°55′N	28°12′E
Kadamatt Island, i., India	236	11°13′N	72°47′E
Kadan Kyun, i., Mya.	246-47	12°30′N	98°22′E
Kadéï, stm., Afr.	260-61	3°31′N	16°03′E
Kadina, Austl.	276	33°58′S	137°43′E
Kadiyevka, Ukr. *see* Stakhanov	202-03	48°34′N	38°40′E
Kadoma, Zimb.	264-65	18°21′S	29°54′E
Kaduna, Nig. (kä-dōō′nä)	260-61	10°32′N	7°25′E
Kaduna, stm., Nig. (kä-dōō′nä)	260-61	8°45′N	5°48′E
Kāduqlī, Sudan	266	10°60′N	29°43′E
Kadzherom, Russia	186-87	64°41′N	55°55′E
Kaédi, Maur. (kä-ā-dē′)	258-59	16°10′N	13°29′W
Kaesŏng, Kor., N. (kä′ĕ-sŭng) (kĭ′jō)	243	37°59′N	126°34′E
Kafue, stm., Zam. (kä′fōō)	264-65	15°56′S	28°57′E
Kafue National Park, n.p., Zam. (kä′fōō năsh′ŭn-ăl pärk)	264-65	15°22′S	25°25′E
Kaga Bandoro, C.A.R.	262-63	6°59′N	19°12′E
Kagera, stm., Afr. (kä-gā′rà)	267	0°56′S	31°47′E
Kagoshima, Japan (kä′gō-shē′mà)	245	31°36′N	130°33′E
Kagoshima-wan, b., Japan (kä′gō-shē′mä wän)	245	31°24′N	130°38′E
Kahama, Tan.	267	3°49′S	32°36′E
Kahayan, stm., Indon.	248-49	3°16′S	114°06′E
Kahemba, D.R.C.	262-63	7°18′S	18°59′E
Kaho'olawe, i., Hi., U.S. (kä-hōō-lä′wē)	127a	20°33′N	156°37′W
Kahoka, Mo., U.S. (kà-hō′kà)	120-21	40°26′N	91°43′W
Kahramanmaraş, Tur.	186-87	37°35′N	36°57′E
Kahuku Point, c., Hi., U.S. (kä-hōō′kōō point)	127a	21°43′N	157°59′W
Kai, Kepulauan, is., Indon.	224-25	5°35′S	132°45′E
Kaibab Indian Reservation, ind. res., Az., U.S. (kä′ē-bäb ĭn′dĭ-ăn rĕ-sĕr-vā′shĕn)	118-19	36°55′N	112°40′W
Kaidu, stm., China (kī-dōō)	222-23	41°58′N	86°44′E
Kaifeng, China (kī-fŭŋ)	238-39	34°47′N	114°21′E
Kaijo, Kor., N. *see* Kaesŏng	243	37°59′N	126°34′E
Kai Kecil, i., Indon.	224-25	5°46′S	132°43′E
Kailas, mtn., China *see* Kangrinboqê Feng	234-35	31°04′N	81°18′E
Kailas Range, mts., China (kī-läs rānj) *see* Gangdisê Shan	234-35	31°0′N	82°00′E
Kailu, China	240-41	43°36′N	121°19′E
Kailua, Hi., U.S. (kä′ē-lōō′ä)	127a	21°24′N	157°45′W
Kailua, Hi., U.S. (kä′ē-lōō′ä)	127a	19°39′N	155°58′W
Kailua Kona, Hi., U.S. *see* Kailua	127a	19°39′N	155°58′W
Kaiping, China	238-39	22°22′N	112°37′E
Kairouan, Tun.	184-85	35°41′N	10°07′E
Kaiserslautern, Ger. (kī-zĕrs-lou′tĕrn)	194-95	49°26′N	7°45′E
Kaiyuan, China (kī-yuän)	243	42°32′N	124°02′E
Kaiyuan, China (kū-yuän)	238-39	23°42′N	103°14′E
Kajaani, Fin. (kä′yà-nĕ)	184-85	64°14′N	27°45′E
Kaka, Turkmen.	232-33	37°20′N	59°37′E
Kakabia, Pulau, i., Indon.	248-49	6°54′S	122°13′E
Kakamas, S. Afr.	264-65	28°46′S	20°36′E
Kakamega, Kenya	267	0°17′N	34°45′E
Kakhovka, Ukr. (kä-kôf′kà)	202-03	46°49′N	33°30′E
Kakhovka Reservoir, res., Ukr *see* Kakhovs'ke vodoskhovyshche	202-03	47°28′N	34°06′E
Kakhovs'ke vodoskhovyshche, res., Ukr.	202-03	47°28′N	34°06′E
Kakhul, Mol. *see* Cahul	202-03	45°55′N	28°12′E
Kākināda, India	236	16°57′N	82°15′E
Kakshaal-Too, mts., Asia	226	41°0′N	78°00′E
Kaktovik, Ak., U.S. (kăk-tō′vĭk)	126	70°08′N	143°38′W
Kakuma, Kenya	267	3°42′N	34°52′E
Kalaallit Nunaat, dep., N.A. *see* Greenland	85	70°0′N	40°00′W
Kalabahi, Indon.	248-49	8°15′S	124°32′E
Kalach, Russia (kà-làch′)	186-87	50°25′N	41°00′E
Kalachinsk, Russia	226	55°02′N	74°35′E
Kalach-na-Donu, Russia	186-87	48°43′N	43°28′E
Kalae, c., Hi., U.S.	127a	18°55′N	155°41′W
Kalahari Desert, des., Afr. (kä-lä-hä′rē dĕs′ĕrt)	264-65	24°0′S	21°30′E
Kalahari Gemsbok National Park, n.p., S. Afr.	264-65	25°30′S	20°30′E
Kalama, Wa., U.S. (kà-lăm′à)	112-13	46°01′N	122°50′W
Kalamáta, Grc.	200-01	37°03′N	22°07′E
Kalamazoo, Mi., U.S. (kăl-à-mà-zōō′)	116-17	42°17′N	85°35′W
Kalamazoo, stm., Mi., U.S. (kăl-à-mà-zōō′)	116-17	42°40′N	86°12′W
Kalanchak, Ukr. (kä-län-chäk′)	202-03	46°15′N	33°18′E
Kalao, Pulau, i., Indon.	248-49	7°18′S	120°58′E
Kalaotoa, Pulau, i., Indon.	248-49	7°22′S	121°47′E
Kalāt, Pak. (kŭ-lät′)	232-33	29°02′N	66°35′E
Kalaw, Mya.	246-47	20°38′N	96°34′E
Kalbarri, Austl.	270-71	27°42′S	114°10′E
Kaledupa, Pulau, i., Indon.	248-49	5°32′S	123°47′E
Kalemie, D.R.C.	267	5°55′S	29°11′E
Kalemyo, Mya.	246-47	23°13′N	94°07′E
Kalevala, Russia	186-87	65°11′N	31°11′E
Kalewa, Mya.	246-47	23°12′N	94°18′E
Kalgoorlie-Boulder, Austl. (kăl-gōōr′lē-bōld′ĕr)	270-71	30°44′S	121°27′E
Kalibo, Phil.	250	11°43′N	122°23′E
Kalima, D.R.C.	262-63	2°36′S	26°37′E
Kalimantan, i., Asia *see* Borneo	248-49	0°30′N	114°00′E
Kālimpang, India	234-35	27°04′N	88°28′E
Kaliningrad, Russia (kä-lē-nēn′grät)	194-95	54°43′N	20°30′E
Kalisch, Pol. *see* Kalisz	194-95	51°46′N	18°06′E
Kalispell, Mt., U.S. (kăl′ĭ-spĕl)	112-13	48°12′N	114°19′W
Kalisz, Pol. (kä′lēsh)	194-95	51°46′N	18°06′E
Kalixälven, stm., Swe.	184-85	65°53′N	23°03′E
Kalmar, Swe. (käl′mär)	192-93	56°40′N	16°22′E
Kalmarsund, strt., Swe. (käl′mär)	192-93	56°40′N	16°25′E
Kal'mius, stm., Ukr. (käl′myōōs)	202-03	47°05′N	37°34′E
Kalmykia, state, Russia	186-87	46°30′N	45°30′E
Kalmykiya, state, Russia *see* Kalmykia	186-87	46°30′N	45°30′E
Kalpeni Island, i., India	236	10°05′N	73°38′E
Kalsūbai, mtn., India	234-35	19°36′N	73°43′E
Kaluga, Russia (kà-lō′gä)	202-03	54°32′N	36°17′E
Kalundborg, Den. (kà-lòn′′bôr′)	192-93	55°41′N	11°07′E
Kalush, Ukr. (kä′lòsh)	194-95	49°02′N	24°22′E
Kalyān, India	236	19°16′N	73°08′E
Kalyazin, Russia (käl-yá′zēn)	202-03	57°14′N	37°54′E
Kálymnos, i., Grc.	200-01	37°0′N	27°00′E
Kama, stm., Russia (kä′mä)	186-87	55°35′N	51°29′E
Kamaishi, Japan (kä′mä-ē′shē)	244	39°16′N	141°53′E
Kamakura, Japan (kä′mä-kōō′rä)	245	35°19′N	139°33′E
Kama Reservoir, res., Russia (kä′mä rĕ′sĕr-vwär) *see* Kamskoye Vodokhranilishche	186-87	58°52′N	56°15′E
Kambarka, Russia	186-87	56°15′N	54°13′E
Kamchatka, Poluostrov, pen., Russia *see* Kamchatka Peninsula	218-19	56°0′N	160°00′E
Kamchatka Peninsula, pen., Russia (kăm-chăt′kà pĕ-nĭn′sūlà)	218-19	56°0′N	160°00′E
Kamenjak, Rt, c., Cro. (kä′mĕ-nyäk)	200-01	44°46′N	13°55′E
Kamenka, Russia	186-87	53°11′N	44°03′E
Kamen'-na-Obi, Russia (kä-mĭny′nŭ ô′bē)	226	53°48′N	81°20′E
Kāmet, mtn., Asia	234-35	30°54′N	79°37′E
Kam'ianets'-Podil's'kyi, Ukr.	194-95	48°40′N	26°36′E
Kamina, D.R.C.	262-63	8°44′S	25°00′E
Kaminak Lake, l., Nu., Can.	130-31	62°09′N	95°07′W
Kamino-shima, i., Japan	243	34°35′N	129°25′E
Kaminuriak Lake, l., Nu., Can.	130-31	62°59′N	95°35′W
Kamituga, D.R.C.	267	3°02′S	28°14′E
Kamloops, B.C., Can. (kăm′lōōps)	132-33	50°40′N	120°20′W
Kampala, nat. cap., Ug. (käm-pä′lä)	267	0°19′N	32°34′E
Kampar, stm., Indon. (käm′pär)	246-47	0°14′N	102°42′E
Kamphaeng Phet, Thai.	246-47	16°28′N	99°32′E
Kâmpóng Cham, Camb.	246-47	12°0′N	105°27′E
Kâmpóng Chhnăng, Camb.	246-47	12°15′N	104°40′E
Kâmpóng Saôm, Camb.	246-47	10°38′N	103°31′E
Kâmpóng Saôm, Chhâk, b., Camb.	246-47	10°50′N	103°32′E
Kâmpóng Thum, Camb. (kŏm′pŏng-tŏm)	246-47	12°42′N	104°54′E
Kâmpôt, Camb. (käm′pōt)	246-47	10°37′N	104°11′E
Kampuchea, nation, Asia *see* Cambodia	206-07	13°0′N	105°00′E
Kamsack, Sk., Can. (kăm′săk)	134-35	51°34′N	101°54′W
Kamskoye Vodokhranilishche, res., Russia	186-87	58°52′N	56°15′E
Kamuela, Hi., U.S. *see* Waimea	127a	20°02′N	155°40′W
Kámuk, Cerro, mtn., C.R. (sĕ′r-rô-kä-mōō′k)	149	9°17′N	83°01′W
Kamyshin, Russia (kä-mwēsh′ĭn)	186-87	50°07′N	45°24′E
Kanaaupscow, stm., Qc., Can.	130-31	53°40′N	76°44′W
Kanab, Ut., U.S. (kăn′ăb)	118-19	37°03′N	112°32′W
Kanab Plateau, plat., U.S. (kăn′ăb plä-tō′)	118-19	36°36′N	112°45′W
Kanagawa, state, Japan (kä′nä-gä′wä)	245	35°30′N	139°15′E
Kananga, D.R.C.	262-63	5°54′S	22°25′E
Kanash, Russia	186-87	55°31′N	47°29′E
Kanawha, stm., W.V., U.S. (kà-nô′wà)	116-17	38°50′N	82°09′W
Kanazawa, Japan (kä′nà-zä′wà)	245	36°34′N	136°39′E
Kanchanjanggā, mtn., Asia *see* Kānchenjunga	234-35	27°41′N	88°10′E
Kānchenjunga, mtn., Asia (kĭn-chĭn-jŏn′gà)	234-35	27°41′N	88°10′E
Kānchipuram, India	236	12°50′N	79°43′E
Kandahār, Afg.	232-33	31°37′N	65°43′E
Kandalaksha, Russia (kàn-dà-làk′shà)	184-85	67°09′N	32°24′E
Kandangan, Indon.	248-49	2°48′S	115°16′E
Kandavu, i., Fiji	279f	19°00′S	178°11′E
Kandy, Sri L. (kän′dē)	236	7°18′N	80°38′E
Kane, Pa., U.S. (kān)	116-17	41°40′N	78°48′W
Kāne'ohe, Hi., U.S. (kä-nā-ō′hā)	127a	21°25′N	157°48′W
Kanevskaya, Russia (kà-nyĕf′skà)	202-03	46°05′N	38°58′E
Kangar, Malay.	246-47	6°27′N	100°12′E
Kangaroo Island, i., Austl. (kăŋ-gà-rō′ ī′lănd)	276	35°50′S	137°05′E

ăt; finăl; rāte; senâte; ärm; àsk; sofà; fâre; ch-choose; dh-as th in other; bē; ēvent; bĕt; recĕnt; cratĕr; g-gō; gh-guttural g; bĭt; ĭ-short neutral; rīde; κ-guttural k as ch in German ich;

PRONOUNCING INDEX

Kangāvar – Kazym 343

Feature (Pronunciation)	Page	Lat.	Long.
Kangāvar, Iran (kŭŋ´gā-vär)	228-29	34°30'N	47°58'E
Kangding, China	238-39	30°04'N	102°01'E
Kangean, Kepulauan, is., Indon. (käŋ´gē-än)	248-49	6°55'S	115°30'E
Kangean, Pulau, i., Indon.	248-49	6°54'S	115°20'E
Kanggye, Kor., N. (käng´gyĕ)	243	40°58'N	126°36'E
Kangiqsliniq, Nu., Can. see Rankin Inlet	128-29	62°49'N	92°10'W
Kangiqsualujjuaq, Qc., Can.	128-29	58°42'N	65°59'W
Kangiqsujuaq, Qc., Can.	128-29	61°35'N	71°58'W
Kangirsuk, Qc., Can.	128-29	60°02'N	70°01'W
Kangnŭng, Kor., S. (käng´nô ng)	243	37°46'N	128°54'E
Kango, Gabon (käɴ-gō)	260-61	0°11'N	10°05'E
Kangrinboqê Feng, mtn., China	234-35	31°04'N	81°18'E
Kangto, mtn., Asia	234-35	27°52'N	92°30'E
Kanhsien, China see Ganzhou	238-39	25°53'N	114°55'E
Kaniama, D.R.C.	262-63	7°33'S	24°10'E
Kanin, Poluostrov, pen., Russia	186-87	68°0'N	45°00'E
Kanin Nos, Mys, c., Russia	186-87	68°39'N	43°17'E
Kankakee, Il., U.S. (kăŋ-kȧ-kē´)	116-17	41°07'N	87°51'W
Kankan, Gui. (käɴ-käɴ) (kän-kän´)	260-61	10°23'N	9°18'W
Kankō, Kor., N. see Hamhŭng	243	39°55'N	127°32'E
Kanmaw Kyun, i., Mya.	246-47	11°40'N	98°28'E
Kannapolis, N.C., U.S. (kăn-ăp´ô-lĭs)	124-25	35°29'N	80°37'W
Kannur, India see Cannanore	236	11°52'N	75°22'E
Kano, Nig. (kä´nō)	260-61	12°01'N	8°30'E
Kānpur, India (kän´pûr)	234-35	26°28'N	80°19'E
Kansas, state, U.S. (kăn´zȧs)	108-09	38°45'N	98°15'W
Kansas City, Ks., U.S. (kăn´zȧs sĭ´tê)	120-21	39°07'N	94°38'W
Kansas City, Mo., U.S. (kăn´zȧs sĭ´tê)	120-21	39°06'N	94°34'W
Kansk, Russia	218-19	56°12'N	95°43'E
Kansu, state, China see Gansu	240-41	37°0'N	103°00'E
Kantang, Thai. (kän´täng´)	246-47	7°24'N	99°32'E
Kanton, i., Kir. see Canton	280-81	2°49'S	171°41'W
Kantunilkin, Mex. (kän-tōō-nēl-kē´n)	148	21°06'N	87°29'W
Kanye, Bots.	264-65	24°59'S	25°19'E
Kaohsiung, Tai. (kä-ô-syŏng´)	225a	22°38'N	120°17'E
Kaoko Veld, plat., Nmb.	264-65	20°0'S	14°00'E
Kaolack, Sen.	260-61	14°09'N	16°04'W
Kaoma, Zam.	264-65	14°47'S	24°48'E
Kapenguria, Kenya	267	1°09'N	35°01'E
Kapfenberg, Aus. (kȧp´fĕn-bĕrgh)	194-95	47°27'N	15°17'E
Kapingamarangi, at., Micron.	280-81	1°04'N	154°46'E
Kapit, Malay.	248-49	2°00'N	112°56'E
Kapoeta, Sudan	267	4°47'N	33°35'E
Kaposvár, Hung. (kô´pôsh-vär)	194-95	46°22'N	17°48'E
Kapuas, stm., Indon.	248-49	0°09'S	109°08'E
Kapuas Hulu, Pegunungan, mts., Asia see Upper Kapuas Mountains	248-49	1°15'N	113°30'E
Kapuas Hulu, Pergunungan, mts., Asia see Upper Kapuas Mountains	248-49	1°15'N	113°30'E
Kapuskasing, On., Can.	136-37	49°25'N	82°25'W
Kapuskasing, stm., On., Can.	136-37	49°38'N	82°16'W
Kara, Togo	260-61	9°33'N	1°12'E
Kara, stm., Russia (kärȧ)	186-87	69°07'N	64°45'E
Kara-Balta, Kyrg.	226	42°48'N	73°51'E
Karabogaz, Turkmen.	186-87	41°32'N	52°35'E
Kara-Bogaz-Gol Gulf, b., Turkmen. (kȧ-rä´ bŭ-gäs´ gôl gŭlf)	232-33	41°15'N	53°24'E
Karabük, Tur.	186-87	41°13'N	32°37'E
Karachay, state, Russia see Cherkessia	227	44°0'N	42°00'E
Karachay-Cherkessia, state, Russia see Cherkessia	227	44°0'N	42°00'E
Karachayevo-Cherkesiya, state, Russia see Cherkessia	227	44°0'N	42°00'E
Karachev, Russia (kȧ-rȧ-chôf´)	202-03	53°07'N	34°59'E
Karāchi, Pak. (kȧ-rä´chē)	232-33	24°54'N	67°01'E
Kara Deniz, s., see Black Sea	186-87	43°0'N	35°00'E
Karaginskiy, Ostrov, i., Russia	218-19	58°50'N	164°00'E
Karaginskiy Zaliv, b., Russia	218-19	58°50'N	164°00'E
Karaj, Iran	232-33	35°50'N	50°59'E
Karakax, stm., China	226	38°03'N	80°32'E
Karakelong, Pulau, i., Indon.	248-49	4°16'N	126°49'E
Karakol, Kyrg.	226	42°29'N	78°23'E
Karakoram Range, mts., Asia (kä´rä kō´rŏm rănj)	234-35	35°30'N	77°00'E
Karakorum, hist., Mong.	240-41	47°14'N	102°50'E
Karakorum Shan, mts., Asia see Karakoram Range	234-35	35°30'N	77°00'E
Kara Kum, des., Turkmen. (kärä-kōōm´)	226	39°0'N	60°00'E
Kara-Kum Canal, can., Turkmen. (kärä-kōōm´ kȧ´năl)	232-33	37°34'N	65°41'E
Karakumy, des., Turkmen. see Kara Kum	226	39°0'N	60°00'E
Karaman, Tur. (kä-rä-män´)	186-87	37°11'N	33°13'E
Karamay, China (kär-äm-ā)	226	45°36'N	84°51'E
Karamea Bight, b., N.Z. (kȧ-rȧ-mē´ȧ bīt)	278	41°30'S	171°40'E
Karasburg, Nmb.	264-65	28°01'S	18°45'E
Kara Sea, s., Russia (kärȧ sē)	218-19	76°0'N	80°00'E
Karasuk, Russia	226	53°43'N	78°03'E
Karatau Range, mts., Kaz.	226	43°36'N	68°52'E
Karatsu, Japan (kä´rȧ-tsōō)	245	33°26'N	129°59'E
Karawang, Indon.	248-49	6°18'S	107°18'E
Karbalā', Iraq	228-29	32°37'N	44°02'E
Karcag, Hung. (kär´tsäg)	194-95	47°19'N	20°56'E
Kardeljevo, Cro.	200-01	43°04'N	17°26'E
Kärdla, Est. (kĕrd´lȧ)	192-93	58°60'N	22°45'E
Kargasok, Russia	218-19	59°04'N	80°50'E
Kargopol', Russia (kär-gō-pōl´)	186-87	61°30'N	38°58'E
Kariba, Zimb.	264-65	16°31'S	28°48'E
Kariba, Lake, res., Afr.	264-65	17°0'S	28°00'E
Karimata, Kepulauan, is., Indon. (kä-rē-mä´tȧ)	246-47	1°25'S	109°05'E
Karimata, Pulau, i., Indon.	246-47	1°36'S	108°55'E
Karimata, Selat, strt., Indon.	248-49	2°05'S	108°40'E
Karīmnagar, India	236	18°26'N	79°09'E
Karimunjawa, Kepulauan, is., Indon. (kä´rē-mōōn-yä´vä)	248-49	5°50'S	110°25'E
Karisimbi, Volcan, vol., Afr.	267	1°30'S	29°27'E
Karkar Island, i., Pap. N. Gui. (kär´kär ī´lȧnd)	277	4°40'S	146°00'E
Karkūk, Iraq see Kirkuk	228-29	35°28'N	44°24'E
Karleby, Fin. see Kokkola	184-85	63°50'N	23°09'E
Karl-Marx-Stadt, Ger. see Chemnitz	194-95	50°50'N	12°56'E
Karlovac, Cro. (kär´lô-vȧts)	200-01	45°29'N	15°33'E
Karlovo, Blg. (kär´lô-vō)	200-01	42°39'N	24°48'E
Karlovy Vary, Czech Rep. (kär´lô-vê vä´rê)	194-95	50°14'N	12°53'E
Karlshamn, Swe. (kärls´häm)	192-93	56°09'N	14°51'E
Karlskrona, Swe. (kärls´krô-nä)	192-93	56°10'N	15°36'E
Karlsruhe, Ger. (kärls´rōō-ĕ)	194-95	49°01'N	8°23'E
Karlstad, Swe. (kärl´städ)	192-93	59°23'N	13°31'E
Karmøy, i., Nor. (kärm-ûe)	192-93	59°15'N	5°15'E
Karnāl, India	234-35	29°41'N	76°59'E
Karnātaka, state, India	236	14°0'N	76°00'E
Karonga, Malawi (kȧ-rōŋ´gȧ)	264-65	9°55'S	33°56'E
Kárpathos, i., Grc.	188-89	35°41'N	27°09'E
Karpaty, mts., Eur. see Carpathian Mountains	186-87	48°0'N	24°00'E
Karpinsk, Russia (kär´pĭnsk)	186-87	59°46'N	60°00'E
Karpogory, Russia	186-87	64°00'N	44°23'E
Karratha, Austl.	270-71	20°43'S	116°48'E
Kars, Tur. (kärs)	227	40°36'N	43°05'E
Karshi, Uzb. (kär´shē) see Qarshi	232-33	38°52'N	65°48'E
Karskoye More, s., Russia see Kara Sea	218-19	76°0'N	80°00'E
Kartaly, Russia (kȧr´tȧ lê)	226	53°03'N	60°39'E
Karumba, Austl.	277	17°28'S	140°51'E
Karūr, India	236	10°57'N	78°05'E
Kārwār, India	236	14°48'N	74°08'E
Kasai, stm., Afr.	262-63	3°02'S	16°56'E
Kasama, Zam. (kȧ-sä´mȧ)	264-65	10°12'S	31°11'E
Kasar, Ras, c., Afr. see Kasr, Ra's	266	18°01'N	38°34'E
Kasba Lake, lk., Can.	130-31	60°18'N	102°07'W
Kasba-Tadla, Mor. (käs´bȧ-täd´lȧ)	269a	32°37'N	6°16'W
Kaschau, Slvk. see Košice	194-95	48°43'N	21°16'E
Kasenga, D.R.C. (kȧ-seŋ´gȧ)	262-63	10°22'S	28°37'E
Kasese, Ug.	267	0°10'N	30°05'E
Kāshān, Iran (kä-shän´)	232-33	33°59'N	51°26'E
Kashgar, China (käsh-gär) see Kashi	226	39°28'N	75°59'E
Kashi, China (kä-shr)	226	39°28'N	75°59'E
Kashihara, Japan (kä´shē-hä´rä)	245	34°30'N	135°48'E
Kashin, Russia (kä-shēn´)	202-03	57°22'N	37°37'E
Kashira, Russia (kä-shē´rȧ)	202-03	54°51'N	38°10'E
Kashiwazaki, Japan (kä´shē-wä-zä´kē)	245	37°22'N	138°33'E
Kāshmar, Iran	232-33	35°13'N	58°28'E
Kasia, India	234-35	26°45'N	83°55'E
Kasimov, Russia (kȧ-sē´môf)	186-87	54°56'N	41°23'E
Kaskaskia, stm., Il., U.S. (kăs-kăs´kĭ-ȧ)	120-21	37°58'N	89°57'W
Kaskattama, stm., Mb., Can. (kăs-kȧ-tä´mȧ)	134-35	57°03'N	90°05'W
Kasongo, D.R.C. (kä-sôŋ´gō)	262-63	4°27'S	26°40'E
Kasongo-Lunda, D.R.C.	262-63	6°29'S	16°50'E
Kaspīy Mangy oypaty, pl., see Caspian Depression	186-87	48°0'N	52°00'E
Kaspiysk, Russia	227	42°53'N	47°38'E
Kaspiyskiy, Russia	186-87	45°24'N	47°21'E
Kaspiyskoye More, lk., see Caspian Sea	226	41°18'N	50°59'E
Kasr, Ra's, c., Afr.	266	18°01'N	38°34'E
Kassa, Slvk. see Košice	194-95	48°43'N	21°16'E
Kassalā, Sudan	266	15°27'N	36°23'E
Kassel, Ger. (käs´ĕl)	194-95	51°19'N	9°29'E
Kasserine, Tun.	184-85	35°09'N	8°50'E
Kasson, Mn., U.S. (kăs´ŭn)	114-15	44°02'N	92°46'W
Kastamonu, Tur. (kä-stȧ-mō´nōō)	186-87	41°23'N	33°47'E
Kastellorizo, i., Grc. see Megísti	188-89	36°08'N	29°36'E
Kastoría, Grc. (kȧs-tō´rĭ-ȧ)	200-01	40°32'N	21°17'E
Kasulu, Tan.	267	4°34'S	30°06'E
Kasungu, Malawi	264-65	13°03'S	33°28'E
Kasūr, Pak.	232-33	31°07'N	74°27'E
Katahdin, Mount, mtn., Me., U.S. (mount kȧ-tä´dĭn)	117a	45°55'N	68°55'W
Katanda, D.R.C.	267	0°50'S	29°22'E
Katanga, hist. reg., D.R.C. (kȧ-täŋ´gȧ)	262-63	10°0'S	26°00'E
Katanga, stm., Russia	218-19	60°09'N	102°14'E
Katanning, Austl. (kȧ-tăn´ĭng)	270-71	33°42'S	117°33'E
Katchall Island, i., India	246-47	7°55'N	93°23'E
Katha, Mya.	238-39	24°10'N	96°20'E
Katherine, Austl. (kăth´ĕr-ĭn)	270-71	14°29'S	132°16'E
Kāthiāwār Peninsula, pen., India (kä´tyȧ-wär´ pĕ-nĭn´sūlȧ)	234-35	22°0'N	71°00'E
Kāṭhmāṇḍāū, nat. cap., Nepal see Kathmandu	234-35	27°42'N	85°19'E
Kathmandu, nat. cap., Nepal (kät-män-dōō´)	234-35	27°42'N	85°19'E
Katihār, India	234-35	25°33'N	87°34'E
Katima Mulilo, Nmb.	264-65	17°30'S	24°16'E
Ka Tiriti o te Moana, mts., N.Z. see Southern Alps	278	43°30'S	170°30'E
Katmai National Park and Preserve, n.p., Ak., U.S. (kăt´mī năsh´ŭn-ăl pärk ănd prĭ-zûrv´)	126	58°30'N	155°05'W
Kātmāndu, nat. cap., Nepal see Kathmandu	234-35	27°42'N	85°19'E
Katni, India see Murwāra	234-35	23°50'N	80°24'E
Katoomba, Austl.	276	33°43'S	150°18'E
Katowice, Pol.	194-95	50°16'N	19°01'E
Katrineholm, Swe. (kȧ-trē´nĕ-hōlm)	192-93	58°59'N	16°12'E
Katsina, Nig. (kät´sē-nȧ)	260-61	12°60'N	7°36'E
Kattaqo'rg'on, Uzb.	232-33	39°55'N	66°16'E
Kattegat, strt., Eur. (kăt´ĕ-găt)	192-93	57°0'N	11°00'E
Kattegatt, strt., Eur. see Kattegat	192-93	57°0'N	11°00'E
Kattowitz, Pol. see Katowice	194-95	50°16'N	19°01'E
Katun', stm., Russia (kȧ-tōn´)	226	52°26'N	85°00'E
Kaua'i, i., Hi., U.S.	127a	22°0'N	159°30'W
Kaufbeuren, Ger. (kouf´boi-rĕn)	194-95	47°53'N	10°37'E
Kaufman, Tx., U.S. (kôf´măn)	120-21	32°35'N	96°20'W
Kaukauna, Wi., U.S. (kô-kô´nȧ)	116-17	44°16'N	88°16'W
Kaukau Veld, plat., Afr.	264-65	19°30'S	20°30'E
Kaunakakai, Hi., U.S. (kä´ōō-nȧ-kä´kī)	127a	21°06'N	157°01'W
Kaunas, Lith. (kou´nȧs) (kôv´nô)	192-93	54°54'N	23°54'E
Kauriālā, stm., Asia see Ghāghara	234-35	25°45'N	84°48'E
Kau-ye Kyun, i., Mya.	246-47	10°60'N	98°31'E
Kavála, Grc. (kä-vä´lä)	200-01	40°57'N	24°24'E
Kavalerovo, Russia	244	44°16'N	135°03'E
Kavaratti Island, i., India	236	10°34'N	72°38'E
Kavieng, Pap. N. Gui. (kä-vê-ĕng´)	277	2°34'S	150°48'E
Kavīr, Dasht-e, des., Iran (dŭsht-ē-ka-vēr´)	232-33	34°40'N	54°30'E
Kavkasioni, mts., see Caucasus Mountains	227	42°38'N	45°00'E
Kawaguchi, Japan (kä-wä-gōō-chē)	245	35°48'N	139°43'E
Kawambwa, Zam.	264-65	9°48'S	29°05'E
Kawasaki, Japan (kä-wä-sä´kê)	245	35°32'N	139°42'E
Kaxgar, stm., China	226	39°25'N	76°26'E
Kayak Island, i., Ak., U.S.	126	59°54'N	144°27'W
Kayan, stm., Indon.	248-49	2°55'N	117°35'E
Kaycee, Wy., U.S. (kā-sē´)	112-13	43°43'N	106°40'W
Kayes, Mali (kāz)	258-59	14°27'N	11°26'W
Kayoa, Pulau, i., Indon.	248-49	0°04'S	127°24'E
Kayseri, Tur. (kī´sĕ-rē)	186-87	38°44'N	35°29'E
Kayuagung, Indon.	246-47	3°23'S	104°50'E
Kazakh Hills, hills, Kaz. (kä-zäk´ hĭlz)	226	49°0'N	72°00'E
Kazakhstan, nation, Asia (kä-zäk-stän´)	206-07	47°0'N	76°00'E
Kazan', Russia (kȧ-zän´)	186-87	55°51'N	49°04'E
Kazan, stm., Can.	130-31	64°10'N	95°22'W
Kazanka, Ukr. (kȧ-zän´kȧ)	202-03	47°50'N	32°50'E
Kazanlŭk, Blg. (kȧ´zȧn-lêk)	200-01	42°37'N	25°24'E
Kazan-rettō, is., Japan	280-81	25°0'N	141°00'E
Kazbek, Gora, vol., (gȧ-rä´ kȧz-bĕk´)	227	42°42'N	44°31'E
Kāzerūn, Iran	230-31	29°37'N	51°39'E
Kazincbarcika, Hung. (kô´zĭnts-bôr-tsĭ-ko)	194-95	48°15'N	20°39'E
Kazvin, Iran see Qazvīn	232-33	36°16'N	49°58'E
Kazym, stm., Russia (kä-zēm´)	218-19	63°53'N	65°53'E

n-sing; ŋ-baŋk; ɴ-nasalized n; nŏd; cŏmmit; ōld; ôbey; ôrder; oi-boil; fōōd; ŏ-as oo in foot; ou-out; s-soft; sh-dish; th-thin; pūre; ûnite; ûrn; stŭd; circŭs; ü-as in French tu; ´-indeterminate vowel.

n-sing; ŋ-baŋk; N-nasalized n; nŏd; cŏmmit; ōld; ôbey; ôrder; oi-boil; fōōd; ȯ-as oo in foot; ou-out; s-soft; sh-dish; th-thin; pūre; ûnite; ûrn; stŭd; circŭs; ü-as in French tu; ′-indeterminate vowel.

ăt; finăl; rāte; senăte; ärm; àsk; sofá; fâre; ch-choose; dh-as th in other; bē; ĕvent; bĕt; recĕnt; cratĕr; g-gō; gh-guttural g; bĭt; ĭ-short neutral; rīde; ĸ-guttural k as ch in German ich;

Feature (Pronunciation)	Page	Lat.	Long.
Kualakapuas, Indon.	248-49	3°02's	114°25'E
Kuala Lumpur, nat. cap., Malay. (kwä´lä lŏm-pōōr´)	246-47	3°10'N	101°42'E
Kuala Terengganu, Malay.	246-47	5°19'N	103°09'E
Kuandian, China (kûan-dǐen)	243	40°44'N	124°47'E
Kuantan, Malay.	246-47	3°49'N	103°20'E
Kuban', stm., Russia	186-87	45°21'N	37°25'E
Kuching, Malay. (kōō´chǐng)	248-49	1°34'N	110°20'E
Kudat, Malay. (kōō-dät´)	248-49	6°53'N	116°46'E
Kudus, Indon.	248-49	6°48's	110°50'E
Kudymkar, Russia (kōō-dǐm-kär´)	186-87	59°01'N	54°39'E
Kufstein, Aus. (kōōf´shtīn)	194-95	47°35'N	12°10'E
Kugluktuk, Nu., Can.	128-29	67°47'N	115°11'w
Kuiseb, stm., S. Afr.	264-65	22°58's	14°29'E
Kuito, Ang.	264-65	12°23's	16°56'E
Kuiu Island, i., Ak., U.S.	126	56°45'N	134°10'w
Kujū-san, vol., Japan (kōō´jō-sän´)	245	33°05'N	131°15'E
Kula Kangri, mtn., Bhu.	234-35	28°03'N	90°22'E
Kular, Russia	218-19	70°42'N	134°12'E
Kuldīga, Lat. (kŏl´dě-gà)	192-93	56°58'N	21°60'E
Kuldja, China see Yining	226	43°55'N	81°18'E
Kulmbach, Ger. (klŏlm´bäк)	194-95	50°06'N	11°27'E
Kŭlob, Taj.	232-33	37°55'N	69°47'E
Kuloy, Russia	186-87	61°02'N	42°29'E
Kulsary, Kaz.	186-87	46°59'N	53°59'E
Kulundinskaya Ravnina, pl., Asia see Qulyndy Zhazyghy	226	53°0'N	79°00'E
Kulundinskoye, Ozero, lk., Russia	226	53°0'N	79°36'E
Kuma, stm., Russia (kōō´mä)	186-87	44°57'N	46°27'E
Kumamoto, Japan (kōō´mä-mō´tō)	245	32°48'N	130°43'E
Kumanovo, Mac. (kȯ-mä´nȯ-vȯ)	200-01	42°08'N	21°43'E
Kumasi, Ghana (kōō-mä´sě)	260-61	6°41'N	1°38'w
Kumayri, Arm. see Gyumri	227	40°47'N	43°51'E
Kumba, Cam. (kòm´bä)	260-61	4°38'N	9°26'E
Kumbakonam, India (kòm´bŭ-kō´nŭm)	236	10°57'N	79°23'E
Kumertau, Russia	186-87	52°46'N	55°48'E
Kŭm-gang, stm., Kor., S. (kòm gäng´)	243	35°60'N	126°42'E
Kumo, Nig.	260-61	10°01'N	11°13'E
Kumul, China see Hami.	240-41	42°50'N	93°31'E
Kunashir, Ostrov, i., Russia (ŏs-trȯf´ kōō-nŭ-shēr´)	244	44°10'N	146°00'E
Kunashiri-tō, i., Russia see Kunashir, Ostrov	244	44°10'N	146°00'E
Kunene, stm., Afr.	264-65	17°15's	11°45'E
Kungälv, Swe. (kŭng´ělf)	192-93	57°52'N	11°60'E
Kunghit Island, i., B.C., Can.	132-33	52°06'N	131°04'w
Kungsbacka, Swe. (kŭngs´bä-kȧ)	192-93	57°28'N	12°05'E
Kungur, Russia (kòn-gōōr´)	186-87	57°26'N	56°57'E
Kunjirap Daban, p., Asia see Khunjerab Pass	232-33	36°52'N	75°28'E
Kunlun Mountains, mts., China (kōōn-lōōn moun´tĭnz) see Kunlun Shan.	222-23	36°30'N	88°00'E
Kunlun Shan, mts., China (kōōn-lōōn shän)	222-23	36°30'N	88°00'E
Kunming, China (kōōn-mǐŋ)	238-39	25°03'N	102°43'E
Kunsan, Kor., S. (kòn´sän)	243	35°59'N	126°43'E
Kununurra, Austl.	270-71	15°46's	128°44'E
K'uo-k'o-sha-lo Ling, mts., Asia see Kakshaal-Too.	226	41°0'N	78°00'E
Kuopio, Fin. (kȯ-ȯ´pě-ȯ)	184-85	62°54'N	27°43'E
Kupang, Indon.	248-49	10°11's	123°35'E
Kup'ians'k, Ukr.	202-03	49°43'N	37°38'E
Kupino, Russia (kōō-pǐ´nȯ)	226	54°21'N	77°17'E
Kupiškis, Lith. (kȯ-pǐsh´kǐs)	192-93	55°50'N	24°59'E
Kupreanof Island, i., Ak., U.S.	126	56°45'N	133°31'w
Kuqa, China (kōō-chyä)	226	41°11'N	83°28'E
Kür, stm., Asia	227	39°17'N	49°26'E
Kura, stm., Asia	227	39°17'N	49°26'E
Kurashiki, Japan (kōō´rä-shē´kě)	245	34°36'N	133°46'E
Kuraymah, Sudan	266	18°34'N	31°51'E
Kurayoshi, Japan (kōō´rä-yō´shě)	245	35°26'N	133°49'E
Kurchatov, Russia	202-03	51°39'N	35°36'E
Kurdistan, hist. reg., Asia (kûrd´ĭ-stăn)	228-29	37°0'N	45°00'E
Kure, Japan (kōō´rě)	245	34°15'N	132°34'E
Kure Atoll, at., Hi., U.S.	127	28°15'N	178°25'w
Kuressaare, Est. (kȯ´rě-sä´rě)	192-93	58°15'N	22°30'E
Kureyka, stm., Russia.	218-19	66°29'N	87°15'E
Kurgan, Russia (kȯr-gän´)	226	55°27'N	65°20'E
Kurgan-Tyube, Taj. (kȯr-gän´ tyȯ´bě) see Qŭrghonteppa	232-33	37°50'N	68°47'E
Kuria, i., Kir.	280-81	0°12'N	173°24'E
Kuril Islands, is., Russia (kōō´rĭl ī´lăndz)	218-19	47°14'N	152°18'E
Kuril'skiye Ostrova, is., Russia see Kuril Islands	218-19	47°14'N	152°18'E
Kurmuk, Sudan (kȯr´mōōk)	262-63	10°33'N	34°17'E
Kurnool, India (kór-nōōl´)	236	15°50'N	78°02'E
Kuršėnai, Lith. (kȯr´shä-nī)	192-93	55°59'N	22°56'E
Kursk, Russia (kòrsk)	202-03	51°44'N	36°11'E
Kuruman, S. Afr. (kōō-rōō-män´)	264-65	27°28's	23°26'E
Kurume, Japan (kōō´rȯ-mě)	245	33°19'N	130°31'E
Kurunegala, Sri L.	236	7°29'N	80°22'E
Kushiro, Japan (kōō´shē-rō)	244	42°59'N	144°24'E
Kushka, Turkmen. see Guşgy	232-33	35°16'N	62°21'E
Kushtia, Bngl.	234-35	23°55'N	89°08'E
Kushui, China	240-41	42°10'N	94°22'E
Kustanay, Kaz. see Qostanay	226	53°12'N	63°37'E
Kūstī, Sudan	266	13°10'N	32°40'E
Kütahya, Tur. (kû-tä´hyà)	186-87	39°26'N	29°58'E
Kutaisi, Geor. (kōō-tü-ē´sē)	227	42°16'N	42°42'E
Kūt al-Imāra, Iraq see Al-Kūt	228-29	32°30'N	45°49'E
Kutaradja, Indon. see Banda Aceh	246-47	5°33'N	95°19'E
Kutch, Gulf of, b., India see Kachchh, Gulf of	234-35	22°37'N	69°30'E
Kutch, Rann of, reg., Asia	234-35	24°15'N	70°46'E
Kutina, Cro. (kōō´tě-nä)	200-01	45°29'N	16°46'E
Kutno, Pol. (kòt´nȯ)	194-95	52°14'N	19°22'E
Kuujjuaq, Qc., Can.	128-29	58°06'N	68°25'w
Kuusamo, Fin. (kōō´sȧ-mȯ)	184-85	65°59'N	29°10'E
Kuvshinovo, Russia (kȯv-shē´nȯ-vȯ)	202-03	57°01'N	34°11'E
Kuwait, nation, Asia (kōō-wāt´)	206-07	29°30'N	47°45'E
Kuwait, nat. cap., Kuw. (kōō-wāt´)	228-29	29°19'N	47°60'E
Kuybyshev, Russia see Samara.	186-87	53°11'N	50°07'E
Kuybyshev, Russia	218-19	55°27'N	78°18'E
Kuybyshev Reservoir, res., Russia (kōō´ě-bĭ-shĭf rě´sěr-vwär´) see Kuybyshevskoye Vodokhranilishche	186-87	54°30'N	48°30'E
Kuybyshevskoye Vodokhranilishche, res., Russia	186-87	54°30'N	48°30'E
Kuzneck, Russia see Novokuznetsk.	226	53°45'N	87°07'E
Kuznetsk, Russia (kōōz-nyĕtsk´)	186-87	53°07'N	46°36'E
Kuznetsovka, Russia (kȯz-nyĕt´sȯf-kȧ)	192-93	56°19'N	28°34'E
Kvaløya, i., Nor.	184-85	69°40'N	18°30'E
Kwajalein, at., Marsh. Is.	280-81	9°06'N	167°21'E
Kwando, stm., Afr.	264-65	18°30's	23°36'E
Kwangchow, China see Guangzhou	238-39	23°08'N	113°16'E
Kwangju, Kor., S.	243	35°09'N	126°54'E
Kwango, stm., Afr. (kwäng´ō´)	262-63	3°13's	17°23'E
Kwangsi Chuang, state, China see Guangxi	238-39	24°0'N	109°00'E
Kwangtung, state, China see Guangdong	287	23°0'N	113°00'E
Kweichow, state, China see Guizhou	238-39	27°0'N	107°00'E
Kweihwa, China see Hohhot	240-41	40°49'N	111°39'E
Kweiyang, China see Guiyang	238-39	26°35'N	106°43'E
Kwekwe, Zimb.	264-65	18°56's	29°49'E
Kwilu, stm., Afr. (kwē´lōō) see Cuilo.	262-63	5°53's	16°35'E
Kwilu, stm., Afr. (kwē´lōō)	260-61	3°23's	17°23'E
Kyakhta, Russia (kyäк´ta)	240-41	50°21'N	106°27'E
Kyaukpyu, Mya. (chouk´pyoo´)	246-47	19°25'N	93°33'E
Kyauktaw, Mya.	246-47	20°49'N	92°59'E
Kyïv, nat. cap., Ukr. (kē´yěf) see Kiev	202-03	50°26'N	30°30'E
Kyïvs'ke vodoskhovyshche, res., Ukr.	202-03	50°51'N	30°32'E
Kyoga, Lake, lk., Ug.	267	1°30'N	33°00'E
Kyŏmip'o, Kor., N. see Songnim	243	38°44'N	125°38'E
Kyŏngju, Kor., S. (kyŭng´yōō)	243	35°51'N	129°13'E
Kyŏngsŏng, nat. cap., Kor., S. see Seoul	243	37°33'N	127°01'E
Kyōto, Japan (kyō´tō´)	245	34°60'N	135°45'E
Kyrgyz Ala Too, mts., Asia see Kirgiz Range	226	42°29'N	73°50'E
Kyrgyzstan, nation, Asia (kûr´-gǐ-stän´)	226	41°30'N	75°00'E
Kyūshū, i., Japan (kyōō-shōō)	245	33°0'N	131°00'E
Kyustendil, Blg. (kyòs-těn-dīl´)	200-01	42°18'N	22°41'E
Kyzyl, Russia (kĭ´zĭl)	222-23	51°43'N	94°24'E
Kyzylkum, des., Asia see Qyzylqum.	226	42°0'N	64°00'E
Kyzyl-Kyya, Kyrg.	232-33	40°15'N	72°07'E

L

Feature (Pronunciation)	Page	Lat.	Long.
Läänemeri, s., Eur. see Baltic Sea	192-93	57°0'N	19°00'E
Laascaanood, Som.	262-63	8°29'N	47°21'E
La Asunción, Ven. (lä ä-sōōn-syōn´)	164-65	11°01'N	63°52'w
Laayoune, nat. cap., W. Sah. (lä-yōōn´) (lä-yōōn´)	258-59	27°10'N	13°12'w
La Baie, Qc., Can.	136-37	48°20'N	70°53'w
La Banda, Arg. (lä bän´dä)	168-69	27°44's	64°15'w
La Barca, Mex. (lä bär´kä)	146-47	20°17'N	102°33'w
Labé, Gui.	260-61	11°19'N	12°17'w
Labe, stm., Eur. (lä´bě) see Elbe.	194-95	53°53'N	9°01'E
Labian, Tanjong, c., Malay.	248-49	5°19'N	119°16'E
Labinsk, Russia	186-87	44°38'N	40°44'E
Labis, Malay. (läb´ĭs)	246-47	2°23'N	103°01'E
Labouheyre, Fr. (lä-bōō-âr´)	196-97	44°13'N	0°55'w
Laboulaye, Arg. (lä-bô´ōō-lä-yě)	173	34°07's	63°24'w
Labrador City, Nf., Can.	128-29	52°56'N	66°54'w
Labrador Sea, s., N.A. (lăb´rȧ-dôr sē)	86	57°0'N	53°00'w
Lábrea, Braz. (lä-brā´ä)	166-67	7°16's	64°47'w
Labuan, Malay.	248-49	5°17'N	115°15'E
Labuha, Indon.	248-49	0°39's	127°30'E
Labuk, stm., Malay.	248-49	5°53'N	117°30'E
La Calera, Chile (lä kä-lě-rä)	163e	32°46's	71°12'w
Lacantum, stm., Mex. (lä-kän-tōō´m)	148	16°33's	90°41'w
La Carlota, Arg.	173	33°26's	63°17'w
La Carolina, Spain (lä kä-rȯ-lē´nä)	198-99	38°17'N	3°37'w
Laccadive, Minicoy and Amīndīvi Islands, state, India see Lakshadweep.	236	10°0'N	73°00'E
Laccadive Islands, is., India see Lakshadweep.	236	10°0'N	73°00'E
La Ceiba, Hond. (lä sē´bä)	149	15°46'N	86°48'w
Lacha, Ozero, lk., Russia (ô´zĕ-rô lä´chä)	186-87	61°20'N	38°48'E
La Chaux-de-Fonds, Switz. (lä shō dĕ-fôn´)	194-95	47°06'N	6°50'E
Lachlan, stm., Austl. (läk´lăn)	276	34°21's	143°53'E
La Chorrera, Col.	164-65	1°12's	72°55'w
La Chorrera, Pan. (lächȯr-rä´rä)	150	8°53'N	79°47'w
Lachute, Qc., Can. (lä-shōōt´)	136-37	45°39'N	74°21'w
La Ciotat, Fr. (lä syȯtá´)	196-97	43°11'N	5°36'E
Lackawanna, N.Y., U.S. (lak-ȧ-wŏn´ä)	116-17	42°49'N	78°51'w
Lac La Biche, Ab., Can.	132-33	54°46'N	111°58'w
Lac-Mégantic, Qc., Can.	138-39	45°34'N	70°53'w
La Columna, mtn., Ven. see Bolívar, Pico	164-65	8°33'N	71°01'w
Lacombe, Ab., Can.	132-33	52°28'N	113°45'w
Laconia, N.H., U.S. (lä-kō´nĭ-ȧ)	116-17	43°32'N	71°28'w
La Coruña, Spain see A Coruña	198-99	43°22'N	8°25'w
La Crosse, Wi., U.S. (lá-krôs´)	114-15	43°48'N	91°14'w
La Désirade, i., Guad.	143b	16°19'N	61°03'w
Ladispoli, Italy (lä-dē´s-pô-lē)	200-01	41°57'N	12°05'E
Lādīz, Iran	230-31	28°55'N	61°18'E
Ladoga, Lake, lk., Russia (läk lä´-dá-gá)	192-93	61°0'N	31°30'E
La Dorada, Col.	163c	5°27'N	74°41'w
Ladozhskoye Ozero, lk., Russia see Ladoga, Lake	192-93	61°0'N	31°30'E
Ladybrand, S. Afr.	269c	29°11's	27°27'E
Ladysmith, B.C., Can. (lä´dĭ-smǐth)	132-33	48°58'N	123°48'w
Ladysmith, S. Afr. (lä´dĭ-smǐth)	269c	28°34's	29°46'E
Ladysmith, Wi., U.S. (lä´dĭ-smǐth)	114-15	45°28'N	91°06'w
Lae, Pap. N. Gui. (lä´ä)	277	6°43's	146°59'E
Læsø, i., Den.	192-93	57°16'N	11°01'E
La Esperanza, Hond. (lä ĕs-pä-rän´zä)	149	14°19'N	88°11'w
Lafayette, Al., U.S. (lä-fā-yĕt´)	124-25	32°54'N	85°24'w
Lafayette, Co., U.S. (lä-fā-yĕt´)	120-21	39°60'N	105°05'w
Lafayette, In., U.S. (lä-fā-yĕt´)	116-17	40°25'N	86°53'w
Lafayette, La., U.S. (lä-fā-yĕt´)	124-25	30°13'N	92°02'w
Lafia, Nig.	260-61	8°30'N	8°31'E
La Flèche, Fr. (lá fläsh´)	196-97	47°42'N	0°04'w
Lagan, stm., Swe.	192-93	56°33'N	12°56'E
Lågen, stm., Nor. (lô´ghěn)	192-93	59°02'N	10°04'E
Lages, Braz.	168-69	27°49's	50°18'w
Laghouat, Alg. (lä-gwät´)	188-89	33°51'N	2°51'E
Lagoa da Prata, Braz. (lä-gô´ä-dä-prä´tá)	172	20°02's	45°33'w
La Gomera, i., Spain.	199d	28°07'N	17°11'w
Lagos, Nig. (lä´gōs)	260a	6°27'N	3°24'E
Lagos, Port. (lä´gôzh)	198-99	37°06'N	8°40'w
Lagos de Moreno, Mex. (lä´gōs dä mô-rā´nō)	146-47	21°22'N	101°54'w
La Grand'Combe, Fr. (lá grän kaɴb´)	196-97	44°13'N	4°01'E
La Grande, Or., U.S. (lä gränd´)	112-13	45°20'N	118°05'w
La Grande Deux, Réservoir, res., Qc., Can.	130-31	53°40'N	76°55'w
La Grande Quatre, Réservoir, res., Qc., Can.	130-31	54°0'N	73°15'w
Lagrange, Ga., U.S.	124-25	33°02'N	85°02'w
La Grange, Ky., U.S. (lä gränj).	116-17	38°24'N	85°23'w
La Gran Sabana, pl., Ven.	164-65	5°21'N	62°04'w

348 La Guajira, Península de – La Tremblade PRONOUNCING INDEX

Feature (Pronunciation)	Page	Lat.	Long.
La Guajira, Península de, pen., S.A.	**164-65**	12°0'N	71°40'W
Laguna, Braz. (lä-gōō'nä)	**172**	28°28'S	48°47'W
Lagunillas, Bol. (lä-gōō-nēl'yäs)	**168-69**	19°38'S	63°43'W
La Habana, nat. cap., Cuba (lä-ä-bä' nä) *see* Havana	**142-43**	23°06'N	82°27'W
Lahad Datu, Malay.	**250**	5°02'N	118°20'E
Lahaina, Hi., U.S. (lä-hä'ē-nä)	**127a**	20°53'N	156°40'W
Lahat, Indon.	**246-47**	3°48'S	103°32'E
Lāhījān, Iran	**232-33**	37°12'N	50°00'E
Laholm, Swe. (lä'hôlm)	**192-93**	56°31'N	13°03'E
Lahore, Pak. (lä-hōr')	**232-33**	31°35'N	74°20'E
Lahr, Ger. (lär)	**194-95**	48°21'N	7°52'E
Lahti, Fin. (lä'tē)	**192-93**	60°59'N	25°40'E
Laibach, nat. cap., Slvn. *see* Ljubljana	**200-01**	46°03'N	14°31'E
Laibin, China (lī-bĭn)	**238-39**	23°42'N	109°14'E
Laichow Bay, b., China *see* Laizhou Wan	**240-41**	37°20'N	119°19'E
L'Aigle, Fr. (lĕ'gl')	**196-97**	48°46'N	0°38'E
Laiwui, Indon.	**248-49**	1°21'S	127°39'E
Laiyang, China (läī'yäng)	**240-41**	36°58'N	120°43'E
Laizhou Bay, b., China (lī-jō bā) *see* Laizhou Wan	**240-41**	37°20'N	119°19'E
Laizhou Wan, b., China (lī-jō wän)	**240-41**	37°20'N	119°19'E
Lajeado, Braz. (lä-zhĕá'dô)	**168-69**	29°24'S	51°57'W
Lajes, Braz. (lá'zhĕs)	**163d**	5°41'S	36°14'W
Lajinha, Braz. (lä-zhē'nyä)	**172**	20°09'S	41°37'W
La Junta, Co., U.S. (lä hōōn'tà)	**120-21**	37°59'N	103°33'W
Lake Arthur, La., U.S. (lāk är'thŭr)	**122-23**	30°05'N	92°41'W
Lakeba, i., Fiji	**279f**	18°13'S	178°47'W
Lakeba Passage, strt., Fiji	**279f**	17°55'S	178°45'W
Lake Cargelligo, Austl.	**276**	33°19'S	146°22'E
Lake Charles, La., U.S. (lāk chärlz')	**122-23**	30°14'N	93°13'W
Lake City, Fl., U.S. (lāk sĭ'tĭ)	**124-25**	30°12'N	82°38'W
Lake City, Mn., U.S. (lāk sĭ'tē)	**114-15**	44°27'N	92°17'W
Lake City, S.C., U.S. (lāk sĭ'tĭ)	**124-25**	33°52'N	79°45'W
Lake Cowichan, B.C., Can. (lāk kou'ĭ-chăn)	**132-33**	48°50'N	124°03'W
Lake Crystal, Mn., U.S. (lāk krĭs'tăl)	**114-15**	44°07'N	94°13'W
Lake Geneva, Wi., U.S. (lāk jĕ-nē'vȧ)	**116-17**	42°36'N	88°26'W
Lake Harbour, Nu., Can. *see* Kimmirut	**128-29**	62°51'N	69°53'W
Lake Havasu City, Az., U.S. (lāk hăv'ȧ-sōō sĭ'tē)	**118-19**	34°29'N	114°21'W
Lakeland, Fl., U.S. (lāk wûrth')	**125a**	28°03'N	81°58'W
Lake Linden, Mi., U.S. (lāk lĭn'dĕn)	**114-15**	47°12'N	88°24'W
Lake Louise, Ab., Can. (lāk lōō-ēz')	**132-33**	51°27'N	116°13'W
Lake Mills, Ia., U.S. (lāk mĭlz')	**114-15**	43°25'N	93°32'W
Lake Oswego, Or., U.S. (lāk ŏs-wē'go)	**112-13**	45°25'N	122°43'W
Lake Placid, N.Y., U.S. (lāk plăs'ĭd)	**116-17**	44°17'N	73°59'W
Lake Preston, S.D., U.S. (lāk prĕs'tŭn)	**114-15**	44°22'N	97°23'W
Lake Providence, La., U.S. (lāk prŏv'ĭ-dĕns)	**124-25**	32°49'N	91°11'W
Lakeview, Or., U.S.	**112-13**	42°12'N	120°21'W
Lake Village, Ar., U.S. (lāk vĭl'ăj)	**124-25**	33°19'N	91°17'W
Lake Wales, Fl., U.S. (lāk wālz')	**125a**	27°54'N	81°35'W
Lakewood, Co., U.S. (lāk'wȯd)	**120-21**	39°44'N	105°07'W
Lakewood, N.J., U.S. (lāk'wȯd)	**116-17**	40°07'N	74°14'W
Lakewood, Oh., U.S. (lāk'wȯd)	**116-17**	41°29'N	81°48'W
Lakewood, Wa., U.S. (lāk'wȯd)	**112-13**	47°11'N	122°31'W
Lake Worth, Fl., U.S. (lāk wûrth')	**125a**	26°37'N	80°03'W
Lakhdenpokh'ya, Russia (l'ăk-dīe'npōkyȧ)	**192-93**	61°31'N	30°12'E
Lakhīmpur, India	**234-35**	27°57'N	80°47'E
Lakota, N.D., U.S. (lȧ-kō'tȧ)	**114-15**	48°02'N	98°21'W
Lakshadweep, state, India	**236**	10°0'N	73°00'E
Lakshadweep, is., India	**236**	10°0'N	73°00'E
Lakshadweep Sea, s., Asia	**236**	7°0'N	76°00'E
La Libertad, Guat. (lä lē-bĕr-tädh')	**148**	16°47'N	90°07'W
La Ligua, Chile (lä lē'gwä)	**163e**	32°27'S	71°15'W
Lalitpur, India	**234-35**	24°41'N	78°25'E
Lalitpur, Nepal	**234-35**	27°40'N	85°19'E
La Loche, Sk., Can.	**134-35**	56°29'N	109°26'W
La Louvière, Bel. (lȧ lōō-vyâr')	**190-91**	50°29'N	4°12'E
La Luz, Mex. (lä lōōz')	**146-47**	24°12'N	97°52'W
Lama, Ozero, lk., Russia	**218-19**	69°32'N	90°27'E
La Madrid, Arg.	**168-69**	27°39'S	65°15'W
La Malbaie, Qc., Can. (lȧ mäl-bā')	**138-39**	47°40'N	70°09'W
La Mancha, reg., Spain (lä män'chä)	**198-99**	39°21'N	2°28'W
La Manche, strt., Eur. *see* English Channel	**190-91**	50°13'N	2°20'W
Lamar, Co., U.S. (lȧ-mär')	**120-21**	38°05'N	102°37'W
Lamar, Mo., U.S. (lȧ-mär')	**120-21**	37°30'N	94°16'W
La Marmora, Punta, mtn., Italy (pō'n-tä-lä-mä'r-mô-rä)	**200-01**	39°59'N	9°20'E
Lamas, Peru (lä'mȧs)	**170**	6°25'S	76°35'W
Lamballe, Fr. (läɴ-bäl')	**196-97**	48°28'N	2°32'W
Lambayeque, Peru (läm-bä-yā'kå)	**170**	6°41'S	79°54'W
Lambertsbaai, S. Afr. *see* Lambert's Bay	**264-65**	32°06'S	18°19'E
Lambert's Bay, S. Afr.	**264-65**	32°06'S	18°19'E
Lame Deer, Mt., U.S. (lām dēr')	**112-13**	45°39'N	106°41'W
La Méditerranée, s., *see* Mediterranean Sea	**188-89**	35°0'N	20°00'E
Lamego, Port. (lä-mā'gō)	**198-99**	41°06'N	7°49'W
Lamesa, Tx., U.S.	**120-21**	32°45'N	101°58'W
Lamía, Grc. (lȧ-mē'ȧ)	**200-01**	38°54'N	22°26'E
Lamon Bay, b., Phil. (lä-mōn' bā)	**250**	14°28'N	122°01'E
Lamoni, Ia., U.S.	**120-21**	40°38'N	93°56'W
Lamotrek, at., Micron.	**280-81**	7°21'N	146°20'E
La Moure, N.D., U.S. (lȧ mōōr')	**114-15**	46°20'N	98°17'W
Lampang, Thai.	**246-47**	18°17'N	99°29'E
Lampasas, Tx., U.S. (lăm-păs'ȧs)	**122-23**	31°04'N	98°11'W
Lampazos de Naranjo, Mex.	**122-23**	27°02'N	100°31'W
Lamphun, Thai.	**246-47**	18°35'N	99°01'E
Lamu, Kenya (lä'mōō)	**262-63**	2°17'S	40°53'E
Lan', stm., Bela. (lȧn')	**194-95**	52°09'N	27°17'E
Lāna'i, i., Hi., U.S. (lä-nä'ē)	**127a**	20°50'N	156°55'W
Lanark, Scot., U.K. (lăn'ȧrk)	**190-91**	55°41'N	3°47'W
Lancang, stm., Asia *see* Mekong	**246-47**	10°33'N	105°27'E
Lancaster, Eng., U.K.	**190-91**	54°03'N	2°50'W
Lancaster, Ca., U.S. (lăŋ'kăs-tē)	**118-19**	34°42'N	118°08'W
Lancaster, Ky., U.S. (lăŋ'kăs-tē)	**116-17**	37°37'N	84°35'W
Lancaster, Oh., U.S. (lăŋ'kăs-tē)	**116-17**	39°43'N	82°36'W
Lancaster, Pa., U.S.	**116-17**	40°03'N	76°19'W
Lancaster, S.C., U.S. (lăŋ'kăs-tē)	**124-25**	34°43'N	80°46'W
Lancaster, Wi., U.S. (lăŋ'kăs-tē)	**114-15**	42°51'N	90°43'W
Lanchow, China *see* Lanzhou	**240-41**	36°04'N	103°43'E
Lander, Wy., U.S. (lăn'dēr)	**112-13**	42°50'N	108°44'W
Landerneau, Fr. (läɴ-dĕr-nō')	**196-97**	48°27'N	4°16'W
Landes, reg., Fr. (läɴd)	**196-97**	44°10'N	0°52'W
Landsberg, Pol. *see* Gorzów Wielkopolski	**194-95**	52°44'N	15°14'E
Landsberg an der Warthe, Pol. *see* Gorzów Wielkopolski	**194-95**	52°44'N	15°14'E
Land's End, c., Eng., U.K. (ländz ĕnd)	**190-91**	50°03'N	5°44'W
Landshut, Ger. (länts'hōōt)	**194-95**	48°33'N	12°09'E
Landskrona, Swe. (lȧns-krō'nȧ)	**192-93**	55°52'N	12°50'E
Lanett, Al., U.S. (lȧ-nĕt')	**124-25**	32°52'N	85°11'W
La'nga Co, lk., China (läŋ-lä tswo)	**234-35**	30°43'N	81°13'E
Langano Hāyk', lk., Eth.	**269d**	7°36'N	38°46'E
Langdon, N.D., U.S.	**114-15**	48°46'N	98°23'W
Langeland, i., Den.	**192-93**	55°00'N	10°51'E
Langeoog, i., Ger.	**194-95**	53°45'N	7°32'E
Langjökull, ice, Ice. (läng-yû'kōōl)	**190a**	64°42'N	20°12'W
Langkawi, Pulau, i., Malay.	**246-47**	6°24'N	99°50'E
Langley, B.C., Can. (lăng'lĭ)	**132-33**	49°06'N	122°39'W
Langon, Fr. (läɴ-gôɴ')	**196-97**	44°33'N	0°15'W
Langøya, i., Nor.	**184-85**	68°44'N	14°50'E
Langqên, stm., Asia *see* Sutlej	**234-35**	29°21'N	71°02'E
Langres, Fr. (läɴ'gr')	**196-97**	47°52'N	5°19'E
Langsa, Indon. (läng'sȧ)	**246-47**	4°28'N	97°58'E
Lang Son, Viet. (läng'sŏn')	**246-47**	21°51'N	106°45'E
Langzhong, China (läŋ-jôŋ)	**238-39**	31°34'N	105°59'E
Lanigan, Sk., Can. (lăn'ĭ-găn)	**134-35**	51°52'N	105°02'W
Länkäran, Azer. (lĕn-kȯ-rän')	**227**	38°45'N	48°51'E
Lansdale, Pa., U.S. (lănz'dāl)	**116-17**	40°15'N	75°17'W
L'Anse, Mi., U.S. (lȧns)	**114-15**	46°45'N	88°26'W
Lansing, Mi., U.S.	**116-17**	42°45'N	84°33'W
Lanta Yai, Ko, i., Thai.	**246-47**	7°34'N	99°03'E
Lanxi, China	**238-39**	29°12'N	119°28'E
Lanzarote, i., Spain (län-zȧ-rō'tä)	**199d**	29°0'N	13°40'W
Lanzhou, China (län-jō)	**240-41**	36°04'N	103°43'E
Lao, nation, Asia *see* Laos	**206-07**	18°0'N	105°00'E
Laoag, Phil. (lä-wäg')	**250**	18°12'N	120°36'E
Laoang, Phil.	**250**	12°35'N	125°02'E
Lao Cai, Viet.	**246-47**	22°30'N	103°58'E
Laoha, stm., China	**240-41**	43°25'N	120°45'E
Laohekou, China	**238-39**	32°25'N	111°36'E
Laon, Fr. (läɴ)	**196-97**	49°34'N	3°39'E
La Orchila, Isla, i., Ven.	**164-65**	11°48'N	66°09'W
La Oroya, Peru (lä-ô-rō'yä)	**163a**	11°30'S	75°56'W
Laos, nation, Asia (lä-ōs) (lȧ-ōs')	**206-07**	18°0'N	105°00'E
La Palma, Pan. (lä-päl'mä)	**150**	7°42'N	80°11'W
La Palma, Pan.	**150**	8°24'N	78°09'W
La Palma, i., Spain (lä-päl'mä)	**199d**	28°40'N	17°52'W
La Paloma, Ur.	**173**	34°40'S	54°10'W
La Paragua, Ven.	**164-65**	6°51'N	63°19'W
La Paz, Arg. (lä päz')	**173**	30°44'S	59°38'W
La Paz, Arg. (lä päz')	**171**	33°27'S	67°34'W
La Paz, Hond. (lä-pȧ'z)	**149**	14°19'N	87°41'W
La Paz, Mex. (lä-pȧ'z)	**146-47**	23°41'N	100°43'W
La Paz, Mex.	**144-45**	24°10'N	110°18'W
La Paz, nat. cap., Bol. (lä-pȧ'z)	**168-69**	16°30'S	68°09'W
Lapeer, Mi., U.S. (lȧ-pēr')	**116-17**	43°03'N	83°18'W
Lapland, reg., Eur. (lăp'lȧnd)	**184-85**	68°0'N	25°00'E
La Plata, Arg. (lä plä'tä)	**173**	34°55'S	57°57'W
La Plata, Mo., U.S. (lȧ plā'tȧ)	**120-21**	40°02'N	92°29'W
La Pocatière, Qc., Can. (lȧ pô-kȧ-tyâr')	**138-39**	47°22'N	70°02'W
La Porte, In., U.S. (lȧ pōrt')	**116-17**	41°37'N	86°42'W
La Porte City, Ia., U.S. (lȧ pōrt' sĭ'tē)	**114-15**	42°19'N	92°11'W
Lappland, reg., Eur.	**184-85**	68°0'N	25°00'E
Laptev Sea, s., Russia (läp'tyĭf sē)	**208-09**	76°0'N	126°00'E
Laptevykh, More, s., Russia *see* Laptev Sea	**208-09**	76°0'N	126°00'E
La Quiaca, Arg. (lä kē-ä'kä)	**168-69**	22°07'S	65°36'W
L'Aquila, Italy (lä'kē-lä)	**200-01**	42°21'N	13°24'E
Lār, Iran (lär)	**230-31**	27°40'N	54°20'E
Larache, Mor. (lä-räsh')	**269a**	35°12'N	6°09'W
Lārak, Jazīreh-ye, i., Iran	**230-31**	26°52'N	56°22'E
Laramie, Wy., U.S. (lăr'ȧ-mĭ)	**112-13**	41°19'N	105°35'W
Larantuka, Indon.	**248-49**	8°19'S	122°58'E
Larat, Pulau, i., Indon.	**224-25**	7°08'S	131°50'E
Laredo, Spain (lȧ-rā'dhō)	**198-99**	43°25'N	3°25'W
Laredo, Tx., U.S. (lȧ-rā'dhō)	**122-23**	27°31'N	99°28'W
Largo, Cayo, i., Cuba (kä'yō-lär'gō)	**142-43**	21°38'N	81°28'W
Larimore, N.D., U.S. (lăr'ĭ-môr)	**114-15**	47°54'N	97°38'W
La Rioja, Arg. (lä rē-ōhä)	**168-69**	29°25'S	66°51'W
La Rioja, state, Arg. (lä-rē-ô'kä)	**168-69**	30°0'S	67°30'W
Lárisa, Grc. (lä'rē-sȧ)	**200-01**	39°38'N	22°25'E
Larissa, Grc. *see* Lárisa	**200-01**	39°38'N	22°25'E
Lārkāna, Pak.	**232-33**	27°33'N	68°13'E
Larnaca, Cyp. *see* Larnaka	**228-29**	34°55'N	33°38'E
Larnaka, Cyp.	**228-29**	34°55'N	33°38'E
Larned, Ks., U.S. (lär'nĕd)	**120-21**	38°11'N	99°05'W
La Rochelle, Fr. (lȧ rô-shĕl')	**196-97**	46°10'N	1°10'W
La Roche-sur-Yon, Fr. (lȧ rôsh'sûr-yôɴ')	**196-97**	46°40'N	1°26'W
La Roda, Spain (lä rō'dä)	**198-99**	39°12'N	2°09'W
La Ronge, Sk., Can.	**134-35**	55°06'N	105°17'W
La Rubia, Arg.	**173**	30°08'S	61°48'W
Larvik, Nor. (lär'vēk)	**192-93**	59°04'N	10°01'E
La Salle, Il., U.S. (lȧ săl')	**116-17**	41°20'N	89°06'W
La Sarre, Qc., Can.	**136-37**	48°48'N	79°12'W
Las Aves, Isla, i., Ven.	**143b**	15°41'N	63°37'W
Lascano, Ur.	**173**	33°40'S	54°13'W
Las Cruces, N.M., U.S. (läs-krōō'sĕs)	**118-19**	32°19'N	106°47'W
La Selle, Morne, mtn., Haiti (mōrn lä'sĕl')	**142-43**	18°22'N	71°59'W
La Serena, Chile (lä-sĕ-rĕ'nä)	**168-69**	29°54'S	71°15'W
Las Flores, Arg. (läs flo'rĕs)	**173**	36°01'S	59°06'W
Las Heras, Arg.	**171**	46°31'S	68°56'W
Lashio, Mya. (lăsh'ē-ō)	**246-47**	22°57'N	97°45'E
Lashkar, India *see* Gwalior	**234-35**	26°13'N	78°09'E
Las Lajas, Arg.	**171**	38°30'S	70°22'W
Las Lomitas, Arg.	**168-69**	24°43'S	60°36'W
Las Minas, Cerro, mtn., Hond.	**149**	14°33'N	88°39'W
La Solana, Spain (lä-sô-lä-nä)	**198-99**	38°57'N	3°14'W
Las Palmas de Gran Canaria, Spain (läs päl'mäs)	**199d**	28°07'N	15°26'W
La Spezia, Italy (lä-spĕ'zyä)	**200-01**	44°07'N	9°50'E
Las Piedras, Ur. (läs-pyĕ'dräs)	**173**	34°44'S	56°13'W
Las Piedras, stm., Peru	**170**	12°31'S	69°14'W
Las Plumas, Arg.	**171**	43°43'S	67°14'W
Las Rosas, Mex. (läs rō thäs)	**146-47**	16°22'N	92°22'W
Lassen Peak, vol., Ca., U.S. (lăs'ĕn pēk)	**112-13**	40°29'N	121°31'W
Lassen Volcanic National Park, n.p., Ca., U.S. (lăs'ĕn vŏl-kăn'ĭk năsh'ŭn-ăl pärk)	**112-13**	40°30'N	121°27'W
Las Tablas, Pan. (läs tä'bläs)	**150**	7°46'N	80°17'W
Last Mountain Lake, lk., Sk., Can. (låst moun'tĭn lāk)	**134-35**	51°06'N	105°15'W
Las Tórtolas, Cerro, mtn., S.A.	**168-69**	29°57'S	69°53'W
Lastoursville, Gabon (lȧs-tōōr-vēl')	**260-61**	0°48'S	12°42'E
Las Tunas, Cuba	**142-43**	20°58'N	76°57'W
Las Varillas, Arg.	**173**	31°52'S	62°42'W
Las Vegas, N.M., U.S. (läs vā'gäs)	**120-21**	35°36'N	105°13'W
Las Vegas, Nv., U.S. (läs vā'gäs)	**118-19**	36°11'N	115°08'W
Latacunga, Ec. (lä-tä-kòŋ'gä)	**170**	0°56'S	78°36'W
Latakia, Syria	**228-29**	35°31'N	35°48'E
La Teste-de-Buch, Fr. (lä-tĕst-dĕ-büsh)	**196-97**	44°38'N	1°09'W
Lathrop, Mo., U.S. (lā'thrŭp)	**120-21**	39°33'N	94°20'W
La Tortuga, Isla, i., Ven. (ē's-lä-lä-tôr-tōō'gä)	**163b**	10°56'N	65°20'W
Latouche Treville, Cape, c., Austl.	**272-73**	18°28'S	121°50'E
La Tremblade, Fr. (lä-trĕɴ-bläd')	**196-97**	45°46'N	1°08'W

ăt; finăl; rāte; senåte; ärm; ȧsk; sofȧ; fâre; ch-choose; dh-as th in other; bē; ėvent; bĕt; recĕnt; cratēr; g-gō; gh-guttural g; bĭt; ĭ-short neutral; rīde; ᴋ-guttural k as ch in German ich;

Feature (Pronunciation)	Page	Lat.	Long.
Latrobe, Pa., U.S. (lȧ-trōb′)	116-17	40°18′N	79°22′W
La Tuque, Qc., Can. (lȧ′tük′)	136-37	47°26′N	72°47′W
Lātūr, India (lä-to͞or′)	236	18°24′N	76°35′E
Latvia, nation, Eur. (lăt′vē-ȧ)	174-75	57°0′N	25°00′E
Latvija, nation, Eur. see Latvia	174-75	57°0′N	25°00′E
Lauenburg, Pol. see Lębork	194-95	54°32′N	17°46′E
Lau Group, is., Fiji	279f	18°20′S	178°30′W
Lauis, Switz. see Lugano	194-95	46°01′N	8°57′E
Launceston, Austl. (lôn′sĕs-tŭn)	276	41°25′S	147°08′E
La Unión, Chile (lä-o͞o-nyô′n)	171	40°18′S	73°05′W
La Unión, El Sal.	148	13°20′N	87°51′W
La Unión, Mex. (lä o͞on-nyōn′)	146-47	17°58′N	101°49′W
Laura, Austl. (lôrȧ)	277	15°33′S	144°26′E
Laurel, De., U.S. (lô′rĕl)	116-17	38°33′N	75°34′W
Laurel, Md., U.S. (lô′rĕl)	116-17	39°06′N	76°51′W
Laurel, Ms., U.S. (lô′rĕl)	124-25	31°42′N	89°08′W
Laurel, Mt., U.S. (lô′rĕl)	112-13	45°40′N	108°46′W
Laurel, Ne., U.S. (lô′rĕl)	114-15	42°26′N	97°06′W
Laurens, S.C., U.S. (lô′rĕnz)	124-25	34°30′N	82°01′W
Laurentides, Les, plat., Qc., Can.	130-31	48°0′N	71°00′W
Laurinburg, N.C., U.S. (lô′rĭn-bûrg)	124-25	34°47′N	79°28′W
Laurium, Mi., U.S. (lô′rĭ-ŭm)	114-15	47°14′N	88°26′W
Lausanne, Switz. (lō-zȧn′)	194-95	46°31′N	6°38′E
Lausitzer Neiße, stm., Eur. see Neisse	194-95	52°04′N	14°46′E
Laut, Pulau, i., Indon.	248-49	3°40′S	116°10′E
Lautaro, Chile (lou-tä′rô)	171	38°31′S	72°26′W
Laut Kecil, Kepulauan, is., Indon.	248-49	4°49′S	115°44′E
Lava, Nosy, i., Madag.	264-65	14°33′S	47°36′E
Lava Beds National Monument, n.p., Ca., U.S. (lä′vȧ bĕds năsh′ŭn-ăl mŏn′ū-mĕnt)	112-13	41°45′N	121°32′W
Laval, Qc., Can.	136-37	45°33′N	73°44′W
Laval, Fr. (lä-väl′)	196-97	48°04′N	0°46′W
Lāvān, Jazīreh-ye, i., Iran	230-31	26°49′N	53°15′E
Lavapié, Punta, c., Chile	171	37°09′S	73°35′W
La Vega, Dom. Rep. (lä-vĕ′gä)	142-43	19°13′N	70°31′W
Laverton, Austl. (lā′vẽr-tŭn)	270-71	28°37′S	122°24′E
La Victoria, Ven. (lä vēk-tō′rē-ä)	163b	10°13′N	67°20′W
Lavras, Braz. (lä′vräzh)	172	21°14′S	45°00′W
Lavrentiya, Russia	126	65°35′N	171°01′W
Lawas, Malay.	248-49	4°51′N	115°24′E
Lawn Hill National Park, n.p., Austl. see Boodjamulla National Park	277	18°45′S	138°27′E
Lawrence, In., U.S. (lô′rĕns)	116-17	39°50′N	86°01′W
Lawrence, Ks., U.S. (lô′rĕns)	120-21	38°57′N	95°15′W
Lawrence, Ma., U.S. (lô′rĕns)	116-17	42°42′N	71°10′W
Lawrenceburg, In., U.S. (lô′rĕns-bûrg)	116-17	39°05′N	84°52′W
Lawrenceburg, Ky., U.S. (lô′rĕns-bûrg)	116-17	38°03′N	84°54′W
Lawrenceburg, Tn., U.S. (lô′rĕns-bûrg)	124-25	35°15′N	87°20′W
Lawrenceville, Ga., U.S. (lô-rĕns-vĭl)	124-25	33°58′N	83°59′W
Lawrenceville, Il., U.S. (lô-rĕns-vĭl)	116-17	38°43′N	87°41′W
Lawrenceville, Va., U.S. (lô-rĕns-vĭl)	124-25	36°46′N	77°51′W
Lawton, Ok., U.S. (lô′tŭn)	120-21	34°36′N	98°24′W
Lawz, Jabal al-, mtn., Sau. Ar.	228-29	28°40′N	35°18′E
La'youn, nat. cap., W. Sah. see Laayoune	258-59	27°10′N	13°12′W
Laysan Island, i., Hi., U.S.	127	25°50′N	171°50′W
Layton, Ut., U.S. (lā′tŭn)	112-13	41°05′N	111°58′W
Lazarev, Russia	218-19	52°12′N	141°30′E
Lázaro Cárdenas, Mex.	146-47	17°57′N	102°12′W
Lazdijai, Lith. (läzh′dē-yī′)	194-95	54°14′N	23°32′E
Lead, S.D., U.S. (lēd)	114-15	44°21′N	103°46′W
Leader, Sk., Can.	134-35	50°53′N	109°31′W
Leadville, Co., U.S. (lĕd′vĭl)	118-19	39°15′N	106°18′W
Leaf, stm., Ms., U.S. (lēf)	124-25	31°0′N	88°45′W
League City, Tx., U.S. (lēg sĭ′tĭ)	122-23	29°30′N	95°06′W
Leamington, On., Can. (lĕm′ĭng-tŭn)	136-37	42°02′N	82°36′W
Leavenworth, Ks., U.S. (lĕv′ĕn-wûrth)	120-21	39°18′N	94°56′W
Leavenworth, Wa., U.S. (lĕv′ĕn-wûrth)	112-13	47°36′N	120°40′W
Łeba, Pol. (lā′bä)	194-95	54°45′N	17°33′E
Lebak, Phil.	250	6°31′N	124°02′E
Lebanon, In., U.S. (lĕb′ȧ-nŭn)	116-17	40°03′N	86°28′W
Lebanon, Ky., U.S. (lĕb′ȧ-nŭn)	116-17	37°34′N	85°15′W
Lebanon, Mo., U.S. (lĕb′ȧ-nŭn)	120-21	37°41′N	92°40′W
Lebanon, N.H., U.S. (lĕb′ȧ-nŭn)	116-17	43°39′N	72°15′W
Lebanon, Oh., U.S. (lĕb′ȧ-nŭn)	116-17	39°26′N	84°13′W
Lebanon, Or., U.S. (lĕb′ȧ-nŭn)	112-13	44°32′N	122°54′W
Lebanon, Tn., U.S. (lĕb′ȧ-nŭn)	124-25	36°13′N	86°17′W
Lebanon, Va., U.S. (lĕb′ȧ-nŭn)	124-25	36°54′N	82°05′W
Lebanon, nation, Asia (lĕb′ȧ-nŭn)	206-07	34°0′N	36°00′E
Lebedyan', Russia (lyĕ′bĕ-dyän′)	202-03	53°01′N	39°08′E
Lębork, Pol. (lăn-bòrk′)	194-95	54°32′N	17°46′E
Lebrija, Spain (lå-brē′hä)	198-99	36°56′N	6°04′W
Lebu, Chile	171	37°37′S	73°39′W
Lecce, Italy (lĕt′chā)	200-01	40°21′N	18°10′E
Lecco, Italy (lĕk′kō)	200-01	45°51′N	9°23′E
Le Creusot, Fr. (lēkrû-zô)	196-97	46°48′N	4°26′E
Ledo, India	234-35	27°17′N	95°44′E
Ledu, China	240-41	36°28′N	102°24′E
Leduc, Ab., Can. (lĕ-do͞ok′)	132-33	53°15′N	113°32′W
Ledyanaya, Gora, mtn., Russia	218-19	61°53′N	171°09′E
Ledyard Bay, b., Ak., U.S.	126	69°14′N	164°31′W
Leech Lake, lk., Mn., U.S. (lēch lāk)	114-15	47°09′N	94°23′W
Leeds, Eng., U.K. (lēdz)	190-91	53°50′N	1°35′W
Leeds, N.D., U.S. (lēdz)	114-15	48°17′N	99°27′W
Leesburg, Fl., U.S. (lēz′bûrg)	124-25	28°49′N	81°53′W
Leesburg, Va., U.S. (lēz′bûrg)	116-17	39°06′N	77°34′W
Leesville, La., U.S. (lēz′vĭl)	122-23	31°08′N	93°16′W
Leeton, Austl.	276	34°33′S	146°24′E
Leeuwarden, Neth. (lā′wär-dĕn)	190-91	53°12′N	5°47′E
Leeuwin, Cape, c., Austl. (kāp o͞o′wĭn)	272-73	34°23′S	115°08′E
Leeward Islands, is., N.A. (lē′wẽrd ī′lăndz)	143b	17°0′N	63°00′W
Lefkáda, i., Grc.	200-01	38°42′N	20°39′E
Lefkoşa, nat. cap., Cyp. see Nicosia	228-29	35°10′N	33°22′E
Lefroy, Lake, lk., Austl. (lăk lē-froi′)	272-73	31°15′S	121°40′E
Leganés, Spain (lå-gä′nås)	198-99	40°20′N	3°46′W
Legaspi, Phil.	250	13°08′N	123°45′E
Leghorn, Italy see Livorno	200-01	43°34′N	10°19′E
Legnica, Pol. (lĕk-nĭt′sȧ)	194-95	51°13′N	16°10′E
Leh, India (lā)	234-35	34°10′N	77°35′E
Le Havre, Fr. (lē àv′r′)	196-97	49°29′N	0°08′E
Leicester, Eng., U.K. (lĕs′tẽr)	190-91	52°39′N	1°08′W
Leikanger, Nor. (lī′käŋ′gẽr)	192-93	61°12′N	6°50′E
Leine, stm., Ger. (lī′nĕ)	194-95	52°43′N	9°36′E
Leipzig, Ger. (līp′tsĭk)	194-95	51°20′N	12°23′E
Leiria, Port. (lā-rē′ä)	198-99	39°45′N	8°48′W
Leitchfield, Ky., U.S. (lēch′fēld)	116-17	37°29′N	86°18′W
Leizhou Bandao, pen., China (lā-jō bän-dou)	238-39	20°47′N	110°05′E
Leksand, Swe. (lĕk′sänd)	192-93	60°43′N	15°01′E
Leland, Mi., U.S. (lē′lănd)	116-17	45°01′N	85°46′W
Leland, Ms., U.S. (lē′lănd)	124-25	33°25′N	90°54′W
Leli Shan, mtn., China	234-35	33°26′N	81°42′E
Le Maire, Estrecho de, strt., Arg. (ĕs-trĕ′chô-dĕ-lĕ-mī′rĕ)	171	54°50′S	64°60′W
Léman, Lac, lk., Eur. see Geneva, Lake	194-95	46°24′N	6°22′E
Le Mans, Fr. (lē mäɴ′)	196-97	48°00′N	0°12′E
Le Mars, Ia., U.S. (lē märz′)	114-15	42°48′N	96°10′W
Lemesós, Cyp.	228-29	34°41′N	33°03′E
Lemhi Range, mts., Id., U.S. (lĕm′hī rānj)	112-13	44°33′N	113°36′W
Lemmon, S.D., U.S. (lĕm′ŭn)	114-15	45°56′N	102°10′W
Lemnos, i., Grc. see Límnos	200-01	39°55′N	25°18′E
Lempa, stm., N.A. (lĕm′pä)	148	13°15′N	88°49′W
Lena, stm., Russia (lē′nȧ) (lyě′nä)	218-19	72°25′N	126°40′E
Lençóis, Braz.	166-67	12°34′S	41°23′W
Lenexa, Ks., U.S. (lē′nĕx-ă)	120-21	38°58′N	94°44′W
Lenghu, China	220-21	38°50′N	93°26′E
Lenin, Qullai, mtn., Asia see Lenin Peak	232-33	39°20′N	72°55′E
Lenina, Pik, mtn., Asia see Lenin Peak	232-33	39°20′N	72°55′E
Lenin Atyndagy Choku, mtn., Asia see Lenin Peak	232-33	39°20′N	72°55′E
Leningrad, Russia see Saint Petersburg	192-93	59°57′N	30°15′E
Leningradskaya, Russia (lyĕ-nĭn-gräd′skȧ-yȧ)	202-03	46°19′N	39°23′E
Leninogor, Kaz. see Ridder	226	50°21′N	83°30′E
Leninogorsk, Russia	186-87	54°35′N	52°29′E
Lenin Peak, mtn., Asia	232-33	39°20′N	72°55′E
Leninsk, Kaz. see Bayqongyr	226	45°38′N	63°18′E
Leninsk-Kuznetskiy, Russia	218-19	54°41′N	86°12′E
Leninskoye, Russia	240-41	47°60′N	132°38′E
Lennox, S.D., U.S. (lĕn′ŭks)	114-15	43°21′N	96°55′W
Lennox, Isla, i., Chile	171	55°18′S	66°50′W
Lenoir, N.C., U.S. (lē-nōr′)	124-25	35°55′N	81°32′W
Lensk, Russia	218-19	60°44′N	114°56′E
Léo, Burkina	260-61	11°06′N	2°06′W
Leoben, Aus. (lå-ō′bĕn)	194-95	47°22′N	15°06′E
Léogâne, Haiti (lā-ō-gan′)	142-43	18°31′N	72°38′W
Leominster, Ma., U.S. (lĕm′ĭn-stẽr)	116-17	42°32′N	71°45′W
León, Mex. (lå-ōn′)	146-47	21°07′N	101°42′W
León, Nic. (lĕ-ō′n)	149	12°26′N	86°52′W
León, Spain (lĕ-ô′n)	198-99	42°36′N	5°34′W
Leon, Ia., U.S. (lē′ŏn)	114-15	40°45′N	93°44′W
León, hist. reg., Spain (lĕ-ô′n)	198-99	42°0′N	6°00′W
Leon, stm., Tx., U.S. (lē′ŏn)	122-23	30°59′N	97°24′W
León de los Aldamas, Mex. see León	146-47	21°07′N	101°42′W
Leonforte, Italy (lā-ôn-fôr′tā)	200-01	37°38′N	14°23′E
Leonora, Austl.	270-71	28°53′S	121°20′E
Léopold II, Lac, lk., D.R.C. see Mai-Ndombe, Lac	260-61	2°25′S	18°18′E
Leopoldina, Braz. (lā-ō-pôl-dē′nä)	172	21°32′S	42°38′W
Léopoldville, nat. cap., D.R.C. see Kinshasa	262-63	4°21′S	15°18′E
Lepe, Spain (lā′pā)	198-99	37°15′N	7°12′W
Leping, China (lŭ-pĭŋ)	238-39	28°57′N	117°06′E
Le Port, Reu.	265a	20°55′S	55°18′E
Le Puy, Fr. (lē pwē′)	196-97	45°03′N	3°53′E
Lerdo, Mex. (lĕr′dō)	122-23	25°32′N	103°31′W
Lérida, Spain see Lleida	198-99	41°37′N	0°38′E
Lerma, stm., Mex. (lĕr′mä)	146-47	20°13′N	102°41′W
Le Roy, N.Y., U.S. (lē roi′)	116-17	42°58′N	77°59′W
Lerwick, Scot., U.K. (lẽr′ĭk) (lûr′wĭk)	190c	60°09′N	1°09′W
Lesbos, i., Grc. see Lésvos	200-01	39°10′N	26°20′E
Les Cayes, Haiti	142-43	18°12′N	73°45′W
Leshan, China (lŭ-shän)	238-39	29°34′N	103°45′E
Leshukonskoye, Russia	186-87	64°53′N	45°42′E
Leskovac, Serb. (lĕs′kō-vȧts)	200-01	43°01′N	21°57′E
Leslie, Mi., U.S. (lĕz′lĭ)	116-17	42°27′N	84°25′W
Lesosibirsk, Russia	218-19	58°14′N	92°29′E
Lesotho, nation, Afr. (lĕsō′thō)	253	29°30′S	28°30′E
Lesozavodsk, Russia (lyĕ-sô-zȧ-vôdsk′)	244	45°28′N	133°24′E
Les Sables-d'Olonne, Fr. (lā sȧ′bl′dô-lŭn′)	196-97	46°30′N	1°47′W
Les Saintes, is., Guad. (lā-săɴt′)	143b	15°52′N	61°37′W
Lesser Antilles, is., (lĕs′ẽr ăn-tĭ′lēz)	143b	15°0′N	61°00′W
Lesser Caucasus, mts., Asia	227	40°60′N	44°35′E
Lesser Khingan Range, mts., China	240-41	48°45′N	127°00′E
Lesser Slave, stm., Ab., Can. (lĕs′ẽr slāv)	132-33	55°10′N	114°03′W
Lesser Slave Lake, lk., Ab., Can. (lĕs′ẽr slāv lāk)	132-33	55°29′N	115°10′W
Lesser Sunda Islands, is., Asia (lĕs′ẽr so͞on′dȧ ī′lăndz)	248-49	9°0′S	120°00′E
Le Sueur, Mn., U.S. (lē so͞or′)	114-15	44°28′N	93°55′W
Lésvos, i., Grc.	200-01	39°10′N	26°20′E
Leszno, Pol. (lĕsh′nô)	194-95	51°51′N	16°35′E
Lethbridge, Ab., Can. (lĕth′brĭj)	132-33	49°42′N	112°49′W
Lethem, Guy.	164-65	3°23′N	59°48′W
Leti, Kepulauan, is., Indon.	248-49	8°13′S	127°50′E
Leticia, Col. (lĕ-tē′syȧ)	164-65	4°10′S	69°56′W
Leucas, i., Grc. see Lefkáda	200-01	38°42′N	20°39′E
Levanger, Nor. (lĕ-väng′ẽr)	184-85	63°45′N	11°18′E
Leveque, Cape, c., Austl. (kāp lē-vĕk′)	272-73	16°26′S	122°56′E
Leverkusen, Ger. (lĕ′fĕr-ko͞o-zĕn)	194-95	51°03′N	6°59′E
Levice, Slvk. (lā′vēt-sĕ)	194-95	48°13′N	18°37′E
Le Vigan, Fr. (lē vē-gäɴ′)	196-97	43°59′N	3°35′E
Lévis, Qc., Can. (lā-vē′) (lē′vĭs)	136-37	46°48′N	71°11′W
Levittown, Pa., U.S. (lĕ′vĭt-toun)	116-17	40°09′N	74°51′W
Levkosía, nat. cap., Cyp. see Nicosia	228-29	35°10′N	33°22′E
Lewes, De., U.S. (lo͞o′ĭs)	116-17	38°46′N	75°08′W
Lewis, Isle of, i., Scot., U.K. (īl ŏv lo͞o′ĭs)	190-91	58°08′N	6°45′W
Lewisburg, Tn., U.S. (lū′ĭs-bûrg)	124-25	35°27′N	86°48′W
Lewisburg, W.V., U.S. (lū′ĭs-bûrg)	116-17	37°48′N	80°27′W
Lewisporte, Nf., Can. (lū′ĭs-pōrt)	138-39	49°16′N	55°05′W
Lewiston, Id., U.S. (lū′ĭs-tŭn)	112-13	46°24′N	117°00′W
Lewiston, Me., U.S. (lū′ĭs-tŭn)	116-17	44°06′N	70°13′W
Lewistown, Il., U.S. (lū′ĭs-toun)	120-21	40°23′N	90°09′W
Lewistown, Mt., U.S. (lū′ĭs-toun)	112-13	47°04′N	109°26′W
Lexington, Il., U.S. (lĕk′sĭng-tŭn)	116-17	40°38′N	88°46′W
Lexington, Ky., U.S. (lĕk′sĭng-tŭn)	116-17	38°03′N	84°31′W
Lexington, Ma., U.S. (lĕk′sĭng-tŭn)	116-17	42°27′N	71°14′W
Lexington, Mo., U.S. (lĕk′sĭng-tŭn)	120-21	39°11′N	93°53′W
Lexington, N.C., U.S. (lĕk′sĭng-tŭn)	124-25	35°49′N	80°15′W
Lexington, Ne., U.S. (lĕk′sĭng-tŭn)	114-15	40°47′N	99°44′W
Lexington, Oh., U.S. (lĕk′sĭng-tŭn)	116-17	40°41′N	82°34′W
Lexington, Tn., U.S. (lĕk′sĭng-tŭn)	124-25	35°39′N	88°24′W
Lexington, Va., U.S. (lĕk′sĭng-tŭn)	116-17	37°46′N	79°27′W
Leyte, i., Phil. (lā′tā)	250	10°50′N	124°50′E
Leyte Gulf, b., Phil.	250	10°50′N	125°25′E
Leżajsk, Pol. (lĕ′zhä-ĭsk)	194-95	50°16′N	22°26′E
L'gov, Russia (lgôf)	202-03	51°39′N	35°16′E
Lhasa, China (läs′ä)	234-35	29°39′N	91°08′E
Lhasa, stm., China	234-35	29°20′N	90°46′E
Lhokseumawe, Indon.	246-47	5°11′N	97°08′E
Lhorong, China	238-39	30°47′N	95°51′E
Li, stm., China	238-39	29°12′N	112°11′E
Liangzhou, China see Wuwei	240-41	37°56′N	102°38′E
Lianjiang, China (lĭĕn-jyäŋ)	225a	26°12′N	119°31′E
Lianxian, China	238-39	24°47′N	112°21′E
Lianyungang, China (lĭĕn-yòn-gäŋ)	238-39	34°37′N	119°11′E
Lianzhou, China see Hepu	238-39	21°41′N	109°11′E
Liao, stm., China	240-41	40°41′N	122°09′E

n-sing; ŋ-baŋk; ɴ-nasalized n; nŏd; cŏmmit; ōld; ôbey; ôrder; oi-boil; fo͞od; ò-as oo in foot; ou-out; s-soft; sh-dish; th-thin; pūre; ûnite; ûrn; stŭd; circŭs; ü-as in French tu; ′-indeterminate vowel.

350 Liaocheng – Llanes PRONOUNCING INDEX

Feature (Pronunciation)	Page	Lat.	Long.
Liaocheng, China (lïou-chŭŋ)	240-41	36°27'N	115°59'E
Liaodong Bandao, pen., China (lïou-dôŋ bän-dou)	240-41	39°55'N	122°19'E
Liaodong Wan, b., China (lïou-dôŋ wäŋ)	240-41	40°30'N	121°30'E
Liaoning, state, China	243	41°0'N	123°00'E
Liaotung, Gulf of, b., China *see* Liaodong Wan	240-41	40°30'N	121°30'E
Liaotung Peninsula, pen., China *see* Liaodong Bandao	240-41	39°55'N	122°19'E
Liaoyang, China (lyä'ō-yäng')	243	41°16'N	123°10'E
Liaoyuan, China (lïou-yůän)	240-41	42°55'N	125°08'E
Liard, stm., Can. (lē-är')	130-31	61°51'N	121°19'W
Lib, i., Marsh. Is.	280-81	8°19'N	167°25'E
Libagon, Phil.	250	10°18'N	125°03'E
Líbano, Col. (lē'bá-nō)	163c	4°56'N	75°04'W
Libau, Lat. *see* Liepāja	192-93	56°31'N	21°01'E
Libby, Mt., U.S. (lĭb'ē)	112-13	48°23'N	115°33'W
Libenge, D.R.C. (lē-bĕŋ'gā)	262-63	3°39'N	18°38'E
Liberal, Ks., U.S. (lĭb'ēr-ăl)	120-21	37°02'N	100°56'W
Liberec, Czech Rep. (lē'bĕr-ĕts)	194-95	50°46'N	15°04'E
Liberia, C.R.	149	10°37'N	85°26'W
Liberia, nation, Afr. (lī-bē'rĭ-ȧ)	253	6°30'N	9°30'W
Liberty, Ky., U.S. (lĭb'ēr-tĭ)	124-25	37°19'N	84°56'W
Liberty, Mo., U.S. (lĭb'ēr-tĭ)	120-21	39°15'N	94°25'W
Liberty, N.Y., U.S. (lĭb'ēr-tĭ)	116-17	41°48'N	74°44'W
Liberty, S.C., U.S. (lĭb'ēr-tĭ)	124-25	34°47'N	82°42'W
Liberty, Tx., U.S. (lĭb'ēr-tĭ)	122-23	30°04'N	94°48'W
Lībiyā, nation, Afr. *see* Libya	253	27°0'N	17°00'E
Lībīyah, Aṣ-Ṣaḥrā' al-, des., Afr. *see* Libyan Desert	254	24°0'N	25°00'E
Libourne, Fr. (lē-bōōrn')	196-97	44°55'N	0°14'W
Libres, Mex. (lē'brās)	146-47	19°28'N	97°41'W
Libreville, nat. cap., Gabon (lē-br'vēl')	260-61	0°24'N	9°28'E
Libya, nation, Afr. (lĭb'ē-ä)	253	27°0'N	17°00'E
Libyan Desert, des., Afr. (lĭb'ē-ăn dĕs'ērt)	254	24°0'N	25°00'E
Licancábur, Volcán, vol., S.A.	168-69	22°50'S	67°50'W
Licantén, Chile (lē-kän-tě'n)	171	34°59'S	72°06'W
Lichinga, Moz.	264-65	13°17'S	35°15'E
Lichtenburg, S. Afr. (lĭk'tĕn-bĕrgh)	269c	26°10'S	26°10'E
Licking, stm., Ky., U.S. (lĭk'ĭng)	116-17	39°05'N	84°31'W
Licungo, stm., Moz.	264-65	17°38'S	37°22'E
Lida, Bela. (lē'dȧ)	194-95	53°54'N	25°18'E
Lidköping, Swe. (lēt'chû-pĭng)	192-93	58°30'N	13°11'E
Lidzbark, Pol. (lĭts'bärk)	194-95	53°16'N	19°50'E
Liechtenstein, nation, Eur. (lĕk'tĕn-shtīn)	194-95	47°09'N	9°35'E
Liège, Bel.	190-91	50°38'N	5°34'E
Liegnitz, Pol. *see* Legnica	194-95	51°13'N	16°10'E
Lienz, Aus. (lē-ĕnts')	194-95	46°50'N	12°46'E
Liepāja, Lat. (le'pä-yä')	192-93	56°31'N	21°01'E
Lietuva, nation, Eur. *see* Latvia	174-75	56°0'N	24°00'E
Lièvre, stm., Qc., Can.	136-37	45°31'N	75°26'W
Lifou, i., N. Cal.	279g	20°44'S	167°14'E
Ligao, Phil. (lē-gä'ō)	250	13°14'N	123°34'E
Ligonha, stm., Moz. (lē-gō'nyȧ)	264-65	16°53'S	39°08'E
Ligonier, In., U.S. (lĭg-ô-nēr)	116-17	41°28'N	85°34'W
Lihir Group, is., Pap. N. Gui.	277	2°55'S	152°36'E
Līhu'e, Hi., U.S. (lē-hōō'ā)	127a	21°59'N	159°22'W
Liivi laht, b., Eur. *see* Riga, Gulf of	192-93	57°30'N	23°35'E
Lijiang, China (lē-jyäŋ)	238-39	26°52'N	100°14'E
Likasi, D.R.C.	262-63	10°59'S	26°43'E
Likhoslavl, Russia (lyē-kôsläv''l)	202-03	57°07'N	35°28'E
Likouala, stm., Congo	262-63	1°12'S	16°49'E
Lille, Fr. (lēl)	196-97	50°39'N	3°07'E
Lillehammer, Nor. (lēl'ĕ-häm'mĕr)	192-93	61°07'N	10°28'E
Lillesand, Nor. (lēl'ĕ-sän')	192-93	58°15'N	8°24'E
Lillestrøm, Nor. (lēl'ĕ-strûm)	192-93	59°58'N	11°04'E
Lillooet, B.C., Can. (lĭ'lōō-ĕt)	132-33	50°42'N	121°56'W
Lillooet, stm., B.C., Can. (lĭ'lōō-ĕt)	132-33	49°45'N	122°08'W
Lilongwe, nat. cap., Malawi (lē-lô-än)	264-65	13°59'S	33°44'E
Liloy, Phil.	250	8°07'N	122°40'E
Lima, Oh., U.S. (lī'mȧ)	116-17	40°45'N	84°07'W
Lima, nat. cap., Peru (lē'mä)	170	12°04'S	77°03'W
Limassol, Cyp. *see* Lemesós	228-29	34°41'N	33°03'E
Limay, stm., Arg. (lē-mä'ē)	171	38°59'S	68°00'W
Limbaži, Lat. (lēm'bä-zĭ)	192-93	57°31'N	24°43'E
Limeira, Braz. (lē-mā'rä)	172	22°34'S	47°24'W
Limerick, Ire. (lĭm'nǎk)	190-91	52°40'N	8°38'W
Límnos, i., Grc.	200-01	39°55'N	25°18'E
Limoges, Fr.	196-97	45°50'N	1°15'E
Limón, Hond. (lē-mô'n)	149	15°51'N	85°31'W
Limon, Co., U.S. (lī'mŏn)	120-21	39°16'N	103°42'W
Limoux, Fr. (lē-mōō')	196-97	43°04'N	2°12'E
Limpopo, stm., Afr. (lĭm-pō'pō)	264-65	25°12'S	33°31'E
Limpopo, Grande Parque Transfronteiriço do, n.p., Afr. *see* Great Limpopo Transfrontier Park	264-65	23°0'S	31°30'E
Limpopo, Parque Nacional do, n.p., Moz.	264-65	23°21'S	31°54'E
Linapacan Island, i., Phil.	250	11°27'N	119°49'E
Linares, Chile (lē-nä'rās)	171	35°50'S	71°36'W
Linares, Mex.	122-23	24°51'N	99°34'W
Linares, Spain (lē-nä'rĕs)	198-99	38°06'N	3°38'W
Lincoln, Arg. (lĭŋ'kŭn)	173	34°52'S	61°31'W
Lincoln, Eng., U.K. (lĭŋ'kŭn)	190-91	53°14'N	0°33'W
Lincoln, Il., U.S. (lĭŋ'kŭn)	116-17	40°09'N	89°22'W
Lincoln, Ks., U.S. (lĭŋ'kŭn)	120-21	39°02'N	98°09'W
Lincoln, Me., U.S. (lĭŋ'kŭn)	117a	45°22'N	68°31'W
Lincoln, Ne., U.S.	114-15	40°48'N	96°43'W
Lincoln, Mount, mtn., Co., U.S. (mount lĭŋ'kŭn)	118-19	39°21'N	106°07'W
Lincolnton, N.C., U.S. (lĭŋ'kŭn-tŭn)	124-25	35°28'N	81°15'W
Lindale, Ga., U.S. (lĭn'dāl)	124-25	34°12'N	85°11'W
Linden, Guy.	164-65	6°05'N	58°17'W
Linden, Al., U.S. (lĭn'dĕn)	124-25	32°19'N	87°48'W
Linden, Tx., U.S. (lĭn'dĕn)	120-21	33°01'N	94°22'W
Lindesberg, Swe. (lĭn'dĕs-bĕrgh)	192-93	59°36'N	15°13'E
Lindesnes, c., Nor. (lĭn'ĕs-nĕs)	192-93	58°0'N	7°02'E
Lindi, Tan. (lĭn'dē)	264-65	9°60'S	39°42'E
Lindi, stm., D.R.C.	262-63	0°33'N	25°05'E
Lindian, China (lĭn-dĭĕn)	240-41	47°11'N	124°52'E
Lindley, S. Afr. (lĭnd'lē)	269c	27°53'S	27°56'E
Lindsay, On., Can. (lĭn'zē)	136-37	44°21'N	78°44'W
Lindsay, Ok., U.S. (lĭn'zē)	120-21	34°50'N	97°37'W
Line Islands, is., Oc. (līn ī'lȧndz)	280-81	0°05'N	157°00'W
Linfen, China	240-41	36°05'N	111°31'E
Lingao, China (lĭn-gou)	238-39	19°54'N	109°40'E
Lingayen, Phil. (lĭŋ'gä-yān')	250	16°01'N	120°14'E
Lingayen Gulf, b., Phil.	250	16°15'N	120°14'E
Lingen, Ger. (lĭŋ'gĕn)	194-95	52°31'N	7°19'E
Lingga, Kepulauan, is., Indon.	246-47	0°05'S	104°35'E
Lingling, China (lĭŋ-lĭŋ) *see* Yongzhou	238-39	26°13'N	111°37'E
Lingyuan, China (lĭŋ-yůän)	240-41	41°15'N	119°16'E
Linh, Ngoc, mtn., Viet.	246-47	15°04'N	107°59'E
Linhai, China	238-39	28°51'N	121°07'E
Linhe, China (lĭn-hŭ)	240-41	40°49'N	107°30'E
Linjiang, China (lĭn-jyäŋ)	243	41°49'N	126°55'E
Linköping, Swe. (lĭn'chû-pĭng)	192-93	58°25'N	15°37'E
Linkou, China	244	45°19'N	130°16'E
Linqing, China (lĭn-chyĭŋ)	240-41	36°51'N	115°42'E
Linqu, China (lĭn-chyōō)	240-41	36°31'N	118°32'E
Linru, China	238-39	34°10'N	112°50'E
Lins, Braz. (lĕ'ns)	168-69	21°40'S	49°45'W
Lintao, China	240-41	35°22'N	103°51'E
Linton, In., U.S. (lĭn'tŭn)	116-17	39°02'N	87°10'W
Linton, N.D., U.S. (lĭn'tŭn)	114-15	46°16'N	100°14'W
Linxi, China (lĭn-shyē)	240-41	43°36'N	118°03'E
Linxia, China	240-41	35°36'N	103°13'E
Linyi, China (lĭn-yē)	240-41	35°04'N	118°22'E
Linyi, China (lĭn-yē)	240-41	37°11'N	116°52'E
Linz, Aus. (lĭnts)	194-95	48°18'N	14°18'E
Lion, Golfe du, b., Fr.	196-97	43°0'N	4°00'E
Lipa, Phil. (lē-pä')	250	13°56'N	121°10'E
Lipari, Isola, i., Italy (ē'-sō-lä-lē'pä-rē)	200-01	38°29'N	14°56'E
Lipetsk, Russia (lyē'pĕtsk)	202-03	52°37'N	39°37'E
Lípez, Cerro, mtn., Bol.	168-69	21°55'S	66°53'W
Liping, China (lē-pĭŋ)	238-39	26°17'N	108°60'E
Lippe, stm., Ger. (lĭp'ĕ)	194-95	51°39'N	6°37'E
Lippstadt, Ger. (lĭp'shtät)	194-95	51°40'N	8°20'E
Lipu, China (lē-pōō)	238-39	24°25'N	110°29'E
Lira, Ug.	267	2°15'N	32°54'E
Lisakovsk, Kaz.	226	52°32'N	62°33'E
Lisala, D.R.C. (lē-sä'lä)	262-63	2°09'N	21°31'E
Lisboa, nat. cap., Port. (lēzh-bō'ä) *see* Lisbon	198-99	38°43'N	9°08'W
Lisbon, N.D., U.S. (lĭz'bŭn)	114-15	46°26'N	97°41'W
Lisbon, Oh., U.S. (lĭz'bŭn)	116-17	40°46'N	80°46'W
Lisbon, nat. cap., Port. (lĭz'bŭn)	198-99	38°43'N	9°08'W
Lisbon Falls, Me., U.S. (lĭz'bŭn fôlz)	116-17	44°00'N	70°03'W
Lisburn, N. Ire., U.K. (lĭs'bŭrn)	190-91	54°31'N	6°03'W
Lisburne, Cape, c., Ak., U.S.	126	68°52'N	166°14'W
Lishui, China (lĭ'shwĭ')	238-39	28°27'N	119°54'E
Lisianski Island, i., Hi., U.S.	127	26°02'N	174°00'W
Lisichansk, Ukr. *see* Lysychans'k	202-03	48°55'N	38°26'E
Lisieux, Fr. (lē-zyû')	196-97	49°09'N	0°14'E
Liski, Russia (lyēs'kē)	202-03	50°59'N	39°31'E
Lismore, Austl. (lĭz'môr)	276	28°49'S	153°17'E
Litang, China	238-39	23°12'N	109°09'E
Litang, China	238-39	29°60'N	100°16'E
Litang, stm., China	238-39	28°03'N	101°32'E
Litchfield, Il., U.S. (lĭch'fēld)	116-17	39°10'N	89°39'W
Litchfield, Mn., U.S. (lĭch'fēld)	114-15	45°08'N	94°32'W
Lithgow, Austl. (lĭth'gō)	276	33°30'S	150°09'E
Lithuania, nation, Eur. (lĭth-ů-ā-'nĭ-ȧ)	174-75	56°0'N	24°00'E
Litoměřice, Czech Rep. (lē'tô-myĕr'zhĭ-tsĕ)	194-95	50°33'N	14°08'E
Litovko, Russia	240-41	49°15'N	135°10'E
Little Abaco, i., Bah. (lĭt''l ä'bä-kō)	142-43	26°54'N	77°43'W
Little Andaman, i., India (lĭt''l ăn-dȧ-măn')	246-47	10°45'N	92°30'E
Little Belt Mountains, mts., Mt., U.S. (lĭt''l bĕlt moun'tĭnz)	112-13	46°45'N	110°35'W
Little Bighorn, stm., U.S. (lĭt''l bĭg-hôrn)	112-13	45°44'N	107°34'W
Little Bighorn Battlefield National Monument, n.p., Mt., U.S. (lĭt''l bĭg-hôrn băt''l-fēld năsh'ŭn-ăl mŏn'ŭ-mĕnt)	112-13	45°32'N	107°20'W
Little Cayman, i., Cay. Is. (lĭt''l kā'mȧn) (lĭt''l kī-män')	142-43	19°42'N	80°02'W
Little Current, On., Can.	136-37	45°58'N	81°55'W
Little Exuma, i., Bah. (lĭt''l ĕk-sōō'mä)	142-43	23°27'N	75°37'W
Little Falls, Mn., U.S. (lĭt''l fôlz)	114-15	45°59'N	94°22'W
Little Falls, N.Y., U.S. (lĭt''l fôlz)	116-17	43°03'N	74°52'W
Littlefield, Tx., U.S. (lĭt''l-fēld)	120-21	33°55'N	102°20'W
Little Inagua, i., Bah. (lĭt''l ē-nä'gwä)	142-43	21°30'N	72°60'W
Little Karoo, plat., S. Afr.	264-65	33°45'S	21°30'E
Little Karroo, plat., S. Afr. (lĭt''l kä-rōō) *see* Little Karoo	264-65	33°45'S	21°30'E
Little Missouri, stm., U.S. (lĭt''l mĭ-sōō'rĭ)	110-11	47°36'N	102°17'W
Little Nicobar, i., India	246-47	7°20'N	93°40'E
Little Powder, stm., U.S. (lĭt''l pou'dēr)	112-13	45°28'N	105°21'W
Little Rock, Ar., U.S.	120-21	34°43'N	92°19'W
Little Scarcies, stm., Afr.	260-61	8°51'N	13°07'W
Little Sioux, stm., U.S. (lĭt''l sōō)	114-15	41°49'N	96°06'W
Little Smoky, stm., Ab., Can. (lĭt''l smōk'ĭ)	132-33	55°40'N	117°38'W
Littleton, Co., U.S. (lĭt''l-tŭn)	120-21	39°35'N	105°01'W
Littleton, N.H., U.S. (lĭt''l-tŭn)	116-17	44°18'N	71°46'W
Litzmannstadt, Pol. *see* Łódź	194-95	51°47'N	19°31'E
Liuaniua, at., Sol. Is. *see* Ontong Java	279e	5°19'S	159°16'E
Liubliana, nat. cap., Slvn. *see* Ljubljana	200-01	46°03'N	14°31'E
Liubotyn, Ukr.	202-03	49°56'N	35°57'E
Liuchow, China *see* Liuzhou	238-39	24°19'N	109°23'E
Liuyang, China (lyōō'yäng')	238-39	28°08'N	113°38'E
Liuzhou, China (lĭô-jō)	238-39	24°19'N	109°23'E
Live Oak, Fl., U.S. (lĭv ōk)	124-25	30°18'N	82°59'W
Livermore, Ca., U.S. (lĭv'ēr-mōr)	118-19	37°41'N	121°46'W
Livermore, Ky., U.S. (lĭv'ēr-mōr)	116-17	37°29'N	87°08'W
Liverpool, N.S., Can. (lĭv'ēr-pōōl)	138-39	44°03'N	64°43'W
Liverpool, Eng., U.K. (lĭv'ēr-pōōl)	190-91	53°25'N	2°57'W
Liverpool Range, mts., Austl. (lĭv'ēr-pōōl rānj)	276	31°51'S	150°18'E
Lívingston, Guat.	148	15°50'N	88°46'W
Livingston, Al., U.S. (lĭv'ĭng-stŭn)	124-25	32°36'N	88°12'W
Livingston, Mt., U.S. (lĭv'ĭng-stŭn)	112-13	45°40'N	110°34'W
Livingston, Tn., U.S. (lĭv'ĭng-stŭn)	124-25	36°23'N	85°19'W
Livingston, Tx., U.S. (lĭv'ĭng-stŭn)	122-23	30°42'N	94°57'W
Livingston, Lake, res., Tx., U.S.	122-23	30°43'N	95°08'W
Livingstone, Zam. (lĭv-ĭng-stôn)	264-65	17°52'S	25°51'E
Livingstone, Chutes de, wtfl., Afr. *see* Livingstone Falls	260-61	4°51'S	14°29'E
Livingstone Falls, wtfl., Afr.	260-61	4°51'S	14°29'E
Livno, Bos. (lēv'nô)	200-01	43°50'N	17°00'E
Livny, Russia (lēv'nē)	202-03	52°25'N	37°37'E
Livorno, Italy (lē-vôr'nō) (lĕg'hôrn)	200-01	43°34'N	10°19'E
Livramento, Braz. (lē-vrȧ-mĕ'n-tô) *see* Santana do Livramento	173	30°53'S	55°31'W
Lixi, China	238-39	29°15'N	114°47'E
Lixian, China (lē shyĕn)	238-39	29°30'N	111°38'E
Lixian, China (lē shyĕn)	238-39	34°09'N	105°07'E
Lixian, stm., Asia *see* Black	246-47	21°15'N	105°21'E
Lizard Point, c., Eng., U.K. (lĭz'ȧrd point)	190-91	49°58'N	5°13'W
Ljubljana, nat. cap., Slvn. (lyōō'blyä'na)	200-01	46°03'N	14°31'E
Ljungby, Swe. (lyông'bü)	192-93	56°50'N	13°56'E
Ljusdal, Swe. (lyōōs'däl)	192-93	61°50'N	16°06'E
Ljusnan, stm., Swe.	184-85	61°09'N	17°10'E
Llandudno, Wales, U.K. (lăn-düd'nō)	190-91	53°19'N	3°50'W
Llanelli, Wales, U.K. (lȧ-nĕl'ĭ)	190-91	51°41'N	4°09'W
Llanes, Spain (lyä'nås)	198-99	43°25'N	4°45'W

352 Ludhiāna – Magnetic Island PRONOUNCING INDEX

Feature (Pronunciation)	Page	Lat.	Long.
Ludhiāna, India	234-35	30°54'N	75°51'E
Ludington, Mi., U.S. (lŭd'ĭng-tŭn)	116-17	43°57'N	86°26'W
Ludlow, Eng., U.K. (lŭd'lō)	190-91	52°22'N	2°43'W
Ludvika, Swe. (loodh-vē'kȧ)	192-93	60°08'N	15°11'E
Ludza, Lat. (lŏŏd'zȧ)	192-93	56°32'N	27°44'E
Luena, Ang.	264-65	11°47'S	19°54'E
Luena, stm., Ang.	264-65	12°30'S	22°34'E
Lufeng, China	238-39	22°56'N	115°37'E
Lufira, stm., D.R.C. (lōō-fē'rȧ)	262-63	8°21'S	26°26'E
Lufkin, Tx., U.S. (lŭf'kĭn)	122-23	31°20'N	94°43'W
Luga, Russia (lōō'gȧ)	192-93	58°44'N	29°52'E
Luga, stm., Russia (lōō'gȧ)	192-93	59°40'N	28°18'E
Lugano, Switz. (lōō-gä'nō)	194-95	46°01'N	8°57'E
Lugenda, stm., Moz.	264-65	11°25'S	38°29'E
Lugo, Italy (lōō'gô)	200-01	44°25'N	11°55'E
Lugo, Spain (lōō'gō)	198-99	43°01'N	7°33'W
Luhans'k, Ukr.	202-03	48°34'N	39°20'E
Luik, Bel. see Liège	190-91	50°38'N	5°34'E
Luimneach, Ire. see Limerick	190-91	52°40'N	8°38'W
Lukanga Swamp, sw., Zam. (lōō-käŋ'gȧ swŏmp)	264-65	14°25'S	27°45'E
Lukenie, stm., D.R.C. (lōō-kā'ynȧ)	262-63	2°44'S	18°10'E
Lukolela, D.R.C.	262-63	1°04'S	17°11'E
Łuków, Pol. (wŏ'kŏf)	194-95	51°56'N	22°23'E
Lukuga, stm., D.R.C. (lōō-kōō'gȧ)	262-63	5°40'S	26°55'E
Lukula, D.R.C.	262-63	5°22'S	12°57'E
Lulaka, stm., D.R.C.	262-63	0°53'S	20°11'E
Luleå, Swe.	184-85	65°36'N	22°10'E
Lüleburgaz, Tur. (lü'lĕ-bŏr-gäs')	200-01	41°25'N	27°22'E
Lüliang Shan, mts., China	240-41	37°25'N	111°20'E
Luling, Tx., U.S. (lū'lĭng)	122-23	29°41'N	97°39'W
Lulonga, stm., D.R.C.	262-63	0°38'N	18°21'E
Lulua, stm., D.R.C.	262-63	5°02'S	21°06'E
Lumberton, Ms., U.S. (lŭm'bẽr-tŭn)	124-25	31°00'N	89°30'W
Lumberton, N.C., U.S. (lŭm'bẽr-tŭn)	124-25	34°38'N	79°01'W
Lumberton, Tx., U.S. (lŭm'bẽr-tŭn)	122-23	30°14'N	94°12'W
Lund, Swe. (lŭnd)	192-93	55°42'N	13°11'E
Lüneburg, Ger. (lü'nē-bŏrgh)	194-95	53°16'N	10°25'E
Lunel, Fr. (lü-nĕl')	196-97	43°40'N	4°08'E
Lunenburg, N.S., Can. (lōō'nĕn-bûrg)	138-39	44°23'N	64°19'W
Lunéville, Fr. (lü-nȧ-vel')	196-97	48°36'N	6°30'E
Lunga, stm., Zam.	264-65	14°34'S	26°26'E
Lūni, stm., India	234-35	24°37'N	71°17'E
Lunsar, S.L.	260-61	8°41'N	12°32'W
Luo, stm., China	238-39	34°41'N	110°08'E
Luoding, China (lwô-dĭŋ)	238-39	22°47'N	111°33'E
Luohe, China (lwô-hŭ)	238-39	33°34'N	114°02'E
Luoyang, China (lwô-yäŋ)	238-39	34°41'N	112°27'E
Luqu, China	238-39	34°38'N	102°14'E
Luray, Va., U.S. (lū-rā')	116-17	38°39'N	78°28'W
Lurgan, N. Ire., U.K. (lûr'găn)	190-91	54°28'N	6°20'W
Lurín, Peru	163a	12°17'S	76°52'W
Lúrio, stm., Moz.	264-65	13°30'S	40°32'E
Lusaka, nat. cap., Zam. (lȯ-sä'kȧ)	264-65	15°24'S	28°17'E
Lusambo, D.R.C. (lōō-säm'bō)	262-63	4°57'S	23°30'E
Lushan, China	238-39	30°15'N	102°58'E
Lu Shan, mtn., China	238-39	29°31'N	115°58'E
Lüshun, China (lü-shŭn)	240-41	38°49'N	121°15'E
Lusk, Wy., U.S. (lŭsk)	114-15	42°46'N	104°27'W
Lūt, Dasht-e, des., Iran (dăsht-ē-lōōt)	232-33	32°0'N	58°00'E
Lutherstadt Wittenberg, Ger.	194-95	51°52'N	12°39'E
Luton, Eng., U.K. (lū'tŭn)	190-91	51°53'N	0°25'W
Lutong, Malay.	248-49	4°28'N	113°60'E
Luts'k, Ukr.	194-95	50°45'N	25°20'E
Lutzow-Holm Bay, b., Ant.	287	69°10'S	37°30'E
Luverne, Al., U.S. (lū-vûrn')	124-25	31°43'N	86°16'W
Luverne, Mn., U.S. (lū-vûn')	114-15	43°39'N	96°13'W
Luvua, stm., D.R.C.	262-63	6°45'S	26°57'E
Luwegu, stm., Tan.	262-63	8°31'S	37°23'E
Luwuk, Indon.	248-49	0°56'S	122°47'E
Luxembourg, nation, Eur. see Luxemburg	190-91	49°45'N	6°05'E
Luxembourg, nat. cap., Lux.	190-91	49°37'N	6°07'E
Luxemburg, nation, Eur. (lŭk'-sŭm-bûrg)	190-91	49°45'N	6°05'E
Luxi, China	238-39	24°21'N	98°23'E
Luxor, Egypt	268b	25°42'N	32°39'E
Luza, Russia	186-87	60°37'N	47°16'E
Luzern, Switz. (lȯ-tsĕrn)	194-95	47°03'N	8°19'E
Luzhou, China (lōō-jō)	238-39	28°53'N	105°27'E
Luziânia, Braz. (lōō-zyȧ'nēȧ)	168-69	16°15'S	47°55'W
Lužická Nisa, stm., Eur. see Neisse	194-95	52°04'N	14°46'E
Luzon, i., Phil. (lōō-zŏn')	250	16°0'N	121°00'E
Luzon Strait, strt., Asia (lōō-zŏn' strāt)	238-39	20°30'N	121°00'E
L'viv, Ukr.	194-95	49°51'N	24°02'E
Lwów, Ukr. see L'viv	194-95	49°51'N	24°02'E
Lyallpur, Pak. see Faisalābād	232-33	31°25'N	73°05'E
Lycksele, Swe.	184-85	64°36'N	18°41'E
Lydenburg, S. Afr. (lī'dĕn-bûrg)	269c	25°08'S	30°27'E
Lykens, Pa., U.S. (lī'kĕnz)	116-17	40°34'N	76°43'W
Lynchburg, Va., U.S. (lĭnch'bûrg)	124-25	37°25'N	79°09'W
Lyndonville, Vt., U.S. (lĭn'dŭn-vĭl)	116-17	44°32'N	72°00'W
Lynn, Ma., U.S. (lĭn)	116-17	42°28'N	70°57'W
Lynn Lake, Mb., Can. (lĭn lāk)	134-35	56°51'N	101°00'W
Lyon, Fr. (lē-ôN')	196-97	45°45'N	4°49'E
Lyons, Ga., U.S. (lī'ŭnz)	124-25	32°12'N	82°19'W
Lyons, Ks., U.S. (lī'ŭnz)	120-21	38°21'N	98°12'W
Lyons, Ne., U.S. (lī'ŭnz)	114-15	41°56'N	96°29'W
Lysekil, Swe. (lü'sĕ-kĕl)	192-93	58°17'N	11°27'E
Lys'va, Russia (lĭs'vȧ)	186-87	58°06'N	57°48'E
Lysychans'k, Ukr.	202-03	48°55'N	38°26'E
Lyuban', Russia (lyōō'bȧn)	192-93	59°21'N	31°15'E
Lyubertsy, Russia (lyōō'bĕr-tsĕ)	202-03	55°41'N	37°53'E
Lyudinovo, Russia (lū-dē'novō)	202-03	53°52'N	34°28'E

M

Feature (Pronunciation)	Page	Lat.	Long.
Ma, stm., Asia	246-47	19°47'N	105°52'E
Ma'ān, Jord. (mä-än')	228-29	30°12'N	35°44'E
Ma'anshan, China	238-39	31°42'N	118°30'E
Maastricht, Neth. (mäs'trĭĸt)	190-91	50°52'N	5°42'E
Mabank, Tx., U.S. (mā'bănk)	120-21	32°23'N	96°06'W
Macaé, Braz.	172	22°24'S	41°47'W
MacAlpine Lake, lk., Nu., Can.	130-31	66°38'N	102°51'W
Macapá, Braz.	166-67	0°03'N	51°03'W
Macará, Ec.	170	4°22'S	79°56'W
Macau, Braz. (mä-kȧ'ō)	163d	5°07'S	36°38'W
Macclesfield, Eng., U.K. (măk''lz-fēld)	190-91	53°16'N	2°08'W
MacDonnell Ranges, mts., Austl. (măk-dŏn'ĕl rānjĕz)	272-73	23°52'S	133°14'E
MacDowell Lake, lk., On., Can. (măk-dou ĕl lāk)	134-35	52°15'N	92°45'W
Macdui, Ben, mtn., Scot., U.K. (bĕn măk-dōō'ē)	190-91	57°05'N	3°39'W
Macedonia, nation, Eur. (măs-ē-dō'nĭ-ȧ)	174-75	41°50'N	22°00'E
Macedonia, hist. reg., Eur. (măs-ē-dō'nĭ-ȧ)	200-01	41°0'N	23°00'E
Maceió, Braz.	163d	9°40'S	35°43'W
Macerata, Italy (mä-chȧ-rä'tä)	200-01	43°18'N	13°27'E
Macfarlane, Lake, lk., Austl. (lăk măc'fär-lān)	276	31°58'S	136°43'E
Machado, stm., Braz.	166-67	8°02'S	62°53'W
Machagai, Arg.	173	26°56'S	60°02'W
Machakos, Kenya	267	1°31'S	37°16'E
Machala, Ec. (mä-chȧ'lä)	170	3°16'S	79°57'W
Machilīpatnam, India	236	16°11'N	81°09'E
Machiques, Ven.	164-65	10°04'N	72°32'W
Machu Picchu, hist., Peru	170	13°07'S	72°34'W
Măcin, Rom. (mȧ-chēn')	202-03	45°15'N	28°08'E
Mackay, Austl. (mă-kī')	277	21°10'S	149°12'E
MacKay Lake, lk., N.T., Can. (măk-kā' lāk)	130-31	63°54'N	110°23'W
Mackenzie, stm., N.T., Can. (mȧ-kĕn'zĭ)	130-31	58°60'N	111°25'W
Mackenzie Bay, b., Can. (mȧ-kĕn'zĭ bā)	126	69°0'N	136°30'W
Mackenzie Mountains, mts., Can. (mȧ-kĕn'zĭ moun'tĭnz)	130-31	64°0'N	130°00'W
Mackinaw City, Mi., U.S. (măk'ĭ-nô sĭ'tē)	116-17	45°46'N	84°43'W
Maclean, Austl.	276	29°28'S	153°13'E
Macleod, Lake, lk., Austl.	272-73	24°04'S	113°42'E
Macomb, Il., U.S. (mȧ-kōōm')	120-21	40°28'N	90°40'W
Mâcon, Fr. (mä-kôN)	196-97	46°19'N	4°50'E
Macon, Ga., U.S. (mā'kŏn)	124-25	32°50'N	83°38'W
Macon, Mo., U.S. (mā'kŏn)	120-21	39°44'N	92°28'W
Macon, Ms., U.S. (mā'kŏn)	124-25	33°06'N	88°34'W
Macquarie, stm., Austl. (mȧ-kwŏr'ē)	276	30°08'S	147°23'E
Mada, stm., Nig.	260-61	7°59'N	7°58'E
Madagascar, nation, Afr. (măd-ȧ-găs'kȧr)	253	19°0'S	46°00'E
Madagasikara, nation, Afr. see Madagascar	253	19°0'S	46°00'E
Madame, Isle, i., N.S., Can. (ĭl mȧ-dȧm')	138-39	45°33'N	61°02'W
Madang, Pap. N. Gui. (mä-däng')	277	5°17'S	145°45'E
Madawaska, stm., On., Can. (măd-ȧ-wôs'kȧ)	136-37	45°27'N	76°21'W
Madeira, i., Port. (mä-dā'rä)	258-59	32°44'N	17°00'W
Madeira, stm., S.A. (mä-dā'-rȧ)	166-67	3°22'S	58°45'W
Madeira, Arquipélago da, is., Port. (är-kē-pĕ'lä-gō-dä-mädĕy'-rä) see Madeira Islands	258-59	32°40'N	16°45'W
Madeira Islands, is., Port. (mä-dā'rä ī'lȧndz)	258-59	32°40'N	16°45'W
Madeleine, Îles de la, is., Qc., Can.	138-39	47°30'N	61°45'W
Madelia, Mn., U.S. (mȧ-dē'lĭ-ȧ)	114-15	44°03'N	94°25'W
Madhya Pradesh, state, India (mŭd'vŭ prū-dāsh')	234-35	23°0'N	79°00'E
Madidi, stm., Bol.	166-67	12°31'S	66°58'W
Madikeri, India	236	12°25'N	75°45'E
Madill, Ok., U.S. (mȧ-dĭl')	120-21	34°05'N	96°47'W
Madison, Al., U.S. (măd'ĭ-sŭn)	124-25	34°41'N	86°45'W
Madison, Fl., U.S. (măd'ĭ-sŭn)	124-25	30°28'N	83°25'W
Madison, Ga., U.S. (măd'ĭ-sŭn)	124-25	33°36'N	83°28'W
Madison, In., U.S. (măd'ĭ-sŭn)	116-17	38°44'N	85°23'W
Madison, Me., U.S. (măd'ĭ-sŭn)	116-17	44°48'N	69°53'W
Madison, Mn., U.S. (măd'ĭ-sŭn)	114-15	45°01'N	96°12'W
Madison, Ms., U.S. (măd'ĭ-sŭn)	124-25	32°28'N	90°07'W
Madison, N.C., U.S. (măd'ĭ-sŭn)	124-25	36°23'N	79°58'W
Madison, Ne., U.S. (măd'ĭ-sŭn)	114-15	41°50'N	97°27'W
Madison, S.D., U.S. (măd'ĭ-sŭn)	114-15	44°00'N	97°07'W
Madison, Wi., U.S. (măd'ĭ-sŭn)	116-17	43°05'N	89°22'W
Madison, W.V., U.S. (măd'ĭ-sŭn)	116-17	38°04'N	81°49'W
Madisonville, Ky., U.S. (măd'ĭ-sŭn-vĭl)	124-25	37°20'N	87°30'W
Madisonville, Tx., U.S. (măd'ĭ-sŭn-vĭl)	122-23	30°56'N	95°55'W
Madiun, Indon.	248-49	7°37'S	111°31'E
Madoi, China	240-41	34°55'N	98°12'E
Madona, Lat. (mȧ'dō'nȧ)	192-93	56°51'N	26°14'E
Madras, India see Chennai	236	13°06'N	80°15'E
Madras, state, India see Tamil Nādu	236	11°0'N	78°15'E
Madre, Laguna, b., Mex. (lä-ó'nä mä'drȧ)	122-23	25°01'N	97°40'W
Madre, Laguna, b., Tx., U.S.	122-23	26°58'N	97°26'W
Madre, Sierra, mts., Phil. (sē-ĕ'r-rä-mä'drē)	250	16°20'N	122°00'E
Madre de Dios, stm., S.A. (mä'drȧ dā dē-ōs')	166-67	10°24'S	65°24'W
Madre de Dios, Isla, i., Chile (ē's-lä-mȧ'drȧ dā dē-ōs')	171	50°15'S	75°05'W
Madre del Sur, Sierra, mts., Mex. (sē-ĕ'r-rä-mä'drȧ dĕl-sōōr')	146-47	17°0'N	100°00'W
Madre Occidental, Sierra, mts., Mex. (sē-ĕ'r-rä-mȧ'drĕ-äk-sī-dĕn'-tl)	144-45	25°0'N	105°00'W
Madre Oriental, Sierra, mts., Mex. (sē-ĕ'r-rä-mȧ'drĕ ō-rē-ĕn-täl')	144-45	21°26'N	99°50'W
Madrid, nat. cap., Spain (mä-drē'd)	198-99	40°24'N	3°41'W
Madridejos, Spain (mä-dhrē-dhā'hōs)	198-99	39°28'N	3°32'W
Madurai, India (mä-dōō'rä)	236	9°55'N	78°08'E
Maebashi, Japan (mä-ĕ-bä'shē)	245	36°23'N	139°05'E
Mae Hong Son, Thai.	246-47	19°16'N	97°57'E
Mae Klong, stm., Thai.	246-47	13°22'N	99°60'E
Mae Sot, Thai.	246-47	16°43'N	98°35'E
Maestra, Sierra, mts., Cuba (sē-ĕ'r-rȧ-mä-ās'trä)	142-43	20°06'N	76°24'W
Maéwo, i., Vanuatu	279g	15°10'S	168°10'E
Mafeking, S. Afr. (mȧf'ĕ'kĭng) see Mafikeng	264-65	25°53'S	25°39'E
Mafia Island, i., Tan.	262-63	7°50'S	39°50'E
Mafikeng, S. Afr.	264-65	25°53'S	25°39'E
Mafra, Braz. (mä'frä)	168-69	26°08'S	49°49'W
Mafra, Port. (mäf'rȧ)	198-99	38°57'N	9°19'W
Magadan, Russia (mȧ-gȧ-dän')	218-19	59°35'N	150°50'E
Magallanes, Chile see Punta Arenas	171	53°09'S	70°55'W
Magallanes, Estrecho de, strt., S.A.	171	54°0'S	71°00'W
Magangué, Col.	164-65	9°18'N	74°48'W
Magat, stm., Phil. (mä-gät')	250	17°02'N	121°50'E
Magdagachi, Russia	222-23	53°27'N	125°49'E
Magdalena, Bol. (mäg-dä-lā'nä)	166-67	13°20'S	64°08'W
Magdalena, Mex. (mäg-dä-lā'nä)	146-47	20°54'N	103°57'W
Magdalena, N.M., U.S. (mäg-dä-lā'nä)	118-19	34°07'N	107°15'W
Magdalena, stm., Col. (mäg-dä-lā'nä)	164-65	11°06'N	74°51'W
Magdalena, Bahía, b., Mex. (bä-ē'ä-mäg-dä-lā'nä)	144-45	24°35'N	112°00'W
Magdalena, Isla, i., Chile (ē's-lä-mäg-dä-lā'nä)	171	44°40'S	73°10'W
Magdalena de Kino, Mex.	144-45	30°38'N	110°58'W
Magdeburg, Ger. (mäg'dĕ-bŏrgh)	194-95	52°08'N	11°38'E
Magelang, Indon.	248-49	7°28'S	110°13'E
Magellan, Strait of, strt., S.A. (strāt ŭv mȧ-gĕl'-ŭn) see Magallanes, Estrecho de	171	54°0'S	71°00'W
Magerøya, i., Nor.	184-85	71°02'N	25°42'E
Magnesia, Tur. see Manisa	200-01	38°37'N	27°26'E
Magnetic Island, i., Austl.	277	19°08'S	146°50'E

PRONOUNCING INDEX

Magnitogorsk – Manhuaçu 353

Feature (Pronunciation)	Page	Lat.	Long.
Magnitogorsk, Russia (mȧg-nyē´tô-gôrsk)	226	53°26'N	59°04'E
Magnolia, Ar., U.S. (măg-nō´lĭ-ȧ)	120-21	33°16'N	93°15'W
Magnolia, Ms., U.S. (măg-nō´lĭ-ȧ)	124-25	31°09'N	90°28'W
Mago, i., Fiji	279f	17°27'S	179°09'W
Magog, Qc., Can. (mȧ-gŏg´)	136-37	45°16'N	72°09'W
Magpie, stm., On., Can. (Măg´pī)	136-37	47°56'N	84°50'W
Magpie, stm., Qc., Can. (Măg´pī)	138-39	50°19'N	64°27'W
Magpie, Lac, lk., Qc., Can. (lăk măg´pī)	138-39	51°0'N	64°41'W
Maguari, Cabo, c., Braz.	166-67	0°18'S	48°22'W
Magway, Mya.	246-47	20°30'N	94°30'E
Magyarország, nation, Eur. *see* Hungary	174-75	47°0'N	20°00'E
Mahābād, Iran	228-29	36°46'N	45°44'E
Mahagi, D.R.C.	267	2°19'N	31°01'E
Mahajanga, Madag.	264-65	15°43'S	46°19'E
Mahakam, stm., Indon.	248-49	0°35'S	117°17'E
Mahalapye, Bots.	264-65	23°06'S	26°50'E
Mahalla el-Kubra, Egypt *see* El-Mahalla el-Kubra	268b	30°58'N	31°10'E
Mahānadi, stm., India	234-35	20°19'N	86°47'E
Mahanoro, Madag. (mȧ-hȧ-nô´rō)	264-65	19°55'S	48°48'E
Mahārāshtra, state, India	236	19°0'N	76°00'E
Maha Sarakham, Thai.	246-47	16°11'N	103°18'E
Mahbūbnagar, India	236	16°44'N	77°59'E
Mahe, India (mä-ā´)	236	11°42'N	75°32'E
Mahébourg, Mauritius	265a	20°24'S	57°42'E
Mahendra Giri, mtn., India	236	18°58'N	84°21'E
Mahendranagar, Nepal	234-35	28°58'N	80°10'E
Mahenge, Tan. (mä-hĕŋ´gȧ)	267	7°38'S	36°16'E
Mahesāna, India	234-35	23°36'N	72°23'E
Mahilëu, Bela.	192-93	53°56'N	30°21'E
Mahnomen, Mn., U.S. (mô-nō´mĕn)	114-15	47°19'N	95°59'W
Mahón, Spain *see* Maó	198-99	39°53'N	4°16'E
Mahone Bay, b., N.S., Can. (mȧ-hōn´ bā)	138-39	44°30'N	64°15'W
Maicuru, stm., Braz.	166-67	2°12'S	54°18'W
Maiduguri, Nig. (mä´ē-dȧ-gōō´rē)	260-61	11°51'N	13°09'E
Maiko, stm., D.R.C.	262-63	0°11'N	25°32'E
Maikop, Russia *see* Maykop	186-87	44°36'N	40°06'E
Mai-Ndombe, Lac, lk., D.R.C.	260-61	2°25'S	18°18'E
Maine, state, U.S. (mān)	108-09	45°15'N	69°15'W
Maine, Gulf of, b., N.A.	138-39	43°0'N	68°00'W
Mainland, i., Scot., U.K. (mān-lănd)	190c	60°16'N	1°16'W
Maintenon, Fr. (mäN-tē-nôN´)	196-97	48°35'N	1°35'E
Maintirano, Madag. (mä´ēn-tē-rä´nō)	264-65	18°03'S	44°02'E
Mainz, Ger. (mīnts)	194-95	50°00'N	8°16'E
Maio, i., C.V. (mä´yo)	260-61	15°11'N	23°10'W
Maipo, stm., Chile (mī´pô)	163e	33°37'S	71°38'W
Maipo, Volcán, vol., S.A. (vôl-kȧ´n mī´pô)	163e	34°10'S	69°50'W
Maipú, Arg.	173	36°52'S	57°54'W
Maiquetía, Ven. (mī-kĕ-tē´ä)	163b	10°36'N	66°58'W
Maitland, Austl. (māt´lănd)	276	32°44'S	151°33'E
Maitland, Austl. (māt´lănd)	276	34°23'S	137°40'E
Maíz, Islas del, is., Nic.	149	12°15'N	83°00'W
Maizuru, Japan (mä-ī´zōō-rōō)	245	35°28'N	135°24'E
Majene, Indon.	248-49	3°32'S	118°57'E
Majī, Eth.	262-63	6°11'N	35°35'E
Majorca, i., Spain (mȧ-jôr´kȧ) *see* Mallorca	198-99	39°30'N	3°00'E
Majuro, at., Marsh. Is.	280-81	7°05'N	171°09'E
Makanya, Tan. (mä-kän´yä)	267	4°21'S	37°50'E
Makarov, Russia	222-23	48°38'N	142°46'E
Makarska, Cro. (mȧ´kär-skȧ)	200-01	43°17'N	17°01'E
Makasar, Selat, strt., Indon. *see* Makassar Strait	248-49	2°0'S	117°30'E
Makassar, Indon. (mȧ-kä´-sûr)	248-49	5°08'S	119°25'E
Makassar Strait, strt., Indon. (mȧ-kä´-sûr strāt)	248-49	2°0'S	117°30'E
Makatea, i., Fr. Poly.	280-81	15°50'S	148°16'W
Makedonija, nation, Eur. *see* Macedonia	174-75	41°50'N	22°00'E
Makedonija, hist. reg., Eur. *see* Macedonia	200-01	41°0'N	23°00'E
Makeni, S.L.	260-61	8°53'N	12°03'W
Makeyevka, Ukr. *see* Makiïvka	202-03	48°02'N	37°58'E
Makgadikgadi, pl., Bots.	264-65	20°17'S	25°43'E
Makhachkala, Russia (mäk´äch-kä´lä)	227	42°59'N	47°30'E
Makhado, S. Afr.	264-65	23°03'S	29°55'E
Makiïvka, Ukr.	202-03	48°02'N	37°58'E
Makindu, Kenya	267	2°16'S	37°50'E
Makinsk, Kaz.	226	52°39'N	70°25'E
Makkah, Sau. Ar. *see* Mecca	266	21°27'N	39°51'E
Makokou, Gabon (mȧ-kô-kōō´)	260-61	0°35'N	12°51'E
Makona, stm., Afr. *see* Moa	260-61	6°60'N	11°34'W
Makoua, Congo	262-63	0°00'S	15°38'E
Makung, Tai.	225a	23°34'N	119°34'E
Makurdi, Nig.	260-61	7°44'N	8°31'E
Mala, Punta, c., Pan. (pò´n-tä-mä´lä)	150	7°28'N	80°01'W
Malabang, Phil.	250	7°38'N	124°04'E
Malabar Coast, cst., India (măl´ȧ-bär kōst)	236	11°0'N	75°00'E
Malabo, nat. cap., Eq. Gui. (mä-lä´bō)	260-61	3°45'N	8°47'E
Malacca, Malay. *see* Kota Kinabalu	246-47	2°12'N	102°16'E
Malacca, Strait of, strt., Asia (strāt ŭv mȧ-lăk´ȧ)	246-47	2°30'N	101°20'E
Malad City, Id., U.S. (mȧ-lăd´ sĭ´tē)	112-13	42°12'N	112°15'W
Maladzečna, Bela.	194-95	54°19'N	26°52'E
Málaga, Col. (mȧ´lä-gȧ)	164-65	6°42'N	72°44'W
Málaga, Spain (mȧ´lä-gȧ)	198-99	36°44'N	4°25'W
Malagasy Republic, nation, Afr. *see* Madagascar	253	19°0'S	46°00'E
Malaita, i., Sol. Is. (mȧ-lä´ē-tȧ)	279e	9°0'S	161°00'E
Malaka, Malay. *see* Kota Kinabalu	246-47	2°12'N	102°16'E
Malaka, Selat, strt., Asia *see* Malacca, Strait of	246-47	2°30'N	101°20'E
Malakāl, Sudan (mȧ-lȧ-käl´)	262-63	9°31'N	31°39'E
Malakula, i., Vanuatu (mä-lä-kōō´lä)	279g	16°15'S	167°30'E
Malang, Indon.	248-49	7°59'S	112°38'E
Malanje, Ang. (mä-läŋ-gȧ)	264-65	9°32'S	16°20'E
Malanville, Benin	260-61	11°52'N	3°23'E
Mälaren, lk., Swe.	192-93	59°30'N	17°12'E
Malargüe, Arg.	171	35°28'S	69°35'W
Malartic, Qc., Can.	136-37	48°09'N	78°07'W
Malatya, Tur. (mȧ-lä´tyȧ)	186-87	38°21'N	38°18'E
Malawi, nation, Afr. (mä-lä´-wē)	253	13°30'S	34°00'E
Malaŵi, Lake, lk., Afr. (läk mä-lä´-wē) *see* Nyasa, Lake	264-65	12°0'S	34°30'E
Malaya Vishera, Russia	192-93	58°51'N	32°14'E
Malaybalay, Phil.	250	8°09'N	125°08'E
Malay Peninsula, pen., Asia (mȧ-lā´ pĕ-nĭn´sū-lȧ) (mā´lā)	246-47	6°0'N	101°00'E
Malaysia, nation, Asia (mȧ-lā´zhȧ)	206-07	2°30'N	112°30'E
Malbork, Pol. (mäl´bôrk)	194-95	54°02'N	19°02'E
Malden, Mo., U.S. (môl´dĕn)	124-25	36°34'N	89°58'W
Malden, i., Kir. (môl´dĕn)	280-81	4°03'S	154°59'W
Maldive Islands, nation, Asia *see* Maldives	206-07	3°15'N	73°00'E
Maldives, nation, Asia (măl´dīvz) (môl´dēvz)	206-07	3°15'N	73°00'E
Maldonado, Ur. (mäl-dŏ-nȧ´dŏ)	173	34°55'S	54°57'W
Male', nat. cap., Mald. (mä-lā´)	236	4°10'N	73°30'E
Maléas, Ákra, c., Grc.	200-01	36°26'N	23°12'E
Male Atoll, at., Mald.	236	4°25'N	73°30'E
Mālegaon, India	234-35	20°33'N	74°32'E
Malheur Lake, lk., Or., U.S. (mȧ-lōōr´ lăk)	112-13	43°20'N	118°45'W
Mali, nation, Afr. (mä´-lē)	253	17°0'N	4°00'W
Mali, stm., Mya.	238-39	25°43'N	97°31'E
Malik, Wādī al-, stm., Sudan	266	18°03'N	30°58'E
Mali Kyun, i., Mya.	246-47	13°06'N	98°16'E
Malinaltepec, Mex. (mä-lē-näl-tȧ-pĕk´)	146-47	17°05'N	98°39'W
Malindi, Kenya (mä-lēn´dē)	262-63	3°13'S	40°06'E
Malino, Bukit, mtn., Indon.	248-49	0°42'N	120°51'E
Malkara, Tur. (mäl´kȧ-rȧ)	200-01	40°52'N	26°55'E
Malko Tŭrnovo, Blg. (mäl´kō-t'r´nô-vȧ)	200-01	41°59'N	27°32'E
Mallawi, Egypt	268b	27°44'N	30°51'E
Mallery Lake, lk., Nu., Can.	130-31	63°55'N	98°25'W
Mallorca, i., Spain	198-99	39°30'N	3°00'E
Malmö, Swe.	192-93	55°36'N	13°01'E
Maloelap, at., Marsh. Is.	280-81	8°45'N	171°03'E
Malolos, Phil. (mä-lô´lôs)	250	14°51'N	120°49'E
Maloshuyka, Russia	186-87	63°44'N	37°25'E
Måløy, Nor.	184-85	61°56'N	5°08'E
Maloyaroslavets, Russia (mä´lô-yä-rô-slä-vyĕts)	202-03	55°01'N	36°28'E
Malpelo, Isla de, i., Col. (ē´s-lä-dĕ-mäl-pā´lō)	164-65	3°59'N	81°35'W
Malpeque Bay, b., P.E., Can. (môl-pĕk´ bā)	138-39	46°30'N	63°47'W
Malta, Mt., U.S. (môl´tȧ)	112-13	48°21'N	107°52'W
Malta, nation, Eur. (môl´tȧ)	174-75	35°50'N	14°35'E
Malta, i., Malta	200b	35°53'N	14°27'E
Maluku, is., Indon. *see* Moluccas	248-49	2°0'S	128°00'E
Maluku, Laut, s., Indon. *see* Molucca Sea	248-49	0°13'N	125°10'E
Malvern, Ar., U.S. (măl´vērn)	120-21	34°22'N	92°49'W
Malyy Anyuy, stm., Russia	218-19	68°31'N	160°55'E
Malyye Derbety, Russia	186-87	47°58'N	44°43'E
Malyy Kavkaz, mts., Asia *see* Lesser Caucasus	227	40°60'N	44°35'E
Malyy Shantar, Ostrov, i., Russia	218-19	54°30'N	137°36'E
Malyy Taymyr, Ostrov, i., Russia	218-19	78°08'N	107°12'E
Malyy Uzen', stm., Eur. *see* Balaözen	186-87	48°58'N	49°38'E
Mamberamo, stm., Indon.	277	1°35'S	137°52'E
Mambéré, stm., C.A.R.	262-63	3°32'N	16°03'E
Mamburao, Phil. (mäm-bōō´rä-ō)	250	13°15'N	120°35'E
Mammoth Cave National Park, n.p., Ky., U.S. (măm´ŏth kāv năsh´ŭn-ăl pärk)	124-25	37°11'N	86°08'W
Mamoré, stm., S.A.	166-67	10°24'S	65°23'W
Mamoudzou, nat. cap., May.	264-65	12°47'S	45°14'E
Mamry, Jezioro, lk., Pol. (mäm´rī)	194-95	54°07'N	21°44'E
Man, C. Iv.	260-61	7°24'N	7°33'W
Man, Isle of, dep., Eur. *see* Isle of Man	190-91	54°15'N	4°30'W
Manacapuru, Braz.	166-67	3°17'S	60°36'W
Manacor, Spain (mä-nä-kôr´)	198-99	39°34'N	3°12'E
Manado, Indon.	248-49	1°29'N	124°51'E
Managua, nat. cap., Nic. (mä-nä´gwä)	149	12°09'N	86°17'W
Managua, Lago de, lk., Nic. (lȧ´gô-dĕ-mä-nä´gwä)	149	12°20'N	86°20'W
Manakara, Madag. (mä-nä-kä´rŭ)	264-65	22°09'S	48°01'E
Manāli, India	234-35	32°16'N	77°09'E
Manama, nat. cap., Bahr. (mä-nä´mȧ) *see* Al-Manāmah	230-31	26°13'N	50°35'E
Manam Island, i., Pap. N. Gui.	277	4°05'S	145°02'E
Mananara, stm., Madag. (mä-nä-nä´rŭ)	264-65	23°21'S	47°42'E
Mananara Avaratra, Madag.	264-65	16°10'S	49°46'E
Mananjary, Madag. (mä-nän-zhä´rē)	264-65	21°14'S	48°21'E
Manáos, Braz. *see* Manaus	166-67	3°07'S	60°01'W
Mana Pools National Park, n.p., Zimb.	264-65	15°52'S	29°15'E
Manas Hu, lk., China	226	45°43'N	85°54'E
Manassas, Va., U.S. (mȧ-năs´ȧs)	116-17	38°45'N	77°28'W
Manaus, Braz. (mä-nä´ōōzh)	166-67	3°07'S	60°01'W
Mancelona, Mi., U.S. (măn-sē-lō´nȧ)	116-17	44°54'N	85°04'W
Manchester, Eng., U.K. (măn´chĕs-tēr)	190-91	53°27'N	2°15'W
Manchester, Ct., U.S. (măn´chĕs-tēr)	116-17	41°47'N	72°31'W
Manchester, Ga., U.S. (măn´chĕs-tēr)	124-25	32°51'N	84°37'W
Manchester, Ia., U.S. (măn´chĕs-tēr)	114-15	42°29'N	91°28'W
Manchester, Ky., U.S. (măn´chĕs-tēr)	124-25	37°09'N	83°47'W
Manchester, N.H., U.S.	116-17	42°59'N	71°28'W
Manchester, Tn., U.S. (măn´chĕs-tēr)	124-25	35°29'N	86°05'W
Manchuria, hist. reg., China (măn-chōō´rē-ȧ)	240-41	47°0'N	125°00'E
Mand, stm., Iran	230-31	28°09'N	51°16'E
Manda Island, i., Kenya	262-63	2°15'S	40°57'E
Mandal, Nor. (män´däl)	192-93	58°02'N	7°27'E
Mandala, Puncak, mtn., Indon.	277	4°43'S	140°18'E
Mandalay, Mya. (măn´dȧ-lā)	246-47	21°58'N	96°05'E
Mandalgovĭ, Mong.	240-41	45°46'N	106°16'E
Mandalī, Iraq	228-29	33°45'N	45°32'E
Mandan, N.D., U.S. (măn´dăn)	114-15	46°49'N	100°55'W
Mandara, Monts, mts., Afr. *see* Mandara Mountains	260-61	10°45'N	13°40'E
Mandara Mountains, mts., Afr. (män-dä´rä moun´tĭnz)	260-61	10°45'N	13°40'E
Mandeb, Bab el, strt., (băb´ĕl män-dĕb´) *see* Bab el Mandeb	266	12°44'N	43°21'E
Mandera, Kenya	262-63	3°56'N	41°52'E
Mandioli, Pulau, i., Indon.	248-49	0°44'S	127°14'E
Mandla, India	234-35	22°35'N	80°23'E
Mandsaur, India	234-35	24°03'N	75°05'E
Manduria, Italy (män-dōō´rē-ä)	200-01	40°24'N	17°38'E
Māndvi, India (mŭnd´vē)	234-35	22°51'N	69°22'E
Manfalût, Egypt	268b	27°19'N	30°58'E
Manfredonia, Italy (män-frå-dô´nyä)	200-01	41°38'N	15°55'E
Mangabeiras, Chapada das, hills, Braz.	166-67	9°55'S	46°32'W
Mangaia, i., Cook Is.	280-81	21°55'S	157°54'W
Mangalore, India (mŭŋ-gŭ-lōr´)	236	12°52'N	74°51'E
Mangchang, China	238-39	25°08'N	107°31'E
Mangkalihat, Tanjung, c., Indon.	248-49	1°02'N	118°59'E
Mangochi, Malawi	264-65	14°28'S	35°15'E
Mangoky, stm., Madag. (män-gō´kē)	264-65	21°20'S	43°32'E
Mangole, Pulau, i., Indon.	248-49	1°51'S	125°51'E
Mangshi, China *see* Luxi	238-39	24°21'N	98°23'E
Mangueira, Lagoa, b., Braz.	173	33°06'S	52°48'W
Mangum, Ok., U.S. (măŋ´gŭm)	120-21	34°53'N	99°30'W
Mangya, China	220-21	37°40'N	90°50'E
Manhattan, Ks., U.S. (măn-hăt´ăn)	120-21	39°11'N	96°34'W
Manhattan, Mt., U.S. (măn-hăt´ăn)	112-13	45°51'N	111°20'W
Manhuaçu, Braz. (män-ŏŏá´sōō)	172	20°15'S	42°02'W

n-sing; ŋ-baŋk; N-nasalized n; nŏd; cŏmmit; ōld; ôbey; ôrder; oi-boil; fōōd; ŏŏ-as oo in foot; ou-out; s-soft; sh-dish; th-thin; pūre; ûnite; ûrn; stŭd; circŭs; ü-as in French tu; ´-indeterminate vowel.

Feature (Pronunciation)	Page	Lat.	Long.
Manicoré, Braz.	166-67	5°49'S	61°16'W
Manicouagan, stm., Qc., Can.	138-39	49°10'N	68°09'W
Manicouagan, Réservoir, res., Qc., Can.	130-31	51°22'N	68°44'W
Manihiki, at., Cook Is. (mä'nē-hē'kē)	280-81	10°24'S	161°01'W
Manila, nat. cap., Phil. (mȧ-nĭl'ȧ)	250	14°35'N	120°60'E
Manila Bay, b., Phil. (mȧ-nĭl'ȧ bā)	250	14°30'N	120°45'E
Manipa, Pulau, i., Indon.	248-49	3°18'S	127°33'E
Manipur, state, India	234-35	25°0'N	94°00'E
Manisa, Tur. (mä'nē-sȧ)	200-01	38°37'N	27°26'E
Manistee, Mi., U.S. (măn-ĭs-tē')	116-17	44°15'N	86°19'W
Manistique, Mi., U.S. (măn-ĭs-tēk')	116-17	45°58'N	86°14'W
Manitoba, state, Can. (măn-ĭ-tō'bȧ)	128-29	54°0'N	97°00'W
Manitoba, Lake, lk., Mb., Can. (lāk măn-ĭ-tō'bȧ)	134-35	50°47'N	98°43'W
Manitoulin Island, i., On., Can. (măn-ĭ-tōō'lĭn ī'lȧnd)	136-37	45°47'N	82°20'W
Manitou Springs, Co., U.S. (măn'ĭ-tōō sprĭngz)	120-21	38°52'N	104°54'W
Manitowoc, Wi., U.S. (măn-ĭ-tô-wŏk')	116-17	44°06'N	87°39'W
Maniwaki, Qc., Can.	136-37	46°23'N	75°59'W
Manizales, Col. (mä-nē-zä'lås)	163c	5°04'N	75°31'W
Mānjra, stm., India	236	18°49'N	77°52'E
Mankanza, D.R.C.	262-63	1°33'N	19°04'E
Mankato, Ks., U.S. (măn-kā'tō)	120-21	39°47'N	98°13'W
Mankato, Mn., U.S. (măn-kā'tō)	114-15	44°10'N	93°59'W
Manlleu, Spain (män-lyā'ōō)	198-99	42°0'N	2°17'E
Manna, Indon.	246-47	4°28'S	102°55'E
Mannar, Sri L. (mȧ-när')	236	8°59'N	79°55'E
Mannar, Gulf of, b., Asia	236	8°30'N	79°00'E
Mannar Island, i., Sri L.	236	9°03'N	79°50'E
Mannheim, Ger. (män'hīm)	194-95	49°30'N	8°28'E
Manning, S.C., U.S. (măn'ĭng)	124-25	33°42'N	80°13'W
Mannington, W.V., U.S. (măn'ĭng-tŭn)	116-17	39°31'N	80°23'W
Manokwari, Indon. (mȧ-nŏk-wä'rē)	224-25	0°51'S	134°05'E
Manono, D.R.C.	262-63	7°18'S	27°25'E
Manosque, Fr. (mȧ-nôsk')	196-97	43°50'N	5°47'E
Manouane, Lac, res., Qc., Can.	138-39	50°42'N	70°46'W
Manra, at., Kir.	280-81	4°27'S	171°15'W
Manresa, Spain (män-rā'sä)	198-99	41°44'N	1°49'E
Mansa, Zam.	264-65	11°12'S	28°53'E
Mansel Island, i., Nu., Can. (măn'sĕl ī'lȧnd)	130-31	61°60'N	79°50'W
Mansfield, Eng., U.K. (mănz'fēld)	190-91	53°09'N	1°12'W
Mansfield, La., U.S. (mănz'fēld)	122-23	32°02'N	93°43'W
Mansfield, Mo., U.S. (mănz'fēld)	120-21	37°06'N	92°35'W
Mansfield, Oh., U.S. (mănz'fēld)	116-17	40°45'N	82°31'W
Mansfield, Pa., U.S. (mănz'fēld)	116-17	41°48'N	77°04'W
Mansura, Egypt *see* El-Manṣûra	268b	31°02'N	31°23'E
Manta, Ec. (män'tä)	170	0°57'S	80°43'W
Mantes-la-Jolie, Fr. (mänt-ĕ-lä-zhō-lē')	196-97	48°59'N	1°43'E
Mantiqueira, Serra da, mts., Braz.	172	22°14'S	44°53'W
Manturovo, Russia	186-87	58°20'N	44°47'E
Manuae, at., Cook Is.	280-81	19°21'S	158°56'W
Manuae, at., Fr. Poly.	280-81	16°30'S	154°40'W
Manua Islands, is., Am. Sam.	279b	14°13'S	169°35'W
Manuel Rodríguez, Isla, i., Chile	171	52°34'S	73°51'W
Manui, Pulau, i., Indon. (pōō-lou mä-nōō'ē)	248-49	3°35'S	123°08'E
Manukau, N.Z.	278	37°02'S	174°54'E
Manus Island, i., Pap. N. Gui. (mä'nōōs ī'lȧnd)	277	2°05'S	147°00'E
Manyame, stm., Afr.	264-65	15°37'S	30°39'E
Manyara, Lake, lk., Tan.	267	3°35'S	35°50'E
Manych, stm., Russia	186-87	47°15'N	40°15'E
Manyoni, Tan.	267	5°45'S	34°50'E
Manzanillo, Cuba (män'zä-nēl'yō)	142-43	20°21'N	77°07'W
Manzanillo, Mex.	146-47	19°03'N	104°20'W
Manzhouli, China (män-jō-lē)	240-41	49°35'N	117°27'E
Mao, Chad (mä'ō)	258-59	14°07'N	15°19'E
Maó, Spain	198-99	39°53'N	4°16'E
Maoke, Pegunungan, mts., Indon.	277	4°0'S	138°00'E
Maoming, China	238-39	21°41'N	110°51'E
Mapastepec, Mex. (ma-päs-tā-pĕk')	146-47	15°26'N	92°54'W
Mapi, Indon.	277	7°05'S	139°24'E
Mapimí, Mex. (mä-pē-mē')	122-23	25°49'N	103°51'W
Mapimí, Bolsón de, des., Mex. (bôl-sŏ'n-dĕ-mä-pē'mē)	122-23	26°30'N	104°00'W
Maple Creek, Sk., Can. (mā'p'l crēk krēk)	134-35	49°55'N	109°29'W
Maplewood, Mn., U.S. (mā'p'l wŏŏd)	114-15	45°01'N	93°04'W
Mapuera, stm., Braz.	166-67	1°05'S	57°03'W
Maputo, nat. cap., Moz. (mä-pōō'-tō)	264-65	25°58'S	32°35'E
Maqat, Kaz.	186-87	47°39'N	53°22'E
Maquan, stm., China	234-35	29°33'N	84°07'E
Maquinchao, Arg.	171	41°15'S	68°41'W
Maquoketa, Ia., U.S. (mȧ-kō-kē-tȧ)	114-15	42°04'N	90°40'W
Mar, Serra do, mts., Braz. (sĕr'rȧ dò mär')	172	23°30'S	45°30'W
Mara, stm., Afr.	267	1°32'S	33°59'E
Marabá, Braz.	166-67	5°21'S	49°06'W
Maracá, Ilha de, i., Braz.	166-67	2°05'N	50°25'W
Maracaibo, Ven. (mä-rä-kī'bō)	164-65	10°40'N	71°38'W
Maracaibo, Lago de, lk., Ven. (lä'gô-dĕ-mä-rä-kī'bō)	164-65	9°43'N	71°50'W
Maracaibo, Lake, lk., Ven. (lāk mä-rä-kī'bō) *see* Maracaibo, Lago de	164-65	9°43'N	71°50'W
Maracay, Ven. (mä-rä-käy')	163b	10°16'N	67°37'W
Marādah, Libya	188-89	29°13'N	19°12'E
Maradi, Niger (mȧ-rȧ-dē')	258-59	13°29'N	7°06'E
Marāgheh, Iran	228-29	37°23'N	46°15'E
Maragogipe, Braz.	166-67	12°46'S	38°55'W
Marahuaca, Cerro, mtn., Ven.	164-65	3°35'N	65°27'W
Marajó, Baía de, b., Braz.	166-67	1°0'S	48°30'W
Maralal, Kenya	267	1°05'N	36°41'E
Maramasike, i., Sol. Is.	279e	9°32'S	161°27'E
Marand, Iran	227	38°26'N	45°46'E
Maranhão, state, Braz. (mä-rän-youɴ)	166-67	5°0'S	45°00'W
Maranoa, stm., Austl. (mä-rä-nō'ä)	272-73	27°44'S	148°44'E
Marañón, stm., Peru (mä-rä-nyōn')	170	4°29'S	73°30'W
Maraş, Tur. *see* Kahramanmaraş	186-87	37°35'N	36°57'E
Marathon, On., Can. (măr'ȧ-thŏn)	136-37	48°43'N	86°23'W
Marathon, Fl., U.S. (măr'ȧ-thŏn)	125a	24°42'N	81°06'W
Marathon, N.Y., U.S. (măr'ȧ-thŏn)	116-17	42°27'N	76°02'W
Marawwaḩ, i., U.A.E.	230-31	24°17'N	53°15'E
Marble Bar, Austl. (märb''l bär)	270-71	21°10'S	119°45'E
Marble Hall, S. Afr.	269c	24°57'S	29°14'E
Marburg an der Drau, Slvn. *see* Maribor	200-01	46°33'N	15°39'E
Marca, Ponta da, c., Ang.	264-65	16°31'S	11°42'E
Marceline, Mo., U.S. (mär-sē-lēn')	120-21	39°43'N	92°57'W
Marchena, Isla, i., Ec. (ē's-lä-mär-chĕ'nä)	170a	0°21'N	90°29'W
Mar Chiquita, Laguna, lk., Arg. (lä-gōō'nä-mär-chē-kē'tä)	173	30°42'S	62°36'W
Marcus Island, i., Japan (mär'kŭs ī'lȧnd)	280-81	24°18'N	153°58'E
Marcy, Mount, mtn., N.Y., U.S. (mount mär'sē)	116-17	44°07'N	73°56'W
Mardān, Pak.	232-33	34°12'N	72°03'E
Mar del Plata, Arg. (mär dĕl- plä'ta)	173	37°60'S	57°34'W
Mardin, Tur. (mär-dēn')	228-29	37°18'N	40°45'E
Maré, i., N. Cal. (mȧ-rā')	279g	21°30'S	167°59'E
Mareeba, Austl.	277	16°60'S	145°24'E
Marengo, Il., U.S. (mȧ-rĕŋ'gō)	116-17	42°15'N	88°37'W
Marfa, Tx., U.S. (mär'fȧ)	122-23	30°19'N	104°02'W
Margarita, Isla de, i., Ven. (ē's-lä dĕ mä-gȧ-rē'tȧ)	163b	11°0'N	64°00'W
Margate, Eng., U.K. (mär'gāt)	190-91	51°23'N	1°25'E
Margelan, Uzb. *see* Marghilon	232-33	40°28'N	71°44'E
Margherita, Som. *see* Jamaame	262-63	0°01'N	42°42'E
Margherita Peak, mtn., Afr.	267	0°22'N	29°51'E
Marghilon, Uzb.	232-33	40°28'N	71°44'E
Mārgow, Dasht-e, des., Afg.	232-33	30°45'N	63°10'E
Marguerite, Pic, mtn., Afr. *see* Margherita Peak	267	0°22'N	29°51'E
Marhanets', Ukr.	202-03	47°39'N	34°38'E
Maria, Îles, is., Fr. Poly.	280-81	21°44'S	154°38'W
María Cleofas, Isla, i., Mex.	146-47	21°18'N	106°15'W
María Elena, Chile	168-69	22°20'S	69°40'W
Maria Island, i., Austl.	276	42°39'S	148°04'E
María Madre, Isla, i., Mex.	146-47	21°37'N	106°35'W
María Magdalena, Isla, i., Mex.	146-47	21°27'N	106°26'W
Mariana Islands, is., Oc. (mä-ryá'nä ī'lȧndz)	280-81	15°60'N	145°44'E
Marianna, Ar., U.S. (mā-rĭ-ăn'ȧ)	124-25	34°46'N	90°46'W
Marianna, Fl., U.S. (mā-rĭ-ăn'ȧ)	124-25	30°46'N	85°15'W
Mariánské Lázně, Czech Rep. (mär'yán-skĕ'läz'nyĕ)	194-95	49°58'N	12°42'E
Maria Theresiopel, Serb. *see* Subotica	200-01	46°06'N	19°41'E
Mariato, Punta, c., Pan.	150	7°13'N	80°53'W
Maribo, Den. (mä'rē-bô)	194-95	54°46'N	11°31'E
Maribor, Slvn. (mä're-bôr)	200-01	46°33'N	15°39'E
Marīdī, Sudan	267	4°55'N	29°28'E
Marie Byrd Land, reg., Ant.	287	80°0'S	120°00'W
Marie-Galante, i., Guad. (mȧ-rē' gȧ-läɴt')	143b	15°56'N	61°16'W
Mari El, state, Russia	186-87	56°30'N	48°00'E
Marienbad, Czech Rep. *see* Mariánské Lázně	194-95	49°58'N	12°42'E
Marienburg, Pol. *see* Malbork	194-95	54°02'N	19°02'E
Mariental, Nmb.	264-65	24°37'S	17°58'E
Mariestad, Swe. (mä-rē'ĕ-städ')	192-93	58°43'N	13°51'E
Marietta, Ga., U.S. (mā-rĭ'-ĕt'ȧ)	124-25	33°57'N	84°33'W
Marietta, Oh., U.S. (mā-rĭ'-ĕt'ȧ)	116-17	39°25'N	81°28'W
Marietta, Ok., U.S. (mā-rĭ'-ĕt'ȧ)	120-21	33°56'N	97°07'W
Marília, Braz. (mä-rē'lyȧ)	168-69	22°13'S	49°57'W
Marimba, Ang.	262-63	8°22'S	16°59'E
Marinduque, i., Phil. (mä-rēn-dōō'kā)	250	13°24'N	121°58'E
Marine City, Mi., U.S. (mȧ-rēn' sĭ'tē)	116-17	42°43'N	82°29'W
Marinette, Wi., U.S. (mär-ĭ-nĕt')	116-17	45°06'N	87°37'W
Maringá, Braz.	168-69	23°25'S	51°56'W
Maringa, stm., D.R.C. (mä-riŋ'gä)	262-63	1°13'N	19°50'E
Marinha Grande, Port. (mä-rēn'yȧ grän'dĕ)	198-99	39°45'N	8°56'W
Marion, Al., U.S. (măr'ĭ-ŭn)	124-25	32°38'N	87°19'W
Marion, Ar., U.S. (măr'ĭ-ŭn)	124-25	35°13'N	90°12'W
Marion, Ia., U.S. (măr'ĭ-ŭn)	114-15	42°02'N	91°36'W
Marion, Il., U.S. (măr'ĭ-ŭn)	116-17	37°44'N	88°56'W
Marion, In., U.S. (măr'ĭ-ŭn)	116-17	40°33'N	85°39'W
Marion, Ky., U.S. (măr'ĭ-ŭn)	124-25	37°20'N	88°05'W
Marion, N.C., U.S. (măr'ĭ-ŭn)	124-25	35°41'N	82°01'W
Marion, Oh., U.S. (măr'ĭ-ŭn)	116-17	40°35'N	83°07'W
Marion, S.C., U.S. (măr'ĭ-ŭn)	124-25	34°11'N	79°24'W
Marion, Va., U.S. (măr'ĭ-ŭn)	124-25	36°50'N	81°31'W
Marion, Lake, res., S.C., U.S. (lāk măr'ĭ-ŭn)	124-25	33°32'N	80°29'W
Mariquita, Col. (mä-rē-kē'tä)	163c	5°11'N	74°54'W
Mariscal Estigarribia, Para.	168-69	22°02'S	60°37'W
Maritzburg, S. Afr. *see* Pietermaritzburg	264-65	29°36'S	30°23'E
Mariupol', Ukr.	202-03	47°06'N	37°34'E
Mariy-El, state, Russia *see* Mari El	186-87	56°30'N	48°00'E
Marka, Som.	262-63	1°43'N	44°46'E
Markaryd, Swe. (mär'kä-rüd)	192-93	56°28'N	13°35'E
Marked Tree, Ar., U.S. (märkt trē)	124-25	35°32'N	90°25'W
Markha, Russia	218-19	60°36'N	123°19'E
Markha, stm., Russia	218-19	63°27'N	118°53'E
Markham, On., Can. (märk'ȧm)	136-37	43°52'N	79°16'W
Markovo, Russia (mär'kô-vô)	218-19	64°40'N	170°27'E
Marks, Russia	186-87	51°42'N	46°44'E
Marksville, La., U.S. (märks'vĭl)	124-25	31°07'N	92°05'W
Marlette, Mi., U.S. (mär-lĕt')	116-17	43°20'N	83°04'W
Marlin, Tx., U.S. (mär'lĭn)	122-23	31°17'N	96°53'W
Marlinton, W.V., U.S. (mär'lĭn-tŭn)	116-17	38°14'N	80°06'W
Marlow, Ok., U.S. (mär'lō)	120-21	34°38'N	97°58'W
Marmande, Fr. (mȧr-mäɴd')	196-97	44°30'N	0°10'E
Marmara, Sea of, s., Tur. (mär'mȧ-rȧ)	200-01	40°40'N	28°15'E
Marmara Denizi, s., Tur. *see* Marmara, Sea of	200-01	40°40'N	28°15'E
Marmarth, N.D., U.S. (mär'mȧrth)	114-15	46°18'N	103°55'W
Marmelos, stm., Braz.	166-67	6°05'S	61°46'W
Maroa, Ven. (mä-rō'ä)	164-65	2°44'N	67°33'W
Maromokotro, mtn., Madag.	264-65	14°01'S	48°58'E
Marondera, Zimb.	264-65	18°10'S	31°32'E
Marosvásárhely, Rom. *see* Târgu Mureş	194-95	46°33'N	24°34'E
Marotiri, Îles, is., Fr. Poly.	280-81	27°53'S	143°21'W
Maroua, Camrn. (mär'wä)	260-61	10°37'N	14°19'E
Marovoay, Madag.	264-65	16°07'S	46°39'E
Marquesas Islands, is., Fr. Poly. (mär-kĕ'säs ī'lȧndz)	280-81	8°59'S	139°31'W
Marquesas Keys, is., Fl., U.S. (mȧr-kē'zȧs kēs)	125a	24°34'N	82°08'W
Marquette, Mi., U.S.	114-15	46°32'N	87°23'W
Marquises, Îles, is., Fr. Poly. *see* Marquesas Islands	280-81	8°59'S	139°31'W
Marrah, Jabal, vol., Sudan (jĕb'ĕl mär'ä)	262-63	13°03'N	24°21'E
Marrakech, Mor. (mȧr-rä'kĕsh)	269a	31°38'N	8°01'W
Marrakesh, Mor. *see* Marrakech	269a	31°38'N	8°01'W
Marree, Austl. (măr'rē)	276	29°39'S	138°04'E
Marromeu, Moz.	264-65	18°16'S	35°52'E
Marsá al-Burayqah, Libya	188-89	30°23'N	19°36'E
Marsabit, Kenya	267	2°20'N	37°60'E
Marsala, Italy (mär-sä'lä)	200-01	37°48'N	12°26'E
Marseille, Fr. (mȧr-sâ'y')	196-97	43°18'N	5°24'E
Marseilles, Il., U.S. (mär-sĕlz')	116-17	41°20'N	88°42'W
Marshall, Il., U.S. (mär'shăl)	116-17	39°23'N	87°42'W
Marshall, Mi., U.S. (mär'shăl)	116-17	42°16'N	84°57'W
Marshall, Mn., U.S. (mär'shăl)	114-15	44°27'N	95°48'W
Marshall, Mo., U.S. (mär'shăl)	120-21	39°07'N	93°12'W
Marshall, Tx., U.S. (mär'shăl)	120-21	32°33'N	94°22'W

ăt; fināl; rāte; senāte; ärm; ȧsk; sofȧ; fâre; ch-choose; dh-as th in other; bē; ēvent; bĕt; recĕnt; cratẽr; g-gō; gh-guttural g; bĭt; ĭ-short neutral; rīde; ĸ-guttural k as ch in German ich;

PRONOUNCING INDEX

Marshall Islands – Medford 355

Feature (Pronunciation)	Page	Lat.	Long.
Marshall Islands, nation, Oc. (mär'shăl ī'lăndz)	**280-81**	11°0'N	168°00'E
Marshalltown, Ia., U.S. (mär'shăl-toun)	**114-15**	42°03'N	92°54'W
Marshfield, Mo., U.S. (märsh'fēld)	**120-21**	37°20'N	92°54'W
Marshfield, Wi., U.S. (märsh'fēld)	**116-17**	44°40'N	90°10'W
Marsh Harbour, Bah. (mär'sh här'bēr)	**142-43**	26°32'N	77°04'W
Marsh Island, i., La., U.S.	**124-25**	29°35'N	91°53'W
Mart, Tx., U.S. (märt)	**122-23**	31°32'N	96°50'W
Martaban, Gulf of, b., Mya. (gŭlf ŭv mär-tŭ-bän')	**246-47**	16°46'N	97°01'E
Martha's Vineyard, i., Ma., U.S. (mär'thaz vĭn'yard)	**116-17**	41°24'N	70°38'W
Martigny, Switz. (mar-tē-nyē')	**194-95**	46°06'N	7°04'E
Martin, S.D., U.S. (mär'tĭn)	**114-15**	43°10'N	101°44'W
Martin, Tn., U.S. (mär'tĭn)	**124-25**	36°21'N	88°51'W
Martina Franca, Italy (mär-tē'nä fräŋ'kä)	**200-01**	40°42'N	17°20'E
Martinez, Ga., U.S. (mär-tē'nĕz)	**124-25**	33°31'N	82°05'W
Martinique, dep., N.A. (mar-tē-nēk')	**140-41**	14°40'N	61°00'W
Martinique Passage, strt., N.A.	**143b**	15°10'N	61°15'W
Martinsburg, W.V., U.S. (mär'tĭnz-bûrg)	**116-17**	39°27'N	77°57'W
Martinsville, In., U.S. (mär'tĭnz-vĭl)	**116-17**	39°25'N	86°25'W
Martinsville, Va., U.S. (mär'tĭnz-vĭl)	**124-25**	36°41'N	79°52'W
Martin Vaz, Ilhas, is., Braz.	**159**	20°30'S	28°51'W
Martos, Spain (mär'tōs)	**198-99**	37°43'N	3°58'W
Martre, Lac la, lk., N.T., Can. (läk lä märtr)	**130-31**	63°15'N	117°55'W
Marungu, mts., D.R.C.	**267**	7°42'S	30°01'E
Mary, Turkmen. (mä'rē)	**232-33**	37°35'N	61°49'E
Maryborough, Austl. (mā'rĭ-bŭr-ô)	**276**	25°32'S	152°42'E
Maryborough, Austl. (mā'rĭ-bŭr-ô)	**276**	37°03'S	143°44'E
Maryland, state, U.S. (mĕr'ĭ-lănd)	**108-09**	39°0'N	76°45'W
Marystown, Nf., Can. (mâr'ĭz-toun)	**138-39**	47°11'N	55°10'W
Marysville, Ca., U.S.	**118-19**	39°09'N	121°35'W
Marysville, Ks., U.S. (mā'rĭz-vĭl)	**120-21**	39°50'N	96°39'W
Marysville, Oh., U.S. (mā'rĭz-vĭl)	**116-17**	40°14'N	83°22'W
Marysville, Wa., U.S. (mā'rĭz-vĭl)	**112-13**	48°04'N	122°10'W
Maryville, Mo., U.S. (mā'rĭ-vĭl)	**120-21**	40°21'N	94°52'W
Maryville, Tn., U.S. (mā'rĭ-vĭl)	**124-25**	35°46'N	83°58'W
Masai Mara Game Reserve, pk., Kenya	**267**	1°15'S	35°15'E
Masai Steppe, plat., Tan.	**267**	4°45'S	37°00'E
Masaka, Ug.	**267**	0°20'S	31°44'E
Masalembu Besar, Pulau, i., Indon.	**248-49**	5°34'S	114°26'E
Masan, Kor., S. (mä-sän')	**243**	35°12'N	128°34'E
Masatepe, Nic. (mä-sä-tē'pĕ)	**149**	11°54'N	86°09'W
Masaya, Nic. (mä-sä'yä)	**149**	11°58'N	86°06'W
Masbate, Phil. (mäs-bä'tä)	**250**	12°22'N	123°38'E
Masbate, i., Phil. (mäs-bä'tä)	**250**	12°15'N	123°30'E
Mascara, Alg.	**198-99**	35°23'N	0°08'E
Mascareignes, Îles, is., Afr.	**265a**	21°0'S	57°00'E
Mascarene Islands, is., Afr. see Mascareignes, Îles	**265a**	21°0'S	57°00'E
Mascota, Mex. (mäs-kō'tä)	**146-47**	20°31'N	104°47'W
Mascoutah, Il., U.S. (măs-kū'tā)	**120-21**	38°29'N	89°48'W
Maseru, nat. cap., Leso. (măz'ēr-ōō)	**269c**	29°19'S	27°29'E
Mashābih, i., Sau. Ar.	**266**	25°38'N	36°31'E
Mashhad, Iran	**232-33**	36°17'N	59°36'E
Māshkel, Hāmūn-i-, lk., Pak. (hā-mōōn'ē māsh-kĕl')	**232-33**	28°15'N	63°00'E
Masi-Manimba, D.R.C.	**262-63**	4°46'S	17°57'E
Masindi, Ug. (mä-sēn'dē)	**267**	1°41'N	31°43'E
Masira, Gulf of, b., Oman see Maşīrah, Khalīj	**220-21**	20°10'N	58°15'E
Maşīrah, i., Oman	**220-21**	20°27'N	58°48'E
Maşīrah, Khalīj, b., Oman	**220-21**	20°10'N	58°15'E
Masjed-e Soleymān, Iran	**232-33**	31°58'N	49°18'E
Masoala, Saikanosy, pen., Madag.	**264-65**	15°26'S	50°04'E
Mason, Mi., U.S. (mā'sŭn)	**116-17**	42°35'N	84°26'W
Mason, Tx., U.S. (mā'sŭn)	**122-23**	30°45'N	99°15'W
Mason City, Ia., U.S. (mā'sŭn sĭ'tĭ)	**114-15**	43°09'N	93°12'W
Masqaţ, nat. cap., Oman see Muscat	**230-31**	23°36'N	58°32'E
Massa, Italy (mäs'sä)	**200-01**	44°03'N	10°09'E
Massachusetts, state, U.S. (măs-ă-chōō'sĕts)	**108-09**	42°15'N	71°50'W
Massafra, Italy (mäs-sä'frä)	**200-01**	40°35'N	17°08'E
Massakory, Chad	**258-59**	12°60'N	15°44'E
Massawa, Erit.	**266**	15°37'N	39°26'E
Massena, N.Y., U.S. (mă-sē'nă)	**116-17**	44°56'N	74°53'W
Masset, B.C., Can. (măs'ĕt)	**132-33**	54°02'N	132°08'W
Massillon, Oh., U.S. (măs'ĭ-lŏn)	**116-17**	40°48'N	81°31'W
Massinga, Moz. (mä-sĭn'gä)	**264-65**	23°20'S	35°24'E
Massive, Mount, mtn., Co., U.S. (mount măs'ĭv)	**118-19**	39°12'N	106°28'W
Maştağa, Azer.	**227**	40°32'N	49°59'E
Mastung, Pak.	**232-33**	29°48'N	66°52'E
Masuda, Japan (mä-sōō'dä)	**245**	34°41'N	131°51'E
Masulipatam, India see Machilīpatnam	**236**	16°11'N	81°09'E
Masvingo, Zimb.	**264-65**	20°04'S	30°49'E
Matadi, D.R.C. (mä-tä'dē)	**262-63**	5°49'S	13°29'E
Matagalpa, Nic. (mä-tä-gäl'pä)	**149**	12°60'N	85°44'W
Matagami, Qc., Can.	**128-29**	49°45'N	77°39'W
Matagorda Island, i., Tx., U.S.	**122-23**	28°15'N	96°37'W
Mataiva, at., Fr. Poly.	**280-81**	14°53'S	148°40'W
Matamoros, Mex. (mä-tä-mō'rôs)	**122-23**	25°52'N	97°30'W
Matamoros, Mex. (mä-tä-mō'rôs)	**122-23**	25°32'N	103°14'W
Matandu, stm., Tan.	**262-63**	8°43'S	39°22'E
Matane, Qc., Can. (ma-tăn')	**138-39**	48°50'N	67°31'W
Matanzas, Cuba (mä-tän'zäs)	**142-43**	23°03'N	81°34'W
Matanzas, state, Cuba (mä-tän'zäs)	**142-43**	22°40'N	81°20'W
Matapalo, Cabo, c., C.R. (ká'bô-mä-tä-pä'lō)	**149**	8°23'N	83°17'W
Matapan, Cape, c., Grc. see Taínaro, Ákra	**200-01**	36°23'N	22°29'E
Matapédia, Qc., Can. (mă-tá-pā'dē-á)	**138-39**	47°58'N	66°56'W
Matapédia, Lac, lk., Qc., Can. (läk mă-tá-pā'dē-á)	**138-39**	48°33'N	67°33'W
Matara, Sri L. (mä-tä'rä)	**236**	5°57'N	80°34'E
Mataram, Indon.	**248-49**	8°35'S	116°07'E
Mataró, Spain	**198-99**	41°32'N	2°26'E
Matasiri, Pulau, i., Indon.	**248-49**	4°48'S	115°49'E
Matâ'utu, nat. cap., Wal./F.	**280-81**	13°17'S	176°09'W
Matehuala, Mex. (mä-tå-wä'lä)	**146-47**	23°40'N	100°38'W
Matera, Italy (mä-tå'rä)	**200-01**	40°41'N	16°36'E
Mathura, India (mu-tò'rŭ)	**234-35**	27°30'N	77°41'E
Mathurai, India see Madurai	**236**	9°55'N	78°08'E
Matias Barbosa, Braz. (mä-tē'äs-bär-bô-sä)	**172**	21°53'S	43°19'W
Mato, Cerro, mtn., Ven.	**164-65**	7°16'N	65°15'W
Mato Grosso, state, Braz. (mät'ò grōs'ò)	**166-67**	12°0'S	57°00'W
Mato Grosso, Planalto do, plat., Braz. (plä-nál'tô-dô mät'ò grōs'ò)	**166-67**	14°59'S	53°37'W
Mato Grosso do Sul, state, Braz.	**168-69**	20°0'S	55°00'W
Matola, Moz.	**264-65**	25°49'S	32°27'E
Matosinhos, Port.	**198-99**	41°11'N	8°41'W
Maţraḩ, Oman (mā-trä')	**230-31**	23°37'N	58°31'E
Matsue, Japan (mät'sò-ĕ)	**245**	35°28'N	133°04'E
Matsumoto, Japan (mät'sò-mō'tô)	**245**	36°14'N	137°58'E
Matsu Tao, i., Tai.	**225a**	26°09'N	119°56'E
Matsuyama, Japan (mät'sò-yä'mä)	**245**	33°50'N	132°46'E
Mattawa, On., Can. (măt'á-wá)	**136-37**	46°18'N	78°41'W
Matterhorn, mtn., Eur. (mät'ēr-hôrn)	**194-95**	45°59'N	7°43'E
Matthew Town, Bah. (măth'ū toun)	**142-43**	21°01'N	73°42'W
Mattoon, Il., U.S. (mă-tōōn')	**116-17**	39°29'N	88°23'W
Maturín, Ven. (mä-tōō-rēn')	**164-65**	9°44'N	63°11'W
Maubeuge, Fr. (mô-bûzh')	**196-97**	50°17'N	3°58'E
Maués, Braz. (má-wĕ's)	**166-67**	3°22'S	57°43'W
Maui, i., Hi., U.S. (mä'ōō-ē)	**127a**	20°45'N	156°15'W
Maumee, Oh., U.S. (mô-mē')	**116-17**	41°34'N	83°39'W
Maumee, stm., U.S. (mô-mē')	**116-17**	41°42'N	83°27'W
Maun, Bots. (mä-òn')	**264-65**	19°60'S	23°25'E
Mauna Kea, vol., Hi., U.S. (mä'ò-năkă'ä)	**127a**	19°50'N	155°28'W
Mauna Loa, vol., Hi., U.S. (mä'ò-nälō'ä)	**127a**	19°29'N	155°36'W
Maunoir, Lac, lk., N.T., Can.	**130-31**	67°30'N	125°00'W
Maurepas, Lake, lk., La., U.S. (lāk mō-rē-pä')	**124-25**	30°15'N	90°30'W
Mauritania, nation, Afr. (mô-rē-tā'nĭ-á)	**253**	20°0'N	12°00'W
Mauritanie, nation, Afr. see Mauritania	**253**	20°0'N	12°00'W
Mauritius, nation, Afr. (mô-rĭsh'ĭ-ŭs)	**253**	20°17'S	57°33'E
Mauston, Wi., U.S. (môs'tŭn)	**116-17**	43°47'N	90°04'W
Mawlamyaing, Mya. see Mawlamyine	**246-47**	16°30'N	97°38'E
Mawlamyine, Mya.	**246-47**	16°30'N	97°38'E
Maxixe, Moz.	**264-65**	23°52'S	35°21'E
Maya, stm., Russia (mä'yä)	**218-19**	60°25'N	134°34'E
Mayaguana, i., Bah.	**142-43**	22°23'N	72°57'W
Mayagüez, P.R. (mä-yä-gwāz')	**142a**	18°12'N	67°09'W
Mayfield, Ky., U.S. (mā'fēld)	**124-25**	36°45'N	88°38'W
Maykop, Russia	**186-87**	44°36'N	40°06'E
Maymyo, Mya. (mī'myō)	**246-47**	22°02'N	96°28'E
Mayo, Yk., Can. (mä-yō')	**128-29**	63°36'N	135°51'W
Mayodan, N.C., U.S. (mā-yō'dăn)	**124-25**	36°24'N	79°59'W
Mayon Volcano, vol., Phil. (mä-yōn' vŏl-kā'nō)	**250**	13°15'N	123°41'E
Mayotte, dep., Afr. (má-yōt')	**264-65**	12°50'S	45°10'E
Maysville, Ky., U.S. (māz'vĭl)	**116-17**	38°38'N	83°46'W
Mayumba, Gabon	**260-61**	3°22'S	10°40'E
Māyūram, India	**236**	11°06'N	79°39'E
Mayville, N.D., U.S. (mā'vĭl)	**114-15**	47°30'N	97°19'W
Mayville, Wi., U.S. (mā'vĭl)	**116-17**	43°30'N	88°32'W
Mayyit, Al-Baḩr al-, lk., Asia see Dead Sea	**228-29**	31°30'N	35°30'E
Maza, Arg.	**173**	36°48'S	63°20'W
Mazabuka, Zam. (mä-zä-bōō'kä)	**264-65**	15°51'S	27°46'E
Mazagan, Mor. see El-Jadida	**269a**	33°15'N	8°31'W
Mazagão, Braz. (mä-zá-gou'ɴ)	**166-67**	0°07'S	51°17'W
Mazara del Vallo, Italy (mät-sä'rä dĕl väl'lō)	**200-01**	37°39'N	12°36'E
Mazār-e Sharīf, Afg.	**232-33**	36°42'N	67°07'E
Mazarrón, Spain (mä-zär-rô'n)	**198-99**	37°36'N	1°19'W
Mazaruni, stm., Guy.	**164-65**	6°26'N	58°36'W
Mazatenango, Guat. (mä-zä-tå-näŋ'gō)	**148**	14°32'N	91°30'W
Mazatlán, Mex. (mä-zä-tlän')	**146-47**	23°13'N	106°25'W
Mažeikiai, Lith. (má-zhā'kē-ī)	**192-93**	56°19'N	22°21'E
Mazoe, stm., Afr. see Mazowe	**264-65**	16°32'S	33°26'E
Mazowe, stm., Afr.	**264-65**	16°32'S	33°26'E
Mazyr, Bela.	**202-03**	52°03'N	29°16'E
Mbabane, nat. cap., Swaz. (m'bä-bä'nē)	**264-65**	26°20'S	31°09'E
Mbaïki, C.A.R. (m'bá-ē'kē)	**262-63**	3°52'N	17°60'E
Mbala, Zam.	**264-65**	8°51'S	31°22'E
Mbale, Ug.	**267**	1°05'N	34°10'E
Mbandaka, D.R.C.	**262-63**	0°02'N	18°15'E
M'banza Congo, Ang.	**262-63**	6°16'S	14°15'E
Mbanza-Ngungu, D.R.C.	**262-63**	5°14'S	14°53'E
Mbarara, Ug.	**267**	0°36'S	30°38'E
Mbari, stm., C.A.R.	**262-63**	4°36'N	22°44'E
Mbeya, Tan.	**264-65**	8°54'S	33°30'E
Mbinda, Congo	**262-63**	2°07'S	12°53'E
Mbini, stm., Afr.	**260-61**	1°35'N	9°38'E
Mbomou, stm., Afr. (m'bō'mōō)	**262-63**	4°09'N	22°29'E
Mbour, Sen.	**260-61**	14°25'N	16°58'W
Mbuji-Mayi, D.R.C.	**262-63**	6°08'S	23°39'E
Mbuji-Mayi, stm., D.R.C.	**262-63**	6°02'S	23°44'E
McAdam, N.B., Can. (măk-ăd'ăm)	**138-39**	45°35'N	67°20'W
McAlester, Ok., U.S. (măk ăl'ĕs-tēr)	**120-21**	34°56'N	95°46'W
McAllen, Tx., U.S. (măk-ăl'ĕn)	**122-23**	26°12'N	98°14'W
McBride, B.C., Can. (măk-brīd')	**132-33**	53°18'N	120°10'W
McCamey, Tx., U.S. (mă-kā'mĭ)	**122-23**	31°08'N	102°13'W
McCauley Island, i., B.C., Can.	**132-33**	53°40'N	130°15'W
McColl, S.C., U.S.	**124-25**	34°40'N	79°33'W
McComb, Ms., U.S. (má-kōm')	**124-25**	31°14'N	90°27'W
McCook, Ne., U.S. (má-kòk')	**120-21**	40°12'N	100°37'W
McGehee, Ar., U.S. (má-gē')	**124-25**	33°38'N	91°24'W
McGill, Nv., U.S. (má-gĭl')	**118-19**	39°25'N	114°49'W
McGrath, Ak., U.S. (măk'gráth)	**126**	62°58'N	155°38'W
McGregor, Tx., U.S. (măk-grĕg'ēr)	**122-23**	31°26'N	97°24'W
McGregor, stm., B.C., Can. (măk-grĕg'ēr)	**132-33**	54°10'N	122°01'W
McKeesport, Pa., U.S. (má-kez'pōrt)	**116-17**	40°21'N	79°52'W
McKenzie, Tn., U.S. (má-kĕn'zĭ)	**124-25**	36°08'N	88°31'W
McKinley, Mount, mtn., Ak., U.S. (mount má-kĭn'lĭ)	**126**	63°04'N	151°00'W
McKinney, Tx., U.S. (má-kĭn'ĭ)	**120-21**	33°12'N	96°37'W
McLaughlin, S.D., U.S. (măk-lŏf'lĭn)	**114-15**	45°49'N	100°48'W
McLennan, Ab., Can. (măk-lĭn'nán)	**132-33**	55°41'N	116°52'W
McLeod, stm., Ab., Can.	**132-33**	54°09'N	115°42'W
McLoughlin, Mount, mtn., Or., U.S. (mount măk-lŏk'lĭn)	**112-13**	42°27'N	122°19'W
McMinnville, Or., U.S. (măk-mĭn'vĭl)	**112-13**	45°13'N	123°11'W
McMinnville, Tn., U.S. (măk-mĭn'vĭl)	**124-25**	35°41'N	85°47'W
McPherson, Ks., U.S. (măk-fŭr's'n)	**120-21**	38°22'N	97°40'W
McRae, Ga., U.S. (măk-rā')	**124-25**	32°04'N	82°54'W
Mead, Lake, res., U.S. (lāk mēd)	**118-19**	36°08'N	114°26'W
Meade, stm., Ak., U.S.	**126**	70°55'N	156°00'W
Meadow Lake, Sk., Can. (mĕd'ō lāk)	**134-35**	54°08'N	108°26'W
Meadville, Pa., U.S.	**116-17**	41°39'N	80°09'W
Meaford, On., Can. (mē'fērd)	**136-37**	44°36'N	80°35'W
Meaux, Fr. (mō)	**196-97**	48°58'N	2°53'E
Mecca, Sau. Ar. (mĕk'á)	**266**	21°27'N	39°51'E
Mechanic Falls, Me., U.S. (mē-kăn'ĭk fôlz)	**116-17**	44°07'N	70°24'W
Mechanicsburg, Pa., U.S. (mē-kăn'ĭks-bûrg)	**116-17**	40°12'N	77°01'W
Mechanicsville, Va., U.S. (mē-kăn'ĭks-vĭl)	**116-17**	37°36'N	77°22'W
Mecubúri, stm., Moz.	**264-65**	14°10'S	40°32'E
Medan, Indon. (må-dän')	**246-47**	3°35'N	98°41'E
Medanosa, Punta, c., Arg. (pōō'n-tä-mĕ-dä-nô'sä)	**171**	48°06'S	65°55'W
Médéa, Alg.	**269b**	36°12'N	2°51'E
Medellín, Col. (må-dhĕl-yēn')	**164-65**	6°15'N	75°35'W
Medenine, Tun. (mā-dē-nēn')	**188-89**	33°20'N	10°30'E
Medford, Ok., U.S. (mĕd'fērd)	**120-21**	36°49'N	97°43'W
Medford, Or., U.S. (mĕd'fērd)	**112-13**	42°20'N	122°52'W

n-sing; ŋ-baŋk; ɴ-nasalized n; nŏd; cŏmmit; ōld; ôbey; ôrder; oi-boil; fōōd; ò-as oo in foot; ou-out; s-soft; sh-dish; th-thin; pūre; ûnite; ûrn; stŭd; circŭs; ü-as in French tu; '-indeterminate vowel.

356 Medford – Middle Andaman PRONOUNCING INDEX

Feature (Pronunciation)	Page	Lat.	Long.
Medford, Wi., U.S. (mĕd′fẽrd)	116-17	45°08′N	90°20′W
Medgyes, Rom. *see* Mediaș	194-95	46°10′N	24°22′E
Mediaș, Rom. (mĕd-yäsh′)	194-95	46°10′N	24°22′E
Medical Lake, Wa., U.S. (mĕd′ĭ-kăl lāk)	112-13	47°37′N	117°43′W
Medicine Hat, Ab., Can. (mĕd′ĭ-sĭn hăt)	132-33	50°03′N	110°41′W
Medicine Lodge, Ks., U.S. (mĕd′ĭ-sĭn lŏj)	120-21	37°17′N	98°35′W
Medina, Sau. Ar. (mȧ-dē′nȧ)	266	24°28′N	39°37′E
Medina, N.Y., U.S. (mē-dī′nȧ)	116-17	43°13′N	78°23′W
Medina, Oh., U.S. (mē-dī′nȧ)	116-17	41°08′N	81°51′W
Medina del Campo, Spain (mâ-dē′nä dĕl käm′pō)	198-99	41°19′N	4°55′W
Medina de Ríoseco, Spain (mâ-dē′nä dā rē-ô-sā′kô)	198-99	41°52′N	5°02′W
Medinīpur, India	234-35	22°26′N	87°20′E
Medio, Punta, c., Chile	168-69	27°07′S	70°56′W
Mediterranean Sea, s., (mĕd-ĭ-tĕr-ā′nē-ăn sē)	188-89	35°0′N	20°00′E
Méditerranée, Mer, s., *see* Mediterranean Sea	188-89	35°0′N	20°00′E
Mediterráneo, Mar, s., *see* Mediterranean Sea	188-89	35°0′N	20°00′E
Mediterraneo, Mar, s., *see* Mediterranean Sea	188-89	35°0′N	20°00′E
Mediterrània, Mar, s., *see* Mediterranean Sea	188-89	35°0′N	20°00′E
Mednogorsk, Russia	226	51°25′N	57°35′E
Médouneu, Gabon	260-61	0°59′N	10°55′E
Medveditsa, stm., Russia (mĕd-vyĕ′dē tsȧ)	186-87	49°35′N	42°39′E
Medvezhyegorsk, Russia	186-87	62°55′N	34°28′E
Medyn', Russia (mĕ-dēn′)	202-03	54°57′N	35°53′E
Meekatharra, Austl. (mē-kȧ-thăr′ȧ)	270-71	26°35′S	118°30′E
Meeker, Co., U.S. (mēk′ẽr)	118-19	40°03′N	107°55′W
Meelpaeg Lake, res., Nf., Can. (mēl′pȧ-ĕg lāk)	138-39	48°16′N	56°35′W
Meerut, India (mē′rŏŏt)	234-35	28°59′N	77°42′E
Meghālaya, state, India	234-35	25°30′N	91°15′E
Meghna, stm., Bngl.	234-35	22°50′N	90°42′E
Megísti, i., Grc.	188-89	36°08′N	29°36′E
Mehun-sur-Yèvre, Fr. (mē-ŭn-sür-yĕvr′)	196-97	47°09′N	2°13′E
Meiganga, Camrn.	260-61	6°34′N	14°07′E
Meiktila, Mya.	246-47	20°52′N	95°52′E
Meixian, China *see* Meizhou	238-39	24°20′N	116°07′E
Meizhou, China	238-39	24°20′N	116°07′E
Mejillones, Chile (mâ-ĸē-lyō′nås)	168-69	23°06′S	70°27′W
Mek'elē, Eth.	266	13°30′N	39°28′E
Meknès, Mor. (mĕk′nĕs)	269a	33°54′N	5°33′W
Mekong, stm., Asia (mā-kông′)	246-47	10°33′N	105°27′E
Mékôngk, stm., Asia *see* Mekong	246-47	10°33′N	105°27′E
Mékrou, stm., Afr.	260-61	12°24′N	2°50′E
Melaka, Malay.	246-47	2°12′N	102°16′E
Melaka, Selat, strt., Asia *see* Malacca, Strait of	246-47	2°30′N	101°20′E
Melanesia, is., Oc. (mĕl-ȧ-nē′-zhȧ)	280-81	13°0′S	164°00′E
Mélanésie, is., Oc. *see* Melanesia	280-81	13°0′S	164°00′E
Melawi, stm., Indon.	248-49	0°05′N	111°29′E
Melbourne, Austl. (mĕl′bŭrn)	276	37°49′S	144°57′E
Melbourne, Fl., U.S. (mĕl′bŭrn)	125a	28°05′N	80°37′W
Melbourne Island, i., Nu., Can.	130-31	68°30′N	104°45′W
Melchor, Isla, i., Chile	171	45°08′S	73°57′W
Melekeok, nat. cap., Palau	280-81	7°29′N	134°37′E
Meleuz, Russia	186-87	52°58′N	55°56′E
Mélèzes, stm., Qc., Can.	130-31	57°41′N	69°29′W
Melfi, Chad	258-59	11°03′N	17°56′E
Melfort, Sk., Can. (mĕl′fôrt)	134-35	52°52′N	104°36′W
Melilla, Sp. N. Afr. (mā-lēl′yä)	198-99	35°18′N	2°57′W
Melipilla, Chile (må-lē-pē′lyä)	163e	33°41′S	71°13′W
Melita, Mb., Can.	134-35	49°16′N	100°59′W
Melitopol', Ukr. (mā-lē-tô′pôl-y')	202-03	46°51′N	35°21′E
Mellen, Wi., U.S. (mĕl′ĕn)	114-15	46°20′N	90°40′W
Mellerud, Swe. (mål′ĕ-rōōdh)	192-93	58°42′N	12°28′E
Melo, Ur. (mā′lō)	173	32°22′S	54°11′W
Melos, i., Grc. (mē′lŏs) *see* Mílos	200-01	36°41′N	24°28′E
Melrhir, Chott, lk., Alg.	258-59	34°18′N	6°17′E
Melrose, Mn., U.S. (mĕl′rōz)	114-15	45°40′N	94°49′W
Melton Mowbray, Eng., U.K. (mĕl′tŭn mō′brâ)	190-91	52°46′N	0°53′W
Melun, Fr. (mē-lŭɴ′)	196-97	48°32′N	2°40′E
Melville, Sk., Can. (mĕl′vĭl)	134-35	50°55′N	102°48′W
Melville, Cape, c., Austl. (kāp mĕl′vĭl)	277	14°11′S	144°30′E
Melville, Lake, lk., Nf., Can. (lāk mĕl′vĭl)	130-31	53°40′N	59°44′W
Melville Island, i., Austl. (mĕl′vĭl ī′lȧnd)	272-73	11°40′S	131°00′E
Melville Island, i., Can.	86	75°15′N	109°59′W
Melville Peninsula, pen., Nu., Can. (mĕl′vĭl pē-nĭn′sūlȧ)	130-31	68°0′N	84°00′W
Memel, Lith. *see* Klaipėda	192-93	55°43′N	21°08′E
Memel, S. Afr. (mĕ′mĕl)	269c	27°41′S	29°34′E
Memmingen, Ger. (mĕm′ĭng-ĕn)	194-95	47°59′N	10°11′E
Mempawah, Indon.	246-47	0°20′N	108°58′E
Memphis, Mo., U.S. (mĕm′fĭs)	120-21	40°28′N	92°10′W
Memphis, Tn., U.S. (mĕm′fĭs)	124-25	35°09′N	90°03′W
Memphis, Tx., U.S. (mĕm′fĭs)	120-21	34°44′N	100°33′W
Mena, Ukr. (mē-ná′)	202-03	51°31′N	32°14′E
Mena, Ar., U.S. (mē′nȧ)	120-21	34°35′N	94°15′W
Menado, Indon. *see* Manado	248-49	1°29′N	124°51′E
Ménaka, Mali	258-59	15°55′N	2°24′E
Menard, Tx., U.S. (mē-närd′)	122-23	30°55′N	99°47′W
Menasha, Wi., U.S. (mē-năsh′ȧ)	116-17	44°12′N	88°26′W
Mendawai, stm., Indon.	248-49	3°14′S	113°19′E
Mende, Fr. (mäɴd)	196-97	44°30′N	3°30′E
Mendi, Pap. N. Gui.	277	6°10′S	143°40′E
Mendocino, Cape, c., Ca., U.S. (kāp mĕn′dô-sē′nō)	112-13	40°25′N	124°23′W
Mendota, Ca., U.S. (mĕn-dō′tȧ)	118-19	36°46′N	120°23′W
Mendota, Il., U.S. (mĕn-dō′tȧ)	116-17	41°33′N	89°07′W
Mendoza, Arg. (mĕn-dō′sä)	163e	32°53′S	68°49′W
Mendoza, state, Arg. (mĕn-dō′sä)	163e	34°30′S	68°30′W
Mengcheng, China (mŭŋ-chŭŋ)	238-39	33°16′N	116°33′E
Menggala, Indon.	246-47	4°29′S	105°15′E
Menghai, China	238-39	21°59′N	100°27′E
Menindee, Austl. (mĕ-nĭn-dē)	276	32°24′S	142°26′E
Menominee, Mi., U.S. (mē-nŏm′ĭ-nē)	116-17	45°08′N	87°37′W
Menominee, stm., U.S. (mē-nŏm′ĭ-nē)	114-15	45°06′N	87°36′W
Menongue, Ang.	264-65	14°39′S	17°41′E
Menorca, i., Spain (mĕ-nô′r-kä)	198-99	40°0′N	4°00′E
Mentawai, Selat, strt., Indon.	246-47	1°45′S	100°00′E
Menzel Bourguiba, Tun.	184-85	37°10′N	9°48′E
Meoqui, Mex.	122-23	28°16′N	105°29′W
Meppel, Neth. (mĕp′ĕl)	190-91	52°42′N	6°12′E
Meppen, Ger. (mĕp′ĕn)	194-95	52°42′N	7°18′E
Merauke, Indon. (må-rou′kä)	277	8°30′S	140°24′E
Merca, Som. *see* Marka	262-63	1°43′N	44°46′E
Merced, Ca., U.S. (mẽr-sĕd′)	118-19	37°18′N	120°29′W
Mercedario, Cerro, mtn., Arg. (sĕ′r-rô mĕr-så-dhä′rē-ō)	168-69	31°59′S	70°08′W
Mercedes, Arg. (mĕr-sā′dhās)	173	29°11′S	58°03′W
Mercedes, Arg. (mĕr-sā′dhās)	173	34°40′S	59°26′W
Mercedes, Ur.	173	33°15′S	58°02′W
Mercy, Cape, c., Nu., Can.	130-31	64°54′N	63°35′W
Merefa, Ukr. (må-rĕf′á)	202-03	49°51′N	36°05′E
Mergui, Mya. (mẽr-gē′)	246-47	12°26′N	98°37′E
Mergui Archipelago, is., Mya. (mẽr-gē′ är′kĭ-pĕ′-â-gō)	246-47	12°0′N	98°00′E
Mérida, Mex.	148	20°59′N	89°37′W
Mérida, Spain	198-99	38°55′N	6°20′W
Mérida, Ven. (mĕ′rē-dhä)	164-65	8°37′N	71°09′W
Meriden, Ct., U.S. (mĕr′ĭ-dĕn)	116-17	41°32′N	72°48′W
Meridian, Id., U.S. (mē-rĭd-ĭ-ăn)	112-13	43°36′N	116°21′W
Meridian, Ms., U.S. (mē-rĭd-ĭ-ăn)	124-25	32°22′N	88°42′W
Meridian, Tx., U.S. (mē-rĭd-ĭ-ăn)	122-23	31°55′N	97°40′W
Merikarvia, Fin. (mä′rē-kár′vē-å)	192-93	61°51′N	21°30′E
Merín, Laguna, b., S.A. *see* Mirim, Lagoa	173	32°45′S	52°50′W
Merir, i., Palau	280-81	4°19′N	132°19′E
Merkel, Tx., U.S. (mûr′kĕl)	120-21	32°28′N	100°01′W
Merrill, Mi., U.S. (mĕr′ĭl)	116-17	43°25′N	84°20′W
Merrill, Wi., U.S. (mĕr′ĭl)	116-17	45°11′N	89°41′W
Merritt, B.C., Can. (mĕr′ĭt)	132-33	50°06′N	120°46′W
Merryville, La., U.S. (mĕr′ĭ-vĭl)	122-23	30°45′N	93°33′W
Mersa Matruh, Egypt	188-89	31°21′N	27°14′E
Merseburg, Ger. (mĕr′zē-bŏŏrgh)	194-95	51°21′N	11°60′E
Mersin, Tur. *see* İçel	228-29	36°49′N	34°38′E
Merthyr Tydfil, Wales, U.K. (mûr′thẽr tĭd′vĭl)	190-91	51°46′N	3°23′W
Méru, Fr. (mā-rü′)	196-97	49°14′N	2°08′E
Meru, Kenya (mā′rōō)	267	0°03′N	37°39′E
Meru, Mount, vol., Tan.	267	3°14′S	36°45′E
Merzifon, Tur. (mĕr′ze-fōn)	186-87	40°52′N	35°27′E
Mesa, Az., U.S. (mā′sȧ)	118-19	33°24′N	111°49′W
Mesabi Range, hills, Mn., U.S. (mā-sŏb′bē rānj)	114-15	47°30′N	92°50′W
Mesagne, Italy (mā-sän′yå)	200-01	40°34′N	17°49′E
Mesa Verde National Park, n.p., Co., U.S. (mā′sȧ vĕr′dē năsh′ŭn-ăl pärk)	118-19	37°15′N	108°26′W
Mescalero Apache Indian Reservation, ind. res., N.M., U.S. (mĕs-kä-lā′rō ȧ-păch′ē ĭn′dĭ-ăn rĕ-sẽr-vā′shĕn)	120-21	33°12′N	105°40′W
Mesewa, Erit. *see* Massawa	266	15°37′N	39°26′E
Meshchovsk, Russia (myĕsh′chĕfsk)	202-03	54°19′N	35°17′E
Meshed, Iran *see* Mashhad	232-33	36°17′N	59°36′E
Mesogéios Thálassa, s., *see* Mediterranean Sea	188-89	35°0′N	20°00′E
Mesopotamia, hist. reg., Asia	228-29	34°0′N	44°00′E
Mesoyéios Thálassa, s., *see* Mediterranean Sea	188-89	35°0′N	20°00′E
Messalo, stm., Moz.	264-65	11°41′S	40°26′E
Messina, Italy (mĕ-sē′nȧ)	200-01	38°11′N	15°33′E
Messina, Stretto di, strt., Italy (stĕ′t-tô dē mĕ-sē′nȧ)	200-01	38°09′N	15°35′E
Meta, stm., S.A.	164-65	6°11′N	67°28′W
Métabetchouane, stm., Qc., Can. (mĕ-tȧ-bĕt-chōō-än′)	136-37	48°26′N	71°58′W
Meta Incognita Peninsula, pen., Nu., Can.	130-31	62°45′N	68°30′W
Metán, Arg. (mĕ-tá′n)	168-69	25°30′S	64°57′W
Metapán, El Sal. (må-täpän′)	148	14°20′N	89°26′W
Metković, Cro. (mĕt′kô-vĭch)	200-01	43°03′N	17°39′E
Metlakatla, Ak., U.S. (mĕt-lȧ-kăt′lȧ)	126	55°07′N	131°35′W
Metropolis, Il., U.S. (mē-trŏp′ô-lĭs)	124-25	37°09′N	88°44′W
Metter, Ga., U.S. (mĕt′ẽr)	124-25	32°24′N	82°04′W
Metz, Fr. (mĕtz)	196-97	49°08′N	6°10′E
Meulaboh, Indon.	246-47	4°09′N	96°08′E
Mexia, Tx., U.S. (må-hē′ä)	122-23	31°40′N	96°29′W
Mexiana, Ilha, i., Braz.	166-67	0°02′S	49°35′W
Mexicali, Mex. (mâk-sē-kä′lē)	144-45	32°39′N	115°30′W
Mexicana, Altiplanicie, plat., Mex.	20-21	25°29′N	104°00′W
Mexican Hat, Ut., U.S. (mĕk′sĭ-kăn hăt)	118-19	37°12′N	109°52′W
Mexico, Me., U.S. (mĕk′sĭ-kō)	116-17	44°34′N	70°33′W
Mexico, Mo., U.S. (mĕk′sĭ-kō)	120-21	39°10′N	91°53′W
Mexico, nation, N.A. (mĕk′sĭ-kō)	85	23°0′N	102°00′W
México, state, Mex.	146-47	19°20′N	99°45′W
México, Golfo de, b., N.A. *see* Mexico, Gulf of	140-41	25°0′N	90°00′W
Mexico, Gulf of, b., N.A. (gŭlf ŭv mĕk′sĭ-kō)	140-41	25°0′N	90°00′W
Mexico City, nat. cap., Mex. (mĕk′sĭ-kō sĭ′tē)	146-47	19°24′N	99°09′W
Meyersdale, Pa., U.S. (mī′ẽrz-dāl)	116-17	39°49′N	79°02′W
Meymaneh, Afg.	232-33	35°56′N	64°48′E
Mezen', Russia	186-87	65°50′N	44°15′E
Mezen', stm., Russia	186-87	65°53′N	44°09′E
Mézenc, Mont, mtn., Fr. (mōɴ-mā-zĕɴ′)	196-97	44°55′N	4°11′E
Mezha, stm., Russia (myâ′zhȧ)	202-03	55°43′N	31°31′E
Mezhdurechensk, Russia	226	53°41′N	88°07′E
Mezőkövesd, Hung. (mĕ′zû-kû′vĕsht)	194-95	47°48′N	20°35′E
Mezőtúr, Hung. (mĕ′zû-tōōr)	194-95	47°00′N	20°37′E
Mezquital, Mex. (måz-kē-täl′)	146-47	23°29′N	104°22′W
Mfangano Island, i., Kenya	267	0°28′S	34°01′E
M'Goun, Irhil, mtn., Mor.	258-59	31°31′N	6°25′W
Miahuatlán de Porfirio Díaz, Mex.	146-47	16°19′N	96°36′W
Miajadas, Spain (mē-ä-hä′däs)	198-99	39°09′N	5°54′W
Miami, Fl., U.S. (mī-ă′-mē)	125a	25°47′N	80°13′W
Miami Beach, Fl., U.S.	125a	25°48′N	80°08′W
Miāneh, Iran	228-29	37°26′N	47°42′E
Mianyang, China	238-39	31°28′N	104°44′E
Miaoli, Tai. (mē-ou′lĭ)	225a	24°33′N	120°49′E
Miass, Russia (mī-ås′)	226	54°59′N	60°06′E
Michalovce, Slvk. (mē′kä-lôf′tsĕ)	194-95	48°46′N	21°56′E
Michelson, Mount, mtn., Ak., U.S. (mount mĭch′ĕl-sŭn)	126	69°19′N	144°17′W
Michigan, state, U.S. (mĭsh-′ĭ-găn)	108-09	44°0′N	85°00′W
Michigan, Lake, lk., U.S. (lăk mĭsh-′ĭ-găn)	116-17	44°0′N	87°00′W
Michigan City, In., U.S. (mĭsh-′ĭ-găn sĭ′tē)	116-17	41°43′N	86°53′W
Michipicoten Island, i., On., Can.	136-37	47°45′N	85°45′W
Michoacán, state, Mex.	146-47	19°10′N	101°50′W
Michurinsk, Russia (mĭ-chōō-rĭnsk′)	186-87	52°54′N	40°29′E
Micronesia, is., Oc. (mī-krō-nē′zhȧ)	280-81	11°0′N	159°00′E
Micronesia, Federated States of, nation, Oc. (fĕ′ẽr-ā′ĕd stāts ŭv mī-krō-nē′zhȧ)	280-81	5°0′N	152°00′E
Middelburg, S. Afr.	264-65	31°30′S	25°00′E
Middelfart, Den. (mĕd′'l-fărt)	192-93	55°30′N	9°45′E
Middle, stm., B.C., Can. (mĭd′'l)	132-33	54°52′N	125°08′W
Middle Andaman, i., India (mĭd′'l ăn-dȧ-măn′)	246-47	12°30′N	92°50′E

PRONOUNCING INDEX

Middle Caicos – Mococa 357

Feature (Pronunciation)	Page	Lat.	Long.
Middle Caicos, i., T./C. Is.	142-43	21°48'N	71°47'W
Middlesboro, Ky., U.S. (mĭd''lz-bŭr-ô)	124-25	36°36'N	83°43'W
Middlesbrough, Eng., U.K. (mĭd''lz-brŭ)	190-91	54°34'N	1°14'W
Middleton, N.S., Can. (mĭd''l-tŭn)	138-39	44°57'N	65°04'W
Middleton Island, i., Ak., U.S.	126	59°26'N	146°19'W
Middletown, Oh., U.S.	116-17	39°31'N	84°23'W
Midland, On., Can. (mĭd'lănd)	136-37	44°45'N	79°52'W
Midland, Mi., U.S.	116-17	43°36'N	84°14'W
Midland, Tx., U.S.	122-23	32°00'N	102°05'W
Midway, Ky., U.S. (mĭd'wā)	116-17	38°08'N	84°42'W
Midway Islands, dep., Oc. (mĭd'wā ī'lăndz)	280-81	28°13'N	177°22'W
Międzyrzecz, Pol. (myăn-dzŭ'zhěch)	194-95	52°27'N	15°35'E
Mier, Mex. (myâr)	122-23	26°26'N	99°09'W
Mieres, Spain (myā'rās)	198-99	43°16'N	5°46'W
Mier y Noriega, Mex. (myâr'ē nô-rē-ā'gä)	146-47	23°25'N	100°08'W
Miguel Alemán, Presa, res., Mex. (prā'sä-mē-gĕl'-älĕ-mà'n)	146-47	18°13'N	96°32'W
Mikhaylov, Russia (mē-kăy'lôf)	202-03	54°14'N	39°02'E
Mikhaylovka, Russia	186-87	50°04'N	43°15'E
Mikkeli, Fin. (mĕk'ĕ-lĭ)	192-93	61°42'N	27°16'E
Mikun', Russia	186-87	62°22'N	50°05'E
Mikura-jima, i., Japan (mē'kōō-rà jē'mȧ)	244	33°52'N	139°36'E
Milaca, Mn., U.S. (mē-lăk'à)	114-15	45°45'N	93°39'W
Milagro, Arg.	168-69	31°01'S	65°60'W
Milagro, Ec.	170	2°08'S	79°36'W
Milan, Italy (mē-län')	200-01	45°28'N	9°12'E
Milan, Mi., U.S. (mī'lăn)	116-17	42°05'N	83°41'W
Milan, Mo., U.S. (mī'lăn)	120-21	40°12'N	93°07'W
Milan, Oh., U.S. (mī'lăn)	116-17	41°18'N	82°37'W
Milan, Tn., U.S. (mī'lăn)	124-25	35°55'N	88°46'W
Milano, Italy (mē-lä'nō) *see* Milan	200-01	45°28'N	9°12'E
Milâs, Tur. (mē'läs)	200-01	37°19'N	27°47'E
Milbank, S.D., U.S. (mĭl'băŋk)	114-15	45°13'N	96°38'W
Mildura, Austl. (mĭl-dū'rȧ)	276	34°12'S	142°10'E
Mile, China	238-39	24°26'N	103°27'E
Miles, Austl.	276	26°40'S	150°11'E
Miles City, Mt., U.S. (mīlz sĭ'tē)	112-13	46°25'N	105°50'W
Milford, Ct., U.S. (mĭl'fērd)	116-17	41°13'N	73°04'W
Milford, De., U.S. (mĭl'fērd)	116-17	38°55'N	75°26'W
Milford, Ne., U.S. (mĭl'fērd)	114-15	40°46'N	97°03'W
Milford, Ut., U.S. (mĭl'fērd)	118-19	38°24'N	113°01'W
Milford Sound, b., N.Z.	278	44°31'S	167°48'E
Milk, stm., N.A.	112-13	48°03'N	106°19'W
Mil'kovo, Russia	218-19	54°42'N	158°38'E
Millau, Fr. (mē-yō')	196-97	44°06'N	3°05'E
Milledgeville, Ga., U.S. (mĭl'ĕj-vĭl)	124-25	33°05'N	83°14'W
Mille Lacs, Lac des, lk., On., Can. (läk dē mēl läks)	136-37	48°50'N	90°30'W
Mille Lacs Lake, lk., Mn., U.S.	114-15	46°15'N	93°40'W
Millen, Ga., U.S. (mĭl'ĕn)	124-25	32°48'N	81°56'W
Millenium, at., Kir. *see* Caroline	280-81	9°58'S	150°13'W
Miller, S.D., U.S. (mĭl'ēr)	114-15	44°31'N	98°59'W
Millerovo, Russia (mĭl'ĕ-rô-vô)	186-87	48°56'N	40°24'E
Millersburg, Ky., U.S. (mĭl'ērz-bûrg)	116-17	38°18'N	84°09'W
Millersburg, Oh., U.S. (mĭl'ērz-bûrg)	116-17	40°33'N	81°54'W
Millicent, Austl. (mĭl-ĭ-sĕnt)	276	37°36'S	140°20'E
Millinocket, Me., U.S. (mĭl-ĭ-nŏk'ĕt)	117a	45°40'N	68°42'W
Mills Lake, lk., N.T., Can.	130-31	61°30'N	118°10'W
Mílos, i., Grc. (mē'lŏs)	200-01	36°41'N	24°28'E
Milton, On., Can. (mĭl'tŭn)	136-37	43°31'N	79°53'W
Milton, Fl., U.S. (mĭl'tŭn)	124-25	30°38'N	87°02'W
Milton, Pa., U.S. (mĭl'tŭn)	116-17	41°01'N	76°51'W
Milton, Wi., U.S. (mĭl'tŭn)	116-17	42°47'N	88°56'W
Milwaukee, Wi., U.S. (mĭl-wô'kē)	116-17	43°01'N	87°56'W
Min, stm., China (mēn)	222-23	26°04'N	119°33'E
Min, stm., China (mēn)	238-39	28°46'N	104°38'E
Minami-Daitō-jima, i., Japan	222-23	25°50'N	131°15'E
Minami-Iō-jima, i., Japan	280-81	24°14'N	141°28'E
Minami-Tori-shima, i., Japan *see* Marcus Island	280-81	24°18'N	153°58'E
Minas, Cuba (mē'näs)	142-43	21°29'N	77°36'W
Minas, Ur. (mē'näs)	173	34°23'S	55°14'W
Minas Basin, b., N.S., Can. (mī'nȧs bā's'n)	138-39	45°20'N	64°00'W
Minas Channel, strt., N.S., Can. (mī'nȧs chăn'ĕl)	138-39	45°15'N	64°45'W
Minas de Oro, Hond. (mē'näs-dĕ-dĕ-ō-rô)	149	14°46'N	87°20'W
Minas Gerais, state, Braz.	172	18°0'S	44°00'W
Minas Novas, Braz. (mē'näzh nō'väzh)	172	17°15'S	42°36'W
Minatitlán, Mex. (mē-nä-tē-tlän')	146-47	17°59'N	94°32'W
Mindanao, i., Phil. (mĭn-dä-nou')	250	8°0'N	125°00'E
Mindanao Sea, s., Phil. (mĭn-dä-nou' sē) *see* Bohol Sea	250	9°10'N	124°25'E
Mindelo, C.V.	260-61	16°52'N	24°60'W
Minden, Ger. (mĭn'dĕn)	194-95	52°18'N	8°55'E
Mindoro, i., Phil. (mĭn-dō'rō)	250	12°50'N	121°05'E
Mindoro Strait, strt., Phil. (mĭn-dō'rō strāt)	250	12°20'N	120°40'E
Mineiros, Braz.	168-69	17°34'S	52°34'W
Mineola, Tx., U.S. (mĭn-ē-ō'lȧ)	120-21	32°40'N	95°29'W
Mineral'nyye Vody, Russia	227	44°12'N	43°08'E
Mineral Point, Wi., U.S. (mĭn'ēr-ăl point)	116-17	42°52'N	90°10'W
Mineral Wells, Tx., U.S. (mĭn'ēr-ăl wĕlz)	120-21	32°48'N	98°07'W
Minfeng, China	226	37°04'N	82°39'E
Mingäçevir, Azer.	227	40°46'N	47°02'E
Mingäçevir su anbarı, res., Azer.	227	40°55'N	46°48'E
Mingāora, Pak.	232-33	34°49'N	72°21'E
Mingechaur, Azer. *see* Mingäçevir	227	40°46'N	47°02'E
Mingechaur Reservoir, res., Azer. *see* Mingäçevir su anbarı	227	40°55'N	46°48'E
Minicoy Island, i., India	236	8°16'N	73°03'E
Minigwal, Lake, lk., Austl.	272-73	29°35'S	123°12'E
Minle, China	240-41	38°28'N	100°56'E
Minna, Nig. (mĭn'à)	260-61	9°37'N	6°33'E
Minneapolis, Mn., U.S. (mĭn-ē-ăp'ô-lĭs)	114-15	44°59'N	93°17'W
Minnedosa, Mb., Can. (mĭn-ē-dō'sȧ)	134-35	50°14'N	99°49'W
Minneota, Mn., U.S. (mĭn-ē-ō'tȧ)	114-15	44°34'N	96°00'W
Minnesota, state, U.S. (mĭn-ē-sō'tȧ)	108-09	46°0'N	94°15'W
Minnesota, stm., Mn., U.S.	114-15	44°54'N	93°11'W
Minnitaki Lake, lk., On., Can. (mĭ'nĭ-tä'kē lăk)	134-35	49°58'N	92°00'W
Minonk, Il., U.S. (mī'nŏnk)	116-17	40°54'N	89°02'W
Minorca, i., Spain *see* Menorca	198-99	40°0'N	4°00'E
Minot, N.D., U.S.	114-15	48°14'N	101°18'W
Minsk, state, Bela. (mênsk)	194-95	53°45'N	27°45'E
Minsk, nat. cap., Bela. (mênsk)	194-95	53°54'N	27°33'E
Mińsk Mazowiecki, Pol. (mên'sk mä-zô-vyĕt'skĭ)	194-95	52°11'N	21°34'E
Minto, Lac, lk., Qc., Can.	130-31	57°12'N	74°58'W
Minturno, Italy (mēn-tōōr'nō)	200-01	41°16'N	13°45'E
Minxian, China	238-39	34°26'N	104°02'E
Minya, Egypt *see* El-Minya	268b	28°06'N	30°45'E
Minya Konka, mtn., China *see* Gongga Shan	238-39	29°35'N	101°51'E
Min'yar, Russia	186-87	55°03'N	57°33'E
Miracema do Tocantins, Braz.	166-67	9°33'S	48°24'W
Mirador, Braz. (mē-rà-dōr')	166-67	6°22'S	44°22'W
Miraflores, Col. (mē-rä-flō'rās)	164-65	1°25'N	72°17'W
Miramar, Arg.	173	38°16'S	57°51'W
Miramichi, N.B., Can.	138-39	47°02'N	65°28'W
Miramichi Bay, b., N.B., Can. (mĭr'ȧ-mē'shē bā)	138-39	47°08'N	65°08'W
Miranda, stm., Braz.	168-69	19°25'S	57°20'W
Miranda de Ebro, Spain (mē-rà'n-dä-dĕ-ĕ'brô)	198-99	42°42'N	2°56'W
Miranda do Douro, Port. (mē-rän'dä dô-dwĕ'rō)	198-99	41°30'N	6°16'W
Mirandela, Port. (mē-rän-dā'lȧ)	198-99	41°29'N	7°11'W
Mirecourt, Fr. (mēr-kōōr')	196-97	48°18'N	6°08'E
Miri, Malay. (mē'rē)	248-49	4°23'N	113°59'E
Mirim, Lagoa, b., S.A. (là-gô'ä-mē-rēɴ')	173	32°45'S	52°50'W
Mirnyy, Russia	218-19	62°31'N	113°59'E
Mīrpur Khās, Pak. (mēr'pōōr käs)	232-33	25°31'N	69°01'E
Mirzāpur, India (mēr'zä-pōōr)	234-35	25°08'N	82°34'E
Misâha, Bîr, well, Egypt	266	22°12'N	27°57'E
Misantla, Mex. (mē-sän'tlä)	146-47	19°56'N	96°50'W
Miscou Island, i., N.B., Can. (mĭs'kō ī'lănd)	138-39	47°57'N	64°32'W
Mishan, China (mĭ'shän)	244	45°32'N	131°52'E
Mishawaka, In., U.S. (mĭsh-ȧ-wôk'ȧ)	116-17	41°40'N	86°10'W
Mishmi Hills, hills, Asia	238-39	29°0'N	96°00'E
Misima Island, i., Pap. N. Gui.	277	10°42'S	152°45'E
Misiones, state, Arg. (mē-syō'nās)	173	27°0'S	55°00'W
Miskitos, Cayos, is., Nic.	149	14°23'N	82°46'W
Miskolc, Hung. (mĭsh'kôlts)	194-95	48°06'N	20°47'E
Misool, Pulau, i., Indon. (pōō-lou mē-sôl')	224-25	1°52'S	130°10'E
Mişr, nation, Afr. *see* Egypt	253	27°0'N	30°00'E
Mişrātah, Libya	188-89	32°22'N	15°06'E
Missinaibi, stm., On., Can. (mĭs'ĭn-ä'ē-bē)	130-31	50°45'N	81°31'W
Missinaibi Lake, lk., On., Can. (mĭs'ĭn-ä'ē-bē lăk)	136-37	48°21'N	83°43'W
Mission, S.D., U.S. (mĭsh'ŭn)	114-15	43°18'N	100°38'W
Mission, Tx., U.S. (mĭsh'ŭn)	122-23	26°13'N	98°19'W
Mississippi, state, U.S. (mĭs-ĭ-sĭp'ē)	108-09	32°50'N	89°30'W
Mississippi, stm., U.S. (mĭs-ĭ-sĭp'ē)	110-11	28°60'N	89°08'W
Mississippi River Delta, del., La., U.S.	110-11	29°10'N	89°15'W
Mississippi Sound, strt., U.S. (mĭs-ĭ-sĭp'ē sound)	124-25	30°15'N	88°40'W
Missoula, Mt., U.S. (mĭ-zōō'lȧ)	112-13	46°52'N	114°00'W
Missouri, state, U.S. (mĭ-sōō'rē)	108-09	38°30'N	93°30'W
Missouri, stm., U.S. (mĭ-sōō'rē)	110-11	38°49'N	90°07'W
Missouri City, Tx., U.S. (mĭ-sōō'rē sĭ'tĭ)	122-23	29°37'N	95°31'W
Missouri Valley, Ia., U.S. (mĭ-sōō'rē văl'ē)	114-15	41°33'N	95°54'W
Mistassibi, stm., Qc., Can.	136-37	48°53'N	72°14'W
Mistassini, Lac, lk., Qc., Can. (lăk mĭs-tȧ-sĭ'nē)	130-31	51°0'N	73°37'W
Misti, Volcán, vol., Peru	170	16°18'S	71°24'W
Mita, Punta de, c., Mex. (pōō'n-tä-dĕ-mē'tä)	146-47	20°47'N	105°32'W
Mitau, Lat. *see* Jelgava	192-93	56°39'N	23°44'E
Mitchell, Austl.	276	26°29'S	147°58'E
Mitchell, In., U.S. (mĭch'ĕl)	116-17	38°44'N	86°29'W
Mitchell, Ne., U.S. (mĭch'ĕl)	114-15	41°57'N	103°48'W
Mitchell, S.D., U.S. (mĭch'ĕl)	114-15	43°43'N	98°02'W
Mitchell, Mount, mtn., N.C., U.S. (mount mĭch'ĕl)	124-25	35°46'N	82°16'W
Mitiaro, i., Cook Is.	280-81	19°48'S	157°43'W
Mito, Japan	245	36°22'N	140°29'E
Mitsio, Nosy, i., Madag.	264-65	12°54'S	48°36'E
Mitsiwa, Erit. *see* Massawa	266	15°37'N	39°26'E
Mittellandkanal, can., Ger. (mĭt'ĕl-lănd kä-näl')	194-95	52°14'N	11°43'E
Mitú, Col.	164-65	1°08'N	70°03'W
Mitumba, Monts, mts., D.R.C.	267	6°0'S	29°00'E
Mitzic, Gabon	260-61	0°47'N	11°34'E
Miyake-jima, i., Japan (mē'yä-kå jē'mȧ)	244	34°05'N	139°32'E
Miyako, Japan	244	39°38'N	141°57'E
Miyako-jima, i., Japan	279a	24°47'N	125°20'E
Miyakonojō, Japan	245	31°43'N	131°04'E
Miyazaki, Japan	245	31°54'N	131°26'E
Miyazu, Japan	245	35°32'N	135°11'E
Miyoshi, Japan (mē-yō'shē')	245	34°49'N	132°51'E
Miyun, China	240-41	40°22'N	116°50'E
Mizdah, Libya (mēz'dä)	188-89	31°26'N	12°59'E
Mizen Head, c., Ire.	190-91	51°27'N	9°49'W
Mizil, Rom. (mē'zēl)	200-01	44°59'N	26°27'E
Mizoram, state, India	246-47	23°30'N	93°00'E
Mizque, Bol.	168-69	17°57'S	65°20'W
Mjölby, Swe. (myûl'bü)	192-93	58°20'N	15°09'E
Mjøsa, lk., Nor. (myûsä)	192-93	60°40'N	11°00'E
Mkinvartsveri, Mt'a, vol., *see* Kazbek, Gora	227	42°42'N	44°31'E
Mladá Boleslav, Czech Rep. (mlä'dä bô'lĕ-slåf)	194-95	50°25'N	14°54'E
Mlanje Peak, mtn., Malawi *see* Sapitwa	264-65	15°57'S	35°36'E
Mława, Pol. (mwä'vȧ)	194-95	53°07'N	20°22'E
Moa, stm., Afr.	260-61	6°60'N	11°34'W
Moa, Pulau, i., Indon.	248-49	8°10'S	127°56'E
Moab, Ut., U.S. (mō'ăb)	118-19	38°35'N	109°33'W
Moa Island, i., Austl.	277	10°12'S	142°16'E
Moala, i., Fiji	279f	18°36'S	179°53'E
Moanda, Gabon	260-61	1°34'S	13°13'E
Moba, D.R.C.	267	7°04'S	29°44'E
Moberly, Mo., U.S. (mō'bēr-lĭ)	120-21	39°25'N	92°26'W
Mobile, Al., U.S. (mô-bēl')	124-25	30°41'N	88°03'W
Mobile Bay, b., Al., U.S. (mô-bēl' bā)	124-25	30°34'N	87°60'W
Mobridge, S.D., U.S. (mō'brĭj)	114-15	45°32'N	100°26'W
Mobutu Sese Seko, Lac, lk., Afr. *see* Albert, Lake	267	1°40'N	31°00'E
Moca, Dom. Rep. (mô'kä)	142-43	19°24'N	70°31'W
Moçambique, Moz. (mō-säɴ-bē'kĕ) *see* Ilha de Moçambique	264-65	15°02'S	40°41'E
Moçambique, nation, Afr. *see* Mozambique	253	18°15'S	35°00'E
Moçambique, Canal de, strt., Afr. *see* Mozambique Channel	264-65	19°0'S	41°00'E
Moçâmedes, Ang. (mô-zà-mĕ-dĕs) *see* Namibe	264-65	15°12'S	12°10'E
Mocha, Yemen	266	13°19'N	43°15'E
Mocha, Isla, i., Chile	171	38°22'S	73°55'W
Mochudi, Bots. (mō-chōō'dē)	269c	24°23'S	26°09'E
Mocímboa da Praia, Moz. (mô-sē'ĕm-bô-ä prä'ēȧ)	264-65	11°20'S	40°22'E
Môco, Morro de, mtn., Ang.	264-65	12°28'S	15°10'E
Mococa, Braz. (mô-kô'kȧ)	172	21°28'S	46°60'W

n-sing; ŋ-baŋk; ɴ-nasalized n; nŏd; cŏmmit; ōld; ôbey; ôrder; oi-boil; fōōd; ŏŏ-as oo in foot; ou-out; s-soft; sh-dish; th-thin; pūre; ûnite; ûrn; stŭd; circŭs; ü-as in French tu; '-indeterminate vowel.

n-sing; ŋ-bank; N-nasalized n; nŏd; cŏmmit; ōld; ôbey; ôrder; oi-boil; fōōd; ò-as oo in foot; ou-out; s-soft; sh-dish; th-thin; pūre; ûnite; ûrn; stŭd; circŭs; ü-as in French tu; ′-indeterminate vowel.

Feature (Pronunciation)	Page	Lat.	Long.
Muhu, i., Est. (mo͞o′ho͞o)	192-93	58°37′N	23°13′E
Mukacheve, Ukr.	194-95	48°26′N	22°45′E
Mukah, Malay.	248-49	2°54′N	112°06′E
Mukalla, Yemen *see* Al-Mukallā	220-21	14°32′N	49°08′E
Mukden, China *see* Shenyang	243	41°48′N	123°24′E
Mukry, Turkmen.	232-33	37°36′N	65°43′E
Mula, Spain (mo͞o′lä)	198-99	38°03′N	1°30′W
Muladu, i., Mald.	236	7°01′N	72°59′E
Mulchatna, stm., Ak., U.S.	126	59°39′N	157°08′W
Mulhacén, mtn., Spain	198-99	37°03′N	3°19′W
Mulhouse, Fr. (mü-lo͞oz′)	196-97	47°45′N	7°20′E
Muling, China (mo͞o-lĭŋ)	244	44°31′N	130°16′E
Muling, China (mo͞o-lĭŋ)	244	44°56′N	130°32′E
Muling, stm., China (mo͞o-lĭŋ)	244	45°52′N	133°30′E
Mull, Island of, i., Scot., U.K. (ī′l*ă*nd ŏv mŭl)	190-91	56°27′N	6°00′W
Mullan, Id., U.S. (mŭl′*ă*n)	112-13	47°28′N	115°48′W
Muller, Pegunungan, mts., Indon. (mül′ẽr)	248-49	0°40′N	113°50′E
Mullewa, Austl.	270-71	28°33′S	115°31′E
Mullins, S.C., U.S. (mŭl′ĭnz)	124-25	34°12′N	79°15′W
Mulongo, D.R.C.	262-63	7°49′S	26°60′E
Multān, Pak. (mo̤-tän′)	232-33	30°11′N	71°27′E
Mulvane, Ks., U.S. (mŭl-vān′)	120-21	37°28′N	97°15′W
Mumbai, India	236	18°57′N	72°50′E
Mumbwa, Zam. (mo̤m′bwä)	264-65	14°59′S	27°04′E
Mun, stm., Thai.	246-47	15°19′N	105°31′E
Muna, Mex. (mo͞o′nȧ)	148	20°29′N	89°43′W
Muna, stm., Russia	218-19	67°53′N	123°05′E
Muna, Pulau, i., Indon.	248-49	4°53′S	122°27′E
München, Ger. *see* Munich	194-95	48°08′N	11°35′E
Muncie, In., U.S. (mŭn′sĭ)	116-17	40°11′N	85°22′W
Munger, India	234-35	25°23′N	86°28′E
Mungindi, Austl. (mŭn-gĭn′dē)	276	28°59′S	148°59′E
Mungkan Kandju National Park, n.p., Austl.	277	13°32′S	142°37′E
Munich, Ger. (mū′nĭk)	194-95	48°08′N	11°35′E
Munising, Mi., U.S. (mū′nĭ-sĭng)	114-15	46°24′N	86°39′W
Munkács, Ukr. *see* Mukacheve	194-95	48°26′N	22°45′E
Münster, Ger.	194-95	51°57′N	7°37′E
Muntok, Indon. (mo̤n-tŏk′)	246-47	2°04′S	105°10′E
Muonio, Fin.	184-85	67°58′N	23°40′E
Muqayshiṭ, i., U.A.E.	230-31	24°10′N	53°45′E
Muqdisho, nat. cap., Som. *see* Mogadishu	262-63	2°03′N	45°20′E
Muradiye, Tur. (mo͞o-rä′dē-yĕ)	227	38°59′N	43°50′E
Murashi, Russia	186-87	59°24′N	48°58′E
Murat, stm., Tur. (mo͞o-rát′)	227	38°40′N	39°53′E
Murchison, stm., Austl. (mûr′chĭ-s*ŭ*n)	272-73	27°42′S	114°08′E
Murchison Falls, wtfl., Ug. *see* Kabalega Falls	267	2°17′N	31°42′E
Murchison Falls National Park, n.p., Ug.	267	2°15′N	31°50′E
Murcia, Spain (mo͞or′thyä)	198-99	37°59′N	1°08′W
Mur-de-Barrez, Fr.	196-97	44°51′N	2°39′E
Murdo, S.D., U.S. (mûr′dō)	114-15	43°53′N	100°41′W
Muret, Fr. (mü-rĕ′)	196-97	43°28′N	1°19′E
Murfreesboro, N.C., U.S. (mûr′frēz-bŭr-ō)	124-25	36°27′N	77°06′W
Murfreesboro, Tn., U.S. (mûr′frēz-bŭr-ō)	124-25	35°50′N	86°23′W
Murgap, stm., Asia (mo͞or-gäp′)	232-33	38°38′N	61°10′E
Murgon, Austl.	276	26°15′S	151°57′E
Mūrītāniyā, nation, Afr. *see* Mauritania	253	20°0′N	12°00′W
Murmansk, Russia (mo͞or-mänsk′)	184-85	68°58′N	33°05′E
Murom, Russia (mo͞o′rôm)	186-87	55°34′N	42°02′E
Muroran, Japan (mo͞o′rō-rän)	244	42°19′N	140°59′E
Muros, Spain (mo͞o′rōs)	198-99	42°47′N	9°04′W
Murphy, N.C., U.S. (mŭr′fĭ)	124-25	35°05′N	84°02′W
Murphysboro, Il., U.S. (mŭr′fĭz-bŭr-ō)	116-17	37°46′N	89°20′W
Murray, Ky., U.S. (mŭr′ĭ)	124-25	36°37′N	88°19′W
Murray, Ut., U.S. (mŭr′ĭ)	112-13	40°39′N	111°54′W
Murray, stm., Austl. (mŭr′ĭ)	276	35°22′S	139°21′E
Murray, stm., B.C., Can. (mŭr′ĭ)	132-33	55°43′N	121°13′W
Murray, Lake, lk., Pap. N. Gui.	277	7°0′S	141°30′E
Murray Bridge, Austl. (mŭr′ĭ brĭj)	276	35°08′S	139°16′E
Murray Harbour, P.E., Can. (mŭr′ĭ här′bẽr)	138-39	45°60′N	62°32′W
Murray-Sunset National Park, n.p., Austl.	276	34°45′S	141°30′E
Murrumbidgee, stm., Austl. (mŭr-ŭm-bĭd′jē)	276	34°42′S	143°08′E
Murska Sobota, Slvn. (mo͞or′skä sô′bô-tä)	200-01	46°40′N	16°10′E
Murua Island, i., Pap. N. Gui.	277	9°06′S	152°45′E
Murud, Gunong, mtn., Malay.	248-49	3°52′N	115°30′E
Mururoa, at., Fr. Poly.	280-81	21°52′S	138°55′W
Murwāra, India	234-35	23°50′N	80°24′E
Murwillumbah, Austl. (m*ŭ*r-wĭl′l*ŭ*m-b*ŭ*)	276	28°21′S	153°24′E
Murzuq, Libya	258-59	25°56′N	13°55′E
Murzūq, Idhān, des., Libya	258-59	24°30′N	13°00′E
Mürzzuschlag, Aus. (mürts′tso͞o-shlägh)	194-95	47°36′N	15°41′E
Muş, Tur. (mo͞osh)	227	38°43′N	41°29′E
Musala, mtn., Blg.	200-01	42°11′N	23°34′E
Musay'īd, Qatar	230-31	24°59′N	51°33′E
Muscat, nat. cap., Oman (mŭs-kăt′)	230-31	23°36′N	58°32′E
Muscat and Oman, nation, Asia *see* Oman	206-07	22°0′N	58°00′E
Muscatine, Ia., U.S. (mŭs-k*ȧ*-tēn)	114-15	41°25′N	91°02′W
Muscle Shoals, Al., U.S. (mŭs′'l shōlz)	124-25	34°44′N	87°40′W
Mushin, Nig.	260a	6°31′N	3°21′E
Musi, stm., Indon. (mo͞o′sē)	246-47	2°22′S	104°55′E
Muskegon, Mi., U.S. (mŭs-kē′g*ŭ*n)	116-17	43°14′N	86°15′W
Muskegon, stm., Mi., U.S. (mŭs-kē′g*ŭ*n)	116-17	43°13′N	86°19′W
Muskegon Heights, Mi., U.S. (mŭs-kē′g*ŭ*n hīts)	116-17	43°12′N	86°14′W
Muskingum, stm., Oh., U.S. (mŭs-kĭŋ′g*ŭ*m)	116-17	39°24′N	81°28′W
Muskogee, Ok., U.S. (mŭs-kō′gē)	120-21	35°44′N	95°22′W
Muskoka, Lake, lk., On., Can. (lāk mŭs-kō′k*ȧ*)	136-37	45°02′N	79°25′W
Musoma, Tan.	267	1°30′S	33°48′E
Mussau Island, i., Pap. N. Gui. (mo͞o-sä′o͞o ī′l*ă*nd)	277	1°27′S	149°37′E
Musselshell, stm., Mt., U.S. (mŭs′'l-shĕl)	112-13	47°27′N	107°55′W
Mustvee, Est. (mo͞ost′vĕ-ĕ)	192-93	58°51′N	26°56′E
Musu-dan, c., Kor., N. (mo͞o′so͞o dän)	243	40°51′N	129°43′E
Muswellbrook, Austl. (mŭs′w*ŭ*nl-bro͝ok)	276	32°16′S	150°54′E
Mutare, Zimb.	264-65	18°58′S	32°40′E
Mutsamudu, Com.	264-65	12°08′S	44°26′E
Mutsu, Japan	244	41°17′N	141°10′E
Mutsu-wan, b., Japan (mo͞ot′so͞o wän)	244	41°05′N	140°55′E
Mutton Bay, Qc., Can. (mŭt′'n bā)	138-39	50°47′N	59°02′W
Muttra, India *see* Mathura	234-35	27°30′N	77°41′E
Mutum, Braz. (mo͞o-to͞o′m)	172	19°48′S	41°27′W
Muynak, Uzb. *see* Mŭynoq	226	43°46′N	59°02′E
Mŭynoq, Uzb.	226	43°46′N	59°02′E
Muyua Island, i., Pap. N. Gui. *see* Murua Island	277	9°06′S	152°45′E
Muzaffarnagar, India	234-35	29°28′N	77°42′E
Muzaffarpur, India	234-35	26°07′N	85°23′E
Muztag, mtn., China	234-35	36°03′N	80°07′E
Muztag, mtn., China	234-35	36°25′N	87°25′E
Muztaū bīigi, mtn., Asia *see* Belukha, Mount	226	49°51′N	86°29′E
Mwali, i., Com.	264-65	12°18′S	43°42′E
Mwanza, Tan. (mwän′zä)	267	2°31′S	32°54′E
Mweka, D.R.C.	262-63	4°51′S	21°34′E
Mwene-Ditu, D.R.C.	262-63	7°03′S	23°27′E
Mweru, Lake, lk., Afr. (lāk mwā′ro͞o)	262-63	9°0′S	28°45′E
Mweru Wantipa, Lake, lk., Zam.	262-63	8°45′S	29°40′E
Mwokil, at., Micron.	280-81	6°39′N	159°47′E
Myanaung, Mya.	246-47	18°17′N	95°19′E
Myanmar, nation, Asia (myän-mär)	206-07	22°0′N	98°00′E
Myaundzha, Russia	218-19	63°03′N	147°11′E
Myaungmya, Mya.	246-47	16°35′N	94°55′E
Myingyan, Mya. (myĭng-yŭn′)	246-47	21°27′N	95°23′E
Myitkyinā, Mya. (myĭ′chē-nȧ)	238-39	25°23′N	97°24′E
Mykolaïv, Ukr.	202-03	46°58′N	31°59′E
Mymensingh, Bngl.	234-35	24°45′N	90°24′E
Myohyang-san, mtn., Kor., N. (myō′hyang-sän′)	243	40°01′N	126°21′E
Mýrdalsjökull, ice, Ice. (mür′däls-yû′kol)	190a	63°40′N	19°05′W
Myrtle Beach, S.C., U.S. (mûr′t'l bēch)	124-25	33°42′N	78°54′W
Mysore, India (mī-sōr′)	236	12°18′N	76°39′E
Mysore, state, India *see* Karnātaka	236	14°0′N	76°00′E
Mys Shmidta, Russia	126	68°52′N	179°37′W
My Tho, Viet.	246-47	10°22′N	106°22′E
Mytilíni, Grc.	200-01	39°06′N	26°33′E
Mytishchi, Russia (mê-tēsh′chi)	202-03	55°55′N	37°46′E
Mzuzu, Malawi	264-65	11°24′S	33°57′E

N

Feature (Pronunciation)	Page	Lat.	Long.
Naantali, Fin. (nän′tȧ-lē)	192-93	60°30′N	22°04′E
Naberezhnye Chelny, Russia	186-87	55°42′N	52°19′E
Nabeul, Tun. (nā-bûl′)	184-85	36°27′N	10°46′E
Nabī Shu'ayb, Jabal an-, mtn., Yemen	220-21	15°17′N	43°59′E
Nābulus, W.B.	228-29	32°14′N	35°17′E
Nacala, Moz. (nă-kȧ′lȧ)	264-65	14°33′S	40°40′E
Náchod, Czech Rep. (näk′ôt)	194-95	50°25′N	16°11′E
Nacogdoches, Tx., U.S. (năk′ô-dō′chĕz)	122-23	31°35′N	94°39′W
Nacozari de García, Mex.	144-45	30°24′N	109°39′W
Nadadores, Mex. (nä-dä-dō′rās)	122-23	27°02′N	101°35′W
Nadiād, India	234-35	22°41′N	72°52′E
Nador, Mor.	198-99	35°11′N	2°56′W
Nadym, Russia	218-19	65°35′N	72°39′E
Nadym, stm., Russia (ná′dĭm)	218-19	66°13′N	72°00′E
Næstved, Den. (nĕst′vĭdh)	194-95	55°14′N	11°46′E
Naga, Phil. (nä′gä)	250	13°38′N	123°11′E
Nāgāland, state, India	234-35	26°0′N	95°00′E
Nagano, Japan (nä′gä-nô)	245	36°39′N	138°12′E
Nagaoka, Japan (nä′gȧ-ō′kȧ)	245	37°27′N	138°51′E
Nagaon, India	234-35	26°21′N	92°41′E
Nāgappattinam, India	236	10°46′N	79°51′E
Nagarote, Nic. (nä-gä-rô′tĕ)	149	12°16′N	86°34′W
Nagasaki, Japan (nä′gȧ-sä′kē)	245	32°45′N	129°53′E
Nāgaur, India	234-35	27°12′N	73°44′E
Nāgercoil, India	236	8°10′N	77°26′E
Nagorno-Karabakh, hist. reg., Azer. (nu-gôr′n*ŭ*-kŭ-r*ŭ*-bäk′)	227	40°00′N	46°40′E
Nagoya, Japan	245	35°10′N	136°55′E
Nāgpur, India (näg′po͞or)	234-35	21°09′N	79°05′E
Nagqu, China	234-35	31°31′N	92°05′E
Nagua, Dom. Rep. (ná′gwä)	142-43	19°23′N	69°51′W
Naguna, **Île**, i., Vanuatu *see* Nguna, Île	279g	17°27′S	168°21′E
Nagybánya, Rom. *see* Baia Mare	194-95	47°39′N	23°35′E
Nagykanizsa, Hung. (nôd′y′kô′nē-shô)	194-95	46°27′N	16°60′E
Nagykőrös, Hung. (nôd′y′kŭ-rûsh)	194-95	47°02′N	19°46′E
Nagyvarad, Rom. *see* Oradea	194-95	47°04′N	21°56′E
Naha, Japan (nä′hä)	244a	26°13′N	127°42′E
Nāhan, India	234-35	30°32′N	77°17′E
Nahanni National Park Reserve, n.p., N.T., Can.	128-29	61°35′N	125°45′W
Nahe, China	240-41	48°29′N	124°53′E
Nahr al-Urdunn, stm., Asia *see* Jordan	228-29	31°46′N	35°34′E
Nahuel Huapi, Lago, lk., Arg. (lä′gô nä′wĕl wä′pē)	171	40°58′S	71°30′W
Naica, Mex. (nä-ē′kä)	122-23	27°51′N	105°30′W
Nain, Nf., Can. (nīn)	128-29	56°33′N	61°43′W
Nā'īn, Iran	232-33	32°52′N	53°05′E
Naini Tāl, India	234-35	29°24′N	79°26′E
Nairn, Scot., U.K. (nârn)	190-91	57°35′N	3°53′W
Nairobi, nat. cap., Kenya (nī-rō′bē)	267	1°16′S	36°49′E
Naitauba, i., Fiji	279f	17°01′S	179°16′W
Naivasha, Kenya (nī-vä′sh*ȧ*)	267	0°45′S	36°26′E
Najafābād, Iran	232-33	32°38′N	51°22′E
Najasa, stm., Cuba (nä-hä′sä)	142-43	20°43′N	77°59′W
Najd, hist. reg., Sau. Ar.	266	26°07′N	44°40′E
Najin, Kor., N. (nä′jĭn)	243	42°15′N	130°18′E
Naju, Kor., S. (nä′jo͞o′)	243	35°02′N	126°43′E
Nakambé, stm., Afr. *see* White Volta	260-61	8°57′N	1°10′W
Nakanbe, stm., Afr. *see* White Volta	260-61	8°57′N	1°10′W
Nakano-shima, i., Japan	244	29°50′N	129°52′E
Nakhichevan, Azer. *see* Naxçıvan	227	39°13′N	45°25′E
Nakhodka, Russia (nŭ-ĸôt′kŭ)	244	42°49′N	132°53′E
Nakhon Pathom, Thai.	246-47	13°49′N	100°04′E
Nakhon Phanom, Thai.	246-47	17°24′N	104°47′E
Nakhon Ratchasima, Thai.	246-47	14°58′N	102°06′E
Nakhon Sawan, Thai.	246-47	15°42′N	100°06′E
Nakhon Si Thammarat, Thai.	246-47	8°26′N	99°58′E
Nakskov, Den. (näk′skou)	194-95	54°50′N	11°08′E
Nakuru, Kenya	267	0°17′S	36°04′E
Nālanda, India	234-35	25°08′N	85°24′E
Nalchik, Russia (nál-chēk′)	227	43°29′N	43°37′E
Nalgonda, India	236	17°03′N	79°16′E
Nalubaale Dam, d., Ug.	267	0°27′N	33°11′E
Nālūt, Libya (nä-lo͞ot′)	188-89	31°53′N	10°60′E
Namak, Daryācheh-ye, lk., Iran	232-33	34°30′N	51°50′E
Namangan, Uzb. (ná-mán-gän′)	232-33	40°60′N	71°40′E
Namapa, Moz.	264-65	13°42′S	39°49′E
Nambour, Austl. (năm′bo̤r)	276	26°38′S	152°58′E
Namcha Barwa, mtn., China *see* Namjagbarwa Feng	238-39	29°38′N	95°04′E
Nam Co, lk., China (näm tswo)	234-35	30°41′N	90°32′E
Nam Dinh, Viet. (näm dĕnĸ′)	246-47	20°26′N	106°10′E
Namhae-do, i., Kor., S. (näm′hī′)	243	34°48′N	127°57′E
Namhkam, Mya.	238-39	23°50′N	97°41′E

ăt; fin*ă*l; rāte; senāte; ärm; ȧsk; sof*ȧ*; fâre; ch-choose; dh-as th in other; bē; ēvent; bĕt; recĕnt; cratẽr; g-gō; gh-guttural g; bĭt; *ĭ*-short neutral; rīde; ĸ-guttural k as ch in German ich;

n-sing; ŋ-baŋk; N-nasalized n; nŏd; cŏmmit; ōld; ŏbey; ôrder; oi-boil; fŏŏd; ò-as oo in foot; ou-out; s-soft; sh-dish; th-thin; pūre; ŭnite; ûrn; stŭd; circŭs; ü-as in French tu; ´-indeterminate vowel.

ăt; fīnăl; rāte; senăte; ärm; ăsk; sofá; fāre; ch-choose; dh-as th in other; bē; ĕvent; bĕt; recĕnt; cratēr; g-gō; gh-guttural g; bĭt; ĭ-short neutral; rīde; к-guttural k as ch in German ich;

n-sing; ŋ-baŋk; ɴ-nasalized n; nŏd; cŏmmit; ōld; ȯbey; ôrder; oi-boil; fōōd; ȯ-as oo in foot; ou-out; s-soft; sh-dish; th-thin; pūre; ûnite; ûrn; stŭd; circǔs; ü-as in French tu; ´-indeterminate vowel.

364 Nosivka – Oelwein PRONOUNCING INDEX

Feature (Pronunciation)	Page	Lat.	Long.
Nosivka, Ukr. (nô´sôf-kȧ)	202-03	50°56'N	31°36'E
Nosop, stm., Afr.	264-65	26°53'S	20°41'E
Nossob, stm., Afr. (nŏ´sŏb)	264-65	26°53'S	20°41'E
Nosy-Varika, Madag.	264-65	20°35'S	48°32'E
Noteć, stm., Pol. (nô´tĕcn)	194-95	52°44'N	15°25'E
Notodden, Nor. (nōt´ôd'n)	192-93	59°34'N	9°16'E
Noto-hantō, pen., Japan	245	37°20'N	137°00'E
Notozero, Ozero, lk., Russia	186-87	66°28'N	32°05'E
Notre-Dame, Monts, mts., Qc., Can.	138-39	48°10'N	68°00'W
Notre Dame Bay, b., Nf., Can. (nō´t'r dȧm´ bā)	138-39	49°46'N	55°15'W
Nottawasaga Bay, b., On., Can. (nŏt´ȧ-wȧ-sā´gȧ bā)	136-37	44°35'N	80°15'W
Nottingham, Eng., U.K. (nŏt´ĭng-ăm)	190-91	52°57'N	1°07'W
Nottingham Island, i., Nu., Can.	130-31	63°20'N	77°55'W
Nouâdhibou, Maur.	258-59	20°55'N	17°02'W
Nouâdhibou, Râs, c., Afr.	258-59	20°47'N	17°03'W
Nouakchott, nat. cap., Maur. (nü-äk´-shôt)	258-59	18°06'N	15°58'W
Nouméa, nat. cap., N. Cal. (nōō-mā´ä)	279g	22°17'S	166°27'E
Nouvelle, Qc., Can. (nōō-vĕl´)	138-39	48°08'N	66°19'W
Nouvelle-Calédonie, dep., Oc. *see* New Caledonia	279g	21°30'S	165°30'E
Nouvelle-Calédonie, i., N. Cal.	279g	21°33'S	165°42'E
Nouvelle-France, Cap de, c., Qc., Can.	130-31	62°27'N	73°42'W
Nouvelles-Hébrides, nation, Oc. *see* Vanuatu	279g	16°0'S	167°00'E
Nouvelles-Hébrides, is., Vanuatu *see* New Hebrides	279g	16°0'S	167°00'E
Nova Freixo, Moz. *see* Cuamba	264-65	14°47'S	36°32'E
Nova Friburgo, Braz. (nō´vȧ frĕ-bōōr´gô)	172	22°16'S	42°32'W
Nova Goa, India *see* Panaji	236	15°30'N	73°50'E
Nova Iguaçu, Braz. (nō´vä-ē-gwä-sōō´)	172	22°45'S	43°27'W
Nova Kakhovka, Ukr.	202-03	46°45'N	33°25'E
Nova Lima, Braz. (nō´vȧ lē´mä)	172	19°60'S	43°51'W
Nova Lisboa, Ang. *see* Huambo	264-65	12°46'S	15°44'E
Novara, Italy (nô-vä´rä)	200-01	45°27'N	8°37'E
Nova Scotia, state, Can. (nō´vȧ skō´shȧ)	128-29	45°0'N	63°00'W
Novaya Ladoga, Russia (nô´vá-ya lȧ-dô-gȧ)	192-93	60°05'N	32°15'E
Novaya Sibir', Ostrov, i., Russia (ôs-trôf´ nô´vá-ya sē-bēr´)	218-19	75°0'N	149°00'E
Novaya Zemlya, is., Russia (nô´vá-ya zĕm-lyá´)	218-19	74°0'N	57°00'E
Nova Zagora, Blg. (nô´vä zä´gô-rȧ)	200-01	42°30'N	26°01'E
Novelda, Spain (nō-vĕl´dä)	198-99	38°23'N	0°46'W
Nové Zámky, Slvk. (nô´vĕ zȧm´kĕ)	194-95	47°60'N	18°11'E
Novgorod, Russia (nôv´gô-rŏt)	192-93	58°32'N	31°18'E
Novi Pazar, Blg. (nō´vĭ pä-zär´)	200-01	43°21'N	27°12'E
Novi Pazar, Serb. (nō´vĭ pá-zär´)	200-01	43°08'N	20°31'E
Novi Sad, Serb. (nō´vĭ säd´)	200-01	45°15'N	19°50'E
Novoanninskiy, Russia	186-87	50°32'N	42°41'E
Novo Aripuanã, Braz.	166-67	5°08'S	60°21'W
Novocherkassk, Russia (nô´vô-chĕr-kȧsk´)	186-87	47°25'N	40°06'E
Novodvinsk, Russia	186-87	64°25'N	40°49'E
Novohrad-Volyns'kyi, Ukr.	194-95	50°36'N	27°38'E
Novokuybyshevsk, Russia	186-87	53°06'N	49°56'E
Novokuznetsk, Russia (nô´vô-kô´z-nyĕ´tsk)	226	53°45'N	87°07'E
Novo Mesto, Slvn. (nôvô mās´tô)	200-01	45°48'N	15°10'E
Novomoskovsk, Russia (nô´vô-môs-kôfsk´)	202-03	54°05'N	38°13'E
Novomoskovs'k, Ukr. (nō´vô-kô´z-nyĕ´tsk)	202-03	48°38'N	35°12'E
Novorossiysk, Russia (nô´vô-rô-sēsk´)	202-03	44°43'N	37°46'E
Novorzhev, Russia (nô´vô-rzhĕv´)	192-93	57°02'N	29°20'E
Novoshakhtinsk, Russia	202-03	47°48'N	39°54'E
Novosibirsk, Russia (nô´vô-sē-bērsk´)	218-19	55°01'N	82°53'E
Novosibirskiye Ostrova, is., Russia *see* New Siberian Islands	218-19	75°0'N	142°00'E
Novosibirskoye Vodokhranilishche, res., Russia	226	54°35'N	82°35'E
Novosil', Russia (nô´vô-sĭl)	202-03	52°58'N	37°03'E
Novosokol'niki, Russia (nô´vô-sô-kôl´nē-kē)	192-93	56°21'N	30°10'E
Novouzensk, Russia (nô-vô-ô-zĕnsk´)	186-87	50°29'N	48°10'E
Novovolyns'k, Ukr.	194-95	50°44'N	24°08'E
Novozybkov, Russia (nô´vô-zĕp´kôf)	202-03	52°32'N	31°56'E
Nový Jičín, Czech Rep. (nô´vē yē´chĕn)	194-95	49°36'N	18°01'E
Novyy Oskol, Russia (nô´vē ôs-kôl´)	202-03	50°46'N	37°53'E
Novyy Uzen, Kaz. *see* Zhangaözen	186-87	43°19'N	52°47'E
Nowata, Ok., U.S. (nô-wä´tȧ)	120-21	36°42'N	95°38'W
Nowra, Austl. (nou´rȧ)	276	34°53'S	150°36'E
Nowshera, Pak.	232-33	34°01'N	71°59'E
Nowy Dwór Mazowiecki, Pol. (nō´vĭ dvōōr mä-zo-vyĕts´ke)	194-95	52°26'N	20°43'E
Nowy Targ, Pol. (nô´vē tärk´)	194-95	49°28'N	20°03'E
Noxubee, stm., U.S. (nŏks´ū-bē)	124-25	32°50'N	88°10'W
Nsanje, Malawi	264-65	16°58'S	35°12'E
Nsukka, Nig.	260a	6°51'N	7°24'E
Ntem, stm., Afr.	260-61	2°20'N	9°50'E
Ntomba, Lac, lk., D.R.C.	262-63	0°48'S	18°03'E
Nu, stm., Asia (nōō) *see* Salween	208-09	16°33'N	97°40'E
Nubian Desert, des., Sudan (nōō´bĭ-ăn dĕs´ẽrt)	266	20°30'N	33°00'E
Nueces, stm., Tx., U.S. (nů-ā´sȧs)	122-23	27°50'N	97°22'W
Nueltin Lake, lk., Can. (nwĕl´tin lāk)	130-31	60°19'N	99°40'W
Nueva, Isla, i., Chile	171	55°14'S	66°32'W
Nueva Gerona, Cuba (nwä´vä кĕ-rŏ´nä)	142-43	21°53'N	82°48'W
Nueva Imperial, Chile	171	38°44'S	72°57'W
Nueva Palmira, Ur. (nwä´vä päl-mē´rä)	173	33°52'S	58°23'W
Nueva Rosita, Mex. (nŏĕ´vä rô-sē´tä)	122-23	27°57'N	101°13'W
Nueva Toltén, Chile	171	39°12'S	73°13'W
Nueve de Julio, Arg. (nwā´vȧ dā hōō´lyô)	173	35°27'S	60°53'W
Nuevitas, Cuba (nwä-vē´täs)	142-43	21°33'N	77°16'W
Nuevo, Cayo, i., Mex.	146-47	21°51'N	92°06'W
Nuevo, Golfo, b., Arg.	171	42°42'S	64°36'W
Nuevo Casas Grandes, Mex.	144-45	30°25'N	107°55'W
Nuevo Laredo, Mex. (nwā´vô lä-rā´dhō)	122-23	27°28'N	99°31'W
Nuevo León, state, Mex. (nwā´vô lå-ōn´)	122-23	25°40'N	100°00'W
Nuguria Islands, is., Pap. N. Gui.	277	3°21'S	154°41'E
Nui, at., Tuvalu	280-81	7°15'S	177°10'E
Nukha, Azer. *see* Şeki	227	41°10'N	47°10'E
Nuku'alofa, nat. cap., Tonga (nōō´-kōō-ä-lō´-fȧ)	280-81	21°08'S	175°13'W
Nukuoro, at., Micron.	280-81	3°51'N	154°58'E
Nukus, Uzb.	226	42°28'N	59°36'E
Nullarbor Plain, pl., Austl. (nŭ-lär´bôr plān)	272-73	31°0'S	129°00'E
Numara, i., Mald.	236	6°25'N	73°04'E
Numazu, Japan (nōō´mä-zōō)	245	35°06'N	138°52'E
Numedalslågen, stm., Nor. *see* Lågen	192-93	59°02'N	10°04'E
Numfoor, Pulau, i., Indon.	224-25	1°03'S	134°54'E
Nunavut, state, Can.	128-29	70°0'N	95°00'W
Nunivak Island, i., Ak., U.S. (nōō´nĭ-văk ī´lȧnd)	126	60°00'N	166°29'W
Nunjiang, China	240-41	49°10'N	125°14'E
Nuomin, stm., China	240-41	48°13'N	124°31'E
Nuoro, Italy (nwô´rō)	200-01	40°20'N	9°20'E
Nūra, stm., Kaz.	226	50°22'N	69°15'E
Nuremberg, Ger. *see* Nürnberg	194-95	49°27'N	11°04'E
Nürnberg, Ger. (nürn´bĕrgh)	194-95	49°27'N	11°04'E
Nushagak, stm., Ak., U.S. (nū-shȧ-găk´)	126	59°03'N	158°24'W
Nu Shan, mts., China	238-39	27°0'N	99°00'E
Nushki, Pak. (nŭsh´kē)	232-33	29°35'N	66°04'E
Nuuk, nat. cap., Green. *see* Godthåb	284-85	64°11'N	51°44'W
Nuweveldberge, mts., S. Afr.	264-65	32°14'S	21°48'E
Nyahururu Falls, Kenya	267	0°02'N	36°22'E
Nyainqêntanglha Shan, mts., China (nyä-ĭn-chyŭn-tăŋ-lä shän)	234-35	30°0'N	90°00'E
Nyala, Sudan	266	12°03'N	24°54'E
Nyandoma, Russia	186-87	61°40'N	40°13'E
Nyanza, Rw.	267	2°21'S	29°45'E
Nyasa, Lake, lk., Afr. (lāk nyä´sä)	264-65	12°0'S	34°30'E
Nyasaland, nation, Afr. *see* Malawi	253	13°30'S	34°00'E
Nyborg, Den. (nü´bôr´')	192-93	55°19'N	10°47'E
Nybro, Swe. (nü´brô)	192-93	56°45'N	15°55'E
Nyeri, Kenya	267	0°25'S	36°57'E
Nyíregyháza, Hung. (nyē´rĕd-y'hä´zä)	194-95	47°57'N	21°43'E
Nyköping, Swe. (nü´chû-pĭng)	192-93	58°45'N	16°60'E
Nylstroom, S. Afr. (nĭl´strōm) *see* Modimolle	269c	24°42'S	28°25'E
Nynäshamn, Swe. (nü-nĕs-hám'n)	192-93	58°55'N	17°57'E
Nyngan, Austl. (nĭŋ´gȧn)	276	31°33'S	147°10'E
Nyong, stm., Camrn. (nyông)	260-61	3°16'N	9°55'E
Nysa Łużycka, stm., Eur. *see* Neisse	194-95	52°04'N	14°46'E
Nyslott, Fin. *see* Savonlinna	192-93	61°52'N	28°54'E
Nytva, Russia	186-87	57°56'N	55°20'E
Nyunzu, D.R.C.	267	5°58'S	28°02'E
Nyurba, Russia	218-19	63°17'N	118°20'E
Nyuvchim, Russia	186-87	61°23'N	50°36'E
Nyuya, stm., Russia (nyōō´yȧ)	218-19	60°32'N	116°18'E
Nzérékoré, Gui.	260-61	7°45'N	8°49'W
Nzwani, i., Com. (äN-zhwäN)	264-65	12°15'S	44°25'E

O

Feature (Pronunciation)	Page	Lat.	Long.
O'ahu, i., Hi., U.S. (ō-ä´hōō) (ō-ä´hü)	127a	21°30'N	158°00'W
Oahe, Lake, res., U.S.	114-15	45°29'N	100°20'W
Oak Bay, B.C., Can. (ōk bā)	132-33	48°27'N	123°18'W
Oak Creek, Wi., U.S. (ōk krēk´)	116-17	42°52'N	87°54'W
Oakdale, La., U.S. (ōk´dāl)	122-23	30°49'N	92°40'W
Oakes, N.D., U.S. (ōks)	114-15	46°08'N	98°06'W
Oak Grove, Ky., U.S. (ōk grōv)	124-25	36°40'N	87°26'W
Oak Harbor, Wa., U.S. (ōk här´bẽr)	112-13	48°18'N	122°40'W
Oakland, Ca., U.S. (ōk´lănd)	118-19	37°48'N	122°17'W
Oakland, Md., U.S. (ōk´lănd)	116-17	39°24'N	79°24'W
Oakland, Ne., U.S. (ōk´lănd)	114-15	41°50'N	96°28'W
Oak Lawn, Il., U.S. (ōk lôn)	116-17	41°43'N	87°45'W
Oakley, Ks., U.S. (ōk´lĭ)	120-21	39°08'N	100°51'W
Oak Ridge, Tn., U.S. (ōk rĭj)	124-25	36°01'N	84°15'W
Oakville, On., Can. (ōk´vĭl)	136-37	43°27'N	79°40'W
Oakville, Mo., U.S. (ōk´vĭl)	120-21	38°28'N	90°19'W
Oaxaca, state, Mex. (wä-hä´kä)	146-47	17°0'N	96°30'W
Oaxaca de Juárez, Mex.	146-47	17°03'N	96°43'W
Ob', stm., Russia (ōb)	218-19	66°47'N	68°56'E
Oban, Scot., U.K. (ō´băn)	190-91	56°25'N	5°28'W
Oberlin, Ks., U.S. (o´bẽr-lĭn)	120-21	39°49'N	100°32'W
Oberlin, Oh., U.S. (o´bẽr-lĭn)	116-17	41°17'N	82°13'W
Obi, Kepulauan, is., Indon. (ō´bē)	248-49	1°27'S	127°38'E
Obi, Pulau, i., Indon.	248-49	1°30'S	127°45'E
Óbidos, Braz. (ō´bē-dŏzh)	166-67	1°54'S	55°31'W
Obihiro, Japan (ō´bē-hē´rō)	244	42°55'N	143°12'E
Obluchye, Russia	240-41	49°01'N	131°04'E
Obninsk, Russia	202-03	55°06'N	36°37'E
Oboyan, Russia (ŏ-bô-yän´)	202-03	51°13'N	36°17'E
Observatoire, Caye de l', i., N. Cal.	272-73	21°25'S	158°50'E
Obsgchiy Syrt, mts., Eur. *see* Zhalpy Syrt	186-87	52°0'N	51°30'E
Obskaya Guba, b., Russia	218-19	69°0'N	73°00'E
Obuasi, Ghana	260-61	6°13'N	1°41'W
Ocala, Fl., U.S. (ō-kä´lȧ)	124-25	29°11'N	82°08'W
Ocampo, Mex. (ŏ-käm´pō)	144-45	28°11'N	108°23'W
Ocaña, Col. (ŏ-kän´yä)	164-65	8°14'N	73°21'W
Ocaña, Spain (ŏ-kä´n-yä)	198-99	39°57'N	3°30'W
Occidental, Cordillera, mts., Col.	164-65	5°0'N	76°00'W
Ocean City, Md., U.S. (ō´shăn sĭ´tē)	116-17	38°20'N	75°05'W
Ocean City, N.J., U.S. (ō´shăn sĭ´tē)	116-17	39°17'N	74°35'W
Ocean Falls, B.C., Can. (ō´shăn fôlz)	132-33	52°21'N	127°41'W
Ocean Grove, N.J., U.S. (ō´shăn grōv)	116-17	40°13'N	74°00'W
Ocean Island, i., Kir. *see* Banaba	280-81	0°52'S	169°33'E
Oceanside, Ca., U.S. (ō´shăn-sīd)	118-19	33°12'N	117°22'W
Ocean Springs, Ms., U.S. (ō´shăn sprĭngz)	124-25	30°26'N	88°50'W
Ochlockonee, stm., U.S. (ŏk-lô-kō´nē)	124-25	29°59'N	84°26'W
Ocilla, Ga., U.S. (ō-sĭl´ȧ)	124-25	31°36'N	83°15'W
Ockelbo, Swe. (ôk´ĕl-bô)	192-93	60°54'N	16°44'E
Ocmulgee National Monument, n.p., Ga., U.S. (ōk-mŭl´gē năsh´ŭn-ăl mŏn´ū-mĕnt)	124-25	32°43'N	83°38'W
Oconee, stm., Ga., U.S. (ō-kō´nē)	124-25	31°58'N	82°32'W
Oconomowoc, Wi., U.S. (ō-kŏn´ō-mô-wŏk´)	116-17	43°06'N	88°29'W
Oconto, Wi., U.S. (ō-kŏn´tō)	116-17	44°54'N	87°52'W
Oconto Falls, Wi., U.S. (ō-kŏn´tō fôlz)	116-17	44°52'N	88°08'W
Ocosingo, Mex.	148	16°55'N	92°06'W
Ocotal, Nic. (ō-kō-täl´)	149	13°38'N	86°28'W
Ocotlán, Mex. (ō-kō-tlän´)	146-47	20°21'N	102°47'W
Ocotlán de Morelos, Mex. (ō-kō-tlän´ dā mō-rā´lōs)	146-47	16°47'N	96°40'W
Ocracoke Island, i., N.C., U.S.	124-25	35°06'N	75°59'W
October Revolution Island, i., Russia *see* Oktyabr'skoy Revolyutsii, Ostrov	218-19	79°30'N	96°60'E
Ocumare del Tuy, Ven. (ō-kōō-mä´ra del twē´)	163b	10°07'N	66°46'W
Oda, Jabal, mtn., Sudan	266	20°21'N	36°39'E
Odda, Nor. (ôdh-ȧ)	192-93	60°04'N	6°32'E
Odemira, Port. (ō-dȧ-mē´rȧ)	198-99	37°35'N	8°38'W
Ödemiş, Tur. (û´dĕ-mēsh)	200-01	38°14'N	27°59'E
Odendaalsrus, S. Afr. (ō´dĕn-däls-rûs´)	269c	27°52'S	26°42'E
Odense, Den. (ō´dhĕn-sĕ)	192-93	55°24'N	10°23'E
Oder, stm., Eur. (ō´dẽr)	194-95	53°55'N	14°17'E
Odesa, Ukr.	202-03	46°29'N	30°42'E
Odessa, De., U.S. (ŏ-dĕs´ȧ)	116-17	39°27'N	75°40'W
Odessa, Tx., U.S. (ŏ-dĕs´ȧ)	122-23	31°51'N	102°22'W
Odin, Mount, mtn., B.C., Can.	132-33	50°33'N	118°08'W
Odintsovo, Russia (ŏ-dēn´tsô-vô)	202-03	55°40'N	37°16'E
Odra, stm., Eur. (ō´drȧ) *see* Oder	194-95	53°55'N	14°17'E
Odrzywół, Pol.	194-95	51°32'N	20°33'E
Oeiras, Braz. (wȧ-ē-räzh´)	166-67	7°01'S	42°08'W
Oelwein, Ia., U.S. (ōl´wīn)	114-15	42°40'N	91°55'W

ăt; finăl; rāte; senåte; ärm; ȧsk; sofȧ; fâre; ch-choose; dh-as th in other; bē; ēvent; bĕt; recĕnt; cratẽr; g-gō; gh-guttural g; bĭt; ĭ-short neutral; rīde; к-guttural k as ch in German ich;

366 Orani – Pacific Ocean PRONOUNCING INDEX

Feature (Pronunciation)	Page	Lat.	Long.
Orani, Phil. (ō-rä'nē)	250	14°49'N	120°31'E
Oranienburg, Ger. (ō-rä'nē-ĕn-bōrgh)	194-95	52°45'N	13°15'E
Oranje, stm., Afr. *see* Orange	264-65	28°35'S	16°28'E
Oranjemund, Nmb.	264-65	28°34'S	16°28'E
Oranjestad, nat. cap., Aruba	140a	12°32'N	70°01'W
Orăştie, Rom. (ô-rûsh'tyå)	194-95	45°50'N	23°13'E
Oraşul Stalin, Rom. *see* Braşov	194-95	45°39'N	25°37'E
Orbetello, Italy (ôr-bå-tĕl'lō)	200-01	42°27'N	11°13'E
Orbost, Austl. (ôr'bŭst)	276	37°42'S	148°28'E
Ord, Ne., U.S. (ôrd)	114-15	41°36'N	98°56'W
Ordu, Tur. (ôr'dò)	186-87	40°59'N	37°52'E
Ordzhonikidze, Russia *see* Vladikavkaz	227	43°03'N	44°39'E
Örebro, Swe. (û'rē-brō)	192-93	59°17'N	15°12'E
Oregon, state, U.S.	108-09	44°0'N	121°00'W
Oregon City, Or., U.S.	112-13	45°21'N	122°36'W
Orekhovo-Zuyevo, Russia (ôr-yĕ'kô-vô zò'yĕ-vô)	202-03	55°48'N	38°58'E
Orël, Russia	202-03	52°59'N	36°04'E
Orem, Ut., U.S. (ō'rĕm)	118-19	40°16'N	111°41'W
Orense, Spain *see* Ourense	198-99	42°20'N	7°52'W
Organ Pipe Cactus National Monument, n.p., Az., U.S. (ôr'găn pīp kăk'tŭs năsh'ŭn-ăl mŏn'ū-mĕnt)	118-19	32°0'N	112°55'W
Orhon, stm., Mong.	240-41	50°14'N	106°08'E
Oriental, Cordillera, mts., Col. (kôr-dēl-yĕ'rä ō-rē-ĕn-täl')	164-65	6°0'N	73°00'W
Oriental, Cordillera, mts., Peru	170	11°0'S	74°00'W
Orillia, On., Can. (ô-rĭl'ĭ-å)	136-37	44°36'N	79°25'W
Orinoco, stm., S.A. (ō-rĭ-nō'kō)	164-65	8°47'N	60°40'W
Orissa, state, India (ō-rĭs'å)	234-35	20°0'N	84°00'E
Oristano, Italy (ô-rēs-tä'nō)	200-01	39°54'N	8°36'E
Oriximiná, Braz.	166-67	1°45'S	55°52'W
Orizaba, Mex. (ô-rē-zä'bä)	146-47	18°51'N	97°06'W
Orkla, stm., Nor. (ôr'klå)	184-85	63°19'N	9°51'E
Orkney, S. Afr. (ôrk'nĭ)	269c	26°59'S	26°41'E
Orkney Islands, is., Scot., U.K.	190c	59°0'N	3°00'W
Orlando, Fl., U.S. (ôr-lăn'dō)	125a	28°32'N	81°23'W
Orléans, Fr. (ôr-lā-äN')	196-97	47°55'N	1°55'E
Orleans, In., U.S. (ôr-lēnz')	116-17	38°40'N	86°27'W
Ormāra, Pak.	232-33	25°13'N	64°38'E
Ormoc, Phil.	250	11°01'N	124°37'E
Ormond Beach, Fl., U.S. (ôr'mŏnd bēch)	124-25	29°17'N	81°04'W
Örnsköldsvik, Swe. (ûrn'skôlts-vēk)	184-85	63°18'N	18°43'E
Orocué, Col.	164-65	4°49'N	71°20'W
Oroluk, at., Micron.	280-81	7°31'N	155°18'E
Oromocto, N.B., Can.	138-39	45°51'N	66°28'W
Orosháza, Hung. (ô-rôsh-hä'sô)	194-95	46°34'N	20°40'E
Orotukan, Russia	218-19	62°16'N	151°38'E
Oroville, Ca., U.S. (ōr'ô-vĭl)	118-19	39°31'N	121°33'W
Oroville, Wa., U.S. (ōr'ô-vĭl)	112-13	48°56'N	119°26'W
Oroville, Lake, res., Ca., U.S. (lăk ōr'ô-vĭl)	118-19	39°38'N	121°30'W
Orrville, Oh., U.S. (ôr'vĭl)	116-17	40°50'N	81°46'W
Orša, Bela.	192-93	54°31'N	30°25'E
Orsa, Swe. (ōr'sä)	192-93	61°08'N	14°37'E
Orsha, Bela. (ôr'shå) *see* Orša	192-93	54°31'N	30°25'E
Orsk, Russia (ôrsk)	226	51°12'N	58°34'E
Orşova, Rom. (ôr'shô-vä)	200-01	44°43'N	22°25'E
Ortega, Col. (ôr-tĕ'gä)	163c	3°56'N	75°13'W
Ortegal, Cabo, c., Spain (kå'bô-ôr-tå-gäl')	198-99	43°46'N	7°54'W
Orthez, Fr. (ôr-tĕz')	196-97	43°30'N	0°46'W
Orthon, stm., Bol.	166-67	10°49'S	66°04'W
Ortigueira, Spain (ôr-tē-gā'ē-rä)	198-99	43°41'N	7°50'W
Ortonville, Mn., U.S. (ôr-tŭn-vĭl)	114-15	45°19'N	96°27'W
Orūmīyeh, Iran	228-29	37°32'N	45°05'E
Orūmīyeh, Daryācheh-ye, lk., Iran	227	37°40'N	45°30'E
Oruro, Bol. (ō-rōō'rō)	168-69	17°58'S	67°07'W
Orust, i., Swe.	192-93	58°10'N	11°38'E
Orvieto, Italy (ôr-vyâ'tō)	200-01	42°44'N	12°06'E
Orxon, stm., China	240-41	48°56'N	117°46'E
Osa, Península de, pen., C.R. (pĕ-nê'n-sōō-lä ō'sä)	149	8°34'N	83°31'W
Osage, Ia., U.S. (ō'sāj)	114-15	43°17'N	92°49'W
Osage, stm., Mo., U.S. (ō'sāj)	120-21	38°36'N	91°56'W
Ōsaka, Japan (ō'sä-kä)	245	34°41'N	135°31'E
Ōsaka-wan, b., Japan (ō'sä-kä wän)	245	34°30'N	135°18'E
Osakis, Mn., U.S. (ô-sā'kĭs)	114-15	45°52'N	95°09'W
Osceola, Ar., U.S. (ŏs-ē-ō'lå)	124-25	35°43'N	89°58'W
Osceola, Ia., U.S. (ŏs-ē-ō'lå)	114-15	41°02'N	93°46'W
Oscoda, Mi., U.S. (ŏs-kō'då)	116-17	44°25'N	83°19'W
Osh, Kyrg. (ôsh)	232-33	40°32'N	72°48'E
Oshakati, Nmb.	264-65	17°47'S	15°41'E
Oshawa, On., Can. (ŏsh'å-wå)	136-37	43°54'N	78°51'W
Ō-shima, i., Japan (ō'shē'mä)	245	34°44'N	139°25'E
Oshkosh, Ne., U.S. (ŏsh'kŏsh)	114-15	41°25'N	102°21'W
Oshkosh, Wi., U.S. (ŏsh'kŏsh)	116-17	44°00'N	88°33'W
Oshogbo, Nig.	260a	7°46'N	4°33'E
Oshwe, D.R.C.	262-63	3°22'S	19°30'E
Osijek, Cro. (ôs'ĭ-yĕk)	200-01	45°33'N	18°42'E
Osipenko, Ukr. *see* Berdians'k	202-03	46°45'N	36°49'E
Oskaloosa, Ia., U.S. (ŏs-kå-lōō'så)	114-15	41°18'N	92°39'W
Oskarshamn, Swe.	192-93	57°16'N	16°29'E
Oskarström, Swe. (ôs'kärs-strûm)	192-93	56°48'N	12°58'E
Öskemen, Kaz.	226	49°57'N	82°38'E
Oslo, nat. cap., Nor. (ôs'lō)	192-93	59°55'N	10°45'E
Osmānābād, India	236	18°10'N	76°02'E
Osnabrück, Ger. (ôs-nä-brük')	194-95	52°17'N	8°03'E
Osorno, Chile (ô-sō'r-nō)	171	40°35'S	73°07'W
Ossa, Mount, mtn., Austl. (mount ŏså)	276	41°54'S	146°01'E
Osse, stm., Nig.	260a	5°55'N	5°16'E
Osseo, Wi., U.S. (ŏs'sē-ō)	114-15	44°35'N	91°14'W
Ossining, N.Y., U.S. (ŏs'ĭ-nĭng)	116-17	41°10'N	73°52'W
Ossipee, N.H., U.S. (ŏs'ĭ-pē)	116-17	43°42'N	71°07'W
Ossora, Russia	218-19	59°18'N	163°09'E
Ostashkov, Russia (ôs-täsh'kôf)	202-03	57°08'N	33°08'E
Ostende, Bel. *see* Oostende	190-91	51°14'N	2°55'E
Oster, Ukr. (ôs'tĕr)	202-03	50°57'N	30°53'E
Österreich, nation, Eur. *see* Austria	174-75	47°20'N	13°20'E
Östersjön, s., Eur. *see* Baltic Sea	192-93	57°0'N	19°00'E
Østersøen, s., Eur. *see* Baltic Sea	192-93	57°0'N	19°00'E
Östersund, Swe. (ûs'tĕr-sōōnd)	184-85	63°11'N	14°39'E
Östhammar, Swe. (ûst'häm'är)	192-93	60°15'N	18°22'E
Ostrau, Czech Rep. *see* Ostrava	194-95	49°50'N	18°17'E
Ostrava, Czech Rep.	194-95	49°50'N	18°17'E
Ostrogozhsk, Russia (ôs-tr-gôzhk')	202-03	50°52'N	39°04'E
Ostrołęka, Pol. (ôs-trô-woN'kå)	194-95	53°05'N	21°35'E
Ostrov, Russia (ôs-trôf')	192-93	57°21'N	28°20'E
Ostrowiec Świętokrzyski, Pol. (ôs-trō'vyĕts shvyĕN-tō-kzhĭ'ske)	194-95	50°56'N	21°24'E
Ostrów Mazowiecka, Pol. (ôs'trōf mä-zô-vyĕt'skä)	194-95	52°48'N	21°54'E
Ostrów Wielkopolski, Pol. (ôs'trōōf vyĕl-kō-pōl'skē)	194-95	51°39'N	17°48'E
Ostsee, s., Eur. *see* Baltic Sea	192-93	57°0'N	19°00'E
Ostuni, Italy (ôs-tōō'nē)	200-01	40°45'N	17°33'E
Ōsumi-shotō, is., Japan	244	30°29'N	130°39'E
Osuna, Spain (ô-sōō'nä)	198-99	37°14'N	5°06'W
Oswego, N.Y., U.S.	116-17	43°27'N	76°31'W
Otaru, Japan (ô'tå-rò)	244	43°12'N	140°60'E
Otavalo, Ec. (ōtä-vä'lō)	170	0°14'N	78°16'W
Othonoí, i., Grc.	200-01	39°51'N	19°24'E
Oti, stm., Afr.	260-61	8°30'N	0°06'E
Otjiwarongo, Nmb. (ŏt-jē-wå-rôn'gō)	264-65	20°27'S	16°38'E
Otočac, Cro. (ō'tô-chàts)	200-01	44°52'N	15°13'E
Otoskwin, stm., On., Can.	134-35	52°11'N	87°45'W
Otra, stm., Nor.	192-93	58°09'N	8°01'E
Ótranto, Italy (ō'trän-tō) (ô-trän'tō)	200-01	40°09'N	18°28'E
Otranto, Canale d', strt., Eur. *see* Otranto, Strait of	200-01	40°0'N	19°00'E
Otranto, Strait of, strt., Eur. (strāt ŭv ō'trän-tô) (ô-trän'tō)	200-01	40°0'N	19°00'E
Otsego, Mi., U.S. (ŏt-sē'gō)	116-17	42°28'N	85°41'W
Ōtsu, Japan (ō'tsò)	245	35°00'N	135°52'E
Ottawa, Il., U.S. (ŏt'å-wå)	116-17	41°21'N	88°51'W
Ottawa, Ks., U.S. (ŏt'å-wå)	120-21	38°37'N	95°16'W
Ottawa, Oh., U.S. (ŏt'å-wå)	116-17	41°01'N	84°02'W
Ottawa, nat. cap., On., Can. (ŏt'å-wå)	136-37	45°25'N	75°41'W
Ottawa, stm., Can. (ŏt'å-wå)	136-37	45°20'N	73°58'W
Ottawa Islands, is., Nu., Can.	130-31	59°30'N	80°10'W
Ottumwa, Ia., U.S. (ô-tŭm'wå)	114-15	41°01'N	92°24'W
Otway, Cape, c., Austl. (kāp ŏt'wā)	276	38°51'S	143°30'E
Otwock, Pol. (ôt'vôtsk)	194-95	52°07'N	21°16'E
Ou, stm., Laos	246-47	20°03'N	102°13'E
Ouachita Mountains, mts., U.S. (wŏsh'ĭ-tô moun'tĭnz)	120-21	34°40'N	94°25'W
Ouagadougou, nat. cap., Burkina (wä'gå-dōō'gōō)	260-61	12°23'N	1°32'W
Ouahigouya, Burkina (wä-ê-gōō'yä)	260-61	13°35'N	2°25'W
Ouahran, Alg. *see* Oran	198-99	35°41'N	0°39'W
Ouaka, stm., C.A.R.	262-63	4°59'N	19°56'E
Ouandja, stm., C.A.R.	262-63	9°34'N	21°39'E
Ouara, stm., C.A.R.	262-63	5°06'N	24°29'E
Ouarâne, reg., Maur.	258-59	21°0'N	10°30'W
Ouargla, Alg.	188-89	31°56'N	5°22'E
Ouarzazate, Mor.	258-59	30°56'N	6°54'W
Oubangui, stm., Afr. (ōō-bäŋ'gē)	262-63	0°25'S	17°47'E
Oudtshoorn, S. Afr. (outs'hōrn)	264-65	33°36'S	22°12'E
Oued-Zem, Mor. (wĕd-zĕm')	269a	32°52'N	6°35'W
Ouémé, stm., Benin	260a	6°27'N	2°33'E
Ouesso, Congo	262-63	1°37'N	16°04'E
Ouezzane, Mor. (wĕ-zan')	269a	34°48'N	5°34'W
Ouham, stm., Afr.	260-61	9°17'N	18°16'E
Oujda, Mor.	184-85	34°41'N	1°54'W
Oulu, Fin. (ō'lò)	184-85	65°01'N	25°28'E
Oulujärvi, lk., Fin.	184-85	64°18'N	27°08'E
Oulujoki, stm., Fin.	184-85	65°01'N	25°29'E
Oum er Rbia, Oued, stm., Mor.	269a	33°20'N	8°20'W
Ouray, Co., U.S. (ōō-rā')	118-19	38°02'N	107°40'W
Ourense, Spain	198-99	42°20'N	7°52'W
Ourinhos, Braz. (ôò-rē'nyôs)	168-69	22°59'S	49°52'W
Ouro Fino, Braz. (ōŭ-rō-fē'nō)	172	22°17'S	46°22'W
Ouro Preto, Braz. (ō'rò prā'tò)	172	20°23'S	43°30'W
Outaouais, stm., Can. *see* Ottawa	136-37	45°20'N	73°58'W
Outardes, stm., Qc., Can.	138-39	49°03'N	68°30'W
Outlook, Sk., Can.	134-35	51°30'N	107°03'W
Ouvéa, i., N. Cal.	279g	20°33'S	166°34'E
Ouyen, Austl. (ōō-ĕn)	276	35°04'S	142°19'E
Ovalau, i., Fiji	279f	17°40'S	178°48'E
Ovalle, Chile (ō-väl'yä)	168-69	30°36'S	71°12'W
Ovar, Port. (ô-vär')	198-99	40°52'N	8°37'W
Övertorneå, Swe.	184-85	66°23'N	23°39'E
Oviedo, Spain (ō-vē-ā'dhō)	198-99	43°22'N	5°51'W
Owando, Congo	262-63	0°29'S	15°55'E
Owase, Japan (ō'wä-shē)	245	34°04'N	136°12'E
Owego, N.Y., U.S. (ō-wē'gō)	116-17	42°07'N	76°16'W
Owen, Wi., U.S. (ō'ĕn)	114-15	44°57'N	90°33'W
Owen Falls Dam, d., Ug. *see* Nalubaale Dam	267	0°27'N	33°11'E
Owensboro, Ky., U.S. (ō'ĕnz-bŭr-ô)	116-17	37°46'N	87°06'W
Owen Sound, On., Can. (ō'ĕn sound)	136-37	44°34'N	80°56'W
Owen Stanley Range, mts., Pap. N. Gui. (ō'ĕn stăn'lē rānj)	277	9°20'S	147°55'E
Owensville, Mo., U.S. (ō'ĕnz-vĭl)	120-21	38°21'N	91°30'W
Owenton, Ky., U.S. (ō'ĕn-tŭn)	116-17	38°32'N	84°50'W
Owerri, Nig. (ô-wĕr'ē)	260a	5°29'N	7°01'E
Owo, Nig.	260a	7°12'N	5°35'E
Owosso, Mi., U.S. (ô-wŏs'ō)	116-17	42°60'N	84°10'W
Owyhee, stm., U.S. (ô-wī'hē)	112-13	43°48'N	117°02'W
Oxbow, Sk., Can.	134-35	49°14'N	102°11'W
Oxford, N.S., Can. (ŏks'fērd)	138-39	45°43'N	63°53'W
Oxford, Eng., U.K. (ŏks'fērd)	190-91	51°46'N	1°16'W
Oxford, Al., U.S. (ŏks'fērd)	124-25	33°36'N	85°50'W
Oxford, Ms., U.S. (ŏks'fērd)	124-25	34°21'N	89°33'W
Oxford, N.C., U.S. (ŏks'fērd)	124-25	36°19'N	78°35'W
Oxford, Oh., U.S. (ŏks'fērd)	116-17	39°30'N	84°45'W
Oxford Lake, lk., Mb., Can. (ŏks'fērd lāk)	134-35	54°49'N	95°29'W
Oxkutzcab, Mex. (ôx-kōō'tz-käb)	148	20°18'N	89°25'W
Oxnard, Ca., U.S. (ŏks'närd)	118-19	34°12'N	119°11'W
Oxus, stm., Asia *see* Amu Darya	226	44°14'N	59°41'E
Oyapok, stm., S.A. (ō-yå-pŏk')	164-65	4°10'N	51°37'W
Oyem, Gabon	260-61	1°36'N	11°35'E
Oyo, Nig. (ō'yō)	260a	7°50'N	3°56'E
Oyonnax, Fr. (ô-yô-näks')	196-97	46°16'N	5°39'E
Oyyl, stm., Kaz.	226	48°33'N	52°25'E
Ozamis, Phil.	250	8°09'N	123°49'E
Ozark, Al., U.S. (ō'zärk)	124-25	31°28'N	85°38'W
Ozark, Ar., U.S. (ō'zärk)	120-21	35°29'N	93°50'W
Ozark, Mo., U.S. (ō'zärk)	120-21	37°01'N	93°12'W
Ozark Plateau, plat., U.S. (ō'zärk plä-tō')	120-21	37°0'N	93°00'W
Ozarks, Lake of the, res., Mo., U.S. (lāk ŭv thå ō'zärksz)	120-21	38°06'N	92°44'W
Ozernovskiy, Russia	218-19	51°30'N	156°31'E
Ozery, Russia (ô-zyô'rê)	202-03	54°51'N	38°33'E
Ozorków, Pol. (ô-zôr'kôf)	194-95	51°58'N	19°18'E

P

Feature (Pronunciation)	Page	Lat.	Long.
Paama, i., Vanuatu	279g	16°29'S	168°14'E
Paarl, S. Afr. (pärl)	264-65	33°44'S	18°58'E
Pabianice, Pol. (pä-byå-nē'tsĕ)	194-95	51°40'N	19°21'E
Pābna, Bngl.	234-35	24°00'N	89°14'E
Pacaraima, Serra, mts., S.A. (sĕr'rå pä-kä-rä-ē'må) *see* Pakaraima Mountains	164-65	5°06'N	60°39'W
Pacaraima, Sierra de, mts., S.A. *see* Pakaraima Mountains	164-65	5°06'N	60°39'W
Pacasmayo, Peru (pä-käs-mä'yō)	170	7°24'S	79°33'W
Pachmarhi, India	234-35	22°28'N	78°26'E
Pachuca de Soto, Mex.	146-47	20°06'N	98°45'W
Pacific Ocean, oc., (på-sĭf'ĭk ōshŭn)	20-21	10°0'S	150°00'W

PRONOUNCING INDEX

Pacific Ranges – Parker 367

Feature (Pronunciation)	Page	Lat.	Long.
Pacific Ranges, mts., B.C., Can. (pȧ-sĭf´ĭk rānjĕz)	**132-33**	51°11'N	125°33'W
Pacific Rim National Park Reserve, n.p., B.C., Can. (pȧ-sĭf´ĭk rĭm năsh´ŭn-ăl pärk rĭ-zûrv´)	**132-33**	48°45'N	125°06'W
Padang, Indon.	**246-47**	0°57'S	100°22'E
Padang, Indon. (pä-däng´)	**246-47**	1°39'S	108°55'E
Padangsidempuan, Indon.	**246-47**	1°23'N	99°16'E
Paden City, W.V., U.S. (pā´dĕn sĭ´tĭ)	**116-17**	39°37'N	80°51'W
Paderborn, Ger. (pä-dĕr-bôrn´)	**194-95**	51°43'N	8°45'E
Padma, stm., Asia *see* Ganges	**234-35**	21°58'N	90°57'E
Padova, Italy (pä´dô-vä)	**200-01**	45°24'N	11°52'E
Padre Island, i., Tx., U.S. (pä´drā ī´lănd)	**122-23**	27°01'N	97°23'W
Padua, Italy (păd´ū-ȧ) *see* Padova	**200-01**	45°24'N	11°52'E
Paducah, Ky., U.S.	**124-25**	37°05'N	88°37'W
Paektu-san, mtn., Asia (pâk´tōō-sän´)	**243**	41°59'N	128°07'E
Pagadian, Phil.	**250**	7°50'N	123°25'E
Pagalu, i., Eq. Gui. *see* Annobón	**260-61**	1°26'S	5°37'E
Pagan, i., N. Mar. Is.	**280-81**	18°07'N	145°46'E
Pago Pago, nat. cap., Am. Sam. (pän´-gō pän´-gō)	**279b**	14°16'S	170°42'W
Pagosa Springs, Co., U.S. (pȧ-gō´sȧ sprĭngz)	**118-19**	37°16'N	107°02'W
Pāhala, Hi., U.S. (pä-hä´lä)	**127a**	19°12'N	155°28'W
Pahang, stm., Malay.	**246-47**	3°30'N	103°24'E
Pahlevī, Iran *see* Bandar-e Anzalī	**227**	37°28'N	49°28'E
Paide, Est. (pī´dĕ)	**192-93**	58°54'N	25°35'E
Päijänne, lk., Fin. (pĕ´ē-yĕn-nĕ)	**192-93**	61°35'N	25°30'E
Painesville, Oh., U.S. (pānz´vĭl)	**116-17**	41°43'N	81°15'W
Painted Desert, des., Az., U.S. (pānt´ĕd dĕs´ērt)	**118-19**	35°45'N	111°07'W
Paintsville, Ky., U.S. (pānts´vĭl)	**116-17**	37°48'N	82°49'W
Paisley, Scot., U.K. (pāz´lĭ)	**190-91**	55°51'N	4°25'W
Paita, Peru (pä-ē´tä)	**170**	5°06'S	81°06'W
Pajala, Swe.	**184-85**	67°13'N	23°23'E
Pakaraima Mountains, mts., S.A.	**164-65**	5°06'N	60°39'W
Pakistan, nation, Asia (pä´-kĭ-stän)	**206-07**	30°0'N	70°00'E
Pakistan, East, nation, Asia *see* Bangladesh	**206-07**	24°0'N	90°00'E
Pakokku, Mya. (pȧ-kŏk´kò)	**246-47**	21°19'N	95°06'E
Paks, Hung. (pôksh)	**194-95**	46°39'N	18°53'E
Pak Sane, Laos *see* Muang Pakxan	**246-47**	18°25'N	103°39'E
Pakxé, Laos	**246-47**	15°08'N	105°48'E
Pala, Chad	**262-63**	9°21'N	14°54'E
Palacios, Tx., U.S. (pä-lä´syōs)	**122-23**	28°42'N	96°13'W
Palaiseau, Fr. (pȧ-lĕ-zō´)	**196-97**	48°43'N	2°16'E
Palana, Russia	**218-19**	59°05'N	159°59'E
Palangkaraya, Indon.	**248-49**	2°10'S	113°54'E
Palani, India	**236**	10°27'N	77°31'E
Pālanpur, India (pä´lŭn-pōōr)	**234-35**	24°10'N	72°27'E
Palapye, Bots. (pȧ-läp´yĕ)	**264-65**	22°34'S	27°07'E
Palatka, Russia	**218-19**	60°06'N	150°57'E
Palatka, Fl., U.S. (pȧ-lăt´kȧ)	**124-25**	29°39'N	81°39'W
Palau, nation, Oc. (pä-lä´ô)	**280-81**	5°0'N	137°00'E
Palauig, Phil. (pȧ-lou´ēg)	**250**	15°26'N	119°56'E
Palawan, i., Phil. (pä-lä´wȧn)	**250**	9°30'N	118°30'E
Paldiski, Est. (päl´dĭ-skĭ)	**192-93**	59°20'N	24°06'E
Palembang, Indon. (pä-lĕm-bäng´)	**246-47**	2°58'S	104°46'E
Palencia, Spain (pä-lĕ´n-syä)	**198-99**	42°01'N	4°32'W
Palenque, Mex. (pä-lĕn´kā)	**148**	17°31'N	91°57'W
Palenque, hist., Mex.	**148**	17°30'N	91°60'W
Palenque, Punta, c., Dom. Rep. (pōō´n-tä pä-lĕn´kā)	**142-43**	18°15'N	70°09'W
Palermo, Italy (pä-lĕr´mô)	**200-01**	38°07'N	13°21'E
Palesse, reg., Eur. *see* Pripet Marshes	**194-95**	52°0'N	27°00'E
Palestine, Tx., U.S. (păl´ĕs-tīn)	**122-23**	31°45'N	95°38'W
Paletwa, Mya. (pŭ-lĕt´wä)	**246-47**	21°18'N	92°51'E
Pālghāt, India	**236**	10°46'N	76°39'E
Pāli, India	**234-35**	25°47'N	73°20'E
Palikir, nat. cap., Micron.	**280-81**	6°58'N	158°13'E
Pālitāna, India	**234-35**	21°31'N	71°49'E
Palizada, Mex. (pä-lē-zä´dä)	**148**	18°15'N	92°05'W
Palk Strait, strt., Asia (pôk strāt)	**236**	10°0'N	79°45'E
Palliser, Cape, c., N.Z.	**278**	41°37'S	175°17'E
Palma de Mallorca, Spain	**198-99**	39°34'N	2°39'E
Palmares, Braz. (päl-má´rĕs)	**163d**	8°41'S	35°36'W
Palmas, Braz. (päl´mäs)	**168-69**	26°30'S	52°01'W
Palmas, Braz.	**166-67**	10°06'S	48°20'W
Palma Soriano, Cuba (päl´mä-sô-rê-ä´nō)	**142-43**	20°13'N	75°59'W
Palmeira dos Índios, Braz. (pä-mā´rä-dôs-ē´n-dyôs)	**163d**	9°25'S	36°37'W
Palmeirinhas, Ponta das, c., Ang.	**264-65**	9°05'S	12°60'E
Palmer, Ak., U.S. (päm´ẽr)	**126**	61°32'N	149°05'W
Palmerston, at., Cook Is.	**280-81**	18°03'S	163°10'W

Feature (Pronunciation)	Page	Lat.	Long.
Palmerston, Cape, c., Austl.	**277**	21°33'S	149°28'E
Palmerston North, N.Z. (päm´ẽr-stŭn nôrth)	**278**	40°21'S	175°37'E
Palmetto, Fl., U.S. (pȧl-mĕt´ô)	**125a**	27°31'N	82°35'W
Palmi, Italy (päl´mē)	**200-01**	38°21'N	15°51'E
Palmira, Col. (päl-mē´rä)	**163c**	3°33'N	76°18'W
Palm Springs, Ca., U.S.	**118-19**	33°50'N	116°32'W
Palmyra, Syria *see* Tudmur	**228-29**	34°33'N	38°17'E
Palmyra, Mo., U.S. (păl-mī´rȧ)	**120-21**	39°48'N	91°31'W
Palmyra, N.Y., U.S. (păl-mī´rȧ)	**116-17**	43°03'N	77°14'W
Palmyra Atoll, at., Oc.	**280-81**	5°51'N	162°05'W
Palo Alto, Ca., U.S. (pä´lō äl´tō)	**118-19**	37°26'N	122°08'W
Paloe, Pulau, i., Indon.	**248-49**	8°20'S	121°43'E
Palopo, Indon.	**248-49**	3°00'S	120°11'E
Palos, Cabo de, c., Spain (ká´bô-dĕ-pä´lôs)	**198-99**	37°38'N	0°41'W
Palu, Indon.	**248-49**	0°54'S	119°52'E
Palu, Tur. (pä-loo´)	**227**	38°41'N	39°60'E
Paluan, Phil. (pä-lōō´än)	**250**	13°26'N	120°27'E
Pāmban Island, i., India	**236**	9°16'N	79°19'E
Pamekasan, Indon.	**248-49**	7°10'S	113°29'E
Pamiers, Fr. (pȧ-myā´)	**196-97**	43°07'N	1°36'E
Pamir, mts., Asia *see* Pamirs	**232-33**	38°0'N	73°00'E
Pāmīr, Daryā-ye, mts., Asia *see* Pamirs	**232-33**	38°0'N	73°00'E
Pamirs, mts., Asia (pä-mērz)	**232-33**	38°0'N	73°00'E
Pamlico Sound, strt., N.C., U.S. (păm´lĭ-kō sound)	**124-25**	35°20'N	75°55'W
Pampa, Tx., U.S. (păm´pȧ)	**120-21**	35°32'N	100°58'W
Pampa, reg., Arg. (päm´pȧ) *see* Pampas	**173**	35°0'S	63°00'W
Pampanga, stm., Phil. (päm-päŋ´gä)	**250**	14°46'N	120°39'E
Pampas, reg., Arg. (päm´päs)	**173**	35°0'S	63°00'W
Pampas, stm., Peru	**170**	13°25'S	73°13'W
Pampeluna, Spain *see* Pamplona	**198-99**	42°49'N	1°39'W
Pamplona, Col. (päm-plō´nä)	**164-65**	7°22'N	72°38'W
Pamplona, Spain (päm-plô´nä)	**198-99**	42°49'N	1°39'W
Pana, Il., U.S. (pā´nȧ)	**116-17**	39°23'N	89°05'W
Panagyurishte, Blg. (pȧ-nȧ-gyōō´rĕsh-tĕ)	**200-01**	42°30'N	24°12'E
Panaitan, Pulau, i., Indon.	**248-49**	6°36'S	105°12'E
Panaji, India	**236**	15°30'N	73°50'E
Panama, nation, N.A. (păn-ȧ-mä´ sĭ´tĭ)	**85**	9°0'N	80°00'W
Panamá, nat. cap., Pan. (păn-ȧ-mä´)	**150**	8°58'N	79°32'W
Panamá, Golfo de, b., Pan.	**150**	8°0'N	79°30'W
Panama, Gulf of, b., Pan. *see* Panamá, Golfo de	**150**	8°0'N	79°30'W
Panama, Isthmus of, isth., Pan. *see* Panamá, Istmo de	**150**	9°0'N	80°00'W
Panamá, Istmo de, isth., Pan.	**150**	9°0'N	80°00'W
Panama Canal, can., Pan.	**150**	9°23'N	79°56'W
Panama City, Fl., U.S. (păn-ȧ-mä´ sĭ´tĭ)	**124-25**	30°10'N	85°40'W
Panay, i., Phil. (pä-nī´)	**250**	11°15'N	122°30'E
Panay Gulf, b., Phil.	**250**	10°15'N	122°15'E
Pančevo, Serb. (pȧn´chĕ-vô)	**200-01**	44°53'N	20°40'E
Panevėžys, Lith. (pä´nyĕ-vāzh´ēs)	**192-93**	55°44'N	24°23'E
Pangani, stm., Tan. (pän-gä´nē)	**262-63**	5°24'S	38°57'E
Pangkalanbuun, Indon.	**248-49**	2°42'S	111°38'E
Pangkalpinang, Indon. (päng-käl´pē-näng´)	**246-47**	2°08'S	106°06'E
Pangnirtung, Nu., Can.	**128-29**	66°08'N	65°43'W
Pangong Tso, lk., Asia	**234-35**	33°45'N	78°42'E
Panguitch, Ut., U.S. (pän´gwĭch)	**118-19**	37°50'N	112°26'W
Pangutaran Group, is., Phil.	**250**	6°14'N	120°39'E
Panhame, stm., Afr. *see* Manyame	**264-65**	15°37'S	30°39'E
Pānīpat, India	**234-35**	29°23'N	76°58'E
Panj, stm., Asia	**232-33**	37°00'N	68°16'E
Panjgūr, Pak.	**232-33**	26°58'N	64°05'E
Panjim, India *see* Panaji	**236**	15°30'N	73°50'E
Panna, India	**234-35**	24°43'N	80°11'E
Pannirtuuq, Nu., Can. *see* Pangnirtung	**128-29**	66°08'N	65°43'W
Pantar, Pulau, i., Indon. (pōō-lou pän´tär)	**248-49**	8°25'S	124°07'E
Pantelleria, Isola di, i., Italy (ē´sō-lä-dē-pän-tĕl-lå-rē´ä)	**200-01**	36°47'N	12°00'E
Pante Makasar, E. Timor	**248-49**	9°13'S	124°21'E
Pánuco, Mex. (pä´nōō-kô)	**146-47**	22°02'N	98°11'W
Pánuco, stm., Mex. (pä´nōō-kô)	**146-47**	22°16'N	97°47'W
Panxian, China	**238-39**	25°49'N	104°35'E
Panzós, Guat. (pä-zōs´)	**148**	15°24'N	89°39'W
Paoli, In., U.S. (pā-ō´lĭ)	**116-17**	38°33'N	86°28'W
Pápa, Hung. (pä´pô)	**194-95**	47°20'N	17°28'E
Papagayo, Golfo de, b., C.R. (gôl-fô-dĕ-pä-pä-gá´yō)	**149**	10°42'N	85°50'W
Papantla de Olarte, Mex. (pä-pän´tlä dā-ō-lä´r-tĕ)	**146-47**	20°27'N	97°19'W

Feature (Pronunciation)	Page	Lat.	Long.
Papeete, nat. cap., Fr. Poly. (pä-pē´-tē)	**279d**	17°32'S	149°34'W
Papenburg, Ger. (päp´ĕn-bôrgh)	**194-95**	53°06'N	7°24'E
Papua, Gulf of, b., Pap. N. Gui. (gŭlf ŭv păp-ōō-ȧ)	**277**	8°30'S	145°00'E
Papua New Guinea, nation, Oc. (păp-ōō-ȧ nū gĭne)	**277**	6°0'S	147°00'E
Papudo, Chile (pä-pōō´dô)	**163e**	32°31'S	71°28'W
Papun, Mya.	**246-47**	18°04'N	97°27'E
Pará, Braz. *see* Belém	**166-67**	1°27'S	48°29'W
Pará, state, Braz.	**166-67**	4°0'S	53°00'W
Pará, stm., Braz.	**166-67**	1°29'S	48°49'W
Paraburdoo, Austl.	**270-71**	23°12'S	117°44'E
Paracatu, Braz. (pä-rä-kä-tōō´)	**172**	17°14'S	46°52'W
Paracatu, stm., Braz.	**168-69**	16°35'S	45°06'W
Paracel Islands, is., China	**224-25**	15°46'N	112°17'E
Paraćin, Serb. (pá´rä-chēn)	**200-01**	43°52'N	21°25'E
Pāradwīp, India	**234-35**	20°17'N	86°41'E
Paragould, Ar., U.S. (păr´ȧ-gōōld)	**124-25**	36°04'N	90°30'W
Paraguá, stm., Bol.	**166-67**	13°32'S	61°49'W
Paragua, stm., Ven.	**164-65**	6°56'N	62°55'W
Paraguaçu, stm., Braz. (pä-rä-gwä-zōō´)	**166-67**	12°50'S	38°48'W
Paraguay, stm., S.A. (pä-rä-gwä´y)	**173**	27°19'S	58°36'W
Paraguai, stm., S.A. *see* Paraguay	**173**	27°19'S	58°36'W
Paraguaná, Península de, pen., Ven.	**164-65**	11°56'N	70°03'W
Paraguarí, Para.	**168-69**	25°37'S	57°09'W
Paraguay, nation, S.A. (păr´ȧ-gwā)	**158**	23°0'S	58°00'W
Parahyba, Braz. *see* João Pessoa	**163d**	7°07'S	34°52'W
Paraíba, Braz. *see* João Pessoa	**163d**	7°07'S	34°52'W
Paraíba, state, Braz. (pä-rä-ē´bä)	**163d**	7°15'S	36°30'W
Paraíba do Sul, stm., Braz.	**172**	21°37'S	41°02'W
Paraíso, Mex.	**146-47**	18°23'N	93°14'W
Paraiso, Pan. (pä-rä-ē´sō)	**150**	9°03'N	79°38'W
Parakou, Benin (pȧ-rȧ-kōō´)	**260-61**	9°20'N	2°37'E
Paramaribo, nat. cap., Sur. (pȧ-rȧ-má´rē-bō)	**164-65**	5°49'N	55°10'W
Paramirim, Braz.	**166-67**	13°27'S	42°14'W
Paramushir, Ostrov, i., Russia	**218-19**	50°25'N	155°50'E
Paraná, Arg. (pä-ä-nä´)	**173**	31°44'S	60°31'W
Paranã, Braz.	**166-67**	12°33'S	47°52'W
Paraná, state, Braz.	**168-69**	24°0'S	51°00'W
Paranã, stm., Braz.	**166-67**	12°30'S	48°14'W
Paraná, stm., S.A. (pä-ä-nä´)	**168-69**	33°48'S	59°14'W
Paranaguá, Braz.	**172**	25°31'S	48°31'W
Paranaguá, Baía de, b., Braz.	**172**	25°27'S	48°22'W
Paranaíba, Braz. (pä-rä-nȧ-ē´bȧ)	**168-69**	19°41'S	51°11'W
Paranaíba, stm., Braz. (pä-rä-nȧ-ē´bȧ)	**168-69**	20°08'S	51°00'W
Paranapanema, stm., Braz. (pä-rä´nȧ´pä-nĕ-mä)	**168-69**	22°42'S	53°10'W
Paranavaí, Braz.	**168-69**	23°04'S	52°29'W
Parapara, Ven. (pä-rä-pä-rä)	**163b**	9°44'N	67°17'W
Paray-le-Monial, Fr. (pȧ-rĕ´lē-mô-nyäl´)	**196-97**	46°27'N	4°07'E
Pārbati, stm., India	**234-35**	25°51'N	76°33'E
Parbhani, India	**236**	19°16'N	76°46'E
Pardo, stm., Braz. (pär´dō)	**166-67**	15°39'S	38°57'W
Pardo, stm., Braz. (pär´dō)	**172**	20°09'S	48°37'W
Pardubice, Czech Rep. (pär´dò-bĭt-sĕ)	**194-95**	50°02'N	15°46'E
Parece Vela, i., Japan *see* Okino-Tori-shima	**222-23**	20°27'N	136°04'E
Parent, Qc., Can.	**136-37**	47°56'N	74°37'W
Parepare, Indon.	**248-49**	4°01'S	119°38'E
Paria, Golfo de, b., (gôl-fô-dĕ-br-pä-rē-ä) *see* Paria, Gulf of	**140-41**	10°20'N	62°00'W
Paria, Gulf of, b.,	**140-41**	10°20'N	62°00'W
Paricutín, vol., Mex.	**146-47**	19°28'N	102°15'W
Parima, Serra, mts., S.A. (sĕr´rȧ pä-rē´mȧ) *see* Parima, Sierra	**164-65**	3°24'N	64°10'W
Parima, Sierra, mts., S.A.	**164-65**	3°24'N	64°10'W
Pariñas, Punta, c., Peru (pōō´n-tä-pä-rē´n-yäs)	**170**	4°40'S	81°20'W
Parintins, Braz. (pä-rĭn-tĭnzh´)	**166-67**	2°37'S	56°45'W
Paris, Ar., U.S. (păr´ĭs)	**120-21**	35°18'N	93°44'W
Paris, Il., U.S. (păr´ĭs)	**116-17**	39°37'N	87°42'W
Paris, Ky., U.S. (păr´ĭs)	**116-17**	38°12'N	84°16'W
Paris, Mo., U.S. (păr´ĭs)	**120-21**	39°29'N	92°00'W
Paris, Tn., U.S. (păr´ĭs)	**124-25**	36°18'N	88°20'W
Paris, Tx., U.S. (păr´ĭs)	**120-21**	33°40'N	95°33'W
Paris, nat. cap., Fr. (pȧ-rē´)	**196-97**	48°52'N	2°21'E
Parita, Bahía de, b., Pan. (bä-ē´ä-dĕ-pä-rē´tä)	**150**	8°08'N	80°24'W
Park City, Ks., U.S. (pärk sĭ´tĕ)	**120-21**	37°48'N	97°18'W
Parker, Co., U.S. (pär´kẽr pärk)	**120-21**	39°31'N	104°46'W
Parker, S.D., U.S. (pär´kẽr pärk)	**114-15**	43°24'N	97°08'W

n-sing; ŋ-baŋk; ɴ-nasalized n; nŏd; cŏmmit; ōld; ôbey; ôrder; oi-boil; fōōd; ò-as oo in foot; ou-out; s-soft; sh-dish; th-thin; pūre; ûnite; ûrn; stŭd; circŭs; ü-as in French tu; ´-indeterminate vowel.

368 Parkersburg – Perleberg PRONOUNCING INDEX

Feature (Pronunciation)	Page	Lat.	Long.
Parkersburg, W.V., U.S. (pär'kẽrz-bûrg)	116-17	39°15'N	81°33'W
Parkes, Austl. (pärks)	276	33°09'S	148°10'E
Park Falls, Wi., U.S. (pärk fôlz)	114-15	45°56'N	90°26'W
Park Range, mts., Co., U.S. (pärk rānj)	112-13	40°40'N	106°40'W
Park Rapids, Mn., U.S. (pärk răp'ĭdz)	114-15	46°55'N	95°04'W
Park River, N.D., U.S. (pärk rĭv'ẽr)	114-15	48°24'N	97°45'W
Parkston, S.D., U.S. (pärks'tŭn)	114-15	43°24'N	97°59'W
Parla, Spain (pär'lä)	198-99	40°14'N	3°46'W
Parlākimidi, India	236	18°47'N	84°06'E
Parma, Italy (pär'mä)	200-01	44°49'N	10°20'E
Parnaguá, Braz.	166-67	10°13'S	44°38'W
Parnaíba, Braz. (pär-nä-ē'bä)	166-67	2°54'S	41°47'W
Parnaíba, stm., Braz. (pär-nä-ē'bä)	166-67	2°46'S	41°50'W
Parnassós, mtn., Grc.	200-01	38°32'N	22°35'E
Pärnu, Est. (pĕr'nōō)	192-93	58°22'N	24°33'E
Paroo, stm., Austl. (pä'rōō)	276	30°23'S	143°59'E
Parowan, Ut., U.S. (păr'ô-wăn)	118-19	37°51'N	112°50'W
Parral, Chile (pär-rä'l)	171	36°09'S	71°50'W
Parramatta, Austl.	276	33°49'S	151°00'E
Parras de la Fuente, Mex.	122-23	25°27'N	102°10'W
Parrsboro, N.S., Can. (pärz'bŭr-ô)	138-39	45°25'N	64°20'W
Parry, Cape, c., N.T., Can.	130-31	70°08'N	124°24'W
Parry, Mount, mtn., B.C., Can. (mount păr'ĭ)	132-33	52°53'N	128°45'W
Parry Sound, On., Can. (păr'ĭ sound)	136-37	45°20'N	80°02'W
Parsnip, stm., B.C., Can. (pärs'nĭp)	132-33	55°10'N	123°02'W
Parsons, Ks., U.S. (pär's'nz)	120-21	37°20'N	95°16'W
Parsons, W.V., U.S. (pär's'nz)	116-17	39°06'N	79°41'W
Parthenay, Fr. (pár-t'nĕ')	196-97	46°39'N	0°15'W
Partinico, Italy (pär-tē'nē-kô)	200-01	38°03'N	13°07'E
Paru, stm., Braz.	166-67	1°35'S	52°31'W
Parys, S. Afr. (pá-rīs')	269c	26°54'S	27°28'E
Pasadena, Ca., U.S. (păs-à-dē'nà)	118-19	34°09'N	118°09'W
Pasaje, Ec.	170	3°20'S	79°48'W
Pa Sak, stm., Thai.	246-47	14°21'N	100°35'E
Pascagoula, Ms., U.S. (păs-kà-gōō'là)	124-25	30°22'N	88°33'W
Pascagoula, stm., Ms., U.S. (păs-kà-gōō'là)	124-25	30°22'N	88°37'W
Paşcani, Rom. (päsh-kän')	194-95	47°15'N	26°44'E
Pasco, Wa., U.S. (păs'kō)	112-13	46°14'N	119°05'W
Pascua, Isla de, i., Chile	282-83	27°07'S	109°22'W
Pasni, Pak.	232-33	25°16'N	63°27'E
Paso de Indios, Arg.	171	43°51'S	68°56'W
Paso de los Libres, Arg. (pä-sô-dĕ-lôs-lē'brĕs)	173	29°42'S	57°09'W
Paso de los Toros, Ur. (pä-sô-dĕ-lôs tō'rôs)	173	32°49'S	56°31'W
Paso Robles, Ca., U.S. (pă'sō rō'blĕs)	118-19	35°38'N	120°41'W
Passaic, N.J., U.S. (pă-sā'ĭk)	116-17	40°52'N	74°08'W
Passau, Ger. (päsou)	194-95	48°34'N	13°27'E
Passero, Capo, c., Italy (kä'pō päs-sĕ'rô)	200-01	36°40'N	15°09'E
Passo Fundo, Braz. (pä'sō fōn'dō)	168-69	28°15'S	52°25'W
Passos, Braz. (pä's-sōs)	172	20°43'S	46°37'W
Pastaza, stm., S.A. (päs-tä'zä)	170	4°55'S	76°24'W
Pasto, Col. (päs'tô)	164-65	1°12'N	77°16'W
Pasuruan, Indon.	248-49	7°38'S	112°54'E
Pasvalys, Lith. (päs-vä-lēs')	192-93	56°04'N	24°24'E
Patagonia, reg., Arg. (păt-à-gō'nĭ-à)	171	44°0'S	68°00'W
Pātan, India	234-35	23°51'N	72°07'E
Pate Island, i., Kenya	262-63	2°06'S	41°03'E
Paterson, N.J., U.S. (păt'ẽr-sŭn)	116-17	40°55'N	74°10'W
Pathānkot, India	234-35	32°16'N	75°39'E
Pathein, Mya.	246-47	16°46'N	94°44'E
Pathfinder Reservoir, res., Wy., U.S. (păth'fīn-dẽr rĕ'sẽr-vwär)	112-13	42°25'N	106°55'W
Patiāla, India (pŭt-ē-ä'lŭ)	234-35	30°19'N	76°23'E
Pātkai Range, mts., Asia	238-39	27°0'N	96°00'E
Patna, India	234-35	25°36'N	85°07'E
Patnanongan Island, i., Phil. (pät-nä-nôn'gän ī'lànd)	250	14°48'N	122°11'E
Pato Branco, Braz.	168-69	26°14'S	52°41'W
Patos, Braz. (pä'tōzh)	163d	7°01'S	37°16'W
Patos, Lagoa dos, b., Braz. (lä'gō-à dozh pä'tōzh)	168-69	31°06'S	51°15'W
Patos de Minas, Braz. (pä'tōzh dĕ-mē'näzh)	172	18°35'S	46°31'W
Patquía, Arg.	168-69	30°02'S	66°52'W
Pátra, Grc.	200-01	38°14'N	21°44'E
Patricio Lynch, Isla, i., Chile	171	48°37'S	75°26'W
Patrocínio, Braz. (pä-trō-sē'nē-ō)	172	18°56'S	46°60'W
Pattani, Thai. (pät'á-nĕ)	246-47	6°52'N	101°15'E
Patten, Me., U.S. (păt''n)	117a	45°59'N	68°27'W
Patterson, La., U.S. (păt'ẽr-sŭn)	124-25	29°42'N	91°18'W
Patuca, stm., Hond.	149	15°48'N	84°18'W
Patuca, Punta, c., Hond. (pōō'n-tä-pä-tōō'kä)	149	15°49'N	84°18'W
Pátzcuaro, Mex. (päts'kwä-rô)	146-47	19°31'N	101°37'W
Pau, Fr. (pō)	196-97	43°18'N	0°22'W
Pauini, stm., Braz.	166-67	7°47'S	67°05'W
Pauk, Mya.	246-47	21°27'N	94°28'E
Paulding, Oh., U.S. (pôl'dĭng)	116-17	41°08'N	84°35'W
Paulis, D.R.C. *see* Isiro	262-63	2°46'N	27°37'E
Paulistana, Braz.	166-67	8°09'S	41°09'W
Paulo Afonso, Braz.	166-67	9°21'S	38°14'W
Paul Roux, S. Afr. (pôrl rōō)	269c	28°18'S	27°58'E
Pauls Valley, Ok., U.S. (pôlz văl'ē)	120-21	34°44'N	97°13'W
Paungde, Mya.	246-47	18°29'N	95°30'E
Pavia, Italy (pä-vē'ä)	200-01	45°12'N	9°10'E
Pavlodar, Kaz. (pàv-lô-dàr')	226	52°17'N	76°59'E
Pavlovo, Russia	186-87	55°57'N	43°04'E
Pavuvu Island, i., Sol. Is.	279e	9°03'S	159°06'E
Pawan, stm., Indon.	248-49	1°51'S	109°56'E
Pawhuska, Ok., U.S. (pô-hŭs'kà)	120-21	36°40'N	96°20'W
Pawnee, Ok., U.S. (pô-nē')	120-21	36°20'N	96°48'W
Pawnee, stm., Ks., U.S. (pô-nē')	120-21	38°10'N	99°06'W
Pawnee City, Ne., U.S. (pô-nē' sĭ'tē)	120-21	40°07'N	96°09'W
Paw Paw, Mi., U.S. (pô pô)	116-17	42°13'N	85°53'W
Pawtucket, R.I., U.S. (pô-tŭk'ĕt)	116-17	41°53'N	71°23'W
Paxton, Il., U.S. (păks'tŭn)	116-17	40°27'N	88°05'W
Payakumbuh, Indon.	246-47	0°14'S	100°38'E
Payette, Id., U.S. (pâ-ĕt')	112-13	44°05'N	116°56'W
Pay-Khey, Khrebet, mts., Russia	186-87	69°0'N	63°00'E
Paynesville, Mn., U.S. (pānz'vĭl)	114-15	45°23'N	94°43'W
Paysandú, Ur. (pī-sän-dōō')	173	32°20'S	58°05'W
Payson, Az., U.S. (pā's'n)	118-19	34°10'N	111°19'W
Pazardzhik, Blg. (pä-zàr-dzhek')	200-01	42°12'N	24°20'E
Peabody, Ks., U.S. (pē'bŏd-ĭ)	120-21	38°10'N	97°06'W
Peace, stm., Can. (pēs)	130-31	58°60'N	111°25'W
Peace, stm., Fl., U.S. (pēs)	125a	26°58'N	82°01'W
Peace River, Ab., Can. (pēs rĭv'ẽr)	132-33	56°15'N	117°16'W
Pearl, stm., U.S. (pûrl)	124-25	30°11'N	89°32'W
Pearland, Tx., U.S. (pûrl'ănd)	122-23	29°33'N	95°17'W
Pearl and Hermes Atoll, at., Hi., U.S.	127	27°55'N	175°45'W
Pearl Harbor, b., Hi., U.S. (pûrl här'bẽr)	127a	21°22'N	157°59'W
Pearsall, Tx., U.S. (pẽr'sôl)	122-23	28°54'N	99°06'W
Pebble Island, i., Falk. Is.	171	51°20'S	59°34'W
Peçanha, Braz. (pâ-kän'yà)	172	18°32'S	42°34'W
Pechenga, Russia (pyĕ'chĕŋ-gà)	184-85	69°34'N	31°14'E
Pechora, Russia	186-87	65°08'N	57°09'E
Pechora, stm., Russia (pyĕ-chô'rà)	186-87	67°59'N	53°56'E
Pechorskoye More, s., Russia	186-87	70°0'N	54°00'E
Pecos, Tx., U.S. (pā'kôs)	122-23	31°25'N	103°30'W
Pecos, stm., U.S. (pā'kôs)	110-11	29°42'N	101°22'W
Pécs, Hung. (pāch)	194-95	46°04'N	18°13'E
Pedernales, Ven.	143b	9°57'N	62°15'W
Pedra Azul, Braz. (pā'drä-zōō'l)	168-69	15°60'S	41°17'W
Pedreiras, Braz. (pĕ-drā'räs)	166-67	4°34'S	44°39'W
Pedro Afonso, Braz.	166-67	8°60'S	48°10'W
Pedro II, Braz. (pā'drò sĕ-gòn'dò)	166-67	4°25'S	41°28'W
Pedro Juan Caballero, Para. (pĕ'drô hòà'n-kä-bäl-yĕ'rō)	168-69	22°33'S	55°45'W
Peebles, Scot., U.K. (pē'b'lz)	190-91	55°39'N	3°12'W
Peekskill, N.Y., U.S. (pēks'kĭl)	116-17	41°17'N	73°55'W
Peel, stm., Can.	130-31	67°42'N	134°31'W
Pegasus Bay, b., N.Z. (pĕg'à-sŭs bā)	278	43°20'S	173°00'E
Pegu, Mya. *see* Bago	246-47	17°20'N	96°29'E
Peiching, nat. cap., China *see* Beijing	240-41	39°55'N	116°22'E
Peipsi järv, lk., Eur. *see* Peipus, Lake	192-93	58°45'N	27°25'E
Peipus, Lake, lk., Eur. (lāk pī'pŭs)	192-93	58°45'N	27°25'E
Peiraiás, Grc.	200-01	37°57'N	23°39'E
Peixe, stm., Braz.	168-69	21°30'S	51°57'W
Pekalongan, Indon.	248-49	6°53'S	109°40'E
Pekanbaru, Indon.	246-47	0°31'N	101°27'E
Pekin, Il., U.S. (pē'kĭn)	116-17	40°34'N	89°39'W
Peking, nat. cap., China *see* Beijing	240-41	39°55'N	116°22'E
Pelagie, Isole, is., Italy	184-85	35°40'N	12°40'E
Pelat, Mont, mtn., Fr. (môn pē-là')	196-97	44°16'N	6°42'E
Peleduy, Russia (pyĕl-yĭ-dōō'ē)	218-19	59°39'N	112°44'E
Pelée, Montagne, vol., Mart. (môn-pē-lā' pĕ-lē')	143b	14°48'N	61°10'W
Pelee Island, i., On., Can. (pē'lē ī'lànd)	136-37	41°46'N	82°39'W
Peleliu, i., Palau *see* Beliliou	280-81	7°00'N	134°15'E
Peleng, Pulau, i., Indon.	248-49	1°15'S	123°08'E
Pelham, Ga., U.S. (pĕl'hăm)	124-25	31°08'N	84°09'W
Pelican Rapids, Mn., U.S. (pĕl'ĭ-kăn răp'ĭdz)	114-15	46°35'N	96°04'W
Pella, Ia., U.S. (pĕl'à)	114-15	41°25'N	92°55'W
Pellworm, i., Ger. (pĕl'vôrm)	194-95	54°31'N	8°38'E
Pelly, stm., Yk., Can. (pĕl'ĭ)	130-31	62°46'N	137°20'W
Pelly Crossing, Yk., Can.	128-29	62°50'N	136°35'W
Pelly Mountains, mts., Yk., Can. (pĕl'ĭ moun'tĭnz)	130-31	62°0'N	133°00'W
Peloponnesus, pen., Grc.	200-01	37°30'N	22°00'E
Pelopónnisos, pen., Grc. *see* Peloponnesus	200-01	37°30'N	22°00'E
Pelotas, Braz. (pā-lō'tāzh)	173	31°45'S	52°19'W
Pelotas, stm., Braz.	168-69	27°28'S	51°54'W
Pematangsiantar, Indon.	246-47	2°57'N	99°04'E
Pemba, Moz. (pĕm'bá)	264-65	13°01'S	40°32'E
Pemba, i., Tan. (pĕm'bá)	262-63	5°10'S	39°48'E
Pemberton, Austl.	270-71	34°27'S	116°01'E
Pembina, N.D., U.S. (pĕm'bĭ-ná)	114-15	48°58'N	97°15'W
Pembina, stm., Ab., Can. (pĕm'bĭ-ná)	132-33	54°45'N	114°17'W
Pembroke, On., Can. (pĕm'brŏk)	136-37	45°49'N	77°07'W
Pembroke, Cape, c., Nu., Can.	130-31	62°56'N	81°56'W
Pembuang, stm., Indon.	248-49	3°21'S	112°33'E
Peñalara, Pico de, mtn., Spain (pē'kō-dĕ-pā-nyä-lä'rä)	198-99	40°51'N	3°57'W
Penang, Malay. *see* George Town	246-47	5°25'N	100°20'E
Peñarroya-Pueblonuevo, Spain (pĕn-yär-rō'yä-pwĕ'blô-nwĕ'vô)	198-99	38°18'N	5°16'W
Peñas, Cabo de, c., Spain (kå'bô-dĕ-pā'nyäs)	198-99	43°39'N	5°51'W
Penas, Golfo de, b., Chile (gôl-fô-dĕ-pĕ'n-äs)	171	47°22'S	74°50'W
Pender, Ne., U.S. (pĕn'dẽr)	114-15	42°07'N	96°43'W
Pendjari, stm., Afr.	260-61	10°55'N	0°50'E
Pendleton, Or., U.S. (pĕn'd'l-tŭn)	112-13	45°40'N	118°48'W
Pend Oreille, Lake, lk., Id., U.S. (lāk pŏn-dô-rā') (lāk pĕn-dô-rĕl')	112-13	48°10'N	116°17'W
Penedo, Braz. (pâ-nā'dò)	163d	10°16'S	36°35'W
Penetanguishene, On., Can. (pĕn'ē-tăŋ-gĭ-shēn')	136-37	44°46'N	79°56'W
Penganga, stm., India	236	19°54'N	79°10'E
P'enghu, Tai. *see* Makung	225a	23°34'N	119°34'E
P'enghu Ch'üntao, is., Tai.	225a	23°30'N	119°30'E
Penglai, China (pŭŋ-lī)	240-41	37°48'N	120°43'E
Pengshui, China	238-39	29°18'N	108°09'E
Pengxian, China	238-39	30°59'N	103°56'E
Peniche, Port. (pĕ-nē'chå)	198-99	39°21'N	9°22'W
Penida, Nusa, i., Indon.	248-49	8°44'S	115°32'E
Pennines, mts., Eng., U.K. (pĕn-īn')	190-91	54°11'N	2°02'W
Pennsylvania, state, U.S. (pĕn-sĭl-vā'nĭ-à)	108-09	40°45'N	77°30'W
Penn Yan, N.Y., U.S. (pĕn yăn')	116-17	42°40'N	77°03'W
Penobscot, stm., Me., U.S.	117a	44°29'N	68°48'W
Penobscot Bay, b., Me., U.S. (pē-nŏb'skŏt bā)	117a	44°15'N	68°52'W
Penola, Austl.	276	37°23'S	140°50'E
Penonomé, Pan.	150	8°31'N	80°22'W
Penrhyn, at., Cook Is.	280-81	9°0'S	158°00'W
Pensacola, Fl., U.S. (pĕn-sà-kō'là)	124-25	30°25'N	87°13'W
Pensacola Mountains, mts., Ant.	287	84°21'S	47°02'W
Pensilvania, Col. (pĕn-sĕl-vá'nyä)	163c	5°32'N	75°03'W
Pentecost Island, i., Vanuatu (pĕn'tē-kŏst ī'lànd) *see* Pentecôte	279g	15°42'S	168°10'E
Pentecôte, i., Vanuatu	279g	15°42'S	168°10'E
Penticton, B.C., Can.	132-33	49°30'N	119°35'W
Pentland Firth, strt., Scot., U.K. (pĕnt'lànd fûrth)	190-91	58°44'N	3°07'W
Penyu, Kepulauan, is., Indon.	248-49	5°22'S	127°46'E
Penza, Russia (pĕn'zà)	186-87	53°12'N	45°00'E
Penzance, Eng., U.K. (pĕn-zăns')	190-91	50°07'N	5°33'W
Penzhina, stm., Russia (pyĭn-zē-nŭ)	218-19	62°29'N	165°15'E
People's Democratic Republic of Korea, nation, Asia *see* Korea, North	206-07	40°0'N	127°00'E
Peoria, Il., U.S. (pē-ō'rĭ-à)	116-17	40°41'N	89°36'W
Peotone, Il., U.S. (pē'ō-tōn)	116-17	41°20'N	87°47'W
Pequeñas Antillas, is., *see* Lesser Antilles	143b	15°0'N	61°00'W
Perabumulih, Indon.	246-47	3°27'S	104°15'E
Perak, stm., Malay.	246-47	3°58'N	100°53'E
Perdido, Monte, mtn., Spain (mōn-tå-pĕr-dē'dō)	198-99	42°40'N	0°05'E
Pereira, Col. (pā-rā'rä)	163c	4°50'N	75°42'W
Pereslavl'-Zalesskiy, Russia (pâ-râ-slàv''l zá-lyĕs'kĭ)	202-03	56°44'N	38°51'E
Pergamino, Arg. (pĕr-gä-mē'nō)	173	33°54'S	60°35'W
Perham, Mn., U.S. (pẽr'hăm)	114-15	46°36'N	95°35'W
Péribonka, stm., Qc., Can.	130-31	48°46'N	72°03'W
Périgueux, Fr. (pā-rē-gû')	196-97	45°11'N	0°43'E
Perito Moreno, Arg.	171	46°36'S	70°55'W
Perlas, Laguna de, b., Nic. (lä-gò'nä-dĕ-läs-pĕr'läs)	149	12°30'N	83°40'W
Perleberg, Ger. (pĕr'lē-bĕrg)	194-95	53°05'N	11°52'E

ăt; finȧl; rāte; senȧte; ärm; åsk; sofȧ; fâre; ch-choose; dh-as th in other; bē; ėvent; bĕt; recĕnt; cratẽr; g-gō; gh-guttural g; bĭt; ĭ-short neutral; rīde; κ-guttural k as ch in German ich;

PRONOUNCING INDEX

Perm' – Pioner, Ostrov 369

Feature (Pronunciation)	Page	Lat.	Long.
Perm', Russia (pĕrm)	186-87	58°00'N	56°16'E
Pernambuco, Braz. *see* Recife	163d	8°03'S	34°54'W
Pernambuco, state, Braz. (pĕr-näm-bōō´kō)	166-67	8°0'S	37°00'W
Pernik, Blg. (pĕr-nēk´)	200-01	42°37'N	23°03'E
Péronne, Fr. (pā-rôn´)	196-97	49°56'N	2°56'E
Perote, Mex. (pĕ-rô´tĕ)	146-47	19°34'N	97°15'W
Perpignan, Fr. (pĕr-pē-nyän´)	196-97	42°42'N	2°53'E
Perros, Bahía de, strt., Cuba (bä-ē´ä-dĕ-pā´rōs)	142-43	22°21'N	78°31'W
Perry, Fl., U.S. (pĕr´ĭ)	124-25	30°07'N	83°35'W
Perry, Ga., U.S. (pĕr´ĭ)	124-25	32°28'N	83°44'W
Perry, Ia., U.S. (pĕr´ĭ)	114-15	41°51'N	94°07'W
Perry, N.Y., U.S. (pĕr´ĭ)	116-17	42°43'N	78°01'W
Perry, Ok., U.S. (pĕr´ĭ)	120-21	36°17'N	97°17'W
Perrysburg, Oh., U.S. (pĕr ĭz-bûrg)	116-17	41°34'N	83°37'W
Perryton, Tx., U.S. (pĕr´ĭ-tŭn)	120-21	36°23'N	100°49'W
Perryville, Mo., U.S. (pĕr-ĭ-vĭl)	120-21	37°43'N	89°52'W
Persepolis, hist., Iran (pĕr-sĕpô-lĭs)	230-31	29°57'N	52°52'E
Persia, nation, Asia *see* Iran	206-07	32°0'N	53°00'E
Persian Gulf, b., Asia (pûr´zhăn gŭlf)	230-31	27°0'N	51°00'E
Perth, Austl. (pûrth)	270-71	31°57'S	115°51'E
Perth, On., Can. (pûrth)	136-37	44°55'N	76°15'W
Perth, Scot., U.K. (pûrth)	190-91	56°24'N	3°27'W
Perth Amboy, N.J., U.S. (pûrth ăm´boi)	116-17	40°31'N	74°14'W
Pertuis, Fr. (pĕr-tüē´)	196-97	43°42'N	5°30'E
Peru, Il., U.S. (pē-rōō´)	116-17	41°20'N	89°07'W
Peru, In., U.S. (pē-rōō´)	116-17	40°45'N	86°03'W
Peru, nation, S.A. (pē-rōō´)	158	10°0'S	76°00'W
Perugia, Italy (pā-rōō´jä)	200-01	43°07'N	12°22'E
Pervomais'k, Ukr.	202-03	48°03'N	30°51'E
Pervouralsk, Russia (pĕr-vô-ô-rälsk´)	218-19	56°55'N	59°57'E
Pesaro, Italy (pā´zä-rō)	200-01	43°55'N	12°55'E
Pescadores, is., Tai. *see* P'enghu Ch'üntao	225a	23°30'N	119°30'E
Pescara, Italy (päs-kä´rä)	200-01	42°29'N	14°12'E
Peshāwar, Pak. (pĕ-shä´wŭr)	232-33	33°60'N	71°33'E
Peshtigo, Wi., U.S. (pĕsh´tē-gō)	116-17	45°03'N	87°44'W
Pesqueira, Braz.	163d	8°22'S	36°42'W
Pesyakov, Ostrov, i., Russia	186-87	68°45'N	57°41'E
Petacalco, Bahía, b., Mex. (bä-ē´ä-dĕ-pĕ-tä-käl´kô)	146-47	17°56'N	101°57'W
Petah Tiqwa, Isr.	228-29	32°06'N	34°54'E
Petaluma, Ca., U.S. (pĕt-à-lò´mà)	118-19	38°14'N	122°38'W
Petare, Ven. (pĕ-tä´rĕ)	163b	10°29'N	66°49'W
Petatlán, Mex. (pā-tä-tlän´)	146-47	17°31'N	101°16'W
Peterborough, Austl.	276	32°58'S	138°50'E
Peterborough, On., Can. (pē´tĕr-bŭr-ô)	136-37	44°18'N	78°20'W
Peterhead, Scot., U.K. (pē-tĕr-hĕd´)	190-91	57°31'N	1°47'W
Peter Pond Lake, lk., Sk., Can. (pē´tĕr pŏnd lāk)	134-35	56°06'N	109°06'W
Petersburg, Ak., U.S. (pē´tērz-bûrg)	126	56°48'N	132°57'W
Petersburg, Il., U.S. (pē´tērz-bûrg)	120-21	40°00'N	89°50'W
Petersburg, In., U.S. (pē´tērz-bûrg)	116-17	38°29'N	87°17'W
Petersburg, Va., U.S. (pē´tērz-bûrg)	124-25	37°14'N	77°24'W
Petersburg, W.V., U.S. (pē´tērz-bûrg)	116-17	38°59'N	79°08'W
Peter the Great Bay, b., Russia *see* Petra Velikogo, Zaliv	244	42°40'N	132°00'E
Petitcodiac, N.B., Can. (pē-tē-kō-dyåk´)	138-39	45°56'N	65°11'W
Petit-Goâve, Haiti (pĕ-tē´ gô-àv´)	142-43	18°26'N	72°51'W
Petlalcingo, Mex. (pĕ-tläl-sēŋ´gô)	146-47	18°04'N	97°56'W
Peto, Mex. (pĕ´tô)	148	20°08'N	88°54'W
Petorca, Chile (pā-tōr´kä)	163e	32°15'S	70°57'W
Petoskey, Mi., U.S. (pē-tŏs-kĭ)	116-17	45°22'N	84°57'W
Petra Velikogo, Zaliv, b., Russia	244	42°40'N	132°00'E
Petrich, Blg. (pā´trĭch)	200-01	41°24'N	23°13'E
Petrified Forest National Park, n.p., Az., U.S. (pĕt´rĭ-fīd fŏr´ĕst năsh´ŭn-ăl pärk)	118-19	34°54'N	109°47'W
Petrinja, Cro. (pā´trēn-yȧ)	200-01	45°27'N	16°16'E
Petrodvorets, Russia (pyĕ-trô-dvô-ryĕts´)	192-93	59°53'N	29°52'E
Petrolia, On., Can. (pē-trō´lĭ-à)	136-37	42°53'N	82°09'W
Petrolina, Braz. (pĕ-trō-lē´nà)	166-67	9°24'S	40°30'W
Petropavlovsk, Kaz. (pyĕ-trô-päv´lôvsk)	226	54°52'N	69°09'E
Petropavlovsk-Kamchatskiy, Russia (pyĕ-trô-päv´lôvsk käm-chät´skĭ)	218-19	53°01'N	158°41'E
Petrópolis, Braz. (på-trô-pô-lēzh´)	172	22°31'S	43°10'W
Petroșani, Rom.	200-01	45°25'N	23°23'E
Petrovgrad, Serb. *see* Zhovti Vody	200-01	45°23'N	20°24'E
Petrovsk, Russia (pyĕ-trôfsk´)	186-87	52°19'N	45°23'E
Petrovsk-Zabaykal'skiy, Russia (pyĕ-trôfskzä-bī-käl´skĭ)	240-41	51°16'N	108°50'E
Petrozavodsk, Russia (pyā´trô-zà-vôtsk´)	186-87	61°47'N	34°21'E
Petrozsény, Rom. *see* Petroșani	200-01	45°25'N	23°23'E
Petukhovo, Russia	226	55°04'N	67°54'E
Pevek, Russia	218-19	69°41'N	170°21'E
Peza, stm., Russia (pyå´zà)	186-87	65°36'N	44°37'E
Pézenas, Fr. (pā-zē-nä´)	196-97	43°27'N	3°26'E
Pforzheim, Ger. (pfôrts´hīm)	194-95	48°54'N	8°42'E
Pha-an, Mya.	246-47	16°53'N	97°38'E
Phangan, Ko, i., Thai.	246-47	9°45'N	100°01'E
Phangnga, Thai.	246-47	8°27'N	98°32'E
Phanom Dong Rak, Thiu Khao, mts., Asia *see* Phanom Dongrak Range	246-47	14°25'N	103°30'E
Phanom Dongrak Range, mts., Asia	246-47	14°25'N	103°30'E
Phan Rang, Viet.	246-47	11°34'N	108°60'E
Phan Si Pan, mtn., Viet. *see* Fan Si Pan	246-47	22°15'N	103°46'E
Phan Thiet, Viet.	246-47	10°56'N	108°06'E
Phenix City, Al., U.S. (fē´nĭks sĭ´tĭ)	124-25	32°28'N	85°01'W
Phetchabun, Thiu Khao, mts., Thai.	246-47	16°32'N	100°55'E
Philadelphia, Ms., U.S. (fĭl-à-dĕl´phĭ-à)	124-25	32°46'N	89°07'W
Philadelphia, Pa., U.S. (fĭl-à-dĕl´phĭ-à)	116-17	39°57'N	75°10'W
Philip, S.D., U.S. (fĭl´ĭp)	114-15	44°02'N	101°39'W
Philippeville, Alg. *see* Skikda	269b	36°53'N	6°55'E
Philippines, nation, Asia (fĭl´ĭ-pēnz)	206-07	13°0'N	122°00'E
Philippine Sea, s., (fĭl´ĭ-pēn sē)	222-23	20°0'N	135°00'E
Philipsburg, Mt., U.S. (fĭl´lĭps-bĕrg)	112-13	46°20'N	113°18'W
Phillip Island, i., Austl. (fĭl´ĭp ī´lănd)	276	38°29'S	145°14'E
Phillips, Wi., U.S. (fĭl´ĭps)	116-17	45°42'N	90°24'W
Phillipsburg, Ks., U.S. (fĭl´lĭps-bĕrg)	120-21	39°45'N	99°19'W
Phillipsburg, N.J., U.S. (fĭl´lĭps-bĕrg)	116-17	40°42'N	75°11'W
Phitsanulok, Thai.	246-47	16°50'N	100°16'E
Phnom Penh, nat. cap., Camb. (nŏm´pĕn´)	246-47	11°34'N	104°54'E
Phnum Pénh, nat. cap., Camb. (nŏm´pĕn´) *see* Phnom Penh	246-47	11°34'N	104°54'E
Phoenix, Az., U.S. (fē´nĭks)	118-19	33°26'N	112°03'W
Phoenix Islands, is., Kir. (fē´nĭks ī´lăndz)	280-81	4°0'S	172°00'W
Phoenixville, Pa., U.S. (fē´nĭks-vĭl)	116-17	40°08'N	75°31'W
Phôngsali, Laos	246-47	21°43'N	102°07'E
Phra Chedi Sam Ong, p., Asia *see* Three Pagodas Pass	246-47	15°18'N	98°22'E
Phrae, Thai.	246-47	18°08'N	100°09'E
Phra Nakhon, nat. cap., Thai. *see* Bangkok	246-47	13°45'N	100°31'E
Phra Nakhon Si Ayutthaya, Thai.	246-47	14°21'N	100°34'E
Phuket, Thai.	246-47	7°52'N	98°23'E
Phuket, Ko, i., Thai.	246-47	8°0'N	98°22'E
Phu Ly, Viet.	246-47	20°31'N	105°56'E
Phu Quoc, Dao, i., Viet.	246-47	10°12'N	104°00'E
Piacenza, Italy (pyä-chĕnt´sä)	200-01	45°03'N	9°42'E
Piatra-Neamț, Rom.	194-95	46°57'N	26°24'E
Piauí, state, Braz.	166-67	7°0'S	43°00'W
Piazza Armerina, Italy (pyät´så är-må-rē´nä)	200-01	37°23'N	14°22'E
Pic, stm., On., Can. (pĕk)	136-37	48°36'N	86°18'W
Picayune, Ms., U.S. (pĭk´á yōōn)	124-25	30°32'N	89°42'W
Pichanal, Arg.	168-69	23°18'S	64°14'W
Pichilemu, Chile (pē-chē-lĕ´mōō)	163e	34°23'S	72°00'W
Pichucalco, Mex. (pē-chōō-käl´kō)	146-47	17°30'N	93°10'W
Pickle Lake, On., Can.	134-35	51°30'N	90°04'W
Pico, i., Port. (pē´kô)	199c	38°28'N	28°20'W
Pico de Orizaba, Volcán, vol., Mex. (vôl-kà´n-pē´kô-dĕ-ô-rē-zä´bä)	146-47	19°01'N	97°16'W
Picos, Braz. (pē´kōzh)	166-67	7°05'S	41°28'W
Picton, On., Can. (pĭk´tŭn)	136-37	43°60'N	77°08'W
Picton, Isla, i., Chile	171	55°03'S	66°55'W
Pictou, N.S., Can. (pĭk-tōō´)	138-39	45°41'N	62°42'W
Pidurutalagala, mtn., Sri L. (pē´dò-rò-tä´lá-gä´lá)	236	6°60'N	80°46'E
Piedmont, Al., U.S. (pēd´mŏnt)	124-25	33°55'N	85°37'W
Piedmont, Mo., U.S. (pēd´mŏnt)	124-25	37°09'N	90°42'W
Piedra del Águila, Arg.	171	40°03'S	70°03'W
Piedras, Punta, c., Arg. (pōō´n-tä-pyĕ´dräs)	173	35°26'S	57°07'W
Piedras Negras, Mex. (pyā´dräs nā´gräs)	122-23	28°42'N	100°31'W
Pierce, Ne., U.S. (pērs)	114-15	42°12'N	97°32'W
Pierre, S.D., U.S. (pēr)	114-15	44°22'N	100°21'W
Pietarsaari, Fin. *see* Jakobstad	184-85	63°41'N	22°43'E
Pietermaritzburg, S. Afr. (pē-tēr-må-rĭts-bûrg)	264-65	29°36'S	30°23'E
Pietersburg, S. Afr. (pē´tērz-bûrg) *see* Polokwane	269c	23°53'S	29°26'E
Pigeon Lake, lk., Ab., Can. (pĭj´ŭn lāk)	132-33	53°0'N	114°00'W
Pigeon Lake, lk., On., Can. (pĭj´ŭn lāk)	136-37	44°30'N	78°30'W
Piggott, Ar., U.S. (pĭg-ŭt)	124-25	36°23'N	90°12'W
Pigüé, Arg.	173	37°37'S	62°25'W
Pihkva järv, lk., Eur. *see* Pskov, Lake	192-93	58°0'N	28°00'E
Pijijiapan, Mex. (pēkē-kē-ä´pän)	146-47	15°42'N	93°13'W
Pikalëvo, Russia	186-87	59°31'N	34°11'E
Pikes Peak, mtn., Co., U.S. (pīks pēk)	120-21	38°51'N	105°03'W
Piketberg, S. Afr.	264-65	32°55'S	18°46'E
Pikeville, Ky., U.S. (pīk´vĭl)	116-17	37°30'N	82°33'W
Piła, Pol. (pē´là)	194-95	53°09'N	16°44'E
Pilanesberg, hill, S. Afr. (pē´ănsˊbûrg)	269c	25°12'S	27°05'E
Pilar, Arg. (pē´lär)	173	31°26'S	61°16'W
Pilar, Para.	173	26°54'S	58°19'W
Pilcomayo, stm., S.A. (pēl-cō-mī´ô)	168-69	25°17'S	57°40'W
Pili, Phil. (pē´lē)	250	13°32'N	123°17'E
Pīlībhīt, India	234-35	28°38'N	79°48'E
Pilica, stm., Pol. (pē-lēt´sä)	194-95	51°52'N	21°17'E
Pilipinas, nation, Asia *see* Philippines	206-07	13°0'N	122°00'E
Pilsen, Czech Rep. *see* Plzeň	194-95	49°45'N	13°23'E
Pinamalayan, Phil. (pē-nä-mä-lä´yän)	250	13°02'N	121°29'E
Pinang, Malay. *see* George Town	246-47	5°25'N	100°20'E
Pinar del Río, Cuba (pē-när´ dĕl rē´ō)	142-43	22°25'N	83°41'W
Pinar del Río, state, Cuba (pē-när´ dĕl rē´ō)	142-43	22°30'N	83°45'W
Pinatubo, Mount, vol., Phil. (mount pē-nä-tōō´bô)	250	15°08'N	120°21'E
Pincher Creek, Ab., Can. (pĭn´chēr krēk)	132-33	49°29'N	113°57'W
Pinckneyville, Il., U.S. (pĭnk´nĭ-vĭl)	116-17	38°05'N	89°23'W
Pindaré, stm., Braz.	166-67	3°18'S	44°47'W
Píndos Óros, mts., Grc.	200-01	39°49'N	21°14'E
Pindus Mountains, mts., Grc. (pĭn´dŭs moun´tĭnz) *see* Píndos Óros	200-01	39°49'N	21°14'E
Pine, stm., B.C., Can. (pīn)	132-33	56°09'N	120°44'W
Pine Bluff, Ar., U.S. (pīn blŭf)	124-25	34°14'N	92°02'W
Pine City, Mn., U.S. (pīn sĭ´tē)	114-15	45°50'N	92°58'W
Pine Creek, Austl. (pīn crēk krēk)	270-71	13°48'S	131°50'E
Pine Falls, Mb., Can. (pīn fôlz)	134-35	50°34'N	96°14'W
Pinega, stm., Russia (pē-nyĕ´gȧ)	186-87	64°08'N	41°54'E
Pinehouse Lake, lk., Sk., Can.	134-35	55°34'N	106°31'W
Pine Ridge, S.D., U.S. (pīn rĭj)	114-15	43°01'N	102°33'W
Pinerolo, Italy (pē-nâ-rô´lō)	200-01	44°54'N	7°20'E
Pines, Isle of, i., Cuba (īl ŭv pīnz) *see* Juventud, Isla de la	142-43	21°40'N	82°50'W
Pineville, Ky., U.S. (pīn´vĭl)	124-25	36°45'N	83°42'W
Pineville, La., U.S. (pīn´vĭl)	122-23	31°20'N	92°26'W
Ping, stm., Thai.	246-47	15°42'N	100°09'E
Pingdingshan, China	238-39	33°45'N	113°18'E
Pingdu, China (pĭŋ-dōō)	240-41	36°47'N	119°56'E
Pingelap, at., Micron.	280-81	6°13'N	160°42'E
Pingjiang, China	238-39	28°42'N	113°35'E
Pingle, China (pĭŋ-lŭ)	238-39	24°38'N	110°40'E
Pingliang, China (pĭng´lyäng´)	240-41	35°33'N	106°42'E
Pingquan, China (pĭŋ-chyůän)	240-41	40°59'N	118°39'E
Pingtan, China (pĭŋ-tän)	225a	25°31'N	119°47'E
Pingtan Dao, i., China (pĭŋ-tän dou)	225a	25°33'N	119°48'E
P'ingtung, Tai.	225a	22°40'N	120°29'E
Pingwu, China (pĭŋ-wōō)	238-39	32°25'N	104°33'E
Pingxiang, China (pĭŋ-shyäŋ)	238-39	22°08'N	106°44'E
Pingxiang, China (pĭŋ-shyäŋ)	238-39	27°38'N	113°50'E
Pingyao, China	240-41	37°16'N	112°14'E
Pingyi, China (pĭŋ-yē)	240-41	35°30'N	117°38'E
Pingyuan, China (pĭŋ-yůän)	238-39	24°36'N	115°55'E
Pinheiro, Braz.	166-67	2°31'S	45°05'W
Pinnacles National Monument, n.p., Ca., U.S. (pĭn´á-k'lz năsh´ŭn-ăl mŏn´ŭ-mĕnt)	118-19	36°30'N	121°11'W
Pinnaroo, Austl.	276	35°16'S	140°54'E
Pinos, Isla de, i., Cuba *see* Juventud, Isla de la	142-43	21°40'N	82°50'W
Pinrang, Indon.	248-49	3°48'S	119°39'E
Pins, Île des, i., N. Cal.	279g	22°37'S	167°28'E
Pinsk, Bela. (pēn'sk)	194-95	52°07'N	26°07'E
Pinsk Marshes, reg., Eur. *see* Pripet Marshes	194-95	52°0'N	27°00'E
Pinta, Isla, i., Ec.	170a	0°35'N	90°44'W
Pinyug, Russia	186-87	60°15'N	47°47'E
Piombino, Italy (pyôm-bē´nō)	200-01	42°56'N	10°32'E
Pioneer Mountains, mts., Mt., U.S. (pī´ô-nēr´ moun´tĭnz)	112-13	45°31'N	112°60'W
Pioner, Ostrov, i., Russia	218-19	79°50'N	92°30'E

n-sing; ŋ-baŋk; ɴ-nasalized n; nŏd; cŏmmit; ōld; ôbey; ôrder; oi-boil; fōōd; ŏŏ-as oo in foot; ou-out; s-soft; sh-dish; th-thin; pūre; ûnite; ûrn; stŭd; circŭs; ü-as in French tu; ´-indeterminate vowel.

ăt; fin*ă*l; rāte; sen*à*te; ärm; àsk; sof*à*; fåre; ch-choose; dh-as th in other; bē; ĕvent; bĕt; recĕnt; cratēr; g-gō; gh-guttural g; bĭt; ī-short neutral; rīde; ĸ-guttural k as ch in German ich;

n-sing; ŋ-baŋk; ᴎ-nasalized n; nŏd; cŏmmit; ōld; ŏbey; ôrder; oi-boil; fŏŏd; ò-as oo in foot; ou-out; s-soft; sh-dish; th-thin; pūre; ûnite; ûrn; stŭd; circŭs; ü-as in French tu; ′-indeterminate vowel.

372 Princeton – Qazaqtyng usaqshoqylyghy PRONOUNCING INDEX

Feature (Pronunciation)	Page	Lat.	Long.
Princeton, N.J., U.S. (prĭns′tŭn)	116-17	40°22′N	74°39′W
Princeton, W.V., U.S. (prĭns′tŭn)	124-25	37°22′N	81°06′W
Prince William Sound, strt., Ak., U.S. (prĭns wĭl′yăm sound)	126	60°42′N	147°07′W
Príncipe, i., S. Tom./P. (prēn′sē-pě)	260-61	1°37′N	7°25′E
Principe Channel, strt., B.C., Can. (prĭn′sĭ-pē chăn′ĕl)	132-33	53°28′N	130°00′W
Príncipe da Beira, Braz.	166-67	12°25′S	64°25′W
Prineville, Or., U.S. (prīn′vĭl)	112-13	44°18′N	120°51′W
Prinzapolka, stm., Nic. (prēn-zä-pōl′kä)	149	13°24′N	83°34′W
Priozërsk, Russia (prĭ-ô′zĕrsk)	192-93	61°02′N	30°09′E
Pripet Marshes, reg., Eur.	194-95	52°0′N	27°00′E
Priština, Serb. (prēsh′tĭ-nä)	200-01	42°40′N	21°10′E
Pritzwalk, Ger. (prēts′välk)	194-95	53°09′N	12°10′E
Privas, Fr. (prē-väs′)	196-97	44°44′N	4°37′E
Privolzhskaya Vozvyshennost′, plat., Russia	186-87	52°0′N	46°00′E
Privolzhskiy, Russia	186-87	51°24′N	46°02′E
Priyutovo, Russia	186-87	53°53′N	53°56′E
Prizren, Serb. (prē′zrĕn)	200-01	42°13′N	20°45′E
Probolinggo, Indon.	248-49	7°45′S	113°13′E
Proctor, Mn., U.S. (prŏk′tẽr)	114-15	46°44′N	92°14′W
Proddatūr, India	236	14°45′N	78°33′E
Progreso, Mex. (prô-grā′sō)	148	21°16′N	89°39′W
Prokopyevsk, Russia	226	53°54′N	86°44′E
Prokuplje, Serb. (prô′kop′l-yĕ)	200-01	43°14′N	21°36′E
Prome, Mya.	246-47	18°49′N	95°13′E
Pronja, stm., Bela. (prô′nyä)	192-93	53°27′N	31°01′E
Propriá, Braz.	163d	10°13′S	36°50′W
Prosser, Wa., U.S. (prŏs′ẽr)	112-13	46°12′N	119°46′W
Prostějov, Czech Rep. (prôs′tyĕ-yôf)	194-95	49°29′N	17°07′E
Protoka, stm., Russia (prôt′ō-kȧ)	202-03	45°44′N	37°47′E
Providence, R.I., U.S. (prŏv′ĭ-dĕns)	116-17	41°50′N	71°25′W
Providence, Atoll de, at., Sey.	264-65	9°14′S	51°03′E
Providencia, Isla de, i., Col.	164-65	13°21′N	81°22′W
Providenciales, i., T./C. Is.	142-43	21°47′N	72°17′W
Provideniya, Russia (prô-vĭ-dă′nĭ-yȧ)	126	64°23′N	173°18′W
Provo, Ut., U.S. (prō′vō)	118-19	40°13′N	111°38′W
Prudhoe Bay, b., Ak., U.S.	126	70°21′N	148°22′W
Prudnik, Pol. (prod′nĭk)	194-95	50°19′N	17°35′E
Pruszków, Pol. (prosh′kôf)	194-95	52°10′N	20°49′E
Prut, stm., Eur. (pro͞ot)	186-87	45°28′N	28°13′E
Prydz Bay, b., Ant.	287	69°0′S	76°00′E
Pryluky, Ukr.	202-03	50°36′N	32°23′E
Pryor, Ok., U.S. (prī′ẽr)	120-21	36°19′N	95°19′W
Przemyśl, Pol. (pzhĕ′mĭsh′l)	194-95	49°47′N	22°47′E
Przhevalsk, Kyrg. (p′r-zhĭ-välsk′) *see* Karakol	226	42°29′N	78°23′E
Pskov, Russia (pskôf)	192-93	57°49′N	28°22′E
Pskov, Lake, lk., Eur. (lăk pskôf)	192-93	58°0′N	28°00′E
Pskovskoye Ozero, lk., Eur. (p′skôv′skô′yĕ ôzê-rô) *see* Pskov, Lake	192-93	58°0′N	28°00′E
Ptuj, Slvn. (ptoo′ē)	200-01	46°26′N	15°52′E
Pucallpa, Peru	170	8°23′S	74°32′W
Pucheng, China (po͞o-chŭŋ)	238-39	27°55′N	118°32′E
Pucheng, China (po͞o-chŭŋ)	238-39	34°58′N	109°35′E
Puck, Pol. (potsk)	194-95	54°43′N	18°24′E
Pudozh, Russia (po͞o′dôzh)	186-87	61°48′N	36°34′E
Puducherry, India *see* Pondicherry	236	11°56′N	79°50′E
Puducherry, state, India	236	11°56′N	79°50′E
Pudukkottai, India	236	10°23′N	78°49′E
Puebla, state, Mex. (pwā′blä)	146-47	18°50′N	98°00′W
Puebla de Zaragoza, Mex.	146-47	19°03′N	98°12′W
Pueblo, Co., U.S. (pwā′blō)	120-21	38°16′N	104°38′W
Puente Genil, Spain (pwĕn′tå-hå-nēl′)	198-99	37°24′N	4°47′W
Puerto Aisén, Chile (pwĕ′r-tō ä′y-sĕ′n)	171	45°15′S	72°15′W
Puerto Ángel, Mex. (pwĕ′r-tō äŋ′hål)	146-47	15°40′N	96°29′W
Puerto Armuelles, Pan. (pwe′r-tô är-mo͞o-ā′lyās)	150	8°17′N	82°52′W
Puerto Asís, Col.	164-65	0°31′N	76°31′W
Puerto Ayacucho, Ven.	164-65	5°40′N	67°38′W
Puerto Baquerizo Moreno, Ec.	170a	0°54′S	89°36′W
Puerto Barrios, Guat. (pwĕ′r-tô bär′rê-ôs)	148	15°43′N	88°35′W
Puerto Bermúdez, Peru (pwĕ′r-tō bĕr-mo͞o′dāz)	170	10°20′S	74°54′W
Puerto Berrío, Col. (pwĕ′r-tō bĕr-rē′ō)	163c	6°28′N	74°26′W
Puerto Cabello, Ven. (pwĕ′r-tō kä-bĕl′yō)	163b	10°28′N	68°01′W
Puerto Cabezas, Nic. (pwĕ′r-tô kä-bā′zäs)	149	14°01′N	83°23′W
Puerto Carreño, Col.	164-65	6°11′N	67°30′W
Puerto Chicama, Peru (pwĕ′r-tō chē-kä′mä)	170	7°42′S	79°25′W
Puerto Cortés, Hond. (pwĕ′r-tô kôr-tās′)	149	15°51′N	87°57′W
Puerto Cumarebo, Ven. (pwĕ′r-tō ko͞o-mä-rĕ′bô)	164-65	11°29′N	69°21′W
Puerto de la Cruz, Spain	199d	28°23′N	16°33′W
Puerto Deseado, Arg. (pwĕ′r-tō dā-sā-ä′dhō)	171	47°44′S	65°54′W
Puerto Juárez, Mex.	148	21°10′N	86°49′W
Puerto la Cruz, Ven. (pwĕ′r-tō lä kro͞o′z)	163b	10°13′N	64°38′W
Puerto Leguízamo, Col.	164-65	0°11′S	74°46′W
Puerto Libertad, Mex.	144-45	29°55′N	112°41′W
Puerto Limón, C.R.	149	9°59′N	83°02′W
Puertollano, Spain (pwĕ-tôl-yä′nō)	198-99	38°41′N	4°06′W
Puerto Madryn, Arg. (pwĕ′r-tō mä-drēn′)	171	42°46′S	65°03′W
Puerto Maldonado, Peru (pwĕ′r-tō mäl-dō-nä′dô)	170	12°36′S	69°12′W
Puerto Montt, Chile (pwĕ′r-tō mô′nt)	171	41°28′S	72°57′W
Puerto Morazán, Nic.	149	12°50′N	87°11′W
Puerto Natales, Chile (pwĕ′r-tō nä-tá′lĕs)	171	51°42′S	72°29′W
Puerto Padre, Cuba (pwĕ′r-tō pä′drā)	142-43	21°12′N	76°36′W
Puerto Peñasco, Mex. (pwĕ′r-tô pěn-yä′s-kô)	144-45	31°19′N	113°32′W
Puerto Pinasco, Para. (pwĕ′r-tō pē-ná′s-kô)	168-69	22°37′S	57°49′W
Puerto Pirámides, Arg.	171	42°34′S	64°15′W
Puerto Píritu, Ven. (pwĕ′r-tō pē′rē-to͞o)	163b	10°02′N	65°02′W
Puerto Plata, Dom. Rep. (pwĕ′r-tō plä′tä)	142-43	19°45′N	70°39′W
Puerto Princesa, Phil.	250	9°44′N	118°45′E
Puerto Rico, Bol.	166-67	11°06′S	67°32′W
Puerto Rico, dep., N.A. (pwĕr′tô rē′kō)	140-41	18°15′N	66°30′W
Puerto Rico, i., P.R. (pwĕr′tô rē′kō)	142a	18°15′N	66°30′W
Puerto Salgar, Col. (pwĕ′r-tō säl-gär′)	163c	5°28′N	74°39′W
Puerto San José, Guat.	148	13°56′N	90°49′W
Puerto San Julián, Arg.	171	49°18′S	67°43′W
Puerto Santa Cruz, Arg. (pwĕ′r-tō sän′tä kro͞oz′)	171	50°01′S	68°34′W
Puerto Sastre, Para.	168-69	22°02′S	58°01′W
Puerto Suárez, Bol. (pwĕ′r-tō swä′råz)	168-69	18°57′S	57°51′W
Puerto Tejada, Col. (pwĕ′r-tō tĕ-κä′dä)	163c	3°14′N	76°25′W
Puerto Vallarta, Mex. (pwĕ′r-tō väl-yär′tä)	146-47	20°37′N	105°14′W
Puerto Varas, Chile (pwĕ′r-tō vä′räs)	171	41°20′S	72°58′W
Puerto Villamil, Ec.	170a	0°56′S	91°01′W
Puerto Wilches, Col. (pwĕ′r-tō vēl′c-hĕs)	164-65	7°20′N	73°54′W
Pueyrredón, Lago, lk., S.A.	171	47°21′S	71°56′W
Puget Sound, b. Wa., U.S.	112-113	47°49′N	122°27′W
Pugachev, Russia (po͞o′gá-chyôf)	186-87	52°02′N	48°49′E
Puhi-waero, c., N.Z. *see* South West Cape	278	47°17′S	167°28′E
Pukch′ŏng-ŭp, Kor., N.	243	40°14′N	128°19′E
Pukou, China	238-39	32°06′N	118°43′E
Pula, Cro. (po͞o′lä)	200-01	44°52′N	13°51′E
Pulacayo, Bol. (po͞o-lä-kä′yō)	168-69	20°23′S	66°42′W
Pulaski, N.Y., U.S. (pů-lăs′kĭ)	116-17	43°34′N	76°07′W
Pulaski, Tn., U.S. (pů-lăs′kĭ)	124-25	35°12′N	87°02′W
Pulaski, Va., U.S. (pů-lăs′kĭ)	124-25	37°03′N	80°47′W
Puławy, Pol. (po-wä′vě)	194-95	51°25′N	21°59′E
Pullman, Wa., U.S. (pol′măn)	112-13	46°44′N	117°10′W
Pulo Anna, i., Palau	280-81	4°40′N	131°58′E
Pulog, Mount, mtn., Phil. (mount po͞o′lôg)	250	16°36′N	120°54′E
Puma Yumco, lk., China (po͞o-mä yo͞om-tswo)	234-35	28°33′N	90°24′E
Puná, Isla, i., Ec.	170	2°47′S	80°08′W
Punakha, Bhu. (po͞o-nŭk′ŭ)	234-35	27°37′N	89°52′E
Punata, Bol. (po͞o-nä′tä)	168-69	17°33′S	65°50′W
Pune, India	236	18°32′N	73°52′E
Punia, D.R.C.	262-63	1°28′S	26°27′E
Punjab, state, India (pŭn′jäb′)	234-35	31°0′N	75°30′E
Puno, Peru (po͞o′nō)	170	15°51′S	70°02′W
Punta Alta, Arg.	173	38°53′S	62°04′W
Punta Arenas, Chile (po͞o′n-tä-rĕ′näs)	171	53°09′S	70°55′W
Punta de Piedras, Ven. (po͞o′n-tä dĕ pyĕ′dräs)	163b	10°54′N	64°06′W
Punta Gorda, Belize (pon′tä gôr′dä)	148	16°06′N	88°48′W
Punta Gorda, Fl., U.S. (pŭn′tȧ gôr′dȧ)	125a	26°56′N	82°03′W
Puntarenas, C.R. (pont-ä-rä′näs)	149	9°58′N	84°50′W
Punto Fijo, Ven. (po͞o′n-tô fē′kô)	164-65	11°43′N	70°12′W
Punxsutawney, Pa., U.S. (pŭnk-sŭ-tô′nē)	116-17	40°56′N	78°58′W
Puqi, China	238-39	29°43′N	113°53′E
Puquio, Peru (po͞o′kyô)	170	14°42′S	74°09′W
Pur, stm., Russia	218-19	67°21′N	77°55′E
Purcell, Ok., U.S. (pûr-sĕl′)	120-21	35°02′N	97°22′W
Puri, India (po′rē)	234-35	19°48′N	85°51′E
Purificación, Col. (po͞o-rē-fē-kä-syōn′)	163c	3°51′N	74°55′W
Purificación, Mex. (po͞o-rē-fē-kä-syô′n)	146-47	19°43′N	104°36′W
Pūrnia, India	234-35	25°47′N	87°29′E
Pursat, Camb. *see* Poŭthĭsăt	246-47	12°32′N	103°56′E
Purus, stm., S.A.	166-67	3°41′S	61°28′W
Purús, stm., S.A. (po͞o-ro͞o′s)	166-67	3°41′S	61°28′W
Purwokerto, Indon.	248-49	7°25′S	109°14′E
Pusan, Kor., S. (po͞o′sän′)	243	35°05′N	129°03′E
Pushkin, Russia (posh′kĭn)	192-93	59°43′N	30°26′E
Pustoshka, Russia (pûs-tôsh′kȧ)	192-93	56°20′N	29°22′E
Putaendo, Chile (po͞o-tä-ĕn-dô)	163e	32°37′S	70°44′W
Putao, Mya.	238-39	27°21′N	97°24′E
Putian, China (po͞o-tĭĕn)	225a	25°26′N	119°00′E
Puting, Tanjung, c., Indon.	248-49	3°32′S	111°49′E
Putla de Guerrero, Mex. (po͞o′tlä-dĕ-gĕr-rĕ′rō)	146-47	17°00′N	97°54′W
Putnam, Ct., U.S. (pŭt′năm)	116-17	41°55′N	71°54′W
Putorana, Gory, plat., Russia	218-19	69°0′N	95°00′E
Putrajaya, nat. cap., Malay.	246-47	2°56′N	101°43′E
Puttalam, Sri L.	236	8°01′N	79°51′E
Putumayo, stm., S.A. (po-to͞o-mä′yō)	170	3°07′S	67°56′W
Puyallup, Wa., U.S. (pū-ăl′ŭp)	112-13	47°11′N	122°17′W
Puyang, China (po͞o-yäŋ)	240-41	35°42′N	115°00′E
Puyo, Ec.	170	1°29′S	77°59′W
Pweto, D.R.C. (pwā′tō)	262-63	8°28′S	28°54′E
Pyakupur, stm., Russia	218-19	64°56′N	77°44′E
Pyandzh, stm., Asia *see* Panj	232-33	37°00′N	68°16′E
Pyasina, stm., Russia (pyä-sē′nȧ)	218-19	73°52′N	87°09′E
Pyasino, Ozero, lk., Russia	218-19	69°45′N	87°45′E
Pyatigorsk, Russia (pyá-tê-gôrsk′)	227	44°04′N	43°04′E
Pyè, Mya. *see* Prome	246-47	18°49′N	95°13′E
Pyinmana, Mya. (pyĕn-mä′nŭ)	246-47	19°44′N	96°13′E
P′yŏngyang, nat. cap., Kor., N. (pyŭng′gäng′)	243	39°01′N	125°44′E
Pyramid Lake, lk., Nv., U.S. (pĭ′rȧ-mĭd lāk)	118-19	40°01′N	119°35′W
Pyramid Lake Indian Reservation, ind. res., Nv., U.S. (pĭ′rȧ-mĭd lāk ĭn′dĭ-ăn rĕ-sĕr-vā′shĕn)	118-19	40°13′N	119°36′W
Pyrenees, mts., Eur. (pĭr-e-nēz′)	196-97	42°40′N	1°00′E
Pýrgos, Grc.	200-01	37°40′N	21°27′E
Pyritz, Pol. *see* Pyrzyce	194-95	53°09′N	14°53′E
Pyrzyce, Pol. (pĕzhĭ′tsĕ)	194-95	53°09′N	14°53′E

Q

Feature (Pronunciation)	Page	Lat.	Long.
Qā′en, Iran	232-33	33°44′N	59°10′E
Qaidam, stm., China	240-41	36°52′N	95°57′E
Qaidam Pendi, bas., China	222-23	37°0′N	95°00′E
Qal′at Bīshah, Sau. Ar.	266	19°60′N	42°36′E
Qalāt, Afg.	232-33	32°07′N	66°54′E
Qamani′tuaq, Nu., Can. *see* Baker Lake	128-29	64°18′N	95°55′W
Qamar, Ghubbat al-, b., Yemen	220-21	16°0′N	52°30′E
Qamdo, China (chyäm-dwō)	238-39	31°10′N	97°09′E
Qamea, i., Fiji	279f	16°46′S	179°46′W
Qandahār, Afg. *see* Kandahār	232-33	31°37′N	65°43′E
Qandala, Som.	262-63	11°28′N	49°52′E
Qapshaghay, Kaz.	226	43°52′N	77°04′E
Qapshaghay bögeni, res., Kaz.	226	43°49′N	77°42′E
Qaqortoq, Green. *see* Julianehåb	284-85	60°44′N	46°02′W
Qaraghandy, Kaz.	226	49°53′N	73°10′E
Qarataū, Kaz.	226	43°10′N	70°28′E
Qarataū zhotasy, mts., Kaz. *see* Karatau Range	226	43°36′N	68°52′E
Qaraton, Kaz.	186-87	46°26′N	53°31′E
Qarazhal, Kaz.	226	48°01′N	70°49′E
Qarqan, stm., China	222-23	39°26′N	88°22′E
Qarshi, Uzb.	232-33	38°52′N	65°48′E
Qârûn, Birket, lk., Egypt	268b	29°28′N	30°39′E
Qāsh, Nahr al-, stm., Afr. *see* Gash	266	16°45′N	35°54′E
Qatar, nation, Asia (kä′tȧr)	206-07	25°0′N	51°10′E
Qattâra, Munkhafad el-, depr., Egypt *see* Qattara Depression	266	30°0′N	27°30′E
Qattara Depression, depr., Egypt (kä-tä′rȧ dĭ-prĕ′shŭn)	266	30°0′N	27°30′E
Qazaqstan, nation, Asia *see* Kazakhstan	206-07	47°0′N	76°00′E
Qazaqtyng usaqshoqylyghy, hills, Kaz. *see* Kazakh Hills	226	49°0′N	72°00′E

ăt; finȧl; rāte; senâte; ärm; åsk; sofȧ; fâre; ch-choose; dh-as th in other; bē; ēvent; bĕt; recĕnt; cratẽr; g-gō; gh-guttural g; bĭt; ĭ-short neutral; rīde; κ-guttural k as ch in German ich;

Feature (Pronunciation)	Page	Lat.	Long.
Rasht, Iran	228-29	37°17'N	49°35'E
Rasshua, Ostrov, i., Russia	218-19	47°45'N	153°01'E
Rasskazovo, Russia (räs-kä'sô-vô)	186-87	52°40'N	41°53'E
Rastatt, Ger. (rä-shtät)	194-95	48°51'N	8°12'E
Ratangarh, India (rŭ-tŭn'gŭr)	234-35	28°05'N	74°37'E
Rathenow, Ger. (rä'tĕ-nō)	194-95	52°36'N	12°20'E
Rat Islands, is., Ak., U.S. (răt ī'lăndz)	126a	52°0'N	178°00'E
Ratlām, India	234-35	23°20'N	75°02'E
Ratnāgiri, India	236	16°59'N	73°18'E
Raton, N.M., U.S. (rȧ-tōn')	120-21	36°55'N	104°26'W
Rättvik, Swe. (rĕt'vēk)	192-93	60°53'N	15°07'E
Rauch, Arg. (rà'ōōch)	173	36°47'S	59°06'W
Rauma, Fin. (rä'ô-mȧ)	192-93	61°08'N	21°30'E
Raurkela, India	234-35	22°13'N	84°52'E
Ravenna, Italy (rä-vĕn'nä)	200-01	44°25'N	12°12'E
Ravenna, Ne., U.S. (rȧ-vĕn'ȧ)	114-15	41°02'N	98°55'W
Ravensburg, Ger. (rä'vĕns-bōōrgh)	194-95	47°47'N	9°37'E
Ravensthorpe, Austl. (rā'vĕns-thôrp)	270-71	33°35'S	120°03'E
Ravenswood, W.V., U.S. (rā'vĕnz-wŏŏd)	116-17	38°57'N	81°46'W
Rāvi, stm., Asia	232-33	30°37'N	71°53'E
Rawaki, at., Kir.	280-81	3°43'S	170°43'W
Rāwalpindi, Pak. (rä-wŭl-pēn'dē)	232-33	33°36'N	73°04'E
Rawicz, Pol. (rä'vēch)	194-95	51°37'N	16°52'E
Rawlinna, Austl.	270-71	31°02'S	125°18'E
Rawlins, Wy., U.S. (rô'lĭnz)	112-13	41°47'N	107°14'W
Rawson, Arg.	171	43°19'S	65°06'W
Raxaul, India	234-35	26°59'N	84°50'E
Ray, Cape, c., Nf., Can. (kāp rā)	138-39	47°38'N	59°18'W
Raya, Bukit, mtn., Indon.	248-49	0°40'S	112°41'E
Raychikhinsk, Russia	240-41	49°48'N	129°24'E
Raymond, N.H., U.S. (rā'mŭnd)	116-17	43°02'N	71°11'W
Raymond, Wa., U.S. (rā'mŭnd)	112-13	46°41'N	123°44'W
Raymondville, Tx., U.S. (rā'mŭnd-vĭl)	122-23	26°29'N	97°46'W
Rayne, La., U.S. (rān)	122-23	30°14'N	92°16'W
Raytown, Mo., U.S. (rā'toun)	120-21	38°59'N	94°28'W
Rayville, La., U.S. (rā-vĭl)	124-25	32°29'N	91°46'W
Raz, Pointe du, c., Fr. (pwănt dü rä)	196-97	48°03'N	4°44'W
Razdol'noye, Russia (räz-dôl'nô-yĕ)	244	43°30'N	131°49'E
Razlog, Blg. (räz'lôk)	200-01	41°53'N	23°29'E
Razorback Mountain, mtn., B.C., Can. (rā'zēr-băk moun'tĭn)	132-33	51°35'N	124°42'W
Ré, Île de, i., Fr.	196-97	46°12'N	1°24'W
Reading, Eng., U.K. (rĕd'ĭng)	190-91	51°28'N	0°59'W
Reading, Pa., U.S.	116-17	40°20'N	75°56'W
Real, Cordillera, mts., S.A.	168-69	16°50'S	66°34'W
Realicó, Arg.	173	35°02'S	64°14'W
Rebun-tō, i., Japan (rē'bōōn tō)	244	45°23'N	141°02'E
Recife, Braz. (rȧ-sē'fĕ)	166-67	8°03'S	34°54'W
Reconquista, Arg. (rā-kôn-kēs'tä)	173	29°09'S	59°38'W
Recreo, Arg.	168-69	29°17'S	65°04'W
Rector, Ar., U.S. (rĕk'tẽr)	124-25	36°16'N	90°18'W
Rèčyča, Bela.	202-03	52°22'N	30°25'E
Red, stm., Asia (rĕd)	238-39	20°18'N	106°32'E
Red, stm., N.A. (rĕd)	110-11	50°25'N	96°47'W
Red, stm., U.S. (rĕd)	110-11	29°49'N	91°23'W
Red, stm., Ky., U.S. (rĕd)	116-17	37°50'N	84°06'W
Redang, Pulau, i., Malay.	246-47	5°46'N	103°01'E
Red Bank, Tn., U.S. (rĕd băngk)	124-25	35°07'N	85°17'W
Red Bluff, Ca., U.S.	118-19	40°11'N	122°14'W
Red Bluff Reservoir, res., U.S. (rĕd blŭf rē'sẽr-vwär)	122-23	31°57'N	103°56'W
Redcliff, Ab., Can. (rĕd'clĭf)	132-33	50°05'N	110°47'W
Redcliffe, Austl. (rĕd'clĭf)	276	27°14'S	153°07'E
Red Cloud, Ne., U.S. (rĕd kloud)	120-21	40°05'N	98°31'W
Red Deer, Ab., Can. (rĕd dēr)	132-33	52°16'N	113°49'W
Red Deer, stm., Can. (rĕd dēr)	132-33	50°55'N	109°53'W
Red Deer, stm., Can. (rĕd dēr)	134-35	52°59'N	100°52'W
Red Deer Lake, lk., Mb., Can. (rĕd dēr lāk)	134-35	52°56'N	101°20'W
Redding, Ca., U.S.	112-13	40°35'N	122°23'W
Redfield, S.D., U.S. (rĕd'fēld)	114-15	44°52'N	98°31'W
Red Indian Lake, lk., Nf., Can. (rĕd ĭn'dĭ-ăn lāk)	138-39	48°39'N	56°50'W
Red Lake, On., Can. (rĕd lāk)	134-35	51°01'N	93°49'W
Red Lake, lk., On., Can.	134-35	51°01'N	94°05'W
Red Lake Falls, Mn., U.S. (rĕd lāk fôlz)	114-15	47°53'N	96°16'W
Red Lake Indian Reservation, ind. res., Mn., U.S. (rĕd lāk ĭn'dĭ-ăn rĕ-sẽr-vā'shĕn)	114-15	48°03'N	94°59'W
Red Lion, Pa., U.S. (rĕd lī'ŭn)	116-17	39°54'N	76°36'W
Redmond, Or., U.S. (rĕd'mŭnd)	112-13	44°17'N	121°10'W
Redmond, Wa., U.S. (rĕd'mŭnd)	112-13	47°40'N	122°07'W
Red Oak, Ia., U.S. (rĕd ōk)	114-15	41°01'N	95°14'W
Redon, Fr. (rē-dôn')	196-97	47°39'N	2°05'W
Redonda, i., Antig. (rĕ-dŏn'dȧ)	143b	16°56'N	62°21'W
Red Sea, s., (rĕd sē)	266	20°0'N	38°00'E
Red Sucker Lake, lk., Mb., Can. (rĕd sŭk'ēr lāk)	134-35	54°09'N	93°40'W
Red Wing, Mn., U.S.	114-15	44°34'N	92°32'W
Redwood Falls, Mn., U.S. (rĕd'wŏŏd fôlz)	114-15	44°32'N	95°07'W
Redwood National Park, n.p., Ca., U.S. (rĕd'wŏŏd năsh'ŭn-ăl pärk)	112-13	41°20'N	124°02'W
Reed City, Mi., U.S. (rēd sĭ'tē)	116-17	43°53'N	85°32'W
Reed Lake, lk., Mb., Can. (rēd lāk)	134-35	54°38'N	100°30'W
Reedley, Ca., U.S. (rēd'lē)	118-19	36°35'N	119°26'W
Reedsburg, Wi., U.S. (rēdz'bûrg)	116-17	43°32'N	89°60'W
Reedsport, Or., U.S. (rēdz'pōrt)	112-13	43°42'N	124°06'W
Reform, Al., U.S. (rē-fôrm')	124-25	33°23'N	88°01'W
Refugio, Tx., U.S. (rȧ-fōō'hyô) (rĕ-fū'jō)	122-23	28°18'N	97°17'W
Rega, stm., Pol. (rĕ-gä)	194-95	54°09'N	15°17'E
Regensburg, Ger. (rā'ghĕns-bôrgh)	194-95	49°01'N	12°06'E
Reggio di Calabria, Italy (rĕ'jô dē kä-lä'brē-ä)	200-01	38°07'N	15°39'E
Reghin, Rom. (rȧ-gēn')	194-95	46°47'N	24°43'E
Regina, Sk., Can. (rē-jī'nȧ)	134-35	50°27'N	104°38'W
Registan, reg., Afg. *see* Rīgestān	232-33	31°0'N	65°00'E
Rehoboth, Nmb.	264-65	23°19'S	17°05'E
Rehovot, Isr.	228-29	31°54'N	34°49'E
Reidsville, N.C., U.S. (rēdz'vĭl)	124-25	36°21'N	79°40'W
Reims, Fr. (răns)	196-97	49°15'N	4°02'E
Reindeer Lake, lk., Can. (rān'dēr lāk)	134-35	57°16'N	102°15'W
Reinosa, Spain (rā-ē-nō'sä)	198-99	42°60'N	4°08'W
Remada, Tun.	188-89	32°19'N	10°23'E
Remanso, Braz.	166-67	9°37'S	42°07'W
Remedios, Pan. (rĕ-mĕ'dyōs)	150	8°13'N	81°50'W
Remiremont, Fr. (rē-mēr-môn')	196-97	48°01'N	6°36'E
Rendova Island, i., Sol. Is. (rĕn'dô-vȧ ī'lănd)	279e	8°32'S	157°20'E
Rendsburg, Ger. (rĕnts'bôrgh)	194-95	54°18'N	9°40'E
Renfrew, On., Can. (rĕn'frōō)	136-37	45°29'N	76°42'W
Rengo, Chile (rĕn'gō)	163e	34°29'S	70°53'W
Reni, Ukr. (ran')	200-01	45°28'N	28°17'E
Renmark, Austl. (rĕn'märk)	276	34°11'S	140°45'E
Rennell, i., Sol. Is. (rĕn-nĕl')	272-73	11°33'S	160°05'E
Rennes, Fr. (rĕn)	196-97	48°07'N	1°41'W
Reno, Nv., U.S. (rē'nō)	118-19	39°32'N	119°49'W
Reno, Tx., U.S. (rē'nō)	120-21	32°56'N	97°35'W
Renovo, Pa., U.S. (rē-nō'vō)	116-17	41°20'N	77°45'W
Rensselaer, In., U.S. (rĕn'sē-lâr)	116-17	40°57'N	87°09'W
Rensselaer, N.Y., U.S. (rĕn'sē-lâr)	116-17	42°40'N	73°45'W
Renton, Wa., U.S. (rĕn'tŭn)	112-13	47°30'N	122°11'W
Reo, Indon.	248-49	8°19'S	120°29'E
Repetek, Turkmen.	232-33	38°34'N	63°11'E
Republic, Mo., U.S. (rē-pŭb'lĭk)	120-21	37°08'N	93°29'W
República Dominicana, nation, N.A. *see* Dominican Republic	140-41	19°0'N	70°40'W
Republican, stm., U.S. (rē-pŭb'lĭ-kăn)	110-11	39°03'N	96°48'W
Republican, South Fork, stm., U.S. (south fôrk rē-pŭb'lĭ-kăn)	120-21	40°04'N	101°31'W
Republic of Korea, nation, Asia	206-07	36°30'N	128°00'E
République centrafricaine, nation, Afr. *see* Central African Republic	253	7°0'N	21°00'E
Repulse Bay, Nu., Can.	128-29	66°32'N	86°14'W
Repulse Bay, b., Austl. (rē-pŭls' bā)	277	20°36'S	148°43'E
Requena, Spain (rȧ-kā'nä)	198-99	39°29'N	1°06'W
Resht, Iran *see* Rasht	228-29	37°17'N	49°35'E
Resistencia, Arg. (rā-sēs-tĕn'syä)	173	27°27'S	59°00'W
Reșița, Rom. (rā'shē-tȧ)	200-01	45°18'N	21°53'E
Resolution Island, i., Nu., Can. (rĕz-ô-lū'shŭn ī'lănd)	130-31	61°30'N	65°00'W
Resolution Island, i., N.Z. (rĕz-ŏl-ûshûn ī'lănd)	278	45°40'S	166°40'E
Restrepo, Col. (rĕs-trĕ'pô)	163c	3°48'N	76°31'W
Retalhuleu, Guat. (rā-täl-ōō-lān')	148	14°32'N	91°41'W
Rethel, Fr. (r-tĕl')	196-97	49°31'N	4°22'E
Reunion, dep., Afr. (rā-ü-nyôn')	265a	21°06'S	55°36'E
Réunion, dep., Afr. *see* Reunion	265a	21°06'S	55°36'E
Reus, Spain (rā'ōōs)	198-99	41°09'N	1°07'E
Reutlingen, Ger. (roit'lĭng-ĕn)	194-95	48°30'N	9°12'E
Reval, nat. cap., Est. *see* Tallinn	192-93	59°26'N	24°48'E
Revda, Russia (ryâv'dȧ)	186-87	67°58'N	34°34'E
Revelstoke, B.C., Can. (rĕv'ĕl-stōk)	132-33	50°59'N	118°11'W
Revillagigedo, Islas, is., Mex. (ĕ's-läs-rĕ-vēl-yä-hĕ'gĕ-dô)	144-45	18°48'N	112°06'W
Revin, Fr. (rē-văn)	196-97	49°56'N	4°39'E
Rewa, India (rā'wä)	234-35	24°32'N	81°18'E
Rexburg, Id., U.S. (rĕks'bûrg)	112-13	43°50'N	111°47'W
Rey, Isla del, i., Pan. (ē's-lä-dĕl-rā'ē)	150	8°22'N	78°55'W
Rey, Laguna del, lk., Mex. (lä-gô'nä-dĕl-rā')	122-23	27°01'N	103°24'W
Reyes, Bol. (rā'yĕs)	166-67	14°19'S	67°22'W
Reyes, Point, c., Ca., U.S. (point rā'yĕs)	118-19	38°0'N	123°01'W
Reykjanes, pen., Ice. (rā'kyȧ-nĕs)	190a	63°49'N	22°43'W
Reykjavík, nat. cap., Ice. (rā'kyȧ-vēk)	190a	64°08'N	21°56'W
Reynosa, Mex. (rā-ē-nō'sä)	122-23	26°05'N	98°17'W
Reẓā'īyeh, Iran *see* Orūmīyeh	228-29	37°32'N	45°05'E
Rēzekne, Lat. (rā'zĕk-nĕ)	192-93	56°30'N	27°20'E
Rheims, Fr. *see* Reims	196-97	49°15'N	4°02'E
Rhein, stm., Eur. *see* Rhine	194-95	51°53'N	6°02'E
Rheine, Ger. (rī'nĕ)	194-95	52°17'N	7°27'E
Rhin, stm., Eur. *see* Rhine	194-95	51°53'N	6°02'E
Rhine, stm., Eur. (rīn)	194-95	51°53'N	6°02'E
Rhinelander, Wi., U.S. (rīn'lăn-dẽr)	116-17	45°38'N	89°24'W
Rhir, Cap, c., Mor.	258-59	30°38'N	9°53'W
Rhode Island, state, U.S. (rōd ī'lănd)	108-09	41°40'N	71°30'W
Rhodes, Grc. *see* Ródos	200-01	36°26'N	28°14'E
Rhodes, i., Grc. (rōdz) *see* Ródos	200-01	36°10'N	28°00'E
Rhodesia, nation, Afr. *see* Zimbabwe	253	20°0'S	30°00'E
Rhône, stm., Eur. (rōn)	196-97	43°53'N	4°39'E
Riachão, Braz. (rē-ä-choun')	166-67	7°22'S	46°39'W
Riau, Kepulauan, is., Indon.	246-47	1°0'N	104°30'E
Ribe, Den. (rē'bĕ)	192-93	55°20'N	8°46'E
Ribeirão Preto, Braz. (rē-bā-roun-prĕ'tô)	172	21°10'S	47°48'W
Riberalta, Bol. (rē-bȧ-räl'tä)	166-67	11°00'S	66°05'W
Rib Lake, Wi., U.S. (rĭb lāk)	116-17	45°19'N	90°12'W
Rice Lake, Wi., U.S. (rīs lāk)	114-15	45°30'N	91°44'W
Rice Lake, lk., On., Can. (rīs lāk)	136-37	44°08'N	78°13'W
Richards Bay, S. Afr.	264-65	28°47'S	32°05'E
Richardson, Tx., U.S. (rĭch'ērd-sŭn)	120-21	32°58'N	96°44'W
Richardson Mountains, mts., Can. (rĭch'ērd-sŭn moun'tĭnz)	130-31	67°22'N	136°04'W
Richfield, Ut., U.S. (rĭch'fērd)	118-19	38°46'N	112°05'W
Rich Hill, Mo., U.S. (rĭch hĭl)	120-21	38°06'N	94°22'W
Richland, Ga., U.S. (rĭch'lănd)	124-25	32°05'N	84°40'W
Richland, Wa., U.S. (rĭch'lănd)	112-13	46°16'N	119°17'W
Richland Center, Wi., U.S. (rĭch'lănd sĕn'tẽr)	114-15	43°20'N	90°23'W
Richmond, Austl. (rĭch'mŭnd)	277	20°44'S	143°08'E
Richmond, B.C., Can. (rĭch'mŭnd)	132-33	49°09'N	123°10'W
Richmond, Qc., Can. (rĭch'mŭnd)	136-37	45°40'N	72°09'W
Richmond, In., U.S. (rĭch'mŭnd)	116-17	39°49'N	84°54'W
Richmond, Ky., U.S. (rĭch'mŭnd)	116-17	37°45'N	84°18'W
Richmond, Mi., U.S. (rĭch'mŭnd)	116-17	42°49'N	82°45'W
Richmond, Mo., U.S. (rĭch'mŭnd)	120-21	39°17'N	93°59'W
Richmond, Va., U.S. (rĭch'mŭnd)	116-17	37°33'N	77°27'W
Richmond Hill, On., Can. (rĭch'mŭnd hĭl)	136-37	43°52'N	79°26'W
Richwood, La., U.S. (rĭch'wŏŏd)	120-21	32°27'N	92°06'W
Richwood, W.V., U.S. (rĭch'wŏŏd)	116-17	38°13'N	80°34'W
Ridā', Yemen	266	14°38'N	44°54'E
Ridder, Kaz.	226	50°21'N	83°30'E
Riding Mountain National Park, n.p., Mb., Can. (rīd'ĭng moun'tĭn năsh'ŭn-ăl pärk)	134-35	50°55'N	100°25'W
Riesa, Ger. (rē'zȧ)	194-95	51°18'N	13°18'E
Riesco, Isla, i., Chile	171	52°59'S	72°38'W
Rieti, Italy (rē-ā'tē)	200-01	42°24'N	12°52'E
Rif, mts., Mor.	258-59	35°0'N	4°00'W
Rift Valley, val., Afr. (rĭft văl'ē)	254	3°0'S	29°00'E
Rīga, nat. cap., Lat. (rē'gȧ)	192-93	56°57'N	24°06'E
Riga, Gulf of, b., Eur. (gŭlf ŭv rē'gȧ)	192-93	57°30'N	23°35'E
Rīgas jūras līcis, b., Eur. *see* Riga, Gulf of	192-93	57°30'N	23°35'E
Rigby, Id., U.S. (rĭg'bē)	112-13	43°40'N	111°56'W
Rīgestān, reg., Afg.	232-33	31°0'N	65°00'E
Rijeka, Cro. (rĭ-yĕ'kä)	200-01	45°20'N	14°27'E
Rijn, stm., Eur. *see* Rhine	194-95	51°53'N	6°02'E
Rima, stm., Nig.	260-61	13°04'N	5°07'E
Rimatara, i., Fr. Poly.	280-81	22°38'S	152°51'W
Rimavská Sobota, Slvk. (rē'mȧf-skȧ sô'bô-tȧ)	194-95	48°23'N	20°05'E
Rimbo, Swe. (rēm'bô)	192-93	59°45'N	18°22'E
Rimini, Italy (rē'mē-nē)	200-01	44°04'N	12°35'E
Rimouski, Qc., Can. (rē-mōōs'kē)	138-39	48°27'N	68°33'W
Rincón del Bonete, Lago Artificial de, res., Ur.	173	32°43'S	56°01'W
Rincón de Romos, Mex. (rēn-kōn dā rō-mōs')	146-47	22°14'N	102°18'W
Ringkøbing, Den. (rĭng'kûb-ĭng)	192-93	56°05'N	8°15'E
Ringsted, Den. (rĭng'stĕdh)	192-93	55°27'N	11°50'E
Ringvassøya, i., Nor. (rĭng'väs-ûê)	184-85	69°55'N	19°15'E
Rinjani, Gunung, vol., Indon.	248-49	8°24'S	116°28'E
Riobamba, Ec. (rē'ō-bäm-bä)	170	1°40'S	78°39'W

ăt; finăl; rāte; senāte; ärm; ȧsk; sofȧ; fâre; ch-choose; dh-as th in other; bē; ēvent; bĕt; recĕnt; cratẽr; g-gō; gh-guttural g; bĭt; ĭ-short neutral; rīde; ĸ-guttural k as ch in German ich;

PRONOUNCING INDEX

Rio Branco – Rotuma 375

Feature (Pronunciation)	Page	Lat.	Long.
Rio Branco, Braz. (rē´ò brän´kò)	166-67	9°58′S	67°48′W
Río Branco, Ur. (riô brän̄cô)	173	32°36′S	53°23′W
Rio Casca, Braz. (rē´ō-ká´s-kä)	172	20°14′S	42°39′W
Río Chico, Ven. (rē´ō chē´kŏ)	163b	10°18′N	65°59′W
Rio Claro, Braz. (rē´ò klä´rò)	172	22°26′S	47°33′W
Río Colorado, Arg.	173	38°60′S	64°07′W
Río Cuarto, Arg. (rē´ō kwär´tō)	173	33°08′S	64°21′W
Rio de Janeiro, Braz. (rē´ò dā zhä-nâ´ē-rò)	172	22°54′S	43°14′W
Rio de Janeiro, state, Braz. (rē´ò dā zhä-nâ´ē-rò)	172	22°0′S	42°30′W
Rio do Sul, Braz.	168-69	27°13′S	49°39′W
Río Gallegos, Arg. (rē´ō gä-lä´gōs)	171	51°38′S	69°13′W
Río Grande, Arg.	171	53°49′S	67°47′W
Rio Grande, Braz. (rē´ò grän´dĕ)	173	32°02′S	52°06′W
Río Grande, Mex. (rē´ō grän´dā)	146-47	15°59′N	97°27′W
Río Grande, Mex. (rē´ō grän´dā)	146-47	23°50′N	103°03′W
Rio Grande, stm., N.A. (rē´ō grän´dā)	110-11	25°57′N	97°09′W
Rio Grande do Sul, Braz. *see* Rio Grande	173	32°02′S	52°06′W
Rio Grande do Sul, state, Braz. (rē´ò grän´dĕ-dò-sōō´l)	173	30°0′S	54°00′W
Ríohacha, Col. (rē´ō-ä´chä)	164-65	11°33′N	72°55′W
Río Hato, Pan. (rē´ō-ä´tō)	150	8°23′N	80°10′W
Rio Largo, Braz.	163d	9°29′S	35°51′W
Riom, Fr. (rē-ôN´)	196-97	45°54′N	3°07′E
Río Mayo, Arg.	171	45°41′S	70°14′W
Rio Negro, Braz.	168-69	26°06′S	49°47′W
Ríonegro, Col. (rē´ō-nĕ´grō)	163c	6°08′N	75°23′W
Río Negro, state, Arg. (rē´ō nā´grō)	171	40°0′S	67°00′W
Rio Pardo, Braz.	168-69	29°59′S	52°22′W
Rio Pardo de Minas, Braz. (rē´ō pär´dō-dĕ-mē´näs)	168-69	15°37′S	42°33′W
Ríosucio, Col. (rē´ō-sōō´syō)	163c	5°25′N	75°42′W
Ríosucio, Col. (rē´ō-sōō´syō)	164-65	7°25′N	77°06′W
Río Tercero, Arg. (rē´ō dĕr-sĕ´rō)	173	32°11′S	64°07′W
Rio Tinto, Braz.	163d	6°48′S	35°05′W
Rio Verde, Braz. (rē´ō vĕr´dĕ)	168-69	17°47′S	50°55′W
Ríoverde, Mex. (rē´ō-vĕr´då)	146-47	21°56′N	99°59′W
Ripley, Ms., U.S. (rĭp´lē)	124-25	34°45′N	88°57′W
Ripley, Tn., U.S. (rĭp´lē)	124-25	35°45′N	89°32′W
Ripley, W.V., U.S. (rĭp´lē)	116-17	38°48′N	81°44′W
Ripoll, Spain (rē-pōl´´)	198-99	42°12′N	2°12′E
Ripon, Wi., U.S. (rĭp´ŏn)	116-17	43°51′N	88°50′W
Rishiri-tō, i., Japan (rē-shē´rē tō)	244	45°11′N	141°15′E
Rising Sun, In., U.S. (rīz´ĭng sŭn)	116-17	38°57′N	84°52′W
Risør, Nor. (rēs´ûr)	192-93	58°43′N	9°14′E
Rittman, Oh., U.S. (rĭt´năn)	116-17	40°58′N	81°47′W
Ritzville, Wa., U.S. (rĭts´vĭl)	112-13	47°07′N	118°22′W
Rivas, Nic. (rē´väs)	149	11°27′N	85°52′W
Rivera, Ur. (rē-vā´rä)	173	30°54′S	55°33′W
River Falls, Wi., U.S. (rĭv´ēr fôlz)	114-15	44°52′N	92°37′W
Riverhead, N.Y., U.S. (rĭv´ēr hĕd)	116-17	40°55′N	72°40′W
Rivers, Mb., Can. (rĭv´ērz)	134-35	50°02′N	100°14′W
Riverside, Ca., U.S.	118-19	33°58′N	117°21′W
Rivers Inlet, B.C., Can.	132-33	51°42′N	127°15′W
Rivesaltes, Fr. (rēv´zält´)	196-97	42°46′N	2°52′E
Riviera Beach, Fl., U.S. (rĭv-ĭ-ĕr´á bēch)	125a	26°46′N	80°04′W
Rivière-du-Loup, Qc., Can. (rē-vyâr´ dü lōō´)	138-39	47°50′N	69°32′W
Rivne, Ukr.	194-95	50°37′N	26°14′E
Riyadh, nat. cap., Sau. Ar. (rĭ-äd´)	230-31	24°38′N	46°43′E
Rize, Tur. (rē´zĕ)	227	41°01′N	40°31′E
Rjukan, Nor. (ryōō´kän)	192-93	59°53′N	8°35′E
Road Town, nat. cap., Br. Vir. Is. (rōd toun)	143b	18°26′N	64°37′W
Roanne, Fr. (rō-än´)	196-97	46°02′N	4°04′E
Roanoke, Al., U.S. (rō´á-nōk)	124-25	33°09′N	85°22′W
Roanoke, Va., U.S. (rō´á-nōk)	124-25	37°16′N	79°57′W
Roanoke, stm., U.S. (rō´á-nōk)	124-25	35°57′N	76°43′W
Roanoke Rapids, N.C., U.S. (rō´á-nōk răp´ĭdz)	124-25	36°28′N	77°39′W
Roan Plateau, plat., U.S. (rōn plă-tō´)	118-19	39°30′N	109°40′W
Roatán, Hond. (rō-ä-tän´)	149	16°20′N	86°32′W
Roatán, Isla de, i., Hond.	149	16°22′N	86°29′W
Roberval, Qc., Can. (rŏb´ēr-văl) (rô-bĕr-vál´)	136-37	48°31′N	72°14′W
Robinson, Il., U.S. (rŏb´ĭn-sŭn)	116-17	39°01′N	87°45′W
Robinvale, Austl. (rŏb-ĭn´vāl)	276	34°36′S	142°46′E
Roblin, Mb., Can.	134-35	51°15′N	101°23′W
Roboré, Bol.	168-69	18°20′S	59°45′W
Robson, Mount, mtn., B.C., Can. (mount rŏb´sŭn)	132-33	53°07′N	119°09′W
Robstown, Tx., U.S. (rŏbz´toun)	122-23	27°47′N	97°40′W
Roca, Cabo da, c., Port. (ká´bō-dä-rō´kä)	198-99	38°47′N	9°29′W
Roca Partida, Isla, i., Mex.	144-45	19°00′N	112°04′W
Rocha, Ur. (rō´chås)	173	34°30′S	54°19′W
Rochefort, Fr. (rôsh-fôr´)	196-97	45°57′N	0°58′W
Rochelle, Il., U.S. (rô-shĕl´)	116-17	41°55′N	89°04′W
Rochester, In., U.S. (rŏch´ĕs-tēr)	116-17	41°04′N	86°12′W
Rochester, Mn., U.S. (rŏch´ĕs-tēr)	114-15	44°00′N	92°29′W
Rochester, N.H., U.S. (rŏch´ĕs-tēr)	116-17	43°18′N	70°59′W
Rochester, N.Y., U.S.	116-17	43°09′N	77°36′W
Rock, stm., U.S. (rŏk)	114-15	41°29′N	90°38′W
Rockdale, Tx., U.S. (rŏk´dāl)	122-23	30°39′N	97°00′W
Rockefeller Plateau, plat., Ant.	287	80°0′S	135°00′W
Rock Falls, Il., U.S. (rŏk fôlz)	116-17	41°47′N	89°41′W
Rockford, Il., U.S. (rŏk´fērd)	116-17	42°16′N	89°05′W
Rockford, Mi., U.S. (rŏk´fērd)	116-17	43°07′N	85°34′W
Rockhampton, Austl. (rŏk-hămp´tŭn)	277	23°23′S	150°31′E
Rock Hill, S.C., U.S. (rŏk hĭl)	124-25	34°56′N	81°02′W
Rockingham, N.C., U.S. (rŏk´ĭng-hăm)	124-25	34°56′N	79°46′W
Rock Island, Il., U.S. (rŏk ī´lănd)	114-15	41°30′N	90°34′W
Rockland, On., Can. (rŏk´lănd)	136-37	45°33′N	75°17′W
Rockland, Me., U.S.	117a	44°07′N	69°07′W
Rockport, In., U.S. (rŏk´pōrt)	116-17	37°53′N	87°03′W
Rockport, Tx., U.S. (rŏk´pōrt)	122-23	28°01′N	97°03′W
Rock Rapids, Ia., U.S. (rŏk răp´ĭdz)	114-15	43°26′N	96°10′W
Rocksprings, Tx., U.S. (rŏk springs)	122-23	30°01′N	100°12′W
Rock Springs, Wy., U.S. (rŏk springz)	112-13	41°35′N	109°13′W
Rockstone, Guy. (rŏk´stōn)	164-65	5°59′N	58°32′W
Rock Valley, Ia., U.S. (rŏk văl´ĭ văl´ē)	114-15	43°12′N	96°18′W
Rockville, In., U.S. (rŏk´vĭl)	116-17	39°45′N	87°14′W
Rockwell City, Ia., U.S. (rŏk´wĕl sĭ´tē)	114-15	42°24′N	94°38′W
Rockwood, Me., U.S. (rŏk-wŏŏd)	116-17	45°40′N	69°45′W
Rockwood, Tn., U.S. (rŏk-wŏŏd)	124-25	35°52′N	84°41′W
Rocky Ford, Co., U.S. (rŏk´-ē fôrd)	120-21	38°03′N	103°43′W
Rocky Island Lake, res., On., Can. (rŏk´-ē ī´lănd lāk)	136-37	46°56′N	82°57′W
Rocky Mount, N.C., U.S. (rŏk´-ē mount)	124-25	35°57′N	77°48′W
Rocky Mount, Va., U.S. (rŏk´-ē mount)	124-25	37°00′N	79°54′W
Rocky Mountain House, Ab., Can. (rŏk´-ē moun´tĭn hous)	132-33	52°23′N	114°56′W
Rocky Mountain National Park, n.p., Co., U.S. (rŏk´-ē moun´tĭn năsh´ŭn-ăl pärk)	112-13	40°21′N	105°42′W
Rocky Mountains, mts., N.A. (rŏk´-ē moun´tĭnz)	86	48°0′N	116°00′W
Rodeo, Arg.	168-69	30°12′S	69°06′W
Rodeo, Mex. (rô-dā´ō)	122-23	25°11′N	104°34′W
Rodez, Fr. (rô-dĕz´)	196-97	44°21′N	2°34′E
Rodniki, Russia (rôd´nē-kē)	186-87	57°06′N	41°44′E
Ródos, Grc.	200-01	36°26′N	28°14′E
Ródos, i., Grc.	200-01	36°10′N	28°00′E
Roebourne, Austl. (rō´bŭrn)	270-71	20°46′S	117°10′E
Rogagua, Laguna, lk., Bol.	166-67	13°42′S	67°07′W
Rogaguado, Laguna, lk., Bol. (rō´gō-ä-gwä-dō)	166-67	12°52′S	65°43′W
Rogers, Ar., U.S. (rŏj-ērz)	120-21	36°20′N	94°07′W
Rogers, Mount, mtn., Va., U.S.	124-25	36°39′N	81°33′W
Rogers City, Mi., U.S. (rŏj-ērz sĭ´tē)	116-17	45°25′N	83°49′W
Rohtak, India	234-35	28°53′N	76°36′E
Roi Georges, Îles du, is., Fr. Poly.	280-81	14°32′S	145°08′W
Rojas, Arg. (rō´häs)	173	34°12′S	60°44′W
Rojo, Cabo, c., Mex. (ká´bō rō´hō)	146-47	21°33′N	97°20′W
Rojo, Cabo, c., P.R. (ká´bō rō´hō)	142a	17°56′N	67°11′W
Rokan, stm., Indon.	246-47	1°50′N	100°55′E
Rokeby National Park, n.p., Austl. *see* Mungkan Kandju National Park	277	13°32′S	142°37′E
Rokycany, Czech Rep. (rô´kĭ´tsä-nĭ)	194-95	49°45′N	13°36′E
Rolândia, Braz.	168-69	23°18′S	51°23′W
Roldanillo, Col. (rôl-dä-nē´l-yō)	163c	4°24′N	76°09′W
Rolla, Mo., U.S.	120-21	37°57′N	91°46′W
Roma, Austl. (rō´má)	276	26°35′S	148°47′E
Roma, nat. cap., Italy (rō´má) *see* Rome	200-01	41°54′N	12°29′E
Romaine, stm., Can. (rô-mĕn´)	138-39	50°18′N	63°48′W
Roman, Rom. (rō´män)	194-95	46°56′N	26°57′E
Romang, Pulau, i., Indon.	248-49	7°34′S	127°26′E
Romania, nation, Eur. (rō-mā´nē-å)	174-75	46°0′N	25°30′E
Roman-Kosh, hora, mtn., Ukr.	202-03	44°37′N	34°15′E
Romano, Cape, c., Fl., U.S. (kāp rō-mä´nō)	125a	25°50′N	81°41′W
Romano, Cayo, i., Cuba (kä´yō-rō-má´nō)	142-43	22°04′N	77°50′W
Romblon, Phil. (rōm-blōn´)	250	12°34′N	122°16′E
Rome, Ga., U.S. (rōm)	124-25	34°16′N	85°10′W
Rome, N.Y., U.S. (rōm)	116-17	43°13′N	75°28′W
Rome, nat. cap., Italy (rōm)	200-01	41°54′N	12°29′E
Romeo, Mi., U.S. (rō´mē-ō)	116-17	42°48′N	83°00′W
Romilly-sur-Seine, Fr. (rô-mē-yē´sür-sān´)	196-97	48°31′N	3°44′E
Romny, Ukr. (rôm´nĭ)	202-03	50°45′N	33°29′E
Rømø, i., Den. (rûm´û)	192-93	55°08′N	8°31′E
Romorantin-Lanthenay, Fr. (rô-mô-räN-täN´)	196-97	47°22′N	1°44′E
Rona, i., Scot., U.K.	184-85	59°07′N	5°49′W
Ronan, Mt., U.S. (rō´năn)	112-13	47°31′N	114°06′W
Roncador, Serra do, plat., Braz. (sĕr´rá dò rôn-kä-dôr´)	166-67	12°0′S	52°00′W
Ronda, Spain (rōn´dä)	198-99	36°44′N	5°10′W
Rondônia, state, Braz.	166-67	11°0′S	63°00′W
Rondonópolis, Braz.	168-69	16°28′S	54°38′W
Ronge, Lac la, lk., Sk., Can. (läk lä rōnzh)	134-35	55°10′N	105°00′W
Rongelap, at., Marsh. Is.	280-81	11°20′N	166°50′E
Rongjiang, China (rōŋ-jyäŋ)	238-39	25°51′N	108°35′E
Rønne, Den. (rûn´ĕ)	194-95	55°06′N	14°42′E
Ronneby, Swe. (rōn´ĕ-bü)	192-93	56°12′N	15°18′E
Ronuro, stm., Braz.	166-67	11°56′S	53°33′W
Roorkee, India	234-35	29°52′N	77°53′E
Roosendaal, Neth. (rō´zĕn-däl)	190-91	51°32′N	4°28′E
Roosevelt, Ut., U.S. (rōz´´vĕlt)	118-19	40°19′N	109°59′W
Roosevelt, stm., Braz. (rô´sĕ-vĕlt)	166-67	7°34′S	60°41′W
Roper, stm., Austl. (rōp´ēr)	272-73	14°44′S	135°23′E
Roque Pérez, Arg. (rô´kĕ-pĕ´rĕz)	173	35°25′S	59°20′W
Roraima, state, Braz. (rô´rīy-mă)	166-67	1°0′N	61°00′W
Roraima, Monte, mtn., S.A. *see* Roraima, Mount	164-65	5°13′N	60°44′W
Roraima, Mount, mtn., S.A. (mount rô-rä-ē´mä)	164-65	5°13′N	60°44′W
Røros, Nor. (rûr´ôs)	184-85	62°35′N	11°23′E
Ros', stm., Ukr. (rôs)	202-03	49°41′N	31°36′E
Rosales, Mex. (rō-zä´läs)	122-23	28°12′N	105°33′W
Rosamorada, Mex. (rō´zä-mō-rä´dhä)	146-47	22°08′N	105°12′W
Rosario, Arg. (rô-zä´rē-ō)	173	32°57′S	60°40′W
Rosário, Braz. (rô-zä´rē-ò)	166-67	2°57′S	44°14′W
Rosario, Mex. (rô-zä´rē-ō)	146-47	23°00′N	105°52′W
Rosario, Para.	168-69	24°25′S	57°06′W
Rosario, Ur. (rô-zä´rē-ō)	173	34°19′S	57°21′W
Rosario de la Frontera, Arg.	168-69	25°48′S	64°58′W
Rosario de Lerma, Arg.	168-69	24°59′S	65°35′W
Rosário do Sul, Braz. (rô-zä´rē-ò-dô-sōō´l)	173	30°15′S	54°56′W
Rosário Oeste, Braz. (rô-zä´rē-ò ō´ĕst´ĕ)	166-67	14°50′S	56°25′W
Roscoe, Tx., U.S. (rôs´kō)	120-21	32°27′N	100°33′W
Roseau, Mn., U.S. (rô-zō´)	114-15	48°51′N	95°46′W
Roseau, nat. cap., Dom.	143b	15°18′N	61°23′W
Rosebud, stm., Ab., Can. (rōz´bŭd)	132-33	51°25′N	112°37′W
Rosebud Indian Reservation, ind. res., S.D., U.S. (rōz´bŭd ĭn´dĭ-ăn rĕ-sēr-vā´shĕn)	114-15	43°08′N	100°33′W
Roseburg, Or., U.S.	112-13	43°14′N	123°20′W
Rosenheim, Ger. (rō´zĕn-hīm)	194-95	47°52′N	12°08′E
Rosetown, Sk., Can. (rōz´toun)	134-35	51°32′N	108°01′W
Rosetta, Egypt	268b	31°24′N	30°25′E
Roseville, Mn., U.S. (rōz´vĭl)	114-15	45°01′N	93°10′W
Roșiori de Vede, Rom. (rô-shôr´ĕ dĕ vĕ-dĕ)	200-01	44°07′N	24°60′E
Roskilde, Den. (rôs´kĕl-dĕ)	192-93	55°39′N	12°06′E
Roslavl', Russia (rôs´läv'l)	202-03	53°57′N	32°52′E
Rossano, Italy (rô-sä´nō)	200-01	39°35′N	16°39′E
Rossiya, nation, Eur. *see* Russia	174-75	60°0′N	100°00′E
Rossland, B.C., Can. (rôs´lănd)	132-33	49°05′N	117°48′W
Rosso, Maur.	258-59	16°31′N	15°48′W
Rossosh', Russia (rôs´sŭsh)	186-87	50°12′N	39°35′E
Ross River, Yk., Can.	128-29	62°00′N	132°26′W
Ross Sea, s., Ant. (rôs sē)	287	76°0′S	175°00′W
Rossville, Ga., U.S. (rôs´vĭl)	124-25	34°59′N	85°18′W
Rosthern, Sk., Can.	134-35	52°40′N	106°20′W
Rostock, Ger. (rôs´tŭk)	194-95	54°05′N	12°07′E
Rostov, Russia (rôstôv)	202-03	57°11′N	39°25′E
Rostov-na-Donu, Russia (rôstôv-nå-dô-nōō)	202-03	47°13′N	39°43′E
Roswell, Ga., U.S. (rŏz´wĕl)	124-25	34°02′N	84°21′W
Roswell, N.M., U.S. (rŏz´wĕl)	120-21	33°24′N	104°33′W
Rota, i., N. Mar. Is.	279c	14°10′N	145°12′E
Rotherham, Eng., U.K. (rŏdh´ēr-ăm)	190-91	53°25′N	1°23′W
Rothesay, Scot., U.K. (rôth´sā)	190-91	55°50′N	5°03′W
Roti, Pulau, i., Indon. (pōō-lou rō´tē)	248-49	10°45′S	123°10′E
Rotorua, N.Z.	278	38°09′S	176°14′E
Rotterdam, Neth. (rŏt´ēr-däm´)	190-91	51°55′N	4°28′E
Rottweil, Ger. (rōt´vīl)	194-95	48°10′N	8°38′E
Rotuma, i., Fiji	280-81	12°30′S	177°05′E

n-sing; ŋ-baŋk; N-nasalized n; nŏd; cŏmmit; ōld; ōbey; ôrder; oi-boil; fōōd; ŏŏ-as oo in foot; ou-out; s-soft; sh-dish; th-thin; pūre; ûnite; ûrn; stŭd; circŭs; ü-as in French tu; ´-indeterminate vowel.

376 Roubaix – Saint-Denis PRONOUNCING INDEX

Feature (Pronunciation)	Page	Lat.	Long.
Roubaix, Fr. (rōō-bĕ´)	196-97	50°41'N	3°10'E
Rouen, Fr. (rōō-äN´)	196-97	49°27'N	1°07'E
Rouge, stm., Qc., Can. (rōōzh)	136-37	45°38'N	74°42'W
Round Mountain, mtn., Austl.	276	30°27'S	152°14'E
Round Rock, Tx., U.S. (round rŏk)	122-23	30°30'N	97°41'W
Roundup, Mt., U.S. (round´ŭp)	112-13	46°27'N	108°33'W
Rouyn-Noranda, Qc., Can.	136-37	48°14'N	79°01'W
Rovaniemi, Fin. (rô´vȧ-nyĕ´mĭ)	184-85	66°30'N	25°42'E
Rovereto, Italy (rō-vå-rā´tô)	200-01	45°54'N	11°02'E
Rovigo, Italy (rô-vē´gô)	200-01	45°05'N	11°47'E
Rovinj, Cro. (rô´ēn')	200-01	45°05'N	13°38'E
Rovira, Col. (rô-vē´rä)	163c	4°14'N	75°15'W
Rovno, Ukr. *see* Rivne	194-95	50°37'N	26°14'E
Rovuma, stm., Afr.	264-65	10°31'S	40°24'E
Rowley Island, i., Nu., Can.	130-31	69°05'N	78°52'W
Roxas, Phil.	250	11°35'N	122°45'E
Roy, Ut., U.S. (roi)	112-13	41°10'N	112°01'W
Royale, Isle, i., Mi., U.S.	114-15	48°0'N	89°00'W
Royal Oak, Mi., U.S. (roi´ăl ōk)	116-17	42°30'N	83°08'W
Royal Tunbridge Wells, Eng., U.K.	190-91	51°08'N	0°16'E
Royan, Fr. (rwä-yäN´)	196-97	45°38'N	1°01'W
Rožňava, Slvk. (rôzh´nyá-vȧ)	194-95	48°40'N	20°33'E
Rtishchevo, Russia ('r-tĭsh´chĕ-vô)	186-87	52°16'N	43°47'E
Ruaha National Park, n.p., Tan.	267	7°30'S	34°40'E
Ruapehu, Mount, vol., N.Z. (mount r´oo-á-pā´hōō)	278	39°17'S	175°34'E
Rub'al-Khali, des., Asia	220-21	20°0'N	51°00'E
Rubizhne, Ukr.	202-03	49°01'N	38°23'E
Rubondo Island, i., Tan.	267	2°20'S	31°52'E
Rubtsovsk, Russia	226	51°31'N	81°12'E
Ruby Mountains, mts., Nv., U.S. (rōō´bē moun´tĭnz)	118-19	40°25'N	115°31'W
Rudkøbing, Den. (rōōdh´kûb-ĭng)	194-95	54°56'N	10°44'E
Rūdnyy, Kaz.	226	52°59'N	63°07'E
Rudolf, Lake, lk., Afr. (lăk rōō´dôlf)	267	3°30'N	36°00'E
Rudolf Hāyk', lk., Afr. *see* Rudolf, Lake	267	3°30'N	36°00'E
Ruffec, Fr. (rü-fĕk´)	196-97	46°01'N	0°12'E
Rufiji, stm., Tan. (rò-fē´jė)	262-63	7°58'S	39°25'E
Rufino, Arg.	173	34°16'S	62°42'W
Rugao, China (rōō-gou)	238-39	32°24'N	120°33'E
Rugby, Eng., U.K. (rŭg´bē)	190-91	52°23'N	1°16'W
Rugby, N.D., U.S.	114-15	48°22'N	99°60'W
Rügen, i., Ger. (rü´ghĕn)	194-95	54°25'N	13°24'E
Rugufu, stm., Tan.	267	5°30'S	30°01'E
Ruhengeri, Rw.	267	1°30'S	29°38'E
Rui'an, China (rwā-än)	238-39	27°50'N	120°35'E
Ruijin, China	238-39	25°52'N	116°00'E
Ruiz, Mex. (rōē´z)	146-47	21°57'N	105°09'W
Ruiz, Nevado del, vol., Col. (nĕ-vá´dô-dĕl-rōōē´z)	163c	4°53'N	75°20'W
Rūjiena, Lat. (rò´yĭ-ă-nȧ)	192-93	57°54'N	25°20'E
Rukwa, Lake, lk., Tan. (lăk rōōk-wä´)	267	8°0'S	32°25'E
Ruma, Serb. (rōō´mȧ)	200-01	45°00'N	19°49'E
Rumbek, Sudan (rŭm´bĕk)	262-63	6°48'N	29°41'E
Rum Cay, i., Bah. (rŭm kē)	142-43	23°41'N	74°53'W
Rumford, Me., U.S. (rŭm´fērd)	116-17	44°33'N	70°33'W
Rumoi, Japan	244	43°56'N	141°39'E
Runan, China (rōō-nän)	238-39	33°00'N	114°21'E
Runde, stm., Zimb.	264-65	21°18'S	32°24'E
Rundu, Nmb.	264-65	17°55'S	19°45'E
Rŭng, Kaôh, i., Camb.	246-47	10°44'N	103°14'E
Rungwa, stm., Tan.	267	7°37'S	31°49'E
Ruo, stm., China (rwô)	240-41	41°04'N	100°20'E
Ruoqiang, China	220-21	39°01'N	88°11'E
Rupat, Pulau, i., Indon. (pōō-lou rōō´pät)	246-47	1°50'N	101°35'E
Rupert, Id., U.S. (rōō´pērt)	112-13	42°38'N	113°41'W
Rurrenabaque, Bol.	166-67	14°28'S	67°30'W
Rurutu, i., Fr. Poly.	280-81	22°26'S	151°20'W
Rusape, Zimb.	264-65	18°32'S	32°08'E
Ruse, Blg. (rōō´sĕ) (rò´sĕ)	200-01	43°51'N	25°57'E
Rushville, Il., U.S. (rŭsh´vĭl)	120-21	40°07'N	90°33'W
Rushville, In., U.S. (rŭsh´vĭl)	116-17	39°36'N	85°27'W
Rushville, Ne., U.S. (rŭsh´vĭl)	114-15	42°43'N	102°28'W
Rusk, Tx., U.S. (rŭsk)	122-23	31°48'N	95°09'W
Russas, Braz. (rōō´s-säs)	166-67	4°56'S	37°58'W
Russell, Mb., Can. (rŭs´ĕl)	134-35	50°47'N	101°15'W
Russell, Ks., U.S. (rŭs´ĕl)	120-21	38°50'N	98°50'W
Russell, Ky., U.S. (rŭs´ĕl)	116-17	38°31'N	82°42'W
Russell Lake, lk., Mb., Can. (rŭs´ĕl lăk)	134-35	56°15'N	101°32'W
Russellville, Al., U.S. (rŭs´ĕl-vĭl)	124-25	34°30'N	87°44'W
Russellville, Ar., U.S. (rŭs´ĕl-vĭl)	120-21	35°17'N	93°09'W
Russellville, Ky., U.S. (rŭs´ĕl-vĭl)	124-25	36°51'N	86°53'W
Russia, nation, Eur. (rŭ´shȧ)	218-19	60°0'N	100°00'E
Rustavi, Geor.	227	41°32'N	45°02'E
Rustenburg, S. Afr. (rŭs´tĕn-bûrg)	269c	25°40'S	27°15'E
Ruston, La., U.S. (rŭs´tŭn)	120-21	32°32'N	92°38'W
Ruteng, Indon.	248-49	8°36'S	120°29'E
Rutherfordton, N.C., U.S. (rŭdh´ēr-fērd-tŭn)	124-25	35°22'N	81°58'W
Rutland, Vt., U.S.	116-17	43°37'N	72°59'W
Rutog, China	234-35	33°26'N	79°42'E
Rutshuru, D.R.C. (rōōt-shōō´rōō)	267	1°11'S	29°27'E
Ruvuma, stm., Afr.	264-65	10°31'S	40°24'E
Ruwenzori Range, mts., Afr.	267	0°20'N	29°53'E
Ruzayevka, Russia	186-87	54°04'N	44°57'E
Rwanda, nation, Afr. (rü-än´-dȧ)	253	2°0'S	30°00'E
Ryazan', Russia (ryä-zän´')	202-03	54°38'N	39°44'E
Ryazhsk, Russia (ryäzh´sk')	186-87	53°42'N	40°05'E
Rybachiy, Poluostrov, pen., Russia	184-85	69°42'N	32°36'E
Rybachye, Kyrg. *see* Balykchy	226	42°28'N	76°12'E
Rybinsk, Russia	202-03	58°03'N	38°52'E
Rybnik, Pol. (rĭb´nĕk)	194-95	50°06'N	18°33'E
Ryde, Eng., U.K. (rīd)	190-91	50°44'N	1°10'W
Ryeosu, Kor., S. *see* Yŏsu	243	34°44'N	127°44'E
Rylsk, Russia (rĕl´'sk)	202-03	51°34'N	34°42'E
Ryojun, China *see* Lüshun	240-41	38°49'N	121°15'E
Ryōtsu, Japan (ryōt´sōō)	245	38°05'N	138°26'E
Ryukyu Islands, is., Japan (rū-kū ī´lăndz)	244a	25°44'N	126°58'E
Rzeszów, Pol. (zhå-shóf)	194-95	50°03'N	22°01'E
Rzhev, Russia ('r-zhĕf)	202-03	56°17'N	34°19'E

S

Feature (Pronunciation)	Page	Lat.	Long.
Saale, stm., Ger. (sä-lĕ)	194-95	51°57'N	11°55'E
Saalfeld, Ger. (säl´fĕlt)	194-95	50°39'N	11°22'E
Saarbrücken, Ger. (zähr´brü-kĕn)	194-95	49°14'N	6°60'E
Saaremaa, i., Est.	192-93	58°25'N	22°30'E
Saavedra, Arg. (sä-ä-vā´drä)	173	37°46'S	62°21'W
Saba, i., Neth. Ant. (sä´bä)	143b	17°38'N	63°14'W
Šabac, Serb. (shä´bàts)	200-01	44°46'N	19°42'E
Sabadell, Spain (sä-bä-dhål´)	198-99	41°33'N	2°06'E
Sabah, hist. reg., Malay.	248-49	5°20'N	117°10'E
Sabanagrande, Hond. (sä-bä´nä-grä´n-dĕ)	149	13°49'N	87°17'W
Sabanalarga, Col. (sä-bá´nä-lär´gä)	164-65	10°38'N	74°55'W
Sabancuy, Mex. (sä-bäŋ-kwē´)	148	18°58'N	91°11'W
Sabang, Indon. (sä´bäng)	248-49	0°13'N	119°53'E
Sabang, Indon. (sä´bäng)	246-47	5°53'N	95°20'E
Şāberī, Hāmūn-e, lk., Asia	232-33	31°30'N	61°20'E
Sabhā, Libya	258-59	27°01'N	14°28'E
Sabi, stm., Afr. (sä´bē) *see* Save	264-65	20°58'S	35°04'E
Sabinal, Cayo, i., Cuba (kä´yō sä-bē-näl´)	142-43	21°40'N	77°18'W
Sabinas, Mex.	122-23	27°51'N	101°07'W
Sabinas, stm., Mex. (sä-bē´näs)	122-23	26°51'N	99°35'W
Sabinas, stm., Mex. (sä-bē´näs)	122-23	27°29'N	100°40'W
Sabinas Hidalgo, Mex. (sä-bē´näs ē-däl´gō)	122-23	26°30'N	100°10'W
Sabine, stm., U.S.	110-11	30°00'N	93°46'W
Sable, Cape, c., N.S., Can. (kāp sā´b'l)	138-39	43°25'N	65°37'W
Sable, Cape, pen., Fl., U.S. (kāp sā´b'l)	125a	25°12'N	81°05'W
Sable, Île de, i., N. Cal.	272-73	19°15'S	159°56'E
Sable Island, i., N.S., Can.	138-39	43°56'N	59°56'W
Sablé-sur-Sarthe, Fr. (säb-lā-sür-särt´)	196-97	47°50'N	0°20'W
Sabor, stm., Port. (sä-bōr´)	198-99	41°11'N	7°07'W
Sabzevār, Iran	232-33	36°13'N	57°40'E
Sac, stm., Mo., U.S. (sôk)	120-21	38°01'N	93°44'W
Sac City, Ia., U.S. (sŏk sĭ´tė)	114-15	42°25'N	94°60'W
Sachigo, stm., On., Can.	134-35	55°04'N	88°59'W
Sachigo Lake, lk., On., Can. (săch´ĭ-gō lăk)	134-35	53°49'N	92°08'W
Sachsen, hist. reg., Ger. (zäк´sĕn) *see* Saxony	194-95	52°45'N	9°30'E
Sackville, N.B., Can. (săk´vĭl)	138-39	45°54'N	64°22'W
Saco, Me., U.S. (sô´kô)	116-17	43°30'N	70°27'W
Sacramento, Ca., U.S. (săk-rȧ-mĕn´tō)	118-19	38°35'N	121°29'W
Sacramento, stm., Ca., U.S. (săk-rȧ-mĕn´tō)	110-11	38°03'N	121°53'W
Sacramento Mountains, mts., N.M., U.S.	120-21	32°42'N	105°37'W
Şa'dah, Yemen	266	16°49'N	43°48'E
Sadiya, India (sŭ-dē´yä)	234-35	27°50'N	95°40'E
Sado, i., Japan (sä´dō)	245	38°0'N	138°25'E
Saeki, Japan (sä´å-kė) *see* Saiki	245	32°58'N	131°55'E
Safāga, Egypt	268b	26°45'N	33°56'E
Safford, Az., U.S. (săf´fērd)	118-19	32°50'N	109°43'W
Safi, Mor. (sä´fē) (äs´fē)	258-59	32°18'N	9°13'W
Safīd Koh, Selseleh-ye, mts., Afg.	232-33	34°30'N	63°30'E
Safonovo, Russia	202-03	55°07'N	33°15'E
Saga, China	234-35	29°29'N	85°09'E
Saga, Japan	245	33°15'N	130°18'E
Sagaing, Mya.	246-47	21°53'N	95°59'E
Sagami-nada, b., Japan (sä´gä´mē nä-dä)	245	34°60'N	139°30'E
Saganaga Lake, lk., N.A. (să-gȧ-nä´gȧ lăk)	134-35	48°14'N	90°52'W
Sāgar, India	234-35	23°50'N	78°45'E
Sagarmāthā, mtn., Asia *see* Everest, Mount	234-35	27°59'N	86°56'E
Sagavanirktok, stm., Ak., U.S.	126	70°21'N	148°11'W
Saginaw, Mi., U.S. (săg´ĭ-nô)	116-17	43°26'N	83°58'W
Saginaw Bay, b., Mi., U.S. (săg´ĭ-nô bā)	116-17	43°50'N	83°40'W
Sagua de Tánamo, Cuba (sä-gwä dĕ tá´nä-mō)	142-43	20°35'N	75°14'W
Sagua la Grande, Cuba (sä-gwä lä grä´n-dĕ)	142-43	22°49'N	80°04'W
Saguaro National Park, n.p., Az., U.S. (säg-wä´rō năsh´ŭn-ăl pärk)	118-19	32°16'N	111°12'W
Saguenay, stm., Qc., Can. (săg-ē-nā´)	138-39	48°08'N	69°41'W
Sagunt, Spain	198-99	39°41'N	0°16'W
Sagunto, Spain (sä-gōn´tō) *see* Sagunt	198-99	39°41'N	0°16'W
Sa'gya, China	234-35	28°54'N	88°04'E
Sahara, des., Afr. (sȧ-hä´rȧ)	258-59	26°0'N	13°00'E
Sahāranpur, India (sŭ-hä´rŭn-pōōr´)	234-35	29°58'N	77°33'E
Sahel, reg., Afr.	258-59	12°0'N	17°00'E
Sāḩil, reg., Afr. *see* Sahel	258-59	12°0'N	17°00'E
Sāhīwāl, Pak.	232-33	30°40'N	73°06'E
Şaḩrā', des., Afr. *see* Sahara	258-59	26°0'N	13°00'E
Saïda, Alg.	184-85	34°50'N	0°09'E
Saidpur, Bngl.	234-35	25°47'N	88°54'E
Saigon, Viet. *see* Ho Chi Minh City	246-47	10°45'N	106°40'E
Saiki, Japan	245	32°58'N	131°55'E
Saimaa, lk., Fin. (sā´ĭ-mä)	192-93	61°15'N	28°15'E
Saín Alto, Mex. (sä-ēn´ äl´tō)	146-47	23°35'N	103°13'W
Saint Albans, Eng., U.K. (sânt ôl´bănz)	190-91	51°45'N	0°21'W
Saint Albans, Vt., U.S. (sânt ôl´bănz)	116-17	44°49'N	73°05'W
Saint Albans, W.V., U.S. (sânt ôl´bănz)	116-17	38°23'N	81°50'W
Saint Albert, Ab., Can. (sânt ăl´bērt)	132-33	53°38'N	113°38'W
Saint-Amand-Mont-Rond, Fr. (săN´t á-mäN´ môN-rôN´)	196-97	46°43'N	2°30'E
Saint-André, Cap, c., Madag. *see* Vilanandro, Tanjona	264-65	16°12'S	44°28'E
Saint Andrews, Scot., U.K.	190-91	56°20'N	2°48'W
Saint-Anselme, Qc., Can. (săN´ tăN-sĕlm´)	138-39	46°37'N	70°57'W
Saint Anthony, Nf., Can. (săn ăn´thô-nē)	138-39	51°22'N	55°37'W
Saint Anthony, Id., U.S. (sânt ăn´thô-nē)	112-13	43°58'N	111°41'W
Saint-Augustin, Qc., Can.	138-39	51°14'N	58°38'W
Saint Augustine, Fl., U.S. (sânt ô´gŭs-tēn)	124-25	29°54'N	81°19'W
Saint-Barthélemy, i., Guad.	143b	17°54'N	62°50'W
Saint Bees Head, c., Eng., U.K. (sânt bēz´hĕd)	190-91	54°31'N	3°38'W
Saint Bride, Mount, mtn., Ab., Can. (mount sânt brīd)	132-33	51°31'N	115°57'W
Saint-Brieuc, Fr. (săN´ brēs´)	196-97	48°31'N	2°45'W
Saint Catharines, On., Can. (sânt kăth´å-rĭnz)	136-37	43°10'N	79°14'W
Saint-Chamond, Fr. (săN´ shȧ-môN´)	196-97	45°29'N	4°31'E
Saint Charles, Il., U.S. (sânt chärlz´)	116-17	41°55'N	88°19'W
Saint Charles, Md., U.S. (sânt chärlz´)	116-17	38°35'N	76°57'W
Saint Charles, Mi., U.S. (sânt chärlz´)	116-17	43°18'N	84°08'W
Saint Charles, Mn., U.S. (sânt chärlz´)	114-15	43°58'N	92°03'W
Saint Charles, Mo., U.S. (sânt chärlz´)	120-21	38°48'N	90°29'W
Saint Christopher, i., St. K./N.	143b	17°20'N	62°45'W
Saint Christopher and Nevis, nation, N.A. *see* Saint Kitts and Nevis	140-41	17°20'N	62°45'W
Saint Clair, Mi., U.S. (sânt klâr)	116-17	42°50'N	82°29'W
Saint Clair, Mo., U.S. (sânt klâr)	120-21	38°21'N	90°59'W
Saint-Claude, Fr. (săN´ klōd´)	196-97	46°23'N	5°51'E
Saint Cloud, Fl., U.S. (sânt kloud´)	125a	28°15'N	81°17'W
Saint Cloud, Mn., U.S. (sânt kloud)	114-15	45°33'N	94°10'W
Saint Croix, i., V.I.U.S. (sânt kroi´)	143b	17°45'N	64°45'W
Saint Croix, stm., N.A. (sânt kroi´)	138-39	45°10'N	67°09'W
Saint Croix, stm., U.S. (sânt kroi´)	114-15	44°45'N	92°48'W
Saint-Denis, Fr. (săN´dē-nē´)	196-97	48°57'N	2°21'E
Saint-Denis, nat. cap., Reu. (săN´dē-nē´)	265a	20°52'S	55°28'E

ăt; finăl; rāte; senâte; ärm; åsk; sofȧ; fâre; ch-choose; dh-as th in other; bē; ėvent; bĕt; recĕnt; cratẽr; g-gō; gh-guttural g; bĭt; ĭ-short neutral; rīde; κ-guttural k as ch in German ich;

PRONOUNCING INDEX

Saint-Dizier – Sallisaw 377

Feature (Pronunciation)	Page	Lat.	Long.
Saint-Dizier, Fr. (săn dē-zyä´)	196-97	48°39'N	4°57'E
Sainte-Agathe-des-Monts, Qc., Can.	136-37	46°03'N	74°17'W
Sainte-Foy, Qc., Can. (sănt fwä)	136-37	46°47'N	71°17'W
Sainte Genevieve, Mo., U.S. (sānt jĕn´ĕ-vēv)	120-21	37°59'N	90°03'W
Saint Elias, Mount, mtn., N.A. (mount sānt ē-lī´ăs)	126	60°18'N	140°55'W
Saint-Élie, Fr. Gu.	164-65	4°50'N	53°17'W
Sainte-Lucie, Canal de, strt., N.A. *see* Saint Lucia Channel	143b	14°09'N	60°57'W
Sainte-Marguerite, stm., Qc., Can.	138-39	50°09'N	66°36'W
Sainte-Marie, Cap, c., Madag. *see* Vohimena, Tanjona	264-65	25°36'S	45°09'E
Sainte Marie, Nosy, i., Madag.	264-65	16°50'S	49°57'E
Saint-Étienne, Fr.	196-97	45°26'N	4°24'E
Saint-Eustache, Qc., Can. (săn´ tû-stásh´)	136-37	45°34'N	73°55'W
Saint-Félicien, Qc., Can. (săn fā-lē-syăn´)	136-37	48°39'N	72°27'W
Saint-Florent-sur-Cher, Fr. (săn´ flô-răn´sür-shâr´)	196-97	46°59'N	2°15'E
Saint-Flour, Fr. (săn flōōr´)	196-97	45°02'N	3°05'E
Saint Francis, Cape, c., S. Afr.	264-65	34°11'S	24°50'E
Saint-Gaudens, Fr. (săn gō-däns´)	196-97	43°07'N	0°44'E
Saint George, Austl. (sānt jôrj´)	276	28°03'S	148°35'E
Saint George, N.B., Can. (săn jôrj´)	138-39	45°08'N	66°49'W
Saint George, S.C., U.S. (sānt jôrj´)	124-25	33°11'N	80°35'W
Saint George, Ut., U.S. (sānt jôrj´)	118-19	37°06'N	113°34'W
Saint George, Cape, c., Nf., Can. (kāp sānt jôr-jĕz)	138-39	48°29'N	59°15'W
Saint George, Cape, c., Fl., U.S. (kāp sānt jôr-jĕz)	124-25	29°35'N	85°04'W
Saint George Island, i., Fl., U.S.	124-25	29°39'N	84°53'W
Saint-Georges, Fr. Gu.	164-65	3°57'N	51°48'W
Saint George's, nat. cap., Gren. (sānt jôrj´ĕs)	143b	12°04'N	61°45'W
Saint George's Bay, b., Nf., Can. (sānt jôr-jĕz bā)	138-39	48°20'N	59°00'W
Saint Georges Bay, b., N.S., Can. (sānt jôr-jĕz bā)	138-39	45°50'N	61°45'W
Saint George's Channel, strt., Eur. (sānt jôr-jĕz chăn´ĕl)	190-91	52°0'N	6°00'W
Saint-Girons, Fr. (săn zhē-rôn´)	196-97	42°59'N	1°09'E
Saint Helena, dep., Afr. (sānt hē-lē´nȧ)	253	15°57'S	5°42'W
Saint Helena, i., St. Hel. (sānt hē-lē´nȧ)	254	15°57'S	5°43'W
Saint Helens, Or., U.S. (sānt hĕl´ĕnz)	112-13	45°52'N	122°48'W
Saint Helens, Mount, vol., Wa., U.S. (mount sānt hĕl´ĕnz)	112-13	46°12'N	122°11'W
Saint Helier, nat. cap., Jersey (sānt hyĕl´yĕr)	196-97	49°12'N	2°07'W
Saint-Hyacinthe, Qc., Can.	136-37	45°38'N	72°57'W
Saint Ignace, Mi., U.S. (sānt ĭg´nās)	116-17	45°52'N	84°44'W
Saint Ignace Island, i., On., Can. (sānt ĭg´nās ī´lȧnd)	136-37	48°48'N	87°56'W
Saint James, Mn., U.S. (sānt jāmz´)	114-15	43°59'N	94°38'W
Saint James, Mo., U.S. (sānt jāmz´)	120-21	37°60'N	91°37'W
Saint James, Cape, c., B.C., Can. (kāp sānt jāmz´)	132-33	51°56'N	131°01'W
Saint-Jean, Lac, res., Qc., Can. (läk săn´ zhän´)	136-37	48°35'N	72°05'W
Saint-Jean-d'Angély, Fr. (săn-zhän´-dän-zhā-lē´)	196-97	45°57'N	0°31'W
Saint-Jean-de-Luz, Fr. (săn-zhän´ dē lüz´)	196-97	43°24'N	1°39'W
Saint-Jean-sur-Richelieu, Qc., Can.	136-37	45°19'N	73°16'W
Saint-Jérôme, Qc., Can. (săn zhā-rōm´)	136-37	45°47'N	74°00'W
Saint John, N.B., Can. (sānt jŏn)	138-39	45°17'N	66°04'W
Saint John, i., V.I.U.S. (sānt jŏn)	143b	18°20'N	64°45'W
Saint John, stm., N.A. (sānt jŏn)	138-39	45°16'N	66°04'W
Saint John, Cape, c., Nf., Can. (kāp sānt jŏn)	138-39	49°59'N	55°32'W
Saint John's, Nf., Can. (sānt jŏns)	138-39	47°34'N	52°43'W
Saint Johns, Az., U.S. (sānt jŏnz)	118-19	34°30'N	109°22'W
Saint Johns, Mi., U.S. (sānt jŏnz)	116-17	42°60'N	84°33'W
Saint John's, nat. cap., Antig. (sānt jŏnz)	143b	17°07'N	61°51'W
Saint Johns, stm., Fl., U.S. (sānt jŏnz)	125a	30°24'N	81°23'W
Saint Johnsbury, Vt., U.S. (sānt jŏnz´bĕr-ē)	116-17	44°26'N	72°01'W
Saint Joseph, Mi., U.S. (sānt jō´sĕf)	116-17	42°05'N	86°29'W
Saint Joseph, Mo., U.S. (sānt jō´sĕf)	120-21	39°46'N	94°50'W
Saint Joseph, stm., U.S. (sānt jō´sĕf)	116-17	42°06'N	86°29'W
Saint Joseph, Lake, lk., On., Can.	134-35	51°03'N	90°52'W
Saint-Joseph-de-Beauce, Qc., Can. (sĕn zhō-zĕf´ dĕ bōs)	138-39	46°18'N	70°52'W
Saint-Junien, Fr. (săn´zhü-nyăn´)	196-97	45°53'N	0°54'E
Saint Kilda, i., Scot., U.K. (sānt kĭl´dȧ)	190-91	57°49'N	8°36'W
Saint Kitts, i., St. K./N. (sānt kĭtts) *see* Saint Christopher	143b	17°20'N	62°45'W
Saint Kitts and Nevis, nation, N.A. (sānt kĭts ănd nē´vĭs)	140-41	17°20'N	62°45'W
Saint-Laurent, stm., N.A. *see* Saint Lawrence	86	49°14'N	67°01'W
Saint-Laurent, Golfe du, b., Can. *see* Saint Lawrence, Gulf of	138-39	48°0'N	62°00'W
Saint-Laurent du Maroni, Fr. Gu.	164-65	5°28'N	54°02'W
Saint Lawrence, Nf., Can. (sānt lô´rĕns)	138-39	46°56'N	55°24'W
Saint Lawrence, stm., N.A. (sānt lô´rĕns)	86	49°14'N	67°01'W
Saint Lawrence, Gulf of, b., Can. (gŭlf ŭv sānt lô´rĕns)	138-39	48°0'N	62°00'W
Saint Lawrence Island, i., Ak., U.S. (sānt lô´rĕns ī´lȧnd)	126	63°30'N	170°30'W
Saint-Louis, Sen.	260-61	16°01'N	16°29'W
Saint Louis, Mi., U.S. (sānt lōō´ĭs)	116-17	43°24'N	84°36'W
Saint Louis, Mo., U.S. (sānt lōō´ĭs) (lōō´ē)	120-21	38°39'N	90°13'W
Saint Lucia, nation, N.A. (sānt lōō´-shȧ)	140-41	13°53'N	60°58'W
Saint Lucia, Lake, lk., S. Afr.	264-65	28°04'S	32°28'E
Saint Lucia Channel, strt., N.A. (sānt lū´shĭ-ȧ chăn´ĕl)	143b	14°09'N	60°57'W
Saint-Malo, Fr. (săn´ má-lō´)	196-97	48°39'N	2°01'W
Saint-Marc, Haiti (săn´ márk´)	142-43	19°07'N	72°41'W
Saint Maries, Id., U.S. (sānt mā´rēs)	112-13	47°19'N	116°34'W
Saint-Martin, i., N.A. (săn-mär´tĭn)	143b	18°04'N	63°04'W
Saint Martinville, La., U.S. (sānt mär´tĭn-vĭl)	124-25	30°08'N	91°50'W
Saint Marys, Austl. (sānt mā´rēz)	276	41°35'S	148°11'E
Saint Marys, Ga., U.S. (sānt mā´rēz)	124-25	30°44'N	81°33'W
Saint Marys, Oh., U.S. (sānt mā´rēz)	116-17	40°33'N	84°24'W
Saint Marys, Pa., U.S. (sānt mā´rēz)	116-17	41°25'N	78°35'W
Saint Marys, W.V., U.S. (sānt mā´rēz)	116-17	39°23'N	81°12'W
Saint Mary's, Cape, c., Nf., Can.	138-39	46°50'N	54°12'W
Saint Mary's Bay, b., Nf., Can.	138-39	46°50'N	53°47'W
Saint Matthew Island, i., Ak., U.S. (sānt măth´ū ī´lȧnd)	218-19	60°29'N	172°53'W
Saint Matthews, S.C., U.S. (sānt măth´ūz)	124-25	33°40'N	80°47'W
Saint Matthias Group, is., Pap. N. Gui.	277	1°36'S	149°47'E
Saint-Maurice, stm., Qc., Can. (săn´ mô-rēs´) (sānt mô´rĭs)	136-37	46°21'N	72°31'W
Saint Michael, Ak., U.S. (sānt mī´kĕl)	126	63°29'N	162°02'W
Saint-Mihiel, Fr. (săn´ mē-yĕl´)	196-97	48°54'N	5°32'E
Saint-Nazaire, Fr. (săn´ná-zâr´)	196-97	47°17'N	2°13'W
Saint-Omer, Fr. (săn´tô-mâr´)	196-97	50°45'N	2°16'E
Saint Paul, Ab., Can. (sānt pôl´)	132-33	53°60'N	111°17'W
Saint-Paul, Reu.	265a	21°0'S	55°16'E
Saint Paul, Mn., U.S. (sānt pôl)	114-15	44°57'N	93°06'W
Saint Paul, Ne., U.S. (sānt pôl)	114-15	41°13'N	98°28'W
Saint Paul, stm., Lib.	260-61	6°25'N	10°44'W
Saint Pauls, N.C., U.S. (sānt pôls)	124-25	34°49'N	78°58'W
Saint Peter, Mn., U.S. (sānt pē´tĕr)	114-15	44°20'N	93°58'W
Saint Peter Port, nat. cap., Guern. (sānt pē´tĕr pôrt)	196-97	49°28'N	2°33'W
Saint Petersburg, Russia (sānt pē´tĕrz-bûrg)	192-93	59°57'N	30°15'E
Saint Petersburg, Fl., U.S. (sānt pē´tĕrz-bûrg)	125a	27°46'N	82°40'W
Saint-Pierre, Reu.	265a	21°19'S	55°29'E
Saint Pierre, i., Sey.	264-65	9°19'S	50°43'E
Saint-Pierre, nat. cap., St. P./M. (săn´pyâr´)	138-39	46°47'N	56°12'W
Saint Pierre and Miquelon, dep., N.A. (sānt pē-âr´ ănd mĭk-ē-lôn´)	138-39	46°55'N	56°20'W
Saint-Pierre-et-Miquelon, dep., N.A. *see* Saint Pierre and Miquelon	138-39	46°55'N	56°20'W
Saint-Pol-de-Léon, Fr. (săn-pô´dĕ-lā-ôn´)	196-97	48°41'N	3°59'W
Saint-Quentin, Fr. (săn´kän-tăn´)	196-97	49°51'N	3°18'E
Saint-Sébastien, Cap, c., Madag. *see* Anorontany, Tanjona	264-65	12°26'S	48°45'E
Saint Stephen, N.B., Can. (sānt stē´vĕn)	138-39	45°12'N	67°17'W
Saint Thomas, On., Can. (sānt tŏm´ȧs)	136-37	42°47'N	81°11'W
Saint Thomas, i., V.I.U.S.	143b	18°21'N	64°55'W
Saint-Tropez, Fr. (săn trô-pĕ´)	196-97	43°16'N	6°38'E
Saint Vincent, i., St. Vin.	143b	13°15'N	61°12'W
Saint-Vincent, Cap, c., Madag. *see* Ankaboa, Tanjona	264-65	21°55'S	43°18'E
Saint Vincent, Gulf, b., Austl. (gŭlf vĭn´sĕnt)	276	34°47'S	138°06'E
Saint Vincent and the Grenadines, nation, N.A. (sānt vĭn´sĕnt ănd thȧ grĕn´ȧ-dēnz)	140-41	13°15'N	61°12'W
Saipan, i., N. Mar. Is.	280-81	15°12'N	145°45'E
Saitama, state, Japan (sī´tä-mä)	245	36°0'N	139°30'E
Sajama, Nevado, mtn., Bol. (nĕ-vá´dô-sä-há´mä)	168-69	18°06'S	68°54'W
Sak, stm., S. Afr.	264-65	30°06'S	20°42'E
Sakai, Japan (sä´kä-ē)	245	34°35'N	135°29'E
Sakākah, Sau. Ar.	228-29	29°58'N	40°13'E
Sakakawea, Lake, res., N.D., U.S.	114-15	47°44'N	102°18'W
Sakami, Lac, lk., Qc., Can.	130-31	53°15'N	76°45'W
Sakart'velo, nation, Asia *see* Georgia	227	42°0'N	44°00'E
Sakarya, Tur.	186-87	40°47'N	30°24'E
Sakarya, stm., Tur. (sȧ-kär´yȧ)	186-87	41°07'N	30°39'E
Sakata, Japan (sä´kä-tä)	244	38°55'N	139°51'E
Sakha, state, Russia *see* Yakutia	218-19	67°0'N	125°00'E
Sakhalin, i., Russia (sȧ-kȧ-lēn´)	218-19	51°0'N	143°00'E
Šakiai, Lith. (shä´kĭ-ī)	192-93	54°58'N	23°04'E
Sakishima-shotō, is., Japan (sä´kē-shē´ma gôn´tō´)	279a	24°33'N	124°26'E
Sal, i., C.V. (säal)	260-61	16°49'N	22°57'W
Sal, stm., Russia (sȧl)	186-87	47°31'N	40°44'E
Sal, Cay, i., Bah. (kē săl)	142-43	23°43'N	80°25'W
Sala, Swe. (sô´lä)	192-93	59°56'N	16°37'E
Salaberry-de-Valleyfield, Qc., Can.	136-37	45°15'N	74°08'W
Sala Consilina, Italy (sä´lä kôn-sē-lē´nä)	200-01	40°25'N	15°34'E
Salada, Laguna, lk., Mex. (lä-gō´nä-sä-lä´dä)	118-19	32°20'N	115°40'W
Saladas, Arg.	173	28°14'S	58°39'W
Saladillo, Arg. (sä-lä-dēl´yō)	173	35°38'S	59°47'W
Salado, stm., Arg. (sä-lä´dô)	168-69	31°41'S	60°44'W
Salado, stm., Arg. (sä-lä´dô)	173	35°45'S	57°23'W
Salado, stm., Arg. (sä-lä´dô)	171	38°49'S	64°59'W
Salado, stm., Mex. (sä-lä´dô)	122-23	26°52'N	99°19'W
Şalālah, Oman	220-21	17°01'N	54°06'E
Salamanca, Chile (sä-lä-mä´n-kä)	168-69	31°46'S	70°59'W
Salamanca, Mex. (sä-lä-mä´n-kä)	146-47	20°34'N	101°12'W
Salamanca, Spain (sä-lä-mä´n-kȧ)	198-99	40°58'N	5°39'W
Salamanca, N.Y., U.S. (săl-ȧ-măn´kȧ)	116-17	42°10'N	78°43'W
Salamat, Bahr, stm., Chad (bär sä-lä-mät´)	262-63	9°27'N	18°06'E
Salamina, Col. (sä-lä-mē´-nä)	163c	5°25'N	75°29'W
Salatiga, Indon.	248-49	7°20'S	110°31'E
Salavat, Russia	186-87	53°22'N	55°56'E
Salaverry, Peru (sä-lä-vĕ´rē)	170	8°14'S	78°58'W
Salawati, i., Indon. (sä-lä-wä´tē)	224-25	1°07'S	130°52'E
Sala y Gómez, Isla, i., Chile	282-83	26°26'S	105°26'W
Saldanha, S. Afr.	264-65	32°60'S	17°57'E
Saldus, Lat. (säl´dòs)	192-93	56°40'N	22°30'E
Sale, Austl. (sāl)	276	38°07'S	147°04'E
Salé, Mor.	269a	34°03'N	6°48'W
Salebabu, Pulau, i., Indon.	248-49	3°56'N	126°42'E
Salekhard, Russia (sŭ-lyĭ-kärt)	218-19	66°32'N	66°37'E
Salem, India (sä´lĕm)	236	11°39'N	78°10'E
Salem, Il., U.S. (sā´lĕm)	116-17	38°37'N	88°57'W
Salem, In., U.S. (sā´lĕm)	116-17	38°36'N	86°06'W
Salem, Mo., U.S. (sā´lĕm)	120-21	37°39'N	91°32'W
Salem, Oh., U.S. (sā´lĕm)	116-17	40°54'N	80°51'W
Salem, Or., U.S.	112-13	44°56'N	123°01'W
Salem, S.D., U.S. (sā´lĕm)	114-15	43°44'N	97°23'W
Salem, Va., U.S. (sā´lĕm)	124-25	37°18'N	80°03'W
Salem, W.V., U.S. (sā´lĕm)	116-17	39°17'N	80°34'W
Salerno, Italy (sä-lĕr´nô)	200-01	40°41'N	14°47'E
Salerno, Golfo di, b., Italy (gôl-fô-dē-sä-lĕr´nô)	200-01	40°32'N	14°42'E
Salgótarján, Hung. (shôl´gô-tôr-yän)	194-95	48°06'N	19°50'E
Salida, Co., U.S. (sȧ-lī´dȧ)	118-19	38°32'N	105°60'W
Salīmah, Wāḩat, well, Sudan	266	21°22'N	29°19'E
Salina, Ks., U.S. (sȧ-lī´nȧ)	120-21	38°50'N	97°36'W
Salina, Ut., U.S. (sȧ-lī´nȧ)	118-19	38°58'N	111°52'W
Salina, Isola, i., Italy (ē´-sō-lä-sä-lē´nä)	200-01	38°34'N	14°50'E
Salina Cruz, Mex. (sä-lē´nä krōōz´)	146-47	16°11'N	95°11'W
Salinas, Ec.	170	2°13'S	80°57'W
Salinas, Ca., U.S. (sȧ-lē´nȧs)	118-19	36°41'N	121°40'W
Salinas de Hidalgo, Mex.	146-47	22°38'N	101°44'W
Saline, stm., Ar., U.S. (sȧ-lēn´)	120-21	33°09'N	92°08'W
Salisbury, Md., U.S.	116-17	38°22'N	75°36'W
Salisbury, Mo., U.S. (sôlz´bĕ-rē)	120-21	39°26'N	92°48'W
Salisbury, N.C., U.S. (sôlz´bĕ-rē)	124-25	35°40'N	80°28'W
Salisbury, nat. cap., Zimb. (sôlz´bĕ-rē) *see* Harare	264-65	17°50'S	31°03'E
Salisbury Island, i., Nu., Can.	130-31	63°30'N	76°60'W
Salliq, Nu., Can. *see* Coral Harbour	128-29	64°08'N	83°12'W
Sallisaw, Ok., U.S. (săl´ĭ-sô)	120-21	35°28'N	94°48'W

n-sing; ŋ-baŋk; ɴ-nasalized n; nŏd; cŏmmit; ōld; ôbey; ôrder; oi-boil; fōōd; ò-as oo in foot; ou-out; s-soft; sh-dish; th-thin; pūre; ůnite; ûrn; stŭd; circŭs; ü-as in French tu; ´-indeterminate vowel.

378 Salluit – San Joaquín
PRONOUNCING INDEX

Feature (Pronunciation)	Page	Lat.	Long.
Salluit, Qc., Can.	128-29	62°13'N	75°36'W
Salmon, Id., U.S. (săm'ŭn)	112-13	45°11'N	113°54'W
Salmon, stm., B.C., Can. (săm'ŭn)	132-33	54°04'N	122°33'W
Salmon, stm., N.B., Can. (săm'ŭn)	138-39	46°04'N	65°55'W
Salmon, stm., Id., U.S. (săm'ŭn)	112-13	45°51'N	116°47'W
Salmon Arm, B.C., Can. (săm'ŭn ärm)	132-33	50°42'N	119°19'W
Salmon River Mountains, mts., Id., U.S. (săm'ŭn rĭv'ẽr moun'tĭnz)	112-13	44°58'N	114°52'W
Salon-de-Provence, Fr. (så-lôn-dĕ-prô-väns')	196-97	43°39'N	5°05'E
Salonika, Grc. *see* Thessaloníki	200-01	40°38'N	22°59'E
Salsk, Russia (sälsk)	186-87	46°28'N	41°33'E
Salt, stm., Az., U.S. (sôlt)	118-19	33°23'N	112°17'W
Salta, Arg. (säl'tä)	168-69	24°48'S	65°25'W
Salta, state, Arg. (säl'tä)	168-69	25°0'S	64°30'W
Saltillo, Mex. (säl-tēl'yō)	122-23	25°26'N	101°00'W
Salt Lake City, Ut., U.S. (sôlt lāk sĭ'tĭ sĭ'tė)	112-13	40°47'N	111°54'W
Salto, Arg. (säl'tō)	173	34°18'S	60°15'W
Salto, Ur.	173	31°23'S	57°58'W
Salto Grande, Embalse, res., S.A.	173	30°55'S	57°54'W
Salto Grande, Embalse de, res., S.A. *see* Salto Grande, Embalse	173	30°55'S	57°54'W
Salton Sea, lk., Ca., U.S. (sôlt'ŭn sē)	118-19	33°19'N	115°50'W
Saltville, Va., U.S. (sôlt'vĭl)	124-25	36°53'N	81°46'W
Saluda, S.C., U.S. (så-lōō'då)	124-25	34°00'N	81°47'W
Salûm, Egypt	188-89	31°34'N	25°09'E
Saluzzo, Italy (sä-lōōt'sō)	200-01	44°39'N	7°29'E
Salvador, Braz. (säl-vä-dōr')	166-67	12°59'S	38°30'W
Salvador, El, nation, N.A. *see* El Salvador	85	13°50'N	88°55'W
Salvador, Lake, lk., La., U.S. (lăk săl'-vå-dôr lāk)	124-25	29°45'N	90°15'W
Salvatierra, Mex. (säl-vä-tyĕr'rä)	146-47	20°13'N	100°54'W
Salyan, Azer.	227	39°35'N	48°58'E
Salzburg, Aus. (sälts'bòrgh)	194-95	47°49'N	13°03'E
Salzwedel, Ger. (sälts-vā'dĕl)	194-95	52°51'N	11°09'E
Samâlût, Egypt (sä-mä-lōōt')	268b	28°18'N	30°42'E
Samana Cay, i., Bah.	142-43	23°05'N	73°44'W
Samar, i., Phil. (sä'mär)	250	12°0'N	125°00'E
Samara, Russia (så-mä'rå)	186-87	53°11'N	50°07'E
Samara, stm., Russia (så-mä'rå)	186-87	53°10'N	50°04'E
Samara, stm., Ukr. (så-mä'rå)	202-03	48°28'N	35°06'E
Samarai, Pap. N. Gui. (sä-mä-rä'ē)	277	10°36'S	150°42'E
Samarinda, Indon.	248-49	0°30'S	117°09'E
Samarqand, Uzb.	232-33	39°40'N	66°56'E
Sāmarrā', Iraq	228-29	34°11'N	43°53'E
Samaúna, Braz.	166-67	7°56'S	60°01'W
Sambalpur, India (sŭm'bŭl-pòr)	234-35	21°28'N	83°59'E
Sambas, Indon.	246-47	1°19'N	109°16'E
Sambava, Madag.	264-65	14°16'S	50°09'E
Sambhal, India	234-35	28°35'N	78°34'E
Sāmbhar, India	234-35	26°54'N	75°13'E
Sambir, Ukr.	194-95	49°31'N	23°13'E
Samborombón, Bahía, b., Arg. (bä-ē'ä-säm-bô-rôm-bô'n)	173	36°0'S	57°12'W
Samch'ŏk, Kor., S.	243	37°27'N	129°10'E
Samch'ŏnp'o, Kor., S.	243	34°56'N	128°05'E
Same, Tan.	267	4°04'S	37°44'E
Samoa, nation, Oc. (să-mō'ă)	279b	13°55'S	172°00'W
Samoa Islands, is., Oc. (să-mō'ă ī'låndz)	279b	14°0'S	171°00'W
Samoded, Russia	186-87	63°37'N	40°30'E
Samokov, Blg. (sä'mô-kôf)	200-01	42°20'N	23°34'E
Sámos, i., Grc. (să'mŏs)	200-01	37°42'N	26°50'E
Samothrace, i., Grc. *see* Samothráki	200-01	40°29'N	25°36'E
Samothráki, i., Grc.	200-01	40°29'N	25°36'E
Sampit, Indon.	248-49	2°33'S	112°57'E
Sam Rayburn Reservoir, res., Tx., U.S.	122-23	31°13'N	94°17'W
Samsun, Tur. (såm'sōōn')	186-87	41°17'N	36°20'E
Samtredia, Geor. (sàm'trĕ-dė)	227	42°10'N	42°21'E
Samui, Ko, i., Thai.	246-47	9°32'N	100°01'E
San, Mali (sän)	258-59	13°18'N	4°54'W
Sandoy, i., Far. Is.	190b	61°50'N	6°45'W
Şan'ā', nat. cap., Yemen (sän'ä) *see* Sanaa	266	15°21'N	44°12'E
Sanaa, nat. cap., Yemen (sän'ä)	266	15°21'N	44°12'E
Sanaga, stm., Camrn. (sä-nä'gä)	260-61	3°33'N	9°39'E
San Agustin, Cape, c., Phil.	250	6°18'N	126°12'E
Sanana, Pulau, i., Indon.	248-49	2°12'S	125°55'E
Sanandaj, Iran	228-29	35°19'N	47°00'E
San Andreas, Ca., U.S. (săn ăn'drė-ăs)	118-19	38°12'N	120°41'W
San Andrés, Col.	150	12°33'N	81°42'W
San Andrés, Isla de, i., Col. (ė's-lä-dĕ-sän-än-drĕ's)	164-65	12°33'N	81°43'W
San Andres Mountains, mts., N.M., U.S. (săn ăn'drė-ăs moun'tĭnz)	118-19	32°59'N	106°36'W
San Andrés Tuxtla, Mex. (sän-än-drā's-tōōs'tlä)	146-47	18°26'N	95°13'W
San Angelo, Tx., U.S. (săn ăn-jĕ-lō)	122-23	31°29'N	100°26'W
San Antonio, Chile (sän-àn-tō'nyō)	163e	33°36'S	71°36'W
San Antonio, Col. (sän-àn-tō'nyō)	163c	3°55'N	75°29'W
San Antonio, Tx., U.S. (săn ăn-tō'nė-ō)	122-23	29°25'N	98°29'W
San Antonio, stm., Tx., U.S. (săn ăn-tō'nė-ō)	122-23	28°30'N	96°53'W
San Antonio, Cabo, c., Arg.	173	36°40'S	56°42'W
San Antonio, Cabo de, c., Cuba (kå'bô-dĕ-sän-än-tô'nyō)	142-43	21°52'N	84°57'W
San Antonio Bay, b., Tx., U.S. (săn ăn-tō'nė-ō bā)	122-23	28°20'N	96°45'W
San Antonio de los Cobres, Arg. (sän-àn-tō'nyō dā lōs kō'brås)	168-69	24°13'S	66°19'W
San Antonio Oeste, Arg. (sän-nä-tō'nyō ô-ĕs'tå)	171	40°45'S	64°58'W
San Augustine, Tx., U.S. (săn ô'gŭs-tēn)	122-23	31°31'N	94°07'W
San Benedetto del Tronto, Italy (sän bā'nå-dĕt'tô dĕl trōn'tō)	200-01	42°58'N	13°53'E
San Benedicto, Isla, i., Mex.	144-45	19°19'N	110°49'W
San Benito, Guat.	148	16°55'N	89°54'W
San Benito, Tx., U.S. (săn bĕ-nē'tō)	122-23	26°08'N	97°38'W
San Bernardino, Ca., U.S. (săn bûr-när-dē'nō)	118-19	34°06'N	117°17'W
San Bernardino Strait, strt., Phil.	250	12°32'N	124°10'E
San Bernardo, Chile (sän bĕr-när'dō)	163e	33°36'S	70°42'W
San Blas, Mex. (sän bläs')	146-47	21°33'N	105°17'W
San Blas, Mex. (sän bläs')	144-45	26°05'N	108°46'W
San Blas, Cape, c., Fl., U.S. (kāp săn blăs')	124-25	29°40'N	85°22'W
San Borja, Bol.	166-67	14°49'S	66°51'W
San Buenaventura, Mex. (sän bwā'nå-vĕn-tōō'rå)	122-23	27°04'N	101°33'W
San Buenaventura, Ca., U.S. *see* Ventura	118-19	34°17'N	119°17'W
San Carlos, Chile (sän-kå'r-lōs)	171	36°26'S	71°57'W
San Carlos, Mex. (sän kär'lōs)	122-23	29°01'N	100°51'W
San Carlos, Nic. (sän-kä'r-lōs)	149	11°07'N	84°47'W
San Carlos, Phil.	250	10°30'N	123°25'E
San Carlos, Phil.	250	15°56'N	120°21'E
San Carlos, Az., U.S. (săn kär'lōs)	118-19	33°21'N	110°27'W
San Carlos, Ven.	164-65	9°40'N	68°35'W
San Carlos, stm., C.R. (sän kär'lōs)	149	10°47'N	84°12'W
San Carlos de Bariloche, Arg.	171	41°09'S	71°18'W
San Carlos de Bolívar, Arg.	173	36°13'S	61°07'W
San Carlos del Zulia, Ven.	164-65	9°02'N	71°56'W
San Carlos de Río Negro, Ven.	164-65	1°55'N	67°04'W
San Carlos Indian Reservation, ind. res., Az., U.S. (săn kär'lōs ĭn'dĭ-ăn rĕ-sẽr-vā'shĕn)	118-19	33°23'N	110°09'W
San Cataldo, Italy (sän kä-täl'dō)	200-01	37°29'N	13°59'E
Sánchez, Dom. Rep. (sän'chĕz)	142-43	19°14'N	69°37'W
San Clemente, Monte, mtn., Chile *see* San Valentín, Monte	171	46°36'S	73°20'W
San Clemente Island, i., Ca., U.S. (săn klå-mĕn'tå ī'lånd)	118-19	32°54'N	118°29'W
San Cristóbal, Arg.	173	30°19'S	61°13'W
San Cristóbal, Dom. Rep. (sän krēs-tô'bäl)	142-43	18°25'N	70°06'W
San Cristóbal, Ven. (sän krēs-tô'bäl)	164-65	7°45'N	72°13'W
San Cristobal, i., Sol. Is.	279e	10°36'S	161°45'E
San Cristóbal, Isla, i., Ec.	170a	0°50'S	89°26'W
San Cristóbal de las Casas, Mex.	146-47	16°45'N	92°38'W
Sancti Spíritus, Cuba (säŋk'tē spē'rė-tōōs)	142-43	21°56'N	79°27'W
Sancti Spíritus, state, Cuba (säŋk'tē spē'rė-tōōs)	142-43	22°0'N	79°20'W
Sancy, Puy de, mtn., Fr. (pwē-dĕ-sän-sē')	196-97	45°32'N	2°49'E
Sandakan, Malay. (sån-dä'kån)	250	5°51'N	118°06'E
Sandefjord, Nor. (sän'dĕ-fyôr')	192-93	59°08'N	10°14'E
Sanders, Az., U.S. (săn'dẽrz)	118-19	35°14'N	109°20'W
Sanderson, Tx., U.S. (săn'dẽr-sŭn)	122-23	30°09'N	102°24'W
Sandersville, Ga., U.S. (săn'dẽrz-vĭl)	124-25	32°59'N	82°49'W
Sand Hills, hills, Ne., U.S. (sănd hĭlz)	114-15	42°0'N	101°00'W
Sandia, Peru	170	14°16'S	69°27'W
San Diego, Ca., U.S. (săn dė-ā'gō)	118-19	32°43'N	117°08'W
San Diego, Tx., U.S. (săn dė-ā'gō)	122-23	27°46'N	98°14'W
San Diego, Cabo, c., Arg.	171	54°39'S	65°08'W
San Diego de la Unión, Mex. (sän dė-å-gō dā lä ōō-nyōn')	146-47	21°28'N	100°52'W
Sandnes, Nor. (sänd'nĕs)	192-93	58°51'N	5°44'E
Sandomierz, Pol. (sån-dô'myĕzh)	194-95	50°41'N	21°46'E
San Donà di Piave, Italy (sän dô nä' dē pyä'vĕ)	200-01	45°38'N	12°34'E
Sandoway, Mya. (sän-dô-wī')	246-47	18°28'N	94°22'E
Sandpoint, Id., U.S. (sănd point)	112-13	48°17'N	116°33'W
Sand Springs, Ok., U.S. (sănd sprĭngz)	120-21	36°08'N	96°07'W
Sandstone, Mn., U.S. (sănd'stōn)	114-15	46°08'N	92°52'W
Sandusky, Mi., U.S. (săn-dŭs'kė)	116-17	43°25'N	82°49'W
Sandusky, Oh., U.S. (săn-dŭs'kė)	116-17	41°27'N	82°42'W
Sandwich, Il., U.S. (sănd'wĭch)	116-17	41°39'N	88°37'W
Sandy, Ut., U.S. (sănd'ė)	112-13	40°37'N	111°54'W
Sandy Cape, c., Austl.	277	24°42'S	153°16'E
Sandykgaçy, Turkmen.	232-33	36°33'N	62°33'E
Sandy Lake, lk., Nf., Can. (sănd'ė lăk)	138-39	49°16'N	57°00'W
Sandy Lake, lk., On., Can. (sănd'ė lăk)	134-35	53°02'N	93°00'W
Sandy Springs, Ga., U.S. (sănd'ė sprĭngz)	124-25	33°56'N	84°23'W
San Estanislao, Para. (sän ĕs-tä-nēs-lä'ō)	168-69	24°39'S	56°29'W
San Felipe, Chile (sän fĕ-lē'på)	163e	32°45'S	70°43'W
San Felipe, Mex. (sän fĕ-lē'pĕ)	146-47	21°29'N	101°13'W
San Felipe, Mex. (sän fĕ-lē'pĕ)	144-45	31°02'N	114°51'W
San Felipe, Ven. (sän fĕ-lē'pĕ)	164-65	10°20'N	68°44'W
San Felipe, Cayos de, is., Cuba (kä'yōs-dĕ-sän-fĕ-lē'pĕ)	142-43	21°58'N	83°30'W
San Félix, Isla, i., Chile (ė's-lä-dĕ-sän fā-lēks')	159	26°17'S	80°06'W
San Fernando, Chile	163e	34°35'S	70°59'W
San Fernando, Mex. (sän fĕr-nän'dō)	122-23	24°51'N	98°10'W
San Fernando, Phil.	250	15°01'N	120°41'E
San Fernando, Phil.	250	16°37'N	120°19'E
San Fernando, Trin.	143b	10°17'N	61°27'W
San Fernando de Apure, Ven. (sän-fĕr-nä'n-dō-dĕ-ä-pōō'rå)	164-65	7°53'N	67°27'W
San Fernando de Atabapo, Ven. (sän-fĕr-nä'n-dō-dĕ-ä-tä-bä'pō)	164-65	4°02'N	67°41'W
San Fernando del Valle de Catamarca, Arg.	168-69	28°28'S	65°47'W
Sanford, Fl., U.S. (săn'fôrd)	124-25	28°47'N	81°17'W
Sanford, Me., U.S. (săn'fẽrd)	116-17	43°27'N	70°47'W
Sanford, N.C., U.S. (săn'fẽrd)	124-25	35°29'N	79°11'W
San Francisco, Arg. (sän frän'sĭs'kō)	173	31°26'S	62°05'W
San Francisco, Ca., U.S. (săn frăn-sĭs'kō)	118-19	37°47'N	122°25'W
San Francisco del Oro, Mex. (sän frän'sĭs'kō-dĕl ō'rō)	122-23	26°52'N	105°51'W
San Francisco del Rincón, Mex. (sän frän'sĭs'kō-dĕl rēn-kōn')	146-47	21°01'N	101°52'W
San Francisco de Macorís, Dom. Rep. (sän frän'sĭs'kō-dā-mä-kō'rēs)	142-43	19°18'N	70°15'W
San Gabriel Chilac, Mex. (sän-gä-brē-ĕl-chē-läk')	146-47	18°20'N	97°21'W
Sangar, Russia	218-19	63°55'N	127°29'E
Sangarius, stm., Tur. *see* Sakarya	186-87	41°07'N	30°39'E
Sangay, vol., Ec.	170	2°0'S	78°20'W
Sangeang, Pulau, i., Indon.	248-49	8°12'S	119°04'E
Sangerhausen, Ger. (säng'ẽr-hou-zĕn)	194-95	51°28'N	11°18'E
Sanggan, stm., China	240-41	40°21'N	115°25'E
Sanggau, Indon.	248-49	0°07'N	110°35'E
Sangha, stm., Afr.	260-61	1°12'S	16°50'E
Sangihe, Kepulauan, is., Indon.	248-49	3°0'N	125°30'E
Sangihe, Pulau, i., Indon.	248-49	3°35'N	125°32'E
San Gil, Col. (sän-kĕ'l)	164-65	6°33'N	73°08'W
San Giovanni in Fiore, Italy (sän jô-vän'nē ēn fyō'rå)	200-01	39°15'N	16°42'E
Sangju, Kor., S. (säng'jōō')	243	36°25'N	128°10'E
Sāngli, India	236	16°52'N	74°34'E
San Gregorio, Ur.	173	32°38'S	55°50'W
Sangue, stm., Braz.	166-67	10°57'S	58°20'W
Sanibel Island, i., Fl., U.S. (săn'ĭ-bĕl ī'lånd)	125a	26°27'N	82°08'W
San Ignacio, Arg.	173	27°16'S	55°33'W
San Ignacio, Mex.	144-45	27°17'N	112°54'W
San Ignacio de Moxo, Bol.	166-67	14°56'S	65°37'W
San Ignacio de Velasco, Bol.	168-69	16°23'S	60°57'W
San Ildefonso, Cape, c., Phil. (kăp sän-ĕl-dĕ-fōn-sō)	250	16°02'N	122°00'E
San Ildefonso ó la Granja, Spain (sän-ĕl-dĕ-fōn-sō ō lä grän'khä)	198-99	40°54'N	4°00'W
San Isidro, Arg. (sän ē-sē'drō)	173	34°28'S	58°31'W
San Jacinto, Phil. (sän hä-sēn'tō)	250	12°34'N	123°44'E
San Javier, Arg.	173	30°34'S	59°56'W
San Javier, Bol.	168-69	16°20'S	62°38'W
San Joaquín, Bol.	166-67	13°04'S	64°49'W

ăt; finăl; rāte; senâte; ärm; àsk; sofå; fâre; ch-choose; dh-as th in other; bē; ėvent; bĕt; recĕnt; cratẽr; g-gō; gh-guttural g; bĭt; ĭ-short neutral; rīde; κ-guttural k as ch in German ich;

PRONOUNCING INDEX

San Joaquín – Santo Ângelo 379

Feature (Pronunciation)	Page	Lat.	Long.
San Joaquín, stm., Bol.	166-67	13°08'S	63°41'W
San Joaquin Valley, val., Ca., U.S.	118-19	36°55'N	120°29'W
San Jorge, Golfo, b., Arg. (gôl-fô-sän-kô'r-кĕ)	171	46°0'S	67°00'W
San Jorge Island, i., Sol. Is.	279e	8°27'S	159°35'E
San Jose, Phil.	250	12°21'N	121°04'E
San Jose, Ca., U.S.	118-19	37°21'N	121°54'W
San José, nat. cap., C.R. (sän hô-sā')	149	9°56'N	84°05'W
San José, Isla, i., Mex. (ē's-lä-sän кô-sĕ')	144-45	25°00'N	110°38'W
San José, Isla, i., Pan. (ē's-lä-sän hô-sā')	150	8°15'N	79°07'W
San José de Chiquitos, Bol.	168-69	17°50'S	60°44'W
San José de Feliciano, Arg. (sän кô-sĕ' dā lä ĕs-kē'nä)	173	30°23'S	58°45'W
San José de Jáchal, Arg.	168-69	30°14'S	68°45'W
San José del Cabo, Mex.	144-45	23°03'N	109°41'W
San José del Guaviare, Col.	164-65	2°34'N	72°38'W
San José de Mayo, Ur.	173	34°21'S	56°42'W
San Jose Island, i., Tx., U.S.	122-23	28°02'N	96°55'W
San Juan, Arg. (sän hwän')	168-69	31°32'S	68°32'W
San Juan, state, Arg. (sän hwän')	168-69	31°0'S	69°00'W
San Juan, nat. cap., P.R. (sän hwän')	142a	18°28'N	66°07'W
San Juan, stm., Arg.	168-69	32°17'S	67°22'W
San Juan, stm., Mex. (sän-hoo-än')	122-23	26°22'N	98°51'W
San Juan, stm., N.A.	149	10°56'N	83°43'W
San Juan, stm., U.S. (sän hwän')	110-11	37°11'N	110°43'W
San Juan, Pico, mtn., Cuba (pē'kô-sän-kôá'n)	142-43	21°59'N	80°09'W
San Juan Bautista, Para. (sän hwän' bou-tēs'tä)	173	26°53'S	57°01'W
San Juan de la Maguana, Dom. Rep.	142-43	18°48'N	71°13'W
San Juan del Norte, Nic.	149	10°55'N	83°42'W
San Juan de los Morros, Ven. (sän-hoo-än' dĕ-lôs-mô'r-rôs)	163b	9°55'N	67°21'W
San Juan del Río, Mex. (sän hwän del rē'ō)	146-47	20°23'N	100°00'W
San Juan del Río, Mex. (sän hwän del rē'ō)	122-23	24°48'N	104°27'W
San Juan del Sur, Nic. (sän hwän dĕl soor)	149	11°15'N	85°52'W
San Juan Evangelista, Mex. (sän-hoo-ä'n-å-väŋ-kå-lĕs'tä')	146-47	17°54'N	95°07'W
San Juanito, Isla, i., Mex.	146-47	21°46'N	106°41'W
San Juan Mountains, mts., Co., U.S. (san hwän' moun'tĭnz)	118-19	37°32'N	107°31'W
San Justo, Arg. (sän hoos'tô)	173	30°47'S	60°35'W
Sankt Michel, Fin. see Mikkeli	192-93	61°42'N	27°16'E
Sankt Pölten, Aus. (zäŋkt-pûl'tĕn)	194-95	48°12'N	15°37'E
Sankuru, stm., D.R.C. (sän-koo'roo)	262-63	4°17'S	20°24'E
San Lázaro, Cabo, c., Mex. (kå'bô sän-lä'zä-rō)	144-45	24°48'N	112°18'W
Şanlıurfa, Tur.	228-29	37°10'N	38°48'E
San Lorenzo, Arg. (sän lô-rĕn'zô)	173	32°44'S	60°45'W
San Lorenzo, Ec.	170	1°15'N	78°50'W
San Lorenzo, Cabo, c., Ec.	170	1°04'S	80°54'W
San Lorenzo, Isla, i., Peru	163a	12°05'S	77°14'W
Sanlúcar de Barrameda, Spain (sän-loo'kär)	198-99	36°47'N	6°21'W
San Lucas, Bol. (sän loo'kås)	168-69	20°06'S	65°08'W
San Lucas, Cabo, c., Mex.	144-45	22°52'N	109°54'W
San Luis, Arg. (sän lô-ēs')	171	33°18'S	66°21'W
San Luis, Guat. (sän lô-ēs')	148	16°13'N	89°27'W
San Luis, state, Arg. (sän lô-ēs')	171	34°0'S	66°00'W
San Luís, Laguna, lk., Bol.	166-67	13°45'S	64°00'W
San Luis de la Paz, Mex. (sän lô-ēs' då lä päz')	146-47	21°18'N	100°31'W
San Luis Obispo, Ca., U.S. (săn lô-ĕes' ô-bĭs'pō)	118-19	35°17'N	120°40'W
San Luis Potosí, Mex.	146-47	22°09'N	100°59'W
San Luis Potosí, state, Mex.	146-47	22°30'N	100°30'W
San Luis Río Colorado, Mex.	144-45	32°28'N	114°46'W
San Marcos, Mex. (sän mär'kôs)	146-47	16°49'N	99°23'W
San Marcos, Tx., U.S. (săn mär'kôs)	122-23	29°53'N	97°56'W
San Marcos de Colón, Hond. (sän-má'r-kōs-dĕ-kô-lô'n)	149	13°26'N	86°49'W
San Marino, nation, Eur. (sän mēr-ē'nô)	200-01	43°56'N	12°25'E
San Martín, Arg.	163e	33°05'S	68°29'W
San Martín, Col. (sän mär-tē'n)	164-65	3°42'N	73°42'W
San Martín, stm., Bol.	166-67	13°08'S	63°47'W
San Martín, Lago, lk., S.A. (lä'gô sän mär-tē'n)	171	48°53'S	72°39'W
San Martín de los Andes, Arg.	171	40°10'S	71°22'W
San Mateo, Ca., U.S. (săn mā-tā'ô)	118-19	37°34'N	122°19'W
San Mateo, Ven. (sän må-tĕ'ô)	163b	9°45'N	64°33'W
San Matías, Golfo, b., Arg. (gôl-fô-sän-mä-tē'äs)	171	41°30'S	64°15'W
Sanmenxia, China	238-39	34°47'N	111°12'E
San Miguel, El Sal. (sän mē-gål')	148	13°28'N	88°11'W
San Miguel, Mex. (sän mē-gål')	122-23	29°10'N	101°28'W
San Miguel, Pan. (sän mē-gål')	150	8°27'N	78°56'W
San Miguel, stm., Bol. (sän-mē-gĕl')	166-67	13°53'S	63°54'W
San Miguel, Golfo de, b., Pan. (gôl-fô-dĕ-sän mē-gål')	150	8°22'N	78°17'W
San Miguel del Monte, Arg.	173	35°27'S	58°49'W
San Miguel de Tucumán, Arg.	168-69	26°49'S	65°13'W
San Miguel El Alto, Mex. (sän mē-gål' ĕl äl'tô)	146-47	21°01'N	102°19'W
Sannār, Sudan	266	13°34'N	33°33'E
San Nicolas, Phil. (sän nē-kô-läs')	250	18°10'N	120°36'E
San Nicolás, stm., Mex. (sän nē-kô-lä's)	146-47	19°38'N	105°13'W
San Nicolás, Canal de, strt., N.A. see Nicholas Channel	142-43	23°21'N	80°21'W
San Nicolás de los Arroyos, Arg.	173	33°20'S	60°14'W
Sanok, Pol. (sä'nôk)	194-95	49°34'N	22°13'E
San Pablo, Phil. (sän-pä-blô)	250	14°04'N	121°19'E
San Pedro, Arg. (sän pā'drô)	168-69	24°15'S	64°52'W
San Pedro, Arg. (sän pā'drô)	173	33°41'S	59°41'W
San Pedro, Chile (sän pĕ'drô)	163e	33°54'S	71°26'W
San-Pédro, C. Iv.	260-61	4°45'N	6°38'W
San Pedro, Punta, c., Chile	168-69	25°31'S	70°38'W
San Pedro, Volcán, vol., Chile	168-69	21°53'S	68°25'W
San Pedro de Jujuy, Arg. see San Pedro	168-69	24°15'S	64°52'W
San Pedro de las Colonias, Mex. (sän pā'drô dā-läs-kô-lô'nyäs)	122-23	25°46'N	102°59'W
San Pedro de Macorís, Dom. Rep. (sän-pĕ'drō-då mä-kô-rēs')	142-43	18°28'N	69°18'W
San Pedro de Ycuamandiyú, Para.	168-69	24°05'S	57°08'W
San Pedro Sula, Hond. (sän pā'drô soo'lä)	149	15°30'N	88°02'W
San Pietro, Isola di, i., Italy (ē'sō-lä-dē-sän pyā'trô)	200-01	39°08'N	8°16'E
San Quintín, Cabo, c., Mex.	144-45	30°22'N	115°60'W
San Rafael, Arg. (sän rä-fä-äl')	163e	34°37'S	68°20'W
San Ramón de la Nueva Orán, Arg.	168-69	23°09'S	64°20'W
San Remo, Italy (sän rā'mô)	200-01	43°50'N	7°46'E
San Roque, Punta, c., Mex.	144-45	27°11'N	114°25'W
San Saba, Tx., U.S. (săn să'bå)	122-23	31°12'N	98°43'W
San Saba, stm., Tx., U.S. (săn să'bå)	122-23	31°15'N	98°36'W
San Salvador, i., Bah. (săn săl'vå-dôr)	142-43	24°02'N	74°27'W
San Salvador, nat. cap., El Sal. (sän säl-vä-dōr')	148	13°40'N	89°13'W
San Salvador, Isla, i., Ec. (ē's-lä-sän säl-vä-dōr') see Santiago, Isla	170a	0°14'S	90°45'W
San Salvador de Jujuy, Arg.	168-69	24°12'S	65°18'W
San Sebastián, Spain (sän så-bås-tyän') see Donostia-San Sebastián	198-99	43°19'N	1°60'W
San Severo, Italy (sän sĕ-vâ'rō)	200-01	41°41'N	15°23'E
Sanshui, China (sän-shwā)	238-39	23°11'N	112°53'E
San Simon, stm., Az., U.S. (sân sī-mōn')	118-19	32°52'N	109°33'W
Santa, stm., Peru	170	9°01'S	78°38'W
Santa Ana, Bol.	166-67	13°45'S	65°35'W
Santa Ana, El Sal. (sän'tä ä'nä)	148	13°59'N	89°34'W
Santa Ana, Mex. (sän'tä ä'nä)	146-47	24°04'N	100°30'W
Santa Ana, Mex. (sän'tä ä'nä)	144-45	30°32'N	111°07'W
Santa Ana, Ca., U.S. (săn'tå ăn'å)	118-19	33°45'N	117°53'W
Santa Anna, Tx., U.S. (săn'tå ăn'å)	122-23	31°44'N	99°19'W
Santa Bárbara, Hond. (sän-tä-bä'r-bä-rä)	149	14°55'N	88°14'W
Santa Bárbara, Mex. (sän-tä-bä'r-bä-rä)	122-23	26°49'N	105°48'W
Santa Barbara, Ca., U.S. (săn-tă-bă'r-bă-ră)	118-19	34°25'N	119°42'W
Santa Catalina Island, i., Ca., U.S. (săn'tå kă-tå-lē'nå ī'lånd)	118-19	33°23'N	118°24'W
Santa Catarina, Mex. (sän'tå kä-tä-rē'nä)	122-23	25°41'N	100°28'W
Santa Catarina, state, Braz. (sän-tä-kä-tä-rē'nå)	168-69	27°0'S	50°00'W
Santa Catarina, Ilha de, i., Braz.	172	27°36'S	48°30'W
Santa Clara, Cuba (sän'tå klä'rä)	142-43	22°25'N	79°58'W
Santa Cruz, Braz. (sän-tä-kroo's)	163d	6°13'S	36°01'W
Santa Cruz, Ca., U.S. (săn'tå krooz')	118-19	36°59'N	122°02'W
Santa Cruz, stm., Arg. (sän'tå krooz')	171	50°08'S	68°21'W
Santa Cruz, Isla, i., Ec. (ē's-lä-sän-tä-kroo'z)	170a	0°38'S	90°23'W
Santa Cruz de la Palma, Spain	199d	28°41'N	17°46'W
Santa Cruz de la Sierra, Bol.	168-69	17°48'S	63°10'W
Santa Cruz del Sur, Cuba (sän-tä-kroo's-dĕl-sŏ'r)	142-43	20°43'N	77°59'W
Santa Cruz de Tenerife, Spain (sän'tä krooz då tā-nå-rē'fā)	199d	28°28'N	16°15'W
Santa Cruz do Sul, Braz.	168-69	29°43'S	52°26'W
Santa Cruz Islands, is., Sol. Is.	272-73	10°60'S	166°15'E
Santa Fe, Arg. (sän'tä fā')	173	31°38'S	60°42'W
Santa Fe, Spain (sän'tä-fā')	198-99	37°11'N	3°43'W
Santa Fe, N.M., U.S. (săn'tå fā')	118-19	35°41'N	105°59'W
Santa Fe, state, Arg. (sän'tä fā')	173	31°0'S	61°00'W
Santa Fe de Bogotá, nat. cap., Col. see Bogotá	164-65	4°37'N	74°06'W
Santa Fé do Sul, Braz.	168-69	20°13'S	50°56'W
Santai, China (san-tī)	238-39	31°09'N	105°01'E
Santa Inés, Isla, i., Chile (ē's-lä-sän'tä ē-näs')	171	53°46'S	72°44'W
Santa Isabel, Arg.	171	36°15'S	66°56'W
Santa Isabel, i., Sol. Is.	279e	8°0'S	159°00'E
Santa Isabel, nat. cap., Eq. Gui. see Malabo	260-61	3°45'N	8°47'E
Santa Magdalena, Isla, i., Mex.	144-45	24°54'N	112°13'W
Santa Margarita, Isla, i., Mex. (ē's-lä-sän'tå mär-gå-rē'tå)	144-45	24°27'N	111°51'W
Santa Maria, Braz. (sän'tå mä-rē'å)	173	29°41'S	53°49'W
Santa Maria, Ca., U.S. (săn-tå må-rē'å)	118-19	34°57'N	120°26'W
Santa Maria, i., Port. (sän-tä-mä-rē'ä)	199c	36°58'N	25°06'W
Santa Maria, i., Vanuatu	279g	14°14'S	167°28'E
Santa María, stm., Mex. (sän'tä mä-rē'å)	146-47	21°48'N	99°10'W
Santa Maria, Cabo de, c., Ang.	264-65	13°25'S	12°32'E
Santa Maria, Cabo de, c., Port. (kå'bō-dĕ-sän-tä-mä-rē'ä)	198-99	36°58'N	7°54'W
Santa María, Isla, i., Ec.	170a	1°17'S	90°26'W
Santa María del Oro, Mex. (sän'tä-mä-rē'ä-dĕl-ô-rô)	122-23	25°56'N	105°23'W
Santa Marta, Col. (sän'tå mär'tä)	164-65	11°15'N	74°12'W
Santa Monica, Ca., U.S. (săn'tå mŏn'ĭ-kå)	118-19	34°01'N	118°29'W
Santana do Livramento, Braz.	173	30°53'S	55°31'W
Santander, Col. (sän-tän-dĕr')	163c	3°03'N	76°29'W
Santander, Phil.	250	9°25'N	123°20'E
Santander, Spain (sän-tän-dâr')	198-99	43°28'N	3°48'W
Sant'Antioco, Isola di, i., Italy (ē'sō-lä-dē-sän-än-tyŏ'kô)	200-01	39°02'N	8°25'E
Santarém, Braz. (sän-tä-rĕɴ')	166-67	2°26'S	54°43'W
Santarém, Port.	198-99	39°14'N	8°41'W
Santaren Channel, strt., Bah. (săn-tå-rĕn' chăn'ĕl)	142-43	24°0'N	79°30'W
Santa Rita, Hond.	149	15°10'N	87°54'W
Santa Rosa, Arg.	173	36°37'S	64°17'W
Santa Rosa, Braz.	173	27°52'S	54°26'W
Santa Rosa, Ec.	170	3°27'S	79°57'W
Santa Rosa, Ca., U.S.	118-19	38°26'N	122°43'W
Santa Rosa, N.M., U.S. (săn'tå rō'så)	120-21	34°56'N	104°41'W
Santa Rosa de Copán, Hond.	149	14°46'N	88°47'W
Santa Rosalía, Mex. (sän'tä rô-zä'lē-å)	144-45	27°20'N	112°17'W
Santa Rosa Range, mts., Nv., U.S. (săn'tå rō'zå rānj)	112-13	41°35'N	117°40'W
Santa Sylvina, Arg.	173	27°50'S	61°08'W
Santa Vitória do Palmar, Braz. (sän-tä-vē-tô'ryä-dô-päl-mär)	173	33°31'S	53°22'W
Santee, Ca., U.S. (săn tē')	118-19	32°50'N	116°57'W
Santee, stm., S.C., U.S. (săn tē')	124-25	33°14'N	79°28'W
Santiago, Braz. (sän-tyå'gô)	173	29°11'S	54°52'W
Santiago, Pan. (sän-tyå'gô)	150	8°06'N	80°58'W
Santiago, i., C.V.	260-61	15°02'N	23°39'W
Santiago, nat. cap., Chile (sän-tē-å'gô)	171	33°27'S	70°40'W
Santiago, Isla, i., Ec.	170a	0°14'S	90°45'W
Santiago de Compostela, Spain	198-99	42°53'N	8°32'W
Santiago de Cuba, Cuba (sän-tyå'gô-dĕ koo'bå)	142-43	20°02'N	75°49'W
Santiago de Cuba, state, Cuba (sän-tyå'gô-dĕ koo'bå)	142-43	20°10'N	75°55'W
Santiago del Estero, Arg. (sän-tē-å'gô-dĕl ĕs-tā-rô)	168-69	27°47'S	64°16'W
Santiago del Estero, state, Arg. (sän-tē-å'gô-dĕl ĕs-tā-rô)	173	28°0'S	63°30'W
Santiago de los Caballeros, Dom. Rep.	142-43	19°27'N	70°42'W
Santiago Jamiltepec, Mex.	146-47	16°18'N	97°50'W
Santiago Papasquiaro, Mex.	122-23	25°03'N	105°25'W
Santiaguillo, Laguna, lk., Mex. (lä-oô'nä-sän-tē-a-gēl'yō)	122-23	24°45'N	104°48'W
Santo Amaro, Braz. (sän'tô ä-mä'rô)	166-67	12°32'S	38°42'W
Santo André, Braz.	172	23°40'S	46°31'W
Santo Ângelo, Braz. (sän-tô-ä'n-zhĕ-lô)	173	28°16'S	54°16'W

ăt; fināl; rāte; senâte; ärm; ásk; sofá; fâre; ch-choose; dh-as th in other; bē; ĕvent; bĕt; recĕnt; cratẽr; g-gō; gh-guttural g; bĭt; ĭ-short neutral; rīde; к-guttural k as ch in German ich;

n-sing; ŋ-bank; ℵ-nasalized n; nŏd; cŏmmit; ōld; ôbey; ôrder; oi-boil; fōōd; ò-as oo in foot; ou-out; s-soft; sh-dish; th-thin; pūre; ûnite; ûrn; stŭd; circǔs; ü-as in French tu; ´-indeterminate vowel.

382 Shangxian – Sierra Leone PRONOUNCING INDEX

Feature (Pronunciation)	Page	Lat.	Long.
Shangxian, China	238-39	33°52'N	109°56'E
Shangzhi, China (shäŋ-jr)	244	45°13'N	127°59'E
Shanhaiguan, China	240-41	40°01'N	119°45'E
Shannon, stm., Ire. (shăn'ŏn)	190-91	52°35'N	9°41'W
Shansi, state, China *see* Shanxi	240-41	37°0'N	112°00'E
Shantarskiye Ostrova, is., Russia (shän'tär-skyě ôs-trôf')	218-19	54°54'N	137°33'E
Shantou, China (shän-tō)	238-39	23°21'N	116°40'E
Shantung, state, China *see* Shandong	240-41	36°0'N	118°00'E
Shantung Peninsula, pen., China *see* Shandong Bandao	240-41	37°0'N	121°00'E
Shanxi, state, China (shän-shyē)	240-41	37°0'N	112°00'E
Shanxian, China (shän shyĕn)	238-39	34°48'N	116°05'E
Shanyin, China	240-41	39°31'N	112°50'E
Shaoguan, China (shou-gůän)	238-39	24°49'N	113°36'E
Shaowu, China	238-39	27°19'N	117°30'E
Shaoxing, China (shou-shyĭŋ)	238-39	29°59'N	120°34'E
Shaoyang, China	238-39	27°15'N	111°28'E
Shar, Kaz.	226	49°35'N	81°03'E
Sharjah, U.A.E.	230-31	25°22'N	55°24'E
Shark Bay, b., Austl. (shärk bā)	272-73	25°30'S	113°30'E
Sharktooth Mountain, mtn., B.C., Can.	130-31	58°35'N	127°57'W
Sharon, Pa., U.S. (shăr'ŏn)	116-17	41°13'N	80°30'W
Sharon Springs, Ks., U.S. (shăr'ŏn sprĭngz)	120-21	38°54'N	101°45'W
Sharonville, Oh., U.S. (shăr'ŏn vĭl)	116-17	39°16'N	84°25'W
Sharpsburg, Md., U.S. (shărps'bûrg)	116-17	39°27'N	77°45'W
Sharqīyah, Aş-Şaḥrā' ash-, des., Egypt *see* Arabian Desert	266	28°0'N	32°00'E
Sharya, Russia	186-87	58°22'N	45°31'E
Shashe, stm., Afr.	264-65	22°11'S	29°21'E
Shashi, China (shä-shē)	238-39	30°19'N	112°14'E
Shasta, Mount, vol., Ca., U.S. (mount shăs'tȧ)	112-13	41°25'N	122°13'W
Shasta Lake, res., Ca., U.S. (shăs'tȧ lāk)	112-13	40°46'N	122°22'W
Shatt al-Arab, stm., Asia *see* 'Arab, Shaṭṭ al-	228-29	29°57'N	48°33'E
Shattuck, Ok., U.S. (shăt'ŭk)	120-21	36°17'N	99°53'W
Shatura, Russia	202-03	55°34'N	39°32'E
Shaunavon, Sk., Can.	134-35	49°39'N	108°24'W
Shaw, Ms., U.S. (shô)	124-25	33°37'N	90°46'W
Shawano, Wi., U.S. (shȧ-wô'nō)	116-17	44°46'N	88°36'W
Shawinigan, Qc., Can.	136-37	46°33'N	72°45'W
Shawnee, Ks., U.S. (shô-nē')	120-21	39°01'N	94°44'W
Shawnee, Ok., U.S. (shô-nē')	120-21	35°20'N	96°55'W
Shawneetown, Il., U.S. (shô'nē-toun)	116-17	37°42'N	88°11'W
Shaybārā, i., Sau. Ar.	266	25°26'N	36°50'E
Shay Gap, Austl.	270-71	20°30'S	120°05'E
Shaykh, Jabal ash-, mtn., Asia *see* Hermon, Mount	228-29	33°25'N	35°51'E
Shchekino, Russia	202-03	54°01'N	37°31'E
Shchelkovo, Russia (shchĕl'kô-vô)	202-03	55°54'N	38°01'E
Shchigry, Russia (shchē'grē)	202-03	51°52'N	36°55'E
Shchors, Ukr. (shchôrs)	202-03	51°49'N	31°57'E
Shchūchīnsk, Kaz.	226	52°56'N	70°11'E
Sheberghān, Afg.	232-33	36°40'N	65°45'E
Sheboygan, Wi., U.S. (shē-boi'găn)	116-17	43°45'N	87°43'W
Sheboygan Falls, Wi., U.S. (shē-boi'găn fôlz)	116-17	43°44'N	87°48'W
Shediac, N.B., Can. (shĕ'dē-ăk)	138-39	46°12'N	64°34'W
Shedin Peak, mtn., B.C., Can. (shĕd'ĭn pēk)	132-33	55°55'N	127°32'W
Sheenjek, stm., Ak., U.S.	126	66°45'N	144°34'W
Sheffield, Eng., U.K.	190-91	53°23'N	1°28'W
Sheffield, Al., U.S. (shĕf'fēld)	124-25	34°45'N	87°42'W
Shekhūpura, Pak.	232-33	31°42'N	73°59'E
Sheki, Azer. *see* Şeki	227	41°10'N	47°10'E
Shelagyote Peak, mtn., B.C., Can.	132-33	55°58'N	127°12'W
Shelbina, Mo., U.S. (shĕl-bī'nȧ)	120-21	39°41'N	92°03'W
Shelburn, In., U.S. (shĕl'bŭrn)	116-17	39°11'N	87°24'W
Shelburne, N.S., Can.	138-39	43°46'N	65°19'W
Shelby, Mi., U.S. (shĕl'bē)	116-17	43°37'N	86°22'W
Shelby, Ms., U.S. (shĕl'bē)	124-25	33°57'N	90°46'W
Shelby, Mt., U.S. (shĕl'bē)	112-13	48°30'N	111°51'W
Shelby, N.C., U.S. (shĕl'bē)	124-25	35°18'N	81°32'W
Shelby, Oh., U.S. (shĕl'bē)	116-17	40°53'N	82°39'W
Shelbyville, Il., U.S. (shĕl'bē-vĭl)	116-17	39°24'N	88°48'W
Shelbyville, In., U.S. (shĕl'bē-vĭl)	116-17	39°31'N	85°46'W
Shelbyville, Ky., U.S. (shĕl'bē-vĭl)	116-17	38°13'N	85°13'W
Shelbyville, Tn., U.S. (shĕl'bē-vĭl)	124-25	35°29'N	86°27'W
Shelbyville, Lake, res., Il., U.S. (lāk shĕl'bē-vĭl)	116-17	39°30'N	88°43'W
Sheldon, Ia., U.S. (shĕl'dŭn)	114-15	43°11'N	95°51'W
Shelikhova, Zaliv, b., Russia	218-19	60°0'N	158°00'E
Shelikof Strait, strt., Ak., U.S. (shĕ'lē-kôf strāt)	126	57°18'N	155°41'W
Shellbrook, Sk., Can.	134-35	53°14'N	106°23'W
Shelley, Id., U.S. (shĕl'lē)	112-13	43°23'N	112°07'W
Shelton, Ct., U.S. (shĕl'tŭn)	116-17	41°19'N	73°05'W
Shelton, Wa., U.S. (shĕl'tŭn)	112-13	47°12'N	123°06'W
Shemonaīkha, Kaz.	226	50°39'N	81°54'E
Shenandoah, Ia., U.S. (shĕn-ăn-dō'ȧ)	114-15	40°46'N	95°23'W
Shenandoah, Pa., U.S. (shĕn-ăn-dō'ȧ)	116-17	40°49'N	76°12'W
Shenandoah, Va., U.S. (shĕn-ăn-dō'ȧ)	116-17	38°29'N	78°37'W
Shenandoah National Park, n.p., Va., U.S. (shĕn-ăn-dō'ȧ năsh'ŭn-ăl pärk)	116-17	38°34'N	78°20'W
Sheng-li Feng, mtn., Asia *see* Jengish Chokusu	226	42°02'N	80°05'E
Shenkursk, Russia (shĕn-kōōrsk')	186-87	62°07'N	42°53'E
Shenxian, China (shŭn shyĕn)	240-41	38°01'N	115°33'E
Shenyang, China (shŭn-yäŋ)	243	41°48'N	123°24'E
Shenzhen, China	238-39	22°34'N	114°07'E
Shepetivka, Ukr.	194-95	50°11'N	27°04'E
Shepparton, Austl. (shĕp'ăr-tŭn)	276	36°23'S	145°25'E
Sherbro Island, i., S.L.	260-61	7°34'N	12°43'W
Sherbrooke, Qc., Can.	136-37	45°24'N	71°54'W
Sheridan, Ar., U.S. (shĕr'ĭ-dăn)	120-21	34°18'N	92°24'W
Sheridan, Wy., U.S. (shĕr'ĭ-dăn)	112-13	44°48'N	106°58'W
Sherlovaya Gora, Russia	240-41	50°32'N	116°18'E
Sherman, Tx., U.S. (shĕr'măn)	120-21	33°35'N	96°36'W
Sherridon, Mb., Can.	134-35	55°07'N	101°05'W
Sherwood Park, Ab., Can.	132-33	53°31'N	113°18'W
Shetland Islands, is., Scot., U.K. (shĕt'lănd ī'lăndz)	190c	60°25'N	1°39'W
Shexian, China (shŭ shyĕn)	238-39	29°53'N	118°26'E
Sheyenne, stm., N.D., U.S. (shī-ĕn')	114-15	47°01'N	96°50'W
Shiashkotan, Ostrov, i., Russia	218-19	48°52'N	154°10'E
Shibām, Yemen (shē'băm)	220-21	15°54'N	48°40'E
Shidao, China	240-41	36°54'N	122°24'E
Shīeli, Kaz.	226	44°10'N	66°44'E
Shijiazhuang, China (shr-jyä-jůäŋ)	240-41	38°02'N	114°29'E
Shikārpur, Pak.	232-33	27°57'N	68°39'E
Shikoku, i., Japan (shē'kō'kōō)	245	33°45'N	133°30'E
Shikotan, Ostrov, i., Russia	218-19	43°47'N	146°45'E
Shikotan-tō, i., Russia *see* Shikotan, Ostrov	218-19	43°47'N	146°45'E
Shiliguri, India	234-35	26°43'N	88°26'E
Shilka, Russia	222-23	51°52'N	116°02'E
Shilka, stm., Russia (shĭl'kȧ)	222-23	53°21'N	121°27'E
Shillong, India (shĕl-lông')	234-35	25°34'N	91°53'E
Shimanovsk, Russia	222-23	52°00'N	127°41'E
Shimber Berris, mtn., Som. *see* Shimbiris	262-63	10°44'N	47°15'E
Shimbiris, mtn., Som.	262-63	10°44'N	47°15'E
Shimian, China	238-39	29°16'N	102°17'E
Shimla, India	234-35	31°06'N	77°10'E
Shimoga, India	236	13°56'N	75°35'E
Shimonoseki, Japan	245	33°58'N	130°56'E
Shimono-shima, i., Japan	243	34°12'N	129°15'E
Shinano, stm., Japan (shē-nä'nō)	245	37°57'N	139°04'E
Shīndand, Afg.	232-33	33°18'N	62°08'E
Shingishū, Kor., N. *see* Sinŭiju	243	40°06'N	124°24'E
Shingū, Japan	245	33°43'N	136°00'E
Shinyanga, Tan. (shĭn-yäŋ'gä)	267	3°40'S	33°26'E
Shiono-misaki, c., Japan (shē-ô'nō mē'sä-kē)	245	33°26'N	135°46'E
Shiqizhen, China *see* Zhongshan	238-39	22°31'N	113°22'E
Shirati, Tan. (shē-rä'tē)	267	1°07'S	33°60'E
Shīrāz, Iran (shē-räz')	230-31	29°36'N	52°32'E
Shire, stm., Afr. (shē'rā)	264-65	17°42'S	35°19'E
Shiretoko-misaki, c., Japan	244	44°21'N	145°20'E
Shishaldin Volcano, vol., Ak., U.S. (shī-shăl'dĭn vŏl-kā'nō)	126	54°45'N	163°57'W
Shively, Ky., U.S. (shīv'lē)	116-17	38°12'N	85°49'W
Shivpuri, India	234-35	25°25'N	77°39'E
Shizuoka, Japan (shē'zōō'ōkȧ)	245	34°58'N	138°23'E
Shkodër, Alb. (shkō'dûr) (skōō'tärē)	200-01	42°04'N	19°31'E
Shkodra, Alb. *see* Shkodër	200-01	42°04'N	19°31'E
Shmidta, Ostrov, i., Russia	208-09	81°08'N	90°48'E
Shoal Lake, lk., Can. (shōl lāk)	134-35	49°32'N	95°00'W
Shoals, In., U.S. (shōlz)	116-17	38°40'N	86°47'W
Shōdo-shima, i., Japan (shō'dō shē'mä)	245	34°30'N	134°17'E
Shortland Island, i., Sol. Is.	279e	7°04'S	155°43'E
Shoshone, Id., U.S. (shô-shōn'tē)	112-13	42°56'N	114°25'W
Shostka, Ukr. (shôst'kȧ)	202-03	51°52'N	33°29'E
Shouguang, China (shō-gůäŋ)	240-41	36°53'N	118°44'E
Shouxian, China (shō shyĕn)	238-39	32°34'N	116°46'E
Shpola, Ukr. (shpô'lȧ)	202-03	49°00'N	31°24'E
Shqipëria, nation, Eur. *see* Albania	174-75	41°0'N	20°00'E
Shreveport, La., U.S. (shrēv'pôrt)	120-21	32°30'N	93°45'W
Shrewsbury, Eng., U.K. (shrōōz'bēr-ī)	190-91	52°43'N	2°45'W
Shū, Kaz.	226	43°36'N	73°45'E
Shū, stm., Asia	226	45°00'N	67°45'E
Shuajingsi, China	238-39	32°00'N	103°17'E
Shuangcheng, China (shůäŋ-chŭŋ)	240-41	45°22'N	126°19'E
Shuangliao, China	240-41	43°30'N	123°30'E
Shuangyashan, China	244	46°35'N	131°19'E
Shubrâ el-Kheima, Egypt	268b	30°06'N	31°15'E
Shumagin Islands, is., Ak., U.S. (shōō'mȧ-gĕn ī'lăndz)	126	55°06'N	159°43'W
Shumen, Blg.	200-01	43°16'N	26°57'E
Shumerlya, Russia	186-87	55°29'N	46°25'E
Shunde, China (shòn-dŭ)	238-39	22°50'N	113°15'E
Shuqayyiqah, Nafūd, sand, Sau. Ar.	266	25°45'N	43°55'E
Shūshtar, Iran (shōōsh'tŭr)	228-29	32°03'N	48°51'E
Shuswap Lake, lk., B.C., Can. (shōōs'wŏp lāk)	132-33	50°57'N	119°15'W
Shuya, Russia (shōō'yȧ)	186-87	56°51'N	41°23'E
Shuyang, China (shōō yäng)	238-39	34°08'N	118°47'E
Shwangliao, China *see* Liaoyuan	240-41	42°55'N	125°08'E
Shwebo, Mya.	246-47	22°34'N	95°42'E
Shymkent, Kaz.	226	42°18'N	69°36'E
Shyok, stm., Asia	232-33	35°14'N	75°55'E
Siālkot, Pak. (sē-äl'kōt)	232-33	32°31'N	74°33'E
Siam, nation, Asia *see* Thailand	206-07	15°0'N	100°00'E
Siam, Gulf of, b., Asia *see* Thailand, Gulf of	246-47	10°0'N	101°00'E
Sian, China *see* Xi'an	238-39	34°15'N	108°52'E
Siargao Island, i., Phil.	250	9°53'N	126°02'E
Siasi Island, i., Phil.	250	5°33'N	120°51'E
Siau, Pulau, i., Indon.	248-49	2°46'N	125°23'E
Šiauliai, Lith. (shē-ou'lē-ī)	192-93	55°56'N	23°20'E
Sibay, Russia (sē'bāy)	226	52°42'N	58°40'E
Šibenik, Cro. (shē-bā'nēk)	200-01	43°44'N	15°54'E
Siberia, reg., Russia (sī-bĭr'ē-aȧ)	218-19	65°0'N	110°00'E
Sibi, Pak.	232-33	29°33'N	67°53'E
Sibir', reg., Russia *see* Siberia	218-19	65°0'N	110°00'E
Sibiryakova, Ostrov, i., Russia	218-19	72°50'N	79°00'E
Sibiti, Congo (sē-bē-tē')	262-63	3°41'S	13°21'E
Sibiu, Rom. (sē-bĭ-ōō')	194-95	45°47'N	24°09'E
Sibley, Ia., U.S. (sĭb'lē)	114-15	43°24'N	95°45'W
Sibolga, Indon. (sē-bō'gä)	246-47	1°45'N	98°47'E
Sibsāgar, India (sēb-sŭ'gŭr)	234-35	26°59'N	94°39'E
Sibu, Malay.	248-49	2°18'N	111°50'E
Sibut, C.A.R.	262-63	5°44'N	19°05'E
Sibutu Island, i., Phil.	250	4°46'N	119°29'E
Sibuyan Island, i., Phil. (sē-bōō-yän' ī'lănd)	250	12°27'N	122°34'E
Sibuyan Sea, s., Phil. (sē-bōō-yän' sē)	250	12°50'N	122°40'E
Sichuan, state, China (sz-chůän)	238-39	31°0'N	105°00'E
Sicilia, i., Italy *see* Sicily	200-01	37°30'N	14°00'E
Sicily, i., Italy (sĭs'ĭ-lē)	200-01	37°30'N	14°00'E
Sico Tinto, stm., Hond. (sē-kō tēn'tō)	149	15°50'N	85°03'W
Sicuani, Peru	170	14°16'S	71°13'W
Sidhi, India	234-35	24°24'N	81°53'E
Sîdi Barrâni, Egypt	188-89	31°37'N	25°56'E
Sidi Bel Abbès, Alg. (sē'dē-bĕl ȧ-bĕs')	198-99	35°12'N	0°11'W
Sidi-Bennour, Mor.	269a	32°39'N	8°25'W
Sidikalang, Indon.	246-47	2°44'N	98°20'E
Sidney, B.C., Can. (sĭd'nē)	132-33	48°39'N	123°24'W
Sidney, Mt., U.S. (sĭd'nē)	112-13	47°43'N	104°09'W
Sidney, Ne., U.S. (sĭd'nē)	114-15	41°09'N	102°59'W
Sidney, N.Y., U.S. (sĭd'nē)	116-17	42°19'N	75°23'W
Sidney, Oh., U.S. (sĭd'nē)	116-17	40°17'N	84°10'W
Sidney Lanier, Lake, res., Ga., U.S. (lāk sĭd'nē lăn'yēr)	124-25	34°15'N	83°57'W
Sidon, Leb.	228-29	33°34'N	35°23'E
Sidra, Gulf of, b., Libya (gŭlf ŭv sĭ'drȧ) *see* Surt, Khalīj	258-59	31°30'N	18°00'E
Siedlce, Pol. (syĕd''l-tsĕ)	194-95	52°10'N	22°17'E
Siegburg, Ger. (zĕg'bōōrgh)	194-95	50°47'N	7°12'E
Siegen, Ger. (zē'ghĕn)	194-95	50°52'N	8°01'E
Siemiatycze, Pol. (syĕm'yä'tē-chĕ)	194-95	52°26'N	22°52'E
Siĕmréab, Camb.	246-47	13°22'N	103°51'E
Siena, Italy (sē-ĕn'ä)	200-01	43°19'N	11°20'E
Sienyang, China *see* Xianyang	238-39	34°20'N	108°42'E
Sieradz, Pol. (syĕ'rädz)	194-95	51°36'N	18°45'E
Sierpc, Pol. (syĕrpts)	194-95	52°51'N	19°40'E
Sierra Blanca, Tx., U.S. (sē-ĕ'rȧ blaŋ-kä)	122-23	31°11'N	105°21'W
Sierra Blanca Peak, mtn., N.M., U.S. (sē-ĕ'r-rä blăn'kȧ pēk)	120-21	33°23'N	105°48'W
Sierra Colorada, Arg.	171	40°36'S	67°45'W
Sierra Leone, nation, Afr. (sē-ĕr'rä lā-ō'nȧ)	253	8°30'N	11°30'W

ăt; finăl; rāte; senâte; ärm; ȧsk; sofȧ; fâre; ch-choose; dh-as th in other; bē; ēvent; bĕt; recĕnt; cratēr; g-gō; gh-guttural g; bĭt; ĭ-short neutral; rīde; ĸ-guttural k as ch in German ich;

n-sing; ŋ-baŋk; ɴ-nasalized n; nŏd; cŏmmit; ōld; ôbey; ôrder; oi-boil; fōōd; ò-as oo in foot; ou-out; s-soft; sh-dish; th-thin; pūre; ûnite; ûrn; stŭd; circŭs; ü-as in French tu; ´-indeterminate vowel.

384 Sochaczew – Spencer PRONOUNCING INDEX

Feature (Pronunciation)	Page	Lat.	Long.
Sochaczew, Pol. (sô-ĸä′chĕf)	194-95	52°14′N	20°15′E
Sochi, Russia (sôch′ĭ)	227	43°35′N	39°44′E
Société, Archipel de la, is., Fr. Poly. *see* Society Islands	280-81	17°0′S	150°00′W
Society Islands, is., Fr. Poly. (sô-sī′ĕ-tê ī′lȧndz)	280-81	17°0′S	150°00′W
Socoltenango, Mex. (sô-kôl-tĕ-näŋ′gō)	148	16°12′N	92°14′W
Socorro, Col. (sô-kôr′rō)	164-65	6°29′N	73°16′W
Socorro, N.M., U.S. (sŏ-kô′r-rō)	118-19	34°04′N	106°54′W
Socorro, Isla, i., Mex.	144-45	18°45′N	110°58′W
Socotra, i., Yemen (sô-kō′trȧ) *see* Suquṭrā	220-21	12°31′N	53°54′E
Soc Trang, Viet.	246-47	9°36′N	105°58′E
Socuéllamos, Spain (sô-kōō-äl′yä-môs)	198-99	39°17′N	2°47′W
Sodankylä, Fin.	184-85	67°25′N	26°34′E
Soda Springs, Id., U.S. (sō′dȧ sprĭngz)	112-13	42°40′N	111°36′W
Söderhamn, Swe. (sû-dĕr-häm′'n)	192-93	61°19′N	17°05′E
Södertälje, Swe. (sû-dĕr-tĕl′yĕ)	192-93	59°12′N	17°37′E
Sodo, Eth.	269d	6°52′N	37°46′E
Soe, Indon.	248-49	9°52′S	124°17′E
Soerabaja, Indon. *see* Surabaya	248-49	7°15′S	112°45′E
Sofia, nat. cap., Blg. (sô′fê-á)	200-01	42°42′N	23°19′E
Sofia, stm., Madag.	264-65	15°25′S	47°14′E
Sofiya, nat. cap., Blg. (sô′fê-á) *see* Sofia	200-01	42°42′N	23°19′E
Sogamoso, Col. (sô-gä-mô′sō)	164-65	5°44′N	72°56′W
Sognefjorden, b., Nor.	192-93	61°06′N	5°10′E
Sogo Nur, lk., China	240-41	42°17′N	101°14′E
Sog Xian, China	238-39	31°50′N	93°47′E
Sōhu Gan, i., Japan	244	29°49′N	140°21′E
Soissons, Fr. (swä-sôɴ′)	196-97	49°23′N	3°20′E
Sŏjosŏn-man, b., Kor., N.	243	39°20′N	124°50′E
Sokal', Ukr. (sô′käl')	194-95	50°29′N	24°17′E
Sokch'o, Kor., S.	243	38°11′N	128°34′E
Söke, Tur. (sû′kĕ)	200-01	37°45′N	27°24′E
Sokhumi, Geor.	227	43°00′N	41°00′E
Sokodé, Togo	260-61	8°59′N	1°09′E
Sokol, Russia	186-87	59°28′N	40°07′E
Sokółka, Pol. (sô-kōl′kȧ)	194-95	53°24′N	23°31′E
Sokołów Podlaski, Pol. (sô-kô-wôf′ pŭd-lä′skĭ)	194-95	52°24′N	22°15′E
Sokoto, Nig. (sō′kô-tō)	260-61	13°04′N	5°15′E
Sokoto, stm., Nig.	260-61	11°24′N	4°08′E
Solano, Phil. (sō-lä′nō)	250	16°31′N	121°11′E
Solāpur, India	236	17°41′N	75°54′E
Soledad, Col. (sō-lĕ-dä′d)	164-65	10°56′N	74°46′W
Soledad Díez Gutiérrez, Mex.	146-47	22°12′N	100°56′W
Solikamsk, Russia (sô-lē-kȧmsk′)	186-87	59°40′N	56°46′E
Sol'-Iletsk, Russia	186-87	51°09′N	55°00′E
Solimões, stm., S.A. *see* Amazon	164-65	0°04′S	49°15′W
Solingen, Ger. (zô′lĭng-ĕn)	194-95	51°10′N	7°05′E
Sollefteå, Swe.	184-85	63°11′N	17°16′E
Solnechnogorsk, Russia	202-03	56°11′N	36°59′E
Solo, Indon. *see* Surakarta	248-49	7°34′S	110°50′E
Solomon Islands, nation, Oc. (sŏ′lō-mŭn ī′lȧndz)	279e	8°0′S	159°00′E
Solomon Sea, s., Oc. (sŏ′lō-mŭn sē)	277	8°0′S	155°00′E
Solon, China (swo-lōōn)	240-41	46°36′N	121°13′E
Solor, Pulau, i., Indon.	248-49	8°28′S	122°59′E
Solov'yëvsk, Russia	240-41	49°55′N	115°42′E
Soltau, Ger. (sôl′tou)	194-95	52°59′N	9°50′E
Sol'tsy, Russia (sôl′tsê)	192-93	58°07′N	30°20′E
Solvay, N.Y., U.S. (sŏl′vā)	116-17	43°04′N	76°14′W
Sölvesborg, Swe. (sûl′vĕs-bôrg)	192-93	56°03′N	14°35′E
Sol'vychegodsk, Russia (sôl′vê-chĕ-gôtsk′)	186-87	61°20′N	46°55′E
Solway Firth, b., U.K. (sŏl′wā fûrth′)	190-91	54°50′N	3°35′W
Solwezi, Zam.	264-65	12°11′S	26°25′E
Somalia, nation, Afr. (sō-ma′lē-ă)	253	6°0′N	48°00′E
Somaliland, nation, Afr. *see* Somalia	253	6°0′N	48°00′E
Somali Republic, nation, Afr. *see* Somalia	253	6°0′N	48°00′E
Sombor, Serb. (sôm′bôr)	200-01	45°47′N	19°07′E
Sombrerete, Mex. (sōm-brå-rā′tå)	146-47	23°41′N	103°39′W
Sombrero, i., St. K./N.	143b	18°36′N	63°26′W
Somerset, Ky., U.S. (sŭm′ēr-sĕt)	124-25	37°05′N	84°37′W
Somerset, Oh., U.S. (sŭm′ēr-sĕt)	116-17	39°48′N	82°18′W
Somerset East, S. Afr. (sŭm′ēr-sĕt ēst)	264-65	32°44′S	25°35′E
Somersworth, N.H., U.S. (sŭm′ērz-wûrth)	116-17	43°16′N	70°52′W
Somerville, Tn., U.S. (sŭm′ēr-vĭl)	124-25	35°15′N	89°21′W
Somerville, Tx., U.S. (sŭm′ēr-vĭl)	122-23	30°20′N	96°32′W
Somoto, Nic. (sô-mō′tō)	149	13°28′N	86°35′W
Son, stm., India (sōn)	234-35	25°42′N	84°52′E
Sønderborg, Den. (sûn′'er-bôrgh)	194-95	54°55′N	9°48′E
Sonepur, India	234-35	20°49′N	83°54′E
Song Da, stm., Asia *see* Black	246-47	21°15′N	105°21′E
Songea, Tan. (sôn-gā′á)	264-65	10°41′S	35°39′E
Songhua, stm., China	240-41	47°43′N	132°31′E
Songhua Hu, res., China	240-41	43°25′N	127°10′E
Songjiang, China	238-39	31°01′N	121°14′E
Sŏngjin, Kor., N. (sŭng′jĭn′) *see* Kimch'aek	243	40°41′N	129°12′E
Songkhla, Thai. (sông′ĸlä′)	246-47	7°12′N	100°36′E
Songnim, Kor., N.	243	38°44′N	125°38′E
Songo, Moz.	264-65	15°39′S	32°43′E
Sonid Youqi, China	240-41	42°44′N	112°40′E
Sonmiāni Bay, b., Pak.	232-33	25°15′N	66°30′E
Sonneberg, Ger. (sôn′ē-bĕrgh)	194-95	50°21′N	11°11′E
Sonora, Ca., U.S. (sô-nō′rȧ)	118-19	37°59′N	120°22′W
Sonora, Tx., U.S. (sô-nō′rȧ)	122-23	30°34′N	100°39′W
Sonora, state, Mex. (sô-nō′rȧ)	144-45	29°20′N	110°40′W
Sonora, stm., Mex. (sô-nō′rȧ)	144-45	29°05′N	110°54′W
Sonora, Desierto de, des., N.A. *see* Sonoran Desert	144-45	30°0′N	113°00′W
Sonoran Desert, des., N.A.	144-45	30°0′N	113°00′W
Sonsón, Col. (sôn-sôn′)	163c	5°43′N	75°18′W
Sonsonate, El Sal. (sōn-sô-nä′tå)	148	13°43′N	89°43′W
Sonsorol Islands, is., Palau (sŏn-sô-rōl′ ī′lȧndz)	280-81	5°20′N	132°13′E
Son Tay, Viet.	246-47	21°08′N	105°30′E
Soomaaliya, nation, Afr. *see* Somalia	253	6°0′N	48°00′E
Soome laht, b., Eur. *see* Finland, Gulf of	192-93	60°0′N	27°00′E
Sora, Italy (sô′rä)	200-01	41°44′N	13°37′E
Sorell, Cape, c., Austl.	276	42°12′S	145°10′E
Sorel-Tracy, Qc., Can.	136-37	46°03′N	73°05′W
Soria, Spain (sō′rê-ä)	198-99	41°46′N	2°28′W
Sorocaba, Braz. (sô-rô-kä′bȧ)	172	23°30′S	47°28′W
Sorochinsk, Russia	186-87	52°26′N	53°10′E
Sorong, Indon. (sō-rông′)	224-25	0°53′S	131°15′E
Soroti, Ug. (sō-rō′tê)	267	1°43′N	33°36′E
Sørøya, i., Nor.	184-85	70°34′N	22°22′E
Sorrento, Italy (sôr-rĕn′tō)	200-01	40°38′N	14°22′E
Sor Rondane Mountains, mts., Ant.	287	72°0′S	25°00′E
Sorsogon, Phil. (sôr-sôgōn′)	250	12°59′N	124°01′E
Sortavala, Russia (sôr′tä-vä-lä)	192-93	61°42′N	30°40′E
Sosna, stm., Russia (sôs′nȧ)	202-03	52°42′N	38°55′E
Sosnogorsk, Russia	186-87	63°36′N	53°53′E
Sosnowiec, Pol. (sôs-nô′vyĕts)	194-95	50°18′N	19°08′E
Sos'va, stm., Russia (sôs′vȧ)	218-19	59°33′N	62°20′E
Soto la Marina, Barra, i., Mex.	146-47	24°10′N	97°44′W
Soufrière, vol., Guad. (sōō-frê-âr′)	143b	16°04′N	61°40′W
Sŏul, nat. cap., Kor., S. *see* Seoul	243	37°33′N	127°01′E
Sounding Creek, stm., Ab., Can. (soun′dĭng krēk)	132-33	52°06′N	110°28′W
Souris, Mb., Can. (sōō′rē′)	134-35	49°38′N	100°16′W
Souris, P.E., Can. (sōō′rē′)	138-39	46°21′N	62°15′W
Souris, stm., N.A. (sōō′rē′)	130-31	49°40′N	99°35′W
Sousa, Braz.	166-67	6°45′S	38°14′W
Sousse, Tun. (sōōs)	184-85	35°49′N	10°38′E
South, stm., N.C., U.S. (south)	124-25	34°35′N	78°16′W
South Africa, nation, Afr. (south ăf′rĭ-kȧ)	253	30°0′S	26°00′E
South America, cont., (south ȧ-mĕr′ĭ-kȧ)	159	15°0′S	60°00′W
Southampton, Eng., U.K. (south-ămp′tŭn)	190-91	50°55′N	1°24′W
Southampton Island, i., Nu., Can.	130-31	64°20′N	84°40′W
South Andaman, i., India (south ăn-dȧ-măn′)	246-47	11°48′N	92°44′E
South Australia, state, Austl. (south ôs-trā′lĭ-ȧ)	270-71	30°0′S	135°00′E
South Bend, In., U.S. (south bĕnd)	116-17	41°41′N	86°14′W
South Bend, Wa., U.S. (south bĕnd)	112-13	46°40′N	123°46′W
South Boston, Va., U.S. (south bôs′tŭn)	124-25	36°42′N	78°54′W
Southbridge, Ma., U.S. (south′brĭj)	116-17	42°05′N	72°03′W
South Carolina, state, U.S. (south kăr-ô-lī′nȧ)	108-09	34°0′N	81°00′W
South China Sea, s., Asia (south chī′nȧ sē)	224-25	10°0′N	113°00′E
South Dakota, state, U.S. (south dȧ-kō′tȧ)	108-09	44°15′N	100°00′W
South East Cape, c., Austl.	276	43°38′S	146°52′E
South East Point, c., Austl.	276	39°08′S	146°25′E
Southend-on-Sea, Eng., U.K. (south-ĕnd′-ŏn-sē)	190-91	51°33′N	0°45′E
Southern Alps, mts., N.Z. (sŭ-thûrn ălps)	278	43°30′S	170°30′E
Southern Bug, stm., Ukr. (sŭ-thûrn bōōg)	202-03	46°39′N	31°56′E
Southern Cook Islands, is., Cook Is.	280-81	20°0′S	159°00′W
Southern Cross, Austl.	270-71	31°14′S	119°19′E
Southern Indian Lake, lk., Mb., Can. (sŭth′ērn ĭn′dĭ-ăn lāk)	134-35	57°13′N	98°21′W
Southern Ocean, oc., (sŭ-thûrn ōshŭn)	20-21	50°0′S	135°00′E
Southern Pines, N.C., U.S. (sŭth′ērn pīnz)	124-25	35°10′N	79°24′W
Southern Ute Indian Reservation, ind. res., Co., U.S. (sŭth′ērn ūt ĭn′dĭ-ăn rĕ-sēr-vā′shĕn)	118-19	37°05′N	107°45′W
South Georgia, i., S. Geor. (south jôr′jȧ)	287	54°15′S	36°45′W
South Georgia and the South Sandwich Islands, dep., S.A.	287	54°0′S	38°00′W
South Haven, Mi., U.S. (south hāv′'n)	116-17	42°24′N	86°16′W
South Henik Lake, lk., Nu., Can.	130-31	61°30′N	97°27′W
South Indian Lake, Mb., Can.	134-35	56°48′N	98°57′W
Southington, Ct., U.S. (sŭdh′ĭng-tŭn)	116-17	41°36′N	72°53′W
South Island, i., India	236	10°03′N	72°17′E
South Island, i., N.Z. (south ī′lȧnd)	278	43°0′S	171°00′E
South Korea, nation, Asia (south kô-rē′-ȧ)	206-07	36°30′N	128°00′E
South Luangwa National Park, n.p., Zam.	264-65	12°56′S	31°38′E
South Nahanni, stm., N.T., Can.	130-31	61°03′N	123°20′W
South Negril Point, c., Jam. (south nå-grēl′ point)	142-43	18°15′N	78°22′W
South Ogden, Ut., U.S. (south ŏg′dĕn)	112-13	41°12′N	111°59′W
South Orkney Islands, is., Ant.	287	60°35′S	44°07′W
South Paris, Me., U.S. (south păr′ĭs)	116-17	44°13′N	70°31′W
South Pittsburg, Tn., U.S. (south pĭs′bûrg)	124-25	35°01′N	85°43′W
South Platte, stm., U.S. (south plăt)	110-11	41°07′N	100°42′W
Southport, Austl. (south′pōrt)	276	27°58′S	153°25′E
Southport, Eng., U.K. (south′pôrt)	190-91	53°39′N	3°01′W
South River, On., Can.	136-37	45°50′N	79°22′W
South Sandwich Islands, is., S. Geor. (south sănd′wĭch ī′lȧndz)	287	57°31′S	26°37′W
South Saskatchewan, stm., Can. (south sȧs-kach′ĕ-wän)	130-31	53°14′N	105°04′W
South Shetland Islands, is., Ant.	287	62°0′S	58°00′W
South Shields, Eng., U.K. (south shēldz)	190-91	54°60′N	1°25′W
South Sioux City, Ne., U.S. (south sōō sĭt′ê sĭ′tê)	114-15	42°27′N	96°25′W
South Thompson, stm., B.C., Can. (south tŏmp′sŭn)	132-33	50°41′N	120°20′W
South West Africa, nation, Afr. *see* Namibia	253	22°0′S	17°00′E
South West Cape, c., Austl.	276	43°33′S	146°04′E
South West Cape, c., N.Z.	278	47°17′S	167°28′E
Southwest Miramichi, stm., N.B., Can. (south-wĕst′ mĭr ȧ-mê′shē)	138-39	46°58′N	65°34′W
Southwest National Park, n.p., Austl.	276	43°05′S	146°09′E
Sovetsk, Russia (sô-vyĕtsk′)	192-93	55°05′N	21°53′E
Sovetsk, Russia (sô-vyĕtsk′)	186-87	57°35′N	48°58′E
Sovetskaya Gavan, Russia (sŭ-vyĕt′skī-u gä′vŭn')	222-23	48°58′N	140°18′E
Soweto, S. Afr.	269c	26°17′S	27°51′E
Sozopol, Blg. (sôz′ô-pôl')	200-01	42°25′N	27°42′E
Spa, Bel. (spä)	190-91	50°29′N	5°52′E
Spain, nation, Eur. (spān)	174-75	40°0′N	4°00′W
Spanish Fork, Ut., U.S. (spăn′ĭsh fôrk)	118-19	40°08′N	111°39′W
Spanish Sahara, dep., Afr. *see* Western Sahara	253	24°30′N	13°00′W
Spanish Town, Jam.	142-43	17°60′N	76°58′W
Sparks, Nv., U.S. (spärks)	118-19	39°32′N	119°44′W
Sparta, Grc. (spär′tȧ)	200-01	37°05′N	22°26′E
Sparta, Tn., U.S. (spär′tȧ)	124-25	35°56′N	85°28′W
Sparta, Wi., U.S. (spär′tȧ)	114-15	43°56′N	90°48′W
Spartanburg, S.C., U.S. (spär′tăn-bûrg)	124-25	34°57′N	81°56′W
Spartel, Cap, c., Mor. (kăp spär-tĕl′)	269a	35°48′N	5°55′W
Spárti, Grc. *see* Sparta	200-01	37°05′N	22°26′E
Spartivento, Capo, c., Italy (kä′pō spär-tê-vĕn′tô)	200-01	37°55′N	16°04′E
Spartivento, Capo, c., Italy (kä′pō spär-tê-vĕn′tô)	200-01	38°53′N	8°50′E
Spas-Demensk, Russia (spȧs dyĕ-mĕnsk′)	202-03	54°25′N	34°02′E
Spas-Klepiki, Russia (spȧs klĕp′ĕ-kĕ)	202-03	55°08′N	40°12′E
Spassk-Dal'niy, Russia (spŭsk′däl′nyē)	244	44°36′N	132°50′E
Spear, Cape, c., Nf., Can. (kāp spēr)	138-39	47°31′N	52°39′W
Spearfish, S.D., U.S. (spēr′fĭsh)	114-15	44°30′N	103°52′W
Speedway, In., U.S. (spēd′wā)	116-17	39°47′N	86°13′W
Spence Bay, Nu., Can. *see* Taloyoak	128-29	69°32′N	93°31′W
Spencer, Ia., U.S. (spĕn′sēr)	114-15	43°09′N	95°09′W

ăt; finăl; rāte; senāte; ärm; åsk; sofȧ; fâre; ch-choose; dh-as th in other; bē; ēvent; bĕt; recĕnt; cratēr; g-gō; gh-guttural g; bĭt; ĭ-short neutral; rīde; ĸ-guttural k as ch in German ich;

PRONOUNCING INDEX

Spencer – Suining 385

Feature (Pronunciation)	Page	Lat.	Long.
Spencer, In., U.S. (spĕn′sẽr)	**116-17**	39°17′N	86°46′W
Spencer, W.V., U.S. (spĕn′sẽr)	**116-17**	38°47′N	81°22′W
Spencer, Cape, c., Austl.	**276**	35°18′S	136°53′E
Spencer Gulf, b., Austl. (spĕn′sẽr gŭlf)	**272-73**	34°0′S	137°00′E
Speyer, Ger. (shpī′ẽr)	**194-95**	49°20′N	8°26′E
Spezia, Italy *see* La Spezia	**200-01**	44°07′N	9°50′E
Spinazzola, Italy (spē-nät′zô-lä)	**200-01**	40°58′N	16°05′E
Spires, Ger. *see* Speyer	**194-95**	49°20′N	8°26′E
Spirit Lake, Ia., U.S. (spĭr′ĭt lāk)	**114-15**	43°26′N	95°06′W
Spirit Lake, Id., U.S. (spĭr′ĭt lāk)	**112-13**	47°58′N	116°53′W
Spišská Nová Ves, Slvk. (spēsh′skä nō′vä vĕs)	**194-95**	48°57′N	20°34′E
Spitsbergen, i., Nor. (spĭts′bûr-gĕn)	**218-19**	78°45′N	16°00′E
Split, Cro. (splēt)	**200-01**	43°30′N	16°26′E
Split Lake, res., Mb., Can.	**134-35**	56°08′N	96°15′W
Spokane, Wa., U.S. (spōkăn′)	**112-13**	47°39′N	117°24′W
Spokane Indian Reservation, ind. res., Wa., U.S. (spōkăn′ ĭn′dĭ-ăn rĕ-sẽr-vā′shĕn)	**112-13**	47°55′N	118°00′W
Spoleto, Italy (spô-lā′tō)	**200-01**	42°44′N	12°44′E
Spooner, Wi., U.S. (spōōn′ẽr)	**114-15**	45°49′N	91°53′W
Spratly Islands, is., Asia	**224-25**	10°0′N	114°00′E
Springbok, S. Afr. (spring′bŏk)	**264-65**	29°43′S	17°55′E
Springdale, Nf., Can. (spring′dāl)	**138-39**	49°31′N	56°04′W
Springdale, Ar., U.S. (spring′dāl)	**120-21**	36°11′N	94°09′W
Springer, N.M., U.S. (spring′ẽr)	**120-21**	36°22′N	104°36′W
Springfield, Co., U.S. (spring′fēld)	**120-21**	37°24′N	102°37′W
Springfield, Fl., U.S. (spring′fēld)	**124-25**	30°12′N	85°37′W
Springfield, Il., U.S.	**116-17**	39°48′N	89°39′W
Springfield, Ky., U.S. (spring′fēld)	**116-17**	37°41′N	85°13′W
Springfield, Ma., U.S.	**116-17**	42°07′N	72°35′W
Springfield, Mn., U.S. (spring′fēld)	**114-15**	44°14′N	94°59′W
Springfield, Mo., U.S. (spring′fēld)	**120-21**	37°13′N	93°17′W
Springfield, Oh., U.S. (spring′fēld)	**116-17**	39°55′N	83°49′W
Springfield, Or., U.S. (spring′fēld)	**112-13**	44°03′N	123°01′W
Springfield, Tn., U.S. (spring′fēld)	**124-25**	36°30′N	86°53′W
Springfield, Vt., U.S. (spring′fēld)	**116-17**	43°18′N	72°29′W
Springhill, N.S., Can. (spring-hĭl′)	**138-39**	45°39′N	64°03′W
Springs, S. Afr. (springs)	**269c**	26°15′S	28°26′E
Springsure, Austl.	**277**	24°07′S	148°05′E
Spring Valley, Il., U.S. (spring crēk văl′ē)	**116-17**	41°19′N	89°12′W
Spring Valley, Mn., U.S. (spring văl′ē)	**114-15**	43°41′N	92°25′W
Spruce Grove, Ab., Can. (sprōōs grōv)	**132-33**	53°32′N	113°55′W
Spruce Knob, mtn., W.V., U.S.	**116-17**	38°42′N	79°32′W
Squamish, B.C., Can. (skwō′mĭsh)	**132-33**	49°42′N	123°08′W
Squamish, stm., B.C., Can. (skwō′mĭsh)	**132-33**	49°39′N	123°14′W
Srbija, nation, Eur. (sr bē-yä) *see* Serbia	**174-75**	44°0′N	21°00′E
Sredinny Khrebet, mts., Russia	**218-19**	56°0′N	158°00′E
Srednekolymsk, Russia (s′rĕd′nyĕ kô-lêmsk′)	**218-19**	67°27′N	153°40′E
Srednerusskaya Vozvyshennost′, plat., Russia	**202-03**	52°0′N	38°00′E
Śrem, Pol. (shrĕm)	**194-95**	52°05′N	17°02′E
Sremska Mitrovica, Serb. (srĕm′skä mē′trô-vē-tsä′)	**200-01**	44°59′N	19°37′E
Sri Aman, Malay.	**248-49**	1°13′N	111°28′E
Sri Jayewardenepura Kotte, nat. cap., Sri L.	**236**	6°54′N	79°54′E
Srīkākulam, India	**236**	18°18′N	83°54′E
Sri Lanka, nation, Asia (shrē′-län-kȧ) (srē′-län-kȧ)	**206-07**	7°0′N	81°00′E
Srinagar, India	**234-35**	34°05′N	74°48′E
Staaten River National Park, n.p., Austl.	**277**	16°40′S	143°00′E
Stafford, Eng., U.K. (stăf′fẽrd)	**190-91**	52°48′N	2°07′W
Stafford, Va., U.S. (stăf′fẽrd)	**116-17**	38°25′N	77°24′W
Stakhanov, Ukr.	**202-03**	48°34′N	38°40′E
Stalin, Rom. *see* Brașov	**194-95**	45°39′N	25°37′E
Stambaugh, Mi., U.S. (stăm′bô)	**114-15**	46°05′N	88°38′W
Stamford, Eng., U.K. (stăm′fẽrd)	**190-91**	52°39′N	0°29′W
Stamford, Ct., U.S. (stăm′fẽrd)	**116-17**	41°03′N	73°33′W
Stamford, Tx., U.S. (stăm′fẽrd)	**120-21**	32°55′N	99°49′W
Stamps, Ar., U.S. (stămps)	**120-21**	33°22′N	93°30′W
Standerton, S. Afr. (stăn′dẽr-tŭn)	**269c**	26°57′S	29°15′E
Standing Rock Indian Reservation, ind. res., U.S. (stănd′ing rŏk ĭn′dĭ-ăn rĕ-sẽr-vā′shĕn)	**114-15**	45°50′N	101°10′W
Stanford, Ky., U.S. (stăn′fẽrd)	**116-17**	37°31′N	84°41′W
Stanisławów, Ukr. *see* Ivano-Frankivs′k	**194-95**	48°55′N	24°44′E
Stanley, N.D., U.S. (stăn′lē)	**114-15**	48°19′N	102°24′W
Stanley, nat. cap., Falk. Is. (stăn′lē)	**171**	51°43′S	57°49′W
Stanley Falls, wtfl., D.R.C.	**262-63**	0°29′N	25°13′E
Stanovoye Nagor′ye, mts., Russia	**218-19**	56°0′N	114°00′E
Stanovoy Khrebet, mts., Russia (stŭn-ȧ-voi′)	**218-19**	55°48′N	125°34′E
Stanovoy Mountains, mts., Russia (stŭn-ȧ-voi′ moun′tĭnz) *see* Stanovoye Nagor′ye	**218-19**	56°0′N	114°00′E
Stanovoy Range, mts., Russia (stŭn-ȧ-voi′ rānj) *see* Stanovoy Khrebet	**218-19**	55°48′N	125°34′E
Stanthorpe, Austl.	**276**	28°40′S	151°56′E
Stanton, Ky., U.S. (stăn′tŭn)	**116-17**	37°50′N	83°55′W
Stanton, Tx., U.S. (stăn′tŭn)	**122-23**	32°08′N	101°47′W
Staples, Mn., U.S. (stā′p′lz)	**114-15**	46°21′N	94°48′W
Staraya Russa, Russia (stä′rȧ-yȧ rōōsȧ)	**192-93**	57°60′N	31°21′E
Stara Zagora, Blg. (stä′rȧ zä′gô-rȧ)	**200-01**	42°26′N	25°39′E
Starbuck, Mb., Can. (stär′bŭk)	**134-35**	49°46′N	97°37′W
Starbuck, i., Kir.	**280-81**	5°37′S	155°53′W
Staritsa, Russia (stä′rē-tsȧ)	**202-03**	56°30′N	34°56′E
Starke, Fl., U.S. (stärk)	**124-25**	29°57′N	82°07′W
Starkville, Ms., U.S. (stärk′vĭl)	**124-25**	33°27′N	88°49′W
Starodub, Russia (stä-rô-drŏp′)	**202-03**	52°35′N	32°46′E
Starominskaya, Russia (stä′rô mĭn′skȧ-yȧ)	**202-03**	46°32′N	39°02′E
Start Point, c., Eng., U.K. (stärt point)	**190-91**	50°14′N	3°39′W
Staryy Oskol, Russia (stä′rē ôs-kôl′)	**202-03**	51°18′N	37°51′E
Staszów, Pol. (stä′shôf)	**194-95**	50°34′N	21°20′E
State College, Pa., U.S. (stāt kŏl′ĕj)	**116-17**	40°47′N	77°52′W
Staten Island, i., Arg. *see* Estados, Isla de los	**171**	54°48′S	64°33′W
Statesboro, Ga., U.S. (stāts′bŭr-ô)	**124-25**	32°27′N	81°47′W
Statesville, N.C., U.S. (stās′vĭl)	**124-25**	35°47′N	80°54′W
Staunton, Il., U.S. (stôn′tŭn)	**120-21**	39°01′N	89°47′W
Staunton, Va., U.S. (stôn′tŭn)	**116-17**	38°09′N	79°05′W
Staunton, stm., U.S. *see* Roanoke	**124-25**	35°57′N	76°43′W
Stavanger, Nor. (stä′väng′ẽr)	**192-93**	58°58′N	5°45′E
Stavropol′, Russia	**186-87**	45°02′N	41°59′E
Stawell, Austl.	**276**	37°04′S	142°46′E
Steamboat Springs, Co., U.S. (stēm′bōt′ springz)	**112-13**	40°29′N	106°50′W
Steel, stm., On., Can. (stēl)	**136-37**	48°47′N	86°54′W
Steens Mountain, mts., Or., U.S. (stēnz moun′tĭn)	**112-13**	42°35′N	118°40′W
Stefanie, Lake, lk., Afr. *see* Ch′ew Bahir	**267**	4°40′N	36°50′E
Steinamanger, Hung. *see* Szombathely	**194-95**	47°14′N	16°38′E
Steinbach, Mb., Can.	**134-35**	49°31′N	96°41′W
Steinkjer, Nor. (stĕĭn-kyĕr)	**184-85**	64°01′N	11°29′E
Stellarton, N.S., Can. (stĕl′ár-tŭn)	**138-39**	45°33′N	62°39′W
Stendal, Ger. (shtĕn′däl)	**194-95**	52°36′N	11°51′E
Stephens Island, i., B.C., Can.	**132-33**	54°10′N	130°45′W
Stephens Lake, res., Mb., Can.	**134-35**	56°26′N	95°07′W
Stephenville, Nf., Can. (stē′vĕn-vĭl)	**138-39**	48°33′N	58°37′W
Sterling, Ak., U.S. (stûr′lĭng)	**126**	60°32′N	150°48′W
Sterling, Co., U.S. (stûr′lĭng)	**114-15**	40°37′N	103°13′W
Sterling, Il., U.S. (stûr′lĭng)	**116-17**	41°48′N	89°42′W
Sterlitamak, Russia (styĕr′lē-ta-mäk′)	**186-87**	53°37′N	55°58′E
Šternberk, Czech Rep. (shtĕrn′bĕrk)	**194-95**	49°44′N	17°18′E
Stettin, Pol. *see* Szczecin	**194-95**	53°26′N	14°32′E
Steubenville, Oh., U.S. (stū′bĕn-vĭl)	**116-17**	40°22′N	80°38′W
Stevens Point, Wi., U.S.	**116-17**	44°31′N	89°34′W
Stevensville, Mt., U.S. (stē′vĕnz-vĭl)	**112-13**	46°30′N	114°05′W
Stewart, B.C., Can.	**132-33**	55°56′N	129°58′W
Stewart, Isla, i., Chile	**171**	54°52′S	71°12′W
Stewart Island, i., N.Z.	**278**	47°0′S	167°50′E
Steynsrus, S. Afr. (stīns′rōōs)	**269c**	27°57′S	27°34′E
Steyr, Aus. (shtīr)	**194-95**	48°03′N	14°25′E
Stikine, stm., N.A. (stĭ-kēn′)	**130-31**	56°41′N	132°14′W
Stillwater, Ok., U.S. (stĭl′wô-tẽr)	**120-21**	36°08′N	97°05′W
Stillwater Range, mts., Nv., U.S. (stĭl′wô-tẽr rānj)	**118-19**	39°53′N	118°06′W
Štip, Mac. (shtĭp)	**200-01**	41°45′N	22°12′E
Stirling, Scot., U.K. (stûr′lĭng)	**190-91**	56°07′N	3°56′W
Stjørdalshalsen, Nor. (styûr-däls-hälsĕn)	**184-85**	63°29′N	10°56′E
Stockholm, nat. cap., Swe. (stôk′hôlm)	**192-93**	59°20′N	18°03′E
Stockport, Eng., U.K. (stŏk′pôrt)	**190-91**	53°25′N	2°10′W
Stockton, Ca., U.S.	**118-19**	37°57′N	121°17′W
Stockton, Ks., U.S. (stŏk′tŭn)	**120-21**	39°26′N	99°16′W
Stockton Plateau, plat., Tx., U.S. (stŏk′tŭn plă-tō′)	**122-23**	30°30′N	102°30′W
Stœng Tréng, Camb. (stông′trĕng′)	**246-47**	13°31′N	105°58′E
Stoke-on-Trent, Eng., U.K. (stōk-ŏn-trĕnt)	**190-91**	52°60′N	2°10′W
Stolbovoy, Ostrov, i., Russia	**218-19**	74°05′N	136°00′E
Stolin, Bela. (stô′lēn)	**194-95**	51°54′N	26°52′E
Stolp, Pol. *see* Słupsk	**194-95**	54°28′N	17°02′E
Stonehaven, Scot., U.K. (stōn′hā-v′n)	**190-91**	56°58′N	2°13′W
Stonewall, Mb., Can. (stōn′wôl)	**134-35**	50°08′N	97°19′W
Storm Bay, b., Austl.	**276**	43°10′S	147°32′E
Storm Lake, Ia., U.S.	**114-15**	42°39′N	95°13′W
Stornoway, Scot., U.K. (stôr′nô-wā)	**190-91**	58°13′N	6°24′W
Storsjøen, lk., Nor. (stôr-syûĕn)	**192-93**	60°21′N	11°41′E
Storsjön, lk., Swe.	**184-85**	63°12′N	14°18′E
Storuman, Swe.	**184-85**	65°05′N	17°05′E
Stosch, Isla, i., Chile	**171**	49°09′S	75°26′W
Strabane, N. Ire., U.K. (stră-băn′)	**190-91**	54°50′N	7°27′W
Strahan, Austl. (strā′ăn)	**276**	42°09′S	145°19′E
Strakonice, Czech Rep. (strä′kô-nyē-tsĕ)	**194-95**	49°15′N	13°55′E
Stralsund, Ger. (shräl′sònt)	**194-95**	54°19′N	13°05′E
Stranraer, Scot., U.K. (străn-rär′)	**190-91**	54°54′N	5°02′W
Strasbourg, Fr. (strȧs-bōōr′)	**196-97**	48°35′N	7°45′E
Stratford, On., Can. (străt′fẽrd)	**136-37**	43°22′N	80°58′W
Stratford, Ct., U.S. (străt′fẽrd)	**116-17**	41°13′N	73°08′W
Stratford, Tx., U.S. (străt′fẽrd)	**120-21**	36°20′N	102°04′W
Straubing, Ger. (strou′bĭng)	**194-95**	48°53′N	12°35′E
Strausberg, Ger. (strous′bĕrgh)	**194-95**	52°34′N	13°53′E
Streator, Il., U.S. (strē′tẽr)	**116-17**	41°08′N	88°49′W
Strehaia, Rom. (strĕ-kä′yȧ)	**200-01**	44°38′N	23°13′E
Streymoy, i., Far. Is.	**190b**	62°08′N	7°00′W
Strickland, stm., Pap. N. Gui. (strĭk′lănd)	**277**	7°35′S	141°23′E
Strongsville, Oh., U.S. (strôngz′vĭl)	**116-17**	41°18′N	81°50′W
Stronsay, i., Scot., U.K. (strŏn′sā)	**190c**	59°06′N	2°36′W
Stroudsburg, Pa., U.S. (stroudz′bûrg)	**116-17**	40°59′N	75°12′W
Strugi-Krasnyye, Russia (strōō′gĭ krä′s-ny′yĕ)	**192-93**	58°16′N	29°07′E
Strumica, Mac. (strōō′mĭ-tsȧ)	**200-01**	41°26′N	22°37′E
Stryi, Ukr.	**194-95**	49°15′N	23°51′E
Strzelce Opolskie, Pol. (stzhĕl′tsĕ o-pŏl′skyĕ)	**194-95**	50°31′N	18°19′E
Strzelecki Creek, stm., Austl.	**276**	29°21′S	139°48′E
Stuart, Fl., U.S. (stū′ẽrt)	**125a**	27°12′N	80°15′W
Stuart, Ia., U.S. (stū′ẽrt)	**114-15**	41°30′N	94°20′W
Stuart, stm., B.C., Can.	**132-33**	53°59′N	123°33′W
Stuart Island, i., Ak., U.S. (stū′ẽrt ī′lănd)	**126**	63°35′N	162°31′W
Stuart Lake, lk., B.C., Can. (stū′ẽrt lāk)	**132-33**	54°32′N	124°35′W
Stuhlweissenburg, Hung. *see* Székesfehérvár	**194-95**	47°12′N	18°25′E
Stupino, Russia	**202-03**	54°54′N	38°05′E
Sturgeon, stm., On., Can. (stûr′jŭn)	**136-37**	46°16′N	79°56′W
Sturgeon Bay, Wi., U.S. (stûr′jŭn bā)	**116-17**	44°50′N	87°22′W
Sturgeon Bay, b., Mb., Can. (stûr′jŭn bā)	**134-35**	52°0′N	97°50′W
Sturgeon Falls, On., Can. (stûr′jŭn fôlz)	**136-37**	46°22′N	79°55′W
Sturt Stony Desert, des., Austl.	**276**	28°30′S	141°00′E
Stuttgart, Ger. (shtōōt′gärt)	**194-95**	48°48′N	9°11′E
Stuttgart, Ar., U.S. (stŭt′gärt)	**124-25**	34°30′N	91°33′W
Styr, stm., Eur. (stẽr)	**194-95**	52°07′N	26°36′E
Suđuroy, i., Far. Is.	**190b**	61°32′N	6°50′W
Suao, Tai. (sōōou)	**225a**	24°36′N	121°50′E
Subansiri, stm., Asia	**238-39**	26°46′N	93°45′E
Subarnarekha, stm., India	**234-35**	21°34′N	87°23′E
Sūbāţ, stm., Sudan	**262-63**	9°22′N	31°33′E
Subotica, Serb. (sōō′bô′tē-tsȧ)	**200-01**	46°06′N	19°41′E
Suceava, Rom. (sōō-châ-ä′vȧ)	**194-95**	47°40′N	26°17′E
Sucre, nat. cap., Bol. (sōō′krā)	**168-69**	19°02′S	65°16′W
Sudan, nation, Afr. (sōō-dän′)	**253**	15°0′N	30°00′E
Sudan, reg., Afr. (sōō-dän′) *see* Sahel	**258-59**	12°0′N	17°00′E
Sudbury, On., Can. (sŭd′bẽr-ē)	**136-37**	46°29′N	80°59′W
Sudd, reg., Sudan *see* As-Sudd	**262-63**	8°0′N	31°00′E
Sudost′, stm., Eur. (sò-dôst′)	**202-03**	52°20′N	33°23′E
Sudzha, Russia (sòd′zhȧ)	**202-03**	51°11′N	35°18′E
Sue, stm., Sudan	**262-63**	7°40′N	28°02′E
Sueca, Spain (swā′kä)	**198-99**	39°12′N	0°19′W
Suez, Egypt (sōō-ĕz′)	**268b**	29°58′N	32°33′E
Suez, Gulf of, b., Egypt (gŭlf ŭv sōō-ĕz′)	**268b**	29°0′N	32°50′E
Suez Canal, can., Egypt (sōō-ĕz′ kȧ′năl)	**268b**	29°57′N	32°35′E
Suffolk, Va., U.S. (sŭf′ŭk)	**124-25**	36°44′N	76°35′W
Suhag, Egypt	**268b**	26°33′N	31°42′E
Şuḩār, Oman	**230-31**	24°20′N	56°44′E
Sühbaatar, Mong.	**240-41**	50°13′N	106°12′E
Suhl, Ger. (zōōl)	**194-95**	50°36′N	10°41′E
Suid-Afrika, nation, Afr. *see* South Africa	**253**	30°0′S	26°00′E
Suide, China (swā-dŭ)	**240-41**	37°31′N	110°15′E
Suifenhe, China (swā-fŭn-hŭ)	**244**	44°24′N	131°08′E
Suihua, China	**240-41**	46°39′N	126°59′E
Suining, China (sōō′ē-nĭng′)	**238-39**	30°30′N	105°35′E

n-sing; ŋ-baŋk; ɴ-nasalized n; nŏd; cŏmmit; ōld; ôbey; ôrder; oi-boil; fōōd; ŏ-as oo in foot; ou-out; s-soft; sh-dish; th-thin; pūre; ûnite; ûrn; stŭd; circŭs; ü-as in French tu; ′-indeterminate vowel.

386 Suipacha – Taedong-gang PRONOUNCING INDEX

Feature (Pronunciation)	Page	Lat.	Long.
Suipacha, Arg. (swē-pä´chä)	173	34°47′S	59°42′W
Suisse, nation, Eur. see Switzerland	174-75	47°0′N	8°00′E
Suixian, China (swā shyĕn)	238-39	34°26′N	115°04′E
Suizhong, China (swā-jôŋ)	240-41	40°20′N	120°20′E
Suizhou, China	238-39	31°42′N	113°22′E
Sukabumi, Indon.	248-49	6°55′S	106°55′E
Sukagawa, Japan (sōō´kä-gä´wä)	245	37°17′N	140°23′E
Sukarnapura, Indon. see Jayapura	277	2°32′S	140°43′E
Sukarno, Pegunungan, mtn., Indon. see Jaya, Puncak	224-25	4°05′S	137°11′E
Sukhinichi, Russia (sōō´ĸē´nē-chē)	202-03	54°07′N	35°22′E
Sukhona, stm., Russia (sò-ĸô´nà)	186-87	60°45′N	46°18′E
Sukhothai, Thai.	246-47	17°01′N	99°49′E
Sukhumi, Geor. (sò-kòm´) see Sokhumi	227	43°00′N	41°00′E
Sukkozero, Russia	184-85	63°14′N	32°18′E
Sukkur, Pak. (sŭk´ŭr)	232-33	27°42′N	68°52′E
Sūknah, Libya	188-89	29°04′N	15°47′E
Sukumo, Japan (sōō´kò-mō)	245	32°56′N	132°44′E
Sula, i., Nor.	192-93	61°08′N	4°55′E
Sula, stm., Ukr. (sōō-lä´)	202-03	49°38′N	32°43′E
Sula, Kepulauan, is., Indon.	248-49	1°52′S	125°22′E
Sulaimaniya, Iraq see As-Sulaymānīyah	228-29	35°34′N	45°27′E
Sulaimān Range, mts., Pak. (sò-lä-ē-män´ rānj)	232-33	30°30′N	70°10′E
Sulawesi, i., Indon. see Celebes	248-49	2°0′S	121°00′E
Sulawesi, Laut, s., Asia see Celebes Sea	248-49	3°0′N	122°00′E
Sulina, Rom. (sōō-lē´nà)	202-03	45°09′N	29°40′E
Sulitelma, mtn., Eur. (sōō-lē-tyĕl´mà)	184-85	67°08′N	16°24′E
Sulitjelma, mtn., Eur. see Sulitelma	184-85	67°08′N	16°24′E
Sullana, Peru (sōō-lyä´nä)	170	4°54′S	80°41′W
Sulligent, Al., U.S. (sŭl´ĭ-jĕnt)	124-25	33°54′N	88°08′W
Sullivan, Il., U.S. (sŭl´ĭ-văn)	116-17	39°36′N	88°37′W
Sullivan, In., U.S. (sŭl´ĭ-văn)	116-17	39°05′N	87°24′W
Sullivan, Mo., U.S. (sŭl´ĭ-văn)	120-21	38°12′N	91°10′W
Sulmona, Italy (sōōl-mō´nä)	200-01	42°04′N	13°55′E
Sulphur, La., U.S. (sŭl´fŭr)	122-23	30°14′N	93°22′W
Sulphur, Ok., U.S. (sŭl´fŭr)	120-21	34°30′N	96°58′W
Sulphur Springs, Tx., U.S. (sŭl´fŭr springz)	120-21	33°09′N	95°36′W
Sultanabad, Iran see Arāk	232-33	34°05′N	49°41′E
Sulu, Laut, s., Asia see Sulu Sea	250	8°0′N	120°00′E
Sulu Archipelago, is., Phil. (sōō´lōō är´kå-pĕ´-å-gō)	250	6°0′N	121°00′E
Sulūq, Libya	188-89	31°40′N	20°15′E
Sulu Sea, s., Asia (sōō´lōō sē)	250	8°0′N	120°00′E
Sumatera, i., Indon. see Sumatra	246-47	0°05′S	102°00′E
Sumatra, i., Indon. (sò-mä-trà)	246-47	0°05′S	102°00′E
Sumba, i., Indon. (sŭm´bà)	248-49	10°0′S	120°00′E
Sumba, Île, i., D.R.C.	262-63	1°44′N	19°32′E
Sumbawa, i., Indon. (sòm-bä´wä)	248-49	8°49′S	117°56′E
Sumbawa Besar, Indon.	248-49	8°30′S	117°24′E
Sumbawanga, Tan.	267	7°60′S	31°38′E
Sumbe, Ang.	264-65	11°14′S	13°51′E
Sumenep, Indon.	248-49	7°00′S	113°52′E
Summerland, B.C., Can. (sŭ´mĕr-lănd)	132-33	49°36′N	119°41′W
Summerside, P.E., Can. (sŭm´ēr-sīd)	138-39	46°24′N	63°47′W
Summerville, Ga., U.S. (sŭm´ēr-vĭl)	124-25	34°29′N	85°21′W
Summerville, S.C., U.S. (sŭm´ēr-vĭl)	124-25	33°01′N	80°11′W
Summit Lake, B.C., Can.	132-33	54°17′N	122°37′W
Summit Peak, mtn., Co., U.S. (sŭm´mĭt pēk)	118-19	37°21′N	106°42′W
Šumperk, Czech Rep. (shòm´pĕrk)	194-95	49°58′N	16°59′E
Sumqayıt, Azer.	227	40°35′N	49°38′E
Sumter, S.C., U.S. (sŭm´tēr)	124-25	33°55′N	80°21′W
Sumy, Ukr. (sōō´mĭ)	202-03	50°55′N	34°48′E
Sumzom, China	238-39	29°44′N	96°08′E
Sunchales, Arg.	173	30°56′S	61°34′W
Sunch'ŏn, Kor., S.	243	34°57′N	127°30′E
Sunda, Selat, strt., Indon. see Sunda Strait	248-49	6°00′S	105°46′E
Sundance, Wy., U.S. (sŭn´dăns)	114-15	44°24′N	104°23′W
Sunda Strait, strt., Indon. (sōōn´dà strāt)	248-49	6°00′S	105°46′E
Sunderland, Eng., U.K. (sŭn´dēr-lănd)	190-91	54°55′N	1°23′W
Sundsvall, Swe. (sònds´väl)	192-93	62°23′N	17°19′E
Sungaipenuh, Indon.	246-47	2°04′S	101°24′E
Sungari, stm., China see Songhua	240-41	47°43′N	132°31′E
Sungari Reservoir, res., China see Songhua Hu	240-41	43°25′N	127°10′E
Sunne, Swe. (sōōn´ĕ)	192-93	59°50′N	13°10′E
Sunnyvale, Ca., U.S. (sŭn-nē-văl)	118-19	37°22′N	122°01′W
Sunset Crater Volcano National Monument, n.p., Az., U.S. (sŭn-sĕt krā´tēr vŏl-kā´nō năsh´ŭn-ăl mŏn´ū-mĕnt)	118-19	35°22′N	111°31′W
Suntar, Russia (sòn-tär´)	218-19	62°10′N	117°38′E
Sun Valley, Id., U.S.	112-13	43°43′N	114°23′W
Sunyani, Ghana	260-61	7°21′N	2°20′W
Suomenlahti, b., Eur. see Finland, Gulf of	192-93	60°0′N	27°00′E
Suomi, nation, Eur. see Finland	174-75	64°0′N	26°00′E
Suomussalmi, Fin.	184-85	64°53′N	29°02′E
Superior, Az., U.S. (su-pē´rĭ-ēr)	118-19	33°18′N	111°06′W
Superior, Ne., U.S. (su-pē´rĭ-ēr)	120-21	40°01′N	98°04′W
Superior, Wi., U.S. (su-pē´rĭ-ēr)	114-15	46°43′N	92°05′W
Superior, Laguna, b., Mex. (lä-gò´nä sōō-pā-rē-ōr´)	146-47	16°21′N	94°55′W
Superior, Lake, lk., N.A. (lāk su-pē´rĭ-ēr)	114-15	48°0′N	88°00′W
Suphan Buri, Thai.	246-47	14°28′N	100°08′E
Suqian, China (sōō-chyĕn)	238-39	33°57′N	118°18′E
Suquṭrā, i., Yemen	220-21	12°31′N	53°54′E
Ṣūr, Oman	230-31	22°34′N	59°30′E
Sura, stm., Russia	186-87	55°37′N	46°02′E
Surabaja, Indon. see Surabaya	248-49	7°15′S	112°45′E
Surabaya, Indon.	248-49	7°15′S	112°45′E
Surakarta, Indon.	248-49	7°34′S	110°50′E
Sūrat, India (sò´rŭt)	234-35	21°12′N	72°50′E
Surat Thani, Thai.	246-47	9°06′N	99°18′E
Surazh, Russia (sōō-ràzh´)	202-03	53°01′N	32°25′E
Surendranagar, India	234-35	22°43′N	71°38′E
Surgut, Russia (sòr-gòt´)	218-19	61°16′N	73°12′E
Surigao, Phil.	250	9°46′N	125°29′E
Suriname, nation, S.A. (sōō-rē-näm´)	158	4°0′N	56°00′W
Sūrīyah, nation, Asia see Syria	206-07	35°0′N	38°00′E
Sūrmaq, Iran	230-31	31°05′N	52°48′E
Surt, Libya	188-89	31°12′N	16°35′E
Surt, Khalīj, b., Libya	258-59	31°30′N	18°00′E
Suruga-wan, b., Japan (sōō´rōō-gä wän)	245	34°51′N	138°33′E
Susanville, Ca., U.S.	118-19	40°25′N	120°39′W
Susong, China (sōō-sôŋ)	238-39	30°09′N	116°07′E
Susquehanna, Pa., U.S. (sŭs´kwē-hăn´à)	116-17	41°56′N	75°36′W
Susquehanna, stm., U.S. (sŭs´kwē-hăn´à)	116-17	39°32′N	76°05′W
Susques, Arg.	168-69	23°25′S	66°30′W
Sussex, N.B., Can. (sŭs´ĕks)	138-39	45°43′N	65°31′W
Susuman, Russia	218-19	62°46′N	148°10′E
Sutlej, stm., Asia (sŭt´lĕj)	234-35	29°21′N	71°02′E
Sutton, W.V., U.S. (sut´'n)	116-17	38°39′N	80°45′W
Sutton, Monts, mts., N.A. see Green Mountains	116-17	43°45′N	72°45′W
Suva, nat. cap., Fiji (sōō-vä)	279f	18°07′S	178°27′E
Suwałki, Pol. (sò-vou´kē)	194-95	54°06′N	22°56′E
Suwanose-jima, i., Japan	244	29°38′N	129°43′E
Suwarrow, at., Cook Is.	280-81	13°15′S	163°05′W
Suweis, Khalīg el-, b., Egypt see Suez, Gulf of	268b	29°0′N	32°50′E
Suweis, Qanâ el-, can., Egypt see Suez Canal	268b	29°57′N	32°35′E
Suwŏn, Kor., S.	243	37°16′N	127°01′E
Suzdal', Russia (sōōz´dàl)	202-03	56°25′N	40°26′E
Suzhou, China (sōō-jō)	238-39	33°38′N	116°59′E
Suzhou, China (sōō-jō)	238-39	31°18′N	120°37′E
Svalbard, dep., Eur. (sväl´bärt)	208-09	78°0′N	17°00′E
Svay Riĕng, Camb.	246-47	11°04′N	105°49′E
Svelvik, Nor. (svĕl´vēk)	192-93	59°37′N	10°24′E
Svendborg, Den. (svĕn-bôrgh)	194-95	55°04′N	10°37′E
Sverdlovs'k, Ukr.	202-03	48°05′N	39°39′E
Sverige, nation, Eur. see Sweden	174-75	62°0′N	15°00′E
Svetlaya, Russia (svyĕt´lá-yá)	244	46°34′N	138°20′E
Svetlograd, Russia	186-87	45°20′N	42°50′E
Svilengrad, Blg. (svĕl´ĕn-gràt)	200-01	41°46′N	26°13′E
Svir', stm., Russia	186-87	60°30′N	32°48′E
Svishtov, Blg. (svēsh´tôf)	200-01	43°37′N	25°21′E
Svizzera, nation, Eur. see Switzerland	174-75	47°0′N	8°00′E
Svobodnyy, Russia (svô-bôd´nĭ)	222-23	51°23′N	128°08′E
Svolvær, Nor. (svôl´vĕr)	184-85	68°15′N	14°33′E
Swainsboro, Ga., U.S. (swānz´bŭr-ô)	124-25	32°36′N	82°20′W
Swakop, stm., Nmb.	264-65	22°41′S	14°32′E
Swakopmund, Nmb. (svä´kôp-mònt) (swá´kôp-mònd)	264-65	22°40′S	14°32′E
Swan, stm., Can. (swŏn)	134-35	52°34′N	100°45′W
Swan Hill, Austl. (swŏn hĭl)	276	35°21′S	143°33′E
Swan Lake, lk., Mb., Can. (swŏn lăk)	134-35	52°31′N	100°45′W
Swan Range, mts., Mt., U.S. (swŏn rānj)	112-13	47°50′N	113°40′W
Swan River, Mb., Can. (swŏn rĭv´ēr)	134-35	52°05′N	101°16′W
Swansea, Wales, U.K. (swŏn´sē)	190-91	51°38′N	3°58′W
Swaziland, nation, Afr. (swä´zē-lănd)	253	26°30′S	31°30′E
Sweden, nation, Eur. (swē´dĕn)	174-75	62°0′N	15°00′E
Sweetwater, Tn., U.S. (swēt´wô-tēr)	124-25	35°36′N	84°28′W
Sweetwater, Tx., U.S. (swēt´wô-tēr)	120-21	32°28′N	100°24′W
Swellendam, S. Afr.	264-65	34°01′S	20°26′E
Świecie, Pol. (shvyĕn´tsyĕ)	194-95	53°24′N	18°27′E
Swift Current, Sk., Can. (swĭft kûr´ĕnt)	134-35	50°17′N	107°47′W
Swindon, Eng., U.K. (swĭn´dŭn)	190-91	51°34′N	1°47′W
Swinemünde, Pol. see Świnoujście	194-95	53°54′N	14°15′E
Świnoujście, Pol. (shvĭ-nĭ-ô-wēsh´chyĕ)	194-95	53°54′N	14°15′E
Switzerland, nation, Eur. (swĭt´zēr-lănd)	174-75	47°0′N	8°00′E
Sycamore, Il., U.S. (sĭk´á-mōr)	116-17	41°59′N	88°41′W
Sychëvka, Russia (sē-chôf´kà)	202-03	55°49′N	34°17′E
Sydney, Austl. (sĭd´nē)	276	33°52′S	151°13′E
Sydney, N.S., Can. (sĭd´nē)	138-39	46°09′N	60°12′W
Sydney Mines, N.S., Can. (sĭd´nē mīns)	138-39	46°15′N	60°15′W
Syktyvkar, Russia (sük-tüf´kär)	186-87	61°39′N	50°49′E
Sylacauga, Al., U.S. (sĭl-á-kô´gá)	124-25	33°10′N	86°15′W
Sylhet, Bngl.	234-35	24°54′N	91°52′E
Sylvania, Ga., U.S. (sĭl-vā´nĭ-à)	124-25	32°45′N	81°38′W
Sylvester, Ga., U.S. (sĭl-vĕs´tēr)	124-25	31°32′N	83°50′W
Syracuse, Ks., U.S. (sĭr´á-kūs)	120-21	37°59′N	101°45′W
Syracuse, Ne., U.S. (sĭr´á-kūs)	120-21	40°39′N	96°11′W
Syracuse, N.Y., U.S.	116-17	43°03′N	76°09′W
Syrdarīya, stm., Asia see Syr Darya	226	46°04′N	60°04′E
Syr Darya, stm., Asia (sĭr-dä´rē-ä)	226	46°04′N	60°04′E
Syria, nation, Asia (sĭr´ĭ-à)	206-07	35°0′N	38°00′E
Syriam, Mya.	246-47	16°46′N	96°15′E
Syrian Desert, des., Asia	228-29	32°0′N	40°00′E
Sýros, i., Grc.	200-01	37°26′N	24°55′E
Syzran', Russia (sĕz-rän´)	186-87	53°09′N	48°26′E
Szabadka, Serb. see Subotica	200-01	46°06′N	19°41′E
Szamotuły, Pol. (shà-mô-tōō´wĕ)	194-95	52°37′N	16°35′E
Szatmárnémeti, Rom. see Satu Mare	194-95	47°47′N	22°53′E
Szczecin, Pol. (shchĕ´tsĭn)	194-95	53°26′N	14°32′E
Szechwan, state, China see Sichuan	238-39	31°0′N	105°00′E
Szeged, Hung. (sĕ´gĕd)	194-95	46°16′N	20°10′E
Székesfehérvár, Hung. (sā´kĕsh-fĕ´hār-vär)	194-95	47°12′N	18°25′E
Szekszárd, Hung. (sĕk´särd)	194-95	46°21′N	18°43′E
Szentes, Hung. (sĕn´tĕsh)	194-95	46°39′N	20°16′E
Szolnok, Hung.	194-95	47°11′N	20°12′E
Szombathely, Hung. (sòm´bôt-hĕl')	194-95	47°14′N	16°38′E
Szydłowiec, Pol. (shid-wô´vyets)	194-95	51°14′N	20°52′E

T

Feature (Pronunciation)	Page	Lat.	Long.
Ta'izz, Yemen	266	13°35′N	44°01′E
Taal, Lake, lk., Phil. (lăk tä-äl´)	250	13°60′N	121°01′E
Tabaco, Phil. (tä-bä´kō)	250	13°23′N	123°43′E
Tabar Islands, is., Pap. N. Gui.	277	2°45′S	151°57′E
Ṭabas, Iran	232-33	33°36′N	56°55′E
Tabasco, state, Mex. (tä-bäs´kô)	146-47	18°15′N	93°00′W
Taber, Ab., Can.	132-33	49°47′N	112°09′W
Tablas Island, i., Phil. (tä´bläs ī´lănd)	250	12°23′N	122°02′E
Tábor, Czech Rep. (tä´bôr)	194-95	49°25′N	14°41′E
Tabora, Tan. (tä-bō´rä)	267	5°01′S	32°50′E
Tabrīz, Iran (tà-brēz´)	227	38°05′N	46°17′E
Tabuaeran, at., Kir.	280-81	3°51′N	159°18′W
Tabūk, Sau. Ar.	228-29	28°23′N	36°35′E
Tacheng, China (tä-chŭŋ)	226	46°45′N	82°58′E
Tacloban, Phil. (tä-klō´bän)	250	11°14′N	124°60′E
Tacna, Peru (täk´nä)	170	18°01′S	70°15′W
Tacoma, Wa., U.S. (tá-kō´má)	112-13	47°15′N	122°26′W
Taconic Range, mts., U.S. (tá-kŏn´ĭk rānj)	116-17	42°30′N	73°20′W
Tacotalpa, stm., Mex. (tä-kō-täl´pä)	146-47	17°48′N	92°51′W
Tacuarembó, Ur.	173	31°42′S	55°59′W
Tademaït, Plateau du, plat., Alg. (plä-tō´ dü tä-dē-mä´ēt)	258-59	28°20′N	2°47′E
Tadoussac, Qc., Can. (tá-dōō-sák´)	138-39	48°10′N	69°42′W
Tādpatri, India	236	14°54′N	78°00′E
Tadzhikistan, nation, Asia see Tajikistan	232-33	39°0′N	71°00′E
T'aebaek-sanmaek, mts., Asia (tī-bĭk´ sän-mīk´)	243	37°30′N	128°31′E
Taedong-gang, stm., Kor., N. (tī-dŏng gäng´)	243	38°43′N	125°07′E

ăt; fināl; rāte; senāte; ärm; ásk; sofá; fâre; ch-choose; dh-as th in other; bē; ēvent; bĕt; recĕnt; cratēr; g-gō; gh-guttural g; bĭt; ĭ-short neutral; rīde; ĸ-guttural k as ch in German ich;

n-sing; ŋ-baŋk; ɴ-nasalized n; nŏd; cŏmmit; ōld; ŏbey; ôrder; oi-boil; fōͦd; ȯ-as oo in foot; ou-out; s-soft; sh-dish; th-thin; pūre; ûnite; ûrn; stŭd; circŭs; ü-as in French tu; ´-indeterminate vowel.

388 Tarpon Springs – Thanlwin

PRONOUNCING INDEX

Feature (Pronunciation)	Page	Lat.	Long.
Tarpon Springs, Fl., U.S. (tär´pŏn sprĭngz)	125a	28°09'N	82°46'W
Tarquinia, Italy (tär-kwē´nē-ä)	200-01	42°15'N	11°45'E
Tarragona, Spain (tär-rä-gō´nä)	198-99	41°07'N	1°14'E
Tàrrega, Spain	198-99	41°39'N	1°09'E
Tárrega, Spain (tä rå-gä) *see* Tàrrega	198-99	41°39'N	1°09'E
Tarsus, Tur. (tår'sós) (tär´sŭs)	228-29	36°54'N	34°55'E
Tartagal, Arg. (tär-tä-gá´l)	168-69	22°33'S	63°50'W
Tartu, Est. (tär´tōō)	192-93	58°23'N	26°43'E
Ṭarṭūs, Syria	228-29	34°53'N	35°54'E
Tarutao, Ko, i., Thai.	246-47	6°35'N	99°40'E
Tarutung, Indon.	246-47	2°01'N	98°58'E
Taseyeva, stm., Russia	218-19	58°05'N	94°01'E
Tashauz, Turkmen. *see* Daşoguz	226	41°50'N	59°58'E
Ṭashk, Daryācheh-ye, lk., Iran	230-31	29°45'N	53°30'E
Tashkent, nat. cap., Uzb. (tásh´kĕnt)	232-33	41°19'N	69°17'E
Tāshkurghān, Afg. *see* Kholm	232-33	36°41'N	67°42'E
Tashtagol, Russia	226	52°46'N	87°53'E
Tasiilaq, Green. *see* Angmagssalik	284-85	65°35'N	37°50'W
Tasikmalaya, Indon.	248-49	7°20'S	108°13'E
Tasman Bay, b., N.Z. (tăz´măn bā)	278	41°0'S	173°20'E
Tasmania, state, Austl.	276	43°0'S	147°00'E
Tasman Peninsula, pen., Austl. (tăz´măn pĕ-nĭn´sū-lå)	276	43°05'S	147°50'E
Tasman Sea, s., Oc. (tăz´măn sē)	282-83	40°0'S	163°00'E
Tatabánya, Hung.	194-95	47°34'N	18°26'E
Tataouine, Tun.	188-89	32°55'N	10°28'E
Tatarskiy Proliv, strt., Russia	218-19	50°0'N	141°15'E
Tatar Strait, strt., Russia (tá-tär´ strāt) *see* Tatarskiy Proliv	218-19	50°0'N	141°15'E
Tateyama, Japan (tä´tĕ-yä´mä)	245	34°59'N	139°52'E
Tathlina Lake, lk., N.T., Can.	130-31	60°32'N	117°32'W
Tatnam, Cape, c., Mb., Can.	134-35	57°14'N	90°54'W
Tatta, Pak.	232-33	24°45'N	67°56'E
Tatvan, Tur.	227	38°31'N	42°18'E
Tau, i., Am. Sam.	279b	14°15'S	169°29'W
Taunggyi, Mya.	246-47	20°47'N	97°02'E
Taupo, N.Z.	278	38°41'S	176°06'E
Taupo, Lake, lk., N.Z. (läk tä´ōō-pō)	278	38°49'S	175°55'E
Tauragė, Lith. (tou´rá-gā)	192-93	55°15'N	22°17'E
Tauranga, N.Z.	278	37°42'S	176°09'E
Tauroa Point, c., N.Z.	278	35°10'S	173°04'E
Taurus Mountains, mts., Tur. (tôr´ŭs moun´tĭnz)	186-87	37°0'N	33°00'E
Tavastehus, Fin. *see* Hämeenlinna	192-93	60°58'N	24°31'E
Tavda, stm., Russia (táv-dá´)	218-19	57°48'N	67°15'E
Tavira, Port. (tä-vē´rå)	198-99	37°07'N	7°39'W
Tavoy, Mya. *see* Dawei	246-47	14°05'N	98°13'E
Tavşanlı, Tur. (táv´shän-lĭ)	200-01	39°32'N	29°29'E
Tawas City, Mi., U.S. (tô´wás sĭ´tĭ)	116-17	44°16'N	83°31'W
Tawau, Malay.	248-49	4°16'N	117°53'E
Tawitawi Island, i., Phil.	250	5°11'N	119°60'E
Ṭawkar, Sudan	266	18°25'N	37°44'E
Taxco de Alarcón, Mex. (täs´kō dĕ ä-lär-kō´n)	146-47	18°33'N	99°36'W
Taxkorgan Tajik Zizhixian, China	234-35	37°47'N	75°14'E
Tayabas Bay, b., Phil. (tä-yä´bäs bā)	250	13°45'N	121°45'E
Taylor, Tx., U.S. (tā´lẽr)	122-23	30°34'N	97°24'W
Taylorville, Il., U.S. (tā´lẽr-vĭl)	116-17	39°33'N	89°18'W
Taymura, stm., Russia	218-19	63°46'N	98°07'E
Taymyr, Ozero, lk., Russia (ô´zĕ-rô tī-mĭr´)	208-09	74°36'N	102°24'E
Taymyr, Poluostrov, pen., Russia (tī-mĭr´)	218-19	76°0'N	104°00'E
Taymyr Peninsula, pen., Russia (tī-mĭr´ pĕ-nĭn´sū-lå) *see* Taymyr, Poluostrov	218-19	76°0'N	104°00'E
Tayshet, Russia (tī-shĕt´)	218-19	55°56'N	98°00'E
Taytay, Phil.	250	10°49'N	119°31'E
Taz, stm., Russia (táz)	218-19	67°30'N	78°44'E
Taza, Mor. (tä´zä)	184-85	34°14'N	4°01'W
Tazovskiy, Russia	218-19	67°29'N	78°42'E
Tbilisi, nat. cap., Geor. ('tbĭl-yē´sē)	227	41°44'N	44°47'E
Tchad, nation, Afr. *see* Chad	253	15°0'N	19°00'E
Tchad, Lac, lk., Afr. *see* Chad, Lake	258-59	13°03'N	14°33'E
Tchibanga, Gabon (chē-bäŋ´gä)	260-61	2°51'S	11°01'E
Teapa, Mex. (tā-ä´pä)	146-47	17°34'N	92°58'W
Tébessa, Alg.	184-85	35°24'N	8°07'E
Tebingtinggi, Indon.	246-47	3°19'N	99°10'E
Tecalitlán, Mex. (tā-kä-lē-tlän´)	146-47	19°28'N	103°17'W
Techiman, Ghana	260-61	7°36'N	1°56'W
Tecka, Arg.	171	43°28'S	70°50'W
Tecomán, Mex. (tā-kō-män´)	146-47	18°55'N	103°52'W
Tecpan de Galeana, Mex. (tĕk-pän´ dā gä-lā-ä´nä)	146-47	17°13'N	100°36'W
Tecuala, Mex. (tĕ-kwä-lä)	146-47	22°24'N	105°28'W
Tecuci, Rom. (ta-kòch')	202-03	45°51'N	27°26'E
Tecumseh, Mi., U.S. (tē-kŭm´sĕ)	116-17	41°60'N	83°56'W
Tecumseh, Ne., U.S. (tē-kŭm´sĕ)	120-21	40°22'N	96°12'W
Tecumseh, Ok., U.S. (tē-kŭm´sĕ)	120-21	35°15'N	96°56'W
Tees, stm., Eng., U.K. (tēz)	190-91	54°36'N	1°15'W
Tefé, Braz.	166-67	3°23'S	64°43'W
Tefé, stm., Braz.	166-67	3°31'S	64°57'W
Tegal, Indon.	248-49	6°52'S	109°08'E
Tégua, i., Vanuatu	279g	13°15'S	166°37'E
Tegucigalpa, nat. cap., Hond. (tå-gōō-sē-gäl´pä)	149	14°05'N	87°13'W
Tehek Lake, lk., Nu., Can.	130-31	64°56'N	95°37'W
Teheran, nat. cap., Iran *see* Tehrān	232-33	35°40'N	51°25'E
Tehrān, nat. cap., Iran (tĕ-hrän´)	232-33	35°40'N	51°25'E
Tehuacán, Mex. (tā-wä-kän´)	146-47	18°27'N	97°24'W
Tehuantepec, Golfo de, b., Mex. (gôl-fô dĕ tå-wän-tå-pĕk´)	146-47	15°60'N	94°50'W
Tehuantepec, Istmo de, isth., Mex. (ē´st-mô dĕ tå-wän-tå-pĕk´)	146-47	17°0'N	95°00'W
Teide, Pico del, mtn., Spain	199d	28°16'N	16°38'W
Tejen, Turkmen.	232-33	37°22'N	60°31'E
Tejen, stm., Asia	232-33	37°24'N	60°31'E
Tejo, stm., Eur. *see* Tagus	198-99	38°51'N	8°57'W
Tejupan, Punta, c., Mex. (pōō´n-tä-tĕ-kōō-pä´n)	146-47	18°20'N	103°30'W
Tejupilco de Hidalgo, Mex. (tå-hōō-pēl´kô dā ē-dhäl´gō)	146-47	18°54'N	100°09'W
Tekamah, Ne., U.S. (tē-kā´må)	114-15	41°47'N	96°13'W
Tekeli, Kaz.	226	44°48'N	78°51'E
Tekezē, stm., Afr.	266	14°20'N	35°51'E
Tekirdağ, Tur.	200-01	40°60'N	27°31'E
Tekit, Mex. (tĕ-kē´t)	148	20°32'N	89°20'W
Tela, Hond. (tā´lä)	149	15°46'N	87°28'W
Tel Aviv-Jaffa, Isr. *see* Tel Aviv-Yafo	228-29	32°03'N	34°47'E
Tel Aviv-Yafo, Isr. (tĕl-ä-vēv´já´já´fä)	228-29	32°03'N	34°47'E
Telegraph Creek, B.C., Can. (tĕl´ē-gráf krēk)	128-29	57°55'N	131°10'W
Telén, Arg.	171	36°16'S	65°31'W
Telen, stm., Indon.	248-49	0°09'S	116°41'E
Telescope Peak, mtn., Ca., U.S. (tĕl´ē-skōp pēk)	118-19	36°10'N	117°05'W
Teletskoye Ozero, lk., Russia	226	51°38'N	87°40'E
Tell City, In., U.S. (tĕl sĭ´tē)	116-17	37°57'N	86°46'W
Tello, Col. (tĕ´l-yô)	163c	3°04'N	75°08'W
Telluride, Co., U.S. (tĕl´ū-rīd)	118-19	37°57'N	107°48'W
Teloloapan, Mex. (tā´lō-lō-ä´pän)	146-47	18°21'N	99°52'W
Telos, i., Grc. *see* Tílos	200-01	36°26'N	27°23'E
Telsen, Arg.	171	42°27'S	66°58'W
Telšiai, Lith. (tĕl´sha´ē)	192-93	55°59'N	22°15'E
Teluk Intan, Malay.	246-47	4°01'N	101°02'E
Tema, Ghana	260-61	5°38'N	0°01'E
Temagami, Lake, lk., On., Can.	136-37	47°0'N	80°05'W
Temax, Mex. (tĕ´mäx)	148	21°09'N	88°56'W
Tembenchi, stm., Russia	218-19	64°37'N	99°56'E
Tembesi, stm., Indon.	246-47	1°42'S	103°06'E
Tembilahan, Indon.	246-47	0°16'S	103°13'E
Temesvár, Rom. *see* Timișoara	200-01	45°45'N	21°13'E
Temirtaū, Kaz.	226	50°03'N	72°57'E
Tempe, Az., U.S.	118-19	33°24'N	111°55'W
Tempio Pausania, Italy (tĕm´pē-ō pou-sä´nē-ä)	200-01	40°54'N	9°06'E
Temple, Tx., U.S. (tĕm´p'l)	122-23	31°06'N	97°21'W
Tempoal, stm., Mex. (tĕm-pô-ä´l)	146-47	21°46'N	98°27'W
Temryuk, Russia (tyĕm-ryòk´)	202-03	45°16'N	37°22'E
Temuco, Chile (tå-mōō´kō)	171	38°44'S	72°36'W
Tena, Ec.	170	0°59'S	77°49'W
Tenāli, India	236	16°15'N	80°35'E
Tenasserim, Mya. (tĕn-ăs´ẽr-ĭm)	246-47	12°05'N	99°01'E
Ten Degree Channel, strt., India	246-47	10°0'N	93°00'E
Tendrara, Mor.	188-89	33°04'N	2°00'W
Ténéré, des., Niger	258-59	18°43'N	10°51'E
Tenerife, i., Spain (tå-nå-rē´fä) (tĕn-ẽr-ĭf´)	199d	28°19'N	16°34'W
Ténès, Alg. (tā-nĕs´)	198-99	36°30'N	1°18'E
Tengchong, China	238-39	25°01'N	98°30'E
Tenggara, Nusa, is., Asia *see* Lesser Sunda Islands	248-49	9°0'S	120°00'E
Tengiz köli, lk., Kaz.	226	50°22'N	68°56'E
Tengxian, China (tŭŋ shyĕn)	238-39	23°20'N	110°53'E
Tengxian, China (tŭŋ shyĕn)	240-41	35°05'N	117°09'E
Tennant Creek, Austl. (tĕn´ănt krēk)	270-71	19°39'S	134°11'E
Tennessee, state, U.S. (tĕn-ĕ-sē´)	108-09	35°50'N	85°30'W
Tennessee, stm., U.S. (tĕn-ĕ-sē´)	110-11	37°05'N	88°34'W
Teno, stm., Eur.	184-85	70°26'N	28°16'E
Tenom, Malay.	248-49	5°07'N	115°56'E
Tenosique, Mex. (tā-nō-sē´kå)	148	17°29'N	91°26'W
Tenryū, stm., Japan (tĕn´ryōō´)	245	34°40'N	137°48'E
Tensas, stm., La., U.S. (tĕn´sô)	124-25	31°37'N	91°48'W
Tenterfield, Austl. (tĕn´tẽr-fēld)	276	29°04'S	152°01'E
Teocaltiche, Mex. (tā´ô-käl-tē´chå)	146-47	21°26'N	102°34'W
Teófilo Otoni, Braz. (tĕ-ô´fē-lō-tô´nē)	172	17°53'S	41°31'W
Teotihuacán, hist., Mex.	146-47	19°44'N	98°50'W
Tepalcatepec, Mex. (tā´päl-kä-tå´pĕk)	146-47	19°11'N	102°51'W
Tepatitlán de Morelos, Mex. (tā-pä-tē-tlän´ dā mô-rā´los)	146-47	20°48'N	102°44'W
Tepeaca, Mex. (tā-pā-ä´kä)	146-47	18°58'N	97°54'W
Tepic, Mex. (tā-pēk´)	146-47	21°30'N	104°54'W
Tequila, Mex. (tå-kē´lä)	146-47	20°52'N	103°50'W
Tequisquiapan, Mex. (tå-kēs-kē-ä´pän)	146-47	20°32'N	99°54'W
Téra, Niger	258-59	14°00'N	0°46'E
Teraina, i., Kir.	280-81	4°42'N	160°45'W
Teramo, Italy (tā´rä-mô)	200-01	42°40'N	13°42'E
Terceira, i., Port. (tĕr-sā´rä)	199c	38°43'N	24°13'W
Tercero, stm., Arg.	173	32°55'S	62°20'W
Terek, stm., Russia	227	43°44'N	46°33'E
Teresina, Braz. (tĕr-å-sē´nå)	166-67	5°05'S	42°49'W
Teresópolis, Braz. (tĕr-ā-sô´pô-lēzh)	172	22°26'S	42°59'W
Tergüün Bogd uul, mtn., Mong.	240-41	44°57'N	100°15'E
Teriberka, Russia (tyĕr-ĕ-byôr´kå)	186-87	69°07'N	35°08'E
Términos, Laguna de, b., Mex. (lä-gò´nä dĕ ĕ´r-mē-nôs)	148	18°36'N	91°34'W
Termiz, Uzb.	232-33	37°14'N	67°16'E
Termoli, Italy (tĕr´mô-lē)	200-01	42°00'N	14°60'E
Ternate, Indon. (tĕr-nä´tā)	248-49	0°49'N	127°18'E
Terney, Russia	244	45°03'N	136°36'E
Terni, Italy (tĕr´nē)	200-01	42°34'N	12°39'E
Ternopil', Ukr.	194-95	49°33'N	25°37'E
Terpeniya, Mys, c., Russia (mĭs tĕr-pā´nĭ-yá)	218-19	48°39'N	144°44'E
Terpeniya, Zaliv, b., Russia (zä´lĭf tĕr-pā´nĭ-yá)	218-19	49°0'N	143°30'E
Terrace, B.C., Can. (tĕr´ĭs)	132-33	54°32'N	128°35'W
Terracina, Italy (tĕr-rä-chē´nä)	200-01	41°17'N	13°15'E
Terranova di Sicilia, Italy *see* Gela	200-01	37°04'N	14°15'E
Terrebonne, Qc., Can. (tĕr-bŏn´)	136-37	45°42'N	73°37'W
Terre Haute, In., U.S. (tĕr-ē hōt´)	116-17	39°27'N	87°25'W
Teruel, Spain (tå-rōō-ĕl´)	198-99	40°21'N	1°06'W
Tes, stm., Asia	222-23	50°29'N	93°03'E
Teseney, Erit.	266	15°08'N	36°42'E
Tes-Khem, stm., Asia *see* Tes	222-23	50°29'N	93°03'E
Teslin, Yk., Can. (tĕs-lĭn)	128-29	60°11'N	132°43'W
Teslin, stm., Can. (tĕs-lĭn)	130-31	61°34'N	134°53'W
Teslin Lake, lk., Can. (tĕs-lĭn lāk)	130-31	60°15'N	132°57'W
Tessalit, Mali	258-59	20°12'N	1°00'E
Tessaoua, Niger (tĕs-sä´ò-ä)	258-59	13°45'N	7°59'E
Tete, Moz. (tā´tĕ)	264-65	16°09'S	33°36'E
Tetepare Island, i., Sol. Is.	279e	8°43'S	157°33'E
Teterow, Ger. (tā´tĕ-rō)	194-95	53°46'N	12°34'E
Tetiaroa, at., Fr. Poly.	279d	17°00'S	149°34'W
Tetouan, Mor.	269a	35°35'N	5°22'W
Tetovo, Mac. (tā´tô-vô)	200-01	42°00'N	20°59'E
Teuco, stm., Arg.	168-69	25°39'S	60°10'W
Tevere, stm., Italy *see* Tiber	200-01	41°45'N	12°14'E
Texarkana, Ar., U.S. (tĕk-sär-kăn´å)	120-21	33°26'N	94°03'W
Texarkana, Tx., U.S. (tĕk-sär-kăn´å)	120-21	33°26'N	94°04'W
Texas, state, U.S. (tĕk´sŭs)	108-09	31°30'N	99°00'W
Texas City, Tx., U.S. (tĕk´sŭs sĭ´tĭ)	122-23	29°23'N	94°54'W
Texoma, Lake, res., U.S. (lāk tĕk´ō-mă)	120-21	33°54'N	96°37'W
Teykovo, Russia (tĕy-kô-vô)	202-03	56°51'N	40°33'E
Teziutlán, Mex. (tå-zē-ōō-tlän´)	146-47	19°49'N	97°21'W
Tezpur, India	234-35	26°37'N	92°48'E
Thabana-Ntlenyana, mtn., Leso.	264-65	29°28'S	29°16'E
Thabazimbi, S. Afr.	269c	24°37'S	27°24'E
Thai Lan, Vinh, b., Asia *see* Thailand, Gulf of	246-47	10°0'N	101°00'E
Thailand, nation, Asia (tī´ănd)	206-07	15°0'N	100°00'E
Thailand, Gulf of, b., Asia (gŭlf ŭv tī´ănd)	246-47	10°0'N	101°00'E
Thai Nguyen, Viet.	246-47	21°36'N	105°50'E
Thakhek, Laos *see* Muang Khammouan	246-47	17°25'N	104°49'E
Thal, Pak.	232-33	33°22'N	70°33'E
Thames, stm., On., Can. (tĕmz)	136-37	42°19'N	82°27'W
Thames, stm., Eng., U.K. (tĕmz)	190-91	51°27'N	0°21'E
Thāne, India	236	19°14'N	72°59'E
Thanh Hoa, Viet. (tän´hō´á)	246-47	19°48'N	105°46'E
Thanh Pho Ho Chi Minh, Viet. *see* Ho Chi Minh City	246-47	10°45'N	106°40'E
Thanjāvūr, India	236	10°47'N	79°09'E
Thanlwin, stm., Asia *see* Salween	208-09	16°33'N	97°40'E

ăt; finăl; rāte; senâte; ärm; åsk; sofá; fâre; ch-choose; dh-as th in other; bē; ēvent; bĕt; recĕnt; cratẽr; g-gō; gh-guttural g; bĭt; ĭ-short neutral; rīde; κ-guttural k as ch in German ich;

Feature (Pronunciation)	Page	Lat.	Long.
Thann, Fr. (tän)	196-97	47°49'N	7°05'E
Thar Desert, des., Asia (tär dĕs´ērt)	232-33	27°0'N	71°00'E
Thargomindah, Austl. (thár´gō-mĭn´dȧ)	276	28°0'S	143°49'E
Tharrawaddy, Mya.	246-47	17°39'N	95°47'E
Thásos, i., Grc. (thă´sôs)	200-01	40°39'N	24°40'E
Thayer, Mo., U.S. (thâ´ēr)	124-25	36°31'N	91°33'W
Thayetmyo, Mya.	246-47	19°19'N	95°11'E
Thazi, Mya.	246-47	20°51'N	96°04'E
Thebes, Grc. (thēbz) *see* Thíva	200-01	38°20'N	23°19'E
Thebes, hist., Egypt (thēbz)	268b	25°42'N	32°39'E
The Coorong, b., Austl. (thȧ kŏ´rŏng)	276	35°46'S	139°15'E
The Dalles, Or., U.S. (thȧ dălz)	112-13	45°36'N	121°11'W
The Hague, nat. cap., Neth. (thȧ hāg) *see* Hague, The	190-91	52°06'N	4°18'E
The Minch, strt., Scot., U.K.	190-91	58°10'N	5°50'W
Theodore, Austl. (thēō´dôr)	277	24°57'S	150°05'E
Theodore Roosevelt National Park (North Unit), n.p., N.D., U.S. (thē-ŏ-dôr rōō-sȧ-vĕlt năsh´ŭn-ăl pärk)	114-15	47°34'N	103°24'W
Theodore Roosevelt National Park (South Unit), n.p., N.D., U.S. (thē-ŏ-dôr rōō-sȧ-vĕlt năsh´ŭn-ăl pärk)	114-15	46°58'N	103°25'W
The Pas, Mb., Can. (thȧ pä)	134-35	53°49'N	101°13'W
Thermopolis, Wy., U.S. (thēr-mŏp´ō-lĭs)	112-13	43°39'N	108°13'W
The Snares, is., N.Z. *see* Snares Islands	287	48°0'S	166°30'E
Thessaloníki, Grc. (thĕs-sȧ-lō-nē´kē)	200-01	40°38'N	22°59'E
Thetford Mines, Qc., Can. (thĕt´fērd mīns)	136-37	46°05'N	71°18'W
The Valley, nat. cap., Anguilla	143b	18°13'N	63°04'W
Thibodaux, La., U.S. (tē-bŏ-dō´)	124-25	29°48'N	90°49'W
Thief River Falls, Mn., U.S. (thēf rĭv´ēr fôlz)	114-15	48°07'N	96°11'W
Thiers, Fr. (tyâr)	196-97	45°51'N	3°32'E
Thiès, Sen. (tē-ĕs´)	260-61	14°48'N	16°56'W
Thika, Kenya	267	1°03'S	37°04'E
Thimphu, nat. cap., Bhu. (tĭm-pōō´)	234-35	27°28'N	89°39'E
Thingvellir, Ice.	190a	64°16'N	21°07'W
Thionville, Fr. (tyôn-vēl´)	196-97	49°22'N	6°10'E
Thíra, i., Grc.	200-01	36°26'N	25°27'E
Thiruvananthapuram, India	236	8°31'N	76°57'E
Thisted, Den. (tēs´tĕdh)	192-93	56°57'N	8°42'E
Thíva, Grc.	200-01	38°20'N	23°19'E
Thjórsá, stm., Ice. (tyûr´sȧ)	190a	63°55'N	20°40'W
Thomas, Ok., U.S. (tŏm´ăs)	120-21	35°45'N	98°45'W
Thomaston, Ga., U.S. (tŏm´ăs-tŭn)	124-25	32°53'N	84°19'W
Thomasville, Al., U.S. (tŏm´ăs-vĭl)	124-25	31°54'N	87°45'W
Thomasville, Ga., U.S. (tŏm´ăs-vĭl)	124-25	30°50'N	83°59'W
Thomasville, N.C., U.S. (tŏm´ăs-vĭl)	124-25	35°53'N	80°05'W
Thompson, Mb., Can. (tŏm-sŏn)	134-35	55°44'N	97°51'W
Thompson, stm., B.C., Can. (tŏm-sŏn)	132-33	50°14'N	121°35'W
Thompson, stm., U.S. (tŏm-sŏn)	120-21	39°45'N	93°37'W
Thompson Falls, Mt., U.S. (tŏm-sŏn fôlz)	112-13	47°35'N	115°21'W
Thomson, stm., Austl. (tŏm-sŏn)	277	25°11'S	142°50'E
Thomson's Falls, Kenya (tŏm-sŏns fôlz) *see* Nyahururu Falls	267	0°02'N	36°22'E
Thonon-les-Bains, Fr. (tô-nôn´lā-băn´)	196-97	46°23'N	6°29'E
Thorn, Pol. *see* Toruń	194-95	53°01'N	18°37'E
Thorshavn, nat. cap., Far. Is. *see* Tórshavn	190b	62°01'N	6°46'W
Thouars, Fr. (tōō-är´)	196-97	46°59'N	0°13'W
Thrace, hist. reg., Eur. (thrās)	200-01	41°20'N	26°45'E
Thráki, hist. reg., Eur. *see* Thrace	200-01	41°20'N	26°45'E
Three Forks, Mt., U.S. (thrē fôrks)	112-13	45°53'N	111°34'W
Three Gorges Reservoir, res., China	238-39	31°0'N	110°30'E
Three Hummock Island, i., Austl.	276	40°26'S	144°55'E
Three Oaks, Mi., U.S. (thrē ōks)	116-17	41°48'N	86°36'W
Three Pagodas Pass, p., Asia	246-47	15°18'N	98°22'E
Three Points, Cape, c., Ghana	260-61	4°45'N	2°05'W
Three Rivers, Mi., U.S. (thrē rĭv´ērz)	116-17	41°56'N	85°37'W
Thrissur, India	236	10°31'N	76°13'E
Thu, Cu Lao, i., Viet.	246-47	10°32'N	108°57'E
Thule, Green.	288	76°41'N	68°51'W
Thunder Bay, On., Can. (thŭn´dēr bā)	136-37	48°24'N	89°15'W
Thunder Bay, b., On., Can. (thŭn´dēr bā)	136-37	48°24'N	89°00'W
Thursday Island, Austl.	277	10°36'S	142°15'E
Thurso, Scot., U.K.	190-91	58°35'N	3°32'W
Thysville, D.R.C. *see* Mbanza-Ngungu	262-63	5°14'S	14°53'E
Tiandong, China (tĭĕn-dôŋ)	238-39	23°36'N	107°08'E
Tianjin, China (tĭĕn-jyĭ)	240-41	39°08'N	117°11'E
Tianjin, state, China	240-41	39°30'N	117°15'E
Tianjun, China	240-41	37°20'N	98°57'E
Tianmen, China (tĭĕn-mŭn)	238-39	30°39'N	113°10'E
Tian Shan, mts., Asia (tĭĕn shän) *see* Tien Shan	226	42°0'N	80°00'E
Tianshui, China (tĭĕn-shwā)	238-39	34°32'N	105°54'E
Tiantai, China	238-39	29°08'N	121°00'E
Tianzhu, China	240-41	36°60'N	103°07'E
Tiaret, Alg.	198-99	35°28'N	1°21'E
Tibasti, Sarīr, des., Libya	258-59	24°0'N	17°00'E
Tibati, Camn.	260-61	6°27'N	12°37'E
Tiber, stm., Italy (tī´bēr)	200-01	41°45'N	12°14'E
Tiberias, Lake, lk., Isr. *see* Galilee, Sea of	228-29	32°48'N	35°35'E
Tibesti, mts., Afr. (tĭ-bĕs´-tē)	258-59	21°30'N	17°30'E
Tibet, state, China (tĭ-bĕt´)	234-35	32°0'N	88°00'E
Tibet, Plateau of, plat., China (plä-tō´ ŭv tĭ-bĕt´)	222-23	33°0'N	92°00'E
Tibooburra, Austl.	276	29°26'S	142°01'E
Tiburón, Isla, i., Mex.	144-45	29°0'N	112°23'W
Tīchīt, Maur.	258-59	18°29'N	9°28'W
Ticonderoga, N.Y., U.S. (tī-kŏn-dēr-ō´gȧ)	116-17	43°51'N	73°26'W
Ticul, Mex. (tē-kōō´l)	148	20°24'N	89°32'W
Tidaholm, Swe. (tē´dȧ-hōlm)	192-93	58°11'N	13°58'E
Tidjikja, Maur.	258-59	18°33'N	11°25'W
Tidore, Indon.	248-49	0°38'N	127°24'E
Tieli, China	240-41	46°59'N	128°04'E
Tieling, China (tĭĕ-lĭŋ)	243	42°18'N	123°51'E
Tien Giang, stm., Asia *see* Mekong	246-47	10°33'N	105°27'E
Tien Shan, mts., Asia (tĭĕn shän)	226	42°0'N	80°00'E
Tientsin, China *see* Tianjin	240-41	39°08'N	117°11'E
Tientsin, state, China *see* Tianjin	240-41	39°30'N	117°15'E
Tierp, Swe. (tyĕrp)	192-93	60°20'N	17°31'E
Tierra Blanca, Mex. (tyĕ´r-rä-blä´n-kä)	146-47	18°26'N	96°21'W
Tierra del Fuego, i., S.A. (tyĕr´rä dĕl fwā´gō)	171	54°0'S	69°00'W
Tietê, stm., Braz.	168-69	20°37'S	51°34'W
Tiffin, Oh., U.S. (tĭf´ĭn)	116-17	41°06'N	83°10'W
Tifton, Ga., U.S. (tĭf´tŭn)	124-25	31°27'N	83°30'W
Tiga, Île, i., N. Cal.	279g	21°08'S	167°48'E
Tighina, Mol.	202-03	46°50'N	29°29'E
Tigil', Russia	218-19	57°47'N	158°42'E
Tignish, P.E., Can. (tĭg´nĭsh)	138-39	46°58'N	64°02'W
Tigre, stm., Peru	170	4°29'S	74°05'W
Tigris, stm., Asia (tī-grĭs)	208-09	30°60'N	47°27'E
Tihuatlán, Mex. (tē-wä-tlän´)	146-47	20°44'N	97°34'W
Tijuana, Mex. (tē-hwä´nä)	144-45	32°32'N	117°01'W
Tikal, hist., Guat. (tē-käl´)	148	17°15'N	89°39'W
Tikei, Île, i., Fr. Poly.	280-81	14°58'S	144°33'W
Tikhoretsk, Russia (tē-kôr-yĕtsk´)	186-87	45°51'N	40°08'E
Tikhvin, Russia (tēk-vēn´)	192-93	59°39'N	33°32'E
Tikrīt, Iraq	228-29	34°36'N	43°42'E
Tiksi, Russia (tēk-sē´)	218-19	71°39'N	128°48'E
Tilburg, Neth. (tĭl´bûrg)	190-91	51°34'N	5°05'E
Tilemsi, Vallée du, stm., Mali	258-59	16°18'N	0°01'E
Tillamook, Or., U.S. (tĭl´ȧ-mŏŏk)	112-13	45°27'N	123°50'W
Tillsonburg, On., Can. (tĭl´sŭn-bûrg)	136-37	42°52'N	80°43'W
Tílos, i., Grc.	200-01	36°26'N	27°23'E
Tilpa, Austl.	276	30°57'S	144°24'E
Tim, Russia (tēm)	202-03	51°38'N	37°07'E
Timan Ridge, hills, Russia *see* Timanskiy Kryazh	186-87	65°0'N	51°00'E
Timanskiy Kryazh, hills, Russia	186-87	65°0'N	51°00'E
Timaru, N.Z. (tĭm´á-rōō)	278	44°24'S	171°14'E
Timbalier Bay, b., La., U.S. (tĭm´bȧ-lēr bā)	124-25	29°10'N	90°20'W
Timbuktu, Mali *see* Tombouctou	258-59	16°47'N	3°01'W
Timimoun, Alg. (tē-mē-mōōn´)	188-89	29°14'N	0°16'E
Timirist, Râs, c., Maur.	258-59	19°23'N	16°32'W
Timișoara, Rom.	200-01	45°45'N	21°13'E
Timmins, On., Can. (tĭm´ĭnz)	136-37	48°29'N	81°21'W
Timor, i., Asia (tē-mōr´)	248-49	9°0'S	125°00'E
Timor, Laut, s., *see* Timor Sea	272-73	11°0'S	128°00'E
Timor-Leste, nation, Asia *see* East Timor	248-49	8°35'S	126°00'E
Timor Sea, s., (tē-mōr´ sē)	272-73	11°0'S	128°00'E
Timor Timur, nation, Asia *see* East Timor	248-49	8°35'S	126°00'E
Timpanogos Cave National Monument, n.p., Ut., U.S. (tĭ-măn´ō-gōz kāv năsh´ŭn-ăl mŏn´ŭ-mĕnt)	118-19	40°26'N	111°44'W
Tinaca Point, c., Phil.	250	5°34'N	125°20'E
Tindouf, Alg. (tēn-dōōf´)	258-59	27°49'N	8°08'W
Tinghert, Ḥamādat, plat., Afr.	258-59	29°0'N	9°00'E
Tingo María, Peru (tē´ngō-mä-rē´ä)	170	9°10'S	75°56'W
Tingri, China *see* Dinggyê	234-35	28°35'N	86°37'E
Tingsryd, Swe. (tĭngs´rüd)	192-93	56°32'N	14°59'E
Tinian, i., N. Mar. Is.	280-81	15°00'N	145°38'E
Tinkisso, stm., Gui.	260-61	11°21'N	9°11'W
Tinogasta, Arg. (tē-nō-gäs´tä)	168-69	28°03'S	67°34'W
Tínos, i., Grc.	200-01	37°36'N	25°10'E
Tinrhert, Hamada de, plat., Afr.	258-59	29°0'N	9°00'E
Tintina, Arg.	173	27°02'S	62°43'W
Tioman, Pulau, i., Malay.	246-47	2°48'N	104°10'E
Tipitapa, Nic. (tē-pē-tä´pä)	149	12°12'N	86°06'W
Tip Top Mountain, mtn., On., Can.	136-37	48°16'N	85°59'W
Tīrān, i., Sau. Ar.	228-29	27°57'N	34°33'E
Tīrân, Madīq, strt., *see* Tiran, Strait of	228-29	27°58'N	34°28'E
Tiran, Strait of, strt.	228-29	27°58'N	34°28'E
Tirana, nat. cap., Alb. *see* Tiranë	200-01	41°20'N	19°50'E
Tiranë, nat. cap., Alb. (tē-rä´nä)	200-01	41°20'N	19°50'E
Tirano, Italy (tē-rä´nō)	200-01	46°13'N	10°11'E
Tiraspol, Mol.	202-03	46°51'N	29°38'E
Tire, Tur. (tē´rĕ)	200-01	38°06'N	27°45'E
Tiree, i., Scot., U.K. (tī-rē´)	190-91	56°31'N	6°52'W
Tîrgu Mureș, Rom. *see* Târgu Mureș	194-95	46°33'N	24°34'E
Tirich Mīr, mtn., Pak.	232-33	36°15'N	71°50'E
Tirreno, Mar, s., Eur. *see* Tyrrhenian Sea	200-01	40°0'N	12°00'E
Tiruchchirāppalli, India (tĭr´ō-chĭ-rä´pȧ-lĭ)	236	10°49'N	78°42'E
Tirunelveli, India	236	8°44'N	77°41'E
Tiruppur, India	236	11°06'N	77°21'E
Tisa, stm., Eur.	200-01	45°08'N	20°17'E
Tisdale, Sk., Can. (tĭz´dāl)	134-35	52°51'N	104°03'W
Tisisat Falls, wtfl., Eth.	266	11°29'N	37°35'E
T'īs Isat Fwafwatē, wtfl., Eth. *see* Tisisat Falls	266	11°29'N	37°35'E
Tīsta, stm., Asia	234-35	25°31'N	89°42'E
Tisza, stm., Eur. (tē´sä)	200-01	45°08'N	20°17'E
Titicaca, Lago, lk., S.A. (lä´gō-tē-tē-kä´kä)	168-69	15°50'S	69°20'W
Titograd, nat. cap., Mont. *see* Podgorica	200-01	42°27'N	19°16'E
Titov Veles, Mac. (tē´tôv vĕ´lĕs)	200-01	41°43'N	21°47'E
Titusville, Fl., U.S. (tĭ´tŭs-vĭl)	125a	28°37'N	80°49'W
Titusville, Pa., U.S. (tĭ´tŭs-vĭl)	116-17	41°38'N	79°41'W
Tivoli, Italy (tē´vô-lē)	200-01	41°58'N	12°48'E
Tiwanaku, hist., Bol.	168-69	16°33'S	68°41'W
Tizimín, Mex. (tē-zē-mē´n)	148	21°10'N	88°10'W
Tizi Ouzou, Alg. (tē´zē-ōō-zōō´)	269b	36°48'N	4°02'E
Tiznit, Mor. (tēz-nēt)	258-59	29°42'N	9°43'W
Tjörn, i., Swe.	192-93	58°0'N	11°38'E
Tlacotalpan, Mex. (tlä-kō-täl´pän)	146-47	18°38'N	95°40'W
Tlacotepec, Mex. (tlä-kō-tȧ-pĕ´k)	146-47	17°47'N	99°59'W
Tlahualilo de Zaragoza, Mex.	122-23	26°06'N	103°26'W
Tlalnepantla, Mex. (tläl-nȧ-pán´tlä)	146-47	19°32'N	99°12'W
Tlaquepaque, Mex. (tlä-kĕ-pä´kĕ)	146-47	20°39'N	103°19'W
Tlaxcala, state, Mex.	146-47	19°25'N	98°10'W
Tlaxcala de Xicohténcatl, Mex.	146-47	19°19'N	98°14'W
Tlemcen, Alg.	198-99	34°53'N	1°18'W
Toamasina, Madag.	264-65	18°09'S	49°24'E
Tobago, i., Trin. (tō-bā´gō)	143b	11°15'N	60°40'W
Tobejuba, Isla, i., Ven.	143b	9°20'N	60°52'W
Tobelo, Indon.	248-49	1°44'N	128°00'E
Tobi, i., Palau	280-81	3°0'N	131°10'E
Tobol, stm., Asia (tŏ-bôl´)	218-19	58°09'N	68°13'E
Tobol'sk, Russia (tŏ-bôlsk´)	218-19	58°11'N	68°15'E
Tobruk, Libya	258-59	32°05'N	23°57'E
Tobyl, stm., Asia	218-19	58°09'N	68°13'E
Tocantinópolis, Braz. (tō-kän-tē-nō´pō-lĕs)	166-67	6°19'S	47°25'W
Tocantins, state, Braz. (tō-kän-tēns´)	166-67	10°0'S	48°00'W
Tocantins, stm., Braz. (tō-kän-tēns´)	166-67	1°45'S	49°12'W
Toccoa, Ga., U.S. (tŏk´ō-ȧ)	124-25	34°35'N	83°20'W
Tocoa, Hond. (tō-kō´ä)	149	15°38'N	86°01'W
Tocopilla, Chile (tō-kō-pēl´yä)	168-69	22°06'S	70°11'W
Tocuyo de la Costa, Ven. (tô-kōō´yō-dĕ-lä-kōs´tä)	163b	11°02'N	68°22'W
Todos Santos, Bol.	168-69	16°48'S	65°08'W
Toemoek Hoemak Gebergte, mts., S.A. *see* Tumuc-Humac Mountains	164-65	2°19'N	54°35'W
Tofino, B.C., Can. (tō-fē´nō)	132-33	49°08'N	125°54'W
Toga, i., Vanuatu	279g	13°25'S	166°41'E
Togian, Kepulauan, is., Indon.	248-49	0°20'S	122°00'E
Togliatti, Russia	186-87	53°32'N	49°26'E
Togo, nation, Afr. (tō´gō)	253	8°0'N	1°10'E
Tok, Ak., U.S.	126	63°20'N	143°00'W
Tokachi, stm., Japan (tō-kä´chē)	244	42°44'N	143°43'E
Tokat, Tur. (tō-kät´)	186-87	40°19'N	36°34'E
Tokelau, dep., Oc. (tō-kē-lä´ō)	280-81	9°0'S	171°45'W
Tokmok, Kyrg.	226	42°50'N	75°18'E
Tokushima, Japan (tō´kō´shē-mä)	245	34°04'N	134°34'E
Tokuyama, Japan (tō´kō´yä-mä)	245	34°03'N	131°48'E

n-sing; ŋ-baŋk; ɴ-nasalized n; nŏd; cŏmmit; ōld; ōbey; ôrder; oi-boil; fōōd; ŏ-as oo in foot; ou-out; s-soft; sh-dish; th-thin; pūre; ûnite; ûrn; stŭd; circŭs; ü-as in French tu; ´-indeterminate vowel.

Feature (Pronunciation)	Page	Lat.	Long.
Tōkyō, nat. cap., Japan (tō´kē-ō)	245	35°42′N	139°47′E
Tôlañaro, Madag.	264-65	25°02′S	47°00′E
Toledo, Spain (tô-lĕ´dō)	198-99	39°53′N	4°03′W
Toledo, Ia., U.S. (tô-lē´dō)	114-15	41°60′N	92°35′W
Toledo, Oh., U.S. (tô-lē´dō)	116-17	41°39′N	83°33′W
Toledo, Or., U.S. (tô-lē´dō)	112-13	44°38′N	123°56′W
Toledo, Montes de, mts., Spain (mô´n-tĕs-dĕ-tô-lĕ´dô)	198-99	39°33′N	4°20′W
Toledo Bend Reservoir, res., U.S. (tô-lē´dō bĕnd rĕ´sĕr-vwär)	122-23	31°30′N	93°45′W
Toliara, Madag.	264-65	23°22′S	43°40′E
Tolima, Nevado del, vol., Col. (nĕ-vä-dô-dĕl-tô-lē´mä)	163c	4°40′N	75°19′W
Tolitoli, Indon.	248-49	1°02′N	120°49′E
Tolmezzo, Italy (tôl-mĕt´zō)	200-01	46°25′N	13°01′E
Tolo, Teluk, b., Indon. (tō´lō)	248-49	2°0′S	122°30′E
Tolosa, Spain (tô-lō´sä)	198-99	43°09′N	2°05′W
Tolsan-do, i., Kor., S.	243	34°38′N	127°45′E
Toluca, Il., U.S. (tô-lōō´kȧ)	116-17	40°60′N	89°08′W
Toluca, Nevado de, vol., Mex. (nĕ-vä-dô-dĕ-tô-lōō´kä)	146-47	19°05′N	99°44′W
Toluca de Lerdo, Mex.	146-47	19°17′N	99°39′W
Tolyatti, Russia *see* Togliatti	186-87	53°32′N	49°26′E
Tom', stm., Russia	218-19	56°53′N	84°27′E
Tomah, Wi., U.S. (tō´mȧ)	114-15	43°59′N	90°30′W
Tomahawk, Wi., U.S. (tŏm´ȧ-hôk)	116-17	45°28′N	89°44′W
Tomakomai, Japan	244	42°38′N	141°36′E
Tomar, Port. (tō-mär´)	198-99	39°36′N	8°25′W
Tomaszów Lubelski, Pol. (tô-mä´shôf lōō-bĕl´skĭ)	194-95	50°27′N	23°25′E
Tomaszów Mazowiecki, Pol. (tô-mä´shôf mä-zô´vyĕt-skĭ)	194-95	51°33′N	20°01′E
Tomatlán, Mex. (tô-mä-tlä´n)	146-47	19°55′N	105°14′W
Tombador, Serra do, plat., Braz. (sĕr´rȧ dô tŏm-bä-dôr´)	166-67	12°0′S	57°40′W
Tombigbee, stm., U.S. (tŏm-bĭg´bē)	110-11	31°04′N	87°58′W
Tombouctou, Mali	258-59	16°47′N	3°01′W
Tombstone, Az., U.S. (tōōm´stōn)	118-19	31°43′N	110°04′W
Tombstone Mountain, mtn., Yk., Can.	130-31	64°25′N	138°30′W
Tombua, Ang. (ȧ-lĕ-zhän´drĕ)	264-65	15°48′S	11°49′E
Tomé, Chile	171	36°36′S	72°57′W
Tomea, Pulau, i., Indon.	248-49	5°45′S	123°56′E
Tomelilla, Swe. (tô´mĕ-lēl-lä)	192-93	55°33′N	13°57′E
Tomelloso, Spain (tō-mål-lyō´sō)	198-99	39°09′N	3°01′W
Tomini, Indon.	248-49	0°32′N	120°32′E
Tomini, Teluk, b., Indon.	248-49	0°20′S	121°00′E
Tommot, Russia (tŏm-mŏt´)	218-19	58°58′N	126°18′E
Tomo, stm., Col.	164-65	5°19′N	67°50′W
Tom Price, Austl.	270-71	22°41′S	117°48′E
Tomsk, Russia (tŏmsk)	218-19	56°30′N	84°58′E
Tonalá, Mex.	146-47	16°05′N	93°45′W
Tondano, Indon. (tôn-dä´nō)	248-49	1°18′N	124°55′E
Tønder, Den. (tûn´nẽr)	194-95	54°56′N	8°52′E
Tone, stm., Japan (tô´nĕ)	245	35°45′N	140°51′E
Tonga, nation, Oc. (tŏŋ´gȧ)	280-81	20°0′S	175°00′W
Tonga Islands, is., Tonga (tŏŋ´gȧ ī´lȧndz)	280-81	20°0′S	175°00′W
Tong'an, China (tôŋ-än)	225a	24°44′N	118°09′E
Tongatapu, i., Tonga	280-81	21°10′S	175°10′W
Tongbei, China (tôŋ-bā)	240-41	47°46′N	126°46′E
Tongcheng, China	238-39	31°03′N	116°57′E
Tongchuan, China	238-39	35°04′N	109°04′E
Tongguan, China (tôŋ-gūän)	238-39	34°36′N	110°17′E
Tonghai, China	238-39	24°07′N	102°47′E
Tonghe, China (tôŋ-hŭ)	244	45°58′N	128°45′E
Tonghua, China (tôŋ-hwä)	243	41°43′N	125°56′E
Tongjiang, China (tôŋ-jyäŋ)	238-39	31°56′N	107°14′E
Tongjiang, China (tôŋ-jyäŋ)	240-41	47°38′N	132°30′E
Tongjosŏn-man, b., Kor., N.	243	39°30′N	128°00′E
Tongliao, China (tôŋ-lĭou)	240-41	43°37′N	122°17′E
Tongoy, Chile (tōn-goi´)	168-69	30°16′S	71°29′W
Tongren, China (tôŋ-rŭn)	238-39	27°43′N	109°11′E
Tongsa Dzong, Bhu.	234-35	27°31′N	90°30′E
Tongxian, China (tôŋ shyĕn)	240-41	39°54′N	116°39′E
Tongyu, China	240-41	44°48′N	123°05′E
Tongzi, China	238-39	28°09′N	106°49′E
Tonk, India (Tŏŋk)	234-35	26°10′N	75°48′E
Tonkawa, Ok., U.S. (tŏŋ kȧ-wô)	120-21	36°41′N	97°19′W
Tonkin, Gulf of, b., Asia (gŭlf ŭv tôn-kăn´)	246-47	20°0′N	108°00′E
Tônlé Sab, Bœng, lk., Camb. *see* Sap, Tonle	246-47	13°0′N	104°00′E
Tonneins, Fr. (tô-năn´)	196-97	44°23′N	0°19′E
Tonopah, Nv., U.S. (tō-nô-pä´)	118-19	38°05′N	117°13′W
Tønsberg, Nor. (tûns´bĕrgh)	192-93	59°16′N	10°26′E

Feature (Pronunciation)	Page	Lat.	Long.
Tonto National Monument, n.p., Az., U.S. (tôn´tô)	118-19	33°34′N	111°02′W
Tooele, Ut., U.S. (tô-ĕl ē)	118-19	40°32′N	112°18′W
Toowoomba, Austl. (tô wōōm´bȧ)	276	27°34′S	151°57′E
Topeka, Ks., U.S.	120-21	39°02′N	95°41′W
Topol'čany, Slvk. (tô-pôl´chä-nü)	194-95	48°34′N	18°10′E
Topolobampo, Mex. (tō-pō-lô-bä´m-pô)	144-45	25°36′N	109°03′W
Topozero, Ozero, lk., Russia	186-87	65°40′N	32°00′E
Toppenish, Wa., U.S. (tôp´ĕn-ĭsh)	112-13	46°23′N	120°19′W
Torawitan, Tanjung, c., Indon.	248-49	1°45′N	124°60′E
Torbat-e Ḥeydarīyeh, Iran	232-33	35°17′N	59°13′E
Torbat-e Jām, Iran	232-33	35°15′N	60°38′E
Torbay, Nf., Can. (tôr-bā´)	138-39	47°40′N	52°45′W
Torbay, Eng., U.K. *see* Torquay	190-91	50°28′N	3°32′W
Torch, stm., Sk., Can.	134-35	53°52′N	103°06′W
Torch Lake, lk., Mi., U.S. (tôrch lāk)	116-17	45°03′N	85°20′W
Torda, Rom. *see* Turda	194-95	46°34′N	23°47′E
Torez, Ukr.	202-03	48°02′N	38°38′E
Torghay, stm., Kaz.	226	48°02′N	62°34′E
Torghay üstirti, plat., Kaz.	226	51°0′N	64°00′E
Torino, Italy *see* Turin	200-01	45°03′N	7°41′E
Tori Sima, i., Japan	244	30°29′N	140°19′E
Torit, Sudan	267	4°24′N	32°34′E
Tormes, stm., Spain (tōr´mās)	198-99	41°18′N	6°27′W
Torneälven, stm., Eur.	184-85	65°49′N	24°09′E
Torneträsk, lk., Swe. (tôr´nĕ trĕsk)	184-85	68°20′N	19°23′E
Torngat, Monts, mts., Can. *see* Torngat Mountains	130-31	59°0′N	64°00′W
Torngat Mountains, mts., Can.	130-31	59°0′N	64°00′W
Tornio, Fin. (tôr´nĭ-ô)	184-85	65°51′N	24°10′E
Tornionjoki, stm., Eur.	184-85	65°49′N	24°09′E
Tornquist, Arg.	173	38°06′S	62°13′W
Toronto, On., Can. (tô-rŏn´tō)	136-37	43°38′N	79°24′W
Toropets, Russia (tô´rô-pyĕts)	192-93	56°30′N	31°40′E
Tororo, Ug.	267	0°42′N	34°11′E
Toros Dağları, mts., Tur. *see* Taurus Mountains	186-87	37°0′N	33°00′E
Torquay, Eng., U.K. (tôr-kē´)	190-91	50°28′N	3°32′W
Torrance, Ca., U.S. (tŏr´rănc)	118-19	33°51′N	118°20′W
Torrelavega, Spain (tôr-rā´lä-vā´gä)	198-99	43°21′N	4°03′W
Torremaggiore, Italy (tôr´rā mäd-jō´rā)	200-01	41°41′N	15°17′E
Torrens, Lake, lk., Austl. (lāk tŏr-ĕns)	276	31°03′S	137°51′E
Torreón, Mex. (tôr-rå-ōn´)	122-23	25°33′N	103°26′W
Torres, Îles, is., Vanuatu	279g	13°17′S	166°39′E
Torres Islands, is., Vanuatu (tôr´rĕs ī´lȧndz) (tŏr´ĕz ī´lȧndz) *see* Torres, Îles	279g	13°17′S	166°39′E
Torres Novas, Port. (tôr´rĕzh nō´väzh)	198-99	39°28′N	8°32′W
Torres Strait, strt., Oc. (tôr´rĕs strāt)	277	10°25′S	142°10′E
Torres Vedras, Port. (tôr´rĕsh vā´dräzh)	198-99	39°05′N	9°15′W
Torrevella, Spain	198-99	37°59′N	0°41′W
Torrevieja, Spain (tôr-rā-vyā´hä) *see* Torrevella	198-99	37°59′N	0°41′W
Torrington, Ct., U.S. (tŏr´ĭng-tŭn)	116-17	41°48′N	73°07′W
Torrington, Wy., U.S. (tŏr´ĭng-tŭn)	114-15	42°05′N	104°12′W
Torsby, Swe. (tôrs´bü)	192-93	60°08′N	13°01′E
Tórshavn, nat. cap., Far. Is. (tôrs-houn´)	190b	62°01′N	6°46′W
Tortola, i., Br. Vir. Is. (tôr-tō´lä)	143b	18°27′N	64°36′W
Tórtolas, Cerro de las, mtn., S.A. *see* Las Tórtolas, Cerro	168-69	29°57′S	69°53′W
Tortona, Italy (tôr-tō´nä)	200-01	44°54′N	8°52′E
Tortosa, Spain (tôr-tō´sä)	198-99	40°48′N	0°31′E
Tortue, Île de la, i., Haiti (ēl-dĕ-lȧ-tôr-tü´) *see* Tortuga Island	142-43	20°03′N	72°47′W
Tortuga Island, i., Haiti *see* Tortue, Île de la	142-43	20°03′N	72°47′W
Toruń, Pol.	194-95	53°01′N	18°37′E
Tõrva, Est. (t'r´vȧ)	192-93	58°01′N	25°56′E
Torzhok, Russia (tôr´zhôk)	202-03	57°03′N	34°58′E
Toscana, hist. reg., Italy (tôs-kä´nä) *see* Tuscany	200-01	43°25′N	11°00′E
Toshkent, nat. cap., Uzb. *see* Tashkent	232-33	41°19′N	69°17′E
Tosno, Russia (tôs´nô)	192-93	59°33′N	30°52′E
Tostado, Arg. (tôs-tá´dô)	173	29°14′S	61°46′W
Totana, Spain (tô-tä-nä)	198-99	37°46′N	1°30′W
Tot'ma, Russia (tôt´mȧ)	186-87	59°58′N	42°45′E
Totoras, Arg. (tô-tô´räs)	173	32°36′S	61°10′W
Totoya, i., Fiji	279f	18°56′S	179°51′W
Tottori, Japan (tô´tô-rē)	245	35°30′N	134°14′E
Toubkal, Jebel, mtn., Mor.	258-59	31°05′N	7°55′W
Toûil, Oued, stm., Alg. (wĕd tōō-ēl´)	269b	35°33′N	2°36′E
Toul, Fr. (tōōl)	196-97	48°41′N	5°53′E

Feature (Pronunciation)	Page	Lat.	Long.
Toulnustouc, stm., Qc., Can.	138-39	49°35′N	68°25′W
Toulon, Fr. (tōō-lôn´)	196-97	43°08′N	5°56′E
Toulouse, Fr. (tōō-lōōz´)	196-97	43°36′N	1°27′E
Toungoo, Mya. (tō-ŏŋ-gōō´)	246-47	18°56′N	96°26′E
Tourane, Viet. *see* Da Nang	246-47	16°03′N	108°12′E
Tourcoing, Fr. (tōr-kwan´)	196-97	50°43′N	3°09′E
Tours, Fr. (tōōr)	196-97	47°24′N	0°43′E
Toussidé, Pic, vol., Chad (pĭk tōō-sē-dā´)	258-59	21°02′N	16°28′E
Towner, N.D., U.S. (tou´nẽr)	114-15	48°21′N	100°24′W
Townsend, Mt., U.S. (toun´zĕnd)	112-13	46°19′N	111°31′W
Townshend Island, i., Austl.	277	22°15′S	150°30′E
Townsville, Austl. (tounz´vĭl)	277	19°16′S	146°48′E
Towson, Md., U.S. (tou´sŭn)	116-17	39°24′N	76°36′W
Towuti, Danau, lk., Indon. (tô-wōō´tē)	248-49	2°45′S	121°32′E
Toxkan, stm., China	226	41°07′N	80°12′E
Toyama, Japan (tō´yä-mä)	245	36°41′N	137°13′E
Toyohashi, Japan (tō´yô-hä´shē)	245	34°46′N	137°23′E
Tozeur, Tun. (tô-zûr´)	188-89	33°55′N	8°08′E
Trabzon, Tur. (trȧb´zôn)	227	40°60′N	39°44′E
Tracy, Mn., U.S. (trā´sē)	114-15	44°14′N	95°37′W
Trafalgar, Cabo, c., Spain (kȧ´bô-trä-fäl-gä´r)	198-99	36°11′N	6°02′W
Trail, B.C., Can. (trāl)	132-33	49°06′N	117°42′W
Trakiya, hist. reg., Eur. *see* Thrace	200-01	41°20′N	26°45′E
Tranås, Swe. (trän´ôs)	192-93	58°03′N	14°59′E
Trancas, Arg.	168-69	26°13′S	65°17′W
Trang, Thai.	246-47	7°33′N	99°36′E
Trangan, Pulau, i., Indon. (pōō-lou trän´gän)	224-25	6°35′S	134°20′E
Trani, Italy (trä´nē)	200-01	41°16′N	16°25′E
Transylvania, hist. reg., Rom. (trăn-sĭl-vā´nĭ-ȧ)	194-95	46°44′N	23°37′E
Transylvanian Alps, mts., Rom. (trăn-sĭl-vā´nĭ-ăn ălps)	200-01	45°25′N	23°33′E
Trapani, Italy	200-01	38°01′N	12°31′E
Traralgon, Austl. (trā´răl-gŏn)	276	38°12′S	146°32′E
Traverse City, Mi., U.S. (trăv´ẽrs sĭ´tē)	116-17	44°45′N	85°37′W
Travnik, Bos. (träv´nēk)	200-01	44°14′N	17°40′E
Trebinje, Bos. (trå´bēn-yĕ)	200-01	42°43′N	18°23′E
Trebišov, Slvk. (trĕ´bē-shôf)	194-95	48°38′N	21°44′E
Trebizond, Tur. *see* Trabzon	227	40°60′N	39°44′E
Treinta y Tres, Ur. (trå-ēn´tä ē trās´)	173	33°14′S	54°23′W
Trelew, Arg. (trē´lū)	171	43°15′S	65°18′W
Trelleborg, Swe.	192-93	55°23′N	13°11′E
Tremblant, Mont, mtn., Qc., Can.	136-37	46°16′N	74°35′W
Trenčín, Slvk.	194-95	48°54′N	18°04′E
Trenque Lauquen, Arg. (trĕn´kĕ-lá´ô-kĕ´n)	173	35°58′S	62°45′W
Trent, Italy *see* Trento	200-01	46°04′N	11°08′E
Trent, stm., On., Can. (trĕnt)	136-37	44°06′N	77°34′W
Trento, Italy (trĕn´tô)	200-01	46°04′N	11°08′E
Trenton, N.S., Can. (trĕn´tŭn)	138-39	45°37′N	62°38′W
Trenton, On., Can. (trĕn´tŭn)	136-37	44°06′N	77°35′W
Trenton, Mo., U.S. (trĕn´tŭn)	120-21	40°05′N	93°37′W
Trenton, N.J., U.S.	116-17	40°13′N	74°45′W
Trenton, Tn., U.S. (trĕn´tŭn)	124-25	35°59′N	88°57′W
Tres Arroyos, Arg. (trās´är-rō´yōs)	173	38°22′S	60°16′W
Três Corações, Braz. (trĕ´s kō-rä-zô´ĕs)	172	21°42′S	45°15′W
Tres Esquinas, Col.	164-65	0°44′N	75°14′W
Três Lagoas, Braz. (trĕ´s lä-gô´ás)	168-69	20°47′S	51°43′W
Tres Marías, Islas, is., Mex.	146-47	21°32′N	106°32′W
Três Marias, Represa de, res., Braz.	172	18°14′S	45°16′W
Tres Picos, Cerro, mtn., Arg.	173	38°09′S	61°57′W
Tres Puntas, Cabo, c., Arg.	171	47°06′S	65°53′W
Três Rios, Braz. (trĕ´s rē´ōs)	172	22°07′S	43°12′W
Treviglio, Italy (trā-vē´lyô)	200-01	45°32′N	9°36′E
Treviso, Italy (trĕ-vē´sō)	200-01	45°40′N	12°14′E
Trichardt, S. Afr. (trĭ-kärt´)	269c	26°30′S	29°14′E
Trichinopoly, India *see* Tiruchchirāppalli	236	10°49′N	78°42′E
Trichūr, India *see* Thrissur	236	10°31′N	76°13′E
Trieste, Italy (trē-ĕs´tä)	200-01	45°40′N	13°46′E
Triglav, mtn., Slvn.	200-01	46°23′N	13°50′E
Trikora, Puncak, mtn., Indon.	277	4°18′S	138°40′E
Trincomalee, Sri L. (trĭŋ-kô-mȧ-lē´)	236	8°34′N	81°14′E
Trinidad, Bol. (trē-nē-dhädh´)	166-67	14°49′S	64°54′W
Trinidad, Col.	164-65	5°25′N	71°40′W
Trinidad, Cuba (trē-nē-dhädh´)	142-43	21°48′N	79°59′W
Trinidad, Co., U.S. (trĭn´ĭdăd)	120-21	37°10′N	104°30′W
Trinidad, Ur.	173	33°32′S	56°54′W
Trinidad, i., Trin. (trĭn´ĭ-dăd)	143b	10°30′N	61°15′W
Trinidad, Isla, i., Arg.	173	39°10′S	61°57′W
Trinidad and Tobago, nation, N.A. (trĭn´ĭ-dăd ănd tô-bā´gō)	140-41	11°0′N	61°00′W
Trinity, Tx., U.S. (trĭn´ĭ-tē)	122-23	30°56′N	95°23′W
Trinity, stm., Ca., U.S. (trĭn´ĭ-tē)	112-13	41°11′N	123°42′W

ăt; finȧl; rāte; senȧte; ärm; ȧsk; sofȧ; fâre; ch-choose; dh-as th in other; bē; ēvent; bĕt; recĕnt; cratẽr; g-gō; gh-guttural g; bĭt; ĭ-short neutral; rīde; κ-guttural k as ch in German ich;

n-sing; ŋ-bank; ɴ-nasalized n; nŏd; cŏmmit; ōld; ŏbey; ôrder; oi-boil; fŏŏd; ò-as oo in foot; ou-out; s-soft; sh-dish; th-thin; pūre; ûnite; ûrn; stŭd; circŭs; ū-as in French tu; ´-indeterminate vowel.

392 Tuul – Uruguaiana PRONOUNCING INDEX

Feature (Pronunciation)	Page	Lat.	Long.
Tuul, stm., Mong.	240-41	48°56'N	104°48'E
Tuvalu, nation, Oc. (to͞o-vä´-lo͞o)	280-81	8°0'S	178°00'E
Tuvuca, i., Fiji	279f	17°40'S	178°48'W
Ţuwayq, Jabal, mts., Sau. Ar.	220-21	23°0'N	46°00'E
Tuxpan, Mex. (to͞os´pän)	146-47	21°56'N	105°17'W
Tuxpan de Rodríguez Cano, Mex.	146-47	20°58'N	97°24'W
Tuxtepec, Mex. (to̤s-tå-pĕk´)	146-47	18°05'N	96°07'W
Tuxtla Gutiérrez, Mex. (to̤s´tlä go͞o-tyår´rĕs)	146-47	16°45'N	93°06'W
Tuyen Quang, Viet.	246-47	21°50'N	105°11'E
Tuy Hoa, Viet.	246-47	13°05'N	109°19'E
Tuymazy, Russia	186-87	54°36'N	53°43'E
Tuz Gölü, lk., Tur.	186-87	38°45'N	33°25'E
Tuzla, Bos. (to̤z´lå)	200-01	44°33'N	18°40'E
Tver', Russia	202-03	56°52'N	35°55'E
Tvertsa, stm., Russia (tvĕr´tså)	202-03	56°52'N	35°56'E
Tweed, stm., U.K. (twēd)	190-91	55°46'N	1°60'W
Tweeling, S. Afr. (twē´lĭng)	269c	27°39'S	28°30'E
Twin Falls, Id., U.S. (twĭn fôlz)	112-13	42°34'N	114°28'W
Two Rivers, Wi., U.S. (to͞o rĭv´ẽrz)	116-17	44°09'N	87°34'W
Tyan' Shan', mts., Asia *see* Tien Shan	226	42°0'N	80°00'E
Tyler, Mn., U.S. (tī´lẽr)	114-15	44°17'N	96°08'W
Tyler, Tx., U.S. (tī´lẽr)	120-21	32°21'N	95°19'W
Tylertown, Ms., U.S. (tī´lẽr-toun)	124-25	31°07'N	90°09'W
Tym, stm., Russia	218-19	59°26'N	80°01'E
Tymovskoye, Russia	218-19	50°51'N	142°38'E
Tynda, Russia	218-19	55°09'N	124°43'E
Tyndall, S.D., U.S. (tĭn´dål)	114-15	42°60'N	97°52'W
Tyrma, Russia	240-41	50°03'N	132°10'E
Tyrrhenian Sea, s., Eur. (tĭr-rē´nĭ-*ă*n sē)	200-01	40°0'N	12°00'E
Tyrrhénienne, Mer, s., Eur. *see* Tyrrhenian Sea	200-01	40°0'N	12°00'E
Tyul'gan, Russia	186-87	52°24'N	56°14'E
Tyumen', Russia (tyo͞o-mĕn´)	218-19	57°10'N	65°33'E
Tyung, stm., Russia	218-19	63°46'N	121°32'E
Tyva, state, Russia	222-23	52°0'N	95°00'E
Tzaneen, S. Afr.	269c	23°49'S	30°10'E
Tzeliutsing, China *see* Zigong	238-39	29°22'N	104°45'E
Tzucacab, Mex. (tzo͞o-kä-kä´b)	148	20°04'N	89°02'W
Tzupo, China *see* Boshan	240-41	36°29'N	117°51'E

U

Feature (Pronunciation)	Page	Lat.	Long.
Uatumã, stm., Braz.	166-67	2°24'S	57°33'W
Uaupés, stm., S.A.	164-65	0°02'N	67°15'W
Ubá, Braz.	172	21°07'S	42°56'W
Ubangi, stm., Afr. (o͞o-bäŋ´gē)	262-63	0°25'S	17°47'E
Ubatuba, Braz. (o͞o-bå-to͞o´bå)	172	23°26'S	45°04'W
Ube, Japan	245	33°57'N	131°15'E
Úbeda, Spain (o͞o´bå-dä)	198-99	38°01'N	3°22'W
Uberaba, Braz. (o͞o-bå-rä´b*ȧ*)	172	19°46'S	47°56'W
Uberlândia, Braz. (o͞o-bĕr-lá´n-dyä)	172	18°54'S	48°15'W
Ubon Ratchathani, Thai. (o͞o´bŭn rä´chätä-nē)	246-47	15°14'N	104°52'E
Ubrique, Spain (o͞o-brē´kå)	198-99	36°41'N	5°27'W
Ubsu-Nur, Ozero, lk., Asia *see* Uvs Lake	222-23	50°20'N	92°45'E
Ubundu, D.R.C.	262-63	0°21'S	25°25'E
Ucayali, stm., Peru (o͞o´kä-yä´lē)	170	4°30'S	73°30'W
Uchaly, Russia (û-chä´lĭ)	226	54°18'N	59°27'E
Uchiura-wan, b., Japan (o͞o´chē-o͞o´rä wän)	244	42°20'N	140°40'E
Uchiza, Peru	170	8°25'S	76°25'W
Uchur, stm., Russia (o̤-cho̤r´)	218-19	58°47'N	130°36'E
Uda, stm., Russia (o̤´då)	222-23	51°49'N	107°34'E
Uda, stm., Russia (o̤´då)	218-19	54°43'N	135°18'E
Uda, stm., Russia (o̤´då)	218-19	56°02'N	99°38'E
Udachnyy, Russia	218-19	66°29'N	112°15'E
Udagamandalam, India	236	11°25'N	76°42'E
Udai, stm., Ukr. (o̤´då)	202-03	50°04'N	33°07'E
Udaipur, India (o̤-dŭ´ē-po͞or)	234-35	24°35'N	73°42'E
Uddevalla, Swe. (o͞od´dĕ-väl-å)	192-93	58°21'N	11°55'E
Udine, Italy (o͞o´dē-nå)	200-01	46°04'N	13°15'E
Udmurtia, state, Russia	186-87	57°0'N	53°00'E
Udmurtiya, state, Russia *see* Udmurtia	186-87	57°0'N	53°00'E
Udon Thani, Thai.	246-47	17°24'N	102°47'E
Ueda, Japan (wä´dä)	245	36°24'N	138°15'E
Uele, stm., D.R.C. (wä´lå)	262-63	4°07'N	22°26'E
Uelen, Russia	126	66°09'N	169°48'W
Uelzen, Ger. (ült´sĕn)	194-95	52°58'N	10°34'E
Uere, stm., D.R.C.	262-63	3°33'N	25°15'E
Ufa, Russia (o̤´fa)	186-87	54°42'N	55°58'E
Ufa, stm., Russia (o̤´fa)	186-87	54°41'N	56°02'E
Ugab, stm., Nmb. (o͞o´gäb)	264-65	21°11'S	13°38'E
Ugalla, stm., Tan. (o͞o-gä´lä)	267	5°17'S	30°58'E
Uganda, nation, Afr. (o͞o-gän´dä) (û-găn´d*ȧ*)	253	1°0'N	32°00'E
Uglegorsk, Russia (o͞o-glĕ-gôrsk)	218-19	49°04'N	142°03'E
Uglich, Russia (o͞og-lĕch´)	202-03	57°32'N	38°20'E
Ugoma, mtn., D.R.C.	267	4°0'S	28°45'E
Uhrichsville, Oh., U.S. (ū´rĭks-vĭl)	116-17	40°24'N	81°21'W
Uíge, Ang.	262-63	7°38'S	15°04'E
Uina, stm., Camrn. *see* Vina	260-61	7°52'N	15°46'E
Uitenhage, S. Afr.	264-65	33°40'S	25°27'E
Uji, Japan (o͞o´jē)	245	34°54'N	135°49'E
Ujiji, Tan. (o͞o-jē´jē)	267	4°55'S	29°41'E
Uji-yamada, Japan *see* Ise	245	34°30'N	136°42'E
Ujjain, India (o͞o-jŭēn)	234-35	23°11'N	75°47'E
Ujungpandang, Indon. *see* Makassar	248-49	5°08'S	119°25'E
Újvidék, Serb. *see* Novi Sad	200-01	45°15'N	19°50'E
Ukara Island, i., Tan.	267	1°50'S	33°03'E
Ukerewe Island, i., Tan.	267	2°03'S	33°00'E
Ukhta, Russia (o͞ok´tå)	186-87	63°34'N	53°44'E
Ukiah, Ca., U.S.	118-19	39°09'N	123°12'W
Ukiah, Or., U.S. (ū-kī´å)	112-13	45°09'N	118°56'W
Ukkusiksalik National Park, n.p., Nu., Can.	128-29	66°0'N	90°00'W
Ukmergė, Lith. (o̤k´mĕr-ghå)	192-93	55°15'N	24°46'E
Ukraïna, nation, Eur. *see* Ukraine	174-75	49°0'N	32°00'E
Ukraine, nation, Eur. (yo͞o-krān´)	174-75	49°0'N	32°00'E
Ukyr, Russia	240-41	49°28'N	108°52'E
Ulaanbaatar, nat. cap., Mong. (o͞o´län-bä´tôr)	240-41	47°55'N	106°56'E
Ulaangom, Mong.	240-41	49°59'N	92°04'E
Ulaan-Uul, Mong.	240-41	44°23'N	111°12'E
Ulan Bator, nat. cap., Mong. *see* Ulaanbaatar	240-41	47°55'N	106°56'E
Ulanhad, China *see* Chifeng	240-41	42°16'N	118°58'E
Ulanhot, China	240-41	46°04'N	122°04'E
Ulan-Ude, Russia (o͞o´län o͞o´då)	222-23	51°50'N	107°36'E
Ulawa Island, i., Sol. Is.	279e	9°47'S	161°57'E
Ulchin, Kor., S. (o͞ol´chĕn´)	243	36°59'N	129°23'E
Uldz, stm., Asia	240-41	49°55'N	115°33'E
Uldza, stm., Asia *see* Uldz	240-41	49°55'N	115°33'E
Uleåborg, Fin. *see* Oulu	184-85	65°01'N	25°28'E
Ulhāsnagar, India	236	19°14'N	73°08'E
Uliast, Mong.	240-41	48°57'N	91°09'E
Uliastay, Mong.	240-41	47°44'N	96°51'E
Ulindi, stm., D.R.C. (o͞o-lĭn´dē)	262-63	1°40'S	25°52'E
Ulithi, at., Micron.	280-81	9°55'N	139°42'E
Ülkenözen, stm., Eur.	186-87	48°60'N	49°59'E
Ulm, Ger. (o̤lm)	194-95	48°24'N	9°59'E
Ulónguè, Moz.	264-65	14°37'S	34°19'E
Ulricehamn, Swe. (o̤l-rē´sĕ-häm)	192-93	57°48'N	13°25'E
Ulsan, Kor., S. (o͞ol´sän´)	243	35°33'N	129°19'E
Ulúa, stm., Hond. (o͞o-lo͞o´å)	149	15°52'N	87°44'W
Ulul, i., Micron.	280-81	8°36'N	149°40'E
Ulungur, stm., China (o͞o-lo͞on-gûr)	222-23	46°59'N	87°26'E
Ulungur Hu, lk., China	222-23	47°13'N	87°16'E
Uluru, mtn., Austl.	272-73	25°20'S	130°60'E
Ulverstone, Austl. (ŭl´vẽr-st*ŭ*n)	276	41°10'S	146°11'E
Ulyanovsk, Russia (o͞o-lyä´nôfsk)	186-87	54°19'N	48°22'E
Ulysses, Ks., U.S. (ū-lĭs´ēz)	120-21	37°35'N	101°21'W
Umán, Mex. (o͞o-män´)	148	20°53'N	89°45'W
Uman', Ukr. (o̤-mån´)	202-03	48°44'N	30°14'E
'Umān, nation, Asia *see* Oman	206-07	22°0'N	58°00'E
'Umān, Khalīj, b., Asia *see* Oman, Gulf of	230-31	24°30'N	58°30'E
Umarkot, Pak.	232-33	25°22'N	69°45'E
Umatilla Indian Reservation, ind. res., Or., U.S. (ū-må-tĭl´å ĭn´dĭ-*ă*n rĕ-sẽr-vā´shĕn)	112-13	45°41'N	118°31'W
Umba, Russia	186-87	66°41'N	34°18'E
Umboi Island, i., Pap. N. Gui.	277	5°36'S	147°53'E
Umeå, Swe.	184-85	63°50'N	20°16'E
Umeälven, stm., Swe.	184-85	63°47'N	20°19'E
Umm Durmān, Sudan *see* Omdurman	266	15°39'N	32°29'E
Umm Lajj, Sau. Ar.	266	25°07'N	37°16'E
Umm Ruwābah, Sudan	266	12°54'N	31°12'E
Umm Urūmah, i., Sau. Ar.	266	25°46'N	36°33'E
Umnak Island, i., Ak., U.S. (o͞om´nȧ ī´l*ă*nd)	126a	53°25'N	168°10'W
Umpqua, stm., Or., U.S. (ŭmp´kwå)	112-13	43°42'N	124°05'W
'Umrān, Yemen	266	15°58'N	43°58'E
Umtata, S. Afr. (o̤m-tä´tä)	264-65	31°35'S	28°47'E
Umuarama, Braz.	168-69	23°46'S	53°19'W
Unalakleet, Ak., U.S. (ū-nȧ-lăk´lēt)	126	63°53'N	160°47'W
Unalaska, Ak., U.S. (ū-nȧ-lås´kȧ)	126a	53°52'N	166°32'W
Unalaska Island, i., Ak., U.S.	126a	53°45'N	166°45'W
Unauna, Pulau, i., Indon.	248-49	0°10'S	121°35'E
'Unayzah, Sau. Ar.	266	26°05'N	43°59'E
Uncia, Bol. (o͞on´sē-ä)	168-69	18°26'S	66°35'W
Uncompahgre Peak, mtn., Co., U.S. (ŭn-kŭm-pä´grē pēk)	118-19	38°04'N	107°28'W
Unecha, Russia (o̤-nĕ´chȧ)	202-03	52°51'N	32°42'E
Ungava, Baie d', b., Can. *see* Ungava Bay	130-31	59°30'N	67°30'W
Ungava, Péninsule d', pen., Qc., Can.	130-31	60°0'N	74°00'W
Ungava Bay, b., Can. (ŭŋ-gä´vȧ bā)	130-31	59°30'N	67°30'W
Ungava Peninsula, pen., Qc., Can. (ŭŋ-gā´vȧ pĕ-nĭn´sūl*ȧ*) *see* Ungava, Péninsule d'	130-31	60°0'N	74°00'W
Ungvár, Ukr. *see* Uzhhorod	194-95	48°37'N	22°19'E
União, Braz.	166-67	4°35'S	42°52'W
União dos Palmares, Braz.	163d	9°10'S	36°02'W
Unimak Island, i., Ak., U.S. (o͞o-nē-mȧk´ ī´l*ă*nd)	126	54°43'N	164°27'W
Unini, stm., Braz.	166-67	1°41'S	61°31'W
Union, Mo., U.S. (ūn´yŭn)	120-21	38°27'N	91°01'W
Union, S.C., U.S. (ūn´yŭn)	124-25	34°43'N	81°37'W
Union City, In., U.S. (ūn´yŭn sĭ´tē)	116-17	40°11'N	85°00'W
Union City, Mi., U.S. (ūn´yŭn sĭ´tē)	116-17	42°04'N	85°09'W
Union City, Pa., U.S. (ūn´yŭn sĭ´tē)	116-17	41°54'N	79°50'W
Union City, Tn., U.S. (ūn´yŭn sĭ´tē)	124-25	36°25'N	89°03'W
Union Springs, Al., U.S. (ūn´yŭn sprĭngz)	124-25	32°09'N	85°43'W
Uniontown, Al., U.S. (ūn´y*ŭ*n-toun)	124-25	32°27'N	87°31'W
Uniontown, Pa., U.S.	116-17	39°54'N	79°44'W
Unionville, Mo., U.S. (ūn´y*ŭ*n-vĭl)	120-21	40°29'N	93°01'W
United Arab Emirates, nation, Asia (ū-nī´tĕd âr´*ă*b ĕ´mĕr-*ĕ*ts)	206-07	24°0'N	54°00'E
United Arab Republic, nation, Afr. *see* Egypt	253	27°0'N	30°00'E
United Kingdom, nation, Eur. (ū-nī´tĕd kĭng´d*ŭ*m)	174-75	54°0'N	2°00'W
United States, nation, N.A. (ū-nī´tĕd stāts)	85	38°0'N	97°00'W
Unity, Sk., Can.	134-35	52°27'N	109°07'W
Upa, stm., Russia (o̤´på)	202-03	54°02'N	36°21'E
Upata, Ven. (o͞o-pä´tä)	164-65	8°01'N	62°24'W
Upemba, Lac, lk., D.R.C.	262-63	8°36'S	26°26'E
Upington, S. Afr. (ŭp´ĭng-t*ŭ*n)	264-65	28°27'S	21°14'E
Upland, In., U.S. (ŭp´l*ă*nd)	116-17	40°28'N	85°29'W
Upolu, i., Samoa	279b	13°55'S	171°45'W
Upolu Point, c., Hi., U.S. (o͞o-pô´lo͞o point)	127a	20°16'N	155°51'W
Upper Arrow Lake, lk., B.C., Can. (ŭp´ẽr ăr´ō lāk)	132-33	50°31'N	117°56'W
Upper Kapuas Mountains, mts., Asia	248-49	1°15'N	113°30'E
Upper Klamath Lake, lk., Or., U.S. (ŭp´ẽr klăm´*ă*th lāk)	112-13	42°24'N	121°54'W
Upper Red Lake, lk., Mn., U.S. (ŭp´ẽr rĕd lāk)	114-15	48°10'N	94°40'W
Upper Sandusky, Oh., U.S. (ŭp´ẽr săn-dŭs´kē)	116-17	40°49'N	83°17'W
Upper Volta, nation, Afr. *see* Burkina Faso	253	13°0'N	1°30'W
Uppsala, Swe. (o͞op´så-lä)	192-93	59°52'N	17°38'E
Upsala, Swe. *see* Uppsala	192-93	59°52'N	17°38'E
Ural, stm., (o̤-räl´') (ū-rôl)	176-77	46°50'N	51°33'E
Ural Mountains, mts., Russia (o̤-räl´' moun´tĭnz) (ū-rôl moun´tĭnz)	218-19	60°0'N	60°00'E
Ural'skiye Gory, mts., Russia *see* Ural Mountains	218-19	60°0'N	60°00'E
Ura-Tyube, Taj. *see* Istaravshan	232-33	39°54'N	69°00'E
Urbana, Il., U.S. (ûr-băn´å)	116-17	40°07'N	88°13'W
Urbana, Oh., U.S. (ûr-băn´å)	116-17	40°07'N	83°45'W
Urbino, Italy (o͞or-bē´nô)	200-01	43°44'N	12°39'E
Urdinarrain, Arg. (o͞or-dē-när-rȧē´n)	173	32°41'S	58°54'W
Urfa, Tur. *see* Şanlıurfa	228-29	37°10'N	38°48'E
Urganch, Uzb.	232-33	41°33'N	60°38'E
Urgench, Uzb. *see* Urganch	232-33	41°33'N	60°38'E
Urla, Tur. (o̤r´lå)	200-01	38°20'N	26°46'E
Urmi, stm., Russia (o̤r´mē)	240-41	48°36'N	135°01'E
Urmia, Iran *see* Orūmīyeh	228-29	37°32'N	45°05'E
Urmia, Lake, lk., Iran (lāk o̤r´mē*ȧ*) *see* Orūmīyeh, Daryācheh-ye	227	37°40'N	45°30'E
Urrao, Col. (o͞or-rȧ´ô)	163c	6°20'N	76°08'W
Uruapan del Progreso, Mex.	146-47	19°25'N	102°04'W
Urubamba, stm., Peru (o͞o-ro͞o-bäm´bä)	170	10°44'S	73°44'W
Uruguai, stm., S.A.	173	34°10'S	58°18'W
Uruguaiana, Braz.	173	29°46'S	57°04'W

ăt; fin*ă*l; rāte; senåte; ärm; åsk; sof*ȧ*; fâre; ch-choose; dh-as th in other; bē; ēvent; bĕt; recĕnt; cratẽr; g-gō; gh-guttural g; bĭt; ĭ-short neutral; rīde; κ-guttural k as ch in German ich;

PRONOUNCING INDEX

Uruguay – Venadillo 393

Feature (Pronunciation)	Page	Lat.	Long.
Uruguay, nation, S.A. (o͞o-ro͞o-gwī´) (ū´ro͞o-gwā)	158	33°0'S	56°00'W
Uruguay, stm., S.A. (o͞o-ro͞o-gwī´)	173	34°10'S	58°18'W
Urumchi, China *see* Ürümqi	222-23	43°48'N	87°35'E
Ürümqi, China (ů-rům-chyē)	222-23	43°48'N	87°35'E
Urundi, nation, Afr. *see* Burundi	253	3°15'S	30°00'E
Urup, Ostrov, i., Russia (ôs-trôf´ ǒ´rǒp´)	218-19	46°0'N	150°00'E
Uryupinsk, Russia (ǒr´yǒ-pēn-sk´)	186-87	50°48'N	42°01'E
Urzhum, Russia	186-87	57°07'N	50°01'E
Urziceni, Rom. (ǒ-zē-chěn´')	202-03	44°43'N	26°40'E
Usa, stm., Russia (ǒ´sȧ)	186-87	65°58'N	56°57'E
Uşak, Tur. (o͞o´shȧk)	200-01	38°41'N	29°24'E
Usborne, Mount, mtn., Falk. Is.	171	51°41'S	58°50'W
Üshtöbe, Kaz.	226	45°14'N	77°58'E
Ushuaia, Arg. (o͞o-sho͞o-ī´ä)	171	54°47'S	68°19'W
Usinsk, Russia	186-87	65°57'N	57°24'E
Üsküb, nat. cap., Mac. *see* Skopje	200-01	42°00'N	21°28'E
Usman', Russia (o͞os-mán´)	202-03	52°03'N	39°45'E
Uspanapa, stm., Mex. (o͞os-pä-nä´pä)	146-47	17°56'N	94°28'W
Ussel, Fr. (üs´ěl)	196-97	45°33'N	2°18'E
Ussuri, stm., Asia (o͞o-so͞o´rē)	240-41	48°27'N	135°04'E
Ussuriysk, Russia	244	43°48'N	131°59'E
Ust'-Barguzin, Russia	218-19	53°25'N	109°02'E
Ust-Bolsheretsk, Russia	218-19	52°49'N	156°17'E
Ust'-Ilimsk, Russia	218-19	58°00'N	102°40'E
Ústí nad Labem, Czech Rep.	194-95	50°40'N	14°02'E
Ustinov, Russia *see* Izhevsk	186-87	56°50'N	53°12'E
Üstirt, plat., Asia *see* Ust-Urt Plateau	226	43°0'N	56°00'E
Ust-Kamchatsk, Russia	218-19	56°13'N	162°29'E
Ust'-Kut, Russia	218-19	56°47'N	105°43'E
Ust'-Kuyga, Russia	218-19	69°60'N	135°35'E
Ust-Maya, Russia (ǒst má´yá)	218-19	60°25'N	134°30'E
Ust'-Nera, Russia	218-19	64°34'N	143°18'E
Ust'-Omchug, Russia	218-19	61°08'N	149°37'E
Ust-Tsilma, Russia (ǒst tsĭl´má)	186-87	65°25'N	52°05'E
Ust-Urt Plateau, plat., Asia (o͞ost-o͞ort plä-tō´)	226	43°0'N	56°00'E
Ustyurt Platosi, plat., Asia *see* Ust-Urt Plateau	226	43°0'N	56°00'E
Ustyuzhna, Russia (yo͞ozh´ná)	202-03	58°51'N	36°28'E
Usu, China (ů-so͞o)	226	44°26'N	84°41'E
Usulután, El Sal. (o͞o-so͞o-lä-tän´)	148	13°20'N	88°26'W
Usumacinta, stm., N.A. (o͞o´so͞o-mä-sēn´tō)	148	18°23'N	92°39'W
Usumbura, nat. cap., Bdi. *see* Bujumbura	267	3°23'S	29°22'E
Utah, state, U.S. (ū´taw)	108-09	39°30'N	111°30'W
Utah Lake, lk., Ut., U.S. (ū´taw lāk)	118-19	40°13'N	111°49'W
Utembo, stm., Ang.	264-65	17°04'S	21°58'E
Utena, Lith. (o͞o´tā-nä)	192-93	55°30'N	25°37'E
Uthai Thani, Thai.	246-47	15°23'N	100°02'E
Utiariti, Braz.	166-67	13°02'S	58°17'W
Utica, N.Y., U.S.	116-17	43°06'N	75°15'W
Utiel, Spain (o͞o-tyâl´)	198-99	39°34'N	1°13'W
Utila, Isla de, i., Hond. (ē´s-lä-dě-o͞o-tē´lä)	149	16°06'N	86°56'W
Uto, Japan (o͞o´tō´)	245	32°41'N	130°40'E
Utrecht, Neth. (ū´trěkt) (ü´trěkt)	190-91	52°05'N	5°08'E
Utrecht, S. Afr.	269c	27°40'S	30°19'E
Utrera, Spain (o͞o-trā´rä)	198-99	37°11'N	5°47'W
Utsunomiya, Japan (o͞ot´sǒ-nō-mē-yá´)	245	36°33'N	139°54'E
Uttaradit, Thai.	246-47	17°38'N	100°06'E
Uttarakhand, state, India	234-35	30°0'N	79°30'E
Uttaranchal, state, India *see* Uttarakhand	234-35	30°0'N	79°30'E
Uttar Pradesh, state, India (ǒt-tär-prä-děsh)	234-35	27°0'N	80°00'E
Uummannarsuaq, c., Green. *see* Farewell, Cape	86	59°46'N	43°60'W
Uvá, stm., Col.	164-65	3°56'N	68°34'W
Uvalde, Tx., U.S. (ū-văl´dē)	122-23	29°13'N	99°47'W
Uvira, D.R.C. (o͞o-vē´rä)	267	3°23'S	29°09'E
Uvs Lake, lk., Asia	222-23	50°20'N	92°45'E
Uvs nuur, lk., Asia *see* Uvs Lake	222-23	50°20'N	92°45'E
Uwajima, Japan (o͞o-wä´jē-mä)	245	33°13'N	132°34'E
Uwayl, Sudan	262-63	8°46'N	27°24'E
'Uwaynāt, Jabal al-, mtn., Afr.	258-59	21°53'N	25°02'E
Uxmal, hist., Mex. (o͞o´x-mä´l)	148	20°22'N	89°46'W
Uyuni, Bol. (o͞o-yo͞o´nē)	168-69	20°28'S	66°50'W
Uyuni, Salar de, pl., Bol. (sä-lär-dě o͞o-yo͞o´nē)	168-69	20°17'S	68°07'W
Uzbekistan, nation, Asia (o͞oz-běk´-ē--stän´)	232-33	41°0'N	64°00'E
Ŭzbekiston, nation, Asia *see* Uzbekistan	232-33	41°0'N	64°00'E
Uzh, stm., Ukr. (ǒzh)	202-03	51°15'N	30°15'E
Uzhhorod, Ukr.	194-95	48°37'N	22°19'E
Užice, Serb. (o͞o´zhē-tsě)	200-01	43°52'N	19°51'E
Uzlovaya, Russia	202-03	53°59'N	38°11'E

V

Feature (Pronunciation)	Page	Lat.	Long.
Vaal, stm., S. Afr. (väl)	264-65	29°04'S	23°38'E
Vaasa, Fin. (vä´sȧ)	184-85	63°06'N	21°37'E
Vache, Île à, i., Haiti	142-43	18°04'N	73°38'W
Vadodara, India	234-35	22°18'N	73°11'E
Vaduz, nat. cap., Liech. (vä´dǒts)	194-95	47°09'N	9°32'E
Vaga, stm., Russia (va´gȧ)	186-87	62°49'N	42°53'E
Vágar, i., Far. Is.	190b	62°05'N	7°17'W
Vaghena Island, i., Sol. Is.	279e	7°26'S	157°46'E
Váh, stm., Slvk. (väĸ)	194-95	47°45'N	18°09'E
Vaitupu, i., Tuvalu	280-81	7°28'S	178°41'E
Vakh, stm., Russia (váĸ)	218-19	60°49'N	76°48'E
Vākhān, hist. reg., Afg.	232-33	37°0'N	73°00'E
Vakhsh, stm., Taj.	232-33	37°07'N	68°19'E
Valcheta, Arg.	171	40°42'S	66°09'W
Valdai Hills, hills, Russia (vál-dī´ hĭlz) *see* Valdayskaya Vozvyshennost'	202-03	57°0'N	33°30'E
Valday, Russia (vál-dī´)	202-03	57°59'N	33°15'E
Valdayskaya Vozvyshennost', hills, Russia *see* Valdai Hills	202-03	57°0'N	33°30'E
Valdepeñas, Spain (väl-dā-pān´yäs)	198-99	38°46'N	3°23'W
Valdés, Península, pen., Arg. (pě-nē´n-so͞o-lä väl-dě´s)	171	42°30'S	64°00'W
Valdez, Ak., U.S. (văl´děz)	126	61°08'N	146°20'W
Valdivia, Chile (väl-dē´vä)	171	39°49'S	73°13'W
Val-d'Or, Qc., Can.	136-37	48°06'N	77°46'W
Valdosta, Ga., U.S. (văl-dŏs´tȧ)	124-25	30°50'N	83°16'W
Vale, Or., U.S. (vāl)	112-13	43°59'N	117°15'W
Valença, Braz. (vä-lěn´sȧ)	166-67	13°22'S	39°05'W
Valença, Braz. (vä-lěn´sȧ)	172	22°15'S	43°42'W
Valence, Fr.	196-97	44°56'N	4°54'E
València, Spain	198-99	39°28'N	0°22'W
Valencia, Spain *see* València	198-99	39°28'N	0°22'W
Valencia, Ven. (vä-lěn´syä)	163b	10°11'N	68°00'W
Valenciennes, Fr. (vá-län-syěn´)	196-97	50°21'N	3°31'E
Valentine, Ne., U.S. (vá län-tē-nyě´)	114-15	42°53'N	100°33'W
Valera, Ven. (vä-lě´rä)	164-65	9°19'N	70°37'W
Valga, Est. (väl´gȧ)	192-93	57°47'N	26°03'E
Valjevo, Serb. (väl´yȧ-vǒ)	200-01	44°16'N	19°54'E
Valladolid, Mex. (väl-yä-dhō-lēdh´)	148	20°41'N	88°12'W
Valladolid, Spain (väl-yä-dhō-lēdh´)	198-99	41°39'N	4°43'W
Valle de Guanape, Ven. (vä´l-yě-dě-gwä-nä´pě)	163b	9°54'N	65°41'W
Valle de la Pascua, Ven. (väl´yā dā lä-pä´s-ko͞oä)	163b	9°13'N	66°00'W
Valle de Santiago, Mex. (väl´yā dā sän-tē-ä´gō)	146-47	20°24'N	101°12'W
Valledupar, Col. (väl´yā-do͞o-pär´)	164-65	10°28'N	73°15'W
Vallegrande, Bol. (väl´yā grän´dā)	168-69	18°29'S	64°06'W
Vallenar, Chile (väl-yå-när´)	168-69	28°34'S	70°46'W
Valletta, nat. cap., Malta (väl-lět´ä)	200b	35°54'N	14°31'E
Valley City, N.D., U.S. (văl´ē sĭ´tĭ)	114-15	46°56'N	98°00'W
Valleyview, Ab., Can.	132-33	55°05'N	117°17'W
Vallimanca, Arroyo, stm., Arg. (är-rō´yō väl-yē-mä´n-kä)	173	35°44'S	60°08'W
Valls, Spain (väls)	198-99	41°17'N	1°15'E
Valmiera, Lat. (vál´myě-rá)	192-93	57°32'N	25°26'E
Valognes, Fr. (vá-lôn´y')	196-97	49°31'N	1°28'W
Valona, Alb. *see* Vlorë	200-01	40°29'N	19°30'E
Vālpārai, India	236	10°19'N	76°54'E
Valparaíso, Chile (väl´pä-rä-ē´sō)	163e	33°03'S	71°37'W
Valparaíso, Mex.	146-47	22°46'N	103°35'W
Valparaiso, Fl., U.S. (văl-pȧ-rā´zō)	124-25	30°31'N	86°30'W
Valparaiso, In., U.S. (văl-pȧ-rā´zō)	116-17	41°28'N	87°03'W
Valréas, Fr. (vál-rà-ä´)	196-97	44°23'N	4°59'E
Vals, Tanjung, c., Indon.	277	8°24'S	137°38'E
Valuyki, Russia (vá-lǒ-ē´kē)	202-03	50°12'N	38°08'E
Valverde del Camino, Spain (väl-věr-dě-děl-kä-mē´nō)	198-99	37°34'N	6°45'W
Van, Tur. (ván)	227	38°30'N	43°24'E
Van, Lake, lk., Tur. *see* Van Gölü	227	38°33'N	42°46'E
Vanadzor, Arm.	227	40°48'N	44°29'E
Vanavara, Russia	218-19	60°21'N	102°16'E
Van Buren, Ar., U.S. (văn bū´rĕn)	120-21	35°27'N	94°22'W
Van Buren, Me., U.S. (văn bū´rĕn)	117a	47°10'N	67°57'W
Vanceburg, Ky., U.S. (văns´bûrg)	116-17	38°36'N	83°19'W
Vancouver, B.C., Can. (văn-ko͞o´vẽr)	132-33	49°17'N	123°07'W
Vancouver, Wa., U.S. (văn-ko͞o´vẽr)	112-13	45°38'N	122°39'W
Vancouver Island, i., B.C., Can. (văn-ko͞o´vẽr ī´lănd)	130-31	49°45'N	126°00'W
Vancouver Island Ranges, mts., B.C., Can. (văn-ko͞o´vẽr ī´lănd rānjěz)	132-33	49°25'N	125°25'W
Vandalia, Il., U.S. (văn-dā´lĭ-ȧ)	116-17	38°58'N	89°06'W
Vandalia, Mo., U.S. (văn-dā´lĭ-ȧ)	120-21	39°19'N	91°30'W
Vandalia, Oh., U.S. (văn-dā´lĭ-ȧ)	116-17	39°54'N	84°12'W
Vanderbijlpark, S. Afr.	269c	26°42'S	27°50'E
Vanderhoof, B.C., Can.	132-33	54°01'N	124°06'W
Vanderlin Island, i., Austl.	272-73	15°44'S	137°02'E
Van Diemen Gulf, b., Austl. (văn dē´měn gŭlf)	272-73	11°50'S	132°00'E
Vanegas, Mex. (vä-ně´gäs)	146-47	23°53'N	100°56'W
Vänern, lk., Swe.	192-93	58°55'N	13°30'E
Vänersborg, Swe. (vě´něrs-bôr´)	192-93	58°23'N	12°19'E
Vangaindrano, Madag.	264-65	23°21'S	47°36'E
Van Gölü, lk., Tur.	227	38°33'N	42°46'E
Vanikolo, i., Sol. Is.	272-73	11°37'S	166°52'E
Vanimo, Pap. N. Gui.	277	2°44'S	141°20'E
Vankarem, Russia	126	67°50'N	175°50'W
Van Lear, Ky., U.S. (văn lēr´)	116-17	37°47'N	82°48'W
Vannes, Fr. (ván)	196-97	47°39'N	2°46'W
Van Rees, Pegunungan, mts., Indon.	277	2°35'S	138°15'E
Vanua Balavu, i., Fiji	279f	17°14'S	178°57'W
Vanua Lava, i., Vanuatu	279g	13°45'S	167°28'E
Vanua Levu, i., Fiji	279f	16°33'S	179°15'E
Vanuatu, nation, Oc. (vä-no͞o-ä´-to͞o)	279g	16°0'S	167°00'E
Van Wert, Oh., U.S. (văn wûrt´)	116-17	40°52'N	84°35'W
Vārānasi, India	234-35	25°20'N	82°59'E
Varaždin, Cro. (vä´räzh´děn)	200-01	46°18'N	16°20'E
Varberg, Swe. (vär´běrg)	192-93	57°06'N	12°16'E
Vardar, stm., Eur. (vär´där) *see* Axiós	200-01	40°31'N	22°43'E
Vardø, Nor.	184-85	70°21'N	31°01'E
Varėna, Lith. (vä-rā´nȧ)	194-95	54°13'N	24°35'E
Vareš, Bos. (vä´rěsh)	200-01	44°09'N	18°19'E
Varese, Italy (vä-rā´så)	200-01	45°49'N	8°50'E
Varginha, Braz. (vär-zhē´n-yä)	172	21°34'S	45°26'W
Varkaus, Fin. (vär´kous)	184-85	62°19'N	27°54'E
Varna, Blg. (vär´ná)	200-01	43°13'N	27°54'E
Värnamo, Swe. (věr´ná-mô)	192-93	57°11'N	14°03'E
Vasa, Fin. *see* Vaasa	184-85	63°06'N	21°37'E
Vaslui, Rom. (vás-lo͞o´ē)	202-03	46°38'N	27°45'E
Vassar, Mi., U.S. (văs´ẽr)	116-17	43°22'N	83°35'W
Västerås, Swe. (věs´těr-ôs)	192-93	59°37'N	16°33'E
Västervik, Swe. (věs´těr-vēk)	192-93	57°45'N	16°39'E
Vasto, Italy (väs´tō)	200-01	42°07'N	14°43'E
Vasyugan, stm., Russia (vás-yo͞o-gán´)	218-19	59°07'N	80°46'E
Vasyugan'ye, sw., Russia	218-19	58°0'N	77°00'E
Vatican City, nation, Eur. (văt´ĭkăn sĭ´tē)	200-01	41°54'N	12°27'E
Vaticano, Città del, nation, Eur. *see* Vatican City	200-01	41°54'N	12°27'E
Vatnajökull, ice, Ice. (vät´ná-yû-kôl)	190a	64°25'N	16°50'W
Vatra Dornei, Rom. (vät´rá dôr´nå´)	194-95	47°21'N	25°22'E
Vättern, lk., Swe.	192-93	58°24'N	14°36'E
Vatu-i-ra Channel, strt., Fiji	279f	17°17'S	178°31'E
Vaughn, N.M., U.S.	120-21	34°36'N	105°15'W
Vaupés, stm., S.A. (vá´o͞o-pě´s)	164-65	0°02'N	67°15'W
Växjö, Swe. (věks´shû)	192-93	56°53'N	14°49'E
Vaygach, Ostrov, i., Russia (ôs-trôf´ vī-gách´)	186-87	70°0'N	59°30'E
Vedea, stm., Rom. (vå´dyá)	200-01	43°43'N	25°33'E
Vedia, Arg. (vě´dyä)	173	34°30'S	61°33'W
Vega, i., Nor.	184-85	65°39'N	11°50'E
Vegreville, Ab., Can.	132-33	53°30'N	112°03'W
Vejle, Den. (vī´lě)	192-93	55°42'N	9°32'E
Velebit, mts., Cro. (vā´lě-bět)	200-01	44°38'N	15°03'E
Vélez-Málaga, Spain (vā´läth-mä´lä-gä)	198-99	36°47'N	4°06'W
Velhas, stm., Braz.	172	17°13'S	44°49'W
Velikaya, stm., Russia (vå-lē´ká-yá)	192-93	57°52'N	28°09'E
Velikaya, stm., Russia (vå-lē´ká-yá)	218-19	64°35'N	176°12'E
Veliki Bečkerek, Serb. *see* Zhovti Vody	200-01	45°23'N	20°24'E
Velikiye Luki, Russia (vyē-lē´-kyě lo͞o´ke)	192-93	56°20'N	30°33'E
Velikiy Ustyug, Russia (vå-lē´kĭ o͞os-tyǒg´)	186-87	60°45'N	46°19'E
Veliko Tŭrnovo, Blg.	200-01	43°04'N	25°38'E
Velizh, Russia (vå´lēzh)	192-93	55°36'N	31°12'E
Vella Lavella, i., Sol. Is.	279e	7°45'S	156°40'E
Velletri, Italy (věl-lā´trē)	200-01	41°41'N	12°46'E
Vellore, India (věl-lōr´)	236	12°55'N	79°08'E
Vel'sk, Russia (vělsk)	186-87	61°04'N	42°06'E
Venadillo, Col. (vě-nä-dē´l-yō)	163c	4°43'N	74°55'W

n-sing; ŋ-baŋk; ɴ-nasalized n; nŏd; cŏmmit; ōld; ôbey; ôrder; oi-boil; fo͞od; ǒ-as oo in foot; ou-out; s-soft; sh-dish; th-thin; pūre; ûnite; ûrn; stŭd; circŭs; ü-as in French tu; ´-indeterminate vowel.

ăt; finál; rāte; senāte; ärm; àsk; sofá; fâre; ch-choose; dh-as th in other; bē; ĕvent; bĕt; recĕnt; cratĕr; g-gō; gh-guttural g; bĭt; ĭ-short neutral; rīde; ᴋ-guttural k as ch in German ich;

PRONOUNCING INDEX

Virginia Beach – Wapello 395

Feature (Pronunciation)	Page	Lat.	Long.
Virginia Beach, Va., U.S. (vẽr-jĭn´yȧ bēch)	124-25	36°52'N	75°59'W
Virginia City, Nv., U.S.	118-19	39°19'N	119°39'W
Virgin Islands, dep., N.A. (vûr´jĭn ī´lȧndz)	140-41	18°20'N	64°50'W
Viroqua, Wi., U.S. (vĭ-rō´kwȧ)	114-15	43°34'N	90°53'W
Virovitica, Cro. (vē-rô-vē´tē-tsȧ)	200-01	45°50'N	17°24'E
Virrat, Fin. (vĭr´ät)	192-93	62°15'N	23°45'E
Virserum, Swe. (vĭr´sĕ-rôm)	192-93	57°19'N	15°36'E
Virudunagar, India	236	9°35'N	77°57'E
Vis, Otok, i., Cro.	200-01	43°02'N	16°11'E
Visalia, Ca., U.S. (vĭ-sā´lĭ-ȧ)	118-19	36°20'N	119°18'W
Visayan Sea, s., Phil.	250	11°35'N	123°51'E
Visby, Swe. (vĭs´bü)	192-93	57°38'N	18°19'E
Viscount Melville Sound, strt., Can.	86	74°10'N	108°00'W
Višegrad, Bos. (vē´shĕ-gräd)	200-01	43°47'N	19°18'E
Vishākhapatnam, India	236	17°43'N	83°19'E
Vishera, stm., Russia (vĭ´shĕ-rȧ)	186-87	59°54'N	56°26'E
Visoko, Bos. (vē´sô-kô)	200-01	43°59'N	18°11'E
Vistula, stm., Pol. (vĭs´tů-lȧ)	194-95	54°21'N	18°56'E
Vitarte, Peru	163a	12°02'S	76°56'W
Viterbo, Italy (vē-tĕr´bō)	200-01	42°25'N	12°06'E
Viti, nation, Oc. see Fiji	279f	18°0'S	178°00'E
Viti, nation, Oc. see Fiji	279f	18°0'S	178°00'E
Viti Levu, i., Fiji	279f	18°0'S	178°00'E
Vitim, stm., Russia (vē´têm)	218-19	59°28'N	112°35'E
Vitória, Braz. (vē-tō´rē-ä)	166-67	2°53'S	52°00'W
Vitória, Braz.	172	20°19'S	40°21'W
Vitoria, Spain (vē-tô-ryä) see Gasteiz	198-99	42°51'N	2°40'W
Vitória da Conquista, Braz.	166-67	14°51'S	40°51'W
Vitry-le-François, Fr. (vē-trē´lĕ-frän-swȧ´)	196-97	48°44'N	4°36'E
Vivian, La., U.S. (vĭv´ĭ-ȧn)	120-21	32°53'N	93°59'W
Vizcaya, Golfo de, b., Eur. see Biscay, Bay of	196-97	44°0'N	4°00'W
Vize, Ostrov, i., Russia	218-19	79°33'N	76°50'E
Vizianagaram, India	236	18°07'N	83°25'E
Vladikavkaz, Russia	227	43°03'N	44°39'E
Vladimir, Russia (vlȧ-dyē´mēr)	202-03	56°08'N	40°24'E
Vladivostok, Russia (vlȧ-dē-vôs-tŏk´)	240-41	43°08'N	131°56'E
Vlonë, Alb. see Vlorë	200-01	40°29'N	19°30'E
Vlora, Alb. see Vlorë	200-01	40°29'N	19°30'E
Vlorë, Alb.	200-01	40°29'N	19°30'E
Vogel Peak, mtn., Nig. see Dimlang	260-61	8°24'N	11°47'E
Voghera, Italy (vô-gā´rä)	200-01	44°60'N	9°01'E
Vohimena, Tanjona, c., Madag.	264-65	25°36'S	45°09'E
Voi, Kenya	262-63	3°23'S	38°34'E
Voinjama, Lib.	260-61	8°25'N	9°45'W
Voiron, Fr. (vwȧ-rôN´)	196-97	45°22'N	5°35'E
Volcano Islands, is., Japan (vŏl-kā´nō ī´lȧndz) see Kazan-rettō	280-81	25°0'N	141°00'E
Volga, stm., Russia (vôl´gä)	186-87	45°45'N	47°56'E
Volga Upland, plat., Russia (vôl´gä ŭp´lȧnd) see Privolzhskaya Vozvyshennost'	186-87	52°0'N	46°00'E
Volgodonsk, Russia	186-87	47°31'N	42°08'E
Volgograd, Russia (vŏl-gō-grä´t)	186-87	48°44'N	44°25'E
Volgograd Reservoir, res., Russia (vŏl-gō-grä´t rĕ´sĕr-vwär) see Volgogradskoye Vodokhranilishche	186-87	50°18'N	45°49'E
Volgogradskoye Vodokhranilishche, res., Russia	186-87	50°18'N	45°49'E
Volkhov, Russia (vôl´kôf)	192-93	59°55'N	32°19'E
Volksrust, S. Afr.	269c	27°22'S	29°54'E
Vologda, Russia (vô´lôg-dȧ)	186-87	59°14'N	39°55'E
Volokolamsk, Russia (vô-lô-kô-lȧmsk)	202-03	56°02'N	35°58'E
Vólos, Grc.	200-01	39°22'N	22°57'E
Vol'sk, Russia (vôl´sk)	186-87	52°03'N	47°22'E
Volta, stm., Ghana (vôl´tȧ)	260-61	5°46'N	0°40'E
Volta Blanche, stm., Afr. (vôl´tȧ blänsh) see White Volta	260-61	8°57'N	1°10'W
Volta Lake, res., Ghana (vôl´tȧ lăk)	260-61	7°30'N	0°07'E
Volta Noire, stm., Afr. (vôl´tȧ nwär) see Black Volta	260-61	8°41'N	0°60'W
Volta Redonda, Braz. (vōl´tä-rä-dôn´dä)	172	22°32'S	44°07'W
Volzhsk, Russia	186-87	55°52'N	48°21'E
Volzhskiy, Russia	186-87	48°50'N	44°45'E
Vordingborg, Den. (vôr´dĭng-bôr)	194-95	55°01'N	11°55'E
Vóreioi Sporades, is., Grc.	200-01	39°15'N	23°55'E
Vorgashor, Russia	186-87	67°32'N	64°05'E
Vorkuta, Russia (vôr-kōō´tȧ)	186-87	67°29'N	64°03'E
Vormsi, i., Est. (vôrm´sĭ)	192-93	59°00'N	23°15'E
Vorona, stm., Russia (vô-rô´na)	186-87	51°21'N	42°02'E
Voronezh, Russia (vô-rô´nyĕzh)	202-03	51°40'N	39°10'E
Voronezh, stm., Russia (vô-rô´nyĕzh)	186-87	51°32'N	39°06'E
Voronya, stm., Russia (vô-rônyȧ)	186-87	69°00'N	35°42'E
Voroshilov, Russia see Ussuriysk	244	43°48'N	131°59'E
Voroshilovsk, Russia see Stavropol'	186-87	45°02'N	41°59'E
Võru, Est. (vô´rû)	192-93	57°50'N	27°01'E
Voskresensk, Russia (vôs-krĕ-sĕnsk´)	202-03	55°19'N	38°42'E
Voss, Nor. (vôs)	192-93	60°38'N	6°26'E
Vostochno-Sibirskoye More, s., Russia see East Siberian Sea	218-19	74°0'N	166°00'E
Vostok, i., Kir.	280-81	10°06'S	152°23'W
Votkinsk, Russia (vôt-kēnsk´)	186-87	57°03'N	53°59'E
Votuporanga, Braz.	168-69	20°26'S	49°58'W
Voyageurs National Park, n.p., Mn., U.S.	114-15	48°30'N	93°00'W
Voznesens'k, Ukr.	202-03	47°34'N	31°20'E
Vrangelya, Ostrov, i., Russia	218-19	71°14'N	179°21'W
Vranje, Serb. (vrän´yĕ)	200-01	42°34'N	21°55'E
Vratsa, Blg. (vrät´tsȧ)	200-01	43°12'N	23°34'E
Vrbas, Serb. (v'r´bäs)	200-01	45°34'N	19°39'E
Vrchlabí, Czech Rep. (v'r´chlä-bē)	194-95	50°37'N	15°37'E
Vrede, S. Afr. (vrĭ´dĕ)(vrēd)	269c	27°26'S	29°10'E
Vredefort, S. Afr. (vrĭ´dĕ-fôrt)(vrēd´fôrt)	269c	27°00'S	27°22'E
Vrindāvan, India	234-35	27°35'N	77°42'E
Vršac, Serb. (v'r´shäts)	200-01	45°07'N	21°18'E
Vryburg, S. Afr. (vrī´bûrg)	264-65	26°58'S	24°44'E
Vryheid, S. Afr. (vrī´hīt)	264-65	27°46'S	30°48'E
Vsetín, Czech Rep. (fsĕt´yēn)	194-95	49°20'N	18°00'E
Vukovar, Cro. (vŏ´kô-vär)	200-01	45°21'N	19°00'E
Vulcano, Isola, i., Italy (ē´-sō-lä-vōōl-kä´nô)	200-01	38°24'N	14°58'E
Vung Tau, Viet.	246-47	10°21'N	107°05'E
Vyatka, Russia see Kirov	186-87	58°36'N	49°40'E
Vyatka, stm., Russia (vyȧt´kȧ)	186-87	55°35'N	51°29'E
Vyatskiye Polyany, Russia	186-87	56°14'N	51°05'E
Vyazemskiy, Russia (vyȧ-zĕm´skĭ)	240-41	47°33'N	134°46'E
Vyazma, Russia (vyȧz´mȧ)	202-03	55°12'N	34°17'E
Vyazniki, Russia (vyȧz´nē-kē)	186-87	56°15'N	42°08'E
Vychegda, stm., Russia (vê´chĕg-dȧ)	186-87	61°17'N	46°37'E
Vygozero, Ozero, lk., Russia	186-87	63°35'N	34°42'E
Vym', stm., Russia (vwĕm)	186-87	62°13'N	50°24'E
Vyritsa, Russia (vē´rĭ-tsȧ)	192-93	59°24'N	30°20'E
Vyshniy Volochëk, Russia (vêsh´nyĭ vôl-ô-chĕk´)	202-03	57°35'N	34°34'E
Vyškov, Czech Rep. (vêsh´kôf)	194-95	49°17'N	16°60'E
Vysokogornyy, Russia	218-19	50°06'N	139°09'E
Vysokovsk, Russia (vĭ-sô´kôfsk)	202-03	56°19'N	36°34'E
Vytegra, Russia (vû´tĕg-rȧ)	186-87	61°00'N	36°28'E

W

Feature (Pronunciation)	Page	Lat.	Long.
Wa, Ghana	260-61	10°03'N	2°30'W
Wabana, Nf., Can.	138-39	47°39'N	52°57'W
Wabasca, stm., Ab., Can.	130-31	58°21'N	115°20'W
Wabasca-Desmarais, Ab., Can.	132-33	55°58'N	113°52'W
Wabash, In., U.S. (wô´băsh)	116-17	40°48'N	85°49'W
Wabash, stm., U.S. (wô´băsh)	110-11	37°48'N	88°01'W
Wabasha, Mn., U.S. (wä´bȧ-shô)	114-15	44°23'N	92°02'W
Wabē Gestro, stm., Eth.	262-63	4°17'N	42°03'E
Wabē Shebelē, stm., Afr.	262-63	0°10'N	42°46'E
Wabowden, Mb., Can. (wȧ-bō´d'n)	134-35	54°54'N	98°37'W
W.A.C. Bennett Dam, d., B.C., Can.	132-33	56°01'N	122°10'W
Waccasassa Bay, b., Fl., U.S. (wă-kȧ-să´sȧ bā)	124-25	29°06'N	82°52'W
Waco, Tx., U.S. (wā´kō)	122-23	31°33'N	97°09'W
Waddān, Libya	188-89	29°10'N	16°10'E
Waddeneilanden, is., Eur. see Frisian Islands	190-91	53°27'N	5°50'E
Waddington, Mount, mtn., B.C., Can. (mount wŏd´dĭng-tŭn)	132-33	51°22'N	125°16'W
Wadena, Sk., Can.	134-35	51°56'N	103°47'W
Wadena, Mn., U.S. (wŏ-dē´nȧ)	114-15	46°26'N	95°09'W
Wadesboro, N.C., U.S. (wādz´bŭr-ô)	124-25	34°58'N	80°05'W
Wādī Ḩalfā', Sudan	266	21°48'N	31°20'E
Wadley, Ga., U.S. (wŭd´lē)	124-25	32°52'N	82°24'W
Wad Madanī, Sudan (wăd mĕ-dä´nē)	266	14°23'N	33°31'E
Wadsworth, Nv., U.S. (wŏdz´wŭrth)	118-19	39°38'N	119°17'W
Wafangdian, China	240-41	39°37'N	122°01'E
Wagadugu, nat. cap., Burkina see Ouagadougou	260-61	12°23'N	1°32'W
Wager Bay, b., Nu., Can. (wā´jĕr bā)	130-31	65°26'N	88°40'W
Wagga Wagga, Austl. (wôg´ȧ wôg´ȧ)	276	35°07'S	147°21'E
Wagoner, Ok., U.S. (wăg´ŭn-ĕr)	120-21	35°58'N	95°23'W
Wągrowiec, Pol. (vôŋ-grô´vyĕts)	194-95	52°49'N	17°13'E
Wāh Cantonment, Pak.	232-33	33°48'N	72°41'E
Wahoo, Ne., U.S. (wä-hōō´)	114-15	41°13'N	96°37'W
Wahpeton, N.D., U.S. (wô´pē-tŭn)	114-15	46°16'N	96°36'W
Wahrān, Alg. see Oran	198-99	35°41'N	0°39'W
Wai'anae, Hi., U.S. (wä´ē-ȧ-nä´ä)	127a	21°27'N	158°11'W
Waigeo, Pulau, i., Indon. (pōō-lou wä-ē-gā´ô)	224-25	0°10'S	130°55'E
Waikabubak, Indon.	248-49	9°38'S	119°25'E
Waikato, stm., N.Z. (wä´ē-kä´to)	278	37°23'S	174°43'E
Waikerie, Austl. (wā´kĕr-ē)	276	34°11'S	139°59'E
Wailuku, Hi., U.S. (wä´ē-lōō´kōō)	127a	20°54'N	156°30'W
Waimea, Hi., U.S. (wä-ē-mā´ä)	127a	21°58'N	159°40'W
Waimea, Hi., U.S. (wä-ē-mā´ä)	127a	20°02'N	155°40'W
Waimea, Hi., U.S. (wä-ē-mā´ä)	127a	20°02'N	155°40'W
Wainganga, stm., India (wä-ēn-gŭŋ´gä)	234-35	19°37'N	79°48'E
Waingapu, Indon.	248-49	9°40'S	120°16'E
Wainwright, Ab., Can. (wān-rīt)	132-33	52°51'N	110°51'W
Wainwright, Ak., U.S. (wān-rīt)	126	70°39'N	159°59'W
Waitekere, N.Z.	278	36°55'S	174°40'E
Waitsburg, Wa., U.S. (wāts´bûrg)	112-13	46°16'N	118°09'W
Wajima, Japan (wä´jē-mȧ)	245	37°24'N	136°54'E
Wajir, Kenya	262-63	1°45'N	40°04'E
Waka, Eth.	269d	7°10'N	37°21'E
Wakamatsu, Japan see Aizu-wakamatsu	245	37°30'N	139°56'E
Wakasa-wan, b., Japan (wä´kä-sä wän)	245	35°45'N	135°40'E
Wakatipu, Lake, lk., N.Z. (lāk wä-kä-tē´pōō)	278	45°05'S	168°34'E
Wakayama, Japan (wä-kä´yä-mä)	245	34°13'N	135°10'E
WaKeeney, Ks., U.S. (wô-kē´nē)	120-21	39°01'N	99°53'W
Wakefield, Ne., U.S. (wāk-fēld)	114-15	42°16'N	96°52'W
Wake Forest, N.C., U.S. (wāk fŏr´ĕst)	124-25	35°58'N	78°31'W
Wake Island, dep., Oc. (wāk ī´lȧnd)	280-81	19°17'N	166°36'E
Wakhān, hist. reg., Afg. see Vākhān	232-33	37°0'N	73°00'E
Wakkanai, Japan (wä´kä-nä´ē)	244	45°24'N	141°41'E
Wakkerstroom, S. Afr. (vȧk´ĕr-strōm)(wăk´ĕr-strōōm)	269c	27°20'S	30°08'E
Wałbrzych, Pol. (väl´bzhûk)	194-95	50°46'N	16°17'E
Waldenburg, Pol. see Wałbrzych	194-95	50°46'N	16°17'E
Waldorf, Md., U.S. (wăl´dôrf)	116-17	38°37'N	76°54'W
Wales, Ak., U.S. (wālz)	126	65°36'N	168°04'W
Wales, state, U.K. (wālz)	190-91	52°30'N	3°30'W
Wales Island, i., Nu., Can.	130-31	68°0'N	86°43'W
Walgett, Austl. (wôl´gĕt)	276	30°02'S	148°07'E
Walhalla, N.D., U.S. (wŭl-hăl´ȧ)	114-15	48°56'N	97°55'W
Walhalla, S.C., U.S. (wŭl-hăl´ȧ)	124-25	34°46'N	83°04'W
Walikale, D.R.C.	267	1°25'S	28°03'E
Walker, Mi., U.S. (wôk´ĕr)	116-17	42°59'N	85°45'W
Walker, Mn., U.S. (wôk´ĕr)	114-15	47°06'N	94°35'W
Walker Lake, lk., Mb., Can. (wôk´ĕr lāk)	134-35	54°42'N	96°57'W
Walker Lake, lk., Nv., U.S.	118-19	38°44'N	118°43'W
Wallaceburg, On., Can.	136-37	42°36'N	82°23'W
Wallaroo, Austl. (wŏl-ȧ-rōō)	276	33°56'S	137°37'E
Walla Walla, Wa., U.S. (wŏl´ȧ wŏl´ȧ)	112-13	46°04'N	118°19'W
Wallis, Îles, is., Wal./F.	280-81	13°18'S	176°10'W
Wallis and Futuna, dep., Oc. (wŏl´ĭs ănd fōō-tōō´nȧ)	280-81	14°0'S	177°00'W
Wallis et Futuna, dep., Oc. see Wallis and Futuna	280-81	14°0'S	177°00'W
Wallowa Mountains, mts., Or., U.S. (wôl´ô-wȧ moun´tĭnz)	112-13	45°16'N	117°21'W
Walnut Creek, stm., Ks., U.S. (wôl´nŭt krēk)	120-21	38°21'N	98°41'W
Walnut Ridge, Ar., U.S. (wôl´nŭt rĭj)	124-25	36°04'N	90°58'W
Walsall, Eng., U.K. (wôl-sôl)	190-91	52°36'N	1°59'W
Walsenburg, Co., U.S. (wôl´sĕn-bûrg)	120-21	37°37'N	104°47'W
Walters, Ok., U.S. (wôl´tĕrz)	120-21	34°21'N	98°19'W
Walvisbaai, Nmb. see Walvis Bay	264-65	22°57'S	14°31'E
Walvis Bay, Nmb. (wôl´vĭs bā)	264-65	22°57'S	14°31'E
Walworth, Wi., U.S. (wôl´wûrth)	116-17	42°32'N	88°37'W
Wamba, D.R.C.	267	2°09'N	28°00'E
Wamego, Ks., U.S. (wō-mē´gō)	120-21	39°12'N	96°18'W
Wami, stm., Tan. (wä´mē)	262-63	6°15'S	38°51'E
Wanfoxia, China	240-41	40°05'N	95°55'E
Wanganui, N.Z. (wôŋ´gȧ-nōō´ē)	278	39°56'S	175°02'E
Wangaratta, Austl. (wŏŋ´gȧ-răt´ȧ)	276	36°22'S	146°19'E
Wangiwangi, Pulau, i., Indon.	248-49	5°20'S	123°35'E
Wangpan Yang, b., China	238-39	30°30'N	121°46'E
Wanneroo, Austl.	270-71	31°45'S	115°48'E
Wanxian, China (wän-shyĕn)	238-39	30°49'N	108°22'E
Wanzai, China (wän-dzī)	238-39	28°05'N	114°27'E
Wapakoneta, Oh., U.S. (wä´pȧ-kô-nĕt´ȧ)	116-17	40°34'N	84°12'W
Wapawekka Lake, lk., Sk., Can. (wŏ´pă-wĕ´kȧ lāk)	134-35	54°55'N	104°40'W
Wapello, Ia., U.S. (wŏ-pĕl´ō)	114-15	41°10'N	91°12'W

n-sing; ŋ-baŋk; N-nasalized n; nŏd; cŏmmit; ōld; ôbey; ôrder; oi-boil; fōōd; ŏ-as oo in foot; ou-out; s-soft; sh-dish; th-thin; pūre; ûnite; ûrn; stŭd; circŭs; ü-as in French tu; ´-indeterminate vowel.

396 Wapiti – West Point Lake PRONOUNCING INDEX

Feature (Pronunciation)	Page	Lat.	Long.
Wapiti, stm., Can.	**132-33**	55°08'N	118°18'W
Wapusk National Park, n.p., Can.	**128-29**	58°0'N	93°30'W
Warangal, India (wŭ'răṇ-gǎl)	**236**	18°00'N	79°35'E
Warburton Creek, stm., Austl.	**276**	27°59'S	137°25'E
Warden, S. Afr. (wôr'dĕn)	**269c**	27°51'S	28°58'E
Wardha, India (wŭr'dä)	**234-35**	20°45'N	78°37'E
Wardha, stm., India	**234-35**	19°36'N	79°47'E
Warialda, Austl.	**276**	29°33'S	150°35'E
Warmbad, S. Afr. *see* Bela-Bela	**269c**	24°53'S	28°19'E
Warm Baths, S. Afr. *see* Bela-Bela	**269c**	24°53'S	28°19'E
Warm Springs Indian Reservation, ind. res., Or., U.S. (wôrm sprĭngz ĭn'dĭ-ăn rĕ-sĕr-vā'shĕn)	**112-13**	44°53'N	121°23'W
Warrego, stm., Austl. (wôr'ē-gô)	**270-71**	30°25'S	145°21'E
Warren, Ar., U.S. (wŏr'ĕn)	**120-21**	33°37'N	92°04'W
Warren, Mi., U.S. (wŏr'ĕn)	**116-17**	42°30'N	83°02'W
Warren, Mn., U.S. (wŏr'ĕn)	**114-15**	48°12'N	96°47'W
Warren, Oh., U.S. (wŏr'ĕn)	**116-17**	41°14'N	80°49'W
Warrensburg, Mo., U.S. (wŏr'ĕnz-bûrg)	**120-21**	38°46'N	93°44'W
Warrenton, S. Afr.	**264-65**	28°07'S	24°51'E
Warrenton, Mo., U.S. (wŏr'ĕn-tŭn)	**120-21**	38°49'N	91°09'W
Warrenton, Or., U.S. (wŏr'ĕn-tŭn)	**112-13**	46°10'N	123°55'W
Warrenton, Va., U.S. (wŏr'ĕn-tŭn)	**116-17**	38°43'N	77°48'W
Warri, Nig. (wär'ē)	**260a**	5°31'N	5°46'E
Warrnambool, Austl. (wôr'năm-bōōl)	**276**	38°23'S	142°29'E
Warroad, Mn., U.S. (wôr'rōd)	**114-15**	48°54'N	95°19'W
Warsaw, In., U.S. (wôr'sô)	**116-17**	41°14'N	85°51'W
Warsaw, Ky., U.S. (wôr'sô)	**116-17**	38°47'N	84°54'W
Warsaw, Mo., U.S. (wôr'sô)	**120-21**	38°15'N	93°23'W
Warsaw, N.C., U.S. (wôr'sô)	**124-25**	34°59'N	78°05'W
Warsaw, Va., U.S. (wôr'sô)	**116-17**	37°57'N	76°46'W
Warsaw, nat. cap., Pol. (wôr'sô)	**194-95**	52°15'N	21°00'E
Warszawa, nat. cap., Pol. (vár-shä'vá) *see* Warsaw	**194-95**	52°15'N	21°00'E
Warwick, Austl. (wŏr'ĭk)	**276**	28°13'S	152°02'E
Warwick, R.I., U.S. (wŏr'ĭk)	**116-17**	41°43'N	71°23'W
Wasco, Ca., U.S. (wăs'kō)	**118-19**	35°36'N	119°20'W
Waseca, Mn., U.S. (wô-sē'ká)	**114-15**	44°05'N	93°30'W
Washburn, N.D., U.S. (wŏsh'bŭrn)	**114-15**	47°17'N	101°02'W
Washburn, Wi., U.S. (wŏsh'bŭrn)	**114-15**	46°40'N	90°54'W
Washington, Ga., U.S. (wŏsh'ĭng-tŭn)	**124-25**	33°44'N	82°44'W
Washington, Ia., U.S. (wŏsh'ĭng-tŭn)	**114-15**	41°18'N	91°41'W
Washington, Il., U.S. (wŏsh'ĭng-tŭn)	**116-17**	40°42'N	89°25'W
Washington, In., U.S. (wŏsh'ĭng-tŭn)	**116-17**	38°39'N	87°10'W
Washington, Mo., U.S. (wŏsh'ĭng-tŭn)	**120-21**	38°33'N	91°01'W
Washington, N.C., U.S. (wŏsh'ĭng-tŭn)	**124-25**	35°33'N	77°04'W
Washington, state, U.S. (wŏsh'ĭng-tŭn)	**108-09**	47°30'N	120°30'W
Washington, nat. cap., D.C., U.S. (wŏsh'ĭng-tŭn)	**116-17**	38°53'N	77°02'W
Washington, Mount, mtn., N.H., U.S. (mount wŏsh'ĭng-tŭn)	**116-17**	44°16'N	71°18'W
Washington Island, i., Kir. *see* Teraina	**280-81**	4°42'N	160°45'W
Washington Island, i., Wi., U.S. (wŏsh'ĭng-tŭn ī'lănd)	**116-17**	45°22'N	86°54'W
Waskaganish, Qc., Can.	**128-29**	51°29'N	78°45'W
Waskaiowaka Lake, lk., Mb., Can. (wŏ'skă-yō'wŏ-kă lāk)	**134-35**	56°31'N	96°18'W
Watampone, Indon.	**248-49**	4°32'S	120°19'E
Wataru, i., Mald.	**236**	5°43'N	73°23'E
Waterberge, mts., S. Afr. (wôrtĕr'bûrg)	**269c**	24°28'S	27°58'E
Waterbury, Ct., U.S. (wô'tĕr-bĕr-ē)	**116-17**	41°33'N	73°02'W
Waterbury, Vt., U.S. (wô'tĕr-bĕr-ē)	**116-17**	44°20'N	72°45'W
Waterford, Ire. (wô'tĕr-fĕrd)	**190-91**	52°15'N	7°06'W
Waterhen Lake, lk., Mb., Can.	**134-35**	52°06'N	99°34'W
Waterloo, Bel. (wô-tĕr-lōō')	**190-91**	50°43'N	4°24'E
Waterloo, On., Can. (wô-tĕr-lōō')	**136-37**	43°28'N	80°30'W
Waterloo, Qc., Can. (wô-tĕr-lōō')	**136-37**	45°21'N	72°30'W
Waterloo, Ia., U.S. (wô-tĕr-lōō')	**114-15**	42°30'N	92°21'W
Waterloo, Il., U.S. (wô-tĕr-lōō')	**120-21**	38°20'N	90°09'W
Waterton Lakes National Park, n.p., Ab., Can.	**132-33**	49°06'N	114°01'W
Watertown, N.Y., U.S.	**116-17**	43°59'N	75°55'W
Watertown, S.D., U.S. (wô'tĕr-toun)	**114-15**	44°54'N	97°07'W
Watertown, Wi., U.S. (wô'tĕr-toun)	**116-17**	43°11'N	88°43'W
Water Valley, Ms., U.S. (väl'ē văl'ē)	**124-25**	34°10'N	89°38'W
Waterville, Me., U.S.	**117a**	44°33'N	69°38'W
Watervliet, N.Y., U.S. (wô'tĕr-vlēt')	**116-17**	42°44'N	73°43'W
Watford, Eng., U.K. (wŏt'fŏrd)	**190-91**	51°40'N	0°25'W
Watford City, N.D., U.S.	**114-15**	47°48'N	103°18'W
Watling Island, i., Bah. *see* San Salvador	**142-43**	24°02'N	74°27'W
Watonga, Ok., U.S. (wŏ-tôŋ'gá)	**120-21**	35°51'N	98°25'W
Watrous, Sk., Can.	**134-35**	51°41'N	105°27'W
Watsa, D.R.C. (wät'sä)	**267**	3°02'N	29°32'E
Watseka, Il., U.S. (wŏt-sē'ká)	**116-17**	40°46'N	87°44'W
Watson Lake, Yk., Can. (wŏt'sŭn lāk)	**128-29**	60°04'N	128°44'W
Watsonville, Ca., U.S. (wŏt'sŭn-vĭl)	**118-19**	36°55'N	121°45'W
Wauchula, Fl., U.S. (wô-chōō'lá)	**125a**	27°33'N	81°49'W
Waukegan, Il., U.S. (wŏ-kē'găn)	**116-17**	42°21'N	87°51'W
Waukesha, Wi., U.S. (wô'kê-shô)	**116-17**	43°01'N	88°14'W
Waukon, Ia., U.S. (wô kŏn)	**114-15**	43°16'N	91°29'W
Waupaca, Wi., U.S. (wô-păk'á)	**116-17**	44°21'N	89°05'W
Waupun, Wi., U.S. (wô-pŭn')	**116-17**	43°38'N	88°44'W
Waurika, Ok., U.S. (wô-rē'ká)	**120-21**	34°10'N	97°60'W
Wausau, Wi., U.S. (wô'sô)	**116-17**	44°57'N	89°37'W
Wausaukee, Wi., U.S. (wô-sô'kē)	**116-17**	45°23'N	87°59'W
Wauseon, Oh., U.S. (wô'sē-ŏn)	**116-17**	41°33'N	84°08'W
Wautoma, Wi., U.S. (wô-tō'má)	**116-17**	44°04'N	89°18'W
Waverly, Ia., U.S. (wā'vĕr-lē)	**114-15**	42°44'N	92°29'W
Waverly, Ne., U.S. (wā'vĕr-lē)	**114-15**	40°55'N	96°32'W
Waverly, Oh., U.S. (wā'vĕr-lē)	**116-17**	39°07'N	82°59'W
Waverly, Tn., U.S. (wā'vĕr-lē)	**124-25**	36°05'N	87°48'W
Wāw, Sudan	**262-63**	7°41'N	27°59'E
Wawa, On., Can.	**136-37**	47°59'N	84°47'W
Waxahachie, Tx., U.S. (wăk-sá-hăch'ē)	**120-21**	32°24'N	96°51'W
Waya, i., Fiji	**279f**	17°18'S	177°08'E
Wayabula, Indon.	**248-49**	2°18'N	128°12'E
Waycross, Ga., U.S.	**124-25**	31°13'N	82°22'W
Wayne, Ne., U.S. (wān)	**114-15**	42°14'N	97°01'W
Wayne, W.V., U.S. (wān)	**116-17**	38°13'N	82°27'W
Waynesboro, Ga., U.S. (wānz'bŭr-ô)	**124-25**	33°05'N	82°01'W
Waynesboro, Ms., U.S. (wānz'bŭr-ô)	**124-25**	31°40'N	88°39'W
Waynesboro, Pa., U.S. (wānz'bŭr-ô)	**116-17**	39°45'N	77°35'W
Waynesboro, Va., U.S. (wānz'bŭr-ô)	**116-17**	38°04'N	78°53'W
Waynesville, Mo., U.S. (wānz'vĭl)	**120-21**	37°50'N	92°12'W
Waynesville, N.C., U.S. (wānz'vĭl)	**124-25**	35°29'N	82°60'W
Waynoka, Ok., U.S. (wā-nō'ká)	**120-21**	36°35'N	98°53'W
Weagamow Lake, lk., On., Can. (wē'ăg-ă-mou lāk)	**134-35**	52°53'N	91°22'W
Weatherford, Ok., U.S. (wĕ-dhĕr-fĕrd)	**120-21**	35°32'N	98°43'W
Weatherford, Tx., U.S. (wĕ-dhĕr-fĕrd)	**120-21**	32°46'N	97°48'W
Weddell Island, i., Falk. Is.	**171**	51°53'S	61°05'W
Weddell Sea, s., Ant. (wĕd'ĕl sē)	**287**	72°0'S	45°00'W
Wedgeport, N.S., Can. (wĕj'pōrt)	**138-39**	43°45'N	65°60'W
Weed, Ca., U.S. (wēd)	**112-13**	41°25'N	122°23'W
Weenen, S. Afr. (vā'nĕn)	**269c**	28°51'S	30°05'E
Wei, stm., China (wā)	**238-39**	34°37'N	110°17'E
Wei, stm., China (wā)	**240-41**	36°49'N	115°41'E
Weichang, China (wā-chäŋ)	**240-41**	42°00'N	117°40'E
Weifang, China	**240-41**	36°42'N	119°06'E
Weihai, China (wa'hăĭ')	**240-41**	37°30'N	122°07'E
Weilheim, Ger. (vīl'hīm')	**194-95**	47°50'N	11°09'E
Weimar, Ger. (vī'mär)	**194-95**	50°59'N	11°19'E
Weinan, China	**238-39**	34°29'N	109°29'E
Weipa, Austl.	**277**	12°42'S	141°56'E
Weiser, Id., U.S. (wē'zĕr)	**112-13**	44°15'N	116°58'W
Weißenfels, Ger. (vī'sĕn-fĕlz)	**194-95**	51°12'N	11°58'E
Weixi, China (wā-shyē)	**238-39**	27°11'N	99°17'E
Welch, W.V., U.S. (wĕlch)	**124-25**	37°26'N	81°35'W
Welkom, S. Afr. (wĕl'kŏm)	**269c**	27°58'S	26°44'E
Welland, On., Can. (wĕl'ănd)	**136-37**	42°59'N	79°15'W
Wellesley Islands, is., Austl.	**277**	16°42'S	139°30'E
Wellington, Austl. (wĕl'lĭng-tŭn)	**276**	32°34'S	148°57'E
Wellington, Co., U.S. (wĕl'lĭng-tŭn)	**120-21**	40°42'N	104°60'W
Wellington, Ks., U.S. (wĕl'lĭng-tŭn)	**120-21**	37°16'N	97°24'W
Wellington, Oh., U.S. (wĕl'lĭng-tŭn)	**116-17**	41°10'N	82°13'W
Wellington, Tx., U.S. (wĕl'lĭng-tŭn)	**120-21**	34°51'N	100°13'W
Wellington, nat. cap., N.Z. (wĕl'lĭng-tŭn)	**278**	41°18'S	174°46'E
Wellington, Isla, i., Chile (ē's-lä-ŏĕ'lĕng-tŏn)	**171**	49°20'S	74°40'W
Wells, Mn., U.S. (wĕlz)	**114-15**	43°45'N	93°44'W
Wells, Nv., U.S. (wĕlz)	**112-13**	41°07'N	114°58'W
Wells, Lake, lk., Austl. (lāk wĕlz)	**272-73**	26°41'S	123°11'E
Wellsboro, Pa., U.S. (wĕlz'bŭ-rô)	**116-17**	41°45'N	77°17'W
Wellsburg, W.V., U.S. (wĕlz'bûrg)	**116-17**	40°16'N	80°36'W
Wellston, Oh., U.S. (wĕlz'tŭn)	**116-17**	39°07'N	82°32'W
Wellsville, N.Y., U.S. (wĕlz'vĭl)	**116-17**	42°07'N	77°56'W
Wellsville, Oh., U.S. (wĕlz'vĭl)	**116-17**	40°36'N	80°39'W
Wellsville, Ut., U.S. (wĕlz'vĭl)	**112-13**	41°39'N	111°56'W
Wels, Aus. (vĕls)	**194-95**	48°10'N	14°01'E
Welshpool, Wales, U.K. (wĕlsh'pōōl)	**190-91**	52°40'N	3°09'W
Wembere, stm., Tan.	**267**	4°09'S	34°11'E
Wenatchee, Wa., U.S. (wê-năch'ē)	**112-13**	47°25'N	120°19'W
Wenatchee Mountains, mts., Wa., U.S. (wê-năch'ē moun'tĭnz)	**112-13**	47°20'N	120°45'W
Wenchang, China (wŭn-chäŋ)	**238-39**	19°33'N	110°45'E
Wenchow, China *see* Wenzhou	**238-39**	28°01'N	120°38'E
Wendover, Ut., U.S.	**112-13**	40°44'N	114°02'W
Wenlock, stm., Austl.	**277**	12°15'S	141°56'E
Wenshan, China	**238-39**	23°30'N	104°28'E
Wentworth, Austl. (wĕnt'wûrth)	**276**	34°06'S	141°55'E
Wenzhou, China (wŭn-jō)	**238-39**	28°01'N	120°38'E
Werdēr, Eth.	**262-63**	6°58'N	45°21'E
Wesel, Ger. (vā'zĕl)	**194-95**	51°40'N	6°38'E
Weser, stm., Ger. (vā'zĕr)	**194-95**	53°32'N	8°34'E
Wesermünde, Ger. *see* Bremerhaven	**194-95**	53°32'N	8°36'E
Weslaco, Tx., U.S. (wĕs-lā'kō)	**122-23**	26°10'N	97°59'W
Wessel, Cape, c., Austl.	**272-73**	11°02'S	136°45'E
Wessington Springs, S.D., U.S. (wĕs'ĭng-tŭn sprĭngz)	**114-15**	44°05'N	98°34'W
West Allis, Wi., U.S. (wĕst ăl'ĭs)	**116-17**	43°01'N	88°01'W
West Bend, Ia., U.S. (wĕst bĕnd)	**114-15**	42°57'N	94°26'W
West Bend, Wi., U.S. (wĕst bĕnd)	**116-17**	43°25'N	88°10'W
West Bengal, state, India (wĕst bĕn-gôl')	**234-35**	24°0'N	88°00'E
West Branch, Ia., U.S. (wĕst bránch)	**114-15**	41°40'N	91°21'W
West Branch, Mi., U.S. (wĕst bránch)	**116-17**	44°16'N	84°14'W
Westbrook, Me., U.S. (wĕst'brŏŏk)	**116-17**	43°41'N	70°21'W
West Caicos, i., T./C. Is. (wĕst kī'kōs) (wĕst käē'kō)	**142-43**	21°39'N	72°28'W
West Cape, c., N.Z. (wĕst kāp)	**278**	45°55'S	166°25'E
West Chester, Pa., U.S. (wĕst chĕs'tĕr)	**116-17**	39°58'N	75°36'W
West Columbia, S.C., U.S. (wĕst cŏl'ŭm-bē-á)	**124-25**	33°59'N	81°05'W
West Columbia, Tx., U.S. (wĕst cŏl'ŭm-bē-á)	**122-23**	29°09'N	95°39'W
West Des Moines, Ia., U.S. (wĕst dē moin')	**114-15**	41°34'N	93°44'W
West End, Bah. (wĕst ĕnd)	**142-43**	26°42'N	78°59'W
Westerly, R.I., U.S. (wĕs'tĕr-lē)	**116-17**	41°23'N	71°50'W
Western Australia, state, Austl. (wĕst'tĕrn ôs-trā'lĭ-á)	**270-71**	25°0'S	122°00'E
Western Desert, des., Egypt (wĕst'tĕrn dĕs'ĕrt)	**266**	27°0'N	27°00'E
Western Dvina, stm., Eur.	**192-93**	57°04'N	24°03'E
Western Ghāts, mts., India (wĕst'tĕrn ghäts) (wĕst'tĕrn ghôts)	**236**	14°0'N	75°00'E
Westernport, Md., U.S. (wĕs'tĕrn pōrt)	**116-17**	39°29'N	79°03'W
Western Sahara, dep., Afr. (wĕst'tĕrn sá-hä'rá)	**253**	24°30'N	13°00'W
Western Samoa, nation, Oc. *see* Samoa	**279b**	13°55'S	172°00'W
Westerville, Oh., U.S. (wĕs'tĕr-vĭl)	**116-17**	40°07'N	82°55'W
West Falkland, i., Falk. Is.	**171**	51°50'S	59°60'W
Westfield, Ma., U.S. (wĕst'fēld)	**116-17**	42°08'N	72°45'W
Westfield, N.Y., U.S. (wĕst'fēld)	**116-17**	42°19'N	79°35'W
Westfield, Wi., U.S. (wĕst'fēld)	**116-17**	43°53'N	89°30'W
West Frankfort, Il., U.S. (wĕst frăŋk'fŭrt)	**116-17**	37°54'N	88°56'W
West Helena, Ar., U.S. (wĕst hĕl'ĕn-á)	**124-25**	34°33'N	90°39'W
West Indies, is., (wĕst ĭn'dēz)	**140-41**	19°0'N	70°00'W
West Lafayette, In., U.S. (wĕst lä-fā-yĕt')	**116-17**	40°25'N	86°54'W
West Liberty, Ia., U.S. (wĕst lĭb'ĕr-tĭ)	**114-15**	41°34'N	91°16'W
West Liberty, Oh., U.S. (wĕst lĭb'ĕr-tĭ)	**116-17**	40°15'N	83°47'W
Westlock, Ab., Can. (wĕst'lŏk)	**132-33**	54°09'N	113°52'W
Westminster, Co., U.S. (wĕst'min-stĕr)	**120-21**	39°51'N	105°04'W
West Nishnabotna, stm., Ia., U.S. (wĕst nĭsh-ná-bŏt'ná)	**120-21**	40°30'N	95°42'W
Weston, W.V., U.S. (wĕs'tŭn)	**116-17**	39°02'N	80°29'W
Weston-super-Mare, Eng., U.K. (wĕs'tŭn sū'pĕr-mā'rē)	**190-91**	51°21'N	2°58'W
West Palm Beach, Fl., U.S. (wĕst päm bēch)	**125a**	26°44'N	80°08'W
West Pensacola, Fl., U.S. (wĕst pĕn-sá-kō'lá)	**124-25**	30°25'N	87°16'W
West Plains, Mo., U.S. (wĕst-plānz')	**124-25**	36°44'N	91°52'W
West Point, Ga., U.S. (wĕst point)	**124-25**	32°54'N	85°09'W
West Point, Ms., U.S. (wĕst point)	**124-25**	33°36'N	88°39'W
West Point, Ne., U.S. (wĕst point)	**114-15**	41°51'N	96°43'W
West Point, N.Y., U.S. (wĕst point)	**116-17**	41°24'N	73°58'W
West Point, Va., U.S. (wĕst point)	**116-17**	37°32'N	76°48'W
West Point, c., Austl.	**272-73**	35°01'S	135°57'E
West Point Lake, res., U.S. (wĕst point lāk)	**124-25**	32°60'N	85°12'W

ăt; finăl; rāte; senâte; ärm; åsk; sofá; fâre; ch-choose; dh-as th in other; bē; êvent; bĕt; recĕnt; cratĕr; g-gō; gh-guttural g; bĭt; ĭ-short neutral; rīde; ĸ-guttural k as ch in German ich;

n-sing; ŋ-baŋk; ɴ-nasalized n; nŏd; cŏmmit; ōld; ȯbey; ôrder; oi-boil; fŏōd; ȯ-as oo in foot; ou-out; s-soft; sh-dish; th-thin; pūre; ŭnite; ûrn; stŭd; circŭs; ü-as in French tu; ′-indeterminate vowel.

Feature (Pronunciation)	Page	Lat.	Long.
Wisła, stm., Pol. (vēs′wȧ) *see* Vistula	194-95	54°21′N	18°56′E
Wisłoka, stm., Pol. (vēs-wô′kȧ)	194-95	50°27′N	21°24′E
Wismar, Ger. (vĭs′mär)	194-95	53°53′N	11°28′E
Wisner, Ne., U.S. (wĭz′nẽr)	114-15	41°59′N	96°56′W
Wissembourg, Fr. (vē-sän-bōōr′)	196-97	49°02′N	7°57′E
Witbank, S. Afr. (wĭt-bäŋk)	269c	25°53′S	29°14′E
Withlacoochee, stm., U.S. (wĭth-lȧ-kōō′chē)	124-25	30°23′N	83°10′W
Witu Islands, is., Pap. N. Gui.	277	4°45′S	149°19′E
W.J. van Blommestein Meer, res., Sur.	164-65	4°49′N	55°04′W
Wkra, stm., Pol. (f′krȧ)	194-95	52°27′N	20°45′E
Włocławek, Pol. (vwô-tswä′vĕk)	194-95	52°39′N	19°04′E
Włodawa, Pol. (vwô-dä′vä)	194-95	51°33′N	23°34′E
Włoszczowa, Pol. (vwôsh-chô′vä)	194-95	50°51′N	19°58′E
Wodonga, Austl.	276	36°08′S	146°53′E
Wokam, Pulau, i., Indon.	224-25	5°37′S	134°30′E
Woleai, at., Micron.	280-81	7°21′N	143°53′E
Woleu, stm., Afr. *see* Mbini	260-61	1°35′N	9°38′E
Wolf, Volcán, vol., Ec.	170a	0°00′S	91°20′W
Wolf Point, Mt., U.S. (wo͝olf point)	112-13	48°05′N	105°37′W
Wolfsburg, Ger. (vōlfs′bōōrgh)	194-95	52°26′N	10°47′E
Wolfville, N.S., Can. (wo͝olf′vĭl)	138-39	45°05′N	64°22′W
Wollaston, Islas, is., Chile	171	55°45′S	67°37′W
Wollaston Lake, lk., Sk., Can. (wo͝ol′ȧs-tŭn lāk)	130-31	58°15′N	103°20′W
Wollaston Peninsula, pen., Can. (wo͝ol′ȧs-tŭn pĕ-nĭn′sūlȧ)	130-31	70°0′N	115°00′W
Wollongong, Austl. (wo͝ol′ŭn-gŏng)	276	34°25′S	150°54′E
Wołomin, Pol. (vô-wō′mēn)	194-95	52°20′N	21°15′E
Wolseley, Sk., Can.	134-35	50°25′N	103°16′W
Wolverhampton, Eng., U.K. (wo͝ol′vẽr-hămp-tŭn)	190-91	52°35′N	2°08′W
Wondai, Austl.	276	26°19′S	151°53′E
Wŏnju, Kor., S.	243	37°21′N	127°57′E
Wŏnsan, Kor., N. (wŭn′sän′)	243	39°09′N	127°26′E
Wonthaggi, Austl. (wônt-hăg′ē)	276	38°37′S	145°35′E
Woodbine, Ia., U.S. (wo͝od′bīn)	114-15	41°44′N	95°43′W
Woodbridge, Va., U.S. (wo͝od′brĭj′)	116-17	38°39′N	77°15′W
Wood Buffalo National Park, n.p., Can. (wo͝od bŭf′ȧ-lō năsh′ŭn-ăl pärk)	128-29	59°06′N	112°58′W
Woodburn, Or., U.S. (wo͝od′bûrn)	112-13	45°08′N	122°51′W
Woodlark, i., Pap. N. Gui. (wo͝od′lärk) *see* Murua Island	277	9°06′S	152°45′E
Woodroffe, Mount, mtn., Austl. (mount wo͝od′rŭf)	272-73	26°20′S	131°45′E
Woodruff, S.C., U.S. (wo͝od′rŭf)	124-25	34°45′N	82°02′W
Woods, Lake of the, lk., N.A. (lāk ŭv thȧ wo͝odz)	134-35	49°15′N	94°45′W
Woodsfield, Oh., U.S. (wo͝odz-fēld)	116-17	39°46′N	81°07′W
Woodstock, N.B., Can. (wo͝od′stŏk)	138-39	46°09′N	67°34′W
Woodstock, On., Can. (wo͝od′stŏk)	136-37	43°08′N	80°45′W
Woodstock, Il., U.S. (wo͝od′stŏk)	116-17	42°19′N	88°26′W
Woodstock, N.Y., U.S. (wo͝od′stŏk)	116-17	42°03′N	74°07′W
Woodstock, Va., U.S. (wo͝od′stŏk)	116-17	38°53′N	78°30′W
Woodsville, N.H., U.S. (wo͝odz′vĭl)	116-17	44°09′N	72°02′W
Woodville, Ms., U.S. (wo͝od′vĭl)	124-25	31°07′N	91°18′W
Woodville, Tx., U.S. (wo͝od′vĭl)	122-23	30°46′N	94°25′W
Woodward, Ok., U.S. (wo͝od′wôrd)	120-21	36°27′N	99°23′W
Woomera, Austl. (wo͝om′ẽrȧ)	276	31°12′S	136°50′E
Woonsocket, R.I., U.S. (wōōn-sŏk′ĕt)	116-17	42°01′N	71°31′W
Wooramel, stm., Austl.	272-73	25°51′S	114°16′E
Wooster, Oh., U.S. (wo͝os′tẽr)	116-17	40°48′N	81°56′W
Worcester, S. Afr. (wo͝os′tẽr)	264-65	33°39′S	19°27′E
Worcester, Eng., U.K. (wo͝o′stẽr)	190-91	52°11′N	2°14′W
Worcester, Ma., U.S.	116-17	42°16′N	71°48′W
Worden, Mt., U.S. (wôr′dĕn)	112-13	45°58′N	108°13′W
Workington, Eng., U.K. (wûr′kĭng-tŭn)	190-91	54°38′N	3°34′W
Worksop, Eng., U.K. (wûrk′sŏp) (wûr′sŭp)	190-91	53°19′N	1°07′W
Worland, Wy., U.S. (wûr′lȧnd)	112-13	44°01′N	107°57′W
Worms, Ger. (vōrms)	194-95	49°38′N	8°21′E
Worthing, Eng., U.K. (wûr′dhĭng)	190-91	50°49′N	0°23′W
Worthington, In., U.S. (wûr′dhĭng-tŭn)	116-17	39°07′N	86°59′W
Worthington, Mn., U.S. (wûr′dhĭng-tŭn)	114-15	43°38′N	95°36′W
Wotho, at., Marsh. Is.	280-81	10°06′N	166°01′E
Wotje, at., Marsh. Is.	280-81	9°27′N	170°02′E
Wowoni, Pulau, i., Indon. (pōō-lou wō-wō′nē)	248-49	4°08′S	123°06′E
Wrangel Island, i., Russia (răn′gĕl ī′lȧnd) *see* Vrangelya, Ostrov	218-19	71°14′N	179°21′W
Wrangell, Ak., U.S. (răn′gĕl)	126	56°29′N	132°22′W
Wrangell, Cape, c., Ak., U.S. (kāp răn′gĕl)	126a	52°55′N	172°30′E
Wrangell, Mount, mtn., Ak., U.S. (mount răn′gĕl)	126	62°0′N	144°06′W
Wrangell Mountains, mts., Ak., U.S. (răn′gĕl moun′tĭnz)	126	62°0′N	143°00′W
Wrangell-Saint Elias National Park and Preserve, n.p., Ak., U.S.	126	61°37′N	142°57′W
Wrath, Cape, c., Scot., U.K. (kāp răth)	190-91	58°38′N	4°60′W
Wray, Co., U.S. (rā)	120-21	40°05′N	102°14′W
Wrens, Ga., U.S. (rĕnz)	124-25	33°12′N	82°20′W
Wrexham, Wales, U.K. (rĕk′săm)	190-91	53°03′N	2°60′W
Wrightsville, Ga., U.S. (rīts′vĭl)	124-25	32°44′N	82°43′W
Wrigley, N.T., Can.	128-29	63°16′N	123°38′W
Wrocław, Pol. (vrôtsläv) (brĕs′lou)	194-95	51°07′N	17°02′E
Września, Pol. (vzhäsh′nyȧ)	194-95	52°20′N	17°35′E
Wu, stm., China (wōō′)	238-39	24°49′N	113°35′E
Wu, stm., China (wōō′)	238-39	27°11′N	109°48′E
Wuchang, China (wōō-chäŋ)	240-41	44°55′N	127°10′E
Wuchang, China *see* Wuhan	238-39	30°34′N	114°17′E
Wudaoliang, China	234-35	35°12′N	93°05′E
Wudu, China	238-39	33°25′N	104°51′E
Wugang, China	238-39	26°44′N	110°38′E
Wugong Shan, mts., China	238-39	27°21′N	113°50′E
Wuhai, China	240-41	39°40′N	106°48′E
Wuhan, China (wōō-hän′)	238-39	30°34′N	114°17′E
Wuhu, China (wōō′hōō)	238-39	31°21′N	118°22′E
Wūjang, China	234-35	33°37′N	79°48′E
Wukari, Nig.	260-61	7°53′N	9°47′E
Wuliang Shan, mts., China	238-39	24°29′N	100°39′E
Wuliaru, Pulau, i., Indon.	224-25	7°27′S	131°04′E
Wunnummin Lake, lk., On., Can.	134-35	52°55′N	89°10′W
Wupatki National Monument, n.p., Az., U.S.	118-19	35°32′N	111°26′W
Wuppertal, Ger. (vo͝op′ẽr-täl)	194-95	51°17′N	7°11′E
Würzburg, Ger. (vürts′bo͝orgh)	194-95	49°48′N	9°56′E
Wushan, China	238-39	31°06′N	109°50′E
Wushenqi, China	240-41	38°58′N	109°01′E
Wusuli, stm., Asia *see* Ussuri	240-41	48°27′N	135°04′E
Wutai, China	240-41	38°44′N	113°21′E
Wutai Shan, mtn., China	240-41	39°04′N	113°35′E
Wutongqiao, China	238-39	29°24′N	103°49′E
Wutsin, China *see* Changzhou	238-39	31°47′N	119°57′E
Wuvulu Island, i., Pap. N. Gui.	277	1°45′S	142°50′E
Wuwei, China (wōō′wā′)	238-39	31°18′N	117°54′E
Wuwei, China (wōō′wā′)	240-41	37°56′N	102°38′E
Wuxi, China (wōō-shyē)	238-39	31°22′N	109°33′E
Wuxi, China (wōō-shyē)	238-39	31°35′N	120°18′E
Wuxing, China (wōō-shyĭŋ) *see* Huzhou	238-39	30°52′N	120°06′E
Wuyi Shan, mts., China (wōō-yē shän)	238-39	27°42′N	117°09′E
Wuyuan, China	240-41	41°03′N	108°22′E
Wuzhong, China	240-41	37°59′N	106°12′E
Wuzhou, China (wōō-jō)	238-39	23°30′N	111°21′E
Wyandotte, Mi., U.S. (wī′ăn-dŏt)	116-17	42°13′N	83°09′W
Wyandra, Austl.	276	27°16′S	145°59′E
Wymore, Ne., U.S. (wī′mōr)	120-21	40°07′N	96°40′W
Wyndham, Austl. (wĭnd′ăm)	270-71	15°29′S	128°07′E
Wynne, Ar., U.S. (wĭn)	124-25	35°13′N	90°48′W
Wynnewood, Ok., U.S. (wĭn′wo͝od)	120-21	34°39′N	97°10′W
Wynyard, Sk., Can. (wīn′yẽrd)	134-35	51°47′N	104°10′W
Wyoming, Mi., U.S. (wī-ō′mĭng)	116-17	42°55′N	85°43′W
Wyoming, state, U.S. (wī-ō′mĭng)	108-09	43°0′N	107°30′W
Wyong, Austl.	276	33°17′S	151°25′E
Wyszków, Pol. (vēsh′ko͝of)	194-95	52°36′N	21°28′E
Wytheville, Va., U.S. (wĭth′vĭl)	124-25	36°57′N	81°06′W

X

Feature (Pronunciation)	Page	Lat.	Long.
Xaafuun, Raas, c., Som.	262-63	10°26′N	51°25′E
Xaidulla, China	234-35	36°26′N	77°58′E
Xainza, China	234-35	30°55′N	88°40′E
Xai-Xai, Moz.	264-65	25°03′S	33°39′E
Xalapa, Mex.	146-47	19°32′N	96°55′W
Xam, stm., Asia *see* Chu	246-47	19°53′N	105°45′E
Xam Nua, Laos	246-47	20°25′N	104°03′E
Xankändi, Azer.	227	39°49′N	46°45′E
Xapuri, Braz.	166-67	10°39′S	68°31′W
Xar Moron, stm., China	240-41	43°25′N	120°45′E
Xau, Lake, pl., Bots.	264-65	21°18′S	24°44′E
Xäzär, Dänizi, lk., *see* Caspian Sea	226	41°18′N	50°59′E
Xcalak, Mex. (sä-lä′k)	148	18°16′N	87°50′W
Xenia, Oh., U.S. (zē′nĭ-ȧ)	116-17	39°41′N	83°56′W
Xeres, Spain *see* Jerez de la Frontera	198-99	36°42′N	6°08′W
Xi, stm., China (shyē)	238-39	22°20′N	113°18′E
Xi, stm., China (shyē)	240-41	42°25′N	100°55′E
Xiaguan, China *see* Dali	238-39	25°36′N	100°13′E
Xiahe, China	240-41	35°24′N	102°32′E
Xiamen, China	225a	24°27′N	118°07′E
Xi'an, China (shyē-än)	238-39	34°15′N	108°52′E
Xiangfan, China	238-39	32°02′N	112°09′E
Xianggang, China *see* Hong Kong	238-39	22°16′N	114°10′E
Xiangkhoang, Laos	246-47	19°20′N	103°22′E
Xiangquan, stm., Asia *see* Sutlej	234-35	29°21′N	71°02′E
Xiangride, China	240-41	35°60′N	97°59′E
Xiangtan, China (shyäŋ-tän)	238-39	27°51′N	112°54′E
Xiantao, China	238-39	30°22′N	113°27′E
Xianyang, China (shyĕn-yäŋ)	238-39	34°20′N	108°42′E
Xianyou, China	225a	25°22′N	118°40′E
Xiaogan, China	238-39	30°55′N	113°54′E
Xiao Hinggan Ling, mts., China *see* Lesser Khingan Range	240-41	48°45′N	127°00′E
Xiapu, China (shyä-pōō)	238-39	26°52′N	120°01′E
Xibaxa, stm., Asia *see* Subansiri	238-39	26°46′N	93°45′E
Xichang, China	238-39	27°54′N	102°16′E
Xicoténcatl, Mex. (sē-kô-tĕn-kät′l)	146-47	23°00′N	98°56′W
Xifeng, China (shyē-fŭŋ)	240-41	42°44′N	124°43′E
Xigazê, China	234-35	29°16′N	88°54′E
Xilinhot, China	240-41	43°56′N	116°03′E
Ximiao, China	240-41	41°07′N	100°17′E
Xinchang, China (shyĭn-chäŋ)	238-39	29°31′N	120°53′E
Xing'an, China (shyĭŋ-än)	238-39	25°37′N	110°31′E
Xinghua, China (shyĭŋ-hwä)	238-39	32°56′N	119°50′E
Xingkai Hu, lk., Asia *see* Khanka, Lake	244	45°11′N	132°25′E
Xingtai, China (shyĭŋ-tī)	240-41	37°04′N	114°30′E
Xingu, stm., Braz. (zhĕŋ-go͝o′)	166-67	1°30′S	51°50′W
Xingyi, China	238-39	25°05′N	104°54′E
Xinhua, China (shyĭn-hwä)	238-39	27°37′N	111°02′E
Xining, China (shyē-nĭŋ)	240-41	36°38′N	101°50′E
Xinjiang, China	240-41	35°37′N	111°13′E
Xinjiang, state, China (shyĭn-jyäŋ)	220-21	40°0′N	85°00′E
Xinjiulong, China	238-39	22°21′N	114°10′E
Xinmin, China (shyĭn-mĭn)	243	41°59′N	122°50′E
Xinpu, China *see* Lianyungang	238-39	34°37′N	119°11′E
Xintai, China (shyĭn-tī)	240-41	35°54′N	117°46′E
Xinxian, China (shyĭn shyĕn)	240-41	38°24′N	112°44′E
Xinxiang, China (shyĭn-shyäŋ)	240-41	35°18′N	113°52′E
Xinyang, China (shyĭn-yäŋ)	238-39	32°07′N	114°04′E
Xinye, China (shyĭn-yŭ)	238-39	32°33′N	112°21′E
Xiping, China (shyē-pĭŋ)	238-39	33°23′N	114°01′E
Xique-Xique, Braz.	166-67	10°50′S	42°43′W
Xırdalan, Azer.	227	40°28′N	49°46′E
Xisha Qundao, is., China *see* Paracel Islands	224-25	15°46′N	112°17′E
Xishui, China (shyē-shwā)	238-39	30°28′N	115°15′E
Xixian, China (shyē shyĕn)	238-39	32°21′N	114°44′E
Xizang, state, China (shyē-dzäŋ) *see* Tibet	234-35	32°0′N	88°00′E
Xongka, stm., Asia *see* Ca	246-47	18°44′N	105°45′E
Xuancheng, China (shyůän-chŭŋ)	238-39	30°57′N	118°45′E
Xuanhua, China (shyůän-hwä)	240-41	40°36′N	115°02′E
Xuchang, China (shyōō-chäŋ)	238-39	34°02′N	113°49′E
Xun, stm., China (shyo͝on)	238-39	23°26′N	111°30′E
Xuwen, China	238-39	20°20′N	110°11′E
Xuyong, China	238-39	28°10′N	105°25′E
Xuzhou, China	238-39	34°16′N	117°11′E

Y

Feature (Pronunciation)	Page	Lat.	Long.
Yaan, China (yä-än)	238-39	30°01′N	103°04′E
Yablonovy Range, mts., Russia (yȧ-blô-nô-vē′ fănj) *see* Yablonovyy Khrebet	218-19	53°30′N	115°00′E
Yablonovyy Khrebet, mts., Russia	218-19	53°30′N	115°00′E
Yaco, stm., S.A. *see* Iaco	170	9°02′S	68°35′W
Yacuiba, Bol. (yȧ-kōō-ē′bȧ)	168-69	22°02′S	63°42′W
Yacyretá, Isla, i., Para.	173	27°25′S	56°30′W
Yadong, China	234-35	27°29′N	88°54′E
Yafran, Libya	188-89	32°04′N	12°31′E
Yagodnoye, Russia	218-19	62°32′N	149°37′E
Yaguajay, Cuba (yä-guä-hä′ē)	142-43	22°20′N	79°14′W
Yahualica, Mex. (yä-wä-lē′kä)	146-47	21°09′N	102°51′W
Yaitopya, nation, Afr. *see* Ethiopia	253	9°0′N	39°00′E
Yakima, Wa., U.S. (yăk′ĭmȧ)	112-13	46°36′N	120°30′W

n-sing; ŋ-bank; ɴ-nasalized n; nŏd; cŏmmit; ōld; ôbey; ôrder; oi-boil; fōōd; ò-as oo in foot; ou-out; s-soft; sh-dish; th-thin; pūre; ûnite; ûrn; stŭd; circŭs; ü-as in French tu; ′-indeterminate vowel.